FileView1: Combines multiple application resource t 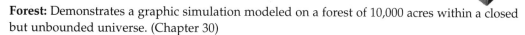 includes operations to read directory and file informa display file contents in a mixed hexadecimal and text

FileView2: Duplicates the FileView1 application usin

Fonts: Demonstrates the use of character fonts. (Chapter 25)

Forest: Demonstrates a graphic simulation modeled on a forest of 10,000 acres within a closed but unbounded universe. (Chapter 30)

GrayImage: Demonstrates printing color images on color printers and converting color images to gray-scale for output on monochrome printers. (Chapter 31)

Jumps: Demonstrates jumping execution from within an exception block. (Chapter 16)

KeyCodes: Provides a view of the actual keyboard-event codes, including status flags, key-down and key-up events, and character events. (Chapter 5)

KeyCodes2: Duplicates the KeyCodes program using the MFC. (Chapter 5)

List: Demonstrates using dynamically allocated arrays and virtual memory functions. (Chapter 17)

MacSock: Demonstrates protocol-specific functionality using the Set Socket Option function. (Chapter 20)

MapDemo: Demonstrates methods of identifying regions within bitmap images based on mouse selection. (Chapter 29)

Modes: Demonstrates standard and custom mapping modes for graphics operations. (Chapter 21)

Mouse1: Demonstrates tracking mouse movement with simple responses to mouse-button clicks. (Chapter 6)

Mouse2: Shows the standard mouse cursor shapes and demonstrates how the mouse cursor can be changed by the application window or by other application conditions. (Chapter 6)

Mouse3: Shows how an application can respond to mouse clicks and correlate the position information to screen/window coordinates. (Chapter 6)

Multimedia: Demonstrates how applications use multimedia extensions. (Chapter 36)

NamePipe: Shows how to use multiple processes with named pipes (shared memory). (Chapter 15)

Nest: Demonstrates nested exceptions. (Chapter 16)

OLE_Client: Demonstrates the simplicity of creating an OLE client (a client with Object Linking and Embedding support) using the MFC and the AppWizard. (Chapter 35)

PainText: Demonstrates the basics of "painting" an application screen, simple font metrics, scrolling, and scrollbar message responses. (Chapter 3)

PainText2: Duplicates the PainText application using the MFC. (Chapter 3)

Parry: Provides a simple OLE server with a distinctively paranoid nature. (Chapter 35)

Continued on page facing CD

NT® 4/Windows 95
Developer's Handbook™

Ben Ezzell
with Jim Blaney

SYBEX

San Francisco · Paris · Düsseldorf · Soest

Associate Publisher: Gary Masters
Acquisitions Manager: Kristine Plachy
Acquisitions & Developmental Editor: Peter Kuhns
Editor: Marilyn Smith
Project Editor: Linda Good
Technical Editor: Doug Langston
Book Design Director: Catalin Dulfu
Book Designer: Suzanne Albertson
Graphic Illustrator: Inbar Berman
Electronic Publishing Specialist: Bill Gibson
Production Coordinators: Alexa Riggs, Grey B. Magauran
Indexer: Matthew Spence
Cover Designer: Design Site
Cover Photographer: Chris Alan Wilton, The Image Bank

Screen reproductions produced with Collage Plus

Library of Congress Card Number: 96-72104
ISBN: 0-7821-1945-X

Manufactured in the United States of America

10 9 8 7 6 5 4 3 2

Software License Agreement: Terms and Conditions

Warranty

SYBEX warrants the enclosed media to be free of physical defects for a period of ninety (90) days after purchase. The Software is not available from SYBEX in any other form or media than that enclosed herein or posted to *www.sybex.com*. If you discover a defect in the media during this warranty period, you may obtain a replacement of identical format at no charge by sending the defective media, postage prepaid, with proof of purchase to:

> SYBEX Inc.
> Customer Service Department
> 1151 Marina Village Parkway
> Alameda, CA 94501
> (510) 523-8233
> Fax: (510) 523-2373
> e-mail: info@sybex.com
> WEB: HTTP//:WWW.SYBEX.COM

After the 90-day period, you can obtain replacement media of identical format by sending us the defective disk, proof of purchase, and a check or money order for $10, payable to SYBEX.

Disclaimer

SYBEX makes no warranty or representation, either expressed or implied, with respect to the Software or its contents, quality, performance, merchantability, or fitness for a particular purpose. In no event will SYBEX, its distributors, or dealers be liable to you or any other party for direct, indirect, special, incidental, consequential, or other damages arising out of the use of or inability to use the Software or its contents even if advised of the possibility of such damage. In the event that the Software includes an online update feature, SYBEX further disclaims any obligation to provide this feature for any specific duration other than the initial posting.

The exclusion of implied warranties is not permitted by some states. Therefore, the above exclusion may not apply to you. This warranty provides you with specific legal rights; there may be other rights that you may have that vary from state to state. The pricing of the book with the Software by SYBEX reflects the allocation of risk and limitations on liability contained in this agreement of Terms and Conditions.

Shareware Distribution

This Software may contain various programs that are distributed as shareware. Copyright laws apply to both shareware and ordinary commercial software, and the copyright Owner(s) retains all rights. If you try a shareware program and continue using it, you are expected to register it. Individual programs differ on details of trial periods, registration, and payment. Please observe the requirements stated in appropriate files.

Copy Protection

The Software in whole or in part may or may not be copy-protected or encrypted. However, in all cases, reselling or redistributing these files without authorization is expressly forbidden except as specifically provided for by the Owner(s) therein.

Over the years, many types of progress have been spurred by many, disparate individuals ... but, very often, these have been individuals whose interest in furthering progress was minimal at best.

For example, when Hotemtep discovered that layered reeds – or, more accurately, thin strips of pith – could be combined to create a flexible surface which held a painted image very nicely, it was Amenat who laughed the loudest while pointing out that this new-fangled papyrus lacked the durability of baked clay, could not be reused (as a wax tablet could), and certainly had no practical value. Moreover, Amenat pointed out, no right-thinking (i.e., wealthy or influential) citizen of the upper- or lower- Nile would have any use at all for such a material, since it would be instantly destroyed by the annual rising of the waters. (You will pardon, I trust, if I do not remember the exact date but the modern calendar also had yet to be invented.)

Much later – and a half-a-world–away – Amenat's successors were equally certain the intelligencia (meaning those with wealth and status) would never – under any circumstances – consider buying these new-fangled 'printed' books. It was simply out of the question. Books should be written – by a trained scribe – and illumi-nated – by a trained artist – on fine parchment, not on cheap, mass-produced paper. Otherwise, very obvi-ously, they were worthless. Besides, there was simply no need for mass-producing books! After all, what earthly use were dozens – much less hundreds – of copies of the same thing.

Photogravure also had its critics – after all, where was the artistry in a system which simply reproduced exactly what you started with?

Moving pictures were even worse – these spelled the death of the theatre ...

And four-color comics? The world was coming to an end, the moral decline of civilization. (But have you tried lately to buy a copy of Action Comics #1.)

And television? The boob-tube? Couldn't possibly have any redeeming value.

Not to mention the Internet – after all, who needs to send a letter halfway around the world in mere seconds. Isn't the mail good enough? What's the rush anyway? Totally worthless. Best that can be hoped for is that it will self-destruct by bringing the national (and international) telephone system to its knees.

Don't take my word for it, just ask Amenat's successors – they've always been available, ready, and willing to point out just how bad each new advance was, how unnecessary and how ruinous these devices, methods, or ideas would be to civilization as we know it.

So, where is the value in Amenat's mental progeny?

Very simple – and we should all listen to them. Really! No joke! After all, the minute Amenat's tribe tells us that something is worthless, destructive of civilization, responsible for the moral decline of modern youth, etc., etc., ... well, that's the time to listen carefully ... because they're pointing the way to our future ... and have provided a certain and reliable guidepost throughout the ages.

Therefore, this book is respectfully dedicated to all the nay-sayers of all the ages who, for those with the wisdom to listen have so reliably pointed the way to the future ...

Say on, dear critics ... we, the malcontents, the recalcitrant, the obstinate, the reactionaries of the world listen with anxious ears for your golden words ...

ACKNOWLEDGMENTS

The fact that an author's name appears on the cover of a book, particularly a technical book, is inherently misleading because no book is produced by the efforts of a single individual. Instead, this book is a product of the efforts of a large group of people and, lacking the facilities to include an "Easter egg" for your amusement and edification, I would like to recognize and thank some of these people here.

Peter Kuhns, developmental editor, puts up with demands that were never in his job description. He has provided invaluable assistance in all phases of preparation of this volume, from its inception to its appearance in your hands. Damnation with faint praise aside, Peter, it has been a real pleasure, and I thank you sincerely for your very able efforts and attentions.

Doug Langston, my technical editor, has ably demonstrated the truism that, if a fool can ask more questions than a wise man can answer, a wise tech editor is even worse. For all your questions, quibbles, and suggestions, please accept my sincere thanks. Your assistance has been invaluable.

Jim Blaney, my co-author, has tackled a number of serious and difficult questions in a competent and accomplished fashion. Hey, guy, now you know what it's like to be on the hotspot. (So, how do you like it?)

Marilyn Smith, my editor, deserves compliments for her patience, her competence, and her careful eye in spotting discrepancies, as well as her efforts in polishing my (our) prose to present the best possible appearance. To an author, a good copy editor is to be prized above pearls.

Linda Good, as project editor, was responsible for putting it all together. I offer a hearty thank you for a job well done. In the publishing business, the project editor is one of the unsung (but often cursed) people who deserve far more credit than they generally receive. (If you don't believe me, just ask one.)

And, not least, the entire Production department at Sybex, who do everything from preparing illustrations to order (surely you didn't think I was the artist?) to pounding masses of paper into a form that will fit between two covers. All of this covers a lot more work than I can describe here, but special nods go to Alexa Riggs and Grey Magauran, the production coordinators, Bill Gibson, the desktop publisher, and Inbar Berman, the graphic illustrator.

In summation, while the author remains responsible for the product—and particularly for any flaws, errors, or mistakes that appear herein—it is a team effort that you are holding in your hands at this point. If the result is pleasing to you and, we trust, helpful, the credit is shared by all; if not, the blame remains mine alone.

Ben Ezzell

CONTENTS AT A GLANCE

TABLE OF CONTENTS

INTRODUCTION

Windows NT and Windows 95 represent both a distinct departure from Windows 3.*x* and a continuation of a familiar programming environment. These new versions of Windows are familiar because they offer essentially the same operations and features that have made earlier versions of Windows so popular. They also retain the capability to execute existing Windows 3.1 applications. Developing applications for Windows NT and 95 is similar to developing applications for Windows 3.1.

But programming for Windows NT and 95 is also different than for earlier versions. This is because they are, themselves, each a complete operating system, rather than a shell operating within DOS's limitations. Windows NT and 95 are able to take advantage of the newer 80386/80486/Pentium CPUs and to provide these same advantages to the user. The differences between the old and new systems are far from cosmetic. Many of the most important changes are not visible at all but still provide extremely important enhancements in operations.

This book will show you how to develop all types of applications to operate under Windows NT and 95. The topics range from the basics of handling keyboard and mouse input to advanced techniques for network and Internet support. You will learn how to take advantage of the Windows NT and 95 features of functions to create programs that look and perform the way that you want.

Who Should Read This Book

Regardless of your previous programming experience, and whether you are an expert or a novice, you will learn the requirements for Windows NT and 95 application development from the topics and examples presented in this book.

For programmers who have never worked with Windows or OS/2, the programs you will find here may present something of a challenge, if only because of the differences between conventional DOS programming and the requirements (and facilities) present in the Windows environment. The topics and explanations in this book, however, are designed to present a clear introduction to event- or message-driven programming, as well as to the demands and capabilities of the Windows API functions. Please realize, however, that some familiarity with C programming is assumed.

Programmers who have previously worked with Windows 3.x will find both similarities and differences between the examples for 32-bit Windows NT and 95 and the equivalent programs for Windows 3.x. The book points out differences between the earlier 16-bit system API calls and the 32-bit system API calls, and includes suggestions for converting programs from Windows 3.x to Windows NT and 95.

Those of you who have worked with OS/2 programming should be familiar with the basic principals of event-driven programming, as well as programming using API function calls. This familiarity will be both an advantage and, to some degree, a disadvantage. The advantage lies in the similarities of the processes and handling in the OS/2 and Windows NT and 95 environments. However, you will need to learn new names, such as those for messages and API functions, and the types and structures Windows uses as parameters.

What This Book Contains

This book demonstrates the principal elements of Windows NT/95 programming, including Windows application resources, using both Borland's C/C++ and Microsoft's Visual C++. All of the topics discussed are illustrated with working examples, with complete listings on the CD accompanying this book. Each of the program examples is complete and can be compiled using either the Borland or Microsoft 32-bit C/C++ compilers.

The book is organized in five parts:

- Introduction to Windows NT/95 Programming

- Windows NT/95 Application Resources

- Advanced Application Designs

- Windows NT/95 Graphics

- Exchanging Information between Applications

Part 1: Introduction to Windows NT/95 Programming

Before you can begin rewriting your application, or designing a new application, the first step is to know how the new operating system works and what your tools and options will be. Therefore, the first chapter in this book begins by looking at the Windows NT/95 environment, including the requirements for working with the operating system. In Chapter 2, we will get to work, starting with a simple program designed to show the basics of application development for NT/95. This chapter also presents a template program, in the form of the Template. I include file, which will be used in other demo programs.

In Chapter 3, we will examine how DOS-based applications can be moved to the NT/95 environment. Chapter 4 deals with the differences between Windows 3.1 and NT/95 application source code, including structure, types, classes, and messages. You'll learn how to convert applications from the earlier to the newer system.

The next three chapters cover the basics of keyboard and mouse handling and window controls. Chapter 5 includes a simple editor program to demonstrate how virtual-key codes are generated and interpreted. Chapter 6 looks at mouse messages and cursors, with a series of demo programs showing how each functions. Chapter 7 introduces child window controls and control buttons.

Part 2: Windows NT/95 Application Resources

Instead of relying on program instructions to create dialog boxes, menus, and window controls, such as buttons and scrollbars, the simpler method is to use a resource editor to draw the desired resource elements for you. Other, less visual, resource elements include keyboard accelerators and strings. Also, elements such as bitmaps, icons, and custom cursors can be created easily with a resource editor.

Part 2 introduces application resources and the resource editors used to create them. Chapter 8 provides an overview of resource types and two popular resource editors. The following chapters discuss bitmap, dialog box, menu, accelerator key, and string resources. Chapter 13 demonstrates the use of resource elements in a single application, named FileView.

Resource elements do not appear in the program source code. Instead, they are created by separate editors and stored, before the application is compiled, as ASCII resource scripts (.RC). Image resources are stored as .BMP, .ICO, or .CUR binary files that are referenced within the resource script. Alternatively, all of these resource elements can be stored in a compiled form in a .RES resource file.

Because all of the program examples in this book have been written for compatibility with both the Borland and Microsoft C compilers (32-bit versions), the application resources for each demo application have been provided as .RC resource scripts (together with, in most cases, external binary .BMP, .CUR, and .ICO image files) rather than .RES compiled resources. The application NMake instruction files each include instructions invoking Microsoft's resource compiler before, finally, linking the compiled .EXE and .RES files to produce the final .EXE executable file.

Part 3: Advanced Application Designs

For those who want to go beyond the basics, Windows NT and 95 offer a variety of tools for more advanced applications. Chapter 14 begins Part 3 with a discussion of multiple-thread programs, which handle asynchronous activity. Programs with multiple windows, for example, generally benefit from creating a thread for each window. Threads can also be used anytime a task can be carried out independently of the main process; for example, threads can be used for controlling external devices.

Chapter 15 continues with this general idea, expanding to using processes and pipes to communicate between independent threads.

Chapter 16 describes how to use NT/95 built-in exception-handling mechanisms in your programs to cope with exceptional conditions that disturb their normal flow of execution.

Chapter 17 covers NT/95 memory management and how processes can share blocks of memory by creating file-mapping objects. The first of the two sample programs constructs a dynamically allocated array using virtual memory functions. The second program lets the user view and edit the contents of shared memory.

The next three chapters cover topics related to connecting to other systems through a network. Chapter 18 discusses the NT/95 security functions, Chapter 19 covers how to include Internet support in your NT/95 applications, and Chapter 20 explains how to build network applications.

Part 4: Windows NT/95 Graphics

Part 4 introduces Windows graphics operations, beginning in Chapter 21 with the Windows device context and mapping modes. Chapter 22 continues with a discussion of colors and palettes and an illustration of the principal ROP drawing modes.

Chapter 23 describes the basic tools for drawing and filling shapes, including curves and polygons as well as pen styles. It concludes with a series of simple business graphs. Chapter 24 covers more drawing tools, including bitmapped brushes, fill modes, predefined bitmap patterns, and device-independent bitmaps (DIBs).

In Chapter 25, the subject is text displays. This chapter examines font selection, alignment, and typefaces, as well as how to modify the device context to control how the text is displayed.

Chapter 26 looks at methods for working with graphics files. It includes a demo program for capturing Windows bitmap images either to the clipboard or to a file and a program for viewing PCX files. Chapter 27 discusses image-enhancement techniques.

In Chapters 28 and 29, you'll learn about graphics selection operations. Chapter 28 describes how to create target overlays, and Chapter 29 demonstrates selection methods for more complex images.

Chapter 30 addresses the topic of graphic simulations. It includes the Forest demo program, which displays a small universe of 10,000 acres, simulating the growth of trees.

The final chapter in this part deals with graphics printing and how to develop gray-scales for outputting color graphics on black-and-white printers.

Part 5: Exchanging Information between Applications

Even in a single-tasking environment such as DOS, where each application stands alone, various methods have been devised to permit an applications to exchange information among themselves. These have ranged from the simplicity of common file formats to more esoteric attempts involving TSRs that paste information into the keyboard buffer for retrieval by the foreground application.

In a multitasking environment such as Windows, information exchange between applications is both practical and, quite often, integral to an application's purpose.

Windows NT and 95 include features that both permit and encourage sharing information, data, or even operations between applications. These processes and mechanisms include:

- Metafiles
- The clipboard
- Dynamic Data Exchange (DDE)
- Object Linking and Embedding (OLE)
- Multimedia

Chapter 32 demonstrates how metafiles can be used to record operations in one application and replay them in another application. Chapter 33 explains how your applications can use clipboard operations.

Chapters 34 and 35 describe the powerful data-sharing tools of DDE and OLE and the Windows NT/95 support for these functions. Chapter 36 finishes this part and the book with an introduction to multimedia application development, showing how multimedia services are used as extensions to other applications.

About the Examples

The examples in this book (and on the accompanying CD) have been written using both Microsoft Visual C++ and Borland C++. In most cases, the source code for any of the applications can be compiled and linked using either compiler. Where exceptions occur, these have been noted in the text, together with suggestions or comments on cross-compiler compatibility. General differences between the two compilers are discussed in Chapter 2.

In no case, however, are the choices of compiler used intended as a recommendation for or against a specific version of C/C++. Compilers are rather like word processors; the best compiler is simply the one that suits you best. If you are more comfortable with CodeView or some other editor/shell that is not even mentioned here, please do not hesitate to continue with whatever development system you find most productive. If you are a command-line compiler user, .MAK files have also been supplied for most of the applications.

With a few exceptions, these applications run under both Windows NT and 95. The exceptions, which are documented and explained in the text, are found in some network and security features that are supported by NT but not recognized by Windows 95.

Although the applications illustrated here have been written by several authors and, therefore, do differ in details of style, these differences are generally unimportant. For simplicity, many of the applications have been written in C (nonobject-oriented); others are fully object-oriented and frequently utilize the Microsoft Foundation Classes (MFC).

Where references to API documentation appear, both in the text and in the source code, they refer to the online documentation commonly supplied on the compiler source CD. The source CD should always be available, either on a local CD or on a shared network drive. The savings in development time realized by having the online documentation available are immeasurable. (And if a brain-dead system manager is responsible for the absence of such documentation, the situation may be corrected by the appropriate application of poison, cement boots, a large club, or a suitably situated bear-trap.)

About the CD

All of the demo applications discussed in this book, together with their resources, NMake files, headers, and relevant source code files, are included on the accompanying CD. Also, a few extra examples that are not discussed in the book or are mentioned only briefly have been included in the CD files.

The source files are arranged in directories, identified by chapter number, where each appear with further subdirectories for each application. In some examples, ..\RES subdirectories, which are generated by MFC and the AppWizard, contain application resource files. Also, in most cases, an .EXE file (or files) is included for each demo program.

Before attempting to compile any of these examples, copy the application directory, all files from the application directory, and any subdirectories to your hard drive.

Because the CD is a read-only device, the file attributes for the CD files are also set to read-only. Many file-management utilities, including the Windows NT/95 Explorer, do not reset the flags for files copied from a CD. Therefore, after copying files to your hard drive, the file attributes should be reset. If this is not done, your compiler/editor will not permit you to edit these files (unless they are saved under a different filename) and, in some cases, may refuse to compile them.

PART I

Introduction to Windows NT/95 Programming

CHAPTER

ONE

1

The 32-Bit Windows Environment

- Hardware requirements for Windows NT and 95 programming

- Disk file systems—16-bit and 32-bit

- Differences between Windows NT and 95

- Dual-boot system installation

If you're reading this book, you're interested in creating applications for Windows NT 4.0, Windows 95, or both. Before you can design and implement applications, however, the first step is to understand the environment in which the application will operate and the requirements necessary to support the environment.

This chapter covers the environment, or environments, created by the Windows NT and Windows 95 operating systems. We'll look at the operating system environment from both a hardware and a software viewpoint.

The Hardware Environment

Although previous versions of both MS-DOS and Windows have tried to provide support for all earlier hardware systems, much of this backward compatibility has been achieved at the expense of limiting functional capabilities. The support for the owners of earlier computer models, including 808x and 80286 CPUs, has prevented programmers from making the best use of newer machines and, of course, placed the end user—knowingly or otherwise—under similar restrictions.

At some future time and in a similar fashion, the restrictions inherent in the Windows NT and 95 operating systems will also be considered archaic, restrictive, and cumbersome, and they will be derided for not providing support for the newest and fastest CPUs and peripherals. When that time comes, NT and 95 in turn, will be replaced by a new operating system.

For now, we're programming for the 32-bit environment and need to meet its requirements. We'll start with the hardware requirements for the computer system, RAM, and hard drive space.

Machine and RAM Requirements

First, and most important, Windows 95 and NT will not operate on an 8080, 8086, or 80286 system. Both operating systems require a minimum platform consisting of an 80386, 80486, or P-5 or equivalent with a minimum of 12MB of RAM, or a MIPS R4000 with 16 MB of RAM. Of course, faster CPU speeds and increased RAM are helpful. Although 12MB of RAM is a minimum requirement, 16MB is recommended. Adding more RAM to your system can boost performance for relatively little expense.

Some early 80386 CPUs incorporating the B0 and B1 steps are not compatible with Windows NT because of protect-mode problems. Systems incorporating these CPU models will require upgrading to at least a C step or, preferably, a contemporary D1 step 80386 CPU. The MS-DOS program `isbstep.exe`, distributed with the Win32 SDK, can be used to detect the presence of a B0 or B1 step machine.

Windows NT operates on the 386, 486, and R4000 systems. However, Windows 95 is limited to Intel-compatible systems. This book concentrates on the 486 and P-5 platforms. Keep in mind that this same material is relevant to R4000 platforms, even though R4000 systems are not explicitly mentioned. Similarly, as support for other CPU designs is added to the 32-bit Windows systems, the Windows NT and 95 API calls and the programs developed using them should run on those systems without requiring conversion, recompilation, or reprogramming.

Hard Drive Space Requirements

A second requirement is hard drive space. Windows NT (together with the SDK tools and examples) requires a minimum of 70MB of hard disk space (typical installations can run over 100MB) plus space for paging (swap) files. Given these requirements, it should be obvious that 120MB hard drives are obsolete, and even 540MB drives are becoming cramped. Fortunately, both memory (RAM) and high-capacity hard drives are considerably cheaper than they have been in the past.

TIP Don't rush to throw that old drive away just because you've bought a newer, higher-capacity drive. Most IDE drives can be ganged as master/slave pairs, even if they're from different manufacturers. And SCSIs are even easier to gang together, with as many as six drives supported by a single SCSI controller.

In a pinch, you may want to use a disk-compression utility to increase the capacity of your existing hard drive. Before installing any compression utility, however, check to ensure that it is not only compatible with Windows NT 4.0 and/or Windows 95, but that it is also compatible with any other operating systems you may be running (using a multi-boot system).

The Software (System) Environment

When it was first introduced, perhaps the biggest advantage of Windows NT over earlier versions of Windows was the change from a 16-bit to a 32-bit operating system. Today, however, with the Windows 95 operating system dominating the new computer market, the introduction of Windows NT 4.0 is a less abrupt change. This version differs from NT 3.1 and 3.51 primarily in the change to the Windows 95–style interface.

Like Windows 95, but unlike earlier versions of Windows, NT is its own operating system and does not rely on the underlying presence of the 16-bit DOS operating system. Unlike Windows 95, NT 3.1, 3.51, and now 4.0 are all true 32-bit operating systems. Windows 95, unfortunately, is a hybrid relying on both 16-bit and 32-bit core code. We'll talk more about the differences between Windows NT and 95 later in the chapter. For now, we need to review the software requirements for creating Windows NT and 95 applications.

Disk File Systems: 16-Bit or 32-Bit?

During installation, Windows NT offers a choice of continuing to use the existing 16-bit file system (the familiar uncompressed MS-DOS or DR DOS FAT file system) or converting the installation hard drive to the new 32-bit NTFS file system. Windows NT operates quite satisfactorily on existing 16-bit file systems, and this selection is strongly recommended at the present time.

There are several potential problems inherent in choosing to convert to the 32-bit file system. There are two principal conflicts in choosing the 32-bit file system:

- Selecting the 32-bit file system means that the dual-boot (multi-boot) option will not be valid because other operating systems, including Windows 95, cannot boot from a drive or access a drive formatted with the NTFS system.

- Existing DOS file-management utilities (such as Drag and File, XTree PRO, PC Tools, and Norton Utilities), as well as various disk optimizers and other DOS, Windows 3.x, and Windows 95 file-intensive applications, will not be able to access the 32-bit file system. This is true even when they are operated from within the Windows NT system (under NT's DOS shell).

You can avoid these conflicts by continuing to use the existing 16-bit file system. If, however, your system will be used to execute only NT and compatible applications, there is probably no reason not to change to the 32-bit file system. In fact, because this change offers an improvement in access times for disk files—particularly for large data files—there may be every reason to change.

Of course, the eventual move to a 32-bit file system is probably inevitable, just as the move from an antiquated 16-bit operating system to a more powerful 32-bit operating system is already occurring. But until 16-bit file-dependent applications are no longer required, and other operating systems can be abandoned entirely in favor of NT and NT-compatible applications, there remain ample reasons to continue to use the existing 16-bit FAT file system.

Also, while the 32-bit file system does promise improvement in disk-access times over the 16-bit file system, faster hard drives, disk-compression utilities, and disk caching usually have more impact on access times.

Path and Directory Requirements

As with DOS, when Windows NT boots, a number of operating parameters are set, using arguments and instructions contained in the Config.NT/Config.SYS and Autoexec.NT/Autoexec.BAT files. However, before going into the contents of these two files, a word of explanation about the file naming is in order.

NOTE If you are running Windows 95 and NT on a dual-boot system, but not running a DOS boot system, not all of the information in this section will apply, but it may still be of some interest. On the other hand, if you are dual-booting Windows 95 and NT, the contents of the Autoexec.BAT and Config.SYS files are essentially irrelevant except when you use the DOS shell feature in either system.

If you are using the Flexboot dual-boot option and boot under DOS, your root directory should show four files:

```
Autoexec.BAT
Autoexec.NT
Config.NT
Config.SYS
```

The two files with .NT extensions are the Windows NT 32-bit autoexecute and configuration files. The other two are the customary DOS boot files. However, when booting for Windows NT, the DOS boot files are renamed as Autoexec.### and Config.###; the two .NT files are renamed .BAT and .SYS, respectively. Curiously, you may also notice that there is still an Autoexec.NT and a Config.NT file listed on the boot drive. Both of these, however, will show a file size of zero (0).

Furthermore, even if Windows NT is interrupted (by a hard reset), when Flexboot is used to boot DOS, the two empty files will be removed, the _.BAT and _.SYS files are renamed as _.NT, and the two _.### files are renamed correctly as Autoexec.BAT and Config.SYS.

If you are not using the Flexboot system, the Config.SYS and Autoexec.BAT files will be simply that: the appropriate autoexecute and configuration files for NT.

> **NOTE**
>
> The Flexboot or dual-boot facility is supplied with the Windows NT installation program and makes it possible for your system to boot two or more different operating systems. Refer to the documentation on the Windows NT CD for details on compatibility and options.

Because of this potential dual nomenclature, the following sections refer to both forms. But keep in mind, the topics discussed pertain to the Windows NT system files, not to the DOS equivalents.

The Config.NT/Config.SYS Instructions

The Windows NT Config.SYS instructions are created by the NT installation program. Although they do not require any particular revisions, some explanation may be helpful.

The first element that you should understand about the Config.SYS file under NT is that the settings supplied here do not affect the NT system itself. The configuration settings supplied here affect only operations in a Windows NT DOS shell; that is, they are used to control DOS emulation but do not affect NT operations otherwise.

The first two lines of the Config.SYS file set the LASTDRIVE and FILES parameters. They were derived as defaults from the existing (DOS) Config.SYS file.

```
LASTDRIVE=Z
FILES=20
```

If you examine your DOS Config.SYS file, you will probably notice several other instructions that have not been copied. These include stack and buffer settings and, most likely, one or more device assignments. The reasons are quite simple: They're not necessary under NT and are not required for DOS emulation.

The next three lines, however, are supplied directly by Windows NT, although they, too, are provided for DOS shell compatibility.

```
DOS=HIGH, UMB
DEVICE=C:\NT\SYSTEM\HIMEM.SYS
SHELL=C:\NT\SYSTEM\COMMAND.COM /P C:\NT\SYSTEM
```

If you will stop for a moment and remember that NT is a 32-bit operating system and uses direct memory addressing of up to 4GB of RAM, you'll realize that it does not require a HIMEM.SYS driver or provisions to load DOS high. The first two instructions here begin to look like a buggywhip socket stuck on a Ferrari. And, in some respects, this simile is not entirely inaccurate. However, there are two important elements to recognize here:

- Setting DOS high and using an upper memory block (UMB) is, again, a simulation for the DOS shell.

- The HIMEM.SYS extended memory driver referenced is not the same HIMEM.SYS driver that you were probably using under DOS because, once more, this is a simulation provided for DOS shell compatibility.

Finally, the SHELL instruction also references NT's version of the Command .COM utility and points to NT's SYSTEM directory, not to the DOS SYSTEM directory. It directs DOS shell operations to use the NT version of Command.COM, not the DOS version.

NOTE   If you compare the \NT\SYSTEM directory with the \DOS directory, you may note that virtually all of the DOS utility programs are duplicated within the NT directory.

The Autoexec.NT/Autoexec.BAT Settings

Like the NT Config.SYS instructions, the NT Autoexec.BAT settings are derived, in part, from the DOS Autoexec.BAT file that exists at the time NT is installed. Also, the settings in the NT Autoexec.BAT file are intended primarily, although not entirely, for use by the NT DOS shell—or more accurately, for use by applications executing under the NT DOS shell.

The first five lines in the NT Autoexec.BAT file were derived directly from the existing DOS Autoexec.BAT file, followed by a three-line remark note supplied by NT.

```
@ECHO OFF
SET TEMP=C:\TEMP
PATH C:\XBAT;C:\QEMM;E:\WINWORD;E:\WINDOWS;C:\;C:\DOS;
PATH %PATH%D:\BC\BIN;C:\UTIL;F:\VIEWER;D:\NORTON
SET NU=D:\NORTON
REM NT will inherit environment variables such as SET and PATH
REM found in this file. TSRs and other programs may also be
REM started here.
```

As the REM comments explain, NT does inherit at least some of the SET and PATH variables that are defined in the Autoexec.BAT file. Unlike the Config.SYS file settings, these settings are not exclusively for use by the DOS shell.

Also, as noted, if any TSRs (terminate-and-stay-resident programs) or other DOS applications are required—for use in the DOS shell, of course—such applications would be invoked at this point.

The next instruction in the Autoexec.BAT file invokes the network redirector. If your system is not installed on a network, you may want to comment out this line.

```
REM Install network redirector (load before dosx.exe)
LH C:\NT\SYSTEM\REDIR
REM Install DPMI support
LH C:\NT\SYSTEM\DOSX
```

Last, the DOSX utility is invoked to load the DOS Protected Mode Interface (DPMI), which supports both the DOS shell and Windows 3.x applications.

WARNING   Before you modify either the Config.NT/Config.SYS or Autoexec.NT/ Autoexec.BAT file, make a backup copy on a different drive or directory, or under a different extension such as .SAV. This way, if your modifications don't work as you intended, you can restore the backup version.

Differences between Windows 95 and NT

The simplest thing to say at this point would be to assert that there are no real differences between Windows 95 and Windows NT 4.0, except that that would be an oversimplification; in truth, there are worlds of differences. From a programming standpoint, however, most of the differences are invisible. Most applications written to run under Windows 95 will also execute under NT, and vice versa. There are exceptions, but they are just that—exceptions.

Sometimes, an application will perform on one system but not on the other because the developers have made use of some tricks that are possible under one operating system but not in the other. In other cases, applications may have been written to depend on operating system–specific features. NT does support some features, such as networking APIs, that are not found under Windows 95. When this is the case, it will be noted in the discussion in the book.

In any case, if you are developing for a cross-system application, the only real solution is simply to periodically try your application on both operating systems. Then, if the application functions on one and not on the other, that's when the fun begins…and best of luck.

Dual-Boot System Operations

Often, the biggest conflict between Windows 95 and NT is not an incompatibility issue but a simple misunderstanding. On a dual-boot system, an application installed under one operating system may be visible under the other (because all of its files are visible on the hard drive), but it will not run on the second operating system. This is usually not because of incompatibility but because the installation needs to be repeated on the second operating system.

Annoying? Yes, but there's a good reason for this annoyance. When an application is installed under either operating system, the installation does more than simply create a directory and copy some files. Sometimes, the installation also copies DLL (dynamic link library) or other special files that are installed in the operating system's /SYSTEM directory. But each operating system has its own /SYSTEM directory, and the contents are not cross-compatible; they cannot be consolidated. Almost always, during installation, entries are made to the operating system's registry. These are also separate and not cross-compatible.

NOTE   Some simple applications, which require no setup at all, can be executed on either operating system without installation. In such cases, the applications are usually self-contained and do not rely on DLLs or registry entries.

Fortunately, the solution is relatively simple. If, for example, you are installing Microsoft Visual C++ and you wish to use it for both Windows 95 and NT on a dual-boot system, follow these steps:

1. Boot either operating system.

2. Perform the installation normally.

3. Reboot the second operating system.

4. Repeat the installation to the same directory.

A dual-installation does not require duplicate directories and duplicate files, except for any files that are copied to each operating system's /SYSTEM directory. What is required is to make duplicate registry entries (and you don't want to try to do these by hand, because it just isn't worth the trouble).

After installation, if the application fails to execute on one or the other operating system for some reason, check the application documentation to see if there are some special requirements or system incompatibilities. Then try the installation a second time.

The hardware and software requirements, as well as the considerations for a dual-boot system if you are running both Windows NT and 95, are basics for NT and 95 programming. In the next chapter, we'll begin by constructing two simple applications. We'll build a Windows version of the traditional "Hello, World" demo program and a template application that can be used as the basis for other applications.

CHAPTER

TWO

2

Application Programming for Windows NT/95

- "Hello World" in Windows NT/95

- A template for Windows application programs

- Conventions used in Windows programming

For DOS programmers, writing applications for Windows NT or Windows 95 constitutes a distinct and abrupt departure from familiar and accepted practices. In fact, this departure is sometimes so abrupt that many programmers find themselves wondering if they have changed languages as well as operating systems. They are surprised to discover distinctly Pascal-like elements appearing in their C code and to find that previously familiar shortcuts and procedures, such as `main()` or `exit(0)`, are either no longer valid or, in some cases, even fatal to the application or the operating system.

Others, particularly those who have worked with previous versions of Windows, or even with OS/2, may find these new practices use familiar techniques, although they sometimes bear new names or have somewhat different syntax. Unfortunately, those who have programmed applications for Windows 3.*x* (either 3.0 or 3.1) may find themselves the most confused of all, because many of the differences are slight; yet in many cases, these very slight differences are also very critical.

So, even if you're an experienced Windows application programmer, you should take the time to study programming practices for Windows NT and 95. Chapter 1 discussed requirements for NT/95 programming. Now it's time to look at the components of a Windows program, beginning, as the White King advised Alice, "at the beginning."

WinHello: An Introductory Windows Program

Traditionally, the introductory C program example has always been a "Hello, World" message, provided by about a half-dozen lines of code. For Windows NT/95, however, the equivalent introductory example will be a bit more complex, requiring some 130+ lines of code, or roughly 20 times longer. This is not so much because NT/95 is that much more complex than DOS, but more a reflection of the fact that any Windows application, even a rudimentary example, operates in a more complex environment than its DOS counterpart. Accordingly, the Windows application requires some minimal provisions to match this environment.

Still, the flip side of this coin does not mean that all applications will be larger and more complex than their DOS counterparts. Instead, more commonly, larger applications will, under Windows, become smaller than their DOS counterparts. This is because many functions and services that are supplied by the application itself under DOS are called externally as system functions under Windows.

NOTE Because Windows applications generally include image (bitmapped) re-sources, which their DOS counterparts lack, direct comparisons of .EXE file sizes are generally not valid. The real differences in size are more readily apparent in comparing source code sizes and development times.

Theory aside, however, the WinHello source example is considerably larger than its DOS counterpart. Its actual size depends on how the application was created. For example, WinHello1, a simple application program using no class definitions, consists of one source file; WinHello2, an MFC (Microsoft Foundation Classes) application created using AppWizard, has 20 source files (WinHello1 and WinHello2 are on the CD that comes with this book).

The Windows.H Header File

The Windows.H header file is the one essential include file required in all Windows source code. The reason for this is simple: Windows.H contains all of the definitions for Windows messages, constants, flag values, data structures, macros, and other mnemonics that permit the programmer to work without needing to memorize thousands of hexadecimal values and their functions.

For earlier versions of Windows, the Windows.H file has been a single, massive text file (about 1000 lines). With NT/95, the Windows.H file itself has shrunk; it now consists principally of a list of other include files, the most important of which is the WinUser.H include file. This include file is the current counterpart of the older Windows.H file and, like its predecessor, is also about 1000 lines in length.

NOTE The following references to definitions, provided by the Windows.H file, are most likely to be found, physically, in either the WinUser.H or Win-Def.H files. Any of these references, however, may be located in other sources listed as include files in Windows.H.

If you are using MFC, the Windows.H header is included in the AppWizard-supplied STDAFX.H header as:

```
#define VC_EXTRALEAN      // Exclude rarely used stuff from Windows
headers
#include <afxwin.h>       // MFC core and standard components
#include <afxext.h>       // MFC extensions
#ifndef _AFX_NO_AFXCMN_SUPPORT
#include <afxcmn.h>       // MFC support for Win95 Common Controls
#endif // _AFX_NO_AFXCMN_SUPPORT
```

The WinMain Procedure

Just as every DOS C program has a procedure titled main at its heart, every Windows program has a similar entry point with the title WinMain (and, yes, this title is case-sensitive). Also, just as a DOS C program may include provisions within the main procedure declaration to retrieve command-line parameters, the WinMain declaration includes a similar provision in the lpszCmdParam parameter, even though command-line parameters are rarely used under Windows.

However, unlike in DOS programming, the declarations used for WinMain are not optional and must be declared exactly in the order and form shown, regardless of whether each specific argument will be used or ignored. Remember, because the application's WinMain procedure is being called only indirectly by the user, with the actual calling format supplied by Windows, the calling format flexibility present in a DOS context is absent under Windows.

Also note that the reserved word PASCAL is used in all exported function declarations, indicating to the compiler that Pascal rather than C ordering is used for all arguments (values) pushed onto the stack. While C commonly uses inverted order, placing the least-significant bytes first on the stack, Windows uses Pascal ordering, which, like Unix, places the most-significant bytes first.

Exported functions are functions that will be called from outside the class, or in the case of a DLL, from other applications outside the unit (library). In a Windows application, where subroutines are called from Windows itself or where a member function in one class is called from outside the class, even if both belong to the same application, the Pascal calling order is necessary. This is a small but crucial difference.

On the other hand, all internal function declarations (functions and subprocedures called directly from other procedures within the application) will expect

As far as the procedure definitions and how argument lists are declared in the definitions, it makes absolutely no difference whether the PASCAL or C calling conventions are being used. These conventions affect only how the arguments are handled internally (on the stack) and do not in any way affect how the programmer constructs the argument lists.

arguments to appear in standard C order and should not be declared using the PASCAL specification.

```
int PASCAL WinMain( HANDLE hInstance,
                    HANDLE hPrevInstance,
                    LPSTR  lpszCmdParam,
                    int    nCmdShow )
```

Of the four calling arguments, the first two are of primary importance. The data type HANDLE refers to a 32-bit, unsigned value; the hInstance and hPrevInstance arguments are unique identifiers supplied by the Windows NT and 95 systems. Unlike DOS applications where only one program (TSRs excepted) is active at a time, multitasking systems require unique identification, not only for each application, but also for each instance of an application that may be executing. Ergo, the hInstance and hPrevInstance parameters are assigned only when an application instance becomes active. They provide the equivalents of the "task ID" and "process ID" values common in other multitasking environments.

The data types used in these declarations may be unfamiliar to DOS programmers. See the introduction to Windows data types later in this chapter for more details. Windows programmers should note that the 16-bit HANDLE used in Windows 3.x is now a 32-bit unsigned value, which is a change that affects a number of aspects of NT/95 programming. These changes will be discussed in detail in Chapter 4.

The hPrevInstance (previous instance) identifier is the hInstance identifier previously assigned to the most recent instance of an application that is already executing. If there is no previous instance of the application currently running, which is frequently the case, this argument will be null (0). The reasons for this second process identifier will be demonstrated presently.

The third parameter, lpszCmdParam, is a long (FAR) pointer to a null-terminated (ASCIIZ) string containing any command-line parameters passed to the program instance. Although the command-line parameters are provided by Windows rather than a conventional (DOS) command line, these can be specified through the Run dialog box invoked from the Program Manager or passed through the File Manager. In general, however, Windows applications rely on dialog boxes for specific input and on .INI entries for default values, rather than expecting command-line parameters.

The fourth calling parameter, nCmdShow, is simply an integer argument indicating whether the newly launched application will be displayed as a normal window or initially displayed as an icon. Usage for the nCmdShow parameter will be shown presently.

Next, following the procedure declaration itself, a brief list of local variable declarations appears.

```
{
    static char szAppName[] = "WinHello";
    HWND        hwnd;
    MSG         msg;
    WNDCLASS    wc;
```

The data types used in the declaration will be covered in more detail later in the chapter. Here's a quick rundown:

- HWND identifies a window handle.

- MSG identifies a message value.

- WNDCLASS refers to a record structure used to pass a number of values relevant to the application's main window.

Registering a Window Class

The first task accomplished within the WinMain procedure depends on the hPrevInstance argument passed. If a previous instance of this application is already active, there's no need to register the window class a second time. But it's more likely, of course, that this is the first instance of the application (hPrevInstance is null) and, therefore, the window class definitions must be assigned and the window class registered.

The wc structure is defined in Windows.H (which must be included in all Windows applications). Of the WNDCLASS record fields, the second (lpfnWndProc) and last (lpszClassName) are the most important. The remainder of the fields can usually remain unchanged from one application to another. (See the source code for Template.C at the end of this chapter for another example.)

The first field is the window-style specification. In this example, it is assigned two style flag values (combined by ORing bitwise). The CS_ flags are defined in Windows.H as 16-bit constants, each with one flag bit set. Here the CS_HREDRAW and CS_VREDRAW flags indicate that the window should be redrawn completely anytime the horizontal or vertical size changes. Thus, for the WinHello demo, if the window size changes, the window display is completely redrawn, with the "Hello, World" message string recentered in the new display.

```
if( ! hPrevInstance )
   {
      wc.style          = CS_HREDRAW | CS_VREDRAW;
      wc.lpfnWndProc    = WndProc;
```

The second field in the WNDCLASS structure, lpfnWndProc, is a pointer to the exported procedure—WndProc, in this example—which will handle all Windows messages for this application. The type prefix lpfn identifies this field as a "long pointer to function." But realize that these prefix conventions are provided for the benefit of the programmer. They are not absolutes, nor do these designations place any constraints on the compiler. However, predefined fields and identifiers can be considered an exception. Although these can be changed, they are best left as defined, if only for the simple reason that redefinitions could easily result in a cascade of changes and confusion.

The next two record fields are integers, which are reserved to specify extra information about the class or window styles. Commonly, neither is required and, by default, both are initialized as zeros (0). (Incidentally, the cb_ prefix stands for count of bytes.)

```
wc.cbClsExtra     = 0;
    wc.cbWndExtra    = 0;
    wc.hInstance     = hInstance;
```

The next field, hInstance, is simply the recipient of the hInstance argument passed by Windows when the program is initially called. This is also one field assignment that can be considered constant for all applications.

The next three data fields currently assign default values for the application's icon, cursor, and background color and pattern.

```
wc.hIcon          = LoadIcon( NULL, IDI_APPLICATION );
wc.hCursor        = LoadCursor( NULL, IDC_ARROW );
wc.hbrBackground  = GetStockObject( WHITE_BRUSH );
```

The default IDI_APPLICATION specification for the icon assigns the predefined image of a white square with a black border. The IDC_ARROW cursor assigns the stock cursor graphic of a slanted arrow.

In the third assignment, the hbrBackground field contains the background color and pattern used for the application's client region. (The hbr stands for handle to brush, where "brush" refers to a pixel pattern used to fill or paint an area.)

Next, since this application does not have a menu assigned, the menu name is entered as a null value. The class name (lpszClassName) is assigned the null-terminated (ASCIIZ) string defined previously.

```
    wc.lpszMenuName  = NULL;
    wc.lpszClassName = szAppName;
    RegisterClass( &wc );
}
```

And last within this conditional subprocess, the RegisterClass function is called with the wc structure passed as a parameter (by address) to register this window class definition with the NT/95 operating system. As mentioned previously, this registration is required only once. Thereafter, the registration and values assigned are available, as long as any instance of the application remains active, to any new instances of the application. Once all instances of the application have closed, the window class registration is discarded, and any future instance will need to execute the class registration process again.

Creating an Application Window

While the previous step, registering a window class, has defined characteristics that are common to all instances of the application, this has not yet created the application window itself. Instead, unlike the RegisterClass function call, which is called only once, every instance of the application must call the CreateWindow function to produce the actual window display.

The handle to the application window that is returned by the CreateWindow function will be used later as an argument in other function calls as a unique identifier for the actual window belonging to the application instance. But, while many properties of the application class have already been defined, other properties specific to this instance of the application have not; they are passed now as parameters to the CreateWindow function.

```
hwnd = CreateWindow(
    szAppName,                    // window class name
    "Hello, World - Windows_NT Style",
                                  // window caption
```

The first two parameters passed are the application class name—the same ASCIIZ string that was used when the class was registered—and the application's initial window caption. Of course, the second of these is optional and, if the window is defined without a caption bar or if no caption is desired, this parameter should be passed as null.

The third parameter defines the window style and, generically, is passed as WS_OVERLAPPEDWINDOW, a value that is a combination of individual flags defined in Windows.H.

```
WS_OVERLAPPEDWINDOW,    // window style
CW_USEDEFAULT,          // initial X position
CW_USEDEFAULT,          // initial Y position
CW_USEDEFAULT,          // initial X size
CW_USEDEFAULT,          // initial Y size
```

The fourth through seventh parameters establish the application window's initial position and size. They can be passed as explicit values or, more often, as CW_USEDEFAULT. This parameter instructs Windows to use the default values for an overlapped window, positioning each successive overlapped window at a stepped horizontal and vertical offset from the upper-left corner of the screen.

The next parameter is passed as null for the simple reason that this application is not associated with a parent window. Alternatively, if this window were to be called as a child process belonging to another application, the parent's window handle would be passed as a parameter here.

```
NULL,                   // parent window handle
NULL,                   // window menu handle
```

The ninth parameter using in calling the CreateWindow function is also passed as null, directing the application to use the default system menu. Note, however, that the menu in question is the window frame's pull-down menu (upper-left icon on most window frames), not the menu bar (or "toolbar"), which is defined as an application resource and assigned during the application class registration.

The tenth calling parameter, which can never be passed as null, is the same instance handle originally supplied by the NT/95 system.

```
hInstance,                  // program instance handle
NULL  );                    // creation parameters
```

The final parameter, again null in this example, may in other cases provide a pointer to additional data for use either by the application window or by some subsequent process. In most examples, however, this will be an empty (null) argument.

Now, after CreateWindow has been called, the application window has been created internally in NT/95's "world view" but does not yet appear on the actual screen display. Therefore, the next step is to call the ShowWindow function, passing as parameters the hwnd value returned by CreateWindow and the nCmdShow argument supplied when WinMain was initially called.

```
ShowWindow( hwnd, nCmdShow );
UpdateWindow( hwnd );
```

The ShowWindow function, however, contrary to what you might assume, does only a portion of the task of creating (painting) the window display. It is principally responsible for creating the window frame, caption bar, menu bar, and minimize/maximize buttons. But what this function does not create is the client window area—the display area specific to the application itself. Therefore, one more function call is necessary before the window display is complete: a call to the UpdateWindow function with the hwnd window handle as an argument (which actually posts a WM_PAINT message to the application instructing it to repaint its own window area—a process that will be discussed in a moment).

And this completes the process of registering a window class, defining and creating the window itself, and updating the screen to show the window. But, while more than a small task, this is also only preparation for the application; the real task has not yet begun, but will momentarily. One last, but very essential, portion of the WinMain function remains: the message-handling loop.

The Message-Handling Loop

Windows creates and manages a separate message queue for each active Windows program instance. Thus, when any keyboard or mouse event occurs, Windows translates this event into a message value. This value is placed in the application's message queue, where it waits until it is retrieved by the application instance, which is precisely the purpose of the message-handling loop.

The message-handling loop begins by calling the GetMessage function to retrieve messages from the application instance's message queue. As long as the message retrieved is not a WM_QUIT message (0x0012), GetMessage will return a TRUE (nonzero) result. The actual message value is returned in the msg structure, which was passed by its address.

```
while( GetMessage( &msg, NULL, 0, 0 ) )
{
```

The syntax for the GetMessage function is defined as:

```
BOOL GetMessage( lpMsg, HWND, wMsgFilterMin, wMsgFilterMax )
```

In most cases, only the first parameter is actually used (to return the message itself). The remaining three parameters are usually passed as null or zero.

The initial parameter is a pointer to a message structure to receive the message information retrieved and, subsequently, to pass this data on through to the TranslateMessage and DispatchMessage functions. And, obviously, without this parameter, there would be little point in calling the GetMessage function at all.

NOTE The second parameter is optional but can be used to identify a specific window (belonging to the calling application) and to restrict retrieval to messages that belong to that window. When passed as null, as in the present example, GetMessage retrieves all messages addressed to any window belonging to the application placing the call. The GetMessage function does not retrieve messages addressed to windows belonging to any other application.

The third and fourth parameters provide filter capabilities, restricting the message types returned. When both parameters are passed as 0, no filtering occurs. Alternatively, constants such as WM_KEYFIRST and WM_KEYLAST could be passed as filter values to restrict message retrieval to keyboard events or, by using WM_MOUSEFIRST and WM_MOUSELAST, to retrieve only mouse-related messages.

Filters and window selection aside, however, the GetMessage function (together with the PeekMessage and WaitMessage functions) has another important characteristic.

Conventionally, loop statements monopolize the system until terminated, thus preempting or preventing other operations for the duration of the loop. And, in other circumstances—remember this as a *caution*—even under Windows, loop operations can tie up system resources.

The GetMessage function, however, has the ability to preempt the loop operation to yield control to other applications when no messages are available for the current application, or when WM_PAINT or WM_TIMER messages directed to other tasks are available. Thus, it can give other applications their share of CPU time to execute.

For the present, when the application receives an event message (other than WM_QUIT), the message value is passed. First, it goes to the Windows Translate-Message function for any keystroke translation that may be specific to the application. Then it is passed to the DispatchMessage handler, where the message information is passed to the next appropriate message-handling procedure (back to Windows, either for immediate handling or, indirectly, for forwarding to the exported WndProc procedure).

```
        TranslateMessage( &msg );
        DispatchMessage( &msg );
    }
```

Finally, when the message-processing loop terminates, the wParam argument from the final message retrieved is, in turn, returned to the calling application—the NT/95 Desktop itself.

```
        return msg.wParam;
    }
```

Messages and Event-Driven Programming

In its simplest form, message-driven programming (also known as *event-driven* programming) is a process by which various subprocesses and/or applications communicate. In Windows, messages are the process used by Windows itself to manage a multitasking system and to share keyboard, mouse, and other resources by distributing information to applications, application instances, and processes within an application.

Thus, under Windows, instead of applications receiving information directly from the keyboard or the mouse driver, the NT/95 operating system intercepts all input information, packaging this information using the MSG message structure (detailed in the following section) and then forwarding the prepared messages to the appropriate recipients. In turn, the recipient applications use Translate-Message for application-specific interpretation (particularly accelerator key assignments) before calling DispatchMessage to forward individual traffic items to their appropriate handlers.

Furthermore, the process described is not limited to keyboard and mouse events. Instead, this includes all input devices (including ports), as well as messages generated by application child and subprocesses, Windows timers, or, quite frequently, by Windows itself.

Abstract descriptions, however, provide only a theoretical outline without really illustrating how these processes function. Therefore, a fuller explanation will be left until subsequent examples in this book can provide both hands-on experience and some practical illustrations (beginning, of course, with messages processed by the WinHello demo).

But first, let's take a look at the message record structure and how messages are organized.

The Message Record Structure

The MSG (message structure) record type is defined in WinUser.H as:

```
typedef struct tagMSG
{  HWND    hwnd;
   UINT    message;
   WPARAM  wParam;
   LPARAM  lParam;
   DWORD   time;
   POINT   pt;} MSG, *PMSG, NEAR *NPMSG, FAR *LPMSG;
```

The POINT data type is defined in WinDef.H as:

```
typedef struct tagPOINT
{  int  x;
   int  y; } POINT, *PPOINT, NEAR *NPPOINT, FAR *LPPOINT;
```

The message-event fields defined are used as:

- hWnd: The handle of the specific window to which the message is directed.

> **NOTE**
>
> Note that each application is itself composed of a series of separate windows. These windows include the frame, the caption bar, the system menu, and minimize and maximize buttons, as well as the application's main display, which is referred to as the *client window* or, occasionally, the *display window*. Normally, only messages directed to the client window will be forwarded, by the DispatchMessage procedure, to the application's WndProc procedure. Messages directed to other application windows are generally handled indirectly (by NT), even though this may result, in turn, in further messages being sent to the client window.

- message: A 16-bit value identifying the message. Constants corresponding to all message values are provided through Windows.H and begin with the WM_ prefix (which stands for window message). For example, a mouse button event message might be identified by the constant WM_LBUTTON_DOWN (left button pressed).

- wParam: A 32-bit (double word) message parameter. The value format and meaning depend on the primary event message type. Variously, the wParam argument might convey a coordinate point pair, use the low-word value to identify a secondary message type, provide some other type of data, or be ignored entirely. In many cases, the wParam value will be treated as two separate word values with different functions.

- lParam: A 32-bit (long) message parameter. The value and meaning of this parameter depend on the primary event message type. Variously, the lParam argument might provide a pointer to a string or record structure; break down as a group of word, byte, or flag values; or, quite frequently, be completely unused.

- time: The double word time value identifies the time the message was placed in the message queue.

- pt: This field contains the mouse coordinates at the time the message was placed in the message queue (irrespective of the message-event type or origin).

Note that these last two fields are not passed to the `WndProc` procedure. Instead, these two fields are used only by NT/95, principally to resolve any conflict over the order of events and, of course, to determine where a specific event should be addressed.

The WndProc Procedure

The `WndProc` procedure is the point where each application actually begins to function. Remember, the `WndProc` procedure receives messages indirectly from the NT/95 operating system, but the `WndProc` procedure determines the application's response to the messages received.

Previously, when the application window class was registered, the address of the `WndProc` subroutine was passed to Windows as:

```
wc.lpfnWndProc = WndProc;
```

And, given this address, Windows calls `WndProc` directly, passing event messages in the form of four parameters, as:

```
long FAR PASCAL WndProc( HWND hwnd,   UINT msg,
                         UINT wParam, LONG lParam )
```

The four calling parameters received correspond to the first four fields of the `MSG` structure described in the previous section, beginning with the `hwnd` parameter identifying the window to which the message is directed. Since most applications have only one client window that will be addressed thus, this parameter may seem superfluous. This parameter will, however, frequently be needed as an argument for use by other processes.

At the present, it's the second calling parameter, `msg`, that is immediately crucial and identifies the window event message. The third and fourth parameters, `wParam` and `lParam`, provide amplifying information to accompany the window event message.

Typically, the `WndProc` procedure does relatively little or nothing itself outside of the `switch...case` responding to the `msg` parameter. In the WinHello demo, local response is provided for only two event messages: the `WM_PAINT` and `WM_DESTROY` messages. All other event messages are handled by default (by the NT/95 operating system).

The first of these two, `WM_PAINT`, is a message that is generally not issued directly. It will be issued indirectly anytime an application window is created, moved, resized, restored from an icon, uncovered by a change in some other application window, or something else has occurred—in this or in some other application—to invalidate the client area of the present application.

The DOS equivalent of the WinHello program would consist principally of a print statement, possibly with an optional clear screen statement. For the Windows version, however, there are differences for two main reasons:

- Because the response to the WM_PAINT message is not a one-time occurrence

- Because a bit more is accomplished than simply dumping the text to the screen

The first requirement, before anything can be written to the client window, is for the application to retrieve a handle (hdc) to the device context (the output device or, in this example, the screen). After the screen update is finished, this handle will be released by calling the EndPaint function.

```
switch( msg )
{
    case WM_PAINT:
        hdc = BeginPaint( hwnd, &ps );
        GetClientRect( hwnd, &rect );
```

After retrieving the device context handle, the GetClientRect procedure is called to retrieve the rect structure with coordinates describing the client window. The rect structure consists of four fields, which report coordinates for the client window. However, the coordinates reported are relative to the client window itself. Therefore, the *left* and *top* fields are returned as zeros, and the *right* and *bottom* fields return the current width and height of the client window (reported in pixels).

Once the window coordinates have been retrieved, the rect structure can be used as an argument in the next step to specify the region where the actual message will be drawn.

```
DrawText( hdc, "Hello, World!", -1, &rect,
    DT_SINGLELINE | DT_CENTER | DT_VCENTER );
```

Since print statements, per se, cannot be used in Windows (because they are unsuited for a graphics display environment), the DrawText function is used instead. DrawText begins with the hdc argument providing access to the active display, followed by the string (text) to be drawn.

The third parameter, -1, indicates that the string argument is a null-terminated string. Alternatively, this parameter could be a value specifying the string length, with the second parameter an indirect reference to a character array.

The fourth argument is the address of the `rect` structure, identifying an area where the string will be drawn. The fifth argument is a combination of flags that set alignment and restrict the text drawn to a single display line. Other elements affecting the display, such as font, size, and color, use the system default settings; although these factors are subject to change, as you will see in future demos.

NOTE The `sprintf` statement can still be used to format text to a buffer array, but direct screen print statements are not allowed.

Last, the `EndPaint` function is called, again with the client window handle and the paint structure (`ps`) as arguments. This function releases the device context and validates the now-restored client area, and incidentally, completes the response to the WM_PAINT message.

```
EndPaint( hwnd, &ps );
return( 0 );
```

The second application message requiring a local response is the WM_DESTROY message, which is issued when the application is ready to close. This message can be generated via several channels, as will be shown later, but for our example, it is issued only if/when the system menu Close option is selected.

```
case WM_DESTROY:
    PostQuitMessage(0);
    break;
```

The WM_DESTROY message is issued to give the application an opportunity to do any necessary cleanup before shutting down. Therefore, as circumstances demand, the application response at this point could include provisions for calling a dialog box to request confirmation, for closing/saving files, or for any other final tasks required for a smooth exit.

Finally (unless, of course, termination is to be aborted), the WM_DESTROY response is completed by calling the `PostQuitMessage` function, which, in turn, places a WM_QUIT message in the application's message queue to terminate the message loop in `WinMain`.

Explicit handling has been provided for only two of the messages that might be sent to this application. Provisions are also required to return to Windows for processing all messages that have not been explicitly handled here, as a default case.

```
        default:                       // if msg unprocessed,
            return(                     //     return to Windows
                DefWindowProc( hwnd, msg, wParam, lParam ) );
    }
    return( NULL );
}
```

This default provision returns the message—precisely as it was originally received—to Windows, then also returns the result from DefWindowProc to the Windows calling process. This final provision should be considered standard for all WndProc message-handler procedures.

For a Windows program, the .C source code is only a part of the story. In most cases, the application will also incorporate an .H header file and, almost always, a .RES resource file. These two elements will be discussed in later chapters. For the present, however, there is one more source file that all Windows application sources require, without exception.

The .DEF File

When a program is compiled, the compiler processes each .C or .CPP source file (and any included .H header files) to produce an .OBJ (object) file bearing the same name. Subsequently, the linker combines .OBJ and .LIB (library) files to produce the executable program.

For DOS applications, this would be essentially all that's required. For Windows applications, however, the linker also expects a .DEF (definition) file. This definition file consists of simple ASCII text, but it contains an essential series of instructions for the linker.

> **TIP**
>
> Applications or DLLs produced using classes defined with the AFX_EXT_CLASS declaration may omit the .DEF definition files. The AFX_EXT_CLASS declaration specifies the entire class as exported and, therefore, available for linking by other applications.

```
;=======================================;
;  WinHello module-definition file      ;
;  used by LINK.EXE                      ;
;=======================================;

NAME           WinHello
DESCRIPTION    'Hello, World ... Windows NT/95 Style'
EXETYPE        WINDOWS
STUB           'WINSTUB.EXE'
CODE   PRELOAD MOVEABLE DISCARDABLE
DATA   PRELOAD MOVEABLE MULTIPLE
HEAPSIZE       1024
STACKSIZE      5120
```

From the top, the .DEF file begins with the application name and a brief description, both of which are optional and could be omitted (however, including a name and description is recommended for clarity and to alleviate future confusion). The third line, EXETYPE, is essentially a binary flag stating either that this is intended to be a Windows executable (WINDOWS) or a dynamic link library (DLL). Alternatively, if this code were being transported to OS/2 for compilation, the specification would be OS2 to identify that operating platform.

The fourth line, STUB, specifies the inclusion, during link, of the WINSTUB.EXE file. The stub program is simply a brief executable that, if the compiled application is called from DOS, displays a warning message stating that the application can be run only from Windows. Similarly, for the OS/2 system, 'OS2STUB.EXE' might be specified, or you might design your own stub program to be referenced as 'MYSTUB.EXE'.

The fifth and sixth lines provide flags identifying how the code and data segments should be treated during execution. Customarily, both the code and data are defined as PRELOAD (load immediately) and MOVEABLE (relocatable in memory). Also as a default, the code segment is normally defined as DISCARDABLE, permitting the memory used by the code segment to be overwritten when memory resources become limited. (Of course, discarding the code segment also means that the application will have to be reloaded from disk before execution can continue.) The MULTIPLE specification for the data segment permits separate data for each active instance of an application. Alternatively, using a SINGLE data specification forces data to be shared between multiple instances.

Next, the HEAPSIZE and STACKSIZE specifications provide default heap and stack memory requirements. The values shown are the suggested defaults and should serve most applications.

The preceding statements can be considered defaults suitable for virtually all applications, and they can be used as a template for future use. The final statements, however, are far more application-specific and, equally, far more important to the application's compiling, linking, and executing correctly.

Last, but certainly important (and perhaps also the least familiar element in the .DEF file), is the EXPORTS statement, together with its subsequent list of export labels.

```
EXPORTS
    WndProc
```

Unlike DOS applications, where the application itself is responsible for all calls to internal procedures, Windows applications depend on exporting principal subprocedures, placing these entry points under the control of the operating system (such as NT), where each will respond to control messages sent by the operating system. For this indirect control to function, the link process must ensure that the addresses of these procedures are known and available; ergo, each must be explicitly exported, which is accomplished by references in the .DEF file.

In this example, only one procedure is exported, WndProc, which provides the principal control structure for the application and forms the absolute minimum required by any Windows application (although the name used may be any valid label desired). However, it is not unusual for applications to have several, dozens, or in very complex situations, even hundreds of exported procedures.

The WinHello.DEF and WinHello.C files provide the minimum necessary to compile an executable NT/95 program. The complete source code for the WinHello program appears at the end of this chapter. Also, for your convenience, WinHello.BAT and WinHello NMake files are included in the complete listings at the end of this chapter.

For future applications, this chapter provides a second program example, which uses a slightly different approach. The next example is provided as a generic template for your own application development, and also to demonstrate a second style for application development.

A Template for NT Application Programs: The Template Program

The Template example, like WinHello, is a simple but functional Windows application. But unlike WinHello, Template has been designed specifically for use as a template for your own application development, and it is also used as the basis for all of the examples in this book.

Unlike familiar DOS programs, which generally have little, if any, source code in common—the `main` procedure aside—most Windows applications have a number of elements in common:

- The same `WinMain` procedure can be used by hundreds of programs, remaining unchanged except for a few string labels identifying the application by name.

- Essentially the same `WndProc` procedure can be used over and over. In this area, the sample provided by the Template application will need to be expanded and altered to provide the specific needs of each separate application.

- Although the About dialog box used in the Template application may not be satisfactory for all purposes, it does provide an example for use in constructing and programming generic dialog boxes.

The Template.C Source Code

The Template.C source code begins with two include statements referencing, the Windows.H header first, and then the Template.H header.

```
#include <windows.h>
#include "template.h"

#define  APP_MENU    "TemplateMenu"
#define  APP_ICON    "Template"

HANDLE hInst;
char    szAppTitle[] = "Application Template";
char    szAppName[]  = "Template";
```

In the WinHello program, only one string identifier was declared—in the `WinMain` procedure for the `szAppClass`—and all the other string references were entered directly as required.

For the Template application, two strings and two defines are declared, global to the entire program. This format was chosen for two reasons:

- Because the instructions referencing these strings are contained in an include file, not in the main source file

- Because this provides a convenient means to change these lines to match other applications without needing to search through the entire program for their occurrence

In some cases, the menu and icon names could also be declared as string variables. This format uses `#define` statements because there are circumstances where a `NULL` argument may be needed instead of strings (as you will see in Chapter 3).

In later examples, additional references will appear, similar to one of these two declaration styles, and generally for the same reasons.

The balance of the Template.C source code is quite brief and contains only three functions: `WinMain`, `WndProc`, and `AboutProc`. The latter two are exported procedures and declared as such in Template.DEF.

The first of these, `WinMain`, is much briefer than its equivalent in the WinHello demo, even though both accomplish the same tasks. In Template's version of the `WinMain` procedure, however, the provisions required to initialize the application class and to initialize application instances have been transferred, as independent subprocedures, to the Template.I include file.

The second procedure, `WndProc` in this example (refer to the complete listings at the end of this chapter), provides skeletal structure for application message handling. In this example, only a few message-response provisions are included: the `WM_COMMAND` and `IDM_ABOUT` subcommand messages, and the `WM_DESTROY` message.

The third procedure, `AboutProc`, parallels the `WndProc` procedure in many respects but provides message handling for the About dialog box.

The Template.I File

The Template.I include file contains the two subprocedures mentioned earlier. These are the `InitApplication` procedure, which initializes the application class (if this task has not already been accomplished) and the `InitInstance` procedure, which initializes each instance of the application. The operations and functions provided by both of the functions are essentially identical to the operations described earlier for the WinHello program.

The Template.H Header File

The WinHello demo program did not require an .H header file, but the Template demo (and all further demos in this book) does require a header. In this case, this requirement is dictated by the need to define a new, application-specific message value. Remember, the Windows.H (or the WinDef.H) header supplies the stock definitions used, but values for any messages that are not already provided must be defined in the application's header file, where these definitions can be accessed by both the Resource Editor(s) and the C compiler.

```
//=============================//
//    Template.H header file   //
//=============================//

#define IDM_ABOUT 100
```

In this case, only one message value is required: `IDM_ABOUT`. However, in later examples, much longer lists of defines will be quite common. Also, in most cases, there is no need to worry about value conflicts between values defined in the application header and values defined in the Windows.H header, since these will be used in different contexts.

It may be useful, however, to avoid values less than 100. Using higher values will avoid confusion with some very common standard button IDs and will help you to group values as much as is practical for your own clarity.

Also, many programmers prefer to include forward function declarations in the application header, as shown in the following code. However, including these declarations is optional and, unless required by your own organization and function ordering, they may be omitted entirely.

```
//==========================================//
// forward function declarations (optional) //
//==========================================//

BOOL InitApplication( HANDLE );
BOOL InitInstance( HANDLE, int );
long FAR PASCAL WndProc( HWND, UINT, UINT, LONG );
BOOL FAR PASCAL AboutProc( HWND, UINT, UINT, LONG );
```

The Template.RC Script

The Template.RC script provides the basic elements required for the Template application. We'll discuss application resources, resource files, and resource scripts in detail in later chapters. In brief, the Template application requires three resources: a menu bar (TemplateMenu), a dialog box (AboutDlg), and an icon image (template.ico). Notice also that the Template.RC script includes a reference to the Template.H header file.

```
//================================//
//    Template.RC Resource Script  //
//================================//

#include "windows.h"
#include "template.h"

TemplateMenu MENU
BEGIN
    POPUP "&Help"
    BEGIN
        MENUITEM "&About Template...", IDM_ABOUT
    END
END
```

This section of the Template.RC script creates a simple menu bar with one pull-down menu titled Help. This menu contains a single item, About Template..., which returns the command message value defined by IDM_ABOUT. Of course, most application menus are considerably more complex. We'll get to these complexities in later chapters.

The IDM_ABOUT command message returned from the menu calls a dialog box that is also described in the resource script, as shown in the following lines:

```
AboutDlg DIALOG 22, 17, 144, 75
STYLE DS_MODALFRAME | WS_CAPTION | WS_SYSMENU
CAPTION "About Template"
BEGIN
    CONTROL "The Template application provides", -1,
            "STATIC",
            SS_CENTER | WS_CHILD | WS_VISIBLE | WS_GROUP,
            14,  7, 115, 8
    CONTROL "a generic template for designing", -1,
            "STATIC",
            SS_CENTER | WS_CHILD | WS_VISIBLE | WS_GROUP,
            14, 18, 115, 8
    CONTROL "Windows NT applications.", -1, "STATIC",
            SS_CENTER | WS_CHILD | WS_VISIBLE | WS_GROUP,
            14, 29, 115, 8
    CONTROL "OK", IDOK, "BUTTON", WS_GROUP, 56, 50, 32, 14
END
```

Figure 2.1 shows the About Template dialog box displayed by this code, along with the single Help menu in the menu bar.

FIGURE 2.1

The About Template dialog box

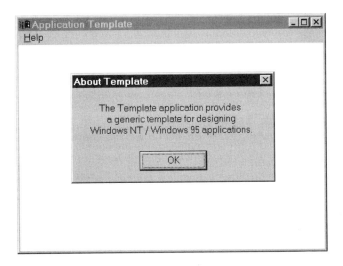

Last, the resource script includes a reference to an .ICO image file, which contains the application icon.

```
Template ICON "template.ico"
```

Since binary images are not readily adaptable to the present format (the printed page), you will need to use an icon editor to create a sample icon image with the Template.ICO file name, or select an appropriate image from any of the many available sources.

A complete listing for the Template program, including the Template.C, Template.DEF, Template.H, Template.BAT, and NMake Template instruction files, appears at the end of this chapter. Because compiled resource files (.RES) are not practical to include as listings, a resource script file (.RC) is included. This resource script file references a Template.ICO (icon image) file, which is a binary file and is included on the CD.

NOTE The Template.I include file that appears here will be referenced by many of the application examples found in this book.

Windows Conventions and Data Types

The following sections describe some Windows NT and 95 conventions for naming, as well as some of the Windows data types, data structures, and handle identifiers.

Variable Names and Hungarian Notation

As programs have become more complex in terms both of size and of the proliferation of data types, many programmers have adopted a variable-naming convention, which is commonly referred to as Hungarian notation (apocryphally named in honor of Microsoft programmer, Charles Simonyi).

Over the past several years, several "standard" versions of Hungarian notation have been proposed and/or published. The version given here is dictated in part by personal preferences and in part by conventions established by Windows in naming constants, variables, and data structure definitions. Since all of these standards are intended as mnemonics for your convenience, you may follow or alter these as desired.

Using Hungarian notation, variable names begin with one or more lowercase letters, which denote the variable type, thus providing an inherent identification. For example, the prefix h is used to identify a handle, as in hWnd or hDlg, referring to window and dialog handles, respectively. In like fashion, the prefix lpsz identifies a long pointer to a null-terminated (ASCIIZ) string. Table 2.1 summarizes the Hungarian notation conventions.

TABLE 2.1   Hungarian Notation Conventions

Prefix	Data type	Prefix	Data type
b	boolean	I	int
by	byte or unsigned char	l	long
c	char	n	short int
cx / cy	short used as size	s	string
dw	DWORD, double word or unsigned long	sz	ASCIIZ null-terminated string
fn	function	w	WORD unsigned int
h	handle	x, y	short used as coordinates

Predefined Constants

Windows also uses an extensive list of predefined constants, which are used as messages, flag values, and other operational parameters. These constant values are always full uppercase, and most include a two- or three-letter prefix set off by an underscore. Here are some examples:

CS_HREDRAW	CS_VREDRAW	CW_USERDEFAULT
DT_CENTER	DT_SINGLELINE	DT_VCENTER
IDC_ARROW	IDI_APPLICATION	WM_DESTROY
WM_PAINT	WS_OVERLAPPEDWINDOW	

In the case of constant identifiers, the prefixes indicate the general category of the constant. Table 2.2 shows the meanings of the prefixes in the examples above.

TABLE 2.2   A Few Constant Prefixes

Prefix	Category	Prefix	Category
CS	Class style	IDI	Icon ID
CW	Create window	WM	Window message
DT	Draw text	WS	Window style
IDC	Cursor ID		

Data Types

Windows also uses a wide variety of new data types and type identifiers, most of which are defined in either the WinDef.H or WinUser.H header files. Table 2.3 lists a few of the more common data types.

Data Structures

Similarly, Windows adds a variety of new data structures. Again, most are defined in either WinDef.H or WinUser.H. The five examples shown in Table 2.4 appear in the WinHello.C program.

TABLE 2.3   A Few Windows Data Types

Data type	Meaning	Data type	Meaning
FAR	Same as far	DWORD	double word, unsigned long int (32 bits)
PASCAL	Same as pascal	LONG	signed long integer (32 bits)
WORD	unsigned integer (16 bits)	LPSTR	long (far) pointer to character string
UINT	unsigned integer, same as WORD		

TABLE 2.4   Five Windows Structures

Structure	Example	Meaning
MSG	msg	Message structure
PAINTSTRUCT	ps	Paint structure
PT	pt	Point structure (mouse position)
RECT	rect	Rectangle structure, two coordinate pairs
WNDCLASS	wc	Window class structure

Handle Identifiers

In like fashion, a variety of handles are defined for use with different Windows elements. Like constants, the handle types use all uppercase identifiers. Table 2.5 shows a few examples.

TABLE 2.5   Four Handle Identifiers

Handle type	Examples	Meaning
HANDLE	hnd or hdl	Generic handle
HWND	hwnd or hWnd	Window handle
HDC	hdc or hDC	Device context handle (CRT)
HBRUSH	hbr or hBrush	Paint brush handle
HPEN	hpen or hPen	Drawing pen handle

You'll see these conventions used throughout the program listings in this book, including the WinHello and Template programs, which follow.

Listing 2.1: The WinHello Application

```
rem ;=======================;
rem ;      WinHello.BAT      ;
rem ;  calls NMAKE utility   ;
rem ;=======================;
nmake -a -f WinHello
del WINHELLO.OBJ


#==================================================#
# Nmake macros for building WinHello application #
#==================================================#

!include <ntwin32.mak>

# instruction allows NMAKE to work

all: winhello.exe

# update object file as necessary
winhello.obj: winhello.c
    $(cc) $(cflags) $(cvars) winhello.c

# update executable file as necessary
winhello.exe: winhello.obj  winhello.def
    $(cvtobj) $(cvtdebug) *.obj
    $(link) $(guiflags) -out:winhello.exe winhello.obj \
            $(guilibs)

# NOTE: no resources are included in this application
# refer also to the Template NMake script


;========================================;
;  WINHELLO.DEF module definition file   ;
;========================================;

NAME          WINHELLO
DESCRIPTION   "Windows Hello, World Program"
EXETYPE       WINDOWS
```

```
;  STUB        "WINSTUB.EXE"
CODE           PRELOAD MOVEABLE DISCARDABLE
DATA           PRELOAD MOVEABLE MULTIPLE
HEAPSIZE    1024
STACKSIZE   5120
EXPORTS     WndProc


//===================================//
//          WinHello.C               //
// HELLO WORLD, Windows_NT Version   //
//===================================//

#include <windows.h>

long FAR PASCAL WndProc( HWND hwnd,   UINT msg,
                         UINT wParam, LONG lParam )
{
   HDC         hdc;
   PAINTSTRUCT ps;
   RECT        rect;

   switch( msg )
   {
     case WM_PAINT:
         hdc = BeginPaint( hwnd, &ps );
         GetClientRect( hwnd, &rect );
         DrawText( hdc, "Hello, World!", -1, &rect,
             DT_SINGLELINE | DT_CENTER | DT_VCENTER );
         EndPaint( hwnd, &ps );
         return( 0L );

     case WM_DESTROY:              // message: window being
        PostQuitMessage(0);       //          destroyed
         break;

     default:                      // if msg unprocessed,
         return(                   //    return to Windows
             DefWindowProc( hwnd, msg, wParam, lParam ) );
   }
   return( 0L );
}
```

```
int PASCAL WinMain( HANDLE hInstance,
                    HANDLE hPrevInstance,
                    LPSTR  lpszCmdParam,
                    int    nCmdShow )
{
    static char szAppClass[] = "WinHello";
    HWND        hwnd;
    MSG         msg;
    WNDCLASS    wc;

    if( ! hPrevInstance )
    {
        wc.style         = CS_HREDRAW | CS_VREDRAW;
        wc.lpfnWndProc   = WndProc;
        wc.cbClsExtra    = 0;
        wc.cbWndExtra    = 0;
        wc.hInstance     = hInstance;
        wc.hIcon         = LoadIcon( NULL, IDI_APPLICATION );
        wc.hCursor       = LoadCursor( NULL, IDC_ARROW );
        wc.hbrBackground = GetStockObject( WHITE_BRUSH );
        wc.lpszMenuName  = NULL;
        wc.lpszClassName = szAppName;
        RegisterClass( &wc );
    }
    hwnd = CreateWindow(
        szAppClass,                    // window class name
        "Hello, World - Windows_NT Style",
                                       // window caption
        WS_OVERLAPPEDWINDOW,           // window style
        CW_USEDEFAULT,                 // initial X position
        CW_USEDEFAULT,                 // initial Y position
        CW_USEDEFAULT,                 // initial X size
        CW_USEDEFAULT,                 // initial Y size
        NULL,                          // parent window handle
        NULL,                          // window menu handle
        hInstance,                     // program instance handle
        NULL  );                       // creation parameters
    ShowWindow( hwnd, nCmdShow );
    UpdateWindow( hwnd );
    while( GetMessage( &msg, NULL, 0, 0 ) )
    {
```

```
        TranslateMessage( &msg );
        DispatchMessage( &msg );
    }
    return msg.wParam;
}
```

Listing 2.2: The Template Application

```
rem ;========================;
rem ;       TEMPLATE.BAT      ;
rem ;   calls NMAKE utility   ;
rem ;========================;
nmake -a -f TEMPLATE
if exist TEMPLATE.OBJ del TEMPLATE.OBJ


#===================================================#
# Nmake macros for building Windows 32-bit apps #
#===================================================#


!include <ntwin32.mak>

# instruction allows NMAKE to work

all: template.exe

# update resource as required
template.res: template.rc template.h
   rc -r -fo template.tmp template.rc
   cvtres -$(CPU) template.tmp -o template.res
   del template.tmp

# update object file as required
template.obj: template.c template.h
   $(cc) $(cflags) $(cvars) template.c

# update executable file if necessary
#   if updated, restore resources
template.exe: template.obj template.res template.def
   $(cvtobj) $(cvtdebug) *.obj
   $(link) $(guiflags) -out:template.exe template.obj \
      template.res $(guilibs)
```

```
;===================================;
;  Template module-definition file  ;
;  used by LINK.EXE                 ;
;===================================;

NAME            Template
DESCRIPTION     'WindowsNT Application Template'
EXETYPE         WINDOWS
STUB            'WINSTUB.EXE'
CODE  PRELOAD MOVEABLE DISCARDABLE
DATA  PRELOAD MOVEABLE MULTIPLE
HEAPSIZE        1024
STACKSIZE       5120

; all functions called by Windows routines
;     must be explicitly exported

EXPORTS
   WndProc
   AboutProc

//===========================//
//   Template.H header file  //
//===========================//

#define IDM_ABOUT 100

//=============================================//
// forward function declarations (optional) //
//=============================================//

BOOL InitApplication( HANDLE );
BOOL InitInstance( HANDLE, int );
long FAR PASCAL WndProc( HWND, UINT, UINT, LONG );
BOOL FAR PASCAL AboutProc( HWND, UINT, UINT, LONG );

//================================//
//   Template.RC Resource Script  //
//================================//

#include "windows.h"
#include "template.h"
```

```
TemplateMenu MENU
BEGIN
   POPUP "&Help"
   BEGIN
      MENUITEM "&About Template...", IDM_ABOUT
   END
END

AboutDlg DIALOG 22, 17, 144, 75
STYLE DS_MODALFRAME | WS_CAPTION | WS_SYSMENU
CAPTION "About Template"
BEGIN
   CONTROL "The Template application provides", -1,
           "STATIC",
           SS_CENTER | WS_CHILD | WS_VISIBLE | WS_GROUP,
           14,  7, 115, 8
   CONTROL "a generic template for designing", -1,
           "STATIC",
           SS_CENTER | WS_CHILD | WS_VISIBLE | WS_GROUP,
           14, 18, 115, 8
   CONTROL "Windows NT applications.", -1, "STATIC",
           SS_CENTER | WS_CHILD | WS_VISIBLE | WS_GROUP,
           14, 29, 115, 8
   CONTROL "OK", IDOK, "BUTTON", WS_GROUP, 56, 50, 32, 14
END

Template ICON "template.ico"

//=============================//
//         Template.C          //
//    Template Example for      //
//   Windows_NT Applications    //
//=============================//

#include <windows.h>
#include "template.h"

#define  APP_MENU    "TemplateMenu"
#define  APP_ICON    "Template"

HANDLE hInst;
char   szAppTitle[] = "Application Template";
char   szAppName[]  = "Template";
```

```
//==========================================================//
//   The AboutProc function requires no initialization
     aside from what                                        //
//   Windows NT supplies by default. AboutProc displays
     a simple                                               //
//   text message, then exits when the OK button is
     clicked.                                               //
//==========================================================//

BOOL FAR PASCAL AboutProc( HWND hDlg,    UINT msg,
                              UINT wParam, LONG lParam )
{
   switch (msg)
   {
      case WM_INITDIALOG:  return( TRUE );
      case WM_COMMAND:
         if( LOWORD( wParam ) == IDOK )
         {
            EndDialog( hDlg, TRUE );
            return( TRUE );
         }
         break;
   }
   return( FALSE );
   UNREFERENCED_PARAMETER( lParam );
}

long FAR PASCAL WndProc( HWND hWnd,    UINT msg,
                           UINT wParam, LONG lParam )
{
   FARPROC lpProc;

   switch( msg )
   {
      case WM_COMMAND:
         switch( LOWORD(wParam) )
         {
            case IDM_ABOUT:
               lpProc = MakeProcInstance(
                        (FARPROC) AboutProc, hInst );
```

```
                DialogBox( hInst,  "AboutDlg",
                            hWnd,  lpProc );
                FreeProcInstance( lpProc );
                break;

            default:
                return( DefWindowProc( hWnd,   msg,
                                         wParam, lParam ) );
        }
        break;

      case WM_DESTROY:
        PostQuitMessage(0);
        break;

      default:
        return( DefWindowProc( hWnd,   msg,
                                 wParam, lParam ) );
    }
    return( 0L );
}


//===========================================================//
//   The Template include file provides subroutines
     to initialize the                                      //
//   application class and instance.                        //
//===========================================================//

#include template.i

//===========================================================//
//   WinMain provides the initial entry point for each
     application and,                                       //
//   in turn, calls the application's initialization
     routines. If either                                   //
//   initialization routine fails, WinMain
     returns FALSE.                                        //
//
//
```

```
//    Next, WinMain executes the loop to retrieve
      and dispatch                                        //
//    messages, terminating when WM_QUIT
      is received (i.e., GetMessage returns               //
//    FALSE). This loop provides the top-level            //
//    control structure for each application. When the
      loop terminates,                                    //
//    WinMain returns the wParam argument from
      PostQuitMessage.                                    //
//============================================================ //

int WinMain( HANDLE hInstance, HANDLE hPrevInstance,
             LPSTR  lpCmdLine, int     nCmdShow    )
{
   MSG    msg;

   if( ! hPrevInstance )
      if( ! InitApplication( hInstance ) )
         return( FALSE );
   if( ! InitInstance( hInstance, nCmdShow ) )
      return (FALSE);
   while( GetMessage( &msg, NULL, NULL, NULL ) )
   {
      TranslateMessage( &msg );
      DispatchMessage( &msg );
   }
   return( msg.wParam );
   UNREFERENCED_PARAMETER( lpCmdLine );
}


//=============================//
//        Template.I          //
//  subprocedure include file  //
//=============================//


//============================================================//
//    InitApplication is called at initialization time
      if, and only if, no                                 //
//    other instances of this
      application are currently running.                  //
```

```
//
//
//    In this example, the window class is initialized
      by assigning                                          //
//    values to the WNDCLASS structure before calling
      RegisterClass().                                      //
//    Because all instances of this application use
      the same window                                       //
//    class, this task is executed only when the
      first application                                     //
//    instance is initialized. //
//=========================================================//

BOOL InitApplication( HANDLE hInstance )
{
   WNDCLASS  wc;

   wc.style = NULL;
   wc.lpfnWndProc = (WNDPROC) WndProc;
   wc.cbClsExtra   = 0;
   wc.cbWndExtra   = 0;
   wc.hInstance    = hInstance;
   wc.hIcon        = LoadIcon( NULL, APP_ICON );
   wc.hCursor      = LoadCursor( NULL, IDC_ARROW );
   wc.hbrBackground = GetStockObject( WHITE_BRUSH );
   wc.lpszMenuName = APP_MENU;
   wc.lpszClassName = szAppName;
   return( RegisterClass( &wc ) );
}


//=========================================================//
//    InitInstance is called at initialization time
      for every instance of                                 //
//    the application executed
      and performs tasks which cannot be                    //
//    shared across multiple instances.                     //
//
//
```

```
//    In this example, InitInstance saves the instance
      handle (using a                                    //
//    static variable) before creating
      and displaying the program's                       //
//    main window.                                       //
//=========================================================//

BOOL InitInstance( HANDLE hInstance, int nCmdShow )
{
   HWND   hWnd;

   hInst = hInstance;
   hWnd = CreateWindow( szAppName, szAppTitle,
                        WS_OVERLAPPEDWINDOW,
                        CW_USEDEFAULT, CW_USEDEFAULT,
                        CW_USEDEFAULT, CW_USEDEFAULT,
                        NULL, NULL, hInstance, NULL   );
   if( ! hWnd ) return( FALSE );
   ShowWindow( hWnd, nCmdShow );
   UpdateWindow( hWnd );
   return( TRUE );
}
```

CHAPTER

THREE

3

From DOS to Windows NT

- Message-handling formats

- WM_PAINT message processing

- Windows font metrics and measurements

- Windowing text output

- Window resizing

Iconic applications are applications that use bitmap images as controls. Because of the migration to graphical environments, iconic applications are convenient and popular. Nevertheless, text, in whatever form, remains an integral and essential part of virtually all applications.

In the conventional text-mode environment, text output is relatively simple, requiring only the `gotoxy` function for position and the `printf` function (or some variation) to format and print the string information.

Even in graphics mode, text output is still relatively simple, particularly if you create a graphics counterpart to the `printf` function.

In both circumstances, your application has complete control of the display and simply writes (or draws) the desired text before forgetting everything and proceeding with the program.

In a Windows environment, however, the environment is shared with other applications, so Windows must remember and be prepared to re-create the display at any time.

DOS text-based applications that run in windows use graphical bitmapped representations of their text-based selves. Such an arrangement relies on a number of Windows calls and functions that are part of a "request"-based execution environment. This chapter shows you the structure of Windows graphical functions and how they are used with windowed DOS applications.

NOTE The distinction between text and graphics modes is quite artificial, originating back when RAM memory was relatively expensive. To save costs, the text-only mode was developed to permit a full-screen display without the need for memory required for a pixel-based display. Some systems, such as the Heath/Zenith Z-100 (with one to three banks of video RAM providing 16 colors), made no distinction between text and graphics modes, permitting ROM-based characters to be displayed on the same screen as pixel graphics. Text-based mode is less sophisticated but became the 'standard' for the time. As memory costs have dropped and overall sophistication has increased, Windows and OS/2-based graphics systems today are quickly supplanting the "text-only" mode—even for text-only applications.

Executing DOS Applications under Windows NT

Since version 3.x, Windows NT has allowed users to run multiple DOS applications in scalable windows. While this is a big plus for those of you who can't live without your favorite DOS programs, NT's DOS capabilities have required programmers to rethink how DOS applications are constructed and run.

Earlier versions of Windows provided a shell or window capable of executing a DOS application, but this DOS window was limited by some restrictions. Only one DOS window could be opened at any time, the DOS window occupied the entire screen, and while the DOS application was active, it effectively prevented Windows applications from executing.

Those of you who are loath to give up some or several of your familiar DOS applications will be happy to know that Windows NT has been able to void the previous DOS window restrictions. It provides us with, effectively, a multitasking DOS environment within the NT environment. Of course, regardless of programmer's dreams and ad agency hype, the DOS windows are not perfect, and some applications may simply not function except under DOS proper. Generally, such incompatibilities are caused by nonstandard file or device I/O, by applications attempting to hog system resources (in a fashion permitted and acceptable under DOS), or occasionally by video-access demands. Overall, however, the compatibility record is excellent, and most DOS applications will execute with little or no difficulty.

NOTE TSR utilities, in general, are not good candidates for DOS window compatibility. Test with care and caution. (The problem with a TSR, even in a DOS window, is that the TSR still expects to install hooks to capture keyboard and/or mouse input—behavior that is very unlikely to be compatible with the Windows system.)

Design for the Unknown

Under DOS, once the screen is written, an application is pretty well free to forget about it and proceed with something else. Under Windows, however, even though an application is limited to its own client window, the display created is not inviolate, and the application must be prepared to re-create the display as required.

Under Windows, because the application does not "own" the display, any application must be prepared for its display to be invalidated—by another window overlaying its display, by its display being resized or shrunk to an icon and restored, or simply because the application window has been moved on the screen. Furthermore, the application itself may invalidate the display by overwriting some portion with a pull-down menu or a pop-up dialog box.

For a text-based display, pop-up dialog boxes and pull-down menus can provide their own screen recovery by saving a memory copy of the existing display and, when finished, can erase themselves by restoring the original display from memory. In text modes, this is relatively simple since less than 4KB are necessary to save an entire screen ($80 \times 25 \times 2$ bytes—character and attribute—per cell).

For a graphics display, however, a similar operation would require nearly 300KB, assuming a screen 640×480 with 16 colors. Of course, for SVGA and true-color displays, memory requirements increase accordingly. Granted, data compression could reduce these requirements to some degree, but until super-fast terabyte memories become common, the saved image approach is not likely to be considered practical for general circumstances.

Instead, under Windows, applications are expected to be able to re-create the screen, in part or entirely, as required.

> **NOTE**
> There are circumstances in which Windows does save overwritten display areas, such as when the display is overwritten by the cursor or when an icon is dragged across a client area. Under these limited circumstances, no screen update is required. But, in all other cases, Windows notifies the application whose screen displays have been invalidated when it is appropriate to re-create the client window while Windows handles restoration of the application's frame.

Message-Handling Formats: Standard versus MFC Classes

For many programmers who began creating applications under DOS (or Unix, CP/M, and so on), the change to Windows' event message programming has required an adjustment in attitude and in their approach to programming. Creating a program as responses to event messages rather a direct flow of actions is a very different milieu.

By now, of course, after several generations and versions of both Windows and OS/2, event-driven programming is not only acceptable and convenient, but often it is the method of choice for triggering an action or activity, even when doing so requires defining and generating custom messages.

In a conventional Windows application, the message responses are normally handled in the WndProc procedure as a switch/case statement, where the various case statements may call subprocedures or may contain the code for the immediate response.

In an MFC-based application, however, the conventional WndProc procedure has been replaced by a message map handler, which directs the event messages to specific class methods that provide the responses. At the same time, the message mapping often also provides interpretation of the conventional message parameters in a more convenient format.

As a brief example, the switch/message handler for the PainText program (conventional version) is shown below, along with the equivalent MFC methods from the PainText2 version.

Conventional	MFC Equivalent
switch(msg)	
{	
case WM_CREATE: …	OnCreate …
case WM_SIZE: …	OnSize …
case WM_PAINT: …	OnDraw …
case WM_VSCROLL: …	OnVScroll …

Conventional	MFC Equivalent

```
case WM_HSCROLL: …   OnHScroll …

case WM_DESTROY: …   (uses default handler)

}
```

While it is perfectly possible and practical, and sometimes necessary, to incorporate an old-style `switch`/`case` statement in an MFC `OnCommand` function, the newer format is more convenient.

In the following sections, the conventional message-handling functions are discussed, referring to the PainText application. The MFC equivalents, from the PainText2 version, are covered primarily where and as they differ or require special responses. You'll find the complete listing of the PainText demo program at the end of this chapter. The listings for both the PainText and PainText2 versions are included on the CD that accompanies this book.

Processing WM_PAINT Messages

The `WM_PAINT` message is posted to an application as notification that the current screen display is invalid, requiring restoration. Thus, a `WM_PAINT` message is issued, notifying the application that it's time to repaint its display, under these conditions:

- When an application window has been hidden, partially or entirely

- When an application window has been resized (assuming the `CS_HREDRAW` and `CS_VREDRAW` flags were set in the style specification)

- When `ScrollWindow` is called to scroll the client area, horizontally or vertically

At the same time, there are circumstances under which the application may wish to issue its own `WM_PAINT` message. For example, during initialization, most applications call the `UpdateWindow` function, which instructs Windows to issue a `WM_PAINT` message addressed to the application's client window. Then, after the message loop begins processing, the `WM_PAINT` message is picked up and forwarded to the WndProc function, and finally, the initial window display is painted.

In other circumstances, the application may choose to use the InvalidateRect or InvalidateRgn functions, both of which explicitly generate WM_PAINT messages, along with information specifying the area requiring repainting. Applications written using MFC may simply call the Invalidate function for the same result.

Now, this may at first appear to be a rather roundabout means of accomplishing what, in other circumstances, would be a fairly straightforward task. After all, instructing Windows to send a message back to the application to request a repaint is a bit like riding 'round Robin Hood's barn (Sherwood Forest).

The reasons, however, are far more than philosophical. For multiple applications to share a computer, as is the case under Windows, they must operate in a fashion permitting others to have access to the system resources. To accomplish this, applications are required to break their operations into a series of subtasks, and instead of initiating these tasks directly, to place requests (that is, messages) in a queue. In this manner, control of the system is passed back to Windows as each task is completed, and if necessary, Windows can then pass control to another application. The result is flexible time-sharing, with Windows offering each application time and resources according to its needs.

The important item to remember is that applications must be prepared to re-create their display space *at any time.* They must be ready to write the screen on demand and to rewrite the screen on demand.

Invalidated Window Regions

Hand in glove with the WM_PAINT message is the PAINTSTRUCT information structure. A separate PAINTSTRUCT record is maintained by Windows for each application with the structure defined as:

```
typedef struct tagPAINTSTRUCT
{   HDC    hdc;
    BOOL   fErase;
    RECT   rcPaint;
    BOOL   fRestore;
    BOOL   fIncUpdate;
    BYTE   rgbReserved[32];
}   PAINTSTRUCT, *PPAINTSTRUCT, *NPPAINTSTRUCT, *LPPAINTSTRUCT;
```

The first three fields in PAINTSTRUCT—hdc, fErase, and rcPaint—are commonly used by applications. The latter three fields are used internally by Windows NT.

> **NOTE**
>
> On conversions from Windows 3.x to Windows NT, if the rgbReserved field is accessed directly, be aware that the size of this field has changed from 16 to 32 bytes.

The hdc field is, of course, simply a handle to the application's device context. Rather than accessing the hdc field from the PAINTSTRUCT field, however, applications should continue to depend on the value returned by the BeginPaint or Get-DC functions called before any screen update operations commence.

The fErase field is a flag value with, confusingly, FALSE instructing Windows to erase the background of an invalidated rectangle, and TRUE indicating that the background has already been erased.

The third field, rcPaint, consists of a RECT structure defined as:

```
typedef  struct tagRECT
{  LONG     left;
   LONG     top;
   LONG     right;
   LONG     bottom;
} RECT,  *PRECT, NEAR *NPRECT, FAR *LPRECT;
```

The rcPaint field is used to keep track of the invalidated region within the application's client window with the four values in the rcPaint field defining the sides of the smallest rectangle enclosing all invalidated areas.

When an application is finished responding to a WM_PAINT message (by calling EndPaint), the rcPaint field is reset, validating the entire client window. Subsequently, when some portion of the client window is overwritten by another application, pull-down menu, or pop-up dialog box, a new invalidated region is calculated. Likewise, when any application is moved, closed, or resized, Windows checks for other applications affected by these changes, resetting the invalidated areas as required and, as appropriate, posting WM_PAINT messages to instruct applications to restore their display areas.

The purpose of the invalidated rectangle is twofold:

- Because paint operations are restricted to the area specified, an application overlapped by another application's window, or even by another of its own display elements, does not overwrite the higher-level display while restoring its own display area.

- This method restricts the area that requires repainting to the minimum actually necessary. While text-based displays can afford less-than-optimum screen updates without being visually apparent, graphics displays, requiring more processing, lack this luxury of action. To present a smooth, visually seamless display, they must use the optimum approach of executing the update in the shortest possible time, which also means within the smallest possible area.

Applications may also need to set their own update areas, a task which is accomplished by calling the InvalidateRect function as:

```
InvalidateRect( hwnd, NULL, TRUE );
```

The first parameter, of course, is the window handle. The second parameter specifies the region to be invalidated. Specifying the region as NULL, as in this example, is the equivalent of specifying the entire client area. Alternatively, you could use an HRGN argument to pass a handle to a data structure containing the precise region coordinates. The third argument, if passed as TRUE, erases the background for the set region or, if FALSE, leaves the current background unchanged.

NOTE   **Applications using MFC do not have direct access to the** PAINTSTRUCT **structure.**

Responding to the WM_PAINT Message

While Windows is responsible for issuing the majority of the WM_PAINT messages, it is solely the application's responsibility to repond to these messages and to create or re-create the application display as necessary. However, before the application can draw anything, even a single pixel, the application must begin by obtaining the device context handle (commonly abbreviated hdc).

In the WinHello demo program presented in Chapter 2, the device context handle was returned by calling the `BeginPaint` function as:

```
hdc = BeginPaint( hwnd, &ps );
```

In this fashion, the application has not only obtained a handle to the device context but, at the same time, has retrieved the PAINTSTRUCT record (`ps`) by passing the address of a local variable of the appropriate type. The form shown is commonly used in response to WM_PAINT messages and is always matched, when the current operations are finished, with a corresponding `EndPaint` function call, thus:

```
EndPaint( hwnd, &ps );
```

If you are using MFC instead of the `BeginPaint` and `EndPaint` instructions, the paint operations are encapsulated in the `OnDraw` method, where the device context is supplied as an argument. Within the `OnDraw` method, however, painting operations proceed in the same fashion as in response to the WM_PAINT message (see the parallel examples in later chapters and on the CD).

In other circumstances, a second method of accessing the device context is:

```
hdc = GetDC( hwnd );
```

Or, using MFC, a third method is used where the `CWnd::GetDC` method is invoked to return a pointer to the device context as:

```
CDC*  pDC;
pDC = GetDC();
```

The `GetDC` function is commonly used in any situation where immediate client window operations are needed without waiting to respond to a WM_PAINT message. For example, a Clock program, responding to a timer event, needs to update its image immediately, and cannot simply wait for a WM_PAINT message to appear in the queue.

The `GetDC` function is not, however, restricted to paint operations; it is also used when an application requires information from a device context. For an example, refer also to the font and text metrics example in Chapter 25.

Like the `BeginPaint` function, the `GetDC` function has its own closing statement as:

```
ReleaseDC( hwnd, hdc );
```

Using MFC, instead of requiring a window handle, the `CWnd::ReleaseDC` method is called as:

```
ReleaseDC( pDC );
```

WARNING
BeginPaint **must always end with** EndPaint. GetDC **is always closed with a** ReleaseDC **function call. Mixing these functions incorrectly will not produce a compiler error but will have serious, or possibly fatal, effects on an application's execution.**

Okay, why two formats? Because each has a different purpose, and each operates in a different fashion.

The BeginPaint/EndPaint process, as mentioned previously, returns and resets the invalidate region data, but it also restricts drawing operations to the region specified.

The GetDC/ReleaseDC process returns a clipping rectangle, which is equal to the entire client window, imposing no restrictions on drawing operations (aside from the inherent limitation to the application's window). At the same time, while End-Paint resets the invalidated region, ReleaseDC does not change existing settings and, therefore, does not clear information that might be needed later to ensure restoration of an invalidated area.

NOTE
While GetDC **permits drawing operations over the entire client window area, Windows itself prevents these operations from overwriting an overlying application's window area, as well as restricting screen operations to the visible or physical portion of the display.**

Last, as will be shown momentarily, the GetDC/ReleaseDC functions are frequently used when only information about a device context—whether the display, a printer, or some other device—is required.

Controlling Graphics Text Displays

Within the Windows environment, four primary factors govern how text is drawn. These are:

- **Position:** The row/column absolute screen positions used in a text environment are replaced, in Windows, with window-relative pixel coordinates. Positioning must also take into account font metrics (text sizing), alignment options, and scroll positioning (vertical and horizontal), as well as variable window sizing.

- **Text size and alignment:** In DOS text mode, characters are a fixed size and positioned automatically by the cursor position or by explicit row/column directions. In Windows, as with other graphics environments, text sizes, styles, and fonts can be mixed and, with the exception of a few fixed-width fonts, individual characters vary in size. Regardless of font, characters and/or strings are positioned by pixel coordinates, not by row and column.

- **Scrolling:** DOS text mode displays, conventionally, are limited to unidirectional vertical scrolling. When horizontal scrolling is permitted, movement is based on character columns. In Windows, both vertical and horizontal scrolling are common, with both adjustments permitted in single-pixel steps. Text displays must take into account offsets from origin points, providing their own vertical (line) calculations. Fortunately, in most cases, horizontal positioning can simply be handled as an offset, without complex calculations.

- **Windows' limits:** DOS text displays can depend on autowrap to prevent strings that are too long from extending beyond the physical display. In Windows, the virtual and physical displays do not share the same limits and, therefore, applications must provide their own length calculations and line breaks. In some applications, text is sized to a phantom, virtual screen's limits, requiring scrolling to view various portions of the virtual window. In other cases, applications may reformat text to accommodate changes in window size.

In the Windows environment, these four elements are not entirely separate considerations. Instead, all of these tend to be interrelated or even synergistic in their effects. And, while these relationships present their own problems for your consideration, Windows shields you from many of the other problems, which otherwise would be part and parcel of the process of sharing a variable-sized display in a multiple-application environment.

And there are advantages as well. For one, since operations are always relative to the window, applications can be moved around the screen without the application requiring special provisions for repositioning. For another, the application itself does not need to recognize the hardware, screen size, and other display constraints and adjust its behavior accordingly. Also, though less commonly a consideration, Windows itself provides a variety of display fonts as well as offering accessibility to additional third-party fonts.

Of course, the real point is simply that Windows applications must take a different approach to writing any type of screen display than a similar application operating in the DOS environment.

Windows Font Metrics and Measurements

The WinHello application (Chapter 2) used the simplest possible text output. It used the `DrawText` function to write a single line centered in the application's client window. However, while the demo was suitable for brief text in a very simple context, most applications will require displays with more than one line of text and/or more sophisticated positioning.

For displays with multiple lines of text, two pieces of data are essential: vertical line spacing and horizontal line length (assuming, of course, a horizontal orientation). But neither of these characteristics are fixed; they both depend on font selection and, without knowing the relevant text metrics, cannot be arbitrarily assumed.

Also, even for system fonts, font characteristics cannot be assumed to be the same for all systems because, during installation, Windows matches fonts to the video display capabilities. At the same time, video board manufacturers and third parties design and distribute their own system fonts as well as specialty fonts.

Thus, regardless of font selection, applications must treat the font metrics as variables and request the current font information through the `GetTextMetrics` function, thus:

```
TEXTMETRICS    tm;

hdc = GetDC( hwnd );
GetTextMetrics( hdc, &tm );
ReleaseDC( hwnd, hdc );
```

This also provides an example of using the `GetDC` function in place of the `Begin-Paint` function. Since no screen paint operations are executed, there's no need for invalidated region information or for `PAINTSTRUCT` data. Thus, for a simple information retrieval, only the `GetDC` operation is necessary.

The TEXTMETRIC structure is defined as:

```
typedef struct tagTEXTMETRIC
{   LONG    tmHeight;
    LONG    tmAscent;            LONG    tmDescent;
    LONG    tmInternalLeading;   LONG    tmExternalLeading;
    LONG    tmAveCharWidth;      LONG    tmMaxCharWidth;
    LONG    tmWeight;            LONG    tmOverhang;
    LONG    tmDigitizedAspectX;  LONG    tmDigitizedAspectY;
    BYTE    tmFirstChar;         BYTE    tmLastChar;
    BYTE    tmDefaultChar;       BYTE    tmBreakChar;
    BYTE    tmItalic;            BYTE    tmUnderlined;
    BYTE    tmStruckOut;         BYTE    tmPitchAndFamily;
    BYTE    tmCharSet;           } TEXTMETRIC;
```

Of these twenty fields, seven that control text spacing are illustrated in Figure 3.1.

FIGURE 3.1

Windows font metrics

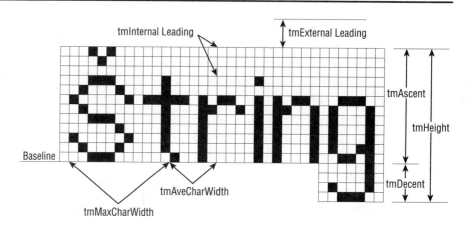

Beginning at the top of Figure 3.1, the TEXTMETRIC fields are:

- tmInternalLeading: This value provides space for accent marks above characters as illustrated by the *S*-umlaut combination shown in Figure 3.1. Although accents are not commonly used in English, many other languages depend heavily on interlinear accent marks. In some cases, these are provided for in international character sets; in other cases, such as Thai, algorithms are employed to correctly combine characters, tone accents, and vowel marks. In all cases, this spacing should be the absolute minimum between lines. See also `tmExternalLeading` described next.

- `tmExternalLeading`: This value is the font designer's suggested interlinear spacing. While optional, white space between text lines increases the readability of the display.

- `tmAscent`: This value specifies the height of an uppercase character, including the `tmInternalLeading` space.

- `tmDescent`: This value provides space for character descenders, as in the characters *g*, *j*, *p*, *q*, and *y*.

- `tmHeight`: This identifies the overall height of the font, including the `tmAscent` and `tmDescent` values but not including the `tmExternalLeading` value.

In the PaintText demo, the vertical line spacing used, `cyChr`, is calculated as:

```
cyChr = tm.tmHeight + tm.tmExternalLeading;
```

The length of a text string is not calculated as simply. `TEXTMETRIC` supplies two values for character widths:

- `tmAveCharWidth`: This value is calculated as the weighted average of the lowercase character widths.

- `tmMaxCharWidth`: This value is the width of the single widest character in the font, usually either the *W* or the *M* character.

If calculating the width of a character string is critical, a third value for the average width of uppercase letters can also be approximated, for most fonts, as 150 percent of the `tmAveCharWidth` value.

Calculating Text Sizing

Since font information will remain unchanged during program execution (unless a new font is selected, of course), the simplest method of calculating text spacing is to retrieve the text metric information when the application is initiated; that is, in response to the WM_CREATE message, the first message WndProc receives. This is accomplished in the PainText demo as:

```
case WM_CREATE:
    hdc = GetDC( hwnd );
    GetTextMetrics( hdc, &tm );
    ReleaseDC( hwnd, hdc );
    cxChr = tm.tmAveCharWidth;
    cxCap = (int)( cxChr * 3 / 2 );
    cyChr = tm.tmHeight + tm.tmExternalLeading;
    break;
```

This provides three basic values for positioning text using the current font: the average lowercase character width, the average uppercase character width, and the vertical line spacing (although only the cxChr and cyChr values are needed in the PainText demo).

In the MFC version of the PainText demo, PainText2, the Create method might appear to be the appropriate location for the corresponding code. However, attempting to call the GetDC function from the Create method will fail, because the appropriate CWnd class has not yet been initialized. Instead, the OnCreate method, which is the equivalent to the WM_CREATE message response, may be used, as in the PainText2 example. Alternatively, the OnInitialUpdate method may be employed.

```
int CPainText2View::OnCreate( LPCREATESTRUCT lpCreateStruct )
{
    if (CView::OnCreate(lpCreateStruct) == -1)
        return -1;
    // TODO: Add your specialized creation code here
    CDC*        pDC;
    TEXTMETRIC  tm;

    pDC = GetDC();
    pDC->GetTextMetrics( &tm );
    m_cxChr = (short) tm.tmAveCharWidth;
    m_cxCap = (short)( ( tm.tmPitchAndFamily & 1 ? 3 : 2 )
                        * m_cxChr / 2 );
    m_cyChr = (short)( tm.tmHeight + tm.tmExternalLeading );
    ReleaseDC( pDC );

    return 0;
}
```

Window Coordinates and Limits

In DOS text mode, the row/column coordinate system is based on the origin point at the upper-left corner of the screen, beginning at 1,1. Under Windows, the default coordinate system used is nominally the same, with three provisions:

- The coordinates are relative to the window.

- The coordinates are in pixel, not row/column, units.

- The origin point is numbered 0,0, not 1,1.

> **NOTE** Windows provides several "modes," each employing different scalar units and different coordinate origins. While alternate mapping modes will be covered in detail in Chapter 21, for text displays, only the default text mapping mode will be required.

Because Windows applications do not write directly to the screen—only indirectly through Windows NT/95 API functions—applications do not need to know where their client windows lie in relationship to the physical screen. Instead, Windows applications simply write to their own virtual screens, using virtual (window-relative) coordinates, and they leave the mapping from the virtual to the physical to Windows.

Applications may, when relevant, limit operations to the present width and height of their client window. Alternatively, if preferable, they may write to an assumed screen of optimum width and/or height (even if this is larger than the active window dimensions) and rely on scrollbar operations to position the viewport (the visible window) over the virtual display, as demonstrated by the PainText application in this chapter.

Outputting Text to a Window

After retrieving the TEXTMETRIC information and deriving the height and width information for the system font, the next obvious step is to write text to the client window (the application's screen display). In the WinHello example in Chapter 2, the DrawText function was sufficient. However, in PainText, a more sophisticated display will be provided using the TextOut function.

Like the WinHello demo, the PainText demo follows the standard response pattern of painting the application screen in response to a WM_PAINT message. But, because the text displayed will be larger than the application window, the client window also has vertical and horizontal scrollbars to position the viewport over a larger virtual window.

The text metric information has already been retrieved when the WM_CREATE message is received, but at this time, there is additional information that the application requires and that can be derived, in part, from the ps paint structure.

```
case WM_PAINT:
    hdc = BeginPaint( hwnd, &ps );
    nFirst = max( 0,          cyPos + ps.rcPaint.top / cyChr );
    nLast  = min( NUM_LINES, cyPos + ps.rcPaint.bottom / cyChr );
```

NOTE cyPos **is calculated in lines of text, not in pixels. In like fashion, the** cxPos **(horizontal) is measured in average character widths.**

In the MFC version (PainText2), since the ps structure is not available in the OnDraw method, we use a CRect instance to retrieve the client window coordinates (window size) and calculate the beginning and ending lines for our display.

```
GetClientRect( cRect );
nFirst = max( 0, m_cyPos );
nLast  = min( NUM_LINES, m_cyPos + cRect.Height() / m_cyChr );
```

The cyPos variable contains the present vertical scrollbar settings (initially set to zero); cyChr is the vertical line spacing. The ps.rcPaint.top and ps.rcPaint.bottom arguments identify the top and bottom, respectively, of the window's invalidated rectangle area (these values are relative to the client window, of course).

In the MFC version (PainText2), the variable designation m_cyPos instead of simply cyPos indicates a member variable; that is, a variable belonging to the class rather than to a local function. Member variables are globally available to all class methods. Local variables are not available outside of the method where they are declared.

Given this information, the nFirst and nLast values to be calculated will provide line numbers identifying text that needs to be repainted, as shown in Figure 3.2.

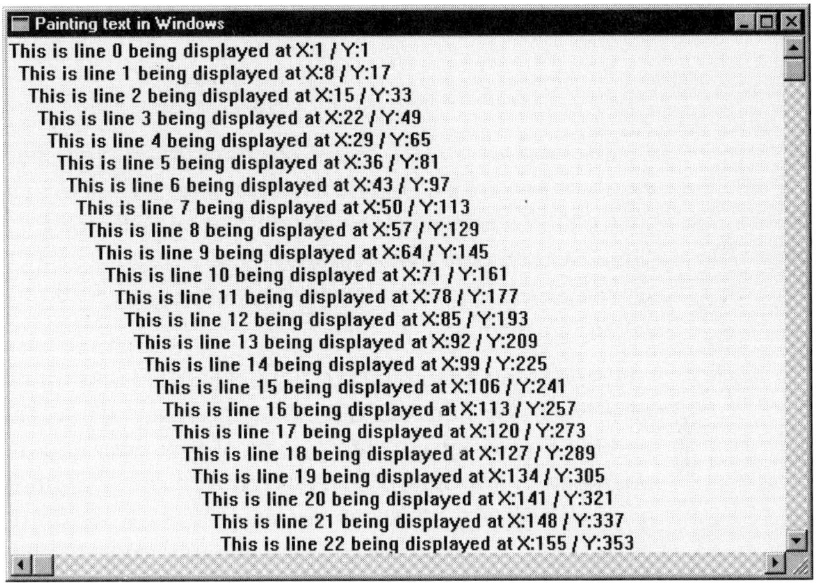

FIGURE 3.2

Displaying multiple text
lines

```
Painting text in Windows
This is line 0 being displayed at X:1 / Y:1
   This is line 1 being displayed at X:8 / Y:17
      This is line 2 being displayed at X:15 / Y:33
         This is line 3 being displayed at X:22 / Y:49
            This is line 4 being displayed at X:29 / Y:65
               This is line 5 being displayed at X:36 / Y:81
                  This is line 6 being displayed at X:43 / Y:97
                     This is line 7 being displayed at X:50 / Y:113
                        This is line 8 being displayed at X:57 / Y:129
                           This is line 9 being displayed at X:64 / Y:145
                              This is line 10 being displayed at X:71 / Y:161
                                 This is line 11 being displayed at X:78 / Y:177
                                    This is line 12 being displayed at X:85 / Y:193
                                       This is line 13 being displayed at X:92 / Y:209
                                          This is line 14 being displayed at X:99 / Y:225
                                             This is line 15 being displayed at X:106 / Y:241
                                                This is line 16 being displayed at X:113 / Y:257
                                                   This is line 17 being displayed at X:120 / Y:273
                                                      This is line 18 being displayed at X:127 / Y:289
                                                         This is line 19 being displayed at X:134 / Y:305
                                                            This is line 20 being displayed at X:141 / Y:321
                                                               This is line 21 being displayed at X:148 / Y:337
                                                                  This is line 22 being displayed at X:155 / Y:353
```

Two macros, min and max, are employed simply as a safeguard against errors in calculation. They are used to ensure that nFirst is never less than 0 and that nLast cannot be greater than NUM_LINES—the maximum number of lines that will be written.

After the beginning and ending points have been determined, the next step before writing anything to the screen is to set the appropriate text alignment. Under DOS, text alignment is fixed, but in almost any graphics context, a choice of alignments is permitted. In this case, the TA_LEFT and TA_TOP settings provide that the text string will be written with the top and left extents aligned with the output coordinates.

```
SetTextAlign( hdc, TA_LEFT | TA_TOP );
for( i = nFirst; i <= nLast; i++ )
{
    x = 1 + cxChr * ( i - cxPos );
    y = 1 + cyChr * ( i - cyPos );
```

Here, the MFC version is virtually identical. The only real difference is how the SetTextAlign function is called.

```
pDC->SetTextAlign( TA_LEFT | TA_TOP );
for( i = nFirst; i <= nLast; i++ )
{
    x = 1 + m_cxChr * ( i - m_cxPos );
    y = 1 + m_cyChr * ( i - m_cyPos );
```

New x-axis and y-axis screen positions (within the client window) are calculated for each line written, together with an x-axis offset to indent successive lines. Normally, the x-axis position used would be one character width (inset from the client window frame). In this case, a progressive offset is used to produce a display that is wider than any normal display terminal can handle and, thus, demonstrating horizontal scrolling.

Also remember that the positions calculated take into account the scrollbar offsets. Thus, either or both values may be negative integers, indicating that the current line begins outside the active client window. This is not an error—screen paint operations may originate at coordinates outside the window, either in the negative or positive directions. When this happens, or when drawing operations extend outside the client window, Windows simply truncates the actual paint operation to the visible region, without requiring the application to make elaborate and complex accommodations.

The alternative, attempting to calculate where a string should be truncated in order to fit the active window and to present the appropriate alignment, is not only cumbersome but, in practical terms, effectively impossible when a variable-width font is being used.

On the other hand, asking the application to begin by writing several hundred lines of text above the visible screen (and hundreds more below), simply to include the visible portion of the display, would be both slow and unnecessarily cumbersome. Ergo, the simplest approach is to allow the application to execute its operations in a virtual space that is as large as necessary horizontally, with Windows providing clipping, but at the same time, provide reasonable begin and end points vertically. This is the approach demonstrated here.

The TextOut Function

In conventional programs, formatted text output is provided directly using the `printf` function (or an equivalent), as:

```
gotoxy( x, y );
```

```
printf( "This is line %d being displayed"
        " at X:%d / Y:%d", i, x, y );
```

In Windows, however, a somewhat different approach is required, as:

```
TextOut( hdc, x, y, szBuffer,
         wsprintf( szBuffer,
                   "This is line %d being displayed"
                   " at X:%d / Y:%d", i, x, y ) );
```

The TextOut function expects five parameters:

- The device context handle (hdc)

- Two screen coordinates (x and y)

- A long pointer (LPSTR) to an ASCIIZ string to be written

NOTE   The term ASCIIZ is shorthand for a null-terminated ASCII string.

- The length of the string (in characters)

These could be provided in a series of separate steps. For example, you could use the sprintf function to format the string to a buffer (an array of char), and then pass the buffer, together with its length, to the TextOut function. However, because the wsprintf function returns the string length directly while writing the text to a buffer, multiple separate instructions can be reduced to a single, longer instruction. (Arguments are always evaluated from left to right; that is, in the same order listed.)

In the MFC version, instead of using a char array, a CString object is used to create the string. We do not need to supply a string length as a separate argument, since the length is included in the CString object.

```
csText.Format( "This is line %d being displayed at"
               " X:%d / Y:%d", i, x, y );
pDC->TextOut( x, y, csText );
```

Notice that in all three cases—whether the printf, wsprintf, or CString::Format functions are used—the arguments and format instructions are the same.

In sum, of course, it's a case of sixes and half-dozens, with little to choose between the three except personal preferences.

Scrollbars and Messages

Scrollbars are a popular control feature normally associated with screen displays for adjusting the horizontal and vertical positioning (although scrollbars are seeing increasing use for other scalar adjustments). Perhaps the only drawback to scrollbars is that they frequently cannot be used without a mouse (many applications implement the arrow and page keys as alternative controls). However, since few (if any) Windows users lack a mouse, there is certainly no reason not to use scrollbars and every reason, including familiarity and programming convenience, to employ them.

Of course, there is always at least one fly in the ointment. For scrollbars, the fly is that the scrollbar operations are not automatic; applications require a few provisions before they can respond to scrollbar messages.

Figure 3.3 illustrates two scrollbars (vertical and horizontal), with labels showing the Windows messages posted when each scrollbar region is clicked with the mouse or released.

Each scrollbar has five active regions (unless it is created in too small a size): the two end arrows (endpads), the scrollbar body to each side of the thumbpad, and the thumbpad itself. When the mouse is clicked or released on any of these areas, each generates a different set of event messages as shown.

Both scrollbars return SB_LINEUP messages when the mouse is clicked (button down) on the top or left endpad; they return SB_LINEDOWN messages when the mouse is clicked on the bottom or right endpad. Alternatively, if the mouse button is held down on any of the endpads, a continuous series of SB_LINEUP or SB_LINEDOWN messages is generated, providing continuous scrolling in the appropriate direction.

The body of the scrollbar—the area between either endpad and the thumbpad— is also an active control. If the mouse hit is above or left of the thumbpad, an SB_PAGEUP message is generated. When the mouse hit is to the right or below the thumbpad, an SB_PAGEDOWN message is generated.

When the mouse button is released anywhere except on the thumbpad itself, an SB_ENDSCROLL message is returned.

The thumbpad itself generates a different type of message. It returns a series of SB_THUMBTRACK messages as long as the mouse button is down. When the mouse button is released, the thumbpad returns a single SB_THUMBPOSITION message, as long as the mouse cursor is still on the scrollbar. If the mouse cursor has moved off the scrollbar, no release message is posted.

FIGURE 3.3

Scrollbar messages

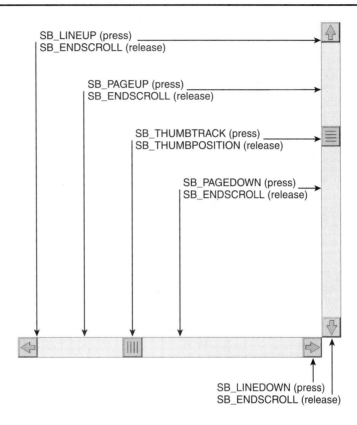

SB_LINEUP (press)
SB_ENDSCROLL (release)

SB_PAGEUP (press)
SB_ENDSCROLL (release)

SB_THUMBTRACK (press)
SB_THUMBPOSITION (release)

SB_PAGEDOWN (press)
SB_ENDSCROLL (release)

SB_LINEDOWN (press)
SB_ENDSCROLL (release)

Also, even if the SB_THUMBTRACK messages are ignored, as long as the mouse button is held down and the mouse remains on the scrollbar, Windows generates a thumbpad outline following the mouse position.

Setting Scrollbar Ranges

In order for scrollbars to report and function correctly, each scrollbar must have both the range and thumbpad positions assigned.

For a standard Windows application, the SetScrollRange function is called with the application window's handle, an integer constant identifying the scrollbar type (horizontal or vertical), two integer arguments setting the minimum and maximum range values, and a Boolean flag directing the scrollbar to be redrawn (if TRUE).

```
SetScrollRange( hwnd, SB_VERT,
                      nRangeMin, nRangeMax, FALSE );
SetScrollPos( hwnd, SB_VERT, nScrollPos, TRUE );
```

After setting, or resetting, the scrollbar range, the scrollbar's thumbpad position remains to be set. Again, `SetScrollPos` is called with the application window's handle and a constant identifying the scrollbar type, followed by the new position and a flag directing the scrollbar to be redrawn, or if FALSE, to be left as is.

The actual scrollbar range adjustment is handled in response to the `WM_SIZE` message. The scrollbar thumbpad position is updated regularly in response to `WM_VSCROLL` or `WM_HSCROLL` messages.

For an MFC-based application, the process is essentially the same, except that the `SetScrollRange` and `SetScrollPos` functions are `CWnd` class methods and do not require the window handle.

Handling Scrollbar Messages

Because the SB_xxxxxx messages posted by scrollbar events are secondary messages, a standard Windows application begins by looking for either a WM_VSCROLL or WM_HSCROLL message, indicating that the mouse event occurred in the vertical or horizontal scrollbar, respectively. The secondary event message is found in the wParam value.

For an MFC-based application, the equivalent is to use the ClassWizard to create two methods: `OnHScroll` and `OnVScroll` in the `CPainText2View` class. Here, however, instead of `wParam` and `lParam` values, three arguments are supplied. Two of these arguments are derived from the standard `wParam` and `lParam` arguments, identifying the type of scroll message and the thumbpad position on the scrollbar. The third argument is a pointer to the `CScrollBar` class instance originating the message.

Since the horizontal and vertical scrollbar responses are quite similar (in the PainText demo program), the `WM_VSCROLL` message handling is used here to illustrate both cases, beginning as:

```
case WM_VSCROLL:
  switch( LOWORD( wParam ) )
    {
```

NOTE

Under earlier Windows versions, the `wParam` argument was commonly accessed as `switch(wParam)` without requiring the `LOWORD` macro. In Windows NT, however, the `wParam` argument has changed from a 16-bit to a 32-bit argument. Despite this change, however, the secondary message value accompanying a `WM_COMMAND`, `WM_VSCROLL`, or `WM_HSCROLL` message (among others) is still a 16-bit value but is now passed as the low word in `wParam`. In many cases, since the high word value will be null, `switch`/`case` handling will function without including the `LOWORD` reference, but you can't depend on this. Ergo, the `LOWORD` macro should always be used to explicitly extract the 16-bit secondary message from the 32-bit argument.

For the MFC version (PainText2), the scrollbar event is already identified in the `nSBCode` parameter and is handled as:

```
switch( nSBCode )
{
```

Since the order in which the scrollbar events are handled is not important, the first two handled will be the endpad messages: `SB_LINEUP` and `SB_LINEDOWN`.

```
case SB_LINEUP:
    cyStep = -1;
    break;

case SB_LINEDOWN:
    cyStep =  1;
    break;
```

Both horizontal and vertical scrollbar cases provide essentially the same response, using a set step value for vertical movement of one line up or down. For the horizontal scrollbar, the equivalent would be a character movement left or right. And, yes, for the present, the graphics text is being treated very much like a row/column text display.

Alternatively, the scrollbar positions themselves could be incremented or decremented at this point. But, for the moment, it's simplest to set a variable at this point, and then later adjust the display and scrollbar positions appropriately.

The next two events are the SB_PAGEUP and SB_PAGEDOWN messages:

```
case SB_PAGEUP:
    cyStep = min( -1, -cyWin / cyChr );
    break;

case SB_PAGEDOWN:
    cyStep = max( 1,  cyWin / cyChr );
    break;
```

In these two instances, the movement range is calculated from the size of the client window (cyWin) and the vertical line spacing (cyChr), with a simple range check to return a minimum line adjustment of 1 (or -1).

While the line and page scroll messages are relatively simple, the SB_THUMBTRACK message requires a different provision. For this event, instead of an incremental adjustment, the scroll step size is the differential between the stored scrollbar position (cyPos) and the new position reported in the low word of the lParam argument.

```
case SB_THUMBPOSITION:
    cyStep = LOWORD( lParam ) - cyPos;
    break;
```

Remember, each scrollbar has already been assigned a range for full-scale movement. Windows, in the low word of lParam, is simply reporting the relative position on the assigned scale. And, at this point, the application is calculating the differential, so that presently another calculation can be made to move the thumbpad to the same position that was reported. Slightly inefficient, isn't it?

Fortunately, execution efficiency isn't important in this particular series of routines. What is important—a smooth, seamless response to dragging the thumbpad—is being accomplished efficiently with a minimum of source code. As always, it's a choice of trade-offs.

Now, if you've realized that no provisions have been made to track the thumbpad, since the SB_THUMBPOSITION event repositions the thumbpad after the mouse button is released and not while it's being dragged, this is a good time to explain that these two forms are generally treated as alternatives, not complements.

Continuously tracking the thumbpad position has one major flaw: it tends to be sluggish, particularly if responding to a change in position requires much calculation or screen activity. Therefore, many applications prefer to use the SB_THUMBPOSITION message and ignore the SB_THUMBTRACK messages.

However, if you wish, the following fragment can be implemented to provide thumbpad tracking:

```
case SB_THUMBTRACK:
    cyStep = LOWORD( lParam ) - cyPos;
    break;
```

For a comparison, try holding the button down on the scrollbar track, generating a series of SB_PAGEDOWN or SB_PAGEUP messages. Then execute a similar scroll using the SB_THUMBTRACK response. Of course, the vertical length of the display is also a factor, but overall, the differences are distinct.

Last, purely as a precaution, a default case is provided to reset the step value:

```
default:
    cyStep = 0;
    break;
```

Before you decide that the default case is redundant, consider for a moment the results if, for example, an SB_PAGEDOWN event is followed by a series of unrecognized SB_THUMBTRACK messages, without resetting cyStep.

Cautionary tales aside, the rest of the story is found after the switch/case statement finishes:

```
if( cyStep = max( -cyPos, min( cyStep, cyMax - cyPos ) ) )
{
    cyPos += cyStep;
```

The first provision is simply a range check, after which the scrollbar position variable is incremented according to the cyStep value (which may be a negative or positive integer).

Having reset the cyPos variable, the next requirements are to adjust the window position to match, and then update the position of the scrollbar's thumbpad.

```
ScrollWindow( hwnd, 0, -cyChr * cyStep, NULL, NULL );
SetScrollPos( hwnd, SB_VERT, cyPos, TRUE );
UpdateWindow( hwnd );
}
```

And, last, the UpdateWindow function is called to ensure that the client window is repainted. This, of course, results in a WM_PAINT message being posted and requires its own response.

Remember, in responding to the ScrollWindow function, Windows has set the invalidate rectangle coordinates to cover the area revealed by the scroll operation.

Therefore, the subsequent WM_PAINT operation is required to paint only a portion of the screen, which is faster than repainting the entire client window.

Sizing and Resizing Windows

While the PaintText demo is deliberately designed to create a display larger than the actual client window, thus necessitating the use of scrollbars, further provisions are also required to respond to changes in the size of the client window.

Any time the client window changes size—vertically or horizontally, larger or smaller—a WM_SIZE message is posted to the application. Also, when the application was first created, a WM_SIZE message preceded the initial WM_PAINT message.

In the WinHello demo in Chapter 2, the WM_SIZE message was left for default handling by Windows instead of being handled by the application itself. The PainText application, however, is intended to be a bit more sophisticated in its response and, for this purpose, several operations are necessary.

The first requirement, in response to a WM_SIZE message, is to retrieve the new cyWin and cxWin values that accompany the WM_SIZE message as the high and low word values in the lParam argument, thus:

```
case WM_SIZE:
    cyWin = HIWORD( lParam );
    cxWin = LOWORD( lParam );
```

In the MFC version, the OnSize function, which is the response to a WM_SIZE message, is called with three parameters: the nType argument, which reports the type of sizing operation but which will be ignored here, and the cx and cy arguments, which report the new client window size.

```
void CPainText2View::OnSize( UINT nType,
                             int cx, int cy)
{
   CView::OnSize(nType, cx, cy);
                     // TODO: Add your message handler code here
   if( m_cxChr > 0 && m_cyChr > 0 )
   {                 // don't do anything unless have text sizes
      m_cyWin = cy;
      m_cxWin = cx;
```

For the MFC version, before responding to the size-change message, the first step is to determine if we have vertical and horizontal character sizes. Using the MFC classes, the sequence of size messages is not quite as clean as it is under a conventional application. A size event will be reported before the system text metrics have been retrieved—depending, of course, on which version is used to test the text metrics. However, to prevent a runtime error caused by a divide-by-zero operation, a simple test is provided.

Also, in the MFC version, the size information is stored in member variables for the `CPainText2View` class rather than in global variables. The effect is the same, but the mechanism is slightly different.

Once the new window size is known, the vertical and horizontal scrollbars should be set to match, beginning by calculating a new value for `cyMax`, taking into account the number of lines that can be displayed in the resized window.

```
cyMax = max( 0, NUM_LINES + 2 - cyWin / cyChr );
cyPos = min( cyPos, cyMax );
```

In like fashion, the scrollbar thumbpad position is also recalculated before next resetting the scrollbar range and thumbpad position.

```
SetScrollRange( hwnd, SB_VERT, 0, cyMax, FALSE);
SetScrollPos(   hwnd, SB_VERT,    cyPos, TRUE );
```

The MFC version follows essentially the same pattern.

And last, a similar treatment is accorded the horizontal scrollbar.

In theory, and according to various documentation, the scrollbar ranges should only require adjustment when the application window is created or resized. Experience, however, has suggested that better results are achieved if the scrollbar range is reset immediately before adjusting the thumbpad position.

The text metric operations demonstrated by the PainText program will be used in a variety of other application examples in this book, as will the scrollbar handling provisions and the text-handling and positioning routines.

The complete source code, .BAT file, and NMake instructions for the PainText demo program follow. Both the PainText and PainText2 versions are included on the accompanying CD.

Listing 3.1: The PainText Application

```
rem ;======================;
rem ;       PAINTEXT.BAT      ;
rem ;  calls NMAKE utility   ;
rem ;======================;
nmake -a -f PAINTEXT
if exist PAINTEXT.OBJ del PAINTEXT.OBJ


#======================================================#
# Nmake macros for building Windows 32-Bit apps #
#======================================================#


!include <ntwin32.mak>

# instruction allows NMAKE to work

all: paintext.exe

# update object file as required
paintext.obj: paintext.c
   $(cc) $(cflags) $(cvars) paintext.c

# update executable file if necessary
paintext.exe: paintext.obj paintext.def
   $(cvtobj) $(cvtdebug) *.obj
   $(link) $(guiflags) -out:paintext.exe paintext.obj \
          $(guilibs)


;=========================================;
;   PainText.DEF module definition file   ;
;=========================================;


NAME        PAINTEXT
DESCRIPTION "Windows Paint Text Program"
EXETYPE     WINDOWS
STUB        "WINSTUB.EXE"
CODE        PRELOAD MOVEABLE DISCARDABLE
DATA        PRELOAD MOVEABLE MULTIPLE
HEAPSIZE    1024
STACKSIZE   8192
EXPORTS     WndProc
```

```
//==========================//
//         PaintText.C      //
//  C++ Windows Paint Text  //
//==========================//

#include <windows.h>

#define APP_ICON   IDI_APPLICATION    // system icon
#define APP_MENU   NULL               // no menu
#define NUM_LINES    99

HANDLE hInst;
char    szAppTitle[] = "Painting text in Windows";
char    szAppName[]  = "PaintText";

long FAR PASCAL WndProc( HWND hwnd,   UINT msg,
                         UINT wParam, LONG lParam )
{
   static short cxChr, cxCap, cyChr, cxWin, cyWin,
                cyPos, cxPos, cyMax, cxMax;
   short        i, x, y, cyStep, cxStep, nFirst, nLast;
   HDC          hdc;
   PAINTSTRUCT  ps;
   TEXTMETRIC   tm;
   RECT         rect;
   char         szBuffer[180];

   switch( msg )
   {
      case WM_CREATE:
          hdc = GetDC( hwnd );
          GetTextMetrics( hdc, &tm );
          cxChr = tm.tmAveCharWidth;
          cxCap = ( tm.tmPitchAndFamily & 1 ? 3 : 2 )
                    * cxChr / 2;
          cyChr = tm.tmHeight + tm.tmExternalLeading;
          ReleaseDC( hwnd, hdc );
          break;

      case WM_SIZE:
          cyWin = HIWORD( lParam );
          cxWin = LOWORD( lParam );
```

```
                  // set up vertical scrollbar
        cyMax = max( 0, NUM_LINES + 2 - cyWin / cyChr );
        cyPos = min( cyPos, cyMax );
        SetScrollRange( hwnd, SB_VERT, 0, cyMax, FALSE );
        SetScrollPos(   hwnd, SB_VERT,    cyPos, TRUE );
                  // set up horizontal scrollbar
        cxMax = max( 0, NUM_LINES + 60 - cxWin / cxChr );
        cxPos = min( cxPos, cxMax );
        SetScrollRange( hwnd, SB_HORZ, 0, cxMax, FALSE );
        SetScrollPos(   hwnd, SB_HORZ,    cxPos, TRUE );
        break;

    case WM_PAINT:
        hdc = BeginPaint( hwnd, &ps );
        nFirst = max( 0, cyPos + ps.rcPaint.top / cyChr );
        nLast  = min( NUM_LINES, cyPos
                       + ps.rcPaint.bottom / cyChr );
        SetTextAlign( hdc, TA_LEFT | TA_TOP );
        for( i = nFirst; i <= nLast; i++ )
        {
            x = 1 + cxChr * ( i - cxPos );
            y = 1 + cyChr * ( i - cyPos );
            TextOut( hdc, x, y, szBuffer,
                     wsprintf( szBuffer,
                         "This is line %d being displayed"
                         " at X:%d / Y:%d", i, x, y ) );
        }
        EndPaint( hwnd, &ps );
        break;

    case WM_VSCROLL:
        switch( LOWORD( wParam ) )
        {
            case SB_LINEUP:
                cyStep = -1;
                break;

            case SB_LINEDOWN:
                cyStep =  1;
                break;
```

```
         case SB_PAGEUP:
            cyStep = min( -1, -cyWin/cyChr );
            break;

         case SB_PAGEDOWN:
            cyStep = max(  1,  cyWin/cyChr );
            break;

         case SB_THUMBPOSITION:
            cyStep = LOWORD( lParam ) - cyPos;
            break;

      //===== for experimental use only =======//
      // case SB_THUMBTRACK:
      //    cyStep = LOWORD( lParam ) - cyPos;
      //    break;
      //========================================//

         default:
            cyStep = 0;
            break;
      }
      if( cyStep = max( -cyPos,
                 min( cyStep, cyMax - cyPos ) ) )
      {
         cyPos += cyStep;
         ScrollWindow( hwnd, 0, -cyChr * cyStep,
                    NULL, NULL );
         SetScrollPos( hwnd, SB_VERT, cyPos, TRUE);
         UpdateWindow( hwnd );
      }
      break;

case WM_HSCROLL:
   switch( LOWORD( wParam ) )
   {
      case SB_LINEUP:
         cxStep = -1;
         break;
```

```
                case SB_LINEDOWN:
                    cxStep =  1;
                    break;

                case SB_PAGEUP:
                    cxStep = min( -1, -cxWin/cxChr );
                    break;

                case SB_PAGEDOWN:
                    cxStep = max(  1,  cxWin/cxChr );
                    break;

                case SB_THUMBPOSITION:
                    cxStep = LOWORD( lParam ) - cxPos;
                    break;

            //===== for experimental use only =========//
            // case SB_THUMBTRACK:
            //     cxStep = LOWORD( lParam ) - cxPos;
            //     break;
            //=========================================//

                default:
                    cxStep = 0;
                    break;
            }
            if( cxStep = max( -cxPos,
                            min( cxStep, cxMax - cxPos ) ) )
            {
                cxPos += cxStep;
                ScrollWindow( hwnd, -cxChr * cxStep, 0,
                            NULL, NULL );
                SetScrollPos( hwnd, SB_HORZ, cxPos, TRUE);
            }
            break;

        case WM_DESTROY:
            PostQuitMessage( 0 );
            break;
```

```
      default:
         return( DefWindowProc( hwnd,   msg,
                                wParam, lParam ) );
   }
   return 0;
}

#include <template.i>

int APIENTRY WinMain( HANDLE hInstance, HANDLE hPrevInstance,
                      LPSTR  lpCmdLine, int    nCmdShow    )
{
   MSG   msg;

   if( ! hPrevInstance )
      if( ! InitApplication( hInstance ) )
         return 0;
   if( ! InitInstance( hInstance, nCmdShow ) )
      return 0;
   while( GetMessage( &msg, NULL, 0, 0 ) )
   {
      TranslateMessage( &msg );
      DispatchMessage( &msg );
   }
   return( msg.wParam );
   UNREFERENCED_PARAMETER( lpCmdLine );
}
```

Converting Windows 3.*x* Programs to NT or 95

- WinMain procedure definition changes

- Differences in message handling

- Simplified dialog box processes

- File and directory handling differences

- Portable API functions

For many programmers, the topic of immediate interest will be how to transport existing applications originally written for Windows 3.x to the Windows NT or 95 environments. Fortunately, such conversions, although sometimes tedious, can be relatively simple.

Because both Windows 3.x and NT/95 follow the same general structural format, use the same messaging systems, and employ the same resource elements, the overall structure being moved from Windows 3.x to NT/95 does not change. For the most part, existing Windows 3.x applications will run directly under NT/95, without requiring recompilation for the 32-bit environment.

This compatibility is provided by a translation feature in NT/95 that interprets 16-bit API function calls and message structures into 32-bit formats, and translates 32-bit messages and data formats into their 16-bit equivalents. The result, as you might expect, is a less efficient program, and depending on circumstances, a slower execution, which may or may not be viewed as acceptable.

Alternatively, you can avoid such problems with 16-bit applications by converting and recompiling them using the Windows NT/95 format with a suitable 32-bit compiler. Still, transforming applications from Windows 3.x 16-bit formats to the NT/95 32-bit format requires more than simply a change of compilers.

Although the tasks accomplished under Windows 3.x and under Windows NT/95 are essentially the same, the manner in which these are executed and the formats in which information is handled present several differences. These differences must be taken into account when you are converting an application from the 16-bit to the 32-bit environment.

This chapter provides an overview of some common programming changes you need to be aware of when you convert programs from Windows 3.x to NT/95. It does not cover *all* the possibilities—just the more common ones you may encounter. No single program can illustrate all the relevant changes necessary, so program fragments have been used to illustrate specific topics. At the end of the chapter, I'll explain how the differences between Borland C and Microsoft's C compilers are handled in the program examples in this book.

The WinMain Procedure

The entry point for any Windows application, whether 3.*x*, NT, or 95, is the
WinMain procedure. Outwardly, this portion of an application has not changed,
at least in most cases. In either version, the WinMain procedure is called as:

```
int PASCAL WinMain( HANDLE hInstance,            // 3.x or NT
                    HANDLE hPrevInstance,
                    LPSTR  lpszCmdParam,
                    int    nCmdShow  )
{
    ... same for Windows 3.x and Windows NT ...
}
```

The body of the WinMain procedure also remains the same for both versions.

What is not apparent to programmers, however, is which definitions have
changed. For example, under Windows 3.*x*, the data type HANDLE has a 16-bit
value; under NT/95, it has a 32-bit value. Still, as long as the function parameters
have not changed, these definition changes are handled by the compiler and, for
the programmer, are not immediately relevant.

In other cases, however, the changes are relevant and are reflected in the format
and parameter declarations. For example, in the WndProc procedure, which (under
this or another name) forms the heart of every Windows program, the 3.*x* and NT/
95 version declarations are similar, but not identical.

For Windows 3.*x*, the WndProc declaration appears as:

```
long FAR PASCAL WndProc( HWND hwnd,    WORD msg,     // 3.x
                         WORD wParam, LONG lParam )
```

For NT/95, the WndProc declaration is slightly different, as:

```
long FAR PASCAL WndProc( HWND hwnd,    UINT msg,     // NT
                         UINT wParam, LONG lParam )
```

In both cases, the WndProc procedure is called with four arguments: hwnd, msg,
wParam, and lParam. The first of these, hwnd, has transparently changed from a
16-bit to a 32-bit argument, because the definition of HWND has changed. The second
and third parameters, however, are declared as WORD values in version 3.*x*;
for NT/95, they become UINT, or 32-bit unsigned integer values. Only the fourth
argument, lParam, remains unchanged as a LONG, or 32-bit signed value. Thus,
where the WndProc procedure under Windows 3.*x* was called with a total of 80

bits (10 bytes) of information, under NT/95, the calling arguments have expanded to a total of 128 bits (16 bytes).

Remember, however, even though the fourth parameter, lParam, remains unchanged and is defined, for consistency, as a long signed integer, this parameter does not determine how this data will be used or in what forms. And, as will be discussed presently, except for the hwnd parameter, each of these 32-bit values may be interpreted as one or more individual arguments.

But, before discussing variations and alternatives in message arguments, there's another element that deserves attention: the message-handling structure.

The Message-Handling Structure

Under Windows 3.x, a common practice in the message handling is to have all message cases end by returning a null or 0. Any messages that are not handled internally are returned via the DefWindowProc procedure. Here is an example of a skeleton WndProc message format:

```
switch( msg )                                    // 3.x
{
    case WM_PAINT:   ...     return( NULL );
    case WM_DESTROY:  ...     return( NULL );
}
return( DefWindowProc( hwnd, msg, wParam, lParam ) );
```

The preceding example is fairly simple. Only two case statements require handling, and all other messages (if any) receive default handling. However, under NT, in some cases, this specific handling has produced some conflicts. A slight variation, shown below, produces much cleaner results.

```
switch( msg )                                    // NT
{
    case WM_PAINT:   ...     break;
    case WM_DESTROY:  ...     break;
    default:
        return( DefWindowProc( hwnd,    msg,
                               wParam, lParam ) );
}
return( FALSE );
```

This variation has the following differences:

- Rather than the individual `case` statements returning immediately, each `case` response ends with a break.

- A default `case` explicitly returns all unhandled messages for processing by NT/95.

- All messages that have been handled within `WndProc` do, in the end, return a FALSE result.

You might have expected a NULL return value here, assuming that NULL and FALSE would have the same value. In one sense, both are a 0 (zero) but, because these do not have the same type, you will get a compiler warning—not an error—by returning a NULL.

But remember, this handling is used only for the `WndProc` procedure. Other exported procedures, such as dialog box handlers and other child window procedures, even though these are called with similar parameters and provide similar message handling, do not use the `DefWindowProc` API call to return any messages. Instead, each message case handled returns TRUE to report having handled the message. Any unhandled messages, by default, return FALSE. The default message handling for all child window processes is just that: provided by default.

Child window message handling is illustrated by the skeletal `DialogProc` procedure, following:

```
BOOL APIENTRY DialogProc( HWND hDlg,    UINT msg,     // NT/95
                          UINT wParam, LONG lParam )
{
    switch( msg )
    {
        case WM_INITDIALOG:   ...   return( TRUE );

        case WM_COMMAND:
            switch( LOWORD( wParam ) )
            {
                case IDOK:      ...   return( TRUE );
                case IDCANCEL:  ...   return( TRUE );
            }
            break;
    }
    return( FALSE );
}
```

Alternatively, if the calling procedure doesn't really care about the response returned by this child window process, the three `return( TRUE )` provisions in the above example could be replaced by `break` statements.

Messages and Accompanying Arguments

Within the `switch...case` message structures, there are several important differences between Windows 3.*x* and NT/95. As a reminder, under Windows 3.*x*, in response to a WM_COMMAND message, the usual handler is a second `switch...case` structure using the `wParam` argument, thus:

```
case WM_COMMAND:                                    // 3.x
    switch( wParam )
    {
        case IDD_FNAME: ...
        case IDD_FPATH: ...
```

Under Windows 3.*x*, the `wParam` value is a 16-bit argument identifying the menu item, accelerator entry, or dialog box control originating the message.

Under NT, the `wParam` argument is a 32-bit value, while the item ID originating the message, which is still a 16-bit argument, is now contained in the low-order word of the `wParam` argument. Therefore, under NT, this item ID value must be extracted from the 32-bit argument, thus:

```
case WM_COMMAND:                                    // NT/95
    switch( LOWORD( wParam ) )
    {
        case IDD_FNAME: ...
        case IDD_FPATH: ...
```

Under NT/95, the high-order word of the `wParam` argument accompanying a WM_COMMAND message is one (1) if the message originates from an accelerator message or zero (0) if the message originated from a menu or control element. Likewise, if the message originates with a menu, the `lParam` argument is null. Alternatively, if the message originates with a control element, `lParam` contains the window handle of the control.

The important element here is that the low-order word of the `wParam` argument must be explicitly used in response to the `WM_COMMAND` message; simply following the Windows 3.x format may or may not produce the appropriate response (depending on whether the high-order word is set or not). Also, in many cases, the high-order word of the `wParam` argument and the `lParam` argument can simply be ignored.

But, remember, this particular format applies only to `WM_COMMAND` messages. Also, it is not always completely valid, as you will see in a moment.

NOTE If you are using MFC, the same restrictions apply to the `wParam` and `lParam` arguments reported to the `CWnd::OnCommand` handler.

Continuing with the `WM_COMMAND` message, consider a message sent from a list box. Under Windows 3.x, the high-order word of the `lParam` argument is tested for the `EN_CHANGE` secondary message, which reports a change in the list box selection.

```
case IDD_FNAME:                                    // 3.x
    if( HIWORD( lParam ) == EN_CHANGE )
```

Under NT, however, the `EN_CHANGE` message has moved. It's now found in the high-order word of `wParam`, not `lParam`, thus:

```
case IDD_FNAME:                                    // NT/95
    if( HIWORD( wParam ) == EN_CHANGE )
```

But this is only part of the information that will be extracted. Next, assuming the `EN_CHANGE` message was sent, the sample application needs to extract information from the list box, which is accomplished by sending a message back to the list box control.

```
EnableWindow( GetDlgItem( hDlg, IDOK ),     // 3.x
        (BOOL) SendMessage( LOWORD( lParam ),
                    WM_GETTEXTLENGTH, 0, 0L ) );
```

Exactly which information is being used in the list box message is irrelevant at the moment. What is relevant is the list box handle which, for Windows 3.x, is found in the low-order word of the 1Param argument, preceding. But in Windows 3.*x*, this handle is only a 16-bit value extracted from a 32-bit argument.

Under NT, the equivalent list box handle is a 32-bit argument and consists of the entire high- and low-order word values of the 1Param argument.

```
EnableWindow( GetDlgItem( hDlg, IDOK ),     // NT/95
         (BOOL) SendMessage( (HWND) lParam,
                             WM_GETTEXTLENGTH, 0, 0L ) );
```

Comparing the two fragments immediately preceding, you should notice the differences in how the two version examples reference control handles. (In the second fragment, the (HWND) typecast is used simply to prevent the Microsoft C compiler from generating an irrelevant warning message.)

Application Class Values

When a Windows application class is defined, normally within the WinMain procedure, several class values are assigned before the window class is registered. Under Windows 3.*x*, several of these are WORD values; under NT/95, DWORD values are used. Following is a fragmentary listing from a WinMain procedure that might belong to either a Windows 3.*x* or an NT/95 application.

```
wc.style          = NULL;
wc.lpfnWndProc    = (WNDPROC) WndProc;
wc.cbClsExtra     = 0;
wc.cbWndExtra     = 0;
wc.hInstance      = hInstance;
wc.hIcon          = LoadIcon( hInstance, APP_ICON );
wc.hCursor        = LoadCursor( NULL, IDC_ARROW );
wc.hbrBackground  = GetStockObject( WHITE_BRUSH );
wc.lpszMenuName   = APP_MENU;
wc.lpszClassName  = szAppName;
return( RegisterClass( &wc ) );
```

However, because the values used are assigned either as constants (wc.lpsz-MenuName and wc.lpszClassName) or by indirect reference (wc.hIcon and wc.hCursor), the question of whether a WORD or DWORD value is being used doesn't really come up (at least not at this time).

But there are other circumstances where an application may quite reasonably desire to change one or more of these window class elements. Under Windows 3.*x*, this is normally accomplished using the `SetClassWord` function, as:

```
SetClassWord( hwnd, GCW_HCURSOR,                    // 3.x
              LoadCursor( hInst, HrGls[11] ) );
```

In this fragmentary example, the constant `GCW_HCURSOR` designates the `wc.hCursor` field as the element to be changed. The `SetClassWord` function, however, explicitly changes a `WORD` value and, for NT, the corresponding field is a `DWORD` or `LONG` value. Therefore, for NT/95 applications, the `SetClassWord` function is replaced by a new function, `SetClassLong`, which is called as:

```
SetClassLong( hwnd, GCL_HCURSOR,                    // NT/95
              LoadCursor( hInst, HrGls[11] ) );
```

Notice also that the `GCW_HCURSOR` constant has been changed to become `GCL_HCURSOR`.

The danger—in this pair of functions and in converting applications from Windows 3.*x* to NT/95—is that the `SetClassWord` function has not been totally superseded by the `SetClassLong` function. Instead, both forms continue to be supported, as are both the `GCW_xxxx` and `GCL_xxxx` constants. And, in some circumstances, the `SetClassWord` function remains valid and useful. However, any applications being translated into NT/95 format that use the `SetWindowWord` function to change window class assignments should be particularly careful to translate these to `SetWindowLong` API function calls, and to replace the `GCW_xxxx` constants with the corresponding `GCL_xxxx` constants.

Child Window and Dialog Box Procedures

Child window dialog boxes are an integral feature of Windows applications, in 3.*x*, NT, and 95. And those converting applications from the older versions to the newer will be happy to know that the `DialogBox` function can be used precisely as it has been in the past. The following subprocedure might be used by either version to call a resource dialog box titled SELECTFILE, with message-handling responses provided by the exported procedure: `FileSelectDlgProc`.

```
int DialogProc( HWND hwnd, HINSTANCE hInst )
{
    static FARPROC  lpProc;                      // 3.x or NT
    int     iReturn;

    lpProc = MakeProcInstance( FileSelectDlgProc, hInst );
    iReturn = DialogBox( hInst, "SELECTFILE",
                         hwnd,  lpProc );
    FreeProcInstance( lpProc );
    return( iReturn );
}
```

NT/95, however, has introduced a few changes that make the preceding code not only unnecessarily verbose, but also wastefully redundant.

The first change is in the MakeProcInstance API function call. While this API call is both functional and necessary under Windows 3.x, under NT/95, MakeProcInstance has become a macro. This macro, quite simply, returns the first argument and does nothing more. Thus, calling MakeProcInstance under NT/95, aside from providing backward compatibility, has the singularly useless effect of making lpProc equal to FileSelectDlgProc.

The upshot of this is that the lpProc variable can be replaced in the DialogBox API call with FileSelectDlgProc reference, without needing to declare the lpProc variable or call MakeProcInstance at all.

The second change has to do with the FreeProcInstance API call. Again, under Windows 3.x, this API function was necessary and operational, used to release memory allocated by the DialogBox API call for the child window dialog box. But under NT/95, the FreeProcInstance call has also been redefined, again to provide backward compatibility, as a macro that does precisely nothing.

Therefore, given these two revisions in MakeProcInstance and FreeProc Instance, the DialogProc function can be rewritten, thus:

```
int DialogProc( HWND hwnd, HINSTANCE hInst )
{
    int     iReturn;                             // NT only

    iReturn = DialogBox( hInst, "SELECTFILE", hwnd,
                         FileSelectDlgProc );
    return( iReturn );
}
```

Given the modification shown, this subprocedure could be simplified even further by omitting the iReturn variable in favor of a direct return. Or, it could be discarded entirely in favor of calling the DialogBox API directly, unless, of course, there were other tasks to be accomplished before or after calling the DialogBox. function. But, in either case, the process of calling a dialog box is much simpler in NT/95 than in Windows 3.x.

Remember, this revision is optional. Windows 3.x subprocedures will still compile and execute under NT/95 without changes.

File Operations

File operations have undergone a distinct change from Windows 3.x to NT/95—perhaps, on the surface, the most distinct changes of all.

Opening and Closing Files and Getting File Sizes

Under Windows 3.x, the usual method of opening and closing a file consists of calling the same fopen and fclose procedures used under DOS, as:

```
hFil = fopen( szFName, "r+b" );                        // 3.x
if( hFil != -1 )
{
    FilSz = filelength( fileno( hFil ) );
    ...
    fclose( hFil );
}
```

In addition to opening and closing the file in this fragmentary example, the filelength function is also invoked to return the file size. This also should be a familiar function both from Windows 3.1 and from DOS applications, but it changes almost beyond recognition in its NT/95 counterpart.

In the NT revision, which follows, very little has remained the same. The hFil variable is still used to retrieve a handle to the file opened, but virtually everything else is now different.

```
hFil = OpenFile( szFName, &FileBuff,                // NT/95
                 OF_CANCEL | OF_PROMPT | OF_READ );
if( hFil != -1 )
{
    FilSz = GetFileSize( (HANDLE) hFil, &FilSzHigh );
    ...
    _lclose( hFil );
}
```

As you can see, the `fopen` procedure has been replaced by the `OpenFile` API call, which uses a quite different selection of parameters. One of these parameters is a pointer to the `FileBuff` structure, which receives information about the file.

The `GetFileSize` function is also a major change from its predecessor, `filelength`. Instead of returning a long value with the file size in bytes, `GetFileSize` returns two `DWORD` values: `FilSz` and `FilSzHigh`. The reason for this particular change is simple: where a signed long value can only report a file size up to about 2GB, a signed double `DWORD` value (64 bits) can handle really large file sizes—up to 1.7×10^{308} bytes. Granted, it may be a year or two before mass-storage facilities provide any real need for reporting files of such size, but it will happen eventually.

The final difference, changing `fclose` to `_lclose`, is almost no change at all.

As an alternative, instead of using the `_lclose` instruction, you can use the `CloseHandle` function to close files, as:

```
hFil = OpenFile( szFName, &FileBuff,                // NT/95
                 OF_CANCEL | OF_PROMPT | OF_READ );
if( hFil != -1 )
{
    FilSz = GetFileSize( (HANDLE) hFil, &FilSzHigh );
    ...
    _CloseHandle( hFil );
}
```

But opening and closing files are only one aspect of file operations. The previously familiar directory operations have also changed, although perhaps not as drastically.

Getting the Current Directory and Changing Directories

Under Windows 3.x, retrieving the current directory or changing directories was accomplished as:

```
getcwd( DirPath, sizeof( DirPath ) );                    // 3.x
...
chdir( DirPath );
```

The equivalent operations, under NT, follow the same general formats, but with a change in the function names, as:

```
GetCurrentDirectory( sizeof( DirPath ), DirPath );       // NT/95
...
    SetCurrentDirectory( DirPath );
```

The reasons for such drastic changes in these preceding file and directory examples, as opposed to the relatively simple changes in many other areas, are a direct consequence of three major factors:

- Changes in the NT file system, which supports both the DOS 16-bit FAT system and the new NT 32-bit file system

- Changes in the FAT file system for both Windows NT and 95, which now supports long filenames (Windows 3.x does not)

- The introduction of the 32-bit Unicode character system, which is available as an alternative to the familiar 16-bit ANSI character system

Also, the Unicode character system is responsible, in part, for the changes in string-handling operations, discussed in the next section.

Here, I've presented only a brief overview of the changes involved in moving file operations from Windows 3.x to NT/95. We'll go into the details in Chapter 13, which contains the FileView application. What you need to keep in mind for now is that both file and directory operations have changed drastically, and for application conversions from Windows 3.x to NT/95, these changes must be taken into account.

Unicode versus ANSI and MBCS

The conventional ANSI character set consists of an 8-bit font (255 characters) and is limited to the Roman alphabet, along with some European variations and an assortment of symbols. The shortcoming of the ANSI character set is that it limits displays to languages using the Roman alphabet. This means that large segments of the world's population are not able to view computer displays in their native language(s).

In contrast, Unicode characters ("wide characters") use 16-bit character descriptors (for 65,535 possible characters). Unicode includes character sets for every language used in the modern world, as well as technical symbols and special publishing characters.

In the past, multibyte characters (MBCS) have been used for a number of international languages, such as for the characters in the Japanese Kanji alphabet. However, the multibyte approach has never been standardized and often requires highly specific firmware and software, while still leaving the operating system itself limited to an English (or Roman-alphabet) display.

Wide characters take more space in memory than multibyte characters, but they also are faster to process. Furthermore, with multibyte encoding, only one locale can be implemented at a time; Unicode representation encompasses all character sets.

The MFC framework is Unicode-enabled throughout, except for the database classes. (ODBC—Open Database Connectivity— is not Unicode enabled.)

Most traditional C or C++ code makes assumptions about character and string manipulation that do not work well for international applications. Both MFC and the runtime library support Unicode or MBCS.

Both Unicode and MBCS are enabled by means of portable data types in MFC function parameter lists and return types. These types are conditionally defined in the appropriate ways, depending on whether your build defines the symbol _UNICODE or _MBCS. Different variants of the MFC libraries are automatically linked with your application, depending on which of these two symbols your build defines.

Class library code uses portable runtime functions and other means to ensure correct Unicode or MBCS behavior. The program must, however, still handle certain kinds of internationalization tasks in the application code. Here are some guidelines to simplify internationalization:

- Use the same portable runtime functions that make MFC portable under either environment.
- Make literal strings and characters portable under either environment using the _T macro.
- MBCS strings require precautions during parsing; these precautions are not necessary under Unicode.
- Both ANSI (8-bit) and Unicode (16-bit) strings can be mixed in an application, but they cannot be mixed in the same string.
- Strings should never be hard-coded in any application. Instead, strings should always be STRINGTABLE resources in the application's .RC file. This allows you to localize an application without changing the source code and recompiling it.

You can find extensive information about Unicode and ANSI character sets in the online documentation included with your compiler.

String Operations

String operations are another area that simply rely on existing DOS C functions under Windows 3.x. Like the other operations we've discussed, NT/95 string operations are supplemented by newer API functions, which are compatible with Unicode strings and with international character sets.

These newer API string functions, however, have not superseded the familiar string functions (continue to use #include <string.h> for old-style string functions). However, applications using Unicode strings should employ the API string functions rather than relying on the conventional string functions. Of course, applications written using the API string functions remain compatible with both Unicode and ANSI strings.

The two following code fragments contrast conventional and Windows NT/95 supplied string functions.

```
strupr( szFPath );                                    // 3.x
if( szFPath[ strlen(szFPath)-1 ] != '\\' )
    strcat( szFPath, "\\" );
strcpy( szFName, fileinfo.ff_name );
```

In most cases, the corresponding NT/95 string functions are distinguished by substituting the form lstr__ for the conventional str__. One exception is the CharUpperBuff function, which replaces the conventional strupr function.

```
CharUpperBuff( szFPath, lstrlen( szFPath ) );   // NT
if( szFPath[ lstrlen(szFPath)-1 ] != '\\' )
    lstrcat( szFPath, "\\" );
lstrcpy( szFName, lpFileInfo->cFileName );
```

Again, these two fragments are provided as illustrations of differences that you may or may not need to take into account when converting applications from Windows 3.x to NT/95.

Obsolete Functions: ANSI/ OEM Character Support

Under earlier Windows versions, a variety of functions were provided to support conversions between and within the ANSI and OEM character sets. Examples include the AnsiUpper, AnsiLower, AnsiUpperBuff, and AnsiLowerBuff functions for conversion within the ANSI character set; the AnsiToOem, AnsiToOemBuff, OemToAnsi, and OemToAnsiBuff functions for conversions between the ANSI and OEM character formats; and the AnsiNext and AnsiPrev functions provided for string-scanning operations.

In most cases, even though these functions are technically obsolete, compatibility for them has been supplied in the form of macros that call the newer function versions. For an example, the old AnsiUpper function is now implemented as a macro invoking the new CharUpper API function. In like fashion, AnsiNext now invokes CharNext, and AnsiToOem invokes the CharToOem API function.

Functionally, each of these operations remains essentially the same as in the earlier Windows version. The singularly important difference is that they are now Unicode-compatible, not just ANSI-compatible.

Portable APIs

Thus far, you've read a lot about API functions that have changed—in major or minor respects—from Windows 3.x to NT/95. At the same time, we've also covered elements that, despite changes, have been retained in one form or another to provide backward compatiblity. There are other API functions, however, that are the same in both Windows 3.x and NT/95, but which have not been generally used by Windows 3.x programmers, simply because other, parallel functions have been the accepted standards.

The following code fragment example is typical of a Windows 3.x application that is setting a graphics mapping mode, nominally in response to a WM_PAINT message.

```
SetMapMode( hdc, nCurMode );                          // 3.x
SetWindowExt( hdc, xWinAspect, yWinAspect );
SetViewportExt( hdc, xViewAspect, yViewAspect );
SetWindowOrg( hdc, xOrg, yOrg );
MoveTo( hdc, xPos, yPos );
```

Except for the first API function, SetMapMode, which remains the same under NT, none of the remaining API functions are supported by NT. But each of the four unsupported API functions has a counterpart, portable API function that differs from the format shown in only minor respects.

The following code fragment shows the same code using the portable API functions and is compatible with both Windows 3.x and NT/95.

```
SetMapMode( hdc, nCurMode );                  // 3.x, NT, or 95
SetWindowExtEx( hdc, xWinAspect, yWinAspect, NULL );
SetViewportExtEx( hdc, xViewAspect, yViewAspect, NULL);
SetWindowOrgEx( hdc, xOrg, yOrg, NULL );
MoveToEx( hdc, xPos, yPos, NULL );
```

As you will notice, each of the four portable APIs has essentially the same function name, with the only difference the addition of the extension Ex to the name. They also have one additional argument, which, in this example, is NULL in each case.

The NULL arguments have been used for compatiblity with the original functional intent, but they could be used as pointers to data structures that return previous settings. For example, for the SetWindowExtEx and SetViewportExtEx API functions, the final argument could be a pointer to a SIZE structure, which would return the previous window or viewport extents. In like fashion, the SetWindowOrgEx and MoveToEx API calls could use a pointer to a POINT structure, which would return the previous origin or the current position.

Remember, for either Windows 3.x or NT/95, the final argument is optional in each of these API functions. If the return information is not needed or wanted, use the NULL argument.

The portable APIs described here are only a few of the portable APIs available, but they are representative of the ones most commonly encountered. If you encounter error messages reporting that a Windows 3.x function is no longer recognized, look for a similar API name. You will probably find a portable API with the same functionality, even though it may have slightly different parameters.

Syntax Differences between the Microsoft and Borland Compilers

Most programmers rely on only one compiler, in general, choosing either the Microsoft C or the Borland C compiler. The applications used in this book for illustrations and examples have been written, as much as possible, for compatibility with either compiler. And, for the most part, the differences between the two compiler versions are slight, requiring only minor provisions for compatibility. Still, there are a few elements that deserve explanation.

Explicit Typecasting

First and most common are provisions for explicit typecasting wherever the compiler would, otherwise, issue a warning message, as in this example:

```
FilSz = GetFileSize( (HANDLE) hFil, &FilSzHigh );
```

Here the variable `hFil` was declared as an integer value to be compatible with the value returned by the `OpenFile` function, but it must be explicitly typecast as a `HANDLE` for compatibility with the `GetFileSize` function. If this typecasting is not performed, the Microsoft C compiler will issue a warning message, even though the two types—`HANDLE` and `int`—are compatible, and either function would operate correctly without this provision.

In the next example, two typecasts are made:

```
EnableWindow( GetDlgItem( hDlg, IDOK ),
    (BOOL) SendMessage( (HWND) lParam,
                        WM_GETTEXTLENGTH, 0, 0L ) );
```

The first typecast, `BOOL`, explicitly converts the `LONG` value returned by the `SendMessage` function to a Boolean True/False result acceptable to the `EnableWindow` function. Without this provision, any nonzero result would be interpreted as True and any zero response interpreted as False, but again, the Microsoft C compiler would report a conversion warning.

In both cases, the Borland C compiler, unless the compiler's default warning flags are explicitly reset to request type conversion reporting, will simply make whatever type conversions are actually required and will not flag or report such minor conversions between compatible types.

In other cases, explicit type conversions are required to prevent actual errors, not just prevent warnings. A relatively extreme example is found in the following code fragment. In this case, the compiler must be explicitly instructed how to treat the numerical results of each step of the calculation in order to ensure that the resulting `BYTE` value has, indeed, been calculated properly through a series of floating-point operations.

```
Gray = (BYTE)
   ((UINT)(float)(((unsigned char)
          (LOBYTE(HIWORD(Color))) * 0.30 ) / 16 ) +
    (UINT)(float)(((unsigned char)
          (HIBYTE(LOWORD(Color))) * 0.59 ) / 16 ) +
    (UINT)(float)(((unsigned char)
          (LOBYTE(LOWORD(Color))) * 0.11 ) / 16 ) );
```

You'll see other examples of typecasting in programs later in this book. In general, typecasting is provided simply to suppress compiler warning messages.

Unused Parameters

Another type of warning message requires a different form of suppression: the parameter not used warning message. Both the Microsoft and Borland C compilers, quite properly, issue a warning message whenever they encounter a subprocedure that is called with an argument that is not actually used within the subprocedure.

Normally, such an occurrence would, indeed, be the result of a programmer error and could be corrected by simply removing the unneeded argument from the function declaration. But, under Windows, there are circumstances where functions are called with arguments that may or may not be used by specific subprocedures.

As a general rule, this circumstance occurs in only exported functions, such as the WndProc procedure and other child window processes. But because Windows (3.x, NT, or 95) always expects to call these functions with the same four parameters, regardless of whether all four will be used, another provision is required to suppress the unused parameter warning messages.

Microsoft C and Borland C have different provisions for suppressing such warning messages. The examples in this book provide both formats but use compiler #ifdef statements to match the suppression provisions to the compiler actually in use.

For the Borland C compiler, the following code fragment, which precedes the subprocedure and affects only the subprocedure immediately following the #pragma instruction, prevents any unused parameter warning messages.

```
#ifdef __BORLANDC__
#pragma argsused    // prevents unused parameter message //
#endif

BOOL APIENTRY FileType( HWND hDlg,   UINT msg,
                        UINT wParam, LONG lParam )
```

The macro definition __BORLANDC__ will be valid if, and only if, the Borland C compiler is used. On the other hand, if the Microsoft C compiler is used, the #pragma instruction will simply be ignored (which is all very well and good because the Microsoft C compiler does not recognize the argsused directive and, otherwise, would flag this as an error).

For the opposite circumstance, using the Microsoft C compiler, a different provision is included within the subprocedure, as:

```
#ifndef __BORLANDC__
    UNREFERENCED_PARAMETER( lpCmdLine );
#endif
```

The UNREFERENCED_PARAMETER instruction, which is not recognized by the Borland C compiler and would be reported as an error, is a dummy macro that does precisely nothing—except for providing an instruction that references an otherwise unused argument.

For your own applications, you may use whichever provision is appropriate for your compiler. And, of course, unless you are writing a book on programming, you can omit both the alternative provision and all of the #ifdef and #ifndef directives.

As one alternative, if you are using the Borland C compiler, you could simply include your own definition for the UNREFERENCED_PARAMETER macro as:

```
#ifndef UNREFERENCED_PARAMETER
#define UNREFERENCED_PARAMETER(P)    (P)
#endif
```

In this chapter, we've covered many of the more common Windows 3.x–to-NT/95 conversions and what types of changes may be necessary. Of course, there are many other possible differences between Windows 3.x and NT/95 that can affect program conversion. You'll see other examples later in the book.

CHAPTER

FIVE

5

Keyboards, Carets, and Characters

- Keyboard event message components

- Virtual-key codes and handling

- Keyboard message responses and handling

- Text caret (cursor) handling

- Event message generation

Even though all types of applications—not just Windows NT and 95 programs—are becoming increasingly mouse-interactive, until such time as either mechanical telepathy or direct neural interfaces become common and reliable, the keyboard will remain the primary system input device. The standard 89-key, the enhanced 101/102-key keyboards, and the newer one-handed key encoders remain the input devices of choice for today's computer user. (Yes, I know that pen-based computers are out there, but can we really take them seriously? Not with my handwriting!)

Because the keyboard is so important, knowing how Windows NT and 95 handle keyboard events is critical. The different languages and character sets used around the world also require different programming considerations. This chapter will show you how to work with keyboard-event management in Windows applications.

The Evolution of Keyboard Character Sets and International Language Support

Originally, PCs recognized a single character set with the character values 0x20 through 0x7E devoted to the English alphabet, the Roman number set, and assorted punctuation. The remaining 128 character values—0x80 through 0xFF—were devoted to the extended ASCII characters, providing a selection of Greek and mathematical symbols and a primitive series of box-drawing characters.

On the whole, this character set was strictly English-chauvinistic. For non-English writers, it provided an exercise in frustration, as they attempted to render their native languages via a restrictive display channel. And, while various approaches attempted to circumvent these limitations, these often innovative experiments have become a matter of historical interest only.

Today, since computers are international in both nature and recognition, a variety of keyboard drivers (with corresponding video and printer character sets) provide support for most, if not all, of the principal languages of man. In some cases, such as the Japanese Kanji alphabet, this support may involve special keyboard layouts. In other cases, such as the Thai alphabet, the familiar keyboard can be adapted (with only a change of key caps for Thai characters), and only special support for the display format is required, along with, of course, an appropriate driver.

Earlier versions of Windows have provided international alphabets, but the 256 characters supported by an 8-bit character code, such as the familiar ANSI ASCII standard, have not proved adequate for true international support. For this reason, a new standard, titled Unicode, has been defined. In Unicode, characters use a 16-bit character (or "wide character") code to support a total of 65,536 characters—quite sufficient to encode all of the world's contemporary alphabets.

Of course, this does not mean that every keyboard will be expected to support the entire Unicode character set. Instead, keyboard drivers access subsets of the Unicode standard for specific languages. Win32 applications have the options of supporting either Unicode or the conventional ASCII character set, or providing mixed support for both.

Although you don't need to worry about Unicode in most cases, sometimes it's important for international support, even on an introductory level. This is demonstrated in the KeyCodes and Editor programs presented in this chapter.

How Windows NT and 95 Handle Keyboard Events

One of the principal strengths of the Windows environment is its international adaptability. During installation, or via the International dialog box of the Control Panel, you can select a variety of keyboard drivers, along with fonts and .DLL libraries that support various international keyboard configurations and character sets.

If you are reading this in English, the probabilities are that the keyboard drivers available with your version of NT/95 are principally those suited to the Germanic/Romance languages. If you are reading a translated version of this book, your version of NT/95 probably supplies a different selection of supported keyboards and alphabets.

But, no matter which keyboard driver you're using, Windows has taken control of your keyboard and is actively trapping all keyboard events, long before they could be received and interpreted by an application. Routines supplied by Windows decode these key events, storing the results as keyboard-event messages in the message queue of the application Windows believes the keyboard input is intended for.

The target application needs to retrieve the keyboard-event messages that Windows has stored in that application's message queue. When control returns to the target application, the GetMessage function (refer to the WinMain routine in Chapter 2) retrieves the keyboard-event message from the queue. After it is retrieved, the application treats the event message as characters received directly from the keyboard, in a fashion similar to how they are handled under DOS.

However, you need to be careful, because *similar* does not mean *identical*. The principal difference between a DOS application receiving keyboard-event messages (which essentially is what the scan and character codes returned by the keyboard buffer are) and a Windows application retrieving keyboard-event messages from the application's message queue is primarily the amount of information that is reported.

Early computers, with their slow CPUs and limited memory, couldn't handle complex information from the keyboard without sacrificing what little speed of execution they were capable of. (Some very early machines did not even recognize, except via special provisions, a difference between uppercase and lowercase characters and handled only 6-bit character codes.) For these systems, the wealth of information available through a modern keyboard would be overwhelming.

Under DOS, when the user presses the *a* key, a DOS keyboard buffer is fed only the single character *a* returned as the character code. The scan code, which identifies the physical key and some aspects of the Shift+Ctrl+Alt flag states, has already been discarded as unnecessary. (For details, see DOS interrupts 16h and 21h.)

But Windows NT and 95 (and, to a lesser degree, earlier versions of Windows) are designed for operation on less limited and less time-constrained CPUs. Under Windows, the same physical event of pressing the *a* key begins by reporting three separate event messages:

- A WM_KEYDOWN event reporting that a key is being pressed

- A WM_CHAR event reporting the character code generated (in the wParam argument)

- A WM_KEYUP event reporting the subsequent key release (unless, of course, the key is held down for auto-repeat)

Each of these three messages is accompanied by wParam and lParam arguments. The WM_CHAR event comprises six separate information fields. Ergo, a total of eight data elements are reported for each message received, resulting in a grand total of twenty-four pieces of data generated by one keystroke!

Fortunately, since applications are not required to use all of the information, or even to recognize its existence, you may feel free to wipe the worried sweat away from your brow and cease considering the keyboard as a potential instrument for hari kari. All of the information is there when needed, but it is not obligatory.

Types of Keyboard-Event Messages

Each keyboard event begins by generating a window message indicating that the event is one of two things: an application message or a system keystroke message. Application messages are WM_KEYDOWN, WM_KEYUP, WM_CHAR, and WM_DEADCHAR. System keystroke messages are WM_SYSKEYDOWN, WM_SYSKEYUP, WM_SYSCHAR, or WM_SYSDEADCHAR.

System keystroke messages, identified as WM_SYS*xxxxx*, are generally events that are more important to Windows than to the application. Normally, they are simply passed by default to DefWindowProc for handling. However, the KeyCodes demo program included in this chapter traps and displays almost all keyboard-event messages, both system and application, together with all of the information accompanying each.

TIP

In some cases, because the event message is interpreted by the system as requiring special actions, Windows takes control after the first of the key event is processed. Thus, a few keyboard events are only partially trapped by this program. The reasons for such event instances should be readily apparent to any programmer familiar with the Windows NT/95 interface. This discontinuity occurs simply because this program loses the input—and, therefore, the subsequent keystrokes—whenever a hot-key combination redirects operations to another application or utility.

System key event messages include Alt-key combinations, such as the Alt+Tab or Alt+Esc combinations, which are used to switch the active window or the system menu accelerators. (Alt-key combinations are discussed in detail in Chapter 12.) In some cases, these may be used by applications directly, but they are normally left for Windows to recognize and handle.

In like fashion, both the application and system *xxx*DEADCHAR messages are also ignored by the application. In general, these are used by non-U.S. keyboards that include special keys for adding accents or diacritics to other letters; to provide other special functions, or in Unicode applications to produce other special selections. Since these messages do not, of themselves, generate characters, they are called "dead" and, for most applications, they can be safely ignored.

Similarly, the WM_KEYUP, WM_SYSKEYUP, WM_KEYDOWN, and WM_SYSKEYDOWN messages can generally be ignored by the application. If circumstances demand, the information these messages hold is available.

After all of these exclusions, the WM_CHAR message remains. This event provides the single keyboard message that applications normally process, because it contains the actual character code identifying the key event.

Elements of Keyboard Messages

In DOS, in addition to the character and scan codes, keyboard shift-state information is also available, and this information can be retrieved separately from the keyboard event itself. The DOS keyboard shift-state information contains the current status of the right and left Shift keys, the right and left (assuming an enhanced keyboard) Ctrl and Alt keys, the Caps Lock and Num Lock keys, and the Scroll Lock and Insert keys (which are usually ignored). Under DOS, however, key-press and key-release events are not normally reported as separate events.

In Windows, the wParam and lParam arguments accompanying each keyboard-event message carry the event character code, the scan code, all of the shift-state information just mentioned and, in addition, an eight-bit key repeat count. Figure 5.1 illustrates the components of the wParam and lParam arguments for WM_CHAR.

The wParam Argument

In previous versions of Windows, the character code was found in the low byte of the wParam argument.

Under Windows NT and 95, the wParam argument has grown to 32 bits, and the character code can be either the low byte of the low word (for 8-bit ANSI ASCII values) or, for 16-bit Unicode character values, the low word itself. Which type of character code is expected is determined by compiler switch settings or by direct references to Unicode/ANSI API functions.

The high-word value in the wParam argument currently remains unused.

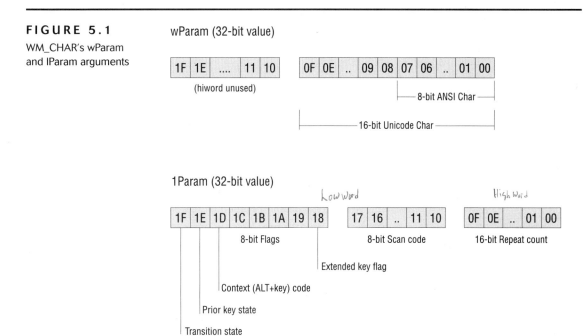

FIGURE 5.1

WM_CHAR's wParam and IParam arguments

The IParam Argument

The `lParam` argument contains a variety of information, as explained in the following sections.

Repeat Count   This 16-bit value reports the number of keystrokes represented by the event message and, normally, is one. However, if a key is held down and the application cannot process the keyboard messages quickly enough (for any reason), Windows will combine multiple WM_KEYDOWN, WM_SYSKEYDOWN, WM_CHAR, and WM_SYSCHAR messages into a single message, incrementing the repeat count appropriately. For WM_KEYUP or WM_SYSKEYUP messages, of course, the repeat count is always one.

One reason that the repeat count value may be higher than one is as a response to a typematic overrun. For example, you may observe typematic overruns while executing the KeyCodes demo program, even on fast machines, simply because of the time required to write a full-line screen message for each key event. You might also generate typematic overruns by selecting a high repeat rate from the Control

Panel. In neither case, however, should this be taken as an indication that typematic overruns are likely in conventional applications.

The PgUp, PgDn, and up and down arrow keys, however, are sometimes sources for typematic overruns, simply because the time required to respond to one instruction may be long enough for additional keystrokes to accumulate and, as a result, often cause applications to overscroll in response. For this reason, many applications prefer to ignore the repeat count value, particularly for specific keys. You should experiment with your own applications to determine whether they should use or ignore the repeat count.

Scan Code   The keyboard scan code is a value generated by the keyboard firmware to identify the actual physical key pressed or released. While the same character code may be generated by different keys—for example, the numeral *1* character can be returned either from the number key at the top of the main keyboard or from the keypad—the scan code is specific to the physical key.

Likewise, right and left Alt and Ctrl keys return separate scan codes, even though neither generates a character code. However, some physical keys may return different scan codes according to the Alt, Ctrl, or Shift states.

Extended Key Flag   This flag is set (1) if the present keystroke was generated by one of the keys specific to the enhanced keyboard. These keys include the non-keypad cursor and page keys, as well as the Insert and Delete keys, the keypad slash key (/), the keypad Enter key, and the Num Lock key.

Context Code Flag   This flag is set (1) if the Alt key is down during the present keystroke or if the current message is WM_SYSKEYUP or WM_SYSKEYDOWN. The context code flag is cleared (0) for all WM_KEYUP and WM_KEYDOWN messages with two exceptions:

- Some non-English keyboards use combinations of the Shift, Ctrl, and Alt keys together with conventional keys to generate special characters. These may have the context code flag set but will not be reported as system keystrokes.

- If the active window is an icon, it does not receive the input focus and, therefore, all keystrokes will generate WM_SYSKEYUP and WM_SYSKEYDOWN messages to prevent the active window (as an icon) from attempting to process these events. In these cases, the context code flag is set only if the Alt key is down.

Prior Key State Flag For `WM_CHAR`, `WM_CHARDOWN`, `WM_SYSCHAR`, and `WM_SYSCHARDOWN` messages, the prior key state flag is set (1) if the same key was previously down or is cleared (0) if the same key was previously up.

For `WM_KEYUP` and `WM_SYSKEYUP` messages, the prior key state flag is always set. Obviously, the key must have been down before it could be released.

Transition State Flag This flag provides redundant information. It is cleared (0) if a key is being pressed, as in a `WM_KEYDOWN` or `WM_SYSKEYDOWN` message. If the key is being released, as in a `WM_KEYUP` or `WM_SYSKEYUP` message, the flag is set (1). For the `WM_CHAR` and `WM_SYSCHAR` messages, the transition flag is cleared (but it's also irrelevant).

Deciphering Keyboard-Event Messages: The KeyCodes Program

The demo program, KeyCodes, provides a window to examine keyboard-event messages in a degree and detail that are not available through conventional handling. Figure 5.2 illustrates a series of key-event messages captured by the Key-Codes program.

NOTE The demo application provides a degree of grouping by including an extra half-line space after each `WM_KEYUP` or `WM_SYSKEYUP` event. However, as you may easily observe, the `_KEYDOWN`, `_CHAR`, and `_KEYUP` messages for a specific key do not always appear in strict sequential order.

The KeyCodes program uses eight `case` statements to respond to the keyboard `WM_xxxxx` messages. The `ShowKey` subprocedure provides the mechanism to decipher and expand the keyboard-event messages.

Let's first look at two provisions in this example that deserve some explanation. First, in the `WndProc` procedure, in response to the `WM_CREATE` message, the following code fragment is used to retrieve text-metric information for the system fixed (monospace) font.

```
case WM_CREATE:
    hdc = GetDC( hwnd );
    SelectObject( hdc, GetStockObject( SYSTEM_FIXED_FONT ) );
    GetTextMetrics( hdc, &tm );
```

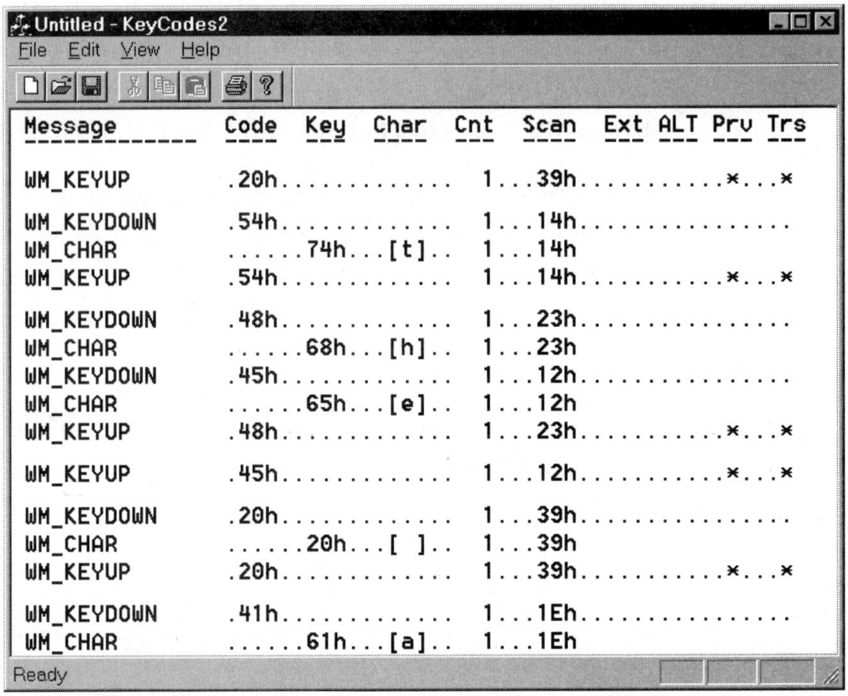

FIGURE 5.2

Keyboard-event messages deciphered through the KeyCodes program

```
Untitled - KeyCodes2                                    _ □ ×
File   Edit   View   Help
┌─────────────────────────────────────────────────┐

Message         Code  Key  Char  Cnt  Scan  Ext ALT Prv Trs
───────         ────  ───  ────  ───  ────  ─── ─── ─── ───

WM_KEYUP        .20h..............  1...39h...........×...×

WM_KEYDOWN      .54h..............  1...14h..............
WM_CHAR         ......74h...[t]..   1...14h
WM_KEYUP        .54h..............  1...14h...........×...×

WM_KEYDOWN      .48h..............  1...23h..............
WM_CHAR         ......68h...[h]..   1...23h
WM_KEYDOWN      .45h..............  1...12h..............
WM_CHAR         ......65h...[e]..   1...12h
WM_KEYUP        .48h..............  1...23h...........×...×

WM_KEYUP        .45h..............  1...12h...........×...×

WM_KEYDOWN      .20h..............  1...39h..............
WM_CHAR         ......20h...[ ]..   1...39h
WM_KEYUP        .20h..............  1...39h...........×...×

WM_KEYDOWN      .41h..............  1...1Eh..............
WM_CHAR         ......61h...[a]..   1...1Eh
Ready
```

```
cxChr = tm.tmAveCharWidth;
cyChr = tm.tmHeight + tm.tmExternalLeading;
ReleaseDC( hwnd, hdc );
rect.top = 2 * cyChr;
```

The tm (text metric) data structure is used to retrieve information about the system fixed font. The character size (in pixels) is then used to set the cxChr and cyChr variables, which will be used to control the format and spacing of the actual display.

NOTE SYSTEM_FIXED_FONT is only one of the many fonts available under Windows NT (fonts are discussed presently). I chose it for the demo program because it provides a simple, monospace font that can be expected to be available on all English/U.S. systems, as well as on most other systems.

The second, parallel provision is found in the response to the WM_PAINT message and in the ShowKeys subprocedure. Before text is written, the same SelectObject and GetStockObject functions are called again. But this time, instead of being called in an information context, they are called as the display font.

```
InvalidateRect( hwnd, NULL, TRUE );
hdc = BeginPaint( hwnd, &ps );
SelectObject( hdc, GetStockObject( SYSTEM_FIXED_FONT ) );
...
EndPaint( hwnd, &ps );
```

Remember, if you arrange spacing to fit a specific font, you also need to be sure that the same font is used for the actual display (unless you aren't particularly concerned about the results).

Last, the switch(msg)... tree provides eight case responses for the eight keyboard-event messages tracked:

```
switch( msg )
{
    ...
    case WM_KEYDOWN:
        ShowKey( hwnd, 0, FALSE, "WM_KEYDOWN", wParam, lParam );
        break;

    case WM_KEYUP:
        ShowKey( hwnd, 0, TRUE,  "WM_KEYUP", wParam, lParam );
        break;

    case WM_CHAR:
        ShowKey( hwnd, 1, FALSE, "WM_CHAR", wParam, lParam );
        break;

    case WM_DEADCHAR:
        ShowKey( hwnd, 1, FALSE, "WM_DEADCHAR", wParam, lParam );
        break;

    case WM_SYSKEYDOWN:
        ShowKey( hwnd, 0, FALSE, "WM_SYSKEYDOWN", wParam, lParam );
        break;

    case WM_SYSKEYUP:
        ShowKey( hwnd, 0, TRUE,  "WM_SYSKEYUP", wParam, lParam );
```

```
            break;

        case WM_SYSCHAR:
            ShowKey( hwnd, 1, FALSE, "WM_SYSCHAR", wParam, lParam );
            break;

        case WM_SYSDEADCHAR:
            ShowKey( hwnd, 1, FALSE, "WM_SYSDEADCHAR",wParam,lParam );
            break;
        . . .
    }
```

In each case, the response is to call the ShowKey subprocedure with the appropriate data for the display shown in Figure 5.2. Beyond this, the remaining provisions for string handling and formatting the text display are fairly straightforward C code, with the possible exception of the TextOut function call. This function appears in text as:

```
TextOut( hdc, cxChr, cyWin - step, szBuff,
            wsprintf( szBuff, szFormat[iType],
                (LPSTR) szMsg, . . .
```

In the ShowKey subprocedure, the wsprintf function is called with an explicit typecasting instruction, (LPSTR), preceding the szMsg reference. LPSTR is defined as a far pointer to a string and is necessary because, in this instance, szMsg has already been passed as a local pointer reference from the WndProc procedure. For clarity (and to prevent a compiler warning message), the explicit redefinition is made from a local to a far pointer.

The remaining parameters, such as the two string references szBuff and szFormat[], are already passed to wsprintf as the expected far pointer references and do not require explicit typecasting. However, when in doubt, including explicit typecasting does no harm; its omission might. See Chapter 4 for more information about explicit typecasting and compiler warning messages.

The complete listing of the KeyCodes program appears on the CD accompanying this book.

Virtual-Key Codes

Under DOS, many applications, particularly TSRs, spend a portion of their time filtering keyboard character codes while waiting for a specific keyboard event to trigger some action. This can be as complex as looking for a Ctrl+Alt+K combination or as common as waiting for an arrow or page key.

> **NOTE**   Hotkey assignments under Windows NT and 95 are not handled in the same fashion as DOS TSRs, nor should they be.

Virtual-key handling is one area where applications moving from DOS to Windows may experience the greatest change, as they shift from filtering characters to simply responding to virtual-key messages. This practice is demonstrated in the Editor demo program included in this chapter.

In the KeyCodes demo program, which we discussed in the previous section, the WM_KEYDOWN, WM_CHAR, and WM_KEYUP messages were introduced, along with five other key-event messages. The accompanying parameters for each message were expanded to show the fields included in the wParam and lParam arguments.

In the KeyCodes demo program, however, all of these key-event messages were given equal weight—a treatment that most applications will not indulge in. In the Editor demo program, for example, only the WM_KEYDOWN and WM_CHAR messages are trapped, leaving the remaining six keyboard-event messages for default handling.

Required Key Codes

Customarily, the WM_KEYDOWN message is trapped while looking for virtual-key messages, each of which is identified by a constant, with the format VK_*xxxxxx*, defined in WinUser.H.

> **TIP**   All the VK_*xxxx* definitions are found in the WinUser.H header file, but many of these are duplicated in the WinRes.H header.

Table 5.1 lists the virtual-key codes you'll encounter during programming for Windows keyboard events.

TABLE 5.1   Virtual-Key Codes Defined in WinUser.H

Constant	Hex	Dec	Req	Keyboard	Comments
VK_LBUTTON	01h	1			Mouse emulation
VK_RBUTTON	02h	2			Mouse emulation
VK_CANCEL	03h	3	*	Ctrl+Break	Same as Ctrl+C
VK_MBUTTON	04h	4			Mouse emulation
	05h .. 07h	5 .. 7			Not assigned
VK_BACK	08h	8	*	Backspace	
VK_TAB	09h	9	*	Tab	
	0Ah .. 0Bh	10 .. 11			Not assigned
VK_CLEAR	0Ch	12		Keypad 5	Num Lock OFF
VK_RETURN	0Dh	13	*	Enter	
	0Eh .. 0Fh	14 .. 15			Not assigned
VK_SHIFT	10h	16	*	Shift	Right or left
VK_CONTROL	11h	17	*	Ctrl	Right or left
VK_MENU	12h	18	*	Alt	Right or left
VK_PAUSE	13h	19		Pause	
VK_CAPITAL	14h	20	*	Caps Lock	

TABLE 5.1 Virtual-Key Codes Defined in WinUser.H (Continued)

Constant	Hex	Dec	Req	Keyboard	Comments
	15h .. 19h	21 .. 25			Reserved for Kanji system
	1Ah	26			Not assigned
VK_ESCAPE	1Bh	27	*	Escape	
	1Ch .. 1Fh	28 .. 31			Reserved for Kanji system
VK_SPACE	20h	32	*	Spacebar	
VK_PRIOR	21h	33	*	PgUp	
VK_NEXT	22h	34	*	PgDn	
VK_END	23h	35		End	
VK_HOME	24h	36	*	Home	
VK_LEFT	25h	37	*	Left Arrow	
VK_UP	26h	38	*	Up Arrow	
VK_RIGHT	27h	39	*	Right Arrow	
VK_DOWN	28h	40	*	Down Arrow	
VK_SELECT	29h	41		Select	OEM specific
VK_PRINT	2Ah	42		Print	OEM specific
VK_EXECUTE	2Bh	43		Execute	OEM specific
VK_SNAPSHOT	2Ch	44		PrtSc	Win 3.0 or later
VK_INSERT	2Dh	45	*	Insert	
VK_DELETE	2Eh	46	*	Delete	
VK_HELP	2Fh	47		Help	OEM specific

TABLE 5.1   Virtual-Key Codes Defined in WinUser.H (Continued)

Constant	Hex	Dec	Req	Keyboard	Comments
VK_0	30h	48	*	0–9 keys	Same as ASCII 0
..	..	..	*		through 9 on main
VK_9	39h	57	*		keyboard
	3Ah	58			Not assigned
	..	..			
	40h	64			
VK_A	41h	65	*	A–Z, a–z keys	Main keyboard
..	..	..	*		
VK_Z	5Ah	90	*		

In Table 5.1 (and in the following Tables 5.2 and 5.3), the column labeled Req (for Required) indicates by asterisks (*) which keys are required for all Windows implementations and which keys will always be available.

Any virtual-key codes that are noted as OEM specific in the Comments column of Table 5.1 (and Table 5.3) may be supported by some keyboard variations but are not standard and should not be relied on except in special circumstances.

Other values, which do not have VK_*xxxxx* constants defined, are noted as not assigned. These are not used and/or supported by any keyboard variations, nor are these assigned for any emulation purposes.

Three values with VK_*xxxxx* constants are identified as mouse emulation. This is not because they will be returned by the mouse as keyboard-event messages, but because these codes are sometimes used to emulate mouse-button events.

Two groups in Table 5.1 are noted as reserved for Kanji system. These values are used with keyboards supporting the Japanese Kanji alphabet.

The virtual-key definitions do not include punctuation and symbols, and they do not distinguish between uppercase and lowercase. Also, applications should not attempt to use virtual-key definitions for text input.

New Windows Keys

The newer "Windows keyboards" include either two or three new keys. These may include two "Windows" keys, right and left, which call the Start menu, and a single Aps key. The function of the Aps key differs according to the active application but, in general, it calls a pop-up menu, in the same fashion as clicking the right mouse button.

These three new keys are defined as shown in Table 5.2.

TABLE 5.2 Virtual-Key Codes for New Windows Keys

Constant	Hex	Dec	Req	Keyboard	Comments
VK_LWIN	5Bh	91		Left Windows key	Not on all keyboards
VK_RWIN	5Ch	92		Right Windows key	Omitted on some portables
VK_APS	5Dh	93		Aps key	Not on all keyboards

NOTE Because of space limitations, many portable computers provide only the left or right "Windows" key, not both.

Function Key and Other Special Key Codes

The function keys, keypad, arrow, Alt, Ctrl, and other special keys common to all keyboards are defined as shown in Table 5.3.

NOTE The left and right Shift, Ctrl, and Alt virtual keys are used only as parameters to the `GetAsyncKeyState` and `GetKeyState` functions. No other API functions or messages distinguish between the left and right keys in this fashion.

TABLE 5.3   Virtual-Key Codes for Function Keys and Other Special Keys

Constant	Hex	Dec	Req	Keyboard	Comments
	5Eh	94			Not assigned
	..	..			
	5Fh	95			
VK_NUMPAD0	60h	96		Keypad 0	Num Lock ON
..	..	..		..	
VK_NUMPAD9	69h	105		Keypad 9	
VK_MULTIPLY	6Ah	106		Keypad *	Enhanced
VK_ADD	6Bh	107		Keypad +	Enhanced
VK_SEPARATOR	6Ch	108			OEM specific
VK_SUBTRACT	6Dh	109		Keypad -	Enhanced
VK_DECIMAL	6Eh	110		Keypad .	Enhanced
VK_DIVIDE	6Fh	111		Keypad /	Enhanced
VK_F1	70h	112	*	Function key F1	Standard
..	..	..	*	..	
VK_F10	79h	121	*	Function key F10	
VK_F11	7Ah	122		Function key F11	Enhanced
VK_F12	7Bh	123		Function key F12	Enhanced
VK_F13	7Ch	124		Function key F13	OEM specific (not
..	..	..		..	available on most
VK_F24	87h	135		Function key F24	keyboards)
	88h	136			Not assigned
	..	..			
	8Fh	143			
VK_NUMLOCK	90h	144	*	Num Lock	
VK_SCROLL	91h	145	*	Scroll Lock	
	92h	146			Not assigned
	..	..			
	9Fh	159			

TABLE 5.3   Virtual-Key Codes for Function Keys and Other Special Keys (Continued)

Constant	Hex	Dec	Req	Keyboard	Comments
VK_LSHIFT	A0h	160		Left Shift key	Enhanced
VK_RSHIFT	A1h	161		Right Shift key	Enhanced
VK_LCONTROL	A2h	162		Left Ctrl key	Enhanced
VK_RCONTROL	A3h	163		Right Ctrl key	Enhanced
VK_LMENU	A4h	164		Left Alt key	Enhanced
VK_RMENU	A5h	165		Right Alt key	Enhanced
	A6h .. E4h	166 .. 288			Not assigned
VK_PROCESSKEY	E5h	229			OEM specific
	E6h .. F5h	230 .. 245			Not assigned
VK_ATTN	F6h	246			OEM specific
VK_CRSEL	F7h	247			OEM specific
VK_EXSEL	F8h	248			OEM specific
VK_EREOF	F9h	249			OEM specific
VK_PLAY	FAh	250			OEM specific
VK_ZOOM	FBh	251			OEM specific
VK_NONAME	FCh	252			OEM specific
VK_PA1	FDh	253			OEM specific
VK_OEM_CLEAR	FEh	254			OEM specific

Of the remaining VK_*xxxxxx* definitions, some are labeled enhanced keyboard and are only supported by enhanced 101/102 keyboards.

NOTE Because the keypad *5* key does not have a "keypad" function (at least not one that is commonly supported), this key returns two different scan codes, depending on whether the Num Lock key is set or cleared. See VK_CLEAR (0x0C).

One additional VK_*xxxxx* definition that may be of interest is the VK_KANA code, defined in AfxVer.H as:

Constant	Hex	Dec	Req	Keyboard	Comments
VK_KANA	15h	21			Used for Kanji

Trapping Virtual-Key Codes: The Editor Program

In the following fragment from the Editor demo program, the Home, End, PgUp, (VK_PRIOR), PgDn (VK_NEXT), and arrow keys are trapped as virtual-key codes in the low word of the wParam argument that accompanies the WM_KEYDOWN message. Each key code exercises the appropriate control over the cursor position:

```
case WM_KEYDOWN:
   switch( LOWORD( wParam ) )
   {
      case VK_HOME:
         xCaret = 0;
         break;

      case VK_END:
         xCaret = cxBuff - 1;
         break;

      case VK_PRIOR:
         yCaret = 0;
         break;

      case VK_NEXT:
         yCaret = cyBuff - 1;
```

```
        break;

        ...

    case VK_DOWN:
        yCaret = min( yCaret+1, cyBuff-1 );
        break;
```

Since the Editor example does not scroll and is limited to the client window display, the PgUp (VK_PRIOR) and PgDn (VK_NEXT) keys move the cursor to the top and bottom text positions within the window, respectively. The complete listing for the Editor program is included at the end of this chapter.

In other applications, almost any key that can be used for control, selection, or activation will be found in the virtual-key list and can be trapped in fashion similar to the preceding example.

Getting Shift-State Data for Virtual Keys

The wParam and lParam arguments accompanying key-event messages carry a considerable amount of information, but they do not provide specific shift-key data other than for alphabetical characters (uppercase or lowercase) and other dual-character keys. To query the current shift states of the Shift, Ctrl, and Alt keys as well as the toggled shift keys, Caps Lock and Num Lock, you can use the Get-KeyState function.

Realize, however, that the shift states reported by this function are the shift states associated with specific keyboard-event messages in the application's message queue—not the physical interrupt-level state at the instant the inquiry is made. Thus, if the string "This is a TEST" were in the application's message buffer, and the next char message to be read was a capital letter (assuming the right or left Shift key was used rather than the Caps Lock key), the API function call GetKeyState (VK_SHIFT) would report the Shift key as down, regardless of the actual physical state of either Shift key at that instant. In like fashion, if the next char message were lowercase, the same inquiry would report both Shift keys were released.

For immediate information about the shift state of any of the shift keys—Shift, Ctrl, or Alt—use the GetAsyncKeyState function with the VK_SHIFT, VK_CONTROL or VK_MENU parameter, respectively. Or, for even more specific information, you could use the VK_Lxxxxx or VK_Rxxxxx parameter to distinguish between the right and left Shift, Ctrl, or Alt key.

NOTE The VK_LBUTTON, VK_RBUTTON, and VK_MBUTTON parameters can also be used with the GetKeyState function to query the mouse-button status. This is generally unnecessary, because the mouse-event messages already contain all the relevant information. See Chapter 6 for more information about mouse-event messages.

Responding to Keyboard Messages

The KeyCodes program, provided to demonstrate interception and reporting for keyboard-event messages, also demonstrates the potential hazards in attempting to process every message received. As mentioned earlier, if an application (or system) is not fast enough to process every keyboard message generated, Windows will combine duplicate messages, incrementing the repeat count appropriately. This approach may seem useful, but keep in mind that processing all—or even most—keyboard messages is neither necessary nor desirable. The reasons for this are threefold:

- The WM_SYS*xxxx* messages are intended for Windows, not the application, to handle. Except under special circumstances, they can safely be left for processing via the DefMessageProc call.

- The WM_KEYDOWN and WM_KEYUP messages are essentially duplicates, and again, except for special circumstances, either or both can be ignored entirely. If, however, they are actually needed, most applications will confine themselves to responding to WM_KEYDOWN events while ignoring WM_KEYUP events.

- Even when WM_KEYDOWN messages are recognized, they are generally confined to cursor and special key events, not to retrieve conventional character key events. For this latter purpose, only the WM_CHAR message should be expected.

Windows NT and 95 applications should not depend on special key combinations, which very well may not be supported by many keyboard drivers and/or physical keyboards (especially non-English versions). Granted, this prohibition does eliminate a number of favorite "tricks." But there are a number of alternatives to using special key combinations. Also, your application will benefit by not relying on deciphering complex key combinations, because the time for processing keyboard messages can be greatly reduced.

Translating Character-Event Messages

Applications dealing with text input depend on the WM_CHAR keyboard-event messages to provide character input (as shown in the Editor demo program in this chapter). However, the WM_CHAR messages may or may not correspond to the familiar ASCII codes. So, how do you ensure that when a key is pressed your application receives the appropriate character code?

Actually, in this respect, there is very little problem because, to match the keyboard drivers generating these messages, Windows also provides translation services that have been incorporated in all of the programming examples. As you may recall, the message loop in the WinMain procedure appears like this:

```
while( GetMessage( &msg, NULL, 0, 0 ) )
{
    TranslateMessage( &msg );
    DispatchMessage( &msg );
}
```

The TranslateMessage function provides the mechanism to convert keystroke-event messages into character messages. These messages are recognized and used by the application because the keyboard, per se, generates only keystroke information. Before this new keystroke information can be used, it must be translated by the keyboard driver into WM_xxxKEYDOWN and WM_xxxKEYUP messages.

This translation process derives the WM_CHAR and WM_DEADCHAR messages from WM_KEYDOWN events, and the WM_SYSCHAR and WM_SYSDEADCHAR messages from WM_SYSKEYDOWN events. The translation service also processes shift-status flags to generate uppercase and lowercase characters.

The important point to remember is that the WM_CHAR message, via the TranslateMessage function, provides character information. The VK_xxxxx message parameters provide all function, cursor, and special key data. Both of these methods are demonstrated by the Editor program. The complete listing of the Editor demo program appears at the end of this chapter.

Keyboard-Event Message Handling Using MFC

If you are using MFC and creating an application using the AppWizard, the conventional message loop is effectively hidden and unavailable. This does not mean, however, that you cannot trap all these message events in the fashion shown in the KeyCodes demo program; it just means that a slightly different approach is required for interception.

The KeyCodes2 application shows how to trap the keyboard events using the `PreTranslateMessage` member function in the `CKeyCodes2View` class. The keyboard-event message is received as an MSG structure, which is defined as:

```
typedef struct tagMSG
{
    HWND    hwnd;
    UINT    message;
    WPARAM  wParam;
    LPARAM  lParam;
    DWORD   time;
    POINT   pt;
}   MSG;
```

The MSG fields are defined as follows:

- `hwnd`: Identifies the handle of the window whose window procedure receives the message.

- `message`: The message number or identifier.

- `wParam`: Provides additional information about the message. The exact meaning depends on the value of the `message` member.

- `lParam`: Provides additional information about the message. The exact meaning depends on the value of the `message` member.

- `time`: Provides the time when the message was posted.

- `pt`: Provides the cursor position, in absolute screen coordinates, at the time the message was posted.

The original KeyCodes demo program is concerned with only the `message`, `wParam`, and `lParam` fields in the MSG structure, and ignores the `hwnd`, `time`, and `pt` fields. The `pt` field would be useful if you were intercepting mouse messages, but it really isn't relevant in this example, which demonstrates handling events generated from the keyboard.

In the KeyCodes2 example `PreTranslateMessage` handler, the `pMsg` structure is handled in the same fashion as the message events are handled in the original Key-Codes program (the non-MFC version). The exception is that, in this case, the `pMsg` structure is provided in place of separate parameters and, therefore, must be decoded before passing the arguments needed to the `ShowKey` function for display.

```
BOOL CKeyCodes2View::PreTranslateMessage(MSG* pMsg)
{
   switch( pMsg->message )
   {
      case WM_KEYDOWN:
         ShowKey( 0, 0, "WM_KEYDOWN", pMsg->wParam, pMsg->lParam );
         break;

      case WM_KEYUP:
         ShowKey( 0, 1, "WM_KEYUP", pMsg->wParam, pMsg->lParam );
         break;

      case WM_CHAR:
         ShowKey( 1, 0, "WM_CHAR", pMsg->wParam, pMsg->lParam );
         break;

      case WM_DEADCHAR:
         ShowKey( 1, 0, "WM_DEADCHAR", pMsg->wParam, pMsg->lParam );
         break;

      case WM_SYSKEYDOWN:
         ShowKey( 0,0,"WM_SYSKEYDOWN",pMsg->wParam, pMsg->lParam );
         break;

      case WM_SYSKEYUP:
         ShowKey( 0, 1, "WM_SYSKEYUP",pMsg->wParam, pMsg->lParam );
         break;

      case WM_SYSCHAR:
         ShowKey( 1, 0, "WM_SYSCHAR",pMsg->wParam, pMsg->lParam );
         break;

      case WM_SYSDEADCHAR:
         ShowKey( 1,0,"WM_SYSDEADCHAR",pMsg->wParam,pMsg->lParam );
         break;
   }
   return CView::PreTranslateMessage(pMsg);
}
```

Notice also that all of the events are returned for default handling by the `Pre-TranslateMessage` function of the parent class. If we had not defined a custom `PreTranslateMessage` handler here, this would have been the default handling provided by MFC.

> **NOTE** Chances are that you will not need to provide this type of handling for any of your own applications. For most key events, MFC provides alternatives that do not need this level of interrogation. Nevertheless, you are still able to intercept keyboard (and other event) messages at the lowest possible level.

Handling Text Input

You already know how important the keyboard is as an input device. What is even more important is the ability of an application to cleanly receive and display text—anything from a few lines to full screens of structured or unstructured text. And, in any case, there are a few basics that apply to all types of text input. Of course, with Windows, there are a few differences as well. As the Walrus said, "the time has come to speak of many things …," but specifically, things governing Windows' ability to display text and to accept inputs.

The Caret versus the Cursor

In Windows, the word *cursor* has been reserved for the mouse cursor. The familiar DOS cursor (from the text-mode display) is now renamed the *caret*. Technically, this term more properly refers to the curious little hat-shaped character (^), which C/C++ commonly recognizes as the bitwise XOR operator, and which other human, European languages use as an accent (as in â, for example).

Of course, the caret displayed has no resemblance to the caret character (thus far, at least, no applications have appeared using a literal caret), any more than the cursor (mouse) resembles the DOS text cursor. Furthermore, in both cases, the displayed symbol for either the cursor or caret pointer device is a graphic, and therefore flexible. Ergo, applications are free to modify both devices, although some standards and conventions do apply.

One standard that does not apply in Windows, however, is the DOS cursor standard of a blinking, underline cursor (caret). This is because Windows supports both flexible font sizes and proportionally spaced fonts, so no fixed character width applies, and the underline caret simply does not serve as an accurate position indicator. Instead, a blinking vertical line, the same height as either the font or the interline spacing, has replaced the blinking underbar in a wide variety of applications. Conventionally, the blinking line is positioned at the point where the next character will begin (or at the first or left-most extent of an existing character).

TIP

For other languages, such as Hebrew (which is written right to left), other conventions apply. For a vertical script such as ancient Chinese ideograms, the solution might be a blinking horizontal bar. Of course, if a bostriphon (literally, as the ox plows) script remains in use anywhere in the world, the alternating right-to-left and left-to-right text would demand its own standards. In fact, this might be a situation where, curiously enough, the caret character, positioned below the line, might serve nicely—certainly much better than a plain underbar.

Changing the Caret Type and Position

Because the caret (text cursor) is a system resource, individual applications are not free to create or destroy the caret any more than they are free to create and destroy the mouse cursor. Applications may, however, borrow the system caret—at least, as long as the application holds the system (input) focus. During this time, an application can change the caret type, as well as control the caret position.

System Focus Messages

The first step, before the caret can be positioned or modified, is for the application to know when it gains or loses the system focus. Two Windows messages are devoted to precisely this function:

- `WM_SETFOCUS` notifies an application that it is receiving the system focus.

- `WM_KILLFOCUS` notifies an application that it is losing the system focus.

The two focus messages are always issued in pairs; that is, a `WM_SETFOCUS` will always be followed at some point by a `WM_KILLFOCUS` message, while the latter message will never be issued except when preceded by the former.

NOTE WM_SETFOCUS and WM_KILLFOCUS are totally independent of the WM_PAINT, WM_SIZE, and other messages that instruct applications to update or adjust their displays. Applications can accomplish these and other appropriate tasks without receiving the system focus or coming to the front of the screen.

At the same time, receipt of a WM_SETFOCUS or WM_KILLFOCUS message does not indicate or suggest that an application is being created or destroyed. It just indicates that the focus is being shifted to or from the present application.

Conversely, a WM_CREATE message is always preceded by a WM_SETFOCUS message. In parallel fashion, a WM_KILLFOCUS message follows a WM_DESTROY message, providing opportunities to create and destroy application carets.

Caret Shape and Position Functions

When an application receives the system focus, as notified by a WM_SETFOCUS message, the immediate response, if applicable, is usually to call the CreateCaret function to assign the desired caret shape, followed by SetCaretPos to position the caret and ShowCaret to make the caret visible:

```
case WM_SETFOCUS:
    CreateCaret( hwnd, (HBITMAP) 1, cxChr, cyChr );
    SetCaretPos( xCaret * cxChr, yCaret * cyChr );
    ShowCaret( hwnd );
    break;
```

The CreateCaret function is called with four parameters: a handle identifying the application window owning the caret, a bitmap handle providing the caret shape, and the width and height of the caret. The bitmap handle may have two default values: null to create a solid caret or one (1) to create a gray caret. In both cases, the caret will be a block (or line) with the dimensions specified by the third and fourth arguments. In the Editor demo program, the caret is a gray block that is the height and width of a single character.

Because any call to CreateCaret destroys any previous caret shape, applications must be prepared to re-create their caret shape anytime the system focus is received. If this is not done, the caret displayed will be whatever shape was set by the last application holding the system focus and defining a caret format.

In addition to creating a caret (text cursor), functions are also provided to set the caret position, find the caret position, and make the caret visible.

The SetCaretPos function is called with the x-axis and y-axis coordinates for the caret position, nominally the position of the upper-left corner of the caret bitmap. If, however, the window was created using the CS_OWNDC class style, these coordinates are mapped to the mapping mode associated with the window, and the caret position (and appearance) are affected accordingly. (Mapping modes will be discussed and illustrated in Chapter 21.) The caret position is set regardless of whether the caret is visible.

The complementary function, GetCaretPos, is called with a long pointer to a POINT structure. It returns the caret's current position (in client window coordinates) or returns FALSE on failure.

The ShowCaret function is called to make the caret visible and has only one parameter: the handle identifying the window owning the caret. If the caret has been hidden two or more times in succession, the ShowCaret function must be called an equal number of times before the caret will become visible. Also, if the handle passed is NULL, the SetCaret function will work only if the caret is owned by a window in the current task (it is, however, very bad form for one application to try to show another application's caret).

NOTE   If the caret has no shape or size, the ShowCaret function will have no effect.

The flip side of the WM_SETFOCUS message is the WM_KILLFOCUS message, which includes the HideCaret function.

```
case WM_KILLFOCUS:
    HideCaret( hwnd );
    DestroyCaret();
    break;
```

The HideCaret function, like its counterpart, ShowCaret, is called with a single parameter identifying the application window owning the caret. Hiding the caret does not destroy the caret shape, which can be restored by the ShowCaret function. Multiple successive calls to the ShowCaret function must be matched by multiple calls to the HideCaret function before the caret will be hidden.

Also, if desired, the `SetCaretBlinkTime` function sets the caret blink rate as elapsed milliseconds between flashes. The function is called with a single argument (`UINT`), specifying both the delay between flashes and the flash duration.

The `GetCaretBlinkTime` function requires no parameters and returns a `UINT` value, specifying the blink time in milliseconds.

Positioning the Caret (Cursor) for a Fixed-Width Font

The Editor demo program uses a gray-block caret, sized to fit the `SYSTEM_FIXED_FONT`, as you can see in Figure 5.3. Since this is a fixed-width font, cursor positioning is quite simple.

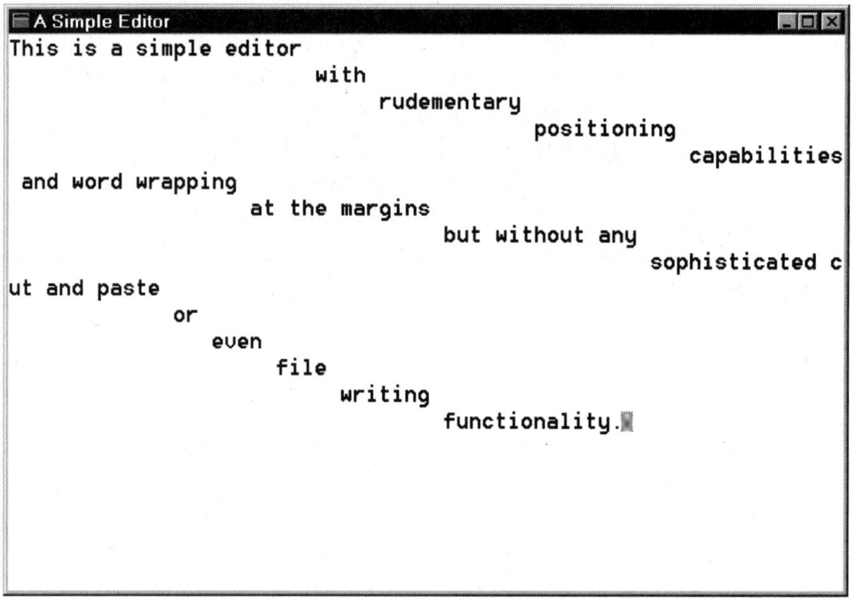

FIGURE 5.3

A simple text-only editor program

With the caret initially located at the upper-left corner of the client window, the caret positioning provisions begin by watching for a `WM_KEYDOWN` message, such as:

```
case WM_KEYDOWN:
    switch( LOWORD( wParam ) )
    {
```

Most of the WM_KEYDOWN messages received will be ignored; a response will be generated only when the wParam argument identifies one of the cursor or page keys (identified by the appropriate VK_*xxxx* virtual-key messages, as explained earlier in the chapter). Since this is a fixed-width font, the appropriate response is simply to increment or decrement the cursor in character (row/column) positions.

```
case VK_HOME:
   xCaret = 0;
   break;

case VK_END:
   xCaret = cxBuff - 1;
   break;

case VK_PRIOR:
   yCaret = 0;
   break;

case VK_NEXT:
   yCaret = cyBuff - 1;
   break;

case VK_LEFT:
   xCaret = max( xCaret-1, 0 );
   break;

case VK_RIGHT:
   xCaret = min( xCaret+1, cxBuff-1 );
   break;

case VK_UP:
   yCaret = max( yCaret-1, 0 );
   break;

case VK_DOWN:
   yCaret = min( yCaret+1, cyBuff-1 );
   break;
```

NOTE

For a variable-width font, such as the the font used for a WYSIWYG ("What You See Is What You Get") editor, the immediate response in most cases would be essentially the same. The application would keep track of the cursor position in terms of line and character positions, and only convert these row/column equivalents to an actual screen position matching the string display position immediately before calling the Set-CaretPos function.

Deleting the Character at the Caret Position

The page and arrow keys are only a few of the VK_*xxxxx* messages to which the editor could respond. In this example, there's only one additional virtual key provided for: the VK_DELETE event, which is handled as:

```
case VK_DELETE:
    for( x = xCaret; x < cxBuff - 1; x++ )
        Buffer( x, yCaret ) = Buffer( x+1, yCaret );
    Buffer( cxBuff-1, yCaret ) = ' ';
```

Here the response is a bit more elaborate than simply changing the cursor position. In this instance, the program deletes the character at the cursor position by shifting the remainder of the line left one character position and appending a blank at the end of the line. (The space ensures that the character, prior to deletion, is overwritten with a blank.) Updating the text buffer is only a part of the necessary response. The display also needs to be updated, which can be done in a couple of ways. For one, the application could simply invalidate the appropriate region, allowing a repaint to repair the screen. Or, as done in this case, an immediate screen update can be executed.

```
HideCaret( hwnd );
hdc = GetDC( hwnd );
SelectObject( hdc,
    GetStockObject( SYSTEM_FIXED_FONT ) );
TextOut( hdc, xCaret * cxChr, yCaret * cyChr,
        &Buffer( xCaret, yCaret ), cxBuff-xCaret );
ShowCaret( hwnd );
ReleaseDC( hwnd, hdc );
```

Notice that, before updating the screen, the `HideCaret` function is called to remove the caret from the display, and after updating, `ShowCaret` restores the text cursor with the position unchanged. Removing the caret is a necessary operation anytime the screen is repainted, simply to ensure that the caret doesn't interfere with the paint operation (similar precautions are generally used when the mouse cursor is active). Feel free to experiment by commenting out both the `HideCaret` and `ShowCaret` API calls and observing the results for yourself.

For a `VK_BACK` (backspace) message, essentially the same response could be used, except the program would also need to decrement the caret position. An alternative is to handle this through a `WM_CHAR` message, as described a bit later in the chapter.

For other possible `VK_xxxxx` messages, quite different responses might be required. For example, suppose provisions were made for the `VK_INSERT` message to toggle between insert and overwrite modes. Should the cursor shape, size, or format change to reflect the current mode?

Still, whatever operations are provided, the last provision within the `VK_KEYDOWN` response is to update the caret position, even though many of the options may not have affected this position at all.

```
SetCaretPos( xCaret * cxChr, yCaret * cyChr );
break;
```

Using the fixed-width font, calculating the position is simple, requiring nothing more than multiplying the row and column position by the character width and line spacing, respectively.

For a variable-width font, a different approach is required. There are several possibilities, but perhaps the best approach might lie in a feature of Windows known as the *current position* or `cp`, described in the next section.

Caret Handling for Variable-Width Fonts

The `cp` is an internal `POINT` structure that can be used by Windows to track drawing operations, with a separate `cp` for each device context. In some cases, `cp` is ignored and is not updated during draw operations.

For example, the `TextOut` function used to write (draw) the text display in the Editor demo program does not, normally, keep track of the `cp`. However, this is subject to change. Calling the `SetTextAlign` function with the `fmode` argument `TA_UPDATECP` will enable current position tracking.

When current position tracking is enabled, the GetCurrentPositionEx function can be called to retrieve the cp coordinates after writing a string or a portion of a string. For example, assume that the string displayed reads, "This is a positioning text," and the caret should be positioned immediately after the *a*. With a proportionally spaced font, the capital *T* will be wider than average, and the two *i*'s will be narrower. Obviously, attempting to estimate character positions from the tmAveCharWidth spacing is not going to produce accurate results. If, however, only a part of the string is drawn ("This is a"), and cp is retrieved before completing the sentence, the retrieved cp will provide the positioning for the caret.

The bad news is that it's not entirely as simple as this illustration suggests. You will need to refer to the SetTextAlign, GetCurrentPositionEx, and TextOut functions for details on how to use each appropriately for the task. And, of course, you will need to do a bit of experimenting.

However, since designing word processors is a topic that would require an entire book of its own, these few hints will have to suffice. Now, we will return to the real topic of this chapter: keyboard operations under Windows.

Handling WM_CHAR Messages

Like WM_KEYDOWN messages, WM_CHAR messages are also subject to a wide variety of processing. Most of the special provisions discussed here can also be handled by virtual-key responses in the WM_KEYDOWN message handling. In fact, in most cases, they would be handled that way. But the WM_CHAR message-handling methods are alternatives that you may want to consider.

 TIP For an exercise in key codes and functions, convert as much as is practical of the WM_CHAR message handling to WM_KEYDOWN handling. Just be sure to test your results carefully.

Repeat Characters

The first step, since the WM_CHAR message may well include a repeat count, is a loop controlled by the low word in the lParam argument.

```
case WM_CHAR:
    for( i = 0; i < (int)LOWORD(lParam); i++ )
    {
```

Within the loop, even though the high word of `wParam` should be simply a null, the `LOWORD` macro is used to discard any potentially conflicting data.

```
switch( LOWORD( wParam ) )
{
```

Backspace

The first character value trapped is the backspace character (\b).

```
case '\b':           // backspace
    if( xCaret > 0 )
    {   xCaret-;
        SendMessage( hwnd, WM_KEYDOWN,VK_DELETE,1L );
    }
    break;
```

The Backspace key is easily handled by simply decrementing the caret position and then issuing a keydown/delete key message. Alternatively, this could be handled as a virtual key (`VK_BACK`) in the preceding `WM_KEYDOWN` handler. In this case, the handling might well be almost exactly the same as shown here.

Tab

The tab character is easily provided for using a `do .. while` loop to insert spaces repeatedly until the desired character position is reached.

```
case '\t':           // tab
    do
        SendMessage( hwnd, WM_CHAR, ' ', 1L);
    while( xCaret % 8 != 0 );
    break;
```

Like the Backspace key, the Tab key can also be trapped by the preceding `WM_KEYDOWN` handler.

Carriage Return and Line Feed

The next two character events are handled here as a pair. The first character watched for is the carriage return (\r or ASCII 0x0D), which resets the horizontal position to the beginning of the line. It is then allowed to fall through to the second case, the line feed, for further response.

```
case '\r':          // carriage return
    xCaret = 0;     // falls through to '\n'

case '\n':          // line feed
    if( ++yCaret == cyBuff )
        yCaret = 0;
    break;
```

The line-feed character ($\backslash n$ or ASCII 0x0A), by convention, does not reset the horizontal position; instead, it is treated as the equivalent of the down arrow. In this example, both of these responses could easily have been written as:

```
case '\r':
    SendMessage( hwnd, WM_KEYDOWN, VK_HOME, 1L );

case '\n':
    SendMessage( hwnd, WM_KEYDOWN, VK_DOWN, 1L );
    break;
```

Notice that the carriage return response is still allowed to fall through to the subsequent line-feed response.

While the practice of responding to one keyboard-event message by issuing other keyboard-event messages may, at first, seem slightly redundant, the overall result is an economy of effort both for the programmer and for the program. After all, instead of duplicating essentially the same response (both as code and executable), this approach allows code and executable to do double duty. In addition, this approach can be (and often is) applied to features other than keyboard responses.

Escape (Esc)

The Escape key (ASCII 0x1B) is another popular "hotkey." In this example, it is used to reset the text buffer and then issue a query for confirmation.

```
case '\x1B':          // escape
    if( MessageBox( hwnd, "Reset text buffer?",
        "Editor Query",
        MB_ICONEXCLAMATION | MB_OKCANCEL |
        MB_DEFBUTTON2 ) == IDOK )
```

The `MessageBox` API call presents a stock dialog box with the caption "Editor Query," the message "Reset test buffer?", and the OK and Cancel buttons. If the OK button is clicked, the function returns TRUE; if the Cancel button is selected, it returns FALSE. This value dictates whether or not the following provisions will be executed.

If the decision is to proceed, then a double loop overwrites the text buffer with blanks, the caret position is reset to the first character position at the upper-left, and last, the InvalidateRect function is called to clear the existing display by issuing a WM_PAINT message.

```
    {
        for( y = 0; y < cyBuff; y++ )
            for( x = 0; x < cxBuff; x++ )
                Buffer( x, y ) = ' ';
        xCaret = 0;
        yCaret = 0;
        InvalidateRect( hwnd, NULL, FALSE );
    }
    break;
```

Other Character Events

As a final response to WM_CHAR messages, the default provision handles all other character events, which are assumed to be conventional alphabetic, numeric, or punctuation characters.

```
    default:                // all other chars
        Buffer( xCaret, yCaret ) =
            (char) LOWORD( wParam );
        HideCaret( hwnd );
        hdc = GetDC( hwnd );
    SelectObject( hdc, GetStockObject
        ( SYSTEM_FIXED_FONT ));
    TextOut( hdc, xCaret * cxChr, yCaret * cyChr,
            &Buffer( xCaret, yCaret ), 1 );
    ShowCaret( hwnd );
    ReleaseDC( hwnd, hdc );
    if( ++xCaret == cxBuff )
    {
        xCaret = 0;
        if( ++yCaret == cyBuff ) yCaret = 0;
    }
    break;
    }   }
```

The handling used is essentially the same as shown earlier for the VK_DELETE message. However, in view of earlier remarks about sharing responses, couldn't the present duplication of code and executable be similarly avoided?

Finally, since some of the preceding responses have affected the caret position, the same closing provision is required here as in the WM_KEYDOWN response.

```
SetCaretPos( xCaret * cxChr, yCaret * cyChr );
break;
```

As you've seen so far, as word processors go, the Editor demo program is both a wimp and an idiot. It includes provisions for nothing except the simplest operations for input, control, and for display. Furthermore, as it stands, Editor does not even toggle between insert and overwrite modes, a feature provided by even the dumbest editors.

Although it's severely lacking, the Editor program does accomplish its objective: not to build a word processor, but to show how keyboard-event messages are handled and to demonstrate the basic caret (text cursor) functions. The complete listing of the Editor program is shown at the end of this chapter.

Before we leave the topics of the keyboard and caret, a couple of other methods used by the KeyCodes and Editor demo programs deserve some explanation.

Generating Event Messages

The flip side of processing keyboard messages (or any other event messages) is being able to generate your own messages to request specific actions. You've seen several brief examples of message generation in the preceding code fragments.

Sending Messages to Applications

The SendMessage function is called with the same four parameters that are passed to the WndProc procedure, as:

```
SendMessage( HWND   hwnd,    UINT msg,
             DWORD wParam, LONG lParam );
```

SendMessage passes its arguments to Windows, which then becomes responsible for placing the message in the message queue for the application identified by the

> **NOTE**
> For sending messages to other applications, `SendMessage` is not the most efficient method. There are simpler ways to exchange information and instructions between applications, as explained in Part 5 of this book.

`hwnd` argument. In this fashion, the destination could be the same application window that originated the message, another window belonging to the same application, or even a window belonging to another application entirely.

PostMessage versus SendMessage

Two functions are provided for passing messages within an application: `SendMessage` and `PostMessage`. These have essentially the same function, except for how messages are dispatched.

`PostMessage` places the message in the messaging queue and then returns immediately, without waiting for the message to be delivered. Using `PostMessage`, the posting procedure can continue operation, and the called procedure, the message recipient, does not act until the message queue delivers.

In contrast, `SendMessage` places a message in the queue but does not return until the message has been processed and delivered to the recepient. In effect, `SendMessage` transfers operational control to another routine—the message recipient—and waits for the recipient to finish its task and return control.

Scrolling with Arrow Keys

In Chapter 3, the PainText program demonstrated how scrollbars are used to respond to mouse-event messages. Even though it is rare to find a computer without a mouse (at least, one that is running Windows), there may be times when using the keyboard for scrolling is more convenient.

To further demonstrate the `SendMessage` function, here is a patch for the Pain-Text program, which allows the arrow keys to simulate mouse operations:

```
switch( msg )
{
    ...
    case WM_KEYDOWN:
        switch( LOWORD( wParam ) )
        {
            case VK_LEFT:
                SendMessage( hwnd, WM_HSCROLL, SB_LINEUP, OL );
                break;

            case VK_RIGHT:
                SendMessage( hwnd, WM_HSCROLL, SB_LINEDOWN, OL );
                break;

            case VK_UP:
                SendMessage( hwnd, WM_VSCROLL, SB_LINEUP, OL );
                break;

            case VK_DOWN:
                SendMessage( hwnd, WM_VSCROLL, SB_LINEDOWN, OL );
                break;
            ...
        }
        break;
    ...
}
break;
...
```

In this fashion, the four arrow keys use the `SendMessage` function to generate scrollbar messages equivalent to clicking on the arrow keys at the ends of the scrollbars. Alternatively, for faster scroll operations, the PgUp (`VK_PRIOR`), PgDn (`VK_NEXT`), Home (`VK_HOME`), and End (`VK_END`) keys can be used to send the appropriate `SB_PAGEUP` and `SB_PAGEDOWN` messages to each scrollbar.

The `SendMessage` function can be used to generate any valid Windows message, not just those shown here. Furthermore, this can be initiated in response to any appropriate circumstance, not just a keyboard (or mouse) event.

In Windows programming, messages are generated in response to a wide variety of circumstances and for a wide variety of purposes. In many senses, the message functions and operations are the heart of Windows applications (actually, life's blood might be a better analogy).

Listing 5.1: The Editor Program

```
rem ;========================;
rem ;        Editor.BAT       ;
rem ;   calls NMAKE utility   ;
rem ;========================;
nmake -a -f EDITOR
if exist EDITOR.OBJ del EDITOR.OBJ



#================================================#
# Nmake macros for building Windows 32-bit apps #
#================================================#

!include <ntwin32.mak>

# instruction allows NMAKE to work

all: editor.exe

# update object file as required
editor.obj: editor.c
   $(cc) $(cflags) $(cvars) editor.c

# update executable file if necessary
editor.exe: editor.obj editor.def
   $(cvtobj) $(cvtdebug) *.obj
   $(link) $(guiflags) -out:editor.exe editor.obj \
           $(guilibs)
```

```
;========================================;
;  Editor.DEF module definition file  ;
;========================================;

NAME          EDITOR
DESCRIPTION   "Windows KeyBoard Program"
EXETYPE       WINDOWS
STUB          "WINSTUB.EXE"
CODE          PRELOAD MOVEABLE DISCARDABLE
DATA          PRELOAD MOVEABLE MULTIPLE
HEAPSIZE      1024
STACKSIZE     5120
EXPORTS       WndProc


//===========================//
//          Editor.C         //
//   C++ Windows Editor Demo //
//===========================//

#include <windows.h>
#include <malloc.h>

#define Buffer( x, y )  *( pBuffer + y * cxBuff + x )
#define MAX_BUFF        65535L
#define APP_ICON        IDI_APPLICATION   // no icon
#define APP_MENU        NULL              // no menu

HANDLE hInst;
char    szAppTitle[] = "A Simple Editor";
char    szAppName[]  = "Editor";

long FAR PASCAL WndProc( HWND hwnd,      UINT msg,
                         UINT wParam, LONG lParam )
{
    static char   *pBuffer = NULL;
    static int    cxChr, cyChr, cxWin, cyWin,
                  cxBuff, cyBuff, xCaret, yCaret;
          int     i, x, y;
    HDC           hdc;
    PAINTSTRUCT   ps;
    TEXTMETRIC    tm;
```

```
switch( msg )
{
   case WM_CREATE:
       hdc = GetDC( hwnd );
       SelectObject( hdc, GetStockObject( SYSTEM_FIXED_FONT ) );
       GetTextMetrics( hdc, &tm );
       cxChr = tm.tmAveCharWidth;
       cyChr = tm.tmHeight + tm.tmExternalLeading;
       ReleaseDC( hwnd, hdc );
       break;

   case WM_SIZE:
       cyWin = HIWORD( lParam );
       cxWin = LOWORD( lParam );
       cxBuff = max( 1, cxWin / cxChr );
       cyBuff = max( 1, cyWin / cyChr );
       if( pBuffer != NULL )
       {
           free( pBuffer );
           pBuffer = NULL;
       }
       if( (LONG) cxBuff * cyBuff > MAX_BUFF ||
           ( pBuffer = malloc( cxBuff * cyBuff ) ) == NULL )
           MessageBox( hwnd, "Insufficient memory -"
                             "Reduce window size ...",
                       "Editor Report",
                       MB_ICONEXCLAMATION | MB_OK );
       else
           for( y=0; y<cyBuff; y++ )
               for( x=0; x<cxBuff; x++ )
                   Buffer( x, y ) = ' ';
       xCaret = 0;
       yCaret = 0;
       if( hwnd == GetFocus() )
           SetCaretPos( xCaret * cxChr, yCaret * cyChr );
       break;

   case WM_SETFOCUS:
       CreateCaret( hwnd, (HBITMAP) 1, cxChr, cyChr );
       SetCaretPos( xCaret * cxChr, yCaret * cyChr );
       ShowCaret( hwnd );
       break;
```

```
case WM_KILLFOCUS:
   HideCaret( hwnd );
   DestroyCaret();
   break;

case WM_KEYDOWN:
   switch( LOWORD( wParam ) )
   {
      case VK_HOME:
         xCaret = 0;
         break;

      case VK_END:
         xCaret = cxBuff - 1;
         break;

      case VK_PRIOR:
         yCaret = 0;
         break;

      case VK_NEXT:
         yCaret = cyBuff - 1;
         break;

      case VK_LEFT:
         xCaret = max( xCaret-1, 0 );
         break;

      case VK_RIGHT:
         xCaret = min( xCaret+1, cxBuff-1 );
         break;

      case VK_UP:
         yCaret = max( yCaret-1, 0 );
         break;

      case VK_DOWN:
         yCaret = min( yCaret+1, cyBuff-1 );
         break;

      case VK_DELETE:
         for( x=xCaret; x<cxBuff-1; x++ )
```

```
                    Buffer( x, yCaret ) = Buffer( x+1, yCaret );
            Buffer( cxBuff-1, yCaret ) = ' ';
            HideCaret( hwnd );
            hdc = GetDC( hwnd );
            SelectObject( hdc,
                GetStockObject( SYSTEM_FIXED_FONT ) );
            TextOut( hdc, xCaret * cxChr, yCaret * cyChr,
                    &Buffer( xCaret, yCaret ), cxBuff-xCaret );
            ShowCaret( hwnd );
            ReleaseDC( hwnd, hdc );
            break;
        }
    SetCaretPos( xCaret * cxChr, yCaret * cyChr );
    break;

case WM_CHAR:
    for( i=0; i<(int)LOWORD(lParam); i++ )
    {
        switch( LOWORD( wParam ) )
        {
        case '\b':          // backspace
            if( xCaret > 0 )
            {
                xCaret--;
                SendMessage( hwnd, WM_KEYDOWN, VK_DELETE, 1L );
            }
            break;

        case '\t':          // tab
            do
                SendMessage( hwnd, WM_CHAR, ' ', 1L);
            while( xCaret % 8 != 0 );
            break;

        case '\r':          // carriage return
            xCaret = 0;     // falls through to '\n'

        case '\n':          // line feed
            if( ++yCaret == cyBuff )
                yCaret = 0;
            break;
```

```
              case '\x1B':        // escape
                 if( MessageBox( hwnd,
                    "Reset text buffer?",
                    "Editor Query",
                    MB_ICONEXCLAMATION | MB_OKCANCEL |
                    MB_DEFBUTTON2 ) == IDOK )
                 {
                    for( y=0; y<cyBuff; y++ )
                       for( x=0; x<cxBuff; x++ )
                          Buffer( x, y ) = ' ';
                    xCaret = 0;
                    yCaret = 0;
                    InvalidateRect( hwnd, NULL, FALSE );
                 }
                 break;

              default:            // all other chars
               Buffer( xCaret, yCaret ) = (char) LOWORD( wParam );
                 HideCaret( hwnd );
                 hdc = GetDC( hwnd );
                 SelectObject( hdc,
                    GetStockObject( SYSTEM_FIXED_FONT ));
                 TextOut( hdc, xCaret * cxChr, yCaret * cyChr,
                          &Buffer( xCaret, yCaret ), 1 );
                 ShowCaret( hwnd );
                 ReleaseDC( hwnd, hdc );
                 if( ++xCaret == cxBuff )
                 {
                    xCaret = 0;
                    if( ++yCaret == cyBuff )
                       yCaret = 0;
                 }
                 break;
           }  }
        SetCaretPos( xCaret * cxChr, yCaret * cyChr );
        break;

     case WM_PAINT:
        hdc = BeginPaint( hwnd, &ps );
        SelectObject( hdc,
           GetStockObject( SYSTEM_FIXED_FONT ) );
        for( y=0; y<cyBuff; y++ )
```

```
            TextOut( hdc, 0, y*cyChr, &Buffer( 0, y ), cxBuff );
         EndPaint( hwnd, &ps );
         break;

      case WM_DESTROY:
         PostQuitMessage( 0 );
         break;

      default: return( DefWindowProc( hwnd, msg, wParam, lParam ) );
   }
   return 0;
}


#include "template.i"

BOOL APIENTRY WinMain( HANDLE hInstance, HANDLE hPrevInstance,
                       LPSTR  lpCmdLine, int    nCmdShow    )
{
   MSG   msg;

   if( ! hPrevInstance )
      if( ! InitApplication( hInstance ) )
         return( FALSE );
   if( ! InitInstance( hInstance, nCmdShow ) )
      return (FALSE);
   while( GetMessage( &msg, NULL, 0, 0 ) )
   {
      TranslateMessage( &msg );
      DispatchMessage( &msg );
   }
   return( msg.wParam );
   UNREFERENCED_PARAMETER( lpCmdLine );
}
```

CHAPTER
SIX

6

Using the Mouse in Windows

- Mouse-event messages

- Mouse-movement tracking

- Mouse cursor shapes

- Mouse-hit testing

If you have read up to this point or have worked on a Windows NT or 95 workstation (who hasn't?), it should be quite obvious that both are totally mouse-oriented. Granted, there are keyboard options for choosing options and switching between windows and applications, but it's quite difficult to accomplish much in Windows without a mouse. At the same time, it is possible that your application could be designed in such a fashion that a mouse was not required—possible, but unlikely.

Besides, is there any real reason—short of some mechao-myomorphicphobia (my version of "fear of mechanical mice") for seeking to avoid these ubiquitous little pseudo-rodents? (Obviously, the question demands a negative response.)

In any case, hypothetical phobias aside, at least a minimal knowledge of mouse operations is essential to any application. Furthermore, knowing how the mouse works may even suggest uses and possibilities relevant to your application design.

The Evolution of the Genus MusMechano

Originally, mouse devices were single-button (left-button equivalent) pointing devices—a primitive form that is still found today on Apple/Macintosh systems but that is virtually obsolete on contemporary DOS, Windows, and OS/2 systems (despite the fact that some sources continue to suggest that a single-button mouse should be considered a minimal standard).

For Windows NT and 95, two standard mouse configurations are supported: the two-button variety typified by the standard Microsoft Mouse and the three-button variety represented by the Logitech Mouse. Support is also provided for some variant forms, such as mouse-emulation by joy sticks and lightpens, which are treated as single-button mice. A variety of less common devices—such as those for use by handicapped persons or special-purpose variations ("un-mouse" pads, touch pads, joy-stick pointers, and so on)—attempt to have their interface indistinguishable from one of the standard interfaces.

Some mouse varieties (mutations, if you prefer) have appeared, sporting dozens of "keys." These keys are usually used for numerical data operations, but in theory, they provide mini-keyboards on a mouse. These varieties require special drivers before any NT interface is possible, and, for present, they can simply be ignored. Virtual devices, such as control gloves that sense spatial motion, are still experimental, and they also can be ignored for now.

The newest "mouse" from Microsoft includes a wheel between the two buttons. The wheel is designed for scrolling through Web pages. For the present, this is another variation that we do need to consider as a "standard" requiring support.

For the moment, only the two standard mouse types require consideration. Even though it can be extremely useful, the third (middle) button on three-button mice will be ignored to concentrate on the minimal standard of two mouse buttons: left and right.

Common usage emphasizes the left mouse button, regardless of the actual number of buttons available, as the equivalent of the Enter key. The right button is often used as the equivalent of the Escape key (southpaws can reverse this by going to the Control Panel, selecting the Mouse icon and swapping the left and right buttons).

NOTE When available, the middle button is often assigned to trigger optional shortcuts. If you are using a Logitech or equivalent mouse—one with a third button—the third button is still active, even if none of your applications respond to the middle-button-down (WM_MBUTTONDOWN) messages.

Is There a Mouse in the House?

Although it is usually safe to assume that a mouse is present, for critical applications, it is possible to query the system to ensure that a mouse is present. This task is accomplished using the GetSystemMetrics function, as:

```
if( GetSystemMetrics( SM_MOUSEPRESENT ) ) ...
```

If a mouse is present (and working), GetSystemMetrics will return TRUE; if no mouse is available, FALSE is reported. If the result is FALSE, mouse-critical applications can report accordingly.

How an application should respond to the absence of a mouse depends entirely on the application and the importance of mouse support. One possibility is to abort the program execution, as demonstrated in the Mouse3 program discussed later in this chapter.

Mouse Actions and Events

Three principal types of mouse actions are possible:

- **Clicking:** Pressing and releasing a mouse button
- **Double-clicking:** Clicking a mouse button twice rapidly
- **Dragging:** Moving the mouse while a mouse button is held down

Other mouse actions may be implemented by an application; these are generally more a feature of the application than a standard mouse activity. For example, instead of dragging an object such as an icon to move it, some applications permit you to simply click once to select it and click again to release it in its new position, without holding down the mouse button. This form (and variations) is popular with many drawing programs and help to reduce "mouse-wrist" injuries (muscle/ tendon strains caused by holding and dragging the mouse in applications requiring fine control for positioning).

Mouse events in Windows are different from mouse events under DOS in several respects:

- In the Windows environment, because the environment is shared, mouse-button events are not always paired. For example, a button-down event can occur in one window while the release event is not reported until the mouse has entered another window. In this fashion, the application receives only one of these event messages, and if it depends on receiving both, may malfunction. For an example, see the discussion of the Mouse2 demo program, later in this chapter.

- It is possible for an application to hold the mouse focus, even after relinquishing the system focus. The application can continue to receive all mouse messages, even though the mouse is outside the client window area.

- If a system modal message or dialog box is active, no other application window can receive any mouse messages. System modal messages and dialog boxes prohibit switching to any other window or application until they are exited.

Special circumstances aside, however, there are normally no restrictions or special provisions required for handling mouse-event messages in Windows.

Mouse-Event Messages

A total of 22 mouse-event messages are defined in WinUser.H. Two of these have values duplicating other mouse messages, and apparently are intended for internal use (or, perhaps, simply for variety). Of the remaining 20, these messages occur in pairs: one for client window events (mouse events occurring within the application's client window) and a corresponding event message for mouse actions that occur outside the client window. Table 6.1 lists these mouse-event messages and their values.

TABLE 6.1   Mouse-Event Messages and Values

Client Window Events	Value	Non-Client Window Events	Value
WM_MOUSEMOVE[1]	0x0200	WM_NCMOUSEMOVE	0x00A0
WM_LBUTTONDOWN	0x0201	WM_NCLBUTTONDOWN	0x00A1
WM_LBUTTONUP	0x0202	WM_NCLBUTTONUP	0x00A2
WM_LBUTTONDBLCLK	0x0203	WM_NCLBUTTONDBLCLK	0x00A3
WM_RBUTTONDOWN	0x0204	WM_NCRBUTTONDOWN	0x00A4
WM_RBUTTONUP	0x0205	WM_NCRBUTTONUP	0x00A5
WM_RBUTTONDBLCLK	0x0206	WM_NCRBUTTONDBLCLK	0x00A6
WM_MBUTTONDOWN	0x0207	WM_NCMBUTTONDOWN	0x00A7
WM_MBUTTONUP	0x0208	WM_NCMBUTTONUP	0x00A8
WM_MBUTTONDBLCLK[2]	0x0209	WM_NCMBUTTONDBLCLK	0x00A9

Note 1: WM_MOUSEFIRST duplicates WM_MOUSEMOVE.
Note 2: WM_MOUSELAST duplicates WM_MBUTTONDBLCLK.

Normally, mouse-movement and mouse-button messages are reported only while the mouse remains within the application's client window. In these cases, the nonclient window mouse events are not issued to the application. However, there are circumstances where an application will request and track mouse events outside its own immediate jurisdiction; for example, a screen-capture application needs this information.

NOTE Because nonclient mouse messages are relevant only under special circumstances, they are not demonstrated in the examples in this chapter. They will be demonstrated in later chapters dealing with graphics.

The most important mouse-event messages for most applications are the nine client-window mouse-button messages listed in Table 6.2:

TABLE 6.2   Mouse Button Messages

Button	Pressed	Released	Double-Clicked
Left	WM_LBUTTONDOWN	WM_LBUTTONUP	WM_LBUTTONDBLCLK
Right	WM_RBUTTONDOWN	WM_RBUTTONUP	WM_RBUTTONDBLCLK
Middle	WM_MBUTTONDOWN	WM_MBUTTONUP	WM_MBUTTONDBLCLK

WM_xBUTTONDOWN and WM_xBUTTONUP messages are issued only once, when a mouse button is pressed or released. A WM_xBUTTONDBLCLK message is issued only when a mouse button is rapidly double-clicked (press–release–press). Unlike keyboard events, no repeating mouse-button messages of any kind are issued by holding a mouse button down, even though WM_MOUSEMOVE messages are issued for all mouse movements regardless of the button states.

The status of both (or all three) mouse buttons may, however, be retrieved from the information accompanying the WM_MOUSEMOVE message, as explained in the "Mouse Messages Information" section, coming up soon.

Double-Click Messages

Because not all applications require (or desire) double-click event messages, provisions are included in Windows to control whether or not double-click events are reported. This provision is controlled by the client window's (or child window's) style definition. WM_*xxxx*DBLCLK messages are generated only if the class style includes the CS_DBLCLKS flag, as:

```
wc.style = CS_HREDRAW | CS_VREDRAW | CS_DBLCLKS;
```

If the CS_DBLCLKS flag is not set, a double-click is simply received as four separate events: WM_*x*BUTTONDOWN, WM_*x*BUTTONUP, WM_*x*BUTTONDOWN, and WM_*x*BUTTONUP. However, when CS_DBLCLKS is enabled, a double-click is received as:

```
WM_xBUTTONDOWN,
WM_xBUTTONUP,
WM_xBUTTONDBLCLK,
WM_xBUTTONUP
```

The double-click message replaces the second-button-pressed message.

In general, responses to a double-click message are designed as continuations or expansions of single-click responses, because before the double-click event is registered, the application has already received a button-pressed/button-released event message pair.

Also, if single- and double-click events are intended to perform quite different tasks, the response processing could become quite complex, because the single-click event message will always be received before the double-click event. On the other hand, you can make this work for you.

As an example, consider the Windows File Manager's handling of a single-click and a double-click on a subdirectory listing. A single-click changes the active directory; a double-click calls a new directory window displaying the selected directory. The result is that accidental entries perform in very much the same fashion, if not precisely the same, as the intended result.

Mouse-Movement Messages

Although many applications require only the mouse-button event messages, the WM_MOUSEMOVE message is issued every time the mouse moves physically. However, this does not necessarily mean that the mouse has moved on the screen, because movement is reported not per screen pixel but per unit of mouse motion.

> **NOTE**
>
> Mouse movement is reported in mickeys. (You already know that all programmers are punsters.) A high-resolution mouse reports 200 to 300 mickeys per inch (without acceleration). The speed of movement is reported as mickeys per second.

Rapid mouse movement may cause WM_MOUSEMOVE messages to be reported irregularly; that is, from noncontiguous screen locations (this effect can be demonstrated by the Mouse1 demo program in this chapter). This effect is produced partially by the effects of the accelerator settings (which multiply distances for rapid mouse movements) and partially by the inability of the system to respond to rapid movement events.

With slower mouse movement, the WM_MOUSEMOVE messages will most likely overlap, resulting in more than one message with the same screen coordinates. Overlapping mouse coordinates, however, ensure a solid series of painted screen coordinates.

Miscellaneous Mouse Messages

Three additional mouse messages are possible, but normally, they are not the direct concern of an application itself and are left to Windows for appropriate handling.

- WM_MOUSEACTIVATE occurs when the cursor is in an inactive window and any mouse button is pressed.

- WM_MOUSEENTER occurs when the mouse enters any window.

- WM_MOUSELEAVE occurs when the mouse leaves any window.

Mouse Messages Information

Each mouse-event message contains, in addition to the event itself, complete mouse button and Shift- and Ctrl-key status data in the wParam argument (as flag information), and mouse coordinate information in the lParam argument. These can be tested as:

```
if( wParam & MK_LBUTTON )...    // left button down
if( wParam & MK_RBUTTON )...    // right button down
if( wParam & MK_MBUTTON )...    // middle button down
if( wParam & MK_CONTROL )...    // Ctrl key pressed
if( wParam & MK_SHIFT )...      // Shift key pressed
```

The mouse coordinate information is in client window pixel coordinates relative to the upper-left corner. This information is found in the lParam argument, with the x-coordinate in the low-order word and the y-coordinate in the high-order word. The MAKEPOINTW macro can be used to convert the lParam argument to a POINTW structure.

Tracking the Mouse: The Mouse1 Program

The Mouse1 program demonstrates how WM_MOUSEMOVE messages are tracked. It plots a single pixel at the coordinates reported with each message received. Plotting is toggled on and off by the left mouse button, beginning plotting with one WM_LBUTTONDOWN message and ending plotting with the next WM_LBUTTONDOWN message. For this example, only the WM_MOUSEMOVE and WM_LBUTTONDOWN messages are provided with responses.

The WM_LBUTTONDOWN message is used to toggle the fPaint variable by XORing fPaint and 1, flipping the value from TRUE to FALSE and vice versa. The value of fPaint was initialized as zero (0).

```
case WM_LBUTTONDOWN:
    fPaint ^= 1;
    MessageBeep(0);
    break;
```

As a minor bonus, the MessageBeep function is called to provide audio feedback.

MessageBeep can be called with a zero argument, although this argument is simply the equivalent of MB_OK and produces the system default sound. Other options are listed in Table 6.3.

TABLE 6.3   MessageBeep Arguments

Argument	Sound
0xFFFFFFFF	Standard beep using the computer speaker
MB_ICONASTERISK	SystemAsterisk
MB_ICONEXCLAMATION	SystemExclamation
MB_ICONHAND	SystemHand
MB_ICONQUESTION	SystemQuestion
MB_OK	SystemDefault

The second response, to the WM_MOUSEMOVE message, depends on the current value in fPaint (TRUE or FALSE). It extracts the mouse's window coordinates from lParam and paints a single black pixel.

```
case WM_MOUSEMOVE:
    if( fPaint )
    {
        hdc = GetDC( hwnd );
      SetPixel( hdc, LOWORD( lParam ), HIWORD( lParam ), 0L );
        ReleaseDC( hwnd, hdc );
    }
    break;
```

For tracking mouse movements, this is sufficient. However, pay particular attention to how different rates of movement affect the dot spacing.

The complete listing for the Mouse1 demo program appears at the end of this chapter.

The Mouse Cursor

Chapter 5 explained how the text pointer is now known as the *caret*, and the term *cursor* is now the property of the mouse pointer. And, while the mouse pointer points at a single pixel rather than a character cell position, the cursor proper is a bitmapped image that is tracked across the display while preserving the background image.

One pixel location within this cursor image is known as the *hotspot,* which is the actual pointer location tracked.

Windows NT provides a series of 14 predefined cursor images (although one of these is blank; and one, which is documented as a duplicate of another, does not appear to function at all), as listed in Table 6.4. By default, Windows uses the slanted arrow (IDC_ARROW). Individual applications are free to define any of these standard cursors as their own default cursor. (Most of the applications demonstrated in this book follow NT in using the slant arrow default.)

TABLE 6.4   Windows Predefined Cursor Shapes

Cursor	Description
IDC_APPSTARTING	A standard arrow and small hourglass combination; used to show that an application is opening
IDC_ARROW	An arrow pointing diagonally up and left; the familiar default cursor
IDC_CROSS	A simple horizontal/vertical cross
IDC_IBEAM	An I-beam cursor; commonly used for word processing
IDC_ICON	An empty shape that can be used to hide the cursor; i.e., no cursor image
IDC_NO	An international negative; i.e., a circle with a diagonal slash
IDC_SIZE	Four arrows, pointing in the four cardinal directions (up, down, left, and right)
IDC_SIZEALL	A four-pointed arrow identical to IDC_SIZE (but currently appears to be nonfunctional)
IDC_SIZENESW	A tilted double-arrow, pointing diagonally up to the right (NE) and down to the left (SW)
IDC_SIZENS	A double-arrow, pointing up and down
IDC_SIZENWSE	A tilted double-arrow, pointing diagonally up to the left (NW) and down to the right (SE)
IDC_SIZEWE	A double-arrow pointing left and right
IDC_UPARROW	Similar to the default cursor, an arrow pointing directly up
IDC_WAIT	An hourglass, or wait, symbol

WARNING

The `IDC_SIZE` and `IDC_SIZEALL` cursors are documented as both producing the identical pointed arrow, the `IDC_SIZEALL` cursor is reportedly available under NT but not under Windows 95. At present, however, the `IDC_SIZEALL` cursor appears to be nonfunctional under both Windows 95 and NT. Thus, for reliability, use `IDC_SIZE` rather than `IDC_SIZEALL`.

Regardless of the default cursor, applications are free to change cursors at any time, as appropriate to specific tasks or to window areas. They also may define their own custom cursors.The predefined cursor shapes (see Table 6.4) are illustrated in the Mouse2 demo program.

Mouse Cursor Shapes: The Mouse2 Program

The Mouse2 demo program subdivides the application client window into 12 child windows, each appearing as a simple outline with a white background. These child windows are secondary to the principal purposes of the example, which are to demonstrate the predefined mouse cursor shapes supplied by Windows NT and 95 and how the mouse cursor is changed by the application. However, these child windows must be created and managed for the example, as described here. See Chapter 7 for more details about child windows and control elements.

Creating the Child Windows

To create these child windows, the first step occurs in the `WinMain` procedure. After registering the window class in `WinMain`, as usual, the `InitApplication` subprocedure is called from the Template.I include file. This subprocedure is used to make another, local set of `wc` assignments to register the child class.

```
if( ! hPrevInstance )
{
   if( ! InitApplication( hInstance ) )
      return( FALSE );
   //*** also register child window class ***//
```

```
wc.style         = CS_HREDRAW | CS_VREDRAW;
wc.cbClsExtra    = 0;
wc.cbWndExtra    = 0;
wc.hInstance     = hInstance;
wc.hbrBackground = GetStockObject( LTGRAY_BRUSH );
wc.lpszMenuName  = NULL;
wc.lpfnWndProc   = ChildWndProc;
wc.hIcon         = NULL;
wc.hCursor       = NULL;            // essential!!! //
wc.lpszClassName = szChildClass;
RegisterClass( &wc );
}
```

This code includes the three critical assignments:

- The pointer to the ChildWndProc

- The assignment of the hCursor field as NULL

- The class name, which is a string defined at the beginning of the source code, following the fashion used for the main window class

Following registration of the child class, the main window is created, as usual, by calling the InitInstance subprocedure and then entering the message loop. Remember, however, that at this point, only the main window instance has been created; while the child window class has been registered, no instances of this class yet exist.

The actual child windows are created in the WndProc procedure, where an array of handles are defined as:

```
static HWND hwndChild[7][2];
```

These are defined as a static array of handles because the values assigned must remain, even when the application exits from this local procedure. Any nonstatic data may be overwritten between messages. This is fine for temporary variables, but the child window handles, once assigned by the CreateWindow function call, must be preserved.

The WM_CREATE message is issued only once: when the application is first created. Therefore, at this time, 14 child window instances are created, each returning a handle, which is stored in the hwndChild array.

```
case WM_CREATE:
  for( x=0; x<7; x++ )
    for( y=0; y<2; y++ )
      hwndChild[x][y] =
        CreateWindow( szChildClass,
          NULL, WS_CHILDWINDOW | WS_VISIBLE,
          0, 0, 0, 0, hwnd,
    (HMENU) ( x | ( y << 8 ) ),
    (HANDLE) GetWindowLong( hwnd, GWL_HINSTANCE ),
    (LPVOID) NULL );
```

Three principal differences from the parallel operation for the parent (application) window exist here:

- Each child window is created using the hwnd handle identifying the parent window. For the parent, the corresponding argument was NULL.

- Each child window requires an ID value that must be unique within this application. In this case, the ID is generated as a word value (x | ($y << 8$)) and is typecast using the HMENU data type. Although HMENU is not the data type you might expect for a window ID, the CreateWindow function is also used to create menus, and this is the type definition expected in the function declaration. The equivalent HWND type will also work, but it will result in a warning message from the Microsoft C compiler. The corresponding ID values will be needed in ChildWndProc to identify specific child windows.

- The child window instance parameter is supplied by calling the GetWindowLong function with the GWL_HINSTANCE argument. When the application's client window was initialized, this argument had been supplied by Windows as the hInstance parameter passed to the WinMain procedure. But now, 12 separate and unique instance handles are needed, and they must be supplied by Windows, indirectly or directly.

NOTE In Windows 3.1, the child window instance parameter is supplied by calling the GetWindowWord function with the GWW_HINSTANCE argument.

There are other differences as well, such as the absence of window titles (identified as NULL) and the differences in the style flag, but these will vary depending on the style and type of child windows desired.

Also, these windows have all been created with both size and position set at zero. While the same was done for the main client window, the main window is sized automatically. The child windows, however, will not be defined as a style that will receive WM_SIZE messages. Therefore, to size and space these dozen children, a provision is required to accomplish this anytime the main client window's size changes.

Ergo, in response to the WM_SIZE message, the WndProc procedure begins by using the current window size in the high and low words in lParam:

```
case WM_SIZE:
    cxWin = LOWORD( lParam ) / 5;
    cyWin = HIWORD( lParam ) / 2;
    for( x=0; x<7; x++ )
    for( y=0; y<2; y++ )
            MoveWindow( hwndChild[x][y], x * cxWin, y * cyWin,
                        cxWin, cyWin, TRUE );
    break;
```

Once cxWin and cyWin hold the appropriate size and spacing for each child window, a double loop calls the MoveWindow function, using the handles in the hwnd-Child array, and sizes and positions each.

Cursor Operations in the Child Windows

As the mouse moves from one child window to another in the Mouse2 demo program, the mouse cursor image is changed for each window. To accomplish this, however, a bit of subterfuge is required. Initially, when the child window style was registered, the cursor was declared NULL, affecting all instances of the child class.

Now, as the mouse moves, each WM_MOUSEMOVE message is directed to whichever child window the mouse happens to occupy, and the response sets the mouse cursor shape appropriate to that child window. However, because there is only one ChildWndProc to handle responses for all of the child windows, in order to assign the appropriate cursor, the WM_MOUSEMOVE response requires one additional piece of information: which child window is currently being handled.

Therefore, the WM_MOUSEMOVE response begins with an inquiry to retrieve the child window ID, as:

```
case WM_MOUSEMOVE:
    switch( GetWindowLong( hwnd, GWL_ID ) )
    {
```

Once the child window ID is known, the `switch`/`case` statement can branch to the appropriate response, as:

```
case 0x0000:
    SetCursor( LoadCursor( NULL, IDC_APPSTARTING ) );
    break;
    . . .
case 0x0106:
    SetCursor( LoadCursor( NULL, IDC_WAIT ) );
    break;
```

Remember, the child window IDs were assigned using the formula $(x \mid (y << 8))$. But here it's simpler just to assign the appropriate constants, especially since formulas are not permitted as `case` statement IDs. Alternatively, a series of mnemonics could have been declared, but this is simple enough for demo purposes.

In the Mouse2 demo program, anytime the left (or primary) mouse button is pressed, the cursor will shift to the default arrow cursor. Likewise, anytime the right (or secondary) mouse button is pressed, the mouse cursor will be hidden until the button is released.

Also, because the changing cursors are assigned (loaded) only in response to a mouse movement, once the selected cursor has been replaced by the default cursor, the selected cursor is reloaded only when another mouse-movement message is received. To avoid this type of interruption, the mouse button messages also need to be handled to ensure that the desired mouse cursor is shown.

Hiding the mouse cursor might be the simplest task of all. It requires only the `ShowCursor` function and an argument specifying whether the cursor is to be hidden or visible.

In Chapter 5, the `ShowCaret` and `HideCaret` functions were used in a similar fashion to hide and reveal the text caret. In that discussion, I mentioned that you could encounter a problem with multiple show or hide calls, because they require equal occurrences of their counterparts before any action occurs.

The same holds for the `ShowCursor` function, except that instead of a corresponding `HideCursor` function, `ShowCursor` accepts a TRUE or FALSE argument. However, if the `ShowCursor(FALSE)` function is called and the mouse is then moved to another child window before a `ShowCursor(TRUE)` call is made, a different problem may occur: the mouse cursor may not be visible again—at least not until the application window is left entirely.

Therefore, to prevent either problem from occurring, a Boolean variable, `Visible`, has been declared. This variable holds the current state of the mouse cursor, and `ShowCursor(FALSE)` is only permitted if `Visible` is TRUE and vice versa. A similar solution, if needed, can be applied to the `ShowCaret`/`HideCaret` functions.

There's also a second solution. Since the `ShowCursor` function returns the new display count resulting from the operation, and the cursor is hidden any time the count is negative and shown whenever the count is zero or higher, the following code lines will increment or decrement the show count until the appropriate value is reached:

```
while( ShowCursor(FALSE) >= 0 );       // hides cursor
while( ShowCursor(TRUE)  <  0 );       // reveals cursor
```

TIP

As an alternative to using predefined cursors, you can include custom cursors in your application. See Chapter 9 for details.

Hit Testing: The Mouse3 Program

The Mouse3 program demonstrates how mouse-click events are registered. It uses a simple cruciform game field, which responds to both the left and right mouse buttons by displaying, respectively, an X or O. Figure 6.1 illustrates the game field.

NOTE

The "game" using this board was originally devised by a young lady of ten. She came up with a rather complex set of rules which, you may be properly relieved to know, are not implemented here.

The actual grid is a 7×7 array, with four elements from each corner flagged as invalid and, therefore, not included in the paint operations. The remaining grid elements each has a corresponding integer flag, which initially is set to 0.

FIGURE 6.1

A cruciform playing
board for mouse-hit
testing

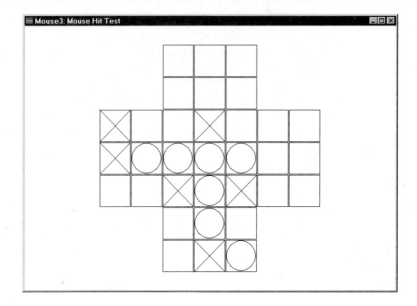

To demonstrate mouse-hit testing, the location of each WM_LBUTTONDOWN and
WM_RBUTTONDOWN message is tested against the grid coordinates, and then shifted
according to the original state and the button clicked before invalidating the specific grid. Conversely, any mouse clicks that fall outside the grid area or on an array
element flagged as invalid produce a warning beep.

As for playing the game, feel free to invent your own rules.

The three programs in this chapter have demonstrated all the principal mouse
operations within the client window area: mouse-event messages, tracking the
mouse, changing the mouse cursor, and mouse hit testing. The complete listing
for the Mouse1 program follows, and all three are included on the CD that
accompanies this book. Since mouse operations are very integral to any Windows application, mouse operations will continue to appear in demo applications in later chapters.

Listing 6.1: The Mouse1 Program

```
rem ;======================;
rem ;        MOUSE1.BAT     ;
rem ;  calls NMAKE utility  ;
rem ;======================;
nmake -a -f MOUSE1
if exist MOUSE1.OBJ del MOUSE1.OBJ
```

```
#===================================================#
# Nmake macros for building Windows 32-Bit apps #
#===================================================#


!include <ntwin32.mak>

# instruction allows NMAKE to work

all: mouse1.exe

# update object file as required
mouse1.obj: mouse1.c
   $(cc) $(cflags) $(cvars) mouse1.c

# update executable file if necessary
mouse1.exe: mouse1.obj mouse1.def
   $(cvtobj) $(cvtdebug) *.obj
   $(link) $(guiflags) -out:mouse1.exe mouse1.obj $(guilibs)
```

```
;====================================;
;  Mouse1.DEF module definition file   ;
;====================================;


NAME          MOUSE1
DESCRIPTION   "Mouse1: Demonstrates Mouse Tracking"
EXETYPE       WINDOWS
STUB          "WINSTUB.EXE"
CODE          PRELOAD MOVEABLE DISCARDABLE
DATA          PRELOAD MOVEABLE MULTIPLE
HEAPSIZE      1024
STACKSIZE     5120
EXPORTS       WndProc
```

```
//===========================//
//          Mouse1.C         //
//   Windows Mouse Tracking  //
//===========================//

#include <windows.h>

#define APP_ICON   IDI_APPLICATION
#define APP_MENU   NULL

HANDLE hInst;
char   szAppTitle[] = "Mouse1: Tracking Demo";
char   szAppName[]  = "Mouse1";

long FAR PASCAL WndProc( HWND hwnd,    UINT msg,
                           UINT wParam, LONG lParam )
{
    HDC         hdc;
    PAINTSTRUCT ps;
    static BOOL fPaint = 0;

    switch( msg )
    {
       case WM_MOUSEMOVE:
          if( fPaint )
          {
             hdc = GetDC( hwnd );
            SetPixel( hdc, LOWORD( lParam ), HIWORD( lParam ), 0L );
             ReleaseDC( hwnd, hdc );
          }
          break;

       case WM_LBUTTONDOWN:
          fPaint ^= 1;
          MessageBeep(0);
          break;

       case WM_PAINT:
          hdc = BeginPaint( hwnd, &ps );
          EndPaint( hwnd, &ps );
          break;
```

```
        case WM_DESTROY:  PostQuitMessage(0);  break;

        default:
            return( DefWindowProc( hwnd, msg, wParam, lParam ) );
    }
    return 0;
}

#include "template.i"

int APIENTRY WinMain( HANDLE hInstance, HANDLE hPrevInstance,
LPSTR  lpCmdLine, int    nCmdShow    )
{
    MSG   msg;

    if( ! hPrevInstance )
        if( ! InitApplication( hInstance ) )
            return( FALSE );
    if( ! InitInstance( hInstance, nCmdShow ) )
        return (FALSE);
    while( GetMessage( &msg, NULL, 0, 0 ) )
    {
        TranslateMessage( &msg );
        DispatchMessage( &msg );
    }
    return( msg.wParam );
    UNREFERENCED_PARAMETER( lpCmdLine );
}
```

CHAPTER

SEVEN

7

Child Windows and Control Elements

- Types of window controls

- Control button styles

- Control button grouping

- Button-event messages

You've already seen examples using child windows. In Chapter 6, two programs include child windows: one to demonstrate different system cursors, and another to respond to mouse-button events by displaying either crosses or circles in child windows.

Generically, child window controls are windows that process mouse (and keyboard) messages. They handle their own responses appropriately and notify the parent window in some suitable fashion as necessary when a control changes the child window's state (for example, a different radio button has been chosen or a scrollbar has been adjusted).

As you will be reassured to know, these tasks can normally be accomplished without the need for elaborate provisions as in the `ChildWndProc` procedures in the demo programs in Chapter 6. Instead, you can use child windows that are predefined window classes. The examples in the chapter demonstrate several of the predefined window classes, and you'll see all the others in the examples throughout the rest of this book.

In Part 2, you'll learn about an easier way of using window control elements. They can be handled as components in dialog boxes, which is accomplished by using a resource editor. But first, you should understand how child windows are handled using direct, rather than indirect, interactions, which is the topic of this chapter.

The Programmer and Child Window Controls

The real use of child windows is in the form of child window controls, although they are not usually referred to as such. Instead, child window controls are commonly referred to by their functions: as buttons, checkboxes, radio buttons, edit boxes, list boxes, scrollbars, and so on.

> **NOTE** We've talked about scrollbars in earlier chapters, but only in one of their many possible forms. As you will see in later chapters, scrollbars can be used for a variety of purposes other than scrolling windows.

If you are familiar with Windows, you've already encountered a wide variety of Windows control elements and know how convenient they are for the user.

Equally important is just how convenient these control elements are for the programmer. The program (and, therefore, the programmer) does not need to be concerned with the mouse driver and mouse-button logic, making control buttons change state, adjusting scrollbars when they are dragged, or any of the other myriad details involved in using these controls. Instead, as the programmer, you are free to use them "as is," like the end user.

As a programmer, the extent of your involvement is simple. You just define the control elements needed and the appropriate responses—then wait. When a control is activated, a WM_COMMAND message is returned, together with additional information identifying the control and, if appropriate, specifics about the state of the control.

For example, in the Mouse2 demo program presented in Chapter 6, a child window class was defined and registered (in this case, in the WinMain procedure). Then, in the WndProc procedure, this child window class was initiated, as individual instances, using the CreateWindow function. Finally, each window was positioned and sized using the MoveWindow function.

The Button1 and Button2 demo programs in this chapter use a similar process, calling the CreateWindow function to create instances of predefined classes before positioning and sizing each using the MoveWindow function. For the predefined window classes, such as buttons and scrollbars, the process becomes much simpler. For these window controls, the classes and their responses are already defined, programmed, and compiled, and they are available as library functions.

The third example discussed in this chapter, Button3, also shows the codes returned by the child window controls. But this example uses MFC to create a dialog box–based application and introduces a wider variety of button styles.

Control Button Types

Windows provides three principal types of control buttons: pushbuttons, checkboxes, and radio buttons. Figure 7.1 shows several examples of each of these three types.

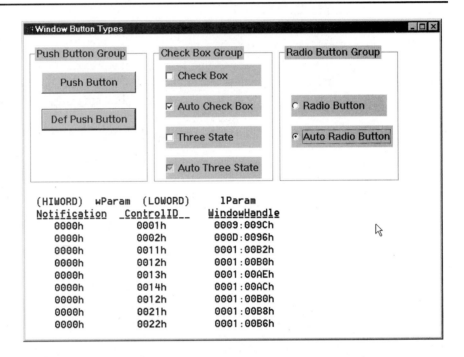

FIGURE 7.1

Standard button control styles

Another child window type also appears in Figure 7.1. A group box contains each of the sets of examples. However, group boxes do not respond to mouse events or issue WM_COMMAND messages. They are used only to visually group other control elements (with or without group labels). Using group boxes for button controls is discussed later in the chapter.

NOTE   Because these child window buttons are "drawn" on a regular white window background, rather than on the halftone gray background common to dialog boxes, here the controls appear unfinished. Because the purpose is to demonstrate messages from child windows, the incomplete appearance shouldn't detract from the buttons' functions. For a more polished version, see the discussion of the Button3 demo program, later in the chapter.

Pushbutton Styles

Generic pushbutton controls are rectangular boxes that have a centered text label and an outline simulating a raised button (3-D shading). When activated, such as by a mouse click, the outline changes to simulate a button that has been physically depressed. This type of control button is commonly used to initiate immediate actions, without retaining or displaying any continuing status information.

For control buttons, the entire active area is enclosed by the button image, although the control button may be any size desired. Two types of pushbutton controls are predefined as:

- BS_PUSHBUTTON is a control button displaying an optional text label. The pushbutton posts a message to the parent window when activated, while briefly changing state to simulate being physically pressed.

- BS_DEFPUSHBUTTON is similar to the BS_PUSHBUTTON control, but with a heavy border. This button represents the default response, and normally accepts the Enter key as equivalent to being pressed. (The heavy border represents the control that currently has the focus.)

NOTE Another Windows button type, BS_PUSHBOX, is defined in Windows 3.*x*, but it is not included in Windows NT or 95. In earlier Windows versions, the BS_PUSHBOX style appears initially as only a text label without a button outline. When selected, the button outline appears (as per BS_PUSHBUTTON) and the label is highlighted, remaining until another pushbutton or control is selected and the input focus is lost.

Checkbox Styles

Checkboxes are small squares with text labels appearing to the right, by default (but you can change them to the left with BS_LEFTTEXT, as explained in the "Special Controls and Modifiers" section). The checked state is shown by a check mark (or an X in MFC) in the box.

Although the box element of the checkbox is fixed in size, the active area, including the optional label, can be any size desired (within practical limits). To select the button, the user can click the mouse anywhere within the checkbox window, not just on the checkbox proper, whether or not the region is visibly delineated.

Four checkbox styles are defined as:

- BS_CHECKBOX displays a bold border when the button is checked. The button state must be set by the owner (application) and is not displayed automatically.

  □ CheckBox

- BS_AUTOCHECKBOX is the same as BS_CHECKBOX, except that the button state is automatically toggled when selected or deselected.

  ☑ Auto Check Box

- BS_3STATE is the same as BS_CHECKBOX, except that three states can be selected: clear, checked, or grayed. The button state must be set by the owner (application) and is not displayed automatically.

  □ Three State Check Box

NOTE The grayed state is typically used to show that a checkbox has been disabled.

- BS_AUTO3STATE is the same as BS_3STATE, except that the checkbox automatically steps through the three states in clear, checked, gray-checked order (unless otherwise explicitly set by the application).

  ☑ Auto Three State

The state (setting) of any of these checkbox controls can be queried or set directly.

Radio Button Styles

Radio buttons are small, circular buttons with optional text labels that appear to the immediate right by default (as with checkbox labels, radio button labels can also be displayed on the left with BS_LEFTTEXT, as explained in the next section).

By custom and intention, radio button controls are used as groups representing mutually exclusive choices. Only one button in a group can be checked at any time. Selecting a radio button a second time (once it is checked) does not change the button status.

MFC also offers the option of creating radio buttons without mutual exclusivity. This is the equivalent of placing each radio button in its own group.

A set radio button is shown with a solid center. Normally, a default or initial choice is selected when the group is initially displayed.

There are two radio button styles:

- BS_RADIOBUTTON displays a bold outline when clicked, but it does not display a set condition or clear set condition until explicitly directed by the owner (application).

- BS_AUTORADIOBUTTON is the same as BS_RADIOBUTTON, except when a button in a group is selected, a BM_CLICKED message notifies the application, the selected button is set automatically, and all other auto-radio buttons in the group are cleared automatically. Any buttons in the group that are not the auto type will not be affected without explicit instructions from the application.

The state of either type of radio button control can be queried directly by the application and can be explicitly set as required.

Special Controls and Modifiers

Three additional BS_xxxx button types are defined for special purposes:

- BS_OWNERDRAW designates an owner-drawn button, but it does not provide any type of image or response. Instead, the parent window is notified when the button is clicked and is expected to supply provisions to paint, invert, and/or disable the button using application-supplied bitmap images.

- BS_GROUPBOX designates a rectangle used to visually group other buttons with or without an optional label, which will be displayed in the rectangle's upper-left corner. The position and size for the group box must be specified appropriately to enclose the controls or area desired. The group box does not respond to mouse events or return any WM_COMMAND messages. (Figure 7.1, shown earlier, includes three group boxes.)

- BS_LEFTTEXT is a flag used in combination with the BS_CHECKBOX, BS_RADIOBUTTON, or BS_3STATE style to shift the label to the left of the checkbox or button. This flag is not valid with pushbuttons.

Button Operations

The button operations demonstrated in the Button1 and Button2 demo programs are less flexible than the usual standards for dialog box button operations, because the only provisions included for these child window operations are to respond to the mouse. No provisions have been made to allow the user to select controls using the Tab or cursor keys, nor do any of these controls, including the default pushbutton, respond to the Enter key.

Likewise, except for the BS_AUTOCHECKBOX, BS_AUTO3STATE, and BS_AUTORADIOBUTTON styles, none of the controls in the demo program display any change of state beyond the immediate selection "flash" when clicked with the mouse.

NOTE   Although this is not obvious in either demo program, the child window controls in the demo programs can obtain the input focus when selected with the mouse. However, they do not subsequently release the input focus to the parent window.

When a button is selected, it sends a WM_COMMAND message to the parent window. In the Button1 program, this message appears below the buttons as a breakdown of the wParam and lParam arguments (see Figure 7.1, shown earlier in the chapter). The table shows, from left to right:

- The notification value (high word in wParam)
- The child window (control) ID (low word in wParam)
- The child window handle value (lParam)

Notification values are described in the section "Button Control Communications: A Two-Way Channel" later in this chapter.

Using CreateWindow for Buttons

The individual control buttons are generated using the same CreateWindow function that we have used to create the application's client window and, in Chapter 6, to create a series of child windows. This time, however, the CreateWindow function is used in a somewhat unusual fashion to create groups of buttons grouped together by a BM_GROUPBOX child window.

The parameters used in calling CreateWindow for this purpose are defined as:

- lpClassName: ASCIIZ character string identifying the window class. This may be a predefined window class or a registered custom class. Note that an error in this field does not cause a compiler error but will not allow an erroneous class object to be displayed.

- lpWindowText: Points to an ASCIIZ character string providing a label for the button or control.

- dwStyle: Double word style identifier, which uses the predefined window and control styles.

- X: Integer specifying the initial x-axis position of the button class (relative to the parent window origin).

- Y: Integer specifying the initial y-axis position of the button class (relative to the parent window origin).

- nWidth: Integer value specifying the control button width (in device units).

- nHeight: Integer value specifying the control button height (in device units).

- hWndParent: Identifies the parent window (owner) of the window or control being created.

- hMenu: Unique value that identifies the child window (in other circumstances this value may identify a menu belonging to the window; the meaning depends on the style definition). Notice that the values used for this field are always cast as HMENU types, regardless of their intended function. This cast is necessary to prevent a compiler warning but does not affect the actual operation.

- hInstance: Identifies the instance creating the window or control.

- lpParam: Pointer used to address extra parameters or, in the Button1 example, to chain a series of window controls. The chain is terminated by passing the final lpParam argument as NULL.

The actual code (which appears in full at the end of this chapter) is rather unwieldy, making the chain structure of these grouped controls difficult to follow. Therefore, the listing following omits most of the parameter arguments in favor of illustrating the links in the declarations.

```
hwndGroup =
    CreateWindow
    (   ... , ... , ... , ... , ... ,
        ... , ... , hwnd, ... , ... ,
    CreateWindow
    (   ... , ... , ... , ... , ... ,
        ... , ... , hwnd, ... , ... ,
    CreateWindow
    (   ... , ... , ... , ... , ... ,
        ... , ... , hwnd, ... , ... ,
    CreateWindow
    (   ... , ... , ... , ... , ... ,
        ... , ... , hwnd, ... , ... ,
    CreateWindow
    (   ... , ... , ... , ... , ... ,
        ... , ... , hwnd, ... , ... ,
        NULL
) ) ) ) )
```

In this diagrammatic example, the `hwndGroup` contains five control window elements, which are chained together in the declaration. The top-most element in this group is the declaration for the group box itself (though this is not an ironclad requirement). The first control button appears as the eleventh parameter in the group box declaration, and so forth.

While there are no firm limits—memory and system limits aside—on such recursive declarations, this is also an awkward programming style. It may appear to produce a result that is not actually accomplished; contrary to what the structure seems to suggest, these control buttons are not grouped by the group box—except visually, both on screen and in the program.

Grouping of Controls

Grouping is not accomplished by the declaration tree (nor by the screen appearance). Instead, a group is declared by first calling `CreateWindow` to create the group box window, and then by using the group box handle (`hwndGroup`) as the owner of the group members when these are declared.

In the tree shown above, of necessity, all of the elements in the declaration tree used the same parent window handle—that of the client window (refer to the complete code listing at the end of the chapter).

In contrast, the Button2 demo program actually does create groups with member controls that are declared and created in the appropriate fashion, even if this is less elaborate.

Here is the Button2 code in skeleton format:

```
hwndPB[0] =
    CreateWindow
    (  ... , ... , BS_GROUPBOX, ... ,
       ... , ... , ... , hwnd,
       ... , ... , NULL );
for( i=1; i<4; i++ )
    hwndPB[i] =
        CreateWindow
        (  ... , ... , BS_xxcontrolxx, ... ,
           ... , ... , ... , hwndPB[0],
           ... , ... , NULL );
```

Here, the first step returns a handle to the group box control, which has the application's client window as a parent/owner. This handle is then used, in the second step within the loop, to provide the owner/parent for the individual control instances. This format creates four child window controls. These belong to the group box and, therefore, are isolated from other controls—a necessary requirement for auto-radio buttons, for example.

However, there's still a fly in the ointment! Because this format, while satisfactory for the present demo purposes, is still not practical for general applications.

Why? Because while the parent window, hwndPB[0], is a group box and does receive messages from the child window processes, it also has no provisions to act on these messages and cannot forward these messages to any other process for action. Ergo, the only actions and responses in the Button2 demo program are those inherent in the button classes themselves.

The real solution is also quite simple and was used, in part, in Chapter 6 in the Mouse2 and Mouse3 programs, when child window processes were first introduced. If you recall, in addition to creating the child windows used in the programs (refer particularly to Mouse3), a subprocess was also created with provisions to respond to messages from the child window. Thus, to use button controls in the fashion illustrated, the group box (whether it's visible or invisible) would be created in similar fashion, complete with the appropriate responses to handle messages from the child window controls (the buttons). Alternatively, instead of a group box, you could use another child window process serving as a parent to the controls.

Now, having been led through this maze of complexity, you can proceed to forget about it—at least for the present. The examples in the following chapters will use a quite different process to create these and other control elements. For the most part, you can create these types of control elements using dialog boxes and dialog box editors, rather than directly within the application code. Be assured, this is a much simpler as well as a much more practical route.

But, before leaving this topic altogether, there are other aspects of child window controls that will be relevant, regardless of how the controls are created.

Button Control Communications: A Two-Way Channel

The Button1 program demonstrates how event messages are received from the button controls elements as WM_COMMAND messages, with amplifying data in the wParam and lParam arguments. The lParam argument, which will generally be ignored, contains the window identifier for the child window control. More immediately important is the wParam argument, which, in the low-order word, reports the control ID assigned by the application when the control was created.

The notification code in the high-order word of wParam is used to inform the parent process precisely what event occurred. This notification code consists of one of the six values shown in Table 7.1.

TABLE 7.1 User Button Notification Codes

Code Constant	Value
BN_CLICKED	0
BN_PAINT	1
BN_HILITE	2
BN_UNHILITE	3
BN_DISABLE	4
BN_DOUBLECLICKED	5

The Button1 program returns only two event types: 0 or 5. The second of these, BN_DOUBLECLICKED, is returned by only the BS_RADIOBUTTON style control (but not by the BS_AUTORADIOBUTTON style control). Control notifications 1 through 4 are returned only by custom control buttons (illustrated in later chapters) to prompt the parent application to take the appropriate action (if any) to update the control's image.

Sending Messages to Controls

The Button2 example demonstrates four group boxes containing groups of child button controls. Unlike in Button1, these group boxes are actually parents to the controls enclosed. Because of this, setting an auto-radio button in one group will not affect settings in another group, but it will reset other buttons in the same group.

However, this demo program is also written to demonstrate other aspects involving messages sent from the application to the control buttons. Five button-specific messages are defined in WinUser.H, each beginning with the prefix BM_ *(button message)*, as shown in Table 7.2.

NOTE

In Windows 3.*x*, the corresponding message values are defined as WM_USER+0 through WM_USER+4. However, if the defined message constants are used, no conversion will be required to move applications from Windows 3.*x* to Windows NT.

TABLE 7.2   Button Control Messages

Code Constant	Value
BM_GETCHECK	00F0h
BM_SETCHECK	00F1h
BM_GETSTATE	00F2h
BM_SETSTATE	00F3h
BM_SETSTYLE	00F4h

The BM_SETCHECK and BM_GETCHECK messages are sent by the parent window to a child window control button to, respectively, retrieve or set the check state of checkboxes and radio buttons (with normal, auto, and three-state versions). In Button2, the BM_SETCHECK message has been used to set three of the checkboxes in the CheckBoxes group, three of the auto-radio buttons in the RadioButtons 1 group, and one of the radio buttons in the RadioButtons 2 group. Figure 7.2 shows the Button2 display.

FIGURE 7.2

Grouped control buttons

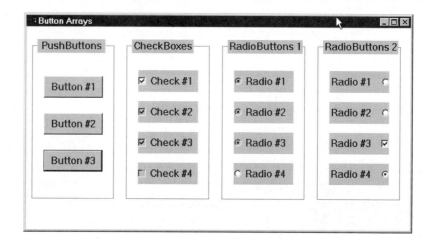

The display in the RadioButtons 1 group, with three auto-radio buttons checked, is definitely anomalous and can only occur (short of bad programming) because of the explicit settings made by the application. Clicking on any of the buttons in this group will correct the situation shown. The BM_SETCHECK message was sent as:

```
SendMessage( hwnd...., BM_SETCHECK, TRUE, OL );
```

Conversely, to clear the check state of a button, another message would be sent as:

```
SendMessage( hwnd...., BM_SETCHECK, FALSE, OL );
```

The first parameter is the child window (control button) handle, followed by the message identifier with the third parameter setting or clearing the flag state. The fourth parameter is unused and is passed as zero.

The BM_SETSTATE message is used to simulate the button "flash" that occurs when a button is clicked with the mouse or otherwise activated. In Figure 7.2, three of the checkboxes (as shown with heavy outlines) have received BM_SETSTATE messages, which were sent in the same fashion as the BM_SETCHECK messages.

The third "set" message provides a means of changing the style of the control button during execution and is demonstrated in Button2 with two examples. First, the BM_SETSTYLE message was used to change the style of the third (bottom) push-button from BS_PUSHBUTTON to BS_DEFPUSHBUTTON as:

```
SendMessage( hwndPB[3], BM_SETSTYLE,
             BStyle | BS_DEFPUSHBUTTON, 1L );
```

Unlike the earlier "set" messages, the BM_SETSTYLE message does use the fourth parameter, passing a nonzero argument to request that the control be redrawn immediately, using the new style settings. A zero argument leaves the control unchanged until some other circumstance causes the control to be redrawn.

Last, one more BM_SETSTYLE message was sent to change the style of the third radio button in the RadioButtons 2 group to a checkbox but, at the same time, did not incorporate the BS_LEFTTEXT flag originally used with all controls in this group. After this was done, the newly styled control button behaves precisely like any other checkbox, but it remains a member of the RadioButtons 2 group.

Querying Control States

The BM_GETCHECK and BM_GETSTATE messages are sent as information requests directed to specific button controls. They return the check or state status as TRUE if the button is checked or depressed (that is, the state flag is set) or FALSE if the appropriate flag is clear. As an example, the following instruction retrieves the check status:

```
fStatus = SendMessage( hwnd..., BM_GETCHECK, 0, 0L );
```

In this inquiry, only two parameters are relevant: the handle identifying the control element and the BM_GETCHECK message.

On the other hand, if the only requirement is to flip the state of a button or check-box, the BM_GETCHECK and BM_SETCHECK instructions can be combined as:

```
SendMessage( hwnd..., BM_SETCHECK,
        (WORD)SendMessage( hwnd...,
                    BM_GETCHECK, 0, 0L), 0L );
```

However, this latter form is generally not required, since the BM_AUTO*xxxxx* styles obviate the need for the application to handle the button state directly.

Button (Window) Labels

One item that applications may wish to change on buttons and controls of all types—whether to present a different series of selections or to update other information types—are the button labels. This also applies to window captions and the window text for any window type. The SetWindowText function is written as:

```
SetWindowText( hwnd, lpszString );
```

The hwnd parameter identifies the window, and the string argument is passed as a long or far pointer to an ASCIIZ string. Button labels are constrained to a single line of text, and line wrapping is not allowed.

> **TIP**
>
> A multiline button can be created using a static text field for the button text and omitting text entirely from the button. The disadvantage of this approach is that the user needs to click on the button itself. Clicking on the text will not set the button, unless the application includes additional code to recognize a hit on the separate label and issue a button message in response.

At the same time, the current text label can be retrieved from any window type using the GetWindowText function, as:

```
nLen = GetWindowText( hwnd, &Buff, sizeof( Buff ) );
```

Obviously, the buffer must be large enough to hold the string information returned. The third parameter places a limit on the length copied. The value returned directly (to nLen) is the actual length copied.

If the length is unknown, the GetWindowTextLength function can be called as:

```
nLen = GetWindowTextLength( hwnd );
```

A More Elaborate Version: Button3

Like Button1, the Button3 program reports the event messages produced when the various buttons are pressed. Unlike the earlier version, however, this variation uses a dialog box–based application window, where the various buttons appear against the appropriate background. Figure 7.3 shows the Button3 demo program.

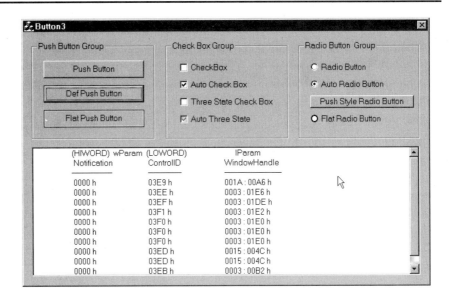

In addition to providing a more complete demo, Button3 also demonstrates three additional button styles: flat pushbutton, push-style radio button, and flat radio button. These styles are provided by MFC, but are not included in the standard defined button styles.

The complete listing for the Button2 and Button3 demo programs is on the CD that accompanies this book. The Button1 listing follows.

Now that you've finished this chapter, you may be tempted to simply forget almost all of it, since these tasks can be accomplished in a simpler fashion. However, whether you use these forms directly or not, a firm understanding of how applications use child window controls is still, if not essential, certainly very valuable. After all, it isn't what you don't know that hurts half as much as what you think you know but actually don't.

Now that you've seen the mechanisms from the inside, in Part 2, we'll look at these same mechanisms (and others) from a higher (and easier to implement) level.

Listing 7.1: The Button1 Program

```
rem ;========================;
rem ;         Button1.BAT         ;
rem ;   calls NMAKE utility   ;
rem ;========================;
nmake -a -f BUTTON1
if exist BUTTON1.OBJ del BUTTON1.OBJ



#==================================================#
# Nmake macros for building Windows 32-bit apps #
#==================================================#


!include <ntwin32.mak>

# instruction allows NMAKE to work

all: button1.exe

# update object file as required
button1.obj: button1.c
   $(cc) $(cflags) $(cvars) button1.c

# update executable file if necessary
#   if updated, restore resources
button1.exe: button1.obj button1.def
   $(cvtobj) $(cvtdebug) *.obj
   $(link) $(guiflags) -out:button1.exe button1.obj \
          $(guilibs)



;====================================;
;  Button1.DEF module definition file  ;
;====================================;


NAME          BUTTON1
DESCRIPTION   "Windows Buttons Program"
EXETYPE       WINDOWS
STUB          "WINSTUB.EXE"
CODE          PRELOAD MOVEABLE DISCARDABLE
DATA          PRELOAD MOVEABLE MULTIPLE
```

```
HEAPSIZE    1024
STACKSIZE   8192
EXPORTS     WndProc


//===========================//
//        Button1.C          //
//  C++ Windows Button Demo  //
//===========================//

#include <windows.h>

#define APP_ICON   IDI_APPLICATION
#define APP_MENU   NULL

#define NUM (sizeof(button) / sizeof(button[0]) )
#define BWidth     16 * cxChr
#define BHeight     7 * cyChr / 4
#define BIndent1    3 * cxChr
#define BIndent2   24 * cxChr
#define BIndent3   45 * cxChr
#define BVStep1     3 * cyChr
#define BVStep2     5 * cyChr / 2
#define BSTYLE      WS_CHILD | WS_VISIBLE

HANDLE  hInst;
char    szAppTitle[] = "Window Button Types";
char    szAppName[]  = "Button1";
char    szClass[]    = "button";
struct { long  style;
         char* name;
         HMENU btnID;  }   button[] =
{
   BSTYLE | BS_GROUPBOX,       "Push Button Group",          NULL,
   BSTYLE | BS_PUSHBUTTON,     "Push Button",      (HMENU) 0x01,
   BSTYLE | BS_DEFPUSHBUTTON,  "Def Push Button",  (HMENU) 0x02,

   BSTYLE | BS_GROUPBOX,       "Check Box Group",            NULL,
   BSTYLE | BS_CHECKBOX,       "Check Box",        (HMENU) 0x11,
   BSTYLE | BS_AUTOCHECKBOX,   "Auto Check Box",   (HMENU) 0x12,
   BSTYLE | BS_3STATE,         "Three State",      (HMENU) 0x13,
   BSTYLE | BS_AUTO3STATE,     "Auto Three State", (HMENU) 0x14,
```

```
        BSTYLE | BS_GROUPBOX,         "Radio Button Group",           NULL,
        BSTYLE | BS_RADIOBUTTON,      "Radio Button",       (HMENU) 0x21,
        BSTYLE | BS_AUTORADIOBUTTON, "Auto Radio Button",   (HMENU) 0x22,
};

long FAR PASCAL WndProc( HWND hwnd,    UINT msg,
                               UINT wParam, LONG lParam )
{
    static char   szBuff[50];
    static HWND   hwndGroup1, hwndGroup2, hwndGroup3;
    static RECT   rect;
    static int    cxChr, cyChr;
    HDC           hdc;
    PAINTSTRUCT   ps;
    TEXTMETRIC    tm;

    switch( msg )
    {
       case WM_CREATE:
          hdc = GetDC( hwnd );
          SelectObject( hdc, GetStockObject( SYSTEM_FIXED_FONT ) );
          GetTextMetrics( hdc, &tm );
          cxChr = tm.tmAveCharWidth;
          cyChr = tm.tmHeight + tm.tmExternalLeading;
          ReleaseDC( hwnd, hdc );

          hwndGroup1 =
             CreateWindow
             (  szClass, button[0].name, button[0].style,
                BIndent1 - 2 * cxChr, cyChr,
                BWidth   + 4 * cxChr, cyChr * 11,
                hwnd, button[0].btnID,
        (HANDLE) ((LPCREATESTRUCT)lParam) -> hInstance,
        (LPVOID) CreateWindow
                (  szClass, button[1].name, button[1].style,
                   BIndent1, BVStep1, BWidth, BHeight,
                   hwnd, button[1].btnID,
            (HANDLE) ((LPCREATESTRUCT)lParam) -> hInstance,
            (LPVOID) CreateWindow
                   (  szClass, button[2].name, button[2].style,
                      BIndent1, BVStep1 * 2, BWidth, BHeight,
```

```
                          hwnd, button[2].btnID,
           (HANDLE) ((LPCREATESTRUCT)lParam) -> hInstance,
                          NULL
                  )
              )
           );


    hwndGroup2 =
       CreateWindow
       (  szClass, button[3].name, button[3].style,
          BIndent2 - 2 * cxChr, cyChr,
          BWidth   + 4 * cxChr, cyChr * 11,
          hwnd, button[3].btnID,
(HANDLE) ((LPCREATESTRUCT)lParam) -> hInstance,
(LPVOID) CreateWindow
          (  szClass, button[4].name, button[4].style,
             BIndent2, BVStep2, BWidth, BHeight,
             hwnd,  button[4].btnID,
     (HANDLE) ((LPCREATESTRUCT)lParam) -> hInstance,
     (LPVOID) CreateWindow
             (  szClass, button[5].name, button[5].style,
                BIndent2, BVStep2 * 2, BWidth, BHeight,
                hwnd,  button[5].btnID,
        (HANDLE) ((LPCREATESTRUCT)lParam) -> hInstance,
        (LPVOID) CreateWindow
                (  szClass, button[6].name, button[6].style,
                   BIndent2, BVStep2 * 3, BWidth, BHeight,
                   hwnd,  button[6].btnID,
           (HANDLE) ((LPCREATESTRUCT)lParam) -> hInstance,
           (LPVOID) CreateWindow
                   (  szClass, button[7].name,
                      button[7].style,
                       BIndent2, BVStep2 * 4, BWidth, BHeight,
                       hwnd,  button[7].btnID,
              (HANDLE) ((LPCREATESTRUCT)lParam) -> hInstance,
                       NULL
                       )
                   )
               )
           )
       );
```

```
                  hwndGroup3 =
                    CreateWindow
                     (  szClass, button[8].name, button[8].style,
                        BIndent3 - 2 * cxChr, cyChr,
                        BWidth   + 4 * cxChr, cyChr * 11,
                        hwnd,  button[8].btnID,
        (HANDLE) ((LPCREATESTRUCT)lParam) -> hInstance,
        (LPVOID) CreateWindow
                     (  szClass, button[9].name, button[9].style,
                        BIndent3, BVStep2 * 2,  BWidth,  BHeight,
                        hwnd,  button[9].btnID,
          (HANDLE) ((LPCREATESTRUCT)lParam) -> hInstance,
          (LPVOID) CreateWindow
                     (  szClass, button[10].name, button[10].style,
                        BIndent3, BVStep2 * 3,  BWidth+cxChr, BHeight,
                         hwnd,  button[10].btnID,
            (HANDLE) ((LPCREATESTRUCT)lParam) -> hInstance,
                       NULL
                     )
                   )
                 );
            break;

    case WM_SIZE:
         rect.left   =  2 * cxChr;
         rect.top    = 15 * cyChr;
         rect.right  = LOWORD( lParam );
         rect.bottom = HIWORD( lParam );
         break;

    case WM_PAINT:
         InvalidateRect( hwnd, &rect, TRUE );
         hdc = BeginPaint( hwnd, &ps );
         SelectObject( hdc,
            GetStockObject( SYSTEM_FIXED_FONT ) );
         SetBkMode( hdc, TRANSPARENT );
         TextOut( hdc, 2*cxChr, 13*cyChr,
            "(HIWORD)  wParam  (LOWORD)      lParam",     37 );
         TextOut( hdc, 2*cxChr, 14*cyChr,
            "Notification   ControlID     WindowHandle", 41 );
         TextOut( hdc, 2*cxChr, 14*cyChr,
            "_____  _____  _____", 41 );
```

```
                  EndPaint( hwnd, &ps );
                  break;

              case WM_COMMAND:
                  ScrollWindow( hwnd, 0, -cyChr, &rect, &rect );
                  hdc = GetDC( hwnd );
                  SelectObject( hdc,
                      GetStockObject( SYSTEM_FIXED_FONT ) );
                  TextOut( hdc, 2*cxChr,
                          cyChr * ( rect.bottom / cyChr - 1 ),
                          szBuff,
                          wsprintf( szBuff,
                              "    %04Xh          %04Xh"
                              "          %04X:%04Xh",
                              HIWORD(wParam), LOWORD(wParam),
                              HIWORD(lParam), LOWORD(lParam) ) );
                  ReleaseDC( hwnd, hdc );
                  ValidateRect( hwnd, NULL );
                  break;

              case WM_DESTROY:
                  PostQuitMessage(0);
                  break;

              default:
                  return( DefWindowProc( hwnd,   msg,
                                      wParam, lParam ) );
      }
      return 0;
}

#include "Template.i"

int APIENTRY WinMain( HANDLE hInstance, HANDLE hPrevInstance,
                    LPSTR  lpCmdLine, int    nCmdShow    )
{
    MSG   msg;

    if( ! hPrevInstance )
      if( ! InitApplication( hInstance ) )
          return( FALSE );
    if( ! InitInstance( hInstance, nCmdShow ) )
```

```
        return (FALSE);
    while( GetMessage( &msg, NULL, 0, 0 ) )
    {
        TranslateMessage( &msg );
        DispatchMessage( &msg );
    }
    return( msg.wParam );
    UNREFERENCED_PARAMETER( lpCmdLine );
}
```

PART II

Windows NT/95
Application
Resources

CHAPTER

EIGHT

8

An Introduction to Application Resources

- Types of application resources

- Types of resource files

- Resource manager functions

Resources in Windows applications appear as a variety of elements. These resources range from text-based menus, to dialog box displays combining graphic and text elements, to purely graphic elements that include bitmaps, cursors, and icons. Individually, applications may use many or all of these elements. For example, an application might include multiple menus and dialog boxes, dozens of bitmaps, and assortments of cursors representing different operations or modes.

In theory, resource elements can be created as part of an application's conventional executable code. Under DOS, this is essentially what is required. Windows, however, provides a different structural approach for executables. The approach used by Windows permits resources to be appended to an application's executable without being embedded within the operational portion of the program.

This chapter provides an overview of the application resources offered by Windows NT and 95. These topics are discussed in detail in the following chapters. In Chapter 13, we'll finish up with an example that uses all the techniques covered in this part: the FileView application.

Advantages of the Windows Approach to Application Resources

When an application is loaded for execution, the resource elements are not loaded. Instead, resources, such as dialog boxes and menus, are loaded only on demand, as required. When a resource is no longer needed, it is discarded. The advantage of loading resources on demand is simple: memory is conserved and expended only for currently operating elements. Memory is not used for storage of elements that may or may not be needed.

For example, one version of a Solitaire program (SOL.EXE) contains 74 bitmaps (52 for the card faces alone), one menu, five dialog boxes, one accelerator, one icon, and one custom resource type—a fairly small load as resource elements go.

In contrast, another application might contain only one resource, the application's icon, and use a series of .DLL files. These .DLL files might contain hundreds of bitmap images, dozens of menus and dialog boxes, multiple accelerator key sets (for different circumstances), a hundred separate cursors, dozens of additional icons, and a huge string table.

In both cases, if these massive assortments of resources needed to be loaded into memory immediately on execution of the application, your system memory would quickly become overloaded. And only a small portion of these resources might actually be used at any time. Instead, since the system loads resources only on demand (when they are needed), memory remains free for other uses.

Another advantage to the approach is that you can edit application resources without needing to recompile the files. While the usual practice is for programmers to edit their own resource files before compiling and linking, executable program resources can also be edited.

> **NOTE** When executables are opened for resource editing, the original resource names do not appear. Instead, all resources are labeled by their identifier values.

However, keep in mind that application resources define only the appearance and organization of the resources, not their functional characteristics. For example, you can change the arrangement or appearance of a dialog box with a resource editor, but you cannot alter how the application responds to the dialog box controls. This means that you can make only cosmetic changes by editing resource elements. If you need to make functional changes, you must revise the application's source code and then recompile it.

Types of Resources

For your Windows NT and 95 applications, the following resources are available:

- **Images:** Three types of image resources are supported as bitmaps (.BMP), cursors (.CUR), and icons (.ICO). Each of these are bit images, but different rules and organizations are applied for the creation of each. You can edit image resources with a bitmap editor. The three bit image resource types are discussed in Chapter 9.

- **Toolbars:** These resources are a specialized bitmap image consisting of one or more individual button images. By default, each button is 16 by 15 pixels, but you can size buttons as desired. Even though toolbars are bitmap images, most resource editors provide a toolbar editor specifically for working with toolbars.

On the Use of Resources

As a programmer, you may have some questions about the use of application resources. Here are some typical concerns, in question-and-answer format:

Q: Exactly what items are considered as resources?

A: List everything that isn't provided directly by your C/C++ source code. In addition to bitmaps, icons, toolbars, dialog templates, hotkey accelerators, string tables, and custom cursors, resources can be data objects (such as a database template), custom controls, sound files (but these are usually external), and any other items you want to include as custom resources.

Q: How much free memory can be used for resources?

A: All of it. In theory, the only limitation under Windows NT is the 4GB limit on addressable memory. You must remember that the operating system is using roughly 12MB of RAM, and that the swap file acts as an extension to system RAM. Therefore, on a 16MB system, somewhere in the neighborhood of 20MB to 30MB of RAM are available for resources. How much you use is entirely up to the design of your application. For Windows 95, the limitations are essentially the same, except that Windows 95 has a 2GB limit on addressable memory instead of 4GB. And, yes, you could use a 2GB or 3GB hard drive as a dedicated swap file if you really need that much space. They're cheap now and relatively fast.

Q: Besides memory, what are the limitations on how many resources you can have loaded at one time?

A: For all practical purposes, memory aside, there are none.

Q: How time-consuming is it to load and unload resources?

A: Actually, it isn't. Resources are part of the application's .EXE file (or .DLL library) and are loaded at the same time the executable runs. If there is insufficient free memory, some part of the executable or DLL is transferred to the swap file, but this is handled by Windows on a demand basis. In this manner, elements that are not needed are off-loaded to a disk image of RAM and are recalled (moved back into active memory) when they are needed. In effect, there is no real way to say what the time constraints are, except to observe that fast hard drives are more responsive than slow ones.

- **Dialog boxes:** These are generally message or input windows, but they also may be child windows used to organize a display. A dialog box editor provides an interactive means of constructing dialog boxes, showing the elements (list boxes, buttons, edit boxes, scrollbars, and so on) exactly as these will appear on screen. Dialog boxes are discussed in Chapter 10.

- **Menus:** These provide lists of program options. The options may immediately execute commands, display submenus, or display dialog boxes for other operations. A menu editor allows you to define and test main and pull-down menus. Menus are discussed in Chapter 11.

- **Accelerators:** These are keyboard resources. An accelerator resource is a key or key combination provided as an alternative to an individual menu item to invoke a command. One common example is pressing the Shift+Ins or Ctrl+V combination as an alternative to pulling down the Edit menu and selecting the Paste option. You can define these hotkey shortcuts for menus with an accelerator editor or a plain text editor. Accelerator resources are discussed in Chapter 12.

- **Strings:** These resources are text strings that are displayed by an application in its menus or dialog boxes, for error messages or other information. By defining text strings as resources, rather than embedding them in the source code, you can conserve memory. This approach also allows you to edit strings for language changes without recompiling. You can create string tables using any plain text editor or a string table editor. String resources are discussed in Chapter 12.

- **Version:** This resource contains information about the application, such as its version number, its intended operating system, and its original filename. The resource is intended to be used with the File Installation library functions. Version resources are discussed in Chapter 12.

Files and File Types

Most resource editors can create, import, export, or edit most resource files used by Windows, including executable files containing resources. A full list of standard resource types appears in Table 8.1.

TABLE 8.1   Resource File Types

File Extension	Type	Description
.EXE	Executable	Executable program code containing application resources and compiled program code
.RES	Resource	Compiled (binary) resource file
.DLL	Executable	Executable (dynamic link library) module, which may contain either executable code, application resources, or both
.H	Source code	Header file containing symbolic names for defined resources
.ICO	Resource	Individual icon image resource file
.CUR	Resource	Individual cursor image resource file
.BMP	Resource	Individual bitmap image file
.DLG	Resource script	Individual dialog box resource script, containing a single dialog box in ASCII text format
.RC	Resource script	ASCII resource script containing one or more resource elements, which may include image resources in hexadecimal format
.DRV	Device driver	Compiled device driver, which may contain resource elements, dialog boxes, etc.

TABLE 8.1   Resource File Types (Continued)

File Extension	Type	Description
.FON	Font library	File containing one or more fonts belonging to a single typeface (not commonly used as a resource element)
.FNT	Font typeface	File containing a single typeface font
.DAT	Resource	Raw data resource, which is used for custom resource types (can be copied, renamed, or deleted but cannot be edited, browsed, or created using a resource editor)

Linking Resources

Normally, the resources are compiled directly to an .RES (binary) file, permitting the linker to link the compiled resources with the compiled .EXE executable. However, when editing an existing .EXE or .DLL source, no .RES file is created. Instead, the resources are written directly to the runtime program.

Using the Microsoft command-line compiler, NMake scripts (.MAK) contain instructions to compile .RC resource scripts before linking the resulting .RES compiled resources. If you are using a resource editor and wish to save resources as binary .RES files, you can modify the NMake scripts to omit the resource compilation.

More commonly, using Borland's IDE (Integrated Development Environment) or Microsoft's Developer Studio (both described later in this chapter), the resource file is linked automatically by including the .RES file in the application's project list.

Note that both resource editors (and most other systems) create an .RC resource script file—a text file—which contains all of the resources that are not images. Image resources, such as bitmaps, icons, cursors, and toolbars, are normally stored as separate image files referenced by the .RC resource script.

Dynamic Link Libraries

A dynamic link library (DLL, sometimes pronounced "dill") is an executable module that may contain both application executables (compiled source code) and application resources. A DLL is similar in construction to a runtime library, except that it is not linked to the application during the compile process. Instead, DLLs

WARNING
Some elements of syntax in the Microsoft and Borland .RC resource scripts differ and may require conversions in order to compile with the other system. These differences are generally minor and can be changed by editing the plain text .RC file. Also note that, even though both the Borland IDE and the Microsoft Developer Studio create .MAK files for application projects, their different versions of .MAK files are incompatible with the other's Make and NMake utilities.

are dynamically linked during execution when library resources—either executable routines or resources—are required.

DLLs have two important strengths:

- A single DLL can be accessed by more than one application without being duplicated within each application.

- Routines in DLLs can be revised and recompiled without modifying the programs using the called routines (assuming, of course, that the call and response format remains unchanged).

NOTE
Just as .EXE resources can be modified without recompilation, .DLL resources can be edited, extracted, or updated without recompilation.

Header Files

All application resources must be identified by numeric values. But, for humans, numeric identifiers are awkward and difficult to remember. Therefore, just as Windows NT and 95 supply mnemonic constants (see the Windows.H and included header files), programmers can also define .H header definition files to provide mnemonics for application resources (or use predefined mnemonics).

When creating resources using the Borland or Microsoft C++ integrated development compilers, the resource identifiers are created automatically and are found in the Resource.H header. Most of the resources appear as scripts in the .RC resource file. All image resources—bitmaps, cursors, and icons—appear as separate .BMP, .CUR, and .ICO files, which are referenced within the .RC script.

Using Resource Editors

Although some resource types, such as dialog boxes, can be designed (however laboriously) by editing script files, image-based resources are difficult to create without using some type of resource editor, such as the Resource Manager in Microsoft's Developer Studio or the Resource Workshop in Borland's IDE. If you prefer, there are a variety of other resource editors available, all of which produce compatible application resources—both image-based and other types.

Both Microsoft and Borland provide a variety of resource editors. Figure 8.1 shows the Microsoft Developer Studio's main screen, and Figure 8.2 shows the Borland IDE's Resource Workshop main screen.

FIGURE 8.1

The Developer Studio Resource Manager's main screen

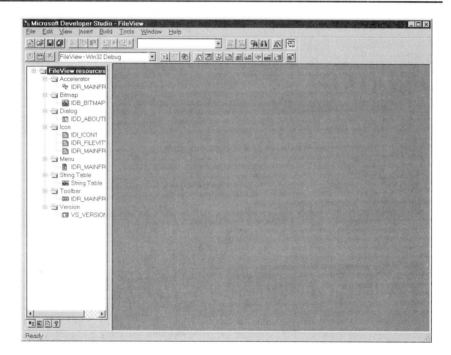

FIGURE 8.2

The Borland IDE
Resource Workshop
main screen

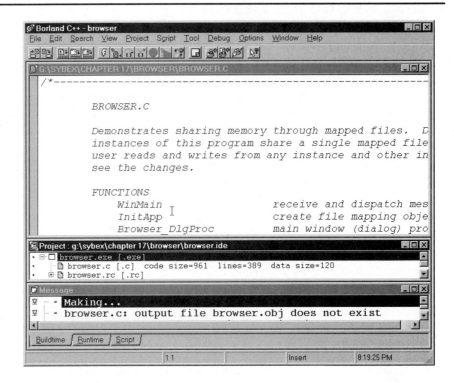

Selecting Options

Like most Windows applications, both the Developer Studio and Resource Work-shop are designed principally for mouse operation. You can activate features by clicking on menu options, buttons, or other controls. However, both the Resource Workshop and Developer Studio also provide hotkey options that allow you to select items by pressing the key corresponding to the underscored letters. Thus, in either system, from the menu, Alt+F selects File, N selects New Project, and a pop-up dialog box or a submenu offers a selection of preferences for creating a new file, a new project, and so on. Similar hotkeys are available in most dialog boxes and menus.

As with many other Windows applications, you can also use the Tab key to cycle through the buttons and/or fields. To select the highlighted option, press the Enter key or spacebar.

Managing Project Resources in the Developer Studio

Since resource elements can be created and stored separately from a project (but are most commonly created within a project), the Developer Studio makes provisions for opening both project and individual resource files. The Developer Studio's File menu has two "open" provisions: Open and Open Workspace.

You can use the Open option to open any type of file, including a project file. But the Open Workspace option provides a shortcut specifically for opening projects. Likewise, the Close Workspace option closes an open workspace and all associated files. When you reopen the workspace, all the files that were previously open are reopened.

On the other hand, if you want to work on an individual resource file or create a new resource file, without opening a project, simply click on New to open the New dialog box, shown in Figure 8.3, and select the file type.

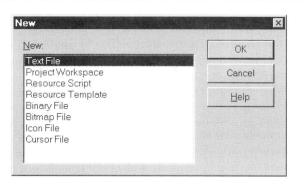

Notice here that there are individual options for bitmap, cursor, and icon files but not for dialog boxes, menus, accelerator keys, and other resources. Instead, all resource types except image resources are covered by the Resource Script option.

If you wish to open an individual resource file, select the Open option to see the dialog box shown in Figure 8.4. Then you can select the type of resource (or other file) from the Files of Type pull-down list.

FIGURE 8.4

Opening a file outside a project

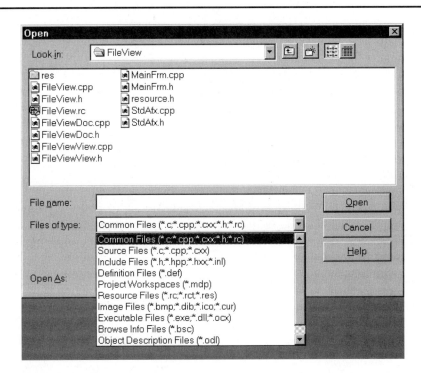

Adding and Editing Resource Elements

Normally, of course, you will be working with a project, and you'll want to create your resources as a part of the project rather than attempting to create individual resource files. For this purpose, instead of opening a new file, select Insert from the main menu, select Resource, and then choose the type of resource to create from the Insert Resource dialog box (by double-clicking on it or highlighting it and clicking on OK), shown in Figure 8.5.

FIGURE 8.5

Adding a resource to a project

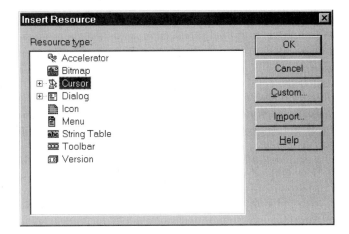

After you select the resource type, a new resource element is added to the project list (at the left) using a default type name such as IDC_CURSOR1. At the same time, the appropriate editor is called to create the new resource element.

To create a custom resource element, select the Custom button, and then enter a name for the custom resource type. You must create custom resources independently, by whatever means are appropriate. The options here only permit you to include a custom resource and custom resource type within a project. You must handle all other provisions yourself, and they must conform to response code within the application or an associated DLL.

You can change default element type names at any time by right-clicking on the appropriate element in the resource list (at the left) to call the pop-up menu. From the menu, select Properties to display the Properties dialog box, shown in Figure 8.6. Then simply enter a new resource name. A corresponding entry will be made in the Resource.H header automatically. This provides a convenient way to replace the default labels supplied when resource elements are generated with new mnemonic resource names.

You can edit an existing resource element simply by double-clicking on it (or highlighting it and pressing Enter) in the project resource list. This brings up the appropriate editor and loads the resource element.

FIGURE 8.6

Entering a new resource name in the Properties dialog box

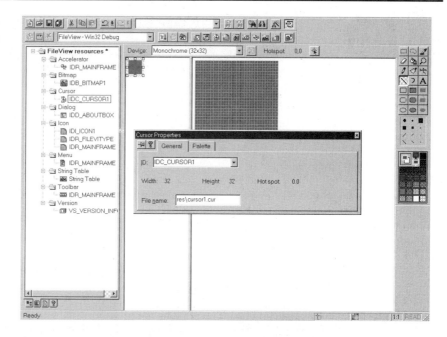

Viewing and Changing Resource Identifiers

To view resource identifiers, select Resource Symbols from the View menu. The Resource Symbols dialog box appears, as shown in Figure 8.7. Here the resource identifiers are listed in alphabetic (not numeric) order.

In the In Use column on the right side of the dialog box, a check mark indicates that an identifier is in use. The Used by box at the bottom of the dialog box shows where the highlighted identifier is used. When an identifier is used by more than one resource, multiple items appear in the Used by list. To view the use of an identifier, click the View Use button.

NOTE

Obsolete or unused identifiers may remain in the Resource.H header but will not be checked. You can delete or change them. However, you should be aware that unchecked identifiers may be mnemonic constants created for special messages. The lack of a check mark simply means that the constant is not used by any resource element.

FIGURE 8.7

Viewing resource
identifiers

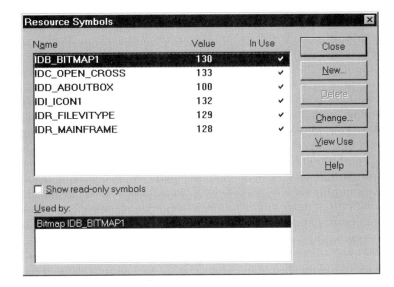

To change an identifier, click on the Change button. If the selected identifier is in use, you will not be able to change that identifier through this dialog box. You can only change an identifier that is in use by changing the properties for the resource element. To edit a resource's properties, use its Properties dialog box, as explained in the previous section.

If the selected identifier is in use, the Delete button will be disabled. You can delete only identifiers that are not in use.

Copying Resource Elements

To duplicate a resource—for example, to use as the basis for creating a different version of the resource—select the resource to duplicate, then use the Copy and Paste options on the Edit menu. A new resource identifier will be created for the duplicated resource.

The Insert menu has a Resource Copy option. This option creates a copy of a resource element that is used only when a special condition is defined, or creates a copy in a second language.

Managing Project Resource Files in the Resource Workshop

The Borland IDE Resource Workshop offers both File and Project menus. Use the File menu to open individual files (either program source files or resource files). Use the Project file to open a project workspace. Once the project is opened, you can select the resource script from the listed project files. Alternatively, you can load the .RC resource file separately from the .IDE project file. To work on a project's resources, use the File option to open the .RC script. Optionally, you may also open any saved binary resource file.

You must, however, have an .RC script open to enable the Resource menu. After opening or creating a resource script, to create a new resource element, select New from the Resource menu, and then select the resource type to create from the list. Figure 8.8 shows this process.

FIGURE 8.8

Creating a new resource in the Resource Workshop

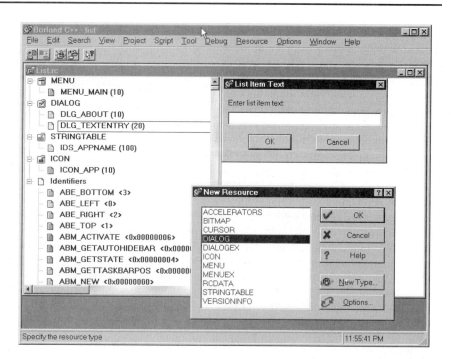

If a project is open when you create a new resource, the resource automatically becomes a part of that project, appearing on the project list (at the left) with a default type name (such as IDC_CURSOR1). At the same time, the appropriate editor is called to create the new resource element.

To create a custom resource element, select the New Type button, and then enter a name for the custom resource type. Custom resources must be created independently, by whatever means are appropriate for the custom resource. The options here permit you to include a custom resource and custom resource type within a project, but you must handle all other provisions yourself, and they must conform to the response code within the application or an associated DLL.

You can change default element type names at any time by right-clicking on the appropriate element in the resource list (at the left) to call the pop-up menu. From the menu, select Resource Attributes to display the dialog box shown in Figure 8.9. Then simply enter a new resource name. The corresponding entry will be made in the Resource.H header automatically. This provides a convenient way to replace the default labels supplied when resource elements are generated with new mnemonic resource names.

FIGURE 8.9

Entering a new resource name in the Resource Attributes dialog box

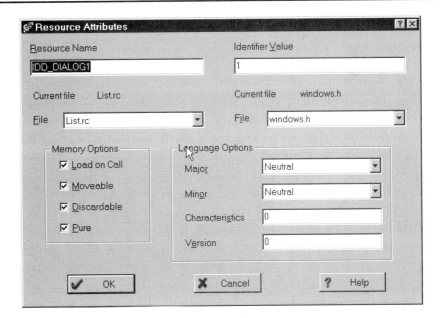

You can edit an existing resource element simply by double-clicking on it (or highlighting it and pressing Enter) in the project resource list. This brings up the appropriate editor and loads the resource element.

To view resource identifiers, select Identifiers from the Resource menu. The Identifiers dialog box appears, as shown in Figure 8.10. Here the resource identifiers are listed in alphabetic (not numeric) order. In the Files column (left), the Identifiers dialog box lists all the sources that provide identifiers that may be used by the application. After you select a source file, the right window lists the identifiers defined in the selected source.

FIGURE 8.10

Viewing resource identifiers in the Resource Workshop

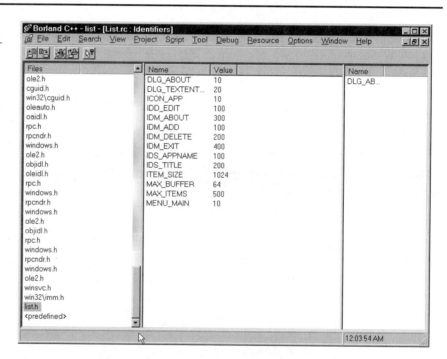

To duplicate a resource—for example, to use as the basis for creating a different version of the resource—select the resource to duplicate, then use the Copy and Paste options from the Edit menu. A new resource identifier will be created for the duplicated resource.

NOTE

Unfortunately, compared with the Visual C++ Resource Identifier utility, this particular Resource Workshop utility is distinctly inferior in several respects. Many individual files in the file list appear two or more times, the listed files are not in any specific order, there is no method of distinguishing global identifiers from project-specific identifiers, and the information that is provided is of minimal usefulness.

As you can see from these descriptions of the Microsoft Developer Studio Resource Manager and the Borland IDE Resource Workshop, both resource editors are easy to use. The individual editors for the various resource types are discussed in the following chapters, explaining how each is used to create resources for the FileView demo program presented in Chapter 13.

CHAPTER
NINE

9

Bit Images and Image Editors

- The three types of image resources

- Two image editors

- Special cursor resource elements

- Some icon guidelines

Bitmap images, icons, and mouse cursors are image resources, which you can manipulate with an image editor. This chapter describes the differences between these types of image resources and the image editors included with two resource managers: Borland's Resource Workshop and Microsoft's Developer Studio.

Types of Image Resources

Although each of the three types of image resources are bit images, different rules and organizations are applied for the creation of each.

Bitmap Images

The simplest bit image type is the bitmap image, which is a pixel image using 2, 16, or 256 colors. Individually, bitmaps may be as large as the full screen (or larger) as in the Jungle.BMP image, medium-sized as in the Solitaire card images, or as small as a few dozen pixels for a checkbox control or radio button. Bitmap images, however, are limited in that they consist only of a foreground image and cannot contain transparent areas.

Of the three image resource types, bitmap images can be created by any paint program and do not differ in any respect from conventional bitmaps. This means that bitmap images can also be imported from external sources. Furthermore, bitmap images can use palettes supporting 2, 16, or 256 colors with no limitations, aside from memory, of course.

Within applications, bitmap images can be used for decorative or informative purposes. They can also be incorporated as graphic controls.

Icon Images

The icon image type is commonly used to represent an application within a Program Manager group or on the Desktop display. You can also include icons as bitmap images within dialog boxes or, with special handling, as menu elements.

Icon images are similar to bitmap images, but they have size limitations supporting only VGA resolution 32x32 (normal) or 64x64 bit image sizes. Like bitmaps, icon palettes can support 2, 16, or 256 colors. Unlike bitmap images, however, icons can interact with their background and can include transparent areas or areas that invert background pixels.

Cursor Images

The third bit image type is the cursor, which, unlike the bitmap and icon types, always interacts with the background image.

A cursor bit image consists of two 32x32 bit images: the first is a mask that interacts with the cursor background, and the second is the cursor pattern itself, which overlays the mask/background combination. Cursors are restricted to a default palette consisting of only four colors: black, white, transparent, and inverted.

Also, unlike other images, a cursor contains a *hotspot*, which is a pixel location within the image that defines the cursor's position. For example, the familiar arrow cursor's hotspot is located at the tip of the arrowhead.

Unfortunately, animated cursors (.ANI) are not currently supported by resource editors, even though Windows NT ships with a set of sample animated cursors. You'll need to use specialized facilities to create these types of cursors. Animated cursors are discussed in more detail later in the chapter.

A Choice of Bitmap Editors

Both Borland's Resource Workshop image editor and Microsoft's Developer Studio image editor support bitmap, icon, and cursor images. Borland's editor is part of its IDE Resource Workshop; Microsoft's editor is part of its Developer Studio Resource Manager. Both editors are illustrated with the WinNT256 bitmap image.

Only the icon and cursor image types require the specialized formats provided by these resource editors. Bitmap images can be created by a wide variety of other paint utilities (many of which are better suited for general illustration than either of these resource editors).

Although these two image editors appear quite different—in their menus, palettes, and toolbars—both accomplish essentially the same tasks. The principal difference between the two is that Borland's editor offers both a full 256-color palette (Microsoft's editor will allow you to choose additional colors) and a split window display with independent zoom capabilities.

Custom Fonts

At one time, custom fonts represented a fourth type of bitmapped resource. Application fonts, however, were limited to bitmapped font images. These are no longer supported as resource elements.

Today, with a few exceptions, bitmapped fonts have been replaced by vectored character fonts. These have several advantages: they are resizable, adaptable to different screen resolutions, and generally cleaner and easier to read, as well as more attractive.

Vectored fonts, however, are not application resources; that is, they are not included as an integral part of the application. Instead, vectored fonts are used as system resources, available to all applications. These types of fonts are not intended to be application-specific.

To create custom fonts, consider using any of the numerous font editors available on the market (such as Fontographer or Adobe Font Manager). However, requiring a custom font or fonts for your application is not a recommended practice and should be done only under special circumstances.

Using the Borland C++ Image Editor

Borland's image editor consists of a split window display, a horizontal palette bar, and a vertical toolbar. Figure 9.1 shows this editor's main screen. Initially, the split window display divides the workspace equally. You can drag the bar dividing the two sections to the left or right to resize the shared display. Also, you can size the bitmap display within each area independently, as in Figure 9.1, by using the View menu options.

The palette bar appears as a horizontal bar with the 256 palette colors. The current foreground and background color selections are shown on the toolbar at the bottom. To select a new foreground color, click on it with the left (primary) mouse button. To pick a different background color, click on it with the right (secondary) mouse button.

The toolbar appears at the bottom of the workspace. At the top of the toolbar, tools are illustrated by icons. You can select a tool with the mouse; the active tool

FIGURE 9.1

The Borland Resource
Workshop image editor

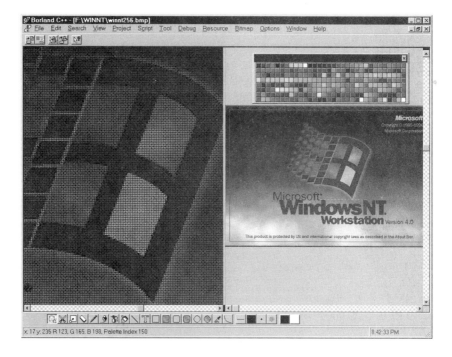

is shown as a depressed button. The tools are the standard ones provided with most paint programs. The Text tool, identified by the T icon, allows you to enter text into an image. The Bitmap menu option offers alignment settings for this text and summons a font selection dialog box, including font sizing options.

Also on the toolbar, the buttons on the right show the current brush shape, airbrush brush shape, the line thickness, and the current pattern using the active (foreground) drawing color.

The drawing operations are essentially the same as in other familiar paint programs, such as in the Paint program distributed with Windows.

TIP

The tools in both the Borland and Microsoft image editors should be familiar to anyone who has used a paint program. For explanations about how the individual tools function, use the editor's Help menu options.

Using Microsoft's Image Editor

Microsoft's Developer Studio image editor is shown in Figure 9.2. This editor supplies split windows for only smaller images. Unfortunately, the zoom capabilities are quite limited, particularly when working with icon or cursor images (a flaw probably favored only by greedy opticians). In the example in Figure 9.2, because of the size of the image, only one window was supported but zoom was allowed.

FIGURE 9.2

The Microsoft Developer Studio image editor

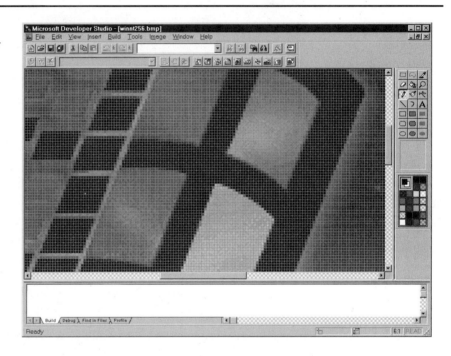

The palette bar appears (in the lower right in Figure 9.2) with 16 basic and 12 dithered palette colors. The foreground and background colors are shown at the upper left of the palette bar. To select a color, click on it with the appropriate mouse button: left-click for the foreground color and right-click for the background. To change any palette entry, double-click on that entry to bring up the Windows common dialog box for color selection.

The toolbar appears as a vertical, triple-column bar (in the upper right in Figure 9.2), with 21 tools illustrated by icons. When you select a brush, pen, airbrush, or similar tool, the rectangle below the tool buttons offers a choice of weights or tool shapes.

As with the Borland image editor, the drawing operations are essentially the same as in other familiar paint programs, such as the Paint program distributed with Windows.

For more complex bitmap images, a wide variety of paint programs are available, and any .BMP or .DIB image can be imported as an application resource.

Cursor Resources

Cursor resources (mouse pointers) are a specialized form of bitmap. Unlike other bitmap images, the bitmap images used for cursors do not replace the underlying background images. Instead, cursor images are intended to interact with the background but leave the underlying image unchanged after the cursor moves.

For maximum visibility, cursor images are normally created as outlines using the inverted pixels for contrast or highlighting. The transparent pixels are simply used for areas where the background is allowed to show through.

Cursor Elements

Cursors provide three principal elements:

- **Pointer image:** The cursor image shows the mouse location and also frequently indicates the general function currently being executed.

- **Screen image:** The screen image is a mask governing the interaction between the cursor (pointer) image and the underlying screen image. This image is generated automatically to fit the pointer image.

- **Hotspot:** The hotspot is a location within the cursor image that corresponds to the mouse's absolute screen position and is assigned by the cursor's designer.

As with previous Windows versions, only black-and-white cursor images are supported, and cursor pixels are composed of four colors: black, white, transparent, and inverted. (Animated cursors, which do permit color, are not considered a standard cursor image.)

Figure 9.3 shows a simple hand cursor with a pointing finger. The hand is drawn in black, then outlined in white, and finally, filled using "inverted" pixels. All these elements were designed to maximize the appearance of the image against any background—light, dark, or mixed. The hotspot is located at the tip of the extended finger.

TIP

A simpler version of the cursor shown in Figure 9.3 could be drawn using only inverted pixels for the image and leaving the rest of the field transparent. Alternatively, you could draw the image in black and use an inverted outline.

FIGURE 9.3

A sample cursor image

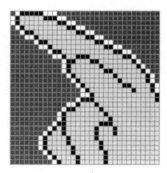

Animated Cursors

Animated cursors are a specialized format using the .ANI extension. They consist of a series of images that provide simple visual animation. A variety of interesting examples are distributed with Windows NT. A few examples include an hourglass with the sand pouring through, walking dinosaurs, and galloping horses.

Neither the Borland nor Microsoft C++ compiler suite provides support for creating or editing animated cursors, nor can they be readily imported as application resources. There are, however, third-party utilities available for animated cursor creation, if you are so inclined.

Alternatively, you could create your own animation by using a separate thread to load a series of cursor images, which is essentially what an animated cursor does in any case.

Icon Resources

Icon resources are used to represent applications, system resources, subsystems, or controls within an application. Icons are commonly displayed by the Program Manager to represent available programs or on the main screen to represent minimized programs. Some applications, such as the Clock program distributed with NT, create their own dynamic icons. Such custom icons aside, however, conventional icons are simply small bitmaps presenting a symbol representing the application.

Icon Design

Designing an icon is largely a matter of personal taste. Icons can be as colorful and gaudy as you can design or as starkly plain as you choose. I won't try to give you a course in commercial art design; however, there are a few points you should keep in mind when designing icons:

- Your application is not going to stand or fall on the quality of your icon (unless you have a very unusual application).

- There is always a temptation to put a great deal of detail into an icon, or to reproduce a company logo, or to execute some concept that sounds fantastic in conversation. But remember, an icon is small, and much of the detail will be lost as clutter. In general, a simple icon is best. Its only real purpose is to be recognizable so that it can be selected for its intended purpose.

- Although you can design icons using fine color details, if they are executed on a simple VGA system (or on many laptops), they will be mapped to the nearest available colors in the palette. The result is that all of your careful work, and quite likely the image as well, is lost. On a monochrome system, the results can be even worse, since the colors are dithered down to black and white.

The best rule is simple, as in "keep it simple." If you need contrast, you can always use inverted pixels to ensure that at least some of the icon will be visible regardless of the background.

Two Icons for FileView

The FileView application, which is described in detail in Chapter 13, is used, in part, to illustrate system resources. This application uses two icon images, as illustrated in Figure 9.4. The primary application icon appears at the right; the icon on the left is used only in one of the dialog boxes.

FIGURE 9.4

Two resources for the
FileView application

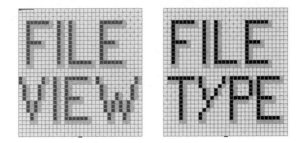

Both icon images were designed to stand out against any background, beginning with a field drawn using the inverse brush. The letters are drawn using the screen (transparent) brush, then outlined in light cyan.

Additional resources used by the FileView application are discussed in the following chapters.

CHAPTER

TEN

10

Dialog Boxes and
Dialog Box Editors

- Microsoft's Developer Studio dialog box editor

- Borland's Resource Workshop dialog box editor

- Dialog box properties

- Dialog box controls

Icons aside, more applications use dialog boxes than any other resource. Of course, since many applications use dozens—or even more—of dialog boxes, the total number of dialog box resources easily exceeds all other resource elements.

Although ASCII scripts can be used to define dialog boxes, dialog box editors provide a much more convenient method. In this chapter, we'll cover the use of two different dialog box editors and describe the various types of dialog box controls.

Introducing Two Dialog Box Editors

Both the Borland and Microsoft dialog box editors provide interactive dialog box design. They provide tools to create and arrange all standard dialog box resource elements, including control buttons, checkboxes, edit fields, list boxes, and radio buttons. Furthermore, the use of both of the dialog box editors is largely intuitive; in many respects, they operate much like a paint program, using drag-and-drop tools to position and size resource elements selected from a toolbar.

For most purposes, either dialog box editor will serve quite well, since they both support the same basic resource elements and controls. However, each of these editors provides a number of features that are not supported by the other. For example, Borland's editor contains the BWCC (Borland Windows Custom Controls) options, which Microsoft does not support; Microsoft's editor contains some MFC controls, which Borland does not support. Both editors, however, in addition to the conventional resource elements, include support for the common control elements provided by Windows NT and 95.

NOTE The illustrations in this chapter are from the Microsoft Developer Studio editor. The resources and dialog boxes created for the FileView1 application may be edited with either system. The FileView2 application files, however, are not compatible with the Borland compiler or resource editors.

The Microsoft Developer Studio Dialog Box Editor

The main screen of the Microsoft Developer Studio dialog box editor is shown in Figure 10.1. Here you see a blank dialog box that contains only two buttons, the Controls toolbar (far right), and the status bar (bottom) with additional operator options and alignment tools.

FIGURE 10.1

The Microsoft Developer Studio dialog box editor

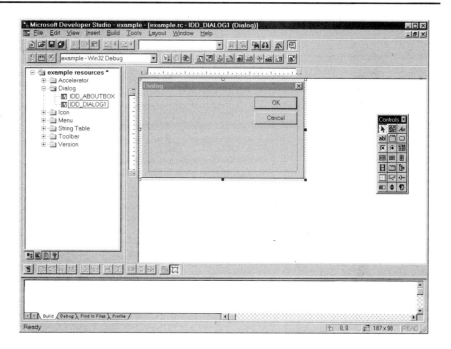

The Developer Studio dialog box editor offers twenty-one icons: one represents the control cursor, nineteen represent the standard dialog box element types, and the last (bottom-right) provides for custom dialog box resource types.

The Layout menu offers options for alignment and layout, which are also on the bottom toolbar. It also offers options for guide settings and tab-order arrangements, which are not found on the toolbar.

The individual tools will be described more fully after we take a look a Borland's dialog box editor.

The Borland Resource Workshop Dialog Box Editor

When you begin to create a new dialog box resource in Borland's Resource Workshop, you'll see a blank dialog box with three buttons, as shown in Figure 10.2. The Resource Workshop dialog box editor uses a tabbed toolbar (upper right) with separate tabs for standard resources, common resources, BWCC (Borland-specific), two data-oriented resource groups, and a custom group. The tabbed toolbar may be either docked (as shown) or free floating. At the bottom, the toolbar offers options for aligning and sizing dialog box resource controls.

FIGURE 10.2

The Resource Workshop Dialog Box Editor

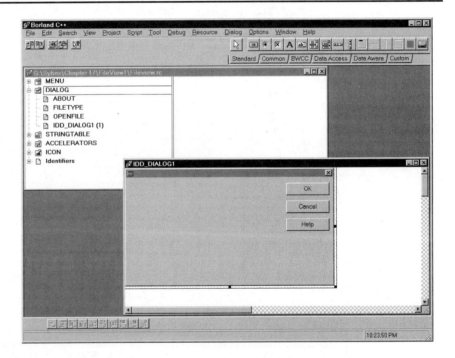

As well as loading dialog boxes from and saving dialog boxes to resource files (.RES), resource scripts (.RC), executable files (.EXE), and dynamic link libraries (.DLL), this editor can also save dialog box designs as dialog box resource scripts (.DLG). At the same time, you can create or edit header (.H) files to provide lists of mnemonic symbols for dialog box resources.

TIP

One advantage of the Borland Resource Workshop over the Microsoft Developer Studio is that the Resource Workshop opens a text window for the .RC script file, as well as providing an interactive editor. The Developer Studio does not readily provide a means of editing the .RC script directly. (As an exception, when an error in the script prevents the script from compiling, editing the text file directly is permitted.)

Dialog Box Properties

With a dialog box editor, you can create a variety of dialog box types and styles. To set the properties for a dialog box with Microsoft's Developer Studio, select Properties from the Edit menu, or right-click on the dialog box in the editor. This brings up the Dialog Properties dialog box, which has tabs for General, Styles, More Styles, and Extended Styles. Figure 10.3 shows the General tab of the Properties dialog box.

FIGURE 10.3

The General tab of the Developer Studio Dialog Properties dialog box

Using the Borland Resource Editor, double-click on the dialog box in the editor, or right-click and select Properties from the pop-up menu to see similar features and control options.

General Properties

The General tab of the Developer Studio Dialog Properties box shows the dialog box ID and caption, along with font information, position information, the dialog menu, and an associated class name. The General tab includes these fields:

- **ID:** A mnemonic symbol defined in the header file. This may be a symbol (the customary default), an integer, or a quoted string.

- **Caption:** Text appearing as the dialog box label. The default dialog box name supplied by the resource editor should be changed to a label identifying the purpose or function of the dialog box.

- **Menu:** An optional resource identifier for a menu to be used in the dialog box.

- **Font Name:** The typeface of the font used in all the controls in the dialog box. The bold version of the typeface is always used.

- **Font Size:** The point size for the font used in all the controls in the dialog box.

- **Font:** Calls a font selection dialog box to change the default typeface or point size used with the dialog box. A sample of the selected typeface and size is shown at the bottom of the dialog box. The Select Dialog Font dialog box is shown in Figure 10.4.

FIGURE 10.4

Choosing a default font for your dialog box

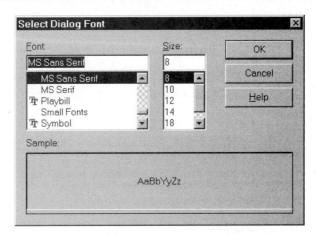

NOTE For applications written using Microsoft Visual C++, only one font may be selected. This font is applied to all controls and text elements in the dialog box. For applications written using Borland's C++ and the BWCC library, individual controls may display different fonts within a single dialog box.

- **X Pos and Y Pos:** The x- and y-coordinates, in dialog box units (DLUs, or dialog logic units), for the upper-left corner of the dialog box.

- **Class Name:** The registered dialog class (a Windows operating system window class, not a C++ class). Provided to support C programming, this element is disabled when using MFC library support.

Dialog Box Styles

The Styles tab of the Developer Studio Dialog Properties box offers controls for the overall appearance and behavior of the dialog box. Figure 10.5 shows this tab.

FIGURE 10.5

The Styles tab of the Developer Studio Dialog Properties dialog box

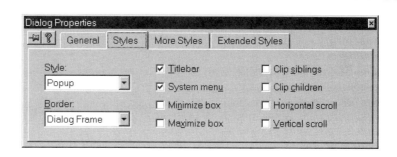

Dialog box styles may have the following values:

- **Style:** You can choose from the following operation styles:

  - Overlapped, which is always a top-level window and should have a caption and a border. Overlapped windows are pop-up windows that can be overlapped by other dialog box windows. Normally, only the main window in an application is defined as Overlapped.

- Popup, which is the default. Pop-up dialog boxes appear only when called by an application in response to a menu selection or some other program instruction.

- Child, which creates a dialog box defined as a child window belonging to another window. These are generally used when several tiled windows are desired within an application, and are displayed at all times (unless, of course, they are covered by another window or application). Child windows belonging to an application are not allowed to overlap.

- **Border:** You can choose from four frame (border) styles, which determine the appearance of the dialog box frame and the presence or absence of a caption bar:

  - None, which displays neither a border nor a caption bar.

  - Thin, which displays a thin, single border without a caption bar.

  - Resizing, which displays a double border without a caption bar.

  - Dialog Frame, the default, which displays a double border with a caption bar.

- **Titlebar:** If checked (the default), the dialog box appears with a title bar.

- **System Menu:** If checked (the default), the dialog box appears with a system menu at the upper-left corner of the frame. The system menu appears only on captioned dialog boxes.

- **Minimize Box:** If checked (unchecked is the default), the dialog box appears with a Minimize box.

- **Maximize Box:** If checked (unchecked is the default), the dialog box appears with a Maximize box.

> **NOTE**
>
> The Minimize Box and Maximize Box options add Minimize and Maximize controls at the upper-right corner of the dialog box frame. However, like the system menu, these controls will appear only if the dialog box is captioned.

- **Clip Siblings:** If checked (unchecked is the default), child windows are clipped relative to each other. Thus, when a particular child window is repainted, all other top-level child windows are clipped from the region of the child window to be updated. If this option is cleared and child windows overlap, drawing in the client area of a child window may draw in the client area of a neighboring child window. This option is for use with child windows only.

- **Clip Children:** If checked (unchecked is the default), this excludes the area occupied by child windows when drawing within the parent window. This option is used only when creating a parent window. Do not use this style if the dialog box contains a group box.

- **Horizontal Scroll:** If checked (unchecked is the default), the dialog box contains a horizontal scrollbar.

- **Vertical Scroll:** If checked (unchecked is the default), the dialog box contains a vertical scrollbar.

WARNING
When a dialog box using the default border style (Dialog Frame) contains scrollbars, the scrollbars are drawn overlapping the borders of the dialog box, rather than inside the frame, and the contents of the dialog box are clipped incorrectly. This is standard Windows behavior. Therefore, to use scrollbars with a dialog box frame, select None, Thin, or Resizing for the Border style. This does not apply to scrollbar controls within the dialog box—only to scrollbars used to scroll the dialog box itself.

More Style Options

The More Styles tab of the Developer Studio Dialog Properties box offers additional controls for the appearance and behavior of the dialog box. Figure 10.6 shows this tab.

This tab offers the following selections, which are all unchecked by default:

- **System Modal:** Makes the dialog box system-modal, prohibiting switching to another window or program while the dialog box is active. This option is used for warnings, queries, and other urgent or immediate messages.

- **Absolute Align:** Aligns the dialog box relative to the upper-left corner of the screen. (By default, the dialog box is aligned relative to its parent window.)

FIGURE 10.6

The More Styles tab
of the Developer Studio
Dialog Properties
dialog box

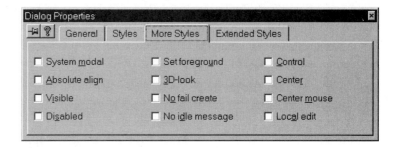

- **Visible:** Makes the dialog box visible when first displayed. This option is applicable to overlapping and pop-up windows. Do not check this option for form views and dialog-bar template resources.

- **Disabled:** Makes the dialog box disabled when it first appears.

- **Set Foreground:** Brings the dialog box to the foreground by, internally, calling the SetForegroundWindow function for the dialog box.

- **3D-look:** Makes the dialog box appear with a nonbold font and draws three-dimensional borders around control windows in the dialog box.

- **No Fail Create:** Creates the dialog box even if errors occur. For example, if a child window cannot be created or if the system cannot create a special data segment for an edit control, the dialog box will still be created.

- **No Idle Message:** Suppresses the WM_ENTERIDLE message ordinarily sent to a dialog box's owner when no more messages are waiting in its message queue. This option is valid only for modal dialog boxes.

- **Control:** Creates a dialog box that works well as a child window of another dialog box, similar to a page in a property sheet. This option permits the user to tab among the control windows of a child dialog box, use its accelerator keys, and so on.

- **Center:** Centers the dialog box in the working area; that is, the area not obscured by the toolbar.

- **Center Mouse:** Centers the mouse cursor in the dialog box on opening.

- **Local Edit:** Specifies that edit-box controls in the dialog box will use memory in the application's data segment. Normally, all edit-box controls in dialog boxes use memory outside the application's data segment. This option should always be used if the application will be using the EM_SETHANDLE or EM_GETHANDLE messages.

Extended Style Options

The Extended Styles tab of the Developer Studio Dialog Properties box offers additional controls for the appearance and behavior of the dialog box. Figure 10.7 shows this tab.

FIGURE 10.7

The Extended Styles tab of the Developer Studio Dialog Properties dialog box

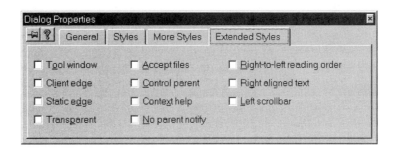

This tab offers the following selections, which are all unchecked by default:

- **Tool Window:** Creates a tool window intended to be used as a floating toolbar. Toolbar windows have a title bar shorter than a normal title bar, and the title is drawn using a smaller font.

- **Client Edge:** Creates a border with a sunken edge around the dialog box.

- **Static Edge:** Creates a border around the dialog box.

- **Transparent:** Creates the dialog box with a transparent window, so that any windows beneath the dialog window are not obscured. The dialog window receives WM_PAINT messages only after all sibling windows beneath it have been updated. This is useful for overlay drawing, but it does not function well when you are attempting to overlay live video.

- **Accept Files:** Allows the dialog box to accept drag-and-drop files. When a file is dropped on a dialog box, a WM_DROPFILES message is sent to the control.

- **Control Parent:** Allows the user to navigate among the dialog child windows using the Tab key. (In either case, navigation using the mouse remains in effect.)

- **Context Help:** Includes the Help question mark icon in the dialog's title bar. When the user clicks on the question mark, the cursor changes to a question mark with a pointer. Then, when a child window is clicked, the child receives a WM_HELP message. The WM_HELP message should be passed to the parent window procedure, which should call the WinHelp function using the HELP_WM_HELP command so that the Help application can display a pop-up window with help information for the child window.

- **No Parent Notify:** Stops the child window from sending the WM_PARENTNOTIFY message to its parent window.

- **Right-to-Left Reading Order:** Displays the dialog box text using right-to-left reading order properties.

- **Right Aligned Text:** Right-aligns text within the dialog box.

- **Left Scrollbar:** Displays the vertical scrollbar (if present) to the left of the client area.

Dialog Box Control Elements

Dialog boxes may contain a wide variety of controls, including buttons, scrollbars, list boxes, edit fields, images, spin buttons, and more. New control varieties are introduced regularly. While it would be literally impossible to describe every type of control, we will attempt to cover most of the standard types here, even though "new" standard types appear almost as often as new custom types.

The dialog box controls are on the dialog box editor's toolbar. Figure 10.8 shows the Microsoft Developer Studio toolbar. These tools, from left to right, are:

Pointer	Picture	Static text
Edit box	Group box	Button
Checkbox	Radio button	Combo box

List box	Horizontal scrollbar	Vertical scrollbar
Animate	Tab control	Tree control
List control	Hotkey	Slider
Progress bar	Spin control	Custom control

Each of these control types can be selected from the toolbar by clicking on the appropriate icon, then positioning the control in the dialog box outline.

FIGURE 10.8

Use the toolbar in the Microsoft Developer Studio dialog box editor to add dialog box controls.

Button Types

Three types of dialog box buttons are provided: pushbuttons, checkboxes, and radio buttons. Buttons are used to define controls that permit user interactions.

Pushbuttons

Buttons (pushbuttons) are the simplest form of dialog box control. Pushbuttons usually contain a text label (caption) identifying their purpose.

Pushbutton controls execute an immediate response when they are clicked on with the mouse, but normally they do not maintain any status information. Default pushbuttons, identified by highlighting (an outline), can also be selected by pressing the Enter key or spacebar. Only one default pushbutton should be defined in any dialog box.

When you choose the button icon on the Microsoft Developer Studio dialog box editor toolbar, you'll see the dialog box shown in Figure 10.9.

FIGURE 10.9

Choosing pushbutton
styles

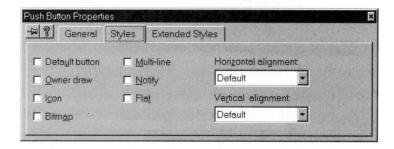

The Push Button Properties dialog box offers the following styles:

- **Default Button:** Makes the control the default button in the dialog box. The default button is drawn with a heavy black border when the dialog box first appears, and it is executed if the user presses Enter without choosing another command in the dialog box. Windows allows only one default button in a dialog box.

> **WARNING**
>
> Unfortunately, the Developer Studio does not prevent more than one button from being created with the Default Button style. The result of having multiple default buttons in a dialog box is generally failure of any of the buttons to respond to the Enter key.

- **Owner Draw:** Used when an application needs to customize the appearance of a control. When this style is selected, Windows does not handle the button appearance. Instead, when the button is activated, the parent window is notified with a request to paint, invert, or disable the button. The application must provide its own OnDrawItem message handler in the owner-window procedure (either the dialog-box procedure or the class derived from MFC class CDialog or CFormView). Owner-draw classes may also be derived from CButton using an override for the CButton::DrawItem method.

- **Icon:** Displays an icon image for the button.

- **Bitmap:** Displays a bitmap image for the button.

- **Multi-line:** Allows the button text to wrap to multiple lines if it is too long to fit on a single line within the button rectangle.

- **Notify:** Sends a notification to the parent window (the dialog box) when a pushbutton is clicked or double-clicked. By default, this option is not selected, and the button functions by generating a message—using the button ID—when selected.

- **Flat:** Creates a flat button without the three-dimensional shading.

- **Horizontal Alignment:** Offers a choice of how the control's caption text is positioned horizontally. Options are Default (centered), Left, Center, or Right.

- **Vertical Alignment:** Offers a choice of how the control's caption text is positioned vertically. Options are Default (centered), Top, Center, or Bottom.

> **TIP**
>
> Borland defines a series of custom pushbuttons, which include bitmap images such as a check mark, X, or question mark. The appearance of the custom pushbuttons is handled by provisions within the BWCC DLL. Similar provisions can be made using the Microsoft compiler by creating bitmap button images.

Radio Buttons

Radio buttons and auto-radio buttons are used to make a selection from a list of mutually exclusive options. Usually, when radio buttons are toggled on, a dot appears inside the button. Labels adjacent to the buttons identify the option or selection. By convention, only one button in any group can be selected at a time, and all other buttons in the same group should be cleared.

Regular radio buttons require provisions within the application to send a set/clear message back to the button to initiate a change of state. Auto-radio buttons, which look just like regular radio buttons, automatically reset their own state and, when selected, also clear any other radio buttons belonging to the same group. Whether radio buttons or auto-radio buttons are used, the application is responsible for setting the initial, default selection in each group when the dialog box is initiated.

When you choose the radio button icon on the Microsoft Developer Studio dialog box editor toolbar, you'll see the dialog box shown in Figure 10.10.

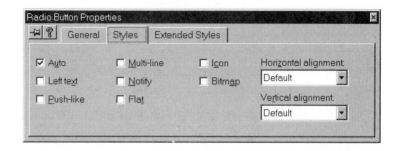

FIGURE 10.10

Choosing radio button styles

The Radio Button Properties dialog box offers the following styles:

- **Auto:** When selected by the user, the radio button automatically displays the checked state. At the same time, any other radio buttons in the group are cleared (deselected). When a group of radio buttons is used with the Dialog Data Exchange, the Auto property must be set. This style is checked by default.

> **NOTE** The Dialog Data Exchange (DDE) is an MFC-based mechanism that provides the exchange of data between dialog box elements and corresponding member variables within the CDialog-derived class. Instead of explicitly generating messages to read or write the state, text, or other values from and to dialog box elements, the UpdateData function is used with DDE. Calling the UpdateData function with a FALSE argument causes all dialog box elements to be updated with the values from their corresponding class members. Calling UpdateData with a TRUE argument retrieves the current values from all the dialog box elements, storing (and validating when appropriate) these values in the member variables.

- **Left Text:** Places the radio button's caption text on the left of the button rather than the right.

- **Push-like:** Gives the radio button the appearance of a conventional pushbutton while still retaining the performance and characteristics of a radio button. A push-like radio button appears raised when unchecked and sunken when checked (pushed).

- **Multi-line:** Allows the radio button text to wrap to multiple lines if it is too long to fit on a single line within the button rectangle.

- **Notify:** Sends a notification to the parent window when a radio button is clicked or double-clicked. Notification is used only when the parent is expected to take immediate action in response to a change rather than waiting to query the button status when the dialog box session concludes.

TIP

> Because radio buttons are customarily used to establish settings or selections that will only become relevant after the dialog box closes and the application returns to its primary tasks, the normal expectation is that the status of a radio button is queried only when the dialog box closes. This is not, however, a rule; it's merely a generality. When an immediate response to a change in state is required, the Notify option should be selected.

- **Flat:** Creates a flat radio button without the three-dimensional shading.

- **Icon:** Displays an icon image for the radio button.

- **Bitmap:** Displays a bitmap image for the radio button.

- **Horizontal Alignment:** Offers a choice of how the control's caption text is positioned horizontally. Options are Default (text to the right of the button), Left, Center, or Right.

- **Vertical Alignment:** Offers a choice of how the control's caption text is positioned. Options are Default (centered), Top, Center, or Bottom.

NOTE

> The Borland's custom, diamond-shaped radio button is supplied by provisions with the BWCC DLL.

Checkboxes

Like radio buttons, checkboxes are usually identified by text labels set to the right or left of the checkbox image. Unlike radio buttons, checkboxes permit selection of none, one, or multiple items. Each checkbox resets its own image by displaying a check mark when selected. A second mouse click on a checkbox cancels selection, resetting the image.

Checkboxes may be grouped but do not interact with others in a group. Each checkbox selection is assumed to be made independently of any other selections.

When you choose the checkbox icon on the Microsoft Developer Studio dialog box editor toolbar, you'll see the dialog box shown in Figure 10.11.

FIGURE 10.11

Choosing checkbox styles

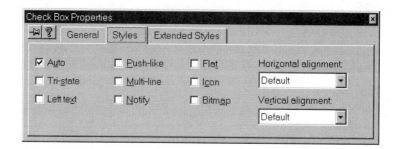

The Check Box Properties dialog box offers the following styles:

- **Auto:** When selected by the user, the checkbox automatically toggles between the checked and unchecked states. When checkboxes are used with the Dialog Data Exchange, this property must be set to True. This style is checked by default.

- **Tri-state:** Allows the checkbox to display three states: checked, cleared, or grayed. A grayed checkbox indicates that the state represented by the control is undetermined or irrelevant (disabled).

- **Left Text:** Places the checkbox's caption text on the left of the checkbox rather than on the right.

- **Push-like:** Gives the checkbox the appearance of a conventional pushbutton, while still retaining the performance and characteristics of a checkbox. A push-like checkbox appears raised when unchecked and sunken when checked (pushed). For a tri-state push-like checkbox, the third state is depressed but grayed.

- **Multi-line:** Allows the button text to wrap to multiple lines if it is too long to fit on a single line within the button rectangle.

- **Notify:** Sends a notification to the parent window when a checkbox is clicked or double-clicked. Notification is used only when the parent is expected to take immediate action in response to a change rather than waiting to query the button status when the dialog box session concludes.

- **Flat:** Creates a flat checkbox without the three-dimensional shading.

- **Icon:** Displays an icon image for the checkbox.

- **Bitmap:** Displays a bitmap image for the checkbox.

- **Horizontal Alignment:** Offers a choice of how the control's caption text is positioned. Options are Default (left), Left, Center, or Right.

- **Vertical Alignment:** Offers a choice of how the control's caption text is positioned. Options are Default (centered), Top, Center, or Bottom.

NOTE

The Borland custom checkmarked checkbox is supplied by provisions within the BWCC DLL.

General Properties for Other Controls

The General tab of the Properties dialog boxes for the text-oriented fields, range and adjustment controls, and other controls is similar for each type. Figure 10.12 shows the General tab of the List Box Properties dialog box.

FIGURE 10.12

The General tab of the List Box Properties dialog box

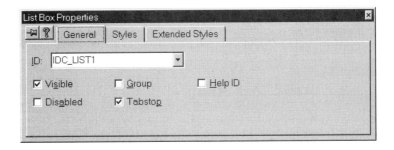

The text-oriented, range and adjustment, and other controls have the following general properties in common:

- **ID:** The default resource ID for the control. You may retain the supplied ID or change to a mnemonic ID by entering the desired identifier. When a new ID is supplied, a value is assigned automatically, and an entry is placed in the Resource.H header. The resource ID may be a symbol, integer, or quoted string.

- **Visible**: Makes the control visible when the application is first run. This option is checked by default.

- **Disabled:** Displays the resource as disabled when the dialog box is created (not relevant to static text controls).

- **Group**: Makes the control the first control of a group of controls, where users can move from one control to the next by using the arrow keys. All controls in the tab order after the first control that have the Group property set to False (unchecked) belong to the same group. The next control in the tab order that has Group set to True (checked) ends the first group of controls and starts the next group. For static text fields, this option is checked by default.

- **Tabstop:** Allows the user to move to this control with the Tab key. This option is checked by default for all text-oriented controls except static text fields. For the other types of controls, it is the default for sliders, hotkeys, and animated controls.

- **Help ID:** Assigns a help ID to the control based on the resource ID (not relevant to static text controls).

Text-Oriented Fields

Six text field types are provided: static text fields, edit boxes, list boxes, combo boxes, list control boxes, and tree controls.

Static Text Fields

Static text fields are used to display labels and other information that cannot be entered or changed by the user. They may show information, ask questions, provide explanations, or simply provide labels for other controls or for edit fields. Static text fields may be formatted as left-justified, right-justified, or centered.

When a static text field is created, the default label "Static" is supplied, and the default identifier IDC_STATIC is assigned. You can enter new text in the General tab of the Text Properties dialog box.

TIP

Static text fields may be assigned unique identifiers if there is any reason to have the displayed text change during execution of the application. After assigning a unique ID, the SetDlgItemText function can be used to assign new text to the static text field.

Along with the properties listed in the previous section, the General tab of the Text Properties dialog box contains a Caption property for the text string to appear in the static text field.

In addition to setting the options on the General tab for a static text field, you can also set the appearance of the control using the Styles tab, shown in Figure 10.13.

WARNING

Static text fields are limited to 255 characters. Multiple static text fields may overlap and conceal portions of other fields.

FIGURE 10.13

Setting static text field styles

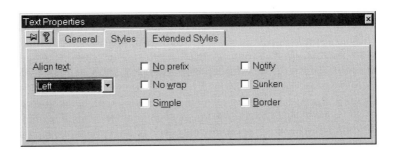

The Styles tab of the Text Properties dialog box has the following options:

- **Align Text:** Controls how text is aligned in the static text control: Left (the default), Center, or Right. This should be set to Left when No Wrap is selected.

- **No Prefix:** Prevents ampersands (&) in the control's text from being interpreted as the mnemonic character. Normally a string containing an ampersand is displayed with the ampersand removed and the next character in the string underlined. The No Prefix style is most often used when filenames or other strings that may contain an ampersand need to be displayed.

- **No Wrap:** Displays text left-aligned; tabs are expanded but text is not wrapped, and any text extending beyond the end of a line is clipped.

- **Simple:** Disables both the No Wrap and Align Text options; text does not wrap and is not clipped. Furthermore, overriding WM_CTLCOLOR in the parent window has no effect on the control.

- **Notify:** Notifies the parent window if a control is clicked or double-clicked (not applicable to static text).

- **Sunken:** Creates a border with a sunken edge around the static text control.

- **Border:** Creates a border around the text control.

> **TIP**
>
> The Borland custom static text control offers the capability of changing the typeface used for the individual control. The custom control requires support from the BWCC DLL.

Edit Boxes

Edit boxes are used for entries and responses, but they may also display information or selections without allowing the user to change the entry. Usually, edit boxes permit the user to enter new text information or to edit existing text information. Although only one type of edit box is listed in the resource editor, these controls can be defined as single- or multiple-line edit fields and may include vertical and/or horizontal scrolling and scrollbars.

When you create an edit box, the resource editor supplies a default ID value: IDC_EDIT*n*. But you can enter a new ID or select one from a list of defined IDs in the General tab of the Edit Properties dialog box. The General tab of the Edit Properties dialog box contains the properties listed earlier, in the section titled "General Properties for Other Controls."

In addition to setting the properties of the General tab, you can also set the appearance of the control using the Styles tab, shown in Figure 10.14.

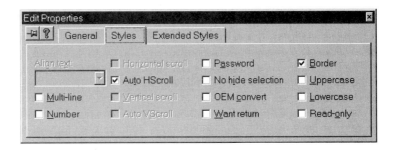

The Styles tab of the Edit Properties dialog box has the following options:

- **Align Text:** Offers a choice of left (the default), centered, or right-aligned text when the Multi-line option is selected.

- **Multi-line:** Creates a multiple-line edit box control. When the multiline edit box is in a dialog box, the default result of pressing the Enter key is to choose the default button. Multiline edit boxes may also have scrollbars and process their own scrollbar messages. They may also process scroll messages sent by the parent window. See also Horizontal Scroll, Auto HScroll, Vertical Scroll, and Want Return.

- **Number:** Restricts input to numeric characters and associated symbols; prevents any nonnumeric characters from being typed.

- **Horizontal Scroll:** Adds a horizontal scrollbar to a multiline control. This option is not available unless the Multi-line option has been selected.

- **Auto HScroll**: Scrolls text right automatically when a character is typed at the right end of the box. This option is checked by default. In a multiline edit box, when Auto HScroll is selected, text automatically scrolls horizontally whenever the caret (text cursor) passes the right edge of the edit box. The Enter key must be pressed to start a new line. If Auto HScroll is not selected, the control automatically wraps words to the beginning of the next line when necessary.

- **Vertical Scroll:** Adds a vertical scrollbar to a multiline edit box control. This option is not available unless the Multi-line option has been selected.

- **Auto VScroll:** In a multiline edit box, automatically scrolls text up one line when the user presses Enter on the last line. This option is not available unless the Multi-line option has been selected.

- **Password:** Displays all characters typed as asterisks (*). This property is not available for multiline edit boxes.

- **No Hide Selection:** Controls how text is displayed when an edit box loses and regains the focus. If this option is selected, selected text remains displayed as selected even when the edit box loses the focus.

- **OEM Convert:** Converts text typed in the edit box from the Windows character set to the OEM character set and then back to the Windows set to ensure proper character conversion when the application calls the `AnsiToOem` function to convert a Windows string in the edit box to OEM characters. This property is most useful for edit box controls containing filenames.

- **Want Return:** Inserts a carriage return when the Enter key is pressed while typing text in a multiline edit box. If Want Return is not set, pressing the Enter key is the same as pressing the dialog box's default pushbutton. Want Return has no effect on single-line edit boxes.

- **Border**: Draws a border around the edit box. This option is checked by default.

- **Uppercase:** Converts all characters typed to uppercase.

- **Lowercase:** Converts all characters typed to lowercase.

- **Read-only:** Prevents users from making changes to the contents of the edit box.

List Boxes

List boxes display text (or icon) lists, allowing one (or more) items to be selected. List box entries are supplied by the application. For example, this type of control might contain a list of filenames. When the list is too long for the allocated space, a scrollbar appears for vertical scrolling.

Custom list boxes can also be defined as owner-drawn list boxes. Custom controls may include graphic as well as text entries, but they require provisions within the application to handle the display material. Custom list boxes begin as standard list boxes, but then you use the Styles tab of the List Box Properties dialog box to select either the Owner Draw Fixed or Owner Draw Variable options. The Owner Draw Fixed style requires that all items in the list box have the same height; the Owner Draw Variable style permits mixing varying item heights.

When you create a list box, the resource editor supplies a default ID value: IDC_LISTn. You can enter a new ID or select one from a list of defined IDs in the General tab of the List Box Properties dialog box (see Figure 10.13, shown earlier). The General tab of the List Box Properties dialog box contains the properties listed earlier, in the section titled "General Properties for Other Controls."

The Styles tab of the List Box Properties dialog box contains options for setting the appearance of the control. Figure 10.15 shows this tab.

FIGURE 10.15

Setting list box styles

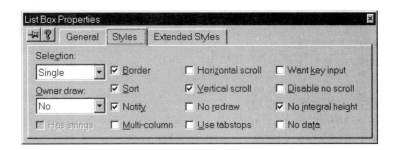

The Styles tab contains the following properties for list boxes:

- **Selection:** Determines how items in a list box can be selected. Possible values are as follows:

  - Single, which allows only one item in a list box to be selected at a time. This is the default selection method.

  - Extended, which allows the Shift and Ctrl keys to be used together with the mouse to select and deselect list-box items, select groups of items, and select nonadjacent items.

- **Owner Draw:** Sets the owner-draw characteristics for the list box using one of the following values:

  - Multiple, which allows more than one list box item to be selected. Clicking or double-clicking on any unselected item selects it. Clicking or double-clicking on any selected item deselects it. The Shift and Ctrl keys have no effect.

- No, which turns off the Owner Draw style, limiting the list box contents to strings. This is the default setting.

- Fixed, which makes the owner of the list box responsible for drawing the contents of the list box. All items in the list box must be the same height. `CWnd::OnMeasureItem` is called when the list box is created, and `CWnd::OnDrawItem` is called when a visual aspect of the list box has changed.

- Variable, which makes the owner of the list box responsible for drawing the contents of the list box. Items in the list box may vary in height. `CWnd::OnMeasureItem` is called for each item in the list when the list box is created, and `CWnd::OnDrawItem` is called when a visual aspect of the list box has changed.

- **Has Strings:** Specifies that an owner-drawn list box contains items consisting of strings. The list box maintains the memory and pointers for the strings, allowing the application to use the `LB_GETTEXT` message to retrieve the text for a particular item. This option is available only if the Owner Draw option is set to either Fixed or Variable. If Owner Draw is set to No, the list box contains strings by default.

- **Border:** Creates a border around the list box. This option is checked by default.

- **Sort:** Sorts the contents of the list box alphabetically. This option is checked by default.

- **Notify:** Sends a notification to the parent window when a list item is clicked or double-clicked. This option is checked by default.

- **Multi-column:** Makes the list box multiple-column. A multicolumn box is scrolled horizontally. Use the `LB_SETCOLUMNWIDTH` message to set the width of the columns.

- **Horizontal Scroll:** Creates a horizontal scrollbar for the list box.

- **Vertical Scroll:** Creates a vertical scrollbar for the list box. This option is checked by default.

- **No Redraw:** Specifies that a list box's appearance is not updated when changes are made. The No Redraw style can be changed via a `WM_SETREDRAW` message or by calling `CWnd::SetRedraw`.

- **Use Tabstops:** Allows a list box to recognize and expand tab characters when drawing its strings. The default tab positions are 32 dialog box units (DLUs).

- **Want Key Input:** Sends the list box owner WM_VKEYTOITEM (when the Has Strings style is used) or WM_CHARTOITEM messages whenever a key is pressed and the list box has the input focus. This option allows an application to perform special processing on the keyboard input.

- **Disable No Scroll:** Displays a disabled vertical scrollbar in the list box when there are not enough items to scroll. By default, no scrollbar appears until the list box contains enough items to scroll.

- **No Integral Height:** Specifies that the size of the list box is exactly the size specified by the application when the list box was created. Normally, the list box is sized so that partial items are not displayed. This option is checked by default.

- **No Data:** Prevents the list box from storing item data.

Combo Boxes

Combo boxes combine the features of edit boxes and list boxes. They permit the user to either select from a list or make an entry directly in the edit field.

Three styles of combo boxes are supported: simple, drop-down, and drop-down list combo boxes (use the Styles tab of the Combo Box Properties dialog box to select these types). Drop-down combo boxes behave essentially the same as simple combo boxes, except that initially only the edit field is displayed. The list box portion appears only when the down arrow at the right of the edit field is clicked. For drop-down combo boxes, the list box area is sized in the same fashion as a simple combo box, but because this field appears only on demand, the area used can also be occupied by other controls. Drop-down combo list boxes are similar to drop-down combo boxes, but they permit only edit field entries that correspond to items already in the list.

You can define custom combo boxes by using the Owner-Draw option in the Styles tab of the Combo Box Properties dialog box.

As with the other resource types, the resource editor supplies a default ID value, IDC_COMBOn, when you create the combo box, but you can enter or select a new ID in the General tab of the Combo Box Properties dialog box. This dialog box contains the properties listed earlier, in the section titled "General Properties for Other Controls," along with one additional property, as shown in Figure 10.16. The Enter

Listbox Items property is available only in resource files using MFC library support. This property allows you to enter the initial selections that will appear in the list portion of the combo box when the dialog box is created. To add entries, press Ctrl+Enter (line feed) at the end of each item to move to the next line.

FIGURE 10.16

Setting general properties of combo boxes

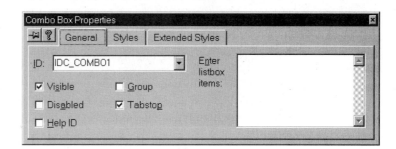

The Styles tab of the Combo Box Properties dialog box allows you to set properties that affect the appearance of the combo box. Figure 10.17 shows this tab.

FIGURE 10.17

Setting combo box styles

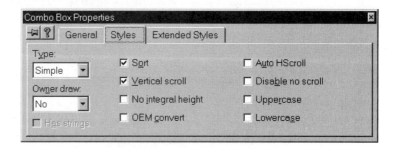

The Styles tab contains the following properties for combo boxes:

- **Type:** Specifies the type of combo box as one of the following:
  - Simple, which creates a simple combo box combining an edit box control for user input with a list box control. The list is visible at all times, with the current selection from the list displayed in the edit box control.

- Dropdown, which creates a drop-down combo box. A drop-down combo box is the same as a simple combo box, except the list is displayed only when the drop-down arrow (at the right of the edit box control portion) is selected. This is the default type.

- Drop List, which is similar to the drop-down style except that edit box control is replaced by a static text item, which does not accept user input, displaying the current list selection.

- **Owner Draw:** Sets the owner-draw characteristics for the combo box using one of the following values:

  - No, which turns off the Owner Draw style, limiting the list box contents to strings. This is the default setting.

  - Fixed, which makes the owner of the combo box responsible for drawing the contents of the list box. All items in the list box must be the same height. `CWnd::OnMeasureItem` is called when the list box is created, and `CWnd::OnDrawItem` is called when a visual aspect of the list box has changed.

  - Variable, which makes the owner of the combo box responsible for drawing the contents of the list box. Items in the list box may vary in height. `CWnd::OnMeasureItem` is called for each item in the list when the list box is created, and `CWnd::OnDrawItem` is called when a visual aspect of the list box has changed.

- **Has Strings:** Specifies that an owner-drawn combo box contains items consisting of strings. The list box maintains the memory and pointers for the strings, allowing the application to use the `LB_GETTEXT` message to retrieve the text for a particular item. This option is available only if the Owner Draw option is set to either Fixed or Variable. If Owner Draw is set to No, the list box contains strings by default.

- **Sort:** Sorts the contents of the combo box alphabetically. This option is checked by default.

- **Vertical Scroll:** Creates a vertical scrollbar for the list box. This item is checked by default.

- **No Integral Height:** Specifies that the size of the combo box is exactly the size specified by the application when the combo box was created. Normally, the combo box is sized so that partial items are not displayed.

- **OEM Convert:** Converts text typed in the combo box control from the Windows character set to the OEM character set and then back to the Windows set to ensure proper character conversion when the application calls the `AnsiToOem` function to convert a Windows string in the combo box to OEM characters. OEM Convert is most useful for combo boxes that contain filenames.

- **Auto HScroll:** Scrolls text right automatically when a character is typed at the right end of the box.

- **Disable No Scroll:** Displays a disabled vertical scrollbar in the list box when there are not enough items to scroll. By default, no scrollbar appears until the list box contains enough items to scroll.

- **Uppercase:** Converts all characters typed to uppercase.

- **Lowercase:** Converts all characters typed to lowercase.

List Control Boxes

List control boxes are an extension of the list box type, with the additional capabilities of displaying either large or small icons, a multiple-column list with icons, or columnar lists with a header (in the Report format). The four styles of list control boxes are illustrated in Figure 10.18.

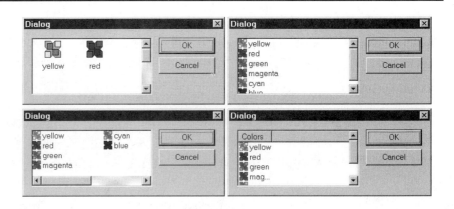

FIGURE 10.18

Four list control box styles

When a list control box is created, the default ID value IDC_LIST*n* (following the same format as a list box) is supplied. You can enter a new ID or select from a list of defined IDs in the General tab of the List Control Properties dialog box. This dialog box contains the properties listed earlier, in the section titled "General Properties for Other Controls."

You can set the appearance of the list control through the Styles tab of the List Control Properties dialog box, shown in Figure 10.19.

FIGURE 10.19

Setting the styles
of list controls

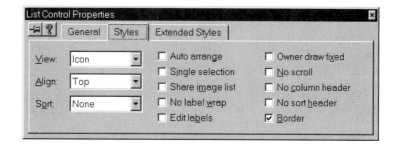

The Styles tab contains the following properties for list controls:

- **View:** Sets the display view for the list control as one of the following:
    - Icon, which sets the large icon view with the icons in a multicolumn arrangement. This is the default view.
    - Small Icon, which sets the small icon view with the icons in a multicolumn arrangement.
    - List, which sets a list view as a single-column display with small icons (optional) along the left.
    - Report, which sets the report view for a multicolumn text display with a column header.
- **Align:** Sets the alignment of icons in the list as one of the following:
    - Top, so that icons are aligned at the top of the view. This is the default alignment.
    - Left, so that icons are aligned at the left of the view.
- **Sort:** Sets the sort order for icons in the list as one of the following:
    - None, so that no sort is applied. This is the default setting.

- Ascending, which sorts items in ascending order based on item text.

- Descending, which sorts items in descending order based on item text.

- **Auto Arrange:** Automatically keeps icons arranged in both the icon and small icon views.

- **Single Selection:** Specifies that only one item at a time may be selected. By default, multiple items may be selected.

- **Share Image List:** Specifies that the list control does not assume ownership of the image lists assigned to it; that is, the image lists are not destroyed when the list control is destroyed. This allows the same image list to be used with multiple list view controls.

- **No Label Wrap:** In icon view, displays item text on a single line. By default, item text may wrap in icon view.

- **Edit Labels:** Allows item labels to be edited in place. To support this, the parent window must process the LVN_ENDLABELEDIT notification message.

- **Owner Draw Fixed:** Allows the owner window to paint items in the Report view. The List view control sends a WM_DRAWITEM message to paint each item but does not send separate messages for each subitem. The itemData member of the DRAWITEMSTRUCT structure contains the item data for the specified List view item.

- **No Scroll:** Disables scrolling, and all items must appear within the client area.

- **No Column Header:** Specifies that no column header is displayed in the Report view.

- **No Sort Header:** Prevents column headers from acting like buttons. Commonly, clicking on a column head is used to sort the list by the column entries, but clicking may be implemented for some other action. If no action is provided as a response to a column header click, setting this option will prevent a screen response.

- **Border:** Creates a border around the List view control. This option is selected by default.

Tree Controls

Tree controls are used to display hierarchical information in a tree format, where branches can be collapsed or expanded. The branches in the tree control may be displayed as a simple indented list or complete with node buttons and lines. Two styles of tree controls are illustrated in Figure 10.20.

FIGURE 10.20

Two formats for tree controls

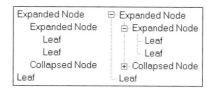

When a tree control box is created, the default ID value IDC_TREE*n* is supplied. You can enter a new ID or select one from a list of defined IDs in the General tab of the Tree Control Properties dialog box. This dialog box contains the properties listed earlier, in the section titled "General Properties for Other Controls."

Through the Styles tab of the Tree Control Properties dialog box, you can set the appearance of the control. Figure 10.21 shows this tab.

FIGURE 10.21

Setting tree control styles

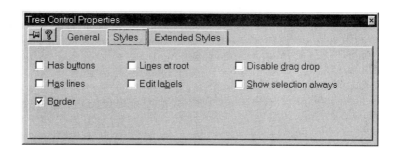

The Styles tab contains the following properties for tree controls:

- **Has Buttons:** Displays plus (+) and minus (–) buttons next to parent items in the tree. These can be used to expand or collapse a parent item's list of child items. To include buttons with items at the root of the tree view, the Lines at Root option must be checked.

- **Has Lines:** Uses lines to show the hierarchy for tree items.

- **Border:** Creates a border around the tree control.

- **Lines at Root:** Uses lines to link items at the root of the tree control. This option is ignored if the Has Lines option is not selected.

- **Edit Labels:** Allows the user to edit the labels of tree items.

- **Disable Drag Drop:** Prevents the tree control from sending `TVN_BEGINDRAG` notification messages.

- **Show Selection Always:** Uses the system highlight colors to draw the selected item.

Range and Adjustment Controls

Standard dialog box features include horizontal and vertical scrollbars. Rather than for scrolling the display within a window, dialog box scrollbars are often used as range slider controls or sometimes as range meters. For example, the Control Panel's Colors dialog box uses scrollbars to adjust the RGB intensities for custom colors. In like fashion, scrollbars might be used in a MIDI control application to set tone, voice, fade, and reverb.

More modern control versions adapted from scrollbars include slider and spin controls. The progress control, while not directly adapted from a scrollbar, does share some of the same characteristics. Figure 10.22 shows some examples of dialog box scrollbars and other range and adjustment controls.

FIGURE 10.22

Scrollbars, sliders, and spin controls

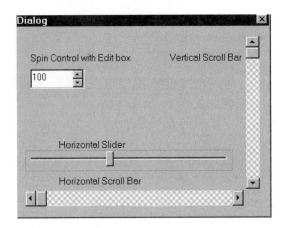

NOTE

Remember, edit boxes, list boxes, and combo boxes supply their own scrollbars. They do not require separate provisions.

Horizontal and Vertical Scrollbars

Even though horizontal and vertical scrollbars are represented by different icons on the dialog box editor's toolbar, these are essentially a single tool differing only in their orientation. Both versions return the same event messages and respond to the same instructions (as do, incidentally, the slider and spin controls). The only real difference between the two forms of scrollbars is whether the SB_HORZ or SB_VERT argument is used when the scrollbar is generated.

When a scrollbar is created, a default ID value is supplied: IDC_SCROLLBARn. You can enter a new ID or select one from a list of defined IDs in the General tab of the Scrollbar Properties dialog box, shown in Figure 10.23.

FIGURE 10.23

The General tab of the Scrollbar Properties dialog box

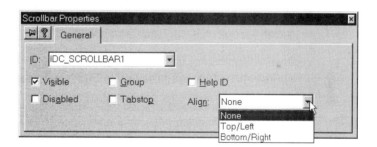

This dialog box contains the properties listed earlier, in the section titled "General Properties for Other Controls," along with one additional property: Align. This property can be one of the following:

- **None:** No special sizing or alignment is performed. The size of the scrollbar is the size specified in the resource script. This is the default alignment.

- **Top/Left:** The scrollbar is set to a standard width (thickness) and aligned with the upper-left corner of the scrollbar window specified in the resource script. The scrollbar length is not changed.

- **Bottom/Right:** The scrollbar is set to a standard width (thickness) and aligned with the lower-right corner of the scrollbar window specified in the resource script. The scrollbar length is not changed.

NOTE Selecting either Top/Left or Bottom/Right alignment sets the thickness of the scrollbar to match the width of the scrollbar's endpads and thumbpad.

Sliders

Slider controls (also called trackbars) are a special case of a scrollbar where the end-pads of the conventional scrollbar are lost and the thumbpad is replaced by a choice of slider tabs. Slider controls may also include tick marks along their length, have the slider tabs pointed to one side or the other, and be vertically or horizontally oriented.

The default resource ID for a new slider control is `IDC_SLIDERn`. You can change this ID and set the other general properties for the slider control through the Slider Properties dialog box. The General tab of this dialog box lists the same properties described earlier, in the section titled "General Properties for Other Controls."

The Styles tab of the Slider Properties dialog box allows you to set orientation, tick marks, and other options. This tab is shown In Figure 10.24.

FIGURE 10.24

Setting slider control styles

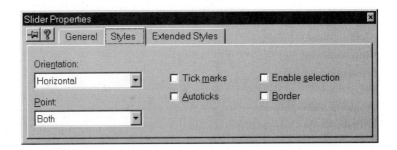

The Styles tab contains the following properties for slider controls:

- **Orientation:** Displays the slider (trackbar) with a horizontal (default) or vertical orientation.

- **Point:** Displays tick marks (if the Tick Marks property is enabled) on either or both sides of the slider and alters the slider knob. The tick marks and knob have the following orientations:
  - Both, which displays tick marks on both sides of the slider. The slider knob is rectangular. This is the default setting.
  - Top/Left, which displays tick marks on the top of a horizontal slider or on the left of a vertical slider. The slider knob changes to point to the selected side.
  - Bottom/Right, which displays tick marks on the bottom of a horizontal slider or on the right of a vertical slider. The slider knob changes to point to the selected side.

- **Tick Marks:** Enables the display of tick marks on a slider.

- **Autoticks:** Sets a tick mark at each increment in the slider's range of values. Tick marks are created automatically by sending the TBM_SETRANGE message.

- **Enable Selection:** Changes the narrow slider (see Figure 10.22) to an open bar that can display a selection range with triangles and a highlighted area.

- **Border:** Creates a border around the slider control.

NOTE Selection limits are not created during dialog box design but may be set during execution. This means, of course, that the triangles and highlight area will not appear during testing with the dialog box editor.

Spin Controls

A spin control is a second variation of the scrollbar. In this adaptation, only the end-pads remain in the form of two buttons; the body of the scrollbar and the thumbpad have vanished. The default form of a spin control is vertically oriented, with up and down arrows on the buttons. The alternative is a horizontal control, with the arrow buttons pointing right and left.

In operation, the spin control has a set range (established by the application). It may wrap values when the limits are reached, or it may simply stop when the limits are encountered.

While a spin control can be used by itself, a common use is to link the spin button to a buddy window, which may be an edit box, as illustrated earlier in Figure 10.22, or a static text field. In these cases, the spin control operations are automatically reflected in the buddy window.

In theory, a spin control could be "buddied" with any other type of control. For example, the label on a button might display the spin control value, or a spin control might serve as a fine control for a slider or scrollbar. In practice, however, you will probably need to write your own provisions to make a spin control interact appropriately with anything except an edit box or static text field.

NOTE When an edit box is used as the buddy window and the `CSpinButton` class is used, changes in the edit box value are automatically reflected in the spin control's value.

Spin controls have the same General tab properties as the other types of controls (see the section titled "General Properties for Other Controls," earlier in the chapter). The default resource ID for a new spin button control is `IDC_SPINn`.

Through the Styles tab of the Spin Properties dialog box, you can specify the control's orientation, alignment, and other options. Figure 10.25 shows this tab.

FIGURE 10.25

Setting spin control styles

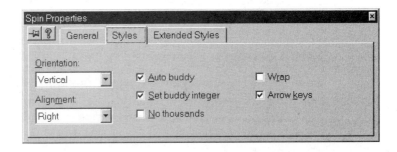

The Styles tab contains the following properties for spin controls:

- **Orientation:** Sets the spin control display as vertical (up-down, the default) or horizontal (right-left).

- **Alignment:** Sets the position where the spin control appears (on execution) relative to the buddy window. If no buddy window is established, alignment is irrelevant. The alignment value can be one of the following:

  - Unattached, so that the spin control is not associated with any other control. This is the default setting.

  - Left, so that on execution, the spin control is positioned next to the left edge of the buddy window. At the same time, the buddy window is moved right and the width adjusted to accommodate the width of the spin control.

  - Right, so that on execution, the spin control is positioned next to the right edge of the buddy window. At the same time, the buddy window is moved left and the width adjusted to accommodate the width of the spin button control.

TIP
Selecting Left or Right alignment does not change the layout of the controls during resource editing. The selected alignment appears only during execution.

- **Auto Buddy:** Automatically selects the previous window in the Z order (tab order) as the spin control's buddy window. In turn, the buddy window displays the values (as text) set by the spin control. Normally, the buddy window will be an edit box or a static text field.

- **Set Buddy Integer:** Sets the text of the buddy window (using the WM_SETTEXT message) when the up or down buttons of the spin control are clicked. The text may have the setting value formatted as a decimal or hexadecimal string.

- **No Thousands:** Prevents the buddy window from inserting a thousands separator between every three digits in decimal format.

- **Wrap:** Wraps the spin control value when it is incremented or decremented beyond the ending or beginning of the range.

- **Arrow Keys:** Automatically increments or decrements the value of the spin control when the up or down arrow keys are pressed. This option is checked by default.

Progress Bars

The progress bar is not a scrollbar derivative per se, even though it does have a similar appearance and, in the past, scrollbars were sometimes used to provide progress bar displays. The progress bar control is not a control in the usual sense. It does not react to user input, nor send messages to the application. Its function is to show the progress of a task. For example, progress bars are commonly used when installing new software products. Figure 10.26 shows an example of a progress bar.

The general properties for a progress bar are the same as those on the General tab of the other Properties dialog boxes for the other controls (see the section titled "General Properties of Other Controls," earlier in the chapter), with the addition of the Border property, which creates a border around the trackbar control. The Border option is checked by default.

Other Control Types

The remaining control features are used to customize the appearance of a dialog box. You can add icons or bitmaps, provide visual grouping, and use shading to enhance the appearance of the dialog box. These include the following types of controls:

- Group boxes
- Hotkey controls
- Tab controls
- Pictures (bitmaps and icons)
- Animated controls
- Custom controls

With the exceptions of animated and custom controls, each of these is illustrated in Figure 10.27.

FIGURE 10.27

Other control features

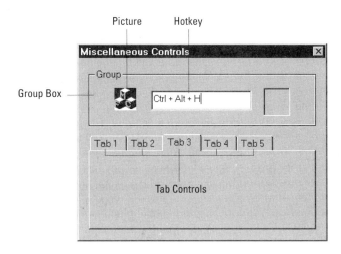

Group Boxes

Group boxes are simply outline boxes used to visually group controls by enclosing one or more controls in an outline with an optional group title.

The general properties for a group box are the same as for the other types of controls (see the section titled "General Properties for Other Controls," earlier in the chapter). However, group boxes also have a Caption property, which provides a label that appears in the upper-left corner of the group box frame.

The default resource ID for a group box is IDC_STATIC. This is the same ID used for a static text field, and for the same reason: A group box normally is not selectable and is not expected to receive or return messages.

Through the Styles tab of the Group Box Properties dialog box, you can set the horizontal alignment, add an icon or a bitmap, and set other properties. Figure 10.28 shows this tab.

The Styles tab contains the following properties for group boxes:

- **Horizontal Alignment:** Sets the position of the group box's caption text to the center, right, or default (left) position.

FIGURE 10.28

Setting group box styles

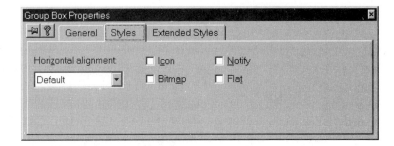

- **Icon:** Indicates that the group box title displays an icon. The Caption field in the General tab identifies the icon to display.

- **Bitmap:** Indicates that the group box title displays an bitmap. The Caption field in the General tab identifies the bitmap to display.

- **Notify:** Notifies the parent window when a group box is clicked or double-clicked.

- **Flat:** Gives the group box a flat appearance rather than the shaded (3-D) format.

Pictures

The picture control is a static control element, which does not respond to mouse selection and, by default, does not return any event messages. Instead, picture controls are customarily used simply to insert a graphic of some form into a dialog box.

Figure 10.29 shows the General tab of the Picture Properties dialog box. This tab has the same general properties as the other types of controls (see the "General Properties of Other Controls" section earlier in the chapter), plus a few extra properties.

The following general properties are specific to pictures:

- **ID:** The default ID for a picture control is IDC_STATIC*n*, and the picture control is treated as an image that does not receive the focus, does not act as a tab stop, and does not return a message. If you want the picture to function as an active control—for example, as a button—the control type should be icon, bitmap, or metafile, and the default ID should be replaced with a unique identifier. The new resource ID may be a symbol, integer, or a quoted string.

FIGURE 10.29

The General tab of
the Pictures Properties
dialog box

- **Type:** Sets the type of static graphic to display as one of the following:

  - Frame, which displays an empty rectangle in the color specified in the Color property. Like a group box, a frame may be used to visually group controls. This is the default type.

  - Rectangle, which displays a filled rectangle in the color specified in the Color property.

  - Icon, which displays an icon in the dialog box. The identifier of the icon is specified in the Image property.

  - Bitmap, which displays a bitmap in the dialog box. The identifier of the bitmap is specified in the Image property.

  - Enhanced Metafile, which displays an enhanced metafile in the dialog box. The application must provide the means of identifying and executing the metafile.

NOTE A metafile is a graphic image recorded as a series of instructions for its creation. Metafiles are discussed in Chapter 32.

- **Image:** Provides the identifier for the icon or bitmap to display.

- **Color:** Sets the color of a frame or rectangle to Black (the default), White, Gray, or Etched. Etched provides a 3-D appearance.

Figure 10.30 shows the Styles tab of the Picture Properties dialog box, which has properties for controlling the appearance of the picture control.

FIGURE 10.30

Setting picture control styles

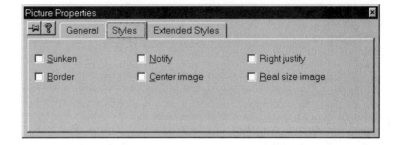

The Styles tab contains the following properties for picture controls:

- **Sunken:** Creates a border with a sunken edge around the picture control.

- **Border:** Creates a border around the picture. This option is selected by default.

- **Notify:** Allows the picture to notify the parent window when clicked or double-clicked.

TIP

Setting the Notify property allows an icon or bitmap image to respond as if it were a button. If you set the Notify property, you should change the default ID to a unique identifier to ensure proper handling and recognition of the message.

- **Center Image:** If the bitmap or icon is smaller than the client area of the picture control, fills the rest of the client area with the color of the pixel in the top-left corner of the bitmap or icon.

- **Right Justify:** Sets the lower-right corner of a picture control to remain fixed when the control is resized; only the top and left sides are adjusted to accommodate the new size.

- **Real Size Image:** Specifies that a static icon or bitmap control will not be resized as it is loaded or drawn. If the image is larger than the destination area, the image is clipped.

> **TIP**
>
> The Borland dialog box tools also provide the horizontal and vertical shade controls, which actually each consist of two separate controls, titled Dip and Bump. In essence, these are simple line elements, which are useful, in combination with the Borland custom group box and shading, to provide vertical and horizontal dividers between items. Although the Microsoft dialog box editor does not provide an equivalent feature, a similar horizontal or vertical line can be created using a very thin frame or rectangle.

Hotkeys

A hotkey control is a simple input box that is used to allow the user to select a hotkey combination to be assigned to a particular task. When the hotkey control is selected, any key combination pressed is displayed as a hotkey combination. Figure 10.27, shown earlier, shows an example where pressing the H key while the Ctrl and Alt keys were down was recognized as Ctrl+Alt+H.

The Ctrl, Alt, and Shift keys may be used in most combinations with any of the following:

Alphanumeric keys	PgUp
Function keys	PgDn
Number pad keys	Right
Caps Lock	Left
Scroll Lock	Home
Num Lock	Up
Insert	End
Delete	Down

Keys or combinations that cannot be used include:

Ctrl+Alt+Delete

Escape

Backspace

Tab

Windows key

System key

Enter on number pad

WARNING The hotkey control does apply minimum validation, and some key combinations will be refused when entered. However, this control does not provide complete validation and, except for certain system hotkey codes, does not check the hotkey assignments against other conflicting assignments. Be careful to avoid assigning the same hotkey twice in a dialog box.

The default resource ID for a group box is IDC_HOTKEY*n*. The general properties for a hotkey control are the same as for the other controls (see the section titled "General Properties for Other Controls," earlier in the chapter), with the addition of a Border property. When the Border property is checked (the default), an outline appears around the hotkey control.

Animation Controls

An animation control is used to play back an animated sequence. This could be a simple sequence of images or a more elaborate video sequence.

WARNING Be aware that AVI sequences take up a lot of space for storage.

The default resource ID for a group box is IDC_ANIMATE*n*. The general properties for an animation control are the same as for other controls, with these additions:

- **Center:** Centers the animation in the animation control window.

- **Transparent:** Draws the animation using a transparent background rather than the background color specified in the animation clip.

- **Autoplay:** Sets the animation to begin playing as soon as the animation clip is opened.

- **Border:** Creates an outline around the animation control. This option is checked by default.

Tab Controls

A tab control (see Figure 10.27, shown earlier) offers a method of arranging groups of controls in a dialog box as a sequence of tabs, with each tab containing a separate set of controls. The tab control may fill the dialog box or may use only a part of the space, leaving the remainder of the space for controls common to all tabs.

The number of tabs in a tab control and the labels for the tabs are set by the application, and tabs may fill more than one row. The contents of the tabs are created as separate dialog boxes without title bars, system menus, and so on, and are then assigned to tabs by the application.

The general properties for a tab control are the same as for the other controls. The default resource ID for a tab control is IDC_TAB*n*.

Through the Styles tab of the Tab Control Properties dialog box, shown in Figure 10.31, you can set the alignment, focus, and other features of the tab control.

FIGURE 10.31

Setting tab control styles

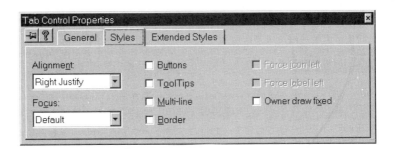

The Styles tab contains the following properties for tab controls:

- **Alignment:** Choose from the following tab control alignments:

  - Right Justify, which adjusts the width of each tab so that each row of tabs fills the entire width of the tab control. This is the default alignment.

  - Fixed Width, which sizes all tabs to the width of the widest label.

  - Ragged Right, which is used with multiline tabs, so that tab widths are not adjusted to fill the rows.

- **Focus:** Determines how tabs are selected, as one of the following:

  - Default, so that keyboard selection may be used to select a tab or a tab may be selected by clicking with the mouse. (And of course, Default is the default setting.)

  - On Button Down, so that tabs receive the input focus (come to the front) when the tab is clicked.

  - Never, so that tabs do not receive the input focus when clicked. Instead, tabs must be selected by the application.

- **Buttons:** Makes the tabs in the control resemble buttons. When tabs are displayed in button format, they should perform the same function as button controls; clicking a tab should carry out a task rather than displaying a tab page.

- **ToolTips:** Creates a tool tip for each tab in the tab control.

- **Multi-line:** Displays multiple rows of tabs.

- **Border:** Creates an outline around the tab control.

- **Force Icon Left:** Left-aligns the icon; the label remains centered.

- **Force Label Left:** Left-aligns both the icon and the label.

WARNING The reference to icons in the Force Icon Left and Force Label Left options is something of a mystery, since selecting either option makes the tabs expand—a feature which is not mentioned—and the icons referred to are unknown. You can experiment for yourself to see how these properties work.

- **Owner Draw Fixed:** Makes the parent window responsible for drawing tabs in the control.

Custom Controls

The custom control is undefined but provides a placeholder—a dark gray rectangle—representing a custom control element. It is the responsibility of the application (or a custom library) to handle the appropriate screen display, to issue and respond to messages, and to handle any other required interactions. The General tab of the Custom Control Properties dialog box is shown in Figure 10.32.

FIGURE 10.32

The Custom Control Properties dialog box

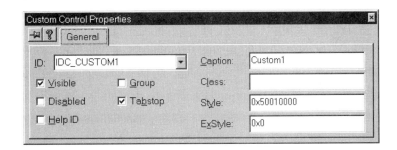

The default resource ID for a custom control is IDC_CUSTOM*n*. The general properties for a custom control are the same as for the other types of controls, with the following additional properties:

- **Caption:** Sets a string entry that appears as a label for the custom control. To make one of the letters in the caption a mnemonic key (hotkey) precede it with an ampersand (&). A default caption name is supplied in the format "Caption" plus a number matching the resource identifier.

- **Class:** Sets the name of the control's Windows class. The named class must be registered before the dialog box containing the control is created. (During execution, the class must be registered first before calling the dialog box.)

- **Style:** Sets a 32-bit hexadecimal value specifying the control's style. This is primarily used to edit the lower 16 bits making up a user control's substyle.

- **ExStyle:** Sets a 32-bit hexadecimal value specifying the control's extended style.

NOTE The Style and ExStyle properties are undefined until a custom control is created. How or if these properties are used depends on the design and functionality of the custom control.

Alignment, Positioning, and Sizing Tools

Both the Microsoft Developer Workshop and the Borland Resource Workshop provide a variety of tools for use in designing dialog box layouts. And they both provide essentially the same tools, but in slightly different arrangements.

You can position and size controls by using the mouse or, in some cases, by entering position and size information directly, but the easiest way to align controls is to use the tools provided by the resource editors. Both dialog box editors offer a toolbar (along the bottom) with an assortment of tools for alignment. The Developer Studio includes sizing tools on the toolbar; the Resource Workshop offers the sizing tools as menu options.

The Developer Studio Toolbar and Options

Using the Microsoft Developer Studio, most of the tools you will want are found on the toolbar itself. Figure 10.33 shows this toolbar, with labels to identify the buttons. The toolbar buttons and other Developer Studio tools are described in the following sections.

The Test Button

Beginning at the left, the toolbar offers the Test button. This allows you to test a dialog box during development—before the dialog box becomes a part of an application.

Alignment Buttons

The four alignment buttons provide left, right, top, and bottom alignment. To align a group of controls, hold down the Shift key while clicking on each of the controls.

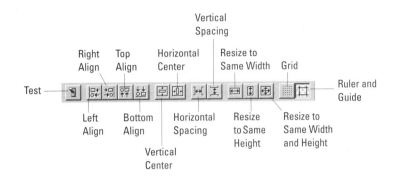

FIGURE 10.33

The Developer Studio toolbar

Dialog Box Testing Tips

When testing a dialog box during development, a few items to check in particular are:

- Tab order for controls. Use the Tab key to move between controls and be sure that the required groups, tab stops, and ordering are appropriate.
- Radio button groups. Be sure that radio button groups function correctly and that buttons reset appropriately. If there is a problem, check the tab order.
- Overlapping elements. Check particularly for static text elements that may be larger than the text they contain and may overlap (and conceal) other elements.

The last control selected will become the reference control, and all other selected controls will be aligned against the position of the reference.

Centering Buttons

The two centering buttons provide vertical and horizontal centering. These can be used to center one or more controls relative to the dialog box itself. If more than one control is selected, the selected controls are centered as a group but retain their positions relative to each other.

Spacing Buttons

The two spacing buttons provide horizontal or vertical spacing. This allows two (or more) controls to be selected and then spaced equally across or down.

For example, if controls are being spaced horizontally, the left-most and right-most extremes are taken as the limits, and all controls are spaced equally between these two limits. At the same time, individual vertical positioning will not be affected.

In like fashion, for vertical spacing, the highest and lowest extremes are taken as limits, and horizontal spacing remains unaffected.

Sizing Buttons

The three sizing buttons are used to resize controls. Again, more than one control must be selected, and the last control selected (identified by the dark handles on the outline) serves as the reference.

Multiple controls may be resized to the same width, to the same height, or with both height and width adjusted at the same time.

Grid Positioning, Rulers, and Guides

The Grid tool provides a background grid of fine dots, which may be used to help align controls. When the grid is enabled, the rule and guides are disabled. Then, when a control is moved, its position is snapped to the grid. Likewise, when a control is resized, the size is snapped to the grid.

The Ruler and Guide option is on by default and provides vertical and horizontal rulers, in dialog box units, plus a guide that appears as a faint blue border or margin around the dialog box. When the guide is enabled, controls moved toward the guides tend to snap to the guide if they are close enough.

From the Layout menu, select the Guide Settings option to change the guide settings and adjust grid spacing.

Tab Ordering

To adjust the tab ordering for dialog box controls, select Tab Order from the Layout menu. When the Tab Order option is selected, all of the dialog box controls are labeled with a tab-order number, as shown in Figure 10.34.

FIGURE 10.34

Selecting the Tab Order
option from the Layout
menu shows the dia-
log box with tab-order
numbers.

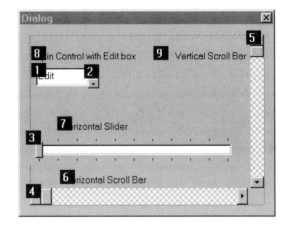

To change the tab order, click on the first control and then continue clicking on
controls in the order desired. The tab-order numbers will change to reflect the new
order. To stop setting the tab order, simply click anywhere except on a control.

The Resource Workshop Toolbar and Options

If you're using the Borland Resource Workshop, most of the tools you will want are
found on the toolbar itself. Figure 10.35 shows this toolbar, with the buttons
labeled. These buttons and other options are described in the following sections.

FIGURE 10.35

The Resource Workshop
toolbar

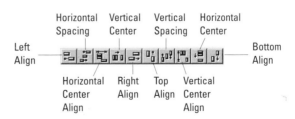

Alignment Buttons

The four alignment buttons provide left, right, top, and bottom alignment. To align a group of controls, hold down the Shift key while clicking on each of the controls. The first control selected will become the reference control, and all other selected controls will be aligned against the position of the reference.

Center Alignment Buttons

The Resource Workshop provides two alignment options not offered by the Developer Studio: the horizontal and vertical center alignment options, which align controls by their centers. As with other alignment options, the first control selected becomes the reference control, and all other selected controls are aligned against the position of the reference.

Centering Buttons

The two centering buttons provide vertical and horizontal centering. These can be used to center one or more controls relative to the dialog box itself. If more than one control is selected, the selected controls are centered as a group but retain their positions relative to each other.

Spacing Buttons

The two spacing buttons provide horizontal and vertical spacing. This allows two (or more) controls to be selected and then spaced equally across or down.

For example, if controls are being spaced horizontally, the left-most and right-most extremes are taken as the limits and all controls are spaced equally between these two limits. At the same time, individual vertical positioning will not be affected.

In like fashion, for vertical spacing, the highest and lowest extremes are taken as limits, and horizontal spacing remains unaffected.

Sizing Options

The Resource Workshop, instead of placing the sizing controls on the toolbar, provides the Size option on the Dialog menu, which presents the Size dialog box shown in Figure 10.36.

FIGURE 10.36

The Resource Workshop
Size dialog box

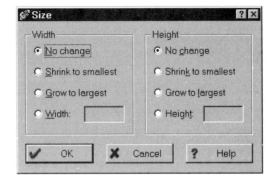

You can change the height or width of controls. Using this dialog box, you can adjust all selected controls to match the smallest or the largest, or to set the sizes to a specific value.

Tab-Ordering Options

To work with tab ordering for dialog box controls, select the Set Creation Order option from the Dialog menu. When this option is selected, all of the dialog controls appear as outlines labeled with a tab-order number, as shown in Figure 10.37.

To change the tab order, click on the first control, and then continue clicking on controls in the order desired. The tab-order numbers will change to reflect the new order. To stop setting the tab order, simply click anywhere except on a control.

NOTE Using the Resource Workshop, you may also want to try the Set Tab Stops and Set Group Flags options on the Dialog menu.

Tab ordering in the
Resource Workshop

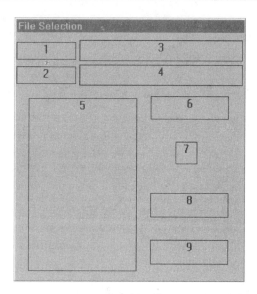

Three Dialog Boxes for the FileView1 Application

The FileView1 program requires three dialog boxes: About, File Type, and Open File. These three dialog boxes are described in the following sections and are included in the FileView1.RC resource script on the CD accompanying this book.

NOTE   In the FileView2 application, where we will use the common dialog File Open facility, there is only one dialog resource: the About dialog. The script for this resource is included on the CD accompanying this book and needs no explanation.

The About Dialog Box

The About dialog box, shown in Figure 10.38, consists of a captioned dialog box without a system menu. The title bar bears the text "About File View." Three dialog box elements appear as a centered text line, an icon box, and a single button.

FIGURE 10.38

A simple About dialog box with an icon

The single button returns a value, IDOK (0x01), which is defined in Windows.H.

The File Type Dialog Box

The File Type dialog box, shown in Figure 10.39, again uses a captioned dialog box with a static text instruction supplementing the caption. In this example, two control buttons appear at the bottom to the right and left of the File Type icon. The left button, as shown by the heavy outline, is the default.

FIGURE 10.39

The File Type dialog box

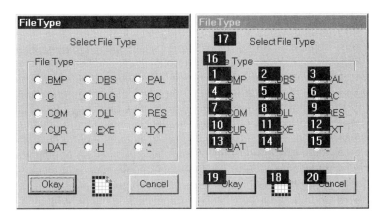

To the right, in Figure 10.39, the File Type dialog box is duplicated showing the mnemonic constants assigned to each control. The corresponding numeric values are 201 through 215, but they could be any values and do not necessarily need to be in order. The static text, group box, and icon, which do not return message values, have control values of –1.

Inside the group box, 15 auto-radio buttons provide the purpose for this dialog box, offering a choice of file extensions. When the dialog box is initialized (by the FileView program), the .* button will be set as the default extension, but this is a provision of the program code, not the dialog box.

Also, even though the auto-radio buttons are enclosed by a group box outline, this is for visual purposes only; the group box does not, in this instance, control the grouping. Instead, the grouping was assigned by setting the Group property for the first item in the group and setting the tab order for all of the buttons.

The File Selection Dialog Box

The File Selection dialog box is the last of the three dialog boxes used by the FileView application, and in some respects, it is also the most complicated and the most important. This dialog box, shown in Figure 10.40, offers two edit entry fields, plus a list box where files matching the file specification will be displayed (together, of course, with directory and drive IDs). Also, in addition to the customary Okay and Cancel buttons, a third button, File Type, is provided to call the File Type dialog box.

FIGURE 10.40

The File Selection dialog box

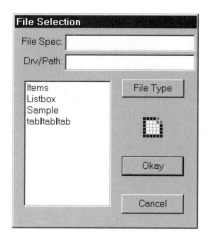

Beginning at the top, the File Spec edit box has been provided with a default test string, "*.*". This text string, however, is superfluous, because when the dialog box is initialized, the application will provide its own string, both here and in the Drv/Path edit box below.

Next, when the dialog box is initialized, the list box at the left will be filled with file, directory, and drive information using the application-assigned default file specification and the current (active) drive/path settings.

Last, the File Type button returns an `IDM_TYPE` message, which is used to instruct the application to load the File Type dialog box.

This completes our discussion of working with dialog box editors. We've covered all types of dialog box controls. Custom dialog box controls have been mentioned only briefly, as alternatives to the standard controls. Fortunately, the majority of applications will not require custom control designs.

Also, as you may have noticed, no mention has been made of adding menus to dialog boxes. This is not because menus are not supported, but because the dialog box editor is not the appropriate mechanism for constructing menus. We'll cover menu editors and menu construction in the next chapter.

CHAPTER

ELEVEN

11

Menus and Menu Editors

- Borland's Resource Workshop menu editor

- Microsoft's Developer Studio menu editor

- Menu item properties

- Menu scripts

For many Windows applications, the primary entry point is a menu bar that offers initial options and access to principal features. In other cases, dialog boxes may use menus to present further choices, or applications may present different primary menus as appropriate to current operations.

In this chapter, we'll look at how menus are constructed and some of the possible arrangements for menus and submenus.

Introducing Two Menu Editors

Menu resources are easy to create, and, in keeping with their text nature, require little more than ASCII scripts for their design. However, the Borland Resource Workshop and the Microsoft Developer Studio provide an easier way to construct and test menus: with a menu editor. Menu editors can generate either an .RC menu script or a compiled .RES resource.

Using the Borland Resource Workshop Menu Editor

The Resource Workshop's menu editor consists of four parts, as shown in Figure 11.1:

- The editor's own menu bar (top)
- The sample or working menu bar (child window at lower right)
- The options window (left)
- The menu script (right)

> **NOTE**
> The menu editor does not recognize an empty menu, so you must add a new item before you can delete the default entries that first appear on the dummy menu. (To delete a menu item, right-click on the entry in the menu window and choose Cut.)

FIGURE 11.1

The Resource Workshop
menu editor

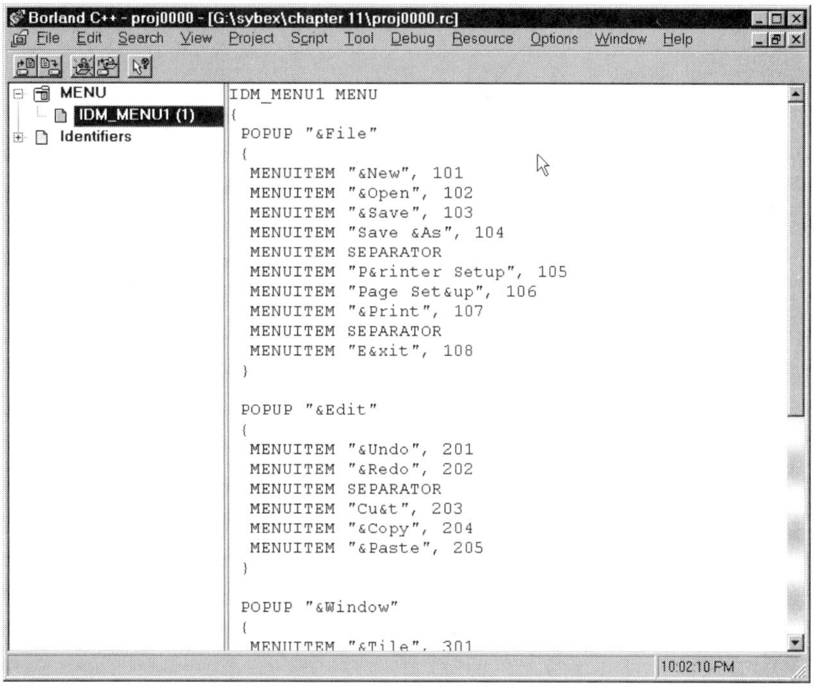

When you start to create a new menu, the menu editor presents a menu containing the standard Windows defaults: the File, Edit, Window, and Help pop-up menus. The assumption is that most applications will want to support these default actions. You can proceed to add new menu selections, remove existing menu options, and make whatever revisions are required.

Figure 11.2 shows a sample menu bar with four primary entries: File, Edit, Window, and Help. The figure also shows the Edit pop-up menu, which consists of five entries: Undo, Redo, Cut, Copy, and Paste. As is standard in Windows menus, hotkeys are identified by underscores; the letters preceded by ampersands in the script are the ones underlined in the menus.

In the menu script, the keywords POPUP and MENUITEM define the menu entry types, and the individual menu entries appear with (optional) indentation showing levels. For example, under Window, the View option calls another pop-up menu with two entries: All and Hidden document list.

FIGURE 11.2

A sample menu in the Resource Workshop editor

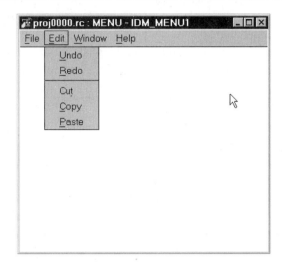

Each POPUP is followed by opening and closing brackets enclosing submenu entries. The menu as a whole begins with the menu name (identifier) IDM_MENU1 and also has opening and closing brackets enclosing the menu.

> **NOTE** The Developer Studio uses BEGIN and END statements rather than brackets. See the "Creating Menu Scripts" section at the end of the chapter for examples.

Within the menu entry definitions, C and C++ programmers should have no difficulty recognizing the \t instruction as a tab character entry, which causes the following text to appear flush right in the menu. See the section "Text for Menu Entries," later in the chapter, for more information about setting up menu entry text.

Menu Hotkeys

In many cases, menu entries have secondary hotkeys identified as Shift+... or Ctrl+.... A second convention uses a simple syntax to identify hotkeys with the caret (^) indicating the Ctrl key. Both conventions are acceptable. However, simply identifying a secondary hotkey in the menu definition does not assign the key definition as a functional hotkey. These hotkey assignments are handled as accelerator keys, as described in the next chapter.

On the other hand, the primary menu hotkeys, which are identified in the menus by the underscore and in the script by the ampersand character (&), are automatic assignments generated when the menu script is compiled.

Within any menu or submenu, you cannot use the same hotkey twice at the same level. Thus Cut, Copy, and Close clipboard—items that are all on the same level— use three different hotkeys (U, C, and L). However, if we added a Search entry as a pop-up menu with a Stop entry under the Search menu, the S hotkey could be used again, because these items are on different levels.

Accelerator hotkeys, which are global, cannot be duplicated within a dialog box or application window, although the same accelerator key combination can be used for different purposes in different menus or different dialog boxes. The use of accelerators is covered in Chapter 12.

Options for Constructing Menus

The Borland menu editor provides the Menu menu option (the semantics are awkward), with options specific to menu construction.

These options work as follows:

- **New Popup (Ctrl+P):** Inserts a new pop-up menu entry at the position highlighted in the menu script, setting the level of the menu element as appropriate for the position.

- **New Menuitem (Ins):** Adds a new item to a menu above the highlighted menu item.

- **New Separator (Ctrl+S):** Adds a separator (a rule between menu entries, such as the one between New Separator and Set Mnemonic in the Menu menu) above the highlighted menu item.

- **Set Mnemonic (Ctrl+&):** Sets a hotkey for the highlighted menu or menu item.

- **Check Duplicates:** Looks for hotkey selections that have been duplicated. It will find any hotkeys that appear in two or more menu entries or conflict with system hotkeys.

- **View as Popup:** Toggles how the working menu is displayed. You can switch between a pop-up menu display or, for development, primary and submenus in a stacked display. Figure 11.3 shows an example of a stacked display.

FIGURE 11.3

A menu displayed in stacked format showing all branches

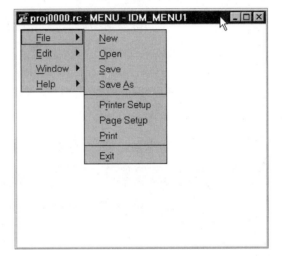

- **Show Property Inspector:** Displays the Property Inspector dialog box for the menu item. Menu properties are discussed later in the chapter.

- **Test Menu:** Creates an application window with a menu bar for the menu being developed, allowing you to experiment with the branches and submenus.

To delete a menu item, right-click on the entry in the sample menu window. From the pop-up menu, select the Cut option. To be safe, select the Copy option before deleting, and you will be able to restore the entry or submenu by pasting. Otherwise, since there is no "undelete" feature, you will need to re-create the entry from scratch if you make a mistake.

WARNING Deleting a menu item for a submenu deletes the entire submenu.

Using the Developer Studio Menu Editor

In some ways, Microsoft's Developer Studio menu editor is much simpler to use than Borland's Resource Workshop menu editor. In the Developer Studio version, the resource script is entirely hidden and only the menu itself is presented. Figure 11.4 shows a menu under construction in this menu editor.

FIGURE 11.4

The Developer Studio menu editor

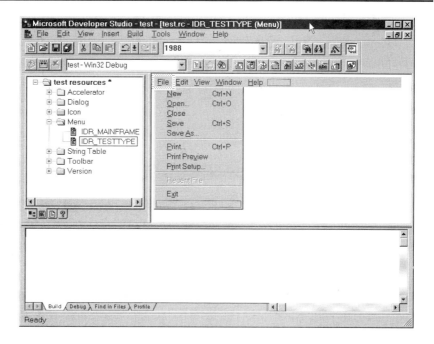

Here you should notice two blank rectangles: one at the end of the primary menu bar and one at the bottom of the pull-down File menu. Neither of these items actually appears in the menu; they are placeholders, ready for your new entries.

To add a menu item, simply double-click on the blank—on the primary level or on the submenu—to call the Menu Item Properties dialog box for the item. In the Properties dialog box, enter an ID and caption (if appropriate) or select an option for the entry. A new blank item will appear as soon as the new caption is entered or the Separator option is checked. See the section titled "Setting Menu Item Properties," later in the chapter, for details.

To move a menu item to a different position in the menu, simply click and drag the entry to the position desired.

To remove a menu item, highlight the item and press the Delete key.

Menu Size Limits

Theoretically, you can create a menu of virtually any size. But in practical terms, too large a menu probably means that you need to rethink your menu organization.

As an unwieldy example, Figure 11.5 shows a primary menu bar with a total of 31 entries, requiring five lines to display on a screen 420 pixels wide.

FIGURE 11.5

An unwieldy primary menu

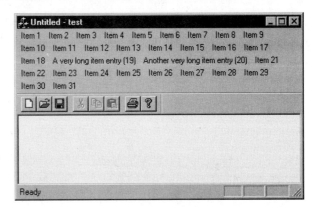

Obviously, there must be some actual limits on the number of menu elements and the number of levels supported, although these real limits have nothing to do with the resource compiler or Windows NT/95. To set practical limits, consider

NOTE   Of course, if the window width is reduced, the menu lines will be rearranged, automatically, to use as many lines as necessary.

how much is too much. At what point does a menu bar become too complex to be comfortable to use? When does it become a liability instead of an asset?

These questions apply not only to the number of primary entries but also to the number of levels and pop-up (pull-down) submenus.

As a general rule of thumb, the primary menu should not exceed one line under normal use, and the number of levels of pop-up submenus should probably not go further than two or three. If your application needs more items than a simple menu structure can supply, consider creating a very simple primary menu, with the menu selections calling a series of dialog boxes to offer the more complex options.

Text for Menu Entries

Individually, menu entries can be as simple as a single word, a brief phrase, or some combination of these. They may or may not include hotkey assignments or accelerator keys.

The text for a menu entry is one of its properties (the Text property in Borland's menu editor and the Caption property in Microsoft's). Type the text exactly as you want it to appear on the actual menu.

By default, Windows uses the first letter in each entry as the hotkey for this entry, but it does not underscore the entry unless a specific instruction is provided. However, the hotkey is not required to be the first character. As mentioned earlier, the ampersand (&) is used as the hotkey identifier in the menu item text. Thus, to select the O in Open... as the hotkey for this entry, type the text as &Open.... (An ellipsis, ..., is often used by convention to indicate that a menu entry will call a dialog box rather than initiating an immediate action.) This will appear in the menu as Open....

You cannot enter a tab character directly by pressing the Tab key while typing in the menu item text. The C convention \t is recognized as a tab instruction and is commonly used to identify accelerator keys by setting them flush right in the menu entry. The \a instruction also causes the text following to be right-justified.

> **TIP**
>
> If more than one ampersand appears in a menu item, only the last ampersand entry is recognized. Alternately, if an actual ampersand is needed in the text, a double ampersand can be entered as "&&" and will appear as "&" but without an underscore. If you want an ampersand to appear as a character in a menu entry, enter it as &&. For example, to create the menu item Search & Replace, enter `Search && Replace`. The ampersand will appear in the item as a single & character, and will not be treated as a hotkey identifier.

Also, as mentioned earlier, for hotkeys, you can type in either the longer version, `Ctrl+...`, or use the simpler syntax convention of the caret (^) to indicate the Ctrl key. And remember, although you can identify a secondary hotkey in the menu definition, you must handle these hotkey assignments as accelerator keys, as described in the next chapter.

Note that no provisions are made for multiple-line menu entries, and carriage returns and line feeds are not supported. Thus, even though the menu editor can accept entries up to 255 characters, this does not mean that the menu can display such strings. Feel free, however, to experiment.

Menu Item Properties

Menu item properties apply to menu items created with either the Resource Workshop or the Developer Studio editor. Only the means of setting these values differ between the two systems.

To set menu properties with Borland's Resource Workshop, choose Show Property Inspector from the Menu menu or right-click on a menu item to display a pop-up options menu. Figure 11.6 shows the Property Inspector dialog box.

FIGURE 11.6

The Resource Workshop Property Inspector dialog box

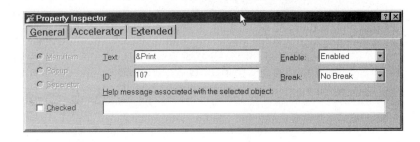

In the Developer Studio, the Properties dialog box will appear when you double-click on the blank in a menu. Figure 11.7 shows an example of a Developer Studio Menu Item Properties dialog box.

FIGURE 11.7

The Developer Studio
Menu Item Properties
dialog box

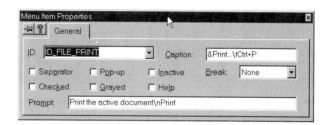

Menu items have the following properties (in Borland's menu editor, some of these elements are found in the Property Inspector's Accelerator or Extended tabs):

- **ID:** Commonly a mnemonic symbol used as an identifier and defined in the header file. Unlike other resources, new menu resources do not get a default ID. However, the prefix `IDM_` is commonly used to identify menu item messages. Pop-up menu items, which are handled internally, do not have ID values and do not return messages when selected. Similarly, menu separators, which cannot be selected, do not require ID values.

- **Caption:** The text entry that appears as the menu item's label. This property is called Text in Borland's Property Inspector. See the previous section, "Text for Menu Entries," for details on how to set up hotkeys and enter text for menu items.

- **Separator:** Specifies that the menu item is a separator. Separator items do not have captions or IDs and cannot be selected.

- **Checked:** Specifies that the menu item is initially checked when the menu opens.

- **Pop-up:** Sets the menu item as a pop-up item; that is, the primary item for a pop-up submenu. This is the default setting for top-level menu items.

- **Grayed:** Sets the menu item as initially inactive and grayed, and also sets the Inactive property. Before an inactive (grayed) menu item can be selected, it must be enabled by the application (see `CMenu::EnableMenuItem`).

- **Inactive:** Sets the menu item as initially inactive (but not grayed). Before an inactive menu item can be selected, it must be enabled by the application (see `CMenu::EnableMenuItem`).

- **Help:** Right-justifies the item on the menu bar at runtime (but not during editing).

- **Break:** Sets the break style as one of the following:

  - None, for no break (the default)

  - Column, so that for a static menu bar item, the item is placed on a new line. For a pop-up menu, the item is placed in a new column with no dividing line between columns. Setting the Column property affects the menu only at runtime, not during editing.

  - Bar, so that for a static menu bar item, the item is placed on a new line. For a pop-up menu, the item is placed in a new column with a vertical dividing line between columns. Setting the Bar property affects the menu only at runtime, not during editing.

- **Prompt:** Supplies text to appear in the status bar when this menu item is selected. The prompt entry is added to the resource string table using the same ID as the menu item. (In Borland's Property Inspector, this item is identified as the Help message.)

NOTE   Unlike toolbar buttons, menu items do not support tool tips. Do not add a tip entry to the prompt string entry.

Creating Menus with Menu Scripts

A menu editor is a convenient tool, but it is not the only way to create a menu script. As an alternative, you can use any plain text editor, such as the Windows Notepad, to create a menu script. As an example, we'll use a script for a simple menu with four primary entries and an assortment of pull-down menus and submenus.

The menu script begins with a name, IDM_MENU1, followed by the resource type identifier, MENU. On the next line, the keyword BEGIN identifies the start of the menu definition.

```
IDM_MENU1 MENU
BEGIN
```

TIP   Earlier in the chapter, opening and closing brackets were used rather than BEGIN and END statements. Both formats are correct, although the Borland and Microsoft compilers may each complain about the other's syntax when moving a resource file from one to the other.

The first menu item is identified by the keyword POPUP and followed by the text for this item. Of course, since the pop-up entry will be followed by at least one sub-entry, another BEGIN/END block is initiated on the next line.

```
POPUP "&Edit"
BEGIN
```

The next few lines define menu entries for the Edit submenu, each beginning with the keyword MENUITEM followed by the entry text, the entry ID, and, optionally, one or more flag arguments controlling how the menu entry is initially displayed.

```
MENUITEM "C&ut\t^U",    201, CHECKED
MENUITEM "&Copy\t^C",   202
MENUITEM "&Paste\t^P",  203, INACTIVE, MENUBARBREAK
```

In this fragment, the first item on this submenu is presented with a check mark (CHECKED). The third item uses the INACTIVE keyword to make the entry unselectable and the MENUBARBREAK keyword to cause a column break with a vertical separator bar.

Next, a new submenu entry is defined as an entry in the Edit submenu. The Search submenu has two entries, without any special features, but it does require a BEGIN/END pair to set off the submenu block.

```
POPUP "&Search\t^S"
BEGIN
   MENUITEM "&Find\t^F",     204
   MENUITEM "&Replace\t^R", 205
END
```

Following the Search submenu, a final entry is made in the Edit submenu but, this time, is disabled using the GRAYED keyword. The MENUBREAK keyword produces a column break but does not produce a vertical separator. The Clear clipboard menu entry is followed by an END statement to close the Edit submenu.

```
        MENUITEM "C&lear clipboard\t^L", 206, GRAYED, MENUBREAK
    END
```

The remaining primary menu level entries are the next MENUITEMS. The Help menu item uses the keyword HELP to set this entry flush right on the main menu bar. The script terminates with a closing END statement.

```
    MENUITEM "&Print", 101
    MENUITEM "&File",  102
    MENUITEM "&Help",  103, HELP
END
```

Now that you've seen the fragments and explanations, the following is the entire Menu_1 script, showing the overall structure and indentations (these indentations are for the programmer's benefit only, and have no effect on how the menu script compiles).

```
IDM_MENU1 MENU
BEGIN
    POPUP "&Edit"
    BEGIN
        MENUITEM "C&ut\t^U",    201, CHECKED
        MENUITEM "&Copy\t^C",   202
        MENUITEM "&Paste\t^P",  203, INACTIVE, MENUBARBREAK
        POPUP "&Search\t^S"
        BEGIN
            MENUITEM "&Find\t^F",    204
            MENUITEM "&Replace\t^R", 205
        END
        MENUITEM "C&lear clipboard\t^L", 206, GRAYED, MENUBREAK
    END
    MENUITEM "&Print", 101
    MENUITEM "&File",  102
    MENUITEM "&Help",  103, HELP
END
```

The one menu script command that does not appear in the preceding example is the horizontal menu separator, SEPARATOR. This command is used in the following script, which is the script for the FileView application menu (the FileView application is presented in Chapter 13).

```
FILEVIEW MENU DISCARDABLE
BEGIN
    POPUP "&File"
    BEGIN
        MENUITEM "&Open...\t^O",  IDM_OPEN     // = 103
        MENUITEM "&Type...\t^T",  IDM_TYPE     // = 104
        MENUITEM SEPARATOR
        MENUITEM "&About",        IDM_ABOUT    // = 102
        MENUITEM "E&xit\t^X",     IDM_QUIT     // = 101
    END
END
```

The FileView2 application menu script, shown below, is slightly different.

```
IDR_MAINFRAME MENU PRELOAD DISCARDABLE
BEGIN
    POPUP "&File"
    BEGIN
        MENUITEM "&Open...\tCtrl+O",          ID_FILE_OPEN
        MENUITEM SEPARATOR
        MENUITEM "E&xit",                     ID_APP_EXIT
    END
    POPUP "&View"
    BEGIN
        MENUITEM "&Toolbar",                  ID_VIEW_TOOLBAR
        MENUITEM "&Status Bar",               ID_VIEW_STATUS_BAR
    END
    POPUP "&Help"
    BEGIN
        MENUITEM "&About FileView2...",       ID_APP_ABOUT
    END
END
```

Notice that both the FileView1 and FileView2 menu scripts are written using mnemonic identifiers rather than actual values. The constants are defined in the FileView.H header file.

While the Menu editor provides a convenient means to create, define, and test application menus, menus can also be created as scripts using any plain text editor such as the Windows Notepad.

Also, in either case, while accelerator keys can be displayed in a menu, these must be defined separately, either using the Accelerator editor or writing an accelerator script, both of which are discussed in Chapter 12.

Accelerators, Strings, Header Files, and Resource Editors

- Accelerators and accelerator editors

- String tables and string table editors

- Header files for resource IDs

- Version resources and version editors

In addition to the more obvious resource types we've discussed so far—images, dialog boxes, and menus—you should know about two other resources: accelerator keys and string resources. Although these are less graphic and less impressive than other resources, they are just as important for the programmer.

Another category of programmer resources is the header definition files, which are also discussed in this chapter. When used properly, header files can prevent a great many errors that would otherwise be difficult to identify.

Version resources, even though they are very simple, provide a convenient location to record version, copyright, and source notes within the application. These types of resources are also explained in this chapter.

Accelerator-Key Resources

Accelerator keys offer a fast shortcut—in the form of keyboard hotkey combinations—for issuing application commands. Although conventional (DOS) programs have often provided similar services, frequently employing TSR utilities to translate individual keystrokes or key combinations into command sequences, accelerator keys take a rather different form.

One of the most important differences is that, unlike DOS-based TSRs, accelerator keys do not depend on interrupt processing by an outside application. Instead, accelerator key processing is handled internally by Windows and is part and parcel of the Windows messaging system.

As explained in Chapter 5, under Windows, keystroke information is not sent directly to the application. Instead, all Windows applications rely on Windows to intercept the hardware keyboard events, translate these as necessary, and then forward them in the form of keyboard messages to the appropriate application. Because of this approach, adding provisions for special key combinations to generate custom messages in place of key-event messages is only a minor change. More important, each application can define its own accelerator-key combinations and the messages to be generated by each.

Still, no matter how convenient or how smooth this translation may be, it remains the programmer's responsibility to define these accelerator hotkey combinations and to prepare this information in a form acceptable to the resource compiler for inclusion in the application's resources.

Defining Accelerator-Key Combinations

An accelerator-key definition consists of two parts:

- A keyboard key or key combination

- A message value to be sent to the application when the key combination is entered

In general, single keystrokes are not used as accelerator keys, simply because these key events have other purposes that take precedence. Instead, accelerator keys are commonly defined as a key combination requiring one conventional key plus one or more of the Ctrl, Alt, or Shift keys. For example, common shortcuts for Edit menu commands are Ctrl+C for Copy, Ctrl+X for Cut, and Ctrl+V for Paste. The conventional key can be defined as either an ASCII key or as a virtual key.

NOTE

In general, an ASCII key refers to any of the alphanumeric keys that produce displayable characters on the screen. These include the punctuation keys and the spacebar.

Virtual versus ASCII Keys

Virtually (the pun is unavoidable) all of the keys on the keyboard (whether a standard or an enhanced keyboard) can be defined as accelerator keys using the virtual-key definitions provided in the WinUser.H header file. These are discussed in detail in Chapter 5.

Not all keys, however, have ASCII equivalents, and a few ASCII keys do not have virtual-key equivalents (such as, for example, the exclamation point!). Furthermore, some virtual-key definitions do not correspond to anything found on the contemporary keyboard (such as the VK_ZOOM or VK_NONAME virtual keys); some refer to a non-keyboard device (such as the VK_MBUTTON virtual key). Table 12.1 lists some of the key codes that shouldn't be used as accelerators.

Virtual-key definitions (all of which begin with the prefix VK_) refer principally to the function, arrow, and keypad keys. Thus, the F1 key is defined as VK_F1, the PgDn key as VK_NEXT, the down arrow key as VK_DOWN, and the left Shift key (on an enhanced keyboard) as VK_LSHIFT. The standard alphanumeric keys, however, are not excluded; they are identified as VK_A through VK_Z and VK_0 through VK_9.

TABLE 12.1   Key Codes Not Recommended for Use as Accelerator Keys

Key codes*	Comments
0Ch, 5Bh..5Dh, 60h..69h	Special requirements, etc.
6Ah..6Bh, 6Dh..7Bh, A0h..A5h	Enhanced keyboards only
29h..2Fh, 2Ah..2Bh, 2Fh, 6Ch, 7Ch..87h, E5h, F6h..FEh	OEM-specific keys
05..07h, 0Ah..0Bh, 0Eh..0Fh, 1Ah, 3Ah..40h, 5Eh..5Fh, 88h..8Fh, 92h..9Fh, A6h..E4h, E6h..F5h	Not assigned
15h..19h, 1Ch..1Fh	Reserved for Kanji system

NOTE   Keep in mind that uppercase and lowercase keys are not differentiated either as virtual keys or when used as accelerator keys employing an ASCII key definition.

Defining an Accelerator-Key Script

Accelerator keys can be defined, in script form, using any plain text editor, such as the Windows Notepad. Here is a sample script for the FileView1 application keyboard accelerators (the FileView application is presented in the next chapter):

```
FILEVIEW ACCELERATORS
BEGIN
    "X", IDM_QUIT, ASCII, CONTROL    // = 101
    "O", IDM_OPEN, ASCII, CONTROL    // = 103
    "T", IDM_TYPE, ASCII, CONTROL    // = 104
END
```

In this example, the three accelerator keys are Ctrl+X, Ctrl+O, and Ctrl+T, returning the values IDM_QUIT, IDM_OPEN, and IDM_TYPE, respectively.

In the following example, the preceding accelerator keys are repeated in a different format, together with five new accelerator keys showing various Ctrl, Alt, and Shift key modifiers.

```
ACCLDEMO ACCELERATORS
BEGIN
    VK_X,   IDM_QUIT, VIRTKEY, CONTROL    // = 101
```

```
VK_O,   IDM_OPEN,  VIRTKEY,  CONTROL     // = 103
VK_T,   IDM_TYPE,  VIRTKEY,  CONTROL     // = 104
VK_F1,  105,       VIRTKEY
VK_F4,  106,       VIRTKEY
VK_F6,  107,       VIRTKEY,            SHIFT
"s",    108,       ASCII,    ALT,      SHIFT
"G",    109,       ASCII,    CONTROL,  SHIFT
END
```

NOTE The spacing is irrelevant to the resource compiler and has been added only to make the various elements of each definition easier to read. Also notice that it does not matter whether the ASCII key definition is entered as uppercase or lowercase, and the Caps Lock status does not affect recognition of the accelerator-key combination.

For non-ASCII keys, this virtual-key definition format is almost essential. However, a more convenient entry method is provided by the accelerator editors in both the Resource Workshop and Developer Studio.

Using a Resource Workshop Editor for Accelerators

Rather than providing a separate accelerator editor, as it did in previous versions, Borland's Resource Workshop simply provides a script editor. Considering the simplicity of accelerator-key definitions, the lack of a more sophisticated editor is not a big deal. The Resource Workshop editor with some accelerators for the File-View application is shown in Figure 12.1.

Using the Developer Studio Accelerator Editor

In contrast to the Resource Workshop, the Developer Studio offers a more elaborate accelerator editor, which includes the Accel Properties dialog box for entering or editing an accelerator table item. Figure 12.2 shows the accelerator editor and Properties dialog box.

FIGURE 12.1

The Resource Work-
shop script editor with
accelerator definitions

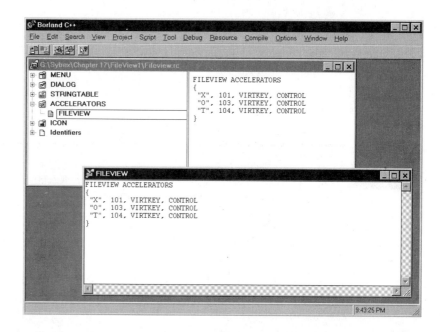

FIGURE 12.2

The Developer Studio
accelerator editor

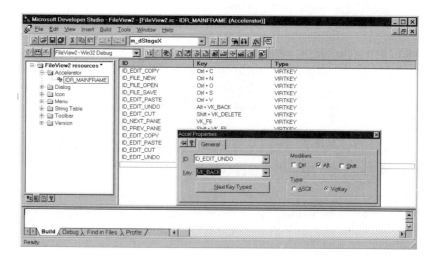

The editor offers the following properties for accelerators:

- **ID:** The resource ID is normally a mnemonic symbol defined in the header file but may also be an integer value or a quoted string.

- **Modifiers:** Indicate whether the accelerator key is a combination formed with the Ctrl, Alt, or Shift keys. If the key value is an ASCII value, the Ctrl and Shift key combinations are not accepted. The defaults are True for Ctrl but False for Alt and Shift.

- **Key**: Specifies the accelerator key. It can be one of the following:

  - Integer, in the range from 0 to 255. Integers are interpreted as ASCII or virtual-key values, depending on the Type property.

NOTE   Any single digit is interpreted as a key value. To enter an ASCII value from 0 to 9, precede the number with two zeros (for example, 006). In like fashion, two-digit codes may be preceded with a single zero, although this is not a firm requirement.

  - Character, for a character value. Optionally, the character value may be preceded by a caret (^) to signify a control character.
  - Virtual Key Identifier, for any virtual-key identifier. Select the desired VK_*xxxx* value from the drop-down list.

- **Type:** Identifies a key value as an ASCII value or a virtual-key (VirtKey) value.

- **Next Key Typed:** Accepts the next key combination typed as the accelerator key. The Key and Modifier values are changed to match. If possible, the key selected is always interpreted as a virtual key. The choice between entering an accelerator-key definition directly or using the Next Key Typed option is purely a matter of personal preference.

String Resources

Treating strings as resources instead of scattering the strings throughout the program code is a distinct departure from conventional programming practices. Most compilers gather such static data together, usually positioning this data toward the end of the .EXE code, along with other static data elements.

Defining strings as resources has three advantages:

- Like other resources, strings are loaded into memory only when and as needed.

- Strings in a string table can be modified more conveniently than strings scattered throughout the source code.

- Multiple string tables can be defined. Each table can provide different language versions and be loaded according to the user's preference.

As with menu and accelerator-key resources, string tables can be created using a plain text editor, such as the Windows Notepad or Unipad (for non-English languages). Alternatively, you can create string tables using the Resource Workshop or Developer Studio string table editor.

Defining Strings

String resources may consist of any type of string data and may be used for any of the same purposes as conventional string data, including window captions, messages, labels, or even brief explanations. The single drawback of string table entries is that they are limited to 255 characters in length.

NOTE String table entries are not usually used for button and control captions or menus, since these text strings can be handled through an image or menu editor.

Individually, each string definition follows C conventions and is enclosed in double quotation marks. Strings also accept C's special embedded characters, such as \n for a line feed, \r for a carriage return, \t for the tab character, \\ for a single backslash, and \' for an embedded double quotation mark.

Constructing String Tables

A typical (if brief) string table might look something like the following (this is excerpted from the FileView1.RC resource script):

```
STRING TABLE
BEGIN
    IDS_NAME,   "FileView"
    IDS_ERROR1, "File size indeterminate"
    IDS_ERROR2, "File too large for present example"
END
```

Each string in a string table is identified by an integer value, placing an upper limit of 65,535 strings in the string table. In this example, the string IDs are provided by constants defined in the FileView.H header.

In the following second version of this string table, the actual values are substituted for the mnemonic constants, and there are a few additional strings.

```
STRING TABLE
BEGIN
     1, "FileView"
     2, "File size indeterminate"
     3, "File too large for present example"
    16, "this string belongs to another group"
    17, "together with this second string"
    32, "and a third group"
END

STRING TABLE
BEGIN
    44, "this string is defined in a second string table"
    45, "as is this second string"
    46, "and this third string"
END
```

In this second example, two string table segments have been defined, but notice that there is nothing in the labels to identify these as separate segments. Instead, in the Resource Workshop, each of these segments would be identified only as the number of the first entry in the table (or as the mnemonic constant).

More immediately important, strings are loaded in groups of 16, with all strings in a group loaded when any one of the strings is required. Groups are identified by their ID number, with numbers 0 through 15 forming the first group, 16 through 31 forming a second group, and so on. Thus, in the examples, strings 1, 2, and 3 form one group, strings 16 and 17 form a second, string 32 is in a group by itself, and strings 44, 45, and 46 form a final group.

The programmer's objective is to group strings so that strings that are needed will be loaded together, without loading unnecessary resources at the same time.

Using a Resource Workshop Editor for String Tables

The Resource Workshop does not provide a separate string table editor. Like accelerators, string table resources are edited as a simple script. String tables have the format:

```
STRING TABLE
{
    IDS_NAME,   "FileView"
    IDS_ERROR1, "File size indeterminate"
    IDS_ERROR2, "File too large for present example"
}
```

Notice that brackets are used by the Borland editor in place of BEGIN and END statements (as in the Resource Workshop's menu editor, described in Chapter 11). Either format, however, is acceptable to either compiler.

Using the Developer Studio String Table Editor

Microsoft's Developer Studio offers a slightly more sophisticated, separate string table editor, as shown in Figure 12.3.

You can work in the Developer Studio string editor as follows:

- Add a string table entry by clicking on the blank entry and entering a new ID and Caption in the Properties dialog box.

- Delete an individual string by selecting the string and pressing the Delete key.

- Move a string from one segment to another by changing the ID values.

FIGURE 12.3

The Developer Studio
string table editor

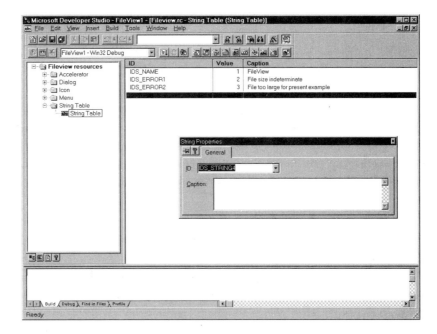

- Move strings from one resource script (.RC) file to another using the Cut and Paste options.

- Change a string or its identifier by editing the entry.

- Add formatting or special characters to a string.

Of course, you can accomplish the same tasks with a plain text editor; the Developer Studio simply offers a more convenient tool for the purpose.

TIP
In the Developer Studio string editor, click the right mouse button to display a pop-up menu of resource-specific commands.

The resource editor does not permit the creation of empty string tables. If a string table is created with no entries, it will be deleted automatically on exiting the Developer Studio.

Header Files

Header files provide a convenient place to define mnemonic constants to be used as a link between resource files and application source code. It's far easier to remember that a radio button labeled IDD_RES, if selected, identifies a request for .RES source files than to remember that this button has a numeric identifier of 213.

Of course, once the .RC resource script has been compiled and linked with the application's executable code, the defined constants will all be replaced, but since the computer does lack a few of the programmer's more human shortcomings, this isn't the point. After all, the header file and the mnemonics are for the programmer's benefit, not the computer's.

Like the other application resources discussed in this chapter, header files can be created using a plain text editor. However, both Borland's Resource Workshop and Microsoft's Developer Studio provide facilities for maintaining ID constants.

Headers and the Resource Workshop

In the Resource Workshop, you can view identifiers by selecting the Identifiers option from the Resources menu. This displays the dialog box shown in Figure 12.4.

As you may guess from the figure, the reported identifiers are drawn not only from the project, but also from all headers in any way associated with the project.

Unfortunately, the Resource Workshop falls short in two respects when trying to examine identifiers:

- It is very slow, as you wait for a host of headers to be opened, examined, and cataloged.

- The sheer volume of identifiers reported results in a massive and confusing overload of information. Programmers are rarely (if ever) looking for any identifiers that are not found in their project headers.

Using the Resource Workshop, it's easier to simply open the header files directly. Or you use a grep utility (a search utility) to search through specific files to find an identifier.

FIGURE 12.4

The Resource Workshop
Identifier dialog box

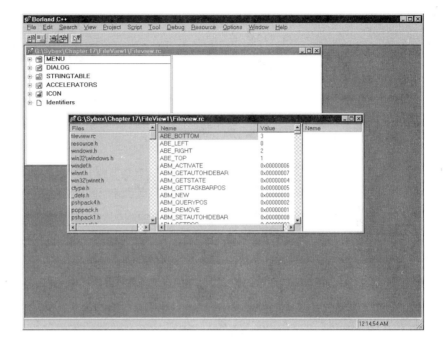

FIGURE 12.4

The Resource Workshop
Identifier dialog box

Headers and the Developer Studio

The Developer Studio handles headers more reasonably than does the Resource Workshop. Choose Resource Symbols from the View menu to see the dialog box shown in Figure 12.5.

The Resource Symbols dialog box displays identifiers specific to the current project. It shows the value of the identifier, whether the identifier is used in the application (unchecked items are often orphaned IDs that could be removed), and where the selected ID is used. If the ID is used in more than one location, which is common, all of the uses will be listed.

When you select a use location and click on the View Use button, the Developer Studio takes you directly to the appropriate source file.

The weakness of the Resource Symbols dialog box is that it does not function well with some non-MFC application source files. For example, using the FileView1 project, where the identifiers are all in the FileView.H header and not in

FIGURE 12.5

The Developer Studio
Resource Symbols
dialog box

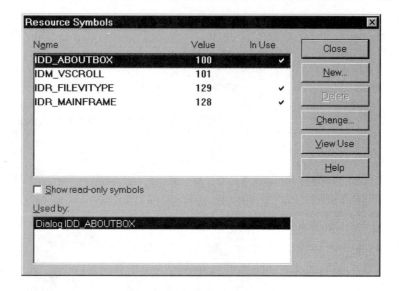

a Resource.H header, the dialog box fails completely. However, in most circumstances, the Resource Symbols dialog box is a very valuable tool.

If you do need to search for an identifier that is defined in one of the multitude of associated library headers, the Find in Files button (or menu option) in the Developer Studio is ideal, and it's far faster and more sophisticated than the Resource Workshop's Identifier feature.

An Example: The FileView1 Header File

The following is the FileView.H header file for the FileView application, presented in Chapter 13, shown in text format:

```
#define   IDS_NAME       1
#define   IDS_ERROR1     2
#define   IDS_ERROR2     3

#define   IDD_FNAME      16
#define   IDD_FPATH      17
#define   IDD_FLIST      18

#define   IDM_QUIT       101
```

```
#define   IDM_ABOUT    102
#define   IDM_OPEN     103
#define   IDM_TYPE     104

#define   IDD_BMP      201
#define   IDD_C        202
#define   IDD_COM      203
#define   IDD_CUR      204
#define   IDD_DAT      205
#define   IDD_DBS      206
#define   IDD_DLG      207
#define   IDD_DLL      208
#define   IDD_EXE      209
#define   IDD_H        210
#define   IDD_PAL      211
#define   IDD_RC       212
#define   IDD_RES      213
#define   IDD_TXT      214
#define   IDD_ANY      215
```

The Version Resource

The Version resource is a structured text block that contains company and product identification, a product release (version) number, and copyright and trademark notifications. A version resource editor allows you to add or delete string blocks or to modify individual string values. Figure 12.6 shows an example of the Developer Studio version resource editor.

NOTE   The Windows standard is for an application to contain only one version resource under the name VS_VERSION_INFO.

To use version information within an application, the GetFileVersionInfo and VerQueryValue functions offer access to the information. Your applications are not required to use a version resource, but it is a convenient location to collect information identifying the application and version.

FIGURE 12.6

The Developer Studio
version resource editor

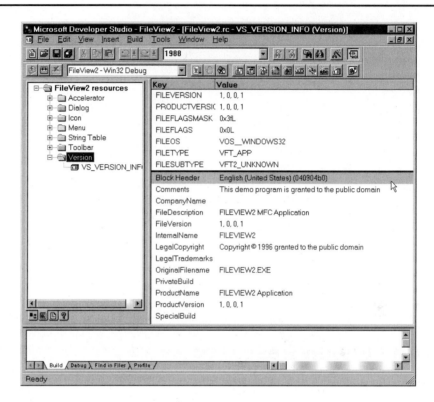

This chapter completes our discussion of individual application resources. In the next chapter, we finally arrive at the FileView application, of which you've seen only fragments so far.

Putting It All Together in a File Finder Application

- Global application resources

- Three dialog box resources for the FileView application

- A common dialog box resource for Windows NT/95 applications

In Chapters 9 through 12, resource elements for the FileView1 and FileView2 applications have been used as examples. Thus far, however, the FileView application itself has been mentioned only in passing. Now it's time to put everything together and create the application that uses these resources.

The FileView1 application is a relatively simple program designed to open a file of any type and display the contents in a columnar, hexadecimal format. It shows the file offset addresses at the right and the corresponding ASCII characters at the left. The main purpose of this application is to demonstrate how the application resources work together with the program.

The FileView2 application performs essentially the same task, but instead of the File Type and File Selection dialog boxes, it uses the common File Open dialog box. Its main purpose is to demonstrate how an application can be revised to take advantage of the MFC libraries.

Using Application Resources: The FileView1 Application

The FileView1 application uses three dialog boxes: About FileView, File Selection, and File Type. Figure 13.1 shows a composite of the application with its three dialog boxes.

Complete program listings for all the FileView1 source files appear at the end of this chapter and are also on the CD accompanying this book.

NOTE   If you do not have the CD that comes with this book, in addition to entering the source code, the two .ICO files must be supplied as binary format files. You can create these using the image editor in Microsoft's Developer Studio or Borland's Resource Workshop. See Chapter 9 for details.

FIGURE 13.1

The completed FileView1 demo program

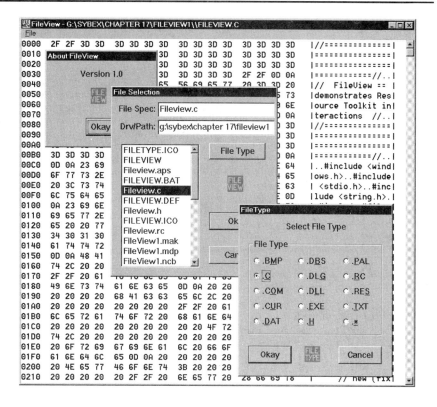

Loading Resources in WinMain

As you've learned, Windows loads application resources only when and as they are required and discards them when they are no longer needed. However, in the FileView demo application, one resource is required during initialization of the first instance of FileView: the application title. This title is contained in the string table, not in the source code. Thus, if no previous instance of FileView is active, during the instance initialization, the LoadString function is called to retrieve the appropriate entry from the string table, as:

```
if( !hPrevInstance ) // if no prev instance, t'is first
{
   LoadString( hInstance, IDS_NAME, (LPSTR) szAppName, 10 );
   wc.lpszClassName = szAppName;
```

In this case, since the application title is global, this string resource will be retained in memory without being discarded. In similar fashion, the application's cursor, icon, and menu are loaded as global resources:

```
wc.hCursor       = LoadCursor( NULL, IDC_ARROW );
wc.hIcon         = LoadIcon( hInstance, szAppName );
wc.lpszMenuName  = (LPSTR) szAppName;
```

This case, however, is not unique to the FileView1 application; a similar set of assignments appears in all Windows NT applications. However, when using an MFC-based application, most of these operations are concealed from the programmer, as you may observe (or not observe) by checking the FileView2 version.

Initializing Variables

Immediately following the instance initialization, provisions are also included to set default values for several global data variables:

```
iFileType = IDD_ANY - IDD_BMP;    // initial file type
lstrcpy( szFileExt, szFileType[iFileType] );
```

The `iFileType` variable is initialized using two symbolic constants, which are defined in the FileView.H header and which are used in the application resources. Once this is done, the `szFileExt` variable is initialized to match. Notice, however, that only global variables are being initialized, and this does not affect the initial settings of the dialog boxes.

Loading the Keyboard Accelerator

Later, but still in the `WinMain` procedure, another set of resources is required, because these, too, are global to the application and cannot be discarded until FileView1 terminates. This is the accelerator resource set, which is loaded immediately after the application has been initialized, as:

```
hAccel = LoadAccelerators( hInst, "FILEVIEW" );
while( GetMessage( &msg, NULL, 0, 0 ) )
{
    if( !TranslateAccelerator( hWndMain, hAccel, &msg ) )
    {
        TranslateMessage( &msg );
        DispatchMessage( &msg );
}   }
```

The `LoadAccelerators` function has returned a handle to the accelerator resource table. However, because this handle is a global variable, elsewhere in the program (as required), the handle could be assigned to a different accelerator table, but it would still be used in the `TranslateAccelerator` call in the `WinMain` message loop.

The `TranslateAccelerator` function filters all of the keyboard-event messages directed to the application, permitting the majority of these to simply pass through without interference. However, when a key combination—or, more accurately, a key event accompanied by the appropriate shift-state flags—matches one of the resource accelerator key events, this keyboard message is trapped or diverted. A new message—the action message defined for the accelerator event—is issued in its place.

Even applications that do not use accelerator keys will still call the message loop, but without the `TranslateAccelerator` invocation, as in:

```
while( GetMessage( &msg, NULL, 0, 0 ) )
{
    TranslateMessage( &msg );
    DispatchMessage( &msg );
}
```

Invoking Dialog Boxes

The three dialog boxes in the FileView1 application were created as dialog box resources and are handled by procedures declared in FileView.DEF as exported.

Once a dialog box has been invoked, the dialog procedure exists as an effectively independent subprogram. The exported procedure receives its own messages from Windows, not directly from the parent application. Thus, declaring a procedure as exported makes the procedure's address available to the Windows NT kernel so that messages can be passed to the dialog.

The three dialog procedures are invoked from instructions in the `WndProc` procedure, with very minimal invocations, as:

```
            case IDM_ABOUT:
                DialogBox( hInst, "ABOUT", hwnd, About );
                break;

            case IDM_TYPE:
                DialogBox( hInst, "FILETYPE", hwnd, FileType );
                break;
```

Long Filenames

The FileView1 demo program can display complete long filenames. It is not limited to the older DOS-style 8.3 filename format, even though it uses only the standard Windows API functions.

Specifically, in Figure 13.1, you can see the long directory names chapter 17 and fileview1, with ten and nine characters respectively, in the Drv/Path edit box, and three filenames with more than eight characters appear in the file list.

If you browse around your hard drive using the FileView1 application, you should notice that all of your long filenames and long directory names—no matter how long they are—appear without any conversions to the archaic 8.3 format.

And, considering that this is accomplished without any special provisions in the code, you may wonder why so many applications that purport to be Windows 95/NT compatible or even "Designed for Win95" remain incapable of displaying anything except the old and obsolete 8.3 filename formats.

A certain amount of ire is a natural response as you go searching through a series of 30 or 40 subdirectories, each rendered as CHAP~nn, trying to find out where your Chapter 17 directory actually is.

And, finally, if you are lucky and persevere, you may discover that Chapter 17 has been hashed to appear as CHAP~11...not exactly how you expected to find it.

Is this the product of a conspiracy of recalcitrant programmers who have banded together to attempt the preservation of the old format in the same fashion that L'Académie Française is attempting to preserve seventeenth century French?

Or is there some special stupidity at work here? It is definitely a mystery! (The solution appears later.)

Exported procedures, discussed in Chapter 2, are simply procedures that need to be visible (accessible) outside their immediate scope; that is, outside the source file or class where they are declared. Procedures that are used only locally do not require export declarations.

Under Windows 3.1, this dialog invocation would have to be somewhat more complex, and would look something like this:

```
case IDM_ABOUT:
    lpProc = MakeProcInstance( About, hInst );
    DialogBox( hInst, "ABOUT", hwnd, lpProc );
    FreeProcInstance( lpProc );
    break;
```

In fact, this format is still acceptable under Windows NT and 95, but it is also unnecessary. The MakeProcInstance procedure from Windows 3.1 is now defined as a macro that simply returns the first argument, with nothing required to create an instance of the procedure. And, since there is no requirement to create a procedure instance, the FreeProcInstance has also been redefined as a macro; this macro does absolutely nothing (aside from preventing the compiler from returning an error message because of an unrecognized term).

When the IDM_OPEN message is received, a slightly different response is used. It begins by initializing a directory path string and a file specification, passing these as arguments to the local CallFileOpen procedure, as:

```
case IDM_OPEN:      // set initial search path
    lstrcpy( szTmpFileSpec, szTmpFilePath );
    lstrcat( szTmpFileSpec, "*" );
    lstrcat( szTmpFileSpec, szFileType[iFileType] );
    if( CallFileOpen( hInst, hwnd,
            szTmpFileSpec, szFileType[iFileType],
            szTmpFilePath, szTmpFileName ) )
    {
```

The CallFileOpen procedure has a few minor tasks of its own before using the same DialogBox API function, which was used to call the preceding two dialogs.

The About dialog does very little except wait for the Okay button to be clicked, after which it returns. There is no return value—or, at least, no response to a returned value—because nothing is decided in this dialog.

The `FileType` and `FileOpen` dialogs, however, are not as simple. Even though they do return Boolean values, the major part of their work involves setting global string variables. This type of information cannot be conveniently treated as a returned value, even under Windows NT. The Boolean value returned by the exported `FileOpen` procedure to the `CallFileOpen` procedure and then to the `WndProc` procedure is used, however, because there is no reason to attempt to open a file if the user hasn't selected one; that is, if the Cancel button was selected instead of the Okay button.

But, before either of these dialogs can return anything, the dialog procedures themselves still have several tasks, including initializing the dialogs before they are displayed.

Initializing Dialogs

The `FileType` and `FileOpen` dialog procedures handle a number of operations, but at the moment, their responses to the `WM_INITDIALOG` messages are the important topic.

The `FileType` dialog procedure has only two important tasks. The first of these tasks is setting the check state of the radio button to match the `iFileType` variable, thus:

```
case WM_INITDIALOG:
    CheckRadioButton( hDlg, IDD_BMP, IDD_ANY,
                      IDD_BMP + iFileType );
    iInitType = iFileType;
    return( TRUE );
```

However, because the dialog buttons used for the 15 file extensions were defined as auto-radio buttons belonging to a single group, there is no requirement to reset the remaining 14; this part of the task is handled automatically.

This leaves the second task: setting the local variable, `iInitType`, equal to the global `iFileType`. Once this is done, the `FileType` dialog is ready for display and waiting for the user's selection.

On the other hand, the `FileOpen` dialog box has a bit more complicated initialization. It begins by retrieving the current or active drive and directory path, then sending the filename list box an initialization instruction setting the length of each entry to a generous 80 characters (just in case we want the long filenames supported by the NTFS file system or by the Windows NT/95 extended filename format).

```
case WM_INITDIALOG:
    GetCurrentDirectory( sizeof(OrgPath), OrgPath );
    SendDlgItemMessage( hDlg, IDD_FNAME, EM_LIMITTEXT,
                        80, 0L );
    DlgDirList( hDlg, szFileSpec, IDD_FLIST, IDD_FPATH,
                wFileAttr );
```

After initializing the list box, the next task is to fill it with entries from the current directory. This task is made almost automatic by the DlgDirList API function. After all, aside from a handle to the dialog box (hDlg), the only requirements are for the application to provide a file specification (szFileSpec), a destination (IDD_FLIST), a directory path specification (IDD_FPATH), and the desired file attribute flags (wFileAttr).

In other circumstances, we might want to use two list boxes: one for filenames and the other for drive and directory information. This is a convenient format used by many Windows applications. For this purpose, the wFileAttr flags for one list would specify files. For the other list, only directory information would be requested using a wDirAttr flag variable.

Finally, as a last step, the current file specification is added to the edit text box above the list box, as:

```
SetDlgItemText( hDlg, IDD_FNAME, szFileSpec );
return( TRUE );
```

Reading the Dialogs

In addition to setting initial information in the two dialog boxes, provisions are also required to retrieve information. And, as mentioned previously, each of these dialog procedures is essentially an independent subprogram.

The File Type Dialog

In the FileType dialog procedure, the important task is tracking the array of radio buttons; fortunately, this is very easily accomplished. Within the FileType dialog procedure, any button selections are tracked using the local variable, iInitType, leaving the global variable, iFileType, unaffected. In this fashion, when any of the

Long Filenames: The Solution

The solution to limiting filenames and directory names to the obsolete 8.3 format is actually quite simple. By specifying a 12-character limit—8 for the filename, 1 for the dot, and 3 for the extension—in the `SendDlgItemMessage` `EM_LIMITTEXT` instruction, the system is forced to report only the old-style filename whenever a longer format filename is encountered.

```
case WM_INITDIALOG:
    GetCurrentDirectory( sizeof(OrgPath), OrgPath );
    SendDlgItemMessage( hDlg, IDD_FNAME, EM_LIMITTEXT, 12, OL );
    DlgDirList( hDlg, szFileSpec,

                IDD_FLIST, IDD_FPATH, wFileAttr );
```

This is definitely a stupid limitation and does not excuse programmers from recognizing (or failing to recognize) new realities.

The guilty parties—and you know who you are—are sentenced to 50 lashes with a wet data stream…and no excuses.

Of course, in all fairness, if any of you are using filenames longer than 80 characters, my FileView1 version will truncate your filenames. But, somehow, I can't find it in my heart to worry unduly about this possibility.

radio buttons are clicked, the array of buttons automatically resets, because these were defined as auto-radio buttons belonging to a single group. The button selected, however, sends an event message to the `FileType` dialog, which is intercepted:

```
case WM_COMMAND:
    switch( LOWORD( wParam ) )
    {
        case IDD_BMP:    case IDD_C:
        case IDD_COM:    case IDD_CUR:
        case IDD_DAT:    case IDD_DBS:
        case IDD_DLG:    case IDD_DLL:
        case IDD_EXE:    case IDD_H:
        case IDD_PAL:    case IDD_RC:
        case IDD_RES:    case IDD_TXT:
        case IDD_ANY:
```

```
iFileType = LOWORD( wParam ) - IDD_BMP;
lstrcpy( szFileExt, szFileType[iFileType] );
return( TRUE );
```

Remember, the wParam argument contains the button identifier, which is a value that will be in the range of 201 to 215. The array of file type extensions, however, has indexes from 0 to 14. Therefore, the constant IDD_BMP is subtracted from the low word in wParam to provide a usable index value.

Last, if the Okay button is pressed, the global variable iFileType can be reset. If the Cancel button is selected instead, the global variable is left unchanged, despite any local selections.

The File Open Dialog

In the FileOpen dialog procedure, the responses are not quite as simple. First, in addition to the Okay and Cancel buttons, a third button is labeled File Type and returns the command message IDM_TYPE if selected. This offers an alternative method of calling the FileType dialog from within the FileOpen dialog. The response provided is very similar to the provisions in the WndProc procedure, as:

```
case IDM_TYPE:
    if( DialogBox( hInst, "FILETYPE",
                    hDlg, FileType ) )
```

If the FileType dialog returns TRUE, meaning that a new file type was selected, the file specification is reset, and the DlgDirList function is called to update the directory list box, much the same as when the dialog was initialized.

The list box, identified as IDD_FLIST, handles most of its own operations automatically, including scrolling, displaying text, and highlighting selections. There are, however, two messages that require handling within the dialog procedure: the LBN_SELCHANGE and LBN_DBLCLK arguments accompanying an IDD_FLIST command message. These arguments are passed as high-word values in the wParam argument and must be tested using the HIWORD macro, as:

```
case IDD_FLIST:
    switch( HIWORD( wParam ) )
    {
        case LBN_SELCHANGE:
```

The LBN_SELCHANGE message simply states that a new item in the list box was selected and, in response, the edit file (IDD_FNAME) should be updated accordingly.

As an alternative, if the dialog box had used a combo list box (combining a list box and edit field in a single feature), this task would be handled automatically, without involving the dialog procedure.

The second `IDD_FLIST` argument, `LBN_DBLCLK`, states that an item in the list box has been double-clicked, indicating an immediate selection. In response, the first step is to call the `DlgDirSelectEx` API function to check if the selected entry is a directory or a file:

```
case LBN_DBLCLK:
    if( DlgDirSelectEx( hDlg, szFileName,
            sizeof(szFileName), IDD_FLIST ) )
    {
        lstrcat( szFileName, szFileSpec );
        DlgDirList( hDlg, szFileName,
                    IDD_FLIST, IDD_FPATH,
                    wFileAttr );
        SetDlgItemText( hDlg, IDD_FNAME,
                        szFileSpec );

    }
```

If `DlgDirSelectEx` reports TRUE, having changed to the new directory, the `DlgDirList` function is called to update the list box and the edit field, and the process proceeds as before.

On the other hand, if a FALSE result is reported, the selection must be a filename rather than a directory and, therefore, the edit field is updated before sending an `IDOK` message to complete the selection process.

```
    else
    {
        SetDlgItemText( hDlg, IDD_FNAME,
                        szFileName );
        SendMessage( hDlg, WM_COMMAND,
                    IDOK, OL );
    }
    return( TRUE );
```

Because the edit field offers the user a chance for direct entry, the `IDD_FNAME` message is also checked for the `EN_CHANGE` argument in the high-word value of the `wParam` argument.

Two final provisions are responses for the `IDOK` and `IDCANCEL` command messages. In the case of an `IDOK` message, the response required is simply to check the edit box and retrieve the current entry before saving this as the selected filename.

```
case IDOK:
    GetDlgItemText( hDlg, IDD_FNAME, szFileName, 80 );
    ...
    EndDialog( hDlg, TRUE );
    return( TRUE );
```

The provisions for parsing the filename and the path/directory information are omitted here. This finishes by closing the dialog with a return message TRUE to indicate to the calling procedure that a filename has been selected.

For the IDCANCEL message, the response is simple. After restoring the original drive/directory, the dialog is closed with a return message of FALSE to report that no selection has been made.

```
case IDCANCEL:
    SetCurrentDirectory( OrgPath );
    EndDialog( hDlg, FALSE );
    return( TRUE );
```

Using the File Open Dialog: The FileView2 Application

The FileView2 version of our demo application has only one resource dialog, the About dialog, because the File Open dialog is a common dialog resource supplied by Windows NT and 95, not by the application. Also, where the FileView1 demo employed a File Type dialog, the FileView2 version omits this resource by loading the list of file types and associated extensions in the File Open dialog, where they appear in the Files of Type pull-down list. Figure 13.2 shows the FileView application with its two dialog boxes.

The main reason for discussing this second version is to show how the File Type and File Selection dialogs were replaced by the common File Open dialog. The heart of this part of the operation occurs in the OnFileOpen method in the CFileView2View class, where we begin by defining a pointer to the CFileDialog class.

```
void CFileView2View::OnFileOpen()
{
    // TODO: Add your command handler code here
    CFileDialog*    pFileDlg;
    CString         csFilter;
```

FIGURE 13.2

The completed FileView2 demo application

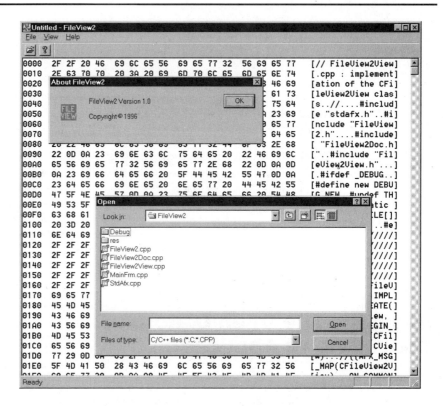

The CFileDialog class encapsulates the Windows common File dialog box, which implements both the File Open and File Save As (or File Save) dialog boxes.

> **TIP**
>
> The File Open and File Save As dialogs can also serve for any other file selection functions. Refer to the CFileDialog class documentation for details.

Defining a pointer to the class rather than an instance of the class provides a handle, which will, in a moment, point to an instance of the class. Before creating an instance of the class, however, there are some preparations.

```
csFilter =
    "Bitmaps (*.bmp)|*.bmp|"
    "C/C++ files (*.C,*.CPP)|*.c;*.cpp|"
    "Com files (*.com)|*.com|"
    "Cursors (*.cur)|*.cur|"
    "Data (*.dat)|*.dat|"
    "DBase files (*.dbs)|*.dbs|"
    "Dialogs (*.dlg)|*.dlg|"
    "Dynamic link libraries (*.dll)|*.dll|"
    "Executables (*.exe)|*.exe|"
    "Headers (*.h,*.hpp)|*.h;*.hpp|"
    "Palettes (*.pal)|*.pal|"
    "Resource scripts (*.rc)|*.rc|"
    "Resource files (*.res)|*.res|"
    "Text files (*.txt)|*.txt|"
    "All files (*.*)|*.*||";
```

The csFilter variable is an instance of the class CString and now contains a complete list of the file types and the file extensions for each type, with the | character used as a separator. Note also the doubled | |, which terminates the string.

NOTE When the csFilter string is passed to the CFileDialog instance, the | characters are interpreted as 0x00—null characters—which serve as delimiters.

Notice that each entry consists of two substrings. The first is the descriptive string, which will be displayed for selection. The second substring contains the file mask. In two cases—C/C++ and header files—two separate file masks are included by separating them with a semicolon (;).

There are no limits on the length of the prompt strings or file masks. Also, since a CString instance is not limited in length, there are no limitations on how many prompts and file masks can be included.

The only real stipulation that we need to observe is that the list provided will be presented in the exact same order; that is, the list of prompts and file masks will not be sorted.

Now, once we have the filter list, the CFileDialog instance can be created thus:

```
pFileDlg = new CFileDialog( TRUE, NULL, NULL,
                            OFN_HIDEREADONLY |
                            OFN_OVERWRITEPROMPT,
                            csFilter );
```

The calling parameters for the CFileDialog are defined as:

```
CFileDialog( BOOL bOpenFileDialog, LPCTSTR lpszDefExt = NULL,
             LPCTSTR lpszFileName = NULL,
             DWORD dwFlags = OFN_HIDEREADONLY |
OFN_OVERWRITEPROMPT,
             LPCTSTR lpszFilter = NULL, CWnd*
             pParentWnd = NULL );
```

The parameters used are defined as:

- bOpenFileDialog: Set to TRUE to construct a File Open dialog box, or to FALSE to construct a File Save As dialog box.

- lpszDefExt: Specifies a default filename extension. If the filename edit box entry does not include an extension when the Open File dialog returns, the lpszDefExt extension will be appended to the filename automatically. If this parameter is NULL, no file extension is appended.

- lpszFileName: Specifies a default filename that will appear in the filename edit box. If NULL, no initial filename appears.

- dwFlags: Specifies flags that are used to customize the dialog box. For a complete list of flags and options, refer to the OPENFILENAME structure in the Win32 SDK documentation.

- lpszFilter: A sequence of string pairs that specify the filters that may be applied to the files. If no filter is supplied, all files are accepted, unless the user supplies a file mask.

- pParentWnd: A pointer to the parent or owner window. If no parent or owner is specified, the Desktop becomes the parent.

Having provided the appropriate parameters, the CFileDialog instance is called using the DoModal method.

```
if( pFileDlg->DoModal() == IDOK )
{
```

Assuming that `DoModal` returns TRUE—meaning that the user has selected the Open (`IDOK`) button rather than the Cancel button—the `GetPathName` method is called to retrieve the selected filename and the complete path/directory specification.

Note that this information is available after the dialog returns but only as long as the `CFileDialog` instance has not closed. And, once we have this information, the `OpenFile` method is called.

```
    m_csFilePath = pFileDlg->GetPathName();
    OpenFile();
}
```

We can call the `OpenFile` method, which is a member of the `CFileView2View` class, without passing any arguments because the file information is contained in another member variable. This is the `CString` member `m_csFilePath`, which is directly available to the `OpenFile` method.

Last, we call the `delete` operator to close the `CFileDialog` instance, as:

```
    delete pFileDlg;
}
```

At this point, even though we're not finished with the file information (the file access and display is handled by other procedures), we are finished with the `CFileDialog` instance. Now we need to clean up, to avoid a memory leak, which may be minor but can cause problems in some cases. In any case, all class instances should be closed when they are no longer needed.

The remainder of the FileView2 demo provisions are quite similar to the ones in the FileView1 program. Its differences are the obvious changes appropriate to using an MFC-based application and some other changes to make appropriate use of object classes, such as `CStrings`, to replace more conventional variable types. If you're interested in the MFC variations, see the `OpenFile`, `FormatLine`, and `PaintFile` methods in the `CFileView2View` class.

Listings for the FileView1 source files follow. The remainder of the FileView application is relatively straightforward programming. This chapter has not explained all the program's operations, since the main point was to demonstrate a few interactions between the program code and the application resources. You can feel free to experiment with the source code listing, where you will find annotations to identify other areas of interest. The complete source files for both FileView1 and FileView2 are included on the CD accompanying this book.

Listing 13.1: The FileView1 Source Files

```
//===============//
//  FileView.H  //
//===============//

#define    IDS_NAME       1
#define    IDS_ERROR1     2
#define    IDS_ERROR2     3

#define    ID_NULL1      -1
#define    ID_NULL2      -2
#define    ID_NULL3      -3

#define    IDD_FNAME     16
#define    IDD_FPATH     17
#define    IDD_FLIST     18

#define    IDM_QUIT      101
#define    IDM_ABOUT     102
#define    IDM_OPEN      103
#define    IDM_TYPE      104

#define    IDD_BMP       201
#define    IDD_C         202
#define    IDD_COM       203
#define    IDD_CUR       204
#define    IDD_DAT       205
#define    IDD_DBS       206
#define    IDD_DLG       207
#define    IDD_DLL       208
#define    IDD_EXE       209
#define    IDD_H         210
#define    IDD_PAL       211
#define    IDD_RC        212
#define    IDD_RES       213
#define    IDD_TXT       214
#define    IDD_ANY       215

//===============//
//  FileView.C  //
//---------------//
```

```
long APIENTRY WndProc( HWND hwnd,   UINT msg,
                       UINT wParam, LONG lParam )
{
    static char szTmpFilePath[64];
    static char szTmpFileExt[5];
    static char szTmpFileSpec[64];
    static char szTmpFileName[64];
    static OFSTRUCT FileBuff;
    char    szBuff[128];
    DWORD   FilSz, FilSzHigh;
    int     hFil;

    switch( msg )
    {
      case WM_CREATE:
          GetCurrentDirectory( sizeof( szTmpFilePath ),
                               szTmpFilePath );
          lstrcat( szTmpFilePath, "\\" );
          lstrcpy( szTmpFileExt,  szFileType[iFileType] );
          lstrcpy( szTmpFileName, "" );
          HDisplay = 16L;
          break;

      case WM_COMMAND:
          switch( LOWORD( wParam ) )
          {
            case IDM_ABOUT:
                DialogBox( hInst, "ABOUT",
                           hwnd,  About );
                break;

            case IDM_TYPE:
                DialogBox( hInst, "FILETYPE",
                           hwnd,  FileType );
                break;

            case IDM_OPEN:      // set initial search path
                lstrcpy( szTmpFileSpec, szTmpFilePath );
                lstrcat( szTmpFileSpec, "*" );
                lstrcat( szTmpFileSpec,
                         szFileType[iFileType] );
```

```
if( CallFileOpen( hInst, hwnd,
      szTmpFileSpec, szFileType[iFileType],
      szTmpFilePath, szTmpFileName ) )
{
   lstrcpy( szFName, szTmpFilePath );
   lstrcat( szFName, "\\" );
   lstrcat( szFName, szTmpFileName );
   wsprintf( szBuff, "%s - %s",
              szAppName, szFName );
   SetWindowText( hwnd, szBuff );
   hFil = OpenFile( szFName, &FileBuff,
            OF_CANCEL | OF_PROMPT | OF_READ );
   if( hFil != -1 )        // get file size
   {
      FilSz = GetFileSize( (HANDLE) hFil,
                            &FilSzHigh );
      if( FilSz == 0xFFFFFFFF )
      {
         ErrorMsg( (char *) IDS_ERROR1 );
         break;
      }
      if( FilSzHigh > 0 )
      {
         ErrorMsg( (char *) IDS_ERROR2 );
         break;
      }
      FilLines =
         (int)(( FilSz + HDisplay - 1L )
              / HDisplay );
      FormatLine( szBuff, szFName,
                  HDisplay, NULL );
                     // get display width
      WndWidth = lstrlen( szBuff );
      vScrlPos = hScrlPos = 0;
      _lclose( hFil );
   }
   else               // if file open failed
   {
      SetWindowText( hwnd, "FileView" );
      FilLines = WndWidth = 0;
   }
   SetScrlRange( hwnd );
```

```
                    InvalidateRect( hwnd, NULL, TRUE );
                    UpdateWindow( hwnd );
            }  break;

        case IDM_QUIT:
            PostMessage( hwnd, WM_CLOSE, 0, 0L );
            break;

        default:
            return( DefWindowProc( hwnd,   msg,
                                   lParam, wParam ) );
    }  break;

case WM_SIZE:
    if( lParam )
    {
        WndY = HIWORD( lParam );   // get vert size
        WndX = LOWORD( lParam );   // get horiz size
        WndY = ( WndY / ChrV + 1 ) * ChrV;
        if( ( WndX / ChrX ) < 60 ) HDisplay =  8L;
                           else HDisplay = 16L;
        FilLines = (int)( ( FilSz + HDisplay-1L )
                        / HDisplay );
        SetScrlRange( hwnd );      // set scroll range
        lParam = MAKELONG( WndX, WndY );
    }  break;

case WM_VSCROLL:
    switch( LOWORD( wParam ) )
    {
        case SB_TOP:
            vInc = -vScrlPos;                        break;
        case SB_BOTTOM:
            vInc =  vScrlMax - vScrlPos;             break;
        case SB_LINEUP:
            vInc = -1;                               break;
        case SB_LINEDOWN:
            vInc =  1;                               break;
        case SB_PAGEUP:
            vInc = -max( 1, WndY / ChrY );           break;
        case SB_PAGEDOWN:
            vInc =  max( 1, WndY / ChrY );           break;
```

```
            case SB_THUMBPOSITION:
                vInc = LOWORD(lParam) - vScrlPos;     break;
            case SB_THUMBTRACK:
                vInc = LOWORD(lParam) - vScrlPos;     break;
            default:
                vInc = 0;
        }
        vInc = max( -vScrlPos,
                    min( vInc, vScrlMax - vScrlPos ) );
        if( vInc )
        {
            vScrlPos += vInc;
            ScrollWindow( hwnd, 0, -ChrY * vInc, 0L, 0L );
            SetScrollPos( hwnd, SB_VERT, vScrlPos, TRUE );
            UpdateWindow( hwnd );
        } break;

    case WM_HSCROLL:
        switch( LOWORD( wParam ) )
        {
            case SB_TOP:
                hInc = -hScrlPos;                       break;
            case SB_BOTTOM:
                hInc =  hScrlMax - hScrlPos;            break;
            case SB_LINEUP:
                hInc = -1;                              break;
            case SB_LINEDOWN:
                hInc =  1;                              break;
            case SB_PAGEUP:
                hInc = -8;                              break;
            case SB_PAGEDOWN:
                hInc =  8;                              break;
            case SB_THUMBPOSITION:
                hInc = LOWORD(lParam) - hScrlPos;     break;
            case SB_THUMBTRACK:
                hInc = LOWORD(lParam) - hScrlPos;     break;
            default:
                hInc = 0;
        }
        hInc = max( -hScrlPos,
                    min( hInc, hScrlMax - hScrlPos ) );
        if( hInc )
```

```
                {
                    hScrlPos += hInc;
                    ScrollWindow( hwnd, -ChrX * hInc, 0, 0L, 0L );
                    SetScrollPos( hwnd, SB_HORZ, hScrlPos, TRUE );
                    UpdateWindow( hwnd );
                } break;

        case WM_KEYDOWN:        // translate keydown messages
            switch( wParam )    //      to scrollbar messages
            {
                case VK_HOME:
                    SendMessage( hwnd, WM_HSCROLL,
                                 SB_TOP,     0L );
                    SendMessage( hwnd, WM_VSCROLL,
                                 SB_TOP,     0L );        break;
                case VK_END:
                    SendMessage( hwnd, WM_HSCROLL,
                                 SB_BOTTOM,  0L );
                    SendMessage( hwnd, WM_VSCROLL,
                                 SB_BOTTOM,  0L );        break;
                case VK_PRIOR:
                    SendMessage( hwnd, WM_VSCROLL,
                                 SB_PAGEUP,   0L );       break;
                case VK_NEXT:
                    SendMessage( hwnd, WM_VSCROLL,
                                 SB_PAGEDOWN, 0L );       break;
                case VK_UP:
                    SendMessage( hwnd, WM_VSCROLL,
                                 SB_LINEUP,   0L );       break;
                case VK_DOWN:
                    SendMessage( hwnd, WM_VSCROLL,
                                 SB_LINEDOWN, 0L );       break;
                case VK_LEFT:
                    SendMessage( hwnd, WM_HSCROLL,
                                 SB_PAGEUP,   0L );       break;
                case VK_RIGHT:
                    SendMessage( hwnd, WM_HSCROLL,
                                 SB_PAGEDOWN, 0L );       break;
            } break;
```

```
        case WM_PAINT:
            PaintFile( hwnd );                              break;

        case WM_CLOSE:
            DestroyWindow( hwnd );                          break;

        case WM_DESTROY:
            CloseFV();   PostQuitMessage(0);                break;

        case WM_QUERYENDSESSION:
            CloseFV();   return( (LONG) TRUE );

        default:
            return( DefWindowProc( hwnd,    msg,
                                   wParam, lParam ) );
    }
    return 0;
}


//=========================================================//
// WinMain - ViewFile main                                 //
//=========================================================//

int PASCAL WinMain( HANDLE hInstance,
                    HANDLE hPrevInstance,
                    LPSTR  lpszCmdLine,
                    int    cmdShow )
{
    MSG        msg;
    HDC        hdc;
    WNDCLASS   wc;
    TEXTMETRIC tm;

    if( !hPrevInstance ) // if no prev instance, t'is first
    {
        LoadString( hInstance, IDS_NAME,
                    (LPSTR) szAppName, 10 );
        wc.lpszClassName = szAppName;
        wc.hInstance     = hInstance;
        wc.lpfnWndProc   = WndProc;
        wc.hCursor       = LoadCursor( NULL, IDC_ARROW );
        wc.hIcon         = LoadIcon( hInstance, szAppName );
```

```
    wc.lpszMenuName   = (LPSTR) szAppName;
    wc.hbrBackground  = GetStockObject( WHITE_BRUSH );
    wc.style          = CS_HREDRAW | CS_VREDRAW;
    wc.cbClsExtra     = 0;
    wc.cbWndExtra     = 0;
    RegisterClass(&wc);
}
iFileType = IDD_ANY - IDD_BMP;      // initial file type
                                    // set default extension
lstrcpy( szFileExt, szFileType[iFileType] );
hInst = hInstance;      // global: save for window procs
hWndMain =
    CreateWindow( szAppName, szAppName,
        WS_OVERLAPPEDWINDOW | WS_HSCROLL | WS_VSCROLL,
        CW_USEDEFAULT,  0, CW_USEDEFAULT,  0,
        NULL, NULL, hInstance, NULL );
hdc = GetDC( hWndMain );
FontLog.lfHeight          = 6;
FontLog.lfWidth           = 6;
FontLog.lfEscapement      = 0;
FontLog.lfOrientation     = 0;
FontLog.lfWeight          = FW_NORMAL;
FontLog.lfItalic          = FALSE;
FontLog.lfUnderline       = FALSE;
FontLog.lfStrikeOut       = FALSE;
FontLog.lfCharSet         = ANSI_CHARSET;
FontLog.lfOutPrecision    = OUT_DEFAULT_PRECIS;
FontLog.lfClipPrecision   = CLIP_DEFAULT_PRECIS;
FontLog.lfQuality         = DEFAULT_QUALITY;
FontLog.lfPitchAndFamily  = FIXED_PITCH | FF_DONTCARE;
lstrcpy( FontLog.lfFaceName, "System" );
NewFont = CreateFontIndirect( (LPLOGFONT) &FontLog );
OrgFont = SelectObject( hdc, NewFont );
GetTextMetrics( hdc, &tm );
ChrX = tm.tmAveCharWidth;
ChrY = tm.tmHeight + tm.tmExternalLeading;
ChrV = tm.tmHeight;
ReleaseDC( hWndMain, hdc );
ShowWindow( hWndMain, cmdShow );
UpdateWindow( hWndMain );
hAccel = LoadAccelerators( hInst, "FILEVIEW" );
while( GetMessage( &msg, NULL, 0, 0 ) )
```

```
    {
      if( !TranslateAccelerator( hWndMain, hAccel, &msg ) )
      {
        TranslateMessage( &msg );
        DispatchMessage( &msg );
    }  }
    return(msg.wParam);
}



//===============================//
//  FileView.RC resource script  //
//===============================//

#include <windows.h>
#include "fileview.h"

FILETYPE ICON "filetype.ico"
FILEVIEW ICON "fileview.ico"

ABOUT DIALOG 10, 35, 89, 67
STYLE DS_MODALFRAME | WS_POPUP | WS_CAPTION
CAPTION "About FileView"
BEGIN
    CONTROL "Version 1.0", 0, "STATIC", SS_CENTER |
                    WS_CHILD | WS_VISIBLE, 0, 6, 89, 12
    ICON "FILEVIEW", 0, 36, 21, 16, 16
    PUSHBUTTON "Okay", IDOK, 32, 45, 24, 14, WS_CHILD |
                    WS_VISIBLE | WS_TABSTOP
END

FILETYPE DIALOG 8, 25, 126, 127
STYLE WS_POPUP | WS_CAPTION
CAPTION "FileType"
BEGIN
    CONTROL ".B&MP", IDD_BMP, "BUTTON", BS_AUTORADIOBUTTON |
            WS_CHILD | WS_VISIBLE, 11, 30, 36, 13
    CONTROL ".&C",   IDD_C,   "BUTTON", BS_AUTORADIOBUTTON |
            WS_CHILD | WS_VISIBLE, 11, 42, 36, 13
    CONTROL ".DL&G", IDD_DLG, "BUTTON", BS_AUTORADIOBUTTON |
            WS_CHILD | WS_VISIBLE, 48, 42, 36, 13
    CONTROL ".&RC",  IDD_RC,  "BUTTON", BS_AUTORADIOBUTTON |
```

```
                    WS_CHILD | WS_VISIBLE, 85, 42, 36, 13
        CONTROL ".C&OM", IDD_COM, "BUTTON", BS_AUTORADIOBUTTON |
                WS_CHILD | WS_VISIBLE, 11, 54, 36, 13
        CONTROL ".D&LL", IDD_DLL, "BUTTON", BS_AUTORADIOBUTTON |
                WS_CHILD | WS_VISIBLE, 48, 54, 36, 13
        CONTROL ".RE&S", IDD_RES, "BUTTON", BS_AUTORADIOBUTTON |
                WS_CHILD | WS_VISIBLE, 85, 54, 36, 13
        CONTROL ".C&UR", IDD_CUR, "BUTTON", BS_AUTORADIOBUTTON |
                WS_CHILD | WS_VISIBLE, 11, 66, 36, 13
        CONTROL ".&EXE", IDD_EXE, "BUTTON", BS_AUTORADIOBUTTON |
                WS_CHILD | WS_VISIBLE, 48, 66, 36, 13
        CONTROL ".&TXT", IDD_TXT, "BUTTON", BS_AUTORADIOBUTTON |
                WS_CHILD | WS_VISIBLE, 85, 66, 36, 13
        CONTROL ".&DAT", IDD_DAT, "BUTTON", BS_AUTORADIOBUTTON |
                WS_CHILD | WS_VISIBLE, 11, 78, 36, 13
        CONTROL ".&H",   IDD_H,   "BUTTON", BS_AUTORADIOBUTTON |
                WS_CHILD | WS_VISIBLE, 48, 78, 36, 13
        CONTROL ".&*",   IDD_ANY, "BUTTON", BS_AUTORADIOBUTTON |
                WS_CHILD | WS_VISIBLE, 85, 78, 36, 13
        CONTROL ".D&BS", IDD_DBS, "BUTTON", BS_AUTORADIOBUTTON |
                WS_CHILD | WS_VISIBLE, 48, 30, 36, 13
        CONTROL ".&PAL", IDD_PAL, "BUTTON", BS_AUTORADIOBUTTON |
                WS_CHILD | WS_VISIBLE, 85, 30, 36, 13
        CONTROL "File Type", -1, "BUTTON", BS_GROUPBOX |
                WS_CHILD | WS_VISIBLE, 7, 19, 111, 76
        CONTROL "Select File Type", -1, "STATIC", SS_CENTER |
                WS_CHILD | WS_VISIBLE, 15, 5, 96, 10
    ICON "FILETYPE", -1, 54, 104, 16, 16
    DEFPUSHBUTTON "Okay", IDOK, 7, 104, 36, 14, WS_CHILD |
            WS_VISIBLE | WS_TABSTOP
    PUSHBUTTON "Cancel", IDCANCEL, 82, 104, 36, 14, WS_CHILD |
            WS_VISIBLE | WS_TABSTOP
END

OPENFILE DIALOG 10, 36, 134, 141
STYLE DS_MODALFRAME | WS_POPUP | WS_CAPTION
CAPTION "File Selection"
BEGIN
    CONTROL "File Spec:", 0, "STATIC", SS_RIGHT | WS_CHILD |
            WS_VISIBLE, 0, 5, 35, 10
    CONTROL "Drv/Path:", 0, "STATIC", SS_RIGHT | WS_CHILD |
            WS_VISIBLE, 0, 19, 35, 10
```

```
            CONTROL "*.*", 16, "EDIT", ES_LEFT | WS_CHILD |
                    WS_VISIBLE | WS_BORDER | WS_TABSTOP, 37, 4, 96, 12
            EDITTEXT 17, 37, 18, 96, 12
            CONTROL "LISTBOX", 18, "LISTBOX", LBS_STANDARD |
                    WS_CHILD | WS_VISIBLE, 7, 37, 64, 99
            ICON "FILEVIEW", 0, 94, 62, 16, 16
            PUSHBUTTON "File Type", IDM_TYPE, 79, 36, 46, 13,
                    WS_CHILD | WS_VISIBLE | WS_TABSTOP
            DEFPUSHBUTTON "Okay", IDOK, 79, 91, 46, 14,
                    WS_CHILD | WS_VISIBLE | WS_TABSTOP
            PUSHBUTTON "Cancel", IDCANCEL, 79, 118, 46, 14,
                    WS_CHILD | WS_VISIBLE | WS_TABSTOP
    END


    STRINGTABLE
    BEGIN
        IDS_NAME,   "FileView"
        IDS_ERROR1, "File size indeterminate"
        IDS_ERROR2, "File too large for present example"
    END


    FILEVIEW MENU
    BEGIN
        POPUP "&File"
        BEGIN
            MENUITEM "&Open...\t^O", 103
            MENUITEM "&Type...\t^T", 104
            MENUITEM SEPARATOR
            MENUITEM "&About", 102
            MENUITEM "E&xit\t^X", 101
        END
    END


    FILEVIEW ACCELERATORS
    BEGIN
        "X", 101, VIRTKEY, CONTROL
        "O", 103, VIRTKEY, CONTROL
        "T", 104, VIRTKEY, CONTROL
    END
```

PART III

Advanced
Application
Designs

CHAPTER

FOURTEEN

14

Creating and Synchronizing Multiple Threads

- How threads work

- Commands for creating and modifying threads

- Mutexes, events, semaphores, and critical sections for synchronizing threads

- A demonstration of threads in action: the Threads demo program

A program of any complexity at all is a maze of instructions that loop and branch, full of forks, jumps, and returns. The processor makes decisions as the program runs, and each decision leads through a different set of instructions. Each time the program executes, the processor follows a different path from start to termination. When Theseus fought the Minotaur, he marked his way through the labyrinth by unwinding a thread behind him. When a Windows NT or 95 program wants to do several things at once, it creates objects called threads, and each thread winds its own way through the program's code.

Another way to look at it is to say that threads let a program be in two places at once. The system keeps a list of all the threads and cycles through them, giving each a slice of time on the processor. When a time slice ends, the system records the current CPU register values in the thread object, including a pointer to whatever instruction the thread was about to execute. The system then selects another thread, restores *its* CPU registers, and resumes execution wherever the thread last left off. A thread marks a location in the program, and by marking several locations with different threads, the program effectively clones itself and seems to execute in many places at the same time.

This chapter begins with a conceptual introduction to threads, then surveys the commands for using threads, and finishes with a sample program demonstrating threads. By the end of this chapter, you will understand when and how to create threads in your programs, how to manage them while they run, and how to synchronize them so they don't interfere with each other. Mutexes, semaphores, events, and critical sections will hold no more mysteries for you.

Thread Concepts

Threads are closely related to processes. A process is a program loaded into memory, complete with all the resources assigned to the program. But a process is static and does nothing by itself.

A thread executes program commands, following a path through the code. Every process possesses one initial thread. Optionally, the initial thread (also called the *primary thread*) may create other threads. All the threads belonging to one process share the assets of that process. They all follow instructions from the same code image, refer to the same global variables, write to the same private address space, and have access to the same objects. A process is a house, which is inhabited by threads.

Life without Threads

While an operation without threads does accomplish similar tasks, the process of doing so is less versatile. For a single-threaded application, initiating a subprocess (or child process) requires temporarily tabling the main process and resuming only when the subprocess is completed.

In earlier versions of Windows, all applications were single-threaded of necessity, even though Windows itself performed something like a multithreaded process, sharing processor time among multiple applications so that each had its own chance to execute.

At the same time, background processes, such as spell-checking, image rendering, or file maintenance, are often relegated to low priority; GUI processes, which are immediately visible to the user, take precedence. Without threads, when tasks of this nature become active, the allocation of resources often results in a slow response from the GUI elements. Threads, although not in themselves a cure-all, do permit a smoother sharing of time in such circumstances.

When to Create Threads and Processes

You should consider creating new threads anytime your program handles asynchronous activity. Programs with multiple windows, for example, generally benefit from creating a thread for each window. Most MDI (Multi-Document Interface) applications create threads for the child windows. A program that interacts with several asynchronous devices creates threads for responding to each device.

A desktop publisher, for example, might assign responsibility for the main window to a single thread of high priority. When the user initiates a lengthy operation, such as pouring text into an empty layout, the program creates a new thread to do the formatting in the background. Meanwhile, the first thread continues to manage the main window and responds quickly to new commands from the user. If the user then asks to cancel the formatting, the input thread can interrupt the formatting thread by terminating it. Threads can also be useful for performing slow disk operations in the background or for communicating with other processes. One thread sends messages, and another waits to receive them.

One example of synchronous activity that might be familiar to many users is using a contemporary word processor with the automatic spell-checker enabled. Here one (or probably more) threads are responsible for responding to the keyboard activity, updating the text on the screen, and managing regular updates of the backup version of the working file. But, at the same time, one thread is busy checking what has been written against the selected dictionary, and when a word is not recognized, sending a message to tell the display thread to highlight the unknown word. As long as the word processor is working smoothly, all of these tasks are occurring synchronously, even though at different rates.

Any thread can create other threads. Any thread can also create new processes. When a program needs to do several things at once, it must decide whether to create threads or processes to share the work. Choose threads whenever you can because the system creates them quickly and they interact with each other easily. Creating a process takes longer because the system must load a new executable file image from the disk. However, a new process has the advantage of receiving its own private address space. You might choose processes over threads as a way of preventing them from interfering, even accidentally, with each other's resources. For more details about processes, see Chapter 15.

Thread Objects

At the system level, a thread is an object created by the Object Manager. Like all system objects, a thread contains data, or attributes, and functions, or methods. Figure 14.1 represents a thread object schematically, listing its attributes and methods.

Most of the thread methods have corresponding Win32 functions. When you call `SuspendThread`, for example, the Win32 subsystem responds by calling the thread's `Suspend` method. In other words, the Win32 API *exposes* the `Suspend` method to Win32 applications.

> **NOTE**
>
> The Win32 API (Application Program Interface) is a library (or libraries) of methods that are called directly or indirectly by applications to request services that are performed by the operating system. For a simple example, asking for a list of files or directories is accomplished through an API call.

FIGURE 14.1

A thread object contains attributes and methods.

STANDARD OBJECT HEADER	
Thread Attributes	**Thread Methods**
Client ID	Create thread
Context	Open thread
Dynamic priority	Query thread information
Base priority	Set thread information
Processor affinity	Current thread
Exicutiontime	Terminate thread
Alert Status	Get context
Suspension count	Set context
Impersonation token	Suspend
Termination port	Resume
Exit status	Alert
	Test alert
	Register termination port

The Thread Context attribute is the data structure for saving the machine state whenever the thread stops executing. We'll explain other attributes as we proceed.

Objects and Handles

Programs that run at the system's user level (as opposed to the more privileged Kernel level) may not directly examine or modify the inside of a system object. Only by calling Win32 API routines can you do anything at all with an object. Windows has always protected some internal structures, such as windows and brushes, from direct manipulation. Windows gives you a handle to identify the object, and you pass the handle to functions that need it. Threads, too, have handles (as do processes, semaphores, files, and many other objects). Windows NT, designed from the ground up to be a secure system, protects its internal structures much more effectively than 16-bit Windows ever did. Only the Object Manager touches the inside of an object.

The function that creates a thread returns a handle to the new object. With the handle, you can do the following:

- Raise or lower the thread's scheduling priority

- Make the thread pause and resume

- Terminate the thread

- Find out what value the thread returned when it ended

Scheduling and Synchronizing Threads

Working with threads requires more than just starting and stopping them. You also need to make threads work together, and effective interaction requires control over timing. Timing control takes two forms: priority and synchronization. Priority controls how often a thread gets processor time. Synchronization regulates threads when they compete for shared resources and imposes a sequence when several threads must accomplish tasks in a certain order.

Process, Base, and Dynamic Priority

When the system scheduler preempts one thread and looks for another to run next, it gives preference to threads of high priority. Some activities, such as responding to an unexpected power loss, always execute at a very high priority. System interrupt handlers have a higher priority than user processes. Every process has a priority rating, and threads derive their base scheduling priority from the process that owns them.

In Figure 14.1, shown earlier, you can see that a thread object's attributes include a base priority and a dynamic priority. When you call commands to change a thread's priority, you change the base priority. You cannot push a thread's priority more than two steps above or below the priority of its process. Threads can't grow up to be very much more important than their parents.

Although a process cannot promote its threads very far, the system can. The system grants a sort of field promotion (dynamic priority) to threads that undertake important missions. When the user gives input to a window, for example, the system always elevates all the threads in the process that owns the window. When a thread waiting for data from a disk drive finally receives it, the system promotes that thread, too. These temporary boosts, added to the thread's current base priority, form the dynamic priority. The scheduler chooses threads to execute based on their dynamic priority. Process, base, and dynamic priorities are distinguished in Figure 14.2.

Dynamic priority boosts begin to degrade immediately. A thread's dynamic priority slips back one level each time the thread receives another time slice and finally stabilizes at the thread's base priority.

How Scheduling Happens

To select the next thread, the scheduler begins at the highest priority queue, executes the threads there, and then works its way down the rest of the list. But the

FIGURE 14.2

How the range of a thread's priority derives from the priority of the process

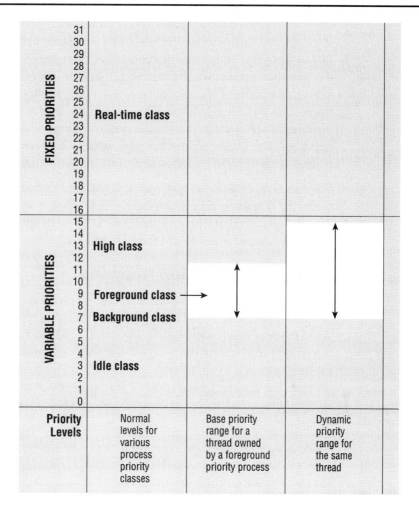

dispatcher ready queue may not contain all the threads in the system. Some may be suspended or blocked. At any moment, a thread may be in one of six states:

- **Ready:** Queued, waiting to execute
- **Standby:** Ready to run next (in the batter's box)
- **Running:** Executing; interacting with the CPU
- **Waiting:** Not executing; waiting for a signal to resume
- **Transition:** About to execute when the system loads its context
- **Terminated:** Finished executing, but the object is not deleted

When the scheduler selects a ready thread from the queue, it loads a *context* for the thread. The context includes a set of values for the machine registers, the Kernel stack, a thread environment block, and a user stack in the address space of the thread's process. (If part of the context has been paged to disk, the thread enters the transition state while the system gathers the pieces.) Changing threads means saving all the pieces of one context and loading into the processor all the pieces of the next one. The newly loaded thread runs for one time slice, which is likely to be on the order of 20 milliseconds. The system maintains a counter measuring the current time slice. On each clock tick, the system decrements the counter; when it reaches 0, the scheduler performs a context switch and sets a new thread running.

For those familiar with how multiple executables function under Windows 3.1, executing threads is very much like executing separate applications. The real difference is simply that single applications are now able to separate tasks for parallel execution instead of executing them in serial fashion.

How Synchronization Happens

To run at all, threads must be scheduled; to run well, they often need to be synchronized. Suppose one thread creates a brush and then creates several threads that share the brush and draw with it. The first thread must not destroy the brush until the other threads finish drawing. Or suppose one thread accepts input from the user and writes it to a file, while another thread reads from the file and processes the text. The reading thread mustn't read while the writing thread is writing. Both situations require a means of coordinating the sequence of actions in several threads.

One solution would be to create a global Boolean variable that one thread uses to signal another. The writing thread might set bDone to TRUE, and the reading thread might loop until it sees the flag change. That would work, but the looping thread wastes a lot of processor time. Instead, Win32 supports a set of synchronization objects:

- A *mutex* object works like a narrow gate for one thread to pass at a time.

- A *semaphore* object works like a multiple-lane toll gate that a limited number of threads can pass through together.

- An *event* object broadcasts a public signal for any listening thread to hear.

- A *critical section* object works just like a mutex but only within a single process.

All are system objects created by the Object Manager. Although each synchronization object coordinates different interactions, they all work in a similar way. A thread that wants to perform some coordinated action waits for a response from one of these objects and proceeds only after receiving it. The scheduler removes waiting objects from the dispatch queue so they do not consume processor time. When the signal arrives, the scheduler allows the thread to resume.

How and when the signal arrives depends on the object. For example, the one essential characteristic of a mutex is that only one thread can own it. A mutex doesn't do anything apart from letting itself be owned by one thread at a time. ("Mutex" stands for *mut*ual *ex*clusion.) If several threads need to work with a single file, you might create a mutex to protect the file. Whenever any thread begins a file operation, it first asks for the mutex. If no one else has the mutex the thread proceeds. If, on the other hand, another thread has just grabbed the mutex for itself, the request fails and the thread *blocks*, becoming suspended while it waits for ownership. When one thread finishes writing it releases the mutex, and the waiting thread revives, receives the mutex, and performs its own file operations.

The mutex does not actively protect anything. It only works because the threads that use it agree not to write to the file without owning the mutex first. Nothing actually prevents all the threads from trying to write at once. The mutex is just a signal, much like the Boolean bDone in our looping example. You might create a mutex to protect global variables, a hardware port, a handle to a pipe, or a window's client area. Whenever several threads share any system resource you should consider whether to synchronize their use of it.

Mutexes, semaphores, and events can coordinate threads in different processes, but critical sections are only visible to threads in a single process. When one process creates a child process, the child often inherits handles to existing synchronization objects. Critical section objects cannot be inherited.

Fundamentally a synchronization object, like other system objects, is simply a data structure. Synchronization objects have two states: signaled and not signaled. Threads interact with synchronization objects by changing the signal or waiting for the signal. A waiting thread is blocked and does not execute. When the signal occurs, the waiting thread receives the object, turns the signal off, performs some synchronized task, and turns the signal back on when it relinquishes the object.

Threads can wait for other objects besides mutexes, semaphores, events, and critical objects. Sometimes it makes sense to wait for a process, a thread, a timer, or a file. These objects serve other purposes as well, but like the synchronization objects they also possess a signal state. Processes and threads signal when they terminate. Timer objects signal when a certain interval passes. Files signal when a read or write operation finishes. Threads can wait for any of these signals.

Bad synchronization causes bugs. For example, a deadlock bug occurs when two threads wait for each other. Neither will end unless the other ends first. A race condition occurs when a program fails to synchronize its threads. Suppose one thread writes to a file, and another thread reads the new contents. Whether the program works depends on which thread wins the race to its I/O operation. If the writing thread wins, the program works. If the reading thread tries to read first, the program fails.

Threads and Multiprocessors

Most of us are still relying on single-CPU systems, but the trend of the future is clear: multiprocessor systems. There are desktop systems available with as many as four CPUs. It is in a multiprocessor environment where threads come into their own.

With multiple processors to handle tasking, the system is able to allocate different threads to different processors. It can spread the load, such as when one application makes heavy demands for CPU resources, across the several CPUs, with different CPUs executing separate tasks simultaneously for different threads.

One area where this will be particularly advantageous is in 3-D modeling and image processing. Different aspects of creating an image can be shared by different threads among two or more CPUs. Another area is in Windows itself, which is required to handle a variety of tasks of its own in addition to supporting applications. Again, a workload shared among several processors makes faster progress than sharing time-slices on a single processor.

About Win32 Object Handles

Under 16-bit Windows, an object has only one handle. The handle may be copied into several variables, but it is still one handle. And when the object is destroyed, all the copies of the handle become invalid. Some of the new objects in Win32, however, work differently. Several threads or processes may have different handles to the same object. Brushes, windows, and device contexts still support only one handle; but a single thread, process, or mutex, for example, may have many different handles. As each finishes with the object, it calls `CloseHandle`. When the last handle closes, the system destroys the object.

> **NOTE** Although the total number of handles in the system is limited only by available memory, no single process may possess more than 65,536 open handles.

Thread-Related Commands

As an introduction to the features of multithreaded programming, this section surveys the parts of the Win32 API that relate to threads. The first half explains commands for creating and modifying threads, and the second half concentrates on commands for synchronizing threads.

Making and Modifying Threads

The life cycle of a thread begins when you call `CreateThread`. Other functions let you examine the thread, suspend or resume it, change its priority, and terminate it.

Creating Threads

Any thread can create another thread by calling `CreateThread`. The arguments to `CreateThread` specify the properties a thread needs to begin life: primarily security privileges and a starting function. The starting function is to a thread what `main` or `WinMain` is to a full program. The thread's life coincides with the life of its main function. When the function returns, the thread ends. A thread can start at any function that receives a single 32-bit parameter and returns a 32-bit value.

The parameter and return value are for your convenience. You need to declare them, but you don't need to use them. `CreateThread` lets you pass a `DWORD` into the starting function. If several threads execute the same function, you might pass each one a different argument. Each might receive a pointer to a different filename, for example, or a different object handle to wait for.

The Parameters   CreateThread takes six parameters:

```
// prototype for the CreateThread function
HANDLE CreateThread(
  LPSECURITY_ATTRIBUTES  lpThreadAttributes,// access privileges
  DWORD                  dwStackSize,       // say 0 for default
  LPTHREAD_START_ROUTINElpStartAddress,     // pointer to function
  LPVOID                 lpParameter,       // value to function
  DWORD                  dwCreationFlags,   // active or suspended
  LPDWORD                lpThreadId );      // system returns ID
```

The first parameter points to a SECURITY_ATTRIBUTES structure that determines who may share the object and whether other processes may be allowed to modify it. The structure contains a security descriptor that assigns access privileges for various system users and groups of users. Most programs simply accept the default descriptor that comes with the current process. The security structure also contains an inheritance flag. If you set the flag to TRUE, any child processes you create will automatically inherit a handle to this object.

```
typedef struct _SECURITY_ATTRIBUTES        /* sa */
{
  DWORD  nLength;                // sizeof(SECURITY_ATTRIBUTES)
  LPVOID lpSecurityDescriptor;   // NULL to accept descriptor
  BOOL   bInheritHandle;         // TRUE if children may inherit
    object
} SECURITY_ATTRIBUTES, *LPSECURITY_ATTRIBUTES;
```

You don't need to create a SECURITY_ATTRIBUTES structure unless you want the thread to be inherited. If you pass NULL as the first parameter to CreateThread, the new thread receives the default descriptor and will not be inherited. If you do want to create a handle with limited access rights to its object, investigate the four SetSecurityDescriptor functions.

The next three parameters give the new thread material to work with. By default, each thread receives a stack the same size as that of the primary thread. You can change the size with the second parameter. If the stack later needs more room, the system expands it automatically. The third parameter points to the function where the thread will start, and the value in the fourth parameter becomes the argument passed to the starting function.

> **WARNING** Beware of using a local variable to pass a value to a new thread. The local variable will be destroyed when its procedure ends, and the thread may not have used it yet. Use global variables, allocate memory dynamically, or make the first thread wait for the new thread to terminate before it returns.

The `dwCreationFlags` parameter may be one of two values: either 0 or `CREATE_SUSPENDED`. A suspended thread does not actually begin to run until you give it a push with `ResumeThread`. A program that creates a number of threads might suspend them, accumulate their handles, and, when ready, start them all off at once. That's what the sample program presented later in the chapter does.

The last parameter points to an empty `DWORD` where `CreateThread` places a number to identify the thread uniquely in the system. A few functions require you to identify threads by their ID number instead of by their handles.

The Return Value   `CreateThread` returns a handle to the new thread. If the thread could not be created, the handle will be NULL. Be aware that the system will create the thread even if the `lpStartAddress` or `lpParameter` values are invalid or point to inaccessible data. In those cases, `CreateThread` returns a valid handle, but the new thread terminates immediately and returns an error code. You can test a thread's viability with `GetExitCodeThread`, which returns `STILL_ACTIVE` if the thread has not ended.

Unless you give `CreateThread` an explicit security descriptor, the new handle comes with full access rights to the new object. In the case of threads, full access means that with this handle you can suspend, resume, terminate, or change the priority of the thread. The handle remains valid even after the thread terminates. To destroy the thread object, close its handle by calling `CloseHandle`. If more than one handle exists, the thread will not be destroyed until the last handle is closed. If you forget to close the handle, the system will do it automatically when your process ends.

Creating Threads Using MFC

An alternative method of creating threads using MFC is to create a class based on the CWinThread class. A skeletal example of the process follows.

```
// CThreadExample

IMPLEMENT_DYNCREATE(CThreadExample, CWinThread)

CThreadExample::CThreadExample()
{
    ...    // class member variables are initialized
}


CThreadExample::~CThreadExample()
{
}

BOOL CThreadExample::InitInstance()
{
    // TODO:  perform any per-thread initialization here
    ...
    // this is the point where non-variable initializations,
    // such as creating instances of other class objects, are
    // handled
    return TRUE;
}


int CThreadExample::ExitInstance()
{
    // TODO:  perform any per-thread cleanup here
    ...
    return CWinThread::ExitInstance();
}


BEGIN_MESSAGE_MAP(CThreadExample, CWinThread)
    //{{AFX_MSG_MAP(CThreadExample)
    // NOTE - ClassWizard will add/remove mapping macros here.
    //}}AFX_MSG_MAP
END_MESSAGE_MAP()
```

A CWinThread object represents an execution thread within an application. Where the application's main thread of execution is normally provided by a

CWinApp-derived object, the CWinApp class itself is derived from CWinThread. Additional CWinThread objects, as shown in the example above, allow multiple threads within the application.

MFC-based applications must use CWinThread-derived classes to ensure that the application is thread-safe. Under MFC, the framework uses thread-local data to maintain thread-specific information for CWinThread-managed objects.

Furthermore, any thread created by the runtime function _beginthreadex cannot use any MFC APIs.

MFC Thread Types   Two general types of threads are supported: working threads and user-interface threads. Working threads do not require a message handler as, for example, a thread performing background calculations in a spreadsheet. Working threads can be derived.

In contrast, user-interface threads must process messages received from the system (from the user) and require a message handler. User-interface threads can be derived from CWinApp or directly from the CWinThread class.

A CWinThread object commonly exists for the duration of the thread, but the behavior of the object may be modified by setting the m_bAutoDelete member to FALSE.

Creating an MFC Thread   Threads are created by calling AfxBeginThread. For a user-interface thread, AfxBeginThread is called with a pointer to the CRuntimeClass of the CWinThread-derived class.

For a worker thread, AfxBeginThread is called with a pointer to the controlling function and the parameter for the controlling function.

For both worker and user-interface threads, additional parameters can be specified to modify the priority, stack size, creation flags, and security attributes for the thread. AfxBeginThread returns a pointer to the new CWinThread object.

Alternatively, a CWinThread-derived object can be constructed and then created by calling the CreateThread function for the class. Using this format permits the CWinThread-derived object to be reused between successive creations and terminations of thread executions.

Changing a Thread's Priority

High-priority threads get more time on the processor, finish their work more quickly, and are more responsive to the user. But making all of your threads high priority entirely defeats the purpose of priorities. If a number of threads have the same priority—whether their priority is high or low—the scheduler must give them equal processor time. One thread can be more responsive only if the others are less responsive. The same rule applies equally to processes. Restrict your threads and processes as much as possible to low or average priority levels, and stay at high levels only as long as you must.

These functions retrieve or modify any thread's base priority:

```
BOOL SetThreadPriority(
    HANDLE hThread                    // a thread to modify
    int    iPriority );               // its new priority level

int GetThreadPriority( HANDLE hThread );
```

SetThreadPriority returns TRUE or FALSE for success or failure. GetThread-Priority returns the thread's current priority. A set of constants names the possible priority values for both functions.

- THREAD_PRIORITY_LOWEST: Two levels below process

- THREAD_PRIORITY_BELOW_NORMAL: One level below process

- THREAD_PRIORITY_NORMAL: Same level as process

- THREAD_PRIORITY_ABOVE_NORMAL: One level above process

- THREAD_PRIORITY_HIGHEST: Two levels above process

- THREAD_PRIORITY_TIME_CRITICAL: Fifteen (in normal user processes)

- THREAD_PRIORITY_IDLE: One (in normal user processes)

The first five values adjust the thread's base priority level with respect to the level of its parent process, as shown earlier in Figure 14.2. The last two, for critical and idle priority, express absolute priority levels at the upper and lower extremes of the parent's priority class. (For real-time priority codes, these extremes are 16 and 31.) The Idle priority level works well for screen-savers, since they should not execute unless nothing else is happening. Use the Time Critical level with extreme caution and only for short periods, because it will starve lower-priority threads of processor time.

Suspending and Resuming a Thread's Execution

A suspended thread stops running and will not be scheduled for processor time. It remains in this state until some other thread makes it resume. Suspending a thread might be useful if, for example, the user interrupts a task. You could suspend the thread while waiting for the user to confirm the cancellation. If the user chooses to continue, the interrupted thread can resume where it left off. The sample program later in this chapter suspends several drawing threads whenever the user resizes the window. When the window is repainted, the threads continue drawing.

A thread calls these functions to make another thread pause and resume:

```
DWORD SuspendThread( HANDLE hThread );
DWORD ResumeThread( HANDLE hThread );
```

A single thread may be suspended several times in succession without any intervening resume commands, but every SuspendThread command must eventually be matched with a ResumeThread command. The system counts the number of pending suspension commands for each thread. (See the Suspension Count attribute in Figure 14.1, shown earlier.) SuspendThread increments the counter, and ResumeThread decrements it. Both functions return in a DWORD the previous value of the counter. Only when the counter returns to 0 does the thread resume execution.

A thread can suspend itself but cannot resume itself. However, a thread can put itself to sleep for a set amount of time. The Sleep command delays execution, removing the thread from the scheduler's queue until some interval passes. Interactive threads that write or draw information for the user often take short naps to give the user time to see the output. Sleep is better than an empty loop because it doesn't use processor time.

A thread calls these functions to pause for a set time:

```
VOID Sleep( DWORD dwMilliseconds );

DWORD SleepEx(
    DWORD dwMilliseconds,  // duration of pause
    BOOL bAlertable );     // TRUE to resume if I/O operation finishes
```

The extended SleepEx function typically works in conjunction with background I/O functions and can be used to initiate a read or write operation without waiting for it to finish. The operation continues in the background. When it finishes, the system notifies the user by invoking a callback procedure from the program. Background I/O (also called overlapping I/O) is particularly helpful in interactive programs that must remain responsive to the user while working with relatively slow devices, such as tape drives and network disks.

The Boolean parameter in SleepEx lets the system wake the thread prematurely if an overlapping I/O operation finishes before the sleep interval expires. If SleepEx is interrupted, it returns WAIT_IO_COMPLETION. SleepEx returns 0 if the interval passes without interruption.

Getting Information about Existing Threads

A thread can easily retrieve the two pieces of its own identity: a handle and an identifier.

These functions return information identifying the current thread:

```
DWORD GetCurrentThreadID( VOID );
HANDLE GetCurrentThread( VOID );
```

The return value from GetCurrentThreadID matches the value in lpIDThread after a CreateThread command. It is the number that identifies the thread uniquely to the system. Although very few of the Win32 API commands require you to know a thread's ID, it can be useful for monitoring threads system-wide without needing to keep handles open for each one. Open handles prevent threads from being destroyed.

The handle that GetCurrentThread returns serves the same purpose as the handle returned from CreateThread. Although it works in the same manner as other handles, it is actually a pseudohandle. A *pseudohandle* is a special constant that the system always interprets a certain way, much as a single dot (.) in DOS always refers to the current directory and this in C++ always points to the current object. The pseudohandle constant returned from GetCurrentThread always refers to the current thread. Unlike real handles, a pseudohandle does not work when passed to other threads. Here's what a thread must do to acquire a real, transferable handle to itself:

```
HANDLE hThread;

hThread = DuplicateHandle(
    GetCurrentProcess(),      // source process
    GetCurrentThread(),       // original handle
    GetCurrentProcess(),      // destination process
```

```
&hThread,              // new duplicate handle
0,                     // access rights (overridden by last param)
FALSE,                 // children do not inherit the handle
DUPLICATE_SAME_ACCESS ); // copy rights from original handle
```

CloseHandle has no effect on a pseudohandle, but the handle Duplicate-Handle creates is real and must eventually be closed. Using pseudohandles lets GetCurrentThread work more quickly, because it assumes a thread should have full access to itself and returns its result without bothering about any security considerations.

Terminating the Execution of a Thread

Normally, a thread meets its demise when it comes to the end of the function where it began, just as a Windows program ends when it comes to the end of WinMain. When a thread comes to the end of its starting function, the system automatically calls ExitThread, as:

```
VOID ExitThread( DWORD dwExitCode );
```

Although the system calls ExitThread automatically, you may call it directly yourself if some condition forces a thread to an untimely end:

```
DWORD ThreadFunction( LPDWORD lpdwParam )
{
    HANDLE hThread = CreateThread( <parameters> );

    // initialization chores happen here
    // test to see if there was a problem

    if( <error condition> )
    {
        ExitThread( ERROR_CODE );   // cancel the thread
    }
    //
    // no error, work continues
    //
    return( SUCCESS_CODE );         // this line causes the system
}                                   // to call ExitThread
```

ERROR_CODE and SUCCESS_CODE are whatever you define them to be. In this simple example, we could just as easily have canceled with a return command:

```
if( <error condition> )
```

```
    {
        return( ERROR_CODE );                // cancel the thread
    }
```

This `return` command has exactly the same effect as `ExitThread`; in fact, it even results in a call to `ExitThread`. The `ExitThread` command would be genuinely useful for canceling from within any subroutines `ThreadFunction` calls.

When a thread ends at a return statement, the 32-bit return value becomes the exit code passed automatically to `ExitThread`. After a thread terminates, its exit code is available through this function:

```
// one thread calls this to find out how another ended
BOOL GetExitCodeThread( HANDLE hThread, LPDWORD lpdwExitCode );
```

`GetExitCodeThread` returns FALSE if an error prevents it from determining the return value.

`ExitThread`, whether called explicitly or as an implicit consequence of `return`, permanently removes a thread from the dispatch queue and destroys the thread's stack. It does not, however, destroy the thread object. That's why you can still ask about the thread's exit status even after the thread stops running. When possible, you should close thread handles explicitly (call `CloseHandle`) to avoid wasting space in memory. The system destroys a thread when its last handle is closed. The system will not destroy a running thread, even if all its handles are closed. (In that case, the thread is destroyed when it stops running.) If a process leaves handles open when it terminates, the system closes them automatically and removes orphaned objects no longer held by any process.

With `ExitThread`, a thread stops itself gracefully at a place of its own choosing. Another function allows one thread to stop another abruptly and arbitrarily:

```
// one thread calls this to stop another
BOOL TerminateThread( HANDLE hThread, DWORD dwExitCode );
```

A thread cannot protect itself from termination. Anyone with a handle to the thread can force the thread to stop immediately, regardless of its current state (providing, of course, that the handle allows full access to the thread). Using the default security attributes in `CreateThread` produces a handle with full access privileges.

`TerminateThread` does not destroy the thread's stack, but it does provide an exit code. Both `ExitThread` and `TerminateThread` set the thread object to its signaled state so that any other threads waiting for this one to end may proceed. After either command, the thread object lingers until all its handles have been closed.

Equivalent C Runtime Functions

Several C runtime library commands duplicate some of the Win32 thread commands:

```
unsigned long _beginthread(
    void( *start_address )( void * ),  // starting function
    unsigned stack_size,               // initial stack size
    void *arglist );                   // parameter for starting function

void _endthread( void );
void _sleep( unsigned long ulMilliseconds );
```

_beginthread performs some internal initialization for a new thread that other C runtime functions, such as signal, depend on. The rule is consistency: If your program manipulates threads with C runtime functions, then use only C runtime functions wherever you have a choice. If your program uses Win32 functions with its threads, then stick to CreateThread and ExitThread. Also, if the thread calls C runtime functions, then create it with the C functions rather than the Win32 API. A few C routines require the initialization that _beginthread performs.

Threads and Message Queues

Each window a program creates belongs to the thread that creates it. When a thread creates a window, the system gives it a message queue, and the thread must enter a message loop to read from its queue. If a single thread creates all of a program's windows, the program needs only a single message loop. Conversely, any thread that wants to receive messages must create a window for itself, even if the window remains hidden. Only threads that create windows get message queues.

Synchronizing Threads

To work with threads, you must be able to coordinate their actions. Sometimes coordination requires ensuring that certain actions happen in a specific order. Besides the functions to create threads and modify their scheduling priority, the Win32 API contains functions to make threads wait for signals from objects, such as files and processes. It also supports special synchronization objects, such as mutexes and semaphores.

The functions that wait for an object to reach its signaled state best illustrate how synchronization objects are used. With a single set of generic waiting commands, you can wait for processes, threads, mutexes, semaphores, events, and a few other objects to reach their signaled states. This command waits for one object to turn on its signal:

```
DWORD WaitForSingleObject( HANDLE hObject, // object to wait for
                           DWORD dwMilliseconds ); // maximum wait time
```

`WaitForSingleObject` allows a thread to suspend itself until a specific object gives its signal. In this command, a thread also states how long it is willing to wait for the object. To wait indefinitely, set the interval to `INFINITE`. If the object is already available, or if it reaches its signal state within the designated time, `WaitForSingleObject` returns 0 and execution resumes. If the interval passes and the object is still not signaled, the function returns `WAIT_TIMEOUT`.

WARNING   Beware when setting the interval to `INFINITE`. If for any reason the object never reaches a signaled state, the thread will never resume. Also, if two threads establish a reciprocal infinite wait, they will deadlock.

To make a thread wait for several objects at once, call `WaitForMultipleObjects`. You can make this function return as soon as any one of the objects becomes available, or you can make it wait until all the requested objects finally reach their signaled states. An event-driven program might set up an array of objects that interest it and respond when any of them signals.

```
DWORD WaitForMultipleObjects(
    DWORD    dwNumObjects,      // number of objects to wait for
    LPHANDLE lpHandles,         // array of object handles
    BOOL     bWaitAll,          // TRUE, wait all; FALSE, wait any
    DWORD    dwMilliseconds );  // maximum waiting period
```

Again, a return value of `WAIT_TIMEOUT` indicates that the interval passed and no objects were signaled. If `bWaitAll` is FALSE, a successful return value—with a flag from any one element—indicates which element of the `lpHandles` array has become signaled. (The first element is 0, the second is 1, and so on.)

If `bWaitAll` is TRUE, the function does not respond until all flags (all threads) have completed.

Two extended versions of the wait functions add an alert status allowing a thread to resume if an asynchronous read or write command happens to end during the wait. In effect, these functions say, "Wake me up if the object becomes available, if a certain time passes, or if a background I/O operation runs to completion."

```
DWORD WaitForSingleObjectEx(
    HANDLE hObject,         // object to wait for
    DWORD  dwMilliseconds,  // maximum time to wait
    BOOL   bAlertable );    // TRUE to end wait if I/O completes

DWORD WaitForMultipleObjectsEx(
    DWORD    dwNumObjects,    // number of objects to wait for
    LPHANDLE lpHandles,      // array of object handles
    BOOL     bWaitAll,       // TRUE wait all; FALSE wait any
    DWORD    dwMilliseconds, // maximum waiting period
    BOOL     bAlertable );   // TRUE to end wait if I/O completes
```

Successful wait commands usually modify the awaited object in some way. For example, when a thread waits for and acquires a mutex, the wait function restores the mutex to its unsignaled state so other threads will know it is in use. Wait commands also decrease the counter in a semaphore and reset some kinds of events.

Wait commands do not modify the state of the specified object until all objects are simultaneously signaled. For example, a mutex can be signaled, but the thread does not receive ownership immediately; it must wait until the other objects are also signaled, and therefore cannot modify the object. Furthermore, while waiting, the mutex may come under the ownership of another thread, which will further delay the completion of the wait condition.

Of course, you must create an object before you can wait for it. We'll start with mutexes and semaphores, because they have parallel API commands to create the objects, acquire or release them, get handles to them, and destroy them.

Creating Mutexes and Semaphores

The creation functions for mutexes and semaphores need to be told what access privileges you want, some initial conditions for the object, and an optional name for the object.

```
HANDLE CreateMutex(
    LPSECURITY_ATTRIBUTES lpsa,  // optional security attributes
    BOOL bInitialOwner           // TRUE if creator wants ownership
    LPTSTR lpszMutexName )       // object's name

HANDLE CreateSemaphore(
    LPSECURITY_ATTRIBUTES lpsa,  // optional security attributes
    LONG lInitialCount,          // initial count (usually 0)
    LONG lMaxCount,              // maximum count (limits # of threads)
    LPTSTR lpszSemName );        // name of the semaphore (may be NULL)
```

If the security descriptor is NULL, the returned handle will possess all access privileges and will not be inherited by child processes. The names are optional and useful for identification only when several different processes want handles to the same object.

By setting the `bInitialOwner` flag to TRUE, a thread creates and acquires a mutex both at once. The new mutex remains unsignaled until the thread releases it.

Only one thread at a time may acquire a mutex, but a semaphore remains signaled until its acquisition count reaches `iMaxCount`. If any more threads try to wait for the semaphore, they will be suspended until some other thread decreases the acquisition count.

Acquiring and Releasing Mutexes and Semaphores

Once a semaphore or a mutex exists, threads interact with it by acquiring and releasing it. To acquire either object, a thread calls `WaitForSingleObject` (or one of its variants). When a thread finishes whatever task the object synchronizes, it releases the object with one of these functions:

```
BOOL ReleaseMutex( HANDLE hMutex );

BOOL ReleaseSemaphore(
    HANDLE hSemaphore,
    LONG lRelease,          // amount to increment counter on release
                            // (usually 1)
    LPLONG lplPrevious ); // variable to receive the previous count
```

Releasing a mutex or a semaphore increments its counter. Whenever the counter rises above 0, the object assumes its signaled state, and the system checks whether any other threads were waiting for it.

Only a thread that already owns a mutex—in other words, a thread that already waited for the mutex—can release it. `ReleaseSemaphore`, however, can be called by any thread and can adjust the acquisition counter by any amount up to its maximum value. Changing the counter by arbitrary amounts lets you vary the number of threads that may own a semaphore as your program runs. You may have noticed that `CreateSemaphore` allows you to set the counter for a new semaphore to something other than its maximum value. You might, for example, create it with an initial count of 0 to block all threads while your program initializes and then raise the counter with `ReleaseSemaphore`.

Remember to release synchronization objects. If you forget to release a mutex, for example, any threads that wait for it without specifying a maximum interval will deadlock. They will not be released.

A thread may wait for the same object more than once without blocking, but each wait must be matched with a release. This is true of mutexes, semaphores, and critical sections.

Working with Events

An event is the object a program creates when it requires a mechanism for alerting threads if some action occurs. In its simplest form, a manual reset event, the event object turns its signal on and off in response to the two commands `SetEvent` (signal on) and `ResetEvent` (signal off). When the signal is on, all threads that wait for the event will receive it. When the signal is off, all threads that wait for the event become blocked. Unlike mutexes and semaphores, manual reset events change their state only when some thread explicitly sets or resets them.

You might use a manual reset event to allow certain threads to execute only when the program is not painting its window or only after the user enters certain information. Here are the basic commands for working with events:

```
HANDLE CreateEvent(
   LPSECURITY_ATTRIBUTES lpsa, // security privi.; default, NULL
   BOOL bManualReset,          // TRUE if event must be reset manually
   BOOL bInitialState,      // TRUE to create event in signaled state
   LPTSTR lpszEventName );  // name of event (may be NULL)

BOOL SetEvent( HANDLE hEvent );

BOOL ResetEvent( HANDLE hEvent );
```

With the `bInitialState` parameter, `CreateEvent` allows the new event to arrive in the world already signaled. The Set and Reset functions return TRUE or FALSE to indicate success or failure.

With the `bManualReset` parameter, `CreateEvent` lets you create an automatic reset event instead of a manual reset event. An automatic reset event returns to its unsignaled state after a SetEvent command. ResetEvent is redundant for an auto-reset event. Furthermore, an automatic reset button always releases only a single thread on each signal before resetting. An auto-reset event might be useful for a program where one master thread prepares data for other worker threads. Whenever a new set of data is ready, the master sets the event and a single worker thread is released. The other workers continue to wait in line for more assignments.

Besides setting and resetting events, you can pulse events.

```
BOOL PulseEvent( hEvent );
```

A pulse turns the signal on for a very short time and then turns it back off. Pulsing a manual event allows all waiting threads to pass and then resets the event. Pulsing an automatic event lets one waiting thread pass and then resets the event. If no threads are waiting, none will pass. Setting an automatic event, on the other hand, causes the event to leave its signal on until some thread waits for it. As soon as one thread passes, the event resets itself.

The sample named pipe program in Chapter 15 demonstrates the use of automatic and manual reset events.

Sharing Mutexes, Semaphores, and Events

Processes, even unrelated processes, can share mutexes, semaphores, and events. By sharing objects, processes can coordinate their activities, just as threads do. There are three mechanisms for sharing. One is inheritance, where one process creates another and the new process receives copies of the parent's handles. Only those handles marked for inheritance when they were created will be passed on.

The other methods involve calling functions to create a second handle to an existing object. Which function you call depends on what information you already have. If you have handles to both the source and destination processes, call DuplicateHandle. If you have only the name of the object, call one of the Open functions. Two programs might agree in advance on the name of the object they share, or one might pass the name to the other through shared memory, the DDEML (Dynamic Data Exchange Management Library), or a pipe.

```
BOOL DuplicateHandle(
    HANDLE hSourceProcess, // process that owns the original object
    HANDLE hSource,        // handle to the original object
    HANDLE hTargetProcess, // process that wants a copy of the handle
    LPHANDLE lphTarget,    // place to store duplicated handle
    DWORD fdwAccess,       // requested access privileges
    BOOL bInherit,         // may the duplicate handle be inherited?
    DWORD fdwOptions );    // optional actions, e.g., close handle
```

```
HANDLE OpenMutex(
    DWORD fdwAccess,      // requested access privileges
    BOOL bInherit,        // TRUE if children may inherit this handle
    LPTSTR lpszName );    // name of the mutex

HANDLE OpenSemaphore(
    DWORD fdwAccess,      // requested access privileges
    BOOL bInherit,        // TRUE if children may inherit this handle
    LPTSTR lpszName );    // name of the semaphore

HANDLE OpenEvent(
    DWORD fdwAccess,      // requested access privileges
    BOOL bInherit,        // TRUE if children may inherit this handle
    LPTSTR lpszName );    // name of the event
```

Those LPTSTR variable types are not a misprint, by the way. It's a generic text type that compiles differently depending on whether an application uses Unicode strings or ASCII strings.

Destroying Mutexes, Semaphores, and Events

Mutexes, semaphores, and events persist in memory until all the processes that own them end or until all the object's handles have been closed with CloseHandle.

```
BOOL CloseHandle( hObject );
```

Working with Critical Sections

A critical section object performs exactly the same function as a mutex except that critical sections may not be shared. They are visible only within a single process. Critical sections and mutexes both allow only one thread to own them at a time, but critical sections work more quickly and involve less overhead.

The functions for working with critical sections do not use the same terminology, but they do roughly the same things. Instead of creating a critical section, you *initialize* it. Instead of waiting for it, you *enter* it. Instead of releasing it, you *leave* it. Instead of closing its handle, you *delete* the object.

```
VOID InitializeCriticalSection( LPCRITICAL_SECTION lpcs );
VOID EnterCriticalSection( LPCRITICAL_SECTION lpcs );
VOID LeaveCriticalSection( LPCRITICAL_SECTION lpcs );
VOID DeleteCriticalSection( LPCRITICAL_SECTION lpcs );
```

The variable type LPCRITICAL_SECTION names a pointer (not a handle) to a critical section object. InitializeCriticalSection expects to receive a pointer to an empty object, &cs, which you can allocate like this:

```
CRITICAL_SECTION cs;
```

An Example with Multiple Threads: The Threads Program

The Threads sample program, shown in Figure 14.3, puts into code some of the ideas explained in this chapter. It creates four secondary threads, each of which draws rectangles in a child window until the program ends. The top of the window contains a list box showing information about all four threads. By selecting a thread and choosing a menu command, you can suspend, resume, and change the priority of any thread. From the Options menu, you can also activate a mutex so that only one thread draws at a time.

Initialization Procedures

The initialization procedures register two window classes: one for the main overlapping window and one for the child windows where the threads draw. They also create a timer. At five-second intervals, the list box updates the information about each thread. The CreateWindows function creates and positions all the windows, including the list box that shows information about each thread. The four threads are created during the WM_CREATE message handler.

Note the absence of a PeekMessage loop in WinMain. That's a clear sign that you have entered the world of preemptive multitasking. The threads can draw continuously without monopolizing the processor. Other programs can still run at the same time.

```
/*-----------------------------------------------------------------
   WIN MAIN
      Calls initializing procedures and runs the message loop
   -----------------------------------------------------------------*/

int WINAPI WinMain(  HINSTANCE hinstThis, HINSTANCE hinstPrev,
   LPSTR lpszCmdLine,   int iCmdShow  )
{
```

FIGURE 14.3

The Threads program

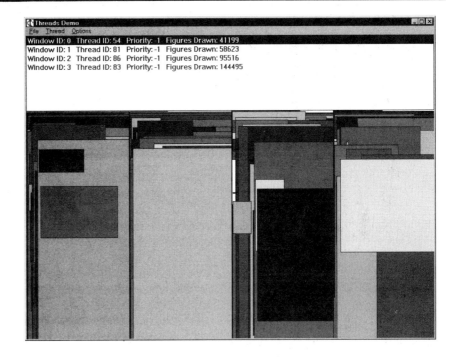

```
MSG msg;

hInst = hinstThis;              // store in global variable
if( ! InitializeApp( ) )
{
   // if the application was not initialized, exit here
   return( 0 );
}
ShowWindow( hwndParent, iCmdShow );
UpdateWindow( hwndParent );
     // receive and forward messages from our queue
while( GetMessage( &msg, NULL, 0, 0 ) )
{
   TranslateMessage( &msg );
   DispatchMessage( &msg );
}
return( msg.wParam );
}
```

In addition to registering the application class and the usual setup procedures, the InitializeApp procedure handles setting up the thread priority and starting each thread in a suspended state.

```
/*--------------------------------------------------------------------
    INITIALIZE APP
        Register two window classes and then create the windows
    ----------------------------------------------------------------*/

BOOL InitializeApp ( void )
{
    ...
        // Mark the initial state of each thread as SUSPENDED.
        // That is how they will be created.
    for( iCount = 0; iCount < 4; iCount++ )
    {
        iState[iCount] = SUSPENDED;
    }
        // make primary thread important to facilitate user i/o
    SetThreadPriority( GetCurrentThread(),
                        THREAD_PRIORITY_ABOVE_NORMAL );
        // create all the windows
    return( CreateWindows( ) );
}
```

The call to SetThreadPriority increases the priority of the primary thread. If all the secondary threads were busy working at the same priority as the main thread, the menus would respond sluggishly. You can test this yourself by raising the priority of the secondary threads as the program runs.

Also, the CreateWindows function is used, in addition to creating the main window, to create a list box and a series of child windows for the threads.

```
/*--------------------------------------------------------------------
    CREATE WINDOWS
        Create the parent window, the list box window, and the four
        child windows.
    ----------------------------------------------------------------*/

BOOL CreateWindows ( void )
{
    char    szAppName[MAX_BUFFER];
    char    szTitle[MAX_BUFFER];
```

```
char    szThread[MAX_BUFFER];
HMENU   hMenu;
int     iCount;

   // load the relevant strings
LoadString( hInst, IDS_APPNAME, szAppName, sizeof(szAppName));
LoadString( hInst, IDS_TITLE,   szTitle,   sizeof(szTitle));
LoadString( hInst, IDS_THREAD,  szThread,  sizeof(szThread));

   // create the parent window
hMenu = LoadMenu( hInst, MAKEINTRESOURCE(MENU_MAIN) );
hwndParent = CreateWindow( szAppName, szTitle,
                    WS_OVERLAPPEDWINDOW | WS_CLIPCHILDREN,
                       CW_USEDEFAULT, CW_USEDEFAULT,
                       CW_USEDEFAULT, CW_USEDEFAULT,
                       NULL, hMenu, hInst, NULL );
if( ! hwndParent )
{
   return( FALSE );
}
   // create the list box
hwndList = CreateWindow( "LISTBOX", NULL,
                    WS_BORDER | WS_CHILD | WS_VISIBLE |
                    LBS_STANDARD | LBS_NOINTEGRALHEIGHT,
                    0, 0, 0, 0, hwndParent, (HMENU)1,
                    hInst, NULL );
if( ! hwndList )
{
   return( FALSE );
}
   // create the four child windows
for( iCount = 0; iCount < 4; iCount++ )
{
   hwndChild[iCount] = CreateWindow( "ThreadClass", NULL,
                          WS_BORDER | WS_CHILD |
                          WS_VISIBLE | WS_CLIPCHILDREN,
                          0, 0, 0, 0, hwndParent, NULL,
                          hInst, NULL );
   if( ! hwndChild ) return( FALSE );
}
return( TRUE );
}
```

Window Procedure and Message Handlers

Most of the message handler functions are simple. `Main_OnTimer` calls a procedure to clear the list box, generate four new strings of information, and display them. The `Main_OnSize` function suspends all the secondary threads while the program repositions the child windows to accommodate the new size. Otherwise, the busy threads would slow down the display operation. `Main_OnCreate`, besides creating threads, creates a mutex.

```
/*-----------------------------------------------------------------
    MAIN_WNDPROC
        All messages for the main window are processed here.
    ------------------------------------------------------------*/
LRESULT WINAPI Main_WndProc( HWND hWnd,          // message address
                             UINT uMessage,      // message type
                             WPARAM wParam,       // message contents
                             LPARAM lParam )       // more contents
{
    switch( uMessage )
    {
        HANDLE_MSG( hWnd, WM_CREATE, Main_OnCreate );
            // create the window and the threads
        HANDLE_MSG( hWnd, WM_SIZE, Main_OnSize );
            // reposition the child windows when the main window changes
        HANDLE_MSG( hWnd, WM_TIMER, Main_OnTimer );
            // update the list box every five seconds
        HANDLE_MSG( hWnd, WM_INITMENU, Main_OnInitMenu );
            // put check by Use Mutex menu item if bUseMutex is TRUE
        HANDLE_MSG( hWnd, WM_COMMAND, Main_OnCommand );
            // process menu commands
        HANDLE_MSG( hWnd, WM_DESTROY, Main_OnDestroy );
            // clean up and quit
        default:
            return( DefWindowProc(hWnd, uMessage, wParam, lParam) );
    }
    return( 0L );
}
```

NOTE

The Threads program uses the message cracker macro, HANDLE_MSG. As a result, the compiler may produce a series of warnings saying, "unreferenced formal parameter" for the message handlers. To avoid these, include the following argsused pragma:

```
#ifdef __BORLANDC__
#pragma argsused
#endif
```

The Main_OnCreate function completes the process of initializing the several threads and setting up the mutex synchronization.

```
/*--------------------------------------------------------------
    MAIN_ONCREATE
        Create the four threads and set the timer
    ------------------------------------------------------------*/
BOOL Main_OnCreate( HWND hWnd, LPCREATESTRUCT lpCreateStruct )
{
    UINT uRet;
    int  iCount;

        // create the four threads, initially suspended
    for( iCount = 0; iCount < 4; iCount++ )
    {
        iRectCount[iCount] = 0;
        dwThreadData[iCount] = iCount;
        hThread[iCount] = CreateThread( NULL, 0,
                (LPTHREAD_START_ROUTINE) StartThread,
                        (LPVOID) ( & ( dwThreadData[iCount] ) ),
                                CREATE_SUSPENDED,
                        (LPDWORD) ( & ( dwThreadID[iCount] ) ) );
        if( ! hThread[iCount] )        // was the thread created?
        {
            return( FALSE );
        }
    }
        // Create a timer with a five-second period.
        // The timer is used to update the list box.
    uRet = SetTimer( hWnd, TIMER, 5000, NULL );
    if( ! uRet )
    {                                   // unable to create the timer
```

```
        return( FALSE );
    }


    // create a mutex synchronization object
    hDrawMutex = CreateMutex( NULL, FALSE, NULL );
    if( ! hDrawMutex )
    {                                  // unable to create mutex
        KillTimer( hWnd, TIMER );   // stop the timer
        return( FALSE );
    }
    // start the threads with a priority below normal
    for( iCount = 0; iCount < 4; iCount++ )
    {
        SetThreadPriority( hThread[iCount],
                        THREAD_PRIORITY_BELOW_NORMAL );
        iState[iCount] = ACTIVE;
        ResumeThread( hThread[iCount] );
    }
        // Now all four threads are running!
    return( TRUE );
}
```

Of course, since we have multiple child windows, and because the main application window is resizable, the Main_OnSize function not only must handle resizing the application window, but also needs to resize (and move) all of the child windows at the same time.

```
/*-------------------------------------------------------------------
    MAIN_ONSIZE
        Position the list box and the four child windows.
-------------------------------------------------------------------*/
void Main_OnSize( HWND hWnd, UINT uState, int cxClient, int cyClient )
{
    char* szText = "No Thread Data";
    int   iCount;

    // Suspend all active threads while the windows
    // resize and repaint themselves. This pause
    // enables the screen to update more quickly.
    for( iCount = 0; iCount < 4; iCount++ )
    {
```

```
        if( iState[iCount] == ACTIVE )
            SuspendThread( hThread[iCount] );
    }
        // place the list box across the top fourth of the window
    MoveWindow( hwndList, 0, 0, cxClient, cyClient / 4, TRUE );
        // Spread the 4 child windows across the bottom 3/4 of the
        // window. (The left border of the first one should be 0.)
    MoveWindow( hwndChild[0], 0, cyClient / 4 - 1, cxClient / 4 + 1,
            cyClient, TRUE );
    for( iCount = 1; iCount < 4; iCount++ )
    {
        MoveWindow( hwndChild[iCount], (iCount * cxClient) / 4,
                cyClient / 4 - 1, cxClient / 4 + 1, cyClient, TRUE );
    }
        // Add the default strings to the list box, and initialize
        // the number of figures drawn to zero
    for( iCount = 0; iCount < 4; iCount++ )
    {
        iRectCount[iCount] = 0;
        ListBox_AddString( hwndList, szText );
    }
    ListBox_SetCurSel(hwndList, 0);
        // reactivate the threads that were suspended while redrawing
    for( iCount = 0; iCount < 4; iCount++ )
    {
        if( iState[iCount] == ACTIVE )
        {
            ResumeThread( hThread[iCount] );
        }
    }
    return;
}
```

A timer message may not be the optimum choice for updating the list box. Ideally, this event would be directed by other operations that were responsible for causing a change that needed to be reported. But here, a timer is a simple provision that accomplishes the task.

```
/*-------------------------------------------------------------------
    MAIN_ONTIMER
        Process the timer message by updating the list box.
-------------------------------------------------------------------*/
```

```
void Main_OnTimer( HWND hWnd, UINT uTimerID )
{
    // update the data shown in the list box
  UpdateListBox();
  return;
}
```

The `Main_OnInitMenu` function is simply used to check (or uncheck) the Use Mutex menu command.

```
/*------------------------------------------------------------------
    MAIN_ONINITMENU
        Check or uncheck the Use Mutex menu item based on the
        value of bUseMutex
------------------------------------------------------------------*/
void Main_OnInitMenu( HWND hWnd, HMENU hMenu )
{
  CheckMenuItem( hMenu, IDM_USEMUTEX, MF_BYCOMMAND |
            (UINT)( bUseMutex ? MF_CHECKED : MF_UNCHECKED ) );
  return;
}
```

The `Main_OnCommand` function is provided to parcel out all messages that have not already been handled by message crackers.

```
/*------------------------------------------------------------------
    MAIN_ONCOMMAND
        Respond to commands from the user
------------------------------------------------------------------*/
void Main_OnCommand( HWND hWnd, int iCmd, HWND hwndCtl, UINT uCode
)
{
  switch( iCmd )
  {
    case IDM_ABOUT:        // display the About box
      MakeAbout( hWnd );
      break;

    case IDM_EXIT:         // exit this program
      DestroyWindow( hWnd );
      break;
```

```
        case IDM_SUSPEND:     // modify priority or state of thread
        case IDM_RESUME:
        case IDM_INCREASE:
        case IDM_DECREASE:
           DoThread( iCmd ); // adjust thread
           break;


        case IDM_USEMUTEX:    // toggle the use of the mutex
          ClearChildWindows( );      // make all thread windows white
          bUseMutex = !bUseMutex;    // toggle mutex setting
          break;

        default:
           break;
    }
    return;
}
```

Modifying the Threads

The DoThread procedure responds to menu commands by modifying whichever thread is currently selected in the list box. DoThread can raise or lower a thread's priority, and suspend or resume threads. The iState array records the current state, either active or suspended, of each thread. The hThreads array holds handles to each of the four secondary threads.

```
/*-----------------------------------------------------------------
    DO THREAD
        Modify a thread's priority or change its state in response
        to commands from the menu.
    -------------------------------------------------------------*/
void DoThread( int iCmd )
{
   int iThread;
   int iPriority;

   // determine which thread to modify
   iThread = ListBox_GetCurSel( hwndList );
   switch( iCmd )
   {
      case IDM_SUSPEND:
```

```
            // if the thread is not suspended, then suspend it
        if( iState[iThread] != SUSPENDED )
        {
            SuspendThread( hThread[iThread] );
            iState[iThread] = SUSPENDED;
        }
        break;

    case IDM_RESUME:
            // if the thread is not active, then activate it
        if( iState[iThread] != ACTIVE )
        {
            ResumeThread( hThread[iThread] );
            iState[iThread] = ACTIVE;
        }
        break;

    case IDM_INCREASE:
            // Increase the thread's priority (unless it is
            // already at the highest level.)
        iPriority = GetThreadPriority( hThread[iThread] );

        switch( iPriority )
        {
            case THREAD_PRIORITY_LOWEST:
                SetThreadPriority( hThread[iThread],
                                   THREAD_PRIORITY_BELOW_NORMAL );
                break;

            case THREAD_PRIORITY_BELOW_NORMAL:
                SetThreadPriority( hThread[iThread],
                                   THREAD_PRIORITY_NORMAL );
                break;

            case THREAD_PRIORITY_NORMAL:
                SetThreadPriority( hThread[iThread],
                                   THREAD_PRIORITY_ABOVE_NORMAL );
                break;

            case THREAD_PRIORITY_ABOVE_NORMAL:
                SetThreadPriority( hThread[iThread],
                                   THREAD_PRIORITY_HIGHEST );
```

```
            break;

        default:        break;
    }                   break;

case IDM_DECREASE:
    // Decrease the thread's priority (unless it is
    // already at the lowest level.)
    iPriority = GetThreadPriority( hThread[iThread] );
    switch( iPriority )
    {
        case THREAD_PRIORITY_BELOW_NORMAL:
            SetThreadPriority( hThread[iThread],
                        THREAD_PRIORITY_LOWEST );
            break;

        case THREAD_PRIORITY_NORMAL:
            SetThreadPriority( hThread[iThread],
                        THREAD_PRIORITY_BELOW_NORMAL );
            break;

        case THREAD_PRIORITY_ABOVE_NORMAL:
            SetThreadPriority( hThread[iThread],
                        THREAD_PRIORITY_NORMAL );
            break;

        case THREAD_PRIORITY_HIGHEST:
            SetThreadPriority( hThread[iThread],
                        THREAD_PRIORITY_ABOVE_NORMAL );
            break;

        default:        break;
    }                   break;
    default:            break;
}
return;
}
```

Thread Procedures

When `Main_OnCreate` constructs the secondary threads, in each call to `Create-Thread` it passes a pointer to the `StartThread` function. `StartThread` becomes the main procedure for all the threads. They begin and end executing here.

If `bUseMutex` is TRUE, then the threads will wait to acquire the mutex before they draw and only one thread will draw at a time.

```
/*----------------------------------------------------------
   START THREAD
      This is called when each thread begins execution
   ------------------------------------------------------*/
LONG StartThread ( LPVOID lpThreadData )
{
   DWORD *pdwThreadID; // pointer to DWORD for storing thread's ID
   DWORD dwWait;       // return value from WaitSingleObject

       // retrieve the thread's ID
   pdwThreadID = lpThreadData;

       // draw continuously until bTerminate becomes TRUE
   while( ! bTerminate )
   {
      if (bUseMutex)        // are we using the mutex?
      {
           // draw when this thread gets the mutex
         dwWait = WaitForSingleObject( hDrawMutex, INFINITE );
         if( dwWait == 0 )
         {
            DrawProc( *pdwThreadID );   // draw rectangles
            ReleaseMutex( hDrawMutex ); // let someone else draw
         }
      }
      else
      {
           // not using mutex; let the thread draw
         DrawProc( *pdwThreadID );
      }
   }
       // This return statement implicitly calls ExitThread.
   return( 0L );
}
```

`DrawProc` draws a batch of rectangles. Because GDI (Graphics Device Interface) calls do not always occur immediately, to avoid the overhead of many small messages between a program and the Win32 subsystem, graphics commands are held in a queue and periodically flushed. These delays somewhat exaggerate the effect of changing priorities in the Threads demo program.

```
/*-------------------------------------------------------------------
    DRAW PROC
        Draw five random rectangles or ellipses
------------------------------------------------------------------*/
void DrawProc ( DWORD dwID )
{
    ...
    if (bUseMutex)
    {
        iTotal = 50;      // If only one thread draws at a time,
    }                     // let it draw more shapes at once.
    else
    {
        iTotal = 1;
    }
        // reseed the random generator
    srand( iRandSeed++ );
        // get the window's dimensions
    bError = GetClientRect( hwndChild[dwID], &rcClient );
    if( ! bError ) return;
    cxClient = rcClient.right - rcClient.left;
    cyClient = rcClient.bottom - rcClient.top;
        // do not draw if the window does not have any dimensions
    if( ( ! cxClient ) || ( ! cyClient ) )
    {
        return;
    }
        // get a device context for drawing
    hDC = GetDC( hwndChild[dwID] );
    if( hDC )
    {
            // draw the five random figures
        for( iCount = 0; iCount < iTotal; iCount++ )
        {
            iRectCount[dwID]++;
                // set the coordinates
```

```
        xStart = (int)( rand() % cxClient );
        xStop  = (int)( rand() % cxClient );
        yStart = (int)( rand() % cyClient );
        yStop  = (int)( rand() % cyClient );
            // set the color
        iRed   = rand() & 255;
        iGreen = rand() & 255;
        iBlue  = rand() & 255;
            // create the solid brush
        hBrush = CreateSolidBrush( // avoid dithered colors
                    GetNearestColor( hDC,
                      RGB( iRed, iGreen, iBlue ) ) );
        hbrOld = SelectBrush( hDC, hBrush );
            // draw a rectangle
      Rectangle( hDC, min( xStart, xStop ), max( xStart, xStop ),
                    min( yStart, yStop ), max( yStart, yStop ) );
            // delete the brush
        DeleteBrush( SelectBrush(hDC, hbrOld) );
    }
        // If only one thread is drawing at a time, clear
        // the child window before the next thread draws
    if( bUseMutex )
    {
        SelectBrush( hDC, GetStockBrush(WHITE_BRUSH) );
        PatBlt( hDC, (int)rcClient.left,  (int)rcClient.top,
                    (int)rcClient.right, (int)rcClient.bottom,
                PATCOPY );
    }
        // release the HDC
    ReleaseDC( hwndChild[dwID], hDC );
  }
  return;
}
```

After you run the Threads program and experiment with priorities, turn the mutex on and off, and suspend and resume a few threads, you might want to try running the Process Viewer that comes with the Win32 SDK. In Figure 14.4 you can see what Process Viewer says about Threads. Note that it shows five threads for the program because it includes the primary thread as well. Browsing with Process Viewer gives you a better sense of how Windows NT and 95 work.

FIGURE 14.4

Examining threads using the Win32 SDK Process Viewer

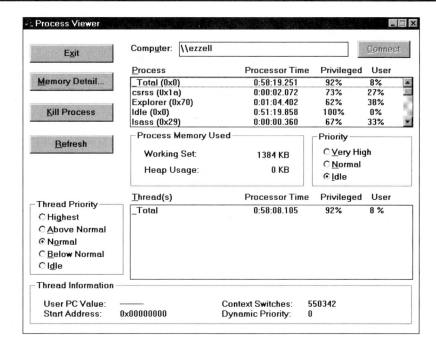

This chapter has explored the use of multiple threads. The Threads program, which is supplied on the CD, gives a practical example of threads in action.

In this discussion, we've mentioned processes and interprocess communication through pipes and shared memory. Chapter 15 explains how to create and manage processes.

Creating Processes and Pipes

- Child and parent processes

- Pipes for communication between processes

- Commands for creating and modifying processes and pipes

- Named and anonymous pipes

In Chapter 14, you saw how one process can create many threads. A program that needs to do several things at once usually creates threads rather than whole new processes. Threads are generally preferable to processes because they are created more quickly with less overhead, they share resources such as handles and variables, and they are easy to synchronize. This chapter shows what happens when you decide instead to divide a task among several distinct processes, each with its own threads and its own private address space.

Processes and pipes are closely related topics. Processes often pass pipe handles to new processes they create in order to establish a channel for exchanging information. Along with the threads and synchronization objects you read about in Chapter 14, pipes and processes form the basic core of tools for multitasking in Windows NT and 95. In this chapter, you'll learn how to launch a new child process, pass it handles, connect the parent to the child with a pipe, and send information through the pipe.

Process and Pipe Concepts

The multitasking capabilities of both Windows NT and 95 depend on the system's handling of processes and threads. Both terms designate ways of dividing labor in the operating system. The term *process* names an executable program and all the program's resources as it runs in the system:

- Its virtual address space
- The access token that assigns it a privilege level
- The resource quotas determined by the user's privilege level
- One or more threads of execution
- Other objects as they are assigned dynamically, such as an open file or a shared memory block

Every process has at least one thread of execution—one path the processor follows through its code. A process can also choose to divide its work into several tasks and create separate threads for each one. *Multitasking* happens when one machine runs several programs at once; *multithreading* happens when one program runs several threads at once. The Process Manager creates and destroys processes and their threads. It also suspends threads and resumes them.

Preemptive versus Permissive Multitasking

The simple difference between Windows 95 and NT is that NT is a preemptive multitasking system, and 95 exercises permissive multitasking. Another example of a preemptive multitasking system is OS/2.

In a *preemptive multitasking* system (NT), the operating system summarily suspends executing threads in order to allow other threads an appropriate time slice for operation. In a *permissive multitasking* system (Windows 95), the operating system depends on the applications to regularly relinquish control of the operating system so that other applications have the opportunity to gain their time slices.

Obviously, a preemptive multitasking system has the ability to provide much smoother execution of multiple tasks and threads. This type of system does not need to depend on the good graces of each program (or the skills of the respective programmers) in surrendering control of the CPU.

Inheritance

The documentation often refers to processes as *parents*, *children*, and *siblings*. A process that creates other processes is called the parent, and the new processes are its children. All the children of a single parent are siblings. Once a parent creates a child, the child no longer depends on the parent. If the parent terminates, the child may continue. The Win32 subsystem does not enforce any strong hierarchical dependence between parents and children.

The familial metaphor extends to one other action: inheritance. A new process *inherits* some attributes from its parent. Inherited attributes include the following:

- An environment block with environment variables

- A current working directory

- Standard input and output handles

- Any other handles the parent may want its children to have

A child of a console process—that is, of a parent that uses the console API for drawing on the screen instead of the Windows GUI—also inherits its parent's console window. A child may inherit handles to processes, threads, mutexes, events, semaphores, pipes, and file-mapping objects. It may also inherit handles created with `CreateFile`, including files, console input buffers, console screen buffers, serial communication devices, and mailslots.

NOTE   Consoles simulate character-based display. The NT command shell, for example, runs in a console window.

When a child inherits a handle, both the parent and the child end up with handles to the same object. Whatever one does to the object affects the other. If a child's thread waits for and acquires a shared mutex, any parent threads that wait for the same object will be blocked. If a parent writes to a file, a child using the same handle will find its file position marker has moved forward, too.

When a child inherits a handle, it really only inherits access to the object. It does not inherit handle variables. When creating a child, the parent must both arrange for inheritance and pass the handles explicitly. These may be passed in several ways: on the command line, through a file, or through a pipe.

An easier but less intuitive option involves the standard I/O channels. Recall that character-based C programs frequently direct their I/O through three standard channels called `stdin`, `stdout`, and `stderr`. Win32 processes automatically possess the same three channels, although they do not have the same predefined names. The standard I/O channels are generally useless to a GUI application because they are not actually connected to any device. (A GUI application may, however, open a console window and use its standard I/O devices there.)

Normally, a child inherits the same standard I/O devices its parent uses, but during creation the parent may specify a different set of handles for the child to receive. The child retrieves its inherited handles with `SetStdHandle`. The parent may also change one or more of its own devices before creating the child. The child inherits the changes.

Children do not inherit all kinds of objects. Memory handles and pseudohandles are excluded from inheritance, for example. Each process has its own address space, so it cannot inherit memory objects from another process. Pseudohandles, such as the value returned by `GetCurrentThread`, are by definition valid only in the place where they originate. Nor do children inherit DLL module handles, GDI handles, or USER handles, including `HBRUSH` and `HWND` objects. Similarly, children do not inherit their parent's priority class. By default a child's priority will be NORMAL_PRIORITY_CLASS. There is one exception: the IDLE_PRIORITY_CLASS is inheritable. By default, parents of very low priority create children of very low priority; the poor stay poor. Parents of any other priority create children of normal priority.

The Life Cycle of a Process

Process resources include an access token, a virtual address space description, and a handle table. Every process has a primary thread, which is the one that begins execution at WinMain, and may create other threads as it runs.

All the threads in one process share a single image of the executable file, but each new process requires the system to map the executable file into a new address space. The command for creating a process asks for the name of an .EXE file. An application that creates child processes to perform part of its work needs to be written and compiled as several distinct programs.

All Win32 processes begin life when some other process invokes them with CreateProcess. The Win32 subsystem starts up all its clients with that command. During CreateProcess, the system sets up a virtual address space, loads an executable file image, and creates a primary thread. CreateProcess returns a handle to the new process and a handle to its primary thread. The parent may close the handles, relinquishing control over its child. Or the parent may keep them in order to change the child's priority class, terminate the child, or read the exit code when the child ends by itself. Like threads, processes remain in memory even after execution stops until all handles to the process have been closed.

A process remains active until its primary thread reaches the end of its starting procedure and stops execution or until any of its threads calls ExitProcess. ExitProcess causes the system to notify all supporting DLLs that this module has stopped. It also causes any other threads in the same process to terminate immediately.

Communication between Processes: Pipes

Sometimes, the processes the user runs have nothing to do with each other. A phone dialer and a paint program probably have little in common. But the ability to exchange information among processes sometimes produces a synergistic effect when their cooperation makes it possible to perform tasks neither program could manage alone. Windows allows many channels of communication, including the clipboard, DDE, and OLE. Windows NT adds new channels. In Chapter 17, for example, you'll see how processes can share memory by opening views onto the same memory-mapped file.

Pipes are another new and easy mechanism for different programs to exchange information. Unlike some other channels, pipes have no formal standards or protocols to govern how information is passed. That makes pipes easier to use and more flexible than, say, DDE conversations, but it also limits them to programs that recognize each other and know how to parse the information they agree to exchange.

A *pipe* is a section of shared memory where processes leave messages for each other. A pipe resembles a file where one program writes and another reads. Because a pipe is dedicated to interprocess communication, the Win32 API can provide a range of commands to facilitate the exchange of information. Conceptually, a pipe is a cross between a computer file and a post office mailslot. One process writes something in the file, and another process looks to see what was left behind.

The Life Cycle of a Pipe

A pipe appears when one program decides to create it. The program that creates a pipe is called the pipe's *server*. Other processes, called *clients*, may connect to the pipe's other end. The server assumes responsibility for the life of the pipe. Any process may be a server or a client, or both at once on different pipes.

After the pipe is created and another process connects to it, either the client or the server, and sometimes both, writes into its end. Anything written at one end is read from the other. Reading and writing operations rely on the same commands you use to work with any file: ReadFile and WriteFile. Typically, a process that expects to receive a series of messages creates a new thread to wait for them. The thread repeatedly calls ReadFile and blocks, remaining suspended until each new message arrives.

Eventually, the server decides the conversation has ended and breaks the connection. To destroy the pipe, the server calls CloseHandle. (The pipe will not actually be destroyed until all handles to it, both the server's and the client's, have been closed.) Alternatively, the server may decide to connect the old pipe with a new client.

Varieties of Pipes

Pipes come in several varieties:

- Inbound, outbound, or duplex
- Byte or message
- Blocking or nonblocking
- Named or anonymous

Most of these attributes are determined when the pipe is created.

Inbound, Outbound, and Duplex Pipes

The first set of terms—inbound, outbound, and duplex—distinguishes the direction information flows through the pipe. *Inbound* and *outbound* describe one-directional pipes, where one side only writes and the other side only reads. An inbound pipe lets the client send and the server receive. An outbound pipe lets the server send and the client receive. A duplex pipe allows both sides to send and receive.

Byte and Message Pipes

What the participants write determines whether the pipe should have a reading mode of type byte or type message. The reading mode helps the system decide when a read operation should stop. With a byte-mode pipe, a read operation stops when it either reaches the last byte of data in the pipe or else fills its reading buffer. With a message-mode pipe, however, a read operation stops when it reaches the end of a single message.

Internally, the system marks messages in a message-mode pipe by prefacing each newly written segment with a header stating its length. The programs on either end of the pipe never see the message headers, but `ReadFile` commands on a message-mode pipe automatically stop when they reach the end of a segment.

Blocking and Nonblocking Pipes

Pipes may also be either blocking or nonblocking. This attribute affects read, write, and connect commands. When any of these commands fails on a nonblocking pipe, the command returns immediately with an error result. On a pipe that allows blocking, the commands do not return until they succeed or an error occurs.

Here is a summary of how blocking and nonblocking mode affect three operations:

Operation	Blocking Mode	Nonblocking Mode
`Connect-NamedPipe`	Blocks until a client connects to the other end.	Returns FALSE immediately.
`ReadFile`	If the pipe is empty, blocks until a message arrives.	If the pipe is empty, returns an error immediately.
`WriteFile`	If the pipe is nearly full, blocks until another process reads from the other end.	If the pipe is nearly full, returns immediately. For a byte-mode pipe, `WriteFile` will write as much as it can first. For a message-mode pipe, `WriteFile` returns TRUE and writes no bytes.

Named and Anonymous Pipes

A pipe may be *named*, in which case the creator has endowed it with an identifying name string, or *anonymous*, meaning it has no name string. Like synchronization objects, such as mutexes and semaphores, a pipe may be given a name to help other processes identify it.

Anonymous pipes require less overhead but perform only a limited subset of the services named pipes can perform. They pass messages in only one direction: either server to client or client to server, but not both. Also, anonymous pipes do not work over networks. The server and client must inhabit the same machine.

Named pipes can do several things that anonymous pipes cannot. They can pass information in both directions through one pipe, connect across a network to a process on a remote machine, exist in multiple instances, and use more pipe modes. The ability to exist in multiple instances permits a named pipe to connect one server with many clients. Each instance is an independent channel of communication. Messages in one instance do not interfere with messages in another instance. Multiple instances of a single pipe result when one or more servers pass the same identifying name to `CreateNamedPipe`.

Process-Related Commands

In many ways, the commands for creating and managing processes resemble the commands for creating and managing threads, which you saw in Chapter 14. To create a process, you specify security attributes and receive a handle. With the handle, you can manage the process; for example, change the priority of the process or terminate it. Even after a process stops running, it continues to exist as long as any handles to it remain open. To destroy a process, close all of its handles.

This section describes the Win32 API commands for creating processes. Two sample programs in the final section of the chapter demonstrate most of the commands explained here.

Making and Modifying Processes

Under NT/95, the `CreateProcess` command starts every new process. The old `WinExec` and `LoadModule` commands still exist for backward compatibility, but internally both now call `CreateProcess`.

```
BOOL CreateProcess(
    LPCTSTR lpszImageName,                // image file (.EXE) name
    LPCTSTR lpszCmdLine,                   // command line for process
    LPSECURITY_ATTRIBUTES lpsaProcess,// how process is shared
    LPSECURITY_ATTRIBUTES lpsaThread,  // how thread is shared
    BOOL bInheritHandles,                  // TRUE to inherit handles
    DWORD fdwCreate,                       // creation flags
    LPVOID lpvEnvironment,           // new environment (default = NULL)
    LPTSTR lpszCurrentDir,            // name of new current directory
    LPSTARTUPINFO lpStartupInfo,      // gives info about new process
    LPPROCESS_INFORMATION lpProcInfo )// receives process info
```

The Parameters

The `CreateProcess` function's parameters permit control over the new process's starting conditions. First, every process requires code to execute. Together, the first two parameters create a complete command line naming a program file and passing it arguments. Here, for example, is a command line you might type at the command prompt:

```
C> qgrep -L -y "ERROR_" *.h
```

Executable and Arguments   The first parameter, `lpszImageName`, must point only to the name of the executable file (for example, `qgrep`). Do not include any arguments. In locating a file named in this parameter, the system does not search the `PATH` directories. The program must be in the current directory, or the string must contain a full path name.

The second parameter, `lpszCmdLine`, may be NULL if you have no arguments to pass. If you do pass arguments, the first item in the `lpszCmdLine` string must be what C programmers call the `argv[0]` value, which is, again, `qgrep` in the example.

The first item is typically, but not necessarily, the name of the program, even if you have already given it in `lpszImageName`. You can omit the path and extension if they appear in the `lpszImageName`, but some item must precede the first argument, just as `qgrep` precedes `-L`.

To make `CreateProcess` search along the environment `PATH` for the file, leave the first parameter blank and pass the complete command line in the second parameter. Here are some examples of using `CreateProcess` parameters:

First Parameter	Second Parameter	Result
`d:\dev\bin\` `qgrep`	NULL	Runs qgrep, without arguments, only if qgrep is found in the \dev\bin directory.
`qgrep.exe`	`qgrep -L-y "ERROR_"` `*.h`	Runs qgrep, with arguments, only if qgrep is in the current directory.
NULL	`qgrep -L-y "ERROR_"` `*.h`	Runs qgrep, with arguments, if it can be found anywhere on the path.

Security Attributes   The next two parameters in `CreateProcess` provide security attributes for both the new process and its primary thread. (Every process receives an initial thread; otherwise, nothing would ever execute.) You saw the same `SECURITY_ATTRIBUTES` structure when we created new threads in Chapter 14, and you will see it often in commands that create new objects. The information in this structure controls what another process may be permitted to do with the object if it opens a duplicate handle. It also controls whether child processes may inherit a handle to the new object. By default, other processes receive full access to the new object and children do not inherit it.

Blocking Inheritance   The `bInheritHandles` parameter of `CreateProcess` gives you a second chance to prevent a child from inheriting other handles you have already created. If `bInheritHandles` is FALSE, the new process inherits no handles, even if they were marked inheritable when they were created. Blocking inheritance is useful because many objects, including threads and processes, persist in memory until all the handles to them are closed. If every new child inherits a full set of handles from its parent, many objects will stay in memory until all the child processes exit and their handles are destroyed. Children should be allowed to inherit only the handles they actually need.

Process Type and Priority   The creation flags in the `fdwCreate` parameter govern the type and priority of the new process. The new process may be initially suspended; it may have a console or a GUI window; it may receive debugging information from its child; and it may receive a particular priority class. Here are some of the values that can be combined in the creation flag parameter:

- `DEBUG_PROCESS`: The parent receives debugging information about the child and any of its children.

- `DEBUG_ONLY_THIS_PROCESS`: The parent receives debugging information about the child but not any of the child's children.

- `CREATE_SUSPENDED`: The primary thread of the new process is initially suspended.

- `DETACHED_PROCESS`: The new process does not use a console window.

- `CREATE_NEW_CONSOLE`: The new process receives its own new console window.

- `IDLE_PRIORITY_CLASS`: The process runs only when the system is idle.

- `NORMAL_PRIORITY_CLASS`: The process has no special scheduling needs.

- `HIGH_PRIORITY_CLASS`: The process preempts all threads of lower priority in order to respond very quickly to some critical situation.

- `REALTIME_PRIORITY_CLASS`: The process preempts even important system tasks.

Environment and Directory Settings   Each process has its own set of environment variables and its own current directory setting. If the `lpszEnvironment` and `lpszCurrentDir` parameters are NULL, the new process copies the block of environment variables and the directory setting from its parent. Environment variables are those defined with the `SET` command at the command prompt, typically in an autoexecute file. Programmers usually define variables, such as `BIN`, `LIB`, and `INCLUDE`, to tell the compiler and linker where to find particular kinds of files.

More generally, environment variables are a convenient way to customize programs by putting information where it is always available. A parent can send information to its children by defining environment variables. To give the child an entirely new environment, the parent should create a buffer and fill it with null-terminated strings of the form *<variable>=<setting>*. The last string must be followed by two null characters. To give the child a slightly modified version of the parent's existing environment, the parent can temporarily modify its own settings with `GetEnvironmentVariable` and `SetEnvironmentVariable`, create the child, and then restore the old settings.

Pointing to Structures   The last two parameters of `CreateProcess` point to structures. The parent fills out the `STARTUPINFO` structure before calling `Create-Process` and receives information about the new process in the `PROCESS_INFORMATION` structure.

```
// You fill this out to describe a new process in advance
typedef struct _STARTUPINFO  /* si */
{
    DWORD   cb;                   // sizeof(STARTUPINFO)
    LPTSTR  lpReserved;           // should be NULL
    LPTSTR  lpDesktop;            // name of Desktop object to run in
    LPSTR   lpTitle;              // caption for console title bar
    DWORD   dwX;                  // upper-left corner for new window
    DWORD   dwY;
    DWORD   dwXSize;              // width of new window
    DWORD   dwYSize;              // height of new window
    DWORD   dwXCountChars;        // width of new console window
    DWORD   dwYCountChars;        // height of new console window
    DWORD   dwFillAttribute;      // text/background colors for console
    DWORD   dwFlags;              // activates fields in this structure
    WORD    wShowWindow;          // iCmdShow parameter value
    WORD    cbReserved2;          // zero
    LPBYTE  lpReserved2;          // NULL
    HANDLE  hStdInput;            // handles for the
    HANDLE  hStdOutput;           //    child's standard
    HANDLE  hStdError;            //    I/O devices
} STARTUPINFO, *LPSTARTUPINFO;
```

You must fill in the first field of the STARTUPINFO structure, but you can initialize all the rest to 0 or NULL to accept default values.

The lpDesktop field is ignored under Windows 95. For NT, lpDesktop points to a zero-terminated string specifying either the name of the Desktop only or the name of both the window station and Desktop for this process. (The Desktop is the background window on which all a user's programs run.) A backslash in the string pointed to by lpDesktop indicates that the string includes both Desktop and window station names. Otherwise, the lpDesktop string is interpreted as a Desktop name. If lpDesktop is NULL, the new process inherits the window station and Desktop of its parent process.

NOTE The current system allows only two Desktops: one for logging on and one for the current user. Several features of the API, such as this lp-Desktop field, suggest that in later releases, NT may allow one user to work with multiple Desktop windows. Until then, Desktop-related fields and parameters serve little purpose. Screen savers run on the logon Desktop for security, to hide the user's data while the machine is idle. NT screen savers do not have access to the user's Desktop.

Many of the other fields in a STARTUPINFO structure matter only for nongraphics processes that will run in console windows instead of regular GUI windows. Most of the fields are ignored unless the values in dwFlags alert the system to use them. dwFlags may contain the following values, each activating a different field or set of fields from the STARTUPINFO structure:

Flag	Field(s) Activated
STARTF_USESHOWWINDOW	wShowWindow
STARTF_USESIZE	dwXSize, dwYSize
STARTF_USEPOSITION	dwX, dwY
STARTF_USECOUNTCHARS	dwXCountChars, dwYCountChars
STARTF_USEFILLATTRIBUTE	dwFillAttribute
STARTF_USESTDHANDLES	hStdInput, hStdOutput, hStdError

You don't need to initialize any of these 11 fields unless you activate them with a flag in dwFlags.

Three additional values for `dwFlags` do not activate specific fields:

- `STARTF_FORCEONFEEDBACK`: Forces the system to display the waiting cursor that gives the user feedback as an application starts up.

- `STARTF_FORCEOFFFEEDBACK`: Forces the system to omit the waiting cursor as an application starts up.

- `STARTF_SCREENSAVER`: Causes a screen-saver program to initialize and terminate at a priority higher than its default idle priority level.

I/O Handles The last three fields allow you to specify standard I/O handles for the child that differ from those of the parent. Normally, the child inherits whatever I/O devices the parent has. The I/O handles provide an easy way to pass the child any handles it needs to receive, such as one end of a pipe. If you use any of the fields, you should set values in all of them. The child receives an invalid handle for any device you leave NULL. Call `GetStdHandle` to copy any of the parent's standard device handles into these fields.

> **NOTE** A process created with the `DETACHED_PROCESS` flag cannot inherit its parent's standard I/O devices. The console program initialization procedures do not correctly receive the devices when the process has no console. Microsoft identified this limitation in an early release and added the handle fields as a work-around. They work for any child but are necessary for detached children.

Return Value

`CreateProcess` returns TRUE if it succeeds in creating the new object or FALSE if an error occurs. If `CreateProcess` returns TRUE, it also returns information about the new process and its primary thread in the final parameter, the `PROCESS_INFORMATION` structure.

```
// CreateProcess fills this out to tell you what it created
typedef struct _PROCESS_INFORMATION  /* pi */
{
    HANDLE hProcess;          // handle to the new process
    HANDLE hThread;           // handle to its primary thread
    DWORD  dwProcessId;       // number identifying new process
    DWORD  dwThreadId;        // number identifying new thread
} PROCESS_INFORMATION;
```

If your program does not make use of the handles for the new process and its primary thread, you should close both right away. Otherwise, even if the PROCESS_INFORMATION structure is a local variable and goes out of scope, abandoning whatever it contained, the two object entries remain in your process's object table and the system counts them as open handles.

The size of physical system memory limits the total number of processes that can be created. Be sure to check for error returns. One of the early beta versions allowed a 16MB machine to create about 40 processes before failing for lack of memory. The limit will vary from version to version and machine to machine, but it is finite. Memory shortage can also cause CreateThread to fail, though threads consume significantly fewer resources than processes.

C Runtime Equivalents

The spawn and exec functions in the C runtime library also create new processes. Internally, however, they map to the same Win32 CreateProcess call. Through its parameters, CreateProcess offers more ways to customize the new process than do the C functions. The C runtime functions _getenv and _putenv, which work with a process's environment variables, also duplicate Win32 API functions.

Getting Information about a Process

Once a process starts up, it can call several commands to find out about itself.

Getting the Handle and ID

Like threads, processes are identified by a handle and an ID number. The parent receives both from the CreateProcess call; the child receives them by calling GetCurrentProcess and GetCurrentProcessId. Like GetCurrentThread, Get-CurrentProcess returns a pseudohandle valid only in the current process. Pseudohandles may not be passed to other processes. To convert a pseudohandle to a real handle, use DuplicateHandle.

```
HANDLE GetCurrentProcess( void );
DWORD GetCurrentProcessId( void );
```

The C runtime function _getpid duplicates GetCurrentProcessId.

Getting the Environment Settings

The next function retrieves the environment settings inherited from the parent.

```
DWORD GetEnvironmentVariable(
    LPTSTR lpszName,     // name of environment variable
    LPTSTR lpszValue,    // address of buffer for variable value
    DWORD  dwValue );    // size of lpszValue buffer in char
```

You fill out the lpszName buffer with a variable name, such as PATH. The function looks up the corresponding value and copies it into lpszValue. The DWORD return value tells how many characters it copied into the lpszValue buffer. It is 0 if the variable was not found.

Getting the Command Line

Another function retrieves a pointer to the command line, but the same information is usually available by other means as well. Console programs written in C can read the command line using argc and argv; GUI programs can retrieve it through the lpszCmdLine parameter of WinMain.

```
LPTSTR GetCommandLine( void )
```

Changing Process Priority

With the creation flags in CreateProcess, the parent can assign one of four base priority classes to a new process:

- IDLE_PRIORITY_CLASS

- NORMAL_PRIORITY_CLASS

- HIGH_PRIORITY_CLASS

- REALTIME_PRIORITY_CLASS

The default priority class is normal. Do not use the high class, and especially not the real-time class, unless you must. Both levels impair the performance of lower-priority processes. Programs that do run at higher priorities should do so only for short periods of time.

Here are the functions to discover and modify a process's priority class:

```
DWORD GetPriorityClass( HANDLE hProcess );

BOOL SetPriorityClass(
    HANDLE hProcess,              // process to modify
    DWORD fdwPriority );          // new priority class
```

The DWORD values in both functions should be one of the four PRIORITY_CLASS flags just listed. The priority class of a process becomes the base priority for all its threads. Refer to the discussion of thread priorities in Chapter 14 to see how the base priority influences a thread's dynamic priority.

Synchronizing Processes

Chapter 14 also explained how threads coordinate their separate tasks by waiting for signals from synchronization objects. Besides the four standard synchronization objects—mutexes, semaphores, events, and critical sections—threads can wait for other threads and for files, timers, and processes. Waiting for a thread or a process means waiting for it to stop execution. A thread waits for a process by passing the process handle to WaitForSingleObject or WaitForMultiple-Objects. When the process terminates, it enters its signaled state, and all threads waiting for it resume execution.

One other synchronization command works only when waiting for processes. Instead of waiting for the process to terminate, you can wait for it to be idle. For this purpose, a process is considered idle when it is finished initializing and no input from the user is waiting to reach it.

```
DWORD WaitForInputIdle(
    HANDLE hProcess,         // process to wait for
    DWORD  dwTimeout );      // time-out time in milliseconds
```

Parents frequently call WaitForInputIdle immediately after creating a new process to allow the child time to establish itself. When the new process initializes and reaches its idle state, the parent can try to communicate with it.

What WaitForInputIdle returns depends on how it ends. It returns 0 for a successful wait when the process becomes idle. If the time-out period elapses before the process idles, WaitForInputIdle returns WAIT_TIMEOUT. To indicate an error, it returns 0xFFFFFFFF.

NOTE WaitForInputIdle tests the child's message queue for pending messages. It is intended only for GUI applications. Character-based console applications, lacking a message queue, are *always* idle by this definition.

Sharing Handles

Like handles to threads and synchronization objects, handles to processes can be shared. Several different processes might possess handles to any one process. As usual, you can't simply pass a handle directly from one process to another. You must instead rely on one of several transfer mechanisms to perform the conversion that makes a handle valid in a new address space. One mechanism is inheritance. If you tell `CreateProcess` to let the child inherit handles, the child receives copies of all the inheritable handles in its own object table. Children cannot use the handles there directly—they must still receive the handle on their command line or through a pipe—but inheritance makes the handle valid when it reaches the child process. If you pass to a child a handle it has not already inherited, the handle will not work.

Making a Handle Copy

Inheritance helps in passing handles only between related processes. To make a handle that can be passed to any other process, related or unrelated, call `Duplicate-Handle`. You saw that function in Chapter 14. Given the original handle and a source and destination process, `DuplicateHandle` creates a new handle valid in the destination process. `DuplicateHandle` also allows you to modify the attributes of a handle you want to keep. If, for example, you want only one of several children to inherit a particular handle, you create the first child, allowing inheritance, and then call `DuplicateHandle` to make a noninheritable copy. Close the original inheritable handle and keep only the copy. Subsequent children will not inherit it.

One of the sample programs in this chapter uses `DuplicateHandle` to control inheritance. Look for the `StartProcess` procedure in the anonymous pipe program.

Opening a Process

Another command allows any process to open a handle to any other process. The usual limits apply: You can open a process only if the security descriptor of your own process endows you with sufficient clearance.

```
HANDLE OpenProcess(
    DWORD fdwAccess,     // desired access privileges
    BOOL  bInherit,      // TRUE for children to inherit the handle
    DWORD dwProcessId ); // number identifying the process
```

`OpenProcess` requires you to identify the process by its ID number. Normally, you know the number only if you created the process or if the process itself, or one of its relatives, passes you the number (through a pipe or a DDE conversation, for example).

Ending a Process

Normally, you don't do anything special to end a process, just as you don't do anything to end a thread. When a thread reaches the `return` instruction at the end of its startup procedure, the system calls `ExitThread` and the thread terminates, leaving an exit code behind. When the primary thread in a process comes to the end of its starting procedure (usually `WinMain`), the system implicitly calls `ExitProcess` instead of `ExitThread`. `ExitProcess` forces all the threads in a process to end, no matter what they may be doing at the time. Any thread, however, may call `ExitProcess` explicitly to end its process at any time.

```
void ExitProcess( UINT fuExitCode );
```

You define the exit code to be whatever you like. Like threads, processes remain in memory even after they terminate until all the handles to them are closed. To determine a process's exit code, keep its handle and call `GetExitCodeProcess`.

```
BOOL GetExitCodeProcess(
    HANDLE  hProcess,         // handle to the process
    LPDWORD lpdwExitCode );   // buffer to receive exit code
```

If the process has not ended, `GetExitCodeProcess` reports the exit code as `STILL_ACTIVE`.

Normally a process ends when its primary thread ends. The primary thread may, however, choose to quit without ending the process. If the primary thread ends with an explicit call to `ExitThread`, the system does not call `ExitProcess`. Other threads in the process continue to execute, and the process runs until any thread calls `ExitProcess` directly or until the last thread ends.

A number of things happen when a process ends:

- All of the process's handles are closed; all of its file handles, thread handles, event handles, and any other handles are destroyed. The objects they point to will also be destroyed, but only if no other processes also possess handles to them.

- Any DLLs the process has called receive notification when the process terminates, giving them a chance to clean up and exit.

- The terminating process acquires an exit code. More specifically, the Exit Status attribute of the process object changes from STILL_ACTIVE to whatever value ExitProcess assigns.

- The process object enters its signaled state, and any threads waiting for it to end resume execution.

Note that when a parent process dies, it does not take its children with it. The children, if any, continue to run independently.

Forcing a Process to Exit

Another command, TerminateProcess, also forces a process to exit. Actually this command brings the process to an abrupt and crashing halt, preventing some of the usual cleanup from happening. DLLs, for example, are not notified when TerminateProcess kills one of their clients. Like TerminateThread, TerminateProcess is abrupt, messy, and best avoided when possible.

```
BOOL TerminateProcess(
    HANDLE hProcess,          // handle to the process
    UINT fuExitCode );        // exit code for the process
```

Pipe-Related Commands

As explained earlier in the chapter, pipes allow two processes to communicate with each other. A pipe is a memory buffer where the system preserves data between the time one process writes it and another process reads it. The API commands ask you to think of the buffer as a pipe, or conduit, through which information flows from one place to another. A pipe has two ends. A one-way pipe allows writing only at one end and reading only at the other; all the information flows from one process to the other. A two-way pipe allows both processes to read and write, so the information flows both ways at once. When you create a pipe, you also decide whether it will be anonymous or named. Anonymous pipes are simpler, so we'll start with them.

Creating Anonymous Pipes

An anonymous pipe passes information in only one direction, and both ends of the pipe must be on the same machine. The process that creates an anonymous pipe receives two handles: one for reading and one for writing. In order to communicate with another process, the server must pass one of the handles to the other process.

```
BOOL CreatePipe(
    PHANDLE phRead,            // variable for read handle (inbound)
    PHANDLE phWrite,           // variable for write handle (outbound)
    LPSECURITY_ATTRIBUTES lpsa, // access privileges
    DWORD   dwPipeSize );      // size of pipe buffer (0=default)
```

The size of the pipe buffer determines how much information the pipe can hold before it overflows. No one can deposit messages in a full pipe until someone makes room by reading the old information from the other end.

If all goes well, CreatePipe returns TRUE and deposits two new valid handles in the variables indicated by the PHANDLE parameters. Next, the creating process usually needs to pass one of the handles to another process. Which handle you give away depends on whether you want the other process to send (write) or receive (read) information through the pipe. You can pass the handle to a child process on its command line or through its standard I/O handles. An unrelated process would need to receive the handle by other means, such as through a DDE conversation or a shared file. Connections through anonymous pipes are easier to arrange when the processes are related.

The following commands work only with named pipes. Do not create an anonymous pipe if you need the functions these commands provide.

CallNamedPipe	ImpersonateNamedPipeClient
ConnectNamedPipe	PeekNamedPipe
CreateFile	RevertToSelf
CreateNamedPipe	SetNamedPipeHandleState
DisconnectNamedPipe	TransactNamedPipe
GetNamedPipeHandleState	WaitNamedPipe
GetNamedPipeInfo	

These commands are discussed in the next section.

Creating Named Pipes

Many NT/95 system objects may be assigned name strings to identify them. Names allow other processes to locate objects more easily. Unnamed objects are known only by their handles, and handles are valid only in the process where they originate. Any process that knows the name of an object, however, can ask the system to search its object name hierarchy. Given a name, the system can find any object on any connected machine.

If a pipe has a name, the client program doesn't need to wait for the server to pass it a handle. Instead, the client can acquire a handle by calling `CreateFile` or `CallNamedPipe`. In either case, the client needs to know only the pipe's name string. A parent might pass the string to a child process on the command line, or any process might pass it to any other through a shared file or a DDE conversation. Most often, however, two processes sharing a named pipe have been written by the same developer, and they simply agree on a name string in advance.

`CreateNamedPipe` makes pipes with names.

```
HANDLE CreateNamedPipe(
    LPTSTR  lpszPipeName,        // string naming new pipe object
    DWORD   fdwOpenMode,         // access, overlap, and write-through
    DWORD   fdwPipeMode,         // type, read, and wait modes
    DWORD   dwMaxInstances,      // maximum number of instances
    DWORD   dwOutBuf,            // outbound buffer size in bytes
    DWORD   dwInBuf,             // inbound buffer size in bytes
    DWORD   dwTimeout,           // time-out interval in milliseconds
    LPSECURITY_ATTRIBUTES lpsa );   // access privileges
```

The Parameters

Because named pipes have more features, `CreateNamedPipe` takes more parameters.

Naming the Pipe   The first parameter points to the string you provide to name the new object. The system stores this name in its hierarchical tree of system object names. Pipe name strings should follow this form:

```
\\.\pipe\<pipename>
```

The first backslash designates the root node of the system's object name hierarchy. The other three backslashes separate the names of subsequent nodes. The dot (.) stands for the local machine. Although pipes can connect with clients on other network servers, a new pipe object always appears on the local server where it was created.

Under the server name is a node called `pipe`, holding the names of all the pipe objects on the local machine. Within the name string, the substring *<pipename>* is the only section the programmer chooses. This substring may be as long as 256 characters and is not case-sensitive (object names are not sensitive to case).

Servers and clients both use the dot (.) to represent the local server, but a client wishing to open a pipe on a remote server must know the server's name. One way to learn remote server names is to enumerate them with the `WNetOpenEnum`, `WNetEnumResource`, and `WNetCloseEnum` functions, but enumeration is slow. We'll suggest a better method in a few pages when we compare pipes to mailslots.

These functions require a pipe's name string as a parameter: `CreateNamedPipe`, `CreateFile`, `WaitNamedPipe`, and `CallNamedPipe`.

Access, Write-through, and Overlapping   The next parameter after the name string, `fdwOpenMode`, combines flags to set several pipe attributes. The most important is the access mode, which determines the direction information flows through the pipe. `fdwOpenMode` must include one of the following three flags:

- `PIPE_ACCESS_OUTBOUND`: The server only writes, and the client only reads.

- `PIPE_ACCESS_INBOUND`: The server only reads, and the client only writes.

- `PIPE_ACCESS_DUPLEX`: Both the server and client may read and write.

You must specify one of the three access flags for `fdwOpenMode`. The other two flags in this parameter are optional:

- `FILE_FLAG_WRITE_THROUGH`: Disables buffering over a network.

- `FILE_FLAG_OVERLAPPED`: Enables asynchronous read and write operations.

For efficiency, when a pipe extends to a remote machine, the system normally does not send every message immediately. Instead it tries to accumulate several short messages in a buffer and send them across the pipe in a single operation. If too much time passes and the buffer remains only partly full, the system eventually sends the buffer anyway. The write-through flag prevents the system from buffering; each new message is sent immediately, and write commands do not return until their output has been transmitted. Turn off the buffering if you expect to send messages only infrequently.

The second optional flag, `FILE_FLAG_OVERLAPPED`, allows read and write commands to return immediately while the action they initiate continues in the background. Read and write operations, because they involve physical devices, are usually slow.

When an NT program reads from a file, for example, it may choose simply to start the read process, name a procedure to be called when the read operation ends, and then continue executing while the system reads in the background. When the read operation finally ends, the system schedules an asynchronous procedure call and invokes the callback function named in the read command. The callback function then processes the newly retrieved information. Making the system do your reading and writing in the background is called *asynchronous I/O* or *overlapping I/O*. Pipes also support overlapping I/O. Overlapping I/O is more difficult to program, because you need to write a callback function, but it's also more efficient.

Type, Read, and Wait   The `fdwPipeMode` parameter combines flags to designate another set of pipe features: the read mode, the type, and the wait flag. The type and the read mode are closely related; they might be better named the write mode and the read mode. Together, they control how information in the pipe is organized and interpreted. Both offer a choice between byte and message modes.

The following are pipe-type (write mode) flags:

- `PIPE_TYPE_BYTE`
- `PIPE_TYPE_MESSAGE`

And these are the read-mode flags:

- `PIPE_READMODE_BYTE`
- `PIPE_READMODE_MESSAGE`

The information in a byte-mode pipe is read and written in the normal binary manner and understood as nothing more than a series of bytes.

Sometimes, it is more convenient to divide the information in a pipe into discrete messages, where the output from each separate write command constitutes a new message. A message-mode pipe automatically and transparently prefaces each new message with an invisible header specifying the length of the message. The header enables a read command to stop automatically when it reaches the end of one message. The recipient recovers messages one at a time, exactly as they were written.

If one program sends to another a long series of integers, for example, it would probably use a byte-mode pipe, because the receiver doesn't care how many integers were written at a time. Everything it retrieves is simply another integer. But if a program were sending commands written in a script language, the receiver would need to retrieve the commands one at a time, exactly as written, in order to parse them. Since each command might be a different length, the two programs would use a message-mode pipe.

The write mode and read mode are designated independently, but not all combinations make sense. Specifically, you can't combine PIPE_TYPE_BYTE and PIPE_READMODE_MESSAGE. A byte-type pipe writes bytes without message headers, so the receiver can't recover message units. On the other hand, you can combine PIPE_TYPE_MESSAGE with PIPE_READMODE_BYTE. In that case, the sender includes message headers but the receiver chooses to ignore them, retrieving the data as a series of undifferentiated bytes. (The receiver still does not see the invisible message headers.)

Besides the flags to set the type and read mode for a pipe, the fdwPipeMode parameter accepts one other flag for the wait mode. The wait mode determines what happens when some condition temporarily prevents a pipe command from completing. For example, what should happen if you try to read from an empty pipe? Some programs might want to forget about reading and move onto the next instruction, but other programs might need to wait for a new message before proceeding.

By default, pipes cause reading threads to block and wait, but you can prevent blocking by adding the PIPE_NOWAIT flag to fdwPipeMode. (The default flag is PIPE_WAIT.) The wait mode affects write commands as well as read commands. A program that tries to write when the pipe buffer is full normally blocks until another program makes room by reading from the other end. The wait mode also affects a server trying to connect with a client. If the ConnectNamedPipe command finds no ready clients, the wait mode determines whether the command waits for a client to connect or returns immediately.

> **TIP**
> The nonblocking mode is provided primarily for compatibility with LANMan 2.0.

Pipe Instances   A server program may wish to open pipes for more than one client. It may not know in advance how many clients it will have. It would be inconvenient to invent a new pipe name for each new client. How would all the clients know in advance what name to use when they open their end of the pipe? To circumvent this problem, Win32 permits the server to create the same pipe over and over.

Each time you call `CreateNamedPipe` with the same name, you get a new instance of the same pipe. Each new instance provides an independent communication channel for another client. The server might begin by creating the same pipe four times. It would receive four different handles, and it could wait for a different client to connect to each one. All the clients would use the same pipe name to request their own handles, but each would receive a handle to a different instance. If a fifth client tried to connect, it would block until the server disconnected one of the first four instances.

The `dwMaxInstances` parameter of the `CreateNamedPipe` command sets an upper limit on the number of instances one pipe will support before `CreateNamedPipe` returns an error. The `PIPE_UNLIMITED_INSTANCES` flag indicates no upper limit. In that case, the maximum number of instances is limited only by system resources. The value of `dwMaxInstances` may not exceed the value of `PIPE_UNLIMITED_INSTANCES`, which our version of Winbase.H defines as 255.

Buffer Sizes   The `dwOutBuf` and `dwInBuf` parameters set the initial size of the buffers that store anything written to the pipe from either end. For an outbound pipe (`PIPE_ACCESS_OUTBOUND`), only the output buffer matters; for an inbound pipe, only the input buffer size is significant.

The limits set by the buffer size parameters are flexible. Internally, every read or write operation on a pipe causes the system to allocate buffer space from the kernel's pool of system memory. The buffer size values are interpreted as a quota limiting these allocations. When the system allocates buffer space for a write operation, it charges the space consumed to the write buffer quota. If the new buffer size fits within the quota, all is well. If it does not, the system allocates the space anyway and charges it to the *process's* resource quota. In order to avoid excessive charges to the process quota, every `WriteFile` operation, that causes the buffer to exceed its quota, blocks. The writing thread suspends operation until the receiving thread reduces the buffer by reading from it.

In estimating buffer sizes, you'll need to take into account the fact that each buffer allocation is slightly larger than you expect because, besides the message contents, it includes an internal data structure of about 28 bytes. The exact size is undocumented and may vary from version to version.

To summarize, the system allocates buffer space dynamically as needed, but threads that frequently exceed their buffer size may block excessively. The sample programs at the end of this chapter leave the buffer size at 0 and suffer no apparent harm. Programs that send frequent messages or that expect the buffers to back up occasionally will benefit from increased buffer sizes.

Time-Out Period   The `dwTimeout` value matters only when a client calls `WaitNamedPipe` to make a connection, and it matters then only if the client accepts the default time-out period. The default period is the number the server sets in the `dwTimeout` parameter of `CreateNamedPipe`, but the client may set a different period in `WaitNamedPipe`.

Security Attributes   The final parameter, a pointer to a `SECURITY_ATTRIBUTES` structure, should look very familiar by now. The values in it determine which operations the new handle allows you to perform on its object, and they also determine whether child processes may inherit the new handle. As usual, if you leave the field NULL, the resulting handle has full access privileges and cannot be inherited.

Summary of Named Pipe Attributes

`CreateNamedPipe` allows you to set many potentially confusing characteristics of the new object. To add to the confusion, some of the characteristics must be exactly the same for every instance of a pipe, but some may vary with each instance. Table 15.1 summarizes these characteristics.

T A B L E 15.1 Summary of Named Pipe Attributes

Characteristics	Parameter	Description	Possible Values	Constant for All Instances
Access mode	`fdwOpen-Mode`	Direction information flows	`PIPE_ACCESS_OUTBOUND` `PIPE_ACCESS_INBOUND` `PIPE_ACCESS_DUPLEX`	Yes
Type (write mode)	`fdwPipe-Mode`	Whether to add a header to each new message	`PIPE_TYPE_BYTE` `PIPE_TYPE_MESSAGE`	Yes
Wait mode	`fdwPipe-Mode`	Whether to block when a command can't work immediately	`PIPE_WAIT` `PIPE_NOWAIT`	No
Overlapped I/O	`fdwOpen-Mode`	Whether to permit asynchronous I/O operations	`FILE_FLAG_OVERLAPPED`	No
Write-through	`fdwOpen-Mode`	Whether to buffer network transmissions	`FILE_FLAG_WRITE_THROUGH`	No

TABLE 15.1 Summary of Named Pipe Attributes (Continued)

Characteristics	Parameter	Description	Possible Values	Constant for All Instances
Read mode	`fdwPipe-Mode`	Whether to end read operations on message boundaries	`PIPE_READMODE_BYTE` `PIPE_READMODE_MESSAGE`	No
Maximum instances	`dwMax-Instances`	Most copies of one pipe allowed simultaneously	Number from 1 to `PIPE_UNLIMITED_INSTANCES`	Yes
Buffer sizes	`dwOutBuf /` `dwInBuf`	Size for buffers that hold messages during transit	Size in bytes (0 for defaults)	No
Time-out period	`dwTimeOut`	Maximum waiting period for commands to succeed	Period in milliseconds	Yes
Security attributes	`lpsa`	Access privileges and inheritability	`SECURITY_ATTRIBUTES` structure or NULL for defaults	No

Anonymous pipes always have the characteristics that are the default state for named pipes: `PIPE_TYPE_BYTE`, `PIPE_READMODE_BYTE`, `PIPE_WAIT`, no overlapping I/O, and network buffering enabled.

Return Value

`CreateNamedPipe` returns a valid handle if it succeeds. If an error occurs, it returns the value `(HANDLE) 0xFFFFFFFF` (also known as `INVALID_HANDLE_VALUE`).

Connecting to an Existing Pipe

After a server opens a named pipe, it must wait for a client to open the other end. A client may open its end in any of several ways, but the most common is `Create-File`. This function not only works with disk files, but also can be used with named pipes, communications devices, and the I/O buffers of a character-based console window. The `ReadFile` and `WriteFile` commands also work with the same set of objects. Using a single unified API for several different objects makes programming easier.

```
HANDLE CreateFile(
    LPCTSTR lpszName,              // name of the pipe (or file)
    DWORD fdwAccess,               // read/write access (must match pipe)
    DWORD fdwShareMode,            // usually 0 (no share) for pipes
    LPSECURITY_ATTRIBUTES lpsa,    // access privileges
    DWORD fdwCreate,               // must be OPEN_EXISTING for pipes
    DWORD fdwAttrsAndFlags,        // write-through and overlap modes
    HANDLE hTemplateFile );        // ignored with OPEN_EXISTING
```

Catching Errors

You may have noticed that many of the functions we've described seem to have very rudimentary error returns. `CreateThread`, `CreateMutex`, `CreateProcess`, `CreatePipe`, and `CreateNamedPipe`, for example, all might fail for a variety of reasons. The system might be low on memory, or a particular mutex might already exist, or a network connection might fail, or a parameter might be invalid. Yet all of these creation functions indicate errors only by returning either FALSE or an invalid handle.

Better diagnostics are available. The system keeps a large set of error messages in a single collective message table and identifies each message with a different number. Whenever a command fails, it stores an error message number for the active thread. Immediately after a function fails, you should call `GetLastError` to retrieve the message number. To translate the number into an explanatory string, suitable for showing in a message box, call `FormatMessage`.

Even functions from the Windows 3.1 API sometimes set error codes under Win32. Microsoft's online help file regularly identifies error-setting commands in the descriptions of their return values: "To get extended error information, use the `GetLastError` function." The sample programs later in this chapter construct a procedure for displaying the appropriate message after any error. Look for `ShowErrorMsg` in the listings.

The pipe name must match the string the server passed to `CreateNamedPipe`. If the server and client programs are connecting over a network, the string must name the network server machine instead of using a dot (.).

The `fdwAccess` parameter tells whether you want to read or write to the pipe. If the pipe was created with the `PIPE_ACCESS_OUTBOUND` flag, you should specify `GENERIC_READ` in CreateFile. For an inbound pipe, the client needs `GENERIC_WRITE` privileges. For a duplex pipe, the client needs `GENERIC_READ | GENERIC_WRITE` privileges.

The `fdwShareMode` should generally be 0 to prohibit sharing the pipe with other processes. Occasionally, however, a client might use the share mode to duplicate the pipe handle for another client. In that case, both clients have handles to the same instance of the same pipe, and they might need to worry about synchronizing their read and write operations.

The security attributes in the `lpsa` parameter should be familiar to you by now. The `fdwCreate` flag must be `OPEN_EXISTING` because `CreateFile` will not create a new pipe. It simply opens existing pipes. Other flags allow `CreateFile` to create new file objects where none existed before, but those flags produce errors when `lpszName` designates a pipe object.

The last two parameters normally govern file attributes, such as hidden, read-only, and archive settings, but `CreateFile` uses the attributes only to create new files. When you open an existing object (with `OPEN_EXIST`), the object keeps whatever attributes it already has. However, there are two exceptions. Two flags in the `fdwAttrsAndFlags` parameters do work when opening an existing named pipe: `FILE_FLAG_WRITE_THROUGH` and `FILE_FLAG_OVERLAPPED`. The client may set flags that differ from the server, enabling or disabling network buffering and asynchronous I/O to suit its own preferences.

Modifying an Existing Pipe

Two ends of the same pipe may have different read or wait modes, but `CreateFile` always copies the original attributes when it opens a handle for a client. Any process, however, can modify its pipe handle with `SetNamedPipeHandleState`.

```
BOOL SetNamedPipeHandleState(
    HANDLE   hNamedPipe,              // handle of named pipe
    LPDWORD  lpdwModes,               // read and wait mode flags
    LPDWORD  lpdwMaxCollect,          // transmission buffer size
    LPDWORD  lpdwCollectDataTimeout );// max time before transmission
```

The first parameter is a handle returned by `CreateNamedPipe` or `CreateFile`.

The second parameter, like the `fdwPipeMode` parameter of `CreateNamedPipe`, combines flags to set several attributes at once. The `lpdwModes` parameter controls whether read operations use the byte or message mode and whether certain commands will block while they wait for the pipe to become available. The read mode may be `PIPE_READMODE_BYTE` or `PIPE_READMODE_MESSAGE`. (Specifying the message read mode for a pipe that was created with `PIPE_TYPE_BYTE` causes an error.) The read-mode pipe may be combined with either `PIPE_WAIT` or `PIPE_NOWAIT`.

The last two parameters matter only for pipes that connect with a remote machine. They control how the system buffers network transmissions. (They have no effect on pipes with the `PIPE_FLAG_WRITE_THROUGH` attribute, which disables network buffering.) Buffering allows the system to combine several messages into a single transmission. It holds outgoing messages in a buffer until either the buffer fills or a set time period elapses. `lpdwMaxCollect` sets the size of the collection buffer, and `lpdwCollectDataTimeout` sets the time period in milliseconds.

Getting Information about an Existing Pipe

Three functions retrieve information about a pipe without changing any of its attributes.

Getting State Information

The first information command is the counterpart of `SetNamedPipeHandleState`, but it retrieves more information than its partner sets:

```
BOOL GetNamedPipeHandleState(
   HANDLE  hNamedPipe,          // handle of named pipe
   LPDWORD lpdwModes,           // read and wait modes
   LPDWORD lpdwCurInstances,    // number of current pipe instances
   LPDWORD lpcbMaxCollect,      // max bytes before remote transmission
   LPDWORD lpdwCollectTimeout,  // max time before remote transmission
   LPTSTR  lpszUserName,        // user name of client process
   DWORD   dwMaxUserNameBuff ); // in char size of user name
```

The `lpdwModes` parameter may contain the `PIPE_READMODE_MESSAGE` and `PIPE_NOWAIT` flags. To indicate the byte mode or wait mode, which are the default states, no flags are set.

`lpdwCurInstances` counts the number of instances that currently exist for a pipe. In other words, it tells how many times the server has called `CreateNamed-Pipe` with the same name string.

The collect and time-out parameters retrieve the same network buffering information that `SetNamedPipeHandleState` controls.

The last two parameters help a server learn about its client. They return the null-terminated string naming the user who is running the client application. User names are the names users give to log in. They are associated with particular configuration and security privileges. The server might want the name for a log or a report, but probably this parameter exists for compatibility with OS/2, which also makes the user name available. The `lpszUserName` parameter must be NULL if `hNamedPipe` belongs to a client; in other words, if it was created with `CreateFile` rather than `CreateNamedPipe`.

Any of the pointer parameters may be set to NULL to ignore the value normally returned in that place.

Getting Fixed Attributes

Another function that returns additional information about a pipe is `GetNamed-PipeInfo`. This function returns attributes that may not be changed. (`GetNamed-PipeHandleState` returns attributes that may change during the life of a pipe.)

```
BOOL GetNamedPipeInfo(
    HANDLE  hNamedPipe,       // handle of named pipe
    LPDWORD lpdwType,         // type and server flags
    LPDWORD lpdwOutBuf,       // size in bytes of pipe's output buffer
    LPDWORD lpdwInBuf,        // size in bytes of pipe's input buffer
    LPDWORD lpdwMaxInstances ); // maximum number of pipe instances
```

The `lpdwType` parameter may contain either or both of two flags: PIPE_TYPE _MESSAGE and PIPE_SERVER_END. If no flags are set, the handle connects to the client end of a pipe that writes in bytes. The input and output buffer sizes are set in `CreateNamedPipe`.

The `lpdwMaxInstances` parameter returns the value `CreateNamedPipe` set as an upper limit for the number of simultaneous instances allowed to exist for one pipe.

Retrieving a Message

Normally, when you read from a pipe, the read operation removes from the buffer the message it retrieves. With `PeekNamedPipe`, however, it is possible to retrieve a message without clearing it from the buffer. The inaptly named `PeekNamedPipe` command works with both named and anonymous pipes.

```
BOOL PeekNamedPipe(
    HANDLE  hPipe,          // handle of named or anonymous pipe
    LPVOID  lpvBuffer,      // address of buffer to receive data
    DWORD   dwBufferSize,   // size in bytes of data buffer
    LPDWORD lpdwBytesRead,  // returns number of bytes read
    LPDWORD lpdwAvailable,  // returns total bytes available
    LPDWORD lpdwMessage );  // returns unread bytes in this message
```

The `lpvBuffer` parameter points to a place for the command to store whatever information it copies from the pipe. `PeekNamedPipe` cannot retrieve more than `dwBufferSize` bytes, even if more information remains in the pipe.

`lpdwBytesRead` returns the number of bytes the function actually did read, and `lpdwMessage` returns the number of bytes remaining in the current message, if any. `lpdwMessage` is ignored if the pipe's read mode is `PIPE_READMODE_BYTE`. In that case, there are no message units to measure. (All anonymous pipes use the byte read mode.)

The total number of available bytes returned in `lpdwAvailable` includes all bytes in all messages. If the buffer currently holds several messages, `*lpdwAvailable` may be greater than the sum of `*lpdwBytesRead` and `*lpdwMessage`.

It is legal to retrieve only a partial set of information by leaving some parameters NULL. You may, for example, set everything to 0 or NULL except the handle and `lpdwAvailable` if all you want to know is how many bytes are waiting in the buffer.

When reading from a pipe set to the message read mode, `PeekNamedPipe` always stops after reading the first message, even if the data buffer has room to hold several messages. Also, `PeekNamedPipe` never blocks on an empty pipe the way `ReadFile` does if `PIPE_WAIT` is set. The wait mode has no effect on `PeekNamedPipe`, which always returns immediately.

Reading and Writing through a Pipe

All the choices you make to create a pipe—named or anonymous, byte or message, blocking or nonblocking—prepare for the moment when you actually send a message through the pipe. One program writes to its handle, and the other program reads from its handle. This most basic transaction typically involves two functions: `WriteFile` and `ReadFile`.

```
BOOL WriteFile(
    HANDLE hFile,                    // place to write (pipe or file)
    CONST VOID *lpBuffer,            // points to data to put in file
    DWORD dwBytesToWrite,            // number of bytes to write
    LPDWORD lpdwBytesWritten,        // returns number of bytes written
    LPOVERLAPPED lpOverlapped );     // needed for asynchronous I/O

BOOL ReadFile(
    HANDLE hFile;                    // source for reading (pipe or file)
    LPVOID lpBuffer;                 // buffer to hold data retrieved
    DWORD dwBytesToRead;             // number of bytes to read
    LPDWORD lpdwBytesRead;           // returns number of bytes read
    LPOVERLAPPED lpOverlapped );     // needed for asynchronous I/O
```

Bytes to Read or Write

The number of bytes to read or write need not be as large as (but should not be larger than) the size of the buffer. If you call ReadFile on a message-mode pipe and give dwBytesToRead a value smaller than the size of the next message, ReadFile reads only part of the message and returns FALSE. A subsequent call to GetLastError discovers an error code of ERROR_MORE_DATA. Call ReadFile again, or PeekNamedPipe, to read the rest of the message. When WriteFile writes to a nonblocking byte-mode pipe and finds the buffer nearly full, it still returns TRUE but the value of *lpdwBytesWritten will be less than dwBytesToWrite.

Blocking

Depending on the pipe's wait mode, both WriteFile and ReadFile may block. WriteFile might have to wait for a full pipe to empty out from the other end; an empty pipe causes ReadFile to block waiting for a new message.

Asynchronous I/O

The final parameter of both commands points to an OVERLAPPED structure that provides extra information for performing asynchronous (or overlapping) I/O. Asynchronous I/O allows the command to return immediately, even before the read or write operation runs to completion. Asynchronous commands do not automatically modify the position of the file pointer, so the OVERLAPPED structure includes an offset pointing to the place in the file where the operation should begin.

The structure also contains a handle to an event object. A thread in the reading program can wait for the event's signal before examining what ReadFile placed in the retrieval buffer. You must supply an OVERLAPPED structure when using file handles that were created with the FILE_FLAG_OVERLAPPED attribute.

Another method of performing asynchronous I/O involves the `ReadFileEx` and `WriteFileEx` commands. Instead of signaling completion with an event, these commands invoke a procedure you provide to be called at the end of each operation.

With respect to pipes, overlapping I/O is a useful strategy for dealing with multiple clients connected to different instances of a single pipe. Synchronous I/O is easier to program, but slow read and write commands might hold up other waiting clients. A server can create a separate thread for each client, as our sample program does for simplicity, but that involves more overhead than the situation actually requires.

A single thread can read and write simultaneously to different pipe instances with asynchronous I/O, because each command always returns immediately, leaving the thread free while the system finishes in the background. With `Wait-ForMultipleObjects`, a thread can arrange to block until any pending operation completes. The efficiency of asynchronous I/O can make a big difference over slow network connections. Also, it is easier to protect program resources when you have fewer threads to synchronize.

Synchronizing Connections

At any time a client may call `CreateFile` to open its end of a named pipe. Two problems, however, may arise:

- The server often needs to know when a client has connected to a pipe. Writing to an unconnected pipe serves little purpose, and `CreateFile` does not tell the server when a connection occurs.

- If all the instances of a pipe are busy, `CreateFile` always immediately returns `INVALID_HANDLE_VALUE` without establishing a connection. The client may prefer to wait for a pipe instance to become available when another client finishes.

In short, both server and client must be able to block while waiting for conditions that permit a connection to occur. To do so, the server calls `ConnectNamedPipe` and the client calls `WaitNamedPipe`.

```
BOOL ConnectNamedPipe(
    HANDLE hNamedPipe,              // handle of available named pipe
    LPOVERLAPPED lpOverlapped );  // info for async operation
```

```
BOOL WaitNamedPipe(
    LPTSTR lpszPipeName,     // points to string naming pipe object
    DWORD dwTimeout );       // maximum wait time in milliseconds
```

These coordinating functions work only with named pipes because a client can-not create its own handle to an anonymous pipe. It must receive a handle directly from the server, and in that case, the connection is already made.

Signaling a Connection

ConnectNamedPipe can respond asynchronously, just as ReadFile and WriteFile can. The lpOverlapped parameter contains an event handle, and the event object signals when a client connects.

How ConnectNamedPipe behaves depends on whether the pipe was created with, or subsequently modified to include, the FILE_FLAG_OVERLAPPING flag and the PIPE_WAIT mode. Its operation is most intuitive on pipes that allow waiting. Here are the possibilities:

Wait Mode	Operation Mode	Results
PIPE_WAIT	Synchronous operation	Does not return until a client connects or an error occurs. Returns TRUE if a client connects after the call begins. Returns FALSE if a client is already connected or an error occurs.
PIPE_WAIT	Asynchronous operation	Returns immediately. Always returns FALSE. GetLastError signals ERROR_IO_PENDING if the wait is in progress.

Wait Mode	Operation Mode	Results
PIPE_NOWAIT	Synchronous operation	Always returns immediately, returning TRUE the first time it is called after a client disconnects. TRUE indicates the pipe is available. Otherwise, the command always returns FALSE. GetLastError indicates ERROR_PIPE_LISTENING if no connection was made or ERROR_PIPE_CONNECTED if a connection has already been made.
PIPE_NOWAIT	Asynchronous mode	Should not be used with a no-wait mode pipe. The no-wait mode exists only for compatibility with LANMan 2.0.

The unintuitive use of TRUE and FALSE returns results from the fact that ConnectNamedPipe returns TRUE only if the pipe begins in a listening state and a client connects after the connect command begins and before it returns. If the pipe is already connected, and if the command responds asynchronously (returns without waiting) or is called for a pipe that does not allow waiting, the command generally returns FALSE.

Client Waiting

The client's wait command, WaitNamedPipe, does not actually create a connection. It returns TRUE when a pipe is or becomes available, but it does not return a handle to the available pipe.

It is common for a client to repeat the wait-then-create cycle in a loop until it acquires a valid handle. Normally, WaitNamedPipe considers a pipe available only when the server calls ConnectNamedPipe to wait for a link. The two commands work together to synchronize server and client. If, however, the server creates a new pipe and has never connected to any client, WaitNamedPipe returns TRUE even without a matching ConnectNamedPipe.

The purpose behind the apparent inconsistency is to guarantee that `WaitNamed-Pipe` connects only at times when the server knows its pipe is available. If a client breaks a connection, the server may not realize it right away; and if another client connected immediately, the server could not know it had a new partner. By recognizing only new pipes and pipes made available through `ConnectNamedPipe`, `WaitNamedPipe` prevents clients from sneaking in to the middle of a running conversation.

NOTE `WaitForSingleObject` **does not work with pipes because pipes do not have signal states.**

Closing a Connection

A client breaks its connection by calling `CloseHandle`. A server may do the same, but sometimes it may prefer to disconnect without destroying the pipe, saving it for later reuse. By calling `DisconnectNamedPipe`, the server forces the conversation to end and invalidates the client's handle.

```
BOOL DisconnectNamedPipe( HANDLE hNamedPipe );
```

If the client tries to read or write with its handle after the server disconnects, the client receives an error result. The client must still call `CloseHandle`, however.

Any data lingering unread in the pipe is lost when the connection ends. A friendly server can protect the last messages by calling `FlushFileBuffers` first.

```
BOOL FlushFileBuffers( HANDLE hFile );
```

When `FlushFileBuffers` receives a handle to a named pipe, it blocks until the pipe's buffers are empty.

Disconnecting a pipe from its client does not destroy the pipe object. After breaking a connection, the server should call `ConnectNamedPipe` to await a new connection on the freed pipe or else call `CloseHandle` to destroy that instance. Clients blocked on `WaitNamedPipe` do not unblock when a client closes its pipe handle. The server must disconnect its end and call `ConnectNamedPipe` to listen for a new client.

Making Transactions

Two more commands facilitate conversations through duplex pipes by combining a read and a write operation into a single *transaction*. Transactions are particularly efficient over networks because they minimize the number of transmissions.

In order to support reciprocal transactions, a pipe must be set up as follows:

- A named pipe
- Use the PIPE_ACCESS_DUPLEX flag
- Set as the message type
- Set to message-read mode

The server sets all those attributes with CreateNamedPipe. The client can adjust the attributes, if necessary, with SetNamedPipeHandleState. The blocking mode has no effect on transaction commands.

Sending a Request

The first command, TransactNamedPipe, sends a request and waits for a response. Clients and servers both may use the command, although clients tend to find it more useful.

```
BOOL TransactNamedPipe(
    HANDLE hNamedPipe,        // handle of named pipe
    LPVOID lpvWriteBuf,       // buffer holding information to send
    DWORD dwWriteBufSize,     // size of write buffer in bytes
    LPVOID lpvReadBuf,        // buffer for information received
    DWORD dwReadBufSize,      // size of read buffer in bytes
    LPDWORD lpdwBytesRead,    // bytes actually read (value returned)
    LPOVERLAPPED lpOverlapped ); // info for asynchronous I/O
```

In spite of its many parameters, the function is straightforward. It writes the contents of lpvWriteBuf into the pipe, waits for the next response, and copies the message it receives into the lpvReadBuf buffer.

The function fails if the pipe has the wrong attributes or if the read buffer is too small to accommodate the entire message. In that case, GetLastError returns ERROR_MORE_DATA, and you should finish the reading with ReadFile or PeekNamedPipe.

`TransactNamedPipe` handles one exchange through a pipe. After establishing a connection, a program might call `TransactNamedPipe` many times before disconnecting.

Single Transactions

Another command, `CallNamedPipe`, works for clients that need a pipe for only a single transaction. `CallNamedPipe` connects, reads from, writes to, and closes the pipe handle.

```
BOOL CallNamedPipe(
    LPTSTR lpszPipeName,     // points to string naming a pipe object
    LPVOID lpvWriteBuf,      // buffer holding information to send
    DWORD dwWriteBuf,        // size of the write buffer in bytes
    LPVOID lpvReadBuf,       // buffer for information received
    DWORD dwReadBuf,         // size of the read buffer in bytes
    LPDWORD lpdwRead,        // bytes actually read (value returned)
    DWORD dwTimeout );       // maximum wait time in milliseconds
```

`CallNamedPipe` expects in its first parameter the name of a pipe that already exists. Only clients call this function. Most of the other parameters supply the buffers needed to perform both halves of a transaction.

`CallNamedPipe` condenses into a single call a whole series of commands: `WaitNamedPipe`, `CreateFile`, `WriteFile`, `ReadFile`, and `CloseHandle`. The final parameter, `dwTimeout`, sets the maximum waiting period for the `WaitNamedPipe` part of this transaction.

If the read buffer is too small to hold an entire message, the command reads what it can and returns FALSE. `GetLastError` reports `ERROR_MORE_DATA`, but because the pipe has already been closed, the extra data is lost.

Disguising the Server

Often, a client sends through a pipe commands or requests for the server to perform some action on its behalf. The client might, for example, ask the server to retrieve information from a file. Because the client and the server are different processes, they may also have different security clearances. A server might want to refuse to perform commands for which the client lacks adequate clearance. The server may temporarily assume the client's security attributes before complying with a request, and then restore its own attributes after responding, using these commands:

```
BOOL ImpersonateNamedPipeClient( HANDLE hNamedPipe );
```

```
BOOL RevertToSelf( void );
```

The impersonation command fails on anonymous pipes, and it will not allow the server to impersonate the client on remote machines. The command temporarily modifies the security context of the thread that calls it.

`RevertToSelf` ends the masquerade and restores the original security context.

Destroying a Pipe

Like most of the objects we've discussed so far, a pipe object remains in memory until all the handles to it are closed. Whenever any process finishes with its end of a pipe, it should call `CloseHandle`. If you forget, the `ExitProcess` command closes all your remaining handles for you.

Distinguishing Pipes and Mailslots

Pipes are similar to another object called a *mailslot*. Like a pipe, a mailslot is a buffer where processes leave messages for each other. Mailslots, however, always work in only one direction, and many applications may open the receiving end of the same mailslot.

A program that opens a handle to receive messages in a mailslot is a *mailslot server*. A program that opens a handle to broadcast messages through a mailslot is the *client*. When a client writes to a mailslot, copies of the message are posted to every server with a handle to the same mailslot.

A pipe takes information from one end and delivers it to the other end. A mailslot takes information from one end and delivers it to many other ends.

Mailslot Commands

Mailslots have string names just as named pipes do. The commands for mailslot operations resemble the pipe API functions:

- To create a server's read-only mailslot handle, call `CreateMailslot`.

- To retrieve or modify its attributes, call `GetMailslotInfo` and `SetMailslotInfo`.

- To create the client's write-only mailslot handle, call `CreateFile`.

- To send and receive mailslot messages, call `WriteFile` and `ReadFile`.

- To destroy a mailslot, close its handles with `CloseHandle`.

Advantages of Mailslots

Besides the advantage of broadcasting a message to multiple recipients, mailslots make it easier to connect with processes over a network. In order for a pipe client to connect with a remote server, the client must first ascertain the name of the server's machine, which may require a slow enumeration of network servers and repeated attempts to connect with each until the pipe is found. But in naming a mailslot for `CreateFile`, the mailslot client may use an asterisk (*) to represent the current network domain.

```
\\*\mailslot\<mailslotname>
```

> **NOTE**   A *domain* is any group of linked workstations and network servers to which an administrator has assigned a common name. One network system may contain a single all-inclusive domain, or it may be divided into several associated domains.

The handle the client receives using a name of that form broadcasts messages to all processes in the current domain that have opened a mailslot using the *<mailslotname>* string. This ability to broadcast across a domain suggests one of the ways mailslots might be used. Processes that want to connect through a remote pipe link may prefer to find each other through a mailslot first, using this procedure:

1. Both processes open a mailslot with the same name.

2. The client broadcasts the name of its pipe, including in the name string the name of its own network server.

3. The recipient uses the broadcast string to connect with the pipe and avoids laboriously enumerating all the available servers.

4. The client and server find each other through a one-way mailslot, and then establish a private two-way pipe to continue the conversation.

Processes Communicating through a Pipe

This chapter presents two versions of a sample program called AnonPipe and NamePipe. In both versions, a parent process creates a child process and communicates with it through a pipe. The first version uses an anonymous pipe, and the second uses a named pipe.

A command on the parent's menu lets the user launch the child process. Once both are running, the user selects shapes, colors, and sizes from the parent program's menu. The parent sends the command information through a pipe, and the client draws the requested shape. In the second version, the user may launch several children, and the parent creates multiple instances of its pipe.

One-Way Communication: The Anonymous Pipe Version

An anonymous pipe is the easiest way to establish single-instance one-way communication between related processes on the same machine. (With two anonymous pipes you can communicate in both directions.)

The parent and child program windows of the anonymous pipe program appear in Figure 15.1. In this example, the user has selected a small red triangle from the parent's menu, and the resulting shape appears in the child's window.

The Parent Process

The files that compose the parent process are Parent.H, Parent.RC, and Parent.C. The child process files are Child.H, Child.RC, and Child.C. The two programs together share an additional header, Global.H, which defines structures and values both processes use to communicate with each other.

FIGURE 15.1

Parent and child windows
of the Process demo
program

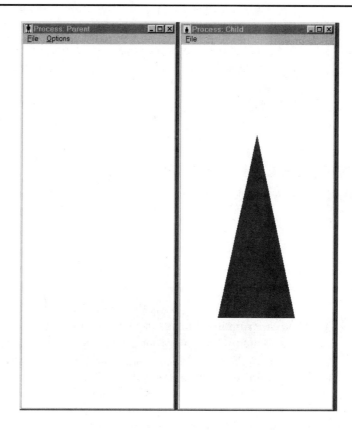

When the parent puts command information into the pipe it uses a descriptive structure called FIGURE. A FIGURE variable holds values that represent commands from the parent's menu. The commands determine the shape, size, and color of the figure the child should draw.

Initializing   The global variables at the top of Parent.C include a handle for the child process, a handle for the pipe, and a FIGURE variable. These are the three pieces of information the parent needs to communicate with its child. WinMain initializes figure to describe a small red rectangle.

```
/*-----------------------------------------------------------------

    PARENT.C   [anonymous pipe version]

    Contains the parent process for the PROCESS demo program.
    In this version, the two processes communicate through
```

```
      an anonymous pipe.
      -----------------------------------------------------------*/

 int WINAPI WinMain( HINSTANCE hinstThis, HINSTANCE hinstPrev,
                     LPSTR lpszCmdLine,   int iCmdShow )
 {
     ...
         // This global FIGURE structure records whatever choices
         // the user makes to choose the shape, size, and color
         // of the figure drawn in the client's window. Here
         // we initialize it to the program's startup defaults.

     figure.iShape = IDM_RECTANGLE; // draw a rectangle
     figure.iSize  = IDM_SMALL;     // don't fill the whole window
     figure.iColor = IDM_RED;       // make the rectangle red
     ...
 }
```

Responding to System Messages   The window procedure looks for only three messages. When the user begins to make a menu choice, the parent program intercepts WM_INITMENU to update the appearance of the menu. If the child process does not exist, the parent disables the commands that work only with the child present, including Terminate and all the shape options. The first message handler, WM_INITMENU, also puts check marks by all the options currently selected.

```
 /*-------------------------------------------------------------
     PARENT_WNDPROC
     This is where the messages for the main window are processed.
     -----------------------------------------------------------*/

 LRESULT WINAPI Parent_WndProc(
     HWND    hWnd,              // message address
     UINT    uMessage,          // message type
     WPARAM  wParam,            // message contents
     LPARAM  lParam )           // more contents
 {
     switch (uMessage)
     {
         HANDLE_MSG( hWnd, WM_INITMENU, Parent_OnInitMenu );
         HANDLE_MSG( hWnd, WM_COMMAND, Parent_OnCommand );
         HANDLE_MSG( hWnd, WM_DESTROY, Parent_OnDestroy );
         default:
             return( DefWindowProc( hWnd, uMessage, wParam, lParam ) );
     }
     return( 0L );
 }
```

The second message handler responds to WM_COMMAND messages from the menu. The user gives commands to start or terminate the child, to modify the shape the child draws, and to close the parent program. If the user makes any selection from the Options menu, SendCommand writes the updated figure variable into the pipe.

The third message handler ends the parent program in response to WM_DESTROY.

The Parent_OnInitMenu procedure provides the handling to check and uncheck the several menu options.

```
/*-----------------------------------------------------------------
    PARENT_ONINITMENU
    Check whether the child process exists and enable or
    disable the Start, Terminate, and Options commands
    accordingly. Also put check marks on the option commands
    that reflect the user's most recent choices.
-------------------------------------------------------------*/

void Parent_OnInitMenu( HWND hWnd, HMENU hMenu )
{
    // While the child process does not exist, some of our
    // menu commands make no sense and should be disabled.
    // These include the Terminate command and the figure
    // options commands.

        // get a handle to the options popup menu
    HMENU hmenuOptions = GetSubMenu( hMenu, 1 );

    if( hProcess )
    { // child process exists; enable Terminate and shape options
      EnableMenuItem( hMenu, IDM_START, MF_GRAYED );
      EnableMenuItem( hMenu, IDM_TERMINATE, MF_ENABLED );
      EnableMenuItem( hmenuOptions, 0, MF_ENABLED | MF_BYPOSITION );
      EnableMenuItem( hmenuOptions, 1, MF_ENABLED | MF_BYPOSITION );
      EnableMenuItem( hmenuOptions, 2, MF_ENABLED | MF_BYPOSITION );
    }
    else
    { // child process does not exist;
      // disable Terminate and shape options
      EnableMenuItem( hMenu, IDM_START, MF_ENABLED );
      EnableMenuItem( hMenu, IDM_TERMINATE, MF_GRAYED );
      EnableMenuItem( hmenuOptions, 0, MF_GRAYED | MF_BYPOSITION );
      EnableMenuItem( hmenuOptions, 1, MF_GRAYED | MF_BYPOSITION );
      EnableMenuItem( hmenuOptions, 2, MF_GRAYED | MF_BYPOSITION );
    }
```

```
      // set a checkmark on one of the three shape commands
  CheckMenuItem( hMenu, IDM_ELLIPSE,
      ( ( figure.iShape == IDM_ELLIPSE) ? (int)MF_CHECKED :
                                          (int)MF_UNCHECKED ) );
  CheckMenuItem( hMenu, IDM_RECTANGLE,
      ( ( figure.iShape == IDM_RECTANGLE) ? (int)MF_CHECKED :
                                            (int)MF_UNCHECKED ) );
  CheckMenuItem( hMenu, IDM_TRIANGLE,
      ( ( figure.iShape == IDM_TRIANGLE) ? (int)MF_CHECKED :
                                           (int)MF_UNCHECKED ) );

      // set a checkmark on one of the two size commands
  CheckMenuItem( hMenu, IDM_SMALL,
      ( ( figure.iSize == IDM_SMALL) ? (int)MF_CHECKED :
                                       (int)MF_UNCHECKED ) );
  CheckMenuItem( hMenu, IDM_LARGE,
      ( ( figure.iSize == IDM_LARGE) ? (int)MF_CHECKED :
                                       (int)MF_UNCHECKED ) );

      // set a checkmark on one of the three color commands
  CheckMenuItem( hMenu, IDM_RED,
      ( ( figure.iColor == IDM_RED ) ? (int)MF_CHECKED :
                                       (int)MF_UNCHECKED ) );
  CheckMenuItem( hMenu, IDM_GREEN,
      ( ( figure.iColor == IDM_GREEN ) ? (int)MF_CHECKED :
                                         (int)MF_UNCHECKED ) );
  CheckMenuItem( hMenu, IDM_BLUE,
      ( ( figure.iColor == IDM_BLUE ) ? (int)MF_CHECKED :
                                        (int)MF_UNCHECKED ) );

  return;
  UNREFERENCED_PARAMETER( hWnd );
}
```

Creating the Pipe and the Child   When the user chooses Start from the File menu, the program calls its StartProcess procedure to create the pipe, launch the child, and send the child its first command. Some complications arise in arranging for the child to inherit one end of the pipe.

The CreatePipe command must not simply accept the default security attributes, because, by default, the new handles cannot be inherited. StartProcess begins by filling out a SECURITY_ATTRIBUTES structure in order to set the bInheritHandle field to TRUE. If the next command were CreateProcess, the new child would automatically inherit copies of both handles, the reading end and the writing end of the pipe.

Unfortunately, that's still not quite what we want to happen. The child needs only one handle. Anonymous pipes work only one way, and our child needs only to read from the pipe. It should not inherit hpipeWrite. The next command, DuplicateHandle, modifies the handle by changing its inheritance attribute. Because the parameter for the copied handle is NULL, the command does not actually make a copy; instead, it modifies the original. Now we have a reading handle that can be inherited and a writing handle that cannot.

Generally, the child should not inherit handles it does not need. Most objects stay open as long as any process holds an open handle to them. If a child inherits an assortment of extraneous handles, many objects may be forced to linger in memory even after the parent ends. Furthermore, in this particular case, if the child owned handles for both ends of the pipe, it would not know when the parent destroyed its end of the pipe. From the child's point of view, the pipe would remain open because someone (itself) still had a handle to the other end.

Normally, when one process closes its end of a pipe, the other process notices because of error results from the read or write commands. That's why we went to the trouble of making sure the child inherits only one of the two pipe handles.

Inheriting a handle is not enough, however, for the handle to be useful. The child still needs to receive the handle explicitly from the parent. In effect, the child inherits only the *right* to use the handle, not the handle itself. More accurately, it receives an entry in its object table but no handle to the entry. The parent must still find a way to pass the handle to the new process. The system considers the inherited object table entry to be an open handle even though the child has no direct access to it. The handle the parent later passes directly to the child connects with the inherited object table entry and does not count as a separate, new handle.

Rather than passing a handle on the command line, we set it in one of the child's standard I/O device channels. The STARTUPINFO procedure passed to CreateProcess contains three standard I/O handles. Two are the default handles returned by GetStdHandle, but the third is the pipe handle. The child will inherit all three devices. (It will use only the pipe handle, but it's best to pass all three handles through STARTUPINFO.)

To summarize, the StartProcess procedure performs these steps:

1. Loads the string that names the child program's executable file (Child.EXE).

2. Creates the pipe with inheritable handles.

3. Modifies the write-only handle with DuplicateHandle so it cannot be inherited.

4. Puts the read-only handle in a STARTUPINFO variable.

5. Creates the child process, which both inherits the read-only handle and receives a copy of the handle as its own stdin device. (The child inherits no other handles from this parent.)

6. Closes the parent's read-only handle to the pipe. The child has its own copy now, and the parent doesn't need it.

The STARTUPINFO structure allows the parent to decide how and where the child's window will appear. Many of the fields, however, apply only to character-based console windows. This child program uses a graphics window, not a character window. Furthermore, because we have set only one activation flag in the dwFlags field, CreateProcess will ignore most of the values anyway. At a minimum, however, you should initialize the cb field, the lpDesktop field, the dwFlags field, and the three reserved fields.

StartProcess checks for errors after almost every command. If any command fails, StartProcess closes all the handles created to that point. The ShowErrorMsg procedure, which comes at the end of Parent.C, displays a message box describing the last error that occurred.

```
/*-----------------------------------------------------------------
   START PROCESS
      In response to the IDM_START command, launch the child
      process and create the pipe for talking to it.
   -----------------------------------------------------------------*/

void StartProcess ( void )
{
char szProcess[MAX_BUFFER];   // name of child process image
   SECURITY_ATTRIBUTES sa;    // security privileges for handles
   STARTUPINFO sui;           // info for starting a process
   PROCESS_INFORMATION pi;    // info returned about a process
   int iLen;                  // return value
   BOOL bTest;                // return value
   HANDLE hpipeRead;          // inbound end of pipe (for client)

      // load name of process image file from resources
   iLen = LoadString( hInst, IDS_PROCESS,
                      szProcess, sizeof(szProcess) );
   if( ! iLen )
   {
      return;
   }
```

```
    // fill SECURITY_ATTRIBUTES struct so handles are inherited
sa.nLength = sizeof(SECURITY_ATTRIBUTES);// structure size
sa.lpSecurityDescriptor = NULL;          // default descriptor
sa.bInheritHandle = TRUE;                // inheritable

    // create the pipe
bTest = CreatePipe( &hpipeRead,    // reading handle
                    &hpipeWrite,   // writing handle
                    &sa,           // lets handles be inherited
                    0 );           // default buffer size

 if( ! bTest )                     // error during pipe creation
 {
    ShowErrorMsg( );
    return;
 }

    // make uninheritable duplicate of outbound handle
bTest = DuplicateHandle( GetCurrentProcess( ),
                         hpipeWrite, // original handle
                         GetCurrentProcess( ),
                         NULL, // don't create new handle
                         0,
                         FALSE, // not inheritable
                         DUPLICATE_SAME_ACCESS );

 if( ! bTest )                 // duplication failed
 {
    ShowErrorMsg( );
    CloseHandle( hpipeRead );
    CloseHandle( hpipeWrite );
    return;
 }

    // fill in the process's startup information
memset( &sui, 0, sizeof(STARTUPINFO) );
sui.cb        = sizeof(STARTUPINFO);
sui.dwFlags   = STARTF_USESTDHANDLES;
sui.hStdInput  = hpipeRead;
sui.hStdOutput = GetStdHandle( STD_OUTPUT_HANDLE );
sui.hStdError  = GetStdHandle( STD_ERROR_HANDLE );
```

```
        // create the drawing process
    bTest = CreateProcess( szProcess,     // .EXE image
                           NULL,          // command line
                           NULL,          // process security
                           NULL,          // thread security
                           TRUE,          // inherit handles--yes
                           0,             // creation flags
                           NULL,          // environment block
                           NULL,          // current directory
                           &sui,          // startup info
                           &pi );         // process info (returned)
        // did we succeed in launching the process?
    if( ! bTest )
    {
        ShowErrorMsg( );                  // creation failed
        CloseHandle( hpipeWrite );
    }
    else                                  // creation succeeded
    {
        hProcess = pi.hProcess;           // save new process handle
        CloseHandle( pi.hThread );        // discard new thread handle
        figure.iShape = IDM_RECTANGLE;    // reset to default shape
        SendCommand( );                   // tell child what to draw
    }
    CloseHandle( hpipeRead );             // discard receiving end
    return;
}
```

If the CreateProcess command succeeds, StartProcess performs several final actions. First, it looks at the two handles returned in the PROCESS_INFORMATION structure. It moves the new process's handle to a global variable. The pi variable also holds a handle to the primary thread of the new child process. Having no use for that handle, the program closes it immediately. Then it closes the handle to the child's end of the pipe and calls SendCommand to tell the child what to draw first.

Resetting the figure variable before SendCommand is very important. The parent process can open and close a child many times in one session. To close the child, the parent puts IDM_TERMINATE in the figure variable and writes that to the pipe. The line that resets figure.iShape to IDM_RECTANGLE ensures that the child will not receive a leftover IDM_TERMINATE command as its first message.

Writing to the Pipe   The parent program sends the child a message immediately after launching the child whenever the user chooses a new shape attribute and when the user chooses Terminate from the Process menu. At each point, the program calls SendCommand to put information in the pipe.

```
/*------------------------------------------------------------------
    SEND COMMAND
        Tell the child program what to draw. Write the current
        contents of the global FIGURE variable into the pipe.

    Return
        TRUE indicates the write operation succeeded. FALSE means
        an error occurred and we have lost contact with the child.
-------------------------------------------------------------------*/

BOOL SendCommand ( void )
{
    BOOL bTest;                     // return value
    DWORD dwWritten;                // number of bytes written to pipe

    // pass the choices to the child through the pipe
    bTest = WriteFile( hpipeWrite,      // anonymous pipe (outbound)
                    &figure,            // buffer to write
                    sizeof(FIGURE),     // size of buffer
                    &dwWritten,         // bytes written
                    NULL );             // overlapping i/o structure
    if( ! bTest )                       // did writing succeed?
    {
        // If the write operation failed because the user has
        // already closed the child program, then tell the user
        // the connection was broken. If some less predictable
        // error caused the failure, call ShowErrorMsg as usual
        // to display the system's error message.

        DWORD dwResult = GetLastError();

        if( ( dwResult == ERROR_BROKEN_PIPE ) ||  // pipe ended
            ( dwResult == ERROR_NO_DAT ) )        // pipe closing
        {
            // presumably the user closed the child
            MessageBox( hwndMain,
                    "Connection with child already broken.",
                    "Parent Message", MB_ICONEXCLAMATION | MB_OK );
        }
        else    // an unpredictable error occurred
        {
            ShowErrorMsg();
        }
    }
```

```
      // If a write error occurred, or if we just sent an
      // IDM_TERMINATE command to make the child quit, then
      // in either case we break
      // off communication with the child process.
      if( ( ! bTest ) || ( figure.iShape == IDM_TERMINATE ) )
      {
         CloseHandle( hProcess );        // forget about the child
         hProcess = NULL;
         CloseHandle( hpipeWrite );      // destroy the pipe
      }
      return( bTest );
   }
```

The WriteFile command may fail for any of several reasons. One likely problem arises if the user closes the child program from the child's menu. The parent does not know the child is gone until it tries to write to the pipe and receives an error. In that case the GetLastError function, which returns a number identifying whatever error last occurred in a given thread, indicates either ERROR_BROKEN_PIPE or ERROR_NO_DATA.

Instead of handling these results like any other error, SendCommand raises a message box explaining that the connection has been broken. If the pipe fails for any reason at all, however, the parent makes no effort to reestablish contact. It closes the pipe handle and the child process handle. The program also resets the process handle to NULL, which CloseHandle does not do. The Parent_OnInitMenu message handler relies on the value of hProcess to determine whether the child still exists.

A separate ShowErrorMsg procedure uses the FormatMessage function to present error messages.

```
/*-------------------------------------------------------------
   SHOW ERROR MESSAGE
-----------------------------------------------------------*/

void ShowErrorMsg ( void )
{
   LPVOID lpvMessage;                   // temporary message buffer

      // retrieve a message from the system message table
   FormatMessage(
     FORMAT_MESSAGE_ALLOCATE_BUFFER | FORMAT_MESSAGE_FROM_SYSTEM,
     NULL,                                 // ignored
     GetLastError(),                       // message ID
     MAKELANGID(LANG_ENGLISH, SUBLANG_ENGLISH_US),
```

```
            // message language
            (LPTSTR) &lpvMessage,      // address of buffer pointer
            0,                         // minimum buffer size
            NULL );                    // no other arguments
        // display the message in a message box
    MessageBox( hwndMain, lpvMessage, "Parent Message",
            MB_ICONEXCLAMATION | MB_OK );
        // release the buffer FormatMessage allocated
    LocalFree( lpvMessage );
    return;
}
```

ShowErrorMsg is built around the FormatMessage command, which chooses a message from the system's internal message table to describe the most recent error. (The most recent error value is maintained separately for each thread.) Given the flags we've set in its first parameter, FormatMessage dynamically allocates a message buffer and puts the address in the lpvMessage variable. Note that FormatMessage wants to receive the *address* of the buffer pointer, not the pointer itself.

The Child Process

The CreateProcess command in the parent's StartProcess procedure launches a program called Child. The parent stores the string "child.exe" in its table of string resources.

Inheriting a Pipe Handle and Creating a Thread   The anonymous pipe version of Child dedicates a secondary thread to the task of waiting for data to arrive through the pipe. The primary thread processes system messages for the program's window. When the secondary thread receives a new command from the parent, it updates the global variables iShape, iSize, and iColor, and then invalidates the window. The primary thread receives a WM_PAINT message and redraws the display using the new shape values. The secondary thread runs in a loop that ends when it reads an IDM_TERMINATE command from the pipe.

The first part of the Child.C listing includes WinMain, the initialization procedures, and the message handlers. The child performs its most important initialization tasks in response to the WM_CREATE message.

Child_OnCreate recovers the pipe handle inherited from the parent and creates a new thread to read from the pipe. If either action fails, the procedure returns FALSE and the process ends.

```
/*--------------------------------------------------------------------
    CHILD_ONCREATE
        On startup open the pipe and start the thread that will
        read from it.
------------------------------------------------------------------*/
BOOL Child_OnCreate( HWND hWnd, LPCREATESTRUCT lpCreateStruct )
{
    // open the pipe for reading
    hpipeRead = GetStdHandle( STD_INPUT_HANDLE );
    if( hpipeRead == INVALID_HANDLE_VALUE )
    {
        ShowErrorMsg( );
        return( FALSE );
    }
        // Create thread that will read from pipe. It is created
        // suspended so its priority can be lowered before it starts.
    hThread = CreateThread( NULL,               // security attributes
                            0,                  // initial stack size
        (LPTHREAD_START_ROUTINE) PipeThread,
                            NULL,               // argument
                            CREATE_SUSPENDED,   // creation flag
                            &dwThreadID );      // new thread's ID
    if( ! hThread )
    {
        ShowErrorMsg( );
        return( FALSE );
    }
        // lower the thread's priority and let it run
    SetThreadPriority( hThread, THREAD_PRIORITY_BELOW_NORMAL );
    ResumeThread( hThread );
    return( TRUE );
    UNREFERENCED_PARAMETER(hWnd);
    UNREFERENCED_PARAMETER(lpCreateStruct);
}
```

To retrieve the pipe handle, the child calls GetStdHandle. This command finds the handle that the parent told CreateProcess to deposit in the child's stdin device slot. The child creates its secondary pipe-reading thread in a suspended state in order to adjust the thread's priority. Because the primary thread responds to user input, we set the secondary thread to a lower priority. The difference ensures that the child will respond quickly to keyboard and menu input.

The paint procedure (not shown here) is long but straightforward. It simply reads the current values of iShape, iSize, and iColor; creates the pens and brushes it needs; and draws an ellipse, a rectangle, or a triangle.

Reading from the Pipe Child_OnCreate designates PipeThread as the main procedure for the secondary thread. The new thread immediately enters a while loop that ends when the global bTerminate flag becomes TRUE. The flag changes when the user chooses Exit from the child's menu, when the parent sends an IDM_TERMINATE command, or if the child encounters an error reading from the pipe. When the while loop finally does end, the thread posts a WM_DESTROY message to the program window. The secondary thread exits, the primary thread receives the destroy command, and the program ends.

```
/*-----------------------------------------------------------------
    PIPE THREAD
        The WM_CREATE handler starts a thread with this procedure
        to manage the pipe connection. This thread waits for
        messages to arrive through the pipe and acts on them.
    ------------------------------------------------------------*/

LONG PipeThread( LPVOID lpThreadData )
{
        // read from named pipe until terminate flag is set to true
    while( ! bTerminate )
    {
        DoRead( );
    }
        // when bTerminate is TRUE, time to end program
    FORWARD_WM_DESTROY( hwndMain, PostMessage );
    return( 0L );                          // implicit ExitThread()
    UNREFERENCED_PARAMETER(lpThreadData);
}
```

The DoRead procedure is responsible for reading from the pipe and for making three decisions:

- It determines if the read is successful or, if not, reports an error.

- Assuming a successful read, the IDM_TERMINATE command is checked to determine if the thread should terminate.

- If the read is successful and it is not a terminate message, the shape, color, and size variables are read from the piped message, and the child window is updated so that a new shape will be drawn.

```
/*--------------------------------------------------------------------
    DO READ
        Read from the pipe and set the figure to be drawn.
--------------------------------------------------------------------*/

void DoRead( void )
{
    FIGURE figure;
    DWORD dwRead;
    BOOL bTest;

        // read from the pipe
    bTest = ReadFile( hpipeRead,        // place to read from
                      &figure,          // buffer to store input
                      sizeof(figure),   // bytes to read
                      &dwRead,          // bytes read
                      NULL );
    if( bTest )
    { // the read command succeeded
        if( figure.iShape == IDM_TERMINATE )
// is new command Terminate?
        { // YES
            bTerminate = TRUE;             // set flag to end this thread
        } // NO
        else // thread continues; draw new shape
        {
                // copy the new shape attributes to global variables
            iShape = figure.iShape;
            iColor = figure.iColor;
            iSize  = figure.iSize;
                // force the parent window to repaint itself
            InvalidateRect( hwndMain, NULL, TRUE );
            UpdateWindow( hwndMain );
        }
    }
    else                                // the read command failed
    {
        ShowErrorMsg( );                // tell user what happened
        bTerminate = TRUE;              // let the child end
    }
    return;
}
```

The `while` loop in the secondary thread does one thing: It calls `DoRead` over and over. The `DoRead` procedure performs one `ReadFile` command, interprets the message, and ends. Each call to `DoRead` retrieves one more message. Since all anonymous pipes use the waiting mode, the thread blocks on each call to `Read-File` until data arrives. `ReadFile` may return immediately if the pipe is full or if an error occurs. For example, it will return immediately if the parent program has already exited and the pipe handle has become invalid.

If the read command succeeds, the child must determine whether it has received a command to terminate or to draw a new shape. If the command fails, the child notifies the user by displaying the system's error message. The child also assumes the connection has been broken and exits.

Although this pipe, like all anonymous pipes, writes and reads in byte mode, the child program still manages to always retrieve exactly one message at a time, even if several messages are waiting. Because the parent always writes exactly `sizeof(FIGURE)` bytes into the pipe, the child knows exactly where one message ends and the next begins.

The Child program's `About_DlgProc` and `ShowErrorMsg` procedures duplicate the corresponding procedures in Parent almost exactly. The full listing of Child appears on the CD accompanying the book.

Multiple Communications: The Named Pipe Version

An anonymous pipe serves the needs of the Parent and Child programs perfectly well. They communicate in only one direction, use only one instance of the pipe at a time, and both run on the same machine. The second version of the demo program, however, allows the parent to create any number of children and communicate with several of them at once. Rather than creating a new anonymous pipe for each client, this version creates two instances of a single named pipe.

If the user launches many child processes, only the first two will connect with the parent. The others will block waiting for one of the existing connections to break. Choosing Terminate from the parent's menu causes all the currently connected children to quit. When the link with one child breaks, that instance of the pipe becomes available for one of the waiting children. In Figure 15.2, the parent process has launched three children. Two are connected and have drawn the currently selected shape, while the third is waiting for an available pipe instance.

The listings that follow are partial and present only the most important changes for the new version, but the CD accompanying the book contains full listings for both versions.

FIGURE 15.2

Parent process with
three children, only two
of which are connected
to instances of the
named pipe

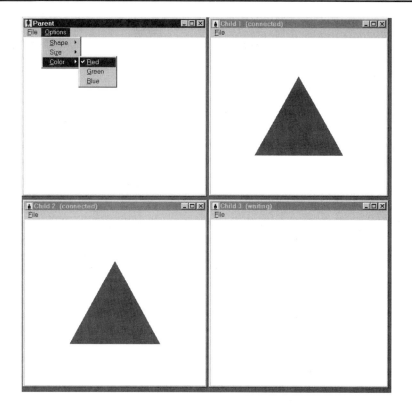

The Parent Process

In order to use a named pipe, both processes must agree on a string to name the pipe they will share. The name string belongs in the string table of both the parent and the child. We've set the string in a shared resource file, Global.STR, and modified both resource scripts to include it. The shared header file, Global.H, adds a new constant to identify the common string resource. Notice that the name string in Global.STR contains double the expected number of backslashes.

```
/*------------------------------------------------------------
    GLOBAL.STR
        Contains a string that should be included in the string
        tables of both the parent and child halves of the
        PROCESS demo program.
------------------------------------------------------------*/
```

```
IDS_PIPE,  "\\\\.\\pipe\\procdemo"      // name of pipe object
```

The resource compiler uses the backslash character to signal the beginning of an ASCII code sequence. Each pair of backslashes inserts a single literal backslash in the resource string.

The new Parent.H header defines the constant NUM_PIPE_INSTANCES, giving it the value of 2. To have the parent create more instances of its pipe and connect with more children simultaneously, modify the definition.

TIP

Figure 15.2 shows three child instances where only two have connected because of the specified NUM_PIPE_INSTANCES limit. When the parent is instructed to close the child processes, the unconnected child will remain open and will assume one of the freed connections.

Creating the Named Pipe   The anonymous pipe parent destroys its pipe each time the child process terminates. If the user launches a new child, the parent creates a new pipe. A named pipe, however, more often lives through several connections with different clients. The named pipe parent creates its pipe instances only once, during initialization. The parent calls its MakePipeInstance procedure twice. Each successive call produces a handle to the program's pipe object and a new thread to support the new instance.

Parent_OnCreate also produces two other important objects, both events. Each event object broadcasts a signal to as many threads as happen to be listening.

```
/*------------------------------------------------------------
    PARENT_ONCREATE
        Create all the pipe instances and the two event objects used
        to synchronize the program's threads
------------------------------------------------------------*/
```

```
BOOL Parent_OnCreate( HWND hWnd, LPCREATESTRUCT lpcs )
{
```

```
int i;
int iNumInstances = 0;                          // counts instances created

   // Create all the instances of the named pipe. The
   // MakePipeInstance command also starts up a new
   // thread to service each pipe instance.

for( i = 1; i <= NUM_PIPE_INSTANCES; i++ )
{
   if( MakePipeInstance() )             // make one instance
   {                                    // if successful,
      iNumInstances++;                  // increment counter
   }
}

if( iNumInstances != NUM_PIPE_INSTANCES )  // did we make all?
{
   char szBuffer[128];
   wsprintf( szBuffer, "Created only %i instances\n\r",
             iNumInstances );
   MessageBox( hwndMain, szBuffer, "Parent Message",
               MB_ICONEXCLAMATION | MB_OK );
   return( FALSE );                     // creation failed
}
   // Create the event object used for signaling the pipe
   // instance threads when the user makes a command.
hCmdEvent = CreateEvent( NULL,   // default security attributes
                         TRUE,   // manual reset event
                         FALSE,  // initially not signaled
                         NULL ); // no name
if( hCmdEvent == NULL )
{
   ShowErrorMsg();                      // event creation failed
   return( FALSE );
}
   // Create the event that coordinates the pipe threads when
   // the program terminates all linked children. The threads
   // block on this event until all the clients have received
   // the IDM_TERMINATE message.
hNotTerminatingEvent =
   CreateEvent( NULL,           // default security attributes
                TRUE,           // manual reset event
                TRUE,           // initially signaled
                NULL );         // no name
if( hNotTerminatingEvent == NULL )
{
```

```
        ShowErrorMsg( );                // event creation failed
        return( FALSE );
    }
    return( TRUE );
    UNREFERENCED_PARAMETER(hWnd);
    UNREFERENCED_PARAMETER(lpcs);
}
```

The Parent program uses one event to notify its pipe threads whenever the user makes a new choice from the menu. In response, the pipe threads send the new command to their clients. This is a manual reset event so that all listening pipes will unblock when the signal arrives. (Automatic reset events unblock only one thread on each signal.)

The other event coordinates the threads while they are sending termination commands to multiple clients. It, too, is a manual reset event. This one, however, begins life already in its signaled state. You'll see why in the code for the pipe instance threads.

Because no other processes have any reason to use either event object, the events need no names.

MakePipeInstance   The MakePipeInstance procedure is used to create a new instance of a named pipe and begins by loading the resource string that names the pipe object. The subsequent call to CreateNamedPipe sets the pipe's attributes.

```
/*-----------------------------------------------------------------
    MAKE PIPE INSTANCE
        Create a new instance of the named pipe.
    Return
        TRUE if the procedure creates a new instance; FALSE if an
        error prevents creation.
    -------------------------------------------------------------*/

BOOL MakePipeInstance ( void )
{
    char szPipe[MAX_BUFFER];        // name of pipe
    int iLen;                       // return value
    HANDLE hPipe;                   // handle to new pipe
    HANDLE hThread;                 // handle to new thread
    DWORD dwThreadID;               // ID of new thread

        // get name to use for sharing pipe
    iLen = LoadString( hInst, IDS_PIPE, szPipe, sizeof(szPipe) );
    if( ! iLen )
```

```
    {
        return( FALSE );
    }
        // Create a new instance of the named pipe. This command will
        // fail if two instances already exist.
    hPipe = CreateNamedPipe( szPipe,                      // name
                        PIPE_ACCESS_OUTBOUND, // open mo0de
                        PIPE_TYPE_BYTE | PIPE_READMODE_BYTE |
                        PIPE_WAIT,
                        NUM_PIPE_INSTANCES, // max instances
                        0,                    // out buffer size
                        0,                    // in buffer size
                        0,                    // time-out value
                    NULL );                // security attributes
    if (hPipe == INVALID_HANDLE_VALUE)
    {
        ShowErrorMsg( );                           // creation failed
        return( FALSE );
    }
    hThread = CreateThread( NULL,              // security attributes
                        0,                    // initial stack size
    (LPTHREAD_START_ROUTINE) PipeInstanceThread,
                (LPVOID) hPipe,          // argument for thread proc
                        CREATE_SUSPENDED,    // creation flag
                        &dwThreadID );      // new thread's ID

    if( ! hThread )
    {
        ShowErrorMsg( );
        CloseHandle( hPipe );
        return( FALSE );                      // thread creation failed
    }
        // lower the thread's priority and let it run
    SetThreadPriority( hThread, THREAD_PRIORITY_BELOW_NORMAL );
    ResumeThread( hThread );
        // let go of the handle, for which we have no further use
    CloseHandle( hThread );
    return( TRUE );
}
```

Because the parent and child send information in only one direction, the program uses a one-way outbound pipe. For clarity, we specify all three mode flags even though the pipe's particular characteristics—byte mode and wait mode—are the default values. We don't need the message mode because the parent's messages are always the same length. NUM_PIPE_INSTANCES prevents Create-NamedPipe from producing more than two handles to this pipe.

The first call to `CreateNamedPipe` sets the pipe's maximum number of instances, and subsequent creation commands will fail if they specify a different number. The zero values for the buffer sizes instruct the system to allocate message space dynamically as needed.

For each pipe handle, `MakePipeInstance` also creates a new thread. The pipe instance thread waits for the user to choose commands from the parent menu and writes the new command into its pipe. We might equally well have stored the pipe handles in an array and created a single thread to write to all the instances on each new command. Again, as with the anonymous pipe child, the program sets secondary threads to a lower priority, reserving normal priority for only the primary thread—the one thread that responds directly to the user.

This time, we pass a parameter to the thread's starting function. A thread function always receives a 32-bit parameter when it starts up, but until now our programs have not used it. Each of our instance threads, however, requires a different pipe handle, so `hPipe` becomes the fourth parameter of `CreateThread`.

Launching the Child   When the user chooses the Start command from the parent's File menu, the program calls `StartProcess`. In this version, the Start command is always enabled, permitting the user to launch any number of children.

As an exercise in using the command line, the parent passes to each child an identifying number. The first child is 1, the second is 2, and so on. To pass arguments to a child on its command line, ignore the first parameter of `CreateProcess` and pass the entire command line, including the program name, in the second parameter. The command-line parameter string looks like this:

```
child.exe 1
```

Use the first parameter, `lpszImage`, when you have no arguments to pass or do not want the system to search for the child's .EXE file along the system PATH.

Because the children can acquire their own pipe handles with `CreateFile`, there is no need to arrange for inheritance. Even if the Parent program had created inheritable handles, the children would not inherit any of them because we pass FALSE as the fifth parameter to `CreateProcess`.

```
/*------------------------------------------------------------------
    START PROCESS
        In response to the IDM_START command, create a new
        child process. The user may create any number of children.
----------------------------------------------------------------*/
```

```
void StartProcess ( void )
{
    static int iChildNum = 1;     // counts child processes
    char szProcess[MAX_BUFFER];   // name of child process image
    STARTUPINFO sui;              // info for starting a process
    PROCESS_INFORMATION pi;       // info returned about a process
    char szCmdLine[MAX_BUFFER];   // child's command line
    int  iLen;                    // return value from LoadString
    BOOL bTest;                   // return value

        // load name of process image file from resources
    iLen = LoadString( hInst, IDS_PROCESS,
                       szProcess, sizeof(szProcess) );
    if( ! iLen )
    {
        return;                   // loading string failed
    }
        // fill in the process's startup information
    sui.cb              = sizeof(STARTUPINFO);
    sui.lpReserved      = NULL; // must be NULL
    sui.lpDesktop       = NULL; // starting desktop
    sui.lpTitle         = NULL; // title for new console window
    sui.dwX             = 0;    // window starting offsets
    sui.dwY             = 0;
    sui.dwXSize         = 0;    // window starting size
    sui.dwYSize         = 0;
    sui.dwXCountChars   = 0;    // console screen buffer size
    sui.dwYCountChars   = 0;
    sui.dwFillAttribute = 0;    // console text colors
    sui.dwFlags         = 0;    // flags to activate startup fields
    sui.wShowWindow     = 0;    // iCmdShow parameter
    sui.cbReserved2     = 0;
    sui.lpReserved2     = NULL;

        // prepare child's command-line argument,
        // a window caption string
    wsprintf( szCmdLine, "%s %i", (LPSTR)szProcess, iChildNum++ );
        // create the drawing process
    bTest = CreateProcess( NULL,        // .EXE image
                       szCmdLine,       // command line
                       NULL,            // process security
                       NULL,            // thread security
                       FALSE,           // inherit handles
                       0,               // creation flags
                       NULL,            // environment block
                       NULL,            // current directory
                       &sui,            // startup info
                       &pi );           // process info (returned)
```

```
   if( ! bTest )
   {
      ShowErrorMsg(); // creation failed
      return;
   }
   WaitForInputIdle( pi.hProcess, 5000 ); // wait for
                                          // child to start up
   CloseHandle( pi.hProcess );            // don't need the handles
   CloseHandle( pi.hThread );
   return;
}
```

Synchronizing the Threads   Whenever the user changes the shape options by choosing a new figure, size, or color, the program must write new commands in all its pipes. The primary thread receives and processes the user's command. It needs a way to make all the pipe instance threads transmit the new information. One of the event objects created during initialization serves this purpose.

When the user picks a new option, the procedures that store the command also pulse the event. The PulseEvent command combines the SetEvent and ResetEvent commands into one operation. The event remains signaled just long enough to unblock all waiting threads and then immediately returns to its unsignaled state.

The ChangeShape procedure incorporates one other modification. When it receives the IDM_TERMINATE command, it saves the old shape value in a global variable, iPrevShape. After all the connected children quit, the parent restores the iPrevShape value to the figure.iShape field. If children are waiting, they will connect immediately to the newly released pipes; if figure.iShape still held IDM_TERMINATE, their first command would shut them down. The iPrevShape variable allows newly connected children to draw immediately whatever shape the user last selected.

```
/*-------------------------------------------------------------------
   CHANGE SHAPE
      Record a shape command from the user. If the user has chosen
      a new shape, send the updated FIGURE structure to the child.
   --------------------------------------------------------------*/

void ChangeShape ( int iCmd )
{
   if( iCmd != figure.iShape )         // new shape?
   {
      // After sending a terminate command, we need to
      // restore the last shape drawn so that newly
      // connected clients can still draw whatever the
```

```
         // user last chose.

         if( iCmd == IDM_TERMINATE )
         {
             iPrevShape = figure.iShape; // save old shape command
         }
         figure.iShape = iCmd;        // record new shape command
         PulseEvent( hCmdEvent );     // tell threads shape has changed
      }
      return;
   }
```

The ChangeSize procedure doesn't have much to do except for recording the new size and then, like the ChangeShape procedure, calling the PulseEvent function to tell the thread that a change has occurred.

```
/*--------------------------------------------------------------------
   CHANGE SIZE
       Record a size command from the user. If the user has chosen
       a new size, send the updated FIGURE structure to the child.
   ----------------------------------------------------------------*/

void ChangeSize( int iCmd )
{
   if( iCmd != figure.iSize )   // new size?
   {
       figure.iSize = iCmd;        // record it
       PulseEvent( hCmdEvent );  // tell threads shape has changed
   }
   return;
}
```

Again, the ChangeColor procedure simply records the new color, then calls the PulseEvent function to tell the thread that a change has occurred.

```
/*--------------------------------------------------------------------
   CHANGE COLOR
       Record a color command from the user. If the user has chosen
       a new color, send the updated FIGURE structure to the child.
   ----------------------------------------------------------------*/

void ChangeColor ( int iCmd )
{
   if( iCmd != figure.iColor )  // new color?
   {
       figure.iColor = iCmd;       // record it
       PulseEvent( hCmdEvent );  // tell threads shape has changed
   }
   return;
}
```

Connecting with Clients   The threads that run each pipe instance begin life at the `PipeInstanceThread` procedure. Each new thread enters an endless loop waiting for clients to connect with its instance of the pipe. When a client does connect, a smaller nested loop begins.

While the connection lasts, the thread waits for command signals from the event object. Each time the event pulses, the thread unblocks, copies the current contents of the global `figure` variable into its pipe, and resumes its wait for a new command.

If, for any reason, the write operation fails, the thread assumes its client process has terminated. The thread calls `DisconnectNamedPipe`, returns to the top of its outer loop, and issues `ConnectNamedPipe` to wait for a new client. The loop also maintains a connection count in the global variable `iNumConnections`. Each time any thread succeeds in connecting, it increments the counter. When the connection breaks, it decrements the counter. The `Parent_OnInitMenu` procedure reads the counter to decide which menu options should be enabled. If the parent has no listening clients, all the shape option commands are disabled.

The outer loop of `PipeInstanceThread` begins with a `while (TRUE)` command, so the loop can never break. The pipe threads stop running when the primary thread reaches the end of `WinMain` and the system calls `ExitProcess`. At our customary -W4 warning level, using a constant for a conditional expression causes the compiler to complain. The `#pragma` commands surrounding the procedure suppress the warning.

```
// Tell the compiler not to complain about the "while (TRUE)" loop
#pragma warning (disable :4127)
```

Adding to the complexity of this procedure is the task of coordinating the threads when they all disconnect their clients in response to a Terminate command from the user. Several potential problems arise along the way. First, the parent should not write its `IDM_TERMINATE` command to the pipe and then disconnect immediately because `DisconnectNamedPipe` destroys any data still lingering in the pipe's buffer. The command could be lost before the child had a chance to read it. `FlushFileBuffers`, when passed a pipe handle, blocks until the receiving program clears the pipe by reading all its contents. Only a program with write access to its pipe may call `FlushFileBuffers`. The command fails when passed a read-only handle.

As each thread disconnects from its terminated client, it returns to the top of the loop and waits for a new connection. As soon as it connects, it sends the client an initial message to make it draw something right away. But if other threads are still terminating their clients, the global `figure` variable still contains the `IDM_TERMINATE` command. The thread will terminate its newly connected client by mistake. We need a way to prevent any thread from sending that initial message to a new client until after all the old clients have been disconnected. The `hNotTerminatingEvent` object solves the problem.

Near the top of the outer loop you'll find a `WaitForSingleObject` command that every thread passes before writing its first message to a new client. Most of the time, the event remains signaled and all threads pass quickly by. As soon as one thread sends a termination command, however, it calls `ResetEvent` to turn off the signal, indicating that a termination sequence has started. Now when any thread finds a new client, it will block before sending the first message. The last thread to terminate its client resets the `figure.iShape` command to `iPrevShape`, the value it last held before the termination began. The last thread also calls `SetEvent` to restore the event signal and unblock the other waiting threads. A thread knows when it is the last to terminate its client because the `iNumConnections` counter reaches 0.

```
LONG PipeInstanceThread ( HANDLE hPipe )
{
    BOOL bConnected;    // true when a client connects to the pipe

    // This loop runs endlessly. When a client disappears, the
    // loop simply waits for a new client to connect. This
    // thread is
    // terminated automatically when the program's
    // primary thread exits.
    while( TRUE )
    {
    // wait for a connection with some client
    ConnectNamedPipe( hPipe, NULL );
```

If other threads are terminating their clients, then `figure.iShape` still holds the `IDM_TERMINATE` command. The thread blocks here until the last client is terminated. The last terminating thread resets `figure.iShape` to its previous value.

```
    WaitForSingleObject( hNotTerminatingEvent, INFINITE );
    // now the connection is made and a command message is ready
    iNumConnections++;    // update global variable
    SendCommand( hPipe );  // give client its first command
    // send another message each time the Command event signals
    bConnected = TRUE;
    while (bConnected)
```

```
    {
      WaitForSingleObject( hCmdEvent, INFINITE );
          // wait for signal
      if( ! SendCommand( hPipe ) )        // send new shape command
        {
          // The connection failed - probably
          // we just sent IDM_TERMINATE or
          // the user exited from the client. Show no error message.
          bConnected = FALSE;
        }
    }
    FlushFileBuffers( hPipe );// wait for child to read message
    DisconnectNamedPipe( hPipe ); // break connection
    iNumConnections--;                 // update global variable
```

The following if condition coordinates threads when they are all terminating
their clients. When a thread discovers it has just sent the IDM_TERMINATE command, it sets the hNotTerminatingEvent object to the nonsignaled state. Other
threads will block until the last thread to disconnect restores the signal. The last
thread also replaces the IDM_TERMINATE command with IDM_RECTANGLE so that all
the threads will have a useful command to send in the first message to their new
clients.

```
    if( figure.iShape == IDM_TERMINATE ) // did we terminate?
    {                                      // have all connections
      if( iNumConnections > 0 )       // been terminated?
        {                                  // no; block other threads
          // while terminating proceeds
          ResetEvent( hNotTerminatingEvent );
        }
      else                               // yes
        {
          figure.iShape = iPrevShape; // restore prev. command
          SetEvent( hNotTerminatingEvent );    // unblock threads
        }
    }
  }
  return( 0L );
}
```

Last, the conditional expression warning is reenabled.

```
// allow the "conditional expression constant" warning again
#pragma warning (default :4127)
```

Writing to the Pipe   Within the `PipeInstanceThread` loops, the program repeatedly calls `SendCommand` to write the current values from `figure` into the pipe. If the connection with the client breaks, the procedure returns FALSE. The connection may break in either of two ways, and each has different consequences for the program's behavior.

The program handles disconnection most gracefully when the user chooses Terminate and the parent breaks the links itself. In that case, `SendCommand` returns FALSE immediately after sending the message, and the program seeks new replacement clients immediately. But if a client closes its handle to the pipe's other end, the server does not know. If the user chooses Exit from the menu of a connected child process, the parent discovers the break only when it later tries to send a new message and `WriteFile` returns an error value. Furthermore, the broken pipe remains technically connected until the server calls `DisconnectNamed-Pipe`. As a consequence, if you end one of the connected child programs while a third child is blocked on `WaitNamedPipe`, the waiting child remains blocked until you issue another command.

Using a two-way duplex pipe would smooth the transition, because the client could send the server a termination message before it exits and the server could disconnect immediately. To accommodate that arrangement, the server would probably dedicate two threads to each pipe instance: one to send and one to receive, or perhaps one thread to do all the writing for all instances and another to do the reading.

```
/*------------------------------------------------------------
    SEND COMMAND
        Tell the child program what to draw. Write the current
        contents of the global FIGURE variable into the pipe.

    Return
        TRUE indicates the write operation succeeded. FALSE means
        an error occurred and we have lost contact with the child.
    ----------------------------------------------------------*/

BOOL SendCommand ( HANDLE hPipe )
{
    BOOL bTest;                 // return value
    DWORD dwWritten;            // number of bytes written to pipe

    // pass the choices to the child through the pipe
    bTest = WriteFile( hPipe,        // named pipe (outbound handle)
                    &figure,         // buffer to write
                    sizeof(FIGURE),  // size of buffer
```

```
                              &dwWritten,     // bytes written
                              NULL );         // overlapping i/o struct.

        if( ! bTest )                         // did writing succeed?
        {
```

If the write operation failed because the user has already closed the child program, then we don't need to do anything special about the error. If, however, some less predictable error caused the failure, call ShowErrorMsg as usual to display the system's error message.

```
        DWORD dwResult = GetLastError();

        if( ( dwResult != ERROR_BROKEN_PIPE ) &&// pipe has ended
            ( dwResult != ERROR_NO_DATA ) )     // pipe closing
        {
            ShowErrorMsg();                     // unpredictable
error
        }
    }
```

SendCommand returns FALSE on errors to indicate that the connection has failed. SendCommand also returns FALSE after it tells a child to quit because that too makes a connection fail.

```
        return( ( bTest ) && ( figure.iShape != IDM_TERMINATE ) );
    }
```

The Child Process

The child process requires fewer changes. One change is visible in Figure 15.2. Because the parent now creates multiple children, we distinguish each with a different number in its window caption. The parent passes each child its own number through the command-line parameter of CreateProcess. The child's window caption also states whether the child is connected to a pipe or waiting for a connection.

```
    BOOL CreateMainWindow ( void )
    {
        char szAppName[MAX_BUFFER];
        char szBuffer[MAX_BUFFER];
        char *pToken;

            // load the relevant strings
        LoadString( hInst, IDS_APPNAME, szAppName,  sizeof(szAppName) );
```

We create the window caption using the command-line string from parent. The basic caption has the form `Child 1 %s`. The identifying number comes from the parent through the command line. We'll use `wsprintf` to insert the phrase "waiting" or "connected" into the title as appropriate.

```
strcpy( szTitle, "Child " );      // begin with "Child "
strtok( GetCommandLine(), " " ); // move past first word
pToken = strtok( NULL, " " );     // get first argument
if( pToken ) // is there one?
{
    strcat( szTitle, pToken );     // append it
}
strcat( szTitle, " %s" );          // append wsprintf format mark
```

During initialization, each child retrieves its assigned number with `GetCommand-Line`. This command returns a pointer to a string containing all the command-line arguments separated by spaces. The first item on the command line should be the name of the program (child.exe), so calling `strtok` twice extracts the child's sequence number, the second item on the command line.

```
    // The global szTitle now contains the base caption.
    // Insert a current status marker in it.
wsprintf( szBuffer, szTitle, (LPSTR)" (waiting)" );
    // create the parent window
hwndMain = CreateWindow( szAppName, szBuffer,
                    WS_OVERLAPPEDWINDOW | WS_CLIPCHILDREN,
                    CW_USEDEFAULT, CW_USEDEFAULT,
                    CW_USEDEFAULT, CW_USEDEFAULT,
                    NULL, NULL, hInst, NULL );
    // return FALSE for an error
return( hwndMain != NULL );
}
```

Creating a Thread and Connecting to the Pipe   Because `CreateMain-Window` has already set the window caption, the new `Child_OnCreate` procedure no longer loads a caption from the resource string table. Because the child has not inherited a pipe handle, this version also omits the original call to `GetStdHandle`. Instead, the new thread function, `PipeThread`, now coordinates all the pipe actions.

`PipeThread` first loads the pipe name string both programs share in the Global.STR file, and then it passes the name to `CreateFile`. The system searches its object name tree and finds the pipe with this name. If an instance of the pipe is available, `CreateFile` returns a handle to it. Because the original pipe was created with the `PIPE_ACCESS_OUTBOUND` flag, the client must request `GENERIC_READ` access rights.

```
LONG PipeThread ( LPVOID lpThreadData )
{
    char szBuffer[MAX_BUFFER];   // used for pipe name, window caption
    int iLen;                    // length of a string
    BOOL bConnected;             // TRUE when we have a pipe handle
    HANDLE hpipeRead;            // receiving handle to 1-way pipe

        // load the string that contains the name of the named pipe
    iLen = LoadString( hInst, IDS_PIPE, szBuffer,
                        sizeof(szBuffer) );
    if( ! iLen )
    {
        return( FALSE );
    }
        // This while loop continues until an instance of the named
        // pipe becomes available. bConnected is a global variable,
        // and while it is FALSE the primary thread paints "Waiting..."
        // in the window's client area. If an unpredictable error
          occurs, the loop sets the bTerminate
        // flag, this procedure ends quickly, and it kills the program
        // on its way out.
    bConnected = FALSE;
```

PipeThread embeds the CreateFile command in a while loop that runs until CreateFile returns a valid handle. The loop begins with a WaitNamedPipe command, causing the thread to block waiting for an available instance. WaitNamed-Pipe does not, however, initiate the connection; CreateFile does that.

```
    while( ! bConnected && ! bTerminate )
    {
            // wait for a pipe instance to become available
        WaitNamedPipe( szBuffer, NMPWAIT_WAIT_FOREVER );
```

Between the execution of the WaitNamedPipe command and the execution of CreateFile, it is possible for the system to schedule another thread that grabs the pipe for itself. If that happens CreateFile will fail even though WaitNamedPipe returned TRUE. If CreateFile fails during PipeThread, the while loop notices the error and tries again. If CreateFile produces an error message indicating any problem other than busy pipes, the loop sets the bTerminate flag, and the process ends a few lines later.

```
            // open the named pipe for reading
        hpipeRead = CreateFile( szBuffer, // name of pipe
                    GENERIC_READ,      // access mode
                    0,                 // share mode
                    NULL,              // security descriptor
```

```
                        OPEN_EXISTING,    // don't create new object
                        FILE_ATTRIBUTE_NORMAL,// file attributes
                        NULL );               // file from which
                                              // to copy attributes
        // check that the pipe's handle is valid
    if( hpipeRead == INVALID_HANDLE_VALUE )
    {
            // If CreateFile failed simply because other
            // waiting threads grabbed pipe, don't bother user
            // with error message.
        if( GetLastError() != ERROR_PIPE_BUSY )
        {
                // an unpredictable error occurred; show message
            ShowErrorMsg();
            bTerminate = TRUE;      // break loop; end program
        }
    }
    else
    {
            bConnected = TRUE;      // succeeded in connecting
    }
}
```

When the client child successfully links to the server parent, the procedure updates the window caption and enters another loop to wait for messages to arrive through the pipe. The receiving loop ends when the user chooses Exit from the child's menu or when the child receives an IDM_TERMINATE command from the parent.

```
        // change window caption to show this window is connected
    wsprintf( szBuffer, szTitle, (LPSTR)" (connected)" );
    SetWindowText( hwndMain, szBuffer );
```

The DoRead procedure calls ReadFile to read messages from the parent. It needs no revisions to work with a named pipe.

```
        // read messages from pipe until receive terminate command
    while( ! bTerminate )
    {
        DoRead( hpipeRead );
    }
        // when bTerminate is TRUE, end the program
    FORWARD_WM_DESTROY( hwndMain, PostMessage );
    return( 0L );                           // implicit ExitThread()
    UNREFERENCED_PARAMETER( lpThreadData );
}
```

The programs discussed here demonstrate how parent and child processes interact, and how pipes allow processes to communicate. The anonymous pipe and named pipe versions of the demo program are on the CD that accompanies the book.

The sample programs in this chapter also introduced the `GetLastError` and `FormatMessage` functions for signaling to the user when something goes wrong. The next chapter explores a more advanced mechanism for dealing with unexpected failures: structured exception handling.

Handling Exceptions

- ■ Structured exception handling

- ■ Termination handling

- ■ Try blocks

- ■ Exception filters

As a program runs, many conditions may disturb its normal flow of execution. The CPU may complain of an improper memory address; the user may interrupt by pressing Ctrl+C; a debugger may halt and resume a program arbitrarily; or an unexpected value may produce an overflow or underflow in a floating-point calculation. Exceptional conditions such as these may arise in user mode or kernel mode, or on a RISC or an Intel chip, and either the hardware or the software may signal their occurrence. Furthermore, each programming language must find a way to cope with them. To unify the processing required for all these different situations, Windows NT and 95 build structured exception-handling mechanisms into the system at a low level.

Different languages, and even different compilers, may choose to expose structured exception handling in different ways. Microsoft's C compilers supply the keywords `try`, `except`, and `finally`, each introducing a new block of code. A `try` block marks code that might raise exceptions. An `except` block contains code to run if an exception occurs. A `finally` block contains code to run when a `try` block ends, even if the try block fails or is interrupted. From the programmer's perspective, these syntax structures conveniently separate code that handles exceptional conditions from code that handles normal tasks.

Exception-Handling Concepts

Exceptions closely resemble interrupts. Both signals cause the CPU to transfer control to some other part of the system; however, interrupts and exceptions are not the same. An interrupt occurs asynchronously, often as a result of some hardware event such as a keypress or serial port input. A program has no control over such interruptions, and they may occur at any time. An exception, on the other hand, arises synchronously, as a direct result of executing a particular program instruction.

Often, exceptions indicate error conditions, and usually they can be reproduced by running the same code again with the same context. These generalizations are useful guidelines, but in practice the distinction is not quite as firm as it might at first appear. The decision to signal some API failures with error returns and others by raising exceptions must sometimes be arbitrary.

Traps and the Trap Handler

Besides switching from thread to thread, the kernel must respond to *interrupts* and *exceptions*. These are signals that arise within the system and interrupt the processor to handle some new condition. When the kernel detects an interrupt or an exception, it preempts the current thread and diverts control to a different part of the system. Which part depends on what condition the signal indicates. The *trap handler* is the part of the kernel invoked to answer interrupts and exceptions. It interprets the signal and transfers control to some procedure previously designated to handle the indicated condition.

Although the system's handling of interrupts will sound familiar to MS-DOS programmers, there are two important differences. First, MS-DOS uses only interrupts, not exceptions. Interrupts are asynchronous, meaning they may occur at any time, and their causes have nothing to do with any code the processor may be executing. Hardware devices, such as a mouse, a keyboard, and a network card, often generate interrupts to feed their input into the processor. Sometimes, software generates interrupts, too. The kernel, for example, initiates a context switch by causing an interrupt.

Exceptions, on the other hand, are synchronous, meaning they arise within a sequence of code as the result of executing a particular instruction. Often, exceptions arise when some piece of code encounters an error it cannot handle. Divide-by-zero errors and memory access violations, for example, cause the system to raise an exception. But not all exceptions are errors. Windows NT also raises an exception when it encounters a call for a system service. In handling the exception, the kernel yields control to the part of the system that provides the requested service.

When it receives an interruption signal, the trap handler first records the machine's current state so it can be restored after the signal is processed. Then it determines whether the signal is an interrupt, a service call, or an exception and passes the signal accordingly to the interrupt dispatcher, the system service dispatcher, or the exception dispatcher. These subsidiary dispatchers locate the appropriate handler routine and transfer control there.

In addition to the trapping of exceptions as well as interrupts, Windows NT differs from MS-DOS in assigning priority levels for each interrupt. The priority assigned to an interrupt is called its *interrupt request level* (IRQL). Do not confuse this with a thread's dynamic priority, which is assigned to a sequence of code; IRQLs are assigned to interrupt sources. The mouse has an IRQL, and its input is processed at one level of priority. The system clock also generates interrupts, and its input is assigned another IRQL.

The CPU also has an IRQL, which changes as the system runs. Changing the CPU's IRQL allows the system to block out interrupts of lower priority. Only kernel-mode services, such as the trap handler, can alter the processor's IRQL. User-mode threads do not have that privilege. Blocked interrupts do not receive attention until some thread explicitly lowers the CPU's level. When the processor runs at the lowest IRQL, normal thread execution proceeds and all interrupts are permitted to occur. When the trap handler calls an *interrupt service routine* (ISR), it first sets the CPU to that interrupt's IRQL. Traps of a lower level are masked while the ISR runs in order to prevent relatively unimportant events, such as device input signals, from interfering with critical operations, such as the power-loss routines. When the processor's IRQL level drops, any interrupts that were masked are drawn from their queue and duly processed. Eventually, the processor returns to the lowest IRQL and the interrupted thread resumes.

To process any interrupt, the trap handler must first locate an appropriate handler routine somewhere in the system. It keeps track of interrupt handlers in the *interrupt dispatch table* (IDT). The IDT has 32 entries, one for each IRQ level. Each entry points to a handler, or possibly to a chain of handlers if several devices happen to use the same IRQL. When new device drivers are loaded into the system, they immediately add their own handlers to the appropriate IDT entry. They do this by creating and connecting an *interrupt object,* a structure containing all the information the kernel needs to augment the IDT. By using an interrupt object, drivers are able to register their interrupt handlers without knowing anything about the interrupt hardware or the structure of the interrupt dispatch table.

Structured Exception Handling

Any exception that arises must be handled, if not by the program then by the system itself. Some code somewhere must respond and clear it. Exception handling, then, means providing blocks of code to respond if an exception occurs. A program is likely to have many small handler blocks guarding different portions of code against different exceptions.

In searching for a block of code prepared to deal with a particular condition, the system looks first in the current procedure, then backward through the stack to other active pending procedures in the same process, and finally to the system's own exception handlers. If the offending process happens to be under the scrutiny of a debugger, then the debugging program also gets a chance to handle the exception.

The provisions for handling errors differ with the subsystem and the programming language. The WOW subsystem, for example, must handle all exceptions directly because its Win16 clients have no way to do it themselves. Also, different languages may choose to expose exception handling through different syntax. But the name *structured exception handling* implies that the language itself must include some control structure for dealing with exceptions.

Basic Exception-Handling Statements

The basic exception-handling statements in C are `try` and `except`. The `try`/`except` structure separates the code for exceptional situations from the code for normal situations.

```
try                             // beginning of try block
{
   <guarded code statements>    // code that may produce exceptions
}
except (<filter>)               // beginning of exception block
{
   <exception handling code>    // execute if exception occurs
}
```

While the Borland C/C++ compiler recognizes the `try`/`except` commands, the equivalent statements for Microsoft C/C++ are the `__try`/`__except` commands. Syntax aside, the two sets of `try`/`except` structures function in the same fashion and, if desired, compiler cross-compatibility can be accomplished by using `#ifdef` and `#define` statements.

In addition to the `try`/`except` conditions, the `try`/`finally` statement is used as well. The Microsoft version appears as `__try`/`__finally`.

The `try`/`finally` statement is an extension to the C and C++ languages that enables 32-bit target applications to guarantee execution of cleanup code when execution of a block of code is interrupted. Cleanup may consist of such tasks as deallocating memory, closing files, and releasing file handles. The `try`/`finally` statement is especially useful for routines that have several places where a check is made for errors which can cause premature return from the routine.

Filtering Exceptions

In any implementation, structured exception handling associates a block of code for handling exceptions with a block of code it is said to guard. If an exception occurs while the guarded block executes, control transfers to the filter expression. Usually, the filter expression asks what the exception is and decides how to proceed. Exceptions that pass through the filter reach the exception-handling code. If the filter blocks an exception, then the handler is not invoked. The system continues to search elsewhere for a handler that will take the exception.

The filter expression may be complex. It may even call a separate function. Sometimes the filter even does the real work of responding to an exception, leaving the `except` block empty.

TIP

While structured exception handling works with Win32 for both C and C++ source files, it is not specifically designed for C++. To ensure portability, use C++ exception handling in the form of the `try`/`catch`/`throw` statements. C++ exception handling is more flexible, in that it can handle exceptions of any type.

Termination Handlers

An exception, by interrupting the execution of a guarded `try` block, may prevent the block from reaching its normal conclusion. If the block normally sets up something at the beginning and takes it down at the end, an exception in the middle may prevent the block from performing its final cleanup instructions. Since exceptions may potentially occur anywhere, no `if` statement can guarantee that cleanup code will execute. That is the job of a termination handler.

The syntax of a termination handler closely resembles that of an exception handler:

```
try                              // beginning of try block
{
    <guarded code statements>    // code that may produce exceptions
}
finally                          // begin termination-handling block
{
    <termination-handling code>  // execute when guarded block ends
}
```

A termination handler contains code that must execute after a guarded block ends, regardless of how the block ends. When the execution path leaves the guarded block, the termination block always runs. It doesn't matter if the guarded block calls `return`, is interrupted by an exception, or simply runs to the end and falls through into the `finally` block. Any of those events triggers the termination handler.

Like the `try`/`except` statement, the compound statement after the __`try` clause is the guarded section, while the compound statement after the __`finally` clause is the termination handler, specifying a set of actions to execute when the guarded section is exited, whether the guarded section is exited by an exception (abnormal termination), or by standard fall-through (normal termination).

Control reaches a __`try` statement by simple sequential execution (fall-through). When control enters the __`try`, its associated handler becomes active. Execution proceeds as follows:

1. The guarded section is executed.

2. The termination handler is invoked.

3. When the termination handler completes, execution continues after the __`finally` statement.

Regardless of how the guarded section ends (for example, via a `goto` out of the guarded body or a `return` statement), the termination handler is executed *before* the flow of control moves out of the guarded section.

A program typically uses termination handlers to guarantee that resources are released. A section of code that waits to own a mutex, for example, might guard itself with a termination handler to ensure the mutex's eventual release. Failure to release a mutex would freeze other waiting threads.

The only way to exit a `try` block without triggering its termination handler is to call `ExitThread` or `ExitProcess` (or `abort`, which calls `ExitProcess` internally).

What Is Exceptional?

Programmers new to structured exception handling sometimes have the false impression that they no longer need to check for error returns after executing each command. An error, however, is not the same thing as an exception. A function can fail without raising an exception. For example, consider these lines of code:

```
hBrush = CreateSolidBrush( RGB(255, 0, 0) );
hOldBrush = SelectObject( hDC, hBrush );
Rectangle( hDC, 0, 0, 100, 100 );
```

If the first command fails and returns NULL for the brush, then `SelectObject` fails, too. The third command still draws a rectangle but does not color it correctly. No exceptions are raised. The only way to protect against those failures is to check the return values. Here's another example:

```
HANDLE hMemory;
char *pData;

hMemory = GlobalAlloc( GHND, 1000 );
pData = (char *)GlobalLock( hMemory );
```

If the allocation fails, then `hMemory` becomes NULL, `GlobalLock` fails, and `pData` becomes NULL, too. Neither failure, however, produces an exception. But the next line does produce an exception when it tries to write to an invalid address:

```
pData[0] = 'a';              // raises exception if pData = NULL
```

An exception is a kind of error that the command can't process. If `GlobalAlloc` can't find enough room, it simply returns NULL. But if the assignment operator has no valid destination to place a value, it can do nothing, not even return an error. It must raise an exception; and if the process cannot handle the exception, the system must close down the process.

The line between exceptions and errors is sometimes difficult to draw. The next chapter, for example, introduces another allocation command, `HeapAlloc`, that can be made to indicate normal failures by generating exceptions instead of returning NULL. The difference between an error and an exception is sometimes a matter of implementation. Recognizing commands that might raise exceptions takes a little practice. Learn which exceptions can arise and then imagine which operations might cause them. The faulty assignment statement causes an *access violation* exception. The list of possible exceptions varies on different machines, but here are some the Windows NT kernel defines universally:

- Data type misalignment
- Debugger breakpoint
- Debugger single step
- Floating-point divide by zero
- Floating-point overflow and underflow
- Floating-point reserved operand
- Guard page violation
- Illegal instruction
- Integer divide by zero
- Integer overflow
- Memory access violation
- Page read error
- Paging file quota exceeded
- Privileged instruction

Frame-Based Exception Handling

The exception-handling mechanisms in Microsoft C are *frame-based*, meaning that each except block is associated with, or framed in, the procedure that contains it. The term *frame* describes a layer in the program stack. Each time a program calls a procedure, the program pushes a new set of information on the stack. The information includes, for example, parameters passed to the new procedure and an address showing where to return when the called procedure ends. If the second procedure calls a third and the third a fourth, each successive call pushes a new frame onto the stack, as you see in Figure 16.1.

Each frame represents an activated procedure waiting for its subroutines to finish before resuming. At any point, it is possible to trace back through the stack frames to discover which procedures have been called. When an exception occurs, the system traces back, looking for exception handlers in each pending procedure.

FIGURE 16.1

Frames in a program stack

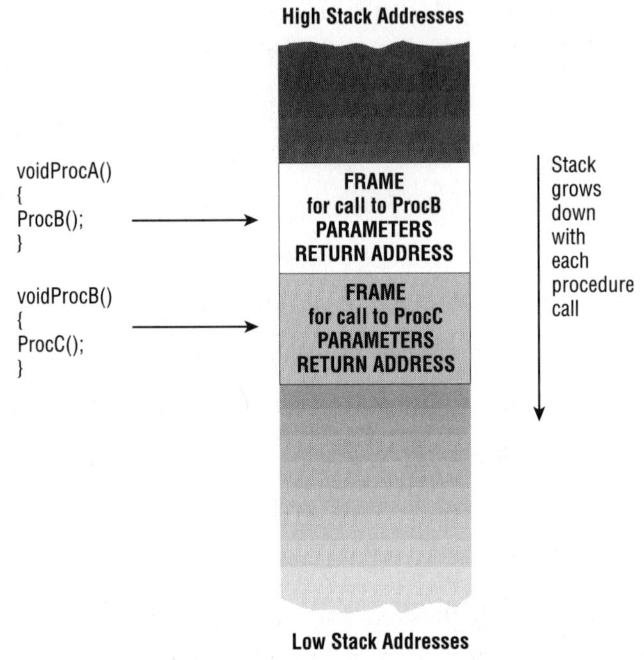

High Stack Addresses

```
voidProcA()
{
  ProcB();
}

voidProcB()
{
  ProcC();
}
```

FRAME
for call to ProcB
PARAMETERS
RETURN ADDRESS

FRAME
for call to ProcC
PARAMETERS
RETURN ADDRESS

Stack grows down with each procedure call

Low Stack Addresses

The internal mechanisms that support exception handling vary from system to system. An MIPS machine, for example, implements handlers through tables, not stacks.

Order of Execution

When an exception arises, the system first saves the machine context of the interrupted thread, just as it does when it performs a context switch for normal multitasking. Depending on how the exception is eventually handled, the system may later use the saved context to resume execution at the beginning of the line where the exception occurred.

In response to an exception, the system generally tries to execute the following pieces of code, in this order:

1. Termination handler

2. Exception filter

3. Exception handler

If the exception arises in code guarded by a `try/finally` structure, the `finally` block executes first. The termination handler performs its duties *before* the system begins to look for an exception handler. Then the system traces backward through the stack looking for an exception filter that accepts the current exception. The system may need to execute several filters in its search.

Exception Handling and Debuggers

The task of finding a handler becomes more involved when a process is being debugged, because the system transfers control to the debugger *before* seeking the program's own exception handlers. Typically, the debugger uses this early alert to handle single-step and breakpoint exceptions, allowing the user to inspect the context before resuming.

If the debugger decides *not* to handle an exception during the early alert, the system returns to the process in search of a handler. If the process also refuses the exception, the system gives the debugger a second chance to handle what has now become a more serious situation. If the debugger refuses a second time, then the system finally gives up and settles for providing its own default response, which is usually to terminate the process.

Exception Handling–Related Commands

This section introduces a few API commands commonly used with exception handlers. It begins with commands useful primarily for gathering information while handling an exception or executing a termination handler. Then it explains how to define custom exceptions to suit the error-handling needs of your own programs.

Filters

The filter expression determines whether or not the handler it accompanies will accept particular exceptions. The filter must ultimately resolve to one of three values:

- `EXCEPTION_EXECUTE_HANDLER`: Yes, do execute the `except` block. When the `except` block ends, execution continues on from its last statement in normal sequential fashion. In other words, if an exception arises in one procedure and is handled in another, the program does not return to where the exception occurred.

- EXCEPTION_CONTINUE_SEARCH: The handler refuses the exception. The `except` block does not execute. The system must continue to search for another handler.

- EXCEPTION_CONTINUE_EXECUTION: The handler accepts the exception but does not execute the `except` block. The system returns control to the point where the exception occurred.

When the system finds a filter that returns EXCEPTION_EXECUTE_HANDLER or EXCEPTION_CONTINUE_EXECUTION, it considers the exception to have been handled. If the system cannot find an interested handler, it displays a message box like the one in Figure 16.2 and terminates the process.

FIGURE 16.2

A system message box with an unhandled exception warning

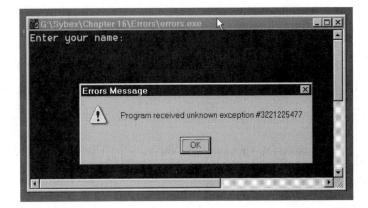

Filter Expressions

In the simplest case, the filter expression may be one of these constants:

```
try
{
    <guarded code statements>
}
except( EXCEPTION_EXECUTE_HANDLER ) // always execute handler code
{
    <exception handling code>
}
```

Of course, that filter expression doesn't really filter anything. It's a poor sentry that lets everyone pass. More flexible filters require a means of determining which exception has just been generated. For that, you need a new command:

```
DWORD GetExceptionCode ( void );
```

The value returned by GetExceptionCode identifies the most recent exception by number. Exception constants are defined in Winbase.H. Here are some of the more commonly encountered exceptions:

- EXCEPTION_ACCESS_VIOLATION: The thread used a memory address for which it is not privileged.

- EXCEPTION_ARRAY_BOUNDS_EXCEEDED: The thread tried to read outside the declared bounds of an array. (Not all hardware supports bounds-checking.)

- EXCEPTION_BREAKPOINT: A debugging breakpoint interrupted the thread.

- EXCEPTION_DATATYPE_MISALIGNMENT: The thread tried to read or write values not evenly aligned on logical address boundaries. (Some systems provide automatic alignment.)

- EXCEPTION_PRIV_INSTRUCTION: The thread tried to execute an instruction illegal in the current running mode.

- EXCEPTION_SINGLE_STEP: A debugging single-step breakpoint interrupted the thread.

- STATUS_NONCONTINUABLE_EXCEPTION: The thread tried to continue after receiving an exception that disallows continuation.

In addition, another set of exceptions signals anomalies in math operations:

- EXCEPTION_FLT_DENORMAL_OPERAND

- EXCEPTION_FLT_DIVIDE_BY_ZERO

- EXCEPTION_FLT_INEXACT_RESULT

- EXCEPTION_FLT_INVALID_OPERATION

- EXCEPTION_FLT_OVERFLOW

- EXCEPTION_FLT_STACK_CHECK

- EXCEPTION_FLT_UNDERFLOW

- EXCEPTION_INT_DIVIDE_BY_ZERO

- EXCEPTION_INT_OVERFLOW

By default, all the floating-point (FLT) exceptions are disabled, and errors announce themselves only by returning infinity or 0. To generate exceptions for any of the floating-point conditions, call _controlfp. These lines, for example, enable exception signals for all errors:

```
int iFPMask = _controlfp( 0 ,0 );          // save old control mask

iFPMask &= ~( EM_OVERFLOW | EM_UNDERFLOW | EM_INEXACT |
              EM_ZERODIVIDE | EM_DENORMAL);

_controlfp( iFPMask, MCW_EM );              // set new control mask
```

Beware, however, when turning on floating-point exceptions because any unhandled exceptions will, as always, cause the program to terminate abruptly.

GetExceptionCode enables a filter expression to execute its handler conditionally. The following example executes its handler only in response to a memory access violation. It refuses other exceptions, forcing the system to continue its search for a handler.

```
try
{
    <guarded code statements>
}
except( ( GetExceptionCode() == EXCEPTION_ACCESS_VIOLATION )
           ? EXCEPTION_EXECUTE_HANDLER : EXCEPTION_CONTINUE_SEARCH )
{
    // this block executes only after an access violation
}
```

Filter Functions

For those occasions when a single line can't hold all the logic of your filter, define your own filter function. A filter function must return one of the three valid filter constants. Microsoft's examples assign the filter function a DWORD return value, but since EXCEPTION_CONTINUE_EXECUTION is defined in Excpt.H as –1, it makes more sense—and avoids a -W4 warning—to return a signed LONG value. This example accepts two different exceptions and refuses all others:

```
try
{
    <guarded code statements>
}
except( MyFilter( GetExceptionCode() ) )
{
```

```
      // this block executes only after an access violation
   }

   LONG MyFilter( DWORD dwException )
   {
      switch( dwException )
      {
         case EXCEPTION_ACCESS_VIOLATION:
         case EXCEPTION_INT_DIVIDE_BY_ZERO:
            return( EXCEPTION_EXECUTE_HANDLER );

         default:
            return( EXCEPTION_CONTINUE_SEARCH );
      }
   }
```

The code in a filter function may be as complex as you care to make it. Note, however, that we did not call GetExceptionCode from within the filter. It works only in the filter expression (on the same line as except) or within the exception-handling block, but not in other procedures, such as MyFilter.

Getting More Information

To discover more about an exception than its identifying number, call GetException-Information instead of GetExceptionCode. GetExceptionInformation returns a pointer to an EXCEPTION_POINTERS structure, which itself holds pointers to two more structures: an EXCEPTION_RECORD and a CONTEXT. The CONTEXT structure contains all the machine-specific information about the state of the CPU at the moment the exception arose. CONTEXT is defined in WinNT.H; its fields vary with the CPU. The structure of an EXCEPTION_RECORD does not vary:

```
   LPEXCEPTION_POINTERS GetExceptionInformation( void );

   typedef struct _EXCEPTION_POINTERS   /* exp */
   {
      PEXCEPTION_RECORD ExceptionRecord;
      PCONTEXT ContextRecord;
   } EXCEPTION_POINTERS;

   typedef struct _EXCEPTION_RECORD   /* exr */
   {
      DWORD ExceptionCode;              // same as GetExceptionCode
      DWORD ExceptionFlags;             // continuable?
      struct _EXCEPTION_RECORD *ExceptionRecord;  // link field
      PVOID ExceptionAddress;           // where exception occurred
```

```
      DWORD NumberParameters;        // no.of params in final array
      DWORD ExceptionInformation[EXCEPTION_MAXIMUM_PARAMETERS];
   } EXCEPTION_RECORD;
```

The `ExceptionFlags` field is most often 0 but, for exceptions so serious that the system will not permit the program to resume the field, this field contains `EXCEPTION_NONCONTINUABLE`. Any attempt to continue executing the program after handling a noncontinuable exception generates a second noncontinuable exception, `STATUS_NONCONTINUABLE_EXCEPTION`.

The `ExceptionRecord` field comes into play when several exceptions occur and accumulate before the system finishes handling any one of them. Traversing the links in this field leads back to records for previous exceptions. The `ExceptionAddress` field is the address of the code instruction where the exception arose. `NumberParameters` tells how many elements of the final `ExceptionInformation` array the current exception actually uses.

Usually `NumberParameters` is 0, but some exceptions do pass information through the array. If the exception code is `EXCEPTION_ACCESS_VIOLATION`, for example, then the first element of the `ExceptionInformation` array tells whether the offending element tried to read or write, and the second element contains the illegal memory address. An exception handler might use the information to fix the problem or to tell the user exactly what happened. Few of the standard system exceptions use the information array, but user-defined exceptions might need it.

`GetExceptionCode` works only when called within a filter or an except block, and `GetExceptionInformation` works only when called within a filter. Neither command works within a filter function; they work only within the filter expression. The restrictions have to do with losing information from the top of the stack when an exception is accepted by a handler. The only useful way to call `GetExceptionInformation` is to pass its result as a parameter to a filter function. If the filter function copies the received values to some other storage, then the exception handler can also read the values.

```
EXCEPTION_RECORD ExceptRecord;              // a global variable

try
{
   <guarded code statements>
}
except( MyFilter( GetExceptionInformation() ) )
{
   // This block can refer to values stored in
```

```
    // the ExceptRecord variable by the filter function.

    if( ExceptRecord.ExceptionCode == EXCEPTION_ACCESS_VIOLATION )
    {
        <code to handle access violations>
    }
}

DWORD MyFilter( LPEXCEPTION_POINTERS lpEP )
{
    // Copy some of the exception information to a place
    // where the exception handler block can read it.
    CopyMemory( &ExceptRecord, lpEP->ExceptionRecord,
                sizeof(EXCEPTION_RECORD) );
    return( EXCEPTION_EXECUTE_HANDLER );
}
```

Abnormal Termination Information

One final information-gathering function works with termination handlers
rather than exception handlers. If from inside a `finally` block you need to know
whether the guarded block reached its natural end or was interrupted, call
`AbnormalTermination`:

```
BOOL AbnormalTermination( void )
```

`AbnormalTermination` works only within a `finally` block. (Placing it elsewhere
produces a compiler error.) It returns FALSE if the guarded `try` block executed its
last line and reached the closing bracket (}). Exiting from any other point is considered abnormal and makes the function return TRUE. Abnormal exits occur when
an exception arises within the block and also as a result of `return`, `break`, `goto`, or
`continue` statements.

Abnormal termination from the first half of a `try`/`finally` structure is costly.
When execution jumps out of a guarded block, the system must trace back through
the stack to see how many termination handlers have been triggered. One jump
can trigger several nested handlers. Tracing back through the stack costs hundreds
of instructions. Wherever possible, design the `try` block of a termination handler
to terminate normally.

To encourage normal termination of `try` blocks wherever possible, Microsoft's
implementation of structured exception handling also includes a keyword called
`leave`. Like the `break` instruction in loops and switches, `leave` jumps immediately
to the closing bracket of a code structure. The `leave` command in this `try` block

skips over intermediate code to exit the block immediately. If the subsequent `finally` block calls `AbnormalTermination`, it receives an answer of FALSE.

```
try
{
   if( <condition> )
   {
      leave;                      // jumps to end of try block
   }
   <more guarded code>
}
finally
{
   <termination-handling code>
}
```

The `__leave` keyword is valid within a `try/finally` statement block. Its effect is to jump to the end of the `try/finally` block, so the termination handler is immediately executed. `leave` is a valid instruction only within a `try` block. Although a `goto` statement could be used to accomplish the same result, a `goto` statement causes stack unwinding. The `__leave` statement is more efficient because it does not involve stack unwinding.

Exiting a `try/finally` statement using the `longjmp` runtime function is considered abnormal termination. It is illegal to jump into a `__try` statement, but legal to jump out of one. All `__finally` statements that are active between the point of departure and the destination must be run. This is called a *local unwind*. The termination handler is not called if a process is killed in the middle of executing a `try/finally` statement.

Do-It-Yourself Exceptions

`RaiseException` generates an exception by hand. It causes the system to step in, save the context, and search for a handler, just as it would for any other exception. `RaiseException` can generate the predefined exceptions you already know, such as access violations, or it can generate exception codes that you define. By incorporating `RaiseException` in your own routines, you can extend the mechanisms of exception handling to structure even more of your code.

```
void RaiseException(
   DWORD dwExceptionCode,    // exception code (you define it)
   DWORD dwExceptionFlags,   // 0 or noncontinuable flag
   DWORD dwNumArgs,          // number of arguments in array
   LPDWORD lpArguments );    // array of optional handler arguments
```

Introducing Console Applications

In order to avoid the extra code necessary for a graphics interface and to concentrate on the mechanisms of structured exception handling, the sample programs presented in this chapter make use of the console application facilities in Windows NT.

A console application does not use the standard graphics features of the Windows interface. It does not create its own windows or run message loops. It automatically receives a single main window that mimics the character-based output of a DOS screen. Console programs follow the traditional structure of C programs, beginning with `main` rather than `WinMain`.

The only special requirements come when linking. The linker must be told to use the console subsystem:

```
link -debug:full -debugtype:cv -subsystem:console example.obj \
    libc.lib ntdll.lib kernel32.lib
```

Changing the subsystem to `console` also changes the default entry point for the `-entry` switch from `WinMainCRTStartup` to `mainCRTStartup`. (It is not necessary to specify the default value on the command line.)

Most console applications do not use routines from Gdi32.LIB and User32.LIB, but they can if they want to. A console program could call `CreateWindow` to create a second drawing area and paint it with GDI commands. It would probably also create a thread to run the window's message loop. Even without creating a GUI window, console applications may still call functions from the Win32 API. They may, for example, have resources, display message boxes, and play multimedia audio.

Exception-Handling Examples

The best way to learn structured exception handling is to read programs that use it. The short programs that follow illustrate a variety of situations that arise when implementing the `try`, `except`, and `finally` structures. We'll consider basic syntax, nested blocks, blocks layered in successive frames, and customized exceptions. The complete source file for these examples appears on the CD accompanying this book.

Nesting Blocks: A Termination Handler

Let's begin with a simple termination handler. A termination handler cleans up when an exception interrupts a block of code, but it does not handle the exception. The `finally` block executes, but the system still must locate an `except` block to process the exception. This short program, for example, never reaches its final line:

```
#include <windows.h>
#include <stdio.h>

int main ( )
{
   char *szText = NULL;

   try
   {
      puts("About to cause an exception." );
      lstrcpy( szText, "Error" );          // writes to NULL string
   }
   finally
   {
      puts( "Termination handler ran." );
   }
      // Because exception is never handled, system terminates
      // the program before it reaches these lines.
   puts( "This line will never print." );
   return( 0 );
}
```

The faulty string copy command generates an exception that is never handled. When the program runs, the `finally` block prints its message, and then the system displays its error message (like the one shown earlier in Figure 16.2) and the program ends. The final message is never printed, as you can see from the program's output.

```
About to cause an exception.
Termination handler ran.
```

Even without an exception handler, a `finally` block can be quite useful, but the two are often paired. The next example nests a termination handler within an exception handler.

```
#include <windows.h>
#include <stdio.h>

int main ( )
```

```
{
    char *szText = NULL;

    try
    {
        try
        {
            puts("About to cause an exception." );
            lstrcpy( szText, "Error" ); // writes to NULL string
        }
        finally
        {
            puts( "Termination handler ran." );
        }
    }
    except( EXCEPTION_EXECUTE_HANDLER )
    {
        puts( "Handling exception." );
    }
    puts( "Program ending normally." );
    return( 0 );
}
```

The `finally` block executes whether or not an exception occurs. If an exception does occur, first the `finally` block executes and then the `except` block. Here's the output:

```
About to cause an exception.
Termination handler ran.
Handling exception.
Program ending normally.
```

As you see, one procedure may contain several `try` blocks. A procedure may contain any number of exception and termination handlers, and they may be nested as these are, or they may appear in succession.

A `finally` block always executes when its `try` block finishes, but it does not execute if an exception interrupts the thread before the `try` block begins. In this revision of the preceding program, for example, the termination handler does *not* execute:

```
#include <windows.h>
#include <stdio.h>

int main ( )
{
    char *szText = NULL;
```

```
try
{
   puts( "About to cause an exception." );
   lstrcpy( szText, "Error" );          // writes to NULL string
   try
   {
      puts( "Entered try block." );
   }
   finally
   {
      puts( "Termination handler ran." );
   }
}
except (EXCEPTION_EXECUTE_HANDLER)
{
   puts( "Handling exception." );
}
puts( "Program ending normally." );
return( 0 );
}
```

The except block handles the exception, but the finally block never runs. The trace message from the termination message does not appear in the output.

```
About to cause an exception.
Handling exception.
Program ending normally.
```

As a further illustration, here's how the Threads program from Chapter 14 should make use of nested exception and termination handlers. Because of the procedure's new exception handler, the thread will continue to run even after an exception occurs (provided the exception permits continuation). The termination handler guarantees that the mutex will be released in any case; no matter what happens to one thread, the others may still acquire the mutex that lets them continue drawing. (A second version of the Threads program, which incorporates exception handling, appears on the CD in the subdirectory for this chapter.)

```
/*-----------------------------------------------------------
   START THREAD
      This is called when each thread begins execution
----------------------------------------------------------*/

LONG StartThread( LPVOID lpThreadData )
{
   DWORD *pdwThreadID;  // pointer to DWORD storing thread's ID
   DWORD dwWait;        // return value from WaitSingleObject
```

```
    // retrieve the thread's ID
pdwThreadID = lpThreadData;

    // draw continuously until bTerminate becomes TRUE
while( ! bTerminate )
{
    if( bUseMutex )
    {
        // draw when this thread gets the mutex
        dwWait = WaitForSingleObject( hDrawMutex, INFINITE );
        if( dwWait == 0 )                   // did wait succeed?
        {
            try
            {
                try
                {
                    DrawProc( *pdwThreadID );
                }
                finally
                {
                    ReleaseMutex( hDrawMutex );
                }
            }
            except (EXCEPTION_EXECUTE_HANDLER)
            {
            MessageBox( hwndParent, "A thread was unable to draw.",
                            "Threads Message",
                            MB_OK | MB_ICONEXCLAMATION );
            }
        }
    }
    else
    {
        // not using mutex; let the thread draw
        DrawProc( *pdwThreadID );
    }
}
    // stop this thread and return
ExitThread(0);                              // now thread is not running
CloseHandle(hThread[*pdwThreadID]);   // now thread is destroyed
return( 0L );
}
```

Back-Stacking: The Unwind Program

We've said that when an exception occurs, the system backtracks through the stack seeking a hospitable handler. The next sample, Unwind, puts three frames on the stack, each with a different handler, and generates exceptions from the bottom level to see where they go.

```c
#include <windows.h>
#include <stdio.h>
#include <float.h>

//  Function prototypes.
//

void MiddleProc( void );            // intermediate function
void InnerProc( void );             // causes various exceptions

// MAIN
//     Program entry point.

int main ( )
{
   puts( "Starting program." );
   try
   {
      MiddleProc();
   }
      // This exception handler responds if anything lower
      // down in the program generates an exception without
      // providing a handler.
   except (EXCEPTION_EXECUTE_HANDLER)
   {
      puts( "Unwind encountered an unknown error." );
   }
   puts( "Program ending normally." );
   return( 0 );
}

// MIDDLE PROC
//     Calls the function that raises exceptions.

void MiddleProc( void )
{
   puts( "Starting MiddleProc." );
   try
   {
```

```
        puts( "In try block of MiddleProc." );
        InnerProc();
    }
    except( ( GetExceptionCode() == EXCEPTION_ACCESS_VIOLATION )
            ? EXCEPTION_EXECUTE_HANDLER : EXCEPTION_CONTINUE_SEARCH )
    {
        puts( "MiddleProc recognized an access violation." );
    }
    puts( "MiddleProc ending normally." );
    return;
}

// INNER PROC
//     Causes exceptions.

void InnerProc( void )
{
    char *szText = NULL;
    int i1;
    int i2 = 0;
    float f1 = FLT_MAX;
    UINT uFPMask;

    puts( "Starting InnerProc." );
    uFPMask = _controlfp( 0, 0 );
    uFPMask &= ~EM_OVERFLOW;
    _controlfp( uFPMask, MCW_EM );
    try
    {
            // This block can produce any of three different
            // exceptions. Comment out some lines to test
            // how the program handles each exception.
        puts( "Forcing an integer divide-by-zero error." );
        i1 = i1 / i2; // handled in InnerProc

    // puts( "Forcing an access violation." );
    // lstrcpy( szText, "Hello" );      // handled in MiddleProc

    // puts( "Forcing a floating point overflow." );
    // f1 = f1 * f1;                    // handled in main

        puts( "This is never printed." );
    }
    except( ( GetExceptionCode() == EXCEPTION_INT_DIVIDE_BY_ZERO )
            ? EXCEPTION_EXECUTE_HANDLER : EXCEPTION_CONTINUE_SEARCH )
    {
```

```
        puts( "InnerProc encountered divide-by-zero error." );
    }
    puts( "InnerProc ending normally." );
    return;
}
```

The innermost procedure, InnerProc, contains statements to generate any of three exceptions. Choose which exception by commenting out the lines you don't want. The handler in the InnerProc frame accepts only the integer divide-by-zero exception. The floating-point and access-violation exceptions must be handled in preceding frames.

The Unwind program issues trace messages as it proceeds, marking its progress through the code. Each of the exceptions produces a different set of trace messages.

The EXCEPTION_INT_DIVIDE_BY_ZERO exception shows these messages:

```
Starting program.
Starting MiddleProc.
In try block of MiddleProc.
Starting InnerProc.
Forcing an integer divide-by-zero error.
InnerProc encountered divide-by-zero error.
InnerProc ending normally.
MiddleProc ending normally.
Program ending normally.
```

The EXCEPTION_ACCESS_VIOLATION exception shows these messages:

```
Starting program.
Starting MiddleProc.
In try block of MiddleProc.
Starting InnerProc.
Forcing an access violation.
MiddleProc recognized an access violation.
MiddleProc ending normally.
Program ending normally.
```

The EXCEPTION_FLT_OVERFLOW exception shows these messages:

```
Starting program.
Starting MiddleProc.
In try block of MiddleProc.
Starting InnerProc.
Forcing a floating point overflow.
Unwind encountered an unknown error.
Program ending normally.
```

The trace messages confirm that an exception handler gains complete control over execution of the program. No matter what procedure generates the exception, execution resumes in the procedure where the exception is handled. For example, when Unwind creates a memory-access exception, `InnerProc` does not terminate normally. Only `main` and `MiddleProc` issue their closing trace messages.

The outer `try` block, the one in `main`, serves as a catchall for any exceptions not handled elsewhere. Because the `except` block comes just before the closing `return` statement, the program terminates whenever this handler runs, but the handler still manages to shield the user from the system's default message box with its cryptic exception addresses.

Incidentally, `InnerProc` would never generate a floating-point exception if it neglected to enable the exception with `_controlfp` first.

Having followed the intricacies of Unwind, you may find it easier now to understand how the system walks the stack for exceptions. An exception handler receives exceptions from only one thread. If a `try` block calls `CreateThread` or `CreateProcess`, the handler will not receive exceptions that arise when the new thread executes its own instructions.

While it is legal to put `return` in the middle of a `finally` block, the result may not be what you intend. When an exception occurs, the system may need to walk back through several frames to find a handler. When it does find one, it goes through the stack again to find and execute all the intervening termination handlers whose `try` blocks the jump interrupts. This is called *unwinding the stack*.

Unwinding proceeds sequentially through all the pending handlers until the system reaches the target frame *or* until one of the `finally` blocks ends with `return`. Executing a `return` statement within a `finally` block halts any unwinding that may be in progress. This is called *colliding the stack*. Handlers and filters still waiting on the stack will be skipped over. Any actions they were expected to perform will not be performed, and that omission could conceivably impede the target handler at the end of the unwind operation.

A Filter Function: Unwind Revised

All the exception handlers in the Unwind program tenaciously transfer execution to their own frames when they execute. Sometimes, it would be useful to determine the cause of the error, modify some data, and try to run the offending instruction again. This snippet revises Unwind's `InnerProc` procedure to modify variables and resume whenever a divide-by-zero exception occurs. Only a filter function can attempt to reexecute code that generated an exception.

```
//   INNER PROC
//   Causes exceptions.

void InnerProc( void )
{
    char *szText = NULL;
    int i1;
    int i2 = 0;
    float f1 = FLT_MAX;
    UINT uFPMask;

    puts( "Starting InnerProc." );

    uFPMask = _controlfp( 0, 0 );
    uFPMask &= ~EM_OVERFLOW;
    _controlfp( uFPMask, MCW_EM );
    try
    {
        // This block can produce any of three different
        // exceptions. Comment out some lines to test
        // how the program handles each exception.
        puts( "Forcing an integer divide-by-zero error." );
        i1 = i1 / i2;                   // handled in InnerProc

//      puts( "Forcing an access violation." );
//      lstrcpy( szText, "Hello" );   // handled in MiddleProc

//      puts( "Forcing a floating-point overflow." );
//      f1 = f1 * f1;                 // handled in main
    }
    except( MyFilter( GetExceptionCode(), &i2 ) )
    {
    };

    puts( "InnerProc ending normally." );
    return;
}

// MY FILTER
//    Filter function for the exception handler in InnerProc

LONG MyFilter( DWORD dwCode, int *i )
{
    if( dwCode == EXCEPTION_INT_DIVIDE_BY_ZERO )
    {
        puts( "MyFilter fixed divide-by-zero exception." );
```

```
        *i = 1;                              // modify offending variable
        return( EXCEPTION_CONTINUE_EXECUTION );
                                             // try that instruction again
    }
    return( EXCEPTION_CONTINUE_SEARCH );
}
```

When this version of Unwind runs, it produces these trace messages:

```
Starting program.
Starting MiddleProc.
In try block of MiddleProc.
Starting InnerProc.
Forcing an integer divide-by-zero error.
MyFilter fixed divide-by-zero exception.
InnerProc ending normally.
MiddleProc ending normally.
Program ending normally.
```

An Error-Handling System:
The Errors Program

The final sample program, Errors, establishes a system for handling program errors. It stores descriptive error strings in a message table, defines two exceptions to signal private events within the program, and builds an exception handler that displays the message corresponding with each exception. The complete listing of Errors appears at the end of the chapter.

The Errors program calls two subroutines. One asks the user to enter a name, and the other echoes the name back to the screen. Each subroutine sometimes raises an exception. GetName raises an exception if the user enters an empty string. For convenience, we assign this exception the same ID number as the message that describes it, namely ERRORS_ERROR_NO_NAME.

```
void GetName( void )
{
    // get name from user
    printf( "Enter your name: " );
    gets( szName );

    // check whether user entered any characters
    if( lstrlen( (LPSTR)szName ) < 1 )
    {
        // user entered nothing; raise an exception
```

```
        DWORD adwArgs[2];      // arguments for exception handler
        char szFile[FILENAME_MAX];  // buffer for source file name

            // store handler arguments in array
        lstrcpy( szFile, __FILE__ );
        adwArgs[0] = (DWORD)szFile;
        adwArgs[1] = __LINE__;

            // call for an exception handler
        RaiseException( ERRORS_ERROR_NO_NAME, 0, 2, adwArgs );
    }
    return;
}
```

The second routine, CheckName, raises an exception if the user happens to enter the name "Moriarty." The symbol identifying this exception is ERRORS_SUCCESS _MASTERMIND. A single exception handler in the main program responds to all exceptions. If the exception ID contains the FACILITY_APP_ERRORS code in its upper half, then the exception handler calls a procedure to display the error message. Any unexpected system exceptions produce a single generic warning message.

```
void CheckName( void )
{
        // did the user enter the name "Moriarty"?
    if( lstrcmp( szName, "Moriarty" ) == 0 )
    {
        DWORD adwArgs[2];          // arguments for exception handler
        char szFile[FILENAME_MAX];  // buffer for source file name

            // store handler arguments in array
        lstrcpy( szFile, __FILE__ );
        adwArgs[0] = (DWORD)szFile;
        adwArgs[1] = __LINE__;

            // call for an exception handler
        RaiseException( ERRORS_SUCCESS_MASTERMIND, 0, 2, adwArgs );
    }
    else
    {
        printf( "Thank you, " );
        printf( szName );
    }
    return;
}
```

Because exceptions beyond those we're expecting to handle may occur, the `MainFilter` procedure tests the exception code against the `FACILITY_APP_ERROR` constant to identify a private exception, which is passed to the `ShowExceptionMsg` procedure. If the exception raised is not a private exception, `MainFilter` also provides handling for any unrecognized exceptions by displaying a message with the exception code.

```c
LONG MainFilter ( LPEXCEPTION_POINTERS lpEP )
{
   DWORD    dwCode   = lpEP->ExceptionRecord->ExceptionCode;
   LPDWORD lpdwArgs = lpEP->ExceptionRecord->ExceptionInformation;

      // is this a private exception?
   if( HIWORD( dwCode & 0x0FFF0000 ) == FACILITY_APP_ERRORS )
   {
         // show a message from the message table
      ShowExceptionMsg( dwCode, lpdwArgs );
   }
   else // not a private exception
   {
      char szMsg[40];

         // tell the user something went wrong
      wsprintf( szMsg, "Program received unknown exception #%lu",
            dwCode );
      MessageBox( NULL, szMsg, "Errors Message",
            MB_ICONEXCLAMATION | MB_OK );
   }
      // resume execution after the except block
   return( EXCEPTION_EXECUTE_HANDLER );
}
```

The `ShowExceptionMsg` function simply displays text appropriate to the exception raised.

```c
void ShowExceptionMsg( DWORD dwMsgCode, LPVOID lpvArgs )
{
   switch( dwMsgCode )
   {
      case ERRORS_ERROR_NO_NAME:
         MessageBox( NULL, "Rats.  Another crook stays nameless.",
               "Errors Message", MB_ICONEXCLAMATION | MB_OK );
         break;

      case ERRORS_SUCCESS_MASTERMIND:
         MessageBox( NULL, "Eureka!  We've found the mastermind.",
```

```
                                  "Errors Message", MB_ICONEXCLAMATION | MB_OK );
                    break;
             }
          return;
       }
```

In a more serious application, a better practice would be to store the message strings as string table resources using the message codes for the string identifiers.

In Figure 16.3 the user entered "Moriarty," and the Errors program raised one of its exceptions.

FIGURE 16.3

Errors program displaying a message in response to a privately defined exception

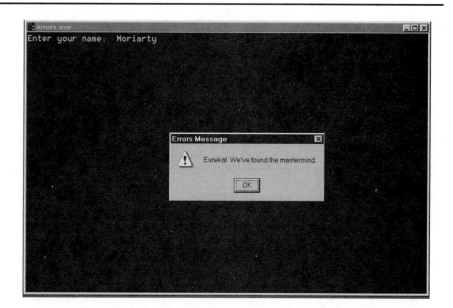

NOTE The lpvArgs argument passed to ShowExceptionMsg is not used in this revision but has been left for compatibility with the original code, which appears as comments in the CD version of this program.

In this chapter, you've seen how the try, except, and finally blocks that perform structured exception handling unify the system's responses to a variety of exceptional conditions. They also clarify code by separating the exceptional from the usual. A program can define private exception values and process its own error conditions in the same structured way it processes other exceptional conditions.

Occasionally, exception-handling mechanisms are more than just convenient. The next chapter focuses on memory management, and one of its sample programs relies on a `try` block to perform a particular memory task in the most efficient way.

Listing 16.1: The Errors Program

```
/*
   Errors.H
   Symbol definitions for the Errors program message table
*/
/*   first message    */
//
//   Values are 32-bit values laid out as follows:
//
//   3 3 2 2 2 2 2 2 2 2 2 2 1 1 1 1 1 1 1 1 1 1
//   1 0 9 8 7 6 5 4 3 2 1 0 9 8 7 6 5 4 3 2 1 0 9 8 7 6 5 4 3 2 1 0
//   +---+-+-+---------------------+---------------------------+
//   |Sev|C|R|Facility             |Code                       |
//
//   where
//
//       Sev -- is the severity code
//
//             00 -- Success
//             01 -- Informational
//             10 -- Warning
//             11 -- Error
//
//       C -- is the customer code flag
//
//       R -- is a reserved bit
//
//       Facility -- is the facility code
//
//       Code -- is the facility's status code
//
// Define the facility codes
#define FACILITY_APP_ERRORS        0x0FFF0000
#define ERRORS_ERROR_NO_NAME       0xCFFF0001L
#define ERRORS_SUCCESS_MASTERMIND  0x0FFF0002L


 /*-------------------------------------------------------------
```

```
        ERRORS.C

        Basic outline for using structured exception handling and
        message tables to process program errors.

        FUNCTIONS
              main                    main routine
              GetName                 ask user to enter a name
              CheckName               see whether user typed "Moriarty"
              MainFilter              interpret exception signals
              ShowExceptionMsg        show messages from message table

        from Mastering Windows NT Programming
        copyright 1993 by Brian Myers & Eric Hamer

        revised 1996 by Ben Ezzell
        remove all dependency on MC script (not supported)


        ------------------------------------------------------------*/

#include <windows.h>
#include <stdio.h>
#include "errors.h"

#define try        __try
#define except     __except


/*-------------------------------------------------------------------
        FUNCTION PROTOTYPES
   -----------------------------------------------------------------*/

void GetName( void );
void CheckName( void );
LONG MainFilter( LPEXCEPTION_POINTERS lpEP );
void ShowExceptionMsg( DWORD dwMsgCode, LPVOID lpvArgs );

/*-------------------------------------------------------------------
        GLOBAL VARIABLE
   -----------------------------------------------------------------*/

char szName[40];                                // string user enters

/*-------------------------------------------------------------------
        MAIN
```

```
            Call two I/O procedures and check for exceptions.
   --------------------------------------------------------------*/

int main ( )
{
    try
    {
        GetName( );                      // get name from user
        CheckName( );                    // see what the user typed
    }
    except (MainFilter( GetExceptionInformation() ))
    {
    }
    return( 0 );
}

/*--------------------------------------------------------------
        GET NAME
        Ask user to enter a name string.
   --------------------------------------------------------------*/

void GetName ( void )
{
    /* get name from user */
    printf( "Enter your name:  " );
    gets( szName );

    /* check whether user entered any characters */
    if (lstrlen((LPSTR)szName) < 1)
    {
        /* user entered nothing; raise an exception */
        DWORD adwArgs[2];    // arguments for exception handler
        char szFile[FILENAME_MAX];  // buffer for source file name

        /* store handler arguments in array */
        lstrcpy( szFile, __FILE__ );
        adwArgs[0] = (DWORD)szFile;
        adwArgs[1] = __LINE__;

        /* call for an exception handler */
        RaiseException( ERRORS_ERROR_NO_NAME, 0, 2, adwArgs );
    }
    return;
}

/*--------------------------------------------------------------
        CHECK NAME
```

```
            Raise an exception of the user typed "Moriarty."
    --------------------------------------------------------------*/

void CheckName ( void )
{
    /* did the user enter the name "Moriarty"? */

    if (lstrcmp( szName, "Moriarty" ) == 0)
    {
        DWORD adwArgs[2];        // arguments for exception handler
        char szFile[FILENAME_MAX];  // buffer for source file name

        /* store handler arguments in array */
        lstrcpy( szFile, __FILE__ );
        adwArgs[0] = (DWORD)szFile;
        adwArgs[1] = __LINE__;

        /* call for an exception handler */
        RaiseException( ERRORS_SUCCESS_MASTERMIND, 0, 2, adwArgs );
    }
    else
    {
        printf( "Thank you, " );
        printf( szName );
    }
    return;
}


/*--------------------------------------------------------------

        MAIN FILTER
        Interpret and respond to exceptions.
    --------------------------------------------------------------*/

LONG MainFilter ( LPEXCEPTION_POINTERS lpEP )
{
    DWORD   dwCode   = lpEP->ExceptionRecord->ExceptionCode;
    LPDWORD lpdwArgs = lpEP->ExceptionRecord->ExceptionInformation;

    /* is this a private exception? */
    if( (dwCode & FACILITY_APP_ERRORS) == FACILITY_APP_ERRORS)
    {
        /* show a message from the message table */
        ShowExceptionMsg( dwCode, lpdwArgs );
    }
    else /* not a private exception */
    {
```

```
        char szMsg[40];

        /* tell the user something went wrong */
        wsprintf( szMsg, "Program received unknown exception #%lu",
                dwCode );
        MessageBox( NULL, szMsg, "Errors Message",
                MB_ICONEXCLAMATION | MB_OK );
    }
        /* resume execution after the except block */
    return( EXCEPTION_EXECUTE_HANDLER );
}


/*------------------------------------------------------------------
        SHOW EXCEPTION MESSAGE
        Display a message box with a string from the program's
        message table.
        --------------------------------------------------------------*/

void ShowExceptionMsg( DWORD dwMsgCode, LPVOID lpvArgs )
{
/*
    LPTSTR lpMessage;

    // pull string from message table and insert formatted arguments
    FormatMessage(
    FORMAT_MESSAGE_FROM_HMODULE |       // take message table string
    FORMAT_MESSAGE_ALLOCATE_BUFFER |// allocate a buffer for it
    FORMAT_MESSAGE_ARGUMENT_ARRAY,  // read lpvArgs as DWORD array
    NULL,                           // message table in this module
    dwMsgCode,                      // code identifying message
    MAKELANGID(LANG_ENGLISH, SUBLANG_ENGLISH_US),   // language
    (LPTSTR)&lpMessage,             // pointer for new buffer
    0,                              // ignored with _ALLOCATE_BUFFER
    lpvArgs );                      // values to insert in string

    // lpvArgs points to the DWORD array containing the location
    // of the source file name string and a line number.FormatMessage
    // inserts those values at the format markers (!s! and !ld!) in
    // the message string.

    // display the message in a message box
    MessageBox( NULL, lpMessage, "Errors Message",
                MB_ICONEXCLAMATION | MB_OK );

    // release the buffer allocated by FormatMessage
    LocalFree( lpMessage );
```

```
    */

    // display the appropriate message for the execption error code
    switch( dwMsgCode )
    {
       case ERRORS_ERROR_NO_NAME:
          MessageBox( NULL, "Rats.  Another crook stays nameless.",
                   "Errors Message", MB_ICONEXCLAMATION | MB_OK );
          break;

       case ERRORS_SUCCESS_MASTERMIND:
          MessageBox( NULL, "Eureka!  We've found the mastermind.",
                   "Errors Message", MB_ICONEXCLAMATION | MB_OK );
          break;
    }
    return;
}
```

CHAPTER

SEVENTEEN

Managing Memory

- How the Virtual Memory Manager handles memory

- Virtual memory commands

- Heap management

- File-mapping objects for sharing memory

Besides the flashy interface and the multitasking, one of Windows' great attractions has always been memory management. From the 8086 target machine of version 1 all the way up through the 80486, 16-bit Windows has always helped programs make full use of whatever resources the system offers. But MS-DOS, the underlying trellis on which Windows grew, is inherently a 1MB system, and much of the potential of a 32-bit processor remained untapped.

With Windows NT and 95, Windows finally transcends the restrictions of DOS. This chapter begins by summarizing the hardware mechanisms and system policies that form the foundation of Windows NT and 95 memory management. It explains the translation from virtual to physical memory and the paging scheme that supports the protected address spaces. A new set of virtual memory API routines gives you control over individual memory pages. Win32 also adds improved heap management and still preserves the old global and local memory functions from the Win16 API.

After discussing these memory-management commands, we'll see how processes in protected address spaces can share blocks of memory by creating file-mapping objects. The first of two sample programs constructs a dynamically allocated array using virtual memory functions. The second program shares a block of memory among instances of a program that lets the user view and edit the contents of the shared memory.

Memory Management Concepts

The Windows NT memory management API, working with an imagined logical address space of 4GB, is supported internally by the Virtual Memory Manager (VMM), which in turn bases its services on the features of advanced 32-bit processors. NT requires its hardware to use 32-bit memory addresses, to map virtual to physical addresses, and to perform memory paging. From these basic capabilities, the Virtual Memory Manager constructs its own mechanisms and policies for managing virtual memory.

Memory Management: NT versus Windows 95

Windows NT and 95 function almost identically in respect to memory management, but there is one discrepancy between the two systems: NT works with an imagined logical address space of 4GB, while Windows 95 is limited to a mere 2GB.

Both of these limits are well in excess of anything we expect to see physically installed in any system (in the near future, at least). For the discussion of memory management in this chapter, we'll use the 4GB limit addressed by NT. If you're programming for Windows 95, just keep the 2GB figure in mind. (No doubt, when RAM in excess of a gigabyte becomes a common feature, some extension will be introduced to allow addressing spaces well in excess of either limit.)

Functionally, this single limit aside, the memory management APIs perform essentially the same for both Windows NT and 95 systems. However, there is another distinction to keep in mind. NT is a true protected-mode system, where attempts to address illegal memory space result in the errant application being terminated. On the other hand, Windows 95 is not so fully protected, and errant applications are more likely to crash the system than to be terminated by the system.

The Virtual Memory Manager

Like virtual reality, virtual memory isn't the real thing but does a good job of pretending to be. The 4GB of memory addresses every NT program commands are in a virtual space. The system does not contain 4GB of physical memory, yet somehow a program is able to use any address in the full range. Obviously, a translator somewhere in the background must silently convert each memory reference into an existing physical address. From this silent conversion, the VMM draws much of its power.

The VMM is the part of the NT system responsible for mapping references to a program's virtual address space into physical memory. It decides where to put each memory object and which memory pages should be written to disk. It also isolates each process in a separate address space by refusing to translate virtual addresses from one process into the physical memory used by another process. It supports the illusion of an idealized, logical space of 4GB, just as the GDI supports the illusion that every program draws to idealized logical display coordinates. The system translates logical addresses or coordinates into physical locations and prevents programs from colliding with each other by trying to use the same resource at the same time.

Pointers and Movable Memory

MS-DOS programmers customarily work with pointers to memory objects. If the object moves to another location, the pointer becomes invalid. On a machine that runs only one program at a time, pointers work fine. But multitasking systems need to manage system memory more actively, loading and discarding pieces on demand and moving pieces to make more room.

The first versions of Windows got around the problem by substituting handles for pointers wherever possible. A handle points to an entry in an object table, and the table remembers where each object actually is at any given moment. When the system moves an object, it updates the table. The handles pointing to the table remain valid even when the object moves because they point to the place where the real pointer is kept, and the system keeps the real pointer current.

Processors running in a protected mode provide a similar layering mechanism for all memory addresses. Instead of working with pointers containing segments and offsets, Intel CPUs work with *selectors* and offsets. A selector is to memory what a handle is to Windows: a pointer to a pointer.

To give a simplified account, the selector, with its offset, refers to a system table that keeps track of memory addresses. In a sense, protected mode has built-in memory handles. The difference is that selectors live at a much lower level in the system than handles do. The hardware knows what a selector is— the CPU can decode them—but only Windows knows what a handle is. Windows can have handles only where Windows itself creates them. You must make an effort to use handles instead of pointers, but protected mode gives you selectors whether you want them or not.

Even when you lock down memory, the system lets you see only the selector, not the physical address. Your program doesn't care. The code that worked with pointers works just as well with selectors, only now it doesn't matter if the system moves what your selector "points" to. The operating system can move objects through memory with impunity as long as it remembers to update the corresponding memory table entry. The entry may change, but the selector does not. The selector always points to the same place in the table, and the table is guaranteed to point to your memory object. As a consequence, you can safely use and preserve a pointer without impeding any other program.

The conversion from a selector and its offset to a physical address involves two stages: a trivial conversion from a logical to a virtual address, and a complex conversion from a linear address to a physical address. The first conversion, from a logical segmented address to a virtual linear address, simply adds an offset to a base address. NT makes this conversion trivial by keeping the base address set to 0. If the segment is constant, only the offset matters. The 32-bit offset may range from 0 to 4GB, exactly the range of the system's flat linear addresses. Under NT, a 32-bit selector addresses all of virtual memory in much the same way that small-model programs address their entire segment with a single near pointer. But a linear address is still not a physical address. In the second and more complex conversion, the VMM parses the linear address into indices for the process's paging tables, which contain physical addresses.

Paging

The use of virtual addresses confers many benefits, among them the illusion of working in a very large space. Windows NT allows the virtual addresses to range from 0 to 4GB, regardless of the physical memory actually installed on the current system. Obviously, a problem arises if all the running programs try to allocate all the virtual memory they think they see all at once. Like a bank, the system goes suddenly broke if all its customers cash in at the same time. Physical memory always imposes some kind of upper limit, but a paging system raises the limit considerably by setting off part of a hard disk to act as additional memory.

The CPUs on which NT runs have built-in memory-paging capabilities. Small blocks of memory called pages can be saved to the disk when not in use to make more room. A page interrupt occurs whenever a program tries to read a part of memory that has been moved to the disk. The program doesn't know the memory is gone; the CPU generates an error, the operating system reloads the missing page, and the program resumes. If blocks of memory can be saved and restored as needed, nothing prevents the system from overcommitting memory. If you have a thousand pages of memory, you could have two thousand pages' worth of code. It can't all be in memory at once, but any block can always be loaded when needed. Of course, disks are slower than RAM. Virtual memory works best if your hard drive is large, fast, and partly empty.

Much of the VMM's energy goes into moving and recovering pages of memory. NT can work with pages of up to 64KB, but the Intel CPU enforces a size of 4KB. A 4KB block of memory aligned on a 4KB boundary is called a *page frame*. The term *page* refers to the data a program stores in a page frame. There are usually more pages than page frames; some of the pages have been saved in the paging file. Although the contents of a page remain the same, those contents may appear in different page frames at different times as the VMM adjusts to the demands of all the current programs.

Page Databases and Tables   In order to satisfy requests for memory, the VMM maintains several data structures. It must be able, for example, to traverse a list of page frames to see which are free and which are full and also to determine which process currently owns any given page. (This also requires each process to occupy some integral number of pages, regardless of their actual requirements.)

The structure that holds this set of information is the *page frame database.* Through the database, the VMM, given any page, can find the process that owns it. Another data structure, called a *page table,* works in the other direction. Every process has at least one page table; given any process, the VMM can find all the pages it owns.

When the VMM assigns physical memory to a process, it updates the database and also adds an entry to a page table. Whenever a process refers to a virtual address, the VMM looks up the address in a page table to find the associated memory. Besides a virtual address and its corresponding physical address, the page table entry records other information about each page, including whether the page is protected (read-only, for example) and whether it is in memory or swapped to the disk. A swapped page is marked invalid, meaning that it resides in the swap file rather than in memory, in the page table.

For the convenience of the hardware, a single page table takes up exactly 4KB. One 4KB page table has room for 1024 different entries. Each entry points to a single page. If one page table can point to 1024 pages and each page is 4KB, then one page table can address 4MB of memory (1024 × 4096). A process that uses more memory receives more page tables.

Each process has a single master table, called a *page directory,* pointing to all its page tables. A page directory also holds up to 1024 entries. With 1024 page tables, each addressing 4MB, a process can reach up to 4GB (4MB × 1024). Because each page directory and page table occupies exactly 4KB, or one page frame, the system can easily swap the directory and tables in and out of memory along with all the other pages as needed.

The diagram in Figure 17.1 should help clarify how page directories point to page tables that point to pages, and at the same time the page frame database keeps a separate list of each page's current status. Most memory operations occur more rapidly than this elaborate indexing scheme seems to allow, because the CPU caches frequently use virtual address translations in a fast hardware buffer called the translation lookaside buffer (TLB).

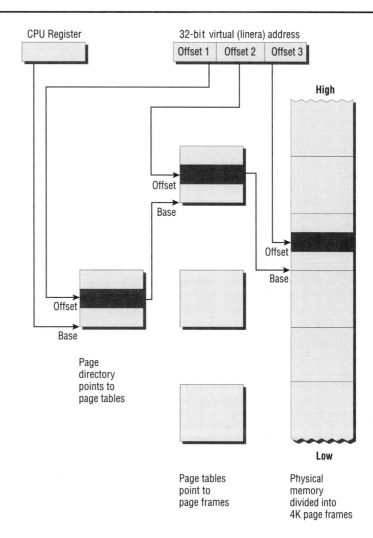

FIGURE 17.1

How the system finds a process's physical memory through the page directory and page tables

Page Frame States   The page frame database records the current state of each page frame. A page frame is always in one of six states (also called status markers):

- **Valid:** Contains a page some process is using. A page table entry points to it.

- **Standby:** Contains a page that was in use, but the VMM has decided to free it for some process. A standby page has been removed from the process's working set.

- **Modified:** Contains a page the VMM wants to discard, but because the process has modified the page, it must first be saved to disk.

- **Free:** A frame that is no longer owned by any process. Anything it contained has been saved to disk.

- **Zeroed:** A frame belonging to no one and full of nothing but zeros. Only zeroed pages may be given to any process.

- **Bad:** A frame that generated a parity error or other hardware error and cannot be used.

Within the page frame database, all the page entries with the same status marker are linked to each other. The VMM can follow a different series of links to find all the zeroed pages, all the free pages, all the standby pages, and so on.

Releasing a page frame involves several steps, and the status marker reflects how far along in the process the VMM has come. When it needs to make room, the VMM looks for frames that haven't been used recently and marks them for later disposal. If the page has not been changed by its process, it is marked Standby. If the process has written to the page so that it needs to be saved to the disk, it is marked Modified. Both markers indicate that the page is ready to be released but has not yet been released. If the owning process tries to use the page while it is still marked Standby or Modified, the system responds quickly to the resulting page fault because it does not need to read the page back from the disk. It simply changes the status back to Valid.

> **NOTE**
>
> One way for a page fault to occur is for an application to attempt to perform its own memory operations and to write to an invalid address (an address that the application or process does not own). Under NT, where operations are very tightly controlled, the usual result is that the process will be terminated by the system. On the other hand, under Windows 95, memory addressing is not so thoroughly policed, and improper addressing may crash the system.

For security reasons, any page frame assigned to a process must be zeroed first. No process may receive memory that still contains information left behind by another program. When the list of available zeroed pages runs low, the memory manager reads through the page frame database following all the links to free pages and zeros them. If memory is still low, the memory manager wakes one of its threads to find Modified pages and save them, slowly and one by one in the background, so as not to interfere with system performance.

Policies and Working Sets

It should be clear by now that the VMM keeps a constant watch over the status of all the system pages. If one process uses more physical memory than allowed in its security quota, the VMM steps in and invalidates some of its pages by marking them Standby or Modified, and eventually their page frames may be released. The group of page frames currently in use by one process is the process's *working set*. Like an embezzler, the VMM sneaks through the system and steals frames out from under processes as they run, hoping no one will notice. When a process begins to complain with a flurry of page faults, the VMM placates it by enlarging its working set. Busy programs end up with bigger sets.

The VMM follows defined policies in deciding when to retrieve swapped pages, where to place restored pages in memory, and what to swap out first when the system needs more room. NT's retrieval policy is called demand paging with clustering. *Demand paging* means the VMM loads pages only when a program asks for them, rather than trying to minimize delays by anticipating what a program will need. The system does try to anticipate to some extent by *clustering;* in response to each demand, the system actually loads several adjacent pages, figuring that memory operations often center on a single region, so nearby pages may be needed soon.

The placement policy determines where reloaded pages are put. The VMM tries to put them on the first zeroed page frames it finds in the page frame database. When it runs out of zeroed frames, it begins searching the lists of frames in other states. When deciding on pages to swap out, the VMM follows a local FIFO replacement policy. *Local* in this context means that the system makes room for one page in a process by dropping another page from the same process. By keeping the working set for each process to a roughly constant size, the system prevents one program from monopolizing resources. *FIFO* means "first in first out." Within one process's working set, the pages that have been in memory longest are the first to go. Pages a program touches often may be marked invalid, but the process will probably recover them from their transitional standby or modified state before the VMM actually saves the contents and zeros the frame.

NOTE If the frame is zeroed, the information is not lost. It has simply been moved to virtual memory (disk swap file) and must be reloaded.

Commitments and Reservations

Now that you know the VMM is sneaky because it steals pages and it's lazy because it often invalidates them without bothering to discard them, perhaps you won't be surprised to learn that it sometimes only pretends to allocate the memory you request.

To allocate memory, the VMM must construct page tables and search the page frame database for suitable zeroed areas. It may even need to find other invalidated pages and prepare them for use, possibly readjusting the working sets of other programs. If a program allocates a large virtual space but ends up using only parts of it, the VMM's efforts will have been largely wasted. Instead of allocating physical memory, the VMM often simply marks part of the process's virtual address space as being in use without securing physical memory to back it up. It *reserves* memory without *committing* it.

Reserving memory is like paying with a promissory note. When a program later tries to use some of the reserved memory, cashing in its IOU, the hardware notices because it can't find a page table entry for the given virtual address. It issues a page fault. The VMM steps in and finally pays its debt, committing physical pages to fulfill an allocation. Of course, even as it commits new page frames for one request, it may be invalidating other pages to make room. The entire sequence of reserving addresses, receiving a page fault, and committing new memory may be invisible to the process.

Virtual Address Descriptors   To support the illusion of a vast address space, the VMM requires yet another data structure. A tree of virtual address descriptors (VADs) records each allocation and suballocation that the process makes in its range of virtual addresses. Whenever a program allocates memory, the VMM creates a VAD and adds it to the tree, as shown in Figure 17.2. A VAD records the range of addresses an allocation claims, the protection status for all pages in the range, and whether child processes may inherit the object contained in the range. If a thread uses an address that falls outside the range of any of its VADs, the VMM knows the address was never reserved and recognizes an access violation.

Constructing a VAD is much simpler than constructing a page table and filling it with valid page frame addresses. Furthermore, the size of the allocation has no effect on the speed of the response. Reserving 2KB is no faster than reserving 2MB; each request produces a single VAD. When a thread actually uses the reserved memory, the VMM commits page frames by copying information from the descriptor into new page table entries.

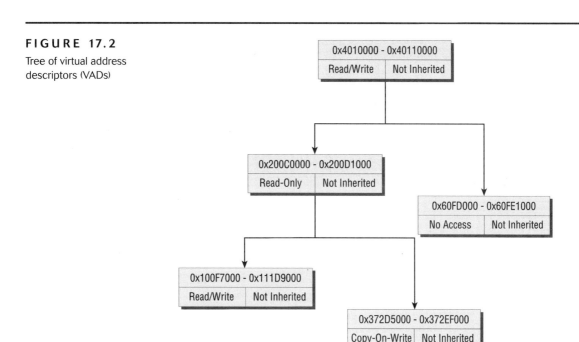

FIGURE 17.2

Tree of virtual address
descriptors (VADs)

Virtual Memory APIs   Often, programs have no need to concern themselves
with the differences between reserved and committed memory. Usually it's enough
to know that memory will be available when you expect it to be. Among its new features, however, Win32 boasts a set of virtual memory APIs that give you precise control over reserving, committing, and protecting pages of memory. By using these
APIs, you can allocate a very large memory object, fill it only partially, and not waste
any memory. The usual example is a spreadsheet because most of its cells are likely
to be empty, with data clustering together in a few areas. If you reserve a large range
of addresses to represent the entire spreadsheet as an array, the VMM commits physical memory only for the areas actually in use, and it still allows convenient access to
any part of the array through a full range of continuous addresses.

The Address Space

Most of what we've explained so far goes on behind the scenes. From the perspective of a running program, what matters most are not the page tables and working
sets but the 4GB of virtual address space. Figure 17.3 shows how the system orga-
nizes the space.

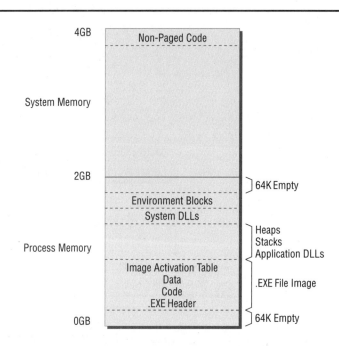

FIGURE 17.3

The virtual addresses the system uses for different entries in the address space of a single process

Although a process does indeed run in a 4GB address space, the process gets to use only 2GB of those addresses. The system reserves the upper half of the addresses for itself. The high half of the address space is the same for every application, but only kernel-mode threads may use it. In other words, it is accessible only to the operating system. At the very highest addresses, the system keeps critical system code that cannot be paged out of memory; for example, the part of the VMM that performs paging operations is stored at the high addresses.

All the pieces of memory over which you have control are mapped into the lower 2GB of the address space. That's where the code and data for a process reside, along with a stack for each thread, at least one default heap, and the program's own DLLs. The system always loads a process's code near the bottom of the address space at the 64KB mark. The 64KB at the top of a process's 2GB space also remain permanently empty. The no-man's-land at either end helps the system identify invalid pointers. For example, 0 is never a valid address.

At the lowest available address is an image of the process's .EXE file, including its header, code, data, and an *image activation table*. The activation table aids in dynamic linking. When the linker finds a `CreateWindow` command in your code, for example, it cannot know in advance where in memory to find the `CreateWindow` code. For all such unresolved dynamic links, the linker creates an entry in the image activation table. When the system loads an executable file, it searches for all the DLL entry points listed in the activation table, locates the appropriate DLL, and fixes the table to include the current entry addresses. The linker speeds loading by guessing where the DLLs will be and providing tentative addresses. The Win32 subsystem always tries to map its system DLLs to the same addresses near the top of the 2GB space. If, on loading a program, the system discovers that the DLLs are indeed in the expected place, then the activation table does not need fixing. (You can specify a preferred loading address for your own DLLs, too.)

The loader may not actually copy an entire .EXE file into memory. It is more likely to reserve virtual addresses for the .EXE file and let the VMM commit physical pages later if the code refers to those addresses. The Win32 subsystem DLLs have been structured to cluster related commands in adjacent addresses. As a result, common calling sequences usually require a minimum of new pages to be loaded.

An application's own DLLs, heaps, and stacks may be allocated anywhere in the address space between the .EXE file image and the system DLLs. Normally, the first allocation begins at 0x00010000, or 64KB.

Mapped Files

Alert readers may already have wondered what happens when a user initiates several instances of a single program. Given that every process has its own secure address space, must the system load a new copy of the .EXE file for each new instance? If not, how do two processes share the block of memory that contains the file image? The situation calls for a new strategy and one widely useful in many other situations as well.

Normally, the VMM protects programs from each other by ensuring that a virtual address from one process never translates to a page frame in use by another process. Because the VMM always translates every virtual address into a physical address, no program reaches memory directly, and the VMM easily routes every memory access to a safe location. The scheme also allows, however, for the VMM to make a single page frame visible in the virtual addresses of different processes. At the operating-system level, a block of shared memory is called a *section object*.

The Win32 subsystem exposes the functionality of section objects to its clients in the form of *memory-mapped files*. Two programs cannot share memory directly, but they can share the same disk file. Of course, most of what the process perceives as physical memory is already in a disk-swapping file. In effect, the VMM lets you retrieve information from the swap file by reading from particular memory addresses. In fact, you can access any disk file the same way, using memory addresses, by creating a memory-mapped file. As an extension of this memory I/O capability, two processes may open the same block of memory as though it were a file, read from it, and write to it. To share memory without creating a new disk file, the programs link the shared object to the system's normal page-swapping file.

When the user launches multiple instances of a program, the system creates a mapped file object to enable all instances to share a single copy of the .EXE file image.

Memory Management Commands

The Win32 memory management commands fall into three main categories: virtual memory functions, heap functions, and the familiar global and local allocation functions. Each set includes commands to allocate and free blocks of memory, but each set manages memory a little differently. We'll survey each group and compare their advantages, and then take a look at the validation commands. Finally, we'll finish this section with the API for memory-mapped files.

Virtual Memory Commands

The virtual memory commands, which have names like VirtualAlloc and VirtualFree, expose some of the VMM's operations that the other two command sets hide. With the virtual memory commands, you can imitate the VMM by reserving addresses without committing memory to support them and by protecting ranges of memory with read-only, read/write, or no-access flags. You can also lock pages in memory to prevent them from being swapped to disk. The other command sets are built on top of the virtual memory commands; these are the basic operations from which the Win32 API builds its other memory services.

Allocating Memory

The VirtualAlloc command is the starting point for managing your own virtual address space. Its parameters tell how much memory to allocate, where in the address space to situate the new block, whether to commit physical memory, and what kind of protection to set.

```
LPVOID VirtualAlloc(
LPVOID lpvAddress,          // desired address for new block
DWORD dwSize,               // size of new memory block
DWORD fdwAllocationType,    // reserve addresses or commit memory
DWORD fdwProtect );         // no access, read-only, or read/write
```

`VirtualAlloc` tries first to find a range of free addresses marking a block of `dwSize` bytes beginning at `lpvAddress`. To do this, it searches the process's tree of VADs. If the requested range is free, the function returns `lpvAddress`. If some part of it is in use, the function searches the entire address space looking for any sufficiently large free block. If it finds one, it returns the starting address. Otherwise it returns NULL.

Most often, programs set the first parameter to NULL and allow `VirtualAlloc` to place the block anywhere. Controlling the placement of a block may occasionally be useful if, for example, you are debugging a DLL that usually loads at a particular address. By using `VirtualAlloc` to reserve that address before the DLL loads, you can force it to another location.

The `fdwAllocationType` parameter may be MEM_RESERVE, MEM_COMMIT, or both. To reserve a range of addresses, `VirtualAlloc` simply makes a new VAD marking an area in use. It does not, however, allocate any physical memory, so the reserved addresses cannot yet be used for anything. Attempts to read or write reserved pages produce access violation exceptions. On the other hand, no other allocation command may use previously reserved addresses, either. `GlobalAlloc` and `malloc`, for example, cannot place new objects in a range that overlaps with reserved space. If you call `VirtualAlloc` to reserve your entire 2GB of address space, all subsequent allocations will fail, even though `VirtualAlloc` has not yet taken up any physical memory.

Reserving addresses has no effect on the system's physical memory. The VMM makes no guarantee that physical pages will be available when you begin to commit a reserved area. Only when you commit memory does the VMM find pages to support it. As a consequence, the system does not charge reserved memory against a process's system resource quotas. Only memory actually in use counts against the quota.

Memory cannot be committed without being reserved. By combining the MEM_RESERVE and MEM_COMMIT flags, you can reserve and commit at the same time.

More often, programs call VirtualAlloc once to reserve a large area and then many times subsequently to commit parts of the area piece by piece.

> **WARNING** A problem arises when you try to write to pages that have been reserved but never committed. The system generates an access violation exception. You might choose to call VirtualQuery before every read or write to be sure the page is committed, but that takes time. The usual practice, demonstrated in the List program in this chapter, is to let the exception arise and provide an exception handler to deal with it. The handler calls VirtualAlloc to commit the required page and lets the program continue.

The fdwProtect flag determines how a page or range of pages may be used. For memory that is only reserved, the flag must be PAGE_NOACCESS. When committing memory, you can optionally change the protection to PAGE_READONLY or PAGE_READWRITE. No other programs can read memory in your address space anyway, so read-only protection guards against bugs in your own program that might accidentally corrupt some important part of your data. Protection levels apply to individual pages. The pages in a single range of memory may have different protection flags. You can, for example, apply PAGE_READONLY to an entire block and temporarily change single pages to allow write access as needed. You cannot write-protect just part of a page. The protection flags apply to entire pages.

VirtualAlloc cannot reserve more than 2GB because a process has control over only the bottom half of its 4GB address space. In fact the actual limit is slightly smaller because of the 64KB free area at either end of a process's 2GB space (see Figure 17.3, earlier in the chapter). Also, VirtualAlloc reserves memory in blocks of 64KB and commits memory in blocks of one page. When reserving memory, VirtualAlloc rounds lpvAddress down to the nearest multiple of 64KB. When committing memory, if lpvAddress is NULL, VirtualAlloc rounds dwSize up to the nearest page size boundary. If lpvAddress is not NULL, VirtualAlloc commits every page containing any bytes in the range lpvAddress to lpvAddress + dwSize. A 2-byte allocation, if it crosses a page boundary, would require the commitment of two entire pages. On most Windows NT systems, a page is 4KB, but if you need to know the size, call GetSystemInfo.

Uses for Reserved Memory

The ability to reserve memory without committing it is useful for dynamically allocated structures and sparse arrays. A thread that expands some structure, perhaps a list, as the program runs can reserve room to prevent other threads from using up addresses the structure may need as it expands.

The reserved area does set an upper limit on the size of the structure because there is no such command as "VirtualReAlloc" to expand a reserved area. Resizing requires allocating a second block, copying the first block into it, and freeing the original. On the other hand, given a 2GB range of possible addresses, you can reasonably set the upper size limit of the original allocation quite high.

Reserved memory also makes it easy to create a sparse array (a large array) with only a few elements full. For example, a spreadsheet is a sparse array of empty cells with only a few positions occupied, and those positions are usually clustered in adjacent areas. With the virtual memory commands, you can reserve a large address space for all the possible cells and commit memory only for the areas in use. Although there are other ways for spreadsheet programs to minimize their allocations, the virtual memory solution to sparse arrays is particularly convenient because you can still address the array as a range of contiguous addresses.

Freeing Memory

When a process ends, the system automatically releases any memory that was still in use. To free memory sooner, call `VirtualFree`.

```
BOOL VirtualFree(
    LPVOID lpvAddress,              // address of memory to free
    DWORD dwSize,                   // size of memory block
    DWORD fdwFreeType );            // decommit or release
```

`VirtualFree` can decommit a set of committed pages leaving their addresses still reserved, or it can release a range of reserved addresses, or both at once. Decommitting can release small blocks, and the blocks may include a mix of both reserved and committed pages.

When you are releasing reserved addresses, you must free the entire range of addresses as originally allocated, and all the pages in the range must be in the same state—either all reserved or all committed. lpvAddress must contain the base address previously returned by VirtualAlloc, and the value of dwSize is ignored because the whole range is freed at once. dwSize matters only when decommitting sections of a range.

Before decommitting a page, be sure no part of it is still in use. Our sample List program, for example, fits four list items on each 4KB page. Deleting one item does not make it safe to delete a page, because the other three items might still be in use.

Programs that use the virtual memory commands usually need some kind of garbage-collection mechanism to decommit pages when they become empty. The mechanism could be a low-priority thread that occasionally cycles through an allocated area looking for entirely empty pages.

Protecting Memory

After reserving address space, you call VirtualAlloc again to commit individual pages and VirtualFree to decommit or release them. When committing pages, VirtualAlloc also changes the protection state from no-access to read-only or read/write. To change the protection for a page already committed, call Virtual-Protect.

```
BOOL VirtualProtect(
    LPVOID  lpvAddress,        // address of memory to protect
    DWORD   dwSize,            // size of area to protect
    DWORD   fdwNewProtect,     // new protection flags
    PDWORD  pfdwOldProtect );  // variable to receive old flags
```

lpvAddress and dwSize indicate the range of addresses to protect. The two flag parameters each contain one of the familiar protection flags: PAGE_NOACCESS, PAGE_READONLY, or PAGE_READWRITE. Flags apply to whole pages. Any page even partially included in the given range will be changed. The pfdwOldProtect parameter returns the previous state of the first page in the range.

VirtualProtect works only with pages already committed. If any page in the range is not committed, the function fails. The pages in the range do not, however, need to have identical protection flags.

The primary advantage of protection is in guarding against your own program bugs. For an example, refer to the revised AddItem and DeleteItem procedures used in the sample List program presented later in this chapter.

Querying Memory Information

Sometimes you need to get information about a block of memory. Before writing to a page, for example, you might want to find out whether the page has been committed. `VirtualQuery` fills a structured variable with information about a given block of memory:

```
DWORD VirtualQuery(
    LPVOID lpvAddress,          // address of area to be described
    PMEMORY_BASIC_INFORMATION pmbiBuffer,
                                // address of description buffer
    DWORD dwLength );           // size of description buffer


typedef struct _MEMORY_BASIC_INFORMATION  /* mbi */
{
    PVOID BaseAddress;        // base address of page group
    PVOID AllocationBase;     // address of larger allocation unit
    DWORD AllocationProtect;  // initial access protection
    DWORD RegionSize;         // size, in bytes, of page group
    DWORD State;              // committed, reserved, free
    DWORD Protect;            // group's access protection
    DWORD Type;               // type of pages (always private)
} MEMORY_BASIC_INFORMATION;

typedef MEMORY_BASIC_INFORMATION *PMEMORY_BASIC_INFORMATION;
```

The `lpvAddress` parameter of `VirtualQuery` points to an arbitrary address. Any given location in memory may be part of two different allocation units. It may be part of a large block of reserved pages, and it may also be part of a smaller region of pages subsequently committed, decommitted, or protected together. A region consists of all contiguous pages with the same attributes.

In the `BaseAddress` field, `VirtualQuery` returns the address of the first page in the smaller region that contains `lpvAddress`. The `AllocationBase` field returns the address of the larger allocation that first reserved `lpvAddress`. `AllocationBase` matches the value returned previously by `VirtualAlloc`. Whatever protection flags the original `VirtualAlloc` applied to the range are returned in `AllocationProtect` (MEM_NOACCESS, MEM_READONLY, or MEM_READWRITE).

The other fields describe the smaller subgroup of like pages, giving its size, current status, and protection flag. The last field always returns MEM_PRIVATE, indicating that other processes cannot share this memory. The existence of this field suggests that Microsoft may later consider adding other mechanisms for processes to share memory.

Although they are not part of the virtual memory command set, two other commands also retrieve information about memory. GlobalMemoryStatus returns the total size and remaining space for physical memory, the page file, and the current address space. GetSystemInfo returns, among other things, the system's physical page size and the lowest and highest virtual addresses accessible to processes and DLLs. (Generally these values are 4KB, 0x00010000, and 0x7FFEFFFF.)

Locking and Unlocking Pages

Two other virtual memory commands lock and unlock pages. A locked page cannot be swapped to disk while your program executes. When your program is not currently executing, however, all of its pages, including locked pages, may be swapped to disk. In effect, locking a page guarantees that it will become a permanent part of the program's working page set. In a busy system, the working set manager may reduce the number of pages a process may lock. The maximum for any process is approximately 30 to 40 pages. The exact value varies slightly with the size of system memory and the application's working set.

Locking memory is discouraged because it constrains the VMM and makes organizing physical memory more difficult. For the most part, only device drivers and other system-level components lock any of their pages. A program that must respond very rapidly to system signals might lock some pages to ensure that unexpected disk reads don't delay the response.

```
BOOL VirtualLock(
    LPVOID lpvAddress,          // beginning of area to lock
    DWORD dwSize );             // size of area to lock

BOOL VirtualUnlock(
    LPVOID lpvAddress,          // beginning of area to unlock
    DWORD dwSize );             // size of area to unlock
```

There is no lock count on virtual memory. VirtualLock commands do not always require a matching VirtualUnlock. You can, for example, lock three contiguous pages with three different commands and then unlock them all with a single command. All the pages must already be locked, but the range does not need to correspond exactly with the range given in any previous lock command.

Before being locked, memory must be committed. When a process ends, the system automatically unlocks any remaining locked pages. `VirtualFree` releases pages even if they are locked.

Be aware that `Globalloc` and `VirtualLock` do very different things. `Globalloc` simply translates handles into pointers. It locks an allocated object into a virtual address but has no effect at all on physical memory. `VirtualLock`, on the other hand, is more severe. It locks pages, not objects, and the locked pages are forced into physical memory whenever the program runs.

Heap Functions

A *heap* is a block of memory from which a program allocates smaller pieces as needed. A 16-bit Windows program draws memory from both a global heap and a local heap. The local heap is faster but limited to 64KB.

NT's flat address space abolishes the difference between global and local and between near and far. The entire address space is a single undifferentiated heap. Even so, working from a smaller heap sometimes still makes sense. Reserving and committing virtual memory has obvious advantages for large dynamic or sparse structures. But what about algorithms that call for many small allocations? The heap memory commands allow you to create one or more private heaps in your address space and suballocate smaller blocks from them.

Creating a Heap

The memory you get from a heap is just like the memory you get any other way. In fact, you can write your own heap implementation using the virtual memory commands; that's exactly what the Windows subsystem does. Heap commands make internal calls to the virtual memory API. To create a heap, you give a starting size and an upper limit:

```
HANDLE HeapCreate(
    DWORD dwOptions,           // heap allocation flag
    DWORD dwInitialSize,       // initial heap size
    DWORD dwMaximumSize );      // maximum heap size
```

Behind the scenes, the Win32 subsystem responds by reserving a block of the maximum size and committing pages to support the initial size. Subsequent allocations make the heap grow from the bottom to the top. If any allocation calls for new pages, the heap commands automatically commit them. Once committed, they remain committed until the program destroys the heap or ends.

The system does not manage the inside of a private heap. It does not compact the heap or move objects within it. Therefore, a heap may become fragmented if you allocate and free many small objects. If allocations fill the heap to its maximum size, subsequent allocations fail. If dwMaximumSize is 0, however, the heap size is limited only by available memory.

The dwOptions parameter allows a single flag to be set: HEAP_NO_SERIALIZE. By default, without this flag (the argument is passed as 0), the heap prevents threads that share memory handles from interfering with each other. A serialized heap disallows simultaneous operations on a single handle. One thread blocks until another finishes. Serialization slows performance slightly. A program's heap does not need to be serialized if the program has only one thread, if only one of its threads uses the heap, or if the program itself protects the heap, perhaps by creating a mutex or a critical section object.

Allocating from a Heap

HeapAlloc, HeapReAlloc, and HeapFree—like the Win16 commands their names recall—allocate, reallocate, and free blocks of memory from a heap. All of them take as one parameter a handle returned from HeapCreate.

```
LPSTR HeapAlloc(
    HANDLE hHeap,           // handle of a private heap
    DWORD dwFlags,          // control flags
    DWORD dwBytes );        // number of bytes to allocate
```

HeapAlloc returns a pointer to a block of the requested size. It may include two control flags:

- HEAP_GENERATE_EXCEPTIONS: This flag influences how the command handles errors. Without the flag, HeapAlloc indicates failure by returning NULL. With the flag, it raises exceptions instead for all error conditions.

- HEAP_ZERO_MEMORY: This flag causes HeapAlloc to initialize the newly allocated block with zeros. If the function succeeds, it allocates at least as much memory as requested and may allocate slightly more to reach a convenient boundary.

To discover the exact size of any block, call HeapSize. Besides the bytes in the block itself, each allocation consumes a few extra bytes for an internal supporting structure. The exact size varies but is near 16 bytes. You need to know this only because it may prevent you from squeezing as many allocations out of one heap as you expect. If you create a 2MB heap and attempt two 1MB allocations, the second one is likely to fail.

To change the size of a memory block after it has been allocated, call `HeapReAlloc`.

```
LPSTR HeapReAlloc(
    HANDLE hHeap,       // handle of a private heap
    DWORD dwFlags,      // flags to influence reallocation
    LPSTR lpMem,        // address of memory block to reallocate
    DWORD dwBytes );    // new size for the memory block
```

Besides the two flags `HeapAlloc` uses to zero memory and to generate exceptions, the `dwFlags` parameter of `HeapReAlloc` accepts one other flag: `HEAP_REALLOC_IN_PLACE_ONLY`. (To the best of our knowledge, five words is a record for Microsoft's manifest constants.) This flag prevents `HeapReAlloc` from moving the memory block to a more spacious area. If other nearby allocations prevent the block from expanding in place, this flag makes `HeapReAlloc` fail rather than relocate. (`HEAP_REALLOC_IN_PLACE_ONLY` would normally be used with one of the other flags.)

Destroying a Heap

When you have no more use for an allocated block, release it with `HeapFree`. When you have no more use for the heap itself, release it with `HeapDestroy`.

```
BOOL HeapFree(
    HANDLE hHeap,       // handle of a private heap
    DWORD  dwFlags,     // unused (must be zero)
    LPSTR  lpMem );     // address of a memory block to free

BOOL HeapDestroy( HANDLE hHeap );
```

Freeing a memory block does not decommit the page it occupied, but it does make the space available for subsequent allocations in the same heap. `Heap-Destroy` decommits and releases all the pages in the heap whether or not the heap still contains allocated blocks. After `HeapDestroy`, the `hHeap` handle is invalid (undefined).

The Heap commands conveniently group allocations together in a small section of the address space. Clustering allocations serves several purposes:

- It can separate and protect related allocations. A program that makes many small allocations that are all the same size can pack memory most efficiently by making them contiguous. A heap allows that.

- If all your linked-list nodes come from one heap and your binary-tree nodes come from another, a mistake in one algorithm is less likely to interfere with the other.

- Memory objects used in conjunction with each other should be grouped together to minimize page swapping. If several addresses happen to reside on the same memory page, a single disk operation retrieves all of them.

Global and Local Memory Commands

In making the transition from 16 to 32 bits, many of the earlier system and memory API commands have been dropped. Most of the obsolete memory commands, such as AllocSelector, refer to low-level features specific to Win16 or to Intel CPUs. For backward compatibility, many of the more familiar memory commands are retained:

GlobalAlloc	LocalAlloc
GlobalDiscard	LocalDiscard
GlobalFlags	LocalFlags
GlobalFree	LocalFree
GlobalHandle	LocalHandle
GlobalLock	LocalLock
GlobalMemoryStatus	LocalReAlloc
GlobalReAlloc	LocalSize
GlobalSize	LocalUnlock
GlobalUnlock	

The Win32 environment forces a few semantic changes. Most important, both sets of commands, global and local, now work with the same heap. On loading, every process receives a default heap, and the old API commands work from that.

It is legal, though confusing, to mix global and local commands in a single transaction. For example, you could, just to be perverse, allocate an object with Global-Alloc and release it with LocalFree. Also, the 32-bit pointer LocalLock now returns is indistinguishable from the 32-bit pointer GlobalLock returns.

The default heap expands as needed, limited only by physical memory. Even the humble LocalAlloc can allocate megabytes. The default heap automatically serializes operations to prevent different threads from corrupting the heap by using the same handle at the same time.

Pages allocated by `GlobalAlloc` or `LocalAlloc` are committed and marked for read/write access. Unlike `HeapFree`, `GlobalFree` checks for empty pages and releases them back to the system. The allocation commands still recognize the flags that make memory fixed or movable, but with NT's paging and virtual addressing, even "fixed" memory moves. The only practical use for `GMEM_FIXED` is to make `GlobalAlloc` return a pointer instead of a handle.

A few of the other flags are now ignored, including `LOWER`, `NOCOMPACT`, `NODISCARD`, `NOT_BANKED`, and `NOTIFY`. More significant than the loss of these minor flags is the loss of `GMEM_DDESHARE`. Like other Win32 object handles, handles to allocated memory refer to the object table of a specific process. A handle passed from one program to another becomes invalid in the new address space. `DuplicateHandle` makes it possible for processes to share some handles, but it fails on memory handles. The `GMEM_DDESHARE` flag still exists (is still defined) because Microsoft apparently plans for it to signal some optimization appropriate for DDE conversations, but the old method of sharing memory handles is simply not supported. Sharing a block of memory now requires a memory-mapped file.

The Win32 global and local memory commands differ from the heap commands in creating movable and discardable objects. Objects created by `HeapAlloc` do not change their virtual address (though their physical address may change). The local and global functions, at the expense of more memory management overhead, do move objects to minimize fragmentation. With a memory manager as flexible as the VMM, discardable memory is less important than it used to be, and a cryptic note in Microsoft's online help file warns that some versions of Win32 may not support it.

The primary advantage of the old API functions is the obvious one: They are portable. To write source code that ports easily from 16 bits to 32 bits, limit yourself to the Win16 memory commands. In Win32, the global and local sets are interchangeable, but you should pick the set that would make the most sense in a Win16 program. For small, fast allocations, use the local functions. For large allocations, use the global functions. Under Windows NT both sets perform alike, but since their advantage is portability, you should use them in a portable fashion.

The heap and virtual memory command sets are faster and more efficient than the older commands. You can allocate from the default heap with less overhead by doing this:

```
HeapAlloc( GetProcessHeap(), 0, dwSize );
```

`GetProcessHeap` returns a handle to the default heap. (Do not pass that handle to `HeapDestroy`.)

System Limits

Because Windows NT does not use the descriptor tables that limited 16-bit Windows to a system-wide total of 8192 handles, the new system supports many more allocations. Nevertheless some limits remain:

- `VirtualAlloc` never reserves an area smaller than 64KB, so allocating 32,767 blocks fills up the 2GB user address space.

- `VirtualAlloc` cannot create more than 32,767 (32K) handles in one process. (`HeapAlloc` has no such limit; Microsoft says it has created over a million handles on a single heap in tests.)

- `GlobalAlloc` and `LocalAlloc` combined cannot create more than 65,535 (64K) handles. The limit applies only to movable objects, however.

TIP

Memory objects allocated using the `GMEM_FIXED` or `LMEM_FIXED` flags do not return handles but, instead, return direct pointers to the memory allocated.

Validation Commands

Another new set of commands tests the validity of pointers. Each receives a virtual address and returns TRUE if the process does not have a particular access privilege. Call these to make programs more robust by testing values before using them.

Function	Argument	Validation Test
`IsBadCodePtr`	Pointer to a function	Tests for read access to the beginning of the function
`IsBadReadPtr`	Pointer to a memory block	Tests for read access to a range of addresses

Function	Argument	Validation Test
IsBadStringPtr	Pointer to a string	Tests for read access to all bytes up to the end of the string
IsBadWritePtr	Pointer to a memory block	Tests for write access to a range of addresses

WARNING Be aware that other threads, and even other processes (such as debuggers), could conceivably change the contents or protection of a memory page between the time an IsBad function confirms validity and the time you try to touch the address yourself.

C Runtime Equivalents

Under Windows NT, the malloc family of C runtime functions calls system heap routines internally. The C routines work perfectly well in Windows 95 and NT, although they do not perform the same suballocations they do in the 16-bit versions.

The runtime memory buffer commands such as memset now have competition from four new Win32 routines:

- CopyMemory
- FillMemory
- MoveMemory
- ZeroMemory

The commands link dynamically to the system DLLs only on an MIPS machine. They are not valid for Windows 95 applications at all. Instead, on an x86 machine, all four map back to the standard C runtime functions: memcopy, memmove, and memset.

Sharing Memory in Mapped Files

For two processes to share a block of memory, they must create a file-mapping object. Such objects have two purposes: They facilitate file I/O and they create a memory buffer processes can share. To explain sharing memory, we need to begin with files.

After opening a disk file, a program may optionally create an associated file-mapping object in order to treat the file as a block of memory. The system reserves a range of addresses from the process's space and maps them to the file instead of to physical memory. The process reads and writes to these addresses as it would to any other memory address, using functions like `lstrcpy` and `FillMemory`. You can even typecast the base address to make an array pointer and retrieve file records by indexing the array. The VMM responds to page faults in a file-mapping object by swapping pages from the disk file rather than the system's paging file.

This ingenious file I/O technique also allows processes to share memory. If two programs can open handles to the same file, what difference does it make if the file happens to be in memory? If the cooperating programs want to share memory but don't need to create a disk file, they can link their shared file-mapping object to the system's paging file. Then the memory in the mapped file is paged exactly the same way all other memory is paged.

Setting up a new mapped file requires three commands:

- `CreateFile`: Opens a disk file.
- `CreateFileMapping`: Returns a handle to a file-mapping object.
- `MapViewOfFile`: Links a region in the file to a range of virtual addresses and returns a pointer.

`CreateFile` should be familiar from Chapter 15, where it was used to open existing named pipes, as well as Chapter 13 where it was used by the FileView application to open conventional files.

`CreateFileMapping` creates a new system object, adds an entry to the process's object table, and returns a handle. The new object creates the potential for parts of the file to be held in memory, but you cannot actually read the file until you also create a view into it.

A *view* is a small section of a larger object, a window into a section of the file. `MapViewOfFile` creates a view by associating positions in the file with positions in the address space. Operations on that range of addresses become operations on the file.

You can create a view big enough to contain the entire file, but in theory, a file can be much larger than your entire address space, so an alternative is necessary. The alternative is to create a smaller view and move it when you need to reach new parts of the file. After creating a file-mapping object, you can map, unmap, and remap your view of it over and over. You can even map several simultaneous views of a single file. Figure 17.4 diagrams the relationship between a file and its view.

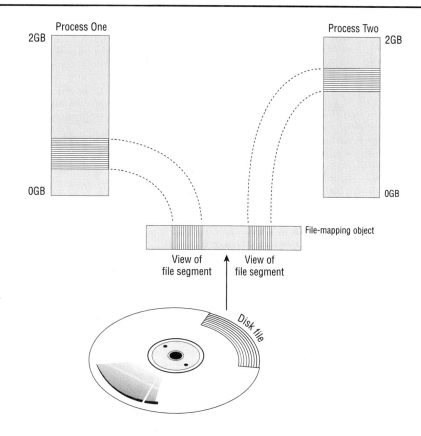

FIGURE 17.4

Two programs with different views of the same file-mapping object

Creating a File-Mapping Object

CreateFileMapping requires a file handle to associate with the new object. Normally you receive the handle from CreateFile. To share memory without creating a separate file, you may instead pass the file handle as (HANDLE) 0xFFFFFFFF. The system then maps from the system paging file.

```
HANDLE CreateFileMapping(
    HANDLE hFile,                    // handle of file to map
    LPSECURITY_ATTRIBUTES lpsa,      // optional security attributes
    DWORD fdwProtect,                // protection for mapping object
    DWORD dwMaxSizeHigh,             // high-order 32 bits of object size
    DWORD dwMaxSizeLow,              // low-order 32 bits of object size
    LPTSTR lpszMapName );            // name of file-mapping object
```

The fdwProtect parameter sets the protection flag for all the memory pages the mapped file uses. It may be PAGE_READONLY, PAGE_READWRITE, or PAGE_WRITECOPY. The first two you know, but PAGE_WRITECOPY is new. We'll say more about it in a moment when we discuss coherent views.

The next two parameters of CreateFileMapping, both DWORDs, together tell the size of the file-mapping object. If the file-mapping object is smaller than the file it maps, not all of the file is accessible through it. The last part of the file is excluded from sharing. The system interprets dwMaxSizeHigh and dwMaxSizeLow as the high and low halves of a single value. The size is an 8-byte quantity to allow for the possibility that disk files may exceed the value of ULONG_MAX (4GB). Programs that work only with files of subastronomical sizes always set dwMaxSizeHigh to 0. Setting both parameters to 0 instructs the system to set the maximum size from the file's current size. If hFile is passed as (HANDLE) 0xFFFFFFFF, however, the size may not be 0. You must set an explicit size in order to work from the system swap file.

The final parameter, lpszMapName, gives the new object a name. lpszMapName is not the name of a disk file; if there is a disk file, its name is passed to CreateFile. lpszMapName assigns a name to the new file-mapping object for the convenience of other processes. Processes use the name to share the object, just as they use pipe names to share pipes. Other processes open their handles to the same object by passing the name string to OpenFileMapping. The name of a file-mapping object may not exceed MAX_PATH characters (currently 260) and may not contain backslashes. (MAX_PATH is defined in Windef.H.)

> **NOTE** The rule against backslashes in mapped file names contrasts with the requirements for naming pipes. Pipe names always begin with the sequence \\.\pipe\ and may contain other backslashes indicating other subnodes. The rules for naming are different because pipes are implemented as a file system, and mapped files belong to the heap management system.

CreateFileMapping returns a valid handle if it succeeds and NULL if it fails. If the name string in lpszMapName designates a mapping object that already exists, and if the requested protection attributes match, CreateFileMapping returns a valid handle to the existing object. That may not be what you want.

A program trying to create a new mapping object may be surprised if another program happens to have used the same name for its own object. To detect whether your new handle belongs to an old object, call `GetLastError` even after `Create-FileMapping` *succeeds* and test for `ERROR_ALREADY_EXISTS`.

Mapping a View

`MapViewOfFile` connects a section of memory with a section of the file. It makes part of the file visible in memory. A mapped file is "mapped" because of what this function does: It associates every byte of the memory range with a corresponding byte in the file.

```
LPVOID MapViewOfFile(
    HANDLE hMapObject,    // mapped file to view
    DWORD fdwAccess,      // access mode
    DWORD dwOffsetHigh,   // high-order 32 bits of file offset
    DWORD dwOffsetLow,    // low-order 32 bits of file offset
    DWORD dwViewSize );   // size of view in bytes
```

The `hMapObject` handle must be created with `CreateFileMapping` or `Open-FileMapping`. The second parameter requests access privileges for the pages within the view. The privileges requested here must not conflict with those already set in the original `CreateFileMapping` command. For example, a file-mapping object created with the `PAGE_READONLY` flag will not support a view with `FILE_MAP_WRITE` access. Many processes may open views to a single file-mapping object. The following are the view access flags:

- `FILE_MAP_WRITE`: Grants write access. Requires `PAGE_READWRITE`.

- `FILE_MAP_READ`: Grants read-only access. Requires `PAGE_READONLY` or `PAGE_READWRITE`.

- `FILE_MAP_ALL_ACCESS`: Synonym for `FILE_MAP_WRITE`. Requires `PAGE_READWRITE`.

- `FILE_MAP_COPY`: Grants copy-on-write access. Requires `PAGE_WRITECOPY`.

When you finish with one view and want to inspect another region of the file, unmap the first view and call `MapViewOfFile` again.

```
BOOL UnmapViewOfFile( LPVOID lpvBaseAddress );
```

`lpvBaseAddress` is the same value received earlier from `MapViewOfFile`. `Unmap-ViewOfFile` writes any modified pages in the view back to the disk and releases the virtual address space reserved for the mapping. (The `FlushViewOfFile` command also forces modifications to be saved.)

Sharing a Mapped-File Object

In order for two processes to share a file-mapping object, both must acquire a handle. Child processes may inherit file-mapping handles from their parents. If the second process is not a child, and if the name string is not coded into both programs, one process must pass the file-mapping object to the other process through a pipe, a mailslot, a DDE conversation, or by some other arrangement. Open-FileMapping converts a name string into a handle for an existing object.

```
HANDLE OpenFileMapping(
    DWORD dwAccess,      // access mode
    BOOL bInheritHandle, // TRUE for children to inherit handle
    LPTSTR lpszName );   // points to name of file-mapping object
```

After receiving its handle, the second process also calls MapViewOfFile to see what the file contains.

Preserving Coherence

If several processes open views on a shared file-mapping object, any changes one makes will be visible to the others. All their view pointers will point to different places in the same coherent object. The file-mapping object coordinates modifications from all its open views. The file may become incoherent, however, if the views derive from two different concurrent file-mapping objects linked to a single file. If the viewers write their changes to different file-mapping objects, they create conflicting versions of the file.

Figure 17.5 shows how two file-mapping objects may contain different versions of the disk file and fall out of sync. Any modifications the first two processes make will be deposited in the first file-mapping object; any modifications made by the third process will be put in the second file-mapping object. If all processes unmap their views and write their changes to the disk, only one set of changes is saved, because one set writes over the other on the disk. When file views become incoherent, he who saves last saves best.

To enforce coherence, Microsoft recommends that the first program to open the file should specify exclusive access (set 0 in the share-mode parameter). Then no other program can open the file to create a second mapping object.

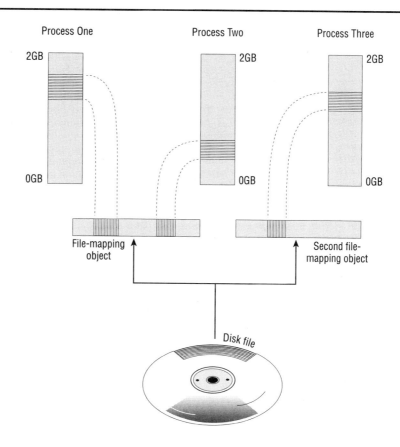

FIGURE 17.5

How deriving views
from different file-
mapping objects pro-
duces incoherence

Three other situations can also produce incoherence:

- Normal I/O performed on a disk file that other processes are viewing as a mapped object causes incoherence. The changes will be lost when the file-mapping object saves its version of the file.

- Processes on different machines may share mapped files, but since they cannot share the same block of physical memory across a network, their views remain coherent only as long as neither process writes to its view.

- A similar situation arises when views are created with copy-on-write protection. If two processes modify a copy-on-write mapped file, they are not writing to the same pages. The modified pages are no longer shared, and the views are not coherent.

Uses of Copy-on-Write Protection

Copy-on-write protection means that when a process tries to write on a page, the system copies the page and writes only to the copy. The original page cannot be modified. In other words, the process has read-only access to the original and gets automatic copies of any parts it decides to change.

Copy-on-write protection can be useful for preserving a buffer's original state until all the changes are final. A half-edited spreadsheet, for example, with all its formulas linking cells, might be useless in its unfinished state. Simply saving changed areas back to the original file could cause problems because the changes in one edited place might invalidate the data in another unedited place. Copy-on-write protection leaves the original buffer and its file intact while editing proceeds. Of course, the problem doesn't arise with unmapped files. In that case, you would need to keep an extra copy of the entire spreadsheet, not just the modified pieces.

Debuggers use copy-on-write protection when altering code to add a breakpoint, for example. If another instance of the process is running outside the debugger, both instances still share all of the source code image except the altered page.

Using Virtual Memory and File-Mapping Objects

Our two sample programs for this chapter, List and Browser, make use of the virtual memory API and file-mapping objects. These are described in the following sections. Full listings of both programs, including two different versions of List, appear on the CD that accompanies the book.

Reserving and Committing Memory:
The List Program

The List program, shown in Figure 17.6, creates a list by reserving virtual memory and committing it as the user enters new items. A list box filling the window's client area displays the entire list. The List menu allows the user to add and delete items.

FIGURE 17.6

The List program accepting a new item entry

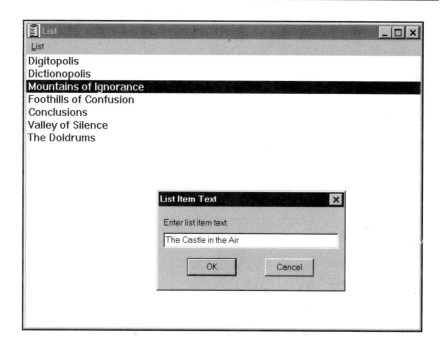

To create a dynamic list of identically sized nodes in 16-bit Windows, you would probably create a structure of linked nodes. Each new entry would require an allocation, using `GlobalAlloc` (or `malloc` with MSC 7.0). An array would be easier to program but much more wasteful since it would allocate more memory than it ever used. Under NT/95, however, the virtual memory commands make a large dynamically allocated array quite practical, and that's how List implements its data structure.

Writing a virtual memory program calls for a decision about how to deal with uncommitted pages. The first version of List uses exception handling to commit pages on demand, as page faults occur. The second version uses a different method, in which the revised procedures query the state of each page before writing. They also keep all pages write-protected except when writing to them.

List Program Header and Resource Files

The header file defines two constants governing the size and structure of the list. Each array element has room for 1024 characters. Because the system's page size (4KB) is a multiple of the element size (1KB), no list item will cross a page boundary; therefore, retrieving an item never requires reading more than a single page from the disk. The program sets the array's maximum size to a mere 500, figuring that filling even that small number will challenge the patience of most readers. Setting the limit to 20,000 would still tie up less than 1 percent of the 2GB user address space.

List Program Initialization

Among the program's global variables are two arrays: iListLookup and bInUse.

```
int  iListLookup[MAX_ITEMS];   // matches index to array position
BOOL bInUse[MAX_ITEMS];        // marks array positions in use
```

The lookup array links lines in the list box to elements in the dynamic array. If iListLookup[4] is 7, then string 5 in the list box is stored in element 7 of the array. (The list box and the array both begin numbering at 0.)

The second array contains a Boolean value for each element in the dynamic array. Whenever the program adds or deletes a string, it changes the corresponding element of bInUse to TRUE for an occupied position and FALSE for an empty position. To add a new string, the program searches bInUse for an empty array element. To delete the currently selected string, the program locates the array element by referring to iListLookup.

When the program starts, the CreateList function is called to reserve memory and initialize the supporting data structures. VirtualAlloc reserves a 1MB range of addresses. Like all reserved pages, these must be marked PAGE_NOACCESS until they are committed.

```
BOOL CreateList ( void )
{
   int i;
      // reserve one meg of memory address space
```

```
      pBase = VirtualAlloc( NULL,              // starting address
(anywhere)
                         MAX_ITEMS * ITEM_SIZE,  // one megabyte
                    MEM_RESERVE,              // reserve; don't commit
                   PAGE_NOACCESS );          // can't be touched
   if( pBase == NULL )
   {
      ShowErrorMsg( __LINE__ );
      return( FALSE );
   }
      // initialize the status variables
   for( i = 0; i < MAX_ITEMS; i++ )
   {
      bInUse[i] = FALSE;                     // show no entries in use
      iListLookup[i] = 0;
   }
   bListEmpty = TRUE;                         // update global flags
   bListFull = FALSE;
   return( TRUE );
}
```

Adding Items

When the user chooses Add Item from the menu, the `AddItem` procedure performs the following steps:

1. Locate the first empty slot in the array (`iIndex`).

2. Ask the user to enter the new string in a dialog box.

3. Copy the new string into the memory allocated during `CreateList`.

4. Update the list box and several global variables.

The first unused position in the array may happen to occupy an uncommitted memory page. In that case, the `lstrcpy` command that tries to put a string there generates an exception. The exception handler around `lstrcpy` looks for the `EXCEPTION_ACCESS_VIOLATION` signal and responds by calling `VirtualAlloc` to commit a single page from the previously reserved range.

```
void AddItem ( void )
{
   char szText[ITEM_SIZE];   // text for one item
```

```
int  iLen;              // string length
int  iIndex;            // position in array
int  iPos;              // position in list box
int  iCount;            // count of entries in list box
BOOL bDone;             // TRUE when free array entry found

    // determine the location of the first free entry
bDone = FALSE;
iIndex = 0;
while( ( ! bDone ) && ( iIndex < MAX_ITEMS ) )
{
   if( ! bInUse[iIndex] )           // is entry in use?
      bDone = TRUE;                  // found an empty entry
   else
      iIndex++;                      // advance to next entry
}

    // ask user for new text string
iLen = GetItemText(szText);
if( ! iLen ) return;
```

The `try` block copies the new text to an empty place in the item array. If that memory page is uncommitted, `lstrcpy` raises an exception. The exception filter commits the page, and the command continues.

```
try
{      // put text in the item
   lstrcpy( &( pBase[iIndex * ITEM_SIZE] ), szText );
}
except( CommitMemFilter( GetExceptionCode(), iIndex ) )
{
      // the filter does all the work
}
   // mark this entry as in use
bInUse[iIndex] = TRUE;
bListEmpty = FALSE;
```

The program adds the new text to the list box. The string is inserted at `iPos`. Then it updates `iListLookup[iPos]` to indicate where in the item array the new entry was stored (`iIndex`).

```
iCount = ListBox_GetCount( hwndList );
iPos = ListBox_InsertString( hwndList, iCount, szText );
```

```
        iCount++;
        ListBox_SetCurSel( hwndList, iPos );
        iListLookup[iPos] = iIndex;
        if (iCount == MAX_ITEMS)      // did we fill the last place?
        {
            bListFull = TRUE;
        }
        return;
}
```

The `CommitMemFilter` function provides an exception-handling filter for the `AddItem` function. If a page fault occurs, `CommitMemFilter` attempts to commit the page and, on success, returns to `lstrcopy` and proceeds. if `CommitMemFilter` fails, the search for an appropriate exception handler continues.

```
LONG CommitMemFilter(
    DWORD dwExceptCode,      // code identifying the exception
    int iIndex )             // array element where fault occurred
{
    LPVOID lpvResult;
        // If the exception was not a page fault, then refuse
        // to handle it.  Make the system keep looking for
        // an exception handler.
    if( dwExceptCode != EXCEPTION_ACCESS_VIOLATION )
    {
        return( EXCEPTION_CONTINUE_SEARCH );
    }
        // Try to commit the missing page.
    lpvResult = VirtualAlloc(
        &( pBase[iIndex * ITEM_SIZE] ), // bottom of area to commit
        ITEM_SIZE,                      // size of area to commit
        MEM_COMMIT,                     // new status flag
        PAGE_READWRITE );               // protection status
    if( ! lpvResult )                   // did allocation fail?
    {
        // if can't commit page, then can't handle the exception
        return( EXCEPTION_CONTINUE_SEARCH );
    }
        // The missing page is now in place.  Tell the
        // system to go back and try again.
    return( EXCEPTION_CONTINUE_EXECUTION );
}
```

Deleting Items

When `DeleteItem` removes an element from the virtual array, it also checks to see whether any other entries remain on the same memory page. If all four entries are empty, it decommits the page, releasing 4KB to the system. The virtual addresses that pointed to the page remain reserved. Whether or not it frees a page, `DeleteItem` then removes the string from the list box and updates the global status variables.

Two other procedures help with these tasks. `GetBasePageEntry` receives an array index and returns the index of the first element on the same page frame. In other words, it rounds down to the nearest multiple of four. `AdjustLookupTable` removes the entry it held for a newly deleted list box string and slides up all the following elements to fill in the gap.

```
void DeleteItem ( void )
{
    int  iCurSel;  // position of current selection in list box
    int  iPlace;   // position of current selection in item array
    int  iStart;   // first position on same page as selection
    int  i;        // loop variable
    BOOL bFree;    // TRUE if all 4 entries on one page are unused
    BOOL bTest;    // for testing return results

      // retrieve the memory offset of the currently selected entry
    iCurSel = ListBox_GetCurSel( hwndList );
    iPlace = iListLookup[iCurSel];
      // zero out the deleted entry
    FillMemory( &(pBase[iPlace * ITEM_SIZE]), ITEM_SIZE, 0 );
      // mark this entry as free
    bInUse[iPlace] = FALSE;
```

We figure out which entry number is first on the current page. If all four entries on the page are empty, we'll uncommit the page to release memory.

```
    iStart = GetPageBaseEntry( iPlace );
    bFree = TRUE;
    for( i = 0; i < 4; i++ )                      // check four entries
    {
        if( bInUse[i + iStart] )                  // in use?
        {
            bFree = FALSE;                        // page is not free
        }
    }
```

If a whole memory page is now unused, we free it.

```
if( bFree )                                    // is page free?
{                                              // yes; release it
   bTest = VirtualFree( &( pBase[iStart * ITEM_SIZE] ),
                        ITEM_SIZE, MEM_DECOMMIT );
   if( ! bTest )
   {
      ShowErrorMsg( __LINE__ );
      ExitProcess( (UINT)GetLastError() );
   }
}
```

Last, we update the list box display and the lookup table array, then check to see if any entries remain in the list.

```
ListBox_DeleteString( hwndList, iCurSel );
AdjustLookupTable( iCurSel );
bListEmpty = TRUE;
i = 0;
while( ( i < MAX_ITEMS ) && ( bListEmpty ) )
{
      // if the item is in use, then the list is not empty
   bListEmpty = !bInUse[i++];
}
   // reposition the selection marker in the list box
if( ! bListEmpty )
{
   if( iCurSel )           // did we delete the first item?
   {                       // no; select item above deletion
      ListBox_SetCurSel( hwndList, iCurSel-1 );
   }
   else                    // deleted item was at top
   {                       // select new top entry
      ListBox_SetCurSel( hwndList, iCurSel );
   }
}
return;
}
```

Deleting a List   The DeleteList function is called when the program ends to delete all the entries in the list and frees the memory the entries occupied.

```
void DeleteList( void )
{
   BOOL bTest;

      // decommit the memory and then release the address space
   bTest = VirtualFree( pBase, 0, MEM_DECOMMIT );
   if( ! bTest )
   {
      ShowErrorMsg( __LINE__ );
   }
   bTest = VirtualFree( pBase, 0, MEM_RELEASE );
   if( ! bTest )
   {
      ShowErrorMsg( __LINE__ );
   }
   return;
}
```

Getting an Entry   Given an index into the list, GetPageBaseEntry figures out which entry is first on the same page by finding the first integer divisible by four and less than or equal to iPlace.

```
int GetPageBaseEntry ( int iPlace )
{
   while( iPlace % 4 )
   {
      iPlace--;
   }
   return( iPlace );
}
```

Adjusting a Lookup Table   When a list box entry is deleted, the array that matches the list box entries and the memory offsets must be updated. The iStart parameter gives the position in the list box from which a string was just deleted.

```
void AdjustLookupTable ( int iStart )
{
   int i;

      // This loop starts at the position where an entry
      // was just deleted and works down the list, scooting
      // lower items up one space to fill in the gap.
```

```
        for( i = iStart; i < MAX_ITEMS - 1; i++ )
        {
            iListLookup[i] = iListLookup[i + 1];
        }

        iListLookup[MAX_ITEMS - 1] = 0;
        return;
    }
```

The remaining procedures run the dialog box where the user enters text, display the About box, and show error messages when something goes wrong. They are included on the CD that accompanies this book.

Write-Protecting the List Pages

Instead of waiting for page faults and scurrying for last-minute commitments, the List program could invest a little overhead and manage its array in a more deliberate fashion. Here are versions of AddItem and DeleteItem that call VirtualProtect before and after each modification to ensure that every page is committed in advance and write-protected afterward.

```
void AddItem( void )
{
  MEMORY_BASIC_INFORMATION MemInfo;// info about a memory block
  char szText[ITEM_SIZE];          // text for one item
  DWORD dwOldState;                // memory status flags
  int iLen;                        // string length
  int iIndex;                      // position in array
  int iPos;                        // position in list box
  int iCount;                      // count of entries in list box
  BOOL bDone;                      // TRUE when free array entry found
  BOOL bTest;                      // for testing return values

      // determine the location of the first free entry
    bDone = FALSE;
    iIndex = 0;
    while( ( ! bDone ) && ( iIndex < MAX_ITEMS ) )
    {
        if( bInUse[iIndex] == 0 )   // is entry in use?
        {
            bDone = TRUE;           // found an empty entry
        }
```

```
        else
        {
            iIndex++;                          // advance to next entry
        }
    }
    iLen = GetItemText(szText);
      // retrieve the text
    if( ! iLen )
    {
        return;
    }
```

We retrieve information about this entry's memory page. If it is committed, we remove the access protection to allow reading and writing. If it is not committed, we allocate it.

```
        // fill out a MEMORY_BASIC_INFORMATION structure
    VirtualQuery( &( pBase[ITEM_SIZE * iIndex] ),
                 &MemInfo, sizeof(MemInfo) );
    if( MemInfo.State == MEM_COMMIT )
    {
```

If the memory has already been committed, we change the access mode to permit reading and writing.

```
        bTest = VirtualProtect(
            &( pBase[ITEM_SIZE * iIndex] ),   // bottom of area to
protect
            ITEM_SIZE,                        // size of area to protect
            PAGE_READWRITE,                   // new protection status
            &dwOldState );                    // old protection status
        if( ! bTest )
        {
            ShowErrorMsg( __LINE__ );         // protection failed
        }
    }
    else                            // this page is not yet committed
    {
```

If memory has not been committed yet, `VirtualAlloc` is called to commit a block at the bottom of the previous memory block.

```
        LPVOID lpvResult;
```

```
    lpvResult = VirtualAlloc(
        &( pBase[iIndex * ITEM_SIZE] ), // bottom of area to commit
        ITEM_SIZE,                      // size of area to commit
        MEM_COMMIT,                     // new status flag
        PAGE_READWRITE );               // protection status
    if( ! lpvResult )
    {
        ShowErrorMsg( __LINE__ );
        return;                         // allocation failed
    }
}
    // put text in the item
lstrcpy( &(pBase[iIndex * ITEM_SIZE]), szText );
    // restore the protection state of this page to read-only
bTest = VirtualProtect(
    &( pBase[iIndex * ITEM_SIZE] ),// bottom of area to protect
    ITEM_SIZE,                      // size of area to protect
    PAGE_READONLY,                  // new protection status
    &dwOldState );                  // previous protection status
if( ! bTest )
{
    ShowErrorMsg( __LINE__ );
}
    // mark this entry as in use
bInUse[iIndex] = 1;
bListEmpty = FALSE;
```

Now we add the new text to the list box, inserting the string at iPos, then update
iListLookup[iPos] to indicate where in the item array the new entry was stored
(iIndex).

```
    iCount = ListBox_GetCount( hwndList );
    iPos = ListBox_InsertString( hwndList, iCount, szText );
    iCount++;
    ListBox_SetCurSel( hwndList, iPos );
    iListLookup[iPos] = iIndex;
    if( iCount == MAX_ITEMS )               // did we fill last place?
    {
        bListFull = TRUE;
    }
    return;
}
```

The `DeleteItem` function removes an item from the list, zeroing the memory previously used. When a page is emptied, it releases the memory for reuse.

```
void DeleteItem ( void )
{
    int iCurSel;      // position of current selection in list box
    int iPlace;       // position of current selection in item array
    DWORD dwOldState; // previous memory-protection flags
    int iStart;      // first position on same memory page as selection
    int i;            // loop variable
    BOOL bFree;       // TRUE if all 4 entries on one page are unused
    BOOL bTest;       // for testing return results

       // retrieve the memory offset of the currently selected entry
    iCurSel = ListBox_GetCurSel( hwndList );
    iPlace = iListLookup[iCurSel];
       // set the protection to read/write and zero out the entry
    bTest = VirtualProtect(
       &( pBase[ITEM_SIZE * iPlace] ),// bottom of area to protect
       ITEM_SIZE,                     // size of area to protect
       PAGE_READWRITE,                // new protection status
       &dwOldState );                 // previous protection status
    if( ! bTest )
    {
       ShowErrorMsg( __LINE__ );
       return;
    }
    FillMemory( &( pBase[iPlace * ITEM_SIZE] ), ITEM_SIZE, 0 );
       // mark this entry as free
    bInUse[iPlace] = 0;
```

Next we figure out which entry number is first on the current page. If all four entries on the page are empty, we'll uncommit the page to release memory.

```
    iStart = GetPageBaseEntry( iPlace );
    bFree = TRUE;
    for( i = 0; i < 4; i++ )              // check four entries
    {
       if( bInUse[i + iStart] )          // in use?
       {
          bFree = FALSE;                 // page is not free
       }
    }
```

If a whole memory page is now unused, free it. If not, we restore its read-only protection.

```
if (bFree)                              // is page free?
{                                       // yes; release it
   bTest = VirtualFree( &( pBase[iStart * ITEM_SIZE] ),
                        ITEM_SIZE, MEM_DECOMMIT );
}
else
{                                       // no; protect it
   bTest = VirtualProtect( &( pBase[ITEM_SIZE * iPlace] ),
                        ITEM_SIZE, PAGE_READONLY, &dwOldState );
}
if( ! bTest )
{
   ShowErrorMsg( __LINE__ );
}
```

Last, the list box display is updated along with the lookup table array, then a check is made to see if any entries remain in the list before repositioning the selection marker.

```
ListBox_DeleteString( hwndList, iCurSel );
AdjustLookupTable( iCurSel );
bListEmpty = TRUE;
i = 0;
while( ( i < MAX_ITEMS ) && ( bListEmpty ) )
{
      // if the item is in use then the list is not empty
   bListEmpty = !bInUse[i++];
}
   // reposition the selection marker in the list box
if( ! bListEmpty )
{
   if( iCurSel )                 // did we delete the first item?
   {                             // no; select item above deletion
      ListBox_SetCurSel( hwndList, iCurSel - 1 );
   }
   else                          // deleted item was at top
   {                             // select new top entry
      ListBox_SetCurSel( hwndList, iCurSel );
   }
}
   return;
}
```

Mapping Memory: A File Browser

Each instance of our next program, Browser, opens a handle to the same file-mapping object and maps a view of it. The object represents a small buffer of only 6KB and is backed by the system's paging file.

A multiline edit box in the program window shows the contents of the shared buffer. A set of six radio buttons permits the user to inspect different sections of the shared buffer. When the user selects a new section, the program copies part of the shared buffer into the edit box, where it can be examined and modified. In Figure 17.7, two instances of Browser have written information to different parts of the same buffer.

FIGURE 17.7

Two instances of the Mapped File Browser program sharing views of the same mapped file

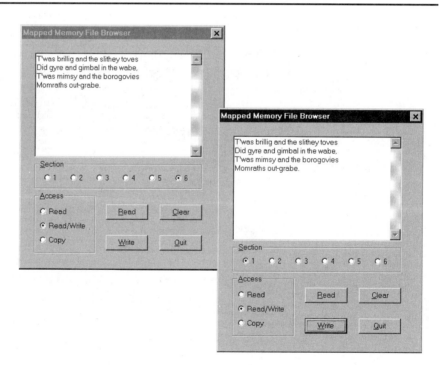

Pushbuttons issue commands to write from the screen back to the buffer, read from the buffer to refresh the screen, clear text from the edit window, and quit the program. Three more radio buttons set the page protection for the current page to

read, read/write, or copy-on-write. If the user clicks on the Write button while viewing a read-only page, the program traps the resulting exception.

Browser Header and Resource Files

Two constants in the header file direct the program in creating and using the mapped file. The program's window has room for six radio buttons across its width, so we want to divide the buffer into six sections. Each section should roughly fill the buffer, so that as the user switches from section to section, new contents come into view. SECTION_SIZE tells how big one section is (1KB), and NUM_SECTIONS tells how many sections there are (6).

The resource script includes a string to name the file-mapping object. Because all instances use the same name string, all receive handles to the same object. Also in the resources is a dialog template describing the program's main window, which is a dialog box. The AUTORADIOBUTTON statement is new in Windows NT and 95, but it duplicates the effect of the old BS_AUTORADIOBUTTON style.

Initializing the Mapped File

Browser keeps information about its file-mapping object in two global variables: hMapFile is a handle to the object, and lpView points to a mapped view of the object.

Because the program's main window is a dialog box, WinMain omits the usual message loop. Instead, it simply calls an initialization procedure and invokes a modal dialog box. When the dialog box quits, WinMain releases its objects and ends.

InitApp creates the file-mapping object and maps a view of it. Because the instances of Browser want only to share memory, not to create a disk file, the CreateFileMapping command passes (HANDLE)0xFFFFFFFF as the file handle. The buffer will be mapped from the system's paging file. If we wanted to create a new disk file for the Browser instances to share, we would need to call Create-File first:

```
    // create the file to be mapped
  hFile = CreateFile( szFileName, // filename string
    GENERIC_READ | GENERIC_WRITE, // access rights
    0,                            // don't share files being mapped
    (LPSECURITY_ATTRIBUTES)NULL,  // default attributes
    CREATE_ALWAYS,                // if file doesn't exist create it
    FILE_ATTRIBUTE_NORMAL,        // no special attributes
    NULL );                       // no special attributes
```

The file-mapping object allows read/write access, but individual views may request different protection flags. PAGE_READWRITE is compatible with all the possible view access flags.

After creating the file-mapping object, InitApp next maps a view of it. Initially, the view allows the user both read and write privileges by specifying FILE_MAP_ ALL_ACCESS. The next two zeros make the beginning of the mapped view begin with the first byte of the file, and the final zero parameter causes the view to extend to the end of the file.

CreateFileMapping sets the file's size to NUM_SECTIONS * SECTION_SIZE, which happens to be 6KB. The size and starting point of the view never change in this program. The starting point can't change because it must be a multiple of 64KB. For a 6KB file, the view must begin at byte 0. To show different sections of the 6KB shared buffer, Browser uses lpView to treat the buffer as an array of characters.

All instances of Browser initialize in the same way. If the program mapped its buffer to an independent disk file, the first instance would need to initialize differently. Only the first instance would call CreateFile, and subsequent instances could be made to call OpenFileMapping rather than repeating the original Create-FileMapping command.

```
    // get a handle for an existing file-mapping object
   hMapFile = OpenFileMapping( FILE_MAP_ALL_ACCESS,// access privi-
   leges
                                FALSE,              // inheritable?
                                szMapFile );        // name of object
   if( ! hMapFile )
   {
      ShowErrorMsg( __LINE__ );                     // initialization failed
      return( FALSE );
   }
```

Because both Windows NT and 95 always pass NULL to WinMain for the hPrev-Instance parameter, Browser requires another mechanism to check for other instances. FindWindow works for overlapping windows, but standard dialog windows don't have a documented class name. (The class for standard dialog windows seems to be #32770, as you can verify with Microsoft's Spy utility, but undocumented features may change in future releases.) Successive instances of Browser could also identify their precedence if the first instance created a named pipe or added a string to the global atom table. Each instance could determine whether it has a predecessor by checking for the existence of the signal object.

Running the Dialog Box

The next procedures receive and respond to messages for the dialog box. The Browser dialog initializes its controls when it receives WM_INITDIALOG. Among other things, Browser_DoInitDialog sets a limit on the number of characters the user may enter in the edit box. The limit prevents the user from entering more text than the current section of the mapped file can hold. Browser_DoCommand calls other procedures to manipulate the mapped file view in response to input from the user.

```
void Browser_DoCommand( HWND hDlg,
                        UINT uCmd )  // control ID of the button pressed
{
    static int iCurSection = 0;
```

The static variable iCurSection records the user's most recent selection from the section's radio buttons.

```
    switch( uCmd )
    {
        case IDD_WRITE:
            DoWrite( hDlg, iCurSection );
            break;

        case IDD_READ:
            DoRead( hDlg, iCurSection );
            break;

        case IDD_CLEAR:
            DoClear( hDlg );
            break;

        case IDD_SECTION1:
        case IDD_SECTION2:
        case IDD_SECTION3:
        case IDD_SECTION4:
        case IDD_SECTION5:
        case IDD_SECTION6:
            iCurSection = uCmd - IDD_SECTION1;// save current choice
            DoClear( hDlg );                  // clear edit box
            DoRead( hDlg, iCurSection );      // show new file section
            break;

        case IDD_READ_ACCESS:
```

```
        case IDD_READWRITE_ACCESS:
        case IDD_WRITECOPY_ACCESS:
            ChangeAccess( uCmd );
            break;

        case IDCANCEL:
        case IDD_QUIT:
            EndDialog( hDlg, TRUE );
            break;
    }
    return;
}
```

Modifying the Shared Object

When the user clicks on the Write, Read, or Clear button, the program calls
DoWrite, DoRead, or DoClear. In response to commands from the Access radio
buttons, the program calls ChangeAccess.

DoWrite and DoRead send WM_GETTEXT and WM_SETTEXT messages to the edit
control. DoWrite copies the contents of the edit buffer to a section of the mapped
file, and DoRead copies a section of the mapped file to the edit control. In both procedures, this expression points to the beginning of the current section of the
mapped view:

```
    &( lpView[ iSection * SECTION_SIZE ] )
```

lpView is type LPSTR, so it points to an array of characters. iSection tells
which radio button is currently checked. The first button is 0, so the result of
iSection*SECTION_SIZE is the number of the first byte in the given file section.
lpView[] evaluates to a character, and &(lpView[]) gives the address of the
character.

```
    void DoWrite( HWND hDlg, int iSection )
    {
            // get the edit control handle
        HWND hwndEdit = GetDlgItem( hDlg, IDD_EDIT );

        if( hwndEdit )
        {
            try
            {
                // copy the text from the edit buffer to the mapped file
```

```
                Edit_GetText( hwndEdit,        // edit control
                              &( lpView[iSection*SECTION_SIZE] ),
                                              // pointer into the view
                              SECTION_SIZE ); // bytes in section
        }
```

The exception handler in DoWrite is designed to catch the error when the user write-protects the mapped view and then tries to use the Write button. We could disable the button, but allowing the error to occur seemed more instructive and a better demonstration of what write protection does.

```
        except( EXCEPTION_ACCESS_VIOLATION )
        {
            // assume the exception was due to read-only access
            MessageBox( hDlg, "Memory is read only.\n\r
                    "No data was written.",
                    "Browser Message", MB_OK | MB_ICONEXCLAMATION );
        }
    }
    return;
}
```

The DoRead function reads text from the mapped file, copying the retrieved text to the edit control buffer.

```
void DoRead( HWND hDlg, int iSection )
{
    HWND hwndEdit;

    // get the edit control handle
    hwndEdit = GetDlgItem( hDlg, IDD_EDIT );
    if( hwndEdit )
    {
        // retrieve the text from memory and display it
        Edit_SetText( hwndEdit,
                    &( lpView[iSection*SECTION_SIZE] ) );
                                            // pointer in view
    }
    return;
}
```

On the other hand, the DoClear procedure does nothing to the mapped file. It clears the text in edit buffer.

```
void DoClear( HWND hWnd )
{
    HWND hwndEdit;
    char *szText = "\0";

        // empty the edit buffer by filling it with a null string
    hwndEdit = GetDlgItem( hWnd, IDD_EDIT );
    if( hwndEdit )
    {
        Edit_SetText( hwndEdit, szText );
    }
    return;
}
```

Last, ChangeAccess unmaps the current view of the file-mapping object in order
to remap it with a different access privilege. Every instance of the program may
choose different access flags, because each has its own independent view of the
object. An instance that uses FILE_MAP_COPY remains synchronized with the other
instances' views until it writes to the buffer. At that moment, the system intervenes
and creates a copy of the protected page for the program to modify. From then on,
the program never sees the original unmodified page again, even though the other
instances do.

```
void ChangeAccess( int iNewAccess )          // requested access
rights
{
    DWORD fdwAccess;                         // new access flag

        // close the previous mapping
    UnmapViewOfFile( lpView );
        // choose new access flag
    switch( iNewAccess )
    {
        case IDD_READWRITE_ACCESS:
            fdwAccess = FILE_MAP_ALL_ACCESS;
            break;

        case IDD_READ_ACCESS:
            fdwAccess = FILE_MAP_READ;
            break;

        default: // IDD_WRITECOPY_ACCESS
```

```
            fdwAccess = FILE_MAP_COPY;
            break;
    }
        // remap the view using the requested access and view number
    lpView = MapViewOfFile( hMapFile, // handle to mapping object
                            fdwAccess,// access privileges
                            0, 0,     // starting offset in file
                0 );                  // view area size (all of file)
    if( lpView == NULL )// error?
    {
        ShowErrorMsg( __LINE__ );      // yes; tell user
    }
    return;
}
```

Since Browser shows the buffer in 1KB sections, four sections fill one page frame. If one instance writes to the first section with copy-on-write protection, it loses synchronization in the first four sections (one page frame). Its view of sections 5 and 6, however, will continue to reflect changes made by other instances. Also, changes the first program makes to its copy-on-write buffer will never be visible to other instances. The copied pages are private.

In this chapter, you've seen some of the new powers of the Windows NT VMM. The virtual memory API passes on to you some of these powers, especially the ability to reserve a range of addresses without immediately committing physical memory to support them. The ability to guarantee that a range of contiguous addresses will be available as an object grows, or as an array slowly fills in, makes working with sparse memory structures easy.

Given the VMM's effectiveness in isolating each process from memory used by any other process, sharing blocks of memory becomes problematic. Programs have moved apart into private address spaces. Gone are the neighborly days of passing memory handles from program to program. In their place are the high-tech miracles of memory-mapped files, and with them come all the modern concerns for protection, coherence, and point of view.

Security and Cryptography

- Security in Windows 95 and NT

- NT security structures

- NT security-related commands

- Encryption methods

- NT's CryptoAPI functions

Windows NT was designed from the ground up to meet rigorous goals for securing data from unauthorized users. In this respect, Windows NT differs significantly from Windows 95. As a programmer, you will find it necessary to have at least a familiarity with how NT's security is implemented and is made available to applications.

Even if you have no interest in incorporating security in your own applications, knowledge of NT's security API is important, because references to security parameters and options keep showing up in many other Win32 API functions, which you will undoubtedly find occasion to use. There is also the danger of inadvertently creating security loopholes, particularly in server applications, when your applications neglect to make use of NT's security APIs properly (or at all).

The importance of data encryption is currently gaining deserved increased attention, thanks in large part to the success of the Internet, as well as blossoming corporate intranets, which together are vastly increasing the volume of information that is accessible online. Data authentication and confidentiality, online financial transactions, and protection from rogue software (virii) are reasons enough to enlist the help of cryptography.

In this chapter, we will first look at how NT's security functions work, with respect to permitting and restricting access to secured objects. Then we will focus on the encryption functions as provided via the CryptoAPI. Finally, we'll wrap up the chapter by looking at some points to consider when you're implementing security in your applications.

Security and Encryption: NT versus Windows 95

One of the main advantages NT has over Windows 95 is its extensive built-in security. There are approximately 80 API functions that pertain to security in Windows NT, not including the Cryptography API (CryptoAPI). Of these security-related functions, only a handful are fully or partially supported under Windows 95.

Of course, as is standard in other areas of the Win32 API, any NT security functions not supported by Windows 95 will at least have function stubs located in an appropriate DLL. Your NT application can at least load on Windows 95 without having linking errors. Your application may *call* any one of these security functions while running on a Windows 95 station, but it better be prepared to check the error-return code, note that the function failed, and take appropriate action.

When designing an application to make use of NT security, it's your responsibility to determine what functionality this application should provide when running under Windows 95—if indeed it should even be permitted to run without security functionality enabled.

Keep in mind that the only correct way to use the NT security API functions is in the context of a server application. While it may be possible to design a server application to run on a Windows 95 station, it would not be possible to do this where the server application needs to implement NT-level security (using the Win32 security API at any rate). The better and simpler approach would probably be to require that the application be run on NT, and simply issue a complaint message and exit if someone tries to run this application on a Windows 95 station.

Having said that, let me also suggest that you may not want to simply perform an operating system version check, and then exit if the version number doesn't seem right. When run on the latest versions of NT, some older Windows applications get confused and complain that they require a newer version of the operating system. Assumptions about what is or isn't an appropriate operating system to run an application, based solely on getting the operating system version number, are prone to errors in certain cases.

A better approach is to look at those categories of functionality needed by your application that currently are not supported by a subset of the operating system, which is otherwise capable of running your application. Then, when your application loads, have it perform checks for any missing functionality, and either exit or else modify its behavior or functionality accordingly.

There is good news, on the other hand, regarding Windows 95's support for encryption. All the functions of the CryptoAPI, except those few functions having to do with data in Unicode format, work the same in Windows 95 and NT. The encryption and decryption demo programs presented later in this chapter will run on both platforms. However, as always, you should verify that anything you write actually does perform exactly as you expect it to on both platforms.

NT Security Concepts

What sorts of applications need to be concerned with NT security? Simply put, anything intended to run on a server is a strong candidate for security implementation. Additionally, at the client level, any applications that will access their own secured objects (shared memory, files, semaphores, the registry, and so on) and most applications that will run as a service will need to make use of at least some NT security functions.

Users and Objects

The first thing to understand about NT security is that it is based on a per-*user* security model. Whenever a user successfully logs on to a trusted server, that user is identified internally (by an access token, as explained shortly), and everything that user then does—from starting applications, to accessing printers and drives, to opening and saving files—is allowed or not allowed based on what rights and privileges are granted that user.

In addition to determining who has access to what, NT's security API also provides system-level and application-level event logging features, so you can later determine who had access to what, and when.

Figure 18.1 shows a simplified representation of how NT's security system keeps track of users versus objects. As each user logs in and is validated by an NT system, that user is given a unique access token, which sticks with them, so to speak, as long as he or she is logged in, and wherever he or she goes within the NT network. Each system object is represented by means of a security descriptor (SD), which holds a number of pieces of security-related information. Whenever a user attempts to access an object, NT's security compares the access token against the permissions in the security descriptor. We'll discuss access tokens and security descriptors in more detail in a bit.

System and User Objects

An NT system object, in the context we are using in this chapter, does not mean a C++ object, an OLE, nor a COM object. A system object is any object created and managed by one of the three main NT subsystems: Kernel, User, or GDI. For various reasons, NT's built-in security is only implemented on Kernel objects. Thus, you are not required (via the API) to worry about security when creating bitmaps, cursors, pens, brushes, icons, metafiles, or window handles, for example. But you

FIGURE 18.1

Each logged-in NT user is represented internally by an access token. Each system object (or user object) in NT is identified by a security descriptor.

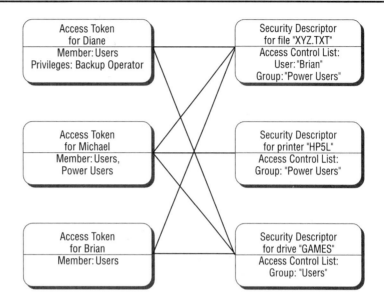

do need to provide at least a security descriptor parameter (or a NULL value) when creating or managing any Kernel object, such as any file, folder, storage device, pipe, mailslot, serial port, registry key, console device, printer queue, and so on.

In addition to system objects, there are also user- or application-defined objects. These are any objects that your application defines, creates, and recognizes. These types of objects can include NT objects from the User and GDI subsystems (if you need to protect a bitmap, for instance), subdivided areas of files, or anything else your application must interact with and control access to—whether it is a piece of data, a menu command, a particular view of a data set, or whatever else you might come up with.

Sometimes, a further distinction is made between NT objects created by NT and NT objects created by the end users, via their use of the system or various applications. This difference becomes important in understanding the difference between System and Discretionary (owner) Access Control Lists, as discussed a bit later in the chapter.

Built-in versus Application Security

When thinking about NT's security, you should keep this distinction between objects in mind:

- Automatically protected objects in NT. NT internally and automatically handles the storage and checking of security settings on its own Kernel system objects. An example of automatic security is the security checking that takes place within the Kernel whenever access attempts occur on files or directories that are located on an NTFS partition.

- Objects you create yourself and must protect by implementing your own security checks. For example, "manual" or "do-it-yourself" security is necessary if you need to prevent unauthorized access to only certain types of functionality within an application or to certain parts of a database file.

Implementing your own security requires several main steps:

1. At the planning stage, create a list of all data objects and/or types of functionality that cannot be open to all users indiscriminately.

2. Devise a logical plan of specific rights or privileges that can be assigned or restricted to the various individuals and/or groups using your system.

3. Add security checks to *every* point in your software where the protected objects or functionality can be accessed.

4. If these objects can possibly be accessed in any way outside your software, (by standard file access, for example), you will need to restrict access here also. This usually can be done by specifying Administrator-only access, for example, on the object, and then have your application run using Administrator privileges so it can access the object itself.

Let me repeat this: Anything not covered by NT's built-in/automatic security, to which you wish to add access restrictions (security), requires that you specify the desired permissions and then check those permissions every time an attempt is made to access your object. NT's security API does give you some help in this regard; its set of functions are the same as those used by NT's own internal security. Therefore, the process you go through to secure your own objects has much in common with what NT does to provide security for its objects.

Of course, if you're creating some object which in turn makes use of one or more system objects, NT may automatically provide some level of security for these system objects. If you store your object in a file, for example, that file will be subject to NT's built-in file security just like any other file (if it's located on an NTFS partition, that is).

This overlap of NT's system security with additional security that you may implement is not only welcome, but is absolutely essential to the proper implementation of security in your application. For example, NT itself knows how to restrict access to files, subdirectories, and drives. However, it doesn't know that part of your database file contains data that should be available to only certain users, while other parts may be appropriate for general access. In this particular case, your database file would actually need to be protected in two ways:

- By your using NTFS's file security to permit direct file access only by system (or database) administrators.

- By writing your database server application so that it takes all the incoming data requests from various users and provides the desired additional level of security based on permissions that you have previously defined at the user or group levels.

This server application, by the way, would itself be able to access the database file directly, because it would run using the Administrator (or other appropriate) access rights.

WARNING When implementing security on any object that might be accessed outside your application, always restrict any and all *direct* access (file, communications, and so on) to this object by also using NT's built-in security attributes, wherever applicable. Typically, this means setting *Administrator-only* access on all "outside" approaches to your object, then having your server application internally make further decisions about granting or denying access on a case-by-case basis.

As you may surmise, it is generally foolhardy to attempt to implement security from within your application when either the application or its data files will end up being stored on a FAT (or other non-NTFS) partition. You could get around this partially by using encryption on your data files, as discussed later in this chapter. However, even with encryption, there are likely to be security loopholes if users are able to directly access your application's data in any way.

Security Is for Servers

When planning your security implementation, always design your application using the *client/server* model! In other words, do not use the security API just anywhere in your Win32 applications; these functions belong only in software that will be run on a *server*.

Split the project into a client application, which individual users will use, and a server application, which runs on a server and handles all incoming requests for secured objects. Why insist on this extra work? There are several reasons:

- The software running on the client side might end up being run under Windows 95 or another operating system that doesn't support security, such as a Web browser.

- This provides a clear division between a server application, which handles all security and therefore "clears" all your secured-object requests, and the client application, which makes use of the objects. The client/server model centralizes the security issues to one machine, rather than several or many, leaving fewer potential security loopholes.

- This separation of function provides you with much greater flexibility down the road, in terms of adding new types of client applications or extending the size of your LAN. You eliminate the hassle of needing to change your server implementation, which would thereby reopen a can of security worms.

> **WARNING**
> Always use the client/server model when designing systems needing NT's security services. The security checking should always (and only!) be performed by an application functioning on a server, or in a server capacity. A client application, running on the user's system, should use any of the standard network communications means to request access to the secured objects from the server application. This technique allows you to combine secure access with the ability to access the objects via workstations that do not internally support NT security (for example, Windows 95 or a Java applet running on somebody's Web browser on a Unix or a Mac machine).

So how is the client application supposed to communicate with the server application? There is more than one right answer to this, however the method you choose must be a secure one. Typically, any of the following means of communicating between client and server applications can be used:

- Named pipes
- Remote procedure calls
- Distributed COM (or DCOM)
- Secure sockets (and supporting Web server)

These are not the only means you could use, of course. However, in most cases, any one or a combination of the above is an excellent choice.

Security Attributes

You cannot do much programming in the Win32 API without running into the many Kernel object-manipulation functions, which always take a pointer to a SECURITY_ATTRIBUTES structure. Take CreateFile, for instance, which is defined as follows:

```
HANDLE CreateFile(
    LPCTSTR  lpFileName,           // pointer to filename
    DWORD    dwDesiredAccess,      // access (read-write) mode
    DWORD    dwShareMode,          // share mode
    LPSECURITY_ATTRIBUTES lpSecurityAttributes,// (see below)
    DWORD    dwCreationDistribution,// create mode
    DWORD    dwFlagsAndAttributes, // open, delete, close attributes
    HANDLE   hTemplateFile         // optional source for attributes
);
```

What! All this—just to create a file? You may take one look at this and decide to go back to using your favorite "normal" means of opening files: fopen, OpenFile, or Delphi's Reset, for example.

CreateFile has far more uses than its name implies. It is the primary means in Win32 of opening all sorts of NT objects in addition to files, including pipes, mailslots, communications sessions, disk devices, and so on. CreateFile is not only used for creating these objects, but can also be used for opening (or reopening), closing, and even deleting files when finished, given the right combinations of flags. As we saw in Chapter 15, CreateFile is also capable of doing both synchronous and asynchronous (overlapped) I/O operations.

Performing any one of these operations on a secured object causes NT's built-in security checking to go to work. The system compares access rights contained in your lpSecurityAttributes structure with any permissions or restrictions that have been placed on the object, and causes your function to succeed or fail, as appropriate.

Typically, you would most often use CreateFile by simply filling in a NULL value for the lpSecurityAttributes. This is fine for routine object access, because when you specify the NULL value, the default set of SECURITY_ATTRIBUTES for the current process is used, which in most cases is appropriate. This is also, by the way, exactly what happens when you open files using `fopen`, `OpenFile`, or any other means of file access under NT. As you might guess, all of these functions behave similarly, because in NT, all of them trace right back to the same code (and security checking) used by `CreateFile` itself.

If you want anything more sophisticated than the default security behavior by using a NULL value for your `SECURITY_ATTRIBUTES` structure, you will need to supply an actual `SECURITY_ATTRIBUTES` structure. Roll up your sleeves and prepare to do some rather strenuous mental exertion.

> **NOTE** When `lpSecurityAttributes` = NULL, whatever the current user's security descriptor happens to be is passed along to `CreateFile`. In other words, there isn't a default security setting per se; rather the default behavior is to use the current user's security descriptor.

The `SECURITY_ATTRIBUTES` structure looks benign and simplistic at first glance:

```
typedef struct _SECURITY_ATTRIBUTES {
    DWORD  nLength; // set this to sizeof( SECURITY_ATTRIBUTES );
    LPVOID lpSecurityDescriptor; // "complex" structure
    BOOL   bInheritHandle; // if child process inherits handle
} SECURITY_ATTRIBUTES;
```

Setting the `nLength` field is simple (and important!). Setting the `bInheritHandle` flag is straightforward enough; it's a Boolean value after all. However, that middle field, which is actually a pointer to a `SECURITY_DESCRIPTOR`, is where the rubber really hits the road, in a security sense.

The security descriptor (SD) is one of the four major data structures used by NT's security API. (`SECURITY_ATTRIBUTES` doesn't count as major, since its purpose is only to be a wrapper for supplying the security descriptor to NT.) As stated earlier, the security descriptor represents an object or a group of objects to NT's security system. It makes sense that the various Win32 API functions dealing with securable objects each takes a `SECURITY_DESCRIPTOR` by encapsulation in the `SECURITY_ATTRIBUTES` structure.

In the following sections, we'll look at each of the four main types of security structures, and then discuss how each is created, initialized, and manipulated using the functions supplied by NT's security API.

The Four Major NT Security Structures

Although these are not the only security-related information structures, the following four structures are certainly the "heavy-hitter" structures used for keeping track of NT security-related information:

- Access tokens
- Security descriptors (SDs)
- Security identifiers (SIDs)
- Access Control Lists (ACLs; also known as SACLs and DACLs)

Although these are structures, you're required to consider them as *opaque*, meaning initializing them and setting their values must be accomplished by means of the appropriate API functions. We'll discuss exactly which functions should be used for manipulating each structure after explaining the structures themselves.

WARNING As the SDK points out, you should never try to manipulate these security structures directly. There are API functions available for you to use to initialize these structures and politely "modify their guts."

Access Tokens

Each user logged on to an NT system is assigned an access token. This token is checked against SDs (security descriptors) of any objects the user is trying to access. Note that the access token contains user privileges, while security descriptors contain access rights.

Security Descriptors (SDs)

Inside the SD are the collected pieces of information that together exactly specify the owner, permitted users and groups, and permissions granted (or denied) to particular users or groups of users of that object.

Rights versus Privileges in NT

What's the difference between rights and privileges? In NT's view of things, a *right* is the ability, given to an individual user or group of users, to access some given object in a particular way. Examples of rights include giving read-only (or read and write) access to a file or folder, to a shared CD-ROM drive, or to some printer on the network. Because rights are attached to objects (but in relation to users), they are stored in the security descriptor (SD) for an object.

Privileges, on the other hand, are the predefined abilities to perform particular operations on the system. Examples of system privileges include being able to shut down or start system services, install or remove system device drivers, or perform backups.

Unlike rights, privileges are stored in the user's access token, primarily because most often a privilege will override otherwise assigned rights. It's much more practical to have this information attached to the user than it would be to update the settings of each object the privilege would affect. Take a typical example: performing system backups. Here, the user must be able to access most or all of the system files in order to perform the backup. Trying to maintain an exceptions list attached to each file that is created in order to keep track of who now has backup privileges is simply not feasible.

Subelements of the SD include the owner and group security identifiers (SIDs), as well as two Access Control Lists (ACLs).

NOTE Again, NT's security API provides an entire array of functions for querying and manipulating the various security structures. Note that since these are *structures*, rather than OOP (object-oriented programming) objects, the way you interact with them is by using appropriate API functions, which expect as a parameter a pointer to a particular type of security structure.

SIDs   An SID is a structure of variable length that uniquely refers to a user or group of users. Internally, an SID contains (among other things) a 48-bit authority value, which is a unique value comprised of a revision level, an identifier-authority value, and a subauthority value.

Once an SID is created, an NT system will not permit it to ever be reused, even if the SID is deleted. The SD of each object contains two SIDs:

- An owner SID, which identifies the current owner of the object

- A Primary Group SID, which identifies that group of users who have specific access rights or restrictions for the given object

Note that SIDs are used in several other areas of NT security. Every access token, for example, contains an SID that identifies the groups that user is a member of. Also, each Access Control Entry (ACE) in an Access Control List (ACL) has its own SID that specifies the individual or group being granted or denied a set of permissions or rights.

ACLs   ACLs are lists of rights or restrictions placed on users or groups for a given object (or group of objects). Each SD can contain two types of ACLs:

- A System ACL (SACL), which keeps track of permissions that are set on an object at the system level. The SACL can be changed only by users who possess system-level access.

- A user or Discretionary ACL (DACL), which keeps track of permissions that are set by the owner of the object. The DACL can be changed by whoever is currently specified as the object's owner ("currently," because one of the rights that can be set on an object is the ability to change who the current owner is).

These ACLs are identical in form. Both types can contain zero or one or more Access Control Entries (ACEs). Each ACE contains three parts: users or groups this ACE pertains to, which rights are affected, and whether the rights are being granted or revoked.

An ACL can be in one of three states: empty, NULL, or containing one or more ACEs. In an ACL's initial state, it is empty, which is in effect the same as saying no access rights have been given for this object, so no users will have access to it. An ACL which is set explicitly to NULL, on the other hand, means *no* security has been assigned to the object, and therefore *all access* is granted. Once you add a single ACE to a previously NULL ACL, the object loses its "general access" (or lack of security) and is available to only those users or groups specified by an ACE.

> **WARNING**
> Do not confuse a NULL DACL with an empty DACL! They are actually opposites in their effect. An empty DACL (the initial state in a new SD) means no *access* has been granted. A NULL DACL means no *restrictions* exist for the object, so it is accessible to all users. A DACL only becomes NULL by being set that way explicitly.

So, you should now understand, at least in theory, how an object's access is specified for any condition: complete access, no access, access granted to some, and access restricted to some.

Self-Relative versus Absolute SDs   SDs can be represented in either absolute or self-relative format. Figure 18.2 illustrates how these two formats differ.

The reason there are two different formats is that there are benefits to storing the data in either way.

Because SDs contain fields (the ACLs) that contain a variable number of entries (ACEs), and each field could either be NULL or empty rather than contain information, it makes the job of updating (adding and removing) entries and settings in an SD much simpler if the SD itself is stored in memory as a structure of pointers (to structures with other pointers, usually). Otherwise, each time anything changed, a larger chunk of memory would need to be allocated, and the entire structure would need to be copied to the new area, along with the new changes. This "update-friendly" format, which makes use of pointers, is called (somewhat confusingly) *absolute* format.

On the other hand, because pointers point to RAM, and RAM is generally only accessible by the computer owning it, it would not work very well to send an SD (in absolute format) across the network (or save it to disk) since you would be sending (or writing) only a set of pointers instead of the various structures themselves. Therefore, the SD can be stored in a second format where the entire structure, including all of its current fields, is stored in one contiguous block of memory. This more "transfer-friendly" format is called *self-relative* format. As you might surmise, this is the format in which SDs are returned to you when you request them from the system. You can look at (read) the SD in this format, but when you need to change (write to) the SD in any way, you must first convert the SD into absolute format.

FIGURE 18.2

SDs come in two flavors: the absolute, which is useful for updating the SD's fields, and the self-relative, which is better suited for transferring the SD to a file, to a different process, or across the network.

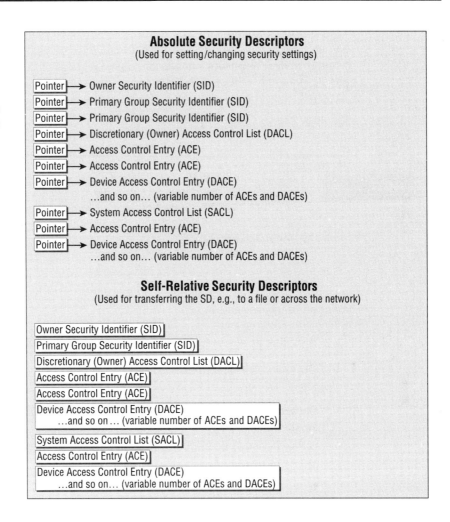

Fortunately, there are two API functions you can use to do this conversion: `Make-AbsoluteSD` and `MakeSelfRelativeSD`. Unfortunately, you will need to use them each and every time you get or put an SD and also need to make changes to it.

Client Impersonation

The procedure whereby a server application checks that a connected client actually has access rights to a requested object is called *client impersonation*. In this process, when the client application makes an object request of the server application, it passes along its access token. The server application uses this access token to log on as the client (impersonate the client), attempting to access the desired object in the same manner that the client is asking for it.

NOTE It is true that the server application could instead look up the security information for the client, and then get the security information for the asked-for object, and see whether the client has the desired permissions that way. However, impersonation is the simpler and more foolproof method of doing this.

Here are the steps a server application might typically take to use client impersonation in implementing server-side security:

1. The client application establishes a connection with the server application.

2. The client application asks the server application for access to a particular object.

3. The server application uses `ImpersonateLoggedOnUser` to obtain an impersonated access token, which it then uses to attempt access in the same manner as the client application.

4. The server application reverts to its own access level, by making a call to `RevertToSelf`, so that it can be available to handle other clients' requests.

5. If the server application's access attempt succeeded, it passes back to the client either an actual handle to the requested object, or to some other prearranged proxy token by which the client application can refer to the requested object in future requests to the server application.

6. Each time the client application wants access (again) to a secured object, the server application should call `ImpersonateLoggedOnUser` again before accessing the object, to ensure that the client's access rights haven't changed during the interim. When the request is handled, the server application again calls `RevertToSelf`.

7. When the client disconnects from the server, the server application can delete the impersonated access token.

Here are some points to keep in mind about client impersonation:

- For private objects, the server and client must establish some consistent means of referring to desired objects. This could be done by using either a handle or token type, which the server assigns and keeps track of. Alternatively, it may be a string or whatever other protocol the server and client applications implement to refer to server-application–managed objects.

- For private objects whose security is being handled by the server application (as opposed to some other server application running on the same or another machine), it is still important to use `ImpersonateLoggedOnUser`, since in the course of handling the client's request, the server may need to open or access objects for which NT does have some level of built-in security assigned. By using impersonation through the entire request-handling section, the server application ensures that it won't inadvertently do something on the client's behalf that is explicitly restricted from that user.

Individual server threads (or processes) can each have a different impersonation access token assigned. This is necessary for permitting simultaneous services to multiple clients.

Checking Access Rights

Whenever an attempt is being made to access an NT-secured object, NT internally calls a function called `AccessCheck`, which compares the user's access token with the access rights contained in the requested object's SD. This either succeeds or fails. In the case of failure, the function that made the access request returns an `ERROR_ACCESS_DENIED` error (traditionally called an error #5, but always use the constant).

In the same way, server applications need to call `AccessCheck` whenever and wherever access to a server-application-protected object is being attempted. If you leave even one place in your code where the server can access an object on behalf of a client without calling `AccessCheck` (and heeding the results!), your server application's security can be compromised, so be careful! It greatly simplifies your implementation if you can make all access to a server-application–protected object occur in the same (one) place in your code.

A similar function, called `PrivilegeCheck`, is useful for checking for required privileges. Also, before calling the checking functions, you may need to create a rights mask containing the appropriate bits set for the requested access rights.

Creating a rights mask from specific or standard rights is simply a matter of ORing the desired rights (constants) together. For example:

```
dwDesiredRights = STANDARD_RIGHTS_EXECUTE | WRITE_OWNER;
```

sets the appropriate bits to allow `dwDesiredRights` to query for the program execution right and the right to change the object's owner. If you're using any generic rights, you must call `MapGenericMask` in order to convert any generic rights bits to appropriate specific or standard rights. Note that since `MapGenericMask` doesn't affect any nongeneric rights bits you may have set, it is safe to call `MapGenericMask` on any rights mask before using it.

Adding New Rights

In addition to the built-in, or predefined system rights that appear in NT's User Manager (or User Manager for Domains), you can create new rights of various types if your application requires them. Rights are stored in a bit field, so individual rights are checked using bit masks and constants.

There are three types of rights:

- **Standard rights:** Those where the assigned bit means the same, or approximately the same thing, across any objects that use them.

- **Specific rights:** Those which could use the same bit values in different objects, but mean different things for different objects. These are the type you would use to define some completely new right, which has not much in common with already existing (predefined) rights.

- **Generic rights:** Rights with very broad meanings, which can be interpreted somewhat differently by different applications. Generic rights can be mapped to specific and standard rights, where there is some similarity of meaning between the name of the general right, and the functionality being mapped to it.

Security-Related Commands

The security functions are grouped here in 12 categories:

Access token functions	Access-checking functions
Impersonation functions	Privileges functions
SD functions	Local Service Authority functions
SID functions	Security information functions
ACL functions	Window station functions
ACE functions	Auditing functions

Note that, in at least a few cases, functions may appear in more than one category, as is appropriate.

TIP

For information about each function's prototype (parameters), see the online help included with your compiler. The online help provides a comprehensive, alphabetized list of all these functions (they are not grouped in categories, as in this chapter). Click on a function to see its prototypes.

The security functions are one of the more complex areas of NT programming, particularly due to the non-object-orientedness of the implementation. Just creating one of the needed structures is usually a multiple-step process. However, security is an important area, and it should not be implemented less often simply because it's more trouble to do so.

The best strategy I can suggest for dealing with these security functions is to learn how they work, then either cut and paste from existing working code or (better yet) wrap up the relative complexity in a tidy object wrapper. You may find that writing an object wrapper for these functions is far preferable to needing to handle allocating and deallocating, initializing, recursing, changing, converting back and forth, and updating these structures.

Access Token Functions

The following are the access token functions:

- `AdjustTokenGroups`: Adjusts the groups in an access token.

- `AdjustTokenPrivileges`: Adjusts privileges for an access token.

- `DuplicateToken`: Creates a new access token identical to one supplied.

- `GetTokenInformation`: Returns user, group, privileges, and other information about a token.

- `SetThreadToken`: Assigns an impersonation token to a given thread.

- `SetTokenInformation`: Modifies user, group, privileges, or other information within a given access token.

- `OpenProcessToken`: Retrieves the access token for a given process.

- `OpenThreadToken`: Retrieves the access token for a given thread.

You retrieve a thread's or a process's access token, respectively, via `OpenProcessToken` or `OpenThreadToken`.

Note that `AdjustTokenGroups` and `AdjustTokenPrivileges` are the obvious "power functions" in this group.

One good use for the `DuplicateToken` function is when you might need to back out (cancel) changes that were just made to an access token. Simply create a copy before making the changes. Then, if necessary, you can use the copy as your backup to restore the token's previous settings.

Impersonation Functions

The following are the client impersonation functions:

- `CreateProcessAsUser`: Identical to `CreateProcess`, but creates the process for a given access token.

- `DdeImpersonateClient`: Allows a DDE server to impersonate a DDE client application, to make system accesses using the client's security.

- `ImpersonateLoggedOnUser`: Lets a calling thread impersonate a given user (takes an access token).

- `ImpersonateNamedPipeClient`: Allows the server end of a named pipe to impersonate the pipe client.

- `ImpersonateSelf`: Returns an access token impersonating that of the calling process (often used for changing access at a thread level).

- `LogonUser`: Allows a server application to acquire an access token for a given user, to use in impersonated access.

- `RevertToSelf`: Terminates the impersonation of a client application.

`LogonUser` isn't included in the online alphabetical list of security functions, but I think it belongs here. You can frequently use it in your server applications to ensure that requests you're fulfilling on the requesting user's behalf match the security settings assigned to that user.

You can log in as a particular user, receive an access token for that user, then use it with calls to `ImpersonateLoggedOnUser` to make your thread have the corresponding access rights for that user. New processes can be created in a similar way for another user by using `CreateProcessAsUser`.

To stop impersonation, use `RevertToSelf`. If you've created a process under a different user access token (with `CreateProcessAsUser`), you may want to use `ImpersonateSelf` instead, if you need to change the access rights for only a particular thread.

Security Descriptor (SD) Functions

The following are the SD functions:

- `MakeAbsoluteSD`: Creates an SD in absolute format, given one in relative format.

- `MakeSelfRelativeSD`: Creates an SD in self-relative format, given one in absolute format.

- `InitializeSecurityDescriptor`: Initializes a new SD for use. This defaults to no rights granted of any kind.

- `IsValidSecurityDescriptor`: Validates an SD by checking the revision level of each part of the SD.

- `GetSecurityDescriptorControl`: Retrieves an SD's control and revision information.

- `GetSecurityDescriptorLength`: Returns the size in bytes for a given SD.

- `GetSecurityDescriptorDacl`: Returns a pointer to the DACL for a given SD.

- `GetSecurityDescriptorGroup`: Returns a pointer to the primary Group SID for a given SD.

- `GetSecurityDescriptorOwner`: Returns a pointer to the owner SID for a given SD.

- `GetSecurityDescriptorSacl`: Returns a pointer to the SACL for a given SD.

- `SetSecurityDescriptorDacl`: Updates a given SD's DACL with new settings.

- `SetSecurityDescriptorGroup`: Updates a given SD's Group SID with new settings.

- `SetSecurityDescriptorOwner`: Updates a given SD's owner SID with new settings.

- `SetSecurityDescriptorSacl`: Updates a given SD's SACL with new settings.

After allocating memory for an SD, you'll need to call `InitializeSecurity-Descriptor` before you can use the SD. Note the `Get` and `Set` functions for the four main parts of each SD: the owner SID, group SID, SACL, and DACL.

Security Identifier (SID) Functions

The following are the SID functions:

- `AllocateAndInitializeSid`: Allocates and initializes an SID with up to eight subauthorities (groups or users).

- `AllocateLocallyUniqueId`: Allocates a locally unique identifier.

- `InitializeSid`: Initializes an SID structure with given number of subauthorities.

- `CopySid`: Returns copy of an SID to a buffer.

- `EqualPrefixSid`: Boolean test of two SIDs' prefix values for equality.

- `EqualSid`: Boolean test of two SIDs' values for equality.

- `FreeSid`: Boolean test of two SIDs' exact equality.

- `GetSidIdentifierAuthority`: Returns a pointer to an SID's top-level authority (in `SID_IDENTIFIER_AUTHORITY`).

- `GetSidLengthRequired`: Returns the length needed, in bytes, to store an SID with a given number of subauthorities.

- `GetSidSubAuthority`: Returns a pointer to the nth subauthority for a given SID.

- `GetSidSubAuthorityCount`: Returns the number of subauthorities in a given SID.

- `GetLengthSid`: Returns the length, in bytes, of a given SID.

- `IsValidSid`: Validates a given SID by verifying that the revision number is within a known range and that the number of subauthorities is below the maximum.

- `LookupAccountSid`: Returns the account name and first domain found for a given SID.

Note that with SIDs, you can allocate and initialize using a single function call. As with SDs, a newly allocated SID needs to be initialized before you can use it.

The `CopySid` function can be used, for example, to retrieve the SID from an access token, and then build a new ACE to be added to an object's DACL.

`EqualSid` is handy for comparing two SIDs.

Access Control List (ACL, DACL, and SACL) Functions

The following are the ACL, DACL, and SACL functions:

- `InitializeAcl`: Creates a new ACL structure.

- `GetAclInformation`: Retrieves information (such as the revision number, size, and ACE count) for a given ACL.

- `IsValidAcl`: Validates a given ACL by checking that the version number is correct, and that the number of ACEs matches the ACE count.

- `SetAclInformation`: Sets information about an ACL.

As explained earlier, ACLs contain all the "ands, buts, ors, and nors," which qualify access to an object for particular users and/or groups. Each entry in the list is an ACE (Access Control Entry). Don't forget to initialize your ACL after allocating and prior to using it.

Access Control Entry (ACE) Functions

The following are the ACE functions:

- `AddAce`: Adds one or more ACEs to a given ACL, at specified index position.

- `AddAccessAllowedAce`: Adds an access-allowed ACE to an ACL, thereby granting access for a particular SID.

- `AddAccessDeniedAce`: Adds an access-denied ACE to an ACL, thereby denying access for a particular SID.

- `AddAuditAccessAce`: Adds a system-audit ACE to an SACL.

- `DeleteAce`: Deletes the *n*th ACE from a given ACL.

- `FindFirstFreeAce`: Returns a pointer to the first free position in an ACL.

- `GetAce`: Returns a pointer to the *n*th ACE for a given ACL.

These functions operate on ACLs (both DACLs and SACLs), permitting you to add permissions or place restrictions as needed. Note that when calling `AddAce` or `DeleteAce`, you must supply an index parameter—the ordering of ACEs in an ACL *matters*. (For more details on ACE-ordering, see the discussion about this in the FileUser demo program, presented later in this chapter.)

The ordering of the ACEs in the list determines the order in which permissions and restrictions are checked. Because ACLs are simply lists of structures (and not some nice OOP collection), when you're adding a new ACE, you must first traverse the list, using `FindFirstFreeAce`, or else insert the ACE into the desired place in the list, using `AddAce`.

Functions for Checking Access

The following are the functions for checking access:

- `AccessCheck`: Used by a server application to check whether a client has access to an object.

- `AccessCheckAndAuditAlarm`: Performs `AccessCheck` and generates corresponding audit messages.

- `AreAllAccessesGranted`: Compares granted with desired rights to see whether *all* specified access rights have been granted.

- `AreAnyAccessesGranted`: Compares granted with desired rights to see whether *any* specified access rights have been granted.

- `PrivilegeCheck`: Tests whether the given access token contains the desired privilege(s).

- `PrivilegedServiceAuditAlarm`: Does `PrivilegeCheck` and generates corresponding audit messages.

- `MapGenericMask`: Maps generic access rights to specific and standard access rights.

`AccessCheck` and `PrivilegeCheck` are the two main functions used for checking whether a given user token has the requested rights or privileges, respectively.

Use `MapGenericMask` to convert generic access rights to rights that apply more specifically to the given object.

NOTE   The `AuditAlarm` functions may not actually generate auditing information on earlier versions of NT.

Keep in mind that overhead (extra time) attaches to each object access while auditing of that object is enabled. How much overhead this incurs depends primarily on how often you will need to access the object. For infrequent access, the auditing overhead isn't a problem, but when you're performing very frequent operations on an object, the overhead required for auditing can noticeably impact performance. The best approach is to test your application with and without auditing enabled, to ensure that with the auditing overhead, performance is still within an acceptable range.

Privileges Functions

The following are the privileges functions:

- `MapGenericMask`: Maps generic access rights of a given mask to specific and standard access rights.

- `PrivilegeCheck`: Tests whether a given access token has the specified privilege(s).

- `LookupPrivilegeDisplayName`: Retrieves the displayable name associated with a particular privilege.

- `LookupPrivilegeName`: Returns the privilege name associated with the given locally unique identifier (LUID).

- `LookupPrivilegeValue`: Returns the LUID associated with a given privilege on a given system.

- `ObjectPrivilegeAuditAlarm`: Generates audit messages when the given user (access token) attempts to perform privileged operations on a particular object.

- `PrivilegedServiceAuditAlarm`: Generates audit messages when the given user (access token) attempts to perform privileged operations.

The two most frequently used functions in this group are `MapGenericMask` and `PrivilegeCheck`.

Note that prior to using `LookupPrivilegeName`, you would need to call `LookupPrivilegeValue`, to obtain the LUID for the privilege. The LUID will (by definition) be completely different from one machine to the next, even though the name of the privilege may be identical to a privilege on another system, so be sure to specify the correct server name when getting the LUID.

Local Service Authority (LSA) Functions

The following are the special LSA functions:

- `InitLsaString`: Creates an `LSA_UNICODE_STRING` for the given privilege name.

- `LsaOpenPolicy`: Opens (or creates) a given policy on target machine.

- `LsaLookupNames`: Returns the account name (and SID) for the given access token.

- `LsaRemoveAccountRights`: Revokes privileges for the specified user(s).

- `LsaAddAccountRights`: Grants privileges to the specified user(s).

- `LsaClose`: Closes a given policy.

- `LsaEnumerateAccountRights`: Enumerates rights or privileges that are currently granted to a given account.

- `LsaEnumerateAccountsWithUserRight`: Enumerates all accounts on a given system that have been granted a given privilege.

These and other LSA functions appear to be part of a larger API category that will be called the Win32 Licensing API (still in beta).

Note that `LsaAddAccountRights` can be used to create a new policy (by name) on a given machine. Currently, these functions support Unicode only. They are supplied via NT's LSAPI32.DLL.

Security Information Functions

The following are the functions that get and set security information:

- `GetFileSecurity`: Obtains the SD for a particular file or directory.

- `GetKernelObjectSecurity`: Obtains the SD for a specified Kernel object.

- `GetPrivateObjectSecurity`: Obtains the SD for a specified private object.

- `GetUserObjectSecurity`: Obtains the SD for a specified user object.

- `SetFileSecurity`: Updates a file or directory's security using the supplied SD.

- `SetKernelObjectSecurity`: Updates a Kernel object's security using the supplied SD.

- `SetPrivateObjectSecurity`: Updates a private object's security using the supplied SD.

- `SetUserObjectSecurity`: Updates a user object's security using the supplied SD.

- `CreatePrivateObjectSecurity`: Allocates and initializes a self-relative SD to be used with a new private object.

- `DestroyPrivateObjectSecurity`: Deletes the given private object's SD.

These functions are the essential tools for getting and setting (changing) the SDs for secured objects.

Note the functions for *private* object security. These are what you'll need whenever you wish to create security restrictions for accessing some object (or class of objects) that your application defines. Don't confuse private objects with user objects, which are simply NT-secured objects created by a user, such as a file that the user has created.

Window Station Functions

A *window station* is a set of one or more Desktops. NT's default window station is WinSta0. A *Desktop* in this context can be thought of as a set of visible windows. The default WinSta0 window station, for example, has three Desktops: logon, screen saver, and application. The SwitchDesktop API function allows you to make a different Desktop visible.

The most typical use of the Desktop functions is when you're writing a service that needs to access a user Desktop in order to visually interact with the user to obtain some input. It comes as no surprise that window stations are another instance of NT system objects that are protected by NT's built-in security. So, to access a particular window station requires appropriate access rights.

There are two window station functions:

- GetProcessWindowStation: Returns a handle to the window station associated with the calling process.

- SetProcessWindowStation: Assigns a given window station to the calling process.

These functions enable a process to access the objects of a particular window station. These objects include a Desktop (containing Desktop objects), a clipboard, and a list of global atoms. (The *global atom table* is a table of up to 37 system-unique strings, typically used to store user-defined clipboard format or message names.)

Auditing Functions

The following are the auditing functions:

- ObjectOpenAuditAlarm: Generates audit messages to log when a user attempts to gain access to an existing object or create a new one.

- ObjectCloseAuditAlarm: Generates audit messages when the handle of an object is closed.

- ObjectDeleteAuditAlarm: Generates audit messages when the handle of an object is deleted.

- ObjectPrivilegeAuditAlarm: Generates audit messages when the given user (access token) attempts to perform privileged operations on a particular object.

- PrivilegedServiceAuditAlarm: Generates audit messages when the given user (access token) attempts to perform privileged operations.

- `AccessCheckAndAuditAlarm`: Performs `AccessCheck` and generates corresponding audit messages.

These functions cause audit messages to be generated whenever the specified type of access is attempted. If you use audit alarms, you should keep in mind that some overhead is added to each object access operation while logging is enabled. Again, for less frequent object access, this isn't a problem. If your application needs to frequently access an audited object, you should experiment with enabling and disabling auditing to determine to what extent auditing will impact your application's performance.

Checking and Updating SDs: The FileUser Program

Our first demo program in this chapter shows how to get a file's current SD, and then update it by adding either an `AccessAllowed` ACE or an `AccessDenied` ACE for a given user. To keep this example simple, we're using a command-line, Win32 console application. The program expects a filename, a user name, and a + (plus sign, specifying access allowed) or – (minus sign, specifying access denied) to be passed from the command line.

The complete source code for this program is available on the accompanying CD.

You'll notice that the only function other than the `main` function in the program is the `Check` function, which simply checks for FALSE return values and displays any resulting errors by calling `GetLastError` and `FormatMessage`. Although this obviously isn't sufficient error handling for shipping software, it works for this simple example.

Allocating Memory for SDs

After checking command-line parameters, the first thing our program does is allocate memory for two SDs. We will use one of these to retrieve the file's current SD. We'll use the other to build the new SD, containing the contents of the current SD plus our new ACE, which we'll be adding to the DACL. This is straightforward:

```
pFileSD     = malloc( FILE_SD_SIZE );
pNewFileSD  = malloc( FILE_SD_SIZE );
```

Note that there are different constants defined for different types of SDs. In this case, we want to use the type `FILE_SD_SIZE`, since we'll be dealing with an SD for a file.

Next, we set a flag, which we'll use shortly to determine which type of ACE to add (an `AccessAllowed` or `AccessDenied` type), based on whether the user enters a + (to allow), or a – (to deny).

```
bAllowAccess = (argv[3][0] == '+');
```

Retrieving the SID

Our next step is to retrieve the SID for the account name specified on the command line (`argv[2]`). Note that we're asking for an `SID_NAME_USE` SID type, because `SIDType` was defined as:

```
SID_NAME_USE           SIDType;
```

`LookupAccountName` will perform a search for the user name on the current server or domain, and if successful, will return the following:

- The domain name (in `szDomainName`) where the user was found

- The length of the domain name returned (in `dwDomainLength`)

- The user's SID (in `UserSID`)

We've defined `UserSID` as a 2KB buffer, which should be enough except in very rare cases.

```
// get the SID of the user (or group)
   Check( LookupAccountName((LPSTR) NULL, argv[2], UserSID,
   dwSIDLength, szDomainName, &dwDomainLength, &SIDType ),
   "LookupAccountName");
```

Getting the File's SD

Next, we need to get the SD for the file. This is done by calling `GetFileSecurity`. If successful, this function will copy the file's SD to `pFileSD`, as well as give us additional security information in `SecInfo`, which is of type `SECURITY_INFORMATION`.

```
// get the file's current SD
   Check( GetFileSecurity(argv[1], SecInfo, pFileSD, dwFileSDLength,
   &dwLengthNeeded ), "GetFileSecurity");
```

Although we've allocated `pNewFileSD`, we have yet to initialize it. This is done next, by calling `InitializeSecurityDescriptor`. The `SECURITY_DESCRIPTOR_REVISION` is defined by the Win32 API, and you should always use it when initializing new SDs. This ensures that the SD will contain the current version number, so that validation functions can work correctly.

```
// initialize a new SD (larger to hold the new user's SID)
Check( InitializeSecurityDescriptor( pNewFileSD,
    SECURITY_DESCRIPTOR_REVISION ),
    "InitializeSecurityDescriptor");
```

We now have a new, valid file SD. Since it's currently empty, we need to copy information from the current file SD and add our new user ACE, before setting this new `pNewFileSD` back as the file's SD. Note that if we were to set this SD "as-is" to the file, no one would have access to the file, since an empty SD means no access rights have been granted. Remember, empty = no; NULL = yes, when it comes to SDs.

Working with the DACL

The next thing we need to do is get the file's current DACL (if it has one). We need the DACL to copy all the ACE entries from it into `pNewFileSD`. This is accomplished using `GetSecurityDescriptorDacl`.

If there is a DACL in `pFileSD`, this function will load `pFileDACL` with the current DACL and set our `bContainsDACL` flag to TRUE. If there isn't a DACL, `bContainsDACL` will be set to FALSE. Also, the flag `bDefaultedDACL` will be set to FALSE if the current DACL was set explicitly by a user, or TRUE if the DACL came from a default DACL source.

```
// get the file's DACL (from the SD)
    Check( GetSecurityDescriptorDacl( pFileSD, &bContainsDACL,
    &pFileDACL, &bDefaultedDACL ),"GetSecurityDescriptorDacl");
```

If we retrieved a DACL, we next need to determine its size, so we can use the size to create a new (and larger) DACL to add our ACE to. `GetAclInformation` fills in our `ACLSizeInfo` structure. Note that we are passing the size of our structure (which is of type `ACL_SIZE_INFORMATION`), and are specifying the `AclSizeInformation` enumerated type, to tell `GetAclInformation` that the information we need is the ACL size.

```
// if file currently has a DACL, get the ACL size info
if (bContainsDACL)
```

```
Check( GetAclInformation( pFileDACL, &ACLSizeInfo,
      sizeof(ACL_SIZE_INFORMATION), AclSizeInformation),
      "GetAclInformation" );
```

Now, we need to calculate the correct size for our new DACL, based on the size of the current DACL plus the new space we'll need for one new ACE. We use the AclSizeInformation enumerated type to tell GetAclInformation that the information we need is the ACL size. AclInfo.AclSizeBytesInUse tells us the current DACL's size.

We'll need to add enough space for either an ACCESS_ALLOWED_ACE or an ACCESS_DENIED_ACE (depending on our bAllowAccess flag). We'll also need to add space for our new user's SID. Finally, we subtract sizeof(DWORD) bytes from our total, which NT evidently adds for a terminating code at the end of a self-relative DACL (and we don't need this counted twice).

```
// calculate size we'll need for current ACL, plus new ACE
dwNewACLSize = ACLSizeInfo.AclBytesInUse + (bAllowAccess?
    sizeof( ACCESS_ALLOWED_ACE ) : sizeof( ACCESS_DENIED_ACE ))
    + GetLengthSid( UserSID ) - sizeof( DWORD );
```

Now that we have calculated the size, we can go ahead and allocate our new DACL.

```
// allocate and initialize new ACL
pNewFileDACL = (PACL) malloc( dwNewACLSize );
```

We now have a pointer to the right amount of memory for a DACL, but it's not really a DACL until we initialize it. Again, don't forget to initialize these structures after allocating!

```
Check( InitializeAcl( pNewFileDACL, dwNewACLSize,
      ACL_REVISION2 ),   "InitializeAcl");
```

For educational purposes, we next call IsValidAcl to make sure that we have a valid DACL. At this point, it should certainly be valid, since there's nothing to it except the revision information.

```
// Verify we've set up our DACL correctly
Check( IsValidAcl( pNewFileDACL ), "IsValidAcl");
```

Adding ACEs

Now, we come to a decision point. If the new ACE we're adding is an ACCESS_DENIED_ACE, we need to add this ACE to the new DACL before copying over all the other ACEs. On the other hand, if we are adding an ACCESS_ALLOWED_ACE, we can wait and add this ACE at the end of the list of other ACEs.

Why does it matter if we add our ACE to the start or end of the list of ACEs? Because of how NT checks the ACLs, ACCESS_DENIED_ACE items should be placed *before* any ACCESS_ALLOWED_ACE items in the list. Otherwise, it's likely that your ACCESS_DENIED_ACE will be ignored, since NT will stop checking if it finds an explicit ACCESS_ALLOWED_ACE first.

So, if we're adding an ACCESS_DENIED_ACE, we need to add it now, before adding the other ACEs to the new DACL.

```
// if DENYING access rights, place new ACE first in new DACL
if (!bAllowAccess)
Check( AddAccessDeniedAce( pNewFileDACL, ACL_REVISION2,
     GENERIC_READ, &UserSID ), "AddAccessDeniedAce");
```

Note that we are specifying GENERIC_READ as the right being allowed or denied. You could experiment by changing this to GENERIC_WRITE (or adding another command-line switch to set the file access) to allow or deny write access to the file.

Next, we need to loop through the current DACL's list of ACEs, copying each in turn to our new DACL. If ACLSizeInfo.AceCount was 0, we can skip this step, because there aren't any ACEs to copy. Each time through the loop, we call GetAce, which fills in our pTempACE pointer with the indexed-to ACE. (Yes, the ACE index is zero-based.) Then, we call AddAce to add the ACE to our pNewFileDACL. Note that we're taking care again to use the current ACL revision number (ACL_REVISION).

```
// copy each existing ACE (if any) over to the new DACL
if (bContainsDACL) { // if current file SD contains a DACL...
   if (ACLSizeInfo.AceCount > 0) { // and if the DACL has any ACEs
   // for each ACE, copy it to our new file DACL
   for (iAceNum=0; iAceNum<ACLSizeInfo.AceCount; iAceNum++) {
      // read ACE from current ACL, write to new ACL
      Check( GetAce(pFileDACL,iAceNum, &pTempACE ), "GetAce");
      Check( AddAce( pNewFileDACL, ACL_REVISION, MAXDWORD,
         pTempACE,((PACE_HEADER) pTempACE)->AceSize ),"AddAce");
      }
   }
}
```

After adding any existing DACLs, we should add the `ACCESS_ALLOWED_ACE`, if that's the type we're adding. Remember, access-denied ACEs should go at the start of the list; access-granted ACEs go at the end.

```
// if GRANTING access rights, add new ACE here at end of the list
    if (bAllowAccess)
        Check( AddAccessAllowedAce( pNewFileDACL, ACL_REVISION2,
            GENERIC_READ, &UserSID ), "AddAccessAllowedAce");
```

Now that we've added all the ACEs we need to our new file DACL, our next step is to set this ACE list to our new file descriptor (`pNewFileSD`). This is done with a call to `SetSecurityDescriptorDacl`. The first Boolean value says that yes, we have a DACL to use, and the second Boolean indicates no, our DACL wasn't arrived at by a default mechanism.

```
// set the new DACL to the new SD
Check( SetSecurityDescriptorDacl( pNewFileSD, TRUE, pNewFileDACL,
    FALSE ), "SetSecurityDescriptorAcl");
```

Setting the New SD

Finally, the time has come to write out our new file SD for the file. The new SD gets set to the file by a call to `SetFileSecurity`, with a `DACL_SECURITY_INFORMATION` flag. This means that we want only the DACL updates, and not any of the other security information (the group and owner SIDs and the SACL).

```
// set our new SD to the object
Check( SetFileSecurity( argv[1], DACL_SECURITY_INFORMATION,
    pNewFileSD ), "SetFileSecurity");
```

> **NOTE**
>
> If we wanted to update the SACL, or owner or group SIDs, we could do this as well. However, setting the SACL would require that we run this program using system-level access; setting the owner or group SIDs would require choosing whether to replace the currently existing user(s) or add our user to them. In the case of the owner SID, we would need to have the right assigned to change the file's ownership as well. As it is, to successfully run this program requires that we have owner access to set the DACL.

The only thing left to do in our code is to clean up, by deallocating the `pNewFile-DACL`, the `pNewFileSD`, and the `pFileSD`, which we allocated earlier.

```
// finally, clean up, prepare to leave
free( pNewFileDACL );
free( pNewFileSD );
free( pFileSD );

return(0);
}
```

This example should give you some understanding of how security is set or modified on an object. You can experiment and modify this sample program to allow no access rights or all access rights, or to change ownership of the file. By changing the DACL type, you can also use this code to modify the security on other types of objects.

Now that we have looked at how data objects (or functionality) can be secured on an NT server application by using the security functions built into NT, we will look at another, complementary approach to securing information: the use of encryption.

Encryption Technology Concepts

Individual packets of data that traverse a network can be intercepted or monitored by anyone who can access the packets at any point along their path from sender to receiver. This means that if you want to exchange data securely over an insecure network, you need to use some form of encryption.

Cryptography is possible without a computer, but most often the information to be encrypted originates (or at least ends up at some point) in machine-readable form—a word processing document, ASCII, EBCDIC, or some other standard computer format. Thus, computers have given rise to the means by which information is most often encrypted, and have also provided a huge and growing population of potential users of encryption.

Secure Communications and the Government

As an interesting conversation topic, one could make the observation that anytime there is competition, the securing and protecting of information becomes an essential strategy. Historically, codes and ciphers were put to use both in commerce and warfare, with governments being the key users (pun intended!) of the information-securing technology of the time. It is only to be expected that governments worldwide would continue to have an active interest in the use (and abuse) of data-securing techniques. Combine that with the fact we're now living in the "information age," particularly with the increasing "Internetization" of all sectors of information, and we find an unprecedented interest in, and growing need for, data-encryption technology by both governments and citizens alike.

At the government level, we find in the United States, for example, that current federal laws categorize most effective encryption technology as *munitions*, making it a felony to export at least the more sophisticated types of data encryption to other countries. France, on the other hand, takes the opposite approach of outlawing the *import* of any encryption technology into France. This is only one good reason why NT's CryptoAPI supports optional use of encryption in a modular framework, permitting third-party encryption provider companies to supply customers with installable encryption algorithms. (The French version of Windows NT, by the way, has no support for built-in encryption.) Even more controversial now in the United States is the government's expressed desire to be "caretaker" of encryption technology (with the Clipper III project and its successors).

It remains to be seen how the tension in various countries between governments and their citizens, in the use of data encryption, plays itself out. Certainly there are important conflicting needs (the maintaining of law and order versus rights to privacy, for example), which will require some sort of ongoing one-legged balancing act.

Meanwhile, because both computers and software continue to grow rapidly in power and sophistication (despite our perennial gripes about bugs and delayed ship dates), it seems certain that any given data-encryption technique is only good for some limited period of time, until a way is found to crack it. Leaving aside the rather philosophical question of whether it is possible to devise unbreakable encryption schemes, I believe one can take the reasonable view that encryption, when used carefully, will generally work for most people's needs, most of the time. At some point soon, various levels of encryption will become ubiquitous in the world of digital information.

Do You Need Encryption?

There are certain costs involved in implementing and using encryption—in terms of development time, the degree to which data throughput is affected, increased complexity for users, and so on. Therefore, the decision of whether or not to use encryption isn't necessarily a "no-brainer."

Here are some pertinent questions you may wish to use as starting points in evaluating whether to use encryption:

- Is this data really worth encrypting?

- How many people need to have access to this information?

- How quickly will the information become outdated (and therefore less sensitive)?

- What do you consider an acceptable level of risk (of information compromise)?

- If the data needs to be exchanged across a network, how secure is the network itself?

- What are the possible repercussions of your secured data falling into the wrong hands (what's the worst that could happen)?

- How valuable (in terms of time, money, or other values) is this information to you?

- How valuable (in the same, or other terms) could this information be to someone else?

- What costs are involved, both in implementing and in using the desired encryption technology?

These are your considerations for the present. As software development tools progress, encryption objects will make built-in support for encryption become almost trivial. End users will find encryption becoming easier to use and more integrated into their software.

Remaining issues regarding encryption costs will probably center more around the degree to which encryption impairs data throughput over networks. With current technology, the degree to which throughput is affected varies from little or negligible impact to extremely significant (factors of a thousand or more times slower than without in some cases!), with the primary determinant being the complexity (and presumably the effectiveness) of the algorithm being used. It will be interesting to see whether using faster computers solves this problem or just elevates it to another level. (I would bet on the latter, since faster computers mean faster ways to attack the algorithms as well.)

Encryption Methods

In recent years, many advances have been made in cryptographic technology and various approaches have been taken. The different approaches achieve varying levels of strength against cracking and incur trade-offs.

Public-Key Encryption

One type of encryption that is quite popular because of its strength and other features is *public-key* encryption.

Public-key encryption involves each party having two keys: one that is kept private to everyone but the owner, and another that can be made very public. This other key can be placed on Web pages, sent in an e-mail message, given out on floppy disks, and so on. Messages (or data) are then encrypted using the private key of the sender plus the public key of the intended recipient. On the other end, the data can only be successfully decrypted using the opposite pair of the sender's public key combined with the recipient's private key.

This type of encryption achieves its high level of security at the expense of speed. It takes several orders of magnitude longer to encrypt and decrypt using public-key technology than using certain other forms of encryption algorithms. This is because public-key encryption usually involves much more bit-crunching to encrypt a given amount of plain text, as compared to symmetric-key encryption, for example.

Digital Signatures and Authentication

The public-key approach provides a second, built-in feature, which is arguably just as important as encryption itself: the ability to "sign" encrypted data in such a way that the recipient can be certain that the decrypted message actually came from the individual whose public key was used in decrypting.

Because two keys are always used, it would be necessary for someone to steal one or the other private key before the thief could "forge" a public-key encrypted message that decrypts successfully using the recipient's private key. Moreover, it is also possible to use the same encryption techniques to get the signature or "verified sender" benefit without needing to encrypt the information. This becomes useful in situations where neither party cares whether the information conveyed is made public. They are only interested in whether the message originated from whom it claims to, and whether the message was altered (accidentally or intentionally) while in transit.

Symmetric-Key Encryption

Another popular form of encryption, called *symmetric-key* encryption, requires using the same key for both encrypting and decrypting. Obviously, this works only if the key used remains undisclosed to anyone but the sender and recipient.

This technique, while not as secure as public-key encryption, is significantly faster in operation—as much as a thousand or more times faster—than using the public-key technology. A disadvantage of the symmetric-key approach is that it requires that the key also be conveyed somehow from sender to recipient.

Combining Public- and Symmetric-Key Encryption

Because, on the one hand, public-key algorithms provide extreme security (plus signatures) at the expense of speed, and symmetric-key algorithms provide speed at the expense of somewhat weaker security, another common approach is to use a combination of both techniques.

A symmetric encryption algorithm is used to encrypt the main body of plain text (or data), and then the symmetric key is encrypted using the stronger but slower public-key encryption. This public-key–encrypted symmetric key can then be safely included along with the body of encrypted text (ciphertext), and allows the symmetric key to be retrieved by the recipient (or recipients) whose public keys were used to encrypt the sender's symmetric key. This combines the benefits of faster encryption for the bulk of the information, with stronger encryption to safeguard the enclosed symmetric key, and also provides the benefit of a digital signature.

In order to safely include a key along with encrypted data, the key itself must be encrypted. The CryptoAPI permits doing this by built-in functionality that can export the encrypted key for you. This encrypted key is called a *key blob*.

Encryption Algorithm Operations

Certain encryption algorithms are designed to operate on streams of data. They take the data a character at a time, and output encrypted data at the same rate. *Block-encryption* algorithms, on the other hand, are designed to encrypt chunks or blocks of data all together. Generally, block encryption is viewed as being somewhat more secure. When this type of algorithm is used, the final block of data will rarely fill the entire block, so padding bytes are usually added to the final block.

Many encryption algorithms generate a residual, or *hash*, value that is continually combined with the current data, producing a new hash, which is again combined with the current hash. A hash value of a certain number of bits is generated by applying some encryption-like algorithm to the data, so that the resulting hash value will be different if even one bit of the source data is lost or tampered with. Obviously, the longer the hash value, the lower the odds are of a hash value equaling another hash value produced from a tampered-with file.

Hashing can be used either by itself or along with encryption. In either case, it provides a value that can be used for digital signing and for error- and tamper-proofing a chunk of data.

NOTE   Virus checkers frequently use a form of hashing on executable files, to determine whether the file has been tampered with. Java code, ActiveX controls, and other software downloaded from the Internet may be subject to similar verification techniques.

Hashing is also used to help ensure that repetitious data does not result in an encryption process producing identical blocks of encrypted data. You do *not* want repetition to show up in the encrypted data, because this can provide enough information to a hacker to completely recover your encryption key. In fact, because of this, some algorithms also allow you to "seed" the hash algorithm periodically by supplying additional random bits, which are incorporated into the encryption algorithm to further scramble the output. These *salt* values, or *salt bits*, as they are called, can be thought of as additional key information, which, like a key, must also be available for successful decrypting.

The CryptoAPI and Cryptographic Service Providers

In recent years, many companies, individuals, and government institutions have devised their own algorithms based on variations of the public-key and symmetric-key approaches. At least for now, the stronger candidates among these methods are quite secure indeed. One remaining problem of using encryption generally has been a lack of standards. Not only are the algorithms used very different, but even with the same published algorithm, software implementations done by different people can result in incompatible encrypted output.

Initiatives such as Microsoft's new CryptoAPI are exciting in their potential, because their modular design addresses the problem of encryption standards. With the CryptoAPI, users can install any third-party cryptographic algorithms as simply as they install a new printer driver. Programmers are free to concentrate on building applications that can make use of whichever algorithms are chosen by the users (subject to certain restrictions, such as the applicability of the algorithm to encryption of streaming versus blocks of data, or key-only types of encryption algorithms).

A *cryptographic service provider* (CSP) is any agency that offers an algorithm, or a set of algorithms, that correspond to the CryptoAPI interface. Through this interface, application software is able to make use of encryption algorithms by selecting them at runtime.

The CryptoAPI Functions

The Microsoft RSA Base Provider (which comes with the CryptoAPI and provides a default Cryptographic Service Provider set of functionality) consists of a software implementation of the PROV_RSA_FULL provider type. The RSA public-key cipher is used for both key exchange and digital signatures, with a key length of

512 bits. The RC2 and RC4 encryption algorithms are implemented with a key length of 40 bits. The MD2, MD5, and SHA hashing algorithms are also provided.

The following sections describe the CryptoAPI functions, grouped in four categories:

- CSP (cryptographic service provider) functions
- Key functions
- Encryption functions
- Hashing functions

More detailed information about each function's parameters and usage is available in the CryptoAPI documentation file, which ships with the CryptoAPI SDK.

CSP Functions

The following are the CSP functions:

- `CryptAcquireContext`: Acquires a handle to the current user's key container within a particular CSP.

- `CryptGetProvParam`: Retrieves attributes of a CSP.

- `CryptReleaseContext`: Releases the handle acquired by `CryptAcquire-Context`.

- `CryptSetProvider`: Specifies the user default CSP for a particular CSP type.

- `CryptSetProvParam`: Specifies attributes of a CSP.

You can consider `CryptAcquireContext` and `CryptReleaseContext` as two bookend functions, which need to go at the start and end, respectively, of the code in your applications that use any of the CryptoAPI functions. Note that `CryptAcquireContext` can be called with a NULL value for the CSP, which results in the default CSP for the current user being used.

Key Functions

The following are the key functions:

- `CryptDestroyKey`: Destroys a given key.

- `CryptExportKey`: Converts a key from the CSP into a key blob that can be safely shared or saved to disk.

- `CryptGenRandom`: Generates some random data. (Used for salt bits.)
- `CryptGetKeyParam`: Retrieves the parameters for a given key.
- `CryptGetUserKey`: Retrieves a handle to an exchange key or a signature key.
- `CryptImportKey`: Converts a key blob into a key usable by a CSP.
- `CryptSetKeyParam`: Sets the parameters for a key.

`CryptGenRandom` is very useful for coming up with keys to be used with symmetric-key algorithms. Remember that you need to save your generated keys somewhere; saving is not done for you automatically. The proper way to save a key is to create an exportable version of it using `CryptExportKey`, then use `CryptImportKey` when you need to read it back from disk.

Encryption Functions

There are two encryption functions:

- `CryptEncrypt`: Encrypts a block or stream of data using the specified encryption key.
- `CryptDecrypt`: Decrypts a block or stream of data using the specified encryption key.

These two functions are the CryptoAPI star players. They perform encryption or decryption using the specified algorithm on a data block or stream.

Hashing Functions

The following are the hashing functions:

- `CryptCreateHash`: Creates an empty hash object.
- `CryptDestroyHash`: Destroys a hash object.
- `CryptGetHashParam`: Retrieves a parameter from a hash object.
- `CryptHashData`: Hashes a block of data and includes the result in a specified hash object.
- `CryptHashSessionKey`: Hashes a session key and includes the result in a specified hash object.
- `CryptSetHashParam`: Sets a parameter of a given hash object.

- `CryptSignHash`: Signs the specified hash object.

- `CryptVerifySignature`: Verifies the digital signature from a signed hash object.

Hashing can be used for verifying both that received data is from an authentic source, and that it hasn't been tampered with. The odds of two different chunks of data randomly happening to have the same hash value is so small as to be *almost* impossible. `CryptHashSessionKey` and `CryptHashData` are useful for creating hashes of keys or data, respectively.

`CryptSignHash` and `CryptVerifySignature` can be used on either end to add a signature to the hash, or to verify that a signature "squares" with a hash value.

Adding Encryption Support to Applications

Our next two sample programs demonstrate how simple the CryptoAPI can make the project of adding support for encryption to your applications. Both programs work fine with Windows 95 as well as NT. But before you can try them out, you need to make sure your system is configured properly to use the CryptoAPI functions.

Getting Started

Because the CryptoAPI is relatively new, before you can use it, you will probably need to do each of the following steps:

- Obtain and install the CryptoAPI SDK.

- Obtain or build import libraries for your compiler.

- Install the CryptoAPI runtime support on the system you will be using.

- Install or create a default CSP and default keys.

Let's take each of these in order.

Obtaining the CryptoAPI SDK

You can get the CryptoAPI SDK either by free download from the Internet (at Microsoft's developer pages) or from the latest MSDN (Microsoft Developer Network) CD-ROM. Or, if you have a very recent compiler, the (Wincrypt.H) header file, help files, and library files may already be included.

Obtaining Import Libraries

Unless you're working with a very recent compiler, you will also need to come up with import libraries (or import units, if you're using Delphi) for the CryptoAPI functions. If you're lucky, your compiler vendor will have made a set of import libraries/units available on its BBS or Web site.

For Microsoft compilers, the import library will be available as part of the CryptoAPI SDK. For Borland C/C++ compilers, it's a simple matter to create import libraries using Implib.EXE. (Simply run `implib dllname`.)

For Delphi/Borland Pascal, you'll need to create an import unit, which is simply a Pascal unit that has function prototypes specified (in Pascal), along with an implementation section that simply specifies which DLL each function is exported from. If you need an example of an import library, see the Delphi Windows import units, which show how this is done.

Installing the CryptoAPI Runtime Support

With future versions of Windows 95 and NT, Crypto support will be built in. But for now, if you write any software that uses the CryptoAPI, you'll need to include the Crypto runtime or make sure that it gets installed on your target systems.

To install the CryptoAPI runtime support, you currently have two options:

- Install Microsoft's Internet Explorer 3.0, which makes use of, and therefore installs, the CryptoAPI.

- Run the Setup applet that comes with the CryptoAPI SDK.

Creating a Default CSP

If you are installing the Crypto runtime, chances are you will also need to create a default CSP and a set of default keys as well, before you can make use of the new API functions. Fortunately, the CryptoAPI SDK comes with a sample applet which, when run, installs these for you. (Look for a file called Inituser.C.)

If you've done all these steps, you should now be ready to begin using the CryptoAPI. The following two programs should get you started.

> **WARNING**
>
> At the time of this writing, CryptoAPI version 2.0 is in public beta, and the examples included here will work with beta version 2.0 (and are backward compatible with CryptoAPI version 1.0). But it's possible you may need to make (minor) changes for these examples to work with the released version CryptoAPI 2.0 or later. Also, since the CryptoAPI is currently in an evolutionary phase (a state of flux), it won't hurt to check out Microsoft's Web pages to be sure there is not a more recent version of the CryptoAPI to download.

Encrypting a File: The Encrypt Program

The Encrypt program shows how to encrypt a file (passed on the command line) using the RC2 block-type encryption (which is one of the algorithms supplied with the CryptoAPI runtime). It demonstrates getting the default user's exchange key, generating an encrypted key, making an exportable key blob, and writing this to disk. Finally, the data from an input file is encrypted and written to an output file.

Let's begin with the #define and #includes.

```
#define _WIN32_WINNT 0x0400
#include <windows.h>
#include <wincrypt.h>
#include <stdio.h>
```

The first thing to note is that we have _WIN32_WINNT defined as 0x0400, for Windows NT version 4.0. The beta Crypto documentation currently incorrectly states that this should be used only for applications running on NT. In fact, it is also necessary for creating Crypto applications that run on Windows 95.

Also note that you'll need to include the Wincrypt.H header file to access the Crypto functions from your C or C++ program. Delphi users may want to check in with Borland; there may be a WINCRYPT import unit available by the time you are reading this. Otherwise, it should not be too hard to write one.

Next, we define the constants we'll use to allocate the two buffers for raw and encrypted data.

```
const IN_BUFFER_SIZE    = 2048;
const OUT_BUFFER_SIZE   = IN_BUFFER_SIZE + 64; // extra padding
```

Note that the OUT_BUFFER_SIZE is slightly larger than the input buffer. This is necessary because the encrypted data could end up being, at most, one encryption block size larger than the data supplied by the input buffer.

Next, we have the main program declaration, followed by our set of variables.

```
int __cdecl main(int argc, char * argv[])
{
    HANDLE      hInFile, hOutFile;
    BYTE            pbBuffer[OUT_BUFFER_SIZE];
```

Note that because CryptEncrypt actually encrypts the data in place, we need only a single buffer (pbBuffer), which we can use both for reading the data in and for encrypting.

Here are the rest of our declared variables:

```
BOOL        finished;
HCRYPTPROV  hProvider = 0;
HCRYPTKEY   hKey = 0, hExchangeKey = 0;
DWORD           dwByteCount, dwBytesWritten;
```

We'll need a handle to a CSP (HCRYPTPROV), and one or more handles to Crypto keys (HCRYPTKEY).

In this example, we'll need two keys: an exchange key and an exportable key. The encryption function, plus ReadFile and WriteFile, will make use of the dwByteCount and dwBytesWritten variables.

Next, if the user hasn't supplied the correct number of parameters, we show a usage message and exit.

```
if (argc != 3) {
    printf("Usage: ENCRYPT infile outfile\n");
    exit(0);
}
```

Now, we're ready to begin the actual steps of the file encryption. The first thing we need to do is retrieve a handle to our default CSP. Specifying NULL rather than an explicit CSP causes the current user's default CSP to be used.

```
    // Get handle for the default provider (use RSA encryption)
    CryptAcquireContext(&hProvider, NULL, NULL,
        PROV_RSA_FULL, 0);
```

Our next step is to open both the input and output files.

```
// Open infile and create outfile
hInFile = CreateFile(argv[1], GENERIC_READ, FILE_SHARE_READ,
    NULL, OPEN_EXISTING, FILE_ATTRIBUTE_NORMAL, NULL);
hOutFile = CreateFile(argv[2], GENERIC_WRITE, FILE_SHARE_READ,
    NULL, CREATE_ALWAYS, FILE_ATTRIBUTE_NORMAL, NULL);
```

We now need to retrieve the exchange key and generate a random, exportable key. The exchange key will be used to encrypt our random key into a blob, which is then saved to include in our encrypted output file.

```
// Generate a random key (in "simple blob" format)
CryptGetUserKey(hProvider, AT_KEYEXCHANGE, &hExchangeKey);
CryptGenKey(hProvider, CALG_RC2, CRYPT_EXPORTABLE, &hKey);
```

Next, we create an exportable key blob with a call to `CryptExportKey`. Note that calling this function with a NULL for the fifth parameter causes the function to simply calculate and return the number of bytes needed for our buffer to hold the exportable key.

```
// The first call to ExportKey with NULL gets the key size
dwByteCount=0;
CryptExportKey(hKey, hExchangeKey, SIMPLEBLOB, 0, NULL,
    &dwByteCount);
CryptExportKey(hKey, hExchangeKey, SIMPLEBLOB, 0, pbBuffer,
    &dwByteCount);
```

We now have an encrypted version of our encryption key, in "simple blob" format. This is safe to write to the output file. We first write the size of this blob, so the decrypt program knows how much data to expect when loading the key blob. Then, we write out the blob itself. The data that immediately follows this blob will be the encrypted data, which we will write out next.

```
// Write key blob size, then key blob itself, to output file
WriteFile(hOutFile, &dwByteCount, sizeof(dwByteCount),
    &dwBytesWritten, NULL);
WriteFile(hOutFile, pbBuffer, dwByteCount, &dwBytesWritten, NULL);
```

Now, we read in a block of data, encrypt it using `CryptEncrypt`, and write it out to the output file, repeating this until we reach the end of the input data. Note the third parameter to `CryptEncrypt` needs to be a Boolean that tells `CryptEncrypt` when we're passing it the last block of data to encrypt.

```
// Now, read data in, encrypt it, and write it to output
do {
    ReadFile(hInFile, pbBuffer, IN_BUFFER_SIZE,
    &dwByteCount,NULL);
    finished = (dwByteCount < IN_BUFFER_SIZE);
        CryptEncrypt(hKey, 0, finished, 0, pbBuffer,
        &dwByteCount, OUT_BUFFER_SIZE);
        WriteFile(hOutFile, pbBuffer, dwByteCount, &dwBytesWritten,
        NULL);
} while (!finished);
```

And we're finished—almost. All we need to do now is clean up. We're finished with both keys at this point, so let's delete them.

```
// Clean up: release handles, close files
CryptDestroyKey(hKey);
CryptDestroyKey(hExchangeKey);
```

We're finished using the CSP handle, so we must release it. We close the input and output files, and we're finished.

```
CryptReleaseContext(hProvider, 0);
CloseHandle(hInFile);
CloseHandle(hOutFile);

return(0);
}
```

The complete listing for the Encrypt program is on the CD that accompanies this book.

NOTE   For clarity in the code, error checking in the Encrypt and Decrypt demo programs is nonexistent. The only thing that is likely to go wrong is that you don't have the default CSP or keys installed. Fortunately, these CryptoAPI functions also return Boolean success/failure results, so you could surround the first few functions with our Check function (from the earlier example in this chapter), if you need some help with debugging your Crypto installation.

Decrypting a File: The Decrypt Program

Much of the code in the Decrypt program is identical to the code in the Encrypt program.

The define and includes are the same as for Encrypt; however, we need only a single buffer size for decrypting. The size of the buffer needs to be a multiple of the encryption block size. Since both RC2 and RC4 encryption (the two block encryption algorithms supplied by the Microsoft base CSP) use 40-bit and 64-bit block sizes, respectively, the program uses a buffer size that is an even multiple of both. This way, you can change the encryption type in both programs without needing to worry about changing the buffer size.

```
#define _WIN32_WINNT 0x0400
#include <windows.h>
#include <wincrypt.h>
#include <stdio.h>

// note: the IN_BUFFER_SIZE used here is purposely an even multiple
of the various possible encryption block sizes, namely 1, 8, and
64 bytes
const BUFFER_SIZE   = 64 * 100; // must be multiple of block size
```

The variables are also almost identical to those in the Encrypt example, except that the buffer being allocated is a different size, as we've just noted.

```
int __cdecl main(int argc, char * argv[])
{
    HANDLE      hInFile, hOutFile;
    BYTE        pbBuffer[BUFFER_SIZE];
    BOOL        finished;
    HCRYPTPROV  hProvider = 0;
    HCRYPTKEY   hKey = 0;
    DWORD       dwByteCount, dwBytesWritten;

    if (argc != 3) {
        printf("Usage: DECRYPT infile outfile\n");
            exit(0);
    }
```

As in the Encrypt program, we first need to get a handle to the default CSP.

```
                // Get handle for the default provider (use RSA encryption)
                CryptAcquireContext(&hProvider, NULL, NULL, PROV_RSA_FULL,
                    0);

                // Open infile and create outfile
        hInFile = CreateFile(argv[1], GENERIC_READ, FILE_SHARE_READ, NULL,
                    OPEN_EXISTING, FILE_ATTRIBUTE_NORMAL, NULL);
        hOutFile = CreateFile(argv[2], GENERIC_WRITE,
                    FILE_SHARE_READ, NULL, CREATE_ALWAYS, FILE_ATTRIBUTE_NORMAL,
                    NULL);
```

We now read in, in the same order as they were written, the key blob size and then the key blob itself.

```
                // Read in key blob size, then key blob itself from input file
                ReadFile(hInFile,&dwByteCount,sizeof(dwByteCount),
                &dwBytesWritten,NULL);
                ReadFile(hInFile, pbBuffer, dwByteCount, &dwBytesWritten,
                    NULL);
```

Now, we convert the key blob back into a key (internally to the CSP), with the call to CryptImportkey.

```
                // Import Key blob into "CSP"
                CryptImportKey(hProvider, pbBuffer, dwByteCount, 0, 0, &hKey);
```

Next, we read encrypted data in, decrypt it using CryptDecrypt, and write the decrypted data to our output file. Like the CryptEncrypt function, CryptDecrypt takes a "finished" Boolean flag to tell it when we're sending it the last buffer to decrypt.

```
                // Read data in, encrypt it, and write it to output file
                do {
                    ReadFile(hInFile, pbBuffer, IN_BUFFER_SIZE,
                        &dwByteCount,NULL);
                    finished = (dwByteCount < IN_BUFFER_SIZE);
                    CryptDecrypt(hKey, 0, finished, 0, pbBuffer,
                        &dwByteCount);
                    WriteFile(hOutFile, pbBuffer,dwByteCount,
                        &dwBytesWritten,NULL);
                } while (!finished);
```

We're finished, so we now delete our key, release the CSP handle, and close the input and output files.

```
            // Clean up: release handles, close files
            CryptDestroyKey(hKey);
            CryptReleaseContext(hProvider, 0);
            CloseHandle(hInFile);
            CloseHandle(hOutFile);

            return(0);
    }
```

The complete listing of the Decrypt program is on the CD that accompanies this book.

Other Security Considerations

The effectiveness of security and encryption is in large part determined by the care with which it is used. Some of the most elaborate data-protecting schemes can be more easily compromised than simpler ones, just because people get lazy (take it for granted) or are insufficiently aware of the weaker points. Here, we'll take a look at some potential pitfalls to be aware of when designing a secure information system.

Exclusive ORing Techniques

One of the simpler encryption techniques is based on exclusive-ORing (XORing) the plain-text data with a key value. If you do this on a file that has lots of blank space or repeated strings of the same character, it's very possible to determine the encryption key. By simply re-XORing the repeated areas with their own value, the plain-text values cancel out, leaving the key.

You might think that with such a weakness, XORing against a key value wouldn't continue to be used. But one advantage of XORing is its extreme speed; XOR is one of the most fundamental computer operations performed.

There are several ways however, to strengthen an XOR algorithm:

- Use a longer, or ideally, an *extremely* long key value.

- Combine additional information, such as the offset position of the character in the file, or the value of the preceding character(s), with the plain-text character before encrypting.

- Use XOR as only one level of a multilevel encryption scheme.

Using Random Keys and Combining Techniques

The discussion of XORing brings up two important points. The first is that, surprisingly, even an operation as simple as XOR can be used to create the strongest type of encryption known, provided the key used is completely random and is equal (or longer) in length than the data stream to be encrypted. How you come up with completely random numbers is another whole matter; entire books can, and have been, written on that subject.

The second point is that combining two or more techniques can result in a much stronger resulting algorithm. Taking this point up at a different level, consider how a system that assigns memorable but unpredictable passwords (or keys) has a significant edge over a system that assigns very difficult to remember passwords. In the second case, it is human nature that a certain number of people will inevitably write down their password on a slip of paper and perhaps even tape it to their monitor!

As a different example on the same theme: Consider the advantage one encrypted e-mail has over another. One was written using couched phrases or only implicitly conveys a message. The other states its content in plain language. The first one stands a good chance of remaining confidential even if the encryption is broken, whereas the second message is cracked at the same time its encryption is breached. This illustrates again how multiple levels, particularly different types of levels, can combine synergistically to achieve a more secure result.

Protecting against Brute Force

Most efforts to break encryption eventually come down to "brute force" approaches—simply trying every possible key value until one fits. Encryption's effectiveness usually depends on the huge range of possible key values to make the chore of guessing take so long as to be impractical.

Many strong encryption algorithms are much stronger in theory than they turn out to be when implemented in software, because the programmer slips up and introduces less randomness in a key value by using pseudorandom (more predictable) computer-generated sources for key values or parts of key values. Such mistakes result in less work required to crack the resulting encryption, because the possible range of key values has been reduced.

Another somewhat more sophisticated version of "brute force" attack uses educated guesses to attempt to narrow down the key value. A password-guesser who starts out by using a person's first and last names, spouse's name, pet's name, and other common sources for passwords is an example of this. In the case of encrypted e-mail, eliminating predictable headers (for example, "Dear Sue,"), and footers ("later, Joe") and compressing blank space (and perhaps also removing the carriage returns and line feeds!) goes a long way toward tightening up the plain text and making it harder for such attacks to gain an easy foothold.

Remember, too, that any encryption scheme is only as strong as its weakest link. It does no good to have an extremely fancy encryption scheme when the decryption keys, for example, are not safeguarded. When saving a key value along with encrypted data, how do you encrypt the key itself? It doesn't hurt to use even stronger encryption for the key value, and to store the key at a random location in the file, or even vary the length of the key used.

Finally, keep in mind that, as the saying goes, there is more than one way to skin a cat. If someone cannot get in through the front door, they may resort to the back door, side door, or window, or rip themselves a hole in your system. Consider the case of a sophisticated encryption algorithm that is snugly packed away in a nice DLL, ActiveX control, or some other dynamic (or even static) code library. If a function in this library takes passwords or key values, or stores them by calling another function, couldn't someone simply replace the code library with his or her own, or (less likely in Windows NT) even intercept or "hook" a function that gets called? The moral is that you should be very, very careful at each stage of the designing and implementation process. Make sure that you haven't inadvertently left a gaping hole.

If all this talk about security and encryption sounds too paranoid for you, then perhaps your system really doesn't have a need for security. But I'll bet even then, you would agree on this point: Security is one area where, if you need it at all, it only makes sense to do it right. The programs discussed in this chapter will give you a good start on designing your own secure applications.

Internet Support

- An overview of Microsoft's Internet support

- The Winsock API functions

- The Internet API functions

- The ActiveX Web Controls

The rapid pace of the technology becoming available for developing Internet-aware software that runs on Windows poses many challenges for any software developer. These challenges involve keeping informed, remaining compatible, and simply leveraging all the technology that is currently available and applicable. On the other hand, the opportunities are richer, and the tools and SDKs currently available are both more powerful and more usable than ever before. They enable the development of many ingenious new solutions for business, commerce, and home use.

In this chapter, we'll begin with a survey of the Internet-related technologies Microsoft has been embracing and introducing over this last year. Next, we'll take a look at some Internet-related concepts of concern to those developing Internet software. Then we will focus on the three chief toolkits or APIs for writing Windows Internet software: Winsock 2.0, the Internet API, and the ActiveX Web Controls. You can think of these as the low-level, medium-level, and high-level Windows Internet toolkits.

A Year's Worth of Progress (at Microsoft)

Only a year or so ago, Internet support in Microsoft operating systems was limited to inclusion of dial-up and Ethernet TCP/IP support, plus a handful of Unix-style command-line utilities, such as ftp, ping, tracert, and the like. Actually, this was not a bad start, since by using the built-in TCP/IP stack and the FTP client, a user could download a Web browser and other Internet software and be set to access the Internet.

In the course of ten months, Microsoft has done an amazing turnabout and embraced Internet technologies on a scale unprecedented even by Microsoft's own previous efforts in other areas. If this sounds even the least bit overdramatic to you, take a look at the software tools and applications listed in Tables 19.1 through 19.6, all of which Microsoft has either adopted or introduced since its "embrace the Internet" announcement made in January 1996.

TABLE 19.1   Improved Internet Connectivity in Operating Systems

Feature	Description
Multi-Channel Modem Binding (for NT 4.0)	Allows two or more modems (or other devices) to be treated as a single network connection—doubling or tripling (or more!) the throughput available to all Internet and/or other network-aware software.
Improved WINS (Windows Internet Name Service) and DHCP (Dynamic Host Control Protocol)	Allows WINS and DHCP to be administered more easily and to work seamlessly with other clients (such as Macintosh clients).
PPTP (Point-to-Point Tunneling Protocol)	Provides a secure way to transparently interconnect wide-area networks across insecure networks such as the Internet, by encapsulating network packets inside a secure packet "envelope."
Windows ISDN	Brings integrated support for internal and external ISDN modems to Windows 95 and NT. Includes support for multiple channel binding.

TABLE 19.2   Tools for Web Page Design and Management

Tool	Description
Microsoft FrontPage	Supports HTML page authoring and Web site management.
Microsoft GIF Animator	Supports creation of GIF and animated GIF files, for use with Web pages.
Microsoft Image Composer	Simplifies creating and manipulating images for placement on Web pages.

TABLE 19.3   Internet Servers

Server	Description
Internet Information Server (IIS)	High-performance Web server with support for WSAPI .DLL extensions, secure Web pages, performance monitoring, and flexible FrontPage Server extensions.
Peer Web Servers (for NT Workstation 4.0)	Provides built-in peer Web, Gopher, and FTP servers.
Catapult Proxy Server	Allows multiple PCs to connect to the Internet via a single server connection, even using other protocols (instead of TCP/IP for the local link, if desired). Also fetches and caches most-often used Web pages for all users.

TABLE 19.3   Internet Servers (Continued)

Server	Description
Internet News Server	Gives companies (or individuals) their own self-managed news groups.
Chat Server	Keeps a running round-table dialog, displayed via Web pages.
White Pages Indexing/ Locator Server	Automatically indexes an entire Web site, providing keyword searches.
Content Replication Server	Assists in porting and/or mirroring part or all of a Web site's content from one server to another.
Server Personalization System	Can be added to IIS to provide Web content customized for each connected user.
Mail Server	Provides sites with POP and SMTP server support (plus MS Mail support).
Merchant Server	Supports "store-front" shopping via Web-pages.

TABLE 19.4   Internet-Related Programmer's Tools

Tool	Description
Visual J++	Provides a Visual Java environment, including Java compiler, debugger, and Windows SDK class libraries.
Jscript (supported in Internet Explorer)	Allows embedding Java script applets in HTML pages.
VBScript (supported in Internet Explorer browsers)	Provides a Visual Basic scripting language for embedding in HTML pages.
Visual C++ 4.2	Provides enhanced support for various Internet APIs, DCOM, ActiveX, etc.

NOTE   Keep in mind that, although we do not cover Java, Jscript, or VBScript here, these also are significant technologies. These tools have entire books devoted to them (Java in particular!).

TABLE 19.5   Internet-Related SDKs and APIs

SDK or API	Description
Winsock 2.0	Provides expanded support for socket-style Internet programming, including AppleTalk, IPX, and other networking protocols in addition to TCP/IP.
Internet API	Simplifies adding TCP/IP support to applications, encapsulating and abstracting Winsock-style functionality.
ActiveX Web Control Pack	Simplifies adding Internet support to applications, via drop-in ActiveX objects. Includes Web browser, FTP, e-mail, and news client objects.
Windows SDK for Java	Provides class libraries for Java applets to access Windows-specific functionality.
Game SDK	Includes support for multiplayer gaming over the Internet.
Crypto API	Provides public and private key encryption and decryption, code and message signing and authentication.
Uploading API	Provides a set of functions to simplify the job of uploading or moving Web pages to and from a Web site.
Ratings API	Provides functions to set content restrictions and query content ratings tags from HTML pages.
Secure Sockets Layer (SSL) for Winsock	Provides encrypted socket-style communications as an extension to Winsock 2.0.
WebPost API	Provides functions to simplify the process of uploading Web pages to a Web site.

In addition to offering the tools and applications listed in these tables, Microsoft has been rushing to include Internet hooks and functionality into *all* of its software applications. Furthermore, it has switched Microsoft Network (MSN) to be Internet-based rather than proprietary, and has moved all of its public (and beta) support forums from CompuServe over to the Internet. Each individual Microsoft product has its own Web page, and there are currently more than 325 public Internet newsgroups run by Microsoft alone, not including many independent newsgroups, which focus, for example, on various elements of Win32 programming.

TABLE 19.6   Other Internet-Related Technologies

Item	Description
Internet Explorer	Web browser, now supports Netscape plug-ins, ActiveX controls, VBScript, Jscript, SSL, code signing and certificates, pop-up menu controls, auto-installation of ActiveX controls, and content ratings system.
Internet Assistants	Export data from Access, Excel, PowerPoint, Word, and Schedule+ to formatted HTML pages.
Data Viewers for Word, PowerPoint, and Excel	Display Word, PowerPoint, and Excel files on stations not equipped with Word, PowerPoint, or Excel.
NetMeeting	Multiuser collaboration tool, supporting text and voice chatting, white boarding, and file transfers.
ISAPI and FrontPage Server Extensions	Support for CGI-like server extensions, with less overhead than an interpreter or the loading and unloading of standard binary executable files.
DCOM (Distributed Component Object Model)	Support for remote object access and execution using TCP/IP (as well as other protocols).
Authenticode	Support for code signing and authentication using certificates.
Cab Files	Initially used for installing Microsoft software, now expanded for simplified downloading of Java source files.

This explosive usage of the Internet has benefited both software end users and software developers. You can find more accessible (and timely) documentation, significant peer support, software upgrades, bug fixes, and enhancements.

And this is a survey of recent developments at only one (admittedly rather huge) company. We could also review (were enough space available) all the Internet work being done by Netscape, Sun, IBM, Symantec, Apple, and literally thousands of other companies. Much of their work also has some bearing on Windows Internet software development.

> **NOTE**
>
> Although we won't go into detail about all of the APIs, you should be aware of their suitability for more specialized uses. The Game SDK includes much more than support for multiplayer game communications over the Internet. DirectPlay, DirectSound, DirectVideo, Direct3D, and related technologies provide speedy access to a wide variety of video, sound, and control hardware. The SSL API is an extension to Winsock 2, providing encrypted data flow through the normal socket architecture. The Ratings API provides access to functions useful for setting, checking, and managing access to classes of information that have been assigned particular ratings, such as for violence and profanity. The CryptoAPI, which is already being used by Microsoft's Internet Explorer, is covered in detail in Chapter 18.

Internet-Related Concepts

Those who are interested in designing Internet software need to aware of the many Internet-related concepts and terms. Here, we will briefly cover IP addressing, Internet protocols, and sockets.

IP Addresses

Most new Internet users quickly become familiar with the fact that they have an e-mail address and an IP address. Setting up a computer for TCP/IP networking (using a TCP/IP protocol stack, as it's sometimes called), typically involves specifying IP addresses for a Domain Name server and network gateway, and entering POP and SMTP server names. IP addresses are typed in using dotted, or dotted-quad notation, where each byte of the 4-byte address is displayed in decimal, and separated from the next byte value with a period. As you probably know, this dotted notation is simply to allow easier reading by human users. Computers and other hardware on the Internet always use the 4-byte (32-bit) values directly.

Because every computer on the Internet has its own IP address (at least while it's connected), and because the number of computers joining the Internet continues to increase rapidly, work is being done to devise a new address scheme using wider network addresses. There are still some issues remaining to be hashed out though, so for the near future, we can continue programming using the 32-bit Internet (IP) addresses.

Internet Protocols

TCP/IP is actually a whole suite of related protocols, some higher-level than others. At the lower levels, for example, are the two main packet protocols that transport data in either sequenced, two-way "conversations" or connectionless "radio-style" (one-way) transmissions: TCP and UDP.

IP (Internet Protocol) is the Internet "delivery system" protocol, which underlies the other Internet protocols. IP itself uses connectionless datagrams, thus IP packets are often called IP datagrams. See the discussion concerning connection-oriented versus connectionless transport for more information.

TCP (Transmission Control Protocol) provides a sequenced, two-way connection-based protocol using byte streams. It is considered "reliable" because it takes responsibility for check-summing each received packet and re-requesting any dropped or damaged packets.

UDP (User Datagram Protocol), on the other hand, is termed "unreliable," in the sense that it provides connectionless transport of data packets, and therefore cannot support built-in error checking. Instead, it acts analogously to a radio signal, which you can be certain was transmitted, but cannot verify whether it was received.

These two approaches are complementary. Connectionless transport is faster, because it does not have the overhead associated with verification of accurate reception and transmission. TCP, with its greater overhead, ensures that data correctly reaches its destination, and thereby makes up for a multitude of potential failure points within the underlying networking hardware (cabling, switching mechanisms, and so on).

At a higher level are a set of protocols with more specialized purposes. These higher-level protocols are the various service-related protocols, which are used to transfer e-mail, files, Web documents, and so on. These protocols include the following:

- **SMTP (Simple Mail Transfer Protocol):** Commonly for sending e-mail to a server.

- **POP3 (Post Office Protocol 3):** Commonly used for retrieving e-mail from a server.

- **FTP (File Transfer Protocol):** Widely used for uploading and downloading files.

- **HTTP (Hypertext Transfer Protocol):** The standard World Wide Web protocol.

- **Telnet (Remote Terminal Access):** Allows remote login and interactive access to remote servers.

Whereas the lower-level transport protocols package their routing information and data using rather complex structures and packet arrangements, the higher-level protocols use techniques that human programmers generally find friendlier to implement. These higher-level service protocols have the following common properties:

- They start with recognizable four-character command strings.

- They assume a client and a server conversation, established via a bi-directional socket.

- They use a numerical scheme for response codes.

TIP

Later in this chapter, we will look at a program that implements SMTP to send an e-mail message to a mail server. You may find it interesting to experiment directly with these protocols by using your Windows 95 or NT Telnet client to send properly formatted protocol strings to an FTP, SMTP, POP3, or HTTP server, and view the incoming replies generated by the server.

Sockets and Winsock

Most Internet programming has traditionally been done using the "sockets" paradigm. In the early days, when TCP/IP became integrated with the Unix operating system, a set of functions, which came to be called the Berkeley sockets standard, was developed. These functions let you create a socket, listen for incoming connections (in the case of a server), connect the socket to a given host computer and port number (as a client), and send and receive data via the socket.

A socket is analogous to a file handle, and on some versions of Unix, can be used directly with the file I/O functions. There are two types of sockets, corresponding to the connected and connectionless protocols:

- TCP sockets require that a connection be established between a socket and a host computer.

- UDP sockets only require that you specify where the data should end up (a specific port number at a specific IP address).

Several years ago, a consortium of individuals and companies got together and came up with a version of socket functions for Windows. Winsock, as it is called, is somewhat different from Berkeley sockets. Because Windows, unlike Unix, was not a true multitasking operating system, certain provisions had to be made. These provisions generally took two approaches. First, functions which might take a while to receive a response or otherwise complete execution could be "blocking," or simply not return until they were finished. Although this worked under Windows, it understandably wasn't considered good programming practice. Using lots of blocking functions in an application can cause the application to become sluggish at best, or completely unresponsive (or crash!) at worst.

Therefore, Winsock also provides a set of asynchronous functions, which notify a Windows application when they finish executing by sending a special message to a specified window. The application then simply needs to call the function, continue other processing, and check for a function return message in the message queue. This works about as well as can be expected, considering 16-bit Windows cannot do preemptive multitasking of Windows applications.

Windows NT, on the other hand, has no problem with multitasking, (although to retain backward compatibility, the 32-bit Winsock functions remain almost unchanged). With NT, an application can use blocking functions in the Unix style of spawning a separate thread, to allow continued execution of the application while the function completes. Certain functions that block for the sake of ease of use in Windows 3.1 don't need to block in NT. Also, by and large, GUI-based NT applications (which have a window to receive notification messages) often continue to use the asynchronous Windows versions of the socket functions, although console applications and some multithreaded applications go with the more "traditional" synchronous socket functions.

The Winsock 2 API Functions

Winsock 2.0 is important for several reasons:

- It supports various protocols.

- It's the best way to produce fast, close-to-the-hardware transport code.

- It's the only way to go when writing servers or when speed and efficiency of throughput are essential (more important than development time, for example).

- It provides more cross-platform support.

In its current version, Winsock 2 maintains most functions of previous Winsock releases and adds a few functions that improve multiprotocol support. Although Winsock is probably most often used for TCP/IP, it also supports socket connections over several other protocols, including IPX, SPX, Banyan VINES, and Apple-Talk. In this chapter, we will be looking at Winsock in its TCP/IP capacity, but keep in mind that socket applications can often be "ported" to use other protocols with little additional work.

Within the Winsock set of functions, there are both a synchronous and an asynchronous batch of socket functions. Additionally, there are some data-conversion functions and database lookup functions.

Socket Functions

The following are the Winsock Socket functions:

- `accept`: Accepts a connection on a given socket.

- `AcceptEx`: Accepts a new connection, returns local and remote addresses, plus the first block of data sent by the client.

- `Bind`: Associates a local address with a socket.

- `closesocket`: Closes a socket.

- `Connect`: Connects a socket with a given peer.

- `GetAcceptExSockaddrs`: Parses data from `AcceptEx` and passes the local and remote addresses, along with the first block of data received upon connection.

- `ioctlsocket`: Gets or sets socket-mode parameters.

- `listen`: Places a given socket in listen mode.

- `recv`: Retrieves data from a given socket.

- `recvfrom`: Retrieves a datagram along with source address.

- `Select`: Determines the status of one or more sockets.

- `Send`: Sends data on a given (connected) socket.

- `Sendto`: Sends data to a given destination.

- `Setsockopt`: Sets a socket option.

- `Shutdown`: Disables sending and/or receiving on a specified socket.

- `Socket`: Creates a socket bound to a given transport service provider.

Data-Conversion Functions

Another set of Winsock functions deals with converting data between *network byte order* and *host byte order*. It is recommended that these functions be used even where it is known that the order is the same on both machines, because this makes for more consistent code, which is more easily portable.

The following are the data-conversion functions:

- `htonl`: Converts a 32-bit value from host to TCP/IP network byte order.

- `htons`: Converts a 16-bit value from host to TCP/IP network byte order.

- `inet_addr`: Converts a dotted IP address string to an unsigned long value.

- `inet_ntoa`: Converts a network address as unsigned long into a dotted IP address string.

- `ntohl`: Converts a 32-bit value from TCP/IP network byte order to host byte order.

- `Ntohs`: Converts a 16-bit value from TCP/IP network byte order to host byte order.

Database Lookup Functions

Another, smaller set of Winsock functions are called the *database lookup* functions. These functions have the duty of looking up correct IP addresses, domain names, service IDs, and protocol port numbers. The database functions behave much like their Unix counterparts. The services information and (usually) a small number of domain names and IP addresses are typically stored in two text files on each host computer. The socket functions make use of these as their first source of information for addresses or service numbers during address or service resolution.

HOSTS and SERVICES Files

Whether on a Unix, NT, or Windows 95 computer, the HOSTS files contains pairs of addresses and host names, and the SERVICES file contains information about "well-known" services, along with their port numbers, the low-level protocol used, and one or more optional alias names. On NT, the SERVICES and HOSTS files can be found in the \WINNT\SYSTEM\DRIVERS\ETC directory. On Windows 95, they are both located in the \WINDOWS directory.

The following is part of a typical SERVICES file (taken from an NT 4.0 station). Note how each entry matches up a service name with a port and protocol type, and one or more optional service name aliases.

```
#          @(#)services    1.16 (Berkeley) 86/04/20
#
# Network services, Internet style
#
#name      port/protocol  aliases
#
echo       7/tcp
echo       7/udp
discard    9/tcp          sink null
discard    9/udp          sink null
systat     11/tcp         users
daytime    13/tcp
daytime    13/udp
netstat    15/tcp
qotd       17/tcp         quote
chargen    19/tcp         ttytst source
chargen    19/udp         ttytst source
ftp        21/tcp
telnet     23/tcp
smtp       25/tcp         mail
time       37/tcp         timserver
time       37/udp         timserver
rlp        39/udp         resource       # resource location
nameserver 42/tcp         name           # IEN 116
whois      43/tcp         nicname
domain     53/tcp         nameserver     # name-domain server
domain     53/udp         nameserver
mtp        57/tcp                        # deprecated
tftp       69/udp
rje        77/tcp         netrjs
finger     79/tcp
link       87/tcp         ttylink
supdup     95/tcp
hostnames  101/tcp        hostname       # usually from sri-nic
ns         105/tcp                       # ph name serve
pop2       109/tcp        postoffice2
pop3       110/tcp        postoffice
```

The following shows a typical HOSTS file. This file is usually kept quite small, with most names being resolved via a DNS (Domain Name Service) server.

```
# HOSTS file used by Microsoft TCP/IP for Windows NT

102.54.94.97      rhino.acme.com        # source server
38.25.63.10       x.acme.com            # x client host
127.0.0.1         localhost
```

In this file, each IP address is matched with a host name. Note the standard address of 127.0.0.1, which is mapped to localhost. By convention, 127.0.0.1 is always a reference to the local host itself. Pinging 127.0.0.1 is sometimes used as a test of one's own IP address.

NOTE On both Windows NT and 95, there is also typically a file similar to the HOSTS file, called LMHOSTS. This performs a similar function, however, the host names are NetBIOS names, and certain extensions are allowed (such as #DOM: to handle NT domains).

Most often, an address lookup will not be resolved by finding a corresponding entry in the HOSTS file. Instead, the lookup request is passed along to the DNS server, which either fills the lookup request, or passes along the request to a first-level DNS server. These IP address and name servers contain many, but by no means all, names and corresponding IP addresses, as registered by InterNIC (InterNIC is responsible, in the United States, for maintaining the DNS entries for all top-level domains, except for the *mil* or military domain). If a match is not found on a first-level server, the request is passed down to the next DNS server in the hierarchy, and so on. This continues until either a match is found or no entry is found (in which case, you may see an error message). The FindAddr program, covered a little later in this chapter, is an example of using host name-to-IP address resolution (as well as IP address-to-host name reverse resolution).

Lookup Functions

The following are the Winsock database lookup functions:

- gethostbyaddr: Gets host information for a given address.

- gethostbyname: Gets host information for a given host name.

- `gethostname`: Returns the standard host name for local machine.

- `getpeername`: Gets the address of the peer connected to a given socket.

- `getprotobyname`: Gets protocol information for a given protocol (name).

- `getprotobynumber`: Gets protocol information.

- `getservbyname`: Gets service information for a given service name and protocol.

- `getservbyport`: Gets service information for a given port number and protocol.

- `getsockname`: Gets the local name for a given socket.

- `getsockopt`: Gets the current value for a specified socket option.

Asynchronous Versions of the Winsock Functions

To do asynchronous Windows socket programming, you use the `WSA` version of a socket function, which typically takes a window handle as a parameter, and posts a status or completion message to that window's message queue when the function completes or needs to communicate information to the application. Because Windows 95 and NT support multithreading, you can also use the synchronous functions by spawning off a separate thread, thus freeing the main application to continue with other processing while waiting for a function to finish executing. Table 19.7 lists the asynchronous functions.

TABLE 19.7   Asynchronous Winsock 2 Functions

Function	Description
WSAAsyncGetHostByAddr	Gets host information for a given address.
WSAAsyncGetHostByName	Gets host information for a given host name.
WSAAsyncGetProtoByName	Gets protocol information for a given protocol name.
WSAAsyncGetProtoByNumber	Gets protocol information for a given protocol number.
WSAAsyncGetServByName	Gets service information for given service name and protocol.

TABLE 19.7 Asynchronous Winsock 2 Functions (Continued)

Function	Description
WSAAsyncGetServByPort	Gets service information for given port number and protocol.
WSAAsyncSelect	Requests Windows message-based notification of network events occurring on specified socket.
WSACancelAsyncRequest	Cancels an (incomplete) asynchronous socket operation.
WSAAccept	Conditionally accepts a connection based on the return value of an (optional) condition function, creating or joining a socket group.
WSAAddressToString	Converts all addresses in a SOCKADDR structure into human-readable string representations.
WSACleanup	Terminates use of Winsock.DLL.
WSACloseEvent	Closes an event object handle.
WSAConnect	Connects to a peer, exchanges connect data, and specifies needed quality of service based on supplied flow specification.
WSACreateEvent	Creates a new event object.
WSADuplicateSocket	Returns a WSAPROTOCOL_INFO structure which can be used to create a new socket descriptor for a shared socket.
WSAEnumNameSpaceProviders	Retrieves information about the available name space providers.
WSAEnumNetworkEvents	Retrieves information about which network events have occurred on a given socket.
WSAEnumProtocols	Retrieves information about available transport protocols.
WSAEventSelect	Specifies an event object to be associated with given FD_*XXX* network events.
WSAGetAddressByName	Resolves an address by name and returns the first available result.

TABLE 19.7   Asynchronous Winsock 2 Functions (Continued)

Function	Description
WSAGetLastError	Returns the error status for the last failed Winsock operation.
WSAGetOverlappedResult	Returns the results of an overlapped operation on the given socket.
WSAGetQOSByName	Initializes a QOS (Quality of Service) structure based on a named template.
WSAGetServiceClassInfo	Retrieves the class information for a service class from a specified name space provider.
WSAGetServiceClassName-ByClassId	Returns the generic service name for a given service type.
WSAHtonl	Converts an unsigned long from host byte order to network byte order.
WSAHtons	Converts an unsigned short from host byte order to network byte order.
WSAInstallServiceClass	Registers a service class schema within a name space.
WSAIoctl	Sets the mode of a given socket.
WSAJoinLeaf	Joins a leaf node into a multipoint session, exchanges connection data, and specifies needed quality of service based on supplied flow specification.
WSALookupServiceBegin	Returns a handle that can be used in further client queries to search for specified service information.
WSALookupServiceEnd	Frees a query handle created by WSALookupServiceBegin.
WSALookupServiceNext	Retrieves next set of service information using given query handle.
WSANtohl	Converts an unsigned long from network byte order to host byte order.
WSANtohs	Converts an unsigned short from network byte order to host byte order.
WSARecv	Receives data from a given socket.

TABLE 19.7 Asynchronous Winsock 2 Functions (Continued)

Function	Description
WSARecvDisconnect	Terminates reception on a given socket, retrieving disconnect data if applicable.
WSARecvFrom	Retrieves a datagram and the source address.
WSARemoveServiceClass	Permanently unregisters a service class schema.
WSAResetEvent	Resets the state of a specified event object to be "non-signaled."
WSASend	Sends data on a connected socket. Permits asynchronous, or overlapped, I/O.
WSASendDisconnect	Initiates termination of a given socket connection and sends disconnect data.
WSASendTo	Sends data to a given destination, using overlapped I/O where applicable.
WSASetEvent	Sets the state of the specified event object to be "signaled."
WSASetLastError	Sets the error code which is returned by subsequent calls to WSASetLastError.
WSASetService	Registers or unregisters a service instance within one or more name spaces.
WSASocket	Creates a socket which is bound to a specific transport service provider, optionally creating or joining a socket group.
WSAStartup	Initiates use of Winsock.DLL by a process.
WSAStringToAddress	Converts a human-readable address string to a socket address structure.
WSAWaitForMultipleEvents	Returns when one or all of the specified event objects are in the signaled state, or when the timeout expires.

An IP Address Lookup Example: The FindAddr Program

The first Winsock sample program we'll look at performs an IP address lookup using a given host name. If this lookup is successful, the program then attempts to use the newly acquired IP address to, in turn, look up the host name. This latter procedure is called a *reverse lookup*. Reverse lookups are used in some TCP/IP server programs, such as e-mail and Web servers, to verify that a given client address is authentic. Web servers usually let you disable this reverse-lookup feature, since performing the lookup will add extra wait time to each incoming client connection. The complete program listing is shown at the end of the chapter.

The program starts out by defining WIN32_LEAN_AND_MEAN to trim excess fat from the executable, then includes the Stdlib.H, Stdio.H, and Winsock2.H header files. Following this, we define version constants that are used to specify the minimum desired Winsock version in the call to WSAStartup.

```
// Insist on at least Winsock version 1.1 (you may use 2.0)
const  VERSION_MAJOR  =  1;
const  VERSION_MINOR  =  1;
```

Although you could set the VERSION_MAJOR to 2 and the VERSION_MINOR to 0, for example, to specify Winsock 2.0, it is best not to do this unless your program specifically needs version 2.0. Rather, your application should request the minimum Winsock version needed to run successfully.

Next, the ShowUsage function is defined, which simply displays the command-line syntax expected, and exits the application.

```
void ShowUsage(void)
{
    printf("usage: FINDADDR some.address.com\n");
    exit(0);
}
```

We next have the start of the main application function, followed by four variable declarations:

```
// Takes string IP address and looks up numeric IP address
int main(int argc, char *argv[])
{
    WSADATA      WSData;
    LPHOSTENT    lpHostEntry;
    DWORD        dwIPAddress;
    LPSTR        szIPAddress;
```

The data type WSADATA is actually a Winsock data structure that is used by WSAStartup to return Winsock information such as the Winsock version number found, the maximum number of sockets that can be opened by the application, the maximum size, in bytes, for a UDP, and other vendor-specific information.

An LPHOSTENT is a long pointer to a HOSTENT structure, or Host Entry structure, which is returned by the gethostbyname function. This program uses szIPAddress to store the mail server's dotted IP address (in string format), which it gets by doing a DNS lookup on the server name. The dotted-address string is converted to a 32-bit value by inet_addr, which is then stored in dwIPAddress.

After the variables section, we check for the expected number of command-line arguments, and if necessary, call ShowUsage.

```
// Check for valid # of command-line arguments
if ( argc != 2 ) ShowUsage();
```

Next, we want to initialize Winsock, which we do with a call to WSAStartup. WSAStartup returns 0 if successful, and fills WSData with information.

```
// Attempt to initialize Winsock (1.1 or later)
if ( WSAStartup(MAKEWORD(VERSION_MAJOR, VERSION_MINOR),
   &WSData) )
{
   printf("Cannot find Winsock (v%d.%d or later)!\n",
      VERSION_MAJOR, VERSION_MINOR);
   return(1);
}
```

Next, we use gethostbyname to look up the mail server's IP address. This causes a DNS lookup to be performed, and the resulting address is returned as a field inside the lpHostEntry structure.

```
lpHostEntry = gethostbyname( argv[1] );
```

Provided the lookup was successful in retrieving an IP address, we next convert the retrieved 32-bit IP address into a more readable dotted-address string so it can be displayed.

```
if ( lpHostEntry == NULL )
   printf("Unable to find %s!\n", argv[1]);
else {
   // Success. Convert address into dotted-notation (string).
   szIPAddress = inet_ntoa( *(LPIN_ADDR)
*(lpHostEntry->h_addr_list) );
```

```
        // Display resolved address.
        printf("Found! IP address is %s\n", szIPAddress );
```

That done, we next attempt a reverse lookup, using the retrieved IP address to look up the corresponding name. To do this, we first need to convert the `szIPAddress` back into a 32-bit value, which is done via a call to `inet_addr`. It's true there's already a copy of this 32-bit value still stored inside the `lpHostEntry` structure, but the sample program uses `inet_addr` to demonstrate how it works.

```
        // Now, let's try reverse lookup
        dwIPAddress = inet_addr( szIPAddress );// Convert to 32-bits
```

The reverse lookup is performed via a call to `gethostbyaddr`, which takes a pointer to our 32-bit IP address value, an address size parameter (specified in bytes), and the `AF_INET` constant, which specifies the TCP/IP protocol family (since Winsock could be used for IPX or other protocols that have different-sized network addresses).

```
lpHostEntry = gethostbyaddr( (LPSTR) &dwIPAddress,
   sizeof( dwIPAddress ), AF_INET);
```

In this example, the `gethostbyaddr` function will usually succeed, since we have already successfully retrieved the IP address using a name. There are some instances, however, where reverse lookup would return a name that is different than the one that was used to look up the IP address. This can happen if the DNS mapping does not contain a reverse-lookup entry, as is often the case with dynamically assigned IP addresses.

```
        // Display reverse-resolved address (or error message)
        if ( lpHostEntry == NULL )
            printf("Hm... Unable to reverse lookup %s\n",
                szIPAddress);
        else
            printf("Successful reverse lookup of %s yields %s\n",
                szIPAddress, lpHostEntry->h_name );
        }
```

The final step in using the Winsock functions is to call `WSACleanup`, to allow Winsock to release any resources allocated for this application, and decrement the usage count on the Winsock DLL.

```
        // Clean up Winsock resources and terminate
        WSACleanup();
        return(0);
    }
```

That completes our look at the FindAddr example. Again, note that in addition to address and domain-name lookup functions, Winsock also has a port lookup function, which returns the port number used for a given TCP/IP protocol or service, which then is used to bind a socket to the desired port. There's an example of this in our second Winsock program, covered next.

Sending E-Mail: The SendMail Program

Our second Winsock example uses not only the TCP stream-oriented protocol, but also the higher-level SMTP to send e-mail. It takes four command-line parameters: mail server-address, from- and to- e-mail addresses, and the name of a text file. The program connects to the specified mail server, and e-mails the text file to the specified "to" address. As a bonus, this program actually has some practical uses! You can write a batch file, for instance, which generates a report file and then e-mails it using SendMail. Or, redirect some program's output to a file, and then e-mail that output file to an e-mail account.

Here's another handy example: Let's say you have an NT workstation or server which runs FTP or Web services and connects to the Internet via a dial-up connection. Most often, this means the IP address will be dynamically assigned, which means you'll have no way of connecting to that station remotely unless you first get someone to go to the station, see what the currently assigned IP address is, and read it to you. Then, you need to repeat this procedure any time the connection breaks. What you can do to solve this problem is write a batch file that looks like this:

```
rasdial MyConnection username password
netstat -r > current-ip
sendmail mailserver me@mydomain.com me@mydomain.com current-ip
```

The net effect (pun intended) of this script is to connect to the Internet, output the currently assigned IP address to a file, and e-mail this file to some account that you have access to. You can use NT's at program (or any other program scheduler) to cause this script to be run at a certain time of day (or week), so that either at connect time or at specified time intervals, you can find out the station's current IP address by simply checking your latest e-mail. You could even add multiple sendmail lines if you want to notify other users of the IP address change. (Of course, you'll get people's permission first, as over time this could generate a number of, perhaps unwanted, e-mail messages.)

TIP   You could write a program similar to SendMail that looks for incoming mail from SendMail and retrieves it from your mail server. A program that reads e-mail would look similar to SendMail, except it would typically use the POP3 protocol to retrieve the e-mail.

Let's look at how SendMail works. The complete program listing is on the CD that accompanies this book.

Note that a few more header files are included this time:

```
#define WIN32_LEAN_AND_MEAN
#include <stdio.h>
#include <stdlib.h>
#include <fstream.h>
#include <iostream.h>
#include <windows.h>
#include <winsock2.h>
```

In particular, we've added the Fstream.H and Iostream.H header files. We implement the text file I/O in this example using a file stream, hence the Fstream.h inclusion. Then, since the program was already using one stream, it made sense to use the C++ standard I/O streams as well. This makes for a bit of variety as well.

As in the FindAddr example, we want to ensure the user is running at least Winsock version 1.1.

```
// Insist on at least Winsock v1.1, can be changed to 2.0
const    VERSION_MAJOR  = 1;
const    VERSION_MINOR  = 1;
```

For clarity, CRLF is defined so we can use it for adding carriage return/line feeds to the SMTP strings and to each line of the outgoing e-mail message.

```
#define  CRLF   "\r\n"   // carriage return/line feed pair
```

As usual, we have a ShowUsage function, but this time, it uses the standard stream I/O to output the usage strings.

```
void ShowUsage(void)
{
    cout << "Usage: SENDMAIL mailserv to_addr from_addr messagefile"
<< endl;
    cout << "Example: SENDMAIL smtp.myisp.com rcvr@elsewhere.com ";
```

```
cout << "my_id@mydomain.com message.txt" << endl;
exit(1);
}
```

Next, there is a short error-checking function. It is designed to be used only with the `send` and `recv` socket functions, because it checks for `SOCKET_ERROR` return codes.

```
// Basic error checking for send() and recv() functions
void Check( int iStatus, char *szFunction )
{
    if (iStatus != SOCKET_ERROR && iStatus != 0) return;

    cerr << "Error during call to " << szFunction << ": ";
    cerr << iStatus << " - " << GetLastError() << endl;
}
```

Now, we start the `main` program declaration and declare needed variables.

```
int main(int argc, char *argv[])
{
    WSADATA      WSData;
    LPHOSTENT    lpHostEntry;
    LPSERVENT    lpServEntry;
    SOCKADDR_IN  SockAddr;
    SOCKET       hServer;
    int          iProtocolPort;
    char         szSmtpServerName[64], szToAddr[64], szFromAddr[64];
    char         szBuffer[4096], szLine[255], szMsgLine[255];
```

Note that the first three variables are identical to those we used in the FindAddr program. A socket address (input) or `SOCKADDR_IN` is necessary for binding our socket to the mail port. The `iProtocolPort` variable stores the mail port number, and `hServer` is the socket we will create to communicate with the mail server.

The next three string variables hold copies of the mail server name, and the e-mail "from" and "to" addresses. The `szBuffer` variable is used to hold incoming socket data, `szLine` is what we read each line of the text file into, and `szMsgLine` is used to format each line of the outgoing e-mail message.

After a standard check for the proper number of command-line parameters, the first three parameters are copied to easier-to-read string variables.

```
// Check for four command-line arguments
if (argc != 5) ShowUsage();

// Load command-line args (for clarity).
lstrcpy( szSmtpServerName, argv[1]);
lstrcpy( szToAddr,         argv[2]);
lstrcpy( szFromAddr,       argv[3]);
```

Next, the text file that will supply the body of our e-mail message is initialized as a file input stream. Note that we just use argv[4] here directly, since it is used right away.

```
// Create input stream for reading e-mail message file
ifstream MsgFile( argv[4] );
```

As in FindAddr, we next prepare to use Winsock by calling the WSAStartup initialization function. If we needed to, we could look at the information returned in the WSData structure, but in this case, we don't need to know, for instance, the maximum number of sockets we can open, since we'll only need one.

```
// Attempt to initialize Winsock (1.1 or later)
if ( WSAStartup(MAKEWORD(VERSION_MAJOR, VERSION_MINOR),
   &WSData) )
{
   cout << "Cannot find Winsock v";
   cout << VERSION_MAJOR << "." << VERSION_MINOR;
   cout << " or later!" << endl;
   return(1);
}
```

If you've studied the FindAddr example, this next step should look familiar as well. We again use gethostbyname to look up the host IP address for the e-mail server.

```
// Look up e-mail server's IP address
lpHostEntry = gethostbyname( szSmtpServerName );
if (lpHostEntry == NULL)
{
   cout << "Cannot find SMTP mail server ";
   cout << szSmtpServerName << endl;
   return(1);
}
```

Next, we need to create a socket. The first parameter specifies that this socket will be used in a TCP/IP context (as opposed to some other network protocol). Next, we want to specify a stream-type socket, because we will be using SMTP, which uses TCP, which is a stream protocol. And, since we don't need a specific protocol type at this point to create the socket, we can specify a zero as the third parameter.

```
// Create a TCP/IP socket, no specific protocol
hServer = socket( PF_INET, SOCK_STREAM, 0);
if (hServer == INVALID_SOCKET)
{
    cout << "Cannot open mail server socket\n";
    return(1);
}
```

The next function finds the port number that has been assigned to the "mail" service, if one exists.

```
// Get the mail service port
lpServEntry = getservbyname( "mail", 0);
```

If there is not a specific entry for the mail service, we'll use the default port number for SMTP.

```
// Use the SMTP default port if no other port is specified
if (lpServEntry == NULL)
    iProtocolPort = htons(IPPORT_SMTP);
else
    iProtocolPort = lpServEntry->s_port;
```

We next need to fill in the family, port, and address fields of the input socket address structure, which will be used to connect to our just-created socket. The socket family is type AF_INET (for TCP/IP), the port number is the mail service port that we've just determined, and the address filled in should be that of the mail server, which we retrieved above in our call to gethostbyname.

```
// Set up a socket address structure
SockAddr.sin_family = AF_INET;
SockAddr.sin_port = iProtocolPort;
SockAddr.sin_addr = *((LPIN_ADDR)*lpHostEntry->h_addr_list);
```

Now, we connect our stream socket to the mail server, at the mail service port. Note that connect returns zero if successful. Also, the third parameter must specify the size of the socket address structure, since the connect function can be used to connect other socket types, and must therefore know what socket-address type it's dealing with. If all goes well, when this function returns, we will have established a "live" socket connection.

```
// Connect the socket
if (connect( hServer, (PSOCKADDR) &SockAddr, sizeof(SockAddr)))
{
    cout << "Error connecting to Server socket.\n";
    return (1);
}
```

Typically, a server will generate some initial response to the client upon connecting. This is always the case with the simple mail protocol, so we must next read this initial response from our socket connection. If you wish to see what this response looks like, you can send `szBuffer` to `cout` or else connect to the mail server using Telnet, and use it to send each string as we do here.

```
// Receive initial response from SMTP server
Check( recv( hServer, szBuffer, sizeof(szBuffer), 0), "recv()Reply");
```

Our next step, according to the simple mail protocol, is literally to say "hello," which is done by sending `HELO` followed by a space, and the client's host name. Terminating every line in this protocol is a carriage-return/line-feed pair.

Note that in this example we are assuming the mail server host name and the client's gateway host name are identical. However, frequently you will have a scenario where you'll want to distinguish these and simply specify the client host name.

```
// Send HELO server.com
sprintf( szMsgLine, "HELO %s%s", szSmtpServerName, CRLF);
Check( send(hServer, szMsgLine, strlen(szMsgLine), 0), "send() HELO");
Check( recv( hServer, szBuffer, sizeof(szBuffer), 0), "recv() HELO");
```

NOTE
It's important to be aware that in the SMTP, every time you send, you need to receive back an acknowledgment. As you'll see shortly, there is one exception to this rule: When you're sending the body of the message, all lines of the message body are sent before reading back any acknowledgment from the mail server.

Note that we aren't doing anything with the data received from the server. We *could* look at it, and in a robust commercial application, particularly when using protocols that are not as lock-step (not as reliant on expected command/reply pairs) as SMTP, we would want to look at and parse the result code from each response. This would allow the application to more gracefully recover from particular error conditions. However, in the case of SMTP, once we are connected, it is very unlikely we will get an unexpected reply. And in the case of a connection error, the Check function will at least give us an indication that we have a problem.

Having sent the HELO to (and received a response from) the server, the next step is to tell the server we have a mail message and indicate the return e-mail address. This is done by sending MAIL FROM:, followed by a space, and the reply-to address in angle brackets. Again, a CRLF pair always terminates each response in SMTP, and after sending, we must read back the server's reply before sending again.

```
// Send MAIL FROM: <sender@mydomain.com>
sprintf( szMsgLine, "MAIL FROM:<%s>%s", szFromAddr, CRLF);
 Check( send( hServer, szMsgLine, strlen(szMsgLine), 0), "send()
    MAIL FROM");
Check( recv( hServer, szBuffer, sizeof(szBuffer), 0), "recv()
    MAIL FROM");
```

Next, we send one (or more, if desired) destination e-mail address, using the form RCPT TO:, followed by a space, and the to-address enclosed in angle brackets. You may send mail to as many recipients as you like this way, but remember to read the server reply after sending each recipient string. Note that if you're attempting to send to many recipients, it is possible to reach the mail server's maximum recipient count, at which point the server would return an error result (which you could detect by checking the result returned each time by recv).

```
// Send RCPT TO: <receiver@domain.com>
sprintf( szMsgLine, "RCPT TO:<%s>%s", szToAddr, CRLF);
Check( send( hServer, szMsgLine, strlen(szMsgLine), 0),
    "send() RCPT TO");
Check( recv( hServer, szBuffer, sizeof(szBuffer), 0),
    "recv() RCPT TO");
```

When we're finished sending the message header information, we signal this to the server by sending DATA (again, followed by a CRLF pair). Note that we could add more optional lines to our header, but the sender and the recipient e-mail addresses are the only parts essential to getting our message delivered.

```
// Send DATA
sprintf( szMsgLine, "DATA%s", CRLF);
```

```
Check( send( hServer, szMsgLine, strlen(szMsgLine),0),"send() DATA");
Check( recv( hServer, szBuffer, sizeof(szBuffer), 0), "recv()DATA");
```

Now, it's time to send each line of the message body text. Since we're sending the contents of a text file, we'll want to read each line, and send it in turn. Note that we do not attempt to read back a reply from the server until we have completed sending all the lines in the message body.

```
// Send all lines of message body (using supplied text file)
MsgFile.getline( szLine, sizeof(szLine)); // get first line
do // for each line of message text...
{
sprintf( szMsgLine, "%s%s", szLine, CRLF);
Check( send( hServer, szMsgLine, strlen(szMsgLine), 0), "send()
    message-line");
MsgFile.getline( szLine, sizeof(szLine)); // get next line
} while ( MsgFile.good() );
```

To signal the server that we're finished sending the body text, we must send a single period on a line by itself. Then, the server issues an acknowledgment reply, which we need to read.

```
// Send blank line and a period
sprintf( szMsgLine, "%s.%s", CRLF, CRLF);
Check( send( hServer, szMsgLine, strlen(szMsgLine), 0), "send()
    end-message");
Check( recv( hServer, szBuffer, sizeof(szBuffer), 0), "recv()
    end-message");
```

At this point, we could either send another e-mail message or quit. Since we don't have anything else to send, we will indicate to the server that we wish to quit. This is done by sending a QUIT string.

```
// Send QUIT
sprintf( szMsgLine, "QUIT%s", CRLF);
Check( send( hServer, szMsgLine, strlen(szMsgLine), 0), "send() QUIT");
Check( recv( hServer, szBuffer, sizeof(szBuffer), 0), "recv() QUIT");
```

Locally, we want to indicate to our user that the message has been sent.

```
// Report message has been sent
cout << "Sent " << argv[4] << " as email message to " << szToAddr
    << endl;
```

And, since we're finished using our server socket, we need to close it.

```
// Close server socket and prepare to exit
```

```
closesocket( hServer );
```

Finally, since we've completed using the Winsock functions, we need to call WSACleanup, which allows Winsock to deallocate any resources it was maintaining for our application. After calling WSACleanup, our application can exit.

```
WSACleanup();

return(0);
}
```

TIP

You may find it interesting to experiment directly with these protocols by using your Windows 95 or NT Telnet client to send properly formatted protocol strings to an FTP, SMTP, POP3, or HTTP server, and view the incoming replies generated by the server. To do this, you will need to locate and download the appropriate protocol specification from the Internet to learn what the command strings and response codes are for a particular protocol. In the Telnet Connect dialog box, enter the corresponding protocol into the Port combo box (yes, many of the protocols are not listed in the combo box, but you can type in whatever you want).

This example should give you a good idea of what is required to write a simple Winsock application. Moreover, it should also give you a basic understanding of how the higher-level TCP/IP protocols communicate information between client and server. POP3, FTP, and HTTP are quite similar in this respect, although in the case of FTP and HTTP, the order in which commands and replies occur is more loosely structured. In SMTP, we can implement sending an e-mail message by means of a very predictable series of send/receive pairs, executing in "see-saw" or lock-step fashion. An HTTP or FTP server requires a more flexible approach, and would be better implemented using a state-table or an event-driven program structure.

The above discussion and examples should help you to understand the issues involved in programming Internet-aware applications by using the Winsock API. Although the socket paradigm is reasonably straightforward and eases the task of communicating via TCP and UDP, it can still be quite tedious to implement the various higher-level protocols in your applications. These protocols vary in their sets of possible states, their message tokens, and behavior. Furthermore, once you have written and debugged your application, you may still need to revisit it periodically to add support for new server implementations, new additions, or changes to the protocol specification. With FTP, for example, although the message tokens are standard, the formats used by various FTP servers to return requested directory listings can vary to some degree.

The recently introduced set of Win32 functions called the Internet API, address these problems. We will look at these functions next.

The Internet API Commands

If you need to write FTP, Gopher, or HTTP client applications, the Internet API may be ideal for your purposes. This set of functions eliminates the need for dealing with TCP/IP implementation details or for using Winsock-related structures and functions. It encapsulates the FTP, HTTP, and Gopher protocols at the task level. Rather than requiring you to open and close sockets, and listen for and accept socket connections, this API lets you manage tasks, such as uploading or downloading files, using a single function call. Moreover, the Internet API encapsulates (hides) the differences in file-listing formats used by different FTP servers, so you can search for files and directories without worrying about which type of FTP server you're connected to.

All the Internet API functions are fully reentrant and thread-safe, so you can use them in multithreaded applications without any problems. Another benefit to using the Internet API is that protocol-specific behavior, which is subject to change, can be isolated from application code and replaced by updating your copy of the Wininet.DLL file (which is the DLL that supplies Internet API functionality).

One drawback to using the Internet API is that it is intended only for Internet *client* applications. Microsoft documentation states clearly that these functions do not provide the appropriate level of control at the protocol or I/O levels to be usable in server implementations. Also, because of the protocol encapsulation and the abstraction of various differences in server behavior, there is likely to be at least a small performance hit as well. But if you need to quickly develop an FTP, Gopher, or HTTP client application, the Internet API will let you get your application up and running in a hurry.

The Internet API functions are listed in the following sections, grouped in nine categories:

- Connect and disconnect functions
- File finding, reading, and writing functions
- FTP-specific functions
- Gopher-specific functions
- HTTP-specific functions
- Cookie functions
- URL-related functions
- Time and date functions
- Error and status functions

> **NOTE** The Internet API automatically caches Internet URLs and recently trans-ferred data. Thus, some functions may return repeated data faster than you might normally expect, because the information does not need to be retrieved again; it is transparently copied from a buffer.

Connect and Disconnect Functions

You interact with the various Internet API functions by using a special Internet handle, called HINTERNET. Unlike the Winsock socket handles, or Win32 handles created using CreateFile, these HINTERNET handles are completely unusable with the normal Win32 handle I/O functions, such as ReadFile or CloseHandle. Instead, you use the Internet API functions, such as InternetReadFile or InternetCloseHandle, to read from an opened resource or to close an opened handle.

HINTERNET handles are created in a hierarchy, or tree. A top-level handle is returned by the InternetOpen function, which you must call before using almost any of the other Internet API functions. Next, you open a connection handle to a particular site, by using InternetConnect. Finally, you open one or more FTP, Gopher, or HTTP file or search handles, which can then be used in calls to InternetReadFile, Internet-FindNextFile, and similar functions.

InternetCloseHandle is used to close HINTERNET handles of any type, includ-ing Internet session, connection, search, and resource handles. Also, because these handles are hierarchical, any lower-level handles will be closed automatically when you close a parent handle. Thus, you could, with a single call to `Internet-CloseHandle` (passing the handle returned from your `InternetOpen` call), close all other handles in your application that were opened using the Internet API functions. For consistency (and good programming practice), however, you may prefer to keep to the habit of closing each handle specifically when you're finished with it.

The following are the Internet API connect and disconnect functions:

- `InternetAttemptConnect`: Attempts to connect to the Internet. Typically, this should be called prior to using the other Internet functions. It returns `ERROR_SUCCESS` if connection is made; otherwise, it returns a Win32 error condition.

- `InternetOpen`: Internet API initialization function. This must be called prior to using the Internet API functions. (Use `InternetCloseHandle` when finished.)

- `InternetConnect`: Connects to the specified FTP, Gopher, or HTTP server, and returns a handle. (Use `InternetCloseHandle` when finished.)

- `InternetCloseHandle`: Closes handles (and subhandles) created by `InternetOpen`, `InternetConnect`, `FtpOpenFile`, `GopherOpenFile`, and `HttpSendRequest`.

File Locating, Reading, and Writing Functions

The following are the Internet API commands for finding, reading, and writing files:

- `InternetFindNextFile`: Continues a search started with `FtpFindFirstFile` or `GopherFindFirstFile`. (And accepts a search handle created by either of these functions.)

- `InternetQueryDataAvailable`: Queries the amount of data available from an HTTP, a Gopher, or an FTP resource.

- `InternetReadFile`: Reads data from a handle opened by `InternetOpenUrl`, `FtpOpenFile`, `GopherOpenFile`, or `HttpOpenRequest`. (See also `FtpGetFile` and `FtpPutFile`.)

- `InternetWriteFile`: Writes data to an open file.

- `InternetSetFilePointer`: Sets the file position for the next `InternetRead-File` call. It returns the current file position if successful; otherwise, it returns a –1. Note that some servers and URL types do not support random access.

FTP-Specific Functions

Finding an FTP (or Gopher) file on a given host connection is very similar to finding a file on a local or network drive using the `FindFirst` and `FindNext` functions. Start searching an FTP (or Gopher) directory with a call to `FtpFindFirstFile` (or `GopherFindFirstFile`), followed by repeated calls to `InternetFindNextFile`, recursing as necessary until you locate the file (or exhaust the available search directories). Remember to close the search handles returned by each `FtpFind-First` (or `GopherFindFirst` call).

The following are the Internet API FTP-related commands:

- `FtpFindFirstFile`: Starts file enumeration or searching in the current server directory. Use this with `InternetFindNextFile` and `InternetCloseHandle`.
- `FtpGetFile`: Retrieves an entire file from the server.
- `FtpPutFile`: Writes an entire file to the server.
- `FtpDeleteFile`: Deletes a file on the server.
- `FtpRenameFile`: Renames a file on the server.
- `FtpOpenFile`: Opens a file on the server for reading or writing. (Use with `InternetQueryDataAvailable`, `InternetReadFile`, `InternetWriteFile`, and `InternetCloseHandle`.)
- `FtpCreateDirectory`: Creates a new directory on the server.
- `FtpRemoveDirectory`: Deletes a directory on the server.
- `FtpSetCurrentDirectory`: Changes the connection's current directory on the server.
- `FtpGetCurrentDirectory`: Returns the connection's current directory on the server.

Gopher-Specific Functions

See the previous section for information about finding a Gopher file on a host connection. The following are the Internet API Gopher-related commands:

- `GopherFindFirstFile`: Starts enumerating a Gopher directory listing. (Use with `InternetFindNextFile` and `InternetCloseHandle`.)

- `GopherOpenFile`: Opens a Gopher object on the server for retrieval. (Use with `InternetQueryDataAvailable`, `InternetReadFile`, `InternetWriteFile`, and `InternetCloseHandle`.)

- `GopherCreateLocator`: Forms a Gopher locator for use in other Gopher function calls.

- `GopherGetAttribute`: Retrieves attribute information on the Gopher object.

HTTP-Specific Functions

The following are the Internet HTTP-specific commands:

- `HttpOpenRequest`: Opens an HTTP request and returns a request handle. (Use `InternetCloseHandle` to close.)

- `HttpAddRequestHeaders`: Adds HTTP request headers to the HTTP request handle.

- `HttpSendRequest`: Sends the specified request to the HTTP server. Use with `InternetQueryDataAvailable` and `InternetReadFile`.

- `HttpQueryInfo`: Retrieves information about an HTTP request.

Cookie Functions

As of the time of this writing, the Internet API is undergoing changes and receiving new API functions. Two functions most recently added deal with setting and retrieving cookie values:

- `InternetGetCookie`: Fills supplied buffer with the cookie data for the specified URL and all its parent URLs. (Intended for interacting with local cookie database.)

- `InternetSetCookie`: Sets cookie data for a given cookie name at a specified URL. (Intended for interacting with local cookie database.)

NOTE

The term *cookie database* refers to the file(s) initially used by Web browsers (but now also by the Internet API) to save cookie values to disk between sessions. Note that Netscape (and other browsers) use their own techniques and file(s) for saving cookie values. Netscape currently stores its cookies in a file called Cookies.TXT. Internet Explorer (and the Internet API) currently store their cookies as separate files, in a directory called \WINNT\COOKIES.

At first glance, this might seem to imply that the Internet API is being expanded to support writing server applications; however, these cookie functions deal only with the cookie database that is located on the client station. You could use these to set or retrieve cookie values that are in memory or have been saved to disk. At least currently, though, you cannot use them to access cookie data stored on a host or peer station.

URL-Related Functions

The URL-related functions are useful for creating, splitting, and combining URLs. These functions are handy for converting between a URL and its component pieces, or for converting between relative and absolute URLs. The following are the Internet API functions associated with URLs:

- `InternetCrackUrl`: Parses a URL string into components.

- `InternetCreateUrl`: Creates a URL string from components.

- `InternetCanonicalizeUrl`: Converts a URL to canonical form. This is used to convert a URL into a server-safe URL, because it converts to escape sequences any spaces or other characters that could be misinterpreted by specific servers.

- `InternetCombineUrl`: Combines base and relative URLs.

- `InternetOpenUrl`: Begins retrieving an FTP, a Gopher, or an HTTP URL.

Time/Date Conversion Functions

The Internet API also supplies functions for converting back and forth between (local) system time and HTTP Internet time strings. HTTP time/date strings are used, for example, in the "Expires:" optional header setting embedded in some HTML documents.

There are two time/date conversion commands:

- `InternetTimeFromSystemTime`: Converts a Win32 SYSTEMTIME structure into a string, formatted according to the HTTP RFC 1.0 time/date string format.

- `InternetTimeToSystemTime`: Converts an HTTP time/date string to a SYSTEMTIME structure.

Error and Status Functions

You can perform error checking by first checking the Boolean return value for each function, and then using the standard `GetLastError` Win32 API function to return a specific error code. More specific information can be retrieved by calling `InternetGetLastResponseInfo`, although in some cases, this tends to return more information than you need. You can also display Internet-specific information using the `InternetErrorDlg` function.

To control protocol-specific settings, use `InternetQueryOption` and `Internet-SetOption`.

The following are the Internet API error and status functions:

- `InternetSetStatusCallback`: Assigns a callback function to be called with status information. This is useful for monitoring functions that take some time to complete.

- `InternetErrorDlg`: Displays predefined dialog boxes for common Internet error conditions.

- `InternetConfirmZoneCrossing`: Detects when your application is moving either from a secure to an insecure URL, or vice versa.

- `InternetQueryOption`: Queries the current setting of a given Internet option.

- `InternetSetOption`: Sets an Internet option.

- `InternetGetLastResponseInfo`: Returns buffer containing data from the last reply; typically used to retrieve more detailed or specialized status or error information.

Simple FTP Transfer: The FtpGet Program

The FtpGet demo program uses the Internet API to perform a simple FTP transfer. As you'll see, in comparison to implementing the FTP protocol directly in your application using Winsock calls, the Internet API is really a breeze to use.

The sample program downloads a given FTP file using the Internet API functions. It starts by calling `InternetOpen` to open an Internet session, then connects to the desired FTP server using `InternetConnect`. If a path has been prepended to the specified filename, this directory is made the current directory on the FTP server, and then the file is downloaded to the client computer using `FtpGetFile`.

To start off, we need to include the necessary header files, including Wininet.H, the Internet API header file.

```
#include <windows.h>
#include <iostream.h>
#include <stdio.h>
#include <wininet.h>
```

> **NOTE**
>
> If your compiler does not yet include the Wininet.H header file and import library, you will need to either download these or otherwise obtain them from Microsoft or your compiler vendor. Currently, you can get the necessary files by downloading the Internet ActiveX SDK—all 10MB of it. It's this size because it includes the Wininet.DLL, .LIB, and .H files, along with other files, including a few sample programs.

Next, we declare two variables to hold the username and password that will be used to log in to the FTP server. For servers permitting anonymous login, the preset values are satisfactory, although you may want to set the password to your own e-mail address, as is customary. For nonanonymous logins, you will definitely need to change both of these values, as appropriate.

```
// Customize login info as appropriate
char  szUsername[64]    = "anonymous";
char  szPassword[64]    = "user@domain.com";
```

This program uses two other global variables. The first, szAppName, is used to hold the name that is passed to the InternetConnect function. The dwBinary variable is a flag that will be needed by the `FtpGetFile` function. Unless you are definitely transferring a text (ASCII) file, be sure to use `FTP_TRANSFER_TYPE_BINARY` to perform a binary file transfer; otherwise, your file will almost certainly fail to transfer the file correctly.

```
// General globals
char      szAppName[20]   = "FtpGet";
DWORD     dwBinary        = FTP_TRANSFER_TYPE_BINARY;
```

In case this application is called from a batch file, here are a set of exit codes for various error conditions that could occur.

```
// Application exit codes
const int    ERR_SUCCESS              = 0;
const int    ERR_USAGE                = 1;
const int    ERR_CONNECTING_INTERNET  = 2;
const int    ERR_CONNECTING_HOST      = 3;
const int    ERR_BAD_DIRECTORY        = 4;
const int    ERR_FTP_TRANSFER         = 5;
```

The `LastErrorMsg` function returns a string containing the error message or status information returned from the last Internet API function call. This information is retrieved by making a call to `InternetGetLastResponseInfo`, and passing it a pointer to the error code, a buffer to fill, and the length of the message buffer. In the event `InternetGetLastResponse` fails (as would happen if there is no Wininet.DLL, for instance), the Win32 `GetLastError` function is called to retrieve whatever Win32 error code might be available.

```
char *LastErrorMsg(void)
{
   static char szErrorMsg[4096];
   ULONG       dwErrorNum, dwLength;

   dwLength = sizeof( szErrorMsg );
   if (!InternetGetLastResponseInfo( &dwErrorNum, (LPSTR)
      szErrorMsg, &dwLength))
   {
      sprintf( szErrorMsg, "Unable to get error information,
      Error# = %d ",
      GetLastError() );
   }
   return( szErrorMsg );
}
```

The main program section starts by declaring the variables that will be used. First listed are two HINTERNET handles. These are "opaque" Internet API handle types, which are allocated by Internet API functions, and are the only handle types suitable for use with the Internet API functions that take a handle as a parameter. (They are "opaque" in that there is no useful information directly accessible inside these handles, and they can only be used with Internet API functions.) Note that HINTERNET handles actually include four types: an "Internet" handle, a session handle, a search handle, and a URL/file handle. The szHost will refer to the FTP server address, and szPath and szFile will contain the path and file, once these have been split apart from the input path/filename supplied to the program.

```
int main( int argc, char *argv[] )
{
    HINTERNET   hInternet, hHost; // handles.
    int         i;
    char        szHost[128];
    char        szPath[MAX_PATH];
    char        szFile[MAX_PATH];
```

Next, the standard usage check, which displays usage information if fewer than two parameters were supplied (remember, zero is always the application name).

```
if (argc < 3)
{
    cout << "Usage: FtpGet ftp.domain.com \\path\\filename (or
        /path/filename)\n";
    return ERR_USAGE;
}
```

Next, we copy the two supplied command-line parameters to szHost and szFile.

```
lstrcpy( szHost, argv[1] );
lstrcpy( szFile, argv[2] );
```

The path default is set to a single slash. We then start at the end of the path/filename, searching for a forward slash or a backslash. If either is found, we know where to split the filename and path; otherwise, we'll assume the entire string is a filename.

```
lstrcpy(szPath, "/"); // Use root as default path
// Get the path if prepended to filename
for (i=strlen(szFile); i>0; --i)
{
```

```
if (szFile[i]=='/' || szFile[i]=='\\')
{
    strncpy(szPath, szFile, ++i);
    szPath[i]= 0; // terminate.
    lstrcpy(szFile, szFile+i);
    break;
}
}
```

Note that we do not need to worry about converting forward slashes to backslashes (or vice versa). This is because the Internet API functions that take filenames know how to convert the slashes and backslashes to the form expected by the server.

Now, we initialize the Internet API for this application, by calling `InternetOpen`. If necessary, the second parameter could be used to tell Wininet that the application needs a proxy server to connect. If the handle returned is zero, an error occurred, and we display an error message and exit.

```
hInternet = InternetOpen( szAppName, LOCAL_INTERNET_ACCESS ,
    NULL, 0, 0 );
if (!hInternet)
{
    cerr << "Error opening Internet: " << LastErrorMsg();
    InternetCloseHandle( hInternet );
    return ERR_CONNECTING_INTERNET;
}
```

NOTE   A *proxy server* is software that permits networked computers to access the Internet via a trusted server. The proxy server usually works with some level of firewall functionality, and sometimes even using network protocols other than TCP/IP, with the appropriate proxy client software.

Having called `InternetOpen`, we are now ready to begin using the other Internet API functions. We first make a call to `InternetConnect`, which establishes a connection to the specified FTP host, using our supplied username and password. If an error occurs at this point, we display an error message and exit.

```
hHost = InternetConnect( hInternet, szHost,
    INTERNET_INVALID_PORT_NUMBER, szUsername,  szPassword,
    INTERNET_SERVICE_FTP, INTERNET_FLAG_PASSIVE , 0);
```

```
if (!hHost)
{
    cerr << "Error connecting to " << szHost << ":
        " << LastErrorMsg();
    InternetCloseHandle( hInternet );
    return ERR_CONNECTING_HOST;
}
```

Next, we set the current directory on the remote server to point to the directory containing the file we're going to download.

```
if (!FtpSetCurrentDirectory( hHost, szPath ))
{
  cerr << "Unable to find remote directory : " << szPath << endl;
    cerr << LastErrorMsg() << endl;
    InternetCloseHandle( hInternet );
    return ERR_BAD_DIRECTORY;
}
```

Now, we're ready to perform the download. This is accomplished in the Internet API via a single call to `FtpGetFile`. The second and third parameters specify the source and destination filenames, respectively. These can be the same, since we've already changed to the correct directory. However, `FtpGetFile` will allow you to include a path name on either (or both) the source and target filenames. If we didn't need to split the filename off for the destination directory, it would have been simpler just to let `FtpGetFile` handle the path name internally.

```
if (!FtpGetFile( hHost, szFile, szFile, FALSE,
    INTERNET_FLAG_RELOAD, dwBinary, 0 ))
{
    cerr << "Unable to transfer file : " << szFile << endl;
    cerr << LastErrorMsg() << endl;
    InternetCloseHandle( hInternet );
    return ERR_FTP_TRANSFER;
}
```

At this point, we want to let our user know the file has finished transferring.

```
cout << "Transferred " << szFile << endl;
```

We can now close the handle to the host (FTP server) connection, and the handle to our Internet connection, signaling the Internet API that we have finished using it in this application.

```
        // Finished, clean up and exit
        InternetCloseHandle( hHost );
        InternetCloseHandle( hInternet );

        return ERR_SUCCESS;
    }
```

> **NOTE** It is possible to set a callback function using the `InternetSetStatus-Callback` function, to be called periodically when Internet API functions that take an extended period of time are busy executing. This would be a nice addition if you need to transfer larger files.

That's it! As you can see, performing an FTP download using the Internet API is really straightforward and quite trivial to implement. The complete listing for this program is on the CD that accompanies this book.

One nice feature you could add to this program would be a searching feature, so that the user would not need to specify the file path on the remote server. This would not be difficult to add; you could use the `FtpFindFirst` and `Internet-FindNext` functions to recursively search each directory for the desired file. Another handy use for these find-first and find-next functions would be to implement a utility that transfers an entire FTP (or Gopher or Web site) from one server to another, by recursing through all directories and copying all files at each level from the host to the client.

Also, note that while this example makes use of the `FtpGetFile` function, you could instead, almost as easily, use the `FtpOpenFile` function, followed by repeated calls to `InternetReadFile`, to read successive blocks from the server. This requires slightly more code but gives you the opportunity to calculate and display a progress indicator as the data is transferring. Or, instead of `FtpOpenFile`, you could use `InternetOpenUrl`. `InternetOpenUrl` has the added benefit of being protocol-independent. It is able to parse different URL types and automatically determine the type of server connection to open. In this way, you can use the same code to open various types of URLs. The protocol-independent data transfer is then performed by making repeated calls to `InternetReadFile`.

The Internet API is a powerful yet easy to use API, and indications are that support for additional protocols is being planned for future versions. Perhaps by the time you read this, there will also be functions for sending and retrieving e-mail. The Internet API has all the earmarks of becoming a widely used Windows API.

If you prefer working with visual controls, you may be especially interested in the Internet Control Pack, which we'll take a look at next.

ActiveX Web Controls

The Microsoft Internet Web Control Pack is a set of ActiveX controls available via Microsoft's Web site (or FTP site). The Control Pack makes building an FTP client, Web browser, news, or e-mail client as easy as dropping the appropriate control onto your form, and adding only a few lines of code. You can use these controls in Delphi, as well as in Visual Basic or even in Visual C++.

In addition to the FTP, HTTP/HTML, news, and e-mail controls, there are also both client and server versions of TCP and UDP Winsock controls, which you can use to create your own specialized, higher-level Internet protocol or build your own Internet server or client. Unlike the Internet API functions, the ActiveX controls encapsulate Winsock functionality in a way that simplifies Winsock programming, yet provides you with enough control over how connections are established to permit building Internet server applications. Again, due to the overhead involved in encapsulating the Winsock functionality inside an ActiveX control, you are not likely to achieve the same performance you would get using the Winsock API itself. On the other hand, the performance hit does not seem very noticeable, and whatever performance these controls sacrifice is well-compensated for by their extreme ease of use.

One Control and One Line of Code

After you install the ActiveX controls, programming is a cinch. For example, it literally requires only placing the HTML control on your application's form and writing a single line of code to initially browse a Web page! For example, this line is all it takes to cause the Web browser to display Microsoft's home page.

```
Html1.RequestDoc('http://www.microsoft.com');
```

Running the application produces a window the size of your HTML control, which establishes a connection to www.microsoft.com. After a few seconds, you should see the resulting HTML page in the control window!

Although you can pass the desired URL through to your application (or recompile each time), a much better approach is to add a combo box to your application, which can be tied to the HTML control and used to supply it with a desired URL. This provides a URL-entry area very similar to that found in any Web browser.

One (rather big!) disadvantage of the Web control is that it currently supports only HTML 2.0. It has no support for frames, Java, ActiveX controls, or any of the other "advanced features" found currently in Netscape and Internet Explorer. Even if Microsoft releases an upgraded version of the Web control, it is unlikely that it would match the features found in commercial browsers, such as Internet Explorer.

Installing Microsoft's Internet ActiveX Controls in Delphi 2.0

For any Delphi users out there, these controls are really a treat. The quick compile time combined with extremely simple visual configuration of the Internet Web Controls will allow you to crank out Internet applications in no time! My first attempts in installing the controls into Delphi led me to believe that Delphi just wasn't compatible with these controls. However, I figured it out and am passing these instructions onto other Delphi users, so you can avoid my mistakes. Here are the steps:

1. Download and install the MS Internet Control Pack.
2. Start Delphi 2.0.
3. From the main menu, select Component/Install.
4. Click on the OCX button.
5. Scroll through the Registered Controls list, until you come to (for example) the Microsoft FTP Client Control. Highlight it.
6. Go down to the Unit File Name field and change the filename to something descriptive but unique. For example, for FTP use MSFTP.PAS; for NNTP, use MSNNTP.PAS; and for HTTP, use MSHTTP.PAS.

(continued on next page)

7. Go to Class Names. Where it says TFTP Control, delete the second word *Control*, plus any blank characters. Be careful not to add any spaces or a carriage return. You will get an "Invalid class name" error message if there are any characters beyond the single-word class name.

8. Click on OK.

Repeat steps 5 through 8 for each OCX control you wish to add.

When finished installing controls, click on OK again. Reply to the message box that asks "Save changes to project?" (most likely you will choose No). At this point, Delphi will rebuild the component library. Depending on how fast your machine is, and the total number of controls installed, it may take anywhere from seconds to minutes to rebuild your component library. After it finishes, you should be able to click on the OCX tab of your component toolbar and see icons for the new Internet controls you've added.

You can find online help files for each control in your \WINDOWS\SYSTEM directory (for Windows 95) or \WINNT\SYSTEM32\ directory (for Windows NT).

The Internet controls are now available for use in Delphi. Have fun!

ActiveX Web Controls in the Internet Control Pack

The Control Pack provides the following controls:

- **FTP Control (client):** Adds support for searching and browsing file listings and downloading files using FTP.

- **HTML Control (client):** Adds support for (simple) Web browsing (an instant Web browser control, as explained earlier).

- **HTTP Control (client):** Adds support for HTTP to your application.

- **NNTP Control (client):** Adds News transport support to your application.

- **POP Control (client):** Adds support for POP to your application, to retrieve e-mail.

- **SMTP Control (client):** Adds support for sending e-mail. You can use it together with the POP control to easily add e-mail send and receive functionality to your application.

- **Winsock TCP and UDP Controls:** Adds TCP/IP or datagram support to your applications. These comes in both client and server versions, and allow you to define your own specialized protocols.

A Simple Web Browser: The WebView Program

The WebView demo program makes use of the HTML control to create a simple but functional Web browser.

> **NOTE**
>
> The example assumes you are using Delphi. If you are using Visual Basic, the online help for the HTML control has a good Visual Basic sample program that you can use instead of the one here.

Here are the steps to follow to make a very simple Web browser in Delphi 2.0:

1. Start a new application. (From the File menu, choose New Application.)

2. Click on the OCX tab in your tools palette, and click on the HTML tool icon.

3. Click on your application form to place a copy of the HTML control on the form.

4. In the Object Inspector window, change the name of this control to **Html**.

5. Select the Events tab, and double-click on the entry-area of the `OnBegin-Retrieval` event.

6. Place the following code under the `HTMLBeginRetrieval` procedure declaration:

```
var  i: integer;  found: boolean;
begin
  found:= FALSE;
  for i:= 0 to UrlBox.Items.Count -1 do
```

```
        if (UrlBox.Items[i] = Html.Url) then begin
          found:= TRUE;
          break;
        end;
      if (not found) then
        UrlBox.Items.Add( Html.Url );
      UrlBox.Text:= Html.Url;
    end;
```

7. Place a combo-box control on your form. This can be positioned just above the HTML control.

8. In the Object Inspector window, change the name of this control to **UrlBox**.

9. Select the Events tab, and double-click on the entry-area for the `OnClick` event.

10. Place the following line inside the `UrlBoxClick` procedure:

```
Html.RequestDoc( UrlBox.Text );
```

11. Back in the Object Inspector window, select the UrlBox's Events tab, and double-click on the entry-area for the `OnKeyDown` event. Place the following line of code inside the `UrlBoxKeyDown` procedure:

```
Html.RequestDoc( Default_Page );
```

12. Double-click on a blank area of your form, and enter the following line into the `FormCreate` procedure:

```
Html.RequestDoc( Default_Page );
```

13. In the Object Inspector window, (and with the main form selected), double-click on the `OnResize` event, and enter the following into the `FormResize` procedure:

```
UrlBox.width:= ClientWidth;
Html.width:= ClientWidth;
Html.height:= ClientHeight - UrlBox.Height;
```

14. Below the `implementation` line, and just above your first procedure declaration, enter the following constant declaration. (Feel free to change to your favorite URL.)

```
CONST

    DEFAULT_PAGE = 'www.webcrawler.com';
```

15. Save your unit1.pas file as **mainwin.pas**, and your project as **webview.pas**. If you like, also rename the main form to **FrmMainWin**. (This last step is not really necessary.)

At this point, you should have an approximately 71-line Delphi program, which looks very similar to the listing for the WebView program shown at the end of the chapter. Try compiling the project. If you have any problems, double-check for syntax errors caused by typos or other mistakes. (To save time, you may want to load the file from the CD that comes with this book, or at least compare your source code with it.)

If the project compiles, try running it. You will need to have an active connection to the Internet (or your intranet) for this application to work. If you have auto-dialing enabled, a connection may be established automatically. Assuming you have a "live" TCP/IP connection to the Internet, your default URL should appear in the browser window within several seconds. To go to a new URL, enter it into the URL area (combo box), and press Enter. To return to a previous URL, select it from the combo-box list.

How WebView Works

As you've probably noticed, the function used to make the HTML control go to a URL and display it is `RequestDoc( SomeURL )`. The `UrlBox` combo box watches each keypress, and when it detects a carriage return (`VK_RETURN`), it feeds its current text into `RequestDoc`. The current URL is added conditionally to `UrlBox` at the start of each page load, when the `BeginRetrieval` event is triggered. The code checks to see if the URL is already in the `UrlBox` list, and if not, it adds it; otherwise, it simply redisplays it.

The HTML control has several other properties, events, and methods. Using more of these and adding more of your own code, you could create a Web browser that is functionally quite similar to Internet Explorer 2.0. You can add Next and Previous buttons, for example, and a menu with configuration options (such as default home page, background color, and link colors). You can add Delphi toolbar buttons to easily change the font size(s), and add bookmarks. Because there are events that are triggered during and at the end of each page load, you could even add a progress indicator, such as a bitmap animation or a progress bar.

Other Uses for Internet Controls

Keep in mind that the HTML control can be used for purposes other than displaying pages. You might also use it to retrieve and parse HTML pages to look for certain search words and follow links—creating a little search "bot," which can search for pages for you and perhaps log each pertinent URL it visits.

Also, don't forget that you can combine different Internet controls or have many of the same Internet controls in your application. You could retrieve mail from one account via a POP control, and forward it to another account using an SMTP control. Also, these controls let you easily Internet-enable other applications you may already have written. For example, you could add an SMTP control, and your application would be able to send you an e-mail message when it's finished processing. Better yet, add an FTP control, and your report application can transfer a copy of that report to any FTP server it has access to.

The UDP and TCP controls can be used for datagram and streaming communications, either as servers or clients (or both). You could even define your own protocol, perhaps modeled after FTP or SMTP, to accomplish some special purpose (such as reading the temperature or remotely controlling a PC). Then you could easily implement it using one of these socket controls (probably a TCP control).

Despite the current state of flux with all things Internet-related, the topics covered here should whet your Internet programming appetite. As you can see, the Internet API and the ActiveX controls make many common Internet tasks practically child's play to implement. And for down-to-the-wire or high-performance-type applications (or for designing more portable Internet software), Winsock 2 provides all the functionality you need, with both synchronous and asynchronous sets of socket functions. The sample FindAddr and WebView programs presented in this chapter follow. The SendMail and FtpGet programs (and all other demos described in this book) are on the CD.

Listing 19.1: The FindAddr Program

```
/*-----------------------------------------------------------------
-----

    FINDADDR.CPP

    Demonstrates using Win32 Winsock "database" functions to perform
    IP address and name lookup. Takes a single parameter, as follows:
```

```
          FINDADDR some.address.com

Attempts to resolve domain name into its assigned IP address us-
ing DNS lookup. If successful, then attempts to reverse-lookup
the domain name using the retrieved IP address. This name may
be different than the name supplied via the command line, and
depends on how the IP address has been mapped.

WINSOCK FUNCTIONS USED:

WSAStartup              Initializes specific winsock version.
gethostbyname           Attempts to lookup host name from IP #.
inet_ntoa               Converts address to dotted format.
inet_addr               Converts dotted address to 32-bits.
gethostbyaddr           Attempts to lookup host IP# from name.
WSACleanup              Deallocates internal winsock resources.


NOTES:

  - This program supports both Windows 95 and NT 4.0, and requires
    Microsoft TCP/IP networking (or another TCP/IP stack) to be
    installed and configured prior to use. (You will also need to
    have a TCP/IP connection established or else have auto-dialing
    enabled).

    written by Jim Blaney
    for NT/95 Developer's Handbook
-------------------------------------------------------------*/

#define WIN32_LEAN_AND_MEAN
#include <winsock2.h>
#include <stdlib.h>
#include <stdio.h>

// Insist on at least Winsock version 1.1 (you may use 2.0)
const  VERSION_MAJOR   =  1;
const  VERSION_MINOR   =  1;

void ShowUsage(void)
```

```
{
   printf("usage: FINDADDR some.address.com\n");
   exit(0);
}

// Takes string IP address and looks up numeric IP address.
int main(int argc, char *argv[])
{
WSADATA      WSData;
   LPHOSTENT    lpHostEntry;
   DWORD        dwIPAddress;
   LPSTR        szIPAddress;

   // Check for valid # of command-line arguments.
   if ( argc != 2 ) ShowUsage();

   // Attempt to initialize Winsock (1.1 or later).
   if ( WSAStartup(MAKEWORD(VERSION_MAJOR, VERSION_MINOR),
      &WSData) )
   {
      printf("Cannot find Winsock (v%d.%d or later)!\n",
        VERSION_MAJOR, VERSION_MINOR);
      return(1);
   }

   lpHostEntry = gethostbyname( argv[1] );

   if ( lpHostEntry == NULL )
      printf("Unable to find %s!\n", argv[1]);
   else {
      // Success. Convert address into dotted-notation (string).
      szIPAddress = inet_ntoa( *(LPIN_ADDR)
        *(lpHostEntry->h_addr_list) );

      // Display resolved address
      printf("Found! IP address is %s\n", szIPAddress );

      // Now, let's try reverse lookup
      dwIPAddress = inet_addr( szIPAddress ); // Convert to 32-bits
lpHostEntry = gethostbyaddr( (LPSTR) &dwIPAddress,
   sizeof(dwIPAddress), AF_INET);
```

```
        // Display reverse-resolved address (or error message).
        if ( lpHostEntry == NULL )
            printf("Hm... Unable to reverse lookup %s\n",
            szIPAddress);
        else
            printf("Successful reverse lookup of %s yields %s\n",
                szIPAddress, lpHostEntry->h_name );
        }

    // Clean up Winsock resources and terminate
    WSACleanup();
    return(0);
}
```

Listing 19.2: The WebView Program

```
    unit MainWin;

    interface

    uses
Windows, Messages, SysUtils, Classes, Graphics, Controls, Forms,
Dialogs, StdCtrls, OleCtrls, MSHTML;

    type
      TfrmMainWin = class(TForm)
        HTML: THTML;
        UrlBox: TComboBox;
        procedure FormResize(Sender: TObject);
        procedure UrlBoxKeyDown(Sender: TObject; var Key: Word;
          Shift: TShiftState);
        procedure HTMLBeginRetrieval(Sender: TObject);
        procedure UrlBoxClick(Sender: TObject);
        procedure FormCreate(Sender: TObject);
      private
        { Private declarations }
      public
        { Public declarations }
      end;
```

```
var
  frmMainWin: TfrmMainWin;

implementation

{$R *.DFM}

CONST
  DEFAULT_PAGE = 'www.webcrawler.com';

procedure TfrmMainWin.FormResize(Sender: TObject);
begin
  UrlBox.width:= ClientWidth;
  Html.width:= ClientWidth;
  Html.height:= ClientHeight - UrlBox.Height;
end;

procedure TfrmMainWin.UrlBoxKeyDown(Sender: TObject; var Key: Word;
  Shift: TShiftState);
begin
  if (key = VK_RETURN) then Html.RequestDoc( UrlBox.Text );
end;

procedure TfrmMainWin.HTMLBeginRetrieval(Sender: TObject);
var  i: integer;  found: boolean;
begin
  found:= FALSE;
  for i:= 0 to UrlBox.Items.Count -1 do
    if (UrlBox.Items[i] = Html.Url) then begin
      found:= TRUE;
      break;
    end;
  if (not found) then
    UrlBox.Items.Add( Html.Url );
  UrlBox.Text:= Html.Url;
end;

procedure TfrmMainWin.UrlBoxClick(Sender: TObject);
begin
  Html.RequestDoc( UrlBox.Text );
end;
```

```pascal
procedure TfrmMainWin.FormCreate(Sender: TObject);
begin
  Html.RequestDoc( Default_Page );
end;

end.
```

CHAPTER

TWENTY

20

Network Programming

- NetBIOS support implementation

- WNet API functions

- LANMan functions

- Winsock 2 for networking applications

- Named pipes and mailslots for networking

- An introduction to RPC and DCON

As Windows has grown up, it has taken a variety of approaches toward network solutions. The good news is that lots of progress has been made. The not-so-good news is that there's enough overlap and partial redundancy of APIs to make it not always obvious which APIs are best suited for a particular purpose. In this chapter, we'll look at the different APIs and their relative merits. By the time you're through, you should be all fired up to go out and learn even more.

Using the NetBIOS Functions

NetBIOS has the distinction of being the only networking API function that was built into DOS. For programmers faced with porting old applications, which made use of NetBIOS DOS interrupt calls, to Win32, the `Netbios` API function can simplify the conversion process. Instead of calling the NetBIOS interrupt, you fill a Network Control Block (NCB) structure and pass a pointer to it in your call to the `Netbios` API.

However, except for the porting scenario, it is unlikely that you will want to use `Netbios` itself in your applications, since a richer set of functions is available via named pipes, RPC, WNet functions, or Winsock, all of which are explained in this chapter. For applications that will never need anything but NetBIOS support, and for programmers already very familiar with it, the `Netbios` API provides an efficient way to implement NetBIOS support.

Here's how the `Netbios` function is defined:

```
UCHAR Netbios
(
   PNCB   pncb    // address of network control block
);
```

The NCB structure is defined as follows:

```
typedef struct _NCB { // ncb
    UCHAR   ncb_command;
    UCHAR   ncb_retcode;
    UCHAR   ncb_lsn;
    UCHAR   ncb_num;
    PUCHAR  ncb_buffer;
    WORD    ncb_length;
    UCHAR   ncb_callname[NCBNAMSZ];
```

```
      UCHAR   ncb_name[NCBNAMSZ];
      UCHAR   ncb_rto;
      UCHAR   ncb_sto;
      void (*ncb_post) (struct _NCB *);
      UCHAR   ncb_lana_num;
      UCHAR   ncb_cmd_cplt;
      UCHAR   ncb_reserve[10];
      HANDLE ncb_event;
} NCB;
```

The ncb_command field must always be set to one of the Netbios function values, which are listed in Table 20.1. ncb_length must always be set to the size of the NCB structure, and certain other fields must be set as appropriate for each function. Upon completion, Netbios returns the status code in ncb_retcode.

TABLE 20.1   NetBIOS Commands

Command	Description
NCBACTION	Enables extensions to the transport interface.
NCBADDGRNAME	Adds a group name to the local name table.
NCBADDNAME	Adds a unique name to the local name table.
NCBASTAT	Retrieves the status of the adapter.
NCBCALL	Opens a session with another name.
NCBCANCEL	Cancels a previous command.
NCBCHAINSEND	Sends the contents of two data buffers to the specified session partner.
NCBCHAINSENDNA	Sends the contents of two data buffers to the specified session partner without waiting for acknowledgment.
NCBDELNAME	Deletes a name from the local name table.
NCBDGRECV	Receives a datagram from any name.
NCBDGRECVBC	Receives a broadcast datagram from any host.
NCBDGSEND	Sends a datagram to a specified name.
NCBDGSENDBC	Sends a broadcast datagram to every host on the LAN.

TABLE 20.1 NetBIOS Commands (Continued)

Command	Description
NCBENUM	Enumerates LAN adapter (LANA) numbers.
NCBFINDNAME	Determines the location of a name on the network.
NCBHANGUP	Closes a specified session.
NCBLANSTALERT	Notifies the user of LAN failures that last for more than one minute.
NCBLISTEN	Enables a session to be opened with another name.
NCBRECV	Receives data from the specified session partner.
NCBRECVANY	Receives data from any session corresponding to a specified name.
NCBRESET	Resets a LAN adapter.
NCBSEND	Sends data to the specified session partner.
NCBSENDNA	Sends data to specified session partner and does not wait for an acknowledgment.
NCBSSTAT	Retrieves the status of the session.
NCBTRACE	Activates or deactivates NCB tracing. Support for this command is optional and system-specific.
NCBUNLINK	Unlinks the adapter.

A few additions and enhancements have been made to the Netbios function for better integration into Windows programs. Functions can be executed asynchronously by either posting (using ncb_post), or using signal-completion events (using ncb_event). In the posting approach, the function specified in ncb_post takes only a single parameter, which (like Netbios) is a pointer to an NCB. This makes your implementation much more consistent and portable across different versions (or platforms) of Windows.

In the events approach, the ncb_event is set to the nonsignaled state when an asynchronous NetBIOS command is requested, and is set to the signaled state when the command has completed.

Using the WNet API

The WNet functions first appeared in Windows for Workgroups, primarily as a higher-level API. Occasionally, these functions, like the LANMan functions, provide an easier API for performing protocol-independent, simple networking tasks. However, most (if not all) the functionality is duplicated (or expanded) in the other Win32 network APIs.

In the WNet way of doing things, any network resource is represented by means of a NETRESOURCE structure, which is defined as follows:

```
typedef struct _NETRESOURCE {
    DWORD   dwScope;
    DWORD   dwType;
    DWORD   dwDisplayType;
    DWORD   dwUsage;
    LPTSTR  lpLocalName;
    LPTSTR  lpRemoteName;
    LPTSTR  lpComment;
    LPTSTR  lpProvider;
} NETRESOURCE;
```

NOTE   In its original form, the WNet functions provided for displaying network dialog boxes that the user could use to browse network resources and connect or disconnect by using the mouse. Although the dialog boxes are still supported in NT 4.0 (and Windows 95), the functions that display them seem to have been phased out. The Win32 SDK documentation discourages using them, and new functions have been added to replace them and provide a similar yet expanded functionality. Win32 programs should make use of the WNetAddConnection2 API function, as shown in this sample program, discussed in a bit. However, you can still display browsable network connect and disconnect dialog boxes, using the WNetConnection-Dialog and WNetDisconnectDialog functions, respectively.

The WNet Functions

The following are the WNet functions.

- `WNetAddConnection`: Connects a local device to a network resource. This creates a persistent connection if successful. This command has been updated to `WNetAddConnection2` and `WNetAddConnection3`.

- `WNetAddConnection2`: More recent version that replaces `WNetAddConnection`.

- `WNetAddConnection3`: Similar to `WNetAddConnection2`, but it also takes a handle to a window that the network provider can use as an owner window for dialog boxes.

- `WNetCancelConnection`: Breaks an existing network connection. This command has been updated to `WNetcancelConnection2`.

- `WNetCancelConnection2`: Replaces `WNetCancelConnection`. It removes persistent network connections that are not currently connected.

- `WNetCloseEnum`: Ends a network-resource enumeration started by the `WNetOpenEnum` function.

- `WNetConnectionDialog`: Starts a general browsing dialog box for connecting to network resources.

- `WNetDisconnectDialog`: Starts a general browsing dialog box for disconnecting from network resources.

- `WNetEnumResource`: Continues a network-resource enumeration started by the `WNetOpenEnum` function.

- `WNetGetConnection`: Retrieves the name of the network resource associated with a local device.

- `WNetGetLastError`: Retrieves the most recent extended error code set by a Windows network function.

- `WNetGetUniversalName`: Takes a drive-based path for a network resource and obtains a data structure that contains a more universal form of the name.

- `WNetGetUser`: Retrieves the current default user name or the user name used to establish a network connection.

- `WNetOpenEnum`: Starts an enumeration of network resources or existing connections.

Mapping a Drive: The WNetDemo Program

The WNet demo is a simple Delphi program that uses the newer `WNetAddConnection2` function to map a user-specified network drive to a specified local name. The complete source code is listed at the end of the chapter.

If you're building this example from scratch, just open a new project in Delphi 2, place a couple edit fields onto your form, add a button, and then add the source code into your button's `buttonclick` method.

In the program, we begin by defining `nr` as a `TNetResource` (or `NETRESOURCE` in C/C++), followed by three string variables that will be used to hold any error message, plus the local and network resource names, as zero- (NULL) terminated strings.

```
var  nr: TNetResource;
     szErrorMessage, szLocalName, szRemoteName: ShortString;
```

Next, we set the hourglass cursor, and start by copying/converting the local and remote resource names (as entered by the end user) from the edit controls to the null-terminated string variables.

```
begin
  // Clear NetResource structure, load local and remote names
  Cursor:= crHourGlass;
  Button1.Cursor:= Cursor;
  fillchar(nr, sizeof(nr), #0);
  strpcopy(@szLocalName, Edit2.Text);
  strpcopy(@szRemoteName, Edit1.Text);
```

Then, we fill in the `NETRESOURCE` fields, as required for a call to `WNetAddConnect2`. First, `dwType` is set to specify that we want to attach to a disk-type network device. The local and remote resource names are filled in, and the display type is set to "generic."

```
  // Now, fill NetResource fields
  with nr do
  begin
    dwType:= RESOURCETYPE_DISK;
    lpLocalName:= @szLocalName;
    lpRemoteName:= @szRemoteName;
  end;
```

In Delphi, the @ symbol is equivalent to the address-of & symbol in C and C++.

Now the call to WNetAddConnection2 can be made. Note that parameters two and three could specify another user name and password. This example simply uses NIL, which defaults to using the current user's password and name.

```
// Call WNetAddConnection2, using default user name and password
if (WNetAddConnection2( nr, NIL, NIL, 0) <> NO_ERROR) then
```

As with some of the C++ examples, if an error occurs, we use FormatMessage to retrieve the Win32 system error message corresponding to the return code provided by GetLastError. ShowMessage suffices to display this message in a dialog box.

```
begin
  // If error occurred, retrieve system error text and display it.
  FormatMessage( FORMAT_MESSAGE_FROM_SYSTEM, NIL, GetLastError,
    LANG_SYSTEM_DEFAULT, @szErrorMessage,
    sizeof(szErrorMessage), NIL);
  ShowMessage('Error attempting connection: '
    '+strpas(@szErrorMessage));
end
else
  ShowMessage(Edit1.Text
    +' has been successfully connected and mapped to
    '+Edit2.Text);
```

Finally, we restore the hourglass cursor to the normal or default cursor. Note that because each object on the form can have its own cursor setting, we set both the form's cursor and the button's cursor, to make sure the user sees the cursor change when pressing the button.

```
Cursor:= crDefault;
Button1.Cursor:= Cursor;
```

That's it! These WNet functions are quite easy to use. You simply set and/or retrieve fields in a NETRESOURCE structure and let the function (or your end user!) make the desired connection.

Using the LANMan Functions

The LAN Manager API has been around since Microsoft's LAN Manager, predating Windows NT. The function set has been modified and expanded with each consecutive version of NT. For the most part, these functions are duplicated in various other Win32 API functions, which often include additional features and parameters. For example, if you read the section on the security API in Chapter 18, you may have noticed that the user and group security functions provided in the LANMan function set are simpler to use, but they leave out important aspects of NT security. There are no parameters, for instance, which take the ACCESS_TOKEN or allow you to impersonate a user. On the other hand, if you do not need these aspects of security, you may want to take advantage of the LANMan functions' ease of use.

> **NOTE**
>
> You may be wondering (because of the functionality overlap with other parts of the API) whether the LANMan functions are on the way out. In fact, this does not appear to be the case. There is no mention in the SDK documentation of these functions being phased out. Moreover, a couple functions were even added in the NT 4.0 release.

You might want to use these functions where convenient in smaller applications. But before you do, check if there is a better alternative provided elsewhere in the Win32 API; this will often be the case. Additionally, when you're implementing security, some things can only be done using the security API. For consistency, it is probably better to avoid mixing calls to both types of security functions in the same program.

If you decide to use the LANMan functions, keep in mind that, at least currently (in NT 4.0), the functions that use strings always use Unicode-style strings. You'll need to convert strings back and forth using the `MultiByteToWideChar` and related string-conversion functions.

The following sections list the LANMan functions, grouped into 17 categories:

Network share and connection	Group security
Server information	User security
Server transport	Workstation
Service management	Message
Network session	Access check
Drive/directory replication	Configuration
Alert, auditing, and error log	Network buffer allocation
Network file	Miscellaneous networking
Job scheduling	

Network Share and Connection Functions

The following are the LANMan share and connection functions:

- `NetShareAdd`: Shares a server resource.

- `NetShareCheck`: Checks whether or not a server is sharing a device.

- `NetShareDel`: Deletes a share name from a server's list of shared resources, disconnecting all connections to the shared resource.

- `NetShareEnum`: Retrieves information about each shared resource on a server. (Win32-based applications should use the `WNetEnumResource` function.)

- `NetShareGetInfo`: Retrieves information about a particular shared resource on a server.

- `NetShareSetInfo`: Sets the parameters of a shared resource.

- `NetStatisticsGet`: Retrieves operating statistics for a service.

- `NetUseAdd`: Establishes a connection between a local or NULL device name and a shared resource by redirecting the local or NULL (UNC) device name to the shared resource. (Win32-based applications should use the `WNetAddConnection2` function.)

- `NetUseDel`: Ends a connection to a shared resource. (Win32-based applications should use the `WNetCancelConnection2` function.)

- `NetUseEnum`: Lists all current connections between the local computer and resources on remote servers. (Win32-based applications should use the `WNetEnumResource` function.)

- `NetUseGetInfo`: Retrieves information about a connection to a shared resource. (Win32-based applications should use the `WNetGetConnection` function.)

Server Information Functions

The following are the LANMan server information functions:

- `NetServerDiskEnum`: Retrieves a list of disk drives on a server.

- `NetServerEnum`: Lists all servers of the specified type(s) that are visible in the specified domain(s).

- `NetServerGetInfo`: Retrieves information about the specified server.

- `NetServerSetInfo`: Sets a server's operating parameters; it can set them individually or collectively. (Settings remain in effect after server is restarted.)

Server Transport Functions

The following are the LANMan server transport functions:

- `NetServerTransportAdd`: Binds the server to the transport.

- `NetServerTransportDel`: Unbinds the transport from the server.

- `NetServerTransportEnum`: Supplies information about transports that are managed by the server.

Service Management Functions

- `NetServiceControl`: Controls the operations of network services.

- `NetServiceEnum`: Retrieves information about all started services, including paused services.

- `NetServiceGetInfo`: Retrieves information about a particular started service.

- `NetServiceInstall`: Starts a network service.

Network Session Functions

The following are the LANMan session functions:

- `NetSessionDel`: Ends a session between a server and a workstation.

- `NetSessionEnum`: Provides information about all current sessions.

- `NetSessionGetInfo`: Retrieves information about a session established between a particular server and workstation.

Drive/Directory Replication Functions

The following are the LANMan drive and directory replication functions:

- `NetReplExportDirAdd`: Registers an existing directory in the export path to be replicated.

- `NetReplExportDirDel`: Deregisters a replicated directory.

- `NetReplExportDirEnum`: Lists the replicated directories in the export path.

- `NetReplExportDirGetInfo`: Retrieves a replicated directory's control information.

- `NetReplExportDirLock`: Locks a replicated directory (increments the lock count) so that replication from it can be suspended.

- `NetReplExportDirSetInfo`: Modifies the control information of a replicated directory.

- `NetReplExportDirUnlock`: Unlocks a directory (decrements the lock count) so that replication from it can resume.

- `NetReplGetInfo`: Retrieves the Replicator service configuration information.

- `NetReplImportDirAdd`: Registers an existing directory in the import path to receive replication from a master.

- `NetReplImportDirDel`: Deregisters a directory so that it no longer receives updates from the master.

- `NetReplImportDirEnum`: Lists the replicated directories in the import path.

- `NetReplImportDirGetInfo`: Retrieves the status information on a client replicated directory.

- `NetReplImportDirLock`: Locks a replicated directory so that replication to it can be suspended.

- `NetReplImportDirUnlock`: Unlocks a directory so that replication to it can resume.

- `NetReplSetInfo`: Modifies the Replicator service configuration information.

Alert, Auditing, and Error Log Functions

The following are the LANMan alert, auditing, and error log functions:

- `NetAlertRaise`: Notifies all registered clients that a particular event occurred.

- `NetAlertRaiseEx`: Simplifies the raising of an administrator alert.

- `NetAuditClear`: Clears the audit log on a server and, optionally, saves the entries in a backup file.

- `NetAuditRead`: Reads from the audit log on a server.

- `NetErrorLogClear`: Clears the error log and optionally saves the entries in a backup file.

- `NetErrorLogRead`: Reads from the specified error log.

Network File Functions

The following are the LANMan file functions:

- `NetFileClose`: Forces a resource to close. This function can be used when an error prevents closure by other means.

- `NetFileEnum`: Supplies information about some or all open files on a server, allowing the user to supply a resume handle and get required information through repeated calls to the function.

- `NetFileGetInfo`: Retrieves information about a particular opening of a server resource.

Job-Scheduling Functions

The following are the LANMan job-scheduling functions:

- `NetScheduleJobAdd`: Submits a job to run at a computer at a specified time and date in the future.

- `NetScheduleJobDel`: Deletes a range of jobs queued to run at a computer.

- `NetScheduleJobEnum`: Lists the jobs queued on a specified computer.

- `NetScheduleJobGetInfo`: Retrieves information about a particular job queued on a specified computer.

NOTE These job scheduling functions require the NT Schedule service to be started.

Group Security Functions

The following are the LANMan group security functions:

- `NetGroupAdd`: Creates a global group in the security database.

- `NetGroupAddUser`: Gives an existing user account membership in an existing global group.

- `NetGroupDel`: Deletes a global group account from the accounts database.

- `NetGroupDelUser`: Removes a user from a particular global group in the user account database.

- `NetGroupEnum`: Retrieves information about each global group account.

- `NetGroupGetInfo`: Retrieves information about a particular global group account on a server.

- `NetGroupGetUsers`: Retrieves a list of the members of a particular global group in the user account database.

- `NetGroupSetInfo`: Sets the parameters of a global group account.

- `NetGroupSetUsers`: Sets (users of) the global group membership for the specified global group.

- `NetLocalGroupAdd`: Creates a local group in the security database.

- `NetLocalGroupAddMember`: Gives an existing user account or global group membership in an existing local group.

- `NetLocalGroupAddMembers`: Adds one or more existing user accounts or global groups as members of an existing local group.

- `NetLocalGroupDel`: Deletes a local group account and all of its members from the accounts database.

- `NetLocalGroupDelMember`: Removes a member from a particular local group in the security database.

- `NetLocalGroupDelMembers`: Removes one or more members from an existing local group.

- `NetLocalGroupEnum`: Retrieves information about each local group account.

- `NetLocalGroupGetInfo`: Retrieves information about a particular local group account on a server.

- `NetLocalGroupGetMembers`: Retrieves a list of the members of a particular local group in the security database.

- `NetLocalGroupSetInfo`: Sets the parameters of a local group.

- `NetLocalGroupSetMembers`: Sets the local group membership for the specified local group.

User Security Functions

The following are the LANMan user security functions:

- `NetUserAdd`: Adds a user account.

- `NetUserChangePassword`: Changes a user's password for a specified network server or domain. This function is new in Windows NT.

- `NetUserDel`: Deletes a user account from the accounts database.

- `NetUserEnum`: Provides resumable enumeration of information about each user account in a domain.

- `NetUserGetGroups`: Retrieves a list of global groups to which a specified user belongs.

- `NetUserGetInfo`: Retrieves information about a particular user account on a server.

- `NetUserGetLocalGroups`: Retrieves a list of local groups to which a specified user belongs.

- `NetUserModalsGet`: Retrieves global information for all users and global groups in the user account database.

- `NetUserModalsSet`: Sets global information for all users and global groups in the user account database.

- `NetUserSetGroups`: Sets global group memberships for a specified user account.

- `NetUserSetInfo`: Sets the parameters of a user account.

Workstation Functions

The following are the LANMan workstation functions:

- `NetWkstaGetInfo`: Returns information about the configuration elements for a workstation.

- `NetWkstaSetInfo`: Configures a workstation. This information is stored in such a manner that it remains in effect after the system has been reinitialized.

- `NetWkstaTransportAdd`: Binds the redirector to the transport.

- `NetWkstaTransportDel`: Unbinds the transport from the redirector.

- `NetWkstaTransportEnum`: Supplies information about transports that are managed by the redirector.

- `NetWkstaUserEnum`: Lists information about all current users on the workstation.

- `NetWkstaUserGetInfo`: Returns the user-specific information about the configuration elements for a workstation.

- `NetWkstaUserSetInfo`: Sets the user-specific information about the configuration elements for a workstation.

Message Functions

The following are the LANMan message functions:

- `NetMessageBufferSend`: Sends a buffer of information to a registered message alias.

- `NetMessageNameAdd`: Registers a message alias in the message name table.

- `NetMessageNameDel`: Deletes a message alias from the table of message aliases on a computer.

- `NetMessageNameEnum`: Lists the message aliases that will receive messages on a specified computer.

- `NetMessageNameGetInfo`: Retrieves information about a particular message alias in the message name table.

Access Check Functions

The following LANMan access check functions are obsolete. They are provided only for backward compatibility with 16-bit Windows. Instead, use `AccessCheck` `GetFileSecurity`, `SetFileSecurity`, and related functions from the Win32 security API, which is covered in Chapter 18.

- `NetAccessCheck`

- `NetAccessDelNetAccessEnum`

- `NetAccessGetInfo`

- `NetAccessGetUserPerms`

- `NetAccessSetInfo`

Configuration Functions

The LANMan API contains three configuration functions:

- `NetConfigGet`: Retrieves the value of a single specified entry for a particular component on the local computer or on a remote server.

- `NetConfigGetAll`: Retrieves all the configuration information for a given component on a local or a remote computer.

- `NetConfigSet`: Sets the value of a single specified entry for a particular component on the local computer or on a remote server.

Network Buffer Allocation Functions

The following are the LANMan network buffer allocation functions:

- `NetApiBufferAllocate`: Allocates `ByteCount` bytes of memory from the heap.

- `NetApiBufferFree`: Frees the memory allocated by `NetApiBufferAllocate`.

- `NetApiBufferReallocate`: Changes the size of a buffer allocated with `NetApiBufferAllocate`.

- `NetApiBufferSize`: Returns the size in bytes of the buffer allocated via `NetApiBufferAllocate`.

Miscellaneous Networking Functions

The following are other LANMan networking-related functions:

- `NetConnectionEnum`: Lists all connections made to a shared resource on the server or all connections established from a particular computer. (Win32-based applications should use the `WNetEnumResource` function.)

- `NetGetDCName`: Returns the name of the primary domain controller (PDC) for the specified domain.

- `NetGetDisplayInformationIndex`: Gets the index of the first display information entry whose name begins with or alphabetically follows a specified string. (You can use this function to determine a starting index for subsequent calls to the `NetQueryDisplayInformation` function.)

- `NetQueryDisplayInformation`: Returns user, computer, or group account information.

- `NetRemoteTOD`: Returns a server's time of day.

Using the Winsock 2.0 API

Although Winsock started life as a means of unifying different vendors' implementations of TCP/IP for the Windows platforms, one of the stated goals of the Winsock consortium was to make Winsock be protocol-independent. With Winsock 2.0, this has largely been accomplished. I say "largely" only because there are certain protocol-specific details you must still be aware of, although admittedly, these have to do with things such as dealing with different network address sizes, which differ among the different network protocols. Also, areas of functionality that are unique to certain protocols are supported by using Winsock's protocol-dependent constants and structures, typically defined in an extra protocol-specific header file.

In reality, Winsock 2.0 is probably as network-independent as you can get; that is, without taking some form of lowest-common-denominator approach. In each protocol, you communicate by sending and receiving data using the sockets model. Initializing and querying of protocol-specific information is done via common functions, but by making use of protocol-specific structures and settings. Additional protocol-specific functionality is accessed by using the `setsockopt` (set socket option) function, as you'll see in the MacSock demo program.

> **TIP**
>
> **Winsock version 1.1 shipped with Windows 95 and earlier versions of NT. Winsock 2 ships with NT 4.0, and is automatically upgraded in Windows 95 installations by installation of the Win95 Service Pack or certain other upgrade files that are available for download via Microsoft's Web site (www.microsoft.com).**

New Features of Winsock 2

New features of Winsock 2 include the following:

- Faster performance using overlapped I/O

- Protocol-independent multipoint/multicase support

- Quality of service (QoS)

- Simultaneous support for multiple network protocols

Just as `CreateFile, ReadFile`, and `WriteFile` can be used to do overlapped (or asynchronous and concurrent) file or pipe I/O, Winsock sockets can also be read from and written to asynchronously, with (if you wish) multiple sockets transferring data simultaneously. This permits each socket to transfer data at its own rate of speed, unencumbered by any throughput problems on other network protocols or hardware connections.

The built-in protocols supported by Winsock 2 currently include TCP, UDP, Net-Ware IPX and SPX, NetBEUI (using NetBIOS), AppleTalk, and TP4. Support for additional protocols can be added by other vendors who conform to Winsock's Service Provider's Interface (SPI) specification.

The transport protocol annex of Winsock 2 handles the area of additional protocol-specific functionality. The SPI allows network service providers to supply their own name space resolution code and supports simultaneous network communications via multiple protocols.

QoS is another new feature that allows applications to adjust for throughput speeds and connection quality, and to request changes in connection quality (such as by opening another ISDN channel when necessary).

Winsock 2 and AppleTalk: The MacSock Program

Chapter 19 included a couple examples of using Winsock for TCP programming. Here, we'll go though a simple example of using the Winsock API to do AppleTalk programming. This example demonstrates how Winsock handles other protocols gracefully. The complete source code for this example is included on the CD that accompanies this book.

NOTE You will need the AppleTalk protocol installed, plus one or more Macintosh computers on your network, in order to actually run the MacSock demo program. If you don't have a Mac, you can still follow along with the example to see how it works.

The sample application simply creates an NBP (Name Binding Protocol) Apple-Talk datagram socket, binds it to an AppleTalk address, then registers a network name on a specific AppleTalk zone.

As with some of the other examples, we use stream I/O to output program information to stdout. Thus, Iostream.H is included, as well as Winsock2.H (which replaces the older Winsock.H header file) Since this application uses the AppleTalk protocol, we also need to include the Atalkwsh.H header file, which defines AppleTalk-specific structures and constants.

```
#include <iostream.h>
#include <winsock2.h>
#include <atalkwsh.h> // Appletalk-specific definitions
```

This application will insist on at least version 2.0 of Winsock. (At the time of this writing, the latest Winsock specification is actually version 2.2.)

```
const VERSION_MAJOR  =  2;  // Winsock 2.0 required by this app.
const VERSION_MINOR  =  0;
```

Inside the `main` application function, we define the five variables that will be used:

- `iStatus` to hold result (or error) status codes from the various Winsock functions

- `SOCKET` for the AppleTalk socket that is created

- `WSData`, a standard Winsock initialization structure

- `SockAddr`, defined as an AppleTalk-specific socket address structure

- `RegName`, an AppleTalk-specific structure that is used for registering a name in a given zone on the network

```
main (int argc, char *argv[])
{
    int        iStatus;    // Error result
    SOCKET     hSocket;    // The socket that gets opened
    WSADATA    WSData;     // Winsock initialization structure

    SOCKADDR_AT        SockAddr; // AppleTalk address struct.
    WSH_REGISTER_NAME  RegName;  // Name registration structure
```

The `WSAStartup` call initializes Winsock and checks to be sure the Winsock version is 2.0 or later.

```
    // Initialize Winsock API (require version 2.0 or later!)
    if ( WSAStartup(MAKEWORD(VERSION_MAJOR, VERSION_MINOR),
        &WSData) )
    {
```

```
        cout << "Cannot find Winsock version ";
        cout << VERSION_MAJOR << "." << VERSION_MINOR << " or
            later!\n";
        return(1);
    }
```

Next, we attempt to open an AppleTalk NBP datagram socket. Note the protocol family specifier is set to PF_APPLETALK. We flush the output stream after each section to ensure that the status is visible at each point in the program; otherwise, all the text written to stdout would be buffered until the end of the program.

```
    cout << "Attempting to open AppleTalk socket: ";

    // Open an AppleTalk NBP datagram socket
    hSocket = socket(PF_APPLETALK, SOCK_DGRAM, DDPPROTO_NBP);
    if ( iStatus == SOCKET_ERROR )
    {
        cout << "Failed - " << WSAGetLastError() << endl;
        goto Cleanup;
    }
    else
        cout << "Success!\n";
    cout << flush;
```

NOTE   Er... is that a *label* I used, in the event of an error? Yes, indeed it is. I've come to the conclusion this actually makes the code easier to read, in this particular case. My philosophy on using labels has mutated slightly over the years. I used to go to great lengths never to use a single label, but I now find on rare occasions that a single label can sometimes simplify code that needs to perform cleanup duties that are performed within the same function.

Assuming that we've successfully opened a socket, the next step is to prepare a SockAddr structure (remember, this is an AppleTalk-specific socket address structure). If you're testing this application on a large AppleTalk network, you may need to set the network and node numbers to something more specific than zero.

```
// Prepare SockAddr strucure to bind to the socket
   SockAddr.sat_family  = PF_APPLETALK;   // AppleTalk family
   SockAddr.sat_net     = 0;         // network number SET THIS!
   SockAddr.sat_node    = 0;          // the node number
   SockAddr.sat_socket  = hSocket;      // the AppleTalk socket
```

Next, we need to bind the socket to the address specified in our `SockAddr` structure. Note that the third parameter to bind specifies the size of `SockAddr`, which, in this case, will be different than a "normal" TCP address structure. In a similar way, if we were binding to an IPX socket, we would use a different-sized address structure that is unique to IPX.

```
cout << "Attempting to bind address to socket: ";

// Attempt to bind address to socket.
iStatus = bind( hSocket, (LPSOCKADDR)&SockAddr,
   sizeof(SockAddr));
if ( iStatus == SOCKET_ERROR )
{
   cout << "Failed - " << WSAGetLastError() << endl;
   goto Cleanup;
}
else
   cout << "Success!\n";
cout << flush;
```

Now the `RegName` structure is filled with an object name, type name, and zone name. The object name and type can be what you want, but you will need to set the zone name to a valid zone on your AppleTalk network, if you are actually running this application. Each corresponding string length field also must be set accordingly.

```
// Prepare RegName struct. for registering our name on net.

// Set name strings.
strcpy(RegName.ObjectName, "MacSock Server"); // name on net.
strcpy(RegName.TypeName,   "Winsock2 Type");  // name type
strcpy(RegName.ZoneName,   "Granny Smith");   // zone name

// Set corresponding string lengths in RegName structure
RegName.ObjectNameLen  = strlen(RegName.ObjectName);
RegName.TypeNameLen    = strlen(RegName.TypeName);
RegName.ZoneNameLen    = strlen(RegName.ZoneName);
```

Now we use the Winsock `setsockopt` call to register our name on the specified AppleTalk zone. The second parameter specifies that the option we're requesting is part of the "AppleTalk level," and the third parameter specifies that we want the "register name" option. Parameter four is a pointer to our option structure. The fifth parameter specifies the size of this structure.

Incidentally, this function call may take as long as ten seconds (or perhaps longer) to execute, so be patient!

```
cout << "Attempting to register name: " << flush;

    // Attempt to register name.
    iStatus = setsockopt(
        hSocket,                      // Appletalk socket
        SOL_APPLETALK,                // option level
        SO_REGISTER_NAME,             // option value requested
        (char *)&RegName,             // pointer to option buffer
        sizeof(WSH_REGISTER_NAME)     // size of option request buffer
    );
    if ( iStatus == SOCKET_ERROR )
        cout << "Failed - " << WSAGetLastError() << endl;
    else
        cout << "Success!\n";
    cout << flush;
```

At this point, we can close the socket and call `WSACleanup`, to tell Winsock we're finished.

```
Cleanup:

    closesocket( hSocket );
    WSACleanup();

    return 0;
}
```

That's it, as far as this example goes. In "real life," you would obviously proceed to do something on the network—as either a client or a server (or perhaps both). You should get a successful return code when registering the name, but instead of exiting immediately, you would go onto do something else, then eventually deregister your name when finished, and finally exit.

Because Winsock 2 not only supports other protocols, but also supports using multiple protocols in the same application simultaneously, you could create a server application that serves Apple, NetWare, and TCP/IP clients, perhaps using some new user-level protocol you've devised. Or, you could use Winsock to build a software router, reading stream or datagram data from one network type, and forwarding it over a second protocol. Depending on the combination of protocols used, however, this could mean needing to convert different-sized data packets that would require using an intermediate packet-repackaging strategy.

Using Named Pipes and Mailslots

Named pipes, and their cousins the mailslots, initially made their appearance in OS/2, and continue to be an excellent high-level means of passing data and messages between NT stations connected on a network. Mailslots and named pipes are similar in the way that they are created, read from, and written to. They differ in the respect that mailslots are one-way and connectionless; named pipes can be two-way and require that a connection be established on each end prior to use. If you're familiar with TCP/IP, mailslots are analogous to UDP—both are used for connectionless, datagram transfers. Named pipes are analogous to TCP—both of these are used for connection-oriented message or stream I/O.

One drawback to using named pipes is that currently Windows 95 (and also Windows for Workgroups) supports only client-side pipes. This means that any server applications you write that use named pipes must run on an NT workstation or server. Another drawback is that pipe and mailslot communications are only as dependable as the network protocol that is being used to support them. In most cases, this should not be a problem, but for transferring very large amounts of data completely error-free, NT's file system functions, for example, would provide better data integrity.

On the other hand, there are several benefits to using pipes and mailslots: they are easy to implement, protocol-independent, and can transfer data asynchronously using overlapped I/O. Since they are implemented as devices in the operating system, they can also be used to redirect I/O to or from other devices, either locally or across a network.

> **NOTE**
>
> There are also unnamed (or anonymous) pipes, which work very much like named pipes and can be used for interprocess and interapplication communication on the same workstation. They differ from named pipes in that they can only be read from and written to locally, on the station that creates them. Use the `CreatePipe` function to create an anonymous pipe. See Chapter 15 for details.

Pipes and mailslots are discussed in Chapter 15. The following sections summarize the Win32 API functions that are pertinent to creating and using pipes and mailslots.

Pipe-Specific Functions

The following are the Win32API functions for working with named pipes:

- `CreateNamedPipe`: Creates the first or a new instance of a named pipe.

- `CallNamedPipe`: Combines connecting, reading from or writing to, and closing a message-type pipe, in one operation.

- `ConnectNamedPipe`: Enables a named pipe server process to wait for a client process to connect to an instance of the named pipe.

- `DisconnectNamedPipe`: Disconnects the server end of a named pipe, leaving the pipe intact.

- `GetNamedPipeHandleState`: Retrieves information about a specified named pipe handle, including the handle's state.

- `GetNamedPipeInfo`: Retrieves information about the specified named pipe.

- `PeekNamedPipe`: Copies data from (or information about) a pipe to a buffer without removing the data from the pipe.

- `SetNamedPipeHandleState`: Sets the read mode and blocking mode of the specified named pipe.

- `TransactNamedPipe`: Combines writing to and reading from a message-type pipe in a single operation.

- `WaitNamedPipe`: Waits for an instance of the specified named pipe to become available, or until a specified time-out interval elapses.

Mailslot-Specific Functions

The following are the Win32 API functions related to mailslots:

- `CreateMailslot`: Creates and returns a handle to a mailslot with the specified name.

- `GetMailslotInfo`: Retrieves information about the specified mailslot.

- `SetMailslotInfo`: Sets the time-out value used for read operations on the specified mailslot.

Standard I/O Functions Supporting Pipes and Mailslots

Several I/O functions support pipes and mailslots:

- `CreateFile`: Can be used to create a pipe or mailslot.

- `ReadFile`: Can be used to read from a pipe or mailslot.

- `WriteFile`: Can be used to write to a pipe or mailslot.

- `ReadFileEx`: Can be used for overlapped (asynchronous) reading from a pipe or mailslot.

- `WriteFileEx`: Can be used for overlapped (asynchronous) writing to a pipe or mailslot.

- `CloseHandle`: Can be used to close a handle to a pipe or mailslot.

Using Remote Procedure Calls (RPC)

RPC provides a mechanism that makes it possible for programs or code located on one computer to call functions and procedures located on another computer, and to do so in a way that makes the calling syntax exactly like calling procedures located in a standard DLL on the local station.

With the debut of DCOM in Windows NT 4.0, RPC is taking on significance not only in its own right, but also because it is the means used by Microsoft to make the Windows implementation of COM (Component Object Model) work remotely across networks (called DCOM). In other words, it is worth your while to learn RPC, not only to be able to make remote procedure calls, but also to be able to make and access remote *objects*.

The RPC "glue" implemented in Windows NT (and Windows 95) conforms to the Open Software Foundation (OSF) specifications. This means that conforming to RPC (or DCOM) in your application ensures that functions you call can be located on a remote computer running a completely different operating system or, conversely, that procedures or object methods you've implemented on NT or Windows 95 can be accessed by applications running on other operating systems—even using different bit-size hardware or a different byte-ordering scheme.

Along with these benefits, as you might guess, comes a measure of added complexity. Currently, implementing RPC or DCOM into your application is really more difficult than it needs to be, at least for normal use. Nonetheless, here we will see how RPC and DCOM work, and show you how to get started with implementing these technologies into your applications.

NOTE
As this is being written, the next wave of compiler tools are being worked on at Borland, Microsoft, and elsewhere. Rumor has it that at least one of these tools may make DCOM programming as transparent as normal OOP.

RPC Concepts

Before going into the details of what you'll need to use RPC, you should understand some RPC-related concepts and terms. These include UUID, GUID, interface class, and marshalling.

UUIDs and GUIDs

A UUID is a *universally unique identifier*, also known as a *globally unique identifier*, or GUID. In Window systems, a UUID or GUID is used to ensure that RPC *interfaces* and COM *classes* are absolutely, positively guaranteed to have a unique identifier entry in the system Registry. (The system Registry, among other things, maintains settings information for each interface and class that is registered with the system.)

UUIDs or GUIDs are guaranteed to be unique, provided all RPC and (D)COM programmers abide by two simple rules:

- Every interface and class must be assigned a separate and unique UUID. This UUID is always a 128-bit (16-byte) value, which you can produce either by running a program such as UUIDGEN or GUIDGEN, or by submitting a request to Microsoft for a "block of UUIDs." (Microsoft has a fairly quick turn around, and you typically get a block of 100 UUIDs, via e-mail or floppy.)

- Anytime you change an interface definition (or a COM or DCOM class), you must leave the old interface intact, and define a new interface with a new UUID.

Provided every programmer follows these rules, UUIDs or GUIDs are extremely unlikely to conflict in the Registry. This is good, because the system Registry in NT (and Windows 95) would become very confused if two or more interfaces (or classes) tried to refer to themselves using the same identifier.

> **NOTE**
>
> In case you're wondering, the UUIDs are generated via an algorithm that mixes together the address of your Ethernet network adapter (which for other reasons, is also supposed to be completely unique; every network card manufacturer is assigned a different range of such addresses to draw from), plus system information. This algorithm produces a number that is extremely unlikely to ever occur twice, on either the same or different machines.

Interface Classes

An RPC/COM interface is a group of one or more related functions. RPC applications usually have only a single interface, although they could have more. COM classes also have at least one interface, and they most frequently have at least two or three. Again, each interface is one group of one or more related functions.

Each interface can have a string name as well as the UUID. The string name you assign an interface is not nearly as important as the unique UUID that you give it. However, to keep things simple, you should try to assign descriptive string names for your interfaces as well as unique UUIDs.

For example, if you needed to implement an RPC server that could execute a set of mathematical functions and also some string-manipulation functions, you might implement a `mymath` interface and a `mystring` interface. In this case, the client RPC application would then use either the `mymath` interface to access your math functions or the `mystring` interface to access your string functions. An application can certainly use both interfaces, but each interface can only be used to access functions that are part of that particular interface.

Marshalling

The way RPC differs from local procedure calling is primarily in the extra steps that are required to package (and unpack) the function parameters so they can be shipped across the network each time a function is called. At runtime, these parameter-handling steps are performed by a set of functions that have been linked into your client (or server) application. These functions know all about the function prototypes being called and how to pack and unpack the parameters correctly. This process of packaging and unpackaging function parameters for transport across the network is called *marshalling*. As you'll see, much of the work involved in implementing RPC has to do with the steps required to create the marshalling code stubs that are linked into your application.

Marshalling includes taking care of pointer and string parameters so that they work as expected on both ends. If you think about it, passing a pointer to a string across a network means that the string itself needs to be sent across the network. A new chunk of RAM must be allocated for the string on the other computer, the string contents need to be copied into this new RAM, and a new pointer variable must be created. This pointer variable has the same data type as the original pointer, but points to this new string copy. If this pointer-to-a-string parameter is defined in our IDL files as an `[in, out]` parameter (as described , shortly), then the string-copy process needs to happen a second time, to send the (presumably) modified string back to the original client program. Finally, marshalling code on the client side needs to copy this version of the pointed-to string back into the original string pointed to by the client's string pointer.

As you can see, RPC (and for the same reason, COM and DCOM) completely changes the normal perception of pointers as a very efficient way to pass parameters. When sent remotely, pointers are actually very inefficient! But the bit of time and network traffic eaten up by passing this parameter (and copying it) are the price for the flexibility and power that remote procedure calling (and DCOM) provide.

That said, it is still best to take more than the normal care when designing functions that will be called over RPC. Engineer them for efficient parameter passing across the network. In addition to decreasing the amount of data passed in parameters, you should also look for opportunities to reduce the number of times individual functions are called. This may mean packing several function calls together into one function, perhaps passing an array or structure of parameters, rather than using more function calls with fewer parameters. This is a strategy Windows NT uses when it packages several GDI calls together before sending them into the kernel for processing.

Preparing Your Compiler for RPC and DCOM

If you do not currently have tools configured in your compiler/editor environment for generating UUIDs, compiling IDL files, and registering .REG files, you may find the going a bit easier if you follow the procedures presented here to add these tools to your Tools menu. These specific procedures are the steps needed for adding the tool entries to Visual C++ 4.*x*.

If you're using a different vendor's compiler that also supports adding custom tool entries, you should not have any trouble adapting these steps to what works for your IDE. For Borland C++ 4.*x* or 5.0 users, we'll go over the general steps required to add a tool in Borland C++. Then we'll cover the specific procedures for VC++.

Adding a Tool in Borland C++

Here are the basic steps for adding a custom tool to the Borland compiler's Tools menu:

1. From the main IDE menu, select Options.

2. Select Tools to bring up a Tools dialog box.

3. Click on the New button.

4. Enter the path, program name, and command-line arguments in the corresponding fields.

5. Enter a descriptive name for the tool in the Menu Text field.

6. When you're finished, click on the OK button. This should add the new tool to your Tools menu.

Adding a Generate UUID Tool in VC++

Here are the steps for adding a tool for generating UUIDs in Visual C++:

1. From the main menu, select Tools.

2. Select Customize to bring up a Customize dialog box.

3. Click on the Tools tab.

4. Click on the Add button.

5. When it asks for the command, enter **UUIDGEN**.

NOTE If you have Borland's tools, you may prefer to use the GUIDGEN tool, which has a graphical interface. If so, just make sure GUIDGEN.EXE is in your path, and then enter it as the command. Then click on the OK button.

6. For UUIDGEN (or GUIDGEN), no command-line arguments are needed. Otherwise, you would enter these in the Arguments field.

7. In the Menu Text field, enter **Generate UUID.**

8. If you are using UUIDGEN, place a check in the checkbox labeled Redirect to Output Window. (If using GUIDGEN, this option should not be available.)

9. The new tool should now be installed. Leave the Tools dialog box open, so you can add the other two tools, as described next.

Adding a Compile IDL File Tool in VC++

Assuming you've just added the UUID tool, you should still have the Customize/ Tools tabbed dialog box open. If not, follow steps 1 through 3 in the previous section. Then continue as follows:

1. Click on the Add button.

2. Enter **MIDL** as the command. If you don't have a path to it, add the complete path. A typical installation directory you may find it in would be C:\MSDEV\BIN\.

NOTE
> The MIDL.EXE program is Microsoft's IDL compiler. It is called a compiler, although probably it would be more accurately called a translator, since it outputs an .H and two .C files.

3. In the Arguments field, enter:

   -ms_ext -char unsigned -env win32 -c_ext $(FileName)

      $(FileExt)

4. In the Initial Directory field, enter:

   $(FileDir)

5. For Menu Text, enter

   Compile IDL file

6. Place a check in the checkbox labeled Redirect to Output Window.

Adding a Register .REG File Tool in VC++

You should still have the Customize/Tools tabbed dialog opened. If not, repeat steps 1 through 3 in the section titled "Adding a Generate UUID Tool in VC++." Then continue as follows:

1. Click on the Add button.

2. Enter **REGEDIT** as the command. Note that you should not need to add a path to this, because it should be located in your \WINNT (for NT) or \WINDOWS (on Windows 95) directory.

3. In the Arguments field, enter the following:

   -s $(FileName)$(FileExt)

4. In the Initial Directory field, enter:

   $(FileDir)

5. For Menu Text, enter:

   Register .REG File

6. Click on the Close button at the bottom of the Customize dialog box.

At this point, all three tools should be added and should be visible from your Tools menu. These will come in handy when you are writing RPC, COM, ActiveX, or DCOM applications.

> **NOTE** For the sample RPC program, the Registry tool is not used. You may decide to postpone installing it, although it will still be useful in other projects.

The next sections describe how to create each of the files needed to build the RPC client and server applications.

Writing Mathlib.CPP: A Function Library

Before you can write an application that uses RPC, you need to come up with the set of functions that will be called remotely. These do not need to be in a separate file, but it is very wise to set them up that way. This lets you test and debug the functions in a "normal" program, before you begin implementing the RPC portions of your client and server programs.

The RPC demo applications discussed a little later in this chapter use a very simplistic set of math functions. These are placed in a separate source file, which is named Mathlib.CPP. A complete listing for this program is shown at the end of this chapter.

> **NOTE** Obviously, the small amount of work these simple math functions do wouldn't justify the overhead of using RPC. But in choosing the functions for this demo, my goal was to keep them as simple as possible, yet include both passing and receiving of integer values, plus sending and receiving of strings.

The first thing to note about the math library is that it includes the Rpc.H header file. Initially when debugging your functions, you may want to comment this out, because you'll presumably be statically linking the functions to your test program.

The Mathlib.H header file bears mention also. Initially, you will want this to be a normal function prototype header file, which you can easily make just as you would any other normal header file. (By simply copying the function header from your source file and placing semicolons at the end of each.) Once you've verified that each function works correctly, you will want to rename this header file to get it out of the way, since one of the steps to building an RPC application results in generating a new header file for this set of functions. However, it's a good idea to save your "normal" header file, in case you need to do further debugging down the road.

```
#include <iostream.h>
#include <rpc.h>
#include "mathlib.h"
```

The first of the functions declared simply prints to standard output the client name that is passed to it. Remember that eventually these functions will execute on the RPC server, so the client will call SendClientName, passing a string, and the server will actually execute the call.

```
void SendClientName( char *pszClientName )
{
    cout << endl << "Client: " << pszClientName << endl;
    cout << flush;
}
```

As with previous applications, the output stream is flushed here, because otherwise you would not see the display update immediately as each function is called.

The next function returns a string back to the calling program. Again, this will be the RPC client application, although the function will actually execute on the server.

```
char *GetMathServerName( void  )
{
    static char szServerName[64];

    strcpy( szServerName, "Name of Server" );

    return szServerName;
}
```

Next, we have the four math functions, which each take two long integers, perform a simple calculation with them, and return a long result value back to the calling program. These examples are simple, but you can make your RPC functions perform as much complex number crunching (or other processing) as you wish. Perhaps the server machine will have a coprocessor, or multiple CPUs, or MMX support, which the client machine can take advantage of by offloading to it the most CPU-intensive functions.

```
long Add(long lNum1, long lNum2)
{
    cout << "Call to Add(" << lNum1 << ", " << lNum2 << ")\n";
    cout << flush;

    return( lNum1 + lNum2 );
}

long Subtract(long lNum1, long lNum2)
{
    cout << "Call to Subtract(" << lNum1 << ", " << lNum2 << ")\n";
    cout << flush;

    return( lNum1 - lNum2 );
}

long Multiply(long lNum1, long lNum2)
{
    cout << "Call to Multiply(" << lNum1 << ", " << lNum2 << ")\n";
    cout << flush;

    return( lNum1 * lNum2 );
}

long Divide(long lNum1, long lNum2)
{
    cout << "Call to Divide(" << lNum1 << ", " << lNum2 << ")\n";
    cout << flush;

    return( lNum1 / lNum2 );
}
```

Incidentally, another thing this demo does that you may want to avoid in a real application is update the display in each function call. In real applications, at least when your functions are likely to get called many times, it might make sense to move any function-related display updating to a different thread (or eliminate it altogether). Anything that can be done to increase the speed of your function execution will allow the function result to be returned back to the calling program that much sooner.

This completes the file that defines the functions that will ultimately get called via RPC. Again, for testing and debugging, execution profiling, and other maintenance, you will usually find it much easier to prepare a normal header file and call these functions directly, without further complicating things by using RPC. Once your functions are working to your satisfaction, you can switch back to using RPC quite easily. In fact, you may want to use your RPC client application as the test program that calls your functions statically in "test" mode, and via RPC in "deployment" mode.

Writing Mathlib.IDL: The IDL Function Interface Definition

In order to create the code that will "know" how to properly pack and unpack the function parameters (which then get sent over the network), it is necessary to create an IDL file. The IDL file gets its name from the abbreviation for the Interface Definition Language, which it is written in. Why do these functions need to be declared using IDL rather than C or C++? Well, one answer is because that's what the OSF stipulates in its distributed computing specifications. Another answer is that perhaps a bit more information is needed to be known about each function than C or C++ normally provides. In fact, if you look at an IDL file, it closely resembles C function prototypes, but with the addition of zero, one, or more attributes enclosed inside square brackets, which precede various function parameters and return values. These attributes most frequently simply identify whether the parameter is an input and/or output parameter:

- An input parameter is signified by [in]

- An output parameter is signified [out]

- A parameter that is passed in and is modified is signified by [in, out]

The attribute information might also include additional data-typing information, as we'll see with the string parameters in our example.

Furthermore, starting out the IDL file is a header that includes a UUID. In the case of our Mathlib example, the corresponding IDL file starts with a header that looks like this:

```
[
uuid (E1CA13A0-388B-11d0-B0C6-0000C0FBDC5A),
version(1.0),
pointer_default(unique)
]
```

The blank space (and blank lines) between the various parts enclosed between the square brackets is optional, but typically is used to make the header more human-readable.

At this point, if your compiler IDL tool is configured as described in the previous sections (and if you have a network adapter installed), you should be able to go to your Tools menu, select the Generate GUID option, and have a new GUID appear. Each time you do this, note that a somewhat different identifier appears. This is how you generate new interface and class GUIDs.

NOTE The number in brackets after the `uuid` was created by my copy of GUIDGEN, running on my computer. So if you compile the RPC demo programs here and change anything, go ahead and generate a new GUID and replace mine with yours each place it appears in all the files discussed in this section. Don't worry—it doesn't appear in too many places, although references to it are used more often.

The second part of the Mathlib.IDL file is the interface definition. Again, this looks very much like a C++ class definition, except that you'll notice there are square brackets containing *attribute* information, preceding certain parameters or variables. The [unique, string], for example, makes it clear that the GetMath-ServerName function returns a string type, and that the string value is to be treated as a unique value (not copied into a string-duplicates table that replaces identical strings with duplicate references, for example). The [in, string] makes it clear that the parameter being passed to SendClientName is a string and can be ignored after the function executes. If it included the out attribute, additional code would be generated that would copy the string back again after the function executed, and then send that string value back to the client. (If you're wondering *who* is generating *what* code, we'll get to that shortly.)

```
interface mathlib
{
    [unique, string] char *GetMathServerName ( void );
    void   SendClientName ( [in, string] char *string );
    long   Add            ( long lNum1, long lNum2 );
    long   Subtract       ( long lNum1, long lNum2 );
    long   Multiply       ( long lNum1, long lNum2 );
    long   Divide         ( long lNum1, long lNum2 );
}
```

The MIDL compiler will use the Mathlib.IDL file to create Mathlib.H and a marshalling stub file for the RPC server and client applications. But before we can use Mathlib.IDL, we need to also create a file called Mathlib.ACF, which is what we'll do next.

Writing Mathlib.ACF: The Marshalling Interface Handle File

The next thing we need to do is create a marshalling interface handle file. For our example, we'll use an automatic interface handle. You could define your own interface handle, but this would require that you write your own marshalling code as well. Since we are using "standard" data types, we can use automatic marshalling for this project, and our .ACF file should contain the following interface handle declaration:

```
[auto_handle]
interface mathlib
{
}
```

If we were planning to support multiple RPC interfaces in our project, we would need to add multiple interface declarations, rather than just the `mathlib` one we've declared in this file.

Using MIDL to Create Mathlib.H, Mathlib_c.C, and Mathlib_s.C

Armed with the Mathlib.IDL and Mathlib.ACF, plus our MIDL Tool entry, we are now ready to "compile" the `mathlib` interface definition to produce an RPC header file and client and server proxy stubs.

Assuming there are no typos in either the Mathlib.IDL or Mathlib.ACF file, you should be able to do this easily. Open the Mathlib.IDL file in your C++ IDE and, make sure it's the selected window. Then choose Compile IDL File from the Tools menu. If all goes well, you should get three new files:

- **Mathlib.H header file:** An "RPC-icized" header file that the RPC client and server applications will need to include.

- **Mathlib_c.C file:** The client proxy stub that needs to be added to the RPC client application.

- **Mathlib_s.C file:** The server proxy stub that needs to be included in the RPC server project.

The Mathlib_c.C and Mathlib_s.C files contain the code that makes the RPC mechanism properly handle the parameters being sent out and received back in each function call. When the client and server applications link with these files, they think the function is being linked locally, but in reality, hooks to the RPC mechanism are set up to be invoked to process each function call at runtime. The listing of the header file that is generated is included on the CD that accompanies this book. Note that outside of adding __RPC_x entries to type the arguments and return values in some of the functions, the header file looks pretty much the way you would expect.

The client and server proxy stubs are lengthier; also these two source listings are included on the CD that accompanies this book. You can look at those listings, or generate the code with the MIDL compiler, to see what the proxy stub code looks like. Fortunately, it's not necessary to understand this code in order to compile and link it into your client and server application projects.

NOTE The RPC application presented in this chapter will run only under Windows NT, not Windows 95.

Writing the Client Application: The RPClient Program

The next step in putting together this RPC project is to write the RPC client application. This is reasonably straightforward, although it does require a few noteworthy observations. First, we include the Mathlib.H file, which was generated by compiling the .IDL file. The project file does *not* include the Mathlib.CPP file, but does need to include the Mathlib_c.C file (which essentially fools the compiler into thinking we're linking to these functions locally).

```
#include <iostream.h>
#include <rpc.h>
#include "..\mathlib.h"
```

Another thing we need to do in both the client and server applications is define a pair of memory allocation and freeing functions, which will be called at runtime by the RPC mechanism, when it needs to create local storage for parameters. This is how the RAM pointed to by the RPC pointer copies can have valid addresses inside the client (or server) processes. It actually *is* allocated by the process whenever RPC makes the allocation or deallocation calls.

```
void __RPC_FAR *__RPC_API midl_user_allocate( size_t len )
{
    return( malloc(len) );
}

void __RPC_API midl_user_free( void __RPC_FAR *ptr )
{
    free( ptr );
}
```

The __RPC_API, __RPC_FAR, and _CRTAPI1 should be included just as they are here, although, oddly when you look these up in the Rpc.H header file, it appears that they are defined to nothing. Nevertheless, the use of these in the SDK examples suggests that it is wise to follow their lead for future and/or backward compatibility.

```
void _CRTAPI1 main(void)
{
    int a = 100;
    int b =  25;
```

Inside the main function, the a and b variables are defined and initialized. These will be the two integer parameters in calls to the RPC server Mathlib functions.

Next, we have what looks like the start of exception-handling code, except we use RpcTryExecpt. This is exception handling, but done RPC style. Exception handling is optional in standard C++ Win32 programs, but it is *mandatory* in RPC client programs. Leave out RpcTryExcept, and you won't have a working RPC application.

```
RpcTryExcept

    SendClientName( "Client's name" );
    cout << "Connected to Math Server " << GetMathServerName()
       << ".\n";

    cout << a << " plus        " << b << " = " << Add(a, b)
       << endl;
    cout << a << " minus       " << b << " = " << Subtract(a, b)
       << "\n";
    cout << a << " times       " << b << " = " << Multiply(a, b)
       << "\n";
    cout << a << " divided by " << b << " = " << Divide(a, b)
       << "\n";
```

After the `RpcTryExcept`, the client application tries out each of the `mathlib` interface's functions, displaying the results of each call. If any RPC runtime exceptions occur, they will be handled by the code after `RpcExcept`, which simply displays an error message in this example.

```
RpcExcept(1)

    cout << "RPC Runtime error occurred.\n";

    RpcEndExcept
}
```

Finally, `RpcEndExcept` ends the exception handling, and the client RPC program terminates.

> **TIP**
>
> For debugging purposes, you may want to make a DebugRpc.H header file, which defines the RPC exception handling as empty macros. If you then add the Mathlib.CPP source into the client project and temporarily remove the Mathlib_c.C file from the project, the resulting application will let you run, test, and debug the functions locally.

The complete RPClient program listing appears on the CD that accompanies this book.

Writing the Server Application: The RPCServ Program

The last source file that must be written is the RPC server. This program may strike you as rather odd, in that nowhere are any of the Mathlib functions being called, as far as is apparent. Actually, the server application's primary duties are to register its existence with the RPC mechanism, specify what network protocol(s) it will use to listen, and then wait around for clients to connect and make RPC calls. The actual calls are then intercepted via the RPC mechanism, which causes the Mathlib functions exported by the server application to be called.

```
#include <iostream.h>
#include <rpc.h>
#include "..\mathlib.h"
```

```
void _CRTAPI1 main(int argc, char *argv[])
{
   RPC_STATUS            status;
   RPC_BINDING_VECTOR    *pBindingVector;
```

As with the client application, we include Iostream.H and Rpc.H header files, plus the Mathlib.H header file, which was generated via the MIDL compile. The `RPC_BINDING_VECTOR` can be thought of as a table of function pointers to all the functions defined in the `mathlib` interface. However `pBindingVector` will not be initialized until several steps into our program.

```
UCHAR *pszProtocolSequence = (UCHAR *) "ncacn_np";
WORD   wMinCalls           = 1;
WORD   wMaxCalls           = 30;
UCHAR *pszEndPoint         = (UCHAR *) "\\pipe\\auto";
WORD   fWaitFlag           = FALSE;
UCHAR *pszEntryName        = (UCHAR *)" /.:/Autohandle_mathlib";
```

The `pszProtocolSequence` variable specifies that named pipes are the method this RPC server will use to accept RPC client calls. The `wMinCalls` and `wMaxCalls` specify the minimum and maximum simultaneous calls this server will handle. The `pszEndPoint` variable specifies the name of the pipe used to listen for client calls, which uses the named pipe of `auto` for automatic marshalling.

The `fWaitFlag` will be used to tell RPC not to let this server terminate, but to wait, listening for client calls. The `pszEntryName` variable contains the name server entry which the `mathlib` interface will be registered as, so that it can be located by name.

The first RPC function is a call to `RpcServerUseProtseqEp`, which in unabbreviated form means "use specified protocol sequence and endpoint" for incoming RPC calls. So in this case, we're specifying that we want a named pipe for clients to connect through.

```
status = RpcServerUseProtseqEp(
      pszProtocolSequence,    // protocol sequence
      wMaxCalls,              // maximum concurrent calls
      pszEndPoint,            // end point (using pipe)
      NULL );                 // security (default used)

   if (status)
   {
      cout << "error "<< status << " setting endpoint!\n";
      exit;
   }
```

Next, we need to register the `mathlib` interface via a call to `RpcServerRegisterIf`. The first parameter is the interface ID defined by the MIDL compiler. The NULL second parameter specifies to use a nil-type manager UUID. This and the NULL third parameter set the server to use the default manager and entry-point vector as generated by our MIDL-compiled proxy stub.

```
status = RpcServerRegisterIf(
   mathlib_v1_0_s_ifspec, // Interface
   NULL,                   // Default/nil MgrTypeUUID
   NULL );                 // MIDL-generated Entry-point vector

if (status)
{
   cout << "error "<< status << " registering server!\n";
   exit;
}
```

Then we request a pointer to the binding handles (vector table), through which RPC calls can be received.

```
status = RpcServerInqBindings( &pBindingVector );

if (status)
{
   cout << "error "<< status << " retrieving bindings!\n";
   exit;
}
```

The final preparatory function we need to call is `RpcNsBindingExport`, which establishes an entry in the name-service database that includes the binding handles we've just retrieved in the previous call.

```
status = RpcNsBindingExport(
      RPC_C_NS_SYNTAX_DEFAULT,  // name syntax type
      pszEntryName,             // Name Service name
      mathlib_v1_0_s_ifspec,    // interface handle
      pBindingVector,           // binding vector (we received)
      NULL );                   // UUID object vectors (none)

if (status)
{
   cout << "error "<< status << " Exporting bindings!\n";
   exit;
}
```

Having registered and advertised our RPC interface "service," we now only need to tell the RPC runtime library to listen for incoming RPC calls.

```
cout << "Listening for RPC calls..." << endl << flush;

status = RpcServerListen(
    1,                          // minimum calls
    30,                         // maximum calls
    FALSE );                    // wait value (FALSE = DO wait)

if (status)
{
    cout << "error "<< status << " during listen!\n";
    exit;
}
```

If we call RpcServerListen and tell it to return immediately, then the following code needs to execute instead, to prevent this server application from exiting before RPC calls arrive. With the last parameter set to FALSE, however, the following section of code can be ignored.

```
if ( fWaitFlag )
{
    status = RpcMgmtWaitServerListen();

    if (status)
    {
        cout << "error "<< status << " during listen!\n";
        exit;
    }
}
```

The final code in the server is again a pair of memory allocation and freeing functions, identical to those defined in the RPC client. The RPC runtime code calls these functions when it needs to allocate local memory for copying buffers, arrays, strings, and pointers.

```
// These get called by MIDL

void __RPC_FAR *__RPC_API midl_user_allocate( size_t len )
{
    return( malloc(len) );
```

```
    }

    void __RPC_API midl_user_free( void __RPC_FAR *ptr )
    {
        free( ptr );
    }
```

This concludes the server source file. The complete listing appears on the CD that accompaies this book. After compiling both the server and client applications, we can test them.

Testing the RPC Client and Server Examples

Assuming the compiling went as planned, testing these two programs should be very easy. Just start up the RPCServ application in one prompt window, and start RPClient in another. The client should locate the server, display the results of each function call, and terminate. Figure 20.1 shows an example of the client screen output. The server should display each RPC call coming in, then wait for more calls. Figure 20.2 shows an example of an RPC server screen.

FIGURE 20.1

An RPC client screen

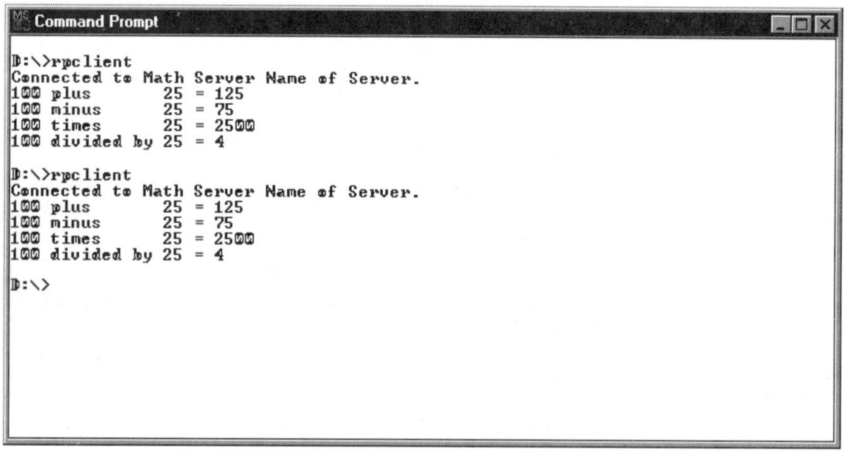

```
D:\>rpclient
Connected to Math Server Name of Server.
100 plus       25 = 125
100 minus      25 = 75
100 times      25 = 2500
100 divided by 25 = 4

D:\>rpclient
Connected to Math Server Name of Server.
100 plus       25 = 125
100 minus      25 = 75
100 times      25 = 2500
100 divided by 25 = 4

D:\>
```

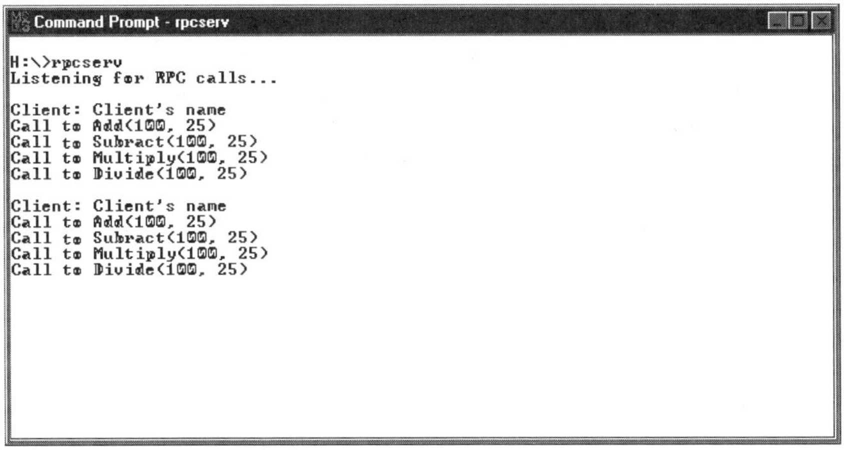

FIGURE 20.2

An RPC server screen

```
Command Prompt - rpcserv                                    [_][口][X]

H:\>rpcserv
Listening for RPC calls...

Client: Client's name
Call to Add(100, 25)
Call to Subract(100, 25)
Call to Multiply(100, 25)
Call to Divide(100, 25)

Client: Client's name
Call to Add(100, 25)
Call to Subract(100, 25)
Call to Multiply(100, 25)
Call to Divide(100, 25)
```

If the test works correctly, then once you remove the default security restrictions on named pipes, you should be able to run the client and server programs on different stations. There are three ways to do this:

- Make an entry in the Registry file corresponding to the `auto` named pipe, and then allow access to this pipe via the NT User Manager (or User Manager for Domains).

- On an NT domain, you could test by using the identical login account on both systems.

- Apply the information in Chapter 18 concerning creating a NULL DACL (Device Access Control List), attach this to an SD, and then use this SD rather than NULL in the security parameter for the `auto` named pipe.

NOTE   As explained in Chapter 18, security by default is enabled, and it takes explicit removal of restrictions before a device can be accessible to some (or all) users. If you attach a NULL DACL to your device's SD, this tells NT to permit access by all users.

An Introduction to DCOM

The good news is that if you understand how to write client and server applications using RPC, then you already understand the *D* in DCOM. On the other hand, understanding how the *COM* (Component Object Model) part of DCOM works truly requires an entire book in itself. Here, we'll just outline the basic concepts required for writing and using DCOM objects.

Just as RPC is defined by the OSF to be a cross-platform means of interprocess and interapplication procedure calling, COM (and DCOM) is defined by OSF to be a cross-platform object model. In a nutshell, DCOM provides the ability to do remote, cross-platform, object-oriented programming. As more and more DCOM objects come online (literally!), it will probably become commonplace to have various parts of an application spread out across a network, over even the Internet, executing on a motley assortment of different operating systems and computer hardware. This is the goal for DCOM, as stated by Microsoft.

DCOM made its debut with the release of Windows NT 4.0. Then Microsoft made DCOM for Windows 95 available as a download from the Internet. At the moment, ASG (from Germany) and a consortium of other companies are working to port DCOM to several flavors of Unix, and a beta version for the Apple operating system has been announced.

> **NOTE**
>
> At the moment, DCOM (and COM) programming require significantly more "under the hood" knowledge of the mechanics of COM than is needed for normal OOP. Whether this remains the case depends on the current work being done at Borland, Microsoft, and elsewhere. Within a year, we should see component writing in general, (and DCOM specifically) being greatly simplified by a number of new programming tools.

COM, OLE, and OCX Controls

COM, as it is implemented by Microsoft, is very similar to OLE (object linking and embedding). OLE was originally built on a set of COM classes, and the many built-in OLE interfaces were defined in terms of COM interfaces. If you've read the previous section on RPC, then you need only to understand the technology underlying OLE to know almost everything necessary to write a DCOM component or to use one from a DCOM client application.

As you explore the underpinnings of the Windows 95 (and now NT 4.0) interface, you will discover that most of the user interface has been implemented as a set of OCXs. The OCX controls, which now are called ActiveX controls, also derive their "objectness" from COM technology. In fact, with the growing use of ActiveX controls on the Internet, Microsoft has permitted ActiveX to return more to its COM roots; you no longer need to include a number of OLE interfaces to build a valid ActiveX component. Moreover, there is now a newly formed quasi-independent ActiveX standards body, which purportedly will assist in making DCOM more platform- and vendor-independent.

Remote Servers

Before NT 4.0 (and the recently released DCOM for Windows 95), COM could be either an *in-process* or *out-of-process* server. In-process servers had their proxy code implemented in a DLL, which when loaded by a calling application, resulted in the COM objects being created within the client process's address space. Out-of-process servers, on the other hand, implemented the proxy code in a separate executable file, which meant that the COM objects were created in a separate address space from the client application. With the arrival of distributed COM, the former out-of-process servers are referred to as *local servers*. Servers implementing DCOM, and therefore running on remote stations, are called *remote servers.* So we now have three types of servers: in-process, local, and remote.

Because DCOM is really an incremental technology that leverages COM through the technology of RPC, it is possible to reverse-implement DCOM on already existing COM objects (also called COM components) without making any changes to the original binary COM object. This means that OLE server applications, out-of-process COM servers, OCX controls, and ActiveX controls all benefit in the same way: Their methods can be accessed across the network! All that is needed to make any of these available for remote calling is to create the required Registry entry that tells the client which server should be used to access instances of that object.

COM Objects, Classes, and Interfaces

COM objects are also referred to as COM *classes*. More often, a COM class refers to an uninstantiated class, which is made available by a COM server. Each COM class has a GUID, just as each RPC interface does. Unlike RPC interfaces, which don't need to be registered in the system Registry, COM classes are registered in the system Registry. Their GUID ensures that they have a unique Registry entry and can be located via that GUID and by any client program that desires to create an instance of the object.

Although it's not a requirement, COM classes can also have a string identifier (name), which allows them to be referred to by name rather than GUID. COM objects also have a Registry entry that contains the module name and complete path location for an in-process and/or local server that knows how to create this class of COM object. With the arrival of DCOM, a third Registry entry is supported, to allow the module name and path to be specified for a remote server. The path can specify the remote server via UNC, through an IP address, or even by an Internet-style domain name.

Class Factories

Servers that know how to create COM objects of a certain class are referred to as *class factories*. A COM server is a class factory for each class it knows how to instantiate. Client applications seeking to create instances of a given COM object follow this procedure:

- The application makes a COM or OLE call that performs a Registry (and/or network name space) lookup first to determine where the class factory "lives."

- Assuming the calling application has sufficient security rights to access this object, the appropriate class factory module is loaded (if it is not already running).

- One or more classes are instantiated.

COM Interfaces

COM objects always possess at least one, and usually more, COM interfaces. An abstract definition of an interface (RPC or COM) is a collection of related functions. A lower-level explanation is that each interface is a vector table, or *vtable*, of pointers to functions. One entry exists in an interface's vtable for each function contained in that interface. In RPC, the vtable is usually created "behind the scenes," by the RPC runtime library and the proxy stub code that is generated by the IDL compiler, and linked into the application. Calls to functions in a particular interface are simply made in the calling program with the same syntax as calling "normal" functions. Again, behind the scenes, each call is traced to the corresponding interface's vtable, and the correct function is called.

With COM objects, the process is similar, but instead of the vtable being completely hidden from the programmer, it is made available as a C++ style collection of class methods. In other words, each COM interface is made available to the calling client as if it were a C++ object (or a C++ class, which is the same thing). In fact, the vtable that is used in COM (and indirectly by RPC) exactly matches the virtual method table used by C++ compilers to implement C++ classes, or objects.

COM Functions

Because each COM interface in a COM class is actually implemented for all practical purposes as a C++ class, you might think that making use of a particular COM interface would be quite easy. Unfortunately, it isn't quite that simple. The complications arise because, when COM was designed, the designers decided it also needed to be capable of supporting multiple platforms, different byte orders, and different programming languages (not just C or C++, for instance). Furthermore, it had to help applications be robust—something that it wouldn't do if programmers could simply call into the internal guts of any object without verifying they had the correct interface class or function prototype, for example.

NOTE

The price for COM's flexibility and robustness, in most folk's assessment, is obtuseness and difficulty of implementation. COM is an interesting approach to addressing a variety of important issues regarding software reuse, extensibility, and inheritance. It also tackles the cross-platform issues—at least in theory. Unfortunately, it has yet to have a released implementation on any platform outside Windows 95 or NT.

The way robustness of the interfaces is implemented—or put another way, the means used to enforce interface-type checking prior to all interface function access—is through an intermediate step whereby a calling program asks for a desired interface specifically, before attempting to call functions of that particular interface.

By calling a function called `QueryInterface`, and specifying the desired interface GUID, the client application can receive an "officially approved" interface pointer, which can then be used as a normal pointer to a C++ class instance to access any function that really is part of that interface.

The complication here is that `QueryInterface` itself is a method of an interface; specifically, it is a function (or method) of the `IClassFactory` interface. So, in order to call `QueryInterface` on an object, you must first call `CoCreateInstance` to create an instance of the COM class, which contains the `ClassFactory` method appropriate for creating the COM class you're interested in. If this succeeds, you then call `Query-Interface` to retrieve the `IClassFactory` interface pointer. You can then use this pointer in a call to `CreateInstance`, whereby you specify the interface GUID you want to be able to use, which should (if all goes well) finally return an interface pointer to the desired interface of the desired object. You can now use this interface pointer to make function calls to the various functions within that interface. But if you need to access other functions in other interfaces of that object, then you must call `Query-Interface` again and retrieve an interface pointer to the new interface.

Fortunately, a recent function addition, `CoCreateInstanceEx`, permits several of these steps to be packaged together into one function call. With this function, an array of structures containing pointers to multiple interface classes can be returned in one fell swoop.

After you're finished with a COM object, you must release the object. Releasing the object decrements the object's reference counter so that it can be safely automatically unloaded from the server as soon as all users have released it (and the usage counter or reference counter) reaches zero.

OOP, COM Style

One key aspect of COM objects is they actually support the key object-oriented attributes of extensibility, inheritance, and polymorphism. Inheritance arises from the fact you can take a COM object and add one or more new interfaces to it. Inheritance (even multiple inheritance) arises from the fact that you can define a new COM object that uses COM interfaces from multiple other COM objects. Polymorphism comes from the fact that the same interface can be implemented in many different COM objects.

TIP

To learn more about COM programming, pick up a copy of the classic *Inside OLE*, by Kraig Brockschmidt (Microsoft Press) and digest that material. Then go over the few examples that are provided in the Microsoft SDK.

Other Network Programming Approaches

In addition to DCOM, RPC, and the various built-in Win32 networking APIs, there are also other, vendor-specific networking APIs, which you may find useful or necessary. Windows 95 and NT are both great networking clients, running a variety of networking protocols right out of the box. As a programmer, however, you may sometimes need to go beyond the common-level functionality provided by the approaches described in this chapter.

If you're primarily interested in network communications, your best bet is to first look at using Winsock. Winsock 2 provides efficient access to protocol-specific features for several protocols now, including Banyan VINES, Apple-Talk, DEC, and NetWare IPX and SPX. Unless you need to do really esoteric stuff, Winsock 2 provides just the right mix of fast, close-to-the-wire control with higher-level, protocol-independent socket programming.

If you need more than this, you'll need to contact individual network vendors (Banyan, Novell, or Apple, for instance) for information about any networking toolkits that they might provide or recommend.

Both Windows 95 and NT include a rather limited NetWare API. You can find them in the NWAPI32.DLL file, located in either the \WINDOWS\SYSTEM (for Windows 95), or \WINNT\SYSTEM32 directory (for NT). Note that the Windows 95 version of this DLL includes only 25 functions, approximately the same number found in previous versions of the NT DLL. The NT version 4.0 DLL includes approximately 115 functions, although many seem to be duplicate or triplicate versions of the same behavior. Novell's NetWare client for NT includes NCPWIN32.DLL, which exports hundreds of NCP (NetWare Core Protocol) functions.

> **TIP**
>
> If you need to write low-level NetWare client software for NT that makes use of the NCP functions, check out Sven Schreiber's November 1996 article in *Dr. Dobb's Journal*, "Undocumented Windows NT and the NetWare Core Protocol." In this article, Mr. Schreiber explains how you can use the undocumented `NwlibMakeNcp` function (included in both Windows 95 and NT) to implement your own NCP function library.

In addition to all the network-related APIs, you may need to devise other methods, based on combinations of these techniques or involving your own approaches. A combination approach would work well, for instance, in an RPC client application that needs to locate all available RPC servers on a network. Although RPC itself provides a mechanism for working with different protocols, you might find it easier to locate these available servers using `WNetEnumResource`, or initially establishing communications using named pipes or mailslots.

You might also choose to take advantage of the fact that the Windows 95 and NT I/O functions themselves are endowed with networking abilities. In fact, because it's so simple, you might easily overlook the fact that file I/O functions can be used in a completely platform- and protocol-independent way to convey information. Your application could, for example, open a dozen files using `CreateFile`, with each file existing on a different host computer, which is running a different operating system and using different networking protocols. As long as you specify the file's location, your application can access these files as easily as if they were located on a local drive.

Network communications using files have the advantages of being fast, simple to implement, easy to debug, and network protocol-independent. In fact, not only is this approach *completely* network-independent, it is even operating system-independent (except for byte-ordering); it does not even require any changes to be made to either the client or server programs in order to add support for new platforms or network protocols. Simply define your communications file structure, devise a means of identifying "completed" message files, and you're set to begin implementing. If you need to deal with different byte-ordering schemes, it is not difficult to create a set of conversion functions (similar in fact to those used in Winsock programming).

Another variation on this approach is to use databases to communicate between running processes or applications. Again, this has the advantages of being network-independent plus at least partially platform-independent. It requires only that all communicating stations be able to access the same database file. This approach works best in asynchronous, message-based communication, such as logging, broadcasting, or the queuing of job requests.

This chapter has covered a relatively large amount of technology in a relatively short space. The main goal was to give you an idea of what network programming options are out there for you as a Windows application developer to use. The listing for the sample WNet Demo program discussed in this chapter follows. All the programs presented in this and the other chapters in the book are on the CD.

Listing 20.1: Delphi Source Code for the WNetDemo Program

```
unit mainwin;

interface

uses
 Windows, Messages, SysUtils, Classes, Graphics, Controls, Forms,
Dialogs, StdCtrls;

type
  TfrmMainWin = class(TForm)
    Button1: TButton;
    Edit1: TEdit;
    Edit2: TEdit;
    Label1: TLabel;
    Label2: TLabel;
    procedure Button1Click(Sender: TObject);
  private
    { Private declarations }
  public
    { Public declarations }
  end;

var
  frmMainWin: TfrmMainWin;

implementation

{$R *.DFM}

procedure TfrmMainWin.Button1Click(Sender: TObject);
var  nr: TNetResource;
     szErrorMessage, szLocalName, szRemoteName: ShortString;
begin
  // Clear NetResource structure, load local and remote names
  Cursor:= crHourGlass;
  fillchar(nr, sizeof(nr), #0);
  strpcopy(@szLocalName, Edit2.Text);
  strpcopy(@szRemoteName, Edit1.Text);

  // Now, fill NetResource fields
```

```
with nr do
begin
  dwType:= RESOURCETYPE_DISK;
  lpLocalName:= @szLocalName;
  lpRemoteName:= @szRemoteName;
  dwDisplayType:= RESOURCEDISPLAYTYPE_GENERIC;
end;

// Call WNetAddConnection2, using default user name and password.
if (WNetAddConnection2( nr, NIL, NIL, 0) <> NO_ERROR) then
begin
 // If error occurred, retrieve system error text and display it.
  FormatMessage( FORMAT_MESSAGE_FROM_SYSTEM, NIL, GetLastError,
    LANG_SYSTEM_DEFAULT, @szErrorMessage,
        sizeof(szErrorMessage), NIL);
  ShowMessage('Error attempting connection: '+strpas
        (@szErrorMessage));
end
else
  ShowMessage(Edit1.Text
    +' has been successfully connected and mapped to
        +Edit2.Text);

  Cursor:= crDefault;
end;

end.
```

PART IV

Windows NT/95 Graphics

CHAPTER
TWENTY-ONE

21

The Windows Graphics Device Interface

- Device context access

- Information context access

- Device capability information

- Windows mapping modes

- The viewport versus the window

This chapter provides an introduction to the Windows Graphics Device Interface (GDI). It begins with the topic of the device context (DC), which is the heart of the GDI. Then it covers the device context information that can be retrieved. Finally, you'll learn about the Windows mapping modes, as well as the viewport versus window coordinates and sizes.

Two demo programs are presented here. The first example demonstrates how device (hardware) information can be retrieved for the Windows device drivers. The second demonstrates the mapping modes supported by the Windows GDI to provide various resolutions for graphics display operations.

The Device Context

Unlike in DOS, where applications simply own the entire display, printer, or other device, under Windows, the output device is a shared resource. The *device context* is a method of permitting peaceful coexistence between applications sharing the resource.

Device Context Handles

Before a Windows application can draw anything to the screen, the application must begin by gaining access to the GDI, which means obtaining a handle to the device context. Asking Windows for a handle to a device context (hDC or hdc) is the equivalent of asking permission to share the output resource. And, in like fashion, including the handle in subsequent calls to GDI output functions not only tells Windows which output device is being addressed, but also assures the GDI that permission has been granted to access the shared device.

The hdc is not only a handle to the device context, but also to a virtual device that has been allocated to the application. The virtual device provides a private space for the application's own display operations. Furthermore, the device context handle is not only a pointer to a virtual space, but is also a pointer to a data structure detailing device (graphic) settings.

For example, when a call is made to the TextOut function, font and color information are not included in the call because attributes have already been set for the device context (default settings are provided if no other selections are made). Thus, TextOut requires only string data and coordinates as parameters for each output

> **NOTE**
>
> After the contents of the virtual display are mapped by the GDI to the physical display, the virtual display can be discarded, at least until further screen operations are needed.

operation. In like fashion, other device contexts used by other applications have their own attribute settings, which are independent of the current device context.

Device Context Handles in MFC

Using MFC-based programming, you usually handle screen updates and drawing operations only in response to calls to the `OnPaint` function (even when you generate these calls indirectly using an `Invalidate` instruction). You usually expect the MFC shell to pass a handle to the device context to you. Or, more accurately, it passes a pointer to a `CDC` class instance, which you subsequently pass on to your specialized paint or drawing routines.

However, don't become too complacent about expecting this level of service and lapse into not attempting any graphics operations except when you have been passed a pointer to the device context class. Remember that whether you use a handle to the device context or an instance of the `CDC` class, the device context is available at any point. You are not required to "wait" for permission to draw! You can, instead, demand permission.

Why Query a Device Context?

The attribute settings for a device context can include color palettes, mapping modes, alignment settings, and so on. These settings can be queried or changed by calling other API functions, called with the appropriate `hdc` parameter to identify the proper device context.

By querying a device context, you can get various information, such as the following:

- Information about supported palettes (colors)

- Font-sizing information (what fonts are available for display and in which sizes)

- Available printer fonts

- Printer resolutions (for optimizing bitmapped images)

- The presence or absence of special hardware capabilities

Accessing the Device Context

To access the device context, you use either the `BeginPaint` or `GetDC` functions to retrieve the `hdc`. It's important to emphasize that no application should attempt to hold on to a device context beyond the immediate operation. Under Windows, device context handles are a limited resource and must be shared among executing applications. Use the `EndPaint` or `ReleaseDC` functions when you're finished with the device context handle.

NOTE   In like fashion, if you're using an instance of the `CDC` class rather than the `BeginPaint` or `GetDC` functions to access a device handle, you should also conclude by closing the instance when finished. However, when you're using a class instance, the device context is released automatically by the class destructor when the class goes out of scope. By all means, use the convenience inherent in the class, but keep in mind what is happening behind the scenes.

A device context should always be released or deleted as soon as the immediate output operation is completed. Of course, once the device context handle is released, the device context itself is no longer valid.

The PAINTSTRUCT Structure

To obtain a handle to the device context, the `BeginPaint` function is called with two parameters, and when finished, the `EndPaint` function accepts the same pair.

```
hdc = BeginPaint( hwnd, &ps );
    . . .
    EndPaint( hwnd, &ps );
```

Here, two calling parameters are included:

- The `hwnd` argument identifying the application accessing the device context

- A pointer to the `ps` structure, a structured variable of type `PAINTSTRUCT`, which contains information specifying which portion of the screen should be repainted (`rcPaint`), whether the background (existing image) should be erased (`fErase`), and so on

The `PAINTSTRUCT` structure is defined in WinUser.H as:

```
typedef struct tagPAINTSTRUCT
{   HDC    hdc;
    BOOL   fErase;
    RECT   rcPaint;
    BOOL   fRestore;
    BOOL   fIncUpdate;
    BYTE   rgbReserved[32];
} PAINTSTRUCT, *PPAINTSTRUCT, *NPPAINTSTRUCT, *LPPAINTSTRUCT;
```

The `BeginPaint/EndPaint` functions are commonly used in response to `WM_PAINT` messages when only a portion of a screen should be updated (which is faster than repainting an entire screen).

In a similar fashion, the `GetDC` and `ReleaseDC` functions are used when operations are required over the entire client window area.

Other Device Context Accesses

There are several other methods of accessing the device context:

- `GetWindowDC`: Unlike `GetDC`, provides access to the entire window, including the window frame, caption, and menu bar. Access is restricted, however, to the current application's window.

- `CreateDC`: Obtains a device context that allows operations outside an application's client window area, such as for a screen-capture utility.

- `CreateIC`: Obtains a handle to an information context as opposed to a device context. An information context, unlike a device context, does not provide a handle for output operations. Instead, the handle returned can be used to obtain information about an output device without actually outputting anything. The use of `CreateIC` is described in the next section.

Acquiring an Information (Device) Context

In most cases, when access to a device such as the video display is required, the `GetDC` function in invoked to return a handle (`hDC`) to the device context. In the DC demo program presented in this chapter, however, two device context handles are declared: hDC and hDCInfo. Since either handle could be used for either purpose, this is slightly redundant. On the other hand, using two handles makes it clear that two quite different device contexts are being used: a conventional *hardware* device context and an *information* device context.

The difference between these two contexts is simple. Unlike the conventional device context, which is used for output, the information context, provided by CreateIC, allows you to access information about the context but does not provide any output capabilities. The information context requires less overhead and is perfectly sufficient for retrieving information.

The first requirement in using the CreateIC function is to determine the device for which you are requesting information. For the video display, the video device is accessed using the default specification "DISPLAY".

```
hdc = CreateIC( "DISPLAY", NULL, NULL, NULL );
```

Under Windows 3.*x*, the WIN.INI file, normally found in the Windows directory, contained printer device information that you could extract with the Get-ProfileString function and use to create an information device context. For Windows NT and 95, however, the information previously found in the WIN.INI file has, for the most part, been replaced by a less-readable storage format. Therefore, the printer device context is no longer available in this fashion and must be accessed via a different route.

NOTE As a general rule, access to a printer-specific information context shouldn't be necessary. One of the strengths of Windows (any version) is being able to let the system handle device-specific details, such as the resolution and capabilities of a printer.

The string information needed to describe the printer can be returned by calling the EnumPrinterDrivers and EnumPrinters procedures. With this information, the CreateIC function and subsequent processes are carried out in the same fashion as demonstrated for the display device in the DC demo program presented in this chapter.

In the example, we've provided a simple routine to query the system and return a list of printer devices. Figure 21.1 shows an example of the Printer Selection dialog box.

FIGURE 21.1

The Printer Selection
dialog box displayed by
the DC program

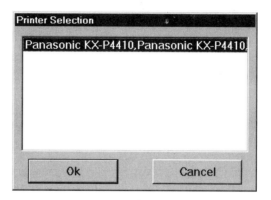

NOTE   Examples of the `EnumPrinterDrivers` and `EnumPrinters` procedures can be found in the EnumPrt.C program (part of the Printer.C demo) distributed with the Windows NT toolkit, located in the x:\MSTOOLS\SAMPLES\WIN32\PRINTER directory.

The Printer Selection dialog box is called in a fashion slightly different from most dialog boxes. In the `WndProc` procedure, under the `msg`/`WM_COMMAND` response, you'll find the following handler:

```
case IDM_PRINTER:
    CheckMenuItem( hMenu, IDM_DISPLAY,
                   MF_UNCHECKED );
    CheckMenuItem( hMenu, IDM_PRINTER,
                   MF_CHECKED );
```

The first two provisions are simple. They show which type of device is being selected by making sure that the Display menu option is unchecked and that the Printer menu option is checked.

```
if( DialogBox( hInst, "PRINTER", hwnd, PrinterProc ) )
    InvalidateRect( hwnd, NULL, TRUE );
break;
```

The third provision creates the dialog box and passes a reference to the `Printer-Proc` procedure, which contains the handler and the provisions to query the available printers. If the `DialogBox` procedure returns TRUE (meaning that a selection has been made), then we invalidate the client window so that it will be redrawn with new information.

The important part at this point is the `PrinterProc` procedure.

```
BOOL APIENTRY PrinterProc( HWND hDlg,    UINT msg,
                            UINT wParam, LONG lParam )
{
    DWORD cbPrinters = 4096L, cbNeeded, cReturned;
    char  szPrinter[40] = "\0";
    int   i, j;

    switch( msg )
    {
```

The first step in handling the query is to initialize the dialog box, beginning by allocating a buffer to hold the information we're about to request.

```
    case WM_INITDIALOG:
        if( ! ( gpPrinters = (PPRINTER_INFO_1)
           LocalAlloc( LMEM_FIXED | LMEM_ZEROINIT, cbPrinters )))
            {
                ErrorMsg( "gpPrinters local alloc failed." );
                return( FALSE );
            }
```

After allocating the buffer, and assuming success, we proceed by issuing a query requesting that the system printers be enumerated.

```
        if( ! EnumPrinters( PRINTER_ENUM_LOCAL, NULL, 1,
                  (LPBYTE) gpPrinters, cbPrinters,
                        &cbNeeded,  &cReturned ) )
            {
```

Note that we have also anticipated the failure of this query, giving full consideration to the possibility that the buffer provided will not be large enough.

```
            if( GetLastError() == ERROR_INSUFFICIENT_BUFFER )
                {
```

However, if the buffer isn't big enough, the response is simple: Free the allocated buffer and then allocate a new buffer using the size requirement reported by the original query.

```
                    LocalFree( (LOCALHANDLE) gpPrinters );
                    gpPrinters = (PPRINTER_INFO_1)
                    LocalAlloc( LMEM_FIXED | LMEM_ZEROINIT, cbNeeded );
                    cbPrinters = cbNeeded;
```

And, after reallocating the buffer using the new information, we query the printer list a second time.

```
                if( ! EnumPrinters( PRINTER_ENUM_LOCAL, NULL, 1,
                            (LPBYTE) gpPrinters, cbPrinters,
                                    &cbNeeded,  &cReturned ) )
                {
                    ErrorMsg( "Can't enumerate printers" );
                    return( FALSE );
                }
            }
            else
            {
                ErrorMsg( "Can't enumerate printers" );
                return( FALSE );
            }
        }
```

The second (and first) queries conclude with report provisions to cover complete failure—just in case.

Assuming that one of our queries has been successful, we check the `cReturned` count. If `cReturned` is zero, we simply report that there are no printers installed and then return.

```
        if( ! cReturned )
        {
            ErrorMsg( "No printers installed" );
            EndDialog( hDlg, FALSE );
            return( FALSE );
        }
```

Otherwise, since at least one printer has been reported, we copy the reported printers to the dialog list box and then set the current selection to the first item (with the zero index).

```
            for( i=0; i<(INT)cReturned; i++ )
                SendDlgItemMessage( hDlg, IDM_PRINTLIST,
                                LB_ADDSTRING, 0,
```

```
                              (LPARAM) gpPrinters[i].pDescription );
            SendDlgItemMessage( hDlg, IDM_PRINTLIST, LB_SETCURSEL,
                              0, 0 );
            return( TRUE );
```

The final provision occurs when the OK button is clicked. (No provisions have been included to handle a double-click on a selection.)

```
        case WM_COMMAND:
            switch( LOWORD( wParam ) )
            {
                case IDOK:
// LB_GETCURSEL message retrieves the index of currently
// selected item, if any, in a single-selection list box
                    i = SendDlgItemMessage( hDlg,
                            IDM_PRINTLIST, LB_GETCURSEL, 0, 0 );
// LB_GETTEXT message retrieves a string from a list box
                    SendDlgItemMessage( hDlg, IDM_PRINTLIST,
                        LB_GETTEXT, (WPARAM) i,
                        (LPARAM)(LPCTSTR) szPrinter );
// Parse the string into device, driver and port names
                    j = 0;
                    i = -1;
                    while( szPrinter[++i] != ',' )
                        gszDeviceName[i] = szPrinter[i];
                        gszDeviceName[i] = '\0';
                    while( szPrinter[++i] != ',' )
                        gszDriverName[j++] = szPrinter[i];
                        gszDriverName[j] = '\0';
                    j = 0;
                    while( szPrinter[++i] != '\0')
                        gszPort[j++] = szPrinter[i];
                        gszPort[j] = '\0';
                    EndDialog( hDlg, TRUE );
                    return( TRUE );
```

Clicking on the OK button simply copies the selection information to the local buffers for further use before closing the dialog box. If no selection has been made and provisions are included for a default selection, the dialog box will refuse to close.

Alternatively, if the Cancel button is clicked, the dialog box simply closes without supplying a printer specification.

```
              case IDCANCEL:
                  EndDialog( hDlg, FALSE );
                  return( FALSE );
            }
            break;
      }
      return 0;
}
```

Once we have retrieved a device specification, we have a wealth of information available—probably more than we're likely to want at any one time.

Device Context Information

Device context information describes the resolution and capacities of hardware output devices such as the video display, a printer or plotter, a camera device, or even a metafile (a file of GDI function calls in binary format).

GDI Identifier Constants

The device context contains a variety of information that can be requested via the identifier constants defined in WinGDI.H. Many of these inquiries return integer values; others return word values composed of bit flags that can be broken down, again using flag constants defined in WinGDI.H. Most of these constants are demonstrated in the DC demo program. Table 21.1 summarizes the GDI information indexes and flag constants.

TABLE 21.1   GDI Information Indexes and Flag Constants

GDI Information Index and Flags	Description
Driver Version and Device Types	
DRIVERVERSION	Device driver version
TECHNOLOGY	Device classification
DT_PLOTTER	Vector plotter

TABLE 21.1   GDI Information Indexes and Flag Constants (Continued)

GDI Information Index and Flags	Description
DT_RASDISPLAY	Raster display
DT_RASPRINTER	Raster printer
DT_RASCAMERA	Raster camera
DT_CHARSTREAM	Character-stream, PLP
DT_METAFILE	Metafile, VDM
DT_DISPFILE	Display file

Device Dimensions

HORZSIZE	Horizontal size (millimeters)
VERTSIZE	Vertical size (millimeters)
HORZRES	Horizontal width (pixels)
VERTRES	Vertical width (pixels)
ASPECTX	Pixel width
ASPECTY	Pixel height
ASPECTXY	Pixel hypotenuse
LOGPIXELSX	Pixels/logical inch (width)
LOGPIXELSY	Pixels/logical inch (height)

Device Color Capabilities

BITSPIXEL	Bits per pixel (color)
PLANES	Color planes
NUMBRUSHES	Device-specific brushes
NUMPENS	Device-specific pens
NUMMARKERS	Device-specific markers
NUMFONTS	Device-specific fonts
NUMCOLORS	Device-specific colors
SIZEPALETTE	Entries in physical palette
NUMRESERVED	Reserved entries in palette
COLORRES	Actual color resolution

Miscellaneous

PDEVICESIZE	Device descriptor size required

TABLE 21.1 GDI Information Indexes and Flag Constants (Continued)

GDI Information Index and Flags	Description
Printer-Related Device Capabilities*	
PHYSICALWIDTH	Width (device units)
PHYSICALHEIGHT	Height (device units)
PHYSICALOFFSETX	x-margin, printable area
PHYSICALOFFSETY	y-margin, printable area
SCALINGFACTORX	x-axis scaling factor
SCALINGFACTORY	y-axis scaling factor
Graphics, Image, and Font-Handling Capabilities	
CURVECAPS	Curve capabilities
CC_NONE	Curves not supported
CC_CIRCLES	Does circles
CC_PIE	Does pie wedges
CC_CHORD	Does chord arcs
CC_ELLIPSES	Does ellipses
CC_WIDE	Does wide lines
CC_STYLED	Does styled lines
CC_WIDESTYLED	Does wide styled lines
CC_INTERIORS	Does interiors
CC_ROUNDRECT	Does rounded rectangles
LINECAPS	Line capabilities
LC_NONE	Lines not supported
LC_POLYLINE	Does polylines
LC_MARKER	Does markers
LC_POLYMARKER	Does polymarkers
LC_WIDE	Does wide lines
LC_STYLED	Does styled lines
LC_WIDESTYLED	Does wide styled lines
LC_INTERIORS	Does interiors
POLYGONALCAPS	Polygonal capabilities
PC_NONE	Polygonals not supported
PC_POLYGON	Does polygons

TABLE 21.1   GDI Information Indexes and Flag Constants (Continued)

GDI Information Index and Flags	Description
PC_RECTANGLE	Does rectangles
PC_WINDPOLYGON	Does winding polygons
PC_TRAPEZOID	Does trapezoids
PC_SCANLINE	Does scan lines
PC_WIDE	Does wide borders
PC_STYLED	Does styled borders
PC_WIDESTYLED	Does wide styled borders
PC_INTERIORS	Does interiors
TEXTCAPS	Text capabilities
TC_OP_CHARACTER	Character output precision
TC_OP_STROKE	Stroke output precision
TC_CP_STROKE	Stroke clip precision
TC_CR_90	Character rotation, 90 degree
TC_CR_ANY	Character rotation, any angle
TC_SF_X_YINDEP	x/y independent scaling
TC_SA_DOUBLE	Double scaling
TC_SA_INTEGER	Integer scaling
TC_SA_CONTIN	Continuous scaling
TC_EA_DOUBLE	Embolden ability (double weight)
TC_IA_ABLE	Italics capable
TC_UA_ABLE	Underline capable
TC_SO_ABLE	Strike-out capable
TC_RA_ABLE	Supports raster fonts
TC_VA_ABLE	Supports vector fonts
TC_RESERVED	Reserved
CLIPCAPS	Clipping capabilities
CP_NONE	No output clipping supported
CP_RECTANGLE	Output clipped to rectangle
CP_REGION	Output clipped to region
RASTERCAPS	Raster/bitblt (bit block transfer) capabilities
RC_NONE**	No raster capablities supported
RC_BITBLT	Does standard block transfer
RC_BANDING	Device requires banding support

TABLE 21.1   GDI Information Indexes and Flag Constants (Continued)

GDI Information Index and Flags	Description
RC_SCALING	Device requires scaling support
RC_BITMAP64	Device can support bitmap > 64KB
RC_GDI20_OUTPUT	Has 2.0 output calls
RC_GDI20_STATE	Function not documented
RC_SAVEBITMAP	Function not documented
RC_DI_BITMAP	Supports DIB (device-independent bitmap) to memory
RC_PALETTE	Palette support
RC_DIBTODEV	Supports DIB to device
RC_BIGFONT	Supports fonts > 64KB
RC_STRETCHBLT	StretchBlt supported
RC_FLOODFILL	FloodFill supported
RC_STRETCHDIB	StretchDIBits supported
RC_OP_DX_OUTPUT	Function not documented
RC_DEVBITS	Function not documented

* These replace the appropriate Escapes from earlier versions.

** If RC_NONE is not defined in WinGDI.H, do not attempt to use this constant (it really isn't necessary anyway).

Reporting Device Capabilities: The DC Program

The DC program uses a single function, GetDeviceCaps, to retrieve a list of integer values describing specific device capabilities. In many cases, the information returned is an integer value, such as the supported vertical or horizontal pixel size. In other cases, the value returned is a flag value that must be deciphered, as individual bits, to identify the presence or absence of specific capabilities.

GetDeviceCaps is called with two parameters: a device context handle (hDC), which identifies a specific device such as a video display or printer, and an integer argument, which specifies the information requested.

In most cases, the capabilities reported by the GetDeviceCaps function are provided by graphics coprocessor devices incorporated in the output devices themselves. In a video display, this would be a coprocessor found on the video card.

NOTE

In the DC program, you will find that the information available has been grouped in related categories, principally for display convenience. Conventionally, these values would not be displayed at all; they would only be requested as needed for use by an application. Or, far more often, this information would not be requested at all, except by the GDI to determine how to best map an application's display (or other output) to the available device. In general, neither programmer nor application should be concerned with any aspect of the physical device, leaving these to be handled by Windows' GDI.

In hard-copy devices, the presence or absence of a graphics coprocessor depends partially on the age of the device and partially on the sophistication (and price) of the model. For example, older laser printers, thought still capable of excellent print quality, often predate the development of graphics coprocessors. Other, more modern devices, such as ink-jet printers, may lack not only coprocessors but also sufficient memory for full-page graphics and, therefore, may require banding (downloading page images in bands) support provided by Windows.

Device Palette (Color) Capabilities

The basic capabilities reported for the video display are shown in Figure 21.2. Figure 21.3 shows the capabilities reported for a printer device.

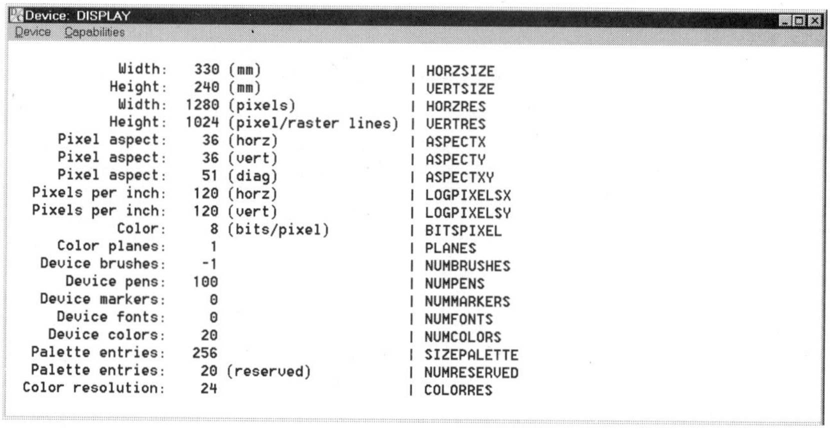

FIGURE 21.2

An example of CRT device information (SVGA)

```
Device: DISPLAY
Device  Capabilities

              Width:    330 (mm)                     | HORZSIZE
             Height:    240 (mm)                     | VERTSIZE
              Width:   1280 (pixels)                 | HORZRES
             Height:   1024 (pixel/raster lines)     | VERTRES
       Pixel aspect:     36 (horz)                   | ASPECTX
       Pixel aspect:     36 (vert)                   | ASPECTY
       Pixel aspect:     51 (diag)                   | ASPECTXY
     Pixels per inch:   120 (horz)                   | LOGPIXELSX
     Pixels per inch:   120 (vert)                   | LOGPIXELSY
              Color:      8 (bits/pixel)             | BITSPIXEL
       Color planes:      1                          | PLANES
     Device brushes:     -1                          | NUMBRUSHES
        Device pens:    100                          | NUMPENS
     Device markers:      0                          | NUMMARKERS
       Device fonts:      0                          | NUMFONTS
      Device colors:     20                          | NUMCOLORS
     Palette entries:   256                          | SIZEPALETTE
     Palette entries:    20 (reserved)               | NUMRESERVED
   Color resolution:     24                          | COLORRES
```

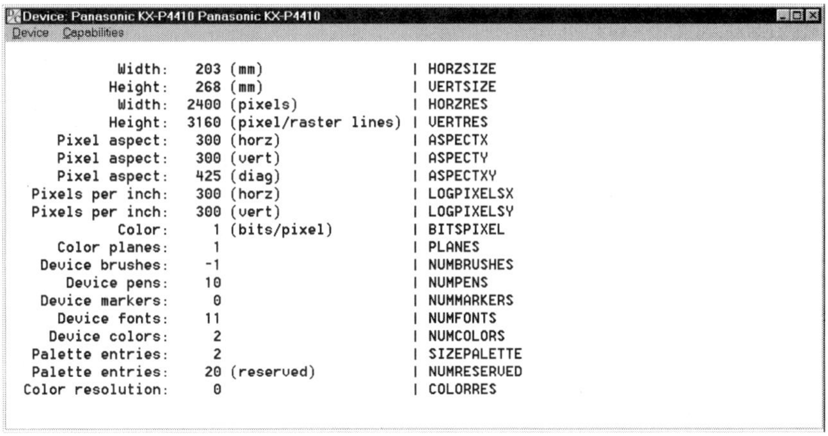

FIGURE 21.3

An example of printer
device information

```
Device: Panasonic KX-P4410 Panasonic KX-P4410                    _□✕
 Device  Capabilities

             Width:    203 (mm)                | HORZSIZE
            Height:    268 (mm)                | VERTSIZE
             Width:   2400 (pixels)            | HORZRES
            Height:   3160 (pixel/raster lines)| VERTRES
     Pixel aspect:     300 (horz)              | ASPECTX
     Pixel aspect:     300 (vert)              | ASPECTY
     Pixel aspect:     425 (diag)              | ASPECTXY
  Pixels per inch:     300 (horz)              | LOGPIXELSX
  Pixels per inch:     300 (vert)              | LOGPIXELSY
            Color:       1 (bits/pixel)        | BITSPIXEL
     Color planes:       1                     | PLANES
   Device brushes:      -1                     | NUMBRUSHES
      Device pens:      10                     | NUMPENS
   Device markers:       0                     | NUMMARKERS
     Device fonts:      11                     | NUMFONTS
    Device colors:       2                     | NUMCOLORS
  Palette entries:       2                     | SIZEPALETTE
  Palette entries:      20 (reserved)          | NUMRESERVED
 Color resolution:       0                     | COLORRES
```

In general, when speaking of device palette capabilities, the first thought that comes to mind is of video display capabilities. And, in most cases, this is accurate. However, hard-copy devices that support palettes with more than two colors (black and white) are becoming increasing popular. Therefore, even if we tend to speak of palettes as if we were referring only to the video device, remember that the video display is not the only color device available. It is, however, generally the most sophisticated device.

As a general rule, the DC program reports video palettes in two elements: bits per pixel (BITSPIXEL) and color planes (PLANES). Also, in most cases, one of these two elements will be reported as value 1, and only the remaining element is relevant in determining the device's supported color range. This limitation (or context, if you prefer) is mostly a matter of how the hardware's device driver is written and not a matter of how the actual physical device operates.

There is, however, a third reported element: device colors (NUMCOLORS), which, to some degree, saves calculations. Figure 21.2 shows the device capabilities reported by the DC program for a Matrox Pulsar video device which (deliberately, because of requirements set by other system uses) is restricted to a 256-color palette. Table 21.2 shows how the reported results vary according to equipment capabilities for different types of devices.

You may note a few discrepancies in the table report, such as the fact that the SVGA palette size is calculated as 256 colors while the reported palette size is only 20. No, this is not an error; the reported palette size is the number of palette entries

TABLE 21.2 Comparing Device Color Capabilities

Device Type	Color Planes	Bits/ Pixel	Calculated Palette Size	Reported Palette Size	Possible Colors
EGA/VGA	4	1	16	16	256
SVGA	1	8	256	20	16,777,216
Printer	1	1	2	2	2
Plotter	1	1	2	8	N/A

that are predefined, not the number of possible (calculated) palette entries. Thus, for an SVGA system, the palette size is 256 color entries, of which 20 have been reserved by the system (Windows) for standard palette colors. The remaining 236 palette entries are undefined and must be defined either by the application or, in some cases, by the user.

Another discrepancy appears in the Plotter device, where a calculated palette size of two is at odds with the reported palette size of eight. This discrepancy occurs because the plotter reported in this table is a pen-carousel plotter, which has eight color pens but still has only one color plane and one bit per pixel. Instead of sending color information in terms of planes or bits per pixel, for the plotter, a specific instruction is required to select a color pen, and all subsequent instructions until another pen is selected are essentially monochromatic.

Incidentally, you may also be wondering where the count of possible colors (rightmost column) is determined since this last piece of information is not inherent in the reported device capabilities. The details of color ranges are covered in Chapter 22. Just note now that the raw data is essentially correct.

When you are reviewing device information, keep in mind that the information reported by the system for a specific device can be useful, but you must understand how these facts are derived and reported.

Version and Device Types

The DRIVERVERSION and TECHNOLOGY index arguments request the device driver version number and the device type. Driver version numbers are reported as word values in hexadecimal format. For example, a version number reported as 0x0103 identifies version 1, revision 3.

Seven device types are defined: vector plotter, raster display (CRT), raster printer (laser-jet or ink-jet), raster camera, character stream, metafile, and display file. Normally, of course, the video device will be a raster display. Depending on the equipment and configuration, however, the reported hard-copy device could be a vector plotter, raster printer, raster camera, or even a metafile or display device.

Size and Resolution

Device size and resolution cover a variety of elements, including physical size, pixel or dot resolutions, colors and palettes, and pixel or dot aspect ratios—in effect, all salient information about a device's reproduction capabilities. In Table 21.3, size and resolution data are compared for four devices.

TABLE 21.3   Comparing Basic Device Resolutions

Data	Matrox Pulsar (Millenium SVGA) Video	Panasonic KX-P4400	HP LaserJet IID Printer	HP PaintJet XL Printer (standard)
Width (mm)	330	203	203	203
Width (pixels/dots)	1280	2395	2400	1440
Height (mm)	240	268	266	260
Height (pixel/raster lines/ dots)	1024	3160	3150	1846
Horizontal (pixel/dot aspect)	36	300	300	180
Vertical (pixel/dot aspect)	36	300	300	180
Diagonal (pixel/dot aspect)	51	425	425	255
Pixels per inch/dots per inch (horiz)	120	300	300	180
Pixels per inch/dots per inch (vert)	120	300	300	180
Color (bits per pixel)	8	1	1	1
Color (planes)	1	1	1	1
Device brushes	-1	-1	-1	-1

TABLE 21.3 Comparing Basic Device Resolutions (Continued)

Data	Matrox Pulsar (Millenium SVGA) Video	Panasonic KX-P4400	HP LaserJet IID Printer	HP PaintJet XL Printer (standard)
Device pens	100	100	10	40
Device fonts	0	0	0	0
Device markers	0	4	0	0
Device colors	20	2	2	8
Palette entries	256	0	2	16
Palette entries (reserved)	20	0	2	16
Color resolution (bits per pixel)	24	0	0	0

Notice that the numbers shown do not always tell the entire story. For example, the PaintJet printer reports 1 color bit per pixel, 1 color plane, and 8 device colors...but, finally and correctly, reports a 16-color palette.

TIP What the PaintJet report does not tell you is that these 16 palette colors can be assigned from a much wider range using RGB specifications. See Chapter 22 for details.

Raster Capabilities

Because most output devices are raster devices (yes, this includes laser printers), the RASTERCAPS reports on general device capabilities such as banding (device memory dependent), bitmap handling, fill operations, scaling, and device palettes. Table 21.4 shows raster capabilities for some different devices.

Raster capabilities typically receive more sophisticated support from video devices than from printers. In either case, support may be partially determined by the amount of memory available to the device; that is, on the video card or in the printer. Because all of the printers used for our example have more than adequate memory for full-page graphics, no banding support is required for any of these. In like fashion, the video card represented has 2MB of RAM and supports large bitmaps as well as large fonts, even though, in general, large fonts are not sent directly to display devices (normally, bitmapped images of text are transferred instead).

TABLE 21.4   Comparing Raster Capabilities

RASTERCAPS	Matrox Pulsar (Millenium SVGA) Video	Panasonic KX-P4400	HP LaserJet IID Printer	HP PaintJet XL Printer (standard)
Banding support required		✓		
Bitmap transfer	✓	✓	✓	✓
Bitmaps >= 64K	✓	✓	✓	✓
SetDIBits and GetDIBits	✓	✓		
SetDIBitsToDevice	✓	✓		
Floodfill	✓			
Windows 2.0 features	✓	✓		
Palettes	✓			
Scaling	✓			
Fonts >= 64K	✓	✓		
StretchBlt	✓	✓	✓	✓
StretchDIBits	✓	✓	✓	✓

TIP

The choice between downloading a font versus sending a bitmapped text image is determined by the printer type and, of course, the printer driver. Fortunately, in normal circumstances, this decision does not need to be made by the programmer. If you are designing printer drivers, however, some experimentation may be necessary to decide when and where the trade-offs occur.

Clip Capabilities

Clipping capabilities, which are reported by the CLIPCAPS request, define the ability of a device to clip drawing instructions to a specified region. Most devices have rectangular clipping capabilities. Region-clipping capabilities, permitting a more complex area definition, are also possible. Table 21.5 shows clipping capabilities for several devices.

Bitmap Operations

In the `GetDeviceCaps` function, bitmap operations are reported as capabilities under the heading of raster capabilities. From a graphics operation standpoint, however, these operations are also probably the most important device capabilities available. Bitmaps inherently require more than a little handling to write to the screen or to move, superimpose, or manipulate in any other fashion.

Characters, whether bitmapped or stroked, are commonly written to the screen as foreground images only and, therefore, generally leave the greater portion of the screen unaffected. A rough estimate suggests that 20 percent or less of the screen pixels are actually written during text operations. Because of this, character operations are inherently faster than bitmapped image operations, which require writing all pixels within the image area.

To offset this speed discrepancy, sophisticated graphics coprocessors include special hardware functions that are devoted to fast bitmap transfers, handling of bitmaps larger than 64KB, and bitmap-scaling operations. If any of these capabilities are supported, the end result is that most common graphics operations are executed at much higher speeds than with unsupported video equipment (or printers).

TABLE 21.5   Comparing Clip Capabilities

CLIPCAPS	Matrox Pulsar (Millenium SVGA) Video	Panasonic KX-P4400	HP LaserJet IID Printer	HP PaintJet XL Printer (standard)
No output clipping support				
Output clipped to rectangle	✓	✓	✓	✓
Output clipped to region				

Curve Capabilities

The curve capability flags (CURVECAPS) report the capabilities of the output device to handle its own curve definitions. These may include circles, arcs, pie wedges, and ellipses, as well as special borders. Table 21.6 shows the curve capabilities of several devices.

TABLE 21.6 Comparing Curve Capabilities

CURVECAPS	Matrox Pulsar (Millenium SVGA) Video	Panasonic KX-P4400	HP LaserJet IID Printer	HP PaintJet XL Printer (standard)
Curves not supported				
Circles	✓		✓	✓
Pie wedges			✓	✓
Chord arcs			✓	✓
Ellipses	✓		✓	✓
Wide borders			✓	✓
Styled borders			✓	✓
Wide and styled borders			✓	✓
Interiors	✓		✓	✓
Rounded rectangles				

Line Capabilities

Line capability flags (LINECAPS) report on line-style support and some interior-fill operations. As with curve capabilities, line capabilities are widely (if not universally) supported. Although it's less calculation-intensive than curve operations, providing external support for line-drawing calculations still increases throughput for both display and hard-copy devices. Table 21.7 shows the line capabilities of some devices.

TABLE 21.7   Comparing Line Capabilities

LINECAPS	Matrox Pulsar (Millenium SVGA) Video	Panasonic KX-P4400	HP LaserJet IID Printer	HP PaintJet XL Printer (standard)
Lines not supported				
Polylines	✓	✓	✓	✓
Markers			✓	✓
Polymarkers			✓	✓
Wide lines			✓	✓
Styled lines	✓	✓	✓	✓
Wide and styled lines			✓	✓
Interiors			✓	✓

Polygon Capabilities

Polygon capability flags (POLYGONALCAPS) report on device capabilities for executing alternate and winding fill operations on polygon figures, as well as plain and style borders and interiors.

NOTE   A winding fill operation is slower than an alternate fill but also fills enclosed areas that might otherwise be omitted. The difference between alternate and winding fill operations is demonstrated in Chapter 23 in the PenDraw3 demo.

Again, as with curve and line capabilities, polygon support is common but not universal. In terms of the calculations required, support for polygon capabilities probably falls somewhere between those for curves and lines, although the fill algorithms may run a close second to curves in terms of the CPU's workload. Again, external support for these tasks does increase throughput and display or output speed.

Table 21.8 shows the polygon capabilities of some devices.

TABLE 21.8   Comparing Polygonal Capabilities

POLYGONALCAPS	Matrox Pulsar (Millenium SVGA) Video	Panasonic KX-P4400	HP LaserJet IID Printer	HP PaintJet XL Printer (standard)
Polygonals not supported				
Alternate fill polygon	✓		✓	✓
Rectangles	✓		✓	✓
Winding fill polygon			✓	✓
Scan lines	✓	✓	✓	✓
Styled borders			✓	✓
Wide and styled borders			✓	✓
Interiors	✓		✓	✓

Text Capabilities

Text capability flags (TEXTCAPS) report device capabilities for character output, including stroked output, character rotation and scaling, and clipping precision, as well as italic, boldface, underlining, and strikeout. Also reported are the handling capabilities for both raster and vector fonts.

In general, printers provide more sophisticated text capabilities than video cards. For either type of device, however, the text source may be more important than the device itself. A WYSIWYG editor, such as Microsoft Word or CorelDraw, may provide character rotation regardless of the display or printer support. If such support is provided by the output device, the result is simply faster output operation, not new or different capabilities.

Table 21.9 shows text capabilities for some devices.

NOTE   Note that these are device capabilities, not font characteristics. For font characteristics, refer to the LOGFONT structure for a specific font. See Chapter 25 for information about fonts.

TABLE 21.9   Comparing Text Capabilities

TEXTCAPS	Matrox Pulsar (Millenium SVGA) Video	Panasonic KX-P4400	HP LaserJet IID Printer	HP PaintJet XL Printer (standard)
Character output precision			✓	✓
Stroke output precision			✓	✓
Stroke clip precision	✓		✓	✓
90-degree character rotation				
Any character rotation				
Independent x/y scaling				
Doubled character scaling				
Integer multiple scaling				
Any multiple scaling				
Double-weight characters				✓
Italic				
Underlining			✓	✓
Strikeout			✓	✓
Raster fonts	✓			
Vector fonts			✓	✓

Working with Mapping Modes

Under DOS, all graphics operations (with some rare exceptions) use a single mapping mode in which the logical unit is the screen pixel. The screen origin—the 0,0 point—is located in the upper-left corner, which is a convention established by and held over from text display and video memory-mapping conventions. Although applications might create both text and graphics windows, this same mapping-mode convention was almost as inevitable as the sun rising in the east.

Things have changed under Windows. Windows supports eight separate mapping modes, each providing a different set of conventions appropriate for different circumstances. Furthermore, while each uses different scalar (logical) units, except for the MM_TEXT mode corresponding to the DOS standard, each mode also uses the lower-left corner—not the upper-left—as the default screen origin or uses a variable origin point.

Windows Mapping Modes

The eight mapping modes under Windows are listed in Table 21.10, along with their values, logical units, and default origins.

TABLE 21.10 Windows Mapping Modes

Mapping Mode	Value	Logical Units	Default Origins x-axis	y-axis
MM_TEXT	1	Pixel	Left	Top
MM_LOMETRIC	2	0.1 mm	Left	Bottom
MM_HIMETRIC	3	0.01 mm	Left	Bottom
MM_LOENGLISH	4	0.01 inch	Left	Bottom
MM_HIENGLISH	5	0.001 inch	Left	Bottom
MM_TWIPS	6	$^1/_{1440}$ inch	Left	Bottom
MM_ISOTROPIC	7	Variable $(x=y)$	Variable	Variable
MM_ANISOTROPIC	8	Variable $(x!=y)$	Variable	Variable

The Default Text Mode

Beginning with the familiar, the MM_TEXT mode (default) corresponds to the DOS graphics modes, allowing the application to operate in terms of pixel positions (virtual or physical device pixels). In the MM_TEXT mode, the default origin lies at the upper-left corner of the screen with the x- and y-axis coordinates increasing to the right and down. Figure 21.4 illustrates the MM_TEXT mode.

FIGURE 21.4

The MM_TEXT mode

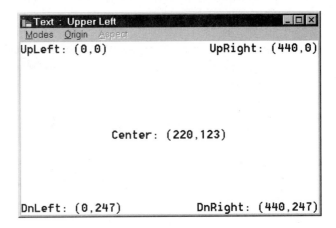

The MM_TEXT mode is used by default if no other mapping mode has been selected and, as the name might suggest, is optimized for text displays—that is, for text displays following European/American conventions with the text flowing from left to right and top to bottom. There is, however, nothing requiring other types of applications to change modes to perform their specific tasks. If you are content performing the necessary coordinate conversions yourself, any operation can be accomplished in MM_TEXT mode, just not always as conveniently. Still, convenience is no small consideration and is the real reason for providing such a variety of mapping modes.

The Cartesian Coordinate Modes

The MM_HIENGLISH, MM_HIMETRIC, MM_LOENGLISH, MM_LOMETRIC, and MM_TWIPS modes all follow the familiar Cartesian coordinate system, with coordinate values increasing up and to the right of the origin point. These five modes differ, however, in their logical units. They provide measurements appropriate to applications that need to draw in physically meaningful units: English, metric, or typesetting units.

The MM_HIMETRIC and MM_LOMETRIC modes use logical units of 0.01 and 0.1 millimeters, respectively, to provide high- and low-resolution imaging. Figure 21.5 shows an example of the MM_LOMETRIC mode. Similarly, the MM_HIENGLISH and MM_LOENGLISH mapping modes use units of 0.01 and 0.001 inches, again providing high and low resolution. Together, these four modes adequately provide for a wide variety of circumstances to suit the needs of engineers, scientists, and artists. (Scaling, of course, can be applied as necessary.)

FIGURE 21.5
The MM_LOMETRIC
mode

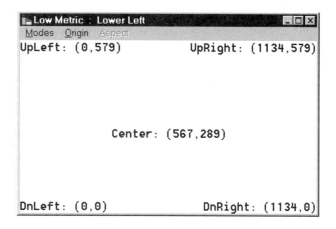

The fifth mapping mode, MM_TWIPS, requires a bit more explanation. The logical units are $1/1440$ inch which, while unfamiliar to an engineer or scientist, just happens to be one-twentieth of a printer's point (72 points = 1 inch). Using MM_TWIPS mode, a 10-point typeface can be drawn 200 logical units in height, providing sufficient detail to render even the most complex typeface, regardless of whether the actual display device can support a similar resolution.

The Isotropic and Anistotropic Modes

The MM_ISOTROPIC and MM_ANISOTROPIC modes provide both variable logical units and variable origin points. They can be adapted to provide any scale or arrangements that might arise and that are not covered by one of the standard modes.

For example, using the MM_ANISOTROPIC mode, where the x- and y-axes can be assigned different scales, the vertical direction might be mapped in thousands of dollars (or the numerical equivalent), and the horizontal direction could represent dates to create a business graph. Equally practical, the MM_ISOTROPIC mode could be used with measurements defined as astronomical units with the 0,0 origin at the center to plot the orbital path of a comet on its passage through the solar system. In both cases, the GDI would provide conversions from the internal modal units to the actual physical display and would not require these conversions to be handled by the application.

Remember, however, that the MM_ISOTROPIC mode has the same logical units assigned to both the x- and y-axes. This mode is useful when preserving the exact shape of an image is important. Figure 21.6 shows an example of the MM_ISOTROPIC mode. The MM_ANISOTROPIC mode may have each axis scaled differently. Furthermore, both modes may have the origin point located anywhere within the application window or even somewhere outside the application window entirely.

FIGURE 21.6

The MM_ISOTROPIC mode

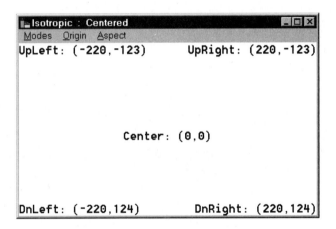

Setting and Getting Mapping Modes

The SetMapMode and GetMapMode functions are provided to set or retrieve the eight defined mapping modes.

```
SetMapMode( hdc, nMapMode );
nMapMode = GetMapMode( hdc );
```

The nMapMode argument used to call SetMapMode would, normally, be one of the predefined constants, but it could be simply an integer argument in the corresponding range. The value returned by SetMapMode reports the previous (existing) mapping mode.

As with `SetMapMode`, the value returned by `GetMapMode` will correspond to one of the defined mapping modes, or if there is an error, will return as zero. Until a different mapping mode is explicitly selected, the initial (default) mode will always be `MM_TEXT`, mapped in pixels with the 0,0 origin at the upper-left corner of the application window, just as in DOS.

After a different mapping mode is selected, the values returned by `SetMapMode` and `GetMapMode` will correspond to that mode. For example, after `MM_LOMETRIC` is selected, the origin point is now at the lower-left corner of the application window, with coordinates increasing up and right. At the same time, instead of specifying coordinates in pixels, coordinates are specified in 0.1 millimeter increments, which on the average SVGA monitor provides a full-screen vertical resolution of 1560 units and 2080 units horizontally (assuming the 208-by-156 millimeter display reported by the DC program).

Remember, however, that the actual physical display mode, assuming standard SVGA resolution, is only 640 pixels wide and 480 pixels high. This means that, horizontally and vertically, 3.25 logical units are mapped to each physical unit, or in overall terms, a total of 10.56 (3.25^2) logical pixels are mapped to each physical pixel.

Table 21.11 shows the logical size and corresponding inches and millimeters for several output devices and modes, arranged in descending order of magnitude.

TABLE 21.11 Device/Mode Resolutions

Device	Logical Size	Unit	Inches	Millimeters
EGA video (H/V)	640 / 350	Pixels	0.012795 / 0.017547	0.3250 / 0.4457*
VGA video (H/V)	640 / 480	Pixels	0.012795	0.3250
MM_LOENGLISH	0.01	Inches	0.010000	0.2540
SVGA video (H/V)	1024 / 768	Pixels	0.079960	0.2031
MM_LOMETRIC	0.1	MM	0.003940	0.1000
LaserJet printer	300	DPI	0.003333	0.0846
MM_HIENGLISH	0.001	Inches	0.001000	0.0254
High-resolution SVGA	1280 / 1024	Pixels	0.008515	0.0191

TABLE 21.11 Device/Mode Resolutions (Continued)

Device	Logical Size	Unit	Inches	Millimeters
MM_TWIPS	$1/20$	Points	0.000694	0.0176
Typesetter	2000	DPI	0.000500	0.0127
MM_HIMETRIC	0.01	MM	0.000394	0.0100

* The physical measurements (inches and millimeters) for video modes are based on standard monitor screen sizes as specified by the manufacturers, with a display area approximately 10.9 inches wide and 7.9 inches high (a nominal 14-inch monitor). Because actual physical units may vary, depending both on monitor adjustments and on larger physical screen sizes, the values shown are for comparative resolutions only.

However, mapping the logical, virtual display to the physical display is not the application's concern because all relevant operations are handled by the GDI. What is the application's concern—or, more properly, the programmer's—is to select the mapping mode appropriate to the task's requirements and, of course, to set the origins and window and viewport extents accordingly.

Coordinate Translations: Viewport versus Window

Under Windows, each application is contending with two separate coordinate systems which, combined, form the client window display. These two reference systems have been given the titles *viewport* and *window*—a nomenclature that is responsible for more than a little confusion.

The term *window* is used to refer to the application's client window, meaning the area of the screen where the application's display actually appears. And, for an even longer time, the term *viewport* has been used, particularly in non-Windows contexts, to refer to a clipping region or a boundary restricting graphics operations.

Under Windows, and specifically when referring to mapping modes, the term *viewport* does, indeed, refer to the screen display where the physical device coordinates must and do apply. When referring to *viewport* coordinates on the screen, the reference is in terms of pixels, and the origin is always at the upper-left corner (just like under DOS).

The term *window*, however, refers to the virtual space where the application is executing its drawing operations. The window coordinates are expressed in logical coordinates. Furthermore, all GDI functions accept coordinates as logical, not physical, units.

The mapping modes are simply a description of how Windows (the system) translates coordinates from the *window,* which is using logical coordinates, to the *viewport,* which uses device (hardware) coordinates. The conversion from window coordinates (*xWindow,yWindow*) to viewport (screen) coordinates (*xViewport,yViewport*) uses two formulas:

```
                                                      xViewExt
    xViewport = xViewOrg + ( ( xWindow - xWinOrg )  *  -------- )
                                                      xWinExt

                                                      yViewExt
    yViewport = yViewOrg + ( ( yWindow - yWinOrg )  *  -------- )
                                                      yWinExt
```

The additional parameters used in these formulas are the variables describing the selected mapping mode:

- The _ViewOrg arguments describe the viewport origin in device or screen coordinates.

- The _WinOrg arguments describe the window origin in local, logical coordinates.

- The _ViewExt and _WinExt parameters define a conversion ratio between "size" in virtual units of the window and an equally fictional "size" for the viewport expressed in device units.

If both the viewport and window were using the same scalar coordinate systems (pixel units) and origin points (0,0 at upper left), these formulas could be greatly simplified as:

```
    xViewport = xViewOrg + xWindow

    yViewport = yViewOrg + yWindow
```

However, such a simplification would destroy the very flexibility that Windows has introduced by using mapping modes (although, essentially, this relationship is found in the default MM_TEXT mode).

Also, when an application does require conversion from the application's coordinate context to the physical device context (or vice versa), Windows provides two functions: DPtoLP and LPtoDP.

The DPtoLP function converts device points to logical points.

```
    DPtoLP( hdc, &Points, 1 );
```

The `Points` argument is an array of `POINT` structures to be converted. The `hdc` argument specifies the device context and the third parameter indicates how many points should be converted.

The reverse process, from logical points to device points, is accomplished by calling the `LPtoDP` function, which has the same arguments:

```
LPtoDP( hdc, &Points, 1 );
```

As another example, assume that an application needs to convert the client window rectangle to device coordinates. This would be accomplished as:

```
GetClientRect( hwnd, &rect );
LPtoDP( hdc, (LPPOINT) &rect, sizeof(rect) / sizeof(POINT) );
```

Remember that most of the time, Windows will provide all the translation required between the viewport and window coordinate systems without application provisions. But if you need to handle these, conversion functions are available.

Setting Window and Viewpoint Origins

Under Windows, all mapping modes have variable origin points, even though six of these modes conventionally use the default origins indicated in Table 21.10. These defaults can be changed by using the `SetViewportOrgEx` and `SetWindow-OrgEx` functions.

The `SetViewportOrgEx` function sets the viewport (device context) origin and is invoked as:

```
SetViewportOrgEx( hdc, xPos, yPos, &Point );
```

The `xPos` and `yPos` arguments are in device context units (pixels for the video device). `Point` is returned reporting the previous origin coordinates, with the y-coordinate in the high-order word and the x-coordinate in the low-order word. Optionally, this fourth parameter can be passed as NULL if no return value is desired.

The `SetWindowOrgEx` function provides a similar flexibility within the virtual context and is invoked as:

```
SetWindowOrgEx( hdc, xPos, yPos, &Point );
```

But this time, `xPos` and `yPos` are expressed in logical units appropriate to the mapping mode selected. Again, an optional Point returns the previous origin coordinates.

NOTE In Windows 3.*x*, similar services are supplied by the `SetViewportOrg` and `SetWindowOrg` functions. However, these have different calling parameters and return values.

Remember, however, that changing the viewport or window origins has no effect on the position of the client window on the screen. Each is, in effect, a fiction providing an adjustable offset that affects how and which portion of an application's display is mapped from the virtual to the physical display. (To change the window position on the screen, use the `SetWindowPos` function.) Also, in general, only one of these two functions is used at any time, since they perform what are, in essence, redundant tasks.

Setting the Window and Viewport Extents

The `SetWindowExtEx` and `SetViewportExtEx` functions are used to set the window and viewport extents. They set the scale and offset sizes, which provide the mapping ratios (see the formulas shown earlier). These ratios determine how an application's client window image is mapped to the physical (device) viewport context. These two functions are valid only when the mapping mode is set to `MM_ISOTROPIC` or `MM_ANISOTROPIC`; they are ignored if any other mapping mode is in effect.

The `SetWindowExtEx` function specifies the window size in logical units and is called as:

```
SetWindowExtEx( hdc, xSize, ySize, &OldSize );
```

The second and third parameters specify the window extent (size) in logical units. The fourth parameter (`OldSize`) is returned with the previous window extent. If the original settings are not needed, this argument can be passed as NULL, and nothing will be returned.

The `SetViewportExtEx` function is called in similar fashion to specify the viewport extent in device units.

```
SetViewportExtEx( hdc, xSize, ySize, &OldSize );
```

Two constraints apply when the `MM_ISOTROPIC` mapping mode is in effect:

- `SetWindowExtEx` must be called before calling `SetViewportExtEx`.

- The `ySize` parameter is ignored by both functions in favor of the `xSize` setting.

In MM_ANISOTROPIC mode, the xSize and ySize parameters can be specified independently, setting different scales along each axis.

The ratios between the x- and y-viewport extents and the x- and y-window extents define how much the GDI should stretch or compress units in the logical coordinate system to fit units in the device (physical) coordinate system. In isotropic mode, the x- and y-axes always maintain the same ratios; in anisotropic mode, these ratios can be determined independently.

As an example, consider an application window using the anisotropic mode with the window x-extent set to 200 and the viewport x-extent at 400. In this situation, the GDI would map two logical units (along the x-axis) to four device units. Continuing with the assumption that the window y-extent is also set at 200 and the viewport y-extent at 100, the GDI would map two logical units to one device unit along the y-axis.

However, since no provision has been made to alter this, the y-axis in the window increases from bottom to top; the same y-axis in the viewport increases from top to bottom. The result is that the image mapped is, in effect, inverted. Of course, if this is not desired, either the viewport or window y-axis can be assigned a negative value, thus inverting the inversion. On the other hand, if both are negative, the situation remains unchanged.

How Modes Affect Window Size: The Modes Demo

The Modes program demonstrates how the mapping modes affect the window's size (in logical units) as well as the window's origin point for each. Figures 21.4, 21.5, and 21.6, shown earlier in the chapter, are from the Modes program.

The main menu offers three selections:

- **Modes:** Displays a submenu listing the eight mapping modes.

- **Origin:** Offers the origin choices of upper-left, center, or lower-left.

- **Aspect:** When the isotropic or anisotropic mode has been selected, displays the dialog box shown in Figure 21.7, which allows you to change the horizontal and vertical viewport and window extents. With other modes, this option is grayed.

FIGURE 21.7

The dialog box displayed
by the Modes program's
Aspect option

FIGURE 21.7

The dialog box displayed
by the Modes program's
Aspect option

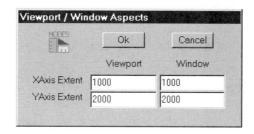

The Modes program demonstrates two menu-handling procedures that you may find useful. The first checks and unchecks menu items according to selection; the second changes the grayed state of the Aspects menu item, enabling this selection only when the isotropic or anisotropic mapping modes are selected.

The demo programs presented in this chapter, DC and Modes, provide an introduction to the GDI. Their source code for these programs is on the CD that accompanies this book. Because the DC program is intended simply to show how device capabilities can be queried, this program is provided only in a conventional Windows C-code format and no MFC/C++ equivalent is provided. In actual applications, a call querying a specific device capability might be made at any time, for the purpose of setting some internal handling, but would not normally involve reporting the capabilities discovered back to the user.

The next chapters continue to demonstrate aspects of the GDI.

CHAPTER

TWENTY-TWO

22

Colors and Color Palettes

- The Windows standard palette

- How dithering works

- Custom color palettes

- Windows color drawing modes

- Color-to-gray-scale conversions

Handling colors under Windows is a distinct departure from the color procedures under DOS. In part, this causes some additional complexity for the programmer, but overall, it provides greater flexibility. The application programmer no longer needs to make separate provisions for various hardware capabilities. Rather, you are free to devote your time to the application's principal objectives instead of writing code for a multitude of display systems.

For the application developer, one of the most important reasons to use color is to provide information in forms more readily recognizable than a simple monochrome display. Even for such simple tasks as viewing spreadsheets or editing program code, the addition of color to highlight various elements provides additional, easily-recognized information that could be lost on a simple black-and-white (or black-and-amber or black-and-green) display. With color, when an accountant says that a company is in the red, he can be speaking quite literally, without needing to reach for a red pen to make an entry in a ledger sheet.

In part, the use of color (or even shades of gray) simply presents a display with the appearance of greater depth and detail than a monochrome display. And, even though first impressions are hardly an appropriate basis for judging an application's design and usefulness, they are still important. Your current and prospective clients will take that first look, and decide how much consideration to give to your application and how much effort they will expend in discovering the real strengths of your design.

Of course, there's also a flip side to this coin. Excessively elaborate graphics or absurdly garish color choices may have precisely the opposite of the desired effect: a bad first impression or, worse, general confusion while operating an application. Thus, restraint is also appropriate.

This is not, however, a lecture on the aesthetics of design (regardless of how relevant the topic might be). Instead, the present topic is how colors *can* be used. How you choose to use them remains up to you.

Windows Palettes

The earliest video cards provided video RAM (VRAM) on the order of 32KB to 64KB, enough for simple displays with limited colors. Today, even an inexpensive video card is expected to provide at least 1MB of RAM—enough for a 1024-by-768 display with a 256 color palette. And many video cards include twice this amount of RAM or more.

Using DOS, the video palette was defined in a relatively restrictive fashion with a fixed palette of 16 colors. These colors were defined using the RGBI flag system, where the flag bits controlled the red, green, and blue color guns together with a single intensity flag.

With the introduction of the EGA/VGA video boards, the palette expanded to 64 colors by exchanging the single intensity bit for three separate intensity bits: one each for the red, green, and blue color guns.

Today, both of these color specification systems have been supplanted by the Windows 32-bit color specification, where each color value is defined as a DWORD value in the format 0x00BBGGRR. In this format, the least-significant byte (eight bits) holds the value for red, the second byte is green, and the third byte is blue. The fourth, most-significant byte remains zero.

You may wonder why this is a 32-bit color specification when we've been talking about 24-bit color. The remaining 8 bits in the DWORD value are used for a different purpose, which we'll discuss later.

Table 22.1 shows the CGA, EGA/VGA, and Windows equivalents for a 16-color palette.

TABLE 22.1   System Color Definitions

Color Names	CGA Colors		EGA/VGA Colors		Windows Equivalents*
	binary	iRGB	binary	rgbRGB	0x..BB GG RR
Black	0000	. . . .	000000	. . . . . .	0x00 00 00 00
Dark Blue	0001	. . . B	000001	. . . . . B	0x00 77 00 00
Dark Green	0010	. . G .	000010	. . . . G .	0x00 00 77 00
Dark Cyan	0011	. . G B	000011	. . . . G B	0x00 77 77 00
Dark Red	0100	. R . .	000100	. . . R . .	0x00 00 00 77
Dark Magenta	0101	. R . B	000101	. . . R . B	0x00 77 00 77

TABLE 22.1   System Color Definitions (Continued)

Color Names	CGA Colors		EGA/VGA Colors		Windows Equivalents*
	binary	iRGB	binary	rgbRGB	0x..BB GG RR
Brown	0110	.RG.	000110	...RG.	0x00 00 77 77
Light Gray	0111	.RGB	000111	...RGB	0x00 77 77 77
Dark Gray	1000	i...	111000	rgb...	0x00 3F 3F 3F
Light Blue	1001	i..B	111001	rgb..B	0x00 FF 00 00
Light Green	1010	i.G.	111010	rgb.G.	0x00 00 FF 00
Light Cyan	1011	i.GB	111011	rgb.GB	0x00 FF FF 00
Light Red	1100	iR..	111100	rgbR..	0x00 00 00 FF
Light Magenta	1101	iR.B	111101	rgbR.B	0x00 FF 00 FF
Yellow	1110	iRG.	111110	rgbRG.	0x00 00 FF FF
White	1111	iRGB	111111	rgbRGB	0x00 FF FF FF

* In a Windows color specification, the most-significant byte is used, in other circumstances, as a flag value indicating the type of color reference.

In the Windows color specification system, each primary color (red, green, or blue) has a possible range of 0 to 255, and individual colors are identified by 24-bit combinations of the RGB components, yielding a total of 16,777,216 possible hues.

However, because video boards (with the exception of the newest 24-bit video board) cannot support individual pixel color specifications, these 24-bit values are written to a color palette. The pixels in the image map itself consist of 8-bit index references to the color palette.

Thus, while an SVGA video card can support 24-bit color specifications, it can only do so as a palette containing 256 entries. Furthermore, partially in support of earlier 16-color standards, Windows reserves 20 of these palette entries, leaving 236 colors for custom use.

The Standard Palette

In DOS, the standard palette consisted of the 16 colors originally defined by EGA video cards or their VGA/SVGA equivalents.

Windows defines a standard palette of 20 static colors (the default palette). On an EGA or VGA system, where only 16 of the 20 colors are actually available on the display, Windows emulates the remaining 4 colors by dithering (a process which will be demonstrated in a moment). On contemporary SVGA systems, where the hardware does support a device palette of 256 colors, the 20 default entries appear as individual hues without adjustments. Table 22.2 shows the RGB color values for each of the standard palette's 20 colors.

TABLE 22.2   The Windows Default Palette Values

Index	Color	R	G	B	Index	Color	R	G	B
0	Black	0	0	0	10	Off-White	266	251	240
1	Dark Red	128	0	0	11	Med. Gray	160	160	164
2	Dark Green	0	128	0	12	Dark Gray	128	128	128
3	Gold	128	128	0	13	Red	255	0	0
4	Dark Blue	0	0	128	14	Green	0	255	0
5	Violet	128	0	128	15	Yellow	255	255	0
6	Dark Cyan	0	128	128	16	Blue	0	0	255
7	Light Gray	192	192	192	17	Magenta	255	0	255
8	Pale Green	192	220	192	18	Light Cyan	0	255	255
9	Pale Blue	166	202	240	19	White	255	255	255

Technically, these 20 standard colors belonging to the stock system palette are inviolable and cannot be altered by an application, even when the application defines its own color values for corresponding palette entries. Because color priority is given to the foreground application, however, and the application's palette takes priority over the standard palette, background displays may be remapped. They may appear in whichever application colors provide the closest match to the standard colors, even when this results in a distinct change in the screen appearance.

In some cases, the color difference may be quite striking, such as when a 256-color bitmap is used as wallpaper and an application has defined its own 256-color palette. The ViewPCX demo program in Chapter 26 can provide a striking example of this effect. As ViewPCX is loading an image from a file (having already defined a new palette), the background image is displayed using the ViewPCX palette.

But, once the new image is displayed, the background colors should return to their original palette colors. Similar effects can be observed using a paint program (such as ZSoft's PhotoFinish) when multiple images are loaded, or while switching between images when a few moments are required to change between two quite different palettes.

Painting with the Standard Palette: The Color1 Program

The Color1 program was created to demonstrate the Windows standard color palette. As you can see in Figure 22.1, except for an optional icon, Color1 has no menu, dialog boxes, or other resources. Execution occurs entirely within the exported WndProc procedure, with a minimum of operations.

FIGURE 22.1

The Color1 program's display of the Windows standard palette

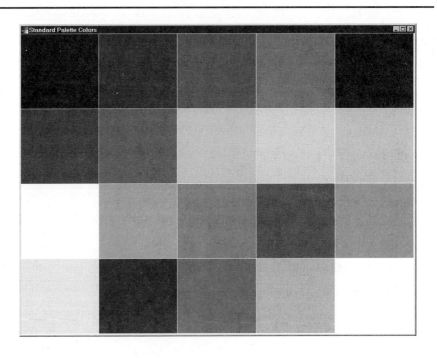

Because all that we intend to do in this demo program is to paint squares using the palette entries, we take the simpler course of defining a macro, which we can use to specify a color as a palette index.

```
#define  PalIndex  0x01000000 + i + ( j * xSteps )
```

The `PalIndex` macro assigns the value 1 to the most-significant byte in a DWORD value. At the same time, it writes an index—from 0 to 19—as the least-significant byte.

As mentioned earlier, the most-significant byte in this 32-bit DWORD value is used for purposes other than specifying an RGB value. In this case, we are not specifying an RGB value at all. Instead, by setting the high byte to 1, we can use the resulting value to instruct the system to use a specific existing palette entry.

The heart of the operation occurs in the WM_PAINT response.

```
case WM_PAINT:
    hdc = BeginPaint( hwnd, &ps );
    for( j=0; j<ySteps; j++ )
        for( i=0; i<xSteps; i++ )
        {
```

It begins with a double-loop used to divide the client window into 20 rectangles, one for each palette entry in the default palette. The size for `xSteps` and `ySteps` is calculated—in response to a WM_SIZE message—to divide the client window into five segments horizontally and four sections vertically.

For each section, the `PalIndex` macro is used as the color specification in calls to `CreatePen` and `CreateSolidBrush` to create both a pen and a brush using the stock color.

```
hPen = SelectObject( hdc,
            CreatePen( PS_SOLID, 1, PalIndex ) );
            hBrush = SelectObject( hdc,
            CreateSolidBrush( PalIndex ) );
Rectangle( hdc, i * xSize, j * ySize,
        ( i + 1 ) * xSize - 1,
        ( j + 1 ) * ySize - 1 );
```

After selecting the pen and brush, the `Rectangle` function draws a rectangle in the indexed color.

Last, both the brush and pen are deleted.

```
        DeleteObject( hPen );
        DeleteObject( hBrush );
    }
EndPaint( hwnd, &ps );
break;
```

The complete listing for the Color1 program appears at the end of this chapter. This is a fairly simple process, but it does demonstrate the standard palette colors. It also leads to an explanation of three types of RGB color specifications.

Types of RGB Color Specifications

Three types of RGB color specifications are demonstrated in the Color1 program: absolute, palette-index, and palette-relative values.

Absolute RGB COLORREF Values

Both the CreatePen and CreateBrush functions are called with a color reference parameter. Conventionally, this parameter is an RGB long integer (DWORD) following the form 0x00BBGGRR, as shown in Table 22.1. Thus, for a white brush, the color value would be specified as 0x00FFFFFF; for black, 0x00000000.

In all cases, the most-significant byte is 0; the red, green, and blue values are each specified by byte (8-bit) values in the range 0 to 255. If necessary for display, the system will map the specified color to the nearest available color in the active palette.

Palette Index RGB COLORREF Values

In the Color1 example, instead of using absolute RGB values, a second COLORREF format is used. In this format, the color parameter is a palette index identifying an existing palette value. For palette-index entries, the COLORREF value takes the form 0x0100xxxx. with the low word (16 bits) providing an index to a logical palette or, in this case, the system palette.

Palette-Relative RGB COLORREF Values

Windows also supports a third format for specifying COLORREF values: the palette-relative RGB value. For this format, the high-order byte value is 2 and the COLOR-REF value takes the format 0x02BBGGRR. This format is used for output devices that support logical palettes, allowing Windows to match a palette-relative RGB value to the nearest actual color supported by the output device.

Alternatively, if the output device doesn't support a logical palette, Windows treats the palette-relative value as if it were an absolute RGB value; that is, instead of palette mapping, Windows attempts to handle the RGB value directly.

Using Dithered Colors

Although individual palette colors can be assigned to any of the 16 million possible hues, this does not guarantee that the physical device is capable of displaying such a wide range of colors. As explained previously, this limitation is imposed by the graphics video card's limits more than by the video monitor's. Most monitors are capable of near-infinite color resolution.

Limitations imposed by the graphics hardware can be circumvented through a process known as *dithering*. The Sunday newspaper comic pages and comic books don't use the same precise techniques, but the end results are very similar. In the comics and in colored ads, a fairly wide range of colors is produced by combining three or four primary colors to create what the eye perceives as many gradations of color.

The computer (or TV) screen creates colors by combining red, green, and blue light against a black background. Printed materials use a white background (the paper) and combine light-absorbing inks consisting of cyan, magenta, yellow, and black (CMYK). In this fashion, a strong brown, for example, is produced by placing dots of black or magenta and cyan over a nearly solid yellow background; a softer brown consists of a halftone of yellow with fewer blacks. Similarly, pinks of various shades combine yellow and magenta with the white paper showing through; dark colors use greater or lesser degrees of black.

On the computer screen, the same principle applies, except that the lights—the pixels—in primary colors are used rather than their complements as inks.

A Dithering Demonstration: The Color2 Program

The Color2 demo demonstrates this principle on an SVGA graphics system by setting the background color to a specific color configuration. Because the requested color is not provided as a palette color, Windows attempts to render the requested color by dithering entries from the default 20 color entries.

As shown in Figure 22.2, three scrollbars are used to select color settings for a single colored area, which displays dithered colors created from the standard palette. The listing for the Color2 program is included on the CD.

FIGURE 22.2

Creating dithered colors

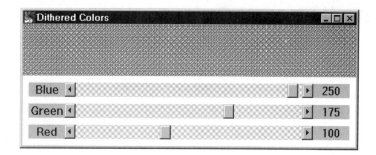

NOTE

If your system is set for 24-bit color (true color) or for anything greater than a 256-color palette, the Color2 demo will render solid hues rather than dithered mixes. To execute the Color2 demo, you must select a 256-color palette system.

Figure 22.3 shows a series of dithered color samples (unfortunately, rendered here in black and white).

FIGURE 22.3

Dithered samples

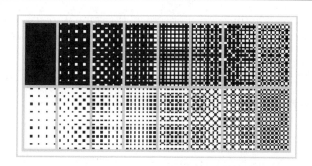

Characteristics of Dithered Colors

Although dithered color patterns are a feature provided by Windows and do not require nor demand your attention, you should note the following characteristics:

- Dithered colors are always an 8-by-8 pattern, spreading the simulated color over a minimum area of 64 pixels.

- Dithering cannot be used for lines that are always drawn using a primary hue supported by the display device.

- Even though 20 (or more) individual hues are available, dithered colors are composed of 4 individual colors. (These are not, of course, the same 4 shades in all cases.)

- Although dithered colors will fill irregular outlines, individual pixels in the fill may combine (visually) with outlines or borders, creating some appearances of irregularity.

Dithering is not limited to color systems. It is also applied to monochrome and gray-scale displays, as will be discussed presently.

Creating Custom Colors

In many cases, whether the resulting color specification appears as a solid hue or as a dithered pattern is irrelevant and makes no difference to your application. In other cases, however, precise color control can be a very important element. When this is the case, dithered colors just aren't in the running; it's either precise color control or nothing!

Changing Palette Colors

When exact colors are required, the solution is to reset one or more palette entries to produce the desired hues. Although this sounds simple enough, in practice, there are a few requirements and limitations.

The primary limitation is physical. Windows, no matter how sophisticated, cannot change the physical characteristics of the system video card. If the physical device supports a palette of only 16 colors, then only 16 custom colors can be displayed and all remaining palette entries will be mapped to the 16 supported physical colors. In like fashion, on an SVGA system, a physical palette limitation of 256 colors may be imposed by the system hardware.

Of course, if you are using one of the new true-color video cards that supports 24 bits of color information per pixel instead of palettes, all of this becomes moot, and you're free to write any information desired to the screen. This particular freedom, however, applies to very few programmers. For the rest of us, we'll assume that our programs are still bound by hardware limitations.

Creating a Custom Color Palette: The Color3 Program

The Color3 demo program creates a new palette using custom color settings, which can be adjusted using the same scrollbar controls illustrated in Color2. Figure 22.4 shows the Color3 display.

FIGURE 22.4

The Color3 program's display of a custom color palette

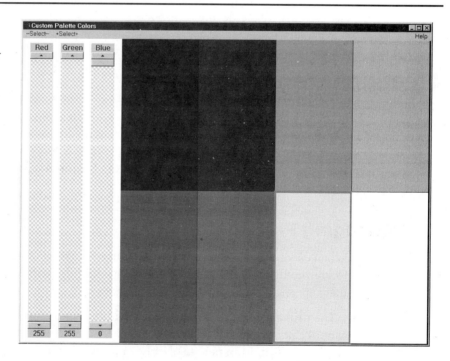

For demonstration purposes, the custom palette used in this example is limited to eight entries. This is a range supported by all graphics cards. It's also large enough to compare several color samples but still small enough to present a clean display.

In the Color3 program, the three scrollbars control the red, green, and blue color specifications and also show the present levels for the selected color sample. The –Select– and +Select+ menu items step through the eight palette entries, identifying the active selection with a gray outline.

The first step in creating a custom palette requires a few declarations:

```
long APIENTRY WndProc( ... )
{
    static LPLOGPALETTE   lPal;
    ...
    HPALETTE      NewPal;
    HBRUSH        NewBrush,  OldBrush;
    HPEN          NewPen,    OldPen;
    ...
```

The lPal variable is a static pointer to a logical palette structure. The remaining variables provide handles (pointers) to two palettes, two brushes, and two pens, all of which will be used presently. Also defined, but not shown here, is an array of eight RGB color values that are used to initialize the color palette and to track changes in the color palette settings.

The logical palette structure (LOGPALETTE) referenced by lPal is defined in WinGDI.H as:

```
typedef struct tagLOGPALETTE
{
    WORD          palVersion;          // windows version (0x0300)
    WORD          palNumEntries;       // size of array
    PALETTEENTRY palPalEntry[1];       // array of palette entries
} LOGPALETTE;
```

The version number is always 0x0300 (version 3.0), regardless of the version of Windows (3.1, 3.11, 95, or NT) being used.

The palPalEntry field specifies an array of PALETTEENTRY data structures defining the actual color entries. The PALETTEENTRY structure is defined as:

```
typedef struct tagPALETTEENTRY
{
    BYTE peRed;
    BYTE peGreen;
    BYTE peBlue;
    BYTE peFlags;
} PALETTEENTRY;
```

The three color bytes accept values in the range 0 to 255. The peFlags field accepts a flag value identifying how the palette entry will be used, or may be NULL. The following are the valid flag values:

- PC_EXPLICIT: Identifies the palette entry as a hardware palette index, allowing the application to use the display driver's palette. The RGB color specification will be used to find the nearest matching device palette entry.

- PC_NOCOLLAPSE: Specifies that the color will be placed in an unused entry in the system palette rather than being matched to an existing palette entry. If no unused entries are available, the color is matched normally. Once a new color entry has been made, further palette entries can be matched to this entry.

- PC_RESERVED: Indicates that the logical palette entry will be used for animation and, therefore, is changeable. As such, other palette entries should not be matched to this entry. If no unused palette entries are available for this color specification, the color specification is not matched to any other existing entries and is not available for animation.

If the peFlags field is NULL, the palette entry is added to the palette if space is available. If not, the entry is matched to the nearest system palette entry.

Much of the processing in Color3 should be familiar to you from earlier examples in this and preceding chapters. The principal elements here are found in the WndProc procedure's message-handling provisions.

The initial color-processing provision is found in the response to the WM_CREATE message. Here, memory allocation is performed for the lPal palette structure and two initial values are assigned: the palette version and the number of palette entries.

```
        switch( msg )
        {
            case WM_CREATE:    // initialize the logical palette
```

```
lPal = (LPLOGPALETTE)
   LocalAlloc( LMEM_FIXED | LMEM_ZEROINIT,
           sizeof(LOGPALETTE) + sizeof(PALETTEENTRY) * 8 );
lPal->palVersion = 0x300;
lPal->palNumEntries = 8;
break;
```

Next, in response to the WM_COMMAND message, the IDM_PLUS (+Select+) and IDM_MINUS (–Select–) instructions step through the palette entries. As they step through the entries, they update the positions of the three scrollbars and the text displays for each to correspond to the current (active) palette settings.

```
case WM_COMMAND:
   switch( LOWORD( wParam ) )
   {
      case IDM_PLUS:
         nPal++;
         if( nPal >= 8 ) nPal = 0;
         for( i=0; i<3; i++ )
         {
            SetScrollPos( hwndScrl[i], SB_CTL,
                          CVal[i][nPal],
                          TRUE );
            SetWindowText( hwndVal[i], itoa( CVal[i][nPal],
                           szBuff, 10 ) );
         }
         InvalidateRect( hwnd, 0L, TRUE );
         break;

      case IDM_MINUS:
         nPal--;
         if( nPal < 0 ) nPal = 7;
         for( i=0; i<3; i++ )
         {
            SetScrollPos( hwndScrl[i], SB_CTL,
                          CVal[i][nPal],
                          TRUE );
            SetWindowText( hwndVal[i], itoa( CVal[i][nPal],
                           szBuff, 10 ) );
         }
         InvalidateRect( hwnd, 0L, TRUE );
         break;
```

```
            case IDM_HELP: ...
        }
        break;
```

The scrollbars used for controls in both the Color2 and Color3 demos are the Windows analog of a vernier or sliding potentiometer control and should be familiar to you from many Windows applications. Their use here demonstrates how scrollbars can be used in any context where a variable control is needed.

> **TIP**
>
> Normally, to select a color specification, instead of placing scrollbars (or sliders or other types of controls) in the main application or in a resource dialog box, the common dialog class CColorDialog would be used.

Handling for the three scrollbars is found in three separate locations: one in the WinMain procedure, where the scrollbars are created, and two in the message responses in the WndProc procedure.

The first provision in the WinMain procedure, occurring at the same time the three scrollbars are created, is to assign a range to each scrollbar, consisting of a minimum and a maximum value. In each of the scrollbars used, the range assigned is 0 to 255, which is the range of the RGB color values. Initial values, or thumbpad positions, are also assigned at this time.

```
for( i=0; i<=2; i++ )
{
    hwndScrl[i] = CreateWindow( "scrollbar", 0L,
                        CHILD_STYLE | WS_TABSTOP | SBS_HORZ,
                            0, 0, 0, 0, hwnd,
                            (HMENU) i, hInst, 0L );
    hwndTag[i]  = CreateWindow( "static", szColorLabel[i],
                        CHILD_STYLE | SS_CENTER, 0, 0, 0, 0,
                            hwnd, (HMENU)(i+4), hInst, 0L );
    hwndVal[i]  = CreateWindow( "static",
                            itoa( CVal[i], szBuff, 10 ),
                        CHILD_STYLE | SS_CENTER, 0, 0, 0, 0,
                            hwnd, (HMENU)(i+7), hInst, 0L );
    SetScrollRange( hwndScrl[i], SB_CTL, 0, 255, 0 );
    SetScrollPos( hwndScrl[i], SB_CTL, CVal[i], 0 );
}
```

Next, in the response to the WM_SIZE message, the scrollbars are positioned within the application window and sized to fit appropriately.

```
case WM_SIZE:
    cxWnd = LOWORD( lParam );
    cyWnd = HIWORD( lParam );

    hdc = GetDC( hwnd );
    GetTextMetrics( hdc, &tm );
    cyChr = tm.tmHeight;
    cxChr = tm.tmAveCharWidth;
    ReleaseDC( hwnd, hdc );
    xOffset = cxChr * 26;

    xSize = ( cxWnd - xOffset ) / xSteps;
    ySize =  cyWnd / ySteps;
    MoveWindow( hwndRect, 0, 0, cxChr * 26, cyWnd, TRUE );
    for( i=0; i<=2; i++ )
    {
        MoveWindow( hwndTag[i], cxChr * ( ( i * 8 ) + 2 ),
                    (INT)(cyChr * 0.5), cxChr * 6, cyChr, TRUE );
        MoveWindow( hwndVal[i], cxChr * ( ( i * 8 ) + 2 ),
                    cyWnd - (INT)( cyChr * 1.5 ),
                    cxChr * 6,   cyChr, TRUE );
        MoveWindow( hwndScrl[i], cxChr * ( ( i * 8 ) + 2 ),
                    (INT)(cyChr * 1.5), cxChr * 6,
                    cyWnd - ( 3 * cyChr ), TRUE );
    }
    SetFocus( hwnd );
    break;
```

Last, in the response to the WM_HSCROLL message in the Color2 demo (with horizontal scrollbars) or the WM_VSCROLL in the Color3 demo (with vertical scrollbars), the position of each scrollbar's thumbpad is adjusted according to where the scrollbar was clicked or where the thumbpad was dragged.

```
case WM_VSCROLL:
    i = GetWindowLong( (HWND) lParam, GWL_ID );
    switch( LOWORD( wParam ) )
    {
        case SB_PAGEDOWN:
            CVal[i][nPal] += 15;        // no break!
```

```
        case SB_LINEDOWN:
            CVal[i][nPal]   = MIN( CVal[i][nPal] );
            break;

        case SB_PAGEUP:
            CVal[i][nPal] -= 15;        // no break!

        case SB_LINEUP:
            CVal[i][nPal]   = MAX( CVal[i][nPal] );
            break;

        case SB_TOP:
            CVal[i][nPal]   =   0;
            break;

        case SB_BOTTOM:
            CVal[i][nPal]   = 255;
            break;

        case SB_THUMBPOSITION:
        case SB_THUMBTRACK:
            CVal[i][nPal] = HIWORD( wParam );
            break;
    }
    SetScrollPos( hwndScrl[i], SB_CTL, CVal[i][nPal], TRUE );
    SetWindowText( hwndVal[i],
                    itoa( CVal[i][nPal], szBuff, 10 ) );
    InvalidateRect( hwnd, 0L, TRUE );
    break;
```

The CVal variable array consists of a 3-by-8 array of byte values containing the RGB color values for the eight palette entries used.

The real work of displaying the palette begins in response to the WM_PAINT message. It starts, as usual, with a BeginPaint instruction. However, before painting anything, a loop is used to read the present values from the CVal array into the palette entries indicated by lPal.

```
        case WM_PAINT:
            hdc = BeginPaint( hwnd, &ps );
            for( i=0; i<8; i++ )
            {
                lPal->palPalEntry[i].peRed   = CVal[0][i];
                lPal->palPalEntry[i].peGreen = CVal[1][i];
```

```
            lPal->palPalEntry[i].peBlue  = CVal[2][i];
            lPal->palPalEntry[i].peFlags = PC_RESERVED;
        }
    NewPal = CreatePalette( lPal );
    SelectPalette( hdc, NewPal, FALSE );
    RealizePalette( hdc );
```

After initializing the palette values in memory, the CreatePalette function creates a new logical palette before SelectPalette makes NewPal the current (active)
palette. Optionally, SelectPalette returns a handle to the old (default) palette.

Last, RealizePalette is called to activate the newly selected palette; that is,
to make this the current drawing palette within the present device-context
handle (hdc).

At this point, the device-context handle is ready for drawing using the new palette. The next segment of code consists of provisions to draw the eight rectangles
composing the palette display.

```
    for( i=0; i<8; i++ )
    {
        j = i % 4;
        k = (int) i / 4;
        if( i == nPal )
            NewPen = CreatePen( PS_SOLID, 5, 0x007F7F7F );
        else
            NewPen = CreatePen( PS_SOLID, 1, PALETTEINDEX(i) );
        OldPen = SelectObject( hdc, NewPen );

        NewBrush = CreateSolidBrush( PALETTEINDEX(i) );
        OldBrush = SelectObject( hdc, NewBrush );

        Rectangle( hdc, xOffset + j * xSize, k * ySize,
                   xOffset + ( j + 1 ) * xSize - 1,
                   ( k + 1 ) * ySize - 1 );
```

Notice that within the loop, a parallel to the CreatePalette/SelectPalette
provisions occurs as the CreatePen/CreateSolidBrush and SelectObject
instructions create and select a pen and brush to draw each rectangle. The original
(default) pen and brush have been saved as the OldPen and OldBrush handles.

```
    SelectObject( hdc, OldBrush );
    DeleteObject( NewBrush );
    SelectObject( hdc, OldPen );
    DeleteObject( NewPen );
```

After each pen and brush is used, the original pen and brush are reselected and the new pen and brush deleted.

Once the paint operation is completed, the new palette is deleted.

```
        }
        EndPaint( hwnd, &ps );
        DeleteObject( NewPal );
        break;
```

Each of these closing provisions is every bit as important as creating the palette, pens, and brushes in the first place. As stressed in Chapter 21, Windows can support only a finite number of handles to logical devices, so you must release handles when you no longer need them.

As a final provision, the new palette is deleted before the WM_PAINT message response concludes. The memory allocated for the palette structure and the pointer lPal is not released, however, and remains available for further use. This memory will be needed the next time the window is updated. All that has been lost is a temporary palette, a temporary pen, and a temporary brush. The originals have been restored, leaving the Windows system in the proper condition for other applications or for other actions by the present application.

WARNING
Remember: Restoring the original condition is not just good manners—it's essential! If these handles are not released when they are no longer needed—immediately after use—and the originals restored, not only can the current application fail suddenly but Windows itself can be left in a very hazardous state. If you wish to experiment, simply comment out the restoration provisions (but be sure to save your work before trying the results).

There is one more element of cleanup required. This last bit is only necessary when the application exits and is handled in response to the WM_DESTROY message:

```
        case WM_DESTROY:
            LocalFree( lPal );
            PostQuitMessage(0);
            break;
```

The `WM_DESTROY` message is an application's opportunity for a final cleanup before exiting. In previous examples, it has responded simply by posting a quit message to notify any child processes of an impending exit (a standard default provision even when there are no child processes). In this case, however, this is the appropriate point in time to release the memory allocated for the palette structure, as shown above, before notifying `WinMain`'s message loop to exit, completing the shutdown.

All special brushes and pens and the logical palette have already been taken care of within the paint procedure, and this concludes cleanup for the application. The complete listing for the Color3 program is on the CD.

Custom Brushes and Color Messages

In the Color2 demo, a custom color was demonstrated by changing the background color. Then, in the Color3 demo, custom colors were demonstrated by creating solid color brushes.

In both the Color2 and Color3 demos, an interesting addition would be to color the three scrollbars using the individual red, green, and blue settings. This is something you can try on your own. However, to facilitate the experiment, a few comments and suggestions follow.

In Windows 3.1, when a window control needs to be redrawn, the parent window is sent a `WM_CTLCOLOR` message with the high word in the `lParam` argument containing the control type and the low word containing the control element's ID value. Both values, of course, are 16 bits.

Under Windows NT and 95, where control elements are now 32-bit rather than 16-bit, the `WM_CTLCOLOR` message has been replaced by a series of seven `WM_CTLCOLORxxxxxx` messages, which explicitly identify the control element type, as shown in Table 22.3.

TABLE 22.3 CTLCOLOR Messages

Message Constant	Control Type
`WM_CTLCOLORMSGBOX`	Message box
`WM_CTLCOLOREDIT`	Edit control
`WM_CTLCOLORLISTBOX`	List box control

TABLE 22.3   CTLCOLOR Messages (Continued)

Message Constant	Control Type
WM_CTLCOLORBTN	Button control
WM_CTLCOLORDLG	Dialog box
WM_CTLCOLORSCROLLBAR	Scrollbar control
WM_CTLCOLORSTATIC	Static control

Accompanying the WM_CTLCOLORxxxxxx message, the wParam argument contains a handle to the display context for the child window (the control to be repainted). The lParam argument contains the 32-bit child window handle.

There are a few cautions involved with using these messages. First, when an application explicitly processes any of these messages, the application must return a handle to a brush to paint the control background. If this is not done, the application will most probably crash. A fragmentary example follows:

```
case WM_CTLCOLORxxxxxx:
    hCtrlBrush = GetWindowLong( lParam, GWL_ID );
    DeleteObject( hCtrlBrush );
    RGBColor = RGB( rVal, gVal, bVal );
    hCtrlBrush = CreateSolidBrush( RGBColor );
    UnrealizeObject( hCtrlBrush );
    return( hCtrlBrush ); // return the handle to the GDI
```

Another, less critical precaution, is to make sure that the application aligns the brush origin with the upper-left corner of the child window. If you don't accomplish this, particularly when you're using patterned brushes, the control may not be painted properly.

The MFC OnCtlColor Method

In applications using MFC classes, the corresponding operation is the OnCtlColor method, which is called when a child control is about to be drawn. Most controls send this message to their parent (usually a dialog box) to prepare the pDC for drawing the control using the correct colors.

In the OnCtlColor method, to change the text color used by a control, call the SetTextColor member function with the desired red, green, and blue values. To change the background color of a single-line edit control, the brush handle is set in both the CTLCOLOR_EDIT and CTLCOLOR_MSGBOX message codes. Also, in response to the CTLCOLOR_EDIT code, call the CDC::SetBkColor function.

Because the list box in a drop-down combo box is actually a child window belonging to the combo box but is not a child of the window, the OnCtlColor is not called for the list box. Thus, to change the color of the drop-down list box, create a custom CComboBox class that includes an override of OnCtlColor that checks for CTLCOLOR_LISTBOX in the nCtlColor parameter. In this handler, the SetBkColor member function must be used to set the background color for the text.

NOTE
The OnCtlColor member function is called by the framework to allow an application to handle a Windows message. The parameters passed to the function reflect the parameters received by the framework when the message was received. If the baseclass implementation of this function is called, the implementation will use the parameters originally passed with the message and not any of the custom parameters supplied.

Resetting with the UnrealizeObject Function

The UnrealizeObject function, called with a handle to an object, is used to reset the origin of the object. In the preceding example, this was the handle to a brush that would be used to paint a control object's background. When this is done, the GDI is directed to reset the origin of an object, such as a brush, when the object is next selected.

WARNING
The UnrealizeObject function should not be called while a drawing object, such as a brush or pen, is currently selected in a device context.

The UnrealizeObject function is also used with logical palettes as an instruction to the GDI to remap the logical palette to the system palette. And, cautions aside, in this case, the palette specified may be the currently selected palette in a device context.

Destroying Brushes and Other Objects

During execution of the Color2 demo program, each time a WM_HSCROLL message is received, the existing background brush is deleted before a new brush (using the new color settings) is created. But before the application exits, a final call to the DeleteObject function is needed:

```
case WM_DESTROY:
    DeleteObject( (HGDIOBJ)
        GetClassLong( hwnd, GCL_HBRBACKGROUND ) );
    PostQuitMessage(0);
    break;
```

If provisions to paint the scrollbars or other controls were included, these brushes would also need provisions to delete each object before exiting. In earlier examples, the only objects used were standard objects—brushes, pens, and such—and so no special provisions for cleanup were needed. However, custom brushes, as well as other custom objects, require some memory and, if not deleted prior to exit, will continue to occupy memory (at least, until the computer is rebooted).

> **NOTE**
>
> An advantage of using C++ object classes, such as the MFC classes, lies in the fact that class objects are self-destroying and delete themselves when they go out of scope, thus relieving the programmer of some of the cleanup tasks.

Color Drawing Modes

Under DOS, only one graphics drawing mode is supported. In this mode, each pixel drawn (including pixels comprising lines and the like) simply overwrites or replaces the existing pixels using the current drawing color.

In contrast, Windows supports multiple drawing modes in which the image is combined with the existing (background) image in a variety of fashions. These drawing modes are referred to variously as *bitwise Boolean operations* or, in Windows, as *raster operations*.

Windows ROP2 Operations

Since the drawing-mode operations involve two pixel patterns—the object image and the screen image—they are also referred to as *ROP2 operations.* In WinGDI.H, they are identified by R2_*xxxx* constants. Sixteen ROP2 operations are defined, as shown in Table 22.4.

TABLE 22.4 Binary Raster Operations

Mode Constant	Operation	Resulting Image
R2_NOP	Screen	Screen not affected (no operation)
R2_NOT	~Screen	Existing screen inverted
R2_COPYPEN	Pen	Pen overwrites screen (default)
R2_NOTCOPYPEN	~Pen	Inverted pen overwrites screen
R2_MASKPEN	Pen & Screen	Pen ANDed with screen
R2_MASKNOTPEN	~Pen & Screen	Inverted pen ANDed with screen
R2_MASKPENNOT	Pen & ~Screen	Pen ANDed with inverted screen
R2_NOTMASKPEN	~(Pen & Screen)	Pen ANDed with screen, result inverted
R2_MERGEPEN	Pen | Screen	Pen ORed with screen
R2_MERGENOTPEN	~Pen | Screen	Inverted pen ORed with screen
R2_MERGEPENNOT	Pen | ~Screen	Pen ORed with inverted screen
R2_NOTMERGEPEN	~(Pen | Screen)	Pen ORed with screen, result inverted
R2_XORPEN	Pen ^ Screen	Pen XORed with screen

TABLE 22.4   Binary Raster Operations (Continued)

Mode Constant	Operation	Resulting Image
`R2_NOTXORPEN`	~(Pen ^ Screen)	Pen XORed with screen, result inverted
`R2_BLACK`	0	Black line (drawing color ignored)
`R2_WHITE` `(R2_LAST)`	1	White line (drawing color ignored)

The ROP2 constants listed are ordered according to function, not according to integer values. Thus, the first ROP2 mode listed, R2_NOP, has no effect on the screen image at all. However, it is still useful, since the current position (cp) is updated by LineTo or LineRel operations when using the R2_NOP mode.

The second ROP2 mode, R2_NOT, draws by inverting the existing image (for example, white becomes black) using bit-wise color inversion. This is useful for two reasons:

- It ensures absolute screen visibility (with the exception of screen areas that are approximately 50 percent gray).

- The original screen can be restored by executing a second, identical drawing operation.

The third ROP2 mode, R2_COPYPEN, is the default drawing mode, corresponding to the conventional DOS drawing mode discussed previously.

The next 11 ROP2 modes produce varying effects, which are more readily demonstrated by the PenDraw1 program—coming up next—than by description.

The last two ROP2 modes, R2_BLACK and R2_WHITE, draw lines using complete black or white, respectively, regardless of the current drawing color.

Demonstrating Drawing Modes: The PenDraw1 Program

The PenDraw1 program begins by writing labels along the right side of the screen before drawing a background. The background drawing starts at the left with five vertical gray bars ranging from 0 percent black (white) to 100 percent black; then continuing with six color bars in blue, green, cyan, red, magenta, and yellow.

Against this background, 16 horizontal lines are drawn using the 16 drawing modes (in the functional order listed in Table 22.4, not in numerical order), each employing the active drawing color. A range of eight drawing colors can be selected from the menu. Figure 22.5 shows an example of the PenDraw1 display.

FIGURE 22.5

Binary raster operations

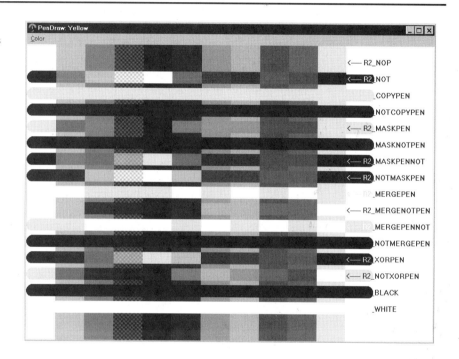

Notice in Figure 22.5 and when executing the PenDraw1 demo that the default white background is not treated in the same fashion as a white background drawn by a brush or as background to the text display. This is easily observed by selecting the yellow drawing color and observing the effects where the lines overlap the labels: R2_NOT, R2_MASKPEN, and R2_NOTXORPEN. Because the lines drawn are slightly wider than the text labels, a thin section of background white appears above and below the labels.

Converting from Color to Gray-Scale

Windows has its own provisions for handling most gray-scale conversions for color programs executing on monochrome video systems. On some plasma and LCD screens (displays that are virtually an endangered species), even though the display is technically monochrome, the video system still accepts color input information, translating the color data into 16, 32, or 64 gray levels.

In both of these situations, not only is the process of converting colors to gray-scale handled without the programmer's participation, but the programmer is effectively forbidden to intervene (except, of course, for offering palette choices that produce optimum contrast and clarity).

Even though most gray-scale conversions are handled by Windows, there may be some circumstances where you must supply your own conversions. For example, you might need to show how a color image would appear on a monochrome printer (see Chapter 31). How this is done depends on the circumstances, the equipment, and the desired results. There are no hard and fast rules, nor are there any absolutes.

Following are a few opinions and provisions that can be used to produce color-to-gray-scale conversions. These methods were directed originally toward hard-copy devices, such as printers, but the same techniques can also be applied to monitors.

Creating Gray-Scale Palettes

One popular method of accomplishing gray-scale conversion is to create a palette of grays suitable for mapping the original color palette. For example, assume a palette of 16 colors (as per EGA/VGA) ranging from white to black. The obvious gray-scale for correspondence would be a 4-by-4 pixel (or dot) pattern, as shown in Figure 22.6.

Here, the 16-bit patterns range from solid black to one-sixteenth black. (Reduced views of the same patterns appear at the lower right.) As an alternative, one of the intermittent patterns could be dropped to adjust the gray-scale from solid black to solid white.

FIGURE 22.6

A 16-bit gray scale

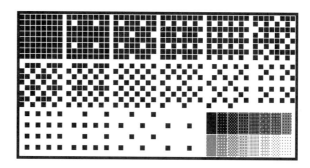

But remember, dithered colors use an 8-by-8 pattern. Applying similar patterns in black and white would offer a possible scale of 64 grays, providing a wider range of grays or a finer texture for hard-copy output.

WARNING Adjacent elements in a 64-level, gray-scale palette can be very difficult to distinguish. Select carefully.

The gray-scale patterns suggested in Figure 22.5 form a uniform range that is about the best that can be accomplished with only 16 elements. Moving up to a 64-bit pattern, presents the possibility of matching the gray-scale density to the intensity (or darkness) of the color being mapped.

To do so, the first step is to understand a few basic principles of color perception. The human eye does not perceive all colors equally, in terms of absolute intensity. Of the three primary colors—red, green, and blue—the eye perceives green almost twice as strongly as red. In turn, the eye's response to blue is approximately one-third the response to red. Thus, an approximate gray-scale formula reflecting the perception curve of the human eye is:

```
Intensity = Red * 0.30 + Green * 0.59 + Blue * 0.11
```

Thus, since Windows uses the RGB values in the range 0 to 255, the gray equivalent matching a 24-bit color specification becomes:

```
      R * 0.30      G * 0.59      B * 0.11
W = (--------) + (--------) + (--------)
        255           255           255
```

Using this formula, if the R, G, and B are all at maximum (255), resulting in white on the screen, the formula yields a value of 100 percent white and 0 percent black.

On the other hand, for a soft blue with an RGB value of 43, 128, 210, here's the formula:

```
      `43 * 0.30    128 * 0.59     210 * 0.11
W =(---------)+(----------)+(----------)
        255            255            255
```

and the equivalent proportions of white to black become:

```
W = ( 0.050 ) + ( 0.296 ) + ( 0.090 ) = 43.6% white (or 56.4% black)
```

Calculating a gray-scale using an 8-by-8 pattern, the optimum gray would be 36 black pixels (or dots) to 28 white.

The problem, however, in converting colors to grays is that quite distinct colors can yield the same gray values simply because they have the same relative intensities. For this problem, there is no simple cure.

On the other hand, optimizing printing a color image by creating 8-by-8 blocks for each pixel in the image is a rather frustrating process, if only in the annoyances involved in creating the 64 dot patterns needed. Instead, there is a simpler approach.

Rather than creating an elaborate system of dots, an easier approach is to simply convert the color image to a gray image by mapping the color pixels to their gray-intensity equivalents. For this, we can use the original formula as:

```
I = ( R * 0.30 ) + ( G * 0.59 ) + ( B * 0.11 )
```

Once I has been calculated, the equivalent gray palette entry would be created as:

```
RGB( I, I, I )
```

Or, even easier, begin by creating a palette with gray scale entries as:

```
for( i=0; i<256; i++ )
{
    lPal->palPalEntry[i].peRed   = i;
    lPal->palPalEntry[i].peGreen = i;
    lPal->palPalEntry[i].peBlue  = i;
    lPal->palPalEntry[i].peFlags = PC_RESERVED;
}
```

```
NewPal = CreatePalette( lPal );
SelectPalette( hdc, NewPal, FALSE );
RealizePalette( hdc );
```

This code fragment would create and realize a palette with 256 shades of gray ranging from black to white. And, to convert a color image to gray, the only real requirement would be to calculate the intensity, using the perception response formula, for each pixel and then assign the intensity as the pixel's palette index.

Once this is done, simply printing to any hard-copy device, which has its own routines to print gray equivalents, results in a black-and-white image that maintains the intensities of the original.

Gray-Scales and Plaiding

There is one hazard inherent in using gray-scale on black-and-white output devices: plaiding can occur when the gray-scale pattern is not matched to the device resolution. Figure 22.7 shows an example of plaiding deliberately produced on the screen, showing that video devices are no more immune than printers to this problem. The illustration in Figure 22.7 is an excerpt from Figure 22.6, enlarged to show the mismatch between the image's dot pattern and the screen resolution.

FIGURE 22.7

Plaiding in gray-scales

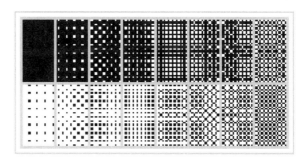

TIP
As a simple rule of thumb, to prevent plaiding, make sure that the pixel dimension of the image (or dot-dimension on a printer) after conversion to gray-scale is an even multiple of the dot resolution of the reproduction size.

For example, assume a 200-by-150 pixel bitmap is converted to a 16-shade gray-scale. After conversion, the result is 800-by-600 pixels. To reproduce this image on a laser printer with a resolution of 300 dpi, without plaiding, the minimum size would be 2.666 inches wide by 2 inches high. Or, for a larger image, a print size of 8 inches wide by 6 inches high would also fit with the image scaled to 2400-by-1800 pixels.

Alternatively, if the image used a 64-shade gray-scale, the smallest acceptable image would be 5.333 inches by 4 inches.

How you employ gray-scaling is up to you and your requirements. Moreover, if you are content with the conversion capabilities provided by Windows and many output devices, you'll probably have little need for this facility. But if you do, you now know the basics of color-to-gray-scale conversion.

Gray-Scale-to-Color Conversions

A less common requirement than color to gray-scale is converting a gray-scale to color. This process is commonly referred to as *false-color conversion*. Normally, this is not an attempt to reproduce a color image from a monochrome source, since there simply is not enough information for that task to be accomplished automatically. The automatic gray-to-color (false-color) conversion is an attempt to render an image where the only information is gray to a form in which colors are used to make differences in intensity stand out.

Exotic examples include radio-star maps rendered in full glorious false color, or topological or meteorological maps, where color enhances readability. In infrared images, false-color assignments make it possible to print thermographic maps where temperatures are easily recognized as ranges of color.

Implementation of false coloration is simple. Just decide on a color range and what levels of intensity to depict, and then construct a palette where the intensity levels (as palette indexes) have the appropriate color values.

Regardless of the number of levels in the original, it is often a good idea to restrict the false-color palette to a reasonably small number of hues, such as 20 or 32, rather than implementing a large palette of 256 shades. Experimentation is recommended.

This process can be applied to virtually any type of information. There is just one thing that you must remember: The color information applied is purely arbitrary and should be chosen only for ease of recognition, not for artistic whim. Producing an image in alternating shades of chartreuse and puce may get you into the Guggenheim, but it's not a good way to convey information (unless you're trying to tell the world that you're color blind).

This chapter has covered color palettes, custom colors, and gray-scale conversions. The Color1 and PenDraw1 program listings follow. (The Color2 and Color3 listings are on the CD that accompanies this book.) In the next chapter, we'll talk about Windows drawing tools.

Listing 22.1: The Color1 Program

```
//=======================//
//        Color1.C       //
//   C++ Windows Colors  //
//=======================//

#include <windows.h>
#include <stdlib.h>

#define APP_ICON   "Color1"
#define APP_MENU   "Color1"
// note: no cursor assignment
#define   xSteps    5
#define   ySteps    4
#define   PalIndex  0x01000000 + i + ( j * xSteps )

HANDLE hInst;
char   szAppTitle[] = "Standard Palette Colors";
char   szAppName[]  = "Color1";

long APIENTRY WndProc( HWND hwnd,    UINT msg,
                       UINT wParam, LONG lParam )
{
    HBRUSH        hBrush;
    HPEN          hPen;
    HDC           hdc;
    PAINTSTRUCT   ps;
    static int    i, j, xSize, ySize;
```

```
    switch( msg )
    {
        case WM_SIZE:
            xSize = ( LOWORD( lParam ) ) / xSteps;
            ySize = ( HIWORD( lParam ) ) / ySteps;
            InvalidateRect( hwnd, NULL, TRUE );
            break;

        case WM_PAINT:
            hdc = BeginPaint( hwnd, &ps );
            for( j=0; j<ySteps; j++ )
               for( i=0; i<xSteps; i++ )
               {
                   hPen = SelectObject( hdc,
                             CreatePen( PS_SOLID, 1, PalIndex ) );
                   hBrush = SelectObject( hdc,
                             CreateSolidBrush( PalIndex ) );
                   Rectangle( hdc, i * xSize, j * ySize,
                             ( i + 1 ) * xSize - 1,
                             ( j + 1 ) * ySize - 1 );
                   DeleteObject( hPen );
                   DeleteObject( hBrush );
               }
            EndPaint( hwnd, &ps );
            break;

        case WM_DESTROY:
            PostQuitMessage(0);
            break;

        default:
            return( DefWindowProc( hwnd, msg, wParam, lParam ) );
    }
    return 0;
}

#include "template.i"

#ifdef __BORLANDC__
#pragma argsused
```

```
#endif

int APIENTRY WinMain( HANDLE hInstance, HANDLE hPrevInstance,
                      LPSTR  lpCmdLine, int    nCmdShow   )
{
   MSG   msg;

   if( ! hPrevInstance )
      if( ! InitApplication( hInstance ) )
         return( FALSE );
   if( ! InitInstance( hInstance, nCmdShow ) )
      return (FALSE);
   while( GetMessage( &msg, NULL, 0, 0 ) )
   {
      TranslateMessage( &msg );
      DispatchMessage( &msg );
   }
   return( msg.wParam );
#ifndef __BORLANDC__
   UNREFERENCED_PARAMETER( lpCmdLine );
#endif
}



//======================//
//       Color1.RC      //
//======================//

COLOR1 ICON "color1.ico"
```

Listing 22.2: The PenDraw1 Program

```
//===================
//   Pendraw.H
//===================
#define   IDM_SOLID       100
#define   IDM_DASH        101
#define   IDM_DOT         102
#define   IDM_DASHDOT     103
```

```
#define   IDM_DASHDOTDOT     104
#define   IDM_NULL           105
#define   IDM_INSIDEFRAME    106


#define   IDM_BLACK          300
#define   IDM_BLUE           301
#define   IDM_GREEN          302
#define   IDM_CYAN           303
#define   IDM_RED            304
#define   IDM_MAGENTA        305
#define   IDM_YELLOW         306
#define   IDM_WHITE          307



//=======================//
//         PenDraw.C     //
//  C++ Windows Drawing  //
//=======================//

#include <windows.h>
#include <string.h>
#include "pendraw.h"

#define APP_ICON   "PENDRAW"
#define APP_MENU   "PENDRAW"
// note: no cursor assignment

HANDLE hInst;
char   szAppTitle[] = "PenDraw",
       szAppName[]  = "PENDRAW",
     * ColorLabels[8] =
{
   "Black", "Blue",    "Green", "Cyan",
   "Red",   "Magenta", "Yellow", "White"
};

COLORREF lpColor[8] =
{
   RGB(   0,   0,   0 ), RGB(   0,   0, 255 ),  // Black,  Blue   //
   RGB(   0, 255,   0 ), RGB(   0, 255, 255 ),  // Green,  Cyan   //
   RGB( 255,   0,   0 ), RGB( 255,   0, 255 ),  // Red,    Magenta //
   RGB( 255, 255,   0 ), RGB( 255, 255, 255 )   // Yellow, White  //
```

```
};

UINT   DrawModes[16] =
{
    R2_NOP,          R2_NOT,          R2_COPYPEN,
    R2_NOTCOPYPEN,   R2_MASKPEN,      R2_MASKNOTPEN,
    R2_MASKPENNOT,   R2_NOTMASKPEN,   R2_MERGEPEN,
    R2_MERGENOTPEN,  R2_MERGEPENNOT,  R2_NOTMERGEPEN,
    R2_XORPEN,       R2_NOTXORPEN,    R2_BLACK,
    R2_WHITE
};

char * szModes[16] =
{
    " <----- R2_NOP",          " <----- R2_NOT",
    " <----- R2_COPYPEN",      " <----- R2_NOTCOPYPEN",
    " <----- R2_MASKPEN",      " <----- R2_MASKNOTPEN",
    " <----- R2_MASKPENNOT",   " <----- R2_NOTMASKPEN",
    " <----- R2_MERGEPEN",     " <----- R2_MERGENOTPEN",
    " <----- R2_MERGEPENNOT",  " <----- R2_NOTMERGEPEN",
    " <----- R2_XORPEN",       " <----- R2_NOTXORPEN",
    " <----- R2_BLACK",        " <----- R2_WHITE"
};

long APIENTRY WndProc( HWND hwnd,   UINT msg,
                       UINT wParam, LONG lParam )
{
    static  int   nColor = IDM_BLACK;
    HDC           hdc;
    HMENU         hMenu;
    HBRUSH        hBrush;
    HPEN          hPen;
    PAINTSTRUCT   ps;
    RECT          rect;
    int           i, j, HUnits = 60, VUnits = 18;
    char          WinTitle[20];

    switch( msg )
    {
        case WM_COMMAND:
            hMenu = GetMenu( hwnd );
            CheckMenuItem( hMenu, nColor, MF_UNCHECKED );
```

```
    nColor = wParam;
    CheckMenuItem( hMenu, nColor, MF_CHECKED );
    InvalidateRect( hwnd, NULL, FALSE );
    wsprintf( WinTitle, "PenDraw: %s",
              ColorLabels[ nColor-IDM_BLACK] );
    SetWindowText( hwnd, WinTitle );
    break;

case WM_SIZE:
    InvalidateRect( hwnd. NULL, TRUE );
    break;

case WM_PAINT:
    hdc = BeginPaint( hwnd, &ps );
    GetClientRect( hwnd, &rect );
    for( j=0; j<16; j++ )
        TextOut( hdc, rect.right-210,
            (int) ( ( j + .75 ) *
                    ( ( rect.bottom - rect.top ) / VUnits ) ),
                szModes[j], strlen( szModes[j] ) );
    SetMapMode( hdc, MM_ANISOTROPIC );
  SetViewportExtEx( hdc, rect.right-140, rect.bottom, NULL );
    SetWindowExtEx( hdc, HUnits, VUnits, NULL );
     //=== draw gray background bars ===   (white thru black)
    for( i=0; i<5; i++ )
    {
        SetRect( &rect, i*5, 0, i*5+5, VUnits );
        FillRect( hdc, &rect, GetStockObject( i ) );
    }
    i*=5;
     //=== draw color background bars === (blue thru yellow)
    for( j=1; j<7; j++ )
    {
        hBrush = CreateSolidBrush( lpColor[ j ] );
        SetRect( &rect, j*5+i-5, 0, j*5+i, VUnits );
        FillRect( hdc, &rect, hBrush );
    }

    hPen = CreatePen( PS_SOLID, 2,
    lpColor[nColor-IDM_BLACK] );
    for( j=0; j<16; j++ )
    {
```

```
            SetROP2( hdc, DrawModes[j] );
            SelectObject( hdc, hPen );
            MoveToEx( hdc, 1, j+1, NULL );
            LineTo( hdc, HUnits-1, j+1 );
         }
      EndPaint( hwnd, &ps );
      DeleteObject( hPen );
      break;

   case WM_DESTROY:  PostQuitMessage(0);  break;

   default:
      return( DefWindowProc( hwnd, msg, wParam, lParam ) );
   }
   return 0;
}

#include "template.i"

int APIENTRY WinMain( HANDLE hInstance, HANDLE hPrevInstance,
                      LPSTR  lpCmdLine, int    nCmdShow    )
{
   MSG   msg;

   if( ! hPrevInstance )
      if( ! InitApplication( hInstance ) )
         return( FALSE );
   if( ! InitInstance( hInstance, nCmdShow ) )
      return (FALSE);
   while( GetMessage( &msg, NULL, 0, 0 ) )
   {
      TranslateMessage( &msg );
      DispatchMessage( &msg );
   }
   return( msg.wParam );
   UNREFERENCED_PARAMETER( lpCmdLine );
}
```

```
//===============
//  PenDraw1.RC
//===============

#include <windows.h>
#include "pendraw.h"

PENDRAW ICON "pendraw.ico"

PENDRAW MENU
BEGIN
    POPUP "&Color"
    BEGIN
        MENUITEM "&Black",    IDM_BLACK, CHECKED
        MENUITEM "B&lue",     IDM_BLUE
        MENUITEM "&Green",    IDM_GREEN
        MENUITEM "&Cyan",     IDM_CYAN
        MENUITEM "&Red",      IDM_RED
        MENUITEM "&Magenta",  IDM_MAGENTA
        MENUITEM "&Yellow",   IDM_YELLOW
        MENUITEM "&White",    IDM_WHITE
    END
END
```

CHAPTER

TWENTY-THREE

23

Drawing Simple Shapes

- Line styles

- Hatch-fill styles

- Figure-drawing functions

- Business graphs: bar and pie charts

While folk wisdom maintains that a picture has value equal to a thousand words, this same adage has been most honored in dispute, disagreement, sarcastic rebuttal, and jest—not to mention outright subversion by pundits found everywhere from Madison Avenue to the halls of government. Still, the real truth might better be that, more often than not, a picture is preferred to a thousand words.

And, in like fashion, a graphic is often preferred to a thousand words. This preference, despite rumors concerning the literary acuity of CEOs and other board members, is not so much founded in any relative values but is based on the simple fact that a good graphic can convey information in a form more readily understood than many thousands of words or columns of figures.

One popular example of this principal is found in data-generated graphics in which images are created as visual analogs of numerical or scalar data, giving clarity to the relative relationships between elements at the expense of absolute magnitudes. Graphics of this type may be composed of simple shapes, such as are used in pie or bar graphs; may be less structured forms, such as with flow charts, schematics, or other diagrams; or may be composed of bitmapped images, as with the iconized buttons and controls found in any of a variety of Windows applications.

For this chapter, the topic is creating graphics images using the drawing tools supplied by the Windows API functions. But, before we see how these tools work by creating a few working applications, the first step is to take a look at the tools available.

Graphics Tools and Shapes

In Chapter 22, we discussed Windows color palettes and line-drawing modes. These are the simplest of the tools supplied. Windows also offers a wide variety of other drawing features, including a selection of standard shapes, varying line styles, and, for solid figures, a selection of fill styles.

Standard Shapes

Windows provides a series of functions to draw standard shapes, either as solids or outlines. Table 23.1 lists the functions and the shapes they draw.

TABLE 23.1   Standard Shapes

Function	Shape
Arc	Open curve, either elliptical or circular
Chord	Arc with the endpoints connected by a chord
Ellipse	Closed curve, either elliptical or circular
Pie	Arc with endpoints connected to center
Polygon	Any multisided figure
Polypolygon	Multiple multisided figures
Rectangle	Rectangle with square corners
RoundRect	Rectangle with rounded corners

The PenDraw2 demo program illustrates five of these eight shape functions, and the PenDraw3 program demonstrates two others. But, before these shapes can be drawn, a drawing pen is also required.

Logical Pens

Windows defines a selection of logical pens, each with a predefined pattern. The default pen (if no other selection has been made) is a solid, black line with a width of one logical unit. The defined pen (line) styles are listed in Table 23.2.

TABLE 23.2   Pen (Line) Styles

Style ID	Line Type
PS_SOLID	——————
PS_DASH	— — — — — —
PS_DOT	· · · · · · · · · · ·
PS_DASHDOT	— · — · — · — ·
PS_DASH2DOT	— · · — · · — · ·

TABLE 23.2 Pen (Line) Styles (Continued)

Style ID	Line Type
PS_NULL	No line (blank)
PS_INSIDEFRAME	If the pen width is greater than one logical unit, ensures that the line is drawn inside the closed shape. Valid with all primitive shapes except polygons.

NOTE The PS_INSIDEFRAME style may be used in combination with any of the other line styles listed in Table 23.2. If the pen color does not match an available RGB palette color, the pen is drawn with a dithered (logical) color. If the pen width is one, PS_INSIDEFRAME is treated as PS_SOLID.

The initial step in selecting a new logical pen is to call the CreatePen function with specifications for the style, width, and drawing color.

```
hPen = CreatePen( nPenStyle,
                  nPenWidth,
                  RGBColor );
hOldPen = SelectObject( hdc, hPen );
```

After creating a new pen, the SelectObject function is called to associate the new pen with the device context, returning a handle to the previous pen.

Optionally, a selection of pens could be created—for example, as an array of handles—and then selected as needed (using SelectObject). But remember, each pen (or brush) created consumes some memory. When the object is no longer needed, dispose of it via the DeleteObject function.

```
DeleteObject( hPen );
```

One caution: A created pen (or brush) should not be deleted while associated with a device context (unless, of course, the device context is about to be closed). Instead, before deleting a pen (or brush), the SelectObject function can be called to restore the original pen. For example, instead of simply calling DeleteObject with the handle of the pen to delete, use a compound statement:

```
DeleteObject( SelectObject( hdc, hOldPen ) );
```

Logical Brushes

Windows also defines a selection of logical brushes, each with a color specification and using a predefined pattern. (Width, of course, does not apply.) A variety of hatched brushes are provided by Windows NT/95 (identifying constants are defined in WinGDI.H), which correspond to hatch-fill patterns supported by Windows 3.x. The hatch-fill styles are listed in Table 23.3.

TABLE 23.3   Hatch-Fill Patterns

Hatch-Fill Style	Pattern
HS_HORIZONTAL	Horizontal lines
HS_VERTICAL	Vertical lines
HS_FDIAGONAL	Forward diagonal (forward slash mark, approx 45°)
HS_BDIAGONAL	Backward diagonal (backslash marks, approx 45°)
HS_CROSS	Horizontal cross-hatch
HS_DIAGCROSS	Diagonal cross-hatch

NOTE   Windows NT version 3.1 had 13 other hatch-fill patterns, which appear to no longer be supported, as they are no longer defined in WinGDI.H. These are HS_FDIAGONAL1, HS_BDIAGONAL1, HS_SOLID, HS_DENSE1, HS_DENSE2, HS_DENSE3, HS_DENSE4, HS_DENSE5, HS_DENSE6, HS_DENSE7, HS_DENSE8, HS_NOSHADE, and HS_HALFTONE.

A logical hatch-fill brush is created in the same fashion as a logical pen, as explained in the previous section, and is subject to the same restrictions.

```
hBrush = CreateBrush( nHatchStyle, RGBColor );
hOldBrush = SelectObject( hdc, hBrush );
```

And, of course, when the brush is no longer needed, it should be disposed of in the same fashion as the logical pen.

```
DeleteObject( SelectObject( hdc, hOldBrush ) );
```

Unfortunately, you are allowed to create a brush or a pen without the formalities of saving a handle to either the new brush or pen or the old brush or pen; that is, without making any provisions to delete the new object or restore the original. The following code will function without reporting any errors or warnings.

```
SelectObject( hdc,
   CreatePen( nPen-IDM_SOLID, 1, cColor ) );
SelectObject( hdc,
   CreateHatchBrush( nHatch-IDM_HORIZ, cColor ) );
```

But the misfortune is that each `CreateHatchBrush` and `CreatePen` call allocates memory for the brush or pen, which is not disposed of until either Windows is exited or the system is rebooted. The bottom line is simple: There are no guards against this type of error except for your awareness and careful programming practices.

Creating Figures: The PenDraw2 Program

The PenDraw2 program demonstrates five of the eight figure functions: `Rectangle`, `Ellipse`, `Arc`, `Chord`, and `Pie`. This program permits you to select shape, line, and fill styles from a menu. The menu also offers a choice of colors, with a palette of eight shades predefined as RGB color values. An example of the PenDraw2 application appears in Figure 23.1.

Drawing Rectangles

Beginning with the simplest figures, the `Rectangle` function requires only four parameters to specify the coordinates (in device-context terms) for the upper-left and lower-right corners.

```
Rectangle( hdc, xUL, yUL, xLR, yLR );
```

A square is simply a special case of a rectangle and can be provided as:

```
Rectangle( hdc, xUL, yUL,
              xUL + min( xLR-xUL, yLR-yUL ),
              yUL + min( yLR-yUL, xLR-xUL ) );
```

In either case, the figure is drawn using the current color, pen, line style, and fill style.

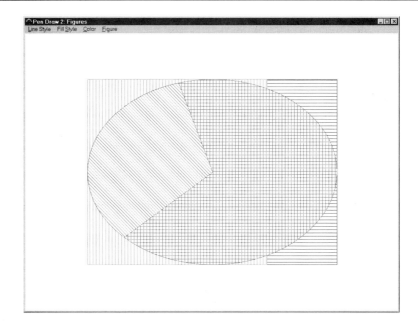

The `RoundRect` function is not demonstrated in PenDraw2, but it operates in the same fashion, except for the addition of two parameters specifying the x and y radii for the ellipse forming the corners.

```
RoundRect( hdc, xUL, yUL, xLR, yLR,
           xRadius, yRadius );
```

In general, `xRadius` and `yRadius` would be equal, making the corner arc circular, but this is not a fixed requirement; the corner ellipse can be elongated in either dimension. Figure 23.2 shows three corner examples: the left with *xRadius* > *yRadius*, the middle with *xRadius* = *yRadius,* and the right with *xRadius* < *yRadius*.

Drawing Ellipses

In other circumstances, ellipses are described in terms of x and y radii and center coordinates. In Windows, however, an ellipse is defined in terms of a theoretical rectangle bounding the ellipse. Thus, the `Ellipse` function is called, in the same fashion as the `Rectangle` function, with four coordinates identifying the upper-left and lower-right corners of a bounding rectangle.

```
Ellipse( hdc, xUL, yUL, xLR, yLR );
```

FIGURE 23.2

Three corners using
RoundRect

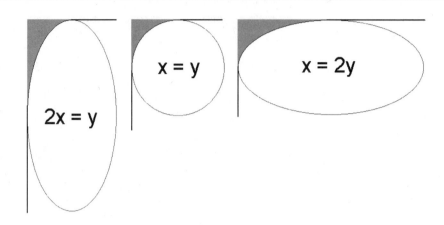

Also, as with the square and the rectangle, a circle is simply a special case of an ellipse in which the x and y radii are equal. This can be provided as:

```
Ellipse( hdc, xUL, yUL,
            xUL + min( xLR - xUL, yLR - yUL ),
            yUL + min( yLR - yUL, xLR - xUL ) );
```

Figure 23.3 shows three elliptical figures together with their bounding rectangles. (These bounding rectangles are not drawn by the Ellipse function but are provided simply as illustration.)

FIGURE 23.3

Three ellipses

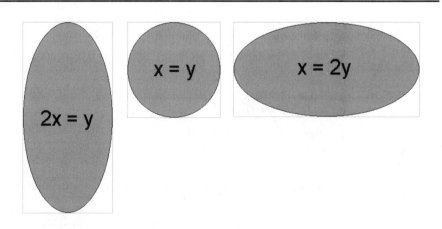

Drawing Arcs, Chords, and Pies

Like the `Ellipse` function, the `Arc`, `Chord`, and `Pie` functions also use coordinate parameters to define a bounding rectangle that determines the shape of the arc, chord, or pie figure. But in addition to the basic curve, each of these functions also requires two pairs of additional coordinate parameters to identify the beginning arc position (`xp1,yp1`) and the ending arc position (`xp2,yp2`). The three functions are called as:

```
Arc(   hdc, xUL, yUL, xLR, yLR,
       xStart, yStart, xEnd, yEnd );
Chord( hdc, xUL, yUL, xLR, yLR,
       xStart, yStart, xEnd, yEnd );
Pie(   hdc, xUL, yUL, xLR, yLR,
       xStart, yStart, xEnd, yEnd );
```

Under DOS, using C++ functions, an arc (or associated shape) would have been drawn by defining a center point, the radius (or x and y radii) and defining the beginning and endpoints as angles, with the 0° angle located horizontally to the right.

In Windows, however, the shape of the arc segment, like the ellipse, is defined by a bounding rectangle. The beginning and endpoints are defined, not by angles, but by points defining radii intersecting the arc.

As shown in Figure 23.4, the arc is drawn counterclockwise, beginning at an angle defined by the `xStart,yStart` coordinates and ending at the angle defined by the `xEnd,yEnd` point.

The `xStart,yStart` point does not necessarily lie on the arc itself (though it may), but identifies a radii drawn from the center of the arc through the point specified. The arc begins at the point where the radii and arc intersect. Or, if you prefer, the `xStart,yStart` point, together with the centerpoint, defines an angle for the arc starting point. In like fashion, the `xEnd,yEnd` point defines a radii setting the endpoint of the arc.

Figure 23.5 shows arc, chord, and pie figures, together with the bounding rectangles and the radii determining the begin and end angles.

For the `Arc` function, the process ends with determining the starting and ending points of the arc. For an arc, the resulting figure is not closed and no fill brush is used, although the arc itself is drawn using the current line style and color.

FIGURE 23.4

Defining arc angles

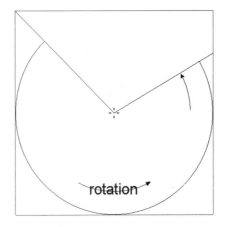

FIGURE 23.5

Arc, chord, and pie
shapes

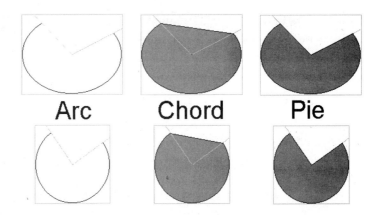

For the Chord function, the endpoints of the arc are connected with a straight line to complete a closed figure, which is filled in the PenDraw2 program using the selected hatch brush.

For the Pie function, the endpoints of the arc are also connected, but instead of a line between the two arc ends, two lines connect the endpoints with the center-point of the arc to create a pie slice. Again, the closed figure is filled using the selected hatch brush.

Remember, for the `Chord` and `Pie` functions, the points used are the endpoints of the arc, not the points passed as arguments to define the radii, which, in turn, determine the arc endpoints. Later, in the PieChart demo program, we'll use conventional trigonometry to calculate points that do lie on the arc (which is easier than calculating points that do not). Just keep in mind that these determining points are not required to lie on the arc itself.

Creating Business Graphs

One useful application for the figure-drawing functions is to create business graphs, such as bar graphs and pie charts. Although business graphs may not be your favorite subjects for programming (and certainly aren't mine), these are common requirements for business applications. So, for practical purposes, the BarGraph and PieGraph programs, personal preferences aside, illustrate how the Rectangle and Pie functions can be used with data sets.

Both the BarGraph and PieGraph demo programs use data arrays that are declared as static information within the program source code. In actual applications, of course, business graphs would use data either read directly from an external source or data calculated from external sources. For demo purposes, however, defining a data format and creating external source files is extraneous to and unnecessary for the actual objective. Do note, however, that both demo programs use the same data sets.

Building a Bar Graph: The BarGraph Program

The BarGraph program displays four years' worth of data broken down into eight categories. Colors are used to identify data by years, and the bars are grouped by category. Optionally, varying fill patterns could also be employed to identify category groups or to replace the year colors (for example, for monochrome displays).

In this application, there are advantages in using separate horizontal and vertical scale ranges and, therefore, the MM_ANISOTROPIC mode is used. A further advantage in using anisotropic mapping is that it allows us to change the vertical scaling to accomodate variations in the maximum values that need to be graphed.

Once the mode is selected, the origin point is set near the lower-left corner of the window but slightly up and to the right, leaving room to accommodate labels below each group of bars. Figure 23.6 illustrates a sample bar graph.

FIGURE 23.6

A sample bar graph

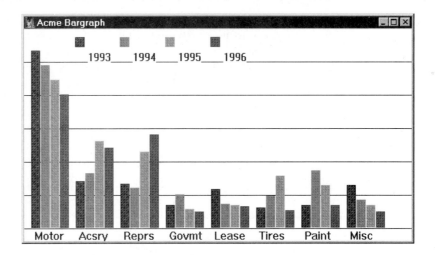

Also, after the client window is painted, the original (entry) mapping mode, which was saved when the MM_ANISOTROPIC mode was set, is restored, as are the original pen and brush sets.

The principal elements specific to the BarGraph program are found in the WM_PAINT response.

```
for( j=0; j<4; j++ )
{
    TextOut( hdc, ( j + 1 ) * 70 + 20,
             -2 * MaxVal - 20, szBuff,
             sprintf( szBuff, "%d", Years[j] ) );
    hPen = CreatePen( PS_SOLID, 1, lpColor[j+1] );
    SelectObject( hdc, hPen );
    hBrush = CreateSolidBrush( lpColor[j+1] );
    SelectObject( hdc, hBrush );
    Rectangle( hdc, (j+1)*70,    2*MaxVal+20,
                    (j+1)*70+15, 2*MaxVal+5 );
```

The outer loop executes for the four years, writing a label to identify each year before creating a small block showing the color used for the year.

The next step executes a loop through the data elements for the year, creating a rectangle for each category using the brush and color created for the current year.

```
for( i=0; i<8; i++ )
    Rectangle( hdc, j * 15 + 1 + i * 70,
               0, ( j + 1 ) * 15 + i * 70,
               2 * Accounts[j][i] );
    DeleteObject( hPen );
    DeleteObject( hBrush );
}
```

Last, the pen and brush objects are deleted because they are no longer necessary. However, compare the present usage to the methods suggested previously where the original pen and brush handles were saved and restored before the new pen and brush objects were deleted.

Building a Pie Graph: The PieGraph Program

The PieGraph demo uses a different approach from the BarGraph program, displaying data for one year at a time in a pie-section format. Of course, pie graphs are generally expected to be round rather than elliptical. Instead of the MM_ANISOTROPIC mode, the PieGraph program uses the MM_ISOTROPIC mode with the viewport origin in the center of the client window—a format selected for the convenience of the application.

Also, because C lacks a predefined value for pi, PI2 is defined as a macro with the value 2.0 * 3.14159, providing a means to convert values to angles (in radians) before using the derived angles to calculate points on the circumference.

The data used for the pie graph is an array of individual values but, before the pie graph can be drawn, they must be converted in proportions of a total (proportions of the total circumference) before they can be converted to angles. Therefore, a loop is used to determine the total for the year, thus:

```
TotVal[0] = 0;
for( i=0; i<8; i++ )
    TotVal[i+1] = TotVal[i] + Accounts[Year][i];
```

Once this has been done, the array TotVal contains the values necessary to calculate an angle for each category (in radians).

Before each pie section is calculated, as with the BarGraph demo program, a new pen and colored brush are created.

```
for( i=0; i<8; i++ )
{
    . . .
    hPen = CreatePen( PS_SOLID, 1, lpColor[i] );
    SelectObject( hdc, hPen );
    hBrush = CreateSolidBrush( lpColor[i] );
    SelectObject( hdc, hBrush );
    . . .
    Pie( hdc, -Radius, Radius, Radius, -Radius,
         (int) ( Radius * cos( PI2 * TotVal[i]
                           / TotVal[8] ) ),
             (int) ( Radius * sin( PI2 * TotVal[i]
                               / TotVal[8] ) ),
             (int) ( Radius * cos( PI2 * TotVal[i+1]
                               / TotVal[8] ) ),
             (int) ( Radius * sin( PI2 * TotVal[i+1]
                               / TotVal[8] ) ) );
```

Because the mapping mode is isotropic and the viewport origin is at the center of the window, the rectangle bounding the pie section (or, more accurately, bounding the circle from which the pie section will be cut) requires no more calculation than the simple coordinate point pairs: -Radius,Radius and Radius,-Radius.

Calculation is required, however, at the point coordinates for the starting and ending points for each pie section. For simplicity, these are calculated as points on the circumference of the pie.

And that's it. Each pie section is created as a fraction of the total circle using a different pen color for the outline and a brush with the corresponding color for the interior. The results are shown in Figure 23.7.

Drawing Polygon Figures

Like the Rectangle, Ellipse, and Pie functions, the Polygon and PolyPolygon functions draw bordered, closed, and filled figures, but with a few differences. The first and principal difference is that the figures drawn by either of the polygon

FIGURE 23.7

A simple pie graph

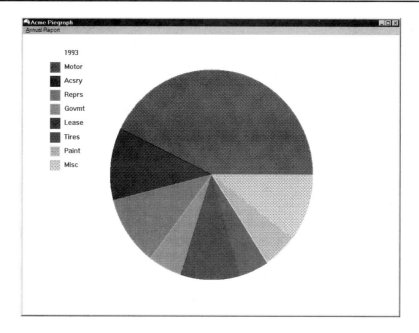

functions can be more complex than a simple rectangle, although the figures created are limited to straight lines and, unlike the `Ellipse` or `Pie` functions, cannot include curves.

The second difference is how the data describing the shape is specified. Where the `Rectangle` function expects a fixed set of coordinates, the `Polygon` function is more flexible and accepts a pointer to an array of coordinates (an array of `POINT`) with a further parameter specifying the number of points in the array.

```
Polygon( hdc, lpPoints, nPoints );
```

Each coordinate pair in the array of `POINT` identifies one vertex in a polygon, which the `Polygon` function uses to create the figure by connecting successive points with straight lines, finishing, if necessary, by connecting the last vertex to the first to close the figure. (For open figures, use the `PolyLine` function.)

Similarly, the `PolyPolygon` function creates a series of closed polygons and is called as:

```
PolyPolygon( hdc, lpPoints, lpPolyCounts, nPolygons );
```

Again, the lpPoints parameter is a pointer to an array of POINT, identifying coordinates for each vertex in the polygon. The next parameter, lpPolyCounts, however, is a pointer to an array of integers, which defines the number of points in each polygon. The final argument, nPolygons, identifies the number of polygons (or, equally, the number of entries in lpPolyCounts).

Unlike the Polygon function, however, the PolyPolygon vertex arrays must be explicitly closed. The final vertex in each polygon must have the same coordinates as the first vertex, because PolyPolygon does not automatically close each figure.

Also, using either function, individual polygons may overlap, but this is not required.

Polygon Fill Modes

The figures we've used so far are simple, closed outlines with contiguous interiors, which require no special handling to fill. However, in the case of many polygon figures, the interior areas may or may not be contiguous; if the area is not contiguous, it requires a different approach for filling.

For this reason, two different fill modes are supported (the names describe the algorithms used to determine which points lie inside the figure and which lie outside):

- **Alternate:** This fill mode considers regions as interior only when they are reached by crossing an odd number of boundaries (1, 3, 5, and so on). Regions reached by crossing an even number of boundaries are not filled.

- **Winding:** This fill mode, although slower to calculate, has the advantage of filling all interior (bounded) regions irrespective of the number of boundaries crossed.

Figure 23.8 shows two polygons, a five- and a seven-pointed star, each of which has been filled using the alternate algorithm. The winding algorithm is available as a menu selection and will fill all interior spaces.

Creating Polygons: The PenDraw3 Program

The PenDraw3 program demonstrates the Polygon function by drawing two figures after calculating the appropriate vertexes, using simple trigonometric functions similar to those employed in the PieGraph program. For the five-pointed star, the vertex coordinates are calculated in the order 0, 2, 4, 1, 3 using the formula

FIGURE 23.8

Polygons and fill modes

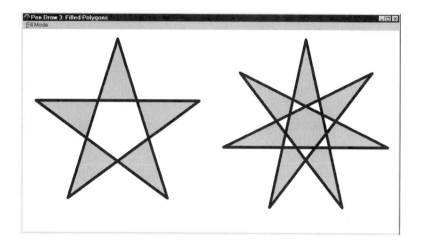

j=(j+2)%5. (If these points were calculated in successive order, the result would be a simple pentagon with a contiguous interior.)

```
for( i=j=0; i<5; i++, j=(j+2)%5 )   // 5 points //
{
    pt[0][i].x =
        (int)( sin( j*PI2/5 ) * 100 ) - 110;
    pt[0][i].y = (int)( cos( j*PI2/5 ) * 100 );
}
```

For the seven-pointed star, the formula j=(j+3)%7 serves the same purpose, with the points calculated in the order 0, 3, 6, 2, 6, 1, 4.

```
for( i=j=0; i<7; i++, j=(j+3)%7 )   // 7 points //
{
    pt[1][i].x =
        (int)( sin( j*PI2/7 ) * 100 ) + 110;
    pt[1][i].y = (int)( cos( j*PI2/7 ) * 100 );
}
```

The constants used—+110 and –110—offset each figure to the right of center and the left of center.

Alternatively, to use the PolyPolygon function, instead of calculating the points for the two figures, a static array of points could be used:

```
static POINT  pts[] =
    {  -110, 100,  -52, -80, -205,  30, -15,  30,
```

```
            -168,  -80,  -110,  100,   110,  100,  153,  -90,
              32,   63,   207,  -22,    13,  -22,  188,   62,
              67,  -90,   110,  100 );
static int poly[] = { 6, 8 };
```

The array `pts` provides the vertexes for the two figures, and the array `poly` declares the number of points in each polygon. With this data available, the `Poly-Polygon` function could be called as:

```
PolyPolygon( hdc, &pt, &poly,
             sizeof(poly) / sizeof(POINT) );
```

Remember, where the `Polygon` function for our example requires only five and seven vertex coordinate points, respectively, the `PolyPolygon` function requires six and eight vertex coordinate pairs. The final coordinate points in each set are the same as the first, thus closing each figure.

We've covered four graphics elements in this chapter: pen styles, fill patterns, drawing functions for regular shapes, and drawing functions for irregular shapes. These are demonstrated in the PenDraw2, BarGraph, PieGraph, and PenDraw3 programs, which are on the CD that accompanies this book.

These are only a few of the graphics functions supported by Windows, and they are also the simplest. More sophisticated graphics functions are demonstrated in the following chapters, beginning in Chapter 24 with bitmap graphics operations.

Brushes and Bitmaps

- Data-array defined bitmaps

- Resource bitmaps

- Old-style bitmaps

- Device-independent bitmaps

In Chapter 23, brushes were introduced as a variety of solid and hatched (or patterned) brushes used to fill figures. In this chapter, you'll learn that any pattern (bitmap), within certain limitations, can be used as a brush pattern.

Of course, fill patterns are only one of many uses for bitmaps. But since bit-mapped brushes provide both a beginning point and one of the simplest uses, they are our first subject.

Using Data-Array Defined Bitmaps

While obvious to the point of being trite, the first step in creating a bitmapped brush is creating the bitmap itself. For a brush, this will be a (minimum) 8-by-8 bit-map image.

A bitmap image could be defined within the source code as an array of BYTE, for example:

```
static BYTE wBricks[] =
    {  0xFF, 0x08, 0x08, 0x08, 0xFF, 0x80, 0x80, 0x80  };
```

> **NOTE** This array defines an 8-by-8 bit pattern similar to the BRICKS image in Figure 24.1, shown a bit later in the chapter, and could be used to pro-duce a pattern brush similar to the one shown in Figure 24.4 (left half of pentagonal star), also presented later in the chapter. However, notice that the preceding statement has been qualified using the condition "similar," because even though the patterns are similar, the array wBricks describes a monochrome pattern; the brush patterns used in the two illustrations are polychrome.

Converting the Array to a Bitmap

In order to use wBricks as a brush pattern, the next step is to call the API function CreateBitmap to convert the value array into a (memory) bitmap image:

```
hBitmap = CreateBitmap( 8, 8, 1, 1, (LPSTR) wBricks );
```

The `CreateBitmap` function creates a device-independent bitmap (in memory) for monochrome images. The parameters work as follows:

- The first two parameters are the width and height specifications.

- The third parameter sets the number of color planes in the bitmap (each plane has `nWidth * nHeight/nBitCount` bits).

- The fourth parameter sets the number of color bits per display pixel. Remember, `wBricks` describes a monochrome image pattern, which is compatible with all video systems.

- The final parameter is a pointer to the array of bytes, which defines the initial bitmap bits. If this argument is NULL, the bitmap will remain uninitialized.

However, creating a device-dependent bitmap is only a part of the process. Next, you must create a brush using the pattern.

Creating a Brush with the Bitmap Pattern

The next step is to use the bitmap handle with a call to `CreatePatternBrush` to actually create a brush using the pattern. This is accomplished as:

```
hBrush = CreatePatternBrush( hBitmap );
SelectObject( hdc, hBrush );
```

Finally, after calling `SelectObject`, the new pattern becomes the current brush object.

Of course, you shouldn't forget, after having created both bitmap and brush, that both should be deleted when they are no longer needed:

```
DeleteObject( hBrush );
DeleteObject( hBitmap );
```

Disadvantages of Bitmaps Defined as Arrays

Even though bitmaps can be defined as arrays of data within the program source code, this approach has three principal drawbacks:

- With the exception of monochrome images, the bitmaps created using `CreateBitmap` are device-dependent. Thus, a bitmap defined for VGA, using four color planes with one color bit per pixel (per plane), will not be compatible with an SVGA system that uses a quite different arrangement.

- Although monochrome bitmaps can be written out as hex data, color bitmaps, in the same format, are a real pain to create.

- Static data arrays within the compiled application, as opposed to resource data elements, waste memory during execution—and do so quite unnecessarily. Granted, under Windows NT/95, this may be less of a problem than with previous Windows versions, but why bother when there are simpler ways.

Using Resource Bitmaps

For each of the disadvantages presented by data-array defined bitmaps, resource bitmaps offer an alternative without the problems.

- Using a bitmap editor (or any other paint program) makes creating bitmaps convenient, regardless of whether they are monochrome or color.

- The bitmaps created are device-independent, whether in monochrome or color, and can be displayed on any video system. Windows supplies any necessary conversions.

- Since the bitmap data is contained in the resource section and only loaded into active memory as needed, the data does not waste memory when not required.

Resource Bitmap Images

For our example of how to use resource bitmaps, we'll use four bitmap images. The first three are for the stripes, diamond and bricks brushes, as shown in Figure 24.1. The fourth is the chains bitmap, shown in Figure 24.2. (These images are included on the CD accompanying this book.)

The three bitmaps in Figure 24.1 are acceptable for use as brushes under both Windows 95 and NT. There is, however, a limit on the bitmap size for brushes: The bitmap pattern cannot be smaller than 8-by-8 pixels. However, under Windows 95 (or Windows 3.1), if the bitmap pattern is larger than 8 pixels square, only the upper-left corner (8×8) of the image is used.

FIGURE 24.1

Three 8×8 bitmap
patterns

FIGURE 24.1

Three 8×8 bitmap
patterns

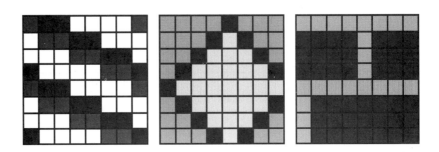

FIGURE 24.2

A 24×24 bitmap pattern

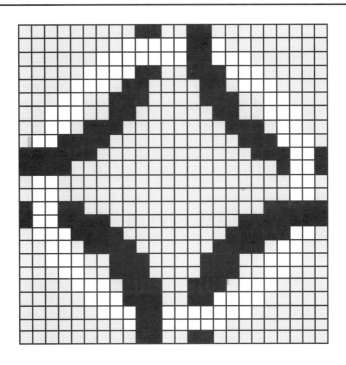

Under Windows NT, there is no limit on bitmap brush size. This is illustrated by the chains bitmap in Figure 24.1, which is 24-by-24 pixels. When you execute the sample PenDraw4 application presented in this chapter under Windows 95 and select the chains bitmap, the resulting brush fill pattern will look like the one shown on the left side of Figure 24.3. When the application is executed under Windows NT and the chains bitmap is selected, the resulting fill pattern uses the entire bitmap image, as shown on the right side in Figure 24.3.

FIGURE 24.3

The chains bitmap under Windows 95 and NT

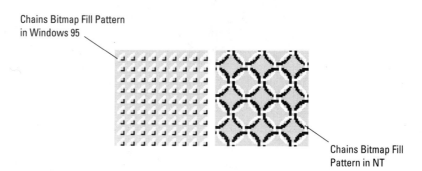

Chains Bitmap Fill Pattern in Windows 95

Chains Bitmap Fill Pattern in NT

After the bitmap images have been created, either a part of a .RES resource or as external .BMP images referenced by a .RC resource script, the linker combines these with the rest of the resources as a part of the .EXE executable. Remember, however, that the resource section of the application is not loaded on execution. Instead, elements from the resource section are loaded on demand as required and discarded when no longer required.

Using Resource Bitmaps to Create Brushes: The PenDraw4 Program

The PenDraw4 demo uses four bitmaps to create four patterned brushes, which are selected from the menu. The brushes are used to draw the same five- and seven-pointed stars demonstrated by PenDraw3 presented in Chapter 23.

There is one other important difference between the PenDraw3 and PenDraw4 programs. In PenDraw3, the two figures are created from calculated data using the `Polygon` function. In PenDraw4, a single static array of coordinates is used together with the `PolyPolygon` function, which was discussed but not demonstrated in Chapter 23.

Figure 24.4 shows a composite of the four bitmapped brushes. In actual practice, only one brush at a time is used.

FIGURE 24.4

Four patterned brushes for
the PenDraw4 program

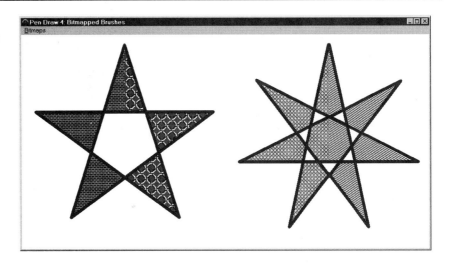

Loading the Bitmaps

Using these bitmaps as resources begins by requiring a LoadBitmap instruction
and, in the PenDraw4 example, this is accomplished in the exported WndProc procedure in response to a WM_CREATE message:

```
static HBITMAP hBitMap[4];

...

switch( msg )
{
   case WM_CREATE:
       hBitMap[0] = LoadBitmap( hInst, "BRICKS"  );
       hBitMap[1] = LoadBitmap( hInst, "CHAINS"  );
       hBitMap[2] = LoadBitmap( hInst, "DIAMOND" );
       hBitMap[3] = LoadBitmap( hInst, "STRIPES" );
       break;
```

The four bitmap images are loaded using a static array of handles (hBitMap[]).
Alternatively, individual bitmaps could be loaded as selected, loaded globally
from the WinMain procedure, or, in another application, loaded when some subprocedure is initiated.

In any case, the LoadBitmap function loads the bitmap resource specified (by the lpBitmapName argument) from the resource section of the executable or, optionally, from some other module specified by the hInst parameter.

Creating and Selecting the Brush

Loading a bitmap is only a part of the task and, in PenDraw4, the next step is executed in response to the WM_PAINT message and consists of creating the brush and selecting the brush as the active object.

```
hBrush = CreatePatternBrush( hBitMap[ nBitMap ] );
SelectObject( hdc, hBrush );
```

And, when finished, DeleteObject is called to cancel the brush handle.

```
DeleteObject( hBrush );
```

Also note that DeleteObject is not called for the bitmaps themselves. This is because these bitmaps are resource elements, and they were not created using the CreateBitmap function.

The complete listing for the PenDraw4 program is included on the CD that accompanies this book.

Using Predefined Bitmaps

In addition to loading resource bitmaps, the LoadBitmap function can access Windows' predefined bitmaps. For this usage, the hInst parameter is specified as NULL, and the lpBitmapName parameter must be one of the values shown in Table 24.1.

TABLE 24.1   Predefined Windows Bitmaps

Win3.x, Win95, or WinNT		WinNT / Win95 Only*	Pre-Windows 3.0**
OBM_CLOSE			OBM_OLD_CLOSE
OBM_UPARROW	OBM_UPARROWD	OBM_UPARROWI	OBM_OLD_UPARROW
OBM_DNARROW	OBM_DNARROWD	OBM_DNARROWI	OBM_OLD_DNARROW
OBM_RGARROW	OBM_RGARROWD	OBM_RGARROWI	OBM_OLD_RGARROW

TABLE 24.1   Predefined Windows Bitmaps (Continued)

Win3.x, Win95, or WinNT		WinNT / Win95 Only*	Pre-Windows 3.0**
OBM_LFARROW	OBM_LFARROWD	OBM_LFARROWI	OBM_OLD_LFARROW
OBM_REDUCE	OBM_REDUCED		OBM_OLD_REDUCE
OBM_ZOOM	OBM_ZOOMD		OBM_OLD_ZOOM
OBM_RESTORE	OBM_RESTORED		OBM_OLD_RESTORE
OBM_MNARROW	OBM_COMBO		
OBM_BTSIZE	OBM_CHECK		
OBM_SIZE	OBM_CHECKBOXES		
OBM_BTNCORNERS			

* These four bitmaps are unique to Windows NT or 95 (i.e., are not supported by Windows 3.x).

** All bitmap names with the form OBM_OLD_*xxxxx* represent bitmaps used by Windows versions prior to version 3.0.

NOTE For an application to use any of the OBM_*xxxxxx* constants, the constant OEMRESOURCE must be defined before including the Windows.H header.

Alternatively, the MAKEINTRESOURCE macro can be used to create a DWORD value with the bitmap ID as the low-order word and the high-order word NULL. If this is done, the resulting value can be used in place of the lpBitmapName argument, serving the same purpose.

The predefined bitmaps listed are used in a variety of Windows resources. For example, the OBM_UPARROW bitmap should be familiar from Windows 3.x, where it appears in the upper-right corner of every application's frame as the Maximize button. For Windows 95 and NT 4.0, the OBM_ZOOM bitmap is the current equivalent. The OBM_CHECK bitmap, as its name might suggest, is a simple checkmark. The OBM_SIZE bitmap provides the diagonal marker that appears in the lower-right corner of a resizable window.

If you would like a simple way to experiment with these, the PenDraw4 application can be modified as shown following:

```
case WM_CREATE:
    hBitMap[0] = LoadBitmap( NULL, MAKEINTRESOURCE( OBM_UPARROW ) );
    hBitMap[1] = LoadBitmap( NULL, MAKEINTRESOURCE( OBM_ZOOM ) );
    hBitMap[2] = LoadBitmap( NULL, MAKEINTRESOURCE( OBM_CHECK ) );
    hBitMap[3] = LoadBitmap( NULL, MAKEINTRESOURCE( OBM_SIZE ) );
    break;
```

Because the PenDraw4 application uses these bitmap resources as brush patterns, you will need to execute it under NT (not Windows 95) for these to be fully visible. (Remember, under Windows 95, only the upper-left 8×8 pixels of the bitmap will be used.)

NOTE   The DeleteObject function must be called to delete each bitmap handle returned by the LoadBitmap function.

Creating Old-Style Bitmaps

The old-style bitmaps originated with Windows 1.0. These bitmaps have the principal drawback of being very device-dependent, which means that old-style bitmaps are structured to match specific display formats and cannot be conveniently transported to other device contexts.

Functions for Old-Style Bitmaps

Windows does, however, provide four principal functions for creating old-style bitmaps:

```
hBitmap = CreateBitmap( cwWidth, cyHeight, nPlanes,
                           nBitsPixel, lpBits );
hBitmap = CreateBitmapIndirect( &bitmap );
hBitmap = CreateCompatibleBitmap( hdc, cxWidth, cyHeight );
hBitmap = CreateDiscardableBitmap( hdc, cxWidth, cyHeight );
```

The `cxWidth` and `cyHeight` arguments define the width and height, in pixels, of the bitmap. And, as described earlier in the chapter, the `CreateBitmap` function accepts specifications for the number of color planes and number of bits per pixel, matching the image to the device context requirements.

As alternatives, in the `CreateCompatibleBitmap` and `CreateDiscardable-Bitmap` functions, the device context handle (`hdc`) permits Windows to access the number of color planes and the color bits per pixel directly. However, both of these functions create uninitialized bitmap images and require the `SetBitmapBits` function to include image information (see the following discussion of the `SetBitmap-Bits` and `GetBitmapBits` functions).

The final function, `CreateBitmapIndirect`, uses the structure `BITMAP` to define the bitmap data, including size, colors, and image, in a fashion paralleling the original `CreateBitmap` function. The `BITMAP` structure is defined, in WinGDI.H, as:

```
typedef struct tagBITMAP
{  LONG    bmType;         // should be 0
   LONG    bmWidth;        // width in pixels
   LONG    bmHeight;       // height in pixels
   LONG    bmWidthBytes;   // width in bytes (must be even)
   WORD    bmPlanes;       // number of color planes
   WORD    bmBitsPixel;    // color bits per pixel
   LPVOID  bmBits;         // pointer to image data
} BITMAP, *PBITMAP, NEAR *NPBITMAP, FAR *LPBITMAP;
```

Setting and Getting Bitmap Data

The `SetBitmapBits` function is used to copy a char (or byte) array into an existing bitmap, usually an unititialized bitmap.

```
SetBitmapBits( hBitmap, dwCount, lpBits );
```

As an alternative, the image data can be retrieved from an existing bitmap via the `GetBitmapBits` function.

```
GetBitmapBits( hBitmap, dwCount, lpBits );
```

The `GetBitmapBits` function copies `dwCount` bits from `hBitmap` to the array addressed as `lpBits`. If the size information is not known, `dwCount` can be calculated by first calling the `GetObject` function to retrieve the bitmap structure data:

```
GetObject( hBitmap, sizeof(BITMAP), (LPSTR) &bm );
```

And, once the data is available in bm, dwCount can be calculated as:

```
dwCount = (DWORD)( bm.bmWidthBytes * bm.bmHeight *
                   bm.bmPlanes );
```

Finally, since these bitmaps are GDI objects, the DeleteObject function should be used to cancel the object when it is no longer needed.

```
DeleteObject( hBitmap );
```

Old-Style Monochrome Bitmaps

Earlier in the chapter, we used the wBricks array to create an 8-by-8 monochrome brush from an array of byte values. For bitmaps not intended simply for use with brushes, the 8-by-8 limitation does not apply, even though each scan line of the bitmap must be an even number of bytes in width (some multiple of 16 bits with zeros used to right-pad the data).

For example, a simple monochrome bitmap consisting of a 9-by-9 square with two diagonals crossing in the center could be defined as:

```
1 1 1 1 1 1 1 1   1 0 0 0 0 0 0 0   =   FFh 80h
1 1 0 0 0 0 0 1   1 0 0 0 0 0 0 0   =   C1h 80h
1 0 1 0 0 0 1 0   1 0 0 0 0 0 0 0   =   A2h 80h
1 0 0 1 0 1 0 0   1 0 0 0 0 0 0 0   =   94h 80h
1 0 0 0 1 0 0 0   1 0 0 0 0 0 0 0   =   88h 80h
1 0 0 1 0 1 0 0   1 0 0 0 0 0 0 0   =   94h 80h
1 0 1 0 0 0 1 0   1 0 0 0 0 0 0 0   =   A2h 80h
1 1 0 0 0 0 0 1   1 0 0 0 0 0 0 0   =   C1h 80h
1 1 1 1 1 1 1 1   1 0 0 0 0 0 0 0   =   FFh 80h
```

To make the bitmap 9-by-9, each scan line requires seven pad bits (zeros), for a total width of 16 bits or two bytes.

To implement this particular image, the corresponding BITMAP structure could be defined as:

```
static BITMAP bm = { 0, 9, 9, 2, 1, 1 };
```

The corresponding image data would be stored in an array of bytes as:

```
static BYTE CheckBox[] =
{  0xFF, 0x80, 0xC1, 0x80, 0xA2, 0x80, 0x94, 0x80, 0x88,
   0x80, 0x94, 0x80, 0xA2, 0x80, 0xC1, 0x80, 0xFF, 0x80  };
```

For old-style bitmaps, the images are coded from the top down. In the new DIB format, images are coded from the bottom up. Of course, since the present example is symmetrical, direction becomes irrelevant.

The simplest method of creating a bitmap from the example data is to use the `CreateBitmap` function.

```
hBitmap = CreateBitmap( 9, 9, 1, 1, CheckBox );
```

Alternatively, the `CreateBitmapIndirect` function can also be used.

```
bm.bmBits = (LPSTR) CheckBox;
hBitmap = CreateBitmapIndirect( &bm );
```

However, there is a potential bug in this format. Because Windows expects to be able to move data around as necessary, the address returned for `CheckBox` may or may not remain valid after it has been assigned. This potential error can be avoided, however, by first creating the bitmap and then transferring the bitmap image to the display (device) context.

```
hBitmap = CreateBitmapIndirect( &bm );
SetBitmapBits( hBitmap, (DWORD) sizeof(CheckBox), CheckBox );
```

Old-Style Color Bitmaps

For color bitmaps, using Windows old-style is both extremely device-dependent as well as quite a bit more complex than for monochrome bitmaps. To illustrate why, following is the 16-color equivalent of `CheckBox`, using only two colors: dark green and white (assuming a standard palette). The bitmap image is calculated as:

```
F F F F F F F F F 0 0 0   =   FFh FFh FFh FFh F0h 00h
F F 2 2 2 2 2 F F 0 0 0   =   FFh 22h 22h 2Fh F0h 00h
F 2 F 2 2 2 F 2 F 0 0 0   =   F2h F2h 22h F2h F0h 00h
F 2 2 F 2 F 2 2 F 0 0 0   =   F2h 2Fh 2Fh 22h F0h 00h
F 2 2 2 F 2 2 2 F 0 0 0   =   F2h 22h F2h 22h F0h 00h
F 2 2 F 2 F 2 2 F 0 0 0   =   F2h 2Fh 2Fh 22h F0h 00h
F 2 F 2 2 2 F 2 F 0 0 0   =   F2h F2h 22h F2h F0h 00h
F F 2 2 2 2 2 F F 0 0 0   =   FFh 22h 22h 2Fh F0h 00h
F F F F F F F F F 0 0 0   =   FFh FFh FFh FFh F0h 00h
```

Again, each scan line is padded to a WORD width by adding three zero (black) pixels at the end of each scan line.

For an EGA/VGA device, this bitmap can be interpreted as a marked checkbox in white against a dark-green background with each four bits representing the color of one pixel. However, if the display device is, for example, an IBM8514/A, where 8 bits are interpreted as the color value for each pixel, not only will the colors be different, but the image will also be quite different. Or, what about the case where a true-color video is used as the display context and 24 bits of color data are expected for each pixel? The solution is found in the newer device-independent bitmap format described in the next section.

Using Device-Independent Bitmaps

The device-independent bitmap (DIB) format originally appeared as an extension of the OS/2 Presentation Manager bitmap format (and, perhaps, the only good element to come out of OS/2 version 1.1). This format presents, as its most important feature, an RGB color table defining all colors used in the bitmap. Most (if not all) bitmap editors or paint programs automatically create DIB image files. However, because device-independent bitmaps have become so common, the .DIB extension is rarely used; files bearing the .BMP extension are almost always device-independent images, not device-dependent.

DIB File Format

The DIB image file format consists of several sections: the DIB header, the BITMAP-INFOHEADER, the color table and the image data. Each of these is described in the following sections.

The DIB File Header

The DIB bitmap file begins with a file header which provides information about the structure of the file itself. The DIB header (defined in WinGDI.H) consists of the 14-byte record shown in Table 24.2.

TABLE 24.2   DIB Header Format

Field	Size	Sample Data	Value	Description
bfType	WORD	42 4D	"BM"	Bitmap ID (constant, all DIBs)
bfSize	DWORD	96 00 00 00	96h	Total file size (example only)
reserved1	WORD	00 00	0h	Set to 0
reserved2	WORD	00 00	0h	Set to 0
bfOffBits	DWORD	76 00 00 00	76h	Offset to bitmap image from first of file (example only)

NOTE   Remember that all data is arranged in `lsb...msb` order. For example, the data bytes 96 00 00 00 represent the value 00000096h, not 96000000h.

The BITMAPINFOHEADER Structure

The file header information is followed by a second data header defined by the BITMAPINFOHEADER structure. This data is shown in Table 24.3.

TABLE 24.3   BITMAPINFOHEADER Data

Field	Size	Sample	Val	Description
biSize	DWORD	28 00 00 00	28h	Size of BITMAPINFOHEADER
biWidth	LONG	08 00 00 00	8h	Bitmap pixel width
biHeight	LONG	08 00 00 00	8h	Bitmap pixel height
biPlanes	WORD	01 00	1h	Color planes (always 1)
biBitCount	WORD	04 00	4h	Color bits per pixel (1, 4, 8, 24)
biCompression	DWORD	00 00 00 00	0h	Compression scheme (0=none)
biSizeImage	DWORD	20 00 00 00	20h	Bitmap image size (used only if compression is set)

TABLE 24.3   BITMAPINFOHEADER Data (Continued)

Field	Size	Sample	Val	Description
biXPelsPerMeter	LONG	00 00 00 00	0h	Horizontal resolution (pixels/meter)
biYPelsPerMeter	LONG	00 00 00 00	0h	Vertical resolution (pixels/meter)
biD1rUsed	DWORD	00 00 00 00	0h	Number of colors used in image
biClrImportant	DWORD	00 00 00 00	0h	Number of important colors

The BITMAPINFOHEADER contains quite a bit of data about the DIB image. However, as you can see from the example, often several of these fields are left blank, especially the horizontal and vertical resolution. The final two fields, identifying the number of colors used and the number of important colors are often used for additional information about custom colors or multiple color palettes; zero values indicate defaults.

Notice also that color is represented only as multiple color bits per pixel, regardless of how a specific device might expect to handle color. Thus, color will be specified as one bit per pixel for monochrome, four for 16-color bitmaps, eight for 256-color bitmaps, or twenty-four for true-color images (16 million colors).

Also, if data compression is used, the data-compression scheme is identified together with the actual size of the uncompressed bitmap (in bytes), thus providing a redundancy check for use in decompressing the image. Four compression schemes are defined, as shown in Table 24.4:

TABLE 24.4   Compression Formats and Identifiers

Constant	Value	Comment
BI_RGB	0	No compression used
BI_RLE8	1	Run-length encoding format
BI_RLE4	2	Run-length encoding format
BI_TOPDOWN	4	

NOTE	Despite provisions for identifying compression formats, many bitmap editors (or paint programs) do not support (or recognize) compressed image data.

The DIB BITMAP Color Table

The DIB color table follows the BITMAPINFOHEADER. This table consists of a series of RGBQUAD structures. These are read, in order, with the first byte blue, the second green, the third red, and the fourth byte in each quad set to zero.

The number of RGBQUAD structures is identified by the biBitCount field. For a monochrome image, this field is set as 1 color bit. Two RGBQUAD records are required to identify the foreground and background colors. If biBitCount is 4, 16 RGBQUAD color identifiers are needed. If biBitCount is 8, 256 RGBQUAD values are required.

If the biClrUsed field is nonzero, this value (instead of the biBitCount field) identifies the number of RGBQUAD structures in the color table.

Table 24.5 shows the default color values for a VGA 16-color palette expressed as RGBQUAD values.

TABLE 24.5   A Sample Color Palette for a DIB Bitmap

Palette Entry	RGBQUAD Data	Color Value			Approximate Color
		R	G	B	
0	00 00 00 00	00	00	00	Black
1	00 00 80 00	80	00	00	Dark Red
2	00 80 00 00	00	80	00	Dark Green
3	00 80 80 00	80	80	00	Gold Green
4	80 00 00 00	00	00	80	Dark Blue
5	80 00 80 00	80	00	80	Purple
6	80 80 00 00	00	80	80	Blue Gray
7	80 80 80 00	80	80	80	Dark Gray

TABLE 24.5 A Sample Color Palette for a DIB Bitmap (Continued)

		Color Value			
Palette Entry	RGBQUAD Data	R	G	B	Approximate Color
8	C0 C0 C0 00	C0	C0	C0	Light Gray
9	00 00 FF 00	FF	00	00	Light Red
10	00 FF 00 00	00	FF	00	Light Green
11	00 FF FF 00	FF	FF	00	Yellow
12	FF 00 00 00	FF	00	00	Light Blue
13	FF 00 FF 00	FF	00	FF	Magenta
14	FF FF 00 00	00	FF	FF	Cyan
15	FF FF FF 00	FF	FF	FF	White

The DIB BITMAP Image

The final section of the bitmap file is the bitmap image itself. The arrangement of this section partly depends on the number of colors (as reported by the `biBit-Count` field), but it is also affected by two other factors, which are constant for all bitmaps:

- Each row of the bitmap image must be a multiple of four bytes (a DWORD multiple). Each data row begins with the left-most pixel of the scan line and is right padded with zeros, as necessary.

- Unlike the original bitmap format (Windows 1.0 or 2.0), the bitmap format for DIBs begins with the bottom scan line in the image, not the top.

For a monochrome bitmap—one color bit per pixel—the bit image begins with the most-significant bit of the first byte in each row. If the bit value is zero (0), the first RGBQUAD color value is used (background). If the bit value is one (1), the second RGBQUAD value is used (foreground).

For a monochrome bitmap, the BRICKS bitmap data would be coded as:

```
80 80 80 FF 08 08 08 FF
```

This data would break down, as a pixel image, as:

```
1 1 1 1 1 1 1 1        // FFh
0 0 0 0 1 0 0 0        // 08h
0 0 0 0 1 0 0 0        // 08h
0 0 0 0 1 0 0 0        // 08h
1 1 1 1 1 1 1 1        // FFh
1 0 0 0 0 0 0 0        // 80h
1 0 0 0 0 0 0 0        // 80h
1 0 0 0 0 0 0 0        // 80h
```

Again, as a reminder, notice that the image data, from left to right, appears in the image from bottom to top, not top down.

For a 16-color bitmap, as used in the Bricks.BMP file with four bits per pixel, each pixel is represented by a four-bit value that serves as an index to the palette entries in the table (as shown in Table 24.5). The color bitmap image appears as:

```
81 11 11 11    81 11 11 11    81 11 11 11    88 88 88 88
11 11 81 11    11 11 81 11    11 11 81 11    88 88 88 88
```

The color image data is decoded as:

```
8 8 8 8 8 8 8 8        // 88h 88h 88h 88h
1 1 1 1 8 1 1 1        // 11h 11h 81h 11h
1 1 1 1 8 1 1 1        // 11h 11h 81h 11h
1 1 1 1 8 1 1 1        // 11h 11h 81h 11h
8 8 8 8 8 8 8 8        // 88h 88h 88h 88h
8 1 1 1 1 1 1 1        // 81h 11h 11h 11h
8 1 1 1 1 1 1 1        // 81h 11h 11h 11h
8 1 1 1 1 1 1 1        // 81h 11h 11h 11h
```

In similar fashion, for a 256-color bitmap, each pixel is represented by a byte value indexing the 256 entries in the color table.

And for a 24-bit-per-pixel color bitmap, with the biClrUsed field specified as zero, instead of a 16 million entry color table (predicating a minimum file size of 64MB just for the color table), no color table is used. Each pixel is represented by a three-byte RGBColor value. If biClrUsed is not zero, a color table is included and pixels are indexed to the table.

OS/2 Bitmaps

OS/2 version 1.1 and later uses a bitmap structure that is very similar to Windows, with only two principal structure changes. First, instead of a BITMAPINFO-HEADER structure, OS/2 uses a BITMAPCOREHEADER structure, which is defined in WinGDI.H as:

```
typedef struct tagBITMAPCOREHEADER
{   DWORD   bcSize;                // offset to color table
    WORD    bcWidth;
    WORD    bcHeight;
    WORD    bcPlanes;
    WORD    bcBitCount;
} BITMAPCOREHEADER, FAR *LPBITMAPCOREHEADER, *PBITMAPCOREHEADER;
```

And, second, instead of a color table consisting of RGBQUAD records, the OS/2 bitmaps use RGBTRIPLE records.

Perhaps the simplest method of identifying the two formats is to check the two byte values in the image file for the value BM, identifying Windows bitmap format. If these two bytes do not identify Windows format, the OS/2 structure can be confirmed by testing the first DWORD value in BITMAPIMAGEHEADER/BITMAPCOREHEADER structures to determine the structure size.

Retrieving Bitmap Dimensions

Windows supplies two bitmap dimension functions: SetBitmapDimensionEx and GetBitmapDimensionEx. However, despite what the names might initially suggest, these two functions do not deal with the pixel dimensions of a bitmap because, once an image is created, the pixel size of the image cannot be changed. Instead, this function pair provides a means of setting or retrieving bitmap dimensions in logical units (the MM_LOMETRIC mode is assumed). These dimensions are not used by the GDI for screen display but may be used by other applications to scale bitmaps that have been exchanged using the clipboard, DDE, or other channels.

The SetBitmapDimensionEx and GetBitmapDimensionEx functions are called as:

```
SetBitmapDimensionEx( hBitmap, xUnits, yUnits, lpSize );
GetBitmapDimensionEx( hBitmap, lpSize );
```

The `lpSize` variable returns with the previous size data (when new dimensions are set) or the current size data (when the `get` function is called). The `SIZE` data structure is defined in WinDef.H as:

```
typedef struct tagSIZE
{  LONG  cx;
   LONG  cy;  } SIZE, *PSIZE, *LPSIZE;
```

NOTE   In general, the two bitmap size fields (`biXPelsPerMeter` / `biYPels-PerMeter`) are set to zero except when needed by special circumstances.

Creating DIBs

Ideally, it would be nice if Windows supplied a simple function to create (or load) and display a bitmap, requiring only a device context, bitmap name, and position. This function might look something like this:

```
DrawBitmap( hwnd, lpBitmapName, xPos, yPos );
```

But, even though bitmaps are both important and integral to Windows, no such basic display function is provided. In place of this omission, Windows provides a series of bitmap primitives which can be used to construct a number of the missing high-level bitmap handlers, beginning with a function titled, appropriately, `DrawBitmap`.

The following sections describe the basic steps required to create and display a DIB.

Step One: Providing a Global Instance Handle

Up to this point, all the program examples have included one provision which, thus far, has not been used, needed, explained, or (most likely) even noticed. The provision in reference, which does have more than a few uses, begins with the global handle declaration:

```
HANDLE  hInst;
```

And, in the `WinMain` procedure, the `hInst` variable is assigned as:

```
hInst = hInstance;
```

Without this provision in the PenDraw4 program, for example, the LoadBitmap instructions in response to the WM_CREATE message in WndProc would need to have been executed in the WinMain procedure using the hInstance handle.

There are, of course, other ways to retrieve an application's instance handle, but since the global instance handle costs a mere 16 bits of overhead memory, why bother with false economies?

And, once the global hInst instance handle is available, the LoadBitmap function can be implemented within our theoretical DrawBitmap function without invoking special provisions to retrieve the application's instance handle.

Step Two: Defining DrawBitmap

Later, other bitmap handlers will be demonstrated, but for a first effort, the basic form will be called with four parameters: the window handle (hwnd), the bitmap name (lpName), and x and y coordinates to position the bitmap. And, as a result, DrawBitmap will display a bitmap at the coordinates specified.

Ergo, the function declaration begins as:

```
BOOL DrawBitmap( HWND hwnd, LPSTR lpName,
                 int   xPos, int    yPos )
{
```

NOTE   DrawBitmap is also provided with the capability to return a Boolean result, reporting success or failure. But as with most C functions, the returned value may be used or ignored, as desired.

A few local variables will be needed, and they are declared as:

```
HDC     hdc, hdcMem;
BITMAP  bm;
HBITMAP hBitmap;
```

Declarations finished, the function is now ready to load a bitmap from the resource segment of the .EXE program. Notice, however, that this is also the point where the global hInst handle becomes essential.

```
if( !( hBitmap = LoadBitmap( hInst, lpName ) ) )
    return( FALSE );
```

Of course, if the load operation fails, `DrawBitmap` will immediately terminate, returning FALSE. This is, however, the only error-check provided.

If successful, once the bitmap is loaded, the next step will be to establish a suitable device context to display the bitmap.

Step Three: Creating the Device Context

Unlike in DOS, where once a graphics mode has been established, anything can be written (drawn) on the screen, under Windows, a bitmap image cannot be drawn (or copied) directly to the display device context. Instead, before the bitmap image can be drawn, a separate device context is created. This is created as a memory device context (with no immediate connection to an output device), using the `hdc-Mem` variable declared local to the `DisplayBitmap` function.

However, the application's actual output device context cannot simply be ignored. Therefore, the next order of business is to retrieve a handle to the application's device context.

```
hdc = GetDC( hwnd );
hdcMem = CreateCompatibleDC( hdc );
```

The trick here is that a reference device context (`hdc`) is needed before the `Create-CompatibleDC` function can be called to create the memory context (`hdcMem`). And the memory device context is simply a block of memory that acts as an analog for the real display context and, for a bitmap, can be used to prepare an image in memory before transferring the image to the display context (to the screen or another output device).

When the memory device context is created, the GDI automatically assigns a "display surface" sized for a 1-by-1 monochrome image; that is, a one-pixel monochrome bitmap. But, while this is hardly sufficient space for any real operations, this deficiency can be corrected immediately by calling `SelectObject` to make the bitmap that was loaded a moment before the active object for the device context, thus:

```
SelectObject( hdcMem, hBitmap );
SetMapMode( hdcMem, GetMapMode( hdc ) );
```

After selecting the bitmap into the memory context, `SetMapMode` assigns the mapping mode used by the active device context (`hdc`) to the memory device context (`hdcMem`), thus making the memory image of the bitmap a suitable match for the output device.

At this point, the bitmap has become the active object for the memory device context, while the memory device has the same mapping mode as the actual device context. But the job isn't done yet; there is still quite a bit of information that needs to be transferred from the source bitmap (hBitmap) to the local bitmap record (bm).

Step Four: Bitmap Data and Mapping Coordinates

The GetObject function can be used to transfer most of the information needed to fill the buffer (bm) to define the logical object (the selected bitmap). For a bitmap, GetObject returns the width, height, and color format information. This function is called as:

```
GetObject( hBitmap, sizeof( BITMAP ), (LPSTR) &bm );
```

But still, the actual image data has not been retrieved yet. This operation comes next.

Step Five: Image Data Transfers

The BitBlt (short for bit-block-transfer and pronounced "bit-blit"), PutBlt, and StretchBlt functions comprise Windows pixel-manipulation power operations. However, while each of these function names implies a block-transfer operation, there's more involved here than simply copying bits from one memory location to another. Instead, there is also a choice of raster operations, as will be explained in a moment.

While not the simplest of the three operations, the BitBlt operation is, for the present purpose, the operation of choice. It is used to complete the task of writing the bitmap image to the client window:

```
BitBlt( hdc, xPos, yPos, bm.bmWidth, bm.bmHeigth,
        hdcMem, 0, 0, SRCCOPY );
```

The BitBlt operation moves the bitmap image from the source device (hdcMem) to the destination device (hdc), with the xSrc and ySrc parameters (0,0 in the example) specifying the origin (in the source device context) of the bitmap to be transferred.

The xPos, yPos, bm.bmWidth, and bm.bmHeight parameters provide the origin and rectangle size (in the destination device context) to be filled by the bitmap image. Unlike many previous operations, instead of RECT rectangular coordinates, the origin point is specified in device context coordinates. The width and height are passed as logical units, not as device coordinates. As demonstrated, these last two values are taken directly from the bitmap data but, optionally, may be assigned on some other basis.

The final parameter is a ternary raster-operation code specifying how the GDI will combine colors between a current brush (pattern), the source image, and any existing destination image. For the `DrawBitmap` operation, the `SRCCOPY` ROP copies the source bitmap image directly to the destination (`hdc`).

The 15 principal ternary raster operations are defined in WinGDI.H and listed in Table 24.6.

TABLE 24.6   Raster Operation Codes (Ternary Raster Ops)

Constant	Operation	Description
SRCCOPY	Dest = Source	Copies source to destination
SRCPAINT	Dest = Source | Dest	Destination is ORed with source
SRCAND	Dest = Source & Dest	Source ANDed with destination
SRCINVERT	Dest = Source ^ Dest	Source XORed with destination
SRCERASE	Dest = Source & !Dest	Destination is inverted before ANDing with source
NOTSRCCOPY	Dest = !Source	Copies inverted source to destination
NOTSR-CERASE	Dest = !Source & !Dest	Inverted destination ANDed with inverted source
MERGECOPY	Dest = Source & Patt	Source ANDed with pattern
MERGEPAINT	Dest = !Source | Dest	Destination ORed with inverted source
PATCOPY	Dest = Patt	Pattern copied to destination
PATPAINT	Dest = Patt | !Source | Dest	Pattern ORed with inverted source, result ORed with destination
PATINVERT	Dest = Patt ^ Dest	Pattern XORed with destination
DSTINVERT	Dest = !Dest	Destination inverted
BLACKNESS	Dest = Black (0)	Destination turns black
WHITENESS	Dest = White (1)	Destination turns white

Raster operations involving monochrome images are fairly straightforward: Bits will be either on or off according to the logical operations selected. For color bitmaps, however, the GDI executes separate operations for each color plane or for each set of color bits, depending on the device context organization. The best way to understand these operations is to experiment, preferably with relatively simple bitmaps and patterns.

Step 6: Cleaning Up

Calling the BitBlt API completed the task of drawing the bitmap, but before DrawBitmap returns, some cleanup is still required. This is accomplished as:

```
ReleaseDC( hwnd, hdc );
DeleteDC( hdcMem );
DeleteObject( hBitmap );
return( TRUE );
```

Initially, three local memory allocations were made, returning three handles as hdc, hdcMem, and hBitmap. The first of these is simply released rather than being deleted; that is, the hdc handle is released, but the application device context is not deleted. The local memory device context, however, is deleted entirely, deallocating all memory involved, not just the memory handle. The locally allocated and loaded bitmap is treated in a similar fashion.

After this cleanup is completed, the DrawBitmap function is free to return, reporting success.

The DrawBitmap function is demonstrated in the PenDraw5 application, which is discussed after we cover one more bitmap operation.

Stretching Bitmaps

Drawing a bitmap using a one-for-one transfer is probably the most common operation. However, another bitmap operation you may find useful is provided by StretchBlt, which permits stretching or distorting a bitmap to fit any (rectangular) space desired. This function moves a bitmap from a source rectangle to a destination rectangle, stretching or compressing the bitmap as appropriate to fit the destination dimensions.

Calling the StretchBlt operation is similar to calling BitBlt, but with two differences:

```
BitBlt( hdc,     xPos, yPos, xWidth,     yHeight,
        hdcMem, xOrg, yOrg,
        dwRasterOp );
StretchBlt( hdc,     xPos, yPos, xWidth,     yHeight,
            hdcMem, xOrg, yOrg, xWidthOut, yHeightOut,
            dwRasterOp );
```

The StretchBlt operation is called with two additional parameters specifying the destination width and height; for the BitBlt operation, source and destination width and height are the same. And it is precisely this difference that instructs StretchBlt to stretch or compress the bitmap during transfer. Since xWidth/xWidthOut and yWidth/yWidthOut are independent, the bitmap could be stretched along one axis and compressed along another.

As with the BitBlt operation, the dwRasterOp specification controls how the source and destination (if any) bitmaps are combined during the StretchBlt operation.

StretchBlt operations, however, are not necessarily limited to resizing images. Instead, StretchBlt can be used to create a mirror image of a bitmap (laterally or vertically) if the signs of the source and destination width or the source and destination height are different. Ergo, if the destination width is negative and the source width positive, StretchBlt creates a mirror image rotated about the vertical axis (swapping left for right). Likewise, for a difference in sign of the height parameters, the image is mirrored along the horizontal axis. If both pairs are opposite in sign, the image is simply rotated 180° but without mirror inversion.

Because the StretchBlt operation resizes a bitmap image, one additional factor controls how data is added or subtracted to create the new image: the StretchBlt mode. The active mode is set by calling the SetStretchBltMode function as:

```
SetStretchBltMode( hdc, nStretchMode );
```

Four StretchBlt modes are defined in WinGDI.H, as described in Table 24.7.

The BLACKONWHITE and WHITEONBLACK modes are typically used to preserve, respectively, the background or foreground pixels in monochrome bitmaps. The COLORONCOLOR and HALFTONE modes are typically used to preserve color in color bitmaps, with the principal difference between the two being that the HALFTONE mode produces higher-image quality but does so at the expense of execution time.

TABLE 24.7   StretchBlt Modes

Constant	Value	Description
BLACKONWHITE	1	Eliminated lines are ANDed with retained lines; preserves black pixels at expense of white
WHITEONBLACK	2	Eliminated lines are ORed with retained lines; preserves white pixels at expense of black
COLORONCOLOR	3	Eliminated lines are deleted without preserving information
HALFTONE	4	Color information in destination approximates source pixels, averaging information from source to destination

Using the Bitmap-Drawing Function: The PenDraw5 Program

The PenDraw5 program demonstrates the DrawBitmap function described earlier, as well as the BitBlt and StretchBlt API functions. PenDraw5 requires five bitmaps, four 16-by-16 images and one 40-by-70 image, as illustrated in Figure 24.5.

FIGURE 24.5

Five bitmap images used in the PenDraw5 demo program

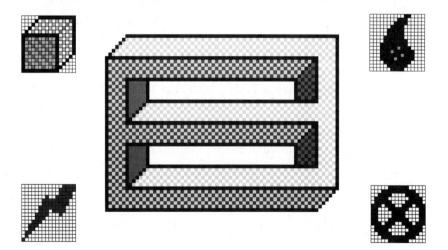

TIP

You can use bitmaps other than the ones shown in Figure 24.5, if you prefer. Just be sure to make the appropriate changes in the source and resource codes.

Initially, the `DrawBitmap` function draws all five bitmaps, placing the four smaller bitmaps at the corners of the client window and the larger bitmap in the center. For each of these, the bitmap is drawn with the upper-left corner of the image at the coordinates specified. Several variations are also used in the demo program:

- `DrawCenBitmap` centers each image (horizontally and vertically) on the coordinate points.

- `LineGraph` uses a brief array of data to position a series of smaller bitmaps in a form appropriate for a simple line graph.

- `StretchBitmap` uses `StretchBlt` API to resize a bitmap to fit a specified rectangle.

- `StretchBitmap2Client` stretches a bitmap to fill the entire client window.

- `MoveBitmap` tracks mouse movement by repositioning a bitmap each time the left mouse button is pressed or, if the button is held down, by tracking the mouse cursor directly.

NOTE

Bitmaps are not well-suited to this last operational format, `MoveBitmap`. This is intended more as a demonstration than as a serious example of practical programming.

Bitmap operations are very powerful tools with a wide variety of uses, extending well beyond the few examples employed in this chapter. For example, bitmaps can be copied from the screen itself, generated or modified off-screen, saved as external files, or cut and pasted from one window to another.

Bitmap files, including .PCX, .IMG, and other formats, are the principal method of storing image data. However, Windows also supports another format, known as a *metafile*, which is a description of an image written as a record of the GDI function calls necessary to create the image. Metafile operations, as used with the Windows clipboard, are discussed further in Chapter 32.

This chapter included two programs to demonstrate bitmap operations: The PenDraw4 program shows how to use resource bitmaps to create brushes, and the PenDraw5 program demonstrates how to work with DIBs (device-independent bitmaps). The listings for these two programs are on the CD that accompanies this book.

Typefaces and Styles

- ■ Text-output features

- ■ Windows' default fonts

- ■ Logical font selection

- ■ Font characteristics

- ■ Font sizing and mapping modes

Windows NT and 95 provide both a selection of typefaces and the capabilities to vary these typefaces with considerable convenience and flexibility. You've seen examples of text operations throughout the examples provided so far. Now it's time to examine a few of the advanced text features, including font selection, font sizing, text justification, character weighting, and other style-related changes.

Before we get to fonts and typefaces, we'll take a closer look at some of Windows' text-output features. There are a few that we haven't covered yet, and they deserve some explanation.

Using Text-Output Features

Thus far in the book, most text display examples have used one of these two general formats:

```
TextOut( hdc, xPos, yPos, lpStr, nCount );

TextOut( hdc, xPos, yPos, szBuff, wsprintf( szBuff,... ) );
```

In the second format, the `wsprintf` function is employed both to return the character count required by the `TextOut` API function and to create a formatted string. But, regardless of the form used, previous examples have, almost exclusively, used the default, flush-left text alignment.

Using the MFC classes, a third format for text display has appeared as:

```
pDC->TextOut( xPos, yPos, csBuff );
```

In this format, no handle to the device context is passed because the `TextOut` function is a member of the `CDC` class. Likewise, since the `CString` instance contains the string-length information, this value is also not required as an argument.

All of these, however, have provided only the simplest form of text display, without alignment, font selection, or special formatting.

Text Alignment

The `SetTextAlign` function provides control not only over the horizontal text alignment, relative to the specified x- and y-coordinate specifications, but also over vertical alignment and current position updating. `SetTextAlign` is called as:

```
SetTextAlign( hdc, wFlags );
```

The SetTextAlign settings affect text displayed using both the TextOut and ExtTextOut functions. The wFlags argument consists of one or more text alignment specifications combined using the OR operator. Eight alignment constants are defined in WinGDI.H. These are listed in Table 25.1.

NOTE The bounding rectangle is a rectangle surrounding the text string, passed as an argument to the TextOut or ExtTextOut function.

TABLE 25.1   Horizontal Text Alignment Flags

Flag ID	Bit Flags	Value	Comments
Vertical Alignment at yPos			
TA_TOP *	0000 0000	0	Aligns with top of bounding rectangle
TA_BASELINE	0001 1000	24	Aligns with baseline of selected font
TA_BOTTOM	0000 1000	8	Aligns with bottom of bounding rectangle
Horizontal Alignment at xPos			
TA_LEFT *	0000 0000	0	Aligns with left side of bounding rectangle
TA_RIGHT	0000 0010	2	Aligns with right side of bounding rectangle
TA_CENTER	0000 0110	6	Aligns with horizontal center of bounding rectangle (current position is not affected)
Current Position Control			
TA_NOUPDATECP *	0000 0000	0	Current position is not updated after TextOut or ExtTextOut calls
TA_UPDATECP	0000 0001	1	Current position is updated after TextOut or ExtTextOut calls
Combined Flags			
TA_MASK	0001 1111	31	TA_BASELINE + TA_CENTER + TA_UPDATECP

* The default flags are TA_LEFT + TA_TOP + TA_NOUPDATECP

Because not all fonts are written horizontally (for example, the Japanese Kanji font is written vertically), two additional flag values substitute for the TA_BASELINE and TA_CENTER flags. These are defined as shown in Table 25.2.

TABLE 25.2   Vertical Text Alignment Flags

Constant	Replaces	Comments
VTA_BASELINE	TA_BASELINE	Reference-point-aligned with baseline of text
VTA_CENTER	TA_CENTER	Reference-point-aligned vertically with center of bounding rectangle

The SetTextAlign function returns an unsigned integer specifying the previous text alignment, or if an error occurs, ERROR is returned.

Extended Text Output Options

The ExtTextOut function expands on the TextOut function. It adds a rectangle specification that can be used for clipping, opaquing, or both and a pointer to an array of data to control character spacing. The ExtTextOut function is called as:

```
ExtTextOut( hdc, xPos, yPos, fOptions, lpRect,
            szString, nCount, lpDx );
```

The hdc, xPos, yPos, szString, and nCount parameters perform in precisely the same fashion as with the TextOut function. The differences are found in the fOptions, lpRect, and lpDx parameters.

- The fOptions parameter may be NULL, or it may be either or both (ORed) of the flag values listed in Table 25.3.

- The lpRect argument points to a RECT structure specifying the enclosing rectangle, or it may be passed as NULL.

- The lpDx argument points to an array of integer values that specify the distance between adjacent character cells in logical units. For example, element lpDx[i] sets the spacing between the origins of the characters szString[i] and szString[i+1]. If lpDx is NULL, the default character spacing is used.

By default, the current position is not updated by calls to ExtTextOut. However, if the SetTextAlign function is called to set TA_UPDATECP, two changes occur.

TABLE 25.3   ExtTextOut Option Flags

Constant	Comments
ETO_CLIPPED	Text is clipped to fit rectangle specification
ETO_OPAQUE	Rectangle is filled using current background color

First, the initial call to ExtTextOut uses the xPos, yPos arguments, updating the current position after drawing the text argument. But, on the second and subsequent calls to ExtTextOut, the xPos and yPos arguments will be ignored and only the current position data will be used. The current position will continue to be updated with the results of each call.

Tabbed Text

Conventionally, graphics text functions have not included any tab provisions, an oversight which is now corrected by the TabbedTextOut function. This function permits an output string to be tabbed according to spacing arguments specified in an lpnTabStopPositions array. The TabbedTextOut function is called as:

```
TabbedTextOut( hdc, xPos, yPos, szString, nCount,
               nTabPositions, lpnTabStopPositions,
               nTabOrigin );
```

The first five arguments are the same as the equivalent arguments in the TextOut function. The difference is that tab characters can be included in the szString argument as embedded \t (or 0x09) characters.

The nTabPositions argument is an integer argument specifying the number of tab stops to be set (the number of entries in the lpnTabStopPositions array) or the number of tab stops to be used. Three variations may be used:

- If nTabPositions is zero (0) and lpnTabStopPositions is NULL, all tabs are expanded to eight times the average character width.

- If nTabPositions is one (1), all tabs are incremented by the first distance specified in the lpnTabStopPositions array.

- If lpnTabStopPositions contains multiple values, subsequent tabs are set according to these values up to the number specified by nTabPositions.

The `lpnTabStopPositions` argument points to an array of tab stops (in increasing order) defined in device units or may be NULL.

The `nTabOrigin` argument is an integer specification, in device units, specifying an initial offset from which the tab specifications are expanded. The `nTabOrigin` argument also allows an application to call `TabbedTextOut` two or more times for a single line, specifying a new offset each time.

Gray Text

The `GrayString` function draws text using a gray brush. It draws gray text by first writing the text in a memory context as a bitmap, graying the bitmap, and then copying the bitmap to the text display. The drawn text is grayed independently of any brush or background color active in the device context used for the display. The font used is the font currently selected in the device context specified by the `hdc` parameter.

The `GrayString` function is called as:

```
GrayString( hdc, hBrush, lpOutputFunct, lpData,
            xPos, yPos, nWidth, nHeight );
```

The `hdc` parameter specifies the device context where the grayed string will be displayed.

The `hBrush` parameter identifies the brush to be used to gray the text.

The `lpOutputFunct` argument is an optional procedure instance address for an application-supplied function to be used to draw the string. If this is specified as NULL, the `TextOut` function will be used.

The `lpData` argument may be a pointer to data to be passed to the `lpOutput-Funct` function, or if `lpOutputFunct` is NULL, must be a pointer to the string to be displayed.

The `xPos` and `yPos` arguments specify, in device coordinates, the starting position of a rectangle bounding the string displayed.

The `nWidth` and `nHeight` arguments specify the width and height, in device units, for the rectangle enclosing the text display. If either parameter is zero (0) and `lpData` is a pointer to a string, `GrayString` calculates the width or height.

A FALSE result is returned if the `GrayString` function fails, if the `lpOutput-Funct` returns failure, or if memory limitations prevent the bitmap from being created.

> **TIP**
>
> You can also draw grayed strings on any device that supports a solid-gray color, without using the `GrayString` function, by using the system color `COLOR_GRAYTEXT`. To do this, call `GetSystColor` to retrieve the color value for `COLOR_GRAYTEXT`. If the result is not zero (0), call `SetTextColor` to select this color before drawing the string directly. If the returned color value is zero, grayed text can only be drawn using the `GrayString` function.

Multiple Text Lines

The `DrawText` function displays formatted text within a specified rectangular area. Unlike the other functions, `DrawText` is specifically designed to display multiple lines, inserting line breaks as required to format the text within the indicated rectangle. The `DrawText` function is called as:

```
DrawText( hdc, szString, nCount, lpRect, wFormat );
```

The `hdc`, `szString`, and `nCount` parameters are used to identify the device context, the string to be printed, and the number of characters in the string. The `lpRect` argument is a pointer to a `RECT` structure identifying a rectangle, in device coordinates, where the text will be drawn.

The fifth argument, `wFormat`, is an unsigned integer and consists of an ORed combination of the flags listed in Table 25.4.

TABLE 25.4   DrawText Format Flags

Constant	Comments
	Horizontal Justification
`DT_LEFT`	Text is aligned flush-left
`DT_CENTER`	Text is centered
`DT_RIGHT`	Text is aligned flush-right

TABLE 25.4 DrawText Format Flags (Continued)

Constant	Comments
	Vertical Justification
DT_TOP	Text is top-justified (single line only)
DT_VCENTER	Text is centered vertically (single line only)
DT_BOTTOM	Text is bottom justified, must be combined with DT_SINGLELINE
	Format and Spacing Instructions
DT_EXTERNALLEADING*	Add font external leading to line spacing
DT_NOCLIP*	Clipping to rectangle disabled (operation is marginally faster)
DT_SINGLELINE	Sets single line only; carriage returns and line feeds do not produce line breaks
DT_WORDBREAK	Enables automatic line breaks at word boundaries as required to fit text to rectangle
DT_EXPANDTABS	Expands tab characters (default is 8 times average character width per tab)
DT_TABSTOP	Sets tab stops using bits 15-8 of the high byte of the low word in wFormat to specify the number of characters for each tab (if zeros, default spacing is used)
DT_NOPREFIX*	Turns off processing of prefix character
DT_INTERNAL*	Not documented
	Automatic Rectangle Calculation
DT_CALCRECT*	Enables automatic calculation of rectangle area but does not draw actual text

* Cannot be used with the DT_TABSTOP flag.

The DT_NOPREFIX flag disables the use of the ampersand (&) character to underline the character immediately following. When DT_NOPREFIX is not set (characters following the ampersand will be underlined), an ampersand can be entered as &&, producing a single & as output.

The DT_CALCRECT flag enables automatic calculation of the rectangle area. If there are multiple lines of text, DrawText uses the rectangle width specified by the lpRect parameter, extending the base of the rectangle to bound the last line of text. If there is only one line of text, DrawText modifies the width (right side) to bound the last character in the line. In both cases, DrawText returns the height of the formatted text but does not draw the actual text.

Device Context Elements

Along with the text-output functions and their flags, the text display is also governed by the active device context. Elements specified by the device context include not only the foreground and background colors, but also how the text display pixels are combined with the existing background image.

By default, when text is drawn, the text background (the area between and around characters) is also filled in using the background color. This drawing mode is the OPAQUE background mode, but it can be changed by calling the SetBkMode function.

```
SetBkMode( hdc, nMode )      // OPAQUE or TRANSPARENT
```

The foreground and background color functions have been used in other examples in this book. In general, they are called as:

```
SetTextColor( hdc, rgbColor );
SetBkColor( hdc, rgbColor );
```

As with pen and brush colors, the rgbColor argument is converted to the nearest solid color supported by the active device. Dithered colors, which are permitted with brushes, are not supported for text or pen displays.

Rather than wondering what colors might be supported, however, the two preceding API calls can be rewritten to request colors that are known to be supported:

```
SetTextColor( hdc, GetSysColor( COLOR_WINDOWTEXT ));
SetBkColor( hdc, GetSysColor( COLOR_WINDOW ));
```

The default colors for the foreground and background are, respectively, black and white. If you want to change these colors, it is also useful to include a provision (in WndProc) to repaint the entire client window when the changes occur. The simplest method, since no system color changes can be made without issuing a notification message to all applications, is to include a WM_SYSCOLORCHANGE response:

```
case WM_SYSCOLORCHANGE:
    InvalidateRect( hwnd );
    break;
```

Using Fonts and Typefaces

An obvious prerequisite for a text display is one or more fonts with which to create the display. In the past, under DOS (in conventional text mode), the system hardware—generally, the video card itself—supplied the display font in the form of a ROM-based, bitmapped character set tailored to the device's display capabilities. Thus CGA video cards supplied one set of bitmaps, EGA video another, and VGA still a third.

Of course, all of this was quite transparent to the software. Applications had no need to ask or to know what the display characteristics consisted of, or even what the display was capable of. Applications simply wrote to the output, in ASCII character codes, and let the hardware take care of the rest. Earlier displays were limited to a single typeface and, essentially, a single type size.

Today, in a graphics environment, the old-style text displays are gone. Graphics displays can not only mix text, graphics, and colors, but can use many different character fonts (typefaces), in many different sizes. Furthermore, they can vary typeface and size in a variety of styles, such as bold and italic, and in many cases, may also vary font widths, slants, and weights.

Programmers now have a wide range of flexibility in handling of graphics text displays. But, to make use of these opportunities, it may help to understand both the origins of type fonts and the characteristics which determine fonts.

Reminiscences of a Printer's Devil

In personal terms (primarily because of a long personal history in the newspaper business beginning long before electronic typesetting), the word *typeface* conjures images of large flat trays of small compartments filled with individual metal characters in an assortment of sizes and typeface designs.

Most of the typesetting, of course, was accomplished by a huge and intricate machine known as a linotype and operated by a highly skilled (and very well paid) individual who knew the precision mechanics of the triple keyboard, as well as the massive armatures and injection molds that for many decades produced newspapers, books, and the bulk of all manner of printed material.

Larger type sizes, such as those used for ads, headlines, and other features, were not supported by the linotype and its banks of molds. These fell to nimble fingers to choose, arrange, and align individual characters from the appropriate trays with a speed which might well have been envied by even expert typists.

Still, by the time I graduated from high school (and, at the same time, completed a 12-year apprenticeship in the mysteries of the newspaper business), it was clear that, soon—at least in technologically historical terms—both the gentle monster and the type trays would be little more than museum exhibits. And, it was not too many years later that both did, indeed, disappear. They were replaced, first, by electronic/optical/photographic processes and then, a scant decade after that, under my own supervision (as a visiting computer consultant), by purely electronic processes.

Today, of course, these are only the memories of a one-time printer's devil. But, even if the old order has passed, the type tray and linotype laid the foundations for the modern world. They are reflected not only in modern fonts and typestyles, but in the terminology that defines font characteristics and in the methods that manipulate their appearance.

A Brief History of Typefaces

When computers were young, typefaces were an embellishment limited to high-end, hard-copy devices, such as daisywheel printers; even then, they were changed only by physically changing the print wheel. For computer monitors, type styles were quite simply firmware built into the system. In general, they consisted of 8-by-8 or 8-by-9 bitmapped (also called *raster*) characters for CGA video systems. These ranged up to 8-by-18 bitmapped characters for VGA systems.

Bitmapped Fonts

Figure 25.1 shows three bitmapped characters in an 8-by-12 format. Bitmapped fonts have some obvious advantages. Since each character's pixel image is already defined, the character can be transferred to the screen by simply copying the bit pattern directly to the video. This process is speedy and places minimal demands on system resources.

FIGURE 25.1

Bitmapped fonts

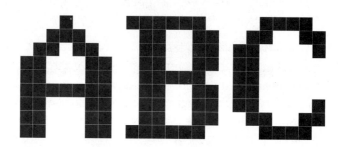

However, there are disadvantages to using bitmapped fonts. They can be resized only as simple multiples and cannot be created in any in-between sizes. When enlarged, the resulting characters tend to be jagged in appearance.

Also, while some systems did offer more than one font, the selection was generally limited to two or three sizes, such as font provisions for a 43- or 50-line display as alternatives to the standard 25 lines, but without offering any variations in style, pitch, or weight. Of course, on early computers, there was little or no demand for larger typefaces or even for varying typefaces. It remained for the advent (and popularity) of graphics display systems to demonstrate the advantages of sizable fonts.

Stroked Fonts

One early approach to creating fonts for a graphics environment involved creating libraries of bitmapped fonts in incremental sizes. As a solution, however, this was never popular for several reasons: because of the sheer mass of data required for the fonts, because of relatively slow response times, and because of the demands on the system memory.

Instead, a different way to define characters was devised (or, more accurately, borrowed from existing typesetting technologies already in use by printers in the newspaper and publishing industries). These are known as *stroked* or *vectored* fonts. In this system, the structure of each character is described by a series of vectors, not by an array of pixels.

There are some disadvantages to the stroked font approach. For small font sizes, the vectored data is, in general, larger than an equivalent bitmapped font and requires more processing to produce each display character. But the disadvantages are minor, placing only minimal demands on modern CPUs and contemporary video systems.

The advantages are tremendous. Stroked fonts can not only be resized, but can be reproportioned, weighted, slanted, rotated, inverted, or otherwise manipulated with minimal effort and maximal effect. And, most important, a single set of font data provides a variety of sizes and styles within a single typeface. Once a font is defined as stroked data, the resulting typeface is available in any size desired—as italics, boldface, or with sufficiently sophisticated processing, as outline, condensed, or extra-bold forms.

Figure 25.2 shows three characters created using a vectored font, sized for 48 points. The *A* shows the vectors defining the character as black lines. The *B* and *C* characters show the outlines after processing.

FIGURE 25.2

A stroked, or
vectored, font

Under the Windows NT system, the older, bitmapped fonts have been largely (but not entirely) discarded in favor of stroked fonts.

Windows Default Fonts

Windows NT and 95 supply the 15 standard fonts shown in Figure 25.3. Each of these fonts appears in its default height, width, and weight (displayed by the Fonts demo program presented in this chapter).

FIGURE 25.3

Fifteen standard fonts

```
The quick brown fox jumps over the lazy red dog. 1234567890
The quick brown fox jumps over the lazy red dog. 1234567890
The quick brown fox jumps over the lazy red dog. 1234567890
The quick brown fox jumps over the lazy red dog. 1234567890
The quick brown fox jumps over the lazy red dog. 1234567890
The quick brown fox jumps over the lazy red dog. 1234567890
The quick brown fox jumps over the lazy red dog. 1234567890
The quick brown fox jumps over the lazy red dog. 123456789
The quick brown fox jumps over the lazy red dog. 1234567890
The quick brown fox jumps over the lazy red dog. 1234567890
Τηε θυιχκ βροων φοξ φυμπσ οπερ τηε λαζψ ρεδ δογ. 1234567890
The quick brown fox jumps over the lazy red dog. 1234567890
The quick brown fox jumps over the lazy red dog
The quick brown fox jumps over the lazy red dog. 1234567890
```

Table 25.5 lists the fonts illustrated, in their order of appearance in Figure 25.3, together with the default height and average width for each. The default weight for all fonts is 400, or normal weight. (See the discussion of the lfWeight field in the "Font Selection Using Logical Fonts" section for more information about font weights.)

TABLE 25.5   Windows Standard Fonts

Font	Height	Avg Width	Comments
Arial	16	6	Proportional sans-serif font; similar to Gothic; True-Type
Courier	16	9	Typewriter or dot-matrix standard (with serifs)
Courier New	16	8	Same as Courier but slightly narrower; True-Type
Fixedsys	15	8	Fixed-width OEM (system) font (sans-serif)

TABLE 25.5 Windows Standard Fonts (Continued)

Font	Height	Avg Width	Comments
Modern	18	10	Proportional sans-serif stroked font
MS Sans Serif	16	7	Another sans-serif with narrower defaults
MS Serif	16	6	Proportional serif font; similar to Times-Roman
Roman	18	11	Serif equivalent of Modern; similar spacing
Script	18	8	Note that Script appears small for point size
Small Fonts	11	5	Small sans-serif font; good for readable fine print; True-Type
Symbol	16	8	Provides Greek, math, and other symbols
System	16	7	Proportional-width system font (sans-serif)
Terminal	16	13	A rather broad san-serif font
Times New Roman	17	6	Popular proportional-width, general-purpose font; True-Type
Wingdings	16	13	Useful symbols; also called Dingbats; True-Type

The Courier, Fixedsys, MS Sans Serif, MS Serif, Small Fonts, System, and Terminal fonts are essentially bitmapped fonts.

Of the remaining eight fonts, the Modern, Roman, and Script fonts consist only of strokes. When they are drawn as enlarged characters (for example, at a height of 400 in text mode), they quite clearly show the strokes comprising each character in a fashion similar to the stroked *A* in Figure 25.1.

The other five fonts—Arial, Courier New, Symbol, Times New Roman, and Wingdings—are stroked outline (or True-Type) fonts. Stroked outline fonts are created as outline strokes with the interiors filled. When these are drawn in larger sizes, they remain fully solid, even though at larger sizes their outlines may begin to show a slight grain or irregularity.

A Note about Typeface Names

Because many of the old-standard typeface names, such as Gothic and Times-Roman, are copyrighted trademarks referring to specific font designs, essentially similar computer-based fonts received new names. For example, the Swiss and Arial fonts are both sans-serif fonts equivalent to the traditional Gothic. Dutch, Roman, and Times New Roman refer to serif fonts similar in design to the popular Times-Roman family of fonts (which, for many decades, were the stock typefaces found in the bulk of all newspaper and magazine text.)

There are, of course, thousands of other typefaces that belong to neither the Gothic nor Roman families. These range from the traditional Old English to the post-modern Avant Gardé. Their names range across the alphabet from Aardvark to Mystical to Zurich-Calligraphic. Their styles range from clarity to obscurity to whimsy.

Font Selection Using Logical Fonts

While you might think of font selection as simply being a matter of requesting a typeface and specifying a character size, for computers, this is a bit too simple. This is not because computers require complexity, but because a font—even a sizable font—still has to match the display characteristics of the device, at least to a minimal degree.

Thus, instead of simply naming a typeface and size, an application makes a request identifying the font name, size, and other characteristics desired. And, for this purpose, the LOGFONT structure is defined in WinGDI.H as:

```
typedef struct tagLOGFONTA
{
    LONG  lfHeight;
    LONG  lfWidth;
    LONG  lfEscapement;
    LONG  lfOrientation;
    LONG  lfWeight;
    BYTE  lfItalic;
    BYTE  lfUnderline;
    BYTE  lfStrikeOut;
    BYTE  lfCharSet;
    BYTE  lfOutPrecision;
    BYTE  lfClipPrecision;
```

```
      BYTE lfQuality;
      BYTE lfPitchAndFamily;
      char lfFaceName[LF_FACESIZE];
   }  LOGFONTA;
```

Two structure definitions are provided: `LOGFONTA`, for use with an ANSI environment, and `LOGFONTW`, for use with a wide, or Unicode, character set. However, since the choice of environment is controlled by a compiler directive, the only source code reference required is `LOGFONT`. Depending on the compiler directive, this will be mapped to either the ANSI or Unicode structure, as appropriate.

The following sections describe the fields in the `LOGFONT` structure.

Height and Width Fields

The `lfHeight` field specifies the desired height of the font in logical units. If the value is positive or negative, the absolute value is transformed to device units and matched against the cell heights of the available fonts.

A 0 (zero) height simply instructs the GDI to select a reasonable (default) height. This is normally the smallest size that will accommodate the strokes comprising the font characters.

In all cases, the font mapper looks for the largest font—the most detailed font (character) description—that does not exceed the requested size. If none match this requirement, the smallest available font is used.

The `lfWidth` field specifies the average width (in logical units) of the characters in the font. If `lfWidth` is zero, the device aspect ratio is matched against the digitization aspect ratio; that is, the width in units that the font will require for display. Selection is based on the closest match, or the smallest absolute difference between the two ratios. In general, a 0 value allows the character width to be matched against the character height.

In actual practice, bitmapped fonts, such as the Courier, Fixedsys, MS Sans Serif, MS Serif, Small Fonts, System, and Terminal fonts (illustrated in Figure 25.3 and listed in Table 25.5) are used, as long as the bitmap size matches the display context relatively well. If any of these are enlarged, however, Windows substitutes a default stroked font, usually Arial, which can be more readily sized. (You can see this in action in the Fonts demo program, presented later in the chapter.)

Weight Field

The lfWeight field specifies the desired weight of the font. This field accepts values in the range 0..1000. If lfWeight is 0, a default weight is used (normal). As you can see in Table 25.6, currently only two weights are actually employed: 400 for normal or 700 for bold. However, future versions (probably with higher-resolution displays) are expected to use a wider range of weights.

TABLE 25.6   Font Weights

Weight Constant	Value	Comments	Alternatives
FW_DONTCARE	0		
FW_THIN	100	Not supported	
FW_EXTRALIGHT	200	Not supported	FW_ULTRALIGHT
FW_LIGHT	300	Not supported	
FW_NORMAL	400	Default weight	FW_REGULAR
FW_MEDIUM	500	Not supported	
FW_SEMIBOLD	600	Not supported	FW_DEMIBOLD
FW_BOLD	700	Boldface	
FW_EXTRABOLD	800	Not supported	FW_EXTRABOLD
FW_HEAVY	900	Not supported	FW_BLACK

Italic, Underline, and Strikeout Fields

The lfItalic field is simply a Boolean flag. If TRUE, the font is created as italics (if possible).

The lfUnderline and lfStrikeOut fields operate in the same fashion.

Character Set Field

The lfCharSet field specifies the character set desired. Seven values are predefined in WinGDI.H, as shown in Table 25.7.

TABLE 25.7 Character Set Constants

Character set	Value	Comments
`ANSI_CHARSET`	0	Default; ANSI characters
`UNICODE_CHARSET`	1	Unicode (32-bit) characters
`SYMBOL_CHARSET`	2	Symbols
`SHIFTJIS_CHARSET`	128	Japanese Kanji characters
`HANGEUL_CHARSET`	129	Non-Roman/Arabic characters
`CHINESEBIG5_CHARSET`	136	Chinese characters
`OEM_CHARSET`	255	Device-dependent characters

WARNING   While fonts supporting character sets other than those defined may be present in a system, no attempt should be made to translate or interpret strings to be rendered with such fonts.

Escapement and Orientation Fields

Both the `lfEscapement` and `lfOrientation` fields are expressed in one-tenth degree increments. The `lfEscapement` value sets the string orientation with an angle of 0 degrees for horizontal alignment, increasing in a counter-clockwise direction.

The `lfOrientation` value determines the angle of the character's baseline relative to horizontal. Thus, for a value of 0, a T or L remains vertical; for a value of 900 (90°), the 'T' will be drawn horizontally and the 'L' will be lying on its back.

Table 25.8 summarizes both the text and character orientation at 90-degree intervals for `lfEscapement` and `lfOrientation`.

Out-Precision, Clip-Precision, and Quality Fields

The `lfOutPrecision`, `lfClipPrecision`, and `lfQuality` fields are used to request specific matches between the fonts selected and the device output capabilities.

TABLE 25.8 Text and Character Orientation

Value	Degrees	lfEscapement (String Orientation)	lfOrientation (Character Orientation)
0	0°	left to right (default)	Normal (vertical, default)
900	90°	vertical, rising	Rotated 90° counter-clockwise
1800	180°	right to left	Inverted
2700	270°	vertical, falling	Rotated 90° clockwise

lfOutPrecision defines how closely the actual output must match the requested font's characteristics, such as height, width, orientation, and pitch. Output precision values are defined as shown in Table 25.9.

TABLE 25.9 Output Precision

Constant	Value	Comments
OUT_DEFAULT_PRECIS	0	
OUT_STRING_PRECIS	1	Maintain string precision
OUT_CHARACTER_PRECIS	2	Maintain character precision
OUT_STROKE_PRECIS	3	Maintain stroke precision
OUT_TT_PRECIS	4	New, not documented; support unknown
OUT_DEVICE_PRECIS	5	New, not documented; support unknown
OUT_RASTER_PRECIS	6	New, not documented; support unknown
OUT_TT_ONLY_PRECIS	7	New, not documented; support unknown
OUT_OUTLINE_PRECIS	8	Maintain outline precision

The lfClipPrecision field specifies how characters that are partially outside the clipping region are clipped. Eight values are defined in WinGDI.H, as shown in Table 25.10.

> **NOTE**
> Several of the flag values for the `lfOutPrecision`, `lfClipPrecision`, and `lfQuality` fields are new and may or may not be fully supported by present versions of Windows NT and/or by present video and output device drivers. Before you rely on a specific precision flag, you should experiment with it. Unimplemented precision flags may be supported later or may be supported by specific device drivers.

TABLE 25.10 Clipping Precision

Constant	Value	Comments
CLIP_DEFAULT_PRECIS	00h	
CLIP_CHARACTER_PRECIS	01h	Clip entire character
CLIP_STROKE_PRECIS	02h	Clip only strokes
CLIP_MASK	0Fh	New, not documented; support unknown
CLIP_LH_ANGLES	10h	New, not documented; support unknown
CLIP_TT_ALWAYS	20h	New, not documented; support unknown
CLIP_EMBEDDED	80h	New, not documented; support unknown

The `lfQuality` field specifies the desired output quality, which is how well the output (physical font) is matched to the requested logical-font attributes. Three values are defined in WinGDI.H, as shown in Table 25.11.

Pitch and Family Field

The `lfPitchAndFamily` field specifies both the pitch (spacing) and the font family. The two low-order bits specify the font spacing, using one of the three values defined in WinGDI.H, as shown in Table 25.12.

The high-order nibble of the `lfPitchAndFamily` byte specifies a family of fonts and can be any of the six values defined in WinGDI.H, as shown in Table 25.13.

TABLE 25.11 Output Quality Specifications

Constant	Value	Comments
DEFAULT_QUALITY	00h	Appearance not important
DRAFT_QUALITY	01h	Appearance of minimal importance; font scaling fully enabled for all GDI fonts; bold, italic, underline, and strikeout synthesized as necessary
PROOF_QUALITY	02h	Character quality more important than matching logical font attributes; GDI font scaling disabled; only closest font sizes chosen; bold, italic, underline, and strikeout synthesized as necessary

TABLE 25.12 Font Pitch

Pitch Constant	Value	Comments
DEFAULT_PITCH	00h	Don't care or don't know
FIXED_PITCH	01h	Fixed spacing (characters per inch)
VARIABLE_PITCH	02h	Variable spacing (proportional)

TABLE 25.13 Font Family

Family Constant	Value	Comments
FF_DONTCARE	00h	Don't care or don't know
FF_ROMAN	10h	Serif, variable character width, such as Times Roman and Century Schoolbook
FF_SWISS	20h	Sans-serif, variable character width, such as Helvetica and Swiss
FF_MODERN	30h	Constant character width, serif or sans-serif, such as Pica, Elite, and Courier
FF_SCRIPT	40h	Cursive, for example
FF_DECORATIVE	50h	Old English, for example

Face Name Field

The `lfFaceName` field contains the address of a null-terminated string specifying the typeface name of the desired font. The string must not exceed 32 characters. If no font name is specified (the argument is NULL), the GDI uses a default typeface such as Arial.

Demonstrating Logical Fonts: The Fonts Program

The Fonts program provides a platform to demonstrate the three principal features of using logical fonts:

- Using the `EnumFonts` function to list available typefaces
- Setting font characteristics (height, width, and so on)
- Showing fonts under different mapping modes

The Fonts program screen is shown in Figure 25.4.

FIGURE 25.4

The Fonts program

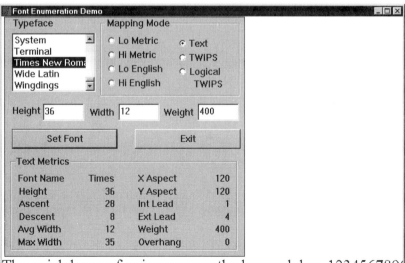

> **NOTE**
>
> A standard font selection dialog box is supplied through the MFC `CFontDialog` class as one of the Windows common dialogs. The advantage of using the standard Fonts dialog is that you do not need to provide your own font-selection mechanisms. For an example of the common font dialog, refer to the FontView demo included with the Visual C++ compiler.

Font Selection

The first feature demonstrated in the Fonts program is the use of the `EnumFonts` function to query the GDI and list all available typefaces, in this case, by loading the font names in a list box.

As a first step, the record type `FONTLIST` requires definition:

```
typedef struct tagFONTLIST
{
    GLOBALHANDLE  hGMem;
    int           nCount;
} FONTLIST;
```

A variable of type `FONTLIST` will be used to record a list of fonts and the number of fonts located.

In most of the other demo programs in this book, the `WndProc` procedure provides the heart of the application. In addition to message handling, this procedure is responsible for a greater or lesser portion of the application's task handling. In contrast, in the Fonts application, the majority of the work is shifted away from the `WndProc` procedure to a modeless dialog box and the `DlgProc` procedure handling messages addressed to the dialog box. The few provisions necessary in `WndProc` for creating `DlgProc` should, at this point, already be familiar to you from many of the previous examples.

The exported `DlgProc` procedure begins by declaring two static variables. One of these is `lpEnumProc`, a pointer to the `FontEnumFunc` procedure, which will actually make the call to the API `EnumProc` function. The other is a `FontList` variable to point to the returned data (the typeface names). A third variable is declared as a long pointer to a string, `lpFontName`, providing a second handle to the font list.

```
BOOL APIENTRY DlgProc( HWND hDlg, UINT msg,
                       UINT wParam, LONG lParam )
```

```
{
    static FARPROC  lpEnumProc;
    static FONTLIST FontList;
    LPSTR           lpFontName;
    HDC             hdc;
    int             i, nSel;
    char            szFont[LF_FACESIZE];
```

In response to the WM_INITDIALOG message, another call is made to the Make-ProcInstance macro to return a handle (lpEnumProc) to the FontEnumFunc procedure. This handle will be used to tell the EnumFonts function where to find the FontEnumFunc callback function.

```
switch( msg )
{
    case WM_INITDIALOG:
        ...
        lpEnumProc = MakeProcInstance( FontEnumFunc, hInst );
        FontList.hGMem = GlobalAlloc( GMEM_MOVEABLE |
                                      GMEM_ZEROINIT, 1L );
        FontList.nCount = 0;
```

The FontList variable also requires initialization by allocating and zeroing one (1) byte, returning the memory pointer to the FontList.hGMem field. Additional memory will be allocated as required, but since the number of fonts is not presently known, it would be pointless to attempt to allocate memory for an unknown number of strings at this time. The FontList.nCount field is also initialized to 0 but will be used presently to track the number of typefaces found.

The next requirement is a device context handle (hdc), which is obtained using GetParent(hDlg) to return a device context for the main application window rather than the dialog window. And, finally, the EnumFonts API function is called using the retrieved device context handle, a pointer to the FontEnumProc function and a pointer to the FontList variable.

```
        hdc = GetDC( GetParent( hDlg ) );
        EnumFonts( hdc, NULL, lpEnumProc, (LPVOID) &FontList );
```

The second parameter, passed as NULL in this example, could have been used, as a long pointer to a string (LPSTR), to specify a particular typeface; in effect, to query if a specific typeface was available. But, by passing this specification as NULL, all available typefaces will be reported.

The FontEnumProc procedure, while not an exported procedure in the usual sense of receiving messages directly from Windows, is used as a callback function by the EnumFonts API function.

The FontEnumProc procedure is called from EnumFonts with four parameters: a pointer to a LOGFONT structure reporting the logical attributes of a font, a pointer to a TEXTMETRIC structure reporting the physical font attributes, a short integer indicating the font type (bit flags), and the same far pointer to FontList that was originally passed to EnumFonts.

```
int APIENTRY FontEnumFunc( LPLOGFONT       lf,
                           LPTEXTMETRIC    tm,
                           short           nFontType,
                           FONTLIST FAR *  FontList )
{
    LPSTR lpFontFace;
```

The first task accomplished in the FontEnumFunc procedure is a GlobalReAlloc to allocate enough additional memory for one more typeface name. If this is successful, GlobalLock is called to ensure that the memory allocated is not moved until the present task is finished.

```
    if( ! GlobalReAlloc( FontList->hGMem,
                         (DWORD) LF_FACESIZE *
                         ( FontList->nCount + 1 ),
                         GMEM_MOVEABLE ) )
        return( FALSE );
    lpFontFace = GlobalLock( FontList->hGMem );
    lstrcpy( lpFontFace + ( ( FontList->nCount ) * LF_FACESIZE ),
            (LPSTR) lf->lfFaceName );
    GlobalUnlock( FontList->hGMem );
    FontList->nCount++;
    return( TRUE );
}
```

Once memory is allocated and locked, the font name (lf->lfFaceName) reported by EnumFonts is copied to the offset of the newly allocated memory, the memory is unlocked, and FontList->nCount is incremented.

NOTE

As you may have already realized, the bulk of the information passed by `EnumFonts` has been discarded; only the font name has been retained. But, in this case, the font name is all that we really need. Actually, there wasn't any choice about what information was passed to the `Fonts-EnumFunc` procedure from the `EnumFonts` API function. The only choice was to select which portion was actually wanted, discarding the excess. (We'll talk about another alternative in a bit.)

The next step is to copy the font list into the list box in the dialog box. And, again, this process begins by globally locking the memory where the data is stored.

```
lpFontName = GlobalLock( FontList.hGMem );
SendDlgItemMessage( hDlg, IDD_FONTLIST, WM_SETREDRAW,
                    (WPARAM) 1, (LPARAM) 0 );
SendDlgItemMessage( hDlg, IDD_FONTLIST,
                    LB_RESETCONTENT, NULL, NULL );
```

Before copying the data, however, as a precaution, two initial messages were sent to the list box to instruct it to be redrawn. These ensure that the new data will be visible. Also, a reset message was sent to clear any contents that the list box might happen to contain.

Once this housekeeping is out of the way, a simple loop, using `FontList.nCount` as the limit, copies the string data. The names are copied one item at a time, using the same offset addresses as before, into the list box.

```
for( i=0; i<FontList.nCount; i++ )
 SendDlgItemMessage( hDlg, IDD_FONTLIST, LB_ADDSTRING, 0,
    (LPARAM)(LPSTR)( lpFontName + ( i * LF_FACESIZE ) ) );
GlobalUnlock( FontList.hGMem );
GlobalFree( FontList.hGMem );
FontList.hGMem = NULL;
FreeProcInstance( lpEnumProc );
ReleaseDC( GetParent( hDlg ), hdc );
```

After the data has been copied over to the list box, the allocated memory (`hGMem`) is no longer required nor is the address variable for the `FontEnumProc` procedure. Therefore, the allocated memory is unlocked and freed, the `lpEnumProc` function handle is freed, and to finish the housekeeping, the device context is released.

Finally, after calling the ShowMetrics function to update the dialog box display, the WM_INITDIALOG response, rather than returning on a break; statement, is allowed to fall through to the WM_SETFOCUS message response, setting the active focus to the dialog box.

```
ShowMetrics( hDlg );   // fall through to SetFocus

case WM_SETFOCUS:
    SetFocus( GetDlgItem( hDlg, IDD_HEIGHT ) );
    break;
```

At this point, the list box in the dialog is primed with a list of available fonts, ready for the user to select the typeface desired. And, when this is done, the dialog box display will be updated to reflect the selection. The main application window will display the sample text string using the chosen typeface.

> **TIP**
>
> If the process of retrieving the font list seems rather round-about, a portion could be simplified. For instance, what about rewriting the FontEnumFunc callback function to load the list box directly? This would simplify matters, wouldn't it? This is an experiment you may want to try.

Varying Font Characteristics

In addition to allowing the user to select typefaces from the list box, the Fonts demo program also provides three edit boxes for entry of height, width, and weight specifications. Values entered in these three edit boxes are used (when the Set Font button is clicked) in the tm (text metric) request that selects the new font (or new size).

The resulting text metrics information reported at the bottom of the dialog box (see Figure 25.4) may or may not provide a precise match for the request parameters. Instead, the resulting text metrics reported represent the best match found by the GDI and reflect the actual font displayed in the application's main window (immediately below the dialog box).

> **TIP** In the Font program's current form, only four of the text metric fields can be edited directly or indirectly; these are the height, width, weight, and typeface. The remaining fields are assigned default values. As another experiment, you could add control features for any or all of the other text metrics.

Font Sizing and Mapping Modes

The Fonts program also includes a provision for selecting the different mapping modes. The principal function of this part of the program is to allow you to see how different fonts appear when resized, how fonts can be changed proportionally by varying the width and height, and how the GDI selects fonts appropriate to the mapping mode and sizes requested. (For more information about mapping modes, see Chapter 21.)

Notice particularly that, when one of the bitmapped fonts is requested in a too-large size, the GDI replaces it with a stroked or outline font, which is more suitable for the purpose.

> **TIP** You may wish to change the defaults assigned to the `lfPitchAndFamily` specification and observe how this affects the GDI's choices. Last, for the adventurous or the dedicated, the `lfEscapement` and `lfOrientation` fields offer ample opportunities for departure from the straight and horizontal. Please feel free to explore the possibilities.

The real test of typeface flexibility, of course, lies in the applications using these facilities. Any shortcomings are more likely to lie in the application design than in the provided resources.

As you have seen, the basic tools permit virtually any degree of text elaboration desired. For those requiring additional typefaces, a variety of fonts are available from third-party sources. You can also find toolkits for designing custom fonts.

The listing for the Fonts program is on the CD that accompanies this book. This should provide you with the basic structure for designing your own font-manipulation facilities. Have fun.

CHAPTER

TWENTY-SIX

26

Graphics Utilities and File Operations

- A screen-capture program for bitmap images

- Bitmap compression techniques

- Commands for handling graphics files

- A PCX file viewer

- Techniques for converting 24-bit color images

A variety of formats have been developed for saving, storing, and displaying graphics images. A number of popular formats predated Windows, including ZSoft's Paintbrush PCX, CompuServe's GIF (Graphics Information Format) and, for more demanding circumstances, Truevision Inc.'s TARGA or TGA formats. And today, Windows has its own native BMP (or bitmap) format.

These formats all have one factor in common: Each is designed for a specific image type or system. TrueVision's TGA images, for example, are designed for video camera images, generally incorporating 16, 24, or 32 bits of color per pixel. In contrast, ZSoft's PCX, CompuServe's GIF, and Windows BMP formats are palette based, encoding images by first including palette color information in the image file and then referencing the individual pixels as palette colors.

In this chapter, we'll take a look at how to handle graphics files. We'll begin with a demo program that captures Windows bitmap images either to the clipboard or to a file. Then we'll cover commands for handling graphics files, treatments for file formats other than the native BMP files, and techniques for converting 24-bit color images.

Capturing and Displaying Screen Images: The Capture Program

Under Windows, where all displays are graphical in nature, a graphics screen-capture utility can be a basic tool for transferring graphics information among applications or for simply saving images for later use. Capturing a screen under Windows is greatly expedited and simplified by procedures inherent within Windows.

Principal among these is the Windows clipboard, a facility that provides both storage and information transfer among Windows applications. (While the clipboard handles several types of information, each with its own format, only the graphics image or bitmap format is relevant to this discussion.)

As an example of the use of the clipboard to store a bitmap, take a look at Figure 26.1. This figure was created using the Capture demo program.

Figure 26.1 is neither a trick nor a composite. It's an actual screen display that begins with loading three instances of the Capture program. Initially, two windows were reduced to icons, and the third window was used to capture the screen to the system clipboard. Note also that during the capture process, the third

FIGURE 26.1

Two captured views

instance has automatically reduces itself to an icon at the bottom of the screen. It resumes normal size after the capture is completed.

When the minimized Capture program returns to normal size, any bitmap image that has been transferred to the clipboard is automatically displayed by all active Capture program windows, as well as the clipboard viewer, if it's active.

In this screen, however, a second instance of the Capture program is also restored to normal size, providing two views of the captured image. One Capture window, in the upper left, is using the Normal display mode; the second window, in the lower-right, is using the Size To Screen option, which in this example shrinks the full-screen image to fit the Capture window. (As you can see, this shrinkage is not always faithful to the original.)

Last, the third Capture instance was called to capture the entire screen containing the first two instances, which were already displaying a previous capture. But this time, rather than capturing the image to the clipboard for display, the image was written directly to a .BMP file. The instance making the capture has reduced

Graphics before Video Monitors

Before computers acquired video monitors (and, yes, there was such a time, although most of us have happily forgotten those benighted days), computer graphics were pretty simple. They generally consisted of graphics ingeniously printed using the standard text characters supported by hard-copy devices. Granted, there were also some rather expensive devices, known as plotters, which even though slow, were somewhat less limited than most printers. Most hard-copy devices, however, were simply glorified typewriters or, for some users, converted teletype machines.

When dot-matrix printers appeared, there was a small but determined stampede of attempts to extend the internal character sets—first in the form of extended ASCII (graphics) characters and then in the form of direct control over the print heads to produce graphics images using dots.

Later, even after video monitors became common, graphics remained fairly restricted, not because of any lack of expertise by the developers, but rather because of the fact that programmers could not depend on the end user's equipment being capable of supporting elaborate graphics displays. Even sophisticated applications relied on the elaborate use of the extended ASCII character set, with or without reverse video, to present semi-graphical title screens.

itself to an icon during capture and, therefore, has lost the active focus, which by default, has reverted to one of the open windows.

Both capture processes, To Clipboard and To File, include a five-second time delay (audible beeps are sounded at one-second intervals during the wait time), during which the operator may use the mouse or keyboard to shift the active focus, to select a different application window, to pull down menus, or to activate other features.

Also, because the third instance has saved the image to a file rather than to the clipboard, the previously displayed image is not replaced. If a different utility were used to capture a bitmap to the clipboard, both of the Capture windows would display that image, or any other image loaded to the clipboard.

The Capture utility stores and retrieves only information that is in bitmap format. Other types of information loaded to the clipboard, such as data, metafiles, or other formats, are ignored.

Capturing Screen Image Information

Screen capture is based on rectangular coordinates that define the area to be copied. For the example, the Capture program simply checks the size of the Desktop (the main screen), using the HWND_DESKTOP window handle, to capture the entire display. Other capture applications could include provisions to select only the active application's display, to select only a specific window, or to use the mouse to select some other rectangular area.

In operation, because the Capture menu offers the To Clipboard and To File choices, two responses are provided for the WM_COMMAND/IDM_CLIP and WM_COMMAND/IDM_FILE messages:

```
case WM_COMMAND:
   switch( LOWORD( wParam ) )
   {
      ...
      case IDM_CLIP:
         Action = TOCLIPBD;
         CloseWindow( hwnd );
         Clock = SetTimer( hwnd, 1, 1000, NULL );
         iSec = 0;
         break;

      case IDM_FILE:
         if( DialogBox( hInst, "GETNAME", hwnd,
                        FileNameDlgProc ) )
         {
            Action = TOFILE;
            CloseWindow( hwnd );
            Clock = SetTimer( hwnd, 1, 1000, NULL );
            iSec = 0;
         }
         break;
```

The two responses are essentially the same. The difference is that before an image can be saved to a file, the `FileNameDlgProc` is invoked, requesting a filename and, optionally, a drive and path specification.

In both responses, the `CloseWindow` API is called to minimize the Capture application before initializing a timer for one-second intervals and setting the seconds counter (`iSec`) to zero.

Subsequently, as `WM_TIMER` messages are received, `iSec` is incremented. Until `iSec` reaches five seconds (or whatever interval is desired), the `MessageBeep` function is called to provide an audible timer signal.

```
case WM_TIMER:
    if( ++iSec == 5 )
        PostMessage( hwnd, WM_COMMAND, IDM_CAPTURE, 0 );
    else
        MessageBeep( MB_ICONEXCLAMATION );
    break;
```

NOTE
The sound (waveform) associated with each `MB_ICONxxxxx` constant may be changed using the Control Panel's Sound dialog box. These assignments, however, are under the control of the user, not the application.

The `MB_ICONEXCLAMATION` argument used here in calling the `MessageBeep` API function is probably more familiar as an argument in a `MessageBox` API call requesting inclusion of the exclamation icon. However, the `MB_ICONEXCLAMATION` constant, as well as the `MB_ICONASTERISK`, `MB_ICONHAND`, `MB_ICONQUESTION`, and `MB_OK` constants, can also be used as parameters to request a system sound that is defined as a .WAV waveform file and reproduced by a sound card, such as Sound Blaster. If no sound card is installed, the system speaker will provide the traditional default beep using the system's internal speaker.

Next, when the `IDM_CAPTURE` message is received, a final beep is issued and the timer process is halted (killed) before either the `SaveBitmap` function is called to create a bitmap file or the `CaptureBitmap` function is called to copy the image to the clipboard.

```
case IDM_CAPTURE:
   MessageBeep( MB_OK );
   KillTimer( hwnd, Clock );
   SetCursor( LoadCursor( NULL, IDC_WAIT ) );
   switch( Action )
   {
      case TOFILE:
         SaveBitmap();             break;
      case TOCLIPBD:
         CaptureBitmap( hwnd ); break;
   }
   SetCursor( LoadCursor( NULL, IDC_ARROW ) );
   OpenIcon( hwnd );
   break;
```

Once the appropriate process is completed, the OpenIcon API function is called to restore the application to its original window size and state. At this time, the application also regains the active focus.

The two capture processes, CaptureBitmap and SaveBitmap, use parallel operations but are not identical.

Capturing to the Clipboard

The CaptureBitmap process begins by calling the GetDC API function but, instead of using the application's window handle (hwnd), the Desktop handle is used as HWND_DESKTOP.

```
int CaptureBitmap( HWND hwnd )
{
   HDC          hdc, hdcMem;
   HBITMAP      hBitmap;
   static int   i, j, CRes, LnWidth, LnPad = 0,
                xSize, ySize;

   SetCursor( LoadCursor( NULL, IDC_WAIT ) );
   hdc = GetDC( HWND_DESKTOP );
   xSize = GetDeviceCaps( hdc, HORZRES );
   ySize = GetDeviceCaps( hdc, VERTRES );
```

Once a handle to the Desktop device context has been retrieved, the GetDevice-Caps function can be used to query the current display resolution. To capture only a specific application's window, the parallel process would be to simply use the application's handle; for example, you could use the GetFocus API function to retrieve a handle for the active application's window.

The next step is to create a memory context that is compatible with the selected device context, and then to create a compatible bitmap.

```
hdcMem = CreateCompatibleDC( hdc );
hBitmap = CreateCompatibleBitmap( hdc, xSize, ySize );
```

Notice that the compatible bitmap created here is not a display bitmap. Rather, hdcMem is a memory device context handle that contains a copy of the display image. This way, the image data can be manipulated without affecting the actual display.

The next step includes a provisional test, before proceeding, to ensure that a valid bitmap handle was returned. If the call to CreateCompatibleBitmap is successful, hBitmap will be non-NULL and the capture process can proceed by calling SelectObject to select the bitmap, hBitmap, into the logical context, hdcMem. However, it is the subsequent StretchBlt instruction that actually transfers the image from the screen to the memory device-context handle.

```
if( hBitmap )
{
    SelectObject( hdcMem, hBitmap );
    StretchBlt( hdcMem, 0, 0, xSize, ySize,
                hdc,    0, 0, xSize, ySize, SRCCOPY );
```

Although both BitBlt and StretchBlt provide a means of copying information between display contexts (hdc and hdcMem in this example), StretchBlt optionally provides the additional capability of stretching (or shrinking) the image to fit the available display space. The BitBlt function simply executes an exact copy.

NOTE Notice that even though StretchBlt is being used for the transfer, the source and destination rectangles are the same size. Thus, no distortion is imposed on the image being copied. The StretchBlt operation is necessary to copy the image pixels from the active device context to the memory context, where they become the bitmap referenced by the hBitmap handle.

The memory device context, however, is not our actual destination for this bitmap. Rather, `hdcMem` is used as an environment where the copy of the original image can be stretched or shrunk to fit the application's display context.

We want to give the bitmap a more permanent storage location and make it accessible to other applications. Calling `OpenClipboard` opens the clipboard for examination. The next instruction, `EmptyClipboard`, gives the current application temporary ownership of the clipboard, dumping the current contents (if any) of the clipboard.

```
OpenClipboard( hwnd );
EmptyClipboard();
SetClipboardData( CF_BITMAP, hBitmap );
CloseClipboard();
```

Next, `SetClipboard` is called to transfer the new material—the bitmap image—to the clipboard, specifying the data type with the `CF_BITMAP` argument. And last, `CloseClipboard` is called, releasing ownership of the clipboard.

> **NOTE**
>
> The preceding sequence is a fairly standard example of clipboard use, beginning with `OpenClipboard` and ending with the `CloseClipboard` command. Between the `Open...` and `Close...` commands, a variety of different actions can be executed. But, remember that control (ownership) of the clipboard is always temporary and should be relinquished as quickly as possible. See Chapter 33 for more information about clipboard operations.

Finally, as with any process, a degree of cleanup is required. It begins, still within the conditional process, by invalidating the application's window to ensure that the application will be repainted after it is restored:

```
InvalidateRect( hwnd, NULL, TRUE );
}
DeleteDC( hdcMem );
ReleaseDC( HWND_DESKTOP, hdc );
return 0;
}
```

The remaining cleanup provisions are not conditional but consist simply of deleting the memory context and releasing the device context.

As you can see, the big advantage in using the clipboard is simplicity. The operations involved are brief and uncomplicated, and in execution are also quite speedy. Unfortunately, the corresponding operations directed toward building a bitmap file are not quite so simple and execute more slowly, although only marginally so.

Painting from the Clipboard

In response to the WM_PAINT message, the Capture program displays any bitmap image contained by the Clipboard, regardless of the source of the image. Again, the first step (after initializing the customary device context) is to open the clipboard. This time, however, the EmptyClipboard function is not called and the application does not assume ownership, only access.

```
case WM_PAINT:
    hdc = BeginPaint( hwnd, &ps );
    OpenClipboard( hwnd );
    if( hBitmap = GetClipboardData( CF_BITMAP ) )
    {
        SetCursor( LoadCursor( NULL, IDC_WAIT ) );
        hdcMem = CreateCompatibleDC( hdc );
        SelectObject( hdcMem, hBitmap );
        GetObject( hBitmap, sizeof( BITMAP ),
                   (LPSTR) &bm );
```

This time, the hBitmap handle is used to retrieve the bitmap from the clipboard. If there is no bitmap image, the process is aborted.

Two methods of displaying a retrieved image are used: either actual-size or sized-to-fit. In the first case, the BitBlt function is used to execute a direct copy to the window. In the second instance, the StretchBlt function is called to copy the bitmap to fit the application window.

```
if( fExpand )
{
    SetStretchBltMode( hdc, iStrMode );
    StretchBlt( hdc, 0, 0, cxWnd, cyWnd,
                hdcMem, 0, 0,
                bm.bmWidth, bm.bmHeight,
                SRCCOPY );
}
else
    BitBlt( hdc, 0, 0, cxWnd, cyWnd,
```

```
                      hdcMem, 0, 0, SRCCOPY );
        SetCursor( LoadCursor( NULL, IDC_ARROW ) );
        DeleteDC( hdcMem );
   }
```

Last, the `CloseClipboard` function must be called before the paint operation concludes:

```
CloseClipboard();
EndPaint( hwnd, &ps );
break;
```

Capturing to a File

Capturing a bitmap to the clipboard is a task well-supported by Windows API functions, making this task almost automatic. In contrast, a similar capture to a file format is less well supported, requiring several specific subtasks to create a .BMP file image.

> **NOTE** The MFC `CBitmap` class does provide some further support. However, this class implementation is also woefully incomplete.

Bitmap Image File Structure

A bitmap image file consists of three parts:

- A file header (`BITMAPFILEHEADER`)
- An information header (`BITMAPINFOHEADER`), which includes color palette information
- The actual image information

Of these, the palette information and the image data vary in structure, depending on the type of color information and the encoding method (or lack thereof) used to store the image data.

Before any of these information structures can be created, however, the first step is to create a device context and to retrieve information about the device context and about parameters, which will be used to describe the bitmap image. As with the process for capturing to the clipboard, this example begins by using the HWND_DESKTOP handle to retrieve a device context handle. It then continues by querying the palette size and bits per pixel, as well as the horizontal and vertical device resolution.

```
int SaveBitmap()
{
    HDC        hdc, hdcMem;
    HANDLE     hBits, hFil;
    HBITMAP    hBitmap;
    HPALETTE   hPal;
    LPVOID     lpBits;
    RGBQUAD    RGBQuad;
    DWORD      ImgSize, plSize, dwWritten;
    int        i, CRes, Height, Width, LnWidth, LnPad;
    BITMAPFILEHEADER    bmFH;
    BITMAPINFO          bmInfo;
    LPLOGPALETTE        lp;

    SetCursor( LoadCursor( NULL, IDC_WAIT ) );
//=== open file for write =================================
    hFil = CreateFile( szFName, GENERIC_WRITE, 0,  NULL,
              CREATE_ALWAYS, FILE_ATTRIBUTE_NORMAL, NULL );
    if( hFil == NULL )
       return( ErrorMsg( "Can't open file" ) );

    hdc = GetDC( HWND_DESKTOP );
    CRes = GetDeviceCaps( hdc, SIZEPALETTE );
    plSize = CRes * sizeof( RGBQUAD );        // palette size
    bmInfo.bmiHeader.biBitCount =
       GetDeviceCaps( hdc, BITSPIXEL );
    Height = GetDeviceCaps( hdc, VERTRES );
    Width  = GetDeviceCaps( hdc, HORZRES );
    if( GetDeviceCaps( hdc, BITSPIXEL ) == 8 )
       LnWidth = Width;
    else
       LnWidth = Width / 2;
    if( LnWidth % sizeof(DWORD) )
       LnPad = sizeof(DWORD) - ( LnWidth % sizeof(DWORD) );
    ImgSize = (DWORD)( (DWORD)( LnWidth + LnPad ) * 480 );
```

As the necessary raw information is retrieved, several local data variables are also calculated, including the raw image size, palette size, and the width of the individual scan lines.

The File Header   The bitmap file begins with a file header defined by the BIT-MAPFILEHEADER structure, which holds information about the type, size, and layout of a DIB (device-independent bitmap) file.

The BITMAPFILEHEADER is defined as:

```
typedef struct tagBITMAPFILEHEADER
{  WORD    bfType;
   DWORD   bfSize;
   WORD    bfReserved1;
   WORD    bfReserved2;
   WORD    bfOffBits;
} BITMAPFILEHEADER;
```

The BITMAPFILEHEADER fields are described in Table 26.1.

TABLE 26.1   BITMAPFILEHEADER Data Fields

Field	Description
bfType	Specifies the file type; must be BM
bfSize	Specifies the file size in DWORD units
bfReserved1	Reserved; must be zero
bfReserved2	Reserved; must be zero
bfOffBits	Offset in bytes from BITMAPFILEHEADER to the start of the actual bitmap in the file

The following code excerpt shows how these fields are set in the Capture program:

```
bmFH.bfType      = 0x4D42;            // Type is "BM"
bmFH.bfReserved1 = 0L;
bmFH.bfReserved2 = 0L;
bmFH.bfOffBits   = plSize +           // bitmap offset
                   sizeof( BITMAPINFO ) +
                   sizeof( BITMAPFILEHEADER );
bmFH.bfSize      = ImgSize +          // file size
                   bmFH.bfOffBits;
WriteFile( hFil, &bmFH, sizeof( bmFH ),
           &dwWritten, NULL );    // write file header
```

The bfOffBits field, which is the offset from the first of the image file to the beginning of the image data, is calculated as the palette size (plSize) plus the size of the BITMAPINFO structure, plus the size of BITMAPFILEHEADER. Once this file header is complete, this block of data is written directly to the file, using the Write-File API function.

The Bitmap Information Structure   Within the DIB file, the BITMAPFILE-HEADER structure is followed immediately by either a BITMAPINFO or BITMAPCORE-INFO data structure. In the Capture example, the BITMAPINFO structure defines the dimensions and color information for a DIB file. BITMAPINFO is defined as follows:

```
typedef struct tagBITMAPINFO
{
    BITMAPINFOHEADER  bmiHeader;
    RGBQUAD           bmiColors[1];
} BITMAPINFO;
```

The BITMAPINFO fields are described in Table 26.2.

TABLE 26.2   BITMAPINFO Data Fields

Field	Description
bmiHeader	BITMAPINFOHEADER containing information about the dimensions and color format of a DIB
bmiColors	An array of RGBQUAD data structures defining the colors in the bitmap

The Bitmap Information Header Structure   The BITMAPINFOHEADER structure provides information about the size and organization of the bitmap image data and is defined as:

```
typedef struct tagBITMAPINFOHEADER
{
    DWORD    biSize;
    DWORD    biWidth;
    DWORD    biHeight;
    DWORD    biPlanes;
    DWORD    biBitCount;
    DWORD    biCompression;
    DWORD    biSizeImage;
    DWORD    biXPelsPerMeter;
    DWORD    biYPelsPerMeter;
    DWORD    biClrUsed;
    DWORD    biClrImportant;
} BITMAPINFOHEADER;
```

Table 26.3 describes the BITMAPINFOHEADER data fields and, where appropriate, the values permitted in the various fields.

TABLE 26.3   BITMAPINFOHEADER Data Fields

Field	Description
biSize	Number of bytes required by the BITMAPINFOHEADER structure
biWidth	Width of the bitmap in pixels
biHeight	Height of the bitmap in pixels
biPlanes	Color planes for target device; must be 1
biBitCount	Bits per pixel; must be 1, 4, 8, or 24 (see Table 26.4)
biCompression	Type of compression for a compressed bitmap (see Table 26.5)
biSizeImage	Image size in bytes
biXPelsPerMeter	Horizontal resolution in pixels per meter of the optimum target device (applications may use this value to select from a resource group a bitmap that best matches the characteristics of the current device)
biYPelsPerMeter	Vertical resolution in pixels per meter of the optimum target device (applications may use this value to select from a resource group a bitmap that best matches the characteristics of the current device)

937

TABLE 26.3   BITMAPINFOHEADER Data Fields (Continued)

Field	Description
biClrUsed	Number of color indexes in the color table used by the bitmap (see Table 26.6)
biClrImportant	Number of color indexes considered important for displaying the bitmap; if 0, all are important

The `biBitCount` field of the `BITMAPINFOHEADER` structure determines the number of bits defining each pixel, as well as the maximum number of colors in the bitmap. This `biBitCount` field may be set to any of the values shown in Table 26.4.

TABLE 26.4   Bitmap Bit Count

Value	Description
1	Monochrome bitmap; `bmiColors` field must contain two entries and each bit in the bitmap array represents one pixel. If the bit is clear (0), the first color entry is used; if set (1), the second color entry is used.
4	Maximum 16 colors; `bmiColors` field must contain the maximum of 16 entries with each pixel in the bitmap represented by a 4-bit index to the color table.
8	Maximum 256 colors; `bmiColors` field contains a maximum of 256 entries with each pixel in the bitmap represented by a byte index to the color table.
24	Maximum 2^{24} colors; `bmiColors` field is NULL. Each pixel in the bitmap is represented by 3 bytes in the data array representing the relative pixel intensities of red, green, and blue.
32	Maximum 2^{24} colors; if `bmiColors` is BI_RGB, `bmiColors` field is NULL. Each pixel in the bitmap is represented by 3 bytes in the data array representing the relative pixel intensities of red, green, and blue. The high byte in each DWORD is ignored.

NOTE In Windows NT, when `biCompression` is BI_BITFIELDS, bits set in each DWORD mask must be contiguous and should not overlap the bits of another mask. All the bits in the pixel do not need to be used. In Windows 95, when `biCompression` is BI_BITFIELDS, only one 32-bit-per-pixel color mask is supported as blue = 0x000000FF, green = 0x0000FF00, red = 0x00FF0000. (The result, of course, is white.)

The biCompression field of the BITMAPINFOHEADER; identifies the compression format used, as listed in Table 26.5. (Bitmap compression formats are discussed later in the chapter.)

TABLE 26.5 Compression Format Identifiers

Field	Description
BI_RGB	Bitmap is not compressed.
BI_RLE8	Run-length encoded format for bitmaps, with 8 bits per pixel; uses a 2-byte format consisting of a count byte followed by a color index byte.
BI_RLE4	Run-length encoded format for bitmaps with 4 bits per pixel; uses a 2-byte format consisting of a count byte followed by a byte containing two color indexes (nibbles).
BI_BITFIELDS	Bitmap is not compressed; color table consists of three DWORD color masks, which specify the red, green, and blue components, respectively, of each pixel. Valid when used with 16- and 32-bit-per-pixel bitmaps.

The biClrUsed field specifies the number of color indexes in the color table that are actually used by the bitmap. If the biClrUsed field is set to 0, the bitmap uses the maximum number of colors corresponding to the value of the biBitCount field, as listed in Table 26.6.

TABLE 26.6 Values for biClrUsed

Value	Description
0	Bitmap uses the maximum number of colors specified in the biBitCount field.
1..15	biClrUsed specifies the actual number of colors accessed by the device driver or graphics image.
16..nn	biClrUsed specifies the size of the color table used to optimize performance for Windows color palettes. If biBitCount is 16 or 32, the optimal color palette starts immediately following the three DWORD color masks.

Colors in the bmiColors table should appear in order of importance, putting the highest frequency colors first. This way, if a bitmapped image is displayed on a device with a lower color resolution, the most important colors are mapped to the high-frequency colors in the palette.

> **NOTE**
> If the bitmap is a packed bitmap—the bitmap array immediately follows the `BITMAPINFO` header and is referenced by a single pointer—the `biClrUsed` member must either be 0 or the actual size of the color table.

In the Capture demo program, the `BITMAPINFOHEADER` assignments are implemented as:

```
bmInfo.bmiHeader.biSize =
    (DWORD) sizeof( BITMAPINFOHEADER );
bmInfo.bmiHeader.biWidth        = Width;
bmInfo.bmiHeader.biHeight       = Height;
bmInfo.bmiHeader.biPlanes       = 1;
bmInfo.bmiHeader.biCompression  = BI_RGB;
bmInfo.bmiHeader.biSizeImage    = 0L;
bmInfo.bmiHeader.biXPelsPerMeter = 0L;
bmInfo.bmiHeader.biYPelsPerMeter = 0L;
bmInfo.bmiHeader.biClrUsed      = 0L;
bmInfo.bmiHeader.biClrImportant = 0L;
WriteFile( hFil, &bmInfo.bmiHeader,
        sizeof( bmInfo.bmiHeader ),
        &dwWritten, NULL );    // write info header
```

Writing the Bitmap Palette

Thus far, only the header information has been written to the bitmap file. Both palette and image information remain to be written. The Capture demo program is set for two types of bitmaps: those with either 16- or 256-color palettes. (For monochrome, 24- or 32-bit-per-pixel bitmaps, additional provisions are necessary, as described earlier in this chapter.)

> **TIP**
> 32-bit-per-pixel color information is essentially the same as 24-bit-per-pixel data except for an 8-bit NULL in each entry used to pad the entry to a DWORD size.

Retrieving Palette Colors   The following excerpt shows the handling for retrieving the palette color information and begins by allocating and locking sufficient memory space to contain the palette information:

```
                // note: GHND = GMEM_FIXED | GMEM_ZEROINIT
        hPal = GlobalAlloc( GHND, sizeof(LOGPALETTE) +
                        ( CRes * sizeof(PALETTEENTRY) ) );
                        // allocate memory for palette
        lp = (LPLOGPALETTE) GlobalLock( hPal );
                        // lock the memory allocated
        lp->palNumEntries = CRes;
        lp->palVersion    = 0x0300;
                        // fill in size and version (3.0)
        GetSystemPaletteEntries( hdc, 0, CRes,
                        lp->palPalEntry );
                        // and get the palette information
```

After allocating space for the palette information, the palette size is initialized (`CRes`) and the version number is set. With this done, the last step is calling `GetSystemPaletteEntries` to retrieve the actual palette color information and fill the `lp->palPalEntry` structure.

Converting Palette Colors   Once the palette information is retrieved, but before the data is stored as part of the bitmap image, the PALETTEENTRY RGB order must be converted to the RGBQUAD format used by bitmap images.

The PALETTEENTRY structure is defined as:

```
typedef struct tagPALETTEENTRY
{
    BYTE    peRed;
    BYTE    peGreen;
    BYTE    peBlue;
    BYTE    peFlags;
} PALETTEENTRY;
```

In contrast, the RGBQUAD structure used by bitmap images is the same size, four bytes, but uses an entirely different ordering for the colors. The RGBQUAD structure is defined as:

```
typedef struct tagRGBQUAD
{
    BYTE    rgbBlue;
```

```
        BYTE   rgbGreen;
        BYTE   rgbRed;
        BYTE   rgbReserved;
    } RGBQUAD;
```

As you can see, the PALETTEENTRY structure uses red-green-blue color order; the RGBQUAD structure uses blue-green-red. Therefore, provisions are necessary to convert the RGB order of the retrieved palette information to the bitmap's order, as shown here:

```
RGBQuad.rgbReserved = 0;
for( i=0; i<=CRes; i++ )
{
    RGBQuad.rgbRed    = lp->palPalEntry[i].peRed;
    RGBQuad.rgbGreen  = lp->palPalEntry[i].peGreen;
    RGBQuad.rgbBlue   = lp->palPalEntry[i].peBlue;
    WriteFile( hFil, &RGBQuad, sizeof( RGBQuad ),
               &dwWritten, NULL );
}
```

As each palette entry is converted to RGBQUAD format, the converted entry is written to the bitmap file. Also, for each entry to the file, the rgbReserved field remains 0.

After looping though the palette information and creating the bitmap palette, the last step is to unlock and free the memory allocated to hold the palette.

```
GlobalUnlock( hPal );    // don't forget to unlock
GlobalFree( hPal );      // and release the memory
```

Still, the task is not finished. Thus far, the bitmap file and information header have been written, followed by the color palette data, but the image data has not been written yet.

Writing the Image Data

Earlier, mention was made of how various color resolutions use specific formats to encode the image data, even ignoring the data-compression formats entirely. As discussed, a 16-color image coded each pixel as a nibble of data (four bits); a 256-color image requires a byte of data for each pixel; and a true-color (24-bit) image expects three bytes of data per pixel.

Rather than providing separate and different encoding methods for each color format, however, the CreateCompatibleBitmap function is used to create a memory device context that is compatible with the hardware device context

(HWND_DESKTOP in the Capture example). Then, by copying the bitmap image to this memory context, the bitmap bits are automatically rendered in the format appropriate to be written to the file.

```
hdcMem = CreateCompatibleDC( hdc );
hBitmap = CreateCompatibleBitmap( hdc, Width, 1 );
hBits = GlobalAlloc( GHND, LnWidth );
lpBits = (LPVOID) GlobalLock( hBits );
SelectObject( hdcMem, hBitmap );
```

Because a large bitmap requires substantial space (increasing with higher color resolutions), a small trick is used here. Instead of allocating memory space to contain the entire image at once, only enough space is allocated to contain one scan line from the image. And, this done, the allocated space is locked and the bitmap selected into the memory context—the buffer, in effect.

The SelectObject function is only a setup for the device context. Although the bitmap has been selected to the context, no image data has yet been assigned to this bitmap. Therefore, in the next loop, the screen is read one scan line at a time, beginning at the bottom and working up, into the memory context; that is, into the bitmap that was sized for a single scan line.

```
for( i = Height - 1; i >= 0; i-- )
{
   BitBlt( hdcMem, 0, 0, Width, 1,
           hdc,    0, i, SRCCOPY );
   GetBitmapBits( hBitmap, Width, lpBits );
   WriteFile( hFil, lpBits, LnWidth, &dwWritten, NULL );
}
```

The whole purpose of this exercise, however, is not to create a bitmap one pixel high, but rather to use the GetBitmapBits function to copy this segment of image, first from the bitmap to the lpBits array and then from the lpBits array to the image file. In this fashion, instead of providing conversions to fit various color resolutions, the BitBlt function provides automatic conversion by writing the data to a memory bitmap. This memory bitmap is sized to match the original image and, therefore, exactly the right size to be written to the file.

Now, once the image has been written, the usual cleanup is necessary to release the various memory allocations and context and handle assignments:

```
GlobalUnlock( hBits );          // don't forget to unlock
GlobalFree( hBits );            // and release the image,
```

```
        hBits = NULL;                        // optional but good form
        DeleteDC( hdcMem );                  // delete and release the
        ReleaseDC( HWND_DESKTOP, hdc );      // device contexts
        CloseHandle( hFil );                 // and close the file
        SetCursor( LoadCursor( NULL, IDC_ARROW ) );
        return( TRUE );
    }
```

Finally, the CloseHandle API function is called to close the completed bitmap image file and the wait cursor is replaced by the default arrow cursor.

> **NOTE** It may have occurred to you that instead of using a loop, all of this could have been done in a single step (even though more memory would be required). What you must remember, however, is that the bitmap file also requires the image to be written from the bottom up. Copying the entire image in a single step would produce an inverted (mirrored) result. By using a loop, in addition to saving memory, we also avoid the necessity of inverting the image before writing the file.

Bitmap Compression Formats

Compression is used with most image formats to reduce both memory and disk storage requirements. In Windows, two compression formats are supported for bitmaps: one for 16-color images with 4 bits per pixel and one for 256-color images with 8 bits per pixel. The bitmap compression format flags are listed in Table 26.5, and the BI_RLE8 and BI_RLE4 formats are described in the following sections.

8-Bit-per-Pixel Bitmap Compression

For 256-color images, using 8 bits per pixel to index pixels to the color palette, the BI_RLE8 format offers two compression modes: encoded or absolute. Both of these modes may occur in the same bitmap (and usually do).

Encoded Mode   Encoded mode uses WORD values, where the first byte in each WORD value specifies some number of consecutive values (01h..FFh) to be drawn using the color index indicated by the second byte. As an exception, the first byte may be set to zero to indicate an escape sequence, with the second byte denoting the end of a scan line, the end of the bitmap, or a delta escape, as listed in Table 26.7.

TABLE 26.7 Compression Escape Sequences

First Byte	Second Byte	Definition
0	0	End of scan line
0	1	End of bitmap
0	2	Delta; the WORD value following the escape sequence contains horizontal (first byte) and vertical (second byte) offsets (relative) to the next pixel position.

Absolute Mode   Absolute mode is indicated by a WORD value, with the first byte set to zero and the second byte in the range 03h..FFh. The second byte represents the number of bytes following that contain absolute color indexes for a single pixel.

Since absolute mode also requires that each run be aligned on a WORD boundary, absolute runs are NULL-padded, by byte, as necessary to end each run on a WORD boundary.

BI_RLE8 Example   Following is an example of hexadecimal WORD values from an 8-bit compressed bitmap, together with the corresponding decompression sequences:

```
0304 0506 0003 4556 6700 0278 0002 0501 0278 0000 091E 0001
```

Compressed	Decompressed Results / Pixel Values
03 04	04 04 04
05 06	06 06 06 06 06
00 03 45 56 67 00	45 56 67 (a single null byte is added for padding for this absolute mode run but is not included in the decompressed image)
02 78	78 78
00 02 05 01	Move 5 pixels right, 1 pixel down
02 78	78 78

Compressed	Decompressed Results / Pixel Values
00 00	End of scan line
09 1E	1E 1E 1E 1E 1E 1E 1E 1E 1E
00 01	End of RLE bitmap

4-Bit-per-Pixel Bitmap Compression

For 4-bit-per-pixel images, the BI_RLE4 format is used. Like BI_RLE8, this format incorporates two modes: encoded or absolute. Both modes may occur anywhere within an individual bitmap (and usually do).

Encoded Mode   In the encoded mode, WORD values are used, and the first byte in each WORD value specifies some number of consecutive values (01h..FFh) to be drawn using the two color indexes contained in the second byte. Since the second byte contains two separate color indexes—one in the high-order nibble and one in the low-order nibble—the pixel sequence is drawn by alternating the two values indicated. With this sequence, the first pixel uses the first color index, the second pixel uses the second color index, the third pixel uses the first color index, and so on, until the indicated number of pixels have been written.

As an exception, the first byte may be set to zero to indicate an escape sequence with the second byte denoting the end of a scan line, the end of the bitmap, or a delta escape (see Table 26.7).

Absolute Mode   In absolute mode, the first byte contains zero, while the second byte specifies the number of absolute color indexes (as nibble values) following. Subsequent bytes contain pairs of color indexes in the high- and low-order nibbles, with four color indexes in each WORD value.

Since absolute mode also requires that each run be aligned on a WORD boundary, absolute runs are NULL-padded, by nibble, as necessary to end each run on a word boundary.

BI_RLE4 Example   Following is an example of hexadecimal WORD values from a 4-bit compressed bitmap, together with the corresponding decompressed sequences. (Single-digit values represent color indexes for single pixels.)

```
0540 0506 0005 4567 8000 0477 0002 0501 0478 0000 091E 0001
```

Compressed	Decompressed Results / Pixel Values
06 40	4 0 4 0 4 0
05 06	0 6 0 6 0
00 05 45 67 80 00	4 5 6 7 8 (three null nibbles are added for padding for this absolute mode run but are not included in the decompressed image)
04 77	7 7 7 7 7 7 7 7
00 02 05 01	Move 5 pixels right, 1 pixel down
04 78	7 8 7 8 7 8 7 8
00 00	End of scan line
09 1E	1 E 1 E 1 E 1 E 1
00 01	End of RLE bitmap

NT/95 Graphics File Operations

Windows 3.*x* and earlier depended on the conventional C/C++ file operators to read and write files using, for example, the familiar `fopen`/`fwrite`/`fclose` functions. Windows NT and 95 have replacements for these old standards in the form of new API function calls, three of which are introduced here as direct replacements.

Opening a File

In any file operation, the first task is to open a file for either input or output. However, instead of the `fopen` function call familiar to C/C++ and Windows 3.1 programmers, the new `CreateFile` API call is used, for example:

```
hFil = CreateFile( szFName, GENERIC_WRITE, 0, NULL,
                   CREATE_ALWAYS, FILE_ATTRIBUTE_NORMAL, NULL );
if( hFil == NULL )
   return( ErrorMsg( "Can't open file" ) );
```

Although the `CreateFile` function is equivalent to the `fopen` function, the calling format, as well as the options and capabilities supported, are different. The `CreateFile` function is defined as:

```
HANDLE CreateFile( LPCTSTR lpszName,
                     DWORD fdwAccess,
                     DWORD fdwShareMode,
        LPSECURITY_ATTRIBUTES lpsa,
                     DWORD fdwCreate,
                     DWORD fdwAttrsAndFlags,
                    HANDLE hTemplateFile  )
```

The `CreateFile` function creates, opens, or truncates a file, returning a handle to the file for subsequent access.

If successful, the `CreateFile` function returns an open handle to the specified file. If the operation fails, the returned value is -1 (0xFFFFFFFF), and the `GetLastError` function may be used to retrieve extended error information.

NOTE The `CreateFile`, `WriteFile`, and `ReadFile` functions can be used with named pipes, mailslots, and communication resources, although some special features or restrictions may need to be observed. For further details, refer to Chapter 15 and to the online API function documentation on pipes.

The Parameters

The calling parameters for the `CreateFile` API function are explained in the following sections.

lpszName   This is the filename argument passed as a pointer to a null-terminated string. The `lpszName` argument specifies the name of a file, pipe, communications resource, or console to be created or opened.

fdwAccess   The `fdwAccess` argument identifies the file access type and may be either or both of the following flag values:

- `GENERIC_READ`: Provides file read access; permits data to be read from the file and the file pointer to be moved.

- `GENERIC_WRITE`: Provides file read/write access; permits data to be read from and written to the file and the file pointer to be moved.

fdwShareMode The `fdwShareMode` parameter specifies if and how the file can be shared and must be some combination of the following flag values:

- 0: File can not be shared

- `FILE_SHARE_READ`: File can be opened for read-only access by other applications; used to open the client end of a mailslot.

- `FILE_SHARE_WRITE`: File can be opened for read/write access by other applications.

lpsa The `lpsa` parameter is a pointer to a SECURITY_ATTRIBUTES data structure specifying file security attributes. The file system, such as NTFS, must support security attributes before these have any effects. (The FAT file system does not support security attributes.)

fdwCreate The `fdwCreate` parameter specifies the action taken when the named file already exists or when no file with this name exists. This parameter must have one of the following values.

- `CREATE_NEW`: Creates a new file, failing if the specified filename already exists.

- `CREATE_ALWAYS`: Creates a new file, overwriting any existing file.

- `OPEN_EXISTING`: Opens an existing file but fails if no file exists.

- `OPEN_ALWAYS`: Opens an existing file or creates a new file if none exists.

- `TRUNCATE_EXISTING`: Opens an existing file, truncating the file to a zero size or failing if the named file does not exist. The file must be opened using `GENERIC_WRITE` access (see the `fdwAccess` argument).

When `CreateFile` creates a new file, if the `fdwAttrsAndFlags` argument is not NULL, the file attributes and flags defined are ORed with the FILE _ATTRIBUTE_ARCHIVE bit (see Table 26.8 in the next section). In like fashion, if an `hTemplateFile` parameter (discussed later) is specified, `CreateFile` copies the extended attributes associated with the specified template file to the newly created file. Otherwise, the security attributes assigned to the new file are specified by the `lpSecurityAttributes` parameter. Last, the newly created file's length is set to zero.

When `CreateFile` is used to open an existing file, the `dwFlagsAndAttributes` and `hTemplateFile` arguments are simply ignored, as is the `lpSecurityDescriptor` member of the `lpSecurityAttributes` argument. However, the remaining flag values in the SECURITY_ATTRIBUTES structure remain valid.

fdwAttrsAndFlags   The `fdwAttrsAndFlags` argument specifies the file attributes and flags assigned to a file. Any combination of the flags and attributes listed in Table 26.8 is acceptable, except that all other flag attributes override the `FILE_ATTRIBUTE_NORMAL` flag.

TABLE 26.8   File Attribute Flags

Attribute Flag	Meaning
`FILE_ATTRIBUTE_ARCHIVE`	Sets archive bit, marking the file for backup.
`FILE_ATTRIBUTE_HIDDEN`	Marks the file as hidden; will not be included in an ordinary directory listing.
`FILE_ATTRIBUTE_NORMAL`	File has no other attribute bits set; valid only if used alone.
`FILE_ATTRIBUTE_READONLY`	Marks file as read-only; cannot be written or deleted.
`FILE_ATTRIBUTE_SYSTEM`	File is part of or used exclusively by the operating system.
`FILE_ATTRIBUTE_TEMPORARY`	Marks file as temporary; applications should write to this file only if absolutely necessary.
`FILE_ATTRIBUTE_ATOMIC_WRITE`	File is an atomic write file; applications should write to the file using atomic write semantics.
`FILE_ATTRIBUTE_XACTION_WRITE`	File is a transaction write file; applications should write to the file using transaction write semantics.
`FILE_FLAG_WRITE_THROUGH`	Instructs system to always write through any intermediate cache and go directly to the file.
`FILE_FLAG_OVERLAPPED`	Instructs system to initialize the file so that `ReadFile`, `WriteFile`, `ConnectNamedPipe`, and `TransactNamedPipe` operations, which take a significant time to process, will return `ERROR_IO_PENDING`. This return may be used to implement flow control.
`FILE_FLAG_NO_BUFFERING`	File is opened without intermediate buffering or caching by the system. All reads and writes are executed on sector boundaries. Useful for rapid reads/writes of large data images.

TABLE 26.8   File Attribute Flags (Continued)

Attribute Flag	Meaning
FILE_FLAG_RANDOM_ACCESS	File is accessed randomly (used by Win32 API to optimize file caching).
FILE_FLAG_SEQUENTIAL_SCAN	File is accessed sequentially from beginning to end; applications should not reposition the file pointer (used by Win32 API to optimize file caching).
FILE_FLAG_DELETE_ON_CLOSE	Instructs system to delete the file immediately after all file handles have been closed.
FILE_FLAG_BACKUP_SEMANTICS	File is being opened or created for a backup or restore operation.
FILE_FLAG_POSIX_SEMANTICS	File is accessed according to POSIX rules. Because POSIX rules allow multiple files with the same name, differing only in case, files created with this flag may not be accessible from DOS, Win16, or Win32 but may be accessed from Windows NT.

NOTE

When FILE_FLAG_OVERLAPPED is specified, the system does not maintain the file pointer. Instead, the file position is passed as part of the OVERLAPPED structure argument to ReadFile and WriteFile calls. When used, the ReadFile and WriteFile functions must also specify an OVERLAPPED structure. The purpose of the FILE_FLAG_OVERLAPPED specification and of the OVERLAPPED structure is to permit separate processes or threads to execute simultaneous operations on a single file. Using the OVERLAPPED structure, each process is responsible for maintaining its own file position pointer and, therefore, is also responsible for updating its own file position pointer.

hTemplateFile   The hTemplateFile parameter specifies a handle with GENERIC_READ access to a template file, which supplies extended attributes for the file being created. Attributes derived from a template file override any attributes supplied as explicit parameters (by the dwFlagsAndAttributes and lpSecurityAttributes arguments).

Writing to a File

The `WriteFile` function is also new with Windows NT and 95 and is defined as:

```
BOOL WriteFile(  HANDLE hFile,
                 CONST VOID *lpBuffer,
                    DWORD nNumberOfBytesToWrite,
                    LPWORD lpNumberOfBytesWritten,
            LPOVERLAPPED lpOverLapped    )
```

Like the `fwrite` function that `WriteFile` replaces, the purpose of the function is to write data to a file, beginning at the position indicated by the file pointer. After the write is completed, the file pointer is adjusted by the number of bytes actually written, except when the file is opened with `FILE_FLAG_OVERLAPPED`. If the file handle was created for overlapped I/O, the application must explicitly adjust the position of the file pointer after the write.

The `WriteFile` function has the following parameters:

- `hFile`: Identifies the file to be written. The file handle must have been created with `GENERIC_WRITE` file access.

- `lpBuffer`: Points to a buffer containing the data to be written to the file.

- `nNumberOfBytesToWrite`: Specifies the number of bytes to be written to the file. A value of 0 is interpreted as a null write.

- `lpNumberofBytesWritten`: Returns the number of bytes actually written to the file and is automatically zeroed before any work is done or any error checking is executed. This argument cannot be NULL and must be the address for a valid `DWORD` variable.

- `lpOverlapped`: Points to an `OVERLAPPED` structure, which is required if the file was opened as `FILE_FLAG_OVERLAPPED`. Otherwise, this argument may simply be passed as NULL. (See the "Overlapped File Operations" section.)

The `WriteFile` function does support a few features not normally encountered or not relevant during DOS file operations, two of which are applicable to conventional disk file operations:

- The `WriteFile` function will fail if the target file is locked by another process and the attempted write overlaps the locked portion.

- If `nNumberOfBytesToWrite` is zero, `WriteFile` does not truncate or extend the file. Instead, the `SetEndOfFile` function can be used.

Truncating a file is usually done to reset a file size to zero preparatory to rewriting the file with new data, but is occasionally used to discard portions of a record file. Extending a file is commonly employed to add space to a file before executing a direct write. In most cases, using conventional file-management techniques, neither of these operations is necessary.

Reading from a File

The ReadFile function, like CreateFile and WriteFile, is new with Windows NT and 95, replacing the traditional and familiar fread functions. The ReadFile function is defined as:

```
BOOL ReadFile(
        HANDLE  hFile,                   // file handle
        LPVOID  lpBuffer,                // address of input buffer
         DWORD  nNumberOfBytesToRead,    // bytes to read
       LPDWORD  lpNumberOfBytesRead,     // count of bytes read
   LPOVERLAPPED  lpOverlapped )          // overlapped I/O structure
```

The ReadFile function reads data from a file, beginning at the position indicated by the file pointer. After the read is completed, the file pointer is adjusted by the number of bytes actually read, except when the file handle has been created with FILE_FLAG_OVERLAPPED. If the file handle was created for overlapped I/O, the application must adjust the position of the file handle after the read.

The following are the ReadFile function's calling parameters:

- hFile: Identifies the file to be read. The file handle must have been created using GENERIC_READ or GENERIC_WRITE file access.

- lpBuffer: Points to the buffer to receive data read from the file.

- nNumberOfBytesToRead: Specifies the number of bytes to read from the file.

- lpNumberOfBytesRead: Returns the number of bytes actually read and is automatically zeroed before any work is done or any error checking is executed. This argument can not be NULL but must be a valid address for a DWORD variable.

- lpOverlapped: Pointer to an OVERLAPPED structure, which is required if the file was opened with FILE_FLAG_OVERLAPPED. Otherwise, this argument may be passed simply as NULL. (See the "Overlapped File Operations" section.)

If the return value is TRUE but the number of bytes read is reported as zero, the file pointer was beyond the current end of the file at the time of the read.

The `ReadFile` function will fail (returning FALSE) if part of the file has been locked by another process and the read overlaps the locked portion.

Overlapped File Operations

The `OVERLAPPED` structure, which remains an optional argument in `ReadFile` calls when file sharing is not enabled, can be used to set a custom file pointer; that is, a custom pointer to a location (offset) within a file.

The `OVERLAPPED` structure is defined as:

```
typedef struct _OVERLAPPED
{
    DWORD  Internal;
    DWORD  InternalHigh;
    DWORD  Offset;
    DWORD  OffsetHigh;
    HANDLE hEvent;
} OVERLAPPED;

typedef OVERLAPPED *LPOVERLAPPED;
```

The structure's fields are defined as follows:

- `Internal`: Reserved for system use; specifies a system-dependent status that is valid only when `GetOverlappedResult` returns without setting the extended error information to `ERROR_IO_PENDING`.

- `InternalHigh`: Reserved for system use; specifies the length transferred; valid only when `GetOverlappedResult` returns TRUE.

- `Offset`: `DWORD` value specifying the low-order 32-bits of the offset address for the transfer. The specification is a file position defined as a byte offset from the start of the file.

- `OffsetHigh`: Optional `DWORD` value specifying the high-order 32-bits of the offset address for the transfer.

- `hEvent`: Identifies an event to be set to the signaled state when the transfer is complete. The `hEvent` argument is optional; however, if an event is used, it must be identified here before calling the `ReadFile`, `WriteFile`, `Connect-NamedPipe`, or `TransactNamedPipe` API functions.

NOTE Both the `Offset` and `OffsetHigh` fields are ignored when reading from and writing to named pipes and communications devices.

Most applications, when opening a file for read or write, will call `CreateFile` without using the `FILE_FLAG_OVERLAPPED` flag. In this case, both `ReadFile` and `WriteFile` calls can be made passing the `lpOverlapped` argument as NULL, initiating the read or write operation at the current file position. If, however, the `lpOverlapped` argument is provided, the read or write operation will be initiated at the file offset specified in the `OVERLAPPED` structure. In either case, neither `ReadFile` nor `WriteFile` will return until the file operation is completed.

Alternatively, if `CreateFile` was called using the `FILE_FLAG_OVERLAPPED` flag, the `lpOverlapped` argument is required to provide the current file position for both read and write operations. If this argument is not provided, both `ReadFile` and `WriteFile` will return FALSE, and `GetLastError` will report `ERROR_INVALID_PARAMETER`.

When a valid `lpOverlapped` argument is supplied, the read or write operation begins at the offset specified. However, either `ReadFile` or `WriteFile` may return before the operation is completed, returning a result of FALSE, and `GetLastError` reports `ERROR_IO_PENDING`. This provision allows the process calling `ReadFile` or `WriteFile` to continue with other tasks as the read or write operation continues independently.

Getting a File Size

The `GetFileSize` API function, new with Windows NT and 95, includes provisions to recognize and report on files that are larger than 4GB, even though such generous file sizes are currently unlikely.

```
DWORD GetFileSize
(
    HANDLE  hFile,           // handle of file to get size of
    LPDWORD lpFileSizeHigh   // address of high word for file size
);
```

The `GetFileSize` function returns a `DWORD` value reporting the low-order 32 bits of the file size. The second argument, `LPDWORD`, is an optional pointer to a second `DWORD` value, which will receive the high-order 32 bits of the file size.

If an error occurs, the return value in the low-order 32 bits will be 0xFFFFFFFF. If the actual file size causes this same value to be returned, a call to the GetLast-Error function will report NO_ERROR. However, in general, even though a maximum file size of 1.8×10^{19} bytes can be reported, for now, most applications can simply ignore the high-order 32-bit value (by using NULL as the calling argument) and assume that the actual file size is smaller than the 4GB still possible.

Closing a File

For file operations, the CloseHandle function replaces the familiar fclose function. The CloseHandle function requires only one argument: the file handle originally returned by the CreateFile function call.

CloseHandle invalidates the specified object handle, decrements the object's handle count, and performs object-retention checks. Once the last handle to an object is closed, the object is removed from the system. The CloseHandle function, however, does not close module objects.

NOTE The CloseHandle function can also be used with handles for console input or output, events, file mapping, mutex, named pipes, processes, semaphores, and threads. See Chapters 14, 15, and 17 for examples.

Working with Image File Formats

Along with the Window's native BMP image format, many other image formats exist. You may need to work with various formats when you are importing and exporting images between applications and into and out of Windows.

Here, we will cover three popular image file formats: .PCX, .GIF, .TIF, and .TGA. Other formats that you may encounter include the GEM/IMG format, used by Ventura Publisher among others; the PIC or MacPaint format, used by the Apple Macintosh computer; and PostScript (.EPS) image formats.

Paintbrush's PCX Format

For a long time, ZSoft's Paintbrush (.PCX) format provided the de facto standard for non-Windows (DOS) bitmapped images. Most graphics programs contain some provision for conversion from their native formats to .PCX formats. Also, the original PBRUSH.EXE program distributed with Windows was written by ZSoft and included .PCX/.BMP conversion facilities.

As graphics devices have become increasingly sophisticated, the .PCX image format has kept pace. Instead of being a single format, the PCX standard comprises a series of formats including 8-, 16-, and 24-bit color formats, as well as true-gray and monochrome formats.

PCX File Structure

All PCX image files begin with a header defined as:

```
typedef struct tagPCXHEAD
{
    char    manufacturer;       // always 0xA0
    char    version;            // version number
    char    encoding;           // should be 1
    char    bits_per_pixel;     // color depth
    short   xmin, ymin;         // image origin
    short   xmax, ymax;         // image dimensions
    short   hres, yres;         // image resolution
    char    palette[48];        // color palette
    char    reserved;
    char    color_planes;       // color planes
    short   bytes_per_line;     // line buffer size
    short   palette_type;       // gray or color palette
    short   hscreensize;        // horizontal screen size
    short   vscreensize;        // vertical screen size
    char    filler[54];         // null filler
} PCXHEAD;
```

> **NOTE**
> Prior to Windows NT and 95, the `xmin, xmax, ymin, ymax, hres, vres,`
> `bytes_per_line, palette_type, hscreensize,` and `vscreensize` fields
> have been commonly defined as `integer`. For 32-bit Windows, because
> `integer` is now defined as a four-byte value, this definition has been
> changed to `short` to preserve the necessary two-byte field length.

The header has the following fields:

- `manufacturer`: A check identifying the file as a Paintbrush format image and should always be `0x0A`.

- `version`: Identifies the version of PC Paintbrush that created the image file. Valid values are 0 (no palette information; Paintbrush 2.5, the earliest incarnation), 2 (valid palette information), 3 (monochrome or the display's default palette), 4 (Paintbrush for Windows), or 5 (Paintbrush 3.0 or later, including 24-bit image files).

- `encoding`: Should always be 1, indicating that PCX's run-length encoding (RLE) has been used. Note, however, that other values may indicate newer versions and newer encoding schemes.

- `bits_per_pixel`: Reports the number of bits to represent each pixel (per color plane). Possible values are 1, 2, 4, 8, or 24.

- `xmin,ymin`: Specify an offset position for the upper-left corner of the image relative to the upper-left corner of the screen (or window). In most cases, no offset is specified, and `xmin` and `ymin` will be 0. (Even when an offset is specified, it is still the prerogative of the application, or programmer, to accept or ignore this offset as desired.)

- `xmax,ymax`: Specify the image dimensions. Note that the sizes indicated by `xmax` and `ymax` are off by 1, because the actual pixel count begins with zero. For example, for an image with a width of 480 pixels, the `xmax` value would be 479. The actual width and height of the image should always be calculated as:

```
width  = ( pcxHead.xmax - pcxHead.xmin ) + 1;
height = ( pcxHead.ymax - pcxHead.ymin ) + 1;
```

- `hres, vres`: Provide the resolution of the device (or video mode) where the image was created; for most purposes, these values may be ignored.

- `palette`: A buffer that contains the palette color information for images with 16 or fewer colors (3 bytes per palette entry or 48 bytes in length). For larger palettes (such as 256-color palettes) this information is appended at the end of the image data. The palette structure used in either case consists of a series of RGB triplets, with the first byte in each defining the red level, the second defining the green level, and the third byte defining the blue level.

- `color_planes`: Defines the image's color planes. The value is 4 for EGA 16-bit color images or 1 for all other images, including monochrome.

- `bytes_per_line`: Reports the number of bytes to allocate for a scan-line plane. This value must be an even number and cannot be calculated by subtracting `xmin` from `xmax`.

- `palette_type`: Originates with the advent of VGA graphics systems with a value of 1 for gray-scale and a value of 2 for full color. This field is ignored in later versions of Paintbrush.

- `hscreensize`, `vscreensize`: Report the horizontal and vertical screen size (of the original system) in pixels. These fields were defined for Paintbrush IV and Paintbrush IV+; for all other versions, these should be NULL.

- `filler`: Pads out the header to 128 bytes and should be filled with NULLs (0s). (Future revisions may redefine the image header by using parts of the `filler` field for new purposes.)

Reading a PCX Image: The ViewPCX Program

The ViewPCX program demonstrates reading a 256-color PCX image and provides an example of a file lookup dialog box to select an image file. Note that no provisions are made for changing the file extension nor for displaying any format of PCX file except one with a 256-color palette.

Since all .PCX images use the same header structure, the first step for reading any .PCX file is to retrieve the header data. The ViewPCX demo program uses the Windows `CreateFile` and `ReadFile` API functions. More important, ViewPCX makes use of the OVERLAPPED structure to maintain a custom file pointer while executing an asynchronous file read.

> **WARNING** The asynchronous file operations used by the ViewPCX demo program are not supported under Windows 95. The ViewPCX demo must be run under Windows NT or converted to synchronous (conventional) file operations.

The first step is to open the file to read:

```
hFile = CreateFile( PCXFile, GENERIC_READ, 0, NULL,
                OPEN_EXISTING, FILE_ATTRIBUTE_NORMAL, NULL );
```

Of course, there's always the need for a provision to report possible errors. If the `CreateFile` function fails, the return value (in `hFile`) will be INVALID _HANDLE_VALUE, which is handled in a relatively typical fashion:

```
if( hFile == INVALID_HANDLE_VALUE )
{
    wsprintf( szBuff, "Error: %d -- unable to open %s!",
              GetLastError(), PCXFile );
    ErrorMsg( szBuff );
    return( FALSE );
}
```

Assuming the file is opened correctly, the image header is retrieved:

```
ReadFile( hFile, &pcxHd, sizeof(PCXHEAD), &fRes, NULL );
if( ( fRes != sizeof(PCXHEAD) ) ||
    ( pcxHd.manufacturer != 0x0A ) )
{
    CloseHandle( hFile );
    ErrorMsg( "Not a valid .PCX file" );
    return( FALSE );
}
```

The `ReadFile` operation is followed by two checks. The first check tests `fRes` (the byte count actually returned) against the expected (and requested) byte size, ensuring that a complete header structure was found and retrieved. The second check tests the identification byte to ensure that it is identified as a PaintBrush PCX format image.

At this point, the image has been identified as, presumably, a proper PCX format. However, there are several possible PaintBrush formats; any further progress depends on the image type and the palette information (if any).

NOTE Decode and display provisions for black-and-white and 16-color palettes can easily be included in the demo program, but are left as an exercise for the reader. For 24-bit color images, slightly more elaborate provisions would be required, beginning, of course, with a 24-bit video card and an appropriate driver. But remember, no palette is included in 24-bit-per-pixel images because each pixel contains its own color information as a three-byte RGB value.

Because 256-color palettes require three bytes per color or a total of 728 bytes to define the palette, the .PCX file header lacks sufficient space to contain the palette information. Instead, the palette information is appended to the end of the PCX image file.

The logical first step, since we are assuming that this is a 256-color image, is to make sure that the image file is large enough to actually contain, at a minimum, the image header, plus a 768-byte palette, plus a 1-byte palette ID. This is easily accomplished thus:

```
fSize = GetFileSize( hFile, NULL );
if( fSize < ( 769 + sizeof(PCXHEAD) ) )
{       // wrong format -- too small for palette
   CloseHandle( hFile );
   ErrorMsg( "Not a 256 color image format" );
   return( FALSE );
}
```

The next logical check is to test the header version number where a value of 5 indicates the presence of a palette. However, the mere presence of a palette of some size does not ensure that the image is a 256-color format. Therefore, the next step is to retrieve the palette information by using a seek to an offset from the end of the file.

Using conventional DOS file operations, this could have been done using the fseek function, thus:

```
fseek, fp, -769L, SEEK_END );
```

However, using the ReadFile API function, a different approach is necessary to accomplish a similar task. In the ViewPCX demo program, an initial offset value is assigned thus:

```
fPos.Offset = fSize - 769;      // seek palette start
fPos.OffsetHigh = 0L;
fPos.hEvent = NULL;
```

The assigned offset is the file size (fSize) minus 769, placing the file pointer one byte ahead of the expected palette. Since a file size greater than 4GB is not anticipated, the fPos.OffsetHigh field is set as zero and will be ignored. Last, the fPos.hEvent field is set as NULL, because no special reports or controls are needed.

After setting the offset, the ReadFile API is called, first to return a single byte that will be tested for the palette identifier. Then, after incrementing the offset to account for the byte just read, ReadFile is called a second time to retrieve the assumed palette information.

```
bResult = ReadFile( hFile, &chPal, 1, &fRes, &fPos );
                                          // get palette ID
fPos.Offset++;
                                          // advance pointer
bResult = ReadFile( hFile, &pcxPal, 768, &fRes, &fPos );
                                          // get palette
```

Last, the version number, palette ID, and returned palette size are tested. If any of these three tests fail, the file is closed, an error message reports that the image was not acceptable, and the process exits:

```
if( ( pcxHd.version != 5 ) ||   // check version number
    ( chPal != 0x000C ) ||      // check palette ID
    ( fRes != 768 ) )           // check palette size
{
    CloseHandle( hFile );
    ErrorMsg( "Not a 256 color image format" );
    return( FALSE );
}
```

Assuming that everything else is acceptable, the retrieved palette information is decoded to a format acceptable to the device context, a logical palette structure.

```
SetCursor( LoadCursor( NULL, IDC_WAIT ) );
//========= create palette ===========================
hPCXPal = GlobalAlloc( GHND, sizeof(LOGPALETTE) +
                       256 * sizeof(PALETTEENTRY ) );
lPal = (LPLOGPALETTE) GlobalLock( hPCXPal );
lPal->palVersion = 0x0300;
lPal->palNumEntries = 256;
for( i=j=0; i<256; ++i )
{
    lPal->palPalEntry[i].peRed   = pcxPal[j++];
    lPal->palPalEntry[i].peGreen = pcxPal[j++];
    lPal->palPalEntry[i].peBlue  = pcxPal[j++];
    lPal->palPalEntry[i].peFlags = PC_NOCOLLAPSE;
    //  use PC_NOCOLLAPSE instead of PC_RESERVED -- //
    //  PC_RESERVED maps to nearest existing color  //
```

```
        //  but no good matches exist for this purpose  //
    }
    hPCXPal = CreatePalette( lPal );
    hOldPal = SelectPalette( hdc, hPCXPal, FALSE );
    RealizePalette( hdc );            // palette is now active
```

After retrieving the image palette information, the application needs to return the image data. Using the DOS file functions, this task would have been accomplished as:

```
    fseek( fp, 128L, SEEK_SET );
```

However, using the ReadFile API, the process reverts to using the OVERLAPPED structure to set the offset, thus:

```
    fPos.Offset = 128;       // set file ptr to image data
```

Because the PCX header, regardless of the image type, is always 128 bytes in length, finding the beginning of the image data is easy. But, if finding the data is easy, decoding the data does require a few provisions.

Also, to simplify the decoding process, the image data is read and decoded one scan line at a time. However, because the image is run-length encoded (RLE), it's hardly practical to determine exactly how many bytes are in a single scan line before reading the data. Therefore, in order to continually update the fPos.Offset value, a new variable, Index, is used during the decode process to determine how many bytes of data have been used and, before the next scan line is read, to increment the offset.

A 256-color PCX image always uses RLE, much the same as in other image formats. Thus, while reading the data, if the two high bits are set (the byte value is greater than 0xC0), then the byte is read as byte count specifying the repeat count for the following byte. For example, the byte value 0xFE indicates that the next byte read will be repeated 0x3E or 62 times (0xFE – 0xC0 = 0x3E).

Now, as you may realize, this also means that individual pixels with palette values in the range 0xC0..0xFF, which make up 75 percent of the total palette, require two bytes, rather than appearing as a single byte. Therefore, a run of pixels with the palette values 0xDE, 0xDF, 0xDF, 0xEA, 0xE2, 0xE7 would be encoded as 0xC1, 0xDE, 0xC2, 0xDF, 0xC1, 0xEA, 0xC1, 0xE2, 0xC1, 0xE7, which is not precisely a savings. This does, however, illustrate the importance of building the palette with the high-frequency color entries appearing first. Still, shortcomings aside, RLE encoding does generally reduce rather than increase file size.

There are still a few tricks involved in decoding an RLE image. For example, the decoding provision used in ViewPCX begins by initializing two values, i and j, before initiating a loop for the scan lines.

```
j = Index = 0;        // initialize position
while( j < depth )
{
    fPos.Offset += Index;
    i = Index = 0;
    ReadFile( hFile, &ImgArray, sizeof(ImgArray),
                &fRes, &fPos );
```

The offset field in fPos is incremented at the beginning of each cycle of the loop; the first time around, however, Index is already zero, so the offset remains at 128 bytes, which is the beginning of the image data. On subsequent cycles, after the offset is adjusted, Index is reset to zero in preparation for the following decode process. At this point, the ReadFile call has read a block of image data, beginning at the specified offset.

After reading the data, a new loop is initialized to handle decoding a single scan line from the image. Within this loop, the first step is a test to determine if the current byte is a repeat value:

```
do
{
    if( ( ImgArray[Index] & 0xC0 ) == 0xC0 )
    {
```

If the current byte is a repeat byte (greater than 0xC0), the count variable is derived, and a new for loop begins to paint the required number of pixels using the next byte in the data array as the palette index.

```
count = ImgArray[Index++] & 0x3F;
for( k=0; k<count; k++ )
{
    SetPixelV( hdc, i++, j,
                PALETTEINDEX( ImgArray[Index] ) );
    if( i >= pcxHd.bytes_per_line ) k = count;
}   // if line is too long just ignore any wraps
}
```

The SetPixelV API function is essentially the same as the customary SetPixel API call, with one difference: Where SetPixel returns the existing color index for the pixel written, SetPixelV is marginally faster because no return value in handled. But remember that the image data is not an RGB value but rather a palette index entry. However, both SetPixel and SetPixelV expect a COLORREF value, supplied here by calling the PALETTEINDEX macro with the palette index as an argument.

Last, purely as a precaution against encoding errors (which are not entirely unknown), if the repeat count extends beyond the scan-line length, the variable k is reset to terminate the inner loop.

If the initial test shows that the byte value is not a repeat count, SetPixelV is called once, as:

```
else
    SetPixelV( hdc, i++, j,
               PALETTEINDEX( ImgArray[Index] ) );
```

In either case, the Index value is incremented once more to point to the next element in the data array:

```
        Index++;
    }
    while( i < pcxHd.bytes_per_line );
    j++;
    i = 0;
}
```

The loop continues until i reaches the length of the scan line, after which, the vertical position (j) is incremented and the horizontal position (i) is reset to the first of the line.

Remember, the variable Index is used both to track the current position within the data array and, after decoding each scan line, to reset the OVERLAPPED offset before reading the next data block.

The complete listing for the ViewPCX program is on the CD that accompanies this book.

Alternatives for Decoding 256-Color PCX Images

Several alternatives are possible for decoding PCX images. The code shown in the ViewPCX demo program is not the most efficient in terms of display; it was chosen to demonstrate using the OVERLAPPED structure.

One alternative is to use a different format to dynamically allocate an array large enough to hold all of the image data returned by a single ReadFile operation. With this method, a DWORD variable, such as Index, would keep track of the position within the data in the same fashion demonstrated within the loop in the ViewPCX program. The advantage, however, is that only one read operation is needed, which would obviously accelerate operations.

A second alternative might be considered because the present method requires reading and decoding the image file every time a WM_PAINT message is received. We could change the handling, reading the image as a PCX file but creating a memory bitmap image from the result. This operation would be done only once, when the image file was selected rather than when the WM_PAINT message was received.

Then when a screen repaint is required, all that would be necessary would be to repaint the screen image using the BitBlt function, which is intrinsically faster than repeatedly reading and decoding the image file. Using the SetPixelV (or the SetPixel) function to paint a bitmap image is also intrinsically slow compared to using BitBlt (or StretchBlt) to simply transfer an image in bulk from a memory context to the screen context.

The basics required for this second alternative can be found in the CaptureBit-map function in the Capture demo program discussed earlier in this chapter (see the complete listing at the end of the chapter or on the CD). Don't forget, however, to set the palette for the memory device as well as the active device context; otherwise, the resulting colors may be interesting but unexpected.

Implementation of either of these alternatives, which could also be combined, is left as an exercise for the reader. However, a code fragment is included in the program listings (on the CD), showing how to create a bitmap from the PCX image data. As you will observe, the PCX image data must be decoded one line at a time before being transferred, using BitBlt, to build up the bitmap image.

Interpreting 24-Bit-per-Pixel PCX Files

When you're working with 24-bit PCX images, remember that they do not contain any palette information. Instead, these images provide full 24-bit color information for each pixel in the image. Identified as version 5 or later, 24-bit PCX images store their data as 8 bits per color plane, in three planes. These are decoded in the same fashion as 16-color images, except that byte values (8 bits) are read as lines of red, green, and blue, in that order.

Therefore, to decode 24-bit PCX images, three scan lines are read as red, green, and blue image lines. After RLE decoding, these lines are treated by combining the first byte of each scan line as an RGB-triplet pixel value, rather than as a palette value. The second pixel uses the second byte from each scan line, and so forth.

Decoding Monochrome PCX Images

For monochrome PCX files, decoding is quite simple. First, if the two high bits of a byte are clear (ANDing with 0xC0), then the six least-significant bits are written to the image as a series of six pixels. (If a bit is set, the pixel is on; otherwise, the pixel is off.)

If the two high bits are set, an index count is created by ANDing the byte with 0x3F and using this count (0..63) to repeat the next byte count number of times, optionally up to a total of 504 pixels (the repeated byte defines an 8-pixel series).

Obviously, the PCX encoding scheme is heavily weighted for use with images containing large contiguous areas. This is not, however, particularly efficient for scanned images (but then, scanners were quite uncommon when the PCX format was created).

Decoding 16-Color PCX Images

Paintbrush PCX images may have 2, 4, 8, or 16 colors before jumping to 256 color images. But, for 16 or fewer colors, the handling remains essentially the same, because the image is treated as four interleaved monochrome images, which is consistent with the EGA video format.

Although this format may sound mysterious, the reason lies in the structure of EGA video cards that were the intended environment for 16-color images. On EGA cards, four 32KB memory pages were treated as layers: one each for red, green, blue, and intensity. (Admittedly, this is an over simplification.) The point is that the four bits selecting a palette color are written 1 bit to each plane, if you're working in machine language and accessing these planes directly.

In this circumstance, however, the question is how to decode the image, not the mechanics of an EGA card. To decode a 16-color PCX image, four scan lines are read and, initially, treated as monochrome masks. To create color (palette) information, the first bit from each scan line is combined after decoding, by shifting the bit from the second scan line one place left, the third scan line two places left, and the fourth scan line three places left to produce a 4-bit nibble.

This sequence of nibbles creates a single scan line for the image and can be written to the screen (or converted to another format) as index values to the 16-color palette.

CompuServe's Graphics Interchange Format (GIF)

Perhaps one of the most popular image formats in general use—in terms of images available on bulletin boards, disk libraries, and CD-ROMs—is the Graphics Interchange Format (GIF). This format was developed by CompuServe as a vehicle for graphics images which could be transferred between different computer systems. Although GIF is copyrighted by CompuServe, a blanket, nonexclusive, limited, royalty-free license has been granted to all developers, permitting free use of the GIF format in computer graphics applications.

The GIF format uses a very effective compression scheme, utilizing variable-length LZW compression (named for its developers: Lempel, Ziv, and Welsh). Although relatively complex to encode and decode, LZW compression has an important advantage over the simpler RLE compression schemes used by BMP and PCX images: reduced size. Images using LZW compression are virtually always considerably smaller than corresponding images created using RLE compression. LZW compression builds tables of patterns from the original, replacing repetitive patterns or pixel sequences with indexes to the table entries. LZW compression is also available in the public domain and is used in a variety of applications and forms, not just for image compression.

Other features supported by the GIF format include provisions for multiple images within a single file, local color tables including 256 colors, and interleaving scan lines (as used in PCX formats). The GIF format also has provisions for user-defined extensions.

GIF images are currently identified by two signatures, GIF87A and GIF89A found in the first six bytes of the image and identifying, respectively, the original 1987 and 1989 revisions.

TIP Current GIF standards and specifications (GIF89A) are readily available on CompuServe (GO GRAPHIC SUPPORT FORUM), as well as from a variety of other online services and private BBSs. A wide variety of GIF display programs, format conversion programs, source code examples, and GIF images are available through these same sources.

Tagged Image File Format (TIFF)

The Tagged Image File Format (TIFF) is perhaps the most complex of the popular formats. This format incorporates a variety of methods for describing images and, depending on the implementation, may provide several different means of data compression.

A second strength of the TIFF image format is that .TIF images, stored in uncompressed format, are capable of tremendous compression using standard file-compression utilities. Compressions of 97 to 99 percent are not uncommon.

This format is popular with typesetting and production graphics applications, partially because it was one of the earlier formats capable of supporting high-resolution images and partially because it provides several subformats optimized for different types of images. The following five classes of TIFF image are supported:

- Class B TIFF files consist of black-and-white images, coded as one bit per pixel and providing three compression formats: none, CCITT Group 3, and PackBits.

- Class G TIFF files are used for gray-scale images consisting of 4 or 8 bits per pixel (16 or 256 shades of gray) and are either uncompressed or use LZW compression.

- Class P TIFF files support color palettes using 1 to 8 bits per pixel and are either uncompressed or use LZW compression.

- Class R TIFF files are used for 24-bit-per-pixel images and, optionally, use LZW compression.

- Class F TIFF files are used for fax images.

TIFF formats can be used as demanded by circumstances. Remember, however, that these are provisions only of the TIFF specification. No actual implementation of the TIFF image software includes all possible formats or compression schemes. There are a number of other TIFF variations in use which do not follow any published standards. In general, these tend to consist of variant compression algorithms but may vary in other ways as well.

Typically, a TIFF encoder/decoder may run five to ten thousand lines of code.

The TIFF file specification and format instructions are available by request from either Aldus or Microsoft. Examples are available for a variety of systems.

Truevision's TARGA (TGA) Format

The TARGA (TGA) file format, originally developed by Truevision, Inc., has been the predominate 24-bit image format used with frame-grabber boards. Truevision markets computer/camera interface boards that are used extensively on machine imaging, as well as for a variety of other applications. Using TARGA cards, or any of a variety of competing brands and models, images are captured directly from video cameras with pixel depths of 16, 24, or 32 bits.

Previously, a TARGA card (or equivalent) was required, usually along with a second, high-resolution monitor, to display TGA images. Today, you can use a single monitor and a wider variety of video cards that are capable of supporting 24-bit-per-pixel images, although these are not yet in widespread use.

All three of the image formats supported (16, 24, or 32 bits per pixel) can be considered true-color formats. And, speaking from personal experience in a color-critical application, I can report that the differences between images using these three formats are quite indistinguishable to the human eye, even tested in side-by-side displays of highly magnified gemstones.

Pixels in the 24-bit image format consist of three 8-bit color values in RGB order. The 32-bit format also contains three 8-bit color values, but also include a fourth 8-bit field, which is NULL and simply ignored, having no purpose except to pad the entry to a DWORD size for convenience in handling and alignment.

The third format, 16 bits per pixel, consists of three 5-bit color values with the sixteenth, high bit treated as an intensity bit. If the high bit is set, the three 5-bit image color values each correspond to the five most-significant bits in the corresponding 8-bit color values. If the high bit is cleared, the three 5-bit values are shifted right one 1 bit, decreasing color intensity.

TARGA image file specifications can be requested from Truevision, Inc, 7340 Shadeland Station, Indianapolis, IN 46256-3919. The phone numbers are 317-841-0332 (voice) and 317-576-7700 (fax).

Converting 24-Bit Color Images

Although 24-bit true-color cards are becoming popular, they are still not common. For the present, SVGA (256-color) cards remain the high-resolution standard and are likely to continue so for at least the next few years. At the same time, the 24-bit video frame-capture systems are also popular but cannot be readily displayed on SVGA systems.

There is a solution: Convert 24-bit color images captured by video cameras to 256-color palette images, which can be displayed on most available systems. (Some graphics programs designed to manipulate 24-bit color images offer just such a palette compression feature under the generic title Posterizing.)

Converting a potential palette of 16 million colors (2^{24} = 16,777,216) to a palette with a mere 256 colors does seem to be a considerable degradation in image quality, but it isn't really quite as bad as it sounds. While the potential palette size of a 24-bit image is over 16 million colors, the actual image (assuming 400x512 pixels) is a total of only 204,800 pixels. Assuming that no individual pixels share the same color, the reduction to a 256-color palette is only an 800-to-1 color reduction rather than 65536-to-1, an improvement of 82:1.

Commonly, however, a typical image will contain a much smaller range of actual colors—perhaps as many as 400 or 500 distinct shades, but usually fewer. And, even when the color variation is high, many shades that are technically different will still be relatively close in hue and can be represented by a single palette entry.

Several methods exist for converting 24-bit images to 256-color palette images. The simplest method, although not necessarily the best approach, is to begin by constructing a 256-color palette containing a range of hues that can be used for a variety of images. The drawback to this method is that the resulting palette does not match any image very well and the resulting displays have a rather cartoon-like quality about them. The following sections suggest some other methods.

Building a Frequency-Ordered Palette

A better method that constructing a simple 256-color palette is to begin by constructing a histogram of the colors represented in a specific image. This entails processing the entire image to construct a frequency record for each individual color in the image.

After this is completed, you can build a custom, frequency-ordered palette from the highest frequency colors with the remaining image pixels mapped to their nearest equivalents from the palette. (Hint: Reserve two of the 256 palette entries: one each for pure white and pure black.)

Next, after constructing a palette of the high-frequency colors, map the original palette values as indexes to their corresponding palette entries or, if no matching palette entries exist, to the closest available palette entry.

Creating a Distributed Palette

Another conversion approach follows the same general pattern of creating a histogram of the actual colors; however, instead of simply taking the 256 (or 254) highest-frequency colors to create the palette, you create a distributed palette.

In this format, after creating a binary tree of color frequencies, the color tree is scanned: for the total number of entries and for the range of differences between colors. If fewer than 256 entries are found in the tree, the palette can be constructed directly, based on frequency.

If more than 256 entries are found in the tree, you need to apply a color-conversion algorithm to find the closest matches in the tree, reducing the branches of the tree by eliminating the lowest frequency entries that have close matches. When the tree is reduced to a suitable number of entries, the remaining entries are used to create the palette.

The first consideration, as mentioned, is simply the number of colors in the tree. If the number of branches (total colors) is, arbitrarily, less than one and a half times the palette size, a distributed palette is probably not necessary. On the other hand, if the number of colors exceeds this arbitrary threshold, a distributed palette may provide a better color spread than a frequency-ordered palette.

There are two considerations in selecting entries for a distributed palette: the uniqueness of the palette entry and the frequency of the color.

Taking the second consideration first, it should be fairly obvious that there's little benefit in devoting a limited resource—a palette entry—to a color that is used by very few pixels in the image. Precisely where this cutoff should be established is arbitrary, but in an image composed of 200,000 pixels, a frequency of 20 pixels is 0.01 percent of the total or 0.25 percent of the average. This value is low enough to suggest that the color in question could be safely mapped to an existing palette entry.

The first consideration, uniqueness of a palette entry, is a different matter. This factor must be calculated carefully, taking all three of the color components (red, green, and blue) into account. The obvious method of comparing two color values is simple: sum the absolute difference of the red, green, and blue components, as:

$$dC = abs(R_1 - R_2) + abs(G_1 - G_2) + abs(B_1 - B_2)$$

The objective here, however, is to emphasize the difference between two colors and to find which colors in the image are the closest to each other and can, therefore, be represented by a single palette entry. The color difference (dC) can be better emphasized using a nonlinear formula:

$$dC = (R_1 - R_2)^2 + (G_1 - G_2)^2 + (B_1 - B_2)^2$$

This second formula shifts the weighting to emphasize differences in a single color component over difference distributed throughout the three color components.

For example, assume three colors, C1, C2, and C3, with RGB values 0x1F2C3B, 0x1F2A3B, and 0x1E2D3A, respectively. Using the first, unweighted formula, C1 and C2 have a color difference of 2 (in the green component); C1 and C3 have a color difference of 3 (1 each in the red, green, and blue values).

Using the second, weighted formula, however, the C1 and C2 entries have a weighted difference of 4 against the weighted difference of 3 for C1 and C3.

Still, as discussed previously when speaking of gray-scaled palettes and converting colors to true-grays, the human eye's response to colors is itself nonlinear. This weighting can be incorporated into a third formula, which calculates the difference between colors using the same weighting as the eye's response:

$$dC = abs((R_1 - R_2) * 0.30) + abs((G_1 - G_2) * 0.59) + abs((B_1 - B_2) * 0.11)$$

Using this third formula, the difference between the C1 and C2 color entries becomes 1.18 versus a difference between C1 and C3 of 1.00. This is a more appropriate result than the first formula yielded, but less distinctive than the second.

However, we can combine the second and third formulas:

$$dC = ((R_1 - R_2) * 0.30)^2 + ((G_1 - G_2) * 0.59)^2 + ((B_1 - B_2) * 0.11)^2$$

The difference between C1 and C2 becomes 1.39 versus a difference between C1 and C3 of 0.45.

This final revision of the weighting formula offers a distinctive difference in results both by incorporating the nonlinear response of the human eye and by emphasizing the difference in one color component over differences spread across all color components.

TIP

A small difference in speed could be achieved in the calculations by converting the percentage weights to integer values (for example, changing 0.30 to 30), thus removing all floating-point operations in favor of integer calculations. In most cases, however, this is not likely to provide a notable change in calculation times.

Experimenting with Color Differences

If you are interested, you can experiment with the Color3 program in Chapter 22 to compare color differences. Here are some points to look for:

- What is the minimum total difference in all color components that can be readily identified by the human eye?
- What is the minimum difference in any one color component that can be readily identified?
- How do differences in each of the three component fields (red, green, and blue) compare?
- How do differences in intensity compare at different absolute intensities (how do absolute differences appear in proportion to absolute intensities)?

Ignoring extreme variations (commonly referred to as color blindness), color perception still varies widely between individuals and may also be affected by age, health, and the use of corrective lenses.

Now that we've covered the subject of bitmap images and file formats, we'll continue in the next chapter with some basic image-processing techniques, including filtering and rudimentary edge-detection

The two demo programs presented in the chapter were Capture, for capturing bitmap images to the clipboard or to a file, and ViewPCX, for displaying PCX files. The complete listing for the Capture program follows. The ViewPCX listing is on the CD that accompanies this book.

Listing 26.1: The Capture Program

```
//================//
//   Capture.H    //
//================//


#define   IDM_EXACT      101
#define   IDM_RESIZE     102
#define   IDM_CLIP       103
#define   IDM_FILE       104
#define   IDM_CAPTURE    105
#define   IDD_FNAME      106


#define   TOCLIPBD       107
#define   TOFILE         108



//==========================//
//          CAPTURE.C       //
//   Screen Capture Program //
//==========================//


#include <windows.h>
#include <stdlib.h>
#include <stdio.h>
#include <math.h>
#include "CAPTURE.h"

#define APP_ICON   "CAPTURE"
#define APP_MENU   "CAPTURE"
// note: no cursor assignment

HANDLE  hInst = NULL;

char    szAppTitle[] = "Screen Capture Demo";
char    szAppName[]  = "CAPTURE";
char    szFName[64]  = "";
int     iSec, Clock;

BOOL ErrorMsg( char * Error )
{
   HWND hwnd = GetFocus();
```

```
            MessageBeep( MB_ICONASTERISK );
            MessageBox( hwnd, Error, "Warning", MB_ICONASTERISK | MB_OK );
            return FALSE;
        }


BOOL APIENTRY FileNameDlgProc( HWND hDlg,   UINT msg,
                                       UINT wParam, LONG lParam )
{
    switch( msg )
    {
      case WM_INITDIALOG:
        SendDlgItemMessage( hDlg, IDD_FNAME, EM_LIMITTEXT, 80, 0 );
          SetDlgItemText( hDlg, IDD_FNAME, szFName );
          return( TRUE );
      case WM_COMMAND:
          switch( LOWORD( wParam ) )
          {
            case IDD_FNAME:
                if( HIWORD( wParam ) == EN_CHANGE )
                   EnableWindow( GetDlgItem( hDlg, IDOK ),
                      (BOOL) SendMessage( (HWND) lParam,
                         WM_GETTEXTLENGTH, 0, 0L ) );
                return( TRUE );

            case IDOK:
                GetDlgItemText( hDlg, IDD_FNAME,
                                  szFName, 80 );
                EndDialog( hDlg, TRUE );
                return( TRUE );

            case IDCANCEL:
                EndDialog( hDlg, FALSE );
                return( TRUE );

            default: return( FALSE );
      }       }
    return( FALSE );
}

int CaptureBitmap( HWND hwnd )
{
    HDC         hdc, hdcMem;
    HBITMAP     hBitmap;
```

```
            static int    i, j, CRes, LnWidth, LnPad = 0,
                          xSize, ySize;

        SetCursor( LoadCursor( NULL, IDC_WAIT ) );
        hdc = GetDC( HWND_DESKTOP );
        xSize = GetDeviceCaps( hdc, HORZRES );
        ySize = GetDeviceCaps( hdc, VERTRES );
        hdcMem = CreateCompatibleDC( hdc );
        hBitmap = CreateCompatibleBitmap( hdc, xSize, ySize );
        if( hBitmap )
        {
            SelectObject( hdcMem, hBitmap );
            StretchBlt( hdcMem, 0, 0, xSize, ySize,
                        hdc,    0, 0, xSize, ySize, SRCCOPY );
            OpenClipboard( hwnd );
            EmptyClipboard();
            SetClipboardData( CF_BITMAP, hBitmap );
            CloseClipboard();
            InvalidateRect( hwnd, NULL, TRUE );
        }
        DeleteDC( hdcMem );
        ReleaseDC( HWND_DESKTOP, hdc );
        return 0;
    }


    int SaveBitmap()
    {
        HDC       hdc, hdcMem;
        HANDLE    hBits, hFil;
        HBITMAP   hBitmap;
        HPALETTE  hPal;
        LPVOID    lpBits;
        RGBQUAD   RGBQuad;
        DWORD     ImgSize, plSize, dwWritten;
        int       i, CRes, Height, Width, LnWidth, LnPad;
        BITMAPFILEHEADER   bmFH;
        BITMAPINFO         bmInfo;
        LPLOGPALETTE       lp;

        SetCursor( LoadCursor( NULL, IDC_WAIT ) );
    //=== open file for write ================================
```

```
        hFil = CreateFile( szFName, GENERIC_WRITE, 0,  NULL,
                CREATE_ALWAYS, FILE_ATTRIBUTE_NORMAL, NULL );
        if( hFil == NULL )
            return( ErrorMsg( "Can't open file" ) );

        hdc = GetDC( HWND_DESKTOP );
        CRes = GetDeviceCaps( hdc, SIZEPALETTE );
        plSize = CRes * sizeof( RGBQUAD );          // palette size
        bmInfo.bmiHeader.biBitCount =
            GetDeviceCaps( hdc, BITSPIXEL );
        Height = GetDeviceCaps( hdc, VERTRES );
        Width  = GetDeviceCaps( hdc, HORZRES );
        if( GetDeviceCaps( hdc, BITSPIXEL ) == 8 )
            LnWidth = Width;
        else
            LnWidth = Width / 2;
        if( LnWidth % sizeof(DWORD) )
            LnPad = sizeof(DWORD) - ( LnWidth % sizeof(DWORD) );
        ImgSize = (DWORD)( (DWORD)( LnWidth + LnPad ) * 480 );

//=== initialize bitmap file header structure ============
        bmFH.bfType      = 0x4D42;                // Type is "BM"
        bmFH.bfReserved1 = 0L;
        bmFH.bfReserved2 = 0L;
        bmFH.bfOffBits   = plSize +              // bitmap offset
                        sizeof( BITMAPINFO ) +
                        sizeof( BITMAPFILEHEADER );
        bmFH.bfSize      = ImgSize +             // file size
                        bmFH.bfOffBits;
        WriteFile( hFil, &bmFH, sizeof( bmFH ),
                &dwWritten, NULL );      // write file header

//=== initialize bitmap info header structure ============
        bmInfo.bmiHeader.biSize =
            (DWORD) sizeof( BITMAPINFOHEADER );
        bmInfo.bmiHeader.biWidth        = Width;
        bmInfo.bmiHeader.biHeight       = Height;
        bmInfo.bmiHeader.biPlanes       = 1;
        bmInfo.bmiHeader.biCompression  = BI_RGB;
        bmInfo.bmiHeader.biSizeImage    = 0L;
        bmInfo.bmiHeader.biXPelsPerMeter = 0L;
```

```
    bmInfo.bmiHeader.biYPelsPerMeter = 0L;
    bmInfo.bmiHeader.biClrUsed       = 0L;
    bmInfo.bmiHeader.biClrImportant  = 0L;
    WriteFile( hFil, &bmInfo.bmiHeader,
               sizeof( bmInfo.bmiHeader ),
               &dwWritten, NULL );        // write info header

//=== add the palette color information ==================
             // note: GHND = GMEM_FIXED | GMEM_ZEROINIT
    hPal = GlobalAlloc( GHND, sizeof(LOGPALETTE) +
                        ( CRes * sizeof(PALETTEENTRY) ) );
                        // allocate memory for palette
    lp = (LPLOGPALETTE) GlobalLock( hPal );
                        // lock the memory allocated
    lp->palNumEntries = CRes;
    lp->palVersion    = 0x0300;
                        // fill in size and version (3.0)
    GetSystemPaletteEntries( hdc, 0, CRes,
                        lp->palPalEntry );
                        // and get the palette information
//========= Structure definitions ====================
// Palette Entry            RGB Quad for Bitmap
//
// typedef struct           typedef struct tagRGBQUAD
// {
//    BYTE   peRed;            BYTE   rgbBlue;
//    BYTE   peGreen;          BYTE   rgbGreen;
//    BYTE   peBlue;           BYTE   rgbRed;
//    BYTE   peFlags;          BYTE   rgbReserved;
// } PALETTEENTRY;          } RGBQUAD;
//
//====================================================
        // record each PALETTEENTRY as RGBQUAD format
    RGBQuad.rgbReserved = 0;
    for( i=0; i<=CRes; i++ )
    {
       RGBQuad.rgbRed   = lp->palPalEntry[i].peRed;
       RGBQuad.rgbGreen = lp->palPalEntry[i].peGreen;
       RGBQuad.rgbBlue  = lp->palPalEntry[i].peBlue;
       WriteFile( hFil, &RGBQuad, sizeof( RGBQuad ),
               &dwWritten, NULL );
```

```
        }
        GlobalUnlock( hPal );      // don't forget to unlock
        GlobalFree( hPal );        // and release the memory
        hPal = NULL;
//====== write image data to file ========================
        hdcMem = CreateCompatibleDC( hdc );
        hBitmap = CreateCompatibleBitmap( hdc, Width, 1 );
        hBits = GlobalAlloc( GHND, LnWidth );
        lpBits = (LPVOID) GlobalLock( hBits );
        SelectObject( hdcMem, hBitmap );
        for( i = Height - 1; i >= 0; i-- )
        {
            BitBlt( hdcMem, 0, 0, Width, 1,
                    hdc,    0, i, SRCCOPY );
            GetBitmapBits( hBitmap, Width, lpBits );
            WriteFile( hFil, lpBits, LnWidth, &dwWritten, NULL );
        }
        GlobalUnlock( hBits );     // don't forget to unlock
        GlobalFree( hBits );       // and release the image
        hBits = NULL;
        DeleteDC( hdcMem );        // delete and release the
        ReleaseDC( HWND_DESKTOP, hdc );   // device contexts
        CloseHandle( hFil );       // and close the file
        SetCursor( LoadCursor( NULL, IDC_ARROW ) );
        return( TRUE );
    }


long APIENTRY WndProc( HWND hwnd,   UINT msg,
                       UINT wParam, LONG lParam )
{
    static  BOOL  fExpand = FALSE;
    static  int   cxWnd, cyWnd, iStrMode, Action;
    BITMAP        bm;
    HBITMAP       hBitmap;
    HDC           hdc, hdcMem;
    PAINTSTRUCT   ps;

    switch( msg )
    {
        case WM_SIZE:
            cxWnd = LOWORD( lParam );
```

```
        cyWnd = HIWORD( lParam );
        InvalidateRect( hwnd, NULL, TRUE );
        break;

case WM_TIMER:
    if( ++iSec == 7 )              // Arbitrary countdown time
        PostMessage( hwnd, WM_COMMAND, IDM_CAPTURE, 0 );
    else MessageBeep( MB_ICONEXCLAMATION );
    break;

case WM_COMMAND:
    switch( LOWORD( wParam ) )
    {
        case IDM_EXACT:
            fExpand = FALSE;
            InvalidateRect( hwnd, NULL, TRUE );
            break;

        case IDM_RESIZE:
            fExpand = TRUE;
            InvalidateRect( hwnd, NULL, TRUE );
            break;

        case IDM_CLIP:
            Action = TOCLIPBD;
            CloseWindow( hwnd );
            Clock = SetTimer( hwnd, 1, 1000, NULL );
            iSec = 0;
            break;

        case IDM_FILE:
            if( DialogBox( hInst, "GETNAME", hwnd,
                           FileNameDlgProc ) )
            {
                Action = TOFILE;
                CloseWindow( hwnd );
                Clock = SetTimer( hwnd, 1, 1000, NULL );
                iSec = 0;
            }
            break;
```

```
              case IDM_CAPTURE:
                 MessageBeep( MB_OK );
                 KillTimer( hwnd, Clock );
                 SetCursor( LoadCursor( NULL, IDC_WAIT ) );
                 switch( Action )
                 {
                    case TOFILE:
                       SaveBitmap();            break;
                    case TOCLIPBD:
                       CaptureBitmap( hwnd ); break;
                 }
                 SetCursor( LoadCursor( NULL, IDC_ARROW ) );
                 OpenIcon( hwnd );
                 break;

              default:
                 return( DefWindowProc( hwnd,    msg,
                                        wParam, lParam ) );
           }
           break;

    case WM_PAINT:
       hdc = BeginPaint( hwnd, &ps );
       OpenClipboard( hwnd );
       if( hBitmap = GetClipboardData( CF_BITMAP ) )
       {
          SetCursor( LoadCursor( NULL, IDC_WAIT ) );
          hdcMem = CreateCompatibleDC( hdc );
          SelectObject( hdcMem, hBitmap );
          GetObject( hBitmap, sizeof( BITMAP ),
                     (LPSTR) &bm );
          if( fExpand )
          {
             SetStretchBltMode( hdc, iStrMode );
             StretchBlt( hdc, 0, 0, cxWnd, cyWnd,
                         hdcMem, 0, 0,
                         bm.bmWidth, bm.bmHeight,
                         SRCCOPY );
          }
          else
             BitBlt( hdc, 0, 0, cxWnd, cyWnd,
```

```
                              hdcMem, 0, 0, SRCCOPY );
               SetCursor( LoadCursor( NULL, IDC_ARROW ) );
               DeleteDC( hdcMem );
            }
            CloseClipboard();
            EndPaint( hwnd, &ps );
            break;

        case WM_DESTROY:
            PostQuitMessage(0);
            break;

        default:
            return( DefWindowProc( hwnd, msg, wParam, lParam ) );
    }
    return 0;
}


#include "template.i"

int APIENTRY WinMain( HANDLE hInstance, HANDLE hPrevInstance,
                      LPSTR lpCmdLine, int    nCmdShow    )
{
    MSG    msg;

    if( ! hPrevInstance )
       if( ! InitApplication( hInstance ) )
          return( FALSE );
    if( ! InitInstance( hInstance, nCmdShow ) )
       return (FALSE);
    while( GetMessage( &msg, NULL, 0, 0 ) )
    {
       TranslateMessage( &msg );
       DispatchMessage( &msg );
    }
    return( msg.wParam );
    UNREFERENCED_PARAMETER( lpCmdLine );
}
```

```
//===============================//
//   Capture.RC                  //
//===============================//

#include <windows.h>
#include "capture.h"

CAPTURE MENU
BEGIN
    POPUP "Capture"
    BEGIN
       MENUITEM "To Clipboard", IDM_CLIP
       MENUITEM "To File", IDM_FILE
    END
    POPUP "Display Mode"
    BEGIN
       MENUITEM "Original Size", IDM_EXACT
       MENUITEM "Size To Window", IDM_RESIZE
    END
END

GETNAME DIALOG 18, 18, 142, 40
STYLE DS_SYSMODAL | DS_MODALFRAME | WS_OVERLAPPED | WS_VISIBLE |
    WS_CAPTION | WS_THICKFRAME
CAPTION "Save Bitmap As"
BEGIN
    CONTROL "TESTFILE.BMP", IDD_FNAME, "EDIT",
       ES_LEFT | ES_UPPERCASE | WS_CHILD | WS_VISIBLE | WS_BORDER |
       WS_TABSTOP, 12, 8, 120, 12
    PUSHBUTTON "Ok", IDOK, 12, 23, 42, 14,
       WS_CHILD | WS_VISIBLE | WS_TABSTOP
    PUSHBUTTON "Cancel", IDCANCEL, 90, 23, 42, 14,
       WS_CHILD | WS_VISIBLE | WS_TABSTOP
END

CAPTURE ICON "capture.ico"
```

CHAPTER
TWENTY-SEVEN

27

Image-Enhancement Techniques

- Data-averaging methods

- Low- and high-pass filters

- Edge-detection algorithms

- Image-processing optimization

The human eye, backed by a sophisticated neural network, can pick out even a deliberately camouflaged shape from a mixed and mottled background. In contrast, teaching a computer to recognize a black square against a white background is more than slightly frustrating. The emphasis is on the computer's ability to *recognize*, which is a quite different process from locating a predefined, fixed pattern. Locating a known shape can be a relatively simple task for an application; recognition is an entirely different matter and a very sophisticated process.

In this chapter, the topic is image enhancement, which is not only integral to pattern recognition—both for computers and for humans—but is also used in image processing for aesthetic purposes.

In Chapter 26, a variety of image formats were discussed. For machine vision, however, the choice of image format is often monochrome and often employing a monochromatic light source. But, when color is used, the choice is simple: 24-bit imaging provides the maximum of data for processing. And, following Sherlock Holmes' caution that "it is a prime mistake to theorize in the absence of data," it's obvious that the more data available, the more information can be derived from that data.

For our present purposes of demonstration, however, a wealth of information also means an excess of processing. Therefore, the demo program in this chapter, Shades, uses 256-color bitmap images, sacrificing the richness of data for simplicity of processing. The demonstrations themselves, of course, are applicable to higher-resolution images and tend to function better as the degree of differentiation within the data increases.

The processes illustrated in this chapter are all public-domain implementations of standard formulas and use only the mathematical tools supplied by standard compilers. For actual machine-vision applications, much better performance can be obtained by using matrix transforms to implement these algorithms, preferably using a good matrix operations library. There are also additional edge-detection algorithms that are not discussed here for the simple reason that they are proprietary and copyrighted. Most of these are available as libraries from a variety of sources.

Nonetheless, the processes demonstrated here (and the suggested matrix libraries) should provide a starting point for your own experimentation in this field.

Converting Images to Maps: Transform Methods

The first step in image processing is to convert a raw image to a map or outline of the principal elements of the image. This process is commonly known as *edge detection*. In image processing, edge detection is simply the identification of abrupt gradients between adjacent pixels. To accomplish this, a variety of processes are available, including the Sobel, smoothed, Laplace, isotropic, and stochastic algorithms (all of these processes will be discussed presently and are included in the Shades demo program).

Too often, what would be a relatively simple process under ideal circumstances is complicated by the presence of noise or other garbage within the original data (image). When this happens, other algorithms, such as high- or low-pass filters or averaging algorithms, can be used to reduce the noise within the data.

Referring to "noise" within an image is not entirely accurate and has connotations that can be misleading. It might be more appropriate to describe the data as "overly complex" and to call the treatment process "simplification." Regardless of the terminology, however, the process is essentially the same: Either a portion of the information is removed or the weight accorded to that portion of the information is decreased.

Data Averaging

Data averaging is precisely what its name suggests: treating each data element or pixel by averaging its value with the value of the surrounding elements. As an example, consider the following array of values:

```
9 9 8 9 9 8 7 6              8 8 8 8 7 7 6 6
9 8 9 9 8 1 6 6      1 1 1   8 8 8 8 7 7 5 6
9 9 9 8 7 6 6 6  X   1 0 1 = 8 8 8 7 6 5 5 6
9 9 8 7 6 7 6 7      1 1 1   8 8 7 7 6 6 6 6
9 8 7 6 6 6 6 6              8 7 7 6 6 6 6 6
```

In the raw data set (on the left), most elements within the sample consist of the values 6..9 with a single noise element appearing with a value of 1. On the right, the sample data set has been "cleaned" using a simple averaging algorithm, the center matrix, and the resulting data set has become considerably more homogeneous than it was originally.

The mask array is applied to each data element in the original set and weighs each element as the average of its neighbors' values while ignoring the element's own value. Thus, the mask is applied to the noise data element as:

```
9 8 7     1 1 1     ((9*1)+(8*1)+(7*1)+
8 1 6  X  1 0 1  =  (8*1)+(1*0)+(6*1)+    = 57/8 = 7.125 = 7
7 6 6     1 1 1     (7*1)+(6*1)+(6*1))/8
```

The resulting value, 7, fits nicely into the original data set. (Later, this same data set will be used to illustrate other filter processes.)

However, although the averaging algorithm demonstrated does serve nicely to remove noise, the original data—with an average range of 9..6—now has a range of 8..6. Both the extreme low and the extreme high have been lost, which means that data has been lost and the entropy of the data set has increased.

> **NOTE**
> This averaging algorithm does not use matrix multiplication but only a simple masking operation. Mathematicians may enjoy applying matrix algebra via a similar algorithm; the results can be very interesting.

Depending on circumstances, a number of different masks can be applied. For example, three useful masks are:

```
1 1 1     1 1 1     1 1 1
1 1 1     1 4 1     1 8 1
1 1 1     1 1 1     1 1 1
```

For these three masks, the normalizing divisors used would be 9, 12, and 16, respectively, and each mask has changed the relative weighting given to the central or target data element. In the prior example, the target element was ignored entirely. In the first of these latter examples, all elements including the target receive equal weighting. Using the second mask, the target element receives one-third weighting against its neighbors' two-thirds weighting. Using the third mask, the target element is weighted equally against the sum of its neighbors. Furthermore, in each case, the severity of the averaging decreases.

Refer back to the previous example and notice that the original data set was only moderately homogeneous. The areas that held predominately nines also held a few eights and, at the lower-right corner of the data set, where the values were predominately sixes, there are also a few scattered sevens.

> **WARNING** Remember: averaging the data also reduces the amount of information contained in the data.

Also, since your attention has been called to the distribution of values, notice a diagonal "edge" consisting of eights and sevens, which forms a transition between the fields consisting predominately of nines and the field consisting predominately of sixes. Later, other algorithms will be applied to this same data set to demonstrate edge detection.

For the moment, however, the subject is averaging or noise removal. What you should particularly note is that the algorithm applied has removed the noisy element and, at the same time, left the remainder of the data essentially unchanged although slightly smoother.

Granted, such a thoroughly "hands-off" selectivity is not a reliable expectation, but the general result is that the homogeneous areas remain relatively unaffected while noisy elements are smoothed out, at least to a degree.

Handling Border Restrictions

With the exception of the color-inversion procedure (discussed later in this chapter), all of the transformation algorithms demonstrated here have a small limitation: The border pixels of the image cannot be included in the convolution.

With a bit of thought, the reason should be obvious: Each pixel (or data element) convoluted requires, using a 3-by-3 array, a border on each side consisting of one column and one row. For the stochastic transform (discussed later), which uses a 5-by-5 or a 7-by-7 mask, the border area increases accordingly.

Also, for the data sets used as illustrations for each of these processes, an appropriate border has been added (but not shown) to permit executing the transforms across the entire data set depicted.

> **NOTE** Adding a "border" to the data is acceptable for demonstration purposes, since the entire data set illustrated was constructed for demonstration in the first place. However, this is not a practice that can be conveniently applied to real data sets.

This may sound like a minor restriction, but it is still an important one. Under Windows, attempts to access data-array elements that are not defined, because they lie outside the data set, will result in a system memory violation. Under DOS, the immediate effects of such errors may be less readily apparent but can still be quite serious. For this reason, the loop calling the transform procedure is always indexed, both vertically and horizontally, with a high and low offset to accommodate the border requirements.

Using an Averaging Procedure

The `DoAveragingTrns` procedure is one of the simpler examples of filtering a data array and will serve to introduce the technique used to implement a variety of other filters.

In the Shades demo program presented in this chapter, `DoAveragingTrns` is called from a procedure that is scanning one copy of an image and writing the results to a second copy. `DoAveragingTrns` is called with an index (DWORD) to a one-dimensional array of data (the image), returning a byte value, which in this case, is the new palette index value.

```
BYTE DoAveragingTrns( DWORD dwPos )
{
   int   TxFrm[3][3] =    // Averaging transformation
         {  1,  1,  1,
            1,  0,  1,
            1,  1,  1  };

   BYTE   RVal,  GVal,  BVal,  m;
   int    RtVal, GtVal, BtVal, i, j, n;
   DWORD  dwOfs;

   RVal = GVal = BVal = 0;
   for( i=-1; i<2; i++ )
      for( j=-1; j<2; j++ )
```

Within `DoAveragingTrns`, a double loop steps through the mask array. Instead of the usual loop from 0..2, a loop from -1..1 is used because the elements for the comparison bracket the target element, appearing before, after, above, and below.

Within the loop, a second process is needed to address the appropriate pixel elements. Thus `dwOfs` is calculated as an offset from `dwPos`. The value `bmScanWidth` was calculated when the image was loaded and, instead of the image width, provides the scan width, which must be an even WORD multiple.

The `DoAveragingTrns` function is not actually implemented in the Shades demo. Instead, a more sophisticated version, `DoSmoothedTrns`, is used. The `DoAveragingTrns` function has the advantages of being simpler to discuss and still providing the same essential elements as the more elaborate version.

```
   {
      dwOfs = (DWORD)( dwPos + i + ( j *bmScanWidth ) );
      m = (BYTE) pMBits[dwOfs];    // get palette index for pixel
```

After determining the appropriate offset (`dwOfs`), `m` retrieves the palette index value from the identified pixel. Since the value contained in `m` is only a palette index, three separate values are extracted from the palette entry itself as red, green, and blue color values, all of which are multiplied by the present mask value.

```
      RtVal += TxFrm[i+1][j+1] * pGLP->palPalEntry[m].peRed;
      GtVal += TxFrm[i+1][j+1] * pGLP->palPalEntry[m].peGreen;
      BtVal += TxFrm[i+1][j+1] * pGLP->palPalEntry[m].peBlue;
   }
```

Obviously, if loop values from -1 to 1 are used to index relative pixels, some correction (as shown) is required to reference the mask array, shifting the values back to the range 0..2.

After the loop completes, one further series of choices is required because provisions have been made to permit operations on only one, any two, or all three of the color planes. But, assuming a color plane is enabled, the total in `_tVal` is divided by eight before typecasting as a `BYTE` value.

```
   if( UseColors[0] ) RVal = (BYTE)( RtVal / 8 );
               else RVal = pGLP->palPalEntry[m].peRed;

   if( UseColors[1] ) GVal = (BYTE)( GtVal / 8 );
               else GVal = pGLP->palPalEntry[m].peGreen;

   if( UseColors[2] ) BVal = (BYTE)( BtVal / 8 );
               else BVal = pGLP->palPalEntry[m].peBlue;
   return( GetNearestPaletteIndex( hGPal,
         RGB((BYTE)RVal,(BYTE)GVal,(BYTE)BVal)));
}
```

Last, the resulting red, green, and blue values are passed to the RGB macro and then to the GetNearestPaletteIndex function to return an appropriate palette index representing the resulting color (or, at least, the closest available match).

Low-Pass Filtering

A second filter process, known as *low-pass filtering* or *two-dimensional Gaussian weighting,* uses a filter matrix. In general, low-pass filters are used for noise smoothing and for interpolating missing or damaged data elements.

The actual Gaussian formula is somewhat more complex than the mask illustrated. However, this matrix does supply a good integer approximation of two-dimensional Gaussian weighting and, for computer processing purposes, is considerably faster than applying the real formula while proving every bit as effective.

Applying the low-pass mask to the data set illustrated previously produces the following results:

```
9 9 8 9 9 8 7 6                   8 8 8 8 8 7 6 6
9 8 9 9 8 1 6 6      1 2 1        8 8 8 8 7 5 5 6
9 9 9 8 7 6 6 6  X   2 4 2  =     8 8 8 7 6 5 5 6
9 9 8 7 6 7 6 7      1 2 1        8 8 7 7 6 6 6 6
9 8 7 6 6 6 6 6                   8 7 7 6 6 6 6 6
```

The results yielded by the low-pass filter are quite similar to the results produced by the averaging filter. The primary difference between the two is simply that the noise elements are not quite as smoothed out as they were when using the averaging filter.

High-Pass Filtering

A third filter process, known as *high-pass filtering,* is essentially the reverse of the low-pass filter. High-pass filters are useful for enhancing contrast and for detecting edges. At the same time, high-pass filters also enhance any noise present within an image.

Following are the effects of applying a high-pass filter to the sample data set:

```
9 9 8 9 9 9 8 7 6                          1    4 -11    3   12   13    5  -6
9 8 9 9 9 8 1 6 6        -1 -2 -1          2  -11    5    7   13  -73    6  -1
9 9 9 8 7 6 6 6 6   X    -2 12 -2    =     1    3    7    1    4    4    3  -2
9 9 8 7 6 7 6 7          -1 -2 -1          1    6    1   -1   -8   11   -4  12
9 8 7 6 6 6 6 6                            6    1   -1   -6   -2   -2   -2  -2
```

In this case, the results no longer fit the range of the original data set. The result of the mask operation could be normalized as shown here:

```
1    4 -11    3   12   13    5  -6                 8 8 7 8 9 9 8 7
2  -11    5    7   13  -73    6  -1                8 8 8 8 9 1 8 7
1    3    7    1    4    4    3  -2   (N1)   =      8 8 8 8 8 8 8 7
1    6    1   -1   -8   11   -4  12                 8 8 8 7 7 8 7 9
6    1   -1   -6   -2   -2   -2  -2                 8 8 7 7 7 7 7 7
```

Normalizing the data, while returning the data to the original range, has also destroyed most of the information gained from the high-pass filter. At the same time, it has blurred the original data.

Range Clipping

More often, a high-pass filter would be used with a different criterion known as *range clipping*. Using range clipping, instead of normalizing all values to maintain the desired range, values rising above the maximum are simply truncated to the maximum, and values falling below the minimum are returned as the minimum.

The effects of range clipping, however, tend to obscure details at both extremes of the range and, therefore, are most useful when the contrasts within a data set (or an image) are relatively low and can be enhanced by this process without losing other important data.

Exercising a normalization of this type has a quite different effect, as shown here:

```
1    4 -11    3   12   13    5  -6                 1 4 0 3 9 9 5 0
2  -11    5    7   13  -73    6  -1                2 0 6 7 9 0 6 0
1    3    7    1    4    4    3  -2   (N2)   =      1 3 7 1 4 4 3 0
1    6    1   -1   -8   11   -4  12                 1 6 1 0 0 9 0 9
6    1   -1   -6   -2   -2   -2  -2                 6 1 0 0 0 0 0 0
```

Employing range clipping does lose some information, in both the highs and the lows; overall, however, it enhances the important contrasts, which, after all, is the entire objective.

High-Pass Filter Variations

A variety of high-pass filters can be applied to produce different degrees of contrast. Discovering the precise effects of variations in high-pass masks is left as an exercise for the reader, but three matrix suggestions follow:

```
-1  -2  -1      -1  -3  -1      -2  -3  -2
-2  16  -2      -3  16  -3      -3  20  -3
-1  -2  -1      -1  -3  -1      -2  -3  -2
```

Notice in each matrix that the sum of the core (center or target) value and the neighbor values is always zero.

Edge-Detection Algorithms

Although high- and low-pass filters are useful, edge-detection algorithms are always an important element of image processing and particularly so in machine-vision applications. It is possible to create a program to measure and identify clearly defined shapes, but such ideal shapes are rarely encountered in actual applications.

More commonly, even good image data generally consists of misaligned images obscured by shadows, highlights, and general noise. In these circumstances, as well as others, edge-detection algorithms become eminently important. Certainly high-pass filters provide some edge detection, but a variety of other functions are expressly designed to detect and identify sharp differentials in intensity and color that identify visually regional boundaries.

As an example, in Figure 27.1, at the top, two modernistic "paintings" appear. (The original images, titled MODERN.BMP and MODERN2.BMP, are included on the CD accompanying this book.) Below each original, in two columns, a series of four transforms appear, each using the Sobel edge-detection algorithm. The first transform uses the red color plane, the second uses the green, and the third uses the blue. Finally, the last transform in each column, employing all three color planes, provides the clearest edge detection, even though this leaves the background color black with edges identified in color according to the degree of slope (color contrast).

Unlike high-pass filters, all edge-detection algorithms are highly directional; that is, a specific convolution matrix will detect slope or edges only in certain orientations. For this reason, edge-detection algorithms commonly use four passes, rotating the matrix in 45-degree steps each time. Or, more commonly, instead of rotating the matrix, a series of four mask rotations are defined and each used in turn.

FIGURE 27.1

Two images before and after edge-detection enhancement

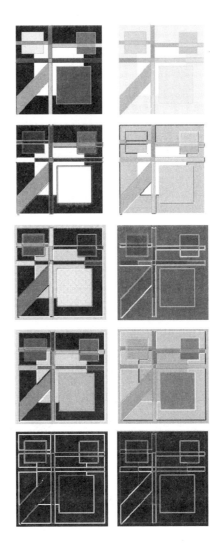

Because each mask will return a positive or a negative value, depending on the direction of the slope encountered, the result of each mask convolution is used as an absolute value. When all four convolutions have been processed, the highest slope of the four detected is returned.

> **NOTE**
> The fact that the Sobel transform was used for the example in Figure 27.1 is unimportant; all of the algorithms demonstrated in the Shades program work equally well with cleanly defined originals. In other circumstances, however, various edge-detection algorithms will differ in efficiency.

Sobel Transforms

The Sobel transform (also called a convolution) is a relatively simple edge-detection algorithm employing four 3-by-3 arrays as shown:

```
-1 -2 -1      0 -1 -2     -1  0  1     -2 -1  0
 0  0  0      1  0 -1     -2  0  2     -1  0  1
 1  2  1      2  1  0     -1  0  1      0  1  2
```

The matrices work as follows:

- The first matrix, at the far left, detects edges that are horizontally oriented.

- The second matrix detects edges slanting diagonally from upper left to lower right.

- The third matrix detects vertical lines.

- The fourth matrix detects diagonals running from lower left to upper right.

The matrix values (and sizes) used by other edge-detection algorithms vary but follow essentially the same principles.

Beginning with the first matrix and applying the Sobel convolution to the data set previously used as an example, the result shows three data points that are identified as an edge element, thus:

```
9 9 8 9 9 8 7 6                          0  2  0  1 10  7  1  4
9 8 9 9 8 1 6 6        -1  0  1          0  1  1  3 19  7  8  1
9 9 9 8 7 6 6 6    X   -2  0  2    =     0  1  4  7 12  4  5  0
9 9 8 7 6 7 6 7        -1  0  1          1  4  7  7  2  1  0  0
9 8 7 6 6 6 6 6                          4  7  7  4  0  0  0  0
```

Next, ignoring the results of the first test and applying the second matrix array, the Sobel convolution detects a very prominent edge running roughly diagonally from the lower left toward the upper right, as shown below. Because this is not a "clean" line, the detected edge varies in width from one to three elements but, given the data set, is the best information available.

```
9 9 8 9 9 8 7 6                              0   1   0   1 18 16 10   6
9 8 9 9 8 1 6 6      -2 -1  0                 0   0   1   4 16 10   0   2
9 9 9 8 7 6 6 6   X  -1  0  1   =            0   2   6 10   8   1 12   1
9 9 8 7 6 7 6 7       0  1  2                 2   6 10 10   5   2   0   0
9 8 7 6 6 6 6 6                              6 10 10   9   2   1   2   1
```

Still, this is only two passes; two further matrices remain to test the data set. Below is the result produced after all convolutions have been processed. The points shown in boldface identify detected edges, or points where the slope or difference between data elements and their neighbors is extreme.

```
0   1   0   1 18 19 13   6
0   2   1   4 16 10   0   2
0   2   6 10   8   1 12   1
2   6 10 10   5   2   0   0
6 10 10   6   2   1   2   1
```

Thus far, the Sobel transform has provided very good contrast, and the detected edges should stand out well from the surrounding data. This contrast can be taken one step further by comparing the new data set with the original and applying three simple rules to create a third data set:

- If the data point after convolution is higher than the data point before convolution, the point is set to a maximum.

- If the data point remains the same or approximately the same, a median value is assigned. What range is considered median can vary according to the application and the data set.

- If the resulting data point is lower than the original, the value is set to a minimum.

Here is the result after maximizing contrasts:

```
0 0 0 0 9 9 9 0
0 0 0 0 9 9 0 0
0 0 0 9 9 0 9 0
0 0 9 9 0 0 0 0
0 9 9 0 0 0 0 0
```

<table>
<tr><td>NOTE</td><td>The maximizing process illustrated here is optional and not implemented in the Shades program; if desired, it can be added conveniently. Remember, however, that comparisons must be made not on the palette index values, but on the actual color values. Furthermore, the red, green, and blue color values must be compared separately, although the values returned for each color plane can be summed for a contrast total.</td></tr>
</table>

Smoothed Transforms

Smoothed (or Hough) transforms operate essentially the same as Sobel transforms except for the matrices used. For a smoothed transform, the four masks used are defined as:

```
-1  0  1      -1 -1  0      -1 -1 -1       0 -1 -1
-1  0  1      -1  0  1       0  0  0       1  0 -1
-1  0  1       0  1  1       1  1  1       1  1  0
```

Aside from the change in values, operations remain the same as the Sobel transform, and the results are also similar.

Laplace Transforms

Laplace transforms are distinctly different from the Sobel and smoothed transforms. The Laplace transform also uses a 3-by-3 array, but this array is symmetrical and only one array is used, making the Laplace transform similar to the high-pass filters discussed earlier.

Although three separate Laplace transforms are provided in the Shades demo program, only one of these matrices will be used at a time, as selected by the degree variable. The three transforms are defined as:

```
 0 -1  0      -1 -1 -1       1 -2  1
-1  4 -1      -1  8 -1      -2  4 -2
 0 -1  0      -1 -1 -1       1 -2  1
```

Notice particularly that the sum of the elements in each mask is zero. The Laplace transform, or Laplace operator, is also known as a *zero-crossing operator* and is useful with photographic (or video) images for outlining areas of constant intensity.

The Isotropic Transform

The isotropic transform parallels the Sobel and smoothed transforms in that it consists of four 3-by-3 masks. Instead of integer values, however, it ideally consists of real values, defined as:

$$
\begin{array}{ccc}
-1 & 0 & 1 \\
-\sqrt{2} & 0 & \sqrt{2} \\
-1 & 0 & 1
\end{array}
\qquad
\begin{array}{ccc}
-\sqrt{2} & -1 & 0 \\
-1 & 0 & 1 \\
0 & 1 & \sqrt{2}
\end{array}
\qquad
\begin{array}{ccc}
-1 & -\sqrt{2} & -1 \\
0 & 0 & 0 \\
1 & \sqrt{2} & 1
\end{array}
\qquad
\begin{array}{ccc}
0 & -1 & -\sqrt{2} \\
1 & 0 & -1 \\
\sqrt{2} & 1 & 0
\end{array}
$$

However, because integer operations are faster than floating-point calculations (and because quite a few operations are required for this process), the transform matrices are defined as:

$$
\begin{array}{ccc}
-100 & 0 & 100 \\
-141 & 0 & 141 \\
-100 & 0 & 100
\end{array}
\qquad
\begin{array}{ccc}
-141 & -100 & 0 \\
-100 & 0 & 100 \\
0 & 100 & 141
\end{array}
\qquad
\begin{array}{ccc}
-100 & -141 & -100 \\
0 & 0 & 0 \\
100 & 141 & 100
\end{array}
\qquad
\begin{array}{ccc}
0 & -100 & -141 \\
100 & 0 & -100 \\
141 & 100 & 0
\end{array}
$$

After these operators are used, the resulting values are simply divided by 100, which is generally a much faster process than floating-point operations.

The Stochastic Transform

Like the isotropic transform, the stochastic transform uses floating-point operations and, again, can be approximated by changing from decimal values to integers in the matrix arrays.

The stochastic transform uses a series of eight masks, each of which is a 5-by-5 array rather than a 3-by-3.

Only one of the eight matrix arrays is illustrated here, using floating-point values:

$$
\begin{array}{ccccc}
0.802 & 0.836 & 0.000 & -0.836 & -0.802 \\
0.845 & 0.897 & 0.000 & -0.897 & -0.845 \\
0.870 & 1.000 & 0.000 & -1.000 & -0.870 \\
0.845 & 0.897 & 0.000 & -0.897 & -0.845 \\
0.802 & 0.836 & 0.000 & -0.836 & -0.802
\end{array}
$$

The principal advantage of the stochastic transform lies in the size of the array, which makes it less susceptible to noise in the data than the other transforms illustrated. Likewise, even large stochastic arrays may be used when necessary, but obviously, processing time will increase proportionally.

A second advantage is that the values used for a stochastic transform can be optimized according to the signal-to-noise ratio in the data set. As an example, for a high signal-to-noise ratio, the preceding array might be rewritten as:

```
0.267   0.364   0.000   -0.364   -0.267
0.373   0.562   0.000   -0.562   -0.373
0.463   1.000   0.000   -1.000   -0.463
0.373   0.562   0.000   -0.562   -0.373
0.267   0.364   0.000   -0.364   -0.267
```

Calculating Values for Matrix Transforms

In each of the examples employing conformal transformations, for both filtering and edge-detection, static arrays have been used. Also, floating-point values have been converted to integers to speed processing, with the resulting values restored to the original ranges.

With the stochastic and isotropic transforms, instead of using static matrices, the size of the arrays used can be adjusted to suit the circumstances, with the necessary values derived by calculation.

Also with stochastic transforms, values for the matrices can be optimized according to the noise levels within the image data or can even be varied according to the noise levels at different areas within an image.

Implementing Image Transformation: The Shades Program

The Shades program demonstrates a variety of convolution transformations. For simplicity, however, Shades also has a few limitations:

- Only uncompressed, 256-color BMP images are accepted. No provisions are included for reading other formats or other image types. (Other formats can be added if desired.)

- Since Windows 32-bit addressing has removed previous memory limits, no provisions are made for the special handling required earlier for large images (those with more than 64KB of image data). Adaptations of these algorithms to other operating systems, however, may require custom handling to access larger images.

- Shades is not intended as a painting program but only as a demonstration of image processing. No provisions have been included to save transformed images back to disk files. This and other drawing options, however, may be added at the discretion of the programmer.

The Shades program offers two principal menu options. The first is Image, which calls a file-selection dialog box to choose and load a bitmap file.

The second option, Transform, calls the dialog box shown in Figure 27.2. Under Operation types, you can choose from seven transform types: pixel averaging, isotropic, color inversion, Laplace, smoothed, Sobel, and stochastic. At the right, the Color Use group box shows three checkboxes for Red, Green, and Blue, permitting operations to be restricted to one, two, or all three color planes (at least one of these color plane options must be selected). The dialog box also has the standard Cancel and Execute buttons.

FIGURE 27.2

Image transformation
options

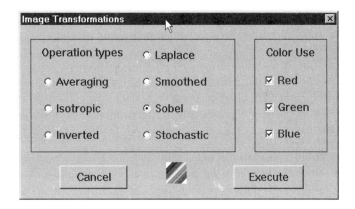

For convenience in programming and to make these routines usable by other applications, all of the image transforms have been placed in the include file Trnsform.I, rather than in the main body of the Shades program code.

Using Memory Bitmaps

As we discussed in Chapter 26, Windows' native image format is the BMP bitmap format, and the Windows internal provisions for handling bitmap images are better than those for other image formats.

WARNING   In any environment, remember not to write the changed information back to the original source until all of the image has been transformed. The results of executing a transform using partially processed results are, at best, undesirable.

Furthermore, regardless of the original bitmap format, all images should be displayed as memory bitmaps rather than being painted to the screen directly. When images are displayed as memory bitmaps, repainting the screen—such as when the window is resized, moved, hidden, or revealed—becomes virtually automatic. As another advantage, the conversion to memory bitmaps is considerably faster than any direct paint operation.

Reading and Displaying the Bitmap

In Shades, the `ReadBitmap` procedure is found in an include file, DIBitMap.I, and is called with two parameters: a handle to the application's window and the name (and drive/path information) of the image file to be loaded for display and processing. The DIBitMap.I include file, and the procedures provided, will be used by other applications as well.

Because `ReadBitmap` may be called repeatedly and, if so, has stored global handles to bitmap and palette information, `ReadBitmap` begins by calling the `Free-GlobalVars` procedure to clean up any existing memory objects before loading a new bitmap from the disk and to reset (zero) variables, as:

```
void FreeGlobalVars()
{       // if old bitmap, delete same
   if( hGBM )   DeleteObject( hGBM );
   if( hGBM )   LocalFree( (HANDLE) hGBM );
   hGBM = NULL;
      // if old palette, delete same
   if( hGPal )  DeleteObject( hGPal );
   if( hGPal )  LocalFree( (HANDLE) hGPal );
   hGPal = NULL;
      // if old palette handle, delete same
   if( hGLP )   DeleteObject( hGLP );
   if( hGLP )   LocalFree( hGLP );
   hGLP = NULL;
   bmWidth = bmHeight = bmImgSize = bmScanWidth = 0;
}
```

Within the `ReadBitmap` procedure, once the global variables have been cleared, the first step is a test to be sure that the named file does exist, which is accomplished by attempting to open the file for read.

```
hFile = _lopen( szFName, OF_READ );
if( hFile == -1 )
{
    sprintf( szBuff, "Can't open %s", szFName );
    return( ErrorMsg( szBuff ) );
}
```

If the file selected does not exist (which is unlikely unless the file selection has been entered directly), an error message is displayed to report the problem before the process returns a FALSE result.

Even assuming that the file does exist, however, there are no assurances that the file is an acceptable image format or even that the file is a bitmap image. Therefore, the next step is to perform a few checks, beginning by reading the file header and checking the two-character key, "BM."

```
SetCursor( LoadCursor( NULL, IDC_WAIT ) );
_lread( hFile, (LPSTR) &bmFH, sizeof(BITMAPFILEHEADER) );
if( bmFH.bfType != 0x4D42 )   // if type isn't "BM" ...
    return( ErrorMsg( "Not a bitmap image" ) );
```

Having identified this as a bitmap file, the next step is to allocate and lock memory space for the bitmap information header before reading the data from the file. This is a more elaborate process than the one used to read the file header but, at this point, the data read needs to be retained (and protected), at least long enough for a few tests and to extract a few facts.

```
hBmIH = LocalAlloc( LMEM_FIXED, sizeof(BITMAPINFOHEADER ) );
pBmIH = (LPBITMAPINFOHEADER) LocalLock( hBmIH );
_lread( hFile, (LPSTR) pBmIH, sizeof(BITMAPINFOHEADER) );
if( (WORD) pBmIH->biBitCount != 8 ) // 2^8 colors = 256
    return( ErrorMsg( "Not a 256 color bitmap"));
if( (DWORD) pBmIH->biCompression != BI_RGB )
    return( ErrorMsg("Compressed images not accepted"));
PalSize = (WORD)( pBmIH->biClrUsed * sizeof(RGBQUAD) );
LocalUnlock( hBmIH );
```

After checking the bit count to ensure that this is a 256-color image, testing to see if the image is compressed, and retrieving the size of the color palette, the bitmap information header is no longer needed and can be released. Remember, memory should be locked only while access is required and should be released entirely when access is no longer needed.

Global Memory Allocation Rules

The memory allocation operations described here use the local heap rather than the global heap, which was required under Windows 3.1. The difference is that, under Windows NT, the global and local heaps are exactly the same thing. However, when using either the global or local heap, all well-behaved applications should observe a few rules:

- Memory must be locked while in use to prevent Windows from relocating data blocks during access.
- Whenever they are not being actively referenced, memory blocks should be unlocked and only relocked when access is required again.
- As with any memory allocation, global memory blocks should be unlocked and freed as soon as the data is no longer needed.

Now that the size of the palette is known, the next step is to allocate memory for both the palette and information header and to set this new pointer back to the just-released information header data:

```
hBmInfo = LocalAlloc( LPTR,
                         PalSize + sizeof(BITMAPINFOHEADER) );
pBmInfo = (LPBITMAPINFO) LocalLock( hBmInfo );
pBmInfo->bmiHeader = *pBmIH;
LocalFree( hBmIH );              // free old memory handle
hBmIH = NULL;
```

Does this sound strange? Releasing the memory and then reallocating it and locking it again? Perhaps this is a bit indirect, but now both the bitmap information header data and the palette data are stored together in a single structure. And, remember, until the information header was read, the palette size was unknown.

Before retrieving the palette data, there is another step that can be executed. By saving the image size and color depth as a series of global variables, we make these values readily accessible to other procedures within this application.

```
bmWidth     = LOWORD( pBmInfo->bmiHeader.biWidth );
bmHeight    = LOWORD( pBmInfo->bmiHeader.biHeight );
//  note width and height saved as WORD, not DWORD
bmBitCount  = (WORD)  pBmInfo->bmiHeader.biBitCount;
bmImgSize   = (DWORD) pBmInfo->bmiHeader.biSizeImage;
bmScanWidth = (DWORD) bmWidth;
while( bmScanWidth % sizeof(WORD) ) bmScanWidth++;
                          // must be an even WORD size !!!
if( pBmInfo->bmiHeader.biSizeImage == 0 )
{
   bmImgSize = ( ( ( ( bmWidth * bmBitCount ) + 31 ) / 32 )
                 * 4 ) * bmHeight;
   pBmInfo->bmiHeader.biSizeImage = bmImgSize;
}
```

Two final provisions are made in the foregoing code. First, the image width (bmWidth) can be any value and can be odd or even. But each scan line in the image must end on a WORD boundary and must be reflected in the bmScanWidth value. Second, just in case the image size wasn't included in the image header data (because not all programs are well-behaved), a provision is included to calculate this essential piece of information.

Now, with these tasks completed, the palette information can be retrieved. Before doing so, however, another test is necessary: checking to see that there is enough data to fill the palette structure, thus:

```
if( _lread( hFile, (LPSTR) pBmInfo->bmiColors, PalSize )
!= PalSize )
{
   GlobalUnlock( hBmInfo );
   LocalFree( hBmInfo );
   pBmInfo = NULL;
   FreeGlobalVars();
   return( ErrorMsg( "Palette read error" ) );
}
```

If the file size is wrong, then the error is reported and the process terminates, returning FALSE.

Assuming that the information was read correctly, memory is allocated for a logical palette structure and the RGBQUAD values read from the BMP file are converted to palette entry structures.

```
pRGB = pBmInfo->bmiColors;
   //===================================================//
   // check for short palette indicated by biClrUsed //
   //===================================================//
if( pBmInfo->bmiHeader.biClrUsed )
   CRes = pBmInfo->bmiHeader.biClrUsed;
if( hGLP != NULL )
   LocalFree( hGLP );
hGLP = LocalAlloc( LPTR, sizeof(LOGPALETTE) +
                     ( ( CRes - 1 ) * sizeof(PALETTEENTRY) ) );
pGLP = (LPLOGPALETTE) LocalLock( hGLP );
              // allocate and lock memory for palette
pGLP->palNumEntries = CRes;        // fill in size and
pGLP->palVersion    = 0x0300;      // version (3.0)
for( i=0; i<CRes; i++ )            // convert colors
{
   pGLP->palPalEntry[i].peRed   = pRGB[i].rgbRed;
   pGLP->palPalEntry[i].peGreen = pRGB[i].rgbGreen;
   pGLP->palPalEntry[i].peBlue  = pRGB[i].rgbBlue;
   pGLP->palPalEntry[i].peFlags = 0;
}
hNewPal = CreatePalette( pGLP );
LocalUnlock( hGLP );
```

Next, CreatePalette is called to create the palette from the color information. Last, the allocated memory is unlocked but not freed.

At this point, all of the information about the bitmap has been retrieved, except for the bitmap itself. Ergo, the next step is to allocate memory for the image data and then to initiate a loop to read blocks of memory until the entire image has been retrieved.

```
hBM = LocalAlloc( LPTR, bmImgSize );
BytesLeft = ReadBytes = bmImgSize;
pBits = (BYTE *) LocalLock( hBM );
```

Allocating and locking the memory required is simple. Under Windows 3.x, however, the process of reading the image data was potentially somewhat more complex. Remember the 64KB limit on data segments? The _lread file function could not read a block greater than 64KB (that is, could not read past a segment boundary) and, therefore, required rather complex provisions to read the appropriate data in smaller segments. The process looked something like this:

```
while( BytesLeft > 0 )
{
   if( BytesLeft > 32767L ) GetBytes = 32768L;
                       else GetBytes = BytesLeft;
      //===========================================//
      // limit block reads to 32K to avoid crossing //
      // segment boundary when calling _lread       //
      //===========================================//
   if( (WORD) _lread( hFile, (LPSTR) pBits,
                    (WORD) GetBytes ) != GetBytes )
   if( ReadBytes <= 0 ) break;
   else
   {
      FreeGlobalVars();
      return( FALSE );
   }
   pBits += GetBytes;
   ReadBytes -= GetBytes;
   BytesLeft -= GetBytes;
}
_lclose( hFile );
```

Notice that this process also required the pBits pointer, the location where the data is stored, to be incremented after each read. Also, if _lread returned fewer bytes than requested, the odds were that a problem had occurred and a check was provided for this possibility.

Under Windows NT, with 32-bit addressing, the question of segment boundaries does not arise—until the file size passes the magic 4GB mark. Although the original code still works, under NT a simpler, single-step operation is possible:

```
ReadFile( hFile, pBits, bmImgSize, &fRes, NULL )
CloseHandle( hFile );
```

In the present example, the earlier version continues to be employed, using the _lread function. Readers, however, are invited to rewrite the ReadBitmap function to use the CreateFile and ReadFile functions to experiment with the newer APIs.

NOTE Remember that Windows 95 does not support attempts to perform asynchronous file access, even though Windows NT does permit overlapped file reads. See Chapter 26 for details.

As long as everything is proceeding normally, the bitmap file can now be closed. But, this does not mean that everything is finished—far from it.

The next step is to make the new palette active by calling the SelectPalette and RealizePalette functions. At this point, if you're using any kind of wallpaper display (unless you are running in true-color mode), you'll probably see the background screen change colors as the new palette is activated; this is usually a temporary effect.

```
hdc = GetDC( GetFocus() );
hOldPal = SelectPalette( hdc, hNewPal, FALSE );
RealizePalette( hdc );
```

After activating the palette, it's time to return to the bitmap itself, beginning by locking the previously allocated memory and then calling CreateDIBitmap (Create Device-Independent Bitmap) to write the bitmap into the device context handle's memory:

```
lpBits = LocalLock( hBM );
hBitmap = CreateDIBitmap( hdc,
    (LPBITMAPINFOHEADER) &pBmInfo->bmiHeader,
                         CBM_INIT,
                         lpBits,
        (LPBITMAPINFO) pBmInfo,
                         DIB_RGB_COLORS );

while( LOBYTE( LocalFlags( hBM ) ) != 0 )
    LocalUnlock( hBM );  // remember, was locked at least twice
```

Once this is done, the memory (hBM) is unlocked again. However, because hBM has been locked twice, a while loop is used to ensure that hBM is unlocked as many times as it was locked. If this is not done, the results can become annoying at a later point.

Also, because this bitmap will be used for a few other purposes aside from the immediate display, global handles to both the bitmap and the palette are assigned. A provision to abort is also included, just in case the bitmap creation failed.

```
if( hBitmap != NULL )
{
    if( hGBM ) DeleteObject( hGBM );     // if exist, delete same
    hGBM = hBitmap;                       // save global handle
    if( hGPal ) DeleteObject( hGPal );  // if exist, delete same
    hGPal = hNewPal;                      // save global handle
}
else
    ErrorMsg( "Bitmap failed" );
```

Next, there's still a bit of cleanup needed, beginning with restoring the original palette and releasing the device context handle. There's still a handle to both the pbmInfo structure (which must also be unlocked) and to the bitmap data itself; both need to be released. The only important elements—global handles to the bit-mapped image and palette—are already set and are not affected by the present actions.

```
if( hOldPal )
    SelectPalette( hdc, hOldPal, FALSE );
ReleaseDC( GetFocus(), hdc );
GlobalUnlock( hBmInfo );
LocalFree( hBmInfo );
pBmInfo = NULL;
LocalFree( hBM );
hBM = NULL;
SetCursor( LoadCursor( NULL, IDC_ARROW ) );
InvalidateRect( hwnd, NULL, TRUE );
return(0);
}
```

Finally, the new palette object can be deleted and the arrow cursor restored. Also, to ensure that the window is redrawn to display the bitmap, an InvalidateRect call is made. But, this completes the task of reading and displaying the bitmap. The complete listing for the Shades program is on the CD that accompanies this book.

> **NOTE**
>
> For other image formats, such as PCX files, the `ReadBitmap` procedure can be modified to read the appropriate image format and to create a corresponding memory bitmap with similar handling.

Optimizing Image Processing

While Windows is, in itself, a graphical environment, it is not necessarily the ideal environment for graphic image processing. Time-sharing, which is inherent in any multitasking environment, increases the time necessary to complete what is already a laborious and computation-intensive task. For this reason, applications requiring intensive image processing may fare better under DOS's single-tasking environment. The presence of a numerical coprocessor, of course, is also an advantage.

Previously the biggest challenge in image processing was simply that both DOS and Windows 3.*x* imposed memory access limitations, resulting in a need to swap sections of an image in and out of extended memory, a process which often required more time than the processing itself. Today, however, using Windows NT or, to a slightly lesser degree, Windows 95, where all memory is treated as flat memory and operations can be executed directly at any memory location within the available RAM, the only real remaining bottleneck is simply the calculation time.

As alternatives, both IBM's OS/2 and the Xenix operating system also offer flat memory, at least, up to 4GB of RAM, but offer no particular advantages over Windows in terms of operating speeds.

Last, but probably most important, the greater the initial information in an image, the better the results after processing. As explained in Chapter 26, 24-bit-per-pixel images are the optimum source images available. The examples use 256-color images because the 24-bit color images are not universally available.

Where speed is a critical requirement, you could move the processing to hardware designed specifically for image processing.

Image-Processing Hardware

However useful, software convolution methods are not always suitable for real-time applications, even if you're using a MIPS RISC system or a fast, multiprocessor Pentium. As you should observe when executing the Shades demo program, processing times run to several seconds even for small images. For slower CPUs, 486s, and the like, execution times increase proportionally.

In real-time applications, instead of using software processing, the optimal choice is to use a hardware *image preprocessor* or an *image postprocessor*. A variety of these boards are available at a variety of prices, but the more economical choices are generally single i860 image processors. More expensive, and correspondingly faster, choices are available using multiple processors.

Image Preprocessors

In general, preprocessors operate in-line with the image source (a video camera). They provide real-time image processing at up to 30 frames per second or more before the image reaches the capture equipment, whether the destination is a computer frame-grabber board or a recording device such as a video camera.

As a general rule, preprocessors are a combination of dedicated graphics processors, frequently with several graphics CPUs operating in tandem. Occasionally, they may use hardware filters similar to those employed in predigital days for audio and radio-frequency signal processing.

One drawback of using such preprocessors is that the only image normally available is a black-and-white or gray-scale; the original color image is lost. The principal reason for this restriction is that a single data set consisting of black-and-white intensity information, instead of separate red, green, and blue color data, requires two-thirds less processing. Another reason is that these devices are commonly designed for machine-vision applications and, in these circumstances, preserving color is generally less important than detecting edges and shapes.

Image Postprocessors

Another approach to hardware image processing is using postprocessors. With this technique, time is less critical; minutes, hours, or even days can be spent processing images after capture. Moreover, given time, much more sophisticated processing can be used, and color information can be preserved.

Postprocessors vary from simple, single-frame (single-image) processors used to enhance individual images to elaborate, sequential-image processors (such as the Video Toaster system from NewTek), which are used not only to enhance images but to edit, modify, and create entire video sequences.

> **TIP**
>
> Hardware processing is a specialized area. If your application requires this type of image processing, consult your local computer dealers (or browse the net) for sources of information and hardware suitable for your application.

Although not every application requires image processing with smoothing or edge-detection algorithms, these techniques are essential in some cases. Unfortunately, these algorithms are also slow and, at the present time, of limited efficiency. Ideally, programmers will eventually discover a tremendous enhancement algorithm that will be able to execute in realtime, in software, with tremendous versatility and with reliability equal to that found in human optical processors (perhaps using a 100-GHz 80986 CPU).

Until then, however, a selection of processing algorithms has been discussed in this chapter. Some of these are demonstrated in the Shades program, which is on the CD that accompanies this book.

CHAPTER

TWENTY-EIGHT

28

Graphics Selection Operations

- Area selection tool features

- Adjustable target overlays

- Custom cursors

- Mouse-hit testing

One aspect of graphics operations that is not commonly mentioned is how to select a section within an image or to select a region of interest. This requirement comes up quite frequently when working with live video applications but is also applicable to static bitmaps.

In this chapter, we will look at a method of creating a nondestructive target overlay on top of an image. The sample program presented here, Target, contains provisions for moving the target, resizing the target, and changing cursors to indicate which operations are being performed.

Creating a Selection Tool

A common requirement in many graphics operations involves selecting an area from either a static bitmap or an active video image. For static bitmaps, selection usually involves creating a tool to select an area, with the selection shown as an outline. For example, the Windows Paint program provides two selection tools: a free-form area tool and a rectangular area tool. Using the rectangular tool, you can select any rectangular region in an image then, subsequently, "pick up" or drag the selection. The free-form selection tool functions in the same fashion, except that you are allowed to "draw" an irregular region for selection.

The first case, rectangular selection, is the more usual and is the type of selection discussed here. Selecting an irregular region involves much the same process, except for keeping a list of boundary points and transferring the selected region as a series of image row sections.

Drawing an Overlay

The simplest way to select an area, and to provide visual feedback to the user, is to draw a rectangle enclosing the area on top of the existing image. Using a conventional drawing operation, however, is destructive to the existing image. Simply drawing a rectangle on top of a bitmap would be fine if we wanted to add the rectangle to the image. But for selection, a different process is needed. We need to draw the rectangle using a method that allows the original image to be restored, without requiring redrawing the entire image.

The simplest method of drawing and then undrawing a figure is to use the ROP2 XOR operation, or `R2_XORPEN`, which is described in Chapter 22. Using the XOR drawing mode, the first time a figure is drawn, the drawing pen (and brush, if any) are XORed with the underlying image. This usually ensures that the drawn figure is optimally visible, regardless of the background image. More important, when the same figure is drawn a second time, the second drawing operation has the effect of canceling the first and, therefore, restoring the original background image, without needing to repaint the entire screen.

Aside from using the XOR drawing mode, the actual process of drawing the overlay is trivial. However, there is one caution: Whatever image or form is used for the overlay, it must be redrawn exactly to erase it before any changes occur in the position or size.

Active Video Image Selection

In the case of active video images, depending on the type of graphics capture card and processor, the selection process may involve capturing a static image first and then manipulating the static bitmap in much the same fashion demonstrated in the Target demo program presented in this chapter.

In other cases, where multiple video planes are supported, the selection process may be accomplished by drawing the area, or other targeting information, in a separate video plane and letting the system combine the targeting information with the active video for presentation.

In the case of multiple video planes, drawing the overlay using the XOR mode still remains the fastest method of repeatedly drawing and removing targeting, selection, or region outline information.

Area Selection Conventions

In many drawing applications, the current convention for area selection is to draw an overlay consisting of a dotted outline with rectangular handles at the corners and centers of the sides. By placing the mouse cursor anywhere within the outline and pressing the mouse button, the selected region can be dragged to another position. On the other hand, by clicking on one of the handles, the outline can be dragged to a new size.

In the case of irregular areas, depending on the application, small "handles" may appear at nodes representing the vertices of a polygon outline. These handles are treated in the same fashion as a rectangular outline, permitting a vertex to be relocated. In other cases, such as in the Windows Paint program, no methods are provided for adjusting a free-form outline.

In the Target demo program, a different set of conventions are used. These involve a set of crosshairs which extend to the window margins and a circle which approximates the target area or region of interest (ROI). An example of a screen in the Target program, with a bitmap displayed behind the target selection overlay, is shown in Figure 28.1.

FIGURE 28.1

Targeting an area in a bitmap

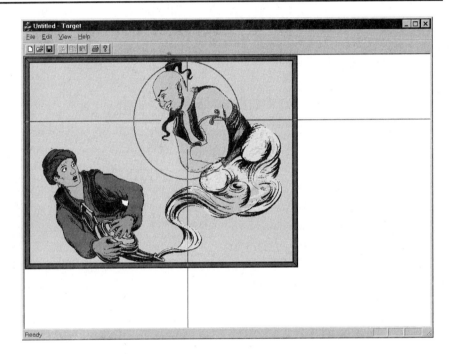

This format is common in machine-vision applications, where the user is selecting an area for examination. Because the crosshairs extend to the margins of the window, they can be used to indicate a position on scales along the sides. The center of the crosshairs is left open, so that the specific target is not obscured. The circular target area marker is used to select an area for closer examination or for action by other associated tools. As an alternative, an elliptical, rather than circular, shape could be used for the target area marker.

In most applications, after a rectangular or irregular region is selected, the selection is actually moved, copied, or otherwise processed. During this processing, the common convention is to show an outline surrounding the selection. While it would be possible to capture or process a circular or irregular area, the usual practice is to process a rectangular image. This simplification is commonly used to show the actual area being processed, as well as to facilitate drag operations.

In the Target program, when the right mouse button is pressed to initiate a capture (though no actual capture is done in this example), the crosshairs and circular target are replaced by a rectangle bounding but outside the region of interest. Figure 28.2 shows an example of the selection rectangle.

FIGURE 28.2

Indicating the selected region of interest

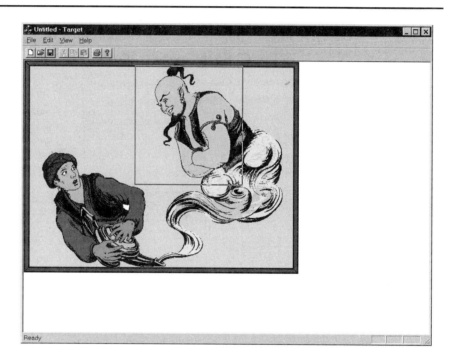

Whether you use these conventions, or any of several others, depends on the needs of your application. There is no single set of conventions that apply to all cases and cover all requirements.

Selecting Parts of an Image: The Target Program

The Target program demonstrates using adjustable target overlays, testing for mouse hits with overlapping targets, and setting custom mouse cursors.

Opening a Bitmap File

The Target demo program provides an option to open a bitmap file for a background image. It uses essentially the same bitmap file and display operations demonstrated in Chapter 26. However, there are a few differences, because the version presented here relies heavily on MFC-defined classes rather than the standard APIs and conventional programming methods.

Also worthy of your attention is the single TRY..CATCH exception handler used when opening a bitmap file, as:

```
TRY
{
   CFile cFile( csFName, CFile::modeRead | CFile::typeBinary );
   SetCursor( LoadCursor( NULL, IDC_WAIT ) );
   . . .
   read the bitmap file here
   . . .
}
CATCH( CFileException, e )
{
   #ifdef _DEBUG
      afxDump << "File access failed: " << e->m_cause << "\n";
   #endif
   return FALSE;
}
END_CATCH
```

The CFile constructor, which is used to open the file for reading, like any class constructor, does not return an error, regardless of what might go wrong. Therefore, to catch an error when opening a file in this fashion, the TRY...CATCH exception handling is required. (Exception handling is discussed in detail in Chapter 16.)

Responding to the Mouse

In the Target program, the selection overlay needs to be able to respond to the mouse in several different fashions, depending on where the mouse is clicked:

- If the mouse is clicked in the center of the target, the target can be dragged to a new position but without changing the size.

- If the mouse is clicked on the left or right side, or on the top or the bottom of the target, the target can be resized horizontally or vertically (but not both) without changing the center position.

- If the mouse is clicked on a corner of the target—upper left, upper right, lower left, or lower right—the target can be resized both horizontally and vertically, again without changing the center position.

In each case, the circular target is the focus of these operations; the crosshairs simply follow the center position of the target. Also, the background image remains unaffected by any of these operations.

Changing the Cursor

While not absolutely necessary to these operations, the Target program includes provisions to change the cursor to reflect the type of operation about to occur, when the left mouse button is pressed. Although the Windows GDI offers a variety of standard cursors, these are not always readily visible against a complex background (see Chapter 9 for more information about Windows cursors). The original program from which Target was derived provides a set of custom cursors, which have been incorporated in the demo program as well.

These five custom cursors appear in Figure 28.3:

- North-south cursor (NS_CURSOR)

- Northeast-southwest cursor (NESW_CURSOR)

- Hand cursor (HAND_CURSOR)

- Northwest-southeast cursor (NWSE_CURSOR)

- East-west cursor (EW_CURSOR)

In each case, the cursor image consists of a white body with a reversed outline. A small mark has been added to each image to identify the position of the cursor's hotspot.

Determining the Hit Position

To manage dragging and resizing operations for the target overlay, the first step is to determine where the mouse hit occurs; that is, where was the mouse positioned when the primary mouse button was pressed.

FIGURE 28.3

Five custom cursors

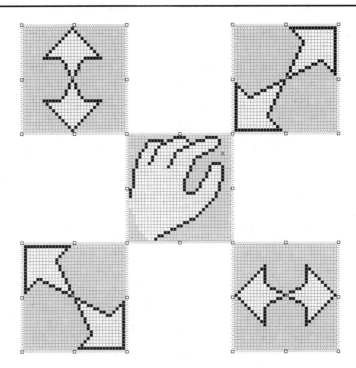

In the `CTargetView` class, the `OnLButtonDown` method is called whenever the left (or primary) mouse button is pressed and receives two parameters: the `nFlags` parameter and the `point` argument. In this case (as in most), we'll ignore the `nFlags` argument, which contains status information, and rely on the `point` information, which tells us where the mouse was, relative to the application client window, when the event occurred.

NOTE   By default, the mouse handler causes an `OnLButtonDown` call when the left mouse button is pressed. If, however, the Mouse utility in the Control Panel has been used to swap the mouse buttons, the `OnLButtonDown` call responds to the right mouse button being pressed. For programming purposes, the primary mouse button always identifies itself with a `WM_LBUTTONxxxxx` message, and the secondary button always reports as `WM_RBUTTONxxxxx`, regardless of which physical mouse button is pressed.

Before any tests are made, the m_nTrack member is initialized as NO_TARGET. Subsequently, if a hit is identified in any target region, m_nTrack will be reassigned a value to identify the correct region.

Also, before any other operations, the SetCapture method is called to ensure that mouse messages from outside the current window will still be received. The mouse capture will be released when the mouse button is released.

```
void CTargetView::OnLButtonDown(UINT nFlags, CPoint point)
{
   m_nTrack = NO_TARGET;
   SetCapture();
```

Next, the m_xRadius and m_yRadius members contain the size of the target ellipse and the m_cPoint member contains the centerpoint. To limit the drag operation to the center of the target area, the first target rectangle is defined using two-thirds of the vertical and horizontal radii. After creating the rectangle, the NormalizeRect function is called, purely as a precaution, to ensure that the bottom coordinate of the rectangle is greater than the top and the right side is greater than the left.

```
   CPoint   cPoint( m_cPoint );
   CRect    cRect( cPoint.x - ( ( m_xRadius / 3 ) * 2 ),
                   cPoint.y - ( ( m_yRadius / 3 ) * 2 ),
                   cPoint.x + ( ( m_xRadius / 3 ) * 2 ),
                   cPoint.y + ( ( m_yRadius / 3 ) * 2 ) );

   cRect.NormalizeRect();
   if( cRect.PtInRect( point ) )
```

The PtInRect method simply returns TRUE if the point argument lies within the rectangle, or FALSE if not. While such a test is not difficult to perform, the provided member function is more convenient than writing a separate operation for each check that is made here.

If PtInRect returns TRUE, the m_nTrack member is set to ALL, meaning that the entire target overlay will be dragged when the next mouse-movement message is received, and the hand cursor is loaded as the active cursor.

```
   {
      m_nTrack = ALL;
      m_hCursor = SetCursor( LoadCursor( theApp.m_hInstance,
                                         "HAND_CURSOR" ) );
   }
```

If the `PtInRect` function returns FALSE, the `OnLButtonDown` method continues through a series of `else` statements, testing each target area in turn. If a hit is found, it sets the `m_nTrack` variable to the appropriate operation and loads the correct cursor.

The real key here is to ensure that the target rectangles are tested in the correct order. Figure 28.4 shows nine overlapping target rectangles, numbered in the order tested.

FIGURE 28.4

The mouse-hit target rectangles

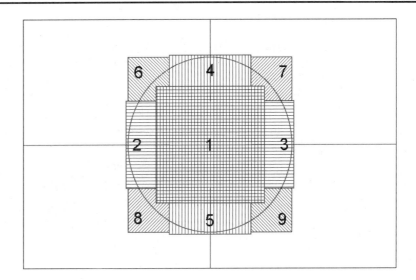

What Figure 28.4 does not show is that region 1 overlaps regions 2, 3, 4, and 5. However, if a hit is found in the first region, no other regions are tested, making the overlapped areas irrelevant.

In like fashion, area 6 is overlapped by areas 1, 2, and 4. But because this area is tested last, a hit will be identified for this area only if it occurs within the irregular region shown. The same holds true for the regions identified as 7, 8, and 9; each is overlapped by three other regions that are tested first.

The point is that it's unnecessary to define complex hit areas when the same task can be accomplished by testing simpler regions in the proper order. On the other hand, when it is absolutely necessary to test complex regions, you can use other methods, such as those demonstrated in Chapter 29.

Last, the CView::OnLButtonDown method is called to provide default handling for the mouse messages.

```
    }
    m_bDrawOverlay = TRUE;
    CView::OnLButtonDown(nFlags, point);
}
```

Since we've already provided complete handling, calling the default method is optional, but still good practice.

Once we've decided where the mouse hit occurred, the next step is to wait for the OnMouseMove function to be called, indicating that the mouse has moved. The OnMouseMove method, like the OnLButtonDown method, is called with nFlags and point arguments, and again, the nFlags argument can simply be ignored as irrelevant.

Before doing anything based on the m_nTrack action flag, the next step is to decide if the mouse is still in the client window. If it is not—if the mouse has been moved outside the application window—then we will release the mouse capture and do nothing.

```
void CTargetView::OnMouseMove(UINT nFlags, CPoint point)
{
    CRect       cRect;

    if( m_bDrawOverlay )
    {
        GetClientRect( cRect );
        if( ! cRect.PtInRect( point ) )// cursor outside client area
        {
            m_nTrack = NO_TARGET;
            SetCursor( m_hCursor );
            ReleaseCapture();
            return;
        }
```

Next, assuming the mouse is still in the window, the response is to call the DrawOverlay method to erase the existing target overlay.

```
        DrawOverlay();                  // erase the overlay target
        switch( m_nTrack )
        {
            case NO_TARGET:             /* no action */
                break;
```

If the m_nTrack member indicates NO_TARGET, then we'll take no action. If m_nTrack is set to ALL, then the m_cPoint member needs to be updated, as:

```
case ALL:
    m_cPoint.x = max( m_xRadius, min( point.x,
                        ( cRect.right - m_xRadius - 2 ) ) );
    m_cPoint.y = max( m_yRadius, min( point.y,
                        ( cRect.bottom - m_yRadius - 2 ) ) );
    break;
```

Alternatively, if m_nTrack is set to TOP, the vertical radius should be adjusted according to the mouse movement:

```
case TOP:
    m_yRadius = max( 30, m_cPoint.y - point.y );
    break;
```

The remaining cases allow adjustments according to the quadrant selected, and the switch statement is followed by a test to ensure that the target is not dragged outside the client window. The bulk of these provisions, however, are routine.

The one important provision remaining is to call DrawOverlay a second time to redraw the target overlay at the changed position or with the changed size.

```
        . . .
        DrawOverlay();                          // redraw the overlay target
    }
    CView::OnMouseMove(nFlags, point);
}
```

Finally, when the mouse button is released, the OnLButtonUp method is called. Here, the same arguments are supplied, but now both nFlags and point can be ignored. We don't really care where the mouse was released or what the flags were; our only interest is that the mouse button has been released. And the response to the mouse button release is simple: Reset the member flags, restore the default cursor, and release the mouse message capture.

```
void CTargetView::OnLButtonUp(UINT nFlags, CPoint point)
{
    m_bDrawOverlay = FALSE;
    m_nTrack = NO_TARGET;
    SetCursor( m_hCursor );
    ReleaseCapture();
    CView::OnLButtonUp(nFlags, point);
}
```

For the right mouse button, the provisions are even simpler: When the right mouse button is pressed, check and see if the event occurred in the target rectangle.

```
void CTargetView::OnRButtonDown(UINT nFlags, CPoint point)
{
/*

   //=== routine to show target areas ===//
   DrawOverlay();
   DrawTargets();
   DrawOverlay();
*/

   CRect cRect( m_cPoint.x - ( ( m_xRadius / 3 ) * 2 ),
                m_cPoint.y - ( ( m_yRadius / 3 ) * 2 ),
                m_cPoint.x + ( ( m_xRadius / 3 ) * 2 ),
                m_cPoint.y + ( ( m_yRadius / 3 ) * 2 ) );

   if( cRect.PtInRect( point ) )            // is cursor in client area?
   {
```

If the mouse event is in the target, set our capture flag, call DrawOverlay to remove the target overlay, and then call DrawROITarget to create the ROI outline.

```
      m_bCapture = TRUE;
      DrawOverlay();
      SetCapture();
      DrawROITarget();
   }
   CView::OnRButtonDown(nFlags, point);
}
```

If we were tracking mouse movement while the right mouse button is down, this would occur in the same OnMouseMove method used to track movement with the primary button down. The only difference would be that we would need to include some provisions, such as the m_bDrawOverlay and m_bCapture flags, to determine which type of event was being tracked. Or, more directly, the nFlags argument accompanying the mouse-movement message could be queried to find out which mouse button was pressed, or if both buttons were pressed.

In this case, we really don't care about movement. All that we're waiting for is for the right mouse button to be released.

```
void CTargetView::OnRButtonUp(UINT nFlags, CPoint point)
{
   if( m_bCapture )
   {
      m_bCapture = ! m_bCapture;
      ReleaseCapture();
      Invalidate();
      DrawOverlay();
   }
   CView::OnRButtonUp(nFlags, point);
}
```

And, once the right mouse button is released, we reset our flag, call the Invalidate function to redraw everything in the window, and then call DrawOverlay to
restore the target overlay. The DrawROITarget function does not use R2_XORPEN;
therefore, there is no easier way to remove the ROI target rectangle.

A Note about Custom Cursors

Some of you may have noticed that the use of the SetCapture method in the
Target program appears rather redundant since, as soon as the mouse
moves outside the client window, ReleaseCapture has been called. Why call
SetCapture and then release it as soon as it becomes useful?

The reason is that by calling SetCapture, we ensure that the cursor we
assign to the mouse remains the active cursor and is not replaced by the
default cursor as soon as the mouse moves.

The explanation for this behavior is found in the notes for the SetCursor
function (from the MFC online documentation):

> "If your application must set the cursor while it is in a window, make
> sure the class cursor for the specified window's class is set to NULL.
> If the class cursor is not NULL, the system restores the class cursor
> each time the mouse is moved."

The trick is how to set the class cursor to NULL. `SetCapture` provides a convenient alternative in this instance. However, the proper way to set custom cursors for a window under MFC is to intercept the `PreCreateWindow` function and to modify the `WNDCLASS` member of the `CREATSTRUCT` argument, setting the `hCursor` member to NULL. The revised `WNDCLASS` structure, however, must be registered before use through the `RegisterClass` function.

The long and the short of this is that setting custom cursors is not conveniently accomplished.

Other Methods of Interest

A provision has also been included in the source code to draw the several target areas used to test for mouse hits. This provision is found in the `DrawTargets` methods and was used to create the illustration in Figure 28.4. This provision can be enabled in the `OnRButtonDown` method.

Also of interest are the `OnFileOpen`, `ReadBitmap`, and `OnDraw` methods used in this demo program. These parallel earlier examples but offer new versions using MFC classes and methods in place of some of the API functions and conventional operations illustrated in previous chapters.

The target drawing and mouse-hit recognition operations are found in the TargetView.H and .CPP files. The complete source code for this application is found on the CD accompanying this volume.

Interactive Images

- Color keying events

- Drunkard's walk algorithm

- Memory map keys

In the previous chapter, we examined some methods for selecting sections, or regions of interest, within a bitmap image. The methods discussed there for responding to mouse clicks work well with simple bitmaps, but they are not suitable for bitmaps that contain more complex shapes. In this chapter, we'll look at several methods of mapping mouse events to complex bitmap regions.

Complex Regions in Interactive Images

A major element, and a major problem, in many graphics applications is identifying the location within an image where an event, such as a mouse click, has occurred. If you're interested in only the window coordinates where the event occurred, this information is supplied in the `lParam` argument accompanying a `WM_xBUTTONxxxx` message or, using MFC, in the `point` argument passed to the `OnxButtonxxxx` and `OnMouseMove` methods. However, determining where a mouse click has occurred in relation to a displayed bitmap or some other region defined on the screen is a more difficult matter, particularly when the region is not conveniently defined by a series of bounding coordinates.

For simple rectangular shapes, the solution is simple. For any other shape, however, the `PtInRect` method, demonstrated in Chapter 28, fails and a new approach is required.

For example, consider Figure 29.1, where three shapes are depicted representing possible screen areas. The first shape, or region, at the left, could be defined using a half-dozen coordinate pairs: one pair for each vertex. A mouse event occurring within the bounded region could be identified by testing the area as two rectangular regions.

FIGURE 29.1

Three bounded regions

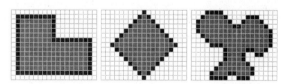

The center region in Figure 29.1 is a simpler shape, with only four vertices. But it is also more complex, because the boundary lines are diagonal rather than rectilinear. In this case, a more complex test is required to calculate where the edges lie in relation to the mouse-click event.

The third region, at the right, is the most complex of all. Following conventional processes, it requires a relatively large number of coordinates describing the convolutions followed by the area's outline.

Methods for Identifying Regions and Enclosures

Although it's possible to create custom algorithms tailored for specific, individual types of images, for a generic mapping process, a different approach to identifying regions and enclosures is desirable. A number of processes can be used for this purpose, as explained in the following sections.

Identifying Regions by Color

One identification approach involves color keying. This approach is demonstrated in the MapDemo program presented in this chapter. The program uses the USMAP01 bitmap.

Identification by color matching relies on the fact that each region (each state) in the United States map depicted by the USMAP01 bitmap possesses a unique color value. Figure 29.2 shows the USMAP01 bitmap image displaying the contiguous United States with Alaska and Hawaii inserted at the lower left.

The MapDemo program contains a lookup table that matches each state's color with the state's name; the color choices themselves are quite arbitrary.

This approach has a few obvious restrictions, including being limited to use on systems with capacities to display more than 16 colors, and requiring that the image consist of areas of continuous color. Also, any two areas with the same color value will be identified as the same region.

Overall, however, it is a practical and useful method of identifying a large number of irregular regions.

FIGURE 29.2

The USMAP01 bitmap

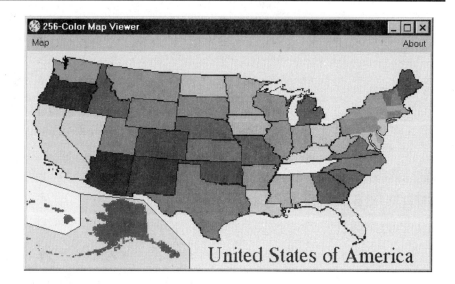

Using a Hidden Color Map

Another identification process involves using a memory map color mask to determine where events have occurred in a bitmap that is not composed of contiguous color regions. This method uses a second color map that is not displayed; that is, it is created in a memory context, not a display context.

This second map contains the color identification values for the primary bitmap that appears on the screen. Then, when the mouse is used to select a point on the displayed bitmap, you look for the pixel value in the hidden bitmap and match this color to the keys.

The Drunkard's Walk Algorithm

An algorithm that is particularly useful for identifying irregular regions is the drunkard's walk algorithm, titled thus because the search pattern follows a trace reminiscent of an inebriated and staggering pedestrian. (This type of motion is also known as Brownian motion, as exhibited by microscopic particles subject to thermal agitation.)

Where a drunkard—or a microscopic particle—simply continues indefinitely, the drunkard's walk algorithm executes a test after each staggering step (rather like a drunkard searching for any lamppost in reach) to determine if it has reached an identifiable point, and halts when such an encounter occurs. These target points are assigned locations within each enclosed region and are indexed to uniquely identify the region.

The drunkard's walk algorithm begins at a point indicated by the mouse click and proceeds in any arbitrary direction until one of these events occurs:

- A boundary is reached

- A random instruction instigates a change in direction.

- The drunkard's search reaches a target coordinate identifying the enclosed region.

In the first case, reaching a boundary identified either by a change in color (or in the MapDemo program, by a specific, preselected border color), the drunkard's path simply bounces or reverses. The drunkard then retraces its path until the second instance, a random change, forces a new direction or until, ultimately, the path intersects an identifiable point.

In the second case, a pseudo-random generator initiates a change in direction, on average, every ten steps. Although in one chance out of eight, this chance is not a change at all, the overall effect is to trace paths with an average length of ten steps (or, in this case, pixels) between changes in direction.

Figure 29.3 shows the same three regions illustrated in Figure 29.1, but this time each has a drunkard's walk trace, which ends at the intersection of the desired target coordinates (shown as a small box outline).

FIGURE 29.3

The drunkard's walk search

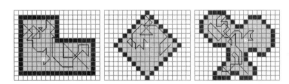

The Recursive Search Algorithm

An alternative to the drunkard's walk algorithm is a recursive search algorithm. This algorithm begins, from the initial coordinates, by initiating a recursive search. For example, the recursive search might begin by searching to the immediate left, then down, then up, and finally to the right, with each point searched initiating a further recursive search in the same direction until a border is reached or the target is found.

For example, assume a recursive search beginning at point 100,100. The recursive process calls itself, first with the coordinates for the point to the immediate left (99,100). When this first search returns, assuming that the target point has not been found, the next search will be up (100,99), then down (100,101), and then right (101,100).

However, the first search at (99,100) initiates its own searches at (98,100), (99,99), (99,101), and (100,100), which is the same point where the search started. And each of these searches executes its own recursive search.

But since each search is looking for either a border, which terminates further recursion in that branch – or the target point, which also terminates recursion, this is not infinitely recursive. But, even with finite recursion, the number of active recursions does increase geometrically. Furthermore, each recursion requires its own register values to be pushed on to the stack, and this can quickly lead to stack overflow. Even if the recursive procedure is very carefully designed, this can still be a problem.

An advantage of this approach is that a well-designed recursive search is absolutely certain. It will find the target location, even if it has to check absolutely every location within a region. But a well-designed recursive search is not necessarily any faster than a drunkard's walk search, and it does consume considerably more of the system's resources. At its worst, the drunkard's walk algorithm is sometimes a bit slower but only rarely and randomly so. In general, the drunkard's walk algorithm tends to be faster, as well as more efficient in overall usage of system resources and, most important, of CPU time.

Finally, on the basis of simple aesthetics, the drunkard's walk algorithm is far more satisfying to the soul (the programmer's, at least, if not the machine's) than the stolidly pedestrian recursive search. After all, getting there is half the fun, isn't it?

Identifying Event Locations in a Bitmap: The MapDemo Program

As explained earlier in the chapter, the MapDemo program uses the USMAP01 bitmap, which is a map of the United States. This program demonstrates the use of the color matching and drunkard's walk algorithm techniques for event identification.

The upper New England states (which appear relatively small in the USMAP01 bitmap) are displayed separately in the USMAP02 bitmap and are used to demonstrate the second area-identification algorithm. The USMAP02 image can be selected either by clicking on the upper New England states in USMAP01 or through the Map menu.

Color Matching

Within the MapDemo program, while the USMAP01 bitmap is displayed, a WM_LBUTTONDOWN message calls the ColorCheckMap function, passing three parameters: the window handle (hwnd) and the two mouse-click coordinates derived from the lParam argument accompanying the mouse-button event message.

```
case WM_LBUTTONDOWN:
    . . .
        CoordCheckMap( hwnd, LOWORD( lParam ),
                             HIWORD( lParam ) );
    break;
```

The mouse-click x-axis coordinate is reported in the low word of lParam, and the high word reports the y-axis coordinate.

The ColorCheckMap function appears to be a simple process, but it does require a bit of finesse to comply with Windows' requirements.

```
void ColorCheckMap( HWND hwnd, WORD xCoord, WORD yCoord )
{
    HDC     hdc;
    DWORD   RColor;
    WORD    SColor;
    int     i;

    . . .
    hdc = GetDC( hwnd );
    RColor = GetPixel( hdc, xCoord, yCoord );
        // need RGB palette-relative color value
    ReleaseDC( hwnd, hdc );
```

The GetPixel function returns a DWORD value containing the RGB color value for the selected pixel in the form 0x00rrggbb. However, while this is the color of the pixel itself, the data identifying the several states consists of the simpler palette index values rather than their RGB equivalents. Ergo, the next task is to match the color returned to the bitmap's palette, retrieving the palette index.

To accomplish this, the first requirement is to lock the pointer to the global palette information (pGLP) and then lock a handle to the logical palette (hGPal) before calling the CreatePalette and RealizePalette functions to temporarily re-create and activate the bitmap palette.

```
LocalLock( hGLP );
LocalLock( hGPal );
        // lock and create palette for reference
hGPal = CreatePalette( pGLP );
if( hGPal == NULL ) ErrorMsg( "Palette not found!" );
        // make palette active for device context
RealizePalette( hdc );
        // get palette index for comparison
SColor = GetNearestPaletteIndex( hGPal, (COLORREF) RColor );
        // unlock everything but don't delete palette
LocalUnlock( hGLP );
LocalUnlock( hGPal );
```

Finally, after the palette is created (or re-created), the GetNearestPaletteIndex function returns the palette index value as SColor. Of course, before finishing, the two memory locks on the global and re-created palettes should be released. Neither, however, should be freed from memory since they may be needed again.

Once the palette index has been retrieved, a pair of simple loops are all that is required to identify the corresponding state or, in the case of the upper New England states, to display the USMAP02 bitmap.

```
for( i=0; i<12; i++ )
   if( SColor == NewEngland[i] )
                // if this is any New England state, switch maps
       PostMessage( hwnd, WM_COMMAND, IDM_MAP2, OL );
   for( i=0; i<=StateColors; i++ )
      if( SColor == CState[i].Color )
         LocationMsg( CState[i].State );
   MessageBeep( MB_ICONASTERISK );
}
```

Once the state or area is identified, a variety of other responses can be implemented as elaborately or simply as desired. In this demo program, however, a simple pop-up dialog box with a "Welcome to the great state of xxxxxx" message is used, identifying the state selected.

The data matching the states and colors is provided by a simple structure listing these by name and palette index. An abbreviated sample follows:

```
ColorState CState[StateColors] =
{   "Arizona",          2,      "New Mexico",        7,
    "Oklahoma",         9,      "Georgia",          11,
    "Oregon",          12,      "Colorado",         13,
    "Missouri",        15,      "South Carolina",   16,
    "Texas",           17,      "Hawaii",           18,
    ...
```

Implementing the Drunkard's Walk Search

Implementing the drunkard's walk search algorithm (CoordCheckMap) is a relatively simple task. As in the ColorCheckMap function, this search is called with three arguments: the window handle, and the x- and y-axis coordinates reported by the mouse-click event message.

```
void CoordCheckMap( HWND hwnd, WORD xCoord, WORD yCoord )
{
    BOOL    Done = FALSE, Reverse;
    HDC     hdc;
    WORD    i;
    int     j, k, x, y;

    ...
    randomize();
    hdc = GetDC( hwnd );
    x = random(3)-1;
    y = random(3)-1;
```

Initially, CoordMapCheck retrieves the device context handle for the window displaying the map and selects step directions (x,y) in the range -1..1. Since these are used to increment the xCoord and yCoord values, the result is a search track beginning in one of eight compass directions (N, NE, E, SE, S, SW, W, NW).

NOTE There is also one chance in nine that the initial search step will be (0,0), which is no search at all. This will, however, correct itself automatically when the next random search direction is selected.

Before the search is initiated, the first step is to check the present coordinates against a loop testing all of the identified coordinate pairs. Also, rather than requiring a perfect hit on the target coordinates, the actual test accepts any point that is within ten pixels of the target (total offset on both axes).

```
do
{
   for( i=0; i<AllCoords; i++ )
   {
      if( ( abs( xCoord - Coord[i].xPos ) +
            abs( yCoord - Coord[i].yPos ) ) < 10 )
      {
         if( i < StateCoords )
             LocationMsg( Coord[i].State );
         else PostMessage( hwnd, WM_COMMAND,
                           IDM_MAP1, 0L );

         Done = TRUE;
      }  }
```

As in a game of horseshoes, close *does* count. An exact match is not required, simplifying the search. If the current coordinates are within a total of ten units of the target coordinates, a match is simply assumed. The hidden assumption here is that no target point is located within ten pixels of a border; otherwise, it could be misidentified by being detected from the wrong side of the border.

In other cases, a closer (or looser) match might be appropriate, with the algorithm adjusted accordingly. For the present, a range of ten pixels is adequate for the purpose.

State coordinate pairs in the MapDemo program are identified, together with the appropriate state names, as a simple structure table:

```
CoordState Coord[AllCoords] =
{  "Connecticut",   267, 208,   "Delaware",     202, 311,
   . . .
   "Vermont",       238, 132,   "RETURN",        14, 337,
   "RETURN",        331, 290,   "RETURN",       122,  81  };
```

In addition to the state coordinates, the program provides three area coordinates that do not fall within a specific state: one below the upper New England states and two in the blank areas surrounding these states. Intersecting any of these three locations sends the application back to the USMAP01 display.

Alternatively, as long as a match is not found, the next test is to determine whether the bitmap borders have been reached:

```
Reverse = FALSE;
if( ( xCoord >= bmWidth-1  ) || ( xCoord <= 1 ) ||
    ( yCoord >= bmHeight-1 ) || ( yCoord <= 1 ) )
  Reverse = TRUE;
```

If, for any reason, the search is approaching the bitmap border, the Boolean `Reverse` flag is set and, subsequently, will reverse the search direction. Without this provision, the usual result under Windows will be a system application error, often trashing the system memory as well.

Next, as long as the search remains away from the bitmap border, a second loop executes a check of the immediate vicinity, searching for pixels identifying a border encounter and, again, reversing direction if a border is found.

```
else
  for( j=-1; j<2; j++ )
    for( k=-1; k<2; k++ )
      if( GetPixel( hdc, xCoord+j, yCoord+k ) == BORDER )
        Reverse = TRUE;
```

A simple, straight-ahead search could be executed, but this would have one fairly dangerous flaw: narrow borders can leak through either single-pixel gaps or diagonal "pores," both of which are illustrated in Figure 29.4.

FIGURE 29.4

Leaky borders using the drunkard's walk algorithm

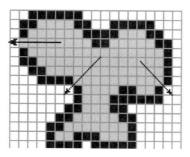

Here, a gap in the left border is one potential leak where a search trace could escape. Two other locations show pores where a diagonal search trace could escape. The remaining potential gaps in the original have been blocked in this version.

Going through a bitmap looking for potential problems of this type, however, is a tedious process and prone to error. Instead, the broad area-checking provisions in the preceding code accommodate a much less rigorous border condition.

Finally, if any of the preceding tests have set the Reverse flag, both the x and y increment variables are inverted by multiplying by –1.

```
if( Reverse )
{
    x *= -1;
    y *= -1;
}
else
if( ! random(10) )
{
    x = random(3)-1;
    y = random(3)-1;
}
```

Alternatively, if no reverse condition has been encountered, a simple random test is used to change the search direction on a one-in-ten chance. Like the original one, the new search direction is selected randomly.

NOTE
A provision has been included in the MapDemo program to render the search trace visible by drawing a white dot at each step. This is implemented quite simply as:
```
//=== option to trace random walk algorithm =========
    SetPixel( hdc, xCoord, yCoord, 0x00FFFFFF );
//=================================================
```
To disable this trace provision, simply comment out this line of code.

Last, the present x and y incremental values are added to the xCoord and yCoord values before the do...while loop continues.

```
    xCoord += x;
    yCoord += y;
}
while( ! Done );
...
return;
}
```

Figure 29.5 shows several drunkard's walk searches executed in various New England states. The illustration was created by having the search paint its own trail markers. After the screen image was captured, the fill colors for each state were replaced by white, and the target points, which appear as small red dots in the map image, were replaced by asterisks for easier identification.

FIGURE 29.5

Drunkard's walk searches in New England

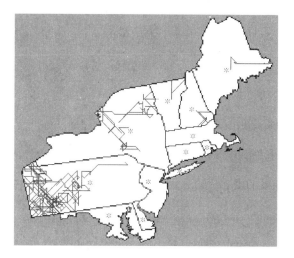

NOTE The drunkard's walk algorithm is not without an occasional shortcoming. Stuart Ozer, who was my technical reviewer for the Windows 3.1 version of an earlier volume, reported finding a starting point on Cape Cod from which the algorithm required ten minutes or more to identify Massachusetts. Such a flaw could be blamed on the geometry of the search versus the boundary configuration, or it could be simple chance produced by bad luck in the pseudo-random number sequence directing the search.

As you can readily see in the traces in Figure 29.5, the drunkard's walk algorithm is not the most efficient search method. Furthermore, as previously mentioned, there are times when this method is indeed ineffective.

For an example, Figure 29.6 shows an enlargement of the search executed in Pennsylvania, with a circle added both to make the target region more visible and to show the nominal target radius. The search shown begins in the northeastern

FIGURE 29.6

Searching Pennsylvania

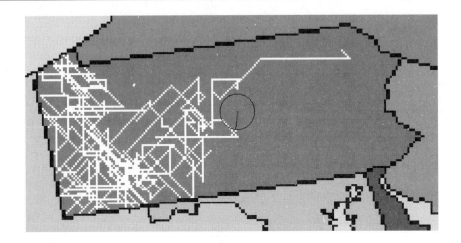

portion of the state, then passes relatively close to the target location, but not quite close enough to trigger a match, before executing a rather massive search of the western region and, finally, returning to the central region to find the target coordinates. On the other hand, since even a complex search like this was executed in a matter of a less than a second, the inefficiency involved was relatively minor.

Also, there are two factors which tend to mask these potential inefficiencies:

- A natural human tendency to click on some point roughly near the center of any area

- The probability that the algorithm will tend to quickly execute an escape from such a region

A third guard can be provided by selecting extra coordinate points within such regions. For an example, see the provisions for New York and Long Island in the MapDemo program. (On the map, the island of Long Island is separate from the remainder of the state and has its own target coordinates.)

Using a Hidden Map

There may be occasions when you want to identify areas without having them visible on the displayed image. For example, in the case of the United States map, you might wish to display a topographic or meteorological map of the country without delineating the states, which would mean no borders.

An alternative approach that will allow you to still be able to identify the states would be to use a second map image—the same size as the first—that does not appear on screen. This second map could be created in a memory context and, when the mouse is used to select a point on the displayed bitmap, the search would be executed from the corresponding point on the hidden bitmap.

Using Direct Coordinate Searches

Although it may appear odd or even inefficient, the drunkard's walk algorithm is, overall, a very fast technique for determining a regional location. There is, however, one alternative which, on first consideration, sometimes appears more efficient: Search the coordinate list for the coordinate pair closest to the starting point, then look for a border between the two points.

The reasons for this second step are simple but are best illustrated by an example. Consider the states of Pennsylvania and New Jersey and assume that the coordinate pairs for each are located at, approximately, Altoona (Pennsylvania) and East Brunswick (New Jersey), placing each location roughly at the center of the state.

A mouse click in the region of Philadelphia (Pennsylvania) would not, however, select the Altoona coordinates as nearest because the East Brunswick coordinates in New Jersey are considerably closer.

Of course, searching for a border between the initial point and the closest target would identify the problem and allow another search for the next closest coordinates (and so on) to proceed. But the search for a border is almost as time-consuming as a simple drunkard's walk and is more difficult to program reliably.

As an alternative to the single border crossing question, suppose that the located coordinate set is correct, that it lies in the same state or region as the mouse click, but that a straight line between the origin and the coordinate point must cross two borders.

Sound unlikely? It isn't. For example, look at Figure 29.5, where the state of Maryland (at the bottom of the map) is virtually split in two by the Chesapeake Bay. At the same time, Long Island and the mainland portion of the state of New York are technically all one region but, physically, are two separate areas on the map. In this instance, neither of the algorithms discussed—he drunkard's walk or the closest points with border-crossing tests—is adequate.

The solution for both the cases of discontinuous or extremely convoluted areas is to provide more than one coordinate point. In the MapDemo program, the USMAP02 provides two coordinate points to identify New York: one on Long Island and one on the mainland.

For Maryland, a second point located across the Chesapeake Bay would simplify searching and would also prevent an error that is present in the current version: Selecting a point across Chesapeake Bay is very likely to locate Delaware, not Maryland.

TIP

It would also be possible to provide a larger number of coordinate point targets in each area, which should ensure very fast searches. The only drawback would be the effort of building tables of points and ensuring that there were no errors in the result. However, since the trade-off in speed is minimal from the user's viewpoint, it hardly seems worth the effort.

In this chapter, we've looked at several methods for working with interactive, complex bitmaps. The MapDemo program, whose listing follows, demonstrates two methods for mapping mouse events to complex bitmap regions. Several other methods were mentioned, which you can experiment with to see how they suit the needs of your applications.

Listing 29.1: The MapDemo Program

```
//=======================//
//       MAPDEMO.H        //
//=======================//
#define  IDM_MAP1    101    // US map
#define  IDM_MAP2    102    // NE map
#define  IDM_EXIT    103


//=======================//
//       MAPDEMO.C        //
//  256-Color Map Viewer  //
//=======================//

#include <windows.h>
#include <stdlib.h>
```

```
#include <string.h>
#include <stdio.h>
#include "mapdemo.h"

#ifndef __BORLANDC__
#define random(x)  ( rand() % (int)( x ) )
#endif

#define StateColors  41
#define StateCoords  13
#define AllCoords    StateCoords+3
#define BORDER       0x00000000
#define APP_ICON     "MAPDEMO"
#define APP_MENU     "MAPDEMO"
#define APP_CURSOR   "MAPDEMO"

char    szAppTitle[] = "256-Color Map Viewer",
        szAppName[]  = "MapDemo";
HANDLE  hInst;
BOOL    bReadColor;

typedef struct { char  *State;
                 short  Color;  } ColorState;

typedef struct { char  *State;
                 short  xPos;
                 short  yPos;  } CoordState;

short NewEngland[12] =
{  60,  61,  65,  67,  69,  70,
   72,  76,  80, 151, 153, 185  };

ColorState CState[StateColors] =
{  "Arizona",         2,      "New Mexico",      7,
   "Oklahoma",        9,      "Georgia",        11,
   "Oregon",         12,      "Colorado",       13,
   "Missouri",       15,      "South Carolina", 16,
   "Texas",          17,      "Hawaii",         18, // 10
   "Virginia",       21,      "Arkansas",       23,
   "Nebraska",       24,      "Illinois",       27,
   "Mississippi",    29,      "Louisana",       35,
   "Ohio",           39,      "California",     40,
```

```
      "Florida",        41,    "Idaho",             52,  // 20
      "Michigan",       56,    "North Carolina",    59,
      "Kansas",         62,    "Washington",        65,
      "Wisconsin",      68,    "West Virginia",     71,
      "Minnesota",      74,    "Kentucky",          77,
      "Iowa",           79,    "Nevada",            81,  // 30
      "Tennessee",      83,    "Utah",             109,
      "South Dakota",  114,    "North Dakota",     121,
      "Wyoming",       142,    "Alabama",          158,
      "Alaska",        180,    "Montana",          189,
      "Indiana",       194,    "Alaska",           248,  // 40
      "Hawaii",        255  };                           // 41

CoordState Coord[AllCoords] =
{   "Connecticut",   267, 208,  "Delaware",        202, 311,
    "Maine",         330,  86,  "Maryland",        148, 305,
    "Maryland",       79, 306,  "Massachusetts",   279, 184,
    "New Hampshire", 276, 144,  "New Jersey",      209, 253,
    "New York",      181, 178,  "New York",        258, 237,
    "Pennsylvania",  119, 256,  "Rhode Island",    300, 201,
    "Vermont",       238, 132,  "RETURN",           14, 337,
    "RETURN",        331, 290,  "RETURN",          122,  81  };

int ErrorMsg( char *Error )
{
    MessageBox( GetFocus(), Error, "Notice", MB_ICONASTERISK |
MB_OK );
    return(0);
}


#include "dibitmap.i"

void LocationMsg( char *State )
{
    char szBuff[80];

    wsprintf( szBuff, "Welcome to the great state of %s", State );
    MessageBox( GetFocus(), szBuff, "Location",
            MB_ICONEXCLAMATION | MB_OK );
    return;
}
```

```
//=== use color matching for the USMAP01 image ===========

void ColorCheckMap( HWND hwnd, WORD xCoord, WORD yCoord )
{
    HDC      hdc;
    DWORD    RColor;
    WORD     SColor;
    int      i;
    char     szBuff[40];

    if( ( xCoord >= ( bmWidth  - 1 ) ) ||
        ( yCoord >= ( bmHeight - 1 ) ) )
    {
        MessageBeep( MB_ICONASTERISK );
        ErrorMsg( "Point selected must\nbe within map bounds" );
        return;
    }
    hdc = GetDC( hwnd );
    RColor = GetPixel( hdc, xCoord, yCoord );
            // need RGB palette-relative color value
    ReleaseDC( hwnd, hdc );
    if( RColor == BORDER )
    {
        MessageBeep( MB_ICONASTERISK );
        ErrorMsg( "Select a point within\na state boundry ..." );
        return;
    }
    LocalLock( hGLP );
    LocalLock( hGPal );
            // lock and create palette for reference
    hGPal = CreatePalette( pGLP );
    if( hGPal == NULL ) ErrorMsg( "Palette not found!" );
            // make palette active for device context
    RealizePalette( hdc );
            // get palette index for comparison
    SColor = GetNearestPaletteIndex( hGPal, (COLORREF) RColor );
            // unlock everything but don't delete palette
    LocalUnlock( hGLP );
    LocalUnlock( hGPal );
    for( i=0; i<12; i++ )
        if( SColor == NewEngland[i] )
```

```
                    // if any New England state, switch maps
                PostMessage( hwnd, WM_COMMAND, IDM_MAP2, OL );
        for( i=0; i<=StateColors; i++ )
            if( SColor == CState[i].Color )
                LocationMsg( CState[i].State );
        MessageBeep( MB_ICONASTERISK );
    }


//=== use drunkard's walk algorithm and coordinate =======
//=== matching for the USMAP02 image ====================

void CoordCheckMap( HWND hwnd, WORD xCoord, WORD yCoord )
{
    BOOL    Done = FALSE, Reverse;
    HDC     hdc;
    WORD    i;
    int     j, k, x, y;
    HCURSOR hOrgCur;

    if( ( xCoord >= ( bmWidth - 1 ) ) ||
        ( yCoord >= ( bmHeight - 1 ) ) )
    {
        MessageBeep( MB_ICONASTERISK );
        ErrorMsg( "Point selected must\nbe within map bounds" );
        return;
    }
#ifdef __BORLANDC__
    randomize();
#endif
    hOrgCur = SetCursor( LoadCursor( NULL, IDC_WAIT ) );
    hdc = GetDC( hwnd );
    x = random(3)-1;
    y = random(3)-1;
    do
    {
        for( i=0; i<AllCoords; i++ )
        {
            if( ( abs( xCoord - Coord[i].xPos ) +
                  abs( yCoord - Coord[i].yPos ) ) < 10 )
            {
                if( i < StateCoords )
```

```
                      LocationMsg( Coord[i].State );
               else
                  PostMessage( hwnd, WM_COMMAND, IDM_MAP1, 0L );
               Done = TRUE;
         }  }
      Reverse = FALSE;
      if( ( xCoord >= bmWidth-1  ) || ( xCoord <= 1 ) ||
          ( yCoord >= bmHeight-1 ) || ( yCoord <= 1 ) )
         Reverse = TRUE;
      else
         for( j=-1; j<2; j++ )
            for( k=-1; k<2; k++ )
               if( GetPixel( hdc, xCoord+j, yCoord+k ) == BORDER )
                  Reverse = TRUE;
      if( Reverse )
      {
         x *= -1;
         y *= -1;
      }
      else
      if( ! random(10) )
      {
         x = random(3)-1;
         y = random(3)-1;
      }
//=== option to trace random walk algorithm =========
      SetPixel( hdc, xCoord, yCoord, 0x00FFFFFF );
//===================================================
      xCoord += x;
      yCoord += y;
   }
   while( ! Done );
   ReleaseDC( hwnd, hdc );
   SetCursor( hOrgCur );
   return;
}

void ResizeWindow( HWND hwnd )
{
   RECT  rMajor, rMinor;
   int   wWidth, wHeight;
```

```
      GetWindowRect( hwnd, &rMajor );
      GetClientRect( hwnd, &rMinor );
      wWidth  = ( rMajor.right - rMajor.left ) -
                ( rMinor.right - rMinor.left ) +
                  bmWidth;
      wHeight = ( rMajor.bottom - rMajor.top ) -
                ( rMinor.bottom - rMinor.top ) +
                  bmHeight;
      MoveWindow( hwnd, 0, 0, wWidth, wHeight, TRUE );
}

#ifdef __BORLANDC__
#pragma argsused
#endif

BOOL APIENTRY AboutProc( HWND hDlg,   UINT msg,
                            UINT wParam, LONG lParam )
{
   switch( msg )
   {
      case WM_INITDIALOG:  return( TRUE );
      case WM_COMMAND:
         switch( LOWORD( wParam ) )
         {
            case IDOK: EndDialog( hDlg, TRUE );
                       return( TRUE );
               default: return( TRUE );
      }    }
   return( FALSE );
}

long APIENTRY WndProc( HWND hwnd, UINT msg, UINT wParam, LONG
lParam )
{
   HDC          hdc, hdcMem;
   PAINTSTRUCT  ps;
   HBITMAP      hBMOld;
   HPALETTE     hPalOld;

   switch( msg )
   {
```

```
case WM_CREATE:
   PostMessage( hwnd, WM_COMMAND, IDM_MAP1, 0L );
   break;

case WM_COMMAND:
   switch( LOWORD( wParam ) )
   {
      case IDM_MAP1:
         ReadBitmap( hwnd, "USMAP01.BMP" );
         bReadColor = TRUE;
         ResizeWindow( hwnd );
         break;

      case IDM_MAP2:
         ReadBitmap( hwnd, "USMAP02.BMP" );
         bReadColor = FALSE;
         ResizeWindow( hwnd );
         break;

      case IDM_ABOUT:
         ErrorMsg( "Calling About" );
         DialogBox( hInst, "ABOUT", hwnd, AboutProc );
         ErrorMsg( "Finished About" );
         break;

      case IDM_EXIT:
         PostMessage( hwnd, WM_CLOSE, 0, 0L );
         break;

      default:
         return( DefWindowProc( hwnd, msg, wParam, lParam ) );
   }
   break;

case WM_LBUTTONDOWN:
   if( bReadColor )
     ColorCheckMap( hwnd, LOWORD(lParam), HIWORD(lParam) );
   else
     CoordCheckMap( hwnd, LOWORD(lParam), HIWORD(lParam) );
   break;
```

```
        case WM_PAINT:
            InvalidateRect( hwnd, NULL, TRUE );
            hdc = BeginPaint( hwnd, &ps );
            if( hGBM )
            {
                hdcMem = CreateCompatibleDC( hdc );
                hBMOld = SelectObject( hdcMem, hGBM );
                if( hGPal )
                    hPalOld = SelectPalette( hdc, hGPal, FALSE );
                BitBlt( hdc, 0, 0, bmWidth, bmHeight,
                        hdcMem, 0, 0, SRCCOPY );
                if( hGPal )
                    SelectPalette( hdc, hPalOld, FALSE );
                SelectObject( hdcMem, hBMOld );
                DeleteDC( hdcMem );
            }
            EndPaint( hwnd, &ps );
            break;

        case WM_DESTROY:
            FreeGlobalVars();
            PostQuitMessage(0);
            break;

        default:
            return( DefWindowProc( hwnd, msg, wParam, lParam ) );
    }
    return( TRUE );
}

#include "template.i"

#ifdef __BORLANDC__
#pragma argsused
#endif

int APIENTRY WinMain( HANDLE hInstance, HANDLE hPrevInstance,
                      LPSTR  lpCmdLine, int    nCmdShow    )
{
    MSG    msg;
```

```
        if( ! hPrevInstance )          // are any other instances running?
          if( ! InitApplication( hInstance ) )
            return( FALSE );
        if( ! InitInstance( hInstance, nCmdShow ) )
          return (FALSE);
        while( GetMessage( &msg, NULL, 0, 0 ) )
        {
          TranslateMessage( &msg );  // translate virtual key codes
          DispatchMessage( &msg );   // dispatch message to window
        }
        return( msg.wParam );           `
#ifndef __BORLANDC__
        UNREFERENCED_PARAMETER( lpCmdLine );
                                        // prevents unused param warning
#endif                                  //    message from compiler
}


//=========================//
//        MAPDEMO.RC        //
//=========================//
#include <windows.h>

MAPDEMO MENU
BEGIN
    POPUP "Map"
    BEGIN
       MENUITEM "United States (All)", 101
       MENUITEM "New England States",  102
       MENUITEM SEPARATOR
       MENUITEM "Exit", 103
    END
    MENUITEM "About", 104, HELP
END

ABOUT DIALOG 39, 40, 126, 84
STYLE DS_MODALFRAME | WS_POPUP | WS_CAPTION
CAPTION "About MapDemo"
BEGIN
    CONTROL "NT Version 1.0", 0, "STATIC",
        SS_CENTER | WS_CHILD | WS_VISIBLE, 38, 44, 50, 12
    ICON "mapdemo", 0, 13, 60, 16, 16
```

```
    CONTROL "Okay", 1, "BorBtn",
        1 | WS_CHILD | WS_VISIBLE | WS_TABSTOP, 46, 60, 33, 20
    CONTROL "MapDemo displays a 256-color map image"
            " allowing selection of states.", -1, "STATIC",
        SS_LEFT | WS_CHILD | WS_VISIBLE | WS_GROUP | WS_TABSTOP,
        4, 4, 118, 16
    CONTROL
        "NOTE: Display is optimized for an SVGA Windows driver.",
        -1, "STATIC",
        SS_LEFT | WS_CHILD | WS_VISIBLE | WS_GROUP | WS_TABSTOP,
        4, 24, 118, 20
      ICON "mapdemo", 0, 95, 59, 16, 16
END

MAPDEMO CURSOR "mapdemo.cur"
MAPDEMO ICON   "mapdemo.ico"
USMAP01 BITMAP "usmap01.bmp"
USMAP02 BITMAP "usmap02.bmp"
```

Graphics Simulations

- A synthetic cosmos for modeling physical interactions

- Variable timing for simulated events

- Choices for simplifying simulations

- Mechanical simulations

- Theoretical system simulations

Over the past two decades, computers have revolutionized more of our world than most people realize. Granted, the Internet is the current buzzword, and most people are aware that computers are used for special effects in movies and commercials on television. Some people are even familiar with using computers to study fluid dynamics, weather patterns, engineering structures, and other technical subjects. All of these, however, are only a few of the areas where computers have radically changed the traditional arts, crafts, and sciences. A complete list of affected areas would fill a large book and would be out-of-date long before it could be published.

But this chapter is not about the computer revolution. It's about an area that did not even exist, with a few modest exceptions, prior to computers: the field of graphics simulations or, more accurately, the mathematical simulation of dynamic systems in general, including both physical and nonphysical systems.

Using Graphics in Simulations

Simulations do not necessarily require graphics and, in some cases, would be slowed down by graphics. We do, however, have a very human desire to see what is happening rather than reading about the results afterwards. As an example, the Forest demo program presented in this chapter displays a small universe of 10,000 acres, simulating the growth of trees.

The simulation begins with bare ground that is randomly seeded with 100 starts. As the simulation progresses, the various wooded areas grow, age, and propagate, spreading trees to new areas.

Of course, if this were the extent of the simulation, the mini-universe would simply fill with trees until there was no bare ground left. The result could be derived simply by calculating the average time necessary to fill the forest. This simulation, however, is not so limited.

Instead, as a defined area of tree population ages, the trees eventually die, rot, and leave a new plot of bare ground. At the same time, in emulation of the real world, the simulated forest is subject to fires. And, once a fire starts, it spreads. The older trees are easiest to ignite, and changing wind patterns affect the spread of the fire.

Overall, if the simulation's only output were a statistical report listing the forested acres for each year, we might learn almost as much. But almost as much is not the same as watching it happen; by watching the forest grow, burn, and reseed, we gain some small measure of understanding of two new and very important elements: the patterns of growth and death, and the way that changing the parameters affects not only the end results but the patterns themselves.

NOTE If you have any doubts about the relative importance of simple statistical results versus patterns, consider the extreme examples of any fractal algorithm. In fractal calculations, such as the Henon Attractor or the Malthusian equation (another famous simulation), statistical results reveal almost nothing; the patterns, visible only when plotted graphically, reveal everything.

Some Background on Computer Simulations

In the ages B.C. (Before Computers), the sheer volume of calculations required for simulations ruled out modeling even the simplest systems unless some measurable physical analog could be employed. In some cases, there were alternatives. Physical erosion was relatively easy to study using a slant box of sand and a water source. Minimal route-mapping problems could be solved using soap films. And many ballistic and navigational problems were attacked using electronic (and some mechanical) analog systems.

As for more general simulations, however, the Life program was played out with paper and pencil, usually by students who might have better spent their time studying. This was roughly the practical limit for an unaided human. (For your amusement, the Life program in electronic form is included on the CD accompanying this book.)

In the Life program, the "world" consists of a grid which, for convenience, is finite but unbounded, and each grid location may be initially "alive" or "dead." Provisions are included in the demo application to "seed" the grid randomly or to create an initial configuration known as a "launcher," which will generate two child "flyers," which will fly across the screen on a diagonal path.

(continued on next page)

At intervals of one-half second, a new generation of Life is calculated according to the current state of the "world" and three simple rules:

1. Any alive location that has more than three neighbors dies of overcrowding in the next generation.

2. Any alive location that has less than two neighbors dies of loneliness in the next generation.

3. Any location, currently alive or dead, that has exactly three neighbors will be alive in the next generation.

Advancing beyond these three simple rules governing the Life program and expanding beyond what is, essentially, a very small universe, the complexity and volume of the calculations required for most simulations have simply overwhelmed both human patience and practical capacities. Some few individuals have accomplished prodigious feats of cogitation and calculation, such as the compilation of the Rudolphine Tables (Kepler) or calculation of the trigonometric functions (Napier), but these are exceptions as well as monumental endeavors. (The Aztec calendar might also qualify but was almost certainly a group effort.)

Thus, for the most part, simulations of any complexity have waited for the advent of our newest and most powerful tool: the computer. Using this tool, we are now able to study—through simulation—systems about which, previously, we could only theorize.

All of this says nothing about the accuracy of our simulations, but it does permit testing our theories against actual performance. Therefore, if your theory holds that playing to fill an inside straight is better than folding on the sixth card, you can create a simulation to test this theory faster and more accurately (as well as more cheaply) than testing the theory at Saturday night poker games. (Of course, this question can also be settled by probability theory without requiring simulations, but we won't go into that here.)

Creating a Dynamic (Memory) Cosmos

The Forest program demonstrates the creation of a synthetic cosmos whose reality is governed by a relatively few and easily defined rules. By intention, the Forest exists only as a shadow, mimicking reality without requiring the complexity of rules (natural laws) that govern what we familiarly consider reality.

Instead, the complex interactions of our reality have been replaced by simpler "shadow" rules that can be manipulated, compressed, and studied. Thus, by analogy and experimentation, we are able to better understand the complexities of reality.

Rather than modeling the growth and complexity of individual trees (along with the weather patterns, soil composition, and myriad other factors) and repeating this for the thousands of acres of trees composing the forest, the forest is calculated as areas following a simple statistical growth pattern with a uniform composition within the area. In this fashion, we *can* see the forest for the trees; we are able to look at the forest as an entity while ignoring the trees themselves.

The Forest Cosmos Size

Our simulated forest exists in a cosmos consisting of a scant 10,000 units (100-by-100) which, for convenience only, are referred to as acres. Because this is a simple simulation, the essential status for each unit is stored in an array of BYTE.

For convenience, two arrays are used, permitting the second array to be updated by reference to the first and to then replace the first array. In this fashion, the first array, which holds the prior status, is not affected by changes that would produce recursive effects.

As you know by now, where DOS and Windows 3.*x* impose limits on array sizes of a mere 64KB, Windows NT and 95, using 32-bit addressing, have revoked this limitation in favor of a theoretical array size of 4GB. Of course, we still face physical limitations imposed by the amount of memory available; even on small systems, however, this is a considerable increase in freedom.

NOTE If you need to use extremely large arrays, in sizes beyond available memory limits, you can use disk files as an extension of RAM. Unfortunately, this approach has the disadvantages of being relatively slow and somewhat cumbersome.

Rules of the Forest Cosmos

Had I been present at the creation, I might have offered the creator much valuable advice.
— remark attributed to Alphonso the YYs.

The Forest cosmos is governed by a series of relatively simple rules, which appear as numerical algorithms within the program:

- The Forest cosmos begins as bare ground and is randomly seeded, initially, with 100 plantings.

- On subsequent cycles (years), the planting age is shown by changing colors.

- After a minimum of five cycles, the forest plots are developed well enough to propagate and, if adjacent plots are bare, may seed these areas, initiating new growth.

- Old-growth acres—arbitrarily those over 11 years old—are susceptible to natural death. A simple simulation provides for old age and other causes. As with natural forests, however, this is a minor element and affects approximately 1 percent of the forest.

- Fire is a major effect in the Forest cosmos, just as it is in real-world forests. For simplicity, only one fire can start during any cycle. Minor fires are not simulated, but a fire may spread to adjacent acreage.

- Fires die out when their fuel is exhausted, but they are also affected by wind direction and speed.

- Fires can spread only to mature acreage; young plots are not affected (under the assumption that young trees are scattered and little deadwood is available to fuel a major burn).

Given these relatively simple rules, the Forest cosmos simulates the same patterns of growth and death exhibited by real forests. And a correspondence in patterns is the hallmark by which a simulation is tested.

Handling Boundary Problems: Creating a Closed, Unbounded Cosmos

Any simulation that re-creates or models a subset of a larger reality is subject to a boundary problem in one form or another. If you'll recall from Chapter 27, when we talked about image enhancements, one form of boundary problem came up when transform operations left a one-pixel border around the original image. Although this border data was used when calculating transformations for adjacent pixels, because these pixels did not themselves have a complete complement of neighbors, they were not included in the transformed image.

In the Forest cosmos, the boundary problem is avoided by the simple expedient of making the cosmos a closed, unbounded universe. What appears to be the left edge of the map actually adjoins the right edge; the top edge of the map joins and continues at the bottom. Topologically, this type of closure is the equivalent of a *toroidal* surface (a doughnut or inner tube provide physical examples of a toroidal surface). Although toroidal surfaces are not commonly encountered in our universe (at least, not on any macrocosmic scale), this is a popular method of avoiding boundary problems in simulations.

There are other, more complex methods for dealing with boundary problems. For example, a method, popular in the physical universe, involves using a spherical surface. Another, even more complicated and computation-intensive approach involves using algorithms to simulate the effects of areas outside the actual simulation boundaries.

For most planar simulations, the toroidal universe provides the simplest approach and the fastest computational results. Furthermore, if your simulated cosmos is not planar but a volume, such as a fluid or gaseous volume, this same practice can be extended to create a hypertoroid in cybernetically four-dimensional space.

The Toroidal Model

The practice of creating or simulating a closed but unbounded cosmos in cyberspace is both simple and complex. On the simple side, because the data describing a simulation is stored in one or more arrays or matrixes, the primary consideration, using the toroidal surface model, is to test all coordinate references (that is, references to array data) and to provide adjustments for references that fall outside the array limits, thus "wrapping" the index back into the array from "the other side."

On the complex side, although simple rectilinear offsets are easily converted, operations involving vectors, angles, or curves are not always easily handled. When operations of this or a similar type are necessary, the simplest approach is to use a separate matrix where the operation can be carried out without crossing a boundary. The results can be mapped, using whatever offsets and adjustments are necessary, into the simulation space.

In spatial terms, the most important element is to make sure all operations that wrap across an array boundary are correctly adjusted for the wrap. Failure to do so can have strange and interesting results that are not always easy to identify or recognize.

Using Colors in Simulations

One principal characteristic of graphic simulations is the use of color to make information clear. In many cases, commonly referred to as *false-color mapping* or *false-color imaging*, color assignments are arbitrary and have no real-world relation to the source or the data.

For example, false-color imaging is often used in astronomy to "translate" radio-frequency images for visual presentation. The translation involved can take several different forms, including using color to represent intensities, radio frequencies, densities, or even gravitational gradations—none of which have any direct correspondence to the visual spectrum.

Another mapping format uses colors that are chosen to represent approximate analogs of the data. An example of this latter approach is used in the Forest simulation. Bare ground is represented by browns, various stages of forest growth by shades of green, fires and embers by reds, and ashy ground by grays.

A combination of both representational color and false-color coding can also be used. This approach generally involves switching between display formats, showing first one information set and then another. For example, we could create a switched display for the Forest program by adding provisions to show simulated rainfall patterns, temperature profiles, or soil composition characteristics (extensions you can experiment with yourself).

Operating the Simulation: The Forest Program

Deciding how to set up a simulation is the first step; coding the simulation is the second. Both steps require provisions for a variety of circumstances.

As an example, Figure 30.1 shows the Forest cosmos some 3868 years after seeding and 30 days into a major burn-off. The illustrated burn began somewhere in the northwest of the display but has not spread too widely, despite a current wind from the north at a strength of 4 (the maximum is 5). Allowing the simulation to continue, the fire revives as the winds change direction and finally burns itself out after 73 days.

FIGURE 30.1

Here, the forest is 3868 years old, 30 days into a burn condition, with the wind from the north at a strength of four.

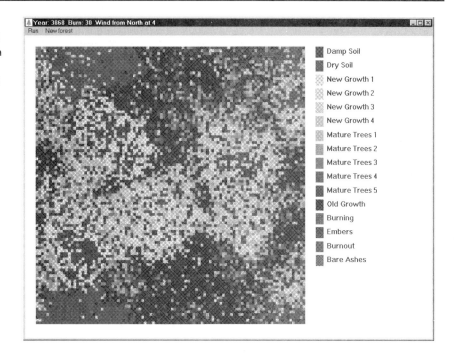

All of these events, of course, exist only in the computer's memory and result from pseudo-random number sequences. Nonetheless, they provide a faithful emulation of patterns of growth and burn-off that have been observed in natural forests.

Defining the Color Palette

In the Forest demo, a palette of 16 colors has been defined. Two of these represent bare ground (light brown and dark brown). Ten shades of green represent trees at various ages. Light and dark red represent fires and embers, respectively. A dark gray is used to represent freshly burnt, ashy ground. A third brown is used for ground left bare by a fire.

The palette colors are defined in Forest.H as RGB values, each with a corresponding integer constant as a convenient identifier. (These latter elements are for the programmer's convenience only—but, then, what is more important?)

However, although these RGB values are defined for each color, this palette is never activated for the device context. Instead, while the RGB colors are referenced as drawing colors, Windows is allowed to dither the existing default palette colors in drawing the simulation map.

> **NOTE** The decision to permit dithering instead of activating the color palette is arbitrary, but this method does show, even on SVGA systems, how a similar display might appear on standard VGA systems. The alternative of activating the defined palette colors is left as an exercise for the reader (and has been demonstrated, numerous times, in other example programs accompanying this book).

Initiating the Cosmos

Lacking the resources to initiate a primal fireball and to then wait for nature to evolve a life form from the first primordial globule, the first provision in the Forest simulation is to set the initial conditions for the simulation. This is accomplished in two steps; beginning in response to the WM_CREATE message.

```
case WM_CREATE:
    randomize();
    ActiveTimer = 0;
    wsprintf( szBuff, szCaption, nYears );
```

```
SetWindowText( hwnd, szBuff );
for( i=0; i<GRID; i++ )            // init world as
    for( j=0; j<GRID; j++ )        // bare ground
        Acres[i][j] = random(2);
break;
```

The randomize function, of course, ensures that new initial conditions (that is, a new pseudo-random number sequence) are used each time the program is executed.

> **NOTE**
>
> If you are using the Microsoft C compiler rather than the Borland C compiler, the randomize function is not available. The function can be provided other ways; for example, by using the system clock (seconds since January 1, 1980) to seed the pseudo-random generator.

The second provision, the double loops, sets the world to a random mixture of damp and dry soils shown by the two browns. Within the program, both are treated simply as fertile ground, without regard to their moisture content. In a more elaborate version, the two browns might be used as different conditions, representing wet and dry ground or high and low terrain. For the current version, two shades of brown are simply not as dull as a single uniform color.

The second stage of initialization occurs only when the New Forest option is selected from the menu. When this option is selected, the program resets the nYears variable to zero and seeds 100 random locations, setting the corresponding array elements as iNewGrowth.

```
case IDM_RESEED:
    randomize();
    nYears = 0;
    for( i=0; i<100; i++ )
    {
        xPos = random(GRID);
        yPos = random(GRID);
        Acres[xPos][yPos] = iNewGrowth;
    }
    EnableMenuItem( GetMenu(hwnd),
                    IDM_STOPTIMER, MF_ENABLED );
    PostMessage( hwnd, WM_COMMAND, IDM_STARTGROWTH, 0L );
    InvalidateRect( hwnd, NULL, FALSE );
    break;
```

The pull-down Run menu has two options, Start and Stop, both of which are initially disabled. After the forest is seeded, the Stop option is enabled, and a message is posted to start the `ID_GROWTH` timer. Last, the `InvalidateRect` function is called to repaint the window.

Setting Variable Time for Events

After the initial conditions for a simulation are set (your cosmos is created), normally the next step is to initiate a sequence of events. In some simulations, such as for plotting fractal algorithms, it is the end result that is important. This type of process is normally carried out as quickly as possible.

More commonly, however, simulations are executed at some regular process rate. Ideally, this rate is fast enough to prevent boredom but slow enough to permit us to observe how the simulation is developing. Generally, for macro simulations such as those in our example, this is compressed time for the simple reason that no one is interested in waiting a year to watch a simulation complete a forest's growth cycle. Alternatively, if we were trying to simulate the first three minutes of the creation of the cosmos, we would probably want to expand time to permit the observation of events that happened too quickly for conventional observation.

In the Forest demo, two different compressed time rates are used, each controlled by a system timer—one for normal growth and another for forest fires.

Forest Growth Simulation

Initially, forest growth is simulated at 1 year = 1 second, with a one-second timer stepping through the growth cycle. Thus, at one-second intervals, the `ID_GROWTH` timer sends a `WM_TIMER` message to the `WndProc` procedure. In response, a number of events are initialized.

```
case WM_TIMER:
    switch( LOWORD( wParam ) )
    {
        case ID_GROWTH:
            wsprintf( szBuff, szCaption, nYears++ );
            SetWindowText( hwnd, szBuff );
            AgeWorld();
            PropogateTrees();
```

The first response is to update the window caption, displaying the current year (the number of cycles since the initial seeding) before calling `AgeWorld` to cycle the forest through a year's growth.

The next step, `PropogateTrees`, calls a subprocedure to seed new areas from existing growth. In this simulation, three factors control the rate of spread of the forest:

- The age of the existing growth (within each plot)
- Selection of a single plot within a range of three plots in any direction (quite arbitrarily)
- Whether the target plot is fertile ground (in this case, any bare soil)

All of these factors could be variables or could be changed arbitrarily to experiment with new environmental conditions. Still, the present settings serve as a good foundation for a forest simulation.

Growth and seeding operations are carried out by writing new values to a copy of the original data array, ensuring that the new conditions do not overwrite the existing conditions used to generate the new ones. However, because of this separation of present and future, the `StepForest` procedure is called to copy this future status back to the present array.

In the current simulation, the potential conflicts between the present and future states of the forest are minimal. The second array could be disposed of, and all operations could be carried out in a single array. In other simulations, however, duplicate arrays may be essential. Moreover, circumstances may require several arrays to store not only present and future, but also various data types, which may include constants (such as terrain) or contain factors affecting larger areas (such as rainfall).

Forest Fire Simulation

After the current state of the forest is updated, the `InitBurns` procedure is called to simulate potential forest fires:

```
StepForest();
InitBurns( hwnd );
InvalidateRect( hwnd, NULL, FALSE );
break;
```

And, when the forest fires (if any) conclude, the display is updated to show the new conditions.

The `InitBurns` procedure begins by selecting an arbitrary location for a fire to start:

```
void InitBurns( HWND hwnd )
{
    int  x, y, NoChance = 20;

    x = random( GRID );
    y = random( GRID );
```

Here, a couple of quite arbitrary conditions have been established:

- Only one fire can be started in any year.

- Any fire that does start completely burns out the affected plot (no plots are partially burned).

- The constant, `NoChance`, is included to adjust the chances for a burn to start.

As with the growth simulation conditions, all of these factors, including the algorithm, can be changed or may include variables to adjust for various ignition potentials.

To actually decide if a fire starts in the targeted area, a simple algorithm is applied:

```
    if( random( iOldGrowth + NoChance ) <= (int) Acres[x][y] )
```

Here, a random value is generated and must be less than the growth state of the plot selected before a fire is initiated. In effect, the older the growth on the target plot, and therefore the more fuel available, the greater the chances of a fire starting.

Assuming that a fire is initiated, another simulation sequence is started, beginning by setting `nDay` to zero and selecting an initial wind direction:

```
    {
        nDays = 0;
        nWind = random(4);
        Acres[x][y] = iBurning;
        PostMessage( hwnd, WM_COMMAND, IDM_STOPGROWTH, OL );
        PostMessage( hwnd, WM_COMMAND, IDM_STARTBURNS, OL );
    }
}
```

Last, to initiate the actual burn simulation sequence, the first timer (`ID_GROWTH`) is turned off and a second timer (`ID_FIRES`) is started.

Because two separate timers are involved in the simulation, and because the Start and Stop menu options are intended to operate either of these independently, a set of purely internal message procedures are used to trigger these options indirectly rather than directly.

After the ID_FIRES timer has been initiated, all subsequent WM_TIMER messages carry the ID_FIRES identifier and are used to control the new simulation sequence.

Because the burn events are an important departure from the normal growth pattern, the MessageBeep function is used to call attention to these changes. Also, the global nWind wind direction is allowed to change at random intervals before calling the TrackFire subprocedure:

```
case ID_FIRES:
    MessageBeep( 0 );
    if( ! random(4) ) nWind = random(4);
    if( ! TrackFire() )
    {
        PostMessage( hwnd, WM_COMMAND,
                     IDM_STOPBURNS, 0L );
        PostMessage( hwnd, WM_COMMAND,
                     IDM_STARTGROWTH, 0L );
    }
    InvalidateRect( hwnd, NULL, FALSE );
    break;

default:
    return( DefWindowProc( hwnd, msg, wParam, lParam ) );
}
break;
```

As long as fires do continue to burn, the TrackFire procedure returns TRUE, and the ID_FIRES timer continues uninterrupted. When there are no remaining fires and a FALSE value is returned, the ID_FIRES timer is killed and the ID_GROWTH timer restarted.

The TrackFire subprocedure accomplishes two tasks:

• It ensures that fires do burn out to embers and then to ashy ground. This is governed by a fairly simple algorithm that allows fires to sustain a long burn initially but, after the fires have been burning, causes later burns to develop swiftly but last only briefly. In effect, after a forest fire is well developed, the fires burn hotter, ignite new areas easier, but burn out faster.

- It provides a means for fires to spread to new areas. This is affected by three factors. The first two, wind direction and wind speed, are relatively obvious. The third is simply a provision to ensure that young acreage does not catch fire and burn off.

The complete listing of the Forest program is on the CD that accompanies this book.

Simulation Design

In the Forest program, the processes involving the growth of a forest have been greatly simplified. For example, no provisions have been made to account for rainfall or, during burn phases, for rains that limit or even extinguish the fire's spread. No provisions have been made for seasonal variations, such as wet springs and dry summers or for longer-term climatic variations. Similarly, only a single, generic species of trees is included, with no other plant life present and with no insect damage or disease damage simulated. Likewise, there are no prevailing winds, rainfall patterns, erosion, or soil fertility variations.

Even so, if all of these factors were included in the simulation, this would still be a very simplified cosmos. The point is that any simulation must be restricted to some degree, if only to allow the computer to handle it in a reasonable time and with reasonable memory requirements.

On the other hand, simplifying the simulation does not mean that the results must be simple. Since the object is to model reality, there is certainly every reason for the results of the simulation to mimic the complexities of reality.

Simplification Choices

The problem of simplification is threefold:

- To decide which elements of reality are essential to the simulation
- To develop algorithms that mathematically mimic reality
- To present the results of the computations in a format that will show what is happening

Because the Forest program was designed solely to demonstrate a graphic simulation and to serve as an example, many elements reflecting reality that would also have increased the complexity of the program were omitted. Instead, two principal factors were selected for representation:

- Propagation rates and patterns for the development of the forest

- Fires to destroy older growth and make room for new additional growth

Given these two principal factors, the resulting simulation (in terms of burn-off and regrowth patterns) still mimics the patterns observed in natural forests quite accurately, which, as an initial objective, is exactly what is desired.

In addition to the propagation and burn patterns, one minor evolutionary provision was added: having older growth die off without burning. In the present simulation, the relatively minor decline of old growth by simple attrition is masked by the larger effect of fires, producing the natural pattern observed in dry-climate forests.

If, however, the burn frequency is decreased or stopped, the old growth decline will become a major rather than a minor effect, producing a pattern typical of wetland forests, where large-scale fires are virtually unknown. And, as you may observe by varying the pattern, such a forest will tend toward a steady-state climax forest, which is quite typical of existing, older wetland forests where older growth dominates and younger growth is sparse.

Extending a Simulation

Once a basic simulation is operating with a satisfactory degree of validity—when the operations correspond somewhat faithfully to reality—further extensions can be added to simulate additional factors. The advantage of a simulation is that any of these additional factors (or any combination of additional factors) can be tested, varied, and tested again to observe how changes in various parameters affect the progress of the overall simulation.

Even our simple Forest program could be expanded to include more factors and used to study the effects of various cutting patterns and the effect on the recovery and long-term management of sustained yield for a real forest. We might include factors such as elevation and erosion effects, rainfall, and leftover debris from cutting operations and its effects on the spread of fires. Other factors that might affect the overall health of a forest, such as insect infestation and disease, might simply be ignored as irrelevant during the tests. But then, if some validity is found for considering further factors—perhaps the cutting of debris provides a breeding ground for the insect population—then these factors should also be included in the model.

Otherwise, the model may show effects that were not anticipated or fail to show effects which were.

How you extend a simulation depends on what you are trying to learn. The real value of a simulation is to reveal how processes occur, how elements interact, or where and how patterns appear within a system.

Simulating Mechanical Systems

Modeling of interactions among living systems is just one of the areas in which simulation is useful. Another fruitful area for simulation design lies in analyzing mechanical systems.

Although CAD systems are commonly thought of as design utilities, simulating how mechanical elements interact is an integral part of any mechanical design process. After all, if a set of gears are going to jam when two driven mechanical arms unexpectedly attempt to pass through the same volume of space, it's considerably cheaper to discover the flaw in an electronic simulation than discovering this same surprise after tooling up to begin production or worse, after building a physical model.

You may be thinking that mechanical modeling certainly could be carried out without any accompanying visual elements. After all, it should be faster to calculate (for example) how two gears mesh than to draw the two gears on screen and to repeatedly redraw them as they turn, right? If the only consideration was the two gears, perhaps. But what about that movement arm driven by the gearing which, in another few seconds of arc, will attempt to pass through one of several mechanical support members? These supports are static and weren't included in the calculated motions; a small oversight, but one that the real universe is not likely to duplicate.

Instead of attempting to calculate the place where every point belonging to every element (both static and dynamic) may potentially interact with some other point, it is simpler to draw the various elements, redrawing each one as often as necessary. This allows the best processors of all, the human eye and brain, to spot the potential conflicts.

WARNING If you are interested or active in mechanical simulations involving human users, please remember that human beings, unlike machine parts, do not come in standard sizes. Not all men are 5 foot 11 inches tall and not all women are 5 foot 2 inches. Design for the taller and smaller people, too.

Mechanical simulations should not be limited to the interactions of cams, gears, and cogs. Instead, as currently implemented in some virtual reality simulations, the humans (or other creatures) using the machines being designed also become part of the simulation process.

Speeding Up Floating-Point Calculations

One problem often encountered in simulations has been slow processing caused by repetitive floating-point calculations. In some cases, floating-point calculations simply cannot be avoided. In these cases, the only solution is a fast CPU with a good math coprocessor. In other cases, however, even when fractional interim values are desired or needed, these can be derived using integer rather than floating-point operations, by the simple expedient of limiting accuracy to what is actually required.

For example, suppose that an algorithm that is called repeatedly (several thousand times per simulation cycle) needs to calculate a radial distance using `pi`. Since the result of the calculation, however, will be cast as an integer and used as an index to a data array, the calculation does not need to be carried out to ten or twelve decimal places, or even three or four places. Therefore, instead of using a floating-point value for π, such as 3.14159, the calculation can be carried out using integer operations (which are faster) using the value 402 (=π * 128), and then dividing the result by simply shifting the value seven places to the right.

The bit-shift operation is considerably faster than any decimal division, and the entire process is markedly faster than floating-point operations, while (within limits) achieving the same result.

Simulating Theoretical Systems

Physical realities, whether they are living systems or mechanical constructs, offer their own physical appearances as a basis for graphic simulation. Other systems, however, which may be theoretical or nonphysical, do not offer quite the same convenience; instead these require imagination and artistry in deciding how to display the information generated by a simulation.

As an example, the operations of a computer chip are often simulated by a computer program, particularly during the design process for a new chip. During design, two quite different elements are taken into consideration: the physical and the electronic layouts for the chip.

Of these, the fabricated layout of the chip is relatively simple: How many circuits can be fabricated within a given area of silicon? The electronic layout, on the other hand, is not only more complex but is also directly affected by the physical layout. In this respect, considerations include the signal path between various elements and, therefore, the signal time between two components; how the components interact electronically; what leakage currents and capacitive effects must be accounted for; and, far from least, how the various components function cybernetically.

So, how is a system this complex simulated? And how is the simulation shown graphically?

First, no single simulation—graphic or otherwise—will suffice (except, possibly for a very simple chip), because of the level of physical complexity in contemporary monolithic integrated circuits. Instead (referring strictly to the physical layout), small portions of the chip might be simulated on the screen. Or, for an overview, color-coded areas might represent repetitive circuit areas or areas dedicated to some specific function.

The electronic functions, however, are not this easily coded. They would probably require several different simulations and displays to handle the various elements. For example, a histogram might be used to show signal-path times for different elements; remember, with today's high-speed chips, even the paths required for clock pulses can be critical, and more than one engineer has vainly expressed a wish for faster electricity. Still other elements are even less easily displayed. Thus, in many cases, instead of attempting to show the simulations directly, only the results of simulations are shown.

Computer chip and other electronic circuitry designs are only one area involving nonphysical simulations. There are other valid areas that have even less connection to traditional physical reality. Some are simply constructs of our own observations. For example, consider a simulation of the population-growth patterns using the Malthusian equation:

$$P_{n+1} = R * P_n * (1 - P_n)$$

where R represents the growth rate for successive populations (P). Okay, population grows linearly, doesn't it? So, wouldn't a simple line graph be appropriate for this equation?

If the whole suggestion sounds like a loaded question, you're right; it is.

First, after a half-dozen initial steps, the equation given is anything but linear. And, second, this particular simulation will yield results unlike anything you might normally expect. In fact, the Malthusian equation is a member of a loose group of formulas referred to as *strange attractors* because of the curves generated over successive reiterations from what initially appear to be only scattered points. The equation produces an interesting simulation, but graphic simulations can show interesting results that would not be visible simply by examining long columns of numbers.

> **TIP**
>
> To experiment with the Malthusian equation, one convenient method is to plot successive points (P_n and P_{n+1}) as x- and y-coordinate pairs. After a few thousand generations, the resulting plots will begin to show an interesting curve. Next, by varying the growth rate R (try the range from 2.3 to 3.8), a single curve becomes an interesting group of curves, complete with inflections and bifurcation points.

In other cases, such as plotting radiation-intensity patterns from a broadcast antenna or reception sensitivity for a receiver, the results are lobes or, in other instances, landscapes ranging from smoothly undulating hills and valleys to fields of jagged peaks and crevasses.

Regardless of the source of the data plotted or the algorithms used for a simulation, the visual presentation is not simply a gimmick to impress board members and visiting bigwigs but a very valuable tool to allow the use of our own most sensitive tools: color eyesight, superior image processing, and unequaled pattern recognition. Graphics can aid in the simulation of all types of dynamic systems, including both physical and nonphysical systems. The Forest program presented in this chapter is a simple example, which you can expand to experiment with various effects.

CHAPTER

THIRTY-ONE

31

Printing Graphics

- Procedures for copying images from a display context to a printer context

- Checks for a color or black-and-white printer

- Gray-scale definition

- Gray-scale printing enhancements

- Considerations for color printing

Being able to print a graphic image is almost as important as (or perhaps more important than) creating the image in the first place. The tools demonstrated in this chapter provide the basis for such facilities using both black-and-white and gray-scale color conversion.

If and how these features are used depends entirely on the needs of your applications. Most likely, you will need to adapt these features and perhaps also add some controls specific to your application. Alternatively, if you require only an occasional screen capture, you might prefer to combine the printer output procedures with one of the screen-capture processes described in an earlier chapter.

Incidentally, if you have access to color-reproduction facilities, you might also consider adding provisions for printing color separations; that is, printing separate red, green, and blue images for use as color screens in conventional printing processes.

Printer Operations

In many ways, Windows has greatly facilitated graphics image handling, with capabilities that range from providing hardware-independent graphics display environments to translating between different image formats. Just as Windows NT and 95 provide support for a wide variety of displays, they also support a wide variety of printers, ranging from dot-matrix printers to all types of laser printers.

Furthermore, provisions exist (using the `BitBlt` or `StretchBlt` function) for copying images from a display context to a printer context, and from there to the printer itself. On the whole, Windows includes almost everything needed to provide hard-copy output of graphics images.

Unfortunately, however, almost is not everything. One fly remains in the ointment: the fact that, although most monitors are color, color printers are still less common than black-and-white printers. And in this last respect, Windows does not offer any automatic solutions. As a general rule, a color image directed to a monochrome printer without any provisions for shading will print all colors, except white, as a solid black, which is generally not a very useful result.

Still, if no automatic solution has been provided, a custom solution is not beyond the realm of the possible and practical, as will be shown momentarily. But before tackling the solution, the first step is to understand the problem and the available mechanisms.

Win.INI versus Up-to-Date Printer Information

During installation, Windows offers an option to select one or more printers. When you choose printers to install, Windows copies the appropriate printer drivers to the Windows directory and lists these drivers in the Registry file, which is a 32-bit Unicode data file that can be accessed via the Registry Editor (RegEdit.EXE).

Under Windows 3.1, the equivalent information was found in the Win.INI file where a series of flag strings were used to locate and identify installed devices. A fragment of a Win.INI file appears following:

```
[windows]
...
device=HP LaserJet Series II,HPPCL,LPT1:
...
[devices]
HP LaserJet Series II=HPPCL,LPT1:
...
[HP LaserJet Series II,LPT1]
Paper Size=1
Number of Cartridges=1
...
[PrinterPorts]
HP LaserJet Series II=HPPCL,LPT1:,15,45
```

Under Windows NT and 95, the old printer-control features continue to be implemented, even though the Win.INI file, itself, is obsolete. However, obsolete does not mean absent, and you probably have a Win.INI file in your Windows 95 directory. The problem is that any application that expects to find printer information in the Win.INI file may very well find that information, but the information may be completely out of date.

For example, in my own Windows 95 system, the Win.INI file identifies my system printer as an HP LaserJet, even though I installed a different printer after I switched to Windows 95, more than two years ago. On the other hand, the version of the Win.INI file in my NT directory, which was not carried forward from an older Windows 3.x installation, does not contain any printer references.

The point is that applications written for Windows 95 or NT should always use the new printer-selection mechanisms and not rely on the old handling methods. Older methods are highly likely to access outdated or incorrect information.

The good news, of course, is that you do not need to write a printer selection process for your applications. Instead, you can use the default printer-selection mechanisms supplied by Windows NT and 95.

> **TIP**
>
> All applications created using Visual C++ and the AppWizard are supplied with a default File menu that contains Print, Print Preview, and Page Setup options, as well as default provisions to connect to the appropriate handlers and dialog boxes. The advantages are that this is all default code, which does not need to be duplicated; a common dialog is provided for printer selection, including capabilities to connect to network printers; and the end user is not faced with needing to decipher a new selection mechanism.

Querying the Printer

The Windows NT/95 system, and the MFC classes, handles the task of getting and listing the available printers for us. However, certain applications may need to get other information about printer capabilities and limitations.

In Chapter 21, a program titled DC (for Device Capacity) demonstrated how to query the system device drivers and obtain information about device capabilities and limitations. In DC's demonstration, all of the information available about a device was shown. To display all of these data elements required a relatively long list of information requests. In other cases, instead of asking for everything available, a more moderate request can be made, restricting queries to only the appropriate or needed data.

Sending a Bitmap to a Printer

The GrayImage program presented in this chapter demonstrates both simple printer access and the gray-scaling of images. A number of the features in GrayImgView.CPP section, such as selecting and displaying a bitmap image, should be familiar from earlier demo programs, such as Shades and ViewPCX. The two processes of interest in GrayImage are for drawing an image to the printer context and for converting an image from black and white to a printed, half-tone gray. For now, we'll begin with the procedures for sending an image to a printer.

Drawing Images to the Printer Context

In previous examples, when a bitmap is presented in the client window, the bitmap image (file) is read (using the procedures demonstrated in earlier chapters). Then, when it's time to update (redraw) the client window, the bitmap palette is selected, a compatible memory device context is obtained, and the handle to the bitmap is used to copy the bitmap to the memory device context. The GrayImage program uses essentially the same procedures to retrieve the bitmap:

```
void CGrayImageView::OnDraw(CDC* pDC)
{
    ...
    if( m_hBitmap )
    {
        if( m_pPal ) pOldPalette = pDC->SelectPalette( m_pPal,
                                        FALSE );
        nBitPxl = pDC->GetDeviceCaps( BITSPIXEL );
        nPlanes = pDC->GetDeviceCaps( PLANES );
        pDCMem = new CDC();
        pDCMem->CreateCompatibleDC( pDC );
        pDCMem->SelectObject( m_hBitmap );
```

In previous examples, once the bitmap is in the memory context, the `BitBlt` function is called to copy the image from the memory context to the display context, the client window.

```
        pDC->BitBlt( 0, 0, m_bmWidth, m_bmHeight, pDCMem,
                        0, 0, SRCCOPY );
```

And, after copying the image to the display, a little bit of cleanup is performed to take care of the palette and the memory device context.

```
        if( m_pPal )
        {
            pDC->SelectPalette( pOldPalette, FALSE );
            pDC->RealizePalette();
        }
        delete pDCMem;
    }
```

Under previous versions of Windows, to copy a bitmap to a printer device, a separate procedure would have been required. Within this print function, provisions would have been needed to query the installed printers, find out what the printer capabilities were, select a printer, get a printer device context, and finally write the image (or other data) to the printer queue.

Now, however, this task is greatly simplified because, when we select the printer icon from the toolbar or select Print from the File menu (assuming the application is being created with the AppWizard or another development tool), the OnDraw method is called with a pointer to a device context for output. For a printer output operation, the only change from refreshing the screen is that the device context provided is a pointer to a printer context instead of a screen context.

Beyond this provision, the OnDraw function is expected to write to the printer in essentially the same fashion as writing to the video. The difference is that some of the output methods preferred for the video may not be compatible with the printer context, even when writing to a color printer.

Checking for a Color or Black-and-White Printer

Given the current popularity of color printers, not anticipating the presence of a color printer could be a serious error. If we simply attempt to provide gray-scaled output for hard-copy and the default color provisions for the video, the result when a color printer is encountered will be a blank sheet of paper.

To understand why this happens, we need to take another look at the default process to copy the image to the screen, shown in the previous code fragment as:

```
//=== copy the bitmap to the screen ==(NORMAL)==========
pDCMem->SelectObject( m_hBitmap );
pDC->BitBlt( 0, 0, m_bmWidth, m_bmHeight, pDCMem,
             0, 0, SRCCOPY );
```

Here, pDCMem is a memory context that is compatible with the device context supplied, pDC, when the OnDraw function is called by Windows. As long as pDC is a video context, pDCMem will be compatible with the HBITMAP object, m_hBitmap.

If pDC is a monochrome printer context, some degree of compatibility is still maintained. However, in most cases, if the SelectObject and BitBlt functions are used, the result will be that all colors (except white) are treated as black—not exactly the printout desired.

You can, however, persuade the monochrome printer to render approximate half-tones (gray-scale) by using the SetDIBitsToDevice function instead of the SelectObject and BitBlt functions. The only conflict with this approach is that the gray-scale image produced will probably be rather coarse, which is the real reason for the gray-scale conversion routine discussed presently.

The next case occurs when the SelectObject and BitBlt functions attempt to print to a color context. The pDC context supplied by Windows for the printer drawing operation is normally a 32-bit-per-pixel scheme, which results in the pDCMem-> SelectObject function failing, simply because the pDCMem context (created to be compatible with pDC) and the bitmap are not compatible. The result is a blank sheet of paper.

However, by using the SetDIBitsToDevice function and a pointer to the bitmap bits instead of a handle to a bitmap, these potential conflicts are resolved. SetDIBitsToDevice can produce a color image on the screen, a native gray-scale image on a monochrome printer, and a color image on a color printer (leaving only the question of producing a better gray-scale image for our specialty routine). These rendering options and devices are summarized in Table 31.1.

TABLE 31.1   Color Image Rendering Functions

Function / Device	SelectObject / BitBlt	SetDIBitsToDevice
Screen	Produces color image	Produces color image
Monochrome Printer	All colors except white treated as black	Colors rendered using native (printer) gray-scale
Color printer	Blank (no image)	Color image

So, why are we still using SelectObject and BitBlt? Simply because, when compatible, these are faster than the SetDIBitsToDevice function. Of course, for most video systems (printers are simply slower in any case) and in most cases, either route is sufficiently fast that the results will be indistinguishable, making the choice a moot point.

The revised OnDraw response begins, as before, by checking the bits per pixel and number of color planes to determine if we have a color or monochrome device.

```
if( ( nBitPxl * nPlanes ) > 1 )
{
    if( m_pPal )
    {
        pOldPalette = pDC->SelectPalette( m_pPal, FALSE );
        pDC->RealizePalette();
    }
```

If this is a color device (either the screen or a printer), we want to select the palette for the image and realize it (make it active).

Our next step is the critical decision. Since we don't know, without awkward tests, whether this is a printer context or a video screen, we can simply attempt the SelectObject operation.

```
if( pDCMem->SelectObject( m_hBitmap ) )
```

If SelectObject succeeds, we know we have a compatible context and assume that this is the video device. In any case, since the context is compatible (the bitmap was selected correctly) calling BitBlt will copy the image to the device.

```
pDC->BitBlt( 0, 0, m_bmWidth, m_bmHeight, pDCMem,
             0, 0, SRCCOPY );
```

The alternative is that SelectObject failed, which probably means that this is a printer device context but still one supporting color. In this case, we want to call SetDIBitsToDevice, supplying the device context handle (hDC) from the supplied device context, specifying the image size and position information, and providing pointers to the bitmap bits and to the bitmap information structure.

```
else
    SetDIBitsToDevice( pDC->m_hDC, 0, 0, m_bmWidth, m_bmHeight,
                       0, 0, 0, m_bmHeight,
                       m_pBits, m_pBmInfo, DIB_RGB_COLORS );
```

The final specification, DIB_RGB_COLORS, simply says how the color data is to be treated; it says that the bitmap information contains RGB colors in the color table. The alternative is DIB_PAL_COLORS suggesting that the device palette should be used, which, normally would not be appropriate.

NOTE In many cases, especially when printing a hard copy of an image, you may want to be able to resize the image. To resize the image on screen, the StretchBlt function is the ideal choice. But for the printer context, just as SelectObject / BitBlt fails, SelectObject / StretchBlt will also fail. Instead, for a printer device context, the choice would be to use the StretchBlt function to copy the image between memory contexts, resizing the image while doing so. Then, after resizing the image, use the SetDIBitsToDevice function to copy the resized image to the printer.

Last, to clean up, `SelectPalette` is called again to restore the original palette.

```
if( m_pPal )
{
    pDC->SelectPalette( pOldPalette, FALSE );
    pDC->RealizePalette();
}

}
else
    ... use gray-scale conversion to monochrome printer
```

Color Printing

In recent years, a variety of color printers have appeared on the market, ranging from paint-jet printers to produce medium-quality color images to dye-diffusion printers producing more expensive but near-photographic quality color images.

Where video uses an RGB color scheme, all printers use the complementary CYM (cyan-yellow-magenta) color scheme. When painting a screen with light, combinations of red, green, and blue lights are sufficient to create an entire range of colors; black is the absence of any colored light, and white is a balanced combination of the three primaries.

To print color, however, the complementary inks are used, which, respectively, absorb everything except cyan, yellow, or magenta. But, by combining yellow and cyan, everything except green is absorbed, and the result is a green image. In like fashion, reds, blues, and all other shades are created by varying the combination and amount of each ink to leave only the desired color reflected. White, of course, is provided by the paper without ink; black uses all three inks to absorb all colors.

To the general relief of programmers, Windows supplies drivers for almost all printer types, including color printers. As for those printers that are not currently supported, most manufacturers are busy developing Windows drivers for them. Of course, there may be a few who are blithely attempting to ignore the new paradigm, but this may also be taken as a benchmark of their probable future and your own future expectations from such companies. Still, the usual cautions apply: Check available support before investing in a specialty printer, not after.

Gray-Scaling an Image

So what do you do when you need to output to a black-and-white printer but want something better than the relatively coarse default gray-scale supplied by most printer devices? The solution is to provide code to create a custom gray-scale by translating each color pixel in the original image to an array of black-and-white pixels. However, this also means that you must enlarge the original. If this is not convenient or practical, there remains the option of using the native gray-scaling.

Translating Colors to Gray Intensities

The first consideration in translating colors to grays is that, for the video display, colors are described by three digital values: red, green, and blue. Thus, using the RGBTriplet format, each of these color components has a value in the range 0 to 255 and the corresponding display ranges from black to full intensity. The result we see on the screen is a combination of the three primary colors. The relative intensities of each primary, as well as the overall intensity, determine the "color" or hue perceived.

But the human eye is not linear. It responds differently to each of the three primaries, with the strongest response (59 percent) to green. Our second strongest response is to red (30 percent), and our response to blue is the weakest (at 11 percent).

Therefore, to translate red, green, and blue intensities into a gray scale, the absolute intensities of the three components must be weighted to match (or, more accurately, the relative darkness of each component must be weighted to produce the appropriate portion of black ink on the page).

> **NOTE** For more details about translating colors to grays and creating gray-scale palettes, see Chapter 22. That chapter covers Windows color handling and color palettes.

Defining Gray-Scale Patterns

Before matching colors to gray equivalents, it will help to have a range of grays for the match. Thus, before writing the matching algorithm, the first step is to create a gray-scale for the printer. For demonstration purposes, a simple 16-step (4×4) gray-scale will be used. However, a 25-step (5×5), 36-step (6×6), 64-step (8×8), or even 256-step (16×16) gray-scale could be implemented.

NOTE The choice of a square gray pattern is dictated by convenience but is not quite an absolute. Using grays that are not squares, however, would require quite different handling and mapping as well as producing distortion in the output image.

Figure 31.1 shows 16 4-by-4 matrices, ranging from full black to complete white. A sample of the resulting gray-scale appears below each 4-by-4 matrix.

FIGURE 31.1

A gray-scale as a matrix series

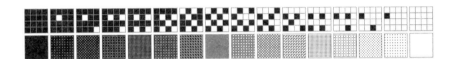

A DWORD hex value providing a binary description of each pattern are: 0x0000, 0x0400, 0x0401, 0x0501, 0x0505, 0x0525, 0xA425, 0xA5A5, 0xA7A5, 0xE5B5, 0xF5B6, 0xF5F5, 0xF5FD, 0xF7FF, 0xFFFF. As you may notice, one possible permutation of blacks and whites—nine black to seven white, distributed among the 16 squares—has been omitted.

These 16 patterns used were selected to provide an even distribution and also to avoid as much as possible any undesired elements, such as lines, herringbone patterns, or other artifacts.

Calculating a Gray Scale

As an alternative to creating a predefined gray-scale, you can create a less rigorous (and somewhat more versatile) gray-scale by calculation. In its simplest form, each color pixel is mapped to a square grid in the printer context, as described in the previous section. However, instead of mapping the color pixel as a predefined pattern, each point in the square for the pixel is assigned a black or white value in proportion to the calculated gray balance and the size of the square. In place of a predetermined pattern, a pseudo-random generator (such as C's random function) is used to assign the appropriate percentage of black and white pixels in an essentially random pattern.

In general, this approach works best with a relatively large matrix for each pixel (8-by-8 or larger) and does not require an exact match between the range of grays used and the size of the pattern matrix. Of course, there are also a few disadvantages, such as a slight loss of edge definition, a need to keep the range of grays used relatively close to the matrix size, and some increase in mapping times because of increased complexity. But overall, the advantages can outweigh the disadvantages when wider ranges of grays are required.

Mapping Color Images to Gray Patterns

The process of mapping color images to gray patterns begins with a requirement for several new variables in the declaration, starting with hTargetBM, which is declared as an HBITMAP and serves as a buffer for the gray-scaled image during conversion. pDCMem and pDCSrc are handles for device contexts used while the color image is converted to a gray-scale image.

```
CDC       *pDCMem, *pDCSrc;
UINT      i, j, m, n;
int       nBitPxl, nPlanes, nGrayWd, nGrayHt;
BYTE      rVal, gVal, bVal, Gray;
DWORD     Color;
HBITMAP   hTargetBM;
WORD      Mask,
          GrayPal[] =                    // gray-scale masks
             { 0x0000, 0x0400, 0x0401, 0x0501,
               0x0505, 0x0525, 0xA425, 0xA5A5,
               0xA7A5, 0xE5B5, 0xF5B6, 0xF5F5,
               0xF5FD, 0xF7FD, 0xF7FF, 0xFFFF };
```

The GrayPal (gray-palette) array (shown earlier in Figure 31.1) is declared here as an array of WORD.

Next, after we have decided that the device context supplied is a monochrome device, the nGrayWd and nGrayHt values are calculated.

```
        else
        {    // if this is a monochrome device - i.e., a printer -
             //     get the max size supported by the device
          nGrayWd = min( (int)(4 * m_bmWidth),
                     pDC->GetDeviceCaps( HORZRES ) );
          nGrayHt = min( (int)(4 * m_bmHeight),
                     pDC >GetDeviceCaps( VERTRES ) );
```

```
//      and create a gray-scaled bitmap to print
hTargetBM = CreateBitmap( nGrayWd, nGrayHt, nPlanes,
                          nBitPxl, NULL );
```

Our only restriction here is that we wish to ensure that the image we print is not larger that the output device supports. But we also need to make the output size 16 times larger than the original, providing space for a 4-by-4 gray pattern for each pixel in the original image.

Having calculated the necessary size, a temporary bitmap, hTargetBM, is defined with the necessary width and height and with the color planes (1) and bits per pixel (1) set for a monochrome image.

Next, if the bitmap creation fails, we simply abort the print operation with a minimal explanation. In your own applications, you would probably want to include a more informative explanation and some alternatives or suggestions for accommodations.

```
if( ! hTargetBM )
{
   ErrorMsg( "Bitmap creation error" );
   return;
}
```

Assuming success, however, we will proceed by calling the SelectObject function to select the (blank) target bitmap into the memory device context, which is compatible with the printer device.

```
pDCMem->SelectObject( hTargetBM );
   // create a device context compatible with the
   // (color) display context, not the printer context
pDCSrc = new CDC();
pDCSrc->CreateCompatibleDC( GetDC() );
   // but select the gray-scaled bitmap to the context
pDCSrc->SelectObject( m_hBitmap );
```

We also need a second, temporary device context, pDCSrc, which is compatible with the screen display. This context is provided by calling Create-CompatibleDC with GetDC as an argument to supply the display context. The original bitmap is simply selected here in a second device context, where we do not need to be concerned about compatibility.

At this point, we have a blank bitmap—four times wider and four times taller than the original—selected in the memory context, pDCMem, and the color bitmap selected in the temporary context, pDCSrc, which is also a memory device context. The actual conversion from color to gray-scale will be carried out working between these two memory device contexts; that is, using pDCSrc as the source and writing the output to pDCMem.

```
for( i=0; i<m_bmHeight; i++ )
    for( j=0; j<m_bmWidth; j++ )
    {
        Color = pDCSrc->GetPixel( j, i );
        rVal = (unsigned char)( LOBYTE(HIWORD( Color ) ) );
        gVal = (unsigned char)( HIBYTE(LOWORD( Color ) ) );
        bVal = (unsigned char)( LOBYTE(LOWORD( Color ) ) );
```

Within a double loop (height and width), the color bitmap is scanned to determine R, G and B values for each pixel. To convert these color values to a gray value, two algorithms are provided: a TrueGray algorithm and an unweighted conversion.

```
if( theApp.m_bTrueGray )
    Gray = (BYTE)
            ( (UINT)(float)( ( rVal * 0.30 ) / 16 ) +
              (UINT)(float)( ( gVal * 0.59 ) / 16 ) +
              (UINT)(float)( ( bVal * 0.11 ) / 16 ) );
else
    Gray = (BYTE)( ( rVal + gVal + bVal ) / 48 );
```

The TrueGray algorithm produces a rather dark printed image; the unweighted algorithm results in a lighter printed image. For a screen display, the TrueGray algorithm offers the better match. For printed output, the unweighted one is preferable.

TIP   As an alternative, the application could use a logarithmic scale to keep blacks black and whites white but shift most colors toward the light end of the scale. You can try implementing this in the sample program if you're interested.

Once a color value has been converted to a gray intensity, the DWORD Mask, from the GrayPal array of predefined patterns, must be written to the output bitmap in pDCMem, as a 4-by-4 array, not as a linear string of bits. Remember, each pixel in the original is being written as a square of pixels in the output.

```
        Mask = GrayPal[Gray];
        //== write gray mask to color bitmap context ========
        for( m=0; m<4; m++ )
            for( n=0; n<4; n++ )
            {
                if( ( Mask >> ((m*4)+n) ) & 0x0001 )
                    pDCMem->SetPixel( (j*4)+m, (i*4)+n,
                                        0x00FFFFFF );
                else
                    pDCMem->SetPixel( (j*4)+m, (i*4)+n,
                                        0x00000000 );

            }
```

To write the output pixels, which are still written as full RGB values, the Mask value is tested bit-wise. The true bits are written as white, and the false bits are written as black.

And, finally, after the output bitmap is prepared, the BitBlt operation is used to copy the image from the memory context, pDCMem, to the printer device context, pDC, where Windows assumes the rest of the task of handling the actual output.

```
        }
        //== now copy from color context to printer context ====
        pDC->BitBlt( 0, 0, nGrayWd, nGrayHt, pDCMem,
                        0, 0, SRCCOPY );
        //== the result is printed as black and white ==========
        DeleteObject( hTargetBM );
        delete pDCSrc;
    }
```

Once the BitBlt operation is handled, a minimum of cleanup is required. We only need to delete the target bitmap, hTargetBM, and the pDCSrc device context.

Overall, perhaps this may appear a rather roundabout fashion to map a color image to a gray-scaled equivalent. Still, this process does have several advantages, including these:

- There is no need for far long pointers to index bitmaps greater than 64KB.

- There is no need to convert palette color indexes into RGB values.

- On the whole, processing times are very fast.

Incidentally, as you may notice, the color-to-gray conversion itself tends to be considerably faster than the process of copying the gray image to the Print Manager.

Figure 31.2 shows an actual printout created using the process described here to convert the 256-color original Modern.BMP to a gray-scaled hard copy. The original output was executed on a 300-dpi laser printer.

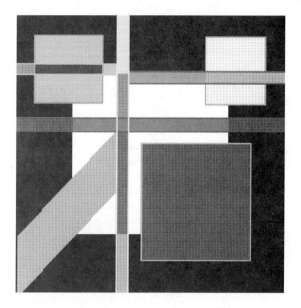

Improved Gray-Scale Printing

In the GrayImage program (in the OnDraw method), the BitBlt API is used to copy a gray image to a monochrome printer. However, the BitBlt API does not include any provisions for resizing the image. As an alternative, the StretchBlt API could be used to create any size output image desired, and you might use CRect coordinates derived from the printer context to size the bitmap to fit the entire page.

However, for several reasons, this may not always be an optimal choice. In actual graphics printing applications, you may want to improve the output in the following ways:

- Allow a specific size

- Preserve the vertical and horizontal proportions

- Avoid plaiding in the printed image

Fortunately, all of these conditions are relatively easy to fulfill.

Precise Sizing

The first objective, a precise size, is simplicity itself. In the `StretchDIBits` operation, replace the page size with the desired image size. Just remember to convert from inches or millimeters (or whatever unit you're using) into logical-device coordinates (pixels or printer dots). For this purpose, as you should recall, device resolution information is available using the `GetDeviceCaps` function.

Preserving Proportions

The second objective, maintaining proportion, is equally easy. For the maximum image size, compare the horizontal and vertical size ratios, and then adjust the greater ratio to maintain image proportions.

Avoiding Plaiding

Avoiding plaiding is perhaps the most difficult objective, simply because this provision is not completely compatible with either of the first two. Even so, in execution, it is not exceedingly difficult.

In practice, the simplest solution is to size the image so that the dots in the output image are some multiple of the original pixel size (or, for gray-scales, some multiple of the gray-scaled pixel size). Thus, for a 200-by-200 pixel image converted into a 16-level gray-scale, the gray image is 800-by-800 pixels and could be printed as 800-by-800, 1600-by-1600, or 2400-by-2400 dots. (Assuming a 300-dpi laser printer, the largest, 2400-dot image would be 8 inches wide.)

NOTE For dot-matrix printers with lower resolutions, of course, the choices and possibilities are more restricted. Typesetting printers and many of the newer laser printer designs offer more versatility.

The only real problem is found with devices that lack a 1-to-1 horizontal-to-vertical aspect ratio. For example, some dot-matrix printers might provide a horizontal resolution of 96 dpi, while their vertical resolution is 180 dpi, for a ratio of 96-to-180 or 8-to-15. This is not an easy ratio to fit without distorting the image proportions. Fortunately, most laser and ink-jet printers do have 1-to-1 aspect ratios.

Printing Gray Images in Color

In some cases, you might need to print a color hard-copy from a gray-scale original. For example, infrared photography images, particularly video images, are captured as gray-scale. In similar fashion, low-light (night-scope) images, NMR, and even CAT scan images do not have inherent color information but are gathered as images scaled by intensity, density, or a synthetic scale.

With infrared images, the problem is that we do not see in this portion of the spectrum, even if we did have printers or monitors capable of displaying these frequencies. But, at the same time, a black-and-white image is less informative than a color image.

In all of these cases, a common solution is to produce a false-color image in which colors are assigned (arbitrarily or otherwise) to various intensity ranges. How colors are assigned is subject to several considerations:

- What is the available range of information? How many gray, intensity, or other levels of information are available in the original image or data?

- How many colors can be displayed? Those who are working with the more sophisticated forms of imaging equipment are rarely limited in their display capabilities and can usually assume at least a 256-color display capacity. However, printers may be more restricted in their color ranges.

- How large a range of color is actually needed? Do you need to use 256 colors or will a simpler palette of 16 colors serve just as well or even better?

- What color palette will best serve to display the information? In general, converting intensity to color is done to make certain characteristics stand out for easy identification and recognition.

As an example, one intensity-to-color development was done as a color printer driver for a company involved in infrared imaging. While the image, which was captured using a special (and expensive) video camera and capture board held a wide range of intensity data (at least 256 levels), the limiting factor was not the video but the printer used. Because the printer employed supported a palette restricted to 16 colors, this became the limiting factor.

Also, the printer palette needed to accommodate a background color that was used for low-temperature areas in the image. This background was not black; it was a light-blue palette entry for a neutral backgrounds. Black was used as a temperature threshold marker. Temperatures (intensities) below a certain level were mapped to violets, blues, and greens, advancing to black, and then to reds and yellows to show the higher intensities.

Printing Color Images

In general, printing a color image is quite similar to printing a monochrome image, as demonstrated in the GrayImage program presented in this chapter. The one difference is that for the monochrome images, no color palette is written to the output device context. For color printers, a palette must be supplied.

Before supplying a palette, you will need to ask the printer what its palette capacity is and supply a palette of the appropriate size. For limited palette sizes, you may need to construct an appropriate palette. Still, you can have a lot of fun simply experimenting, or if you're too busy, turn a teenager (or pre-teen) on the problem and see what he or she comes up with.

The version of the GrayImage program included on the CD accompanying this book provides default handling for a color printer, as well as for gray-scaled output to a monochrome device.

PART V

Exchanging Information between Applications

32

Metafile Operations

■ Advantages of metafiles

■ Metafiles written to a memory context

■ Metafile playback

■ Metafiles written to disk files

■ Temporary metafiles

■ The structure of metafiles

Metafiles, per se, are not a means of storing or exchanging images; they provide a means of storing or exchanging a record of GDI function operations, in a binary format, which create a specific image. As such, the operations recorded in a metafile can be replayed to re-create the original image, in much the same fashion as a CD or tape is replayed to re-create a voice or a piece of music.

But, while all of this may sound interesting, as stated, it does not sound particularly useful. Ergo, what good are metafiles?

As with all simple explanations, the preceding description was both accurate and misleading. We'll begin this chapter by talking about some possible uses of metafiles. Then we'll go into the details of recording and playing back metafiles.

Metafile Uses

One of the principal purposes of metafile operations is to exchange images between applications. This can be done either directly, using the clipboard operations described in Chapter 33, or as demonstrated in this chapter, via file operations.

For example, an accounting program could construct a business graph while recording a metafile of the operations involved, then pass the resulting metafile to a text editor, where the image could be re-created for inclusion in a report. This same metafile can also be "played" directly to the printer, rather than needing to create and copy a bitmap image for the purpose.

Another use for metafiles is to record a calculated graphic (image), permitting it to be re-created or duplicated without the need of repeating the calculations. As an intrinsically calculation-intensive example, consider applying this process to a fractal image. The metafile of the fractal can be replayed in a fraction of the time required for the original calculations.

Another advantage of metafile lies in the storage space required for them versus image files. For example, a scant 150-byte metafile can easily replace a 3970-byte image file. Disk storage may not be a consideration, but even with 28,800-baud modems, image transmission times are still an important factor in more than a few circumstances.

In some cases, metafiles may be preferred over DIB (device-independent bitmap) files. Although DIBs have advantages over conventional image files, metafiles are even less device-dependent and adapt automatically to the device context where they are replayed.

Metafiles are not miracle solutions and will not immediately solve all of your programming problems. But metafiles do offer possibilities, and perhaps this list of uses has already suggested a possibility or two relevant to your own applications. If you don't have any ideas yet, you may by the time you finish reading this chapter.

Recording Metafiles

Because metafile operations are easier to demonstrate than to explain, we'll go through the steps to record a process for a metafile, using an image and a process that should be familiar to you by now. First, we will create the same seven-pointed star that we used in the chapters in Part 4 to illustrate fill and brush operations. Here, we will complete the image by enclosing the star with a circle provided by the Ellipse function.

Creating the Metafile Device Context

The initial requirement is to calculate a series of points describing the seven-pointed star.

```
for( i=j=0; i<7; i++, j=(j+3)%7 )
{
    pt[i].x = (int)( sin( j*PI2/7 ) * 100 );
    pt[i].y = (int)( cos( j*PI2/7 ) * 100 );
}
hdc = BeginPaint( hwnd, &ps );
hPen = CreatePen( PS_NULL, 1, 0L );
SelectObject( hdc, hPen );
SelectObject( hdc, GetStockObject( LTGRAY_BRUSH ) );
Ellipse( hdcMeta, -100, -100, 100, 100 );
```

After calculating the points, creating and selecting a null pen and a standard brush should be familiar operations. With the enclosing circle drawn first, using the null pen and filled by the light-gray brush, the background portion of the image is complete.

Next, still using the null pen, we swap the brush for a dark gray, select the fill mode, and call the Polygon function to draw the star inside the light-gray disk.

```
SelectObject( hdc, GetStockObject( DKGRAY_BRUSH ) );
SetPolyFillMode( hdc, ALTERNATE );
Polygon( hdc, pt, 7 );
DeleteObject( hPen );
EndPaint( hdc, &ps );
```

Finally, we delete the null pen.

Executing this same operation to record the process for a metafile is not much different but requires two new variables, defined as:

```
static HANDLE hMetaFile;
HDC            hdc, hdcMeta;
```

The two new variables are a static handle, hMetaFile, and a device context handle, hdcMeta. The declaration of this latter variable, hdcMeta, may have already suggested a major element of the changes necessary: the substitution of the hdc-Meta device context for the more usual hdc context.

But simply changing the device context ID isn't enough. A more important change appears immediately following:

```
for( i=j=0; i<7; i++, j=(j+3)%7 )
{
    pt[i].x = (int)( sin( j*PI2/7 ) * 100 );
    pt[i].y = (int)( cos( j*PI2/7 ) * 100 );
}
hdcMeta = CreateMetaFile( NULL );
```

Replacing the familiar BeginPaint (or GetDC) instruction, the CreateMetaFile API function provides the metafile equivalent and, in similar fashion, returns a device context handle. The big difference is that this handle is directed to a device context that is not associated with any physical device. At the same time, since the single parameter has been specified as null, the metafile created will exist in memory only; that is, as a temporary memory file.

Later in the chapter, you'll see another form in which the metafile data is written to a physical (disk) file. But, even limited to a memory context, the metafile can still be written to and replayed.

Once the metafile device context has been created, the hdcMeta handle can be substituted for the earlier hdc handle in the drawing instructions, which now appear thus:

```
hPen = CreatePen( PS_NULL, 1, 0L );
SelectObject( hdcMeta, hPen );
SelectObject( hdcMeta, GetStockObject( LTGRAY_BRUSH ) );
Ellipse( hdcMeta, -100, -100, 100, 100 );
SelectObject( hdcMeta, GetStockObject( DKGRAY_BRUSH ) );
SetPolyFillMode( hdcMeta, ALTERNATE );
Polygon( hdcMeta, pt, 7 );
```

Except for the change in the device context, the drawing operations are precisely the same as those previously directed to the screen context. The image itself, however, has not been drawn to the screen; instead, only the GDI operations necessary to draw the image have been recorded.

Closing and Disposing of the Metafile

Last, the `EndPaint` (or `ReleaseDC`) instruction is replaced by a `CloseMetaFile` instruction.

```
hMetaFile = CloseMetaFile( hdcMeta );
DeleteObject( hPen );
```

The call to the `CloseMetaFile` instruction, unlike an `EndPaint` or a `ReleaseDC` instruction, returns a handle, not to a device context but to the metafile itself (which is presently in memory). At this point, this metafile handle can be used to replay the same GDI instructions just calculated.

But, unlike the original image, which would have been drawn to match the display context, the GDI instructions can be played back to any device context and will create an image appropriate to the device context.

Last, even though the metafile has been created only in memory, it is still a logical object and, as such, must be disposed of when no longer required (or, at the very least, before the application closes). In this case, the appropriate point is in response to the `WM_DESTROY` message, thus:

```
case WM_DESTROY:
   DeleteMetaFile( hMetaFile );
   ...
```

Replaying Metafiles

Initially, the drawing instructions for our sample image were presented in the form that would have been used to draw to the screen, nominally in response to a `WM_PAINT` instruction. But, because these were intended for a metafile rather than a display, the instructions were executed in response to the `WM_INITIALIZE` instruction (see the PenDraw6 example at the end of this chapter).

But, now that it's time to replay the metafile instructions, this operation will be carried out in response to a `WM_PAINT` operation, in the same fashion as any other screen refresh.

Providing a Mapping Mode and Extents

However, first, remember that the metafile image was drawn, as GDI instructions, to a memory context. In this form, it lacks any physical device context information, including mapping modes and viewport and window extents. Therefore, before replaying the metafile instructions, we need to provide a physical device context handle, as well as mapping mode and extent settings.

```
case WM_PAINT:
    hdc = BeginPaint( hwnd, &ps );
    SetMapMode( hdc, MM_ANISOTROPIC );
    SetWindowExt( hdc, 1000, 1000 );
    SetViewportExt( hdc, cxWnd, cyWnd );
```

The fact that the metafile does not include mapping mode and extent settings is an advantage, not a disadvantage. Because these are not predefined within the metafile, before a metafile is played back, any mapping mode or window and viewport extents desired can be established and the metafile's GDI operations will be executed accordingly.

Controlling the Image Position

Of necessity, one element is predetermined: the origin point. When the graphics drawing operations were originally executed, the drawing was centered around a (hypothetical) 0,0 origin point, simply because it was convenient. Alternatively, the origin could have been located anywhere in the metaspace, and the resulting operations would be recorded at points relative to this new theoretical origin.

But, while the metafile's origin is known, the viewport and window extents and origins are still undetermined. And, because of these two factors, when the metafile image is replayed, the position of the resulting image can be controlled by changing the window origin.

For the present demonstration, we'll replay the metafile image a total of six times, changing the window origin point each time, to produce an image similar to the screen shown in Figure 32.1. (Because two of the resulting images use the same screen coordinates, only five images appear in the final screen.)

```
for( i=0; i<3; i++ )
{
    SetWindowOrg( hdc, -200 -( i * 300 ), -500 );
    PlayMetaFile( hdc, hMetaFile );
    SetWindowOrg( hdc, -500, -200 -( i * 300 ) );
    PlayMetaFile( hdc, hMetaFile );
}
EndPaint( hwnd, &ps );
break;
```

FIGURE 32.1

Five images produced
by a metafile

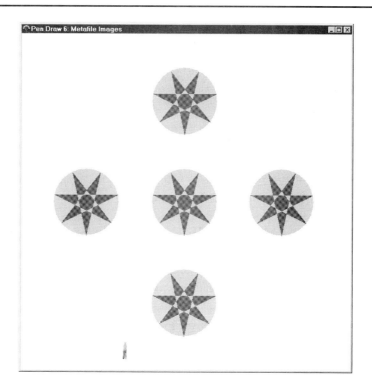

In addition to the metafile drawing operations, other drawing operations could also be carried out, either before or after the metafile is replayed. Also remember that this is not simply an image being copied to the screen; these images are drawn in the same fashion as any other object created by drawing instructions. You should also realize that the metafile may include ROP instructions governing how the recorded drawing operations will interact with existing screen images (see Chapter 24 for more information about ROP instructions.)

Metafiles as Disk Files

The preceding fragmentary examples for both recording and playing back a meta-file assume that the metafile exists only as a memory file. A memory metafile is useful and forms an acceptable format for transfer using clipboard functions. For other purposes, you may want to create a disk metafile, by writing the GDI operation instructions, in a condensed binary format, to an external disk file.

Writing Metafiles to Disk Files

Writing metafiles to disk requires only a minor change in format and could be accomplished, using the preceding examples, by changing one line in the source code, as:

```
hdcMeta = CreateMetaFile( "D:\\METAFILE.WMF" );
```

Neither the filename nor the file extension used here have any particular signif-icance, although the WMF extension (Windows MetaFile) does provide a conve-nient convention.

The `CreateMetaFile` instruction could also be written using an indirect refer-ence, as:

```
hdcMeta = CreateMetaFile( (LPSTR) szMetaFileName );
```

In this form, `szMetaFileName` is a null-terminated string specifying the filename and, as desired, the drive and path specifications.

But, in either case, when the metafile is written to disk, the `DeleteMetaFile` instruction, shown in the previous section in response to the `WM_DESTROY` message, does not affect the metafile disk file. The `DeleteMetaFile` instruction deletes only the local handle to the file. The file itself remains until explicitly erased by other instructions.

As another alternative, you can create a temporary file. This form of storage is more ephemeral than a conventional disk file, but less transitory than a memory file. This is the format used in the PenDraw6 demo program presented in this chapter.

Generating Temporary Files

To create a temporary file, instead of supplying a string constant when calling the `CreateMetaFile` function, we use the `GetTempFileName` function to create a temporary filename and call it, in this example, in response to the `WM_CREATE` function. The `GetTempFileName` function is called as:

```
GetTempFileName( lpszDrivePath, lpszPrefixStr,
                 wUnique, lpszTempFileName );
```

The function's arguments are as follows:

- `lpszDrivePath`: Points to a null-terminated string specifying the drive and directory where the temporary file will be located. If no drive or path are specified, the current drive and directory will be used. (If desired, a call to `GetTempPath` will return the path name of the system's predefined temporary file directory.)

- `lpszPrefixStr`: Points to a null-terminated string to be used as the prefix for a temporary filename. It is limited to three characters in length.

- `wUnique`: An unsigned short integer (`WORD`) used to generate the temporary filename. If this argument is 0, a unique number based on the system time will be generated and will also be returned by `GetTempFileName`. If a file already exists with the generated name, the number will be incremented and the new name tested for conflicts, continuing until a unique filename is found.

- `lpszTempFileName`: Points to a buffer that receives the temporary filename. The return string consists of characters in the OEM-defined character set and should be at least `MAX_PATH` (260) characters in length to allow sufficient room for a complete drive/path/filename specification.

In actual practice (and in the PenDraw6 example), `GetTempFileName` can also be called as:

```
GetTempFileName( NULL, "MFT", 0, (LPSTR) szMetaFileName );
```

The PenDraw6 demo program includes a message box provision that reports the temporary filename generated. As you will observe, the temporary filename created begins with a tilde character (~), followed by the optional prefix ("MFT") and completed with a unique four-character hexadecimal value generated from the `wUnique` parameter. For example, the returned drive/path/filename might be C:\\NT\\TEMP\\~MFT12F3.TMP. Notice that the backslash characters in the path specification are doubled, as required by C-language conventions.

Deleting Temporary Files

Because large numbers of temporary files do tend to clog a hard drive (a fault that, unfortunately, is characteristic of too many existing Windows applications), any applications using temporary files should also include provisions to erase these files when no longer needed.

This task can be accomplished quite easily by minor provisions in response to the WM_DESTROY message.

```
case WM_DESTROY:
    DeleteMetaFile( hMetaFile );
    unlink( szMetaFileName );
    PostQuitMessage(0);
    break;
```

The unlink function erases the temporary file without requiring a file handle or other handling provisions. (Remember that read-only files cannot be unlinked.)

There is one flaw in this system: If an application is interrupted—because of a hang-up requiring a reset, a power interruption, or any other reason—any temporary files created will not be erased and must be cleaned up by manually deleting them from the hard drive. Of course, this can also be done to clean up after other, less-well-behaved applications, and this is also a good reason for using the GetTempPath function. With this last provision, all garbage files will remain in one convenient location where they're easily found and deleted—a small courtesy but also an appreciated one.

Accessing Temporary Metafiles

The principal reasons for creating metafiles are to allow other applications to access the information they contain or so that the application can access metafiles that it created earlier (although a temporary file format would probably not be used in the latter case).

In either case, we need a provision to retrieve or create a metafile handle for a file that was not created by the application or that was previously discarded via the DeleteMetaFile function. This facility is provided by the GetMetaFile function, which is called as:

```
hMetaFile = GetMetaFile( (LPSTR) szMetaFileName );
```

Once the handle has been retrieved, we can access the metafile as before. And, when finished, we should discard the metafile handle using `DeleteMetaFile`.

If the metafile is being created by one application for use by another, the originating application should not call `unlink` to delete the disk file, but the recipient application definitely should.

Metafile Structures

Metafiles, whether in memory or on disk, are simply structured records using the `METARECORD` and `METAHEADER` structures or using the `METAFILEPICT` structure for clipboard operations, which is discussed in Chapter 33.

You do not need to know how to read or decipher metafile instructions in order to use metafile operations. Still, occasionally, being able to do so may prove worthwhile, and they really aren't as difficult to understand as you might assume.

A metafile begins with an 18-byte record header described by the `METAHEADER` structure. This structure is followed by a series of `METARECORD` records, each consisting of a minimum of four `WORD` values, which describe the actual GDI operations.

The Metafile Header Structure

The `METAHEADER` structure is defined, in WinGDI.H, as:

```
typedef struct tagMETAHEADER
{
    WORD     mtType;          // metafile type
    WORD     mtHeaderSize;    // header size (bytes)
    WORD     mtVersion;       // version number
    DWORD    mtSize;          // metafile size (bytes)
    WORD     mtNoObjects;
    DWORD    mtMaxRecord;
    WORD     mtNoParameters;
} METAHEADER;
```

The Metafile Record Structure

The METARECORD structure is defined, also in WinGDI.H, as:

```
typedef struct tagMETARECORD
{
    DWORD  rdSize;         // record size
    WORD   rdFunction;     // function id
    WORD   rdParm[1];      //
} METARECORD;
```

Each METARECORD record records a specific GDI function call and varies in length. The first DWORD value, rdSize, identifies the total size of the individual record. This value is expressed in lsw,msw order, with each word expressed in lsb,msb order.

The second record element, rdFunction, identifies the function to be executed. The low byte identifies the GDI function, and the high byte reports the number of parameters passed to the function. Thus, a hex value 0418 identifies the Ellipse function (18h or META_ELLIPSE), which receives four (04h) parameters, excluding the hdcMeta argument (which is understood).

Metafile operation constants are defined in WinGDI.H. Table 32.1 lists some representative metafile operations.

TABLE 32.1 Representative Metafile Operations

Metafile Operation	Value	Op ID	Arguments
META_SETBKCOLOR	0x0201	01h	2
META_SETBKMODE	0x0102	02h	1
META_SETMAPMODE	0x0103	03h	1
META_SETROP2	0x0104	04h	1
META_SETRELABS	0x0105	05h	1
META_SETPOLYFILLMODE	0x0106	06h	1
META_SETSTRETCHBLTMODE	0x0107	07h	1
META_SETTEXTCHAREXTRA	0x0108	08h	1

TABLE 32.1   Representative Metafile Operations (Continued)

Metafile Operation	Value	Op ID	Arguments
META_SETTEXTCOLOR	0x0209	09h	2
META_SETTEXTJUSTIFICATION	0x020A	0Ah	2
META_SETWINDOWORG	0x020B	0Bh	2
META_SETWINDOWEXT	0x020C	0Ch	2
META_SETVIEWPORTORG	0x020D	0Dh	2
META_SETVIEWPORTEXT	0x020E	0Eh	2
META_OFFSETWINDOWORG	0x020F	0Fh	2
META_SCALEWINDOWEXT	0x0410	10h	4
META_OFFSETVIEWPORTORG	0x0211	11h	2
META_SCALEVIEWPORTEXT	0x0412	12h	4
META_LINETO	0x0213	13h	2
META_MOVETO	0x0214	14h	2
META_EXCLUDECLIPRECT	0x0415	15h	4
META_INTERSECTCLIPRECT	0x0416	16h	4
META_ARC	0x0817	17h	8
META_ELLIPSE	0x0418	18h	4
META_FLOODFILL	0x0419	19h	4
META_PIE	0x081A	1Ah	8
META_RECTANGLE	0x041B	1Bh	4
META_ROUNDRECT	0x061C	1Ch	6

The final element in the METARECORD structure will be one or more bytes containing the arguments required by the GDI operation.

Sample Metafile Instructions

Using the metafile operations recorded by the PenDraw6 demo program, as written to a temporary (disk) metafile, a sample of metafile instructions is shown below. The sample code has been interlineated with the program instructions generating each metafile record, and the META_*xxxxxxx* operation is named at the right. Notice also that, in some cases, a single source code line may generate more than one metafile instruction record.

```
0001 0009 0300 00000004B 0003 00000012 0000      METAHEADER Record

    hPen = CreatePen( PS_NULL, 1, 0L )
00000008 02FA 0005 0001 0000 0000 0000        META_CREATEPENINDIRECT

    SelectObject( hdcMeta, hPen );
00000004 012D 0000                                META_SELECTOBJECT

    SelectObject( hdcMeta, GetStockObject( LTGRAY_BRUSH ) );
00000007 02FC 0000 C0C0 00C0 0000      META_CREATEBRUSHINDIRECT
    (notice that LTGRAY_BRUSH is expressed as an RGB quad)
00000004 012D 0002                                META_SELECTOBJECT

    Ellipse( hdcMeta, -100, -100, 100, 100 );
00000007 0418 0064 0064 FF9C FF9C                     META_ELLIPSE

    SelectObject( hdcMeta, GetStockObject( DKGRAY_BRUSH ) );
00000007 02FC 0000 4040 0040 0000      META_CREATEBRUSHINDIRECT
    (again, DKGRAY_BRUSH is specified as an RGB quad)
00000004 012D 0002                                META_SELECTOBJECT

    SetPolyFillMode( hdcMeta, ALTERNATE );
00000004 0106 0001                            META_SETPOLYFILLMODE

    Polygon( hdcMeta, pt, 7 );
00000012 0324 0007 0000 0064 002B FFA6 FFB2 003E    META_POLYGON
         0061 FFEA FF9F FFEA 004E 003E FFD5 FFA6
    (includes 14 coordinates - 7 points - from pt reference)

    (A 3-byte null record terminates the metafile)
00000003 0000
```

> **NOTE**
>
> If you compare the instructions in the metafile with the complete source code generating these instructions, you may notice a few discrepancies. Where the original instruction was `CreatePen`, the metafile equivalent has become `CreatePenIndirect`. Also, the `DeletePen` instruction in the original source code is not reflected in the metafile instructions. Neither of these are errors but, instead, are simplifications of the original code. Because the `CreatePenIndirect` instruction was used instead of `CreatePen`, the need for a `DeletePen` instruction has been eliminated as has been any requirement to restore the original pen. Thus, in brief—and in the interests of brevity—the metafile translation has improved on the original code.

Again, you do not need to know the structure of a metafile in order to use metafile operations, but the information may prove helpful. Besides, given the preceding breakdown, it really shouldn't be much of a challenge to write a utility to decipher/decode metafile instructions, should it? If you're interested, you can experiment on your own.

Metafile Cautions

Before leaving the subject of metafile operations, there are a few comments and cautions that are worth keeping in mind. Even a cursory awareness of these may assist in preventing future errors, or at least alleviate confusion.

The metafile device context is not a true device context in the sense that it does not correspond to any physical or logical device. As such, the metafile device context does not include a mapping mode, window sizes and origins, or viewport sizes or origins.

All parameters passed to metafiles are actual values, not formulas or references to variable values. Thus variable references used in the generating application's source code are evaluated at the time the metafile is compiled and may or may not contain appropriate values when the metafile is replayed. Thus, an argument such as `cxWnd/2` is recorded as the constant resulting from the calculation and, later, will not reflect changes in window size. (This specific conflict, despite the use of a similar reference, was avoided in the PenDraw6 example by using the isotropic mapping mode.)

Metafile instructions are always interpreted in terms of the existing mapping mode. Metafiles may, however, include instructions to select specific mapping modes.

Also, there are several classes of instructions that are not compatible with metafile operations. The following five categories of GDI instructions are invalid and will not be recorded as metafile operations:

- Any function treating the metafile device context as if it were a physical device context, including operations such as CreateCompatibleBitmap, CreateCompatibleDC, CreateDiscardableBitmap, DeleteDC, PlayMeta-File (self-referential), and ReleaseDC.

- Any function beginning with the form Get..., such as GetDeviceCaps and GetTextMetrics. All data contained in a metafile is preset, and the record structure cannot accommodate information returned by such functions.

- Any function designed to return information to the program, such as DPtoLP and LPtoDP. (However, macros, which are evaluated during compilation, are permitted.)

- Functions requiring handles to brushes, such as FillRect and FrameRect.

- A few of the more complex functions, such as DrawIcon, GrayString, and SetBrushOrg.

If you have any questions about which GDI function calls are permitted in a metafile operation, refer to the list of metafile constants defined in WinGDI.H. All constants begin with the prefix META_. But, remember, some GDI functions do not appear, simply because when the compiler encounters these, it will automatically choose a more compatible variation. For example, a call for the CreatePen function appears in the metafile as META_CREATEPENINDIRECT.

One final caution involves saving the present device context before replaying a metafile and, when finished, restoring the original device context. Because a metafile can change device context settings but cannot record or restore existing device context settings, your applications should include their own provisions for this operation.

Remember, the metafile is free to change drawing and mapping modes, change colors, and make other changes. When the metafile is finished replaying, these changes will remain in effect. Therefore, to save the original device context, before the PlayMetaFile instruction is executed, save the existing device context:

```
SaveDC( hdc );
```

And, after the metafile has been replayed, restore the original device context:

```
RestoreDC( hdc, -1 );
```

Since neither of these instructions involve any operations forbidden to metafiles, and both are supported by metafile instructions, a well-behaved metafile could simply include these provisions within itself. Do remember, however, that every call to SaveDC must have a corresponding RestoreDC call using the -1 argument, and vice versa.

As you've seen in this chapter, metafile operations provide a powerful means to record and replay powerful drawing operations. They can also be used to transfer graphics operations between applications or even between devices (such as from the screen to a printer). In the next chapter, you'll see how metafiles can be used with the clipboard as an alternative to physical (disk) file transfers. The DDE functions detailed in Chapter 24 provide a means for requesting and confirming metafile transfers.

The PenDraw6 example, which is on the accompanying CD, provides a platform for experimentation with metafile operations. To further your expertise and understanding, you might also consider creating two new programs: the first to create a metafile as a disk file and the second to retrieve the metafile from disk, using the GetMetaFile instruction. Then you can replay the graphics under the same or different mapping modes.

Clipboard Data Transfers

- Advantages of using the clipboard

- Clipboard data formats

- Clipboard access

- Private clipboard formats

The Windows Clipboard consists of two quite different entities: the clipboard viewer, Clipbrd.EXE, and the real clipboard. The real clipboard is a feature of the Windows User module. It provides a series of functions designed to facilitate the temporary storage of information in a form permitting retrieval by applications other than the originating application. Of course, the originating application is not prohibited from retrieving its own clipboard information, but the important item to remember is that data passed to the clipboard is public, which means that it is accessible to any application.

The clipboard provides a useful and convenient method for exchanging data of many different types between applications, as explained and demonstrated in this chapter.

Clipboard Uses

The clipboard consists of a series of facilities that provide a platform for the temporary (nondisk) storage of data. Data stored on the clipboard can be transferred between applications or simply retrieved by the application that put it there in the first place.

A source application can copy data to the clipboard using one of the predefined formats or using a custom format (clipboard file formats are discussed later in the chapter). As the data is transferred, the clipboard facilities allocate and manage memory to contain the data.

After the data has been transferred, any application can access the clipboard, inquire what type of data is present, and if desired, retrieve a copy of the data from the clipboard.

When the clipboard viewer (Clipbrd.EXE) is active, the clipboard is queried regularly to determine if any data has been written to the clipboard and, if so, what data type is contained. If possible, the clipboard viewer then retrieves a copy of the data, in its own client window. Note, however, that the clipboard viewer itself does not alter or erase the clipboard contents.

While the clipboard does work very well, it also has a few disadvantages:

- There is only one clipboard.
- All material written to the clipboard is public.
- Any material written to the clipboard is volatile.

Because there is only one clipboard, all applications that want to use the clipboard must share use of this single facility. And sharing can mean conflicts.

For example, suppose that Application A writes a bitmap to the clipboard and then Application B writes a block of text data. However, because Application B quite reasonably begins by clearing the clipboard, the bitmap written by Application A is erased. Now, if the bitmap destination, Application C, has already retrieved the image, everything is fine. But, if Application C has not gotten the bitmap before Application B replaces it with text data, the bitmap is lost.

The public nature of the clipboard also offers opportunities for error. Because the data element written to the clipboard cannot be addressed to a specific recipient, this data can be accessed, by mistake, by another application seeking data of the same type.

The clipboard can contain data of several different types, written by a single application or by different applications. If this is the case, the problem is how to distinguish between the blocks—for example, multiple blocks of text supplied by different sources. For this reason, applications normally begin by clearing the clipboard before writing new material to the clipboard.

These are factors to consider, but they are not serious problems demanding extensive worry and circumvention measures. And, in circumstances where these could become more serious considerations, DDE (Dynamic Data Exchange) techniques, discussed in Chapter 34, provide a more secure channel for the exchange of data.

The Clipboard Viewer

The Clipbrd.EXE program, which is distributed with both Windows NT and Windows 95, is a clipboard viewer that provides a means of checking (viewing) data that has been copied to the User clipboard facilities. As such, the Clipbrd program can be used while testing your own clipboard routines.

The clipboard viewer can also be used to capture (or copy) material transferred to the clipboard facilities by other applications, saving the captured data to a disk file or simply viewing the data.

But remember, the Clipbrd application is only a viewer, not the real clipboard. It cannot affect the contents of the clipboard.

Clipboard Operations

Basically, the clipboard operates by assuming control over globally allocated memory blocks, containing data supplied by applications, by altering memory allocation flags. To copy or write material to the clipboard, an application begins by using the GlobalAlloc function and the GHND flag (defined as GMEM_MOVABLE and GMEM_ZEROINIT) to initialize a memory block which, initially, belongs to the originating application instance.

Under normal circumstances, when the originating application exits or closes, the global memory allocated would be deleted (freed) by Windows. However, when the originating instance calls the SetClipboardData function, using the global handle to the memory block, Windows transfers ownership of the memory block from the application to itself—to the clipboard—by modifying the memory allocation flags for the global memory block.

Ownership of a global memory block is accomplished by the GlobalRealloc function, called as:

```
GlobalRealloc( hMem, NULL, GMEM_MODIFY | GMEM_DDESHARE );
```

Once this is done, the allocated memory no longer belongs to the original application and can now be accessed only through the clipboard using the GetClipboardData function. The GetClipboardData function grants the calling application temporary access to the clipboard data by providing a handle to the global memory block. Ownership, however, remains with the clipboard, not with the application accessing the data.

For this reason, normally, clipboard data can be erased only by calling the EmptyClipboard function. (One exception to this rule will be discussed presently but is not recommended.)

Clipboard Data Formats

Windows supports 14 standard clipboard data formats, defined in WinUser.H as the following:

CF_TEXT	CF_PALETTE
CF_BITMAP	CF_PENDATA
CF_METAFILEPICT	CF_RIFF
CF_SYLK	CF_WAVE

```
CF_DIF                   CF_DIB

CF_TIFF                  CF_UNICODETEXT

CF_OEMTEXT               CF_ENHMETAFILE
```

An additional nine special formats or format flags are also defined, and any application is free to define its own custom clipboard data format. For most purposes, however, the standard formats should suffice.

Text Format

The simplest clipboard data format is the CF_TEXT format, which consists of null-terminated ANSI character strings, each line ending with carriage return (0x0D) / line feed (0x0A). The CF_OEMTEXT and CF_UNICODETEXT formats are similar, but are for the OEM character set and 32-bit Unicode characters, respectively.

Once the text has been transferred to the clipboard, the originating application cannot access the text further except by requesting access from the clipboard.

Bitmap Format

The CF_BITMAP format is used to transfer Windows bitmap images by transferring the bitmap handle to the clipboard. Once the bitmap handle has been transferred to the clipboard, the originating application cannot use the bitmap except by calling the clipboard for access.

Metafile Format

The CF_METAFILEPICT format is used to transfer memory (not disk) metafiles between applications. This format uses the METAFILEPICT structure, defined in WinGDI.H as:

```
typedef struct tagMETAFILEPICT
{
    LONG        mm;
    LONG        xExt;
    LONG        yExt;
    HMETAFILE   hMF;
} METAFILEPICT, FAR *LPMETAFILEPICT;
```

The first three fields show the differences between a clipboard metafile transfer and a disk metafile transfer. The first field, mm, identifies the preferred mapping mode (discussed later) and the second and third fields, xExt and yExt, identify the height and width of the metafile image. The HMETAFILE field is simply a handle to the METAFILE structure introduced in Chapter 32. The use of this data is demonstrated later in the chapter.

The CF_ENHMETAFILE format is the same as the CF_METAFILEPICT format, except that it identifies a metafile using the enhanced metafile format instructions.

Once a metafile is transferred to the clipboard, the originating application should not attempt to use either the global memory block or the original metafile handle, except by requesting access through the clipboard.

DIB Format

The CF_DIB format is used to transfer DIBs (device-independent bitmaps) to the clipboard. The DIB is transferred as a global memory block, beginning with a BITMAPINFO header structure, followed by the bitmap image data. Bitmap structures were introduced in Chapter 24.

> **NOTE** The CF_BITMAP format supported by Windows 2.x and 3.x and identifying device-dependent bitmap formats is not supported by Windows NT but is supported by Windows 95. The preferred CF_DIB format, however, is supported by both Windows NT and 95.

After a bitmap has been transferred to the clipboard, the originating application should not attempt to use either the global memory block or the original bitmap handle except by requesting access through the clipboard.

Palette and Pen Formats

The CF_PALETTE and CF_PENDATA formats are used to transfer a handle to a color palette or a pen, respectively. The palette transfer is often used together with the CF_DIB format to define color palettes used by a bitmap.

Wave Format

The CF_WAVE format is used to transfer audio (waveform) information between applications.

Special-Purpose Formats

Three special-purpose clipboard formats provide support for data formats that were originally designed for use by and between specific applications:

- CF_TIFF: Uses a global memory block to transfer data using the Tagged Image File Format (TIFF). See Chapter 26 for more information about TIFF format.

- CF_DIF: Uses a global memory block to transfer data using the Data Interchange Format (DIF) created by Software Arts, originally for use with the VisiCalc spreadsheet program but now controlled by Lotus Corporation. The format is essentially an ASCII string format with each line terminated by a CR/LF pair.

- CF_SYLK: Uses a global memory block to transfer data using the Microsoft Symbolic Link format, originally designed for data exchanges between Microsoft's Multiplan (spreadsheet), Chart, and Excel applications. The format is an ASCII string format with each line terminated by a CR/LF pair.

Accessing the Clipboard

While many Windows facilities are designed to permit shared access, access to the clipboard is permitted to only one application at a time; this mechanism prevents conflicts.

Opening and Closing the Clipboard

Before any application can access the clipboard to read, write, or clear it, the application must begin by calling the OpenClipboard function, requesting access. The OpenClipboard function returns a Boolean result, with TRUE indicating that the clipboard is available and access is granted or FALSE indicating that access is denied because another application currently holds access rights.

When the application is finished with the clipboard, the CloseClipboard function is called, relinquishing access and freeing the clipboard for access by other applications.

WARNING

Please remember that the OpenClipboard function is *always* matched with a CloseClipboard call. Emphasis on the *ALWAYS*! An application should never, ever attempt to hold the clipboard open, and should always relinquish control of the clipboard as quickly as possible.

Transferring Data to the Clipboard

The Clipboard demo program presented in this chapter provides an example of a clipboard transfer function that copies a memory block to the clipboard.

```
BOOL TransferToClipboard( HWND hwnd, HANDLE hMemBlock,
                                   WORD FormatCB )
{
   if( OpenClipboard( hwnd ) )
   {
      EmptyClipboard();
      SetClipboardData( FormatCB, hMemBlock );
      CloseClipboard();
      return( TRUE );
   }
   return( FALSE );
}
```

The `TransferToClipboard` function begins by requesting access (opening) the clipboard, then copying a single memory block to the clipboard. Last, the clipboard is closed, relinquishing further access.

The `TransferToClipboard` function is quite generic in design, accepting any type of handle (`hMemBlock`). However, it does require the `FormatCB` parameter to specify the format type (the type of data copied to the clipboard).

The term *memory block* does not refer to a specific size; the size of the memory block was set earlier by the `GlobalAlloc` function. A single memory block might contain paragraphs of text, multiple records, or any other data. Each memory block, however, can only contain one data type.

So, what if an application needs to transfer a bitmap, a metafile, a palette, and a text block? The solution is relatively simple. First, each block is copied, separately, to globally allocated memory, retaining a handle to each memory block as, for example, `hBitmap`, `hMetafile`, `hPalette`, and `hText`. With this done, the clipboard is opened and emptied, then each of the handles is transferred to the clipboard as:

```
   if( OpenClipboard( hwnd ) )
   {
      EmptyClipboard();
      SetClipboardData( CF_BITMAP, hBitmap );
      SetClipboardData( CF_PALETTE, hPalette );
      SetClipboardData( CF_METAFILEPICT, hMetafile );
```

```
        SetClipboardData( CF_TEXT, hText );
        CloseClipboard();
    }
```

Last, of course, the clipboard is closed, relinquishing further access to other applications.

In actual practice, the preceding example would be rather cumbersome; providing source code for every possible combination of data types would be more than a little frustrating. But, since the data type identifiers are all WORD values, and the memory block handles are simply that—handles—a simpler form would be to begin by assigning the data types and handle as arrays of WORD and HANDLE, and then calling the transfer function with a further parameter reporting the number of items to transfer. This done, the transfer could be handled as:

```
    if( OpenClipboard( hwnd ) )
    {
        EmptyClipboard();
        for( i=0; i<nCount; i++ )
            SetClipboardData( cfType[i], hData[i] );
        CloseClipboard();
    }
```

Retrieving Clipboard Data

Before attempting to retrieve an item from the clipboard, the first step is to find out if the clipboard holds a particular type of data. Because different data types require different handling after they are retrieved, applications need to know what they're retrieving and to be prepared to handle the result before requesting retrieval.

One method is to simply ask for data of a desired type and see if anything is returned. But this approach does lack a certain elegance, not to mention efficiency.

The more efficient way to find out about the clipboard contents is to use one of the two supplied functions: IsClipboardFormatAvailable or EnumClipboard-Formats.

The IsClipboardFormatAvailable function returns a Boolean result to report if the clipboard contains a desired data format. IsClipboardFormatAvailable is called as:

```
    if( IsClipboardFormatAvailable( CF_xxtypexx ) ) ...
```

The EnumClipboardFormats function queries all available clipboard formats. By initially calling EnumClipboardFormats with a null parameter, a result is returned reporting the first available format and, looping, this value can be returned to request the next available format. Thus, to request a list of all available formats:

```
wFormat = NULL;
OpenClipboard( hwnd );
while( wFormat = EnumClipboardFormats( wFormat ) )
{
    ... code handling various formats ...
}
CloseClipboard();
```

The EnumClipboardFormats function, each time it is called, returns a value reporting the next available format. The formats returned are reported in the same order as the originating application used to paste items to the clipboard. This ordering allows the querying application to respond to the first format acceptable. The originating application can post items in a recommended order; for example, in order of descending data reliability.

If no further formats are available, if the clipboard is empty, or if the clipboard has not been opened, the return result will be zero. The wFormat parameter could be reset to a specific value to repeat the list from that point. Also, the number for formats available in the clipboard can be retrieved by calling:

```
nFormats = CountClipboardFormats();
```

Once an application has determined that the clipboard does contain data of a desired type, retrieving the clipboard data consists of two operations:

- Retrieving a handle to the clipboard data, the memory block

- Doing something with the data after retrieving the handle

The first is quite simple, as illustrated by the RetriveCB function, following:

```
HANDLE RetrieveCB( HWND hwnd, WORD FormatCB )
{
    HANDLE hCB;

    if( ! IsClipboardFormatAvailable( FormatCB ) )
        return( NULL );
    OpenClipboard( hwnd );
    hCB = GetClipboardData( FormatCB );
```

```
        CloseClipboard();
        return( hCB );
    }
```

This example offers a generic subroutine that returns an untyped handle to a clipboard memory block. Or, if the requested type is not available, it returns NULL. (In actual practice, such as in the Clipboard demo program, a slightly different format is used.)

Restrictions on Clipboard Operations

There are a few restrictions on clipboard operations:

- Before an item can be copied to the clipboard, EmptyClipboard must be called to erase the present contents of the clipboard. Remember, simply accessing the clipboard does not transfer ownership of the existing contents. The EmptyClipboard function, however, does assign ownership and, at the same time, clears (releases) any and all existing contents.

- Any application can access the contents of the clipboard, but only the clipboard owner—an application that has called the EmptyClipboard function— can write material to the clipboard. However, because the clipboard can have only one owner, the previous owner's contents are simply erased, even if the same application was the previous owner.

- Although multiple items can be copied to the clipboard, they must all be transferred in a single operation. The clipboard cannot be opened, written, closed, and then reopened again to transfer another item (at least not without erasing the first item transferred).

TIP If an application desires to preserve the original contents of the clipboard while adding new material, the simple solution is to copy the existing contents, clear the clipboard, and then replace the original contents together with whatever new material is desired.

- Only one item of each type can be transferred to the clipboard at any time. This is for the simple reason that there is no method to distinguish between multiple items of a given type. However, when multiple items of different types have been written to the clipboard, an application accessing the clipboard may request only one item, several items, or all items, but it must request each item separately.

The clipboard can be opened repeatedly to request different items or to request the same item a second (or third, fourth, and so on) time. But, in general, when requesting an item from the clipboard, the best option is to make a local copy of the desired item rather than attempting to request the same item more than once. Remember, there are no assurances that the data item requested will remain available locally.

Reading and Writing Different Data Types: The Clipboard Program

The Clipboard program demonstrates writing and reading the clipboard with three different data types: text, bitmap, and metafile. Clipboard uses a simple menu with two primary options: Data To Clipboard and Data From Clipboard, each with a submenu listing equally unimaginative Write and Retrieve options.

The Write Bitmap option includes a simple provision that captures the entire screen (or, at least, a 640-by-480 section of the screen) as a bitmap, writing the image to the clipboard. The Write Metafile option uses the same metafile construct previously demonstrated in the PenDraw6 program presented in Chapter 32. The Write Text option copies a simple text string to the clipboard.

> **NOTE**
> In the Clipboard demo, only one item at a time is written to the clipboard. If you want to experiment, you can try adding a provision to copy multiple items.

Clipboard Text Transfers

Text operations may be the simplest type of clipboard operation, if only because text (string) operations themselves are comfortably familiar and require little explanation.

Writing Text to the Clipboard

For present demonstration purposes, because the Clipboard program will be both source and recipient, the first step is to transfer text information to the clipboard. The text chosen is brief, static string, declared as "The quick brown fox jumps over the lazy red dog." It's not very original, but it serves to demonstrate the principles involved.

The mechanism for handling the text transfer is provided by a subprocedure called with two parameters: a handle to the application (hwnd) and a pointer to the text string (lpText).

```
BOOL TextToClipboard( HWND hwnd, LPSTR lpText )
{
    int             i, wLen;
    GLOBALHANDLE    hGMem;
    LPSTR           lpGMem;
```

Within the TextToClipboard subroutine, four local variables are required, although only the latter two need an explanation. The hGMem variable provides a global handle to a memory block that has not yet been allocated. The second variable, lpGMem, will be used as a pointer into the memory block.

After the wLen variable is initialized with the length of the text parameter, hGMem becomes a pointer to memory globally allocated to hold a copy of the text. Notice, however, that wLen is one larger than the string, providing space allocation for a null terminator. Clipboard text is always stored as an ASCIIZ (or ANSIZ) format:

```
wLen = strlen( lpText );
hGMem = GlobalAlloc( GHND, (DWORD) wLen + 1 );
lpGMem = GlobalLock( hGMem );
```

Last, lpGMem receives the pointer to the memory block returned by the Global-Lock function. But remember, the GHND specification has properly declared this memory block as movable. Also, in addition to returning an address (which could have been obtained several other ways) the GlobalLock function locks the memory block, temporarily preventing it from being moved by Windows.

The second feature provided by the GHND specification is to clear the memory block allocated, filling the memory block with zeros. Thus, the next step is copy the local string, pointed to by lpText, into the memory block.

```
for( i=0; i<wLen; i++ )
    *lpGMem = *lpText++;
```

```
        GlobalUnlock( hGMem );
        return( TransferToClipboard( hwnd, hGMem, CF_TEXT ) );
    }
```

After copying the text information, `GlobalUnlock` is called to release the lock on `hGMem`, making it movable and relocatable. If, however, the memory block had been moved while the local text information was being copied, the `lpGMem` pointer would not have remained valid.

As a last step, the `TransferToClipboard` function (discussed earlier in the chapter) is called with the `hGMem` block, the flag `CF_TEXT`, and the application's window handle to complete the transfer process.

Memory Ownership and the Clipboard

Do not under any circumstances free memory after transferring a data object to the clipboard. For example, if the text-to-clipboard operation was rewritten to include a `GlobalFree` instruction, thus:

```
    for( i=0; i<wLen; i++ )
        *lpGMem = *lpText++;
    GlobalUnlock( hGMem );
    GlobalFree( hGMem );
    return( TransferToClipboard( hwnd, hGMem, CF_TEXT ) );
}
```

the result of calling `GlobalFree` would delete the item from the clipboard. Instead, once a data item has been transferred, ownership of the item has also been transferred, and the local handle should not be used or tampered with further.

Likewise, when a data object is retrieved from the clipboard, the handle to the retrieved data may be locked and unlocked as necessary, but it should not be freed, because the object itself still belongs to the clipboard.

Data objects placed on the clipboard are only freed when an application assumes ownership of the clipboard and calls the `EmptyClipboard` instruction. At this point, all data objects owned by the clipboard are freed by the clipboard itself.

Retrieving Text from the Clipboard

Retrieving text from the clipboard is almost as simple as writing it, but instead of a subroutine, in the Clipboard demo program, the text-retrieval operations are included in the response to the WM_PAINT message. This allows the application to update the window as required. Other applications may, of course, handle this in another fashion.

For retrieval, operations begin by opening the clipboard, continuing by using the GetClipboardData API call to return a handle to the clipboard memory block.

```
OpenClipboard( hwnd );
hTextMem = GetClipboardData( CF_TEXT );
lpText = GlobalLock( hTextMem );
```

Just as was done during the transfer to the clipboard, and for the same reasons, GlobalLock is called to lock the memory block, returning a pointer to the memory address held by lpText. This time, however, instead of a loop, the lstrcpy function is used to copy the string contents from the memory address (lpText) to the local variable, TextStr.

```
lstrcpy( TextStr, lpText );
GlobalUnlock( hTextMem );
CloseClipboard();
```

Last, GlobalUnlock releases the lock on the memory block while CloseClipboard completes the operation. It's important to remember that a memory block should never be left locked; always call GlobalUnlock after calling GlobalLock.

Bitmap Clipboard Transfers

The bitmap demo in Clipboard begins with provisions to capture the existing screen to provide a bitmap for transfer to the clipboard. The screen-capture process itself is peripheral to the present topic; it follows the general form demonstrated in the Capture program presented in Chapter 26.

Figure 33.1 shows the Clipboard demo program (lower right), together with the Windows clipboard viewer, Clipbrd (upper left), in a recursive situation following several screen captures. The current clipboard contents appear in both application windows.

FIGURE 33.1

Two clipboard views

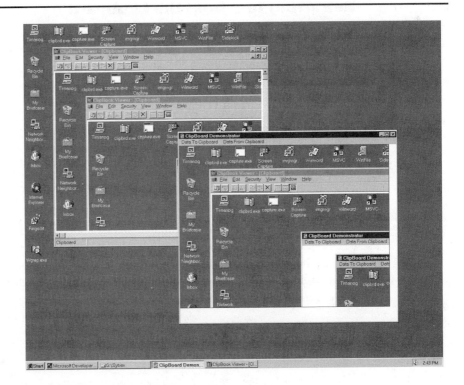

Writing a Bitmap to the Clipboard

The bitmap-to-clipboard transfer process, which is the relevant topic here, begins by first creating a compatible device context, hdcMem, in memory and then creating and selecting a compatible bitmap (also in memory).

```
hdc = GetDC( hwnd );
hdcMem = CreateCompatibleDC( hdc );
hBitmap = CreateCompatibleBitmap( hdc, 640, 480 );
SelectObject( hdcMem, hBitmap );
```

The next step is to copy the bitmap image from the original (source)—in this example, the screen—to the memory context before calling the TransferToClipboard function to compete the transfer.

```
StretchBlt( hdcMem, 0, 0, 639, 479,
            hdc,    0, 0, 639, 479, SRCCOPY );
TransferToClipboard( hwnd, hBitmap, CF_BITMAP );
DeleteDC( hdcMem );
```

Last, as cleanup, the memory device context is deleted, leaving ownership of the bitmap image to the clipboard.

Retrieving a Bitmap from the Clipboard

Retrieving the bitmap image from the clipboard is similar to the process of copying the image to the clipboard. The process begins by opening the clipboard and retrieving a handle to the bitmap (from the clipboard):

```
OpenClipboard( hwnd );
hBitmap = GetClipboardData( CF_BITMAP );
hdcMem = CreateCompatibleDC( hdc );
SelectObject( hdcMem, hBitmap );
```

Again, a compatible device context is required. Then the SelectObject function selects the bitmap.

At this point, there are a few other tasks involved. First, the mapping mode needs to be set, in the memory context, for compatibility with the display context. And second before the bitmap can be copied, the size of the bitmap is needed. The bitmap size is obtained by copying the bitmap header into a local variable, bm.

```
SetMapMode( hdcMem, GetMapMode( hdc ) );
GetObject( hBitmap, sizeof(BITMAP), (LPSTR) &bm );
```

The BITMAP variable (bm) now contains the bitmap header information needed to copy the actual bitmap from the memory context to the device context, this time using the BitBlt function.

```
BitBlt( hdc,      0, 0, bm.bmWidth, bm.bmHeight,
        hdcMem, 0, 0, SRCCOPY );
ReleaseDC( hwnd, hdc );
DeleteDC( hdcMem );
CloseClipboard();
```

All that's left is a bit of cleanup before closing the clipboard, and the job's done. (The clipboard could have been closed earlier, just as soon as a handle had been returned to the image memory block, because closing the clipboard doesn't delete the memory block.)

Metafile Clipboard Transfers

Metafile transfers introduce an element that is not present in text transfers. Although this element is present in bitmap transfers, it is not obtrusively visible, because it was handled virtually without remark. The new element, required for metafile transfers, is information about the file: the mapping mode under which the metafile was originally created and the extent or size information. This data is not necessarily inherent in the metafile itself.

With a text, metric, English, or TWIPS mapping mode, the mapping scale is fixed. The isotropic or anisotropic mapping modes, both of which have advantages for metafile operations, present a need for special information to accompany the metafile instructions.

For metafile clipboard transfers, the METAFILEPICT record is used. This record includes a record of the mapping mode used, size information, and the metafile script itself.

The METAFILEPICT record structure is defined in WinGDI.H as:

```
typedef struct tagMETAFILEPICT
{
    LONG       mm;
    LONG       xExt;
    LONG       yExt;
    HMETAFILE  hMF;
} METAFILEPICT, FAR *LPMETAFILEPICT;
```

The mm field contains the mapping mode. The hMF field is a handle to the metafile instructions. The remaining two fields, xExt and yExt, may contain two different types of information, depending on the mapping mode.

For text, metric, English, or TWIPS mapping modes, the xExt and yExt fields specify the horizontal and vertical size of the metafile picture in units appropriate to the mapping mode.

For the MM_ISOTROPIC or MM_ANISOTROPIC mapping modes, the xExt and yExt fields contain an optional, suggested size expressed in MM_HIMETRIC units, or may be zero if no suggested size is offered. Alternatively, if the xExt and yExt fields are negative, the information is provided as a suggested size ratio, rather than an absolute size.

In the Clipboard demo program, a metafile image is supplied by duplicating the metafile image code from Chapter 32, now in a subroutine titled DrawMetafile.

Much of the `DrawMetafile` procedure should be familiar from previous examples, but it does begin with one new variable declaration:

```
BOOL DrawMetafile( HWND hwnd, int cxWnd, int cyWnd )
{
    LPMETAFILEPICT  lpMFP;
```

Aside from the variable `lpMFP`, which will be used as a pointer to an instance of the `METAFILEPICT` structure, the `DrawMetafile` function proceeds by creating a metafile in memory as demonstrated in Chapter 32. But, after the metafile is created, the next step is to create, in memory, a `METAFILEPICT` structure and, using `GlobalLock`, to return a value to the `lpMFP` pointer.

```
hGMem = GlobalAlloc( GHND, (DWORD) sizeof( METAFILEPICT ) );
lpMFP = (LPMETAFILEPICT) GlobalLock( hGMem );
```

Now that the `METAFILEPICT` structure is allocated and locked, the next steps are to assign values to the mapping mode, provide a suggested size, and assign the metafile handle.

```
lpMFP->mm = MM_ISOTROPIC;
lpMFP->xExt = 200;           // suggested size in //
lpMFP->yExt = 200;           // MM_HIMETRIC units //
lpMFP->hMF = hMetaFile;
```

And, with the assignments completed, all that remains is to unlock the memory before transferring the handle to the clipboard.

```
GlobalUnlock( hGMem );
TransferToClipboard( hwnd, hGMem, CF_METAFILEPICT );
```

Retrieving a Metafile from the Clipboard

Retrieving the metafile from the clipboard begins by opening the clipboard, asking for a handle to the memory block containing the metafile, and locking the block while returning a pointer.

```
OpenClipboard( hwnd );
hGMem = GetClipboardData( CF_METAFILEPICT );
lpMFP = (LPMETAFILEPICT) GlobalLock( hGMem );
```

At this point, the `lpMFP` variable contains a pointer to the metafile memory block or, more accurately, to the `METAFILEPICT` structure, which contains a pointer to the metafile proper.

But, before replaying the metafile itself, there are a couple of other tasks that require attention, beginning by saving the present device context (as suggested in Chapter 32).

```
SaveDC( hdc );
CreateMapMode( hdc, lpMFP, cxWnd, cyWnd );
```

After saving the present device context, because deciphering the mapping mode and size/extent information is moderately complex, the METAFILEPICT information is passed to a subroutine, CreateMapMode, for processing.

CreateMapMode is called with four parameters: the application's device context handle, the METAFILEPICT pointer, and the application window's size.

```
BOOL CreateMapMode( HDC hdc,    LPMETAFILEPICT lpMFP,
                    int cxWnd, int cyWnd )
{
   long   lMapScale;
   int    nHRes, nVRes, nHSize, nVSize;

   SetMapMode( hdc, lpMFP->mm );
   if( lpMFP->mm != MM_ISOTROPIC && lpMFP->mm != MM_ANISOTROPIC )
      return( TRUE );
```

The first task carried out by CreateMapMode is to set the mapping mode specified for the metafile. If the mapping mode is anything except MM_ISOTROPIC or MM_ANISOTROPIC, the function simply returns with nothing more required.

NOTE The image size data could be extracted, but there really isn't any point in doing so in this demo. If desired, you could get the size information and use it to position the metafile image, in a fashion similar to that demonstrated in Chapter 22.

If the metafile mapping mode is MM_ISOTROPIC or MM_ANISOTROPIC, then the CreateMapMode function still has work to do. First, it proceeds by calling the GetDeviceCaps function to query the horizontal and vertical size and resolution.

```
nHRes  = GetDeviceCaps( hdc, HORZRES );
nVRes  = GetDeviceCaps( hdc, VERTRES );
nHSize = GetDeviceCaps( hdc, HORZSIZE );
nVSize = GetDeviceCaps( hdc, VERTSIZE );
```

Three cases may occur, depending on the values passed in the xExt and yExt fields. If the arguments are positive, the values are intended to suggest a size in MM_HIMETRIC units. Therefore, the SetViewportExtEx function is called to set the viewport size appropriately.

```
if( lpMFP->xExt > 0 )
    SetViewportExtEx( hdc,
        (int)((long) lpMFP->xExt * nHRes / nHSize / 100 ),
        (int)((long) lpMFP->yExt * nHRes / nHSize / 100 ),
                    NULL );
```

Alternatively, if negative values have been entered, the arguments are intended as a ratio rather than an absolute size. Therefore, the first step is to calculate a scale to fit the device context.

```
else
if( lpMFP->xExt < 0 )
{
    lMapScale = min( ( 100L * (long) cxWnd * nHSize
                        / nHRes / -lpMFP->xExt ),
                     ( 100L * (long) cyWnd * nVSize
                        / nVRes / -lpMFP->yExt ) );
```

Two scales are calculated: one to fit the x-axis and one to fit the y-axis. But the iMapScale value is chosen as the smaller of the two possible scales to ensure that the resulting image does fit the display. And, once the mapping scale has been calculated, SetViewportExtEx is called again to size the viewport to fit.

```
    SetViewportExtEx( hdc,
        (int)((long) -lpMFP->xExt * lMapScale * nHRes
                        / nHSize / 100 ),
        (int)((long) -lpMFP->yExt * lMapScale * nVRes
                        / nVSize / 100 ),
                    NULL );
}
```

The third alternative that remains is that neither size nor ratio information was supplied and, if so, the remaining solution is simply to set the viewport to match the window size.

```
    else
        SetViewportExtEx( hdc, cxWnd, cyWnd, NULL );
```

Once the `CreateMapMode` function returns, the remainder of the task is simple, requiring nothing more than a call to `PlayMetaFile`, almost exactly as shown previously.

```
PlayMetaFile( hdc, lpMFP->hMF );
RestoreDC( hdc, - 1 );
GlobalUnlock( hGMem );
CloseClipboard();
```

And, after replaying the metafile, the `RestoreDC` function is called with an argument of –1 to restore the original device context, the metafile memory is unlocked, and the clipboard closed.

Using Other Clipboard Formats

The three clipboard formats used in the Clipboard program demonstrate the general processes involved in working with the clipboard, and any of the other clipboard formats should present no special difficulties. However, there are a few clipboard formats that merit some explanation, not because they require special handling as much as because they are defined for special purposes.

Private Clipboard Formats

Windows defines the "private" clipboard formats of `CF_DSPTEXT`, `CF_DSPBITMAP`, `CF_DSPMETAFILEPICT`, and `CF_DSPENHMETAFILE`. These correspond to the `CF_TEXT`, `CF_BITMAP`, `CF_METAFILEPICT`, and `CF_ENHMETAFILE` types, but with the one principal difference: Applications requesting the standard formats will not access these private formats.

There are two assumptions here:

- Data using one of these private formats is intended for exchange between two instances of the same application or two applications specifically designed to operate together.

- Such exchanges may include private information, such as formatting and/or font information used by the Windows Write program.

The term *private* could be misleading. There is nothing to prevent any application from requesting access to one or more of these private formats; these are not designed for security purposes, only to declare nonpublic clipboard transfers.

Also, although two instances of an application, or two related applications, should understand their own private formats, the use of one of these formats does not ensure that the originator is, indeed, another instance of the same application or a companion application. In other words, there is nothing to prevent another, totally unrelated application from using these same format designations.

However, provisions have also been made for this circumstance, and the originator of the clipboard contents can be obtained by calling the `GetClipboardOwner` function, as:

```
hwndCBOwner = GetClipboardOwner();
```

When the `EmptyClipboard` function was called, in preparation for copying materials to the clipboard, the calling application became the new clipboard owner. Other applications accessing the clipboard to retrieve material do not gain ownership of the clipboard, only access. Thus, only the clipboard owner is responsible for originating material on the clipboard, and an application cannot place material on the clipboard without first becoming the clipboard owner and erasing the previous contents. Therefore, any application accessing information in a private format should also query the identity of the clipboard owner to determine if this data is, indeed, in a common format.

Still while the `GetClipboardOwner` function does return a handle identifying the owner, this handle doesn't really tell you very much. But, given the handle, another call can be made to query the application's class name, as:

```
GetClassName( hwndCBOwner, &szClassName, 16 );
```

And, finally, `szClassName` can be compared with the current application's class name or to a list of companion application class names to identify the source of the clipboard information.

Delayed Rendering

Frequently, posting data to the clipboard involves passing a copy of the data to the clipboard while keeping the original intact, which means expending memory on duplicate data blocks. In many circumstances, this may be unimportant, particularly when the memory requirements are small. One obvious solution, which is used in the Clipboard demo program, is to transfer the data without keeping a copy, thus avoiding the problem entirely.

But, there is also another solution, which is particularly appropriate when large amounts of data are involved: delayed rendering of the clipboard data. In delayed rendering, only the format specification is posted to the clipboard and, instead of a global memory block handle, the handle parameter is passed as a null, thus:

```
SetClipboardData( wFormat, NULL );
```

When an application requests a data item that has been posted for delayed rendering, identified by the null in place of the data block, Windows recognizes the use of delayed rendering and calls the clipboard owner (the application that posted the material to the clipboard) with a WM_RENDERFORMAT message, with the requested format specified in wParam.

In response to the WM_RENDERFORMAT message, the application is expected to respond, not with an OpenClipboard and EmptyClipboard call, but with a Set-ClipboardData call, accompanied by the global memory block handle and the format identifier. In this fashion, the actual data is posted only when the recipient is ready to accept it.

When multiple items are to be passed to the clipboard, these may be passed as a mixture of conventional data transfers and delayed rendering transfers.

Special Circumstance Messages

When an application loses ownership of the clipboard, Windows does nothing to prevent this loss but does post a WM_DESTROYCLIPBOARD message to the previous owner, indicating that ownership has been lost. In response, if necessary, an application can resume ownership and post the same material again, but this is not recommended except in special circumstances.

Also, if an application is ready to terminate itself but is also currently the clipboard owner and the clipboard contains null data handles, Windows will send a WM_RENDERALLFORMATS message, without any format specifications, before the application is permitted to terminate. In response, the owner application has two options: clear the clipboard entirely or complete the delayed calls.

Unlike the response to the WM_RENDERFORMAT call, however, the terminating application should not use the SetClipboardData call but should simply clear the clipboard and write new entries entirely, just as if delayed rendering had not been used at all.

Owner-Displayed Clipboard Data

Another, very private, clipboard format is declared as:

```
SetClipboardData( CF_OWNERDISPLAY, NULL );
```

The CL_OWNERDISPLAY type is always passed with the global memory handle specified as null, just as with the delayed rendering format. But, because the clipboard owner is directly responsible for the display, Windows does not send a WM_RENDERFORMAT message when the data is requested. Instead, messages must be sent directly from the clipboard viewer to the clipboard owner. See the discussion of the other private clipboard formats for ways to identify the clipboard owner, using the GetClipboardOwner function. Conversely, the clipboard owner can use the GetClipboardViewer function, if necessary, to identify the viewing application.

To use this private format, the viewer application would post a request to the clipboard owner application, requesting the originating application to provide the actual display and granting the originating application access to the destination application's display. Five messages may be sent from the destination:

- WM_ASKCBFORMATNAME
- WM_HSCROLLCLIPBOARD
- WM_VSCROLLCLIPBOARD
- WM_PAINTCLIPBOARD
- WM_SIZECLIPBOARD

A WM_ASKCBFORMATNAME message is sent by the clipboard viewer to request a copy of the format name from the clipboard owner. Remember, the clipboard itself contains only the CF_OWNERDISPLAY identifier, and the viewer application is still free to decide if it is interested in the actual data type. The WM_ASKCBFORMATNAME message is accompanied by a specification in wParam for the number of bytes to copy. lParam provides a pointer to the buffer where the response should be posted.

A WM_PAINTCLIPBOARD message is sent requesting a repaint of the viewer application's display, probably in response to a WM_PAINT message received by the viewer application. The wParam argument contains a handle to the viewer's window. The lParam argument is a global DDESHARE handle which, when locked, points to a PAINTSTRUCT structure defining the area requiring repainting.

To determine if all or part of the client area requires repainting, the clipboard owner must compare the dimensions of the drawing area reported in the rcpaint field of the PAINTSTRUCT with the dimensions reported in the most recent WM_SIZECLIPBOARD message.

A WM_SIZECLIPBOARD message is sent to indicate the clipboard viewer has changed size. The wParam argument contains a handle to the viewer window. The lParam argument is a global DDESHARE handle pointing to a RECT structure defining the area to be painted.

The WM_HSCROLLCLIPBOARD and WM_VSCROLLCLIPBOARD messages are sent when the viewer application contains a horizontal or vertical scrollbar and a scrollbar event must be reported to the clipboard owner. The wParam argument contains a handle to the viewer's window. The lParam argument contains the same scrollbar messages as would accompany standard WM_HSCROLL or WM_VSCROLL messages.

In response to either of these messages, the clipboard owner should use the InvalidateRect function or repaint the viewer as desired. Of course, the scrollbar positions should also be reset appropriately.

User-Defined Private Formats

Applications may also define their own private clipboard formats, registering a new clipboard format by calling the RegisterClipboardFormat function, as:

```
wFormat = RegisterClipboardFormat( lpszFormatTitle );
```

The returned wFormat identifier will be a value in the range 0xC000..0xFFFF and can subsequently be used as the format parameter in SetClipboardData and Get-ClipboardData calls. Of course, before another application or instance can retrieve clipboard data in this format, it will require the same wFormat ID. This value, however, could be passed via the clipboard using the CD_TEXT format.

Alternatively, the EnumClipboardFormats function, discussed earlier in the chapter, could be used to return all format identifiers, after which the GetClipboardFormat-Name function could be called to return the ASCII name of the format, as:

```
GetClipboardFormatName( wFormat, lpszBuffer, nCharCount );
```

The format identifiers CF_PRIVATEFIRST (0x0200) and CF_PRIVATELAST (0x02FF) may also be used as a range of integer values for private format identifiers. Note, however, that data handles associated with formats in this range will not be freed automatically when another application requests clipboard ownership. Instead, any data handles in this range must be freed by the owner application before the application terminates or when a `WM_DESTROYCLIPBOARD` message is received. Use these latter format IDs with care.

Finally, note that Windows does not require any information about the organization of the data transferred using a private format. It is solely the responsibility of the application to understand the details of the transfer format. All that Windows requires is a format name and a handle to the memory block.

As you've seen in this chapter, a variety of standard and special-purpose clipboard formats are available, or applications can define and register their own special formats. The complete listing for the Clipboard program, which demonstrates working with text, bitmap, and metafile formats, is included on the CD that accompanies this book.

34

Dynamic Data Exchange Operations

- DDE basics

- Client/server transactions

- DDE Management Library (DDEML) functions

- Asynchronous and synchronous transactions

Windows clipboard functions were introduced in Chapter 33 as a means of exchanging data between different applications. This chapter introduces another way to transfer information and instructions between applications: Dynamic Data Exchange (DDE).

DDE is not a system suitable for distributed processing or for intensive data sharing in a situation where speed is the first, second, and third consideration. Instead, the real strength of DDE is that independent applications can exchange data without necessarily having been written explicitly to share with each other. As long as both applications understand how to communicate, are able to request compatible topics and items, and understand each other's formats, the two applications can communicate.

However, unlike clipboard traffic, DDE ensures that messages and data are passed directly between applications sharing a conversation without the data becoming public (accessible to every application) and without the possibility of data being lost (as can happen if the clipboard is preempted by another application). Furthermore, unlike clipboard transfers in which a single service resource must be shared, using DDE, several conversations can be carried on simultaneously between two or more applications, with each conversation independent of the others.

Introducing DDE

DDE is a message-based system, the interapplication equivalent of the internal messaging system that is integral to all Windows applications. As with internal messages, DDE messages are managed by Windows.

Through DDE, independent applications may exchange messages and data. DDE messages may be broadcast (sent to any other applications that may be listening) or may be posted directly to specific applications.

DDE message traffic is a conversation between two (or more) applications and, like a human conversation, includes both protocols and redundancies. But even though both protocols and the inherent redundancies result in a system that, theoretically, is less than 100 percent efficient, like human conversations, the results produce a high degree of surety.

There is one big difference between human conversations and DDE conversations: Unlike humans, using DDE, an application can carry on multiple conversations with different applications or multiple conversations with a single application, all without losing track of the conversations or becoming hopelessly confused. In this respect, instead of conversations, a more reasonable simile would be a chess player who is engaged, by post, in multiple chess games with one or more opponents. In this fashion, even a mediocre player can keep up several "conversations," which, in a more time-intensive situation such as a tournament, would be quite impractical.

And the post versus conversation simile holds in other respects. As with posting letters (or e-mail), the transactions themselves require some overhead and lack the immediacy of a conversation. Furthermore, like the postal-chess players, applications normally are doing other things between reading and responding to message traffic.

DDE Conversation Identifiers

In order to carry on a conversation, DDE applications require three basic identifiers:

- **Application or service name:** In a DDE application, the application name refers to a broad category of information that may be provided by the server. While some servers do supply only one type of information, others may provide several types of data and thus use several *application names*. To avoid confusion, the DDEML (Windows DDE Management Library) uses the term *service name* instead of *application name*.

> **NOTE** Broadcast messages may be addressed to anyone listening (if they choose to pay attention), rather than to a specific application name. This is the equivalent of shouting "Attention, everyone!"

- **Topic:** Any DDE conversation must have at least one topic, even though a single conversation may switch between multiple topics or multiple conversations may be using different topics. In a human conversation, the topic would be the subject; but in a DDL conversation, the topic must be specified and recognized by both parties. The topic name is commonly a filename.

- **Item:** The item name is an identifier within a topic that specifies a particular item of data as the subject of the current exchange. If a member of the conversation does not recognize the topic, the exchange fails and the conversation falters, even though the conversation itself may not fail completely. An item name might identify a page, a string, a bitmap, a spreadsheet cell, or any other data that might be transferred from one program to another.

For example, a spreadsheet might support two service types: *spreadsheet* and *chart*. As topics, each of these services might use filenames to refer to specific spreadsheet data files. The items in the spreadsheet services could be cell ranges or labels used within the spreadsheet. Items in the chart service might be presentation formats such as *pie* or *bar*.

In the DDE sample program presented in this chapter, a relatively limited conversation is carried on between five instances and involves only a few topics and items. In other cases, the topics and items can be quite extensive. These are limited only by the vocabulary that the participants share. Also, like the clipboard data transfers described in Chapter 33, the data elements exchanged can be as simple as integer data, as extensive as a bitmap or metafile, or as complex as an array of record structures. The information may even be any custom data type that all the participants recognize.

Limiting a server to a single service has its own advantages. If the service and the server have the same name, a client who knows one also knows the other. Given the .EXE filename, a client could initiate a conversation.

If the server and service have different names or if there are several services, then client applications (and developers) need additional information before clients can initiate conversations. An alternative is for the server to provide one service, named something like System service, which simply reports the names of the available services to the client applications. (See the section titled "The System Topic" later in this chapter.)

Also, when the client application knows the server (program) name as well as the service name, the client can launch the server, using the `CreateProcess` function, for example, and resume links from the last session.

Types of Transactions

DDEML conversations consist of three types of transactions: link, poke, and execute.

Link Transactions

The link transaction is the commonest type, in which the client requests a data item from the server. The link may be any of three types:

- **Cold link:** This conversation is initiated by a client application that broadcasts a WM_DDE_INITIATE request, identifying both the called application and the type of data requested (either or both of these can be NULL if any available server or subject is acceptable). In turn, as appropriate, one or more servers may respond, identifying themselves for further conversation. If the server does not match the requested name or does not recognize the topic, it will not respond; only affirmative responses are expected. The link ends immediately after receiving the data.

- **Warm link:** This conversation assumes that the client and server "know" each other and that the server has new information it believes the client will find of interest. Normally, the client will have sent a WM_DDE_ADVISE message to the server requesting updates on a topic (and item) as they become available. The server, aside from acknowledging the request, responds only when there is new information available.

- **Hot link:** This conversation is similar to a warm link in that the client requests information but expects acknowledgment and an immediate reply. If the server does not have information available immediately, it will simply respond that the data is not available and will wait for another request. For a hot-link conversation, the server does not volunteer information until the client places a request.

Realize that elements of all three types may occur during a single conversation, and these are quite mutable as well. So mutable, in fact, that it may be difficult to decide where one type starts and another ends.

Poke Transactions

A poke transaction is used to send an item from the client to the server or, more explicitly, to send an unsolicited data item as opposed to responding to a request for data.

Execute Transactions

A command or execute transaction allows the client to send the server a command or series of commands. Execute transactions are discussed presently.

DDE Data Exchange

Trying to explain how DDE exchanges function can quickly degenerate to a Marx Brothers' comedy routine, or perhaps more like the famous Abbot and Costello "Who's On First." A simple overview of a DDE conversation may be of more benefit.

A DDE exchange begins when a client application initiates a conversation and a server application responds. Once a conversation is initiated and until one party or the other terminates (disconnects) from the conversation, the client and server exchange data in one or more of the following fashions:

- The client requests data and the server fills the request.

- The client asks to be informed whenever a specific data item (or items) changes.

- The client requests an automatic update whenever a specific data item (or items) changes.

- The client transmits a command and the server executes the command.

- The client sends unsolicited data to the server.

An important point to remember, however, is that a client application can also be a server, and vice versa. Any application may fill both roles at the same time. The distinction between client and server is artificial and a matter of momentary definition, because either machine can request or supply data.

The DDE Management Library Functions

On its most basic level, a DDE conversation is a detailed and laborious process, involving exacting protocols and acknowledgments. However, because the most important element of programming is a matter of results, not of how much code you slog through to get there, the DDE Management Library (DDEML) provides an alternative. While concealing many of the details involved, the DDEML also conceals much of the labor.

The DDEML is a Windows-supplied library offering high-level API functions to simplify the DDE conversation process. The DDEML maintains a record for each conversation, using the CONVINFO structure, which includes the partners in the conversation, the topics and items requested, and the data format used, as well as type, status, errors, and other details concerning the conversation. Fortunately, most of these elements can simply be ignored by both the application and the programmer and left to the DDEML for handling.

Perhaps most important for developers is the simple fact that DDEML functions are far more transportable between Windows 3.*x* and NT or 95 than the native DDE functions that form the basis for the library routines.

The DDE Initialization Function

DdeInitialize is a DDEML function called to set up a callback function to DDE message traffic. Its use is demonstrated in the DDE_Demo program presented in this chapter.

When a program calls DdeInitialize, the DDEML library notifies other programs by sending an XTYP_REGISTER to their callback functions. These XTYP_REGISTER messages are used by many clients to maintain a list of available services.

The use of an instance identifier in the DdeInitialize call places a new constraint on Windows NT/95 programmers, because the instance identifier is local to a thread and is not inherited by a child process. Furthermore, because most of the DDEML operations require the instance identifier as a parameter, most of the program's DDEML operations for a specific service must be in the same thread where the DdeInitialize call was issued.

In addition, the thread that initialized the DDE session must not terminate until the session ends; otherwise, there is no way to call DdeUninitialize and no graceful way to end the session.

Registering Services

After initialization, server applications should also register the names of the services provided. The DdeNameService function is called with a handle to the string naming the service and an instance identifier for the service. From the instance identifier, the DDEML knows which callback procedure (and thread) supports the service.

```
HDDEDATA DdeNameService (
    DWORD dwInstID,      // instance ID
```

```
HSZ   hsz1,          // string naming service
HSZ   hszRes,        // reserved
UINT  uFlags );      // service name flags
```

The value in `dwInstID` is derived from `DdeInitialize`. The flags in the `uFlags` parameter select registration/unregistration and blocking or receiving connection signals for the registered service:

- `DNS_REGISTER`: Registers the service name.

- `DNS_UNREGISTER`: Unregisters the service name. If the `hsz1` argument is NULL, all services for this server are unregistered.

- `DNS_FILTERON`: Prevents the server from receiving `XTYP_CONNECT` messages for services that have not been registered.

- `DNS_FILTEROFF`: Allows the server to receive `XTYP_CONNECT` messages whenever any DDE program calls `DdeConnect`.

The value returned by `DdeNameService` is actually a Boolean response of 0 for failure or nonzero for success, but it is typed as `HDDEDATA` to allow for possible future improvements in the return indicator.

If the application will support more than one service, each service must be registered separately. Also, it can be advantageous to use a separate thread for each service, maintaining the thread and the thread's instance handle while the service is in use.

The DDE Callback Function

The heart of each DDEML application is found in the `DdeCallback` function. The entry for this function is predefined, complete with a list of eight calling parameters which will be supplied by Windows. However, `DdeCallback` is like the `WndProc` function in that the application is still responsible for filling in the responses. Table 34.1 lists the `DdeCallback` messages and the types of responses they expect.

The DDE Client Transaction Function

Each call to the `DdeClientTransaction` function instructs the DDEML to send a message to the server. The message type differs according to the type of action

TABLE 34.1   DdeCallback Message Types

Message	Response
XTYP_ADVSTART XTYP_CONNECT	Boolean: (TRUE or FALSE)
XTYP_ADVREQ XTYP_REQUEST XTYP_WILDCONNECT	Data handle (or NULL)
XTYP_ADVDATA XTYP_EXECUTE XTYP_POKE	Transaction flag: DDE_FACK, DDE_FBUSY, or DDE_FNOTPROCESSED
XTYP_ADVSTOP XTYP_CONNECT_CONFIRM XTYP_DISCONNECT XTYP_ERROR XTYP_REGISTER XTYP_UNREGISTER XTYP_XACT_COMPLETE	None; notification only

requested by the client. The server's callback function deals with each message in an appropriate fashion. Table 34.2 summarizes the transactions for some message types, which are explained in more detail in the following sections.

TABLE 34.2 Transaction Types

Message	Transaction
XTYP_REQUEST	Cold link: send a single data item
XTYP_ADVISE	Warm or hot link; respond by sending data and updates
XTYP_POKE	Poke (receive) data from the client
XTYP_EXECUTE	Execute a command or perform an action

Request Transaction Handling

When the server receives an XTYP_REQUEST message, it reads the topic and item names from the two string handle parameters and checks the requested data format. If the item is recognized and the format is supported, the server creates a data object for the item's current value and returns a handle to the data object (HDDEDATA). If the item is not supported or the format is not recognized, the server returns NULL.

> **NOTE**
>
> A server that does not support request transactions should set CBF_FAIL_REQUESTS flag in DdeInitialize to avoid receiving unwanted XTYP_REQUEST messages.

The value supplied by the server is returned to the client as the response from the DdeClientTransaction call. Figure 34.1 diagrams a typical interaction in three steps:

1. The client sends a request to the server, via the DDEML.

2. The server deciphers the request and packages the requested data.

3. The client receives and deciphers the response.

Advise Transaction Handling

When the client requests a link with updates, the server's callback procedure receives an XTYP_ADVSTART message. If the server recognizes the topic and item names and supports the requested format, the server returns TRUE to confirm the link, or FALSE to prevent it.

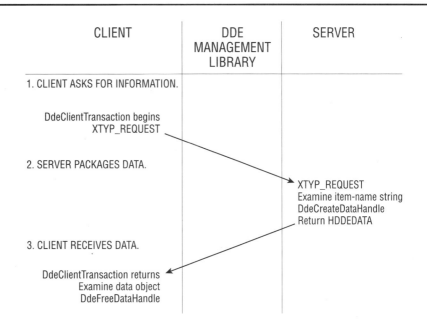

FIGURE 34.1

Sequence of events following a client request for a data item

The following text appears within the figure:

CLIENT

DDE MANAGEMENT LIBRARY

SERVER

1. CLIENT ASKS FOR INFORMATION.

DdeClientTransaction begins
XTYP_REQUEST

2. SERVER PACKAGES DATA.

XTYP_REQUEST
Examine item-name string
DdeCreateDataHandle
Return HDDEDATA

3. CLIENT RECEIVES DATA.

DdeClientTransaction returns
Examine data object
DdeFreeDataHandle

NOTE The XTYP_ADVSTART message does not tell the server whether the link will be warm or hot.

Hot-Link Operations   In a hot link, the server does not return data immediately; it sends data only when the requested data item next changes. In response to XTYP_ADVSTART, the server often sets a flag to remind itself that updates have been requested. Whenever an item changes, the server checks the state of the flag and, if it is set, calls DdePostAdvise to notify the DDEML that new data is available for an interested client.

The server does not need to remember which client has requested a particular item; the DDEML handles this task internally. Given the topic and item name, which is supplied by the server to identify the available item data, the DDEML determines which clients are linked and whether the links are hot or warm.

If the links are hot, the DDEML immediately sends the server an XTYP_ADVREQ message, receives the data from the server, and then posts it to the client in an XTYP_ADVDATA message. Figure 34.2 illustrates the steps in the process:

1. The loop is initiated by the client with the server acknowledging the request with a TRUE response.

2. The server advises the DDEML that new data is available. In turn, the DDEML determines this is a hot link and requests the data, then sends it to the client application. This step will repeat as often as the server has new data available.

3. The client terminates the hot link by sending a XTYP_ADVSTOP message, which the server acknowledges with a NULL response.

FIGURE 34.2

Initiating, executing, and closing a hot-link advise loop

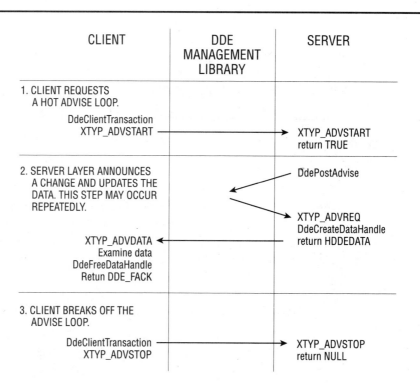

CLIENT	DDE MANAGEMENT LIBRARY	SERVER
1. CLIENT REQUESTS A HOT ADVISE LOOP.		
DdeClientTransaction XTYP_ADVSTART ⟶		XTYP_ADVSTART return TRUE
2. SERVER LAYER ANNOUNCES A CHANGE AND UPDATES THE DATA. THIS STEP MAY OCCUR REPEATEDLY.		DdePostAdvise
		XTYP_ADVREQ DdeCreateDataHandle return HDDEDATA
XTYP_ADVDATA ← Examine data DdeFreeDataHandle Retun DDE_FACK		
3. CLIENT BREAKS OFF THE ADVISE LOOP.		
DdeClientTransaction XTYP_ADVSTOP ⟶		XTYP_ADVSTOP return NULL

Warm-Link Operations   When a warm-link advice operation is requested, the DDEML is still advised when the server's data changes for the requested item, but it does not send a data request message to the server. Instead, the DDEML sends an empty XTYP_ADVDATA message to the client with a NULL data handle.

> **NOTE** A server that does not support advise loops of any kind should set the CBF_FAIL_ADVISES flag in the DdeInitialize operation to avoid receiving unwanted XTYP_ADVSTART and XTYP_ADVSTOP messages.

To see the item's data (to receive a new value), the client must execute a request transaction following the process illustrated in Figure 34.3.

1. The server announces that new data is available.

2. The DDEML notifies the client but the client ignores the notification. In this case, notifications will be sent to the client each time the server data changes, but the client is free to ignore these notifications.

3. The server announces a change in the requested data item.

4. The client responds with a request for the data (XTYP_REQEST).

5. The data request is passed by the DDEML to the server.

6. The server returns the requested data to the client.

Poke and Execute Transaction Handling

Some servers wish to accept data from the client, reversing the usual transfer direction. A client wishing to send data to the server needs an XTYP_POKE transaction. In response to this message, the server checks the topic and item, then, if it wants the information, it reads the data object.

Some servers also accept commands from their clients, receiving the commands in the form of data handles. The server locks the object, parses, the command string contained in the data object, and then performs some action in response. The server must also free the data handle after parsing, but it may duplicate the data string if it will be needed later. Because clients generally expect commands to execute immediately and may expect confirmation, the server should, if possible, execute the command from the callback function prior to returning.

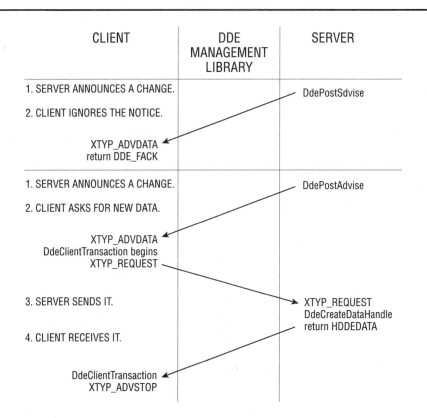

FIGURE 34.3

Initiating, executing, and closing a warm-link advise loop

In response to a poke or execute transaction, the server returns one of three values:

- DDE_FACK: Data received and acknowledged.

- DDE_FBUSY: The server is too busy to process the data or instruction; try again later.

- DDE_FNOTPROCESSED: The data or instruction is refused.

TIP

Both Microsoft Excel and Word accept execute messages where the item string is a command from the application's macro language. For example, a DDEML transaction addressed to the `winword` service on the `system` topic with the string `[file1]` in the data handle, instructs Word to load its most recently used file.

Flags set in the `DdeInitialize` operation can filter out unwanted poke or execute messages for servers not supporting these. `CBF_FAIL_POKES` blocks poke transaction messages. `CBF_FAIL_EXECUTES` blocks execute transaction messages.

The DDE Disconnect Functions

To terminate a DDE conversation, the client or the server calls either `DdeDisconnect` to terminate a specific conversation or `DdeDisconnectList` to terminate all conversations. In both cases, an `XTYP_DISCONNECT` transaction is sent to the other application or applications.

For a single conversation, `DdeDisconnect` is called:

```
DdeDisconnect( hConv );
```

where `hConv` is the conversation handle returned from the `DdeConnect` function.

To disconnect all conversations, `DdeDisconnectList` is called:

```
DdeDisconnectList( hConvList );
```

where `hConvList` is the conversation handle returned from the `DdeConnectList` function.

When the DDEML receives the `XTYP_DISCONNECT` transaction message, any transactions still in progress for the given conversation(s) are abandoned. By convention, only clients are expected to break off conversations. Depending on circumstances, however, servers sometimes must disconnect, such as when the server application is closed.

 Clients and servers alike should be prepared to receive disconnect messages at any time during a conversation and should close data structures accordingly.

The DDE Uninitialize Function

When an application closes, or when it no longer wishes to converse with other applications, the application should uninitialize all DDEML callback procedures.

Calling `DdeUninitialize` removes a service from the DDEML tables, terminates any conversations still in progress, and sends `XTYP_UNREGISTER` messages to all DDEML callback procedures. Figure 34.4 shows the steps involved in breaking off a conversation and withdrawing from the DDEML.

FIGURE 34.4

Closing down a client and a server

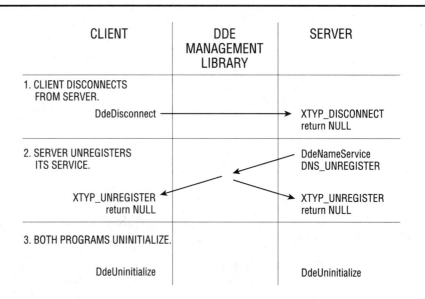

DDE Errors

Normally, when a DDEML function fails, returning either NULL or FALSE, extended error information can be retrieved by calling `DdeGetLastError`:

```
UINT DdeGetLastError( DWORD dwInstID );
```

Because `DdeGetLastError` requires an instance identifier, this function can't be used to return error information if `DdeInitialize` fails. Therefore `DdeInitialize` returns its own extended error codes:

- `DWLERR_NO_ERROR`: Initialization succeeded.

- `DWLERR_DLL_USAGE`: The program is registered as a monitor and cannot use the DDEML for transactions.

- `DWLERR_INVALIDPARAMETER`: A parameter contained invalid information.

- `DWLERR_SYS_ERROR`: An internal error occurred in DDEML.

Using the DDML Functions:
The DDE_Demo Program

The DDE_Demo application uses multiple instances of a single application, with each instance acting as both client and server to all other instances. Structurally, the DDE_Demo application is similar to the previous examples in this book, but it does introduce a few new elements.

The DDE_Demo application is shown in Figure 34.5, with five instances of the application communicating with each other. Individual instances could be minimized (reduced to an icon on the program bar) or even hidden, but despite changes in size, state, or Desktop visibility, they still remain active.

FIGURE 34.5

Five instances communicating via DDE

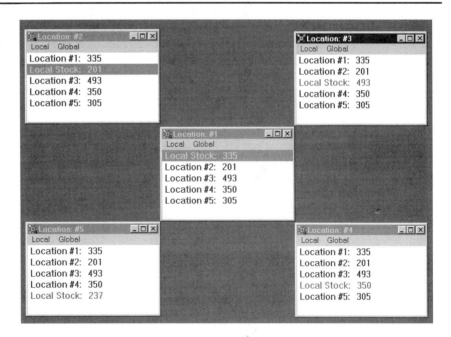

Each instance of the DDE_Demo is communicating with each of the other instances. Each instance is maintaining a local data element, which is listed, in this simulation, as *Local Stock* with the label and amount appearing in red. At the same time, each instance also reports the stock level of all of the other instances, listing these in black.

In Figure 34.5, the instance identified as Location #5 has just updated its own stock level but has not yet reported the change to the remaining instances. Also, the instances identified as Locations #1 and #2 are currently inactive (paused). The screen in Figure 34.5 reflects this by showing its stock level (locally) as a gray bar with light-gray text. Also, even though these two instances are paused, they do continue to report changes made by other locations.

The remaining active instances show their own stock levels in red and display the stock levels of other locations in black.

> **NOTE**
>
> **Keep in mind that this demo program has been written simply to illustrate how DDE data exchanges work and how instructions can be passed between applications or application instances. It uses source code that is both relatively brief and sufficiently structured to be conveniently followed. This is not intended as a practical application and, in fact, is a rather frivolous example.**

Initializing a DDE Application

Within the application, the `WinMain` procedure begins in a familiar enough fashion by initializing itself (by calling the `InitApplication` function from the Template; I include file). Once the application has been initialized, `DdeInitialize`, a DDEML function, is called to set up a callback function to DDE message traffic.

```
int WINAPI WinMain( HINSTANCE hInstance,
                    HINSTANCE hPrevInstance,
                    LPSTR     lpCmdLine,
                    INT       nCmdShow )
{
   ...
   if( DdeInitialize( &idInst,
       (PFNCALLBACK) MakeProcInstance(
             (FARPROC) DdeCallback,
                   hInstance ),
                   APPCMD_FILTERINITS |
                   CBF_SKIP_CONNECT_CONFIRMS |
                   CBF_FAIL_SELFCONNECTIONS |
                   CBF_FAIL_POKES,
                   0 ) )
          return(FALSE);          // fail if error occurs
```

> **NOTE**
>
> The `MakeProcInstance` call is not required by Windows NT but is used here simply for compatibility with Windows 3.*x*.

While establishing the callback function, several conditions are also established. These are a series of filter conditions that restrict the types of message traffic handled:

- `APPCMD_FILTERINITS`: Filter out any applications except those with our own service name.

- `CBF_SKIP_CONNECT_CONFIRMS`: Don't bother to confirm connections.

- `CBF_FAIL_SELFCONNECTIONS`: Don't permit self connections.

- `CBF_FAIL_POKES`: Don't allow `XTYP_POKE` transactions.

Additional filter conditions can be imposed (these are defined in DDEML.H), but these suffice for the present demo application.

Last, if for some reason, the callback function cannot be established, the application returns FALSE and terminates (this is an unlikely event).

Next, the `CreateWindow` function is called in the customary fashion, but in case of failure, provisions are made to call the `DdeUnitialize` function before terminating.

```
hInst = hInstance;
hwnd = CreateWindow( szAppName, szAppTitle,
                     WS_OVERLAPPEDWINDOW,
                     CW_USEDEFAULT, CW_USEDEFAULT,
                     CW_USEDEFAULT, CW_USEDEFAULT,
                     NULL, NULL, hInstance, NULL );
if( ! hwnd )
{
   DdeUninitialize( idInst );
   return( FALSE );
}
```

The next provision is specific to the present demo program. It looks for a command-line parameter, which will be used to identify the separate instances of the application (for our benefit only). Because the initial instance is not expected to have a command-line argument, a default of 1 is also supplied.

```
if( strlen( lpCmdLine ) ) iInst = atoi( lpCmdLine );
                     else iInst = 1;
```

The supplied arguments have nothing to do with the DDE or the management library and will be used only for labeling purposes. The DDEML has other means of identifying each individual instance, using the identification handle supplied by Windows. The origin of the command-line parameters for all but the first instance will be apparent in a moment.

> **NOTE**
>
> If it occurs to you that the `hPrevInstance` argument could be used to determine if this is the first instance of the application, note that Windows NT/95 does not supply an `hPrevInstance` argument. Because each application under NT/95 executes in its own virtual space, this argument is always supplied as NULL, irrespective of how many other instances of an application are executing. The customary test is supplied only for compatibility with Windows 3.*x*.

Pseudo-random number generators are used to supply data but, characteristically, will always generate the same number sequence unless they are seeded (or initialized) to provide a different starting condition. For this purpose, Borland's `randomize` function accesses the system clock. However, because Microsoft C does not supply a `randomize` function, an alternative is supplied to ensure that each instance of the application will generate a different series.

```
#ifdef __BORLANDC__
    randomize();
#else
    for( i=0; i<iInst; i++ ) random( iInst );
#endif
```

The next task, if this is the first instance of the application, is to spawn the remaining four instances by calling the `WinExec` function and supplying the command-line parameter for each.

```
switch( iInst )
{                       // first instance calls four others
    case 1:   xLoc = 195;  yLoc = 125;
              WinExec( "DDE_DEMO 2", SW_SHOW );
              WinExec( "DDE_DEMO 3", SW_SHOW );
              WinExec( "DDE_DEMO 4", SW_SHOW );
              WinExec( "DDE_DEMO 5", SW_SHOW );    break;
    case 2:   xLoc = 0;    yLoc = 0;              break;
```

```
    case 3:    xLoc = 390;    yLoc = 0;          break;
    case 4:    xLoc = 390;    yLoc = 250;        break;
    case 5:    xLoc = 0;      yLoc = 250;        break;
}
```

Also, each instance of the application is supplied with separate xLoc and yLoc coordinates, spacing each around the screen for an optimum display. Again, these provisions are specific to the present demo program, and have nothing to do with DDE functions or the DDEML.

Preparing for Connections

Next, the ShowWindow and UpdateWindow functions are called, in the usual fashion but, before proceeding to the customary message loop, there are a few provisions that the DDE library does require.

```
    hszAppName = DdeCreateStringHandle( idInst, szAppTitle, 0 );
```

The first step, at this point, is to create a string handle for the application title. The idInst argument was supplied earlier by the DDEInitialize function and identifies this instance of the application. The final argument, CP_WINANSI, identifies the default code page. Alternatively, CP_WINUNICODE would be used if the Unicode version of the DDEML library was desired.

Next, a format handle is retrieved by calling the RegisterClipboardFormat function before the present instance attempts to connect to any other matching DDE applications by calling DdeConnectList.

```
    hFormat = RegisterClipboardFormat( szAppTitle );
    hConvList = DdeConnectList( idInst, hszAppName, hszAppName,
                                hConvList, NULL );
```

If there are no DDE applications matching the requested name and topic, that's okay; the conversation list (hConvList) simply remains empty until there is someone to talk to. (Remember, if this is the first instance, self-connection has already been prohibited.)

Last, the DdeNameService function is called to register the current instance, which broadcasts notification to all other DDE applications that the present application instance is available, but it does not force a connection.

```
    DdeNameService( idInst, hszAppName, 0, DNS_REGISTER );
```

Finally, with the DDE connections established, the usual message loop begins and continues until the application instance is ready to terminate.

```
while( GetMessage( &msg, NULL, 0, 0 ) )
{
   TranslateMessage( &msg );
   DispatchMessage( &msg );
}
```

When the application is ready to terminate, a couple of cleanup provisions are desirable, beginning with a call to DestroyWindow and then UnregisterClass to clean up the DDE application.

```
DestroyWindow( hwnd );
UnregisterClass( szAppTitle, hInstance );
```

Responding to Transaction Messages

Although the application is responsible for handling DdeCallback responses, we are not required to respond to all possible transaction types. In the DDE_Demo example, responses are limited to eight XTYP_*xxxx* transactions.

In the demo program, a subprocedure, PostTransaction, is used to handle the details of the transaction (as discussed a bit later in the chapter), but still specifies the transaction type as:

XTYP_REQUEST	Cold link	Transaction ends with receipt of data item.
XTYP_ADVSTART	Hot link	Server sends new data in an XTYP_ADVDATA message whenever the item changes.
XTYP_ADV_START or XTYPF_ADVNODATA	Warm link	Server sends an empty XTYP_ADVDATA message whenever the data item changes.

The first transaction is XTYP_CONNECT. However, because filtering has already been specified (in the DdeInitialize call), any connections that do come through are for the present DDE application and can be accepted by returning TRUE.

```
case XTYP_CONNECT:          return( TRUE );
```

Also, because no provisions have been made for XTYP_WILD_CONNECT transactions, attempts at wildcard connections will fail automatically.

Despite the preceding, when an XTYP_ADVSTART transaction request is received to start a conversation, a test is applied to ensure that we are both (client and server) talking about the same topic and know who we're talking to.

```
case XTYP_ADVSTART:
    return( (UINT) wFmt == hFormat && hszItem == hszAppName );
```

If either calling argument fails, the result returned is FALSE, declining the conversation. Of course, the calling application is free to try again with a different topic (or maybe it really wanted to query a different application and was broadcasting the request).

Since new DDE applications can come in at any time, it would be impractical to attempt to synchronize everybody's initialization. The XTYP_REGISTER transaction notes the new arrival, updates the connection list (hConvList), and then posts a XTYP_ADVSTART transaction back—kind of a "Howdy, neighbor" conversation.

```
case XTYP_REGISTER:
    hConvList =
        DdeConnectList( idInst, hszItem, hszAppName,
                        hConvList, NULL );
    PostTransaction( NULL, 0, hFormat, XTYP_ADVSTART );
    UpdateWindow( hwnd );
    return( TRUE );
```

With a new DDE application in the loop, this is also an appropriate time to update the current instance's window. Alternatively, this could be left to wait for more information (such as a data transaction).

Another event that could occur is that somebody exits from our conversation. But when this happens, there isn't a great deal that the present demo program needs to handle. A simple InvalidateRect instruction to repaint the window is quite sufficient.

```
case XTYP_DISCONNECT:
    InvalidateRect( hwnd, NULL, TRUE );
    break;
```

The next two transaction types are XTYP_ADVREQ (ADVise REQuested) and XTYP_REQUEST, both of which expect a response in the form of a data report. In many DDE applications, this would result in the data being rendered in text format (delimited, usually) to fit the CF_TEXT format. Here, however, a custom format has been used and rendering is not required.

```
case XTYP_ADVREQ:
case XTYP_REQUEST:
    return( DdeCreateDataHandle( idInst, (PBYTE) &DataOut,
                                 sizeof( DataOut ), 0,
                                 hszAppName, hFormat, 0 ) );
```

The DdeCreateDataHandle function is used to provide a handle to the data block. In this case, the data that will be transferred is a UNIT (32-bit unsigned integer), which has the source ID (iInst) in the high byte of the high word and the remainder of the data in the low-order word. Packing this custom format is handled in the WndProc procedure, as described a bit later in the chapter.

When the application is acting as a client rather than a server, the XTYP_ADVDATA (ADVise DATA) transaction handles the other end of the transaction, by calling DdeGetData and DdeSetUserHandle to render the data in a format accessible to the rest of the application.

```
case XTYP_ADVDATA:
    if( DdeGetData( hData, (PBYTE) &DataIn,
                    sizeof(DataIn), 0 ) )
        DdeSetUserHandle( hConv, QID_SYNC, DataIn );
    InvalidateRect( hwnd, NULL, TRUE );
    return( DDE_FACK );
```

The DdeGetData function copies the data to a local buffer (DataIn) before the DdeSetUserHandle function is called to associate the local buffer with a conversation handle (hConv). This process simplifies asynchronous transactions (discussed later in the chapter) and is completed, in the WndProc procedure, when the DdeQueryConvInfo procedure is called in response to the WM_PAINT message.

Also, as you will note in the WndProc procedure, this transaction is initiated, within a loop calling all parties to the present conversation, in response to the WM_PAINT message. This transaction could be initiated for many different reasons under many different conditions—perhaps periodically by a timer or in response to a request for a recalculation of some type—and the current handling was dictated only by the requirements of this demo program.

One transaction type remains in the current demo program: the XTYP_EXECUTE transaction (a request issued by another application or application instance for the present instance to take some particular action). The first step, before we can determine what action is requested, is to access the data by calling DdeAccessData to return a local pointer (local to this instance and procedure) to what is assumed to be string data.

```
case XTYP_EXECUTE:
    pszExec = DdeAccessData( hData, &dwSize );
    if( pszExec )
    {
```

Optionally, the `dwSize` parameter receives the size of the returned string. If the size of the returned data is not required, this argument may be supplied as NULL.

If `pszExec` is not null (it points to a string), the next step is to determine if the string instruction matches anything that we're prepared to respond to.

```
if( ! stricmp( "PAUSE", pszExec ) )
    PauseAutomatic( hwnd );
else
if( ! stricmp( "RESUME", pszExec ) )
    ResumeAutomatic( hwnd );
```

Only two responses have been provided here, triggered by the key strings `"PAUSE"` and `"RESUME"` and each calling a subprocedure. As you will see in the `WndProc` procedure, these same subprocedures are also called in response to menu messages. Incidentally, notice that the string comparison used is case-insensitive.

What is immediately relevant here is that these are instructions that are received from another application or application instance. These instructions originate outside the application but are acted on by the application. In a moment, in the `WndProc` procedure, you will find the matching provisions that permit transmitting such instructions to other applications.

For the moment, however, because `switch`/`case` statements can use only integral arguments, we need a series of `if`/`else` statements for matching strings. And, if more than a few tests are required, this can result in a rather complicated structure.

As an alternative, a loop could be used to match string arguments against string-table entries with a following `switch`/`case` statement using the string-table entry number when a match is found.

DDE Elements in the WndProc Procedure

As usual, the `WndProc` procedure directs the principal activities of the DDE_Demo application, with the obvious exception of responses to instructions received from another application (or instance of this application) via DDE links.

DDE Performance Discrepancies under Windows 95

Although the `DdeAccessData` function performs correctly on the NT system, under Windows 95, the execution string returned (`pszExec`) by the function is not correct. Instead, the returned string has a four-byte error, beginning 0x00, 0x20, 0x0C, 0xDC. To correct this discrepancy, a test routine has been added as follows:

```
case XTYP_EXECUTE:
    pszExec = DdeAccessData( hData, &dwSize );
    if( pszExec[0] <= 0x20 )
        pszExec += 4;
    if( pszExec )
    {
```

You can test this under Windows 95 by placing a break on the `DdeAccess-Data` call and using the watch window to examine the string value returned when issuing a global Pause or Resume instruction.

The same `DdeAccessData` call under NT functions correctly and does not require offsetting the string to compensate for garbage characters.

Also, the `dwSize` value returned by the `DdeAccessData` function under Windows 95 bears no connection to the actual string length nor to the arguments passed in either of the `PostTransaction` instructions:

```
PostTransaction( "RESUME", 7, 0, XTYP_EXECUTE );
PostTransaction( "PAUSE", 6, 0, XTYP_EXECUTE );
```

Under NT, the `dwSize` variable receives the correct values. However, since the `dwSize` argument is not used by the DDE_Demo application, in this case, this error does not require correction. The same, however, cannot be said to apply to all applications.

Also, although less critical, in the DDE_Demo program, breakpoints may not respond to events generated from the first instance of the five client/server instances but will respond to the same events generated by any of the remaining instances. This discrepancy has no effect on the actual instructions being passed between the five instances; it affects only attempts to debug operations. This particular idiosyncrasy applies under both Windows NT and 95 using the Microsoft compiler.

As each instance of the DDE_Demo application is created, the WM_CREATE message provides an opportunity to initialize a timer before sending a WM_SIZE message to size and position the application instance.

The WM_TIMER response is the first location where the DDE functions are actually invoked. It begins by updating the LocalStock variable:

```
case WM_TIMER:
    if( random( 2 ) ) LocalStock += random( 100 );
    else  LocalStock -= min( (UINT) random( 100 ),
                                    LocalStock );
    DataOut = ( iInst << 24 ) + LocalStock;
```

After the LocalStock variable has changed, the DataOut variable, which is used as the custom data format for the actual data transfer, is updated by packing the instance identifier (iInst) in the high byte of the high word with the LocalStock value in the low-order word. A more realistic application might prefer to use a record or data structure at this point but, for demo purposes, this simpler format is sufficient.

Next, now that the data is ready, a DdePostAdvise message is issued to let other applications know that new data is available. This will be received by other parties to the conversation, in the DdeCallback function, as an XTYP_ADVDATA transaction.

```
DdePostAdvise( idInst, hszAppName, hszAppName );
SetRect( &rc, 0, 0, cxText, cyText );
InvalidateRect( hwnd, &rc, TRUE );
UpdateWindow( hwnd );
break;
```

Last, after the DDE transaction has been posted, the application instance issues instructions to update its own window to show the new value. (As you can see in Figure 34.5, shown earlier in the chapter, where Location #5 has been updated but the remaining instances have not, this does not determine which of the DDE clients will be first to update their screens.)

The WM_PAINT message response also executes DDE link transactions. First, if hConvList is not NULL, indicating that the application does have conversation links with other applications or instances, DdeQueryNextServer is called to set hConv to the first conversation on the list.

```
case WM_PAINT:
    ...             // poll other locations and report
    if( hConvList )
```

```
    {
       hConv = DdeQueryNextServer( hConvList, 0 );
       while( hConv )
       {
          ciData.cb = sizeof(CONVINFO);
          DdeQueryConvInfo( hConv, QID_SYNC, &ciData );
```

Once we have a handle to a conversation, `DdeQueryConvInfo` is used to get the latest data. (The actual paint operations used to display this data are ignored; these are not particularly different from those demonstrated in earlier examples.)

Once we've finished with the present conversation, `DdeQueryNextServer` is called again, this time using the current conversation as an argument, to get the next conversation in the list. The loop continues until no further conversations are found.

```
          hConv = DdeQueryNextServer( hConvList, hConv );
       }
    }
```

Before an application can terminate, the `WM_CLOSE` message is always posted and, normally, responds by calling `PostQuitMessage` to terminate. In this application, however, before terminating, there are a few other tasks that need handling. These are primarily to clean up the DDE link, but also to kill the local timer. (Timers may not be the limited resource that they were under Windows 3.1, but they are still not a resource we should waste by leaving them active when no longer needed.)

```
    case WM_CLOSE:
       KillTimer( hwnd, TRUE );
       DdeDisconnectList( hConvList );
       DdeNameService( idInst, 0, 0, DNS_UNREGISTER );
       DdeFreeStringHandle( idInst, hszAppName );
       DdeUninitialize( idInst );
       PostQuitMessage( FALSE );
       break;
```

As for the DDE itself, the first step is to disconnect, then to unregister the service name and free the string handle before, finally, uninitializing the DDE link. And, with this done, the application is finally free to exit.

Other Provisions in WndProc

Aside from direct DDE provisions, the WndProc procedure also processes menu messages. The demo program provides two pull-down menus: Local and Global. Each of these menus offers two options: Resume and Pause. The two Local menu options are used to instruct the local instance to either resume automatic operation or to pause automatic operation. The two Global menu options fall through to the local options.

Before falling though, however, the two Global options are used to broadcast messages to other conversation clients, instructing them to either resume or pause. This is accomplished by calling the PostTransaction procedure, thus:

```
case WM_COMMAND:
    switch( LOWORD( wParam ) )
    {
        case IDG_RESUME:
            PostTransaction( "RESUME", 7, 0, XTYP_EXECUTE );
            // no break - falls through to local selection //

        case IDL_RESUME:
            ResumeAutomatic( hwnd );
            break;

        case IDG_PAUSE:
            PostTransaction( "PAUSE", 6, 0, XTYP_EXECUTE );
            // no break - falls through to local selection //

        case IDL_PAUSE:
            PauseAutomatic( hwnd );
            break;
    }
    break;
```

The PostTransaction procedure is a locally defined operation called with four parameters: pScr, which is a pointer to the instruction string; cbData, with the length (size) of the instruction; fmt, identifying the data format used; and the transaction type, xtyp.

```
VOID PostTransaction( PBYTE pSrc, DWORD cbSize,
                      UINT fmt, UINT xtyp )
{
    HCONV  hConv;
```

```
DWORD   dwResult;
int     iCheck = 0;
```

Locally, the `hConv` variable is a handle to a conversation. The integer `iCheck` is used simply to check to see if any new conversations have been established and, if so, to allow the local instance to update its display. The conversation loop is essentially the same as the one for the `WM_PAINT` message, described in the previous section. The type of conversation, however, differs.

In this situation, the `DdeClientTransaction` API function is called with the instruction, the instruction size (length), the application name (ID), the format, the transaction type, and the `TIMEOUT_ASYNC` instruction identifying this as an asynchronous transaction. Synchronous DDE transactions would specify a timeout in milliseconds.

Last, `dwResult` would receive the results of the transaction but, in this case, we really don't care.

```
if( DdeClientTransaction( pSrc, cbSize, hConv, hszAppName,
    fmt, xtyp, TIMEOUT_ASYNC, &dwResult ) )
    DdeAbandonTransaction( idInst, hConv, dwResult );
```

Because we really don't care about the success or failure of this transaction, and because we don't want to wait for a result to be reported, this is being sent as an asynchronous transaction which returns immediately (automatically returning TRUE). While a subsequent transaction message would report success or failure, no provisions are included to handle success or, in the case of failure, to send the instruction again. Therefore, `DdeAbandonTransaction` is called to terminate this conversation without waiting for a response.

Presumably, however, the posted instruction will be received by the other application instances, in the `DdeCallback` function, and acted on accordingly.

Asynchronous versus Synchronous Transactions

DDEML clients have a choice between synchronous and asynchronous transactions. The DDE_Demo program in this chapter uses asynchronous transactions. The difference between synchronous and asynchronous operations matters only to the client programs. From the server's viewpoint, both types of transactions appear the same.

The advantages of synchronous transactions are that they are faster and easier to program. Asynchronous transactions have advantages for busy programs, which need to perform substantial amounts of processing while interacting with a DDEML server, or for programs that regularly interact with a particularly slow server and need to avoid remaining idle.

Synchronous Transactions

When synchronous transactions are used, the client application waits for an answer from the server after initiating a transaction, whether issuing a request for information or a sending a command for action. If the server makes the client wait longer than the client's time-out period, DdeClientTransaction cancels the transaction and returns.

In a synchronous transaction, you must make provisions for freeing data objects. The DDEML passes the data handle as a return value from DdeClientTransaction and has no way of knowing when the data can be freed. The client owns the data objects received synchronously from DdeClientTransaction and must eventually call DdeFreeDataHandle to release them.

Asynchronous Transactions

For asynchronous operation, when calling DdeClientTransaction, set the timeout period to TIMEOUT_ASYNCH. DdeClientTransaction will return TRUE immediately, returning a transaction ID in the dwResult field. While the client application continues executing other operations, DDEML pursues the transaction in the background.

Then, when the transaction is complete, the DDEML sends an XTYP_XACT_COMPLETE message to the client's callback procedure. This completion message includes the transaction ID in the dwData1 parameter, allowing the client to determine which transaction request is completed.

The DDEML also provides an alternative mechanism for identifying transactions from their completion messages. The client may register a DWORD value of its own to associate with each asynchronous transaction. DdeSetUserHandle accepts a conversation handle, an asynchronous transaction ID, and a custom DWORD value, storing these internally. When the XTYP_XACT_COMPLETE message is received, the client retrieves the private identifier by calling DdeQueryComplete.

While waiting for an asynchronous transaction to complete, `DdeClient-Transaction` enters a modal loop and polls for window messages, allowing the client to continue to respond to user input while waiting. The client may not, however, execute a second DDEML function during this period.

An attempt to call `DdeClientTransaction` also fails if another synchronous operation is already in progress for the same client.

To cancel an asynchronous operation before completion, call the `DdeAbandon-Transaction` function. The DDEML then discards all resources associated with the transaction and discards the result when the server eventually returns. (This is the same process that occurs when a synchronous transaction times out.)

In an asynchronous transaction, the DDEML delivers the data object handle to the client's callback function. When the callback function returns, the DDEML reasonably assumes that the data is no longer needed and frees the data object automatically. If the client needs to preserve the data, the client should make a copy of the data (using `DdeGetData`) before returning.

WARNING The client must not free data handles received asynchronously. Because the server is not yet aware that the data has been received, the server continues to assume ownership of the data package and will take the responsibility for freeing the data when notified that the data was received.

The System Topic

As explained earlier in the chapter, the customary sequence for initiating a conversation requires the client to know in advance which servers and/or topics are required. To make it possible for a client to survey available topics, DDEML servers sometimes include in each service a topic titled System.

Under the System name, support is provided for a set of standard informational items. Through the System topic, a client may obtain information about a specific service.

Strings identifying standard system items are defined in DDEML.H and identified by constants. Three of these in particular should be supported by all server applications:

- SZDDESYS_ITEM_FORMATS: A list of strings, tab-delimited, indicating the clipboard formats supported by the server. (The actual item name string is "Formats".)

- SZDDESYS_ITEM_SYSITEMS: A list of items supported by the server under the System topic. (The item name is "SysItems".)

- SZDDESYS_ITEM_TOPICS: A list of topics supported by the server. (The item name is "Topics".)

In addition to these three items under the System topic, a DDEML server should support another standard item under every topic:

- SZDDE_ITEM_ITEMLIST: A list of items from a topic other than System. (The item name is "TopicItemList".)

In response to requests for these items, the server is expected to concatenate all of the topic, item, or format names into a single, long string using tab characters as delimiters. The server creates a data object from the string, then passes the handle back to the DDEML as the return value in response to the XTYP_REQUEST message. The client then extracts the data from the object, parses the list, and displays the items for the user.

TIP For an example of building an HDDEDATA list containing strings, refer to the TabList.C file on the accompanying CD.

Other DDE Examples

The DDE_Demo application presented in this chapter demonstrates how the DDEML can be used for communications among applications. This program is limited to a single topic and two instructions, and forms little more than a sketch of DDE operations. The complete listing for DDE_Demo is on the CD that accompanies this book.

A second pair of demo applications, named DBServer and DBClient, which use separate client and server programs, is also included on the CD. The database server, DBServer, interacts only with DDEML clients and has a minimal user interface, possesses no menu, and remains permanently iconized. The only options provided to the user are to launch the server application and to close it. The DBServer application maintains a simple address/phone book, with all user interactions supplied by the client application.

The database client, DBClient, offers one menu and four dialog boxes. When DBClient is executed, the Connect option from the Database menu initiates a DDEML conversation with the server. Other menu options are Add, Delete, and Search, each of which brings up a simple dialog box to enter a name or phone number or both, as appropriate for the command. A fourth dialog box appears to show matching records located by the Search command.

For more details and more extensive examples, a variety of sample programs are distributed with the Windows NT SDK as well as the Borland C/C++ compiler. Also, remember, these same DDEML functions are available to 16-bit applications under Windows 3.x, making these far more transportable than the low-level DDE functions themselves.

OLE Client and Server Application Development

- Object Linking and Embedding basics

- OLE library functions

- OLE server registration and selection

- OLE client development

- OLE server application development

Object Linking and Embedding (OLE) provides yet another way for applications to share data. OLE has the advantage of being virtually unlimited in its scope. An OLE application will work perfectly well even if it encounters a server that supplies data in a format Microsoft hasn't anticipated. Microsoft doesn't need to anticipate formats; if a server can handle the data, any client can receive it. A user may well apply OLE programs to tasks the developer never imagined.

Introducing OLE

OLE is a set of protocols and procedures proposed by Aldus Corporation in 1988 to simplify the creation and maintenance of compound documents. A *compound document* is a file belonging to one application (for example, a word processor) that also includes data created by another application (such as a graphics editor). Blocks of foreign data in a compound document are called *objects*. An application that receives data objects and builds compound documents is called an OLE *client*, and one that exports objects for other applications to use is called an OLE *server*.

OLE provides two powerful ways of storing server data in a client's document. The first is *embedding*. Embedding, just like pasting, gives the client a complete and independent copy of the data. An embedded object, however, remembers its origin, and the user can edit an embedded document by double-clicking on it. The double-click invokes the server application, and the editing happens there. When the user closes the server, the client receives the updated object.

The second way of storing objects is to *link* them. Linking does not give the client its own independent copy of the data; instead the client receives a live connection to a piece of the server's document, a kind of window opening into a view of the server's data. If the object is modified in the server, the modifications appear automatically in the client. If several clients link to the same object, an update in one place is visible in all the others.

Whether an application is a client or a server depends on its role in a particular interaction. One application may act simultaneously as a client and a server in different interactions.

Application-Based versus Document-Based Environments

When Microsoft built OLE into Windows, it took a big step toward making the user's work center on documents rather than applications. Traditionally, the user invokes a single application for each new document. Changing from one data format to another—from text to numbers or from pictures to sounds—usually means quitting one application and starting another. Typically, in an application-based environment, a document makes sense only when read by the application that created it.

A document-based environment, on the other hand, lets several applications cooperate in creating a single document. No one application understands all the objects in the document, but as you move from piece to piece the system automatically invokes the appropriate applications. You edit the pieces separately in their native applications, and the master document automatically receives updates from every contributor. You have more freedom to exercise creativity in combining sounds, video, pictures, numbers, and text in a single, integrated document. You can show pictures in your word processor or attach video clips to records in a database.

Compound documents existed in Windows before OLE, but their capabilities were limited. A user would create a compound document by copying data to the clipboard and pasting it into another application. In this common transaction, a data object moves from a server to a client program. But whenever the server subsequently edits its copy of the object, the cut-and-paste operation must be repeated *for all documents into which the object has been pasted.*

To create a document-based environment, the system must offer substantial facilities for coordinating applications. For example, the system must know which applications can operate on which kinds of data. As the user moves from object to object through a document, the system must recognize and support links to various other programs. In Windows, the OLE extension libraries assume these complex chores. The three libraries that implement OLE currently contain a variety of functions to help you create programs that handle virtually any kind of data object through a seamless cooperation with the program that created it.

Linking versus Embedding

An *object* is any set of data from one application treated as a unit. OLE applications create compound documents when they combine several objects in one file. The user sees all the objects from one document displayed together in a single window.

To the client program, each object looks like a black box full of incomprehensible data. The program calls OLE functions to manipulate objects; it does not need to understand them.

When importing an object, a client chooses between linking and embedding. When a document file contains all the data for an object, the object is *embedded*. When a document contains only a reference pointing to data in another document, the object is *linked*.

Both methods produce the same result on the screen, but only linked objects receive updates. Embedded objects are transferred through the equivalent of a cold DDE link; when you copy them into your document, they become independent of their source. By contrast, if you link an object into several documents, changing the object in one place causes it to change in all the others. Linked objects take less space in the document file, but documents that contain only embedded objects can move from system to system, carrying all their data with them, and do not require the OLE server to reside on the destination system. The user can change linked objects into embedded objects at will.

OLE Clients versus OLE Servers

OLE applications come in two basic types: clients and servers. If you embed a Paintbrush picture in a Write document, Paintbrush is the server and Write is the client. Write does not need to understand the data that makes up the image file. Write calls OLE functions to display the data. If the OLE system doesn't know how, it calls on the server, Paintbrush, to display data in the Write window.

Applications such as Word, WordPad, Excel, and Quattro Pro are both clients and servers. Each of these applications both accept OLE objects supplied by other servers and act as OLE servers to other client applications. The Write editor and CardFile programs under Windows 3.x function only as OLE clients and do not offer server services. (Few contemporary applications act as clients without also offering server capabilities.) In contrast, the Windows Paint program is an OLE server and incorporates no client capabilities. Instead, the Paint program limits itself to providing images and image-editing services to client applications.

Because Paint is a stand-alone application as well as an OLE server, Paint is a *full server*. In contrast, a *mini-server* does not operate as a stand-alone application; it does not contain any provisions to open or save files, but it does provide service to OLE client applications.

Servers of either type (*full server* or *mini-server*) may offer more than one type of service. Quattro Pro, for example, offers a choice of Quattro Pro Graph or Quattro Pro Notebook. MS Word offers a choice of Microsoft Word Document or Microsoft Word Picture objects.

Object Classes and Verbs

The type of data a server exports is called an *object class.* Paintbrush, for example, exports objects of the PBrush class. Different classes contain different kinds of data. Excel supports the classes ExcelWorksheet and ExcelChart. Servers register their classes in the system Registry. Only one server may handle each class.

For each of its object classes, a server also registers a set of verbs. A *verb* is something a server can do to an object. Two common verbs are Edit and Play. When the user selects an object in a compound document, the client application retrieves the list of verbs for that object class and makes the verbs available on one of its menus. The user manipulates objects by executing their verbs. Different objects respond to different verbs.

Inserting OLE Objects

The process of adding an object to a container document is simple. From within the client application, the user chooses the type of object to insert. A list box might offer, for example, picture data, spreadsheet data, and video clips; the list varies with the available servers.

If you're running Word and decide to embed a drawing in your document, you might begin by starting Paint, the registered server for bitmap objects. Open a .BMP file, select part of the image, and copy it to the clipboard. Then you enter Write and open the destination file. Pull down the Edit menu, and you'll have a choice of three commands: Paste, Paste Link, and Paste Special. All of them bring the drawing into the text file. The easiest one, Paste, embeds the object. (If Paint did not support OLE, the Paste command would merely copy the object, not embed it.)

Once an object is in the client's document, the client provides ways to activate it. Usually double-clicking activates an object. An activated object performs whatever action is appropriate to its format.

Figure 35.1 shows the process of linking a picture into a Word document, where OLE provides in-place editing (editing the picture directly within the linked document) using the Paint program.

FIGURE 35.1

Linking a picture into a text document and activating the picture to edit it

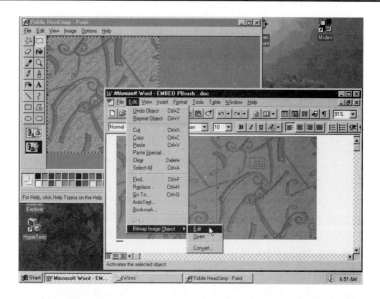

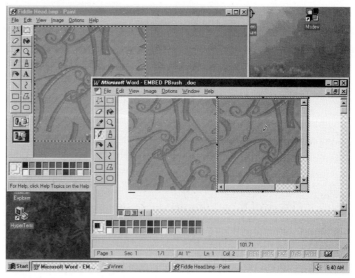

As illustrated, the Edit menu now contains a Bitmap Image Object submenu with three verbs: Edit, Open, and Convert, which are supplied by the Paint application. For a Paint drawing, the default is the verb Edit, which activates in-place editing. For in-place editing, the Paint menu, palette, and toolbars appear inside the Word document frame, allow editing without leaving the document. Selecting Open calls the Paint application with the embedded image, as shown in the lower half of Figure 35.1. Changes made using the Paint program will be reflected in the embedded object in the Word document when the Paint program exits, signaling on termination that the compound document should be updated.

Inserting Object Packages

You can also embed .AVI or .WAV files (multimedia video or sound files) in a compound document. But what does a video clip or sound look like on the screen when you paste it? In this case, the application uses a graphical representation of the data, called a *package*.

Instead of showing a linked or embedded object directly, you can choose to represent it with an icon. A package is an icon that represents an OLE object. When you double-click on the icon, the OLE libraries determine what data the object contains and perform the appropriate verb action.

For some data types, such as .WAV or .AVI files, only packages make sense. By default, the package icon comes from the program that created the data, as shown in Figure 35.2, which shows a sound package and a video package pasted into a WordPad document. The Edit menu, under the Sound Recorder Document Object entry, offers three verbs associated with sound data: Play, Edit, and Open. Since more than one OLE object is embedded in this document, the Wave Sound object must be selected before the Object Properties and Sound Recorder menu options are enabled.

The Clock.AVI file is also an embedded object and, when selected, provides the same three verb entries in the Edit menu under the heading Linked Video Clip Object. Both the .AVI and .WAV files also respond to a double-click: The .AVI object plays the video in a separate .AVI window, and the .WAV object plays the sound waveform through the system sound card (assuming, of course, that a sound card is installed).

TIP Using the Object Packager program that comes with Windows, you can customize both the icon and the label of any package.

FIGURE 35.2

A WordPad document with embedded audio and video clips

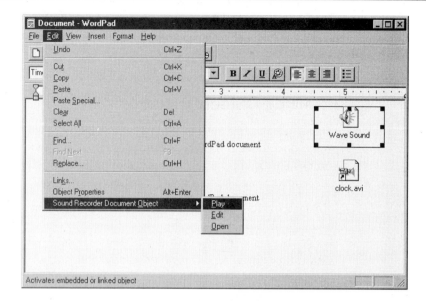

Eventually, with the help of some OLE functions, the client application saves the compound document. The document can then be transferred from user to user and read by the same client application on other computers. If the new system lacks some servers, all the objects will still display correctly because the OLE system itself handles standard clipboard formats like bitmaps and metafiles in any client without calling a server. You can't activate objects without a server, however. You can't do much with .WAV packages, for example, unless you have the Sound Recorder.

Presentation and Native Data Formats

Two of OLE's goals seem to place contradictory demands on data objects. In order to display the object in any application, whether or not the original server is present in the system, the object must contain data in some common, recognizable display format, such as metafiles or bitmaps.

On the other hand, OLE also lets the user continue to edit objects even *after* they are pasted into a new application. In order for the server to edit objects, they must contain whatever data the server uses to represent them internally. Excel, for example, can't continue to edit spreadsheet cells that have been converted for display as a metafile, but neither can client programs—or even the OLE libraries—be expected to understand Excel's internal data well enough to display the cells by themselves on systems where Excel is not installed.

The solution is to supply two copies of the data for every OLE object. You'll read more in a moment about how the server does this, but essentially every OLE object contains data in a *native* format, as the server created it, and in one of several standard *presentation* formats—usually a metafile—so anyone can display it.

The OLE Libraries

Like the DDEML, OLE gives you high-level functions to implement low-level data-sharing processes. The OLE functions reside in three dynamic link libraries. OleCli32.DLL contains all the functions for an OLE client, and OleSvr32.DLL contains the functions for an OLE server. In OLE 1.0, these two libraries exchange data and commands through DDE messages. The third library, Shell32.DLL, maintains a database of servers and data types to ensure that requests for assistance are routed correctly.

Interacting through the OLE Libraries

OLE applications interact with each other through the libraries. When a client decides to edit a picture object, for example, it passes the request to the OleCli DLL. OleCli sends a message to OleSvr. OleSvr locates a server and asks it to begin an editing session. When the user activates an object, the OleSvr library must determine which server application corresponds to the given data format. To identify servers, OleSvr consults the Shell library. The Shell functions manage the system Registry, which maps each data type to a server application name. Servers add their own names to the Registry during their installation.

When the operation has completed, OleSvr passes the results back to OleCli, and OleCli passes them on to the client. The interaction of client and server through the OLE libraries is shown in Figure 35.3.

FIGURE 35.3

How the three OLE librar-
ies interact with client
and server applications

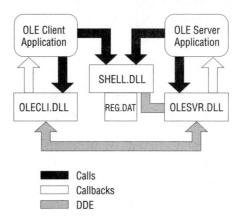

Choosing between the DDE and OLE Libraries

Like the DDEML, the OLE libraries work through the DDE protocol. OLE commands send DDE messages. The underlying DDE processes are invisible to an OLE
application. Because Microsoft developed the DDEML and OLE systems in parallel, neither relies on the other.

To choose between the DDEML and OLE, consider what your application needs
to do. For maintaining many links and updating them all frequently, choose the
DDEML. One DDEML conversation can establish many links, but each OLE conversation transfers only a single object. Although OLE clients can initiate several
conversations with one server, this incurs an overhead that the DDEML avoids.
DDEML links, however, die when either participant terminates.

Choose OLE when you want to support persistent embedding and linking, rendering of common data formats, rendering of specialized data formats through the
server, transferring data through the clipboard and through files, or activating
objects.

Viewing, Selecting, and Registering OLE Servers

When an OLE server is installed on your system or is first executed, it registers itself with the Windows Registry. This registration includes, among other elements, the name and location of the server, as well as the various types of services which it is prepared to supply.

In turn, an OLE client application can query this Registry to find an appropriate server and service. The Registry information can also be accessed directly using the RegEdit (Windows 95) or RegEdt32 (Windows NT) utility located in your \WINDOWS or \WINDOWS\SYSTEM directories.

Using the Registry Editor

Windows 95 and NT do not install the RegEdit utility in a program group or program menu for ready access. This is not an oversight on the part of the designers at Microsoft; it's a deliberate choice to keep the RegEdit utility from being discovered by inexperienced users, because the RegEdit utility is not intended for casual use. Used incorrectly, RegEdit has the ability to literally trash your system. RegEdit provides access to far more than OLE server information. The Registry contains information concerning most of the applications installed on the system, user configuration information, system configuration information, and similar data. Some of these data settings, if changed unwisely or inaccurately, can very easily bring your operating system to its knees.

WARNING Before changing Registry information using the RegEdit utility, *always* make a backup copy of the Registry. The Registry can be copied, using the Registry/Export Registry File option, to another drive or to another directory. Then in the case of a severe error, you can use that backup copy to replace the damaged Registry (SYSTEM.DAT) and restore your previous configuration.

Most of the time, there is no need to access the Registry directly. A number of mechanisms provide indirect access, such as the COleInsertDialog method (discussed shortly), for safe (but restricted) access to Registry information.

Cautions aside, there may still be occasions when you need to access the Registry directly, even if only for information. Figure 35.4 shows the Registry Editor (RegEdit) after using the Edit/Find function to locate the Excel application Registry. Actually, there are quite a few entries for Excel, but the one we want is the class ID. This is found under the branch HKEY_CLASSES_ROOT\CLSID\ and identified by a unique (generated) class ID entry: 00020810-0000-0000-C0000-000000000046. As you might guess, simply looking for this entry by scrolling though the tree would be a rather frustrating task.

FIGURE 35.4

The Registry Editor

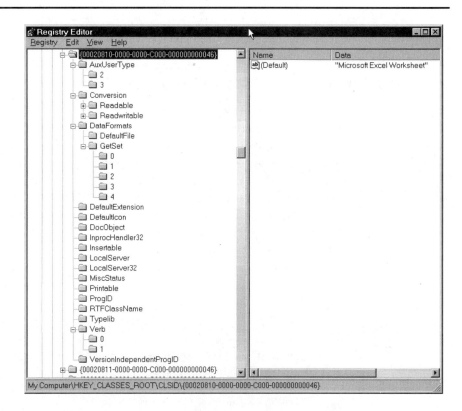

> **NOTE**
>
> As with most Registry entries, this same information can also be found under the entry: HKEY_LOCAL_MACHINE\SOFTWARE\Classes\CLSID as well as other locations. This duplication is not unusual.

For direct access, the only practical method of finding a particular entry (unless you're fairly certain of the location) is to use the Find and Find Next functions to search for a string or another known value.

Once the item desired has been located, a considerable amount of information becomes available. As you can see in Figure 35.4, the available information includes data formats, conversion options, the default extension(s) and icon, the program ID and, not least, which action verbs the OLE server supports.

TIP

Visual C++ includes an application titled OLE2View (located on the VC++ CD in the \MSDEV\Samples\MFC\OLE\OleView directory), which provides another way to view information about OLE applications. Unfortunately, the current version has a few errors requiring some work before the application can be compiled. Despite the errors and the lack of documentation, the OLE2View application does provide an interesting view of a variety of OLE-support functions.

Selecting a Server

Before an OLE client can use server services, the client application must to select an OLE server. How a server is selected varies depending on how the client application chooses to set up the menu options. For the Ole_Client demo application presented in this chapter, the Edit menu's Insert New Object option calls the Insert Object dialog box, shown in Figure 35.5.

FIGURE 35.5

The Insert Object dialog box

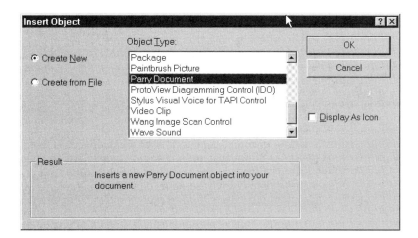

1199

Restoring the Registry

A backup copy of the system Registry is automatically stored as SYSTEM.DA0 (zero) and as USER.DA0 (zero) and can be used to restore damaged Registry files. If your Registry information has become corrupted, follow these steps:

1. Click on the Start button, and then click on Shut Down.

2. Click on Restart The Computer In MS-DOS Mode, and then click on Yes.

3. Change to your Windows directory. For example, if your Windows directory is C:\Windows, type the following:

   ```
   cd c:\windows
   ```

4. Type the following commands, pressing Enter after each one. (Note that SYSTEM.DA0 and USER.DA0. contain the number zero.)

   ```
   attrib -h -r -s system.dat
   attrib -h -r -s system.da0
   copy system.da0 system.dat
   attrib -h -r -s user.dat
   attrib -h -r -s user.da0
   copy user.da0 user.dat
   ```

5. Restart your computer.

Following this procedure will restore your Registry to its state when you last successfully started your computer.

The list box in the Insert Object dialog box lists all of the registered OLE server object types. The Result display below offers a brief explanation of the selected item. The Create New radio button is selected by default.

At the right of the Insert Object dialog box, the Display As Icon checkbox can be selected to insert the object as an icon rather than an active item. The advantage is that an iconized object does not require redrawing and remains inactive until selected.

The Create from File radio button changes the Insert Object dialog box to allow selection of a file of any type for insertion as an OLE object, as shown in Figure 35.6. (Insertion, of course, does not guarantee that there is a supporting server for the file.) Here, you may enter path and filename information directly or click on the Browse button to call the standard file-selection dialog box. After a file is selected, click on OK to insert the file into the application. Files are always inserted with icon representation, regardless of the selection made in the Display As Icon checkbox.

FIGURE 35.6

Inserting a file object

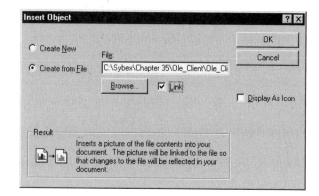

If the Link checkbox is selected, any changes to an OLE file object through external sources, such as when you edit the file through another application, are immediately reflected in the linked object.

> **NOTE**   AppWizard supports full in-place editing for only OLE server objects, not for files. To fully support embedded or linked files, either the client application must be modified to provide support or the Packager option of the Edit menu may be used to call the appropriate support utility.

Registering an OLE Server

You've been introduced to the RegEdit utility for viewing the Registry and to the Insert Object dialog box for selecting a registered server. But how do you register an OLE server?

Full server applications register themselves, automatically, the first time the server application is executed as a stand-alone process by invoking the `COleServerRegister` member. Furthermore, if the application was created using MFC and the AppWizard, the `COleServerRegister` function was installed in the `InitInstance` procedure as a call to the `COleTemplate-Server::RegisterAll` function. These processes are described later in the chapter.

For *mini-server* applications, which cannot run as stand-alone applications, a different approach is necessary. AppWizard provides for registering a mini-server by creating a REG script for the server application:

```
REGEDIT
; This .REG file may be used by your SETUP program.
;    If a SETUP program is not available, the entries below will be
;    registered in your InitInstance automatically with a call to
;    CWinApp::RegisterShellFileTypes and COleObjectFactory::UpdateRegistryAll.

HKEY_CLASSES_ROOT\Parry.Document = Parry Document
HKEY_CLASSES_ROOT\Parry.Document\protocol\StdFileEditing\server = PARRY.EXE
HKEY_CLASSES_ROOT\Parry.Document\protocol\StdFileEditing\verb\0 = &Edit
HKEY_CLASSES_ROOT\Parry.Document\Insertable =
HKEY_CLASSES_ROOT\Parry.Document\CLSID = {C6A0FC60-3173-11D0-93D7-BA6083000000}
HKEY_CLASSES_ROOT\CLSID\{C6A0FC60-3173-11D0-93D7-BA6083000000} = Parry Document
HKEY_CLASSES_ROOT\CLSID\{C6A0FC60-3173-11D0-93D7-BA6083000000}\DefaultIcon =
PARRY.EXE,1
HKEY_CLASSES_ROOT\CLSID\{C6A0FC60-3173-11D0-93D7-BA6083000000}\LocalServer32 =
PARRY.EXE
HKEY_CLASSES_ROOT\CLSID\{C6A0FC60-3173-11D0-93D7-BA6083000000}\ProgId =
Parry.Document
HKEY_CLASSES_ROOT\CLSID\{C6A0FC60-3173-11D0-93D7-BA6083000000}\MiscStatus = 32
HKEY_CLASSES_ROOT\CLSID\{C6A0FC60-3173-11D0-93D7-BA6083000000}\AuxUserType\3 =
Parry
HKEY_CLASSES_ROOT\CLSID\{C6A0FC60-3173-11D0-93D7-BA6083000000}\AuxUserType\2 =
Parry
HKEY_CLASSES_ROOT\CLSID\{C6A0FC60-3173-11D0-93D7-BA6083000000}\Insertable =
HKEY_CLASSES_ROOT\CLSID\{C6A0FC60-3173-11D0-93D7-BA6083000000}\verb\1 =
&Open,0,2
HKEY_CLASSES_ROOT\CLSID\{C6A0FC60-3173-11D0-93D7-BA6083000000}\verb\0 =
&Edit,0,2
HKEY_CLASSES_ROOT\CLSID\{C6A0FC60-3173-11D0-93D7-BA6083000000}\InprocHandler32 =
ole32.dll
```

Normally, when a finished application is installed, the Setup procedure also executes the REG script. For development purposes, however, the RegEdit utility can also be used to execute this script directly. From the Registry menu in RegEdit, select Import Registry Files to open the file-selection dialog box. Select the application's REG script. A few seconds later, RegEdit should inform you that the Registry information has been entered, which is all that is required.

Creating an OLE Client Application

In the past, creating any OLE application was a long and involved process requiring hundreds of lines of code, simply to provide the most rudimentary client capabilities. The good news is that creating an OLE client application using the MFC and the AppWizard (or their equivalent in other compilers) is almost trivial.

Using MFC's AppWizard to build the skeleton for your application, in Step 3 of the AppWizard process, you are presented with an option to include OLE compound document support in your application, as shown in Figure 35.7. (In Step 1 of the AppWizard process, you must select a multi-document application; OLE support does not function for single-document applications.) By default, the None option is checked. To provide OLE client support, simply select the Container option from the list. Following Step 3, continue to specify the remainder of the options required for your application.

WARNING While you are experimenting, there is one restriction to observe in creating an OLE client application. Do not name the application "OLE Client" or "OLEClient" (however, "OLE_Client," with an underscore, is permissible). Using either of these proscribed names results in a `COleClientDoc` class being created as an application class, leading to a conflict with the library class of the same name, which is required to support OLE client operations.

When you complete the AppWizard specifications, MFC creates a multidocument interface with the usual object classes but includes one new object class: the client item, `COle_ClientCntrItem` (container item).

And—SURPRISE!—you now have an OLE client application that is completely ready to compile, link, and execute. More important, the OLE client is ready to operate without any further provisions to support OLE. Granted, this simple

FIGURE 35.7

Adding OLE client support for an application

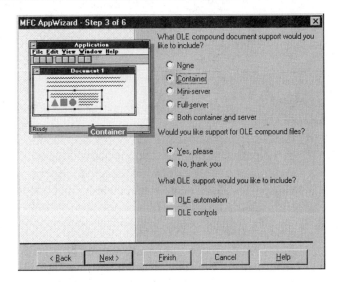

application does not do much other than accept OLE support from server applications. However, given the complexity of creating an OLE client from scratch, this in itself is no small matter.

Client Support and Control Methods

When you create an OLE client application through the AppWizard, it provides classes and functions that handle client support and connections to embedded or linked OLE items.

The COle_ClientView Class

When you instruct AppWizard to provide OLE client support, the `COle_ClientView` class is created, with seven OLE client support functions, which are already fully implemented. These functions are discussed in the following sections.

OnInitialUpdate This function includes a provision to set the member variable `m_pSelection` to NULL where the `m_pSelection` member is a pointer to a `COle_ContainerCntrItem` object.

```
void COle_ClientView::OnInitialUpdate()
{
   CView::OnInitialUpdate();

   m_pSelection = NULL;    // initialize selection
}
```

The default provision shown is adequate for most purposes. However, if you are going to use something besides the default selection mechanisms for variant server classes, you will need to provide the appropriate initialization.

OnDraw   This function, which should be familiar from earlier examples, is expected to draw application-specific data for the client window (the document window). For OLE objects, this is also where the server drawing operations are implemented. Now, according to the stated purposes of OLE, the server application is responsible for doing the actual drawing, right? So, why do we need special provisions in the client's OnDraw function?

The reason is that, before it can carry out its drawing instructions, the OLE server needs to know where to do the drawing operation.

```
void COle_ClientView::OnDraw(CDC* pDC)
{
   COle_ClientDoc* pDoc = GetDocument();
   ASSERT_VALID(pDoc);

   // TODO: add draw code for native data here
   // TODO: also draw all OLE items in the document

   if (m_pSelection == NULL)
   {
      POSITION pos = pDoc->GetStartPosition();
      m_pSelection =
         (COle_ClientCntrItem*)pDoc->GetNextClientItem(pos);
   }
   if (m_pSelection != NULL)
      m_pSelection->Draw(pDC, CRect(10, 10, 210, 210));
}
```

In this default version, the selected OLE object is drawn at an arbitrary position using the rectangle returned by the COle_ClientCntrItem class and an arbitrary drawing rectangle.

When you create a real application, your application must be responsible for positioning the OLE object and for determining the area appropriate for the object's drawing operations (see the description of the OnSize function, later in the chapter).

IsSelected This method performs a test to determine if a specific object corresponds to the m_pSelection object, returning either a TRUE or FALSE response.

```
BOOL COle_ClientView::IsSelected(const CObject* pDocItem) const
{
   // TODO: implement this function that tests for
   // a selected OLE client item
   return pDocItem == m_pSelection;
}
```

As long as the selection is limited to COle_ClientCntrItem objects, no additional provisions are required. If, however, you are planning to handle other types of selection mechanisms, this implementation will require revisions.

OnInsertObject This method serves two functions. The first function is to invoke the standard Insert Object dialog box to select an OLE object (described earlier in the chapter).

```
void COle_ClientView::OnInsertObject()
{
   COleInsertDialog dlg;
   if( dlg.DoModal() != IDOK ) return;
```

If the Insert Object dialog box does not return IDOK, no selection has been made and no further action is necessary.

However, assuming that an OLE object has been selected, OnInsertObject is responsible for connecting the item to the application document. It begins by declaring a new instance of the COle_ClientCntrItem class.

```
   BeginWaitCursor();
   COle_ClientCntrItem* pItem = NULL;
   TRY
   {
      // Create new item connected to this document
      COle_ClientDoc* pDoc = GetDocument();
      ASSERT_VALID(pDoc);
      pItem = new COle_ClientCntrItem(pDoc);
      ASSERT_VALID(pItem);
```

Next, the OLE item must be initialized from the dialog data.

```
if (!dlg.CreateItem(pItem))
    AfxThrowMemoryException();   // any exception will do
```

Assuming that the item was created from the class list (rather than from a file), the object's OLE server is launched to edit the item. In this case, however, editing is simply the method used to create the item's data rather than a process to change the object.

If there is a problem (because of a failure of the server or the system), an exception is thrown and the current TRY loop terminates before the CATCH response (following) takes over to report the failure.

NOTE The phrase *throwing an exception* refers to intercepting an error condition and generating (*throwing*) an exception condition to allow an exception handler to either correct the error or to recover from the error without terminating the application.

Once the object has been created, the server is instructed to show the selected object.

```
ASSERT_VALID(pItem);
if (dlg.GetSelectionType() ==
    COleInsertDialog::createNewItem)
    pItem->DoVerb(OLEIVERB_SHOW, this);
```

Notice that a number of ASSERT_VALID statements are included in the TRY...CATCH loop. These are present only for debugging purposes, and when the application is compiled for release, have no affect. The TRY...CATCH loop, however, is active both in the debug version and the release version.

Last, the default provisions in the OnInsertObject method set the current selection (m_pSelection) to point to the last selected item before calling the document with an UpdateAllViews instruction, which will result in the document (and, therefore, the view) being refreshed.

```
ASSERT_VALID(pItem);
m_pSelection = pItem;   // set selection to last inserted item
pDoc->UpdateAllViews(NULL);
}
```

If you don't want the last selected item to be the current selection, this portion of the code can be revised to create a different selection. However, regardless of how the default selection is made, clicking on an object in the document should still change the object selection.

The CATCH loop simply provides the standard error trapping when an error exception is generated.

```
CATCH(CException, e)
{
    if (pItem != NULL)
    {
        ASSERT_VALID(pItem);
        pItem->Delete();
    }
    AfxMessageBox(IDP_FAILED_TO_CREATE);
}
END_CATCH
EndWaitCursor();
}
```

OnCancelEditCntr   This method provides the standard keyboard UI (User Interface) to cancel an in-place editing session, allowing the client, not the server, to deactivate the operation.

```
void COle_ClientView::OnCancelEditCntr()
{
    // Close any in-place active item on this view.
    COleClientItem* pActiveItem =
      GetDocument()->GetInPlaceActiveItem(this);
    if (pActiveItem != NULL)
    {
        pActiveItem->Close();
    }
    ASSERT(GetDocument()->GetInPlaceActiveItem(this) == NULL);
}
```

OnSetFocus   This method provides the special handling required for an object being edited in-place.

```
void COle_ClientView::OnSetFocus(CWnd* pOldWnd)
{
    COleClientItem* pActiveItem =
```

```
GetDocument()->GetInPlaceActiveItem(this);
if (pActiveItem != NULL &&
    pActiveItem->GetItemState() ==
        COleClientItem::activeUIState)
{
    // need to set focus to this item if it is in the same view
    CWnd* pWnd = pActiveItem->GetInPlaceWindow();
    if (pWnd != NULL)
    {
        pWnd->SetFocus();    // don't call the base class
        return;
    }
}
CView::OnSetFocus(pOldWnd);
}
```

The OnSetFocus method provided is used to check selection and set the focus to the appropriate OLE object. Except for very unusual circumstances, this method should not require revision.

OnSize   This method allows the user to resize an OLE object by selecting the object and dragging the object outline.

```
void COle_ClientView::OnSize(UINT nType, int cx, int cy)
{
    CView::OnSize(nType, cx, cy);
    COleClientItem* pActiveItem =
        GetDocument()->GetInPlaceActiveItem(this);
    if (pActiveItem != NULL)
        pActiveItem->SetItemRects();
}
```

Except for very unusual circumstances, this method should not require revision.

The COle_ClientCntrItem Class

The COle_ClientCntrItem class is derived from the COleClientItem class and is used to provide a connection to an embedded or linked OLE item. The COle_ClientCntrItem class created by AppWizard is a minimal implementation; the real functionality is supplied by the parent COleClientItem class.

> **NOTE** There are more than 70 OLE-handling methods supplied by library and API functions. For more details, refer to the online documentation.

The `COleClientItem` creation methods provide functions to create both embedded and linked items from the clipboard services, from selected files, or by launching an OLE server. The `Implement_Serial` macro generates the basic code required for a `CObject`-derived class, providing runtime access to the class name and base class name defining the class position within the hierarchy. The constructor and destructor methods provided for the derived `COle_ClientCntrItem` class are skeletal and provide no functionality beyond the derived functionality of the parent.

```
IMPLEMENT_SERIAL(COle_ClientCntrItem, COleClientItem, 0)
COle_ClientCntrItem::COle_ClientCntrItem(COle_ClientDoc
                                          * pContainer)
   : COleClientItem(pContainer)
{
   // TODO: add one-time construction code here
}

COle_ClientCntrItem::~COle_ClientCntrItem()
{
   // TODO: add cleanup code here
}
```

The default functionality should be sufficient for most purposes but, if you decide to add custom construction code to `COle_ClientCntrItem`, you need to include corresponding cleanup code in the destructor method.

OnChange   Whenever an OLE item is being edited—whether the editing is occurring in-place or in a fully open server—`OnChange` notifications are sent to the client application to notify the client of changes in the state of the item or changes in the visual appearance of the content. The `OnChange` method allows the client application to update its own appearance.

```
void COle_ClientCntrItem::OnChange(OLE_NOTIFICATION nCode,
                                   DWORD dwParam)
{
   ASSERT_VALID(this);
```

```
COleClientItem::OnChange(nCode, dwParam);
// TODO: invalidate the item by calling UpdateAllViews
//  (with hints appropriate to your application)
GetDocument()->UpdateAllViews(NULL);
    // for now just update ALL views/no hints
}
```

Again, the default functionality will serve for most purposes. However, developers may wish to alter the update performance for special circumstances.

OnChangeItemPosition This function is used during in-place activation to change the position of the in-place window. This may be done because changes to the data in the server document require a change in extent or may be a response to in-place resizing. The default operation is to call the base class `COle-ClientItem::OnChangeItemPosition` with the new in-place window rectangle. In turn, the `COleClientItem::SetItemRects` function is notified to move and/or resize the item to fit the specified rectangle.

```
BOOL COle_ClientCntrItem::OnChangeItemPosition
                          (const CRect& rectPos)
{
    ASSERT_VALID(this);
    if (!COleClientItem::OnChangeItemPosition(rectPos))
        return FALSE;
    // TODO: update any cache of the item's rectangle/extent
    return TRUE;
}
```

If you wish to provide your own resizing implementation, refer to the `Set-Extent` method for embedded OLE items.

OnGetItemPosition This method is called to determine the location of an item during in-place activation. The default implementation provided simply returns a hard-coded rectangle, which was defined by AppWizard.

```
void COle_ClientCntrItem::OnGetItemPosition(CRect& rPosition)
{
    ASSERT_VALID(this);
    // TODO: return correct rectangle (in pixels) in rPosition
    rPosition.SetRect(10, 10, 210, 210);
}
```

For a more sophisticated approach, this rectangle should reflect the current position of the item relative to the view used for activation. To obtain the view, call `COle_ClientCntrItem::GetActiveView`.

OnActivate   This function is used to activate an OLE item in-place by calling the `COleDocument::GetInPlaceActiveItem` function.

```
void COle_ClientCntrItem::OnActivate()
{
    COle_ClientView* pView = GetActiveView();
    ASSERT_VALID(pView);
    COleClientItem* pItem =
        GetDocument()->GetInPlaceActiveItem(pView);
    if (pItem != NULL && pItem != this)
        pItem->Close();
    COleClientItem::OnActivate();
}
```

Only one item (per frame) can be activated at a time.

OnDeactivate   This function is called when an item that was activated in-place is to be deactivated. This restores the container application's user interface to its original state, hiding any menus and other controls that were created for in-place activation.

```
void COle_ClientCntrItem::OnDeactivateUI(BOOL bUndoable)
{
    COleClientItem::OnDeactivateUI(bUndoable);

    DWORD dwMisc = 0;
    m_lpObject->GetMiscStatus(GetDrawAspect(), &dwMisc);
    if (dwMisc & OLEMISC_INSIDEOUT)
        DoVerb(OLEIVERB_HIDE, NULL);
}
```

If `bUndoable` is FALSE, the container should disable the Undo command, in effect discarding the undo state of the container, because it indicates that the last operation performed by the server is not undoable.

Serialize   This method is used to load or store data related to an OLE item within the client document. By default, the data contained within an OLE object is handled by the OLE server and does not require handling by the OLE client. Depending on the type of application you are designing, however, you may need to store references to the linked/embedded items as part of your document storage.

```
void COle_ClientCntrItem::Serialize(CArchive& ar)
{
    ASSERT_VALID(this);
    COleClientItem::Serialize(ar);

    // now store/retrieve data specific to COle_ClientCntrItem
    if (ar.IsStoring())
    {
        // TODO: add storing code here
    }
    else
    {
        // TODO: add loading code here
    }
}
```

Other Methods   There are a host of methods supplied by the parent class, COleClientItem, which may be overwritten when special handling is needed by your application. Status methods provide functions to retrieve OLE item aspects, including the item's class ID, the view aspect, and the OLE type and descriptive string.

The clipboard services support drag-and-drop operations and allow items to be retrieved from the clipboard or passed to the clipboard. Additional methods allow items to be drawn, closed, released, or executed. Object activation is provided by a series of functions handing different aspects of activation. The SetExtent and SetItemRects methods provide resizing. All in all, there are 20 or more functions for various aspects of OLE client operations.

Given these possibilities, you may be properly relieved to know that you do not need to write all of these yourself. For the most part, the default functionality for a client has been supplied. And, when necessary, you can override or extend the default methods.

Creating an OLE Server

Just as you can use the MFC and AppWizard to create an OLE client, these services also provide the means to create a basic OLE server, offering a choice of a mini-server or full-server application.

OLE Server Types

OLE server applications are defined by four base classes: the COleServerDoc and COleServerItem classes used by all server applications, the COleServer class used by mini-servers, and the COleTemplateServer class used by full-server applications.

SDI (Single Document Interface) servers are probably the most common type of OLE servers as well as the simplest to implement. Each SDI server uses a single server object and a single document object but launches a new server instance for each client requesting service. Table 35.1 shows the SDI architecture characteristics. Because mini-servers do not support multiple links, an SDI mini-server offers only one item object. In contrast, a full server supplies multiple item objects when multiple clients are linked to the same document.

TABLE 35.1   SDI Server, Multiple Instances

Class Type	Classes	Mini-Server Objects	Full-server Objects
Server	1	1	1
Document	1	1	1
Item	1	1	Many

MDI (Multiple Document Interface) servers are used when DGROUP (the default data segment) memory constraints preclude multiple-instance servers or when a full server needs to be MDI in stand-alone mode. For mini-servers, there is still only one item per document. Table 35.2 shows characteristics of the MDI server architecture for a single server type, single instance.

Multiple-instance MDI servers include applications such as Excel or Quattro Pro, which provide both charts (graphic objects) and spreadsheets. Each server class has only one document class, and each server object has one document object.

TABLE 35.2 MDI Server, Single Server Type, Single Instance

Class Type	Classes	Mini-Server Objects	Full-Server Objects
Server	1	1	1
Document	1	Many	Many
Item	1	Many	Many

Since full servers support links, each document can provide multiple item objects, and each document class can support multiple item classes. Table 35.3 shows the MDI server characteristics for multiple instances.

TABLE 35.3 MDI Server, Multiple Instances

Class Type	Classes	Full-Server Objects
Server	Many	Many
Document	Many	1
Item	Many	Many

Creating an OLE Server Application Using AppWizard

Just as you are presented with an option to include OLE support in your client application in Step 3 of the AppWizard process, this step also includes selections for a mini-server, full-server or client/server application. In Figure 35.8, a full-server application has been selected.

For OLE support, creating a mini-server and full-server application are essentially the same. Because a full-server application can also run stand-alone, development testing is simply more convenient.

The combined client/server option automatically selects a full server rather than a mini-server, because the client-side insists that the application must run in a stand-alone mode (a mini-server cannot be a client without a user interface).

After you have finished creating your application skeleton, in addition to the application, mainframe, document, and view classes, AppWizard has also created an in-place frame class, CInPlaceFrame, and a server class, CxxNAMExxSrvrItem,

FIGURE 35.8

Adding OLE server sup-
port for an application

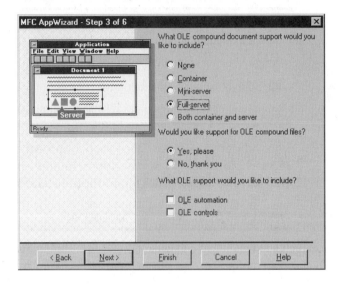

derived from the `COleServerItem` class. For the Parry demo application presented in this chapter, the server class is named `CParrySrvrItem`.

WARNING   When you are creating a full-server application, keep in mind that just because the server works correctly in stand-alone mode, this is no guarantee that it also works as a server. Later, we will discuss at least one point of failure where an application works by itself but fails during client operations.

The Parry OLE Server Application

The Parry program is a relatively simple OLE application that is intended to demonstrate how an OLE application can provide embedded services. The embedded object offers a single menu option and a single toolbar option.

The menu and toolbar entries could be anything desired and could also duplicate the usual system menus, with File, Edit, and Help entries. Remember, however, that options provided by the OLE embedded menu and toolbar, which are presented in the client application when the embedded object is selected, must also be supported by the server application. Because the Parry application does not offer File, Edit, or Help services in the context of the server application, no menu entries for these items have been provided.

The single service provided by the Parry application is the Scan action, which, in true paranoid fashion, looks for enemies (and often finds them). No, this is not a serious application; it was designed with tongue firmly in cheek and for amusement as well as education. But even so, the principals demonstrated in the Parry program still apply to serious server applications.

Table 35.4 lists the main source files used in this demo program. The following sections describe the classes used for the program.

TABLE 35.4   Principal Source Files in the Parry Server Application

Source File(s)	Function
Srvrltem.CPP, .H	Source files for the `CParrySrvrItem` class
MainFrm.CPP, .H	Defines the `CMainFrame` class derived from `CMDIFrameWnd`; controls all MDI frame features
ParryDoc.CPP, .H	Document class files for the server document class; modify these source files to add special document features and implement serialization
IpFrame.CPP, .H	Source files for the in-place frame class derived from the `COleIPFrameWnd` class; controls all frame features when the object is activated in-place
Parry.CPP, .H	Source files for the `CParryApp` application class
ParryView.CPP, .H	Source files for the view class files creating the `CParryView` class; handles in-place editing capabilities
IToolbar.BMP	Bitmap for in-place toolbar
Toolbar.BMP	Bitmap for stand-alone toolbar
Parry.ICO	Icon for stand-alone operation
ParryDoc.ICO	Icon for embedded object
Parry.REG	Registration script used to register the server

The CParrySrvrItem Class

The `CParrySrvrItem` class is derived from `COleServerItem` and provides the link functionality between the server application and the client through the OLE system. The default functionality is provided by the parent class, but there are ample opportunities within the derived class to customize the server's behavior.

The first point where the server can be customized is found in the constructor and destructor methods. The default versions are functional, but they can be modified to provide, for example, additional clipboard formats specific to the item's data source.

```
CParrySrvrItem::CParrySrvrItem(CParryDoc* pContainerDoc)
   : COleServerItem(pContainerDoc, TRUE)
{
   // TODO: add one-time construction code here
}

CParrySrvrItem::~CParrySrvrItem()
{
   // TODO: add cleanup code here
}
```

Serialize   This method is called by the framework when a data item is copied to the clipboard, an action that happens automatically though the OLE callback `OnGetClipboardData`.

The default provisions expect the server object to be embedded and delegate serialization to the document's `Serialize` function. Notice that the `IsLinkedItem` is called and expects a negative response (FALSE) to identify an embedded object.

```
void CParrySrvrItem::Serialize(CArchive& ar)
{
   if( ! IsLinkedItem() )
   {
      CParryDoc* pDoc = GetDocument();
      ASSERT_VALID(pDoc);
      pDoc->Serialize(ar);
   }
}
```

For linked support, additional provisions are needed to serialize only a portion of the server data.

OnGetExtent   This method is designed to check the drawing aspect, returning a `CSize` variable with the appropriate size information.

```
// CParrySrvrItem::OnGetExtent is called to get the extent in
//  HIMETRIC units of the entire item.  The default implemetation
//  here simply returns a hard-coded number of units.

BOOL CParrySrvrItem::OnGetExtent(DVASPECT dwDrawAspect,
                                 CSize& rSize)
{
    if (dwDrawAspect != DVASPECT_CONTENT)
        return COleServerItem::OnGetExtent(dwDrawAspect, rSize);
```

If the drawing aspect is DVASPECT_CONTENT, the parent `OnGetExtent` method is called to retrieve the `rSize` variable. Otherwise, the default implementation provided by the AppWizard simply returns a hard-coded 3000 by 3000 units (in MM_HIMETRIC mode).

```
    CParryDoc* pDoc = GetDocument();
    ASSERT_VALID(pDoc);
        // TODO: replace this arbitrary size
    rSize = CSize(3000, 3000);   // 3000 x 3000 HIMETRIC units
    return TRUE;
}
```

Normally, the server application is expected to handle drawing the content aspect of the item. To support other aspects, such as DVASPECT_THUMBNAIL, you need to override the OnDrawEx function and modify the OnGetExtent function.

The drawing mode, identified by the dwDrawAspect parameter, may be DVASPECT _CONTENT, DVASPECT_THUMBNAIL, DVASPECT_ICON, or DVASPECT_DOCPRINT. To support any modes other than DVASPECT_CONTENT, additional provisions will be required both here and in the OnDraw method.

> **NOTE**   Embedded or linked OLE items are always drawn using HIMETRIC units and a metafile device context. Of course, while the application is executing in stand-alone mode, any drawing mode is acceptable.

OnDraw   This method is provided as a default implementation that sets up the mapping mode and extent in preparation for drawing in a metafile context. But, before you duplicate your entire application's drawing routines, realize that this is not the purpose of the server item's OnDraw method.

When the item is active, it is the View class that is called to provide the drawing operations. The function of the server item's OnDraw method is to act only when the OLE item is active but the client screen still needs to be updated. It might provide instructions for a simple default drawing operation, for drawing an icon view, or for whatever is desired to provide an inactive display.

```
BOOL CParrySrvrItem::OnDraw(CDC* pDC, CSize& rSize)
{
    CParryDoc* pDoc = GetDocument();
    ASSERT_VALID(pDoc);

    // TODO: set mapping mode and extent
    //   (The extent is usually the same as
    // the size returned from OnGetExtent)
    pDC->SetMapMode(MM_ANISOTROPIC);
    pDC->SetWindowOrg(0,0);
    pDC->SetWindowExt(3000, 3000);

    // TODO: add drawing code here. Optionally, fill in
        HIMETRIC extent
    // All drawing takes place in the metafile device context (pDC).

    return TRUE;
}
```

In addition to providing some form of drawing instructions here, the SetWindowExt function call should be rewritten to use the CSize value returned by the OnGetExtent function. Of course, this also assumes that the OnGetExtent function has been rewritten to return something besides the hard-coded values supplied by the AppWizard.

Also, if you want the OLE server view to be drawn both when the item is active and inactive, rather than attempting to provide duplicate code for each operation, a simpler approach is to provide a set of shared drawing functions that are called for both.

Drawing in a Metafile Context   Although both the server item class's and view class's OnDraw methods are called with a pointer to a device context, the supplied device context is not the same in both cases. When the view's OnDraw function is called, the supplied device context is the screen device; when the server item's OnDraw method is invoked (while the item is inactive), the device context supplied is a metafile context.

There are several differences between a screen device context and a metafile context, but the difference you need to be most aware of when designing your OLE server is that a metafile context does not supply the same information as an active screen device context. The information supplied for a metafile context does not include any data that depends on the context actually being a window and an active element in the window hierarchy. This limitation means that functions such as GetTextMetrics, GetDeviceCaps, or many of the other Get*xxxxxxx* functions simply do not operate in a metafile context because there is no connection to any actual physical device context. In like fashion, functions such as CreateCompatibleDC, which might be used to create a bitmap memory context, simply do nothing.

In view of these limitations, the server item's OnDraw function must rely on MM_ANISOTROPIC mode with an extent defined in MM_HIMETRIC units. This selection is based on providing the highest resolution available.

This limitation means that both types of drawing operations must be carried out in MM_HIMETRIC units to make the normal drawing operations compatible with the inactive server drawing operations. Unfortunately, the MM_HIMETRIC mode is not necessarily ideal for this purpose. For example, consider that application fonts must be rendered using MM_HIMETRIC units. (An alternative in this situation is to use conversion functions such as the CFont::CreateFont or CFont::CreateFontIndirect to force a font match based on the relative font size instead of using a font sized according to the metafile context.)

Restrictions aside, most of the output functions, such as MoveTo, TextOut, and DrawText, still remain valid. Also, if necessary, the CDC::HIMETRICtoDP and CDC::DPtoHIMETRIC functions can be used to convert coordinates between the application's format context and device pixels.

The CParryView Class

The OLE application's view class, which is CParryView in this instance, provides the application view in both stand-alone mode and as an active OLE object. As usual, the CParryView class is derived from the CView class.

AppWizard has included one provision in the View class to support server operations: the OnCancelEditSrvr method.

OnCancelEditSrvr   This method parallels `OnCancelEditCntr` in the client application, providing the standard keyboard UI to cancel an in-place editing session. Here, the method allows the server, not the client, to deactivate the operation.

```
void CParryView::OnCancelEditSrvr()
{
    GetDocument()->OnDeactivateUI(FALSE);
}
```

OnDraw   Because the Parry application depends on a dialog box (or a series of dialog boxes) to present information as a pop-up service, the View's `OnDraw` method really doesn't have much to do besides displaying a text string announcing its services.

```
void CParryView::OnDraw(CDC* pDC)
{
    CParryDoc* pDoc = GetDocument();
    ASSERT_VALID(pDoc);

    CString csText = "Paranoid Scanning Services";

    pDC->TextOut( 10, 10, csText );
}
```

However, if we had any graphics information to display (or if we had a more conventional display), this is where the drawing operations would occur, just as they would in any conventional application. Keep in mind, however, that the inactive display for an embedded server item is not drawn in the same context as the active display (see the "Drawing in a Metafile Context" section, earlier in this chapter).

OnScan   In the Parry program, this method is called by the server-supplied menu or the server-supplied toolbar and uses a random-number generator to select the advice message to display. Technically, this is a very minimal application and shouldn't require any particular explanation.

```
void CParryView::OnScan()
{
    CDialog *pDlg;
    UINT     nDlg;
```

```
// Seed the random-number generator with current time so that
// the numbers will be different every time we run.
srand( (unsigned)time( NULL ) );
switch( ( rand() % 10 ) + 1 )
{
    case 1:    nDlg = IDD_DIALOG1;    break;
    case 2:    nDlg = IDD_DIALOG2;    break;
    case 3:    nDlg = IDD_DIALOG3;    break;
    case 4:    nDlg = IDD_DIALOG4;    break;
    case 5:    nDlg = IDD_DIALOG5;    break;
    default:   nDlg = IDD_DIALOG6;    break;
}
if( nDlg != IDD_DIALOG6 )
    MessageBeep( MB_ICONEXCLAMATION );
pDlg = new CDialog( nDlg, NULL );
pDlg->DoModal();
delete pDlg;
}
```

The CInPlaceFrame Class

The CInPlaceFrame class, derived from the COleIPFrame class, creates and positions the frame and control bars for the server window within the client application's document window. The CInPlaceFrame class also handles notifications for embedded COleResizeBar objects whenever an in-place editing window is resized. The parent class provides complete default functionality, but there are still possibilities for customization in the derived class.

The heart of the CInPlaceFrame class is found in two create functions: OnCreate and OnCreateControlBars.

OnCreate   After calling the usual default method from the parent class, this method performs two tasks: setting up a CResizeBar instance to provide for in-place resizing and providing a default drop target.

```
int CInPlaceFrame::OnCreate(LPCREATESTRUCT lpCreateStruct)
{
    if (COleIPFrameWnd::OnCreate(lpCreateStruct) == -1)
        return -1;
    if (!m_wndResizeBar.Create(this))
    {
        TRACE0("Failed to create resize bar\n");
```

```
    return -1;      // fail to create
}
m_dropTarget.Register(this);
return 0;
}
```

The default drop-target does nothing for the frame window but it does prevent drops (as in "drag-and-drop" operations) from falling through to another class that does support drag-and-drop, such as the OLE client.

If your application will be supporting drop operations, then this registration will be necessary anyway—along with provisions to handle drops, naturally.

OnCreateControlBars   This method will be called, as required, by the framework to create control bars for the container application's windows.

```
BOOL CInPlaceFrame::OnCreateControlBars( CFrameWnd* pWndFrame,
                                         CFrameWnd* pWndDoc )
{
    // Set owner to this window, so messages
    // are delivered to correct app
    m_wndToolBar.SetOwner(this);
    // Create toolbar on client's frame window
    if( ! m_wndToolBar.Create(pWndFrame) ||
        ! m_wndToolBar.LoadToolBar(IDR_SRVR_INPLACE) )
    {
        TRACE0("Failed to create toolbar\n");
        return FALSE;
    }
```

The pWndFrame argument is the client application's top-level frame window and is always non-NULL. The pWndDoc argument is the document-level frame window and, if the client is an SDI application, may be NULL. The server application may place control bars on either window but, in this case, the principal task is to create the toolbar and, by default, to dock the toolbar to the client's document window.

```
m_wndToolBar.SetBarStyle( m_wndToolBar.GetBarStyle() |
                          CBRS_TOOLTIPS | CBRS_FLYBY |
                          CBRS_SIZE_DYNAMIC );
        // TODO: Delete these three lines if you don't want the
        // toolbar to be dockable
    m_wndToolBar.EnableDocking(CBRS_ALIGN_ANY);
    pWndFrame->EnableDocking(CBRS_ALIGN_ANY);
```

```
    pWndFrame->DockControlBar(&m_wndToolBar);
    return TRUE;
}
```

The toolbar docking and tool tips provisions, as well as the toolbar button assignments, provide operations only while the OLE item is active in-place. If the OLE item is not active, the toolbar (and menu) will not appear.

The CParryApp Class

The CParryApp class is derived from the CWinApp class. In earlier examples, little attention has been paid to any of the applications' CWinApp-derived classes. We've simply assumed that these classes were there and that they provided, by default, the essentials necessary for initializing and executing our application instances. For our OLE server application, however, the derived CParryApp class continues to supply the same functionality as previous examples but now also offers a few elements that non-OLE applications haven't needed. These elements are described in the following sections.

The CLSID Value   This is the CLSID (CLaSS ID) value used by the system Registry. The CLSID value is defined in the CParry.CPP file as:

```
static const CLSID clsid =
  { 0xc6a0fc60, 0x3173, 0x11d0,
    { 0x93, 0xd7, 0xba, 0x60, 0x83, 0x0, 0x0, 0x0 } };
```

The generated value, C6A0FC60-3173-11D0-93D7-BA6083000000, is statistically unique but may be changed if you want to substitute another identifier.

InitInstance   This function begins by initializing the OLE libraries through a call to AfxOleInit, reporting failure if there is an error.

```
BOOL CParryApp::InitInstance()
{
    // Initialize OLE libraries
    if (!AfxOleInit())
    {
        AfxMessageBox(IDP_OLE_INIT_FAILED);
        return FALSE;
    }
```

Next, as usual, the standard profile settings are loaded, and the document, window, and view class names are assigned.

```
LoadStdProfileSettings();
CSingleDocTemplate* pDocTemplate;
pDocTemplate = new CSingleDocTemplate(
    IDR_MAINFRAME,
    RUNTIME_CLASS(CParryDoc),
    RUNTIME_CLASS(CMainFrame),          // main SDI frame window
    RUNTIME_CLASS(CParryView));
```

Now the `InitInstance` routine departs from the usual routine by calling the `SetServerInfo` function to identify server resources, including menus and accelerator tables, which are used by the server application when an embedded object is activated.

```
pDocTemplate->SetServerInfo( IDR_SRVR_EMBEDDED,
                             // IDR_SRVR_INPLACE,
                             RUNTIME_CLASS(CInPlaceFrame) );
AddDocTemplate(pDocTemplate);
```

The `ConnectTemplate` function is called to connect the server to the document template so that `COleTemplateServer` can use information in the document template to create new documents on behalf of OLE clients.

```
m_server.ConnectTemplate(clsid, pDocTemplate, TRUE);

// SDI applications register server objects only if /Embedding
//   or /Automation is present on the command line.

// Parse command line for standard shell commands, DDE, file open
CCommandLineInfo cmdInfo;
ParseCommandLine(cmdInfo);
```

Finally, after parsing any command-line instructions, a check is made to determine if the application instance is being launched as an OLE server and, if so, to register all of the OLE services as running (`RegisterAll`), allowing the OLE libraries to create objects from other applications.

```
if( cmdInfo.m_bRunEmbedded || cmdInfo.m_bRunAutomated )
{
    COleTemplateServer::RegisterAll();
    return TRUE;
}
```

If the application is being executed as a server rather than as a stand-alone application, the `InitInstance` routine returns TRUE here, so that the application's main window is not created or displayed.

On the other hand, if the application is being run as a stand-alone application, this is a good time to call `UpdateRegistry` to update the system Registry with information about the OLE services before proceeding with normal operations (including starting the command processor and displaying the application window).

```
m_server.UpdateRegistry(OAT_INPLACE_SERVER);
if (!ProcessShellCommand(cmdInfo))
    return FALSE;
return TRUE;
}
```

This chapter has provided an introduction to programming OLE clients and servers. If you are interested in developing OLE applications, you should refer to any of the many books devoted to the topic. For example, *Mastering OLE 2* by Bryan Waters (Sybex, 1995) provides more details about how to provide extended OLE support in your applications. (This book also includes a disk with fun prizes such as code and outrageous OLE tools.) The next, and final, chapter takes a look at another intriguing and growing field for application development: multimedia.

36

Programming for Multimedia

- ■ Windows multimedia features

- ■ Commands for playing waveform sounds

- ■ Multimedia control and file operations functions

- ■ A Sound Recorder demo for playing, recording, and mixing sounds

A guiding principle behind the design of the Windows system has always been integration. Concurrent programs can exchange data, send each other messages and commands, and cooperate in combining linked and embedded objects to create compound documents. Toward this end, the various methods of linking communications and services have occupied the past several chapters and, now, we conclude with multimedia and the multimedia APIs that further the goal of integration by embracing new ranges of data.

Besides text and graphics, audio and video data in many formats now has a place in the general PC market. For about the price of a large hard disk, you can add a sound board and a CD-ROM drive to your computer and play audio CDs, watch movies, record sounds to the disk, and create animation sequences. Multimedia seems to promise most for the education and entertainment fields, but business, too, will appreciate the new flexibility and variety of choices in presenting information.

After explaining the general support Windows provides for multimedia applications, this chapter builds a program modeled on the Windows Sound Recorder. You will learn the high-level commands for operating any multimedia device and the file I/O commands for reading and writing many kinds of multimedia data. You will also see how to play sounds, record them, change their volume, and combine them. The ShowWave demo program introduces basic techniques needed for many multimedia operations.

Windows Multimedia Support

Windows multimedia is a collection of capabilities for dealing with audio and visual peripherals. Its purpose is to allow the integration of many different data formats in a single system environment. Windows' multimedia features include three different components: audio and visual hardware devices, drivers for those devices, and a generalized API that translates programming commands into instructions for any multimedia driver.

Multimedia Devices

Multimedia operations are data-intensive; they make great demands on the CPU to process comparatively large quantities of data rapidly. The devices that store the data must meet certain function and protocol standards in order to work effectively. To encourage the proliferation of multimedia-capable systems, Microsoft consulted with a number of hardware and software companies to develop a Multimedia PC (MPC) specification establishing minimum system capabilities for multimedia computing. Hardware and software products compatible with this standard carry the MPC trademark. For example, to carry the MPC mark, a CD-ROM drive must transfer data at a minimum rate of 150KB per second without utilizing more than 40 percent of the CPU's capacity. It must also have an average seek time of 1 second.

Windows NT and 95 recognize the following types of multimedia devices:

- `animation`: Animation device
- `cdaudio`: Audio CD player
- `dat`: Digital audio tape player
- `digitalvideo`: Digital video (not GDI) in a window
- `other`: Undefined MCI device
- `overlay`: Overlay device (analog video in a window)
- `scanner`: Image scanner
- `sequencer`: MIDI sequencer
- `videodisc`: Videodisc player
- `waveaudio`: Device that plays digitized waveform sounds

The list of drivers suggests the range of hardware and data formats that Windows now expects to encounter, which are devices and data formerly inaccessible to most Intel-based PC users. Besides these drivers, multimedia also brings to Windows enhanced display drivers for high-resolution adapters and gray-scale VGA, the Sound Recorder and Media Player applications, and several applets in the Control Panel for installing devices and setting system sounds.

Multimedia Services

Beyond the hardware and drivers, the multimedia services include a layer of software defining (predictably) a device-independent interface for programs to use multimedia. A single set of commands will, for example, play sounds on any waveform device. Under Windows 3.1, the multimedia services reside in Mmsystem.DLL. Win32 moves them to Winmm.DLL. The layer of Win32 that interprets multimedia commands is called WinMM.

> **NOTE** A program that uses the WinMM commands must include the Mmsystem.H header file and link with the Winmm.LIB library. When porting from Windows 3.1, be sure to change your Makefile to use Winmm.LIB instead of Mmsystem.LIB.

Four Command Sets

The system provides four different ways to manage multimedia services: two high-level command sets, one low-level command set, and a set of file I/O commands.

The low-level and high-level commands control the same multimedia devices. The low-level commands are more powerful, and the high-level commands are more convenient. To record a sound, for example, the low-level functions make you repeatedly send the device an empty buffer and wait for it to come back full. But the low-level functions will also let you mix a new sound with an old sound as you record, scale the pitch and playback rates, change the device volume setting, record a MIDI song, and send custom messages defined by the driver. Also, since all the high-level commands are implemented internally through the low-level commands, you can get better performance by calling the low-level commands directly.

Low-level commands interact with drivers for particular devices. The more generalized high-level commands interact with drivers for logical devices. Windows NT and 95 come with three: a MIDI sequencer, a CD player, and a waveform audio player. These generic drivers translate high-level commands into low-level function calls for particular drivers. The high-level API defined by the generic drivers is called the Multimedia Command Interface (MCI). MCI commands shield you from many small details of managing data streams, but at the expense of some flexibility. The high-level commands give the same kind of control that, for example, `wsprintf` gives for string output. Sometimes you really do need low-level commands like `lstrcat` and `_fcvt`, but the high-level commands are usually much easier to use.

Only specialized programs require the low-level multimedia functions. The high-level functions can play MIDI files, movies, videodiscs, and CD-ROMs, and they can record as well as play waveform sounds.

The MCI supports two parallel sets of high-level MCI functions: a command interface and a message interface. Command strings and command messages do the same thing, but strings are useful for authoring systems where the user writes command scripts to control a device. The function mciSendCommand sends drivers messages like MCI_OPEN and MCI_PLAY. The parallel function mciSendString sends strings like "open c:\sounds\harp.wav" and "play waveaudio to 500".

Besides the low-level commands, the MCI commands, and the MCI strings, a fourth command set facilitates reading and writing with multimedia data files. The Multimedia I/O (MMIO) commands understand the organization of files in the standard RIFF format and also perform buffering, a useful optimization for data-intensive multimedia programs.

The Multimedia Timer

Since timing is often critical in multimedia, particularly for playing MIDI music and for coordinating different devices during a presentation, WinMM also includes enhanced timer services. The multimedia timer does not send WM_TIMER messages; instead, it is based on interrupts. The CPU regularly receives interrupt signals from the computer's timer chip, and the multimedia timer invokes a callback function from your program during those interrupts.

Interrupt-driven timer signals are much more regular because no time is lost waiting for the application's message queue to empty. Furthermore, the multimedia timer is accurate down to about 10 (MIPS) or 16 (Intel) milliseconds, but the smallest effective interval for SetTimer is about 55 milliseconds, and even that resolution isn't guaranteed because of message queue delays. The timer resolution varies from system to system; you can determine the resolution by calling timeGetDevCaps.

> **NOTE** The drawback of real-time interrupt processing is that it can significantly slow other applications and degrade system performance.

Multimedia Animation

WinMM includes animation capabilities. By opening an mmmovie device, you can play animation files called *movies*. Multimedia animation does not provide new GDI functions to create moving images. It works very much like the audio device, translating a data file into output. The movie player reads from a RIFF file (one containing RMMP format chunks).

Movie files can support casts, scores, inks, transitions, palette effects, audio, and other animation structures. You open the movie-player device with the MCI_OPEN command message, play the movie with MCI_PLAY, and finish with MCI_CLOSE. Some other command messages are specific to movie files; MCI_STEP, for example, changes the current position forward or backward a set number of movie frames. MCI_WINDOW sets or adjusts the window where the movie appears. But in general, the MCI commands for movies work the same way as the commands for sound, and when you have learned one set, you can easily learn the other.

> **NOTE**
>
> Creating movie files is more difficult than playing them. You need a high-level tool for designing animation. Microsoft's Video for Windows 3.1 is one choice; the MacroMind Director is another. Although the MacroMind Director runs on the Macintosh, its data files easily convert to Windows' multimedia format. (As of this writing, there is not yet a native Win32 animation tool.)

Sound Data Formats

Digitized sounds for the PC generally come in one of three common forms. One is the Compact Disc-Digital Audio format (also called *Red Book audio*). Commercial CDs use this data-intensive format to store high-quality digitized sound. Each second of sound consumes 176KB of disk space.

Another more compact storage format is defined by the Musical Instrument Digital Interface (MIDI). MIDI is a standard protocol for communication between musical instruments and computers. MIDI files contain instructions for a synthesizer to play a piece of music. MIDI sound files take up less room and produce good-quality sound, but recording them requires MIDI hardware.

A third format, waveform files, produces adequate sound without a synthesizer and consumes less disk space than the CD-Digital Audio format. *Waveform audio* is a technique for re-creating sound waves by sampling the original sound at discrete intervals and recording a digital representation of each sample.

To store sound as waveform data, a digitizer measures the sound at frequent intervals. Each measurement forms a snapshot called a *sample*. With smaller intervals and more frequent samples, the sound quality improves. Sound travels in waves; by sampling frequently we can plot more points on the wave and reproduce it more accurately. WinMM supports three sampling rates: 11.025 kHz, 22.05 kHz, and 44.1 kHz. One kilohertz equals 1000 times per second; 44.1 kHz is 44,100 times per second. In a .WAV file digitized with a sampling rate of 11.025 kHz, each millisecond contains about 11 samples.

The human ear stops perceiving high-pitched sounds when they reach a frequency near 20 kHz. For a recording to capture a sound, it must sample at a rate at least twice the frequency of the sound, so a sampling rate of 44.1 kHz captures the full range of perceptible frequencies. Commercial audio compact discs sample at 44.1 kHz. The lower sampling rates, which are fractions of 44.1, reproduce sound less well but take up less room in storage.

Three Easy Ways to Play Sounds

Waveform files conventionally have the .WAV extension. To produce waveform sounds, most programs will rely on one of three simple commands, which work best with short .WAV files:

- `MessageBeep`: Plays only sounds configured in the Registry for warnings and errors.

- `sndPlaySound`: Plays sounds directly from .WAV files or from memory buffers.

- `PlaySound`: New in Win32, resembles `sndPlaySound` but differs in two respects: It does not play sounds from memory, and it does play sounds stored as resources of type WAVE.

MessageBeep

The `MessageBeep` command takes one parameter naming one of five system sounds configured in the Control Panel. By pairing every call to `MessageBox` with a `MessageBeep`, you can make your program play sounds the user selects to indicate different levels of warning. If `MessageBox` displays the `MB_ICONHAND` icon, `MessageBeep` should pass `MB_ICONHAND` as its parameter. The sound produced depends on the `SystemHand` entry in the system Registry.

TIP
You should allow the user to disable your program's message beeps. If many errors occur, the repeated yellow-alert sirens and broken dishes crashing may become irritating.

Here are the possible parameter values and their corresponding Registry entries:

- 0xFFFFFFFF: Standard Beep through PC speaker

- MB_ICONASTERISK: SystemAsterisk

- MB_ICONEXCLAMATION: SystemExclamation

- MB_ICONHAND: SystemHand

- MB_ICONQUESTION: SystemQuestion

- MB_OK: SystemDefault

Through the Control Panel or the Registry Editor, the user may associate any .WAV file with these signals (see Chapter 35 for more information about the Registry Editor, or RegEdit utility).

Like all the sound functions, MessageBeep requires an appropriate device driver in order to play a waveform sound. The normal PC speaker is not an adequate device for multimedia.

sndPlaySound

With the sndPlaySound command, you can play any system sounds named in the Registry and configured from the Control Panel (there may be others besides the standard five), or you can play .WAV files directly.

```
BOOL sndPlaySound( LPCTSTR lpszSoundName,   // file or Registry key
                   UINT uFlags  );          // SND_ option flags
```

The first parameter names a Registry entry such as SystemStart or System-Question; alternatively, it may contain a full path name pointing to a .WAV file. sndPlaySound requires enough memory to load the full sound into memory. It works best with sound files no larger than about 100KB.

The second parameter expects a flag controlling how the sound is played. Here are some possible values:

- SND_MEMORY: Identifies the first parameter as a pointer to an object in memory and not to a filename or system sound.

- SND_SYNC: Finishes playing sound before returning control to the program.

- SND_ASYNC: Returns control to the program immediately and plays sound in the background.

- SND_ASYNC and SND_LOOP: Return control to the program immediately and play the sound continuously in the background until the program calls sndPlaySound with NULL for the first parameter.

- SND_NODEFAULT: Instructs the function to make no noise at all if for any reason it cannot find or play the sound. Normally, sndPlaySound feels obligated to produce a noise of some sort on every call, and if all else fails, it will at least play the SystemDefault sound.

PlaySound

To play sounds compiled as resources, PlaySound is the best choice. (sndPlaySound can also play sounds from the program's resources, but only if you load them into memory first and set the SND_MEMORY flag.)

```
BOOL PlaySound( LPCTSTR lpszSoundName,   // file or resource name
                HANDLE hModule, // source for resource sounds
                DWORD dwFlags ); // sound type and option flags
```

The function interprets the first parameter according to the option flags.

- SND_ALIAS: Plays a sound from the system Registry. The first parameter is an alias from the Registry, such as SystemAsterisk or SystemHand.

- SND_FILENAME: Plays a sound from a .WAV file, just as sndPlaySound does. The first parameter points to a filename.

- SND_RESOURCE: Plays a sound from a program's resources. The first parameter is a resource ID string, possibly returned from the MAKEINTRESOURCE macro.

These three flags are mutually exclusive. In addition to them, PlaySound recognizes some of the same flags defined for sndPlaySound, such as SND_NODEFAULT and SND_ASYNC. (It does not recognize SND_MEMORY.)

The second parameter, hModule, is ignored unless dwFlags includes SND_RESOURCE, in which case hModule identifies the program whose resources contain the WAVE data named in lpszSoundName. The handle may belong to an instance rather than a module and may be acquired, for example, from GetModuleHandle, LoadLibrary, or GetWindowLong.

Windows NT and 95 do not define a WAVE keyword to use in resource files the way you use ICON or BITMAP, but you can always define your own resource types.

```
<resname> WAVE <filename> // add sound to program's resources
```

`<resname>` is a name you choose for your resource and `<filename>` points to a .WAV file. `PlaySound` always looks for resources identified as type `WAVE`.

But `MessageBeep`, `sndPlaySound`, and `PlaySound` have limits. In order to control where in a sound the playback starts, to record sounds, to mix them and change their volume, and to save new sound files, we need more commands. The Media Control Interface is the easiest way to program for multimedia, as described in the next section.

Media Control Interface (MCI) Operations

MCI operations take the form of command messages sent to devices. Generally, you begin an operation by opening a device; then you send commands, such as `MCI_PLAY` or `MCI_STOP`, to make the device play, stop, record, or rewind; and finally you close the device.

The most important and most versatile of the MCI functions is `mciSendCommand`. This function is to multimedia what `Escape` is to printing: a route for sending any of many possible signals to a device. `mciSendCommand` expects four parameters:

```
MCIERROR mciSendCommand( MCIDEVICEID mciDeviceID,
// MM device identifier
                         UINT uMessage, // command message no.
                         DWORD dwFlags, // flags modifying command
                         DWORD dwParamBlock );// info structure
```

The first parameter addresses a particular device. When you open a device, `mciSendCommand` gives you a device ID; in subsequent commands, the device ID tells Windows where to deliver the message.

The second parameter, `uMessage`, is a constant like `MCI_PLAY` or `MCI_STOP`. ShowWave, the demo program presented in this chapter, sends the following messages:

- `MCI_OPEN`: Opens a device (to begin an interaction).

- `MCI_CLOSE`: Closes a device (to end interaction).

- `MCI SET`: Changes device settings.

- `MCI_PLAY`: Begins playback.

- `MCI_STOP`: Interrupts current action.

- `MCI_RECORD`: Begins recording.

- `MCI_SAVE`: Saves a recorded sound in a file.

Other messages might, for example, make the device pause, seek a location in the device element, or retrieve information about the device.

The third parameter, `dwFlags`, usually combines several bit flags that help Windows interpret the command. The set of possible flags varies for each message, but a few are common to all messages.

For example, `mciSendCommand` normally works asynchronously. When it initiates a device operation, it doesn't wait for the device to finish. It returns immediately and the device continues to operate in the background. If you want to know when the operation ends, setting the `MCI_NOTIFY` flag causes WinMM to send you a termination message. You might, for example, want to close the audio device when a sound finishes playing. On the other hand, sometimes you don't want to proceed until you are certain the device operation succeeded. The `MCI_WAIT` flag forces the command to run synchronously. Program execution stops at `mciSend-Command` until the device finishes the requested task.

The final parameter for `mciSendCommand`, `dwParamBlock`, also varies from message to message. It is always a structured variable holding either information the device may need to execute the command or empty fields for information the device may return after executing the command. Here are the parameter block data structures needed for the ShowWave demo program:

Data Structure	Associated Message
MCI_OPEN_PARMS	MCI_OPEN
MCI_SET_PARMS	MCI_SET
MCI_PLAY_PARMS	MCI_PLAY
MCI_RECORD_PARMS	MCI_RECORD
MCI_SAVE_PARMS	MCI_SAVE

The fields of these structures might hold a filename, positions in the file at which to start or stop playing, a device ID, or the address of a callback function to receive the asynchronous completion message. We'll consider each structure in more detail as we encounter it in the ShowWave program.

> **NOTE**
> One consideration shaping the design of the MCI was clearly extensibility. As other devices and other technologies find their way into Windows PCs, the set of MCI command messages and parameter block structures can easily expand to accommodate them. New drivers can define their own messages and structures.

Multimedia File I/O Functions

Multimedia data files conform to the standard RIFF format. Multimedia programmers need to understand the structure of a RIFF file and to learn the MMIO functions for reading and writing them.

RIFF Files

The Resource Interchange File Format (RIFF) protocol is a tagged file structure, meaning that a file can be divided into a series of irregular sections marked off by *tags,* or short strings. The tags in RIFF files are four-character codes, such as "RIFF", "INFO", and "PAL ". (The fourth character in "PAL " is a space.) Each tag begins a *chunk.* The most important chunks begin with the tag "RIFF". RIFF chunks are allowed to contain other chunks, sometimes called *subchunks.* RIFF files always begin with a RIFF chunk, and all the remaining data is organized as subchunks of the first one.

Every chunk has three parts: a tag, a size, and some binary data. The tag tells what kind of data follows. The size, a DWORD, tells how much data the chunk contains. At the end of the data comes the tag for the next chunk (if any). A waveform file always has at least two subchunks: one for the format and one for the sound data, and may have more. Some chunks might carry copyright and version information; others might hold a list of *cues,* locations in the file that coordinate with events in some other chunk or file.

RIFF chunks differ from most others in that their data fields—the binary data section—always begin with another four-letter code indicating the file's contents. The "RIFF" tag identifies a RIFF file, and the form code tells us to expect subchunks appropriate for a waveform ("WAVE"), a MIDI sound ("RMID"), a DIB ("RDIB"), a movie file ("RMMP"), or a palette file ("PAL").

Since RIFF files need so many of these four-character codes, there's a macro for creating them: mmioFOURCC. This command stores a "RIFF" tag in one field of a chunk information structure:

```
MMCKINFO mmckinfo.ckid = mmioFOURCC( 'R', 'I', 'F', 'F' );
```

The MMCKINFO structure holds information describing a single chunk. When reading data, the system fills out fields describing the current chunk for you. When writing data, you fill out the information for the system to store.

```
typedef struct _MMCKINFO      /* RIFF chunk info data structure */
{
    FOURCC   ckid;                // chunk ID
    DWORD    cksize;              // chunk size
    FOURCC   fccType;             // form type or list type
    DWORD    dwDataOffset;        // offset of data portion of chunk
    DWORD    dwFlags;             // flags used by MMIO functions
} MMCKINFO;
```

FOURCC is a new data type based on the DWORD type. Each character in the code fills one of the 4 bytes in a DWORD. The third field, fccType, is the form tag we said follows every "RIFF" tag. The fccType field is irrelevant for non-RIFF chunks because they don't have forms. Figure 36.1 illustrates parent chunks (or super-chunks) and subchunks in a RIFF file.

FIGURE 36.1
Structure of a RIFF file

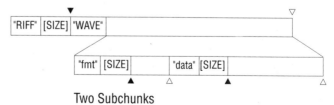

Parent Chunk

Two Subchunks

▲ Descend points
△ Ascend points

The Multimedia File I/O Functions

You've already encountered two sets of file I/O functions, one in the C runtime libraries and one in the Windows API. The WinMM API includes yet another set, having special features for chunky RIFF files. The multimedia file I/O functions understand chunks better than other functions do. In addition, they allow buffered file access. (The Windows NT/95 systems cache file I/O by default, but functions that do their own additional buffering can still improve performance.)

File Operations

The command that opens a file also controls the buffer settings.

```
HMMIO mmioOpen( LPTSTR     lpszFilename,  // name of file to open
                LPMMIOINFO lpmmioinfo,    // place file info
                DWORD      fdwOpen );      // option flags
```

The first parameter names the file, and the second stores information about its current state. Unless you want to change a default setting, such as the size of the I/O buffer (8KB), lpmmioinfo should be NULL. The third parameter contains a variety of option flags. Here are some of them:

- MMIO_READ: Allows reading only.

- MMIO_WRITE: Allows writing only.

- MMIO_READWRITE: Allows reading and writing.

- MMIO_CREATE: Creates a new file.

- MMIO_DELETE: Deletes an existing file.

- MMIO_EXCLUSIVE: Prevents other programs from using the file.

- MMIO_DENYWRITE: Prevents other programs from changing the file.

- MMIO_ALLOCBUF: Enables buffered I/O.

In the C libraries, fopen begins buffered I/O and _open begins unbuffered I/O. The MMIO_ALLOCBUF flag makes the same distinction for the multimedia file I/O procedures. The system responds by allocating a default buffer of 8KB. (To make the buffer larger or smaller, set a value in the MMIOINFO structure or call mmioSetBuffer.)

mmioOpen returns a handle of type HMMIO, meaning a handle to a multimedia file. Multimedia file handles are not compatible with other file handles; don't use them with the other C or Win32 file functions.

The functions `mmioRead`, `mmioWrite`, and `mmioClose` perform easily recognizable file operations.

Chunk Operations

A few other I/O functions deal specifically with RIFF data chunks. To put a new chunk in a file, call `mmioCreateChunk`. This command writes a chunk header, including the tag, the size, and, for RIFF and LIST chunks, a form code as well. It leaves the file pointer on the byte where you will begin writing the chunk's data with `mmioWrite`.

```
MMRESULT mmioCreateChunk( HMMIO hmmio,        // handle of RIFF file
                          LPMMCKINFO lpmmcki, // new chunk
                          UINT uOptions );    // creation options
```

To write a RIFF or LIST superchunk, set an option flag, either `MMIO_CREATERIFF` or `MMIO_CREATELIST`.

Moving the file pointer from chunk to chunk calls for `mmioDescend` and `mmioAscend`. *Descending* into a chunk means advancing the file pointer past the tag and size fields to the beginning of the chunk's binary data. *Ascending* from a chunk means advancing the pointer to the end of its data.

```
MMRESULT mmioDescend( HMMIO hmmio, // RIFF file handle
                      LPMMCKINFO lpmmcki, // place for chunk info
                      LPMMCKINFO lpmmckiParent,// optional struct
                      UINT uSearch ); // search option flags

MMRESULT mmioAscend(  HMMIO hmmio, // RIFF file handle
                      LPMMCKINFO lpmmcki, // place for chunk info
                      UINT uReserved ); // reserved; must be zero
```

After each descent, `mmioDescend` returns information about the chunk through the MMCKINFO parameter. You can also make `mmioDescend` search for a chunk of a certain type and descend into it. To initiate a search, the last parameter should contain `MMIO_FINDCHUNK`, `MMIO_FINDLIST`, or `MMIO_FINDRIFF`. The search begins at the current file position and stops at the end of the file. `mmioAscend`, besides advancing to the end of a chunk, helps build new chunks. Called after you write new data, it pads the chunk to an even byte boundary and writes the data size in the chunk's header.

The PCMWAVEFORMAT Structure

Every waveform in a RIFF file is required to contain a chunk tagged "fmt". (Lower-case tags indicate subchunks in a larger form.) The PCMWAVEFORMAT structure defines the contents of the format subchunk. The ShowWave demo program reads the format information to confirm that the sound is playable. It also remembers the sampling rate (nSamplesPerSecond) for calculating file positions and scrollbar ranges.

```
/* general waveform format (information common to all formats) */
typedef struct waveformat_tag
{
    WORD wFormatTag;          // format type
    WORD nChannels;           // no. of channels (1 = mono; 2 = stereo)
    DWORD nSamplesPerSec;     // sample rate
    DWORD nAvgBytesPerSec;    // for buffer estimation
    WORD nBlockAlign;         // block size of data
} WAVEFORMAT;

/* specific waveform format structure for PCM data */
typedef struct pcmwaveformat_tag
{
    WAVEFORMAT wf;
    WORD wBitsPerSample;
} PCMWAVEFORMAT;
```

Currently, PCM (for pulse control modulation) is the only format category defined for .WAV files, so the value in the wFormatTag field of a WAVEFORMAT structure should be WAVE_FORMAT_PCM.

The PCMWAVEFORMAT structure adds to the general wave data a single field for bits per sample; this describes the space required to hold the data for a single sound sample. The common values on personal computers are 8 and 16 bits. A monaural wave sound sampled for 1 second at 11 kHz and 8 bits per sample contains 11,000 different samples of 8 bits each, for a total of about 11KB. A stereo waveform samples in two channels simultaneously. If each channel records 8 bits at a time, a single full sample is 16 bits. A 1-second 11 kHz stereo waveform with a wBitsPerSample value of 8 would fill 22KB.

A Sound Recorder Clone: The ShowWave Program

The ShowWave demo program imitates the Sound Recorder that comes with Windows NT/95. It reads and writes waveform files, plays and records wave sounds, mixes sounds from several files, and adjusts the volume of a sound. Without a sound card, you can still run the program to open, close, mix, scroll through, and save sound files; however, the program will be deaf and dumb, unable to play or record anything.

ShowWave is made up of several modules. Here they are in the order in which we'll present them:

- **Mci.C:** Sends commands to audio device.

- **Mmio.C:** Reads and writes waveform data.

- **WinMain.C:** Contains `WinMain` and the About box procedure.

- **ShowWave.C:** Responds to dialog box controls.

- **GraphWin.C:** Manages the custom control used for the program's graph.

The first two modules contain general procedures for performing basic sound operations, such as playback and record. WinMain registers and creates the program's window and runs the About box. The fourth module, ShowWave, calls the appropriate functions in response to input from the user. GraphWin manages the sound graph at the center of the program's window, visible in Figure 36.2. When the user scrolls with the scrollbar, the graph display shows the sound wave in different parts of the file. To paint the graph display, we create a custom control and write a window procedure for it. (Another solution would be to subclass a standard control.)

Header Files and Resource Script

Following are the program's header files and resource script. A few oddities may strike you in the main dialog box's resource template. We haven't used the MENU keyword before, but dialog boxes may have menus just as overlapping windows do. Also, the dialog template refers to two custom window classes: `GraphClass` and `ShowWaveClass`. Defining new classes for a dialog control and for the dialog itself makes it possible to assign nonstandard properties to both windows.

FIGURE 36.2

The ShowWave program

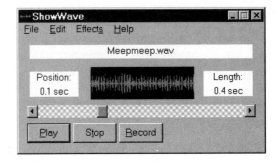

The control in the center of the program window represents the current wave sound as a graph. When the user scrolls through the file, the graph changes to represent different parts of the sound. The custom class for the graph window lets us write the window's paint procedure for graphing the sound. The custom class for the main dialog window lets us assign the dialog an icon to display when minimized.

The MCI Module

In the MCI module, we've isolated all the `mciSendCommand` function calls and built a separate routine for each command message. All the procedures are short, and most follow this basic pattern:

1. Initialize a parameter block.
2. Send a command.
3. Check for errors.
4. Return a value.

The module's eight procedures are described at the top of the Mci.C file:

```
PUBLIC FUNCTIONS
    OpenDevice          open audio device
    CloseDevice         close audio device
    SetTimeFormat       choose millisecond time format
    BeginPlay           begin sound playback
    StopPlay            end sound playback
    BeginRecord         begin recording
    SaveRecord          save recording
```

Opening and Closing a Device

Opening a device is like opening a file; it announces your intention to exchange information with some piece of hardware and tells the system to create whatever internal structures are needed to manage the interaction. The system gives you a device ID number that, like a file handle, identifies your partner in the exchange. When the interaction ends, you close the device, the system releases any related memory resources, and the device ID becomes invalid.

All multimedia devices respond to the MCI_OPEN and MCI_CLOSE messages. (The other three messages to which all drivers must respond are MCI_GETDEVCAPS, MCI_STATUS, and MCI_INFO, all of which request information about the device.)

Every MCI_OPEN command is accompanied by an MCI_OPEN_PARMS structure, defined in Mmsystem.H:

```
    /* parameter block for MCI_OPEN command message */
typedef struct tagMCI_OPEN_PARMS
{
    DWORD dwCallback;          // window handle
    MCIDEVICEID wDeviceID;     // number identifying device
    LPCTSTR lpstrDeviceType;   // type of device to open
    LPCTSTR lpstrElementName;  // input element for device
    LPCTSTR lpstrAlias;        // optional
} MCI_OPEN_PARMS;
```

The dwCallback field appears in all the parameter structures. It works in tandem with the MCI_NOTIFY flag. Any mciSendCommand function call that asks for a notification message must include a window handle in the low-order word of the dwCallback field. This way, when the operation ends, the system can send an MM_MCINOTIFY message to the window you named. You'll see how to answer the notification message when we discuss the ShowWave.C module.

The wDeviceID field must be empty when you open a device; WinMM assigns an ID to the device you open and places the ID in the wDeviceID field. After opening any device, you will want to save the ID number.

The lpcstrDeviceType field names the sort of device you need for your data. The type name comes from the system Registry, where you find entries like these:

```
AVIVideo : REG_SZ : mciavi32.dll
WaveAudio : REG_SZ : mciwave.dll
Sequencer : REG_SZ : mciseq.dll
CDAudio : REG_SZ : mcicda.dll
```

(To find these entries with the Registry Editor, go to HKEY_LOCAL_MACHINE and descend through SOFTWARE to Microsoft to Windows NT to CurrentVersion to MCI and MCI32.)

> **NOTE**
>
> When Microsoft first released the Multimedia Extensions as a separate product enhancing Windows 3.0, the second and third fields were declared to be type WORD. In Windows 3.1, they changed to the polymorphic type UINT, and in Win32, the ID field changed again to the newly defined MCIDEVICEID type. For backward compatibility, however, both fields still incongruously retain the w prefix. In the transition from Windows 3.1 to Windows NT, the MCI_OPEN_PARMS structure has also lost an unused field, wReserved0.

ShowWave requests a device of type WaveAudio in order to play .WAV files.

The lpstrElementName field designates a data source for a compound device. Windows distinguishes between simple devices and compound devices. A *simple device* doesn't need the name of a file in order to operate; a *compound device* does. For example, a program cannot choose what a CD player will play; the player plays only whatever CD the drive contains. A CD player is a simple device. A waveform sound driver, on the other hand, might play any of many different files currently available in the system; you must specify the file. The waveaudio device is always a compound device.

A *device element* is whatever input or output medium your program connects with the device. The device element is usually a file, so the lpstrElementName field usually contains a filename.

The final field, lpstrAlias, allows you to provide a synonym for naming the device you open. Aliases matter only for the MCI string command interface.

You don't need to fill out all the fields in the parameter block. You might, for example, provide only the element name and let the system choose a matching device by looking at the file's extension—a waveaudio device for a .WAV file, a sequencer for a .MID file. Or if you just want information about the device, you might open it by supplying the type without any element. The flags parameter of the mciSendCommand function tells the system which fields to read. Here is an example:

```
/*------------------------------       ---------------------------
OPEN DEVICE
Open a waveaudio device
```

```
------------------------------------------------------------*/
BOOL OpenDevice( HWND hWnd, LPSTR lpszFileName,
                 MCIDEVICEID *lpmciDevice )
{
   DWORD dwRet;
   MCI_OPEN_PARMS mciOpenParms;
      /* open the compound device */
   mciOpenParms.lpstrDeviceType  = "waveaudio";
   mciOpenParms.lpstrElementName = lpszFileName;
   dwRet = mciSendCommand( 0,                              // device ID
                      MCI_OPEN,                            // command
                      MCI_OPEN_TYPE | MCI_OPEN_ELEMENT, // flags
                         (DWORD)(LPVOID)&mciOpenParms );
                                                  // param block
   if( dwRet != 0 )
   {
      ReportMCIError( hWnd, dwRet );
      return( FALSE );
   }
      /* set return values */
   *lpmciDevice = mciOpenParms.wDeviceID;
   return( TRUE );
}
```

The first parameter for mciSendCommand can only be 0 because the device is not open and has not yet been assigned an ID. The third parameter combines two flags. The first, MCI_OPEN_TYPE, tells the system to read the lpstrDeviceType field of the parameter block because we have put a string there. The second flag, MCI_OPEN_ELEMENT, says to read the lpstrElementName field as well. Because we have omitted the MCI_OPEN_ALIAS flag, the system will ignore any value in the lpstrAlias field.

Our OpenDevice procedure returns TRUE or FALSE to indicate its success; if it succeeds, it also returns the device ID in its third parameter. The device ID will be needed for subsequent operations; for example, closing the device:

```
/*------------------------------------------------------------
   CLOSE DEVICE
   Close a multimedia device
------------------------------------------------------------*/
void CloseDevice( HWND hWnd, MCIDEVICEID mciDevice )
{
   DWORD dwRet;
```

```
        dwRet = mciSendCommand( mciDevice, MCI_CLOSE, MCI_WAIT,
                               (DWORD)NULL );
        if( dwRet != 0 )
        {
           ReportMCIError( hWnd, dwRet );
        }
        return;
    }
```

`CloseDevice` expects a device ID as part of its input. No other input is needed; the `MCI_CLOSE` command doesn't even use a parameter block.

Setting the Time Format

When ShowWave asks the `waveaudio` device to play a sound, it always specifies a location in the file from which to begin. With the program's scrollbar, the user can move to any part of the file before starting playback. ShowWave and the driver need to agree on units for measuring the file.

The possible units for waveform files are bytes, samples, and milliseconds. Measuring files in bytes makes intuitive sense. A sample is, as we said, a discrete instance of digitized sound. To measure a file in samples means counting each individual snapshot of the sound wave. Samples are taken at a constant rate, so every millisecond of sound contains the same number of samples. A sound recorded with a sampling rate of 22.5 kHz contains about 22 samples in every millisecond. Because milliseconds mean more to most users than do samples or bytes, Show-Wave chooses the `MM_FORMAT_MILLISECONDS` format. Choosing a format means sending the `MCI_SET` command message with the `MCI_SET_PARMS` parameter block:

```
/* parameter block for MCI_SET command message */
typedef struct tagMCI_SET_PARMS
{
    DWORD dwCallback;        // window for MM_MCINOTIFY message
    DWORD dwTimeFormat;      // time format constant
    DWORD dwAudio;           // audio output channel
} MCI_SET_PARMS;
```

`dwTimeFormat` may be `MM_FORMAT_BYTES`, `MM_FORMAT_SAMPLES`, or `MM_FORMAT_MILLISECONDS`. ShowWave doesn't play stereo, so we ignore the `dwAudio` field.

```
/*-----------------------------------------------------------
    SET TIME FORMAT
    Set time format.  Use milliseconds (not bytes or samples).
-----------------------------------------------------------*/
```

```
BOOL SetTimeFormat( HWND hWnd, MCIDEVICEID mciDevice )
{
    DWORD dwRet;
    MCI_SET_PARMS mciSetParms;

        /* set time format to milliseconds */
    mciSetParms.dwTimeFormat = MCI_FORMAT_MILLISECONDS;
    dwRet = mciSendCommand( mciDevice, MCI_SET,
                            MCI_SET_TIME_FORMAT,
                            (DWORD)(LPVOID)&mciSetParms );
    if( dwRet != 0 )
    {
        ReportMCIError( hWnd, dwRet );
        return( FALSE );
    }
    return( TRUE );                          // success
}
```

The MCI_SET_TIME_FORMAT flag tells the system to read the value in the dwTime-Format field of mciSetParms.

Playing a Sound

For modularity, PlayBack makes no assumptions about the device settings. It resets the time format before each operation. The MCI_PLAY command initiates playback, and its parameter block is called MCI_PLAY_PARMS:

```
/* parameter block for MCI_PLAY command message */
typedef struct tagMCI_PLAY_PARMS
{
    DWORD dwCallback;                // window for MM_MCINOTIFY
    DWORD dwFrom;                    // starting point
    DWORD dwTo;                      // ending point
} MCI_PLAY_PARMS;
```

By default, the Play command starts at the current position in the file and plays to the end, but dwFrom and dwTo, if they are flagged, direct WinMM to start and stop at other points. You may express the starting and stopping points in bytes, samples, or milliseconds, but you should tell the driver in advance which units to expect. (By default, drivers work in milliseconds.)

```
/*------------------------------------------------------------
    BEGIN PLAYBACK
  ----------------------------------------------------------*/
```

```
BOOL BeginPlay ( HWND hWnd, MCIDEVICEID mciDevice, DWORD dwFrom )
{
    DWORD dwRet;
    MCI_PLAY_PARMS mciPlayParms;

        /* set time format to milliseconds */
    if( ! SetTimeFormat( hWnd, mciDevice ) )
    {
        return( FALSE );
    }
        // The callback window will be notified with an MM_MCINOTIFY
        // message when playback is complete.  At that time, the
        // window procedure closes the device.
    mciPlayParms.dwCallback = (DWORD)(LPVOID) hWnd;
    mciPlayParms.dwFrom = dwFrom;
    dwRet = mciSendCommand( mciDevice, MCI_PLAY, MCI_FROM |
                            MCI_NOTIFY,
                            (DWORD)(LPVOID)&mciPlayParms );
    if (dwRet != 0)
    {
        ReportMCIError( hWnd, dwRet );
        return( FALSE );
    }
    return( TRUE );                           // success
}
```

The MCI_FROM flag signals the presence of a value in the dwFrom field. The MCI_NOTIFY flag tells the system to send us a message when the sound stops playing. Sounds can be quite long, so we let WinMM take over and continue to play the sound in the background while ShowWave moves on to the next procedure. When WinMM reaches the end of the .WAV file, it addresses an MM_MCINOTIFY message to the window named in the dwCallback field. Look for an MM_MCINOTIFY message handler when we reach ShowWave_WndProc. It is the completion routine for asynchronous multimedia operations.

The notify message won't arrive until after the wave device reaches the dwTo point or the end of the file. In its wParam, the message carries a result code indicating whether the operation finished normally, was interrupted or superseded by another command to the device, or failed from a device error. The low word of the lParam carries the device ID.

Stopping a Sound

The MCI_STOP command interrupts an operation already in progress. If the user begins playing a long sound and then decides not to listen after all, clicking on the Stop button sends an MCI_STOP command to abort the playback. Like the MCI_CLOSE message, this uses no parameter block.

```
/*----------------------------------------------------------------
    STOP PLAY
    Terminate playback
-------------------------------------------------------------*/
void StopPlay( HWND hWnd, MCIDEVICEID mciDevice )
{
    DWORD dwRet;

    dwRet = mciSendCommand( mciDevice, MCI_STOP, MCI_WAIT,
                            (DWORD)NULL );
    if( dwRet != 0 )
    {
        ReportMCIError( hWnd, dwRet );
    }
    return;
}
```

If we were to send MCI_STOP with MCI_NOTIFY instead of MCI_WAIT, the window procedure would receive *two* notification messages. The first, MCI_NOTIFY_ABORTED, would tell us that playback ended before reaching the terminal point. The second, MCI_NOTIFY_SUCCESSFUL, would indicate successful completion of the Stop command.

Recording a Sound

Sound boards generally include a jack so you can plug a microphone directly into your computer and record straight to disk. The MCI_RECORD message directs the sound device to accept input from a microphone.

```
/* parameter block for MCI_RECORD command message */
typedef struct tagMCI_RECORD_PARMS
{
    DWORD dwCallback;                   // window for MM_MCINOTIFY
    DWORD dwFrom;                       // starting point
    DWORD dwTo;                         // ending point
} MCI_RECORD_PARMS;
```

The dwFrom and dwTo fields name points in an existing file where the recorded information should be written. In a new file, only the dwTo field matters; new files must always begin at 0. Without the MCI_TO flag and a dwTo value, recording continues until either the disk fills up or the driver receives a stop command. To get a new file, give MCI_OPEN a null string ("") for the element name.

```
/*---------------------------------------------------------------
BEGIN RECORD
----------------------------------------------------------------*/
BOOL BeginRecord( HWND hWnd, MCIDEVICEID mciDevice, DWORD dwTo )
{
    DWORD dwRet;
    MCI_RECORD_PARMS mciRecordParms;

        /* set time format to milliseconds */
    if( ! SetTimeFormat( hWnd, mciDevice ) )
    {
        return( FALSE );
    }
        // Begin recording for the specified number of milliseconds.
        // The callback window will be notified with an MM_MCINOTIFY
        // message when recording is complete.  At that time, the
        // window procedure saves the recording and closes the de-
vice.
    mciRecordParms.dwCallback = (DWORD)(LPVOID) hWnd;
    mciRecordParms.dwTo = dwTo;
    dwRet = mciSendCommand( mciDevice, MCI_RECORD, MCI_TO |
                            MCI_NOTIFY,
                            (DWORD)(LPVOID) &mciRecordParms );
    if( dwRet != 0 )
    {
        ReportMCIError( hWnd, dwRet );
        return( FALSE );
    }
    return( TRUE );                               // success
}
```

Saving a Recorded Sound

The MCI_SAVE command instructs a driver to save the current recording to disk. If you record and then close without sending MCI_SAVE, the data will be lost.

```
/* parameter block for MCI_SAVE command message */
typedef struct tagMCI_SAVE_PARMS
{
   DWORD dwCallback;                    // window for MM_MCINOTIFY
   LPCTSTR lpfilename;                  // name of disk file
} MCI_SAVE_PARMS;
```

The string in `lpfilename` names the output file.

```
/*---------------------------------------------------------------
   SAVE RECORD
   Save recording
------------------------------------------------------------*/
BOOL SaveRecord( HWND hWnd, MCIDEVICEID mciDevice, LPSTR
                 lpszFileName )
{
   DWORD dwRet;
   MCI_SAVE_PARMS mciSaveParms;

      // Save the recording to the specified file.  Wait for
      // the operation to complete before continuing.
   mciSaveParms.lpfilename = lpszFileName;
   dwRet = mciSendCommand( mciDevice, MCI_SAVE, MCI_SAVE_FILE |
                           MCI_WAIT,
                           (DWORD)(LPVOID)&mciSaveParms );
   if( dwRet != 0 )
   {
      ReportMCIError( hWnd, dwRet );
      return( FALSE );
   }
   return( TRUE );                              // success
}
```

Handling Errors

The last function in the MCI module handles errors in any of the other functions. It puts up a message box telling the user what happened.

The error procedure needs two strings. The first, the program title for the caption bar, it loads from the string table; the second, an error message, it gets directly from MCI. The `mciGetErrorString` function retrieves a string describing a WinMM error. `mciSendCommand` returns detailed error codes that ShowWave dutifully stores in its dwResult variable. If the return value is not 0, an error has occurred and ShowWave calls ReportMCIError. Given the dwResult error code, mciGetErrorString returns an appropriate string.

The Mmsystem.H file defines about 90 different error codes. Some of them, like MCIERR_INVALID_DEVICE_ID, can happen any time; others, like MCIERR _CANNOT_LOAD_DRIVER, arise only during a specific command (in this case, Open); still others are peculiar to one device. MCIERR_WAVES_OUTPUTSINUSE, for example, indicates that all waveform devices are already busy.

```
/*------------------------------------------------------------------
    REPORT MCI ERROR
    Report given MCI error to the user
---------------------------------------------------------------*/
static void ReportMCIError( HWND hWnd, DWORD dwError )
{
    HINSTANCE hInstance;
    char szErrStr[MAXERRORLENGTH];
    char szCaption[MAX_RSRC_STRING_LEN];

    hInstance = GetWindowInstance( hWnd );
    LoadString( hInstance, IDS_CAPTION, szCaption,
                sizeof(szCaption) );
    mciGetErrorString( dwError, szErrStr, sizeof(szErrStr) );
    MessageBox( hWnd, szErrStr, szCaption,
                MB_ICONEXCLAMATION | MB_OK );
    return;
}
```

The MMIO Module

If ShowWave only played and recorded sounds, it wouldn't need the MMIO module. Several of its functions, however, require the program to manipulate the data in sound files directly. Most obviously, to draw the sound wave it must read samples from the .WAV file. Also, since the user can modify sounds in memory by mixing them or changing the volume, sometimes ShowWave must save data into a new file. The MMIO module contains one function to read wave data, one to write wave data, and one to handle file errors.

Reading the .WAV File

The `ReadWaveData` procedure loads all the data from a .WAV file into memory. It performs the following steps:

1. Opens the file.

2. Finds the `WAVE` chunk.

3. Locates the `fmt` subchunk and confirms that the sound is in a suitable format.

4. Finds the `data` subchunk and loads it into memory.

5. Closes the file.

```
/*-----------------------------------------------------------
    READ WAVE DATA
        Read waveform data from a RIFF file into a memory buffer.

    RETURN
        TRUE if we successfully fill the buffer, otherwise FALSE.
        If the function returns TRUE, then the last three parameters
        return information about the new buffer.
    ---------------------------------------------------------*/
BOOL ReadWaveData( HWND hWnd,
                   LPSTR lpszFileName,
                   LPSTR *lplpWaveData,        // points to buffer
                   DWORD *lpdwWaveDataSize,    // size of buffer
                   DWORD *lpdwSamplesPerSec )  // sampling rate
{
    HMMIO           hmmio;          // file handle
    MMCKINFO        mmckinfoWave;   // description of "WAVE" chunk
    MMCKINFO        mmckinfoFmt;    // description of "fmt " chunk
    MMCKINFO        mmckinfoData;   // description of "data" chunk
    PCMWAVEFORMAT   pcmWaveFormat;  // contents of "fmt " chunk
    LONG            lFmtSize;       // size of "fmt " chunk
    LONG            lDataSize;      // size of "data" chunk
    LPSTR           lpData;         // pointer to data buffer

    /* open the given file for reading using multimedia file I/O */
    hmmio = mmioOpen( lpszFileName, NULL, MMIO_ALLOCBUF | MMIO_READ
);
    if (hmmio == NULL)
```

```
    {
        ReportError( hWnd, IDS_CANTOPENFILE );
        return( FALSE );
    }
```

The `mmioOpen` command takes three parameters: a filename, a structure for extra parameters, and some operation flags. The extra parameters matter only for changing the size of the file I/O buffer, for opening a memory file, or for naming a custom I/O procedure to read the file. Since `ReadWaveData` does none of these, the parameter is NULL.

`MMIO_ALLOCBUF` turns on I/O buffering. The other flag, `MMIO_READ`, opens the file for reading only. `mmioWrite` will return an error for files opened with `MMIO_READ`.

```
        /* locate a chunk with a "WAVE" form type */
        mmckinfoWave.fccType = mmioFOURCC('W','A','V','E');
        if (mmioDescend( hmmio, &mmckinfoWave, NULL, MMIO_FINDRIFF )
            != 0)
        {
            ReportError( hWnd, IDS_NOTWAVEFILE );
            mmioClose( hmmio, 0 );
            return( FALSE );
        }
        /* find the format subchunk */
        mmckinfoFmt.ckid = mmioFOURCC('f','m','t',' ');
        if( mmioDescend( hmmio, &mmckinfoFmt, &mmckinfoWave,
                        MMIO_FINDCHUNK ) != 0)
        {
            ReportError( hWnd, IDS_CORRUPTEDFILE );
            mmioClose( hmmio, 0 );
            return( FALSE );
        }
```

After opening the file, we next locate and verify the data. The first `mmio-Descend` command looks for a "RIFF" tag followed by a WAVE code. If that works, the second command looks for the waveform's format subchunk.

To find the first chunk, we fill out only one field in the chunk information structure: `fccType`. The form type we seek is WAVE. The `ckid` (chunk ID) field should be RIFF, but the `MMIO_FINDRIFF` flag adequately describes that part of our target. The `Descend` command also recognizes three other flags: `MMIO_FINDCHUNK`, `MMIO_FINDRIFF`, and `MMIO_FINDLIST`. In effect, the `FINDCHUNK` flag says to search for whatever is in the `ckid` field, and the other flags say to match the `fccType` field with a `RIFF` or `LIST` chunk.

`mmioDescend` takes four parameters: an `HMMIO` file handle, a description of the target chunk, a description of its parent chunk, and some operation flags. `RIFF` chunks don't have parents, so we leave the third field NULL, but the format chunk is always a subchunk of some parent. Only `RIFF` and `LIST` chunks can have subchunks.

NOTE Pardon the mixed metaphors for chunk relationships. The terminology comes from the Microsoft manuals. Perhaps *superchunk* would be clearer than *parent*.

To find the format subchunk, we put "`fmt`" in the target information structure and "`WAVE`" in the parent information structure. `mmioDescend` will stop looking for "`fmt`" if it reaches the end of the current `WAVE` chunk. In this case, the file is unusable, perhaps corrupted, because you can't interpret a `WAVE` without its format specifications.

The second `Descend` command left the file pointer at the beginning of the data in the format subchunk. Next, we load the format information into memory for verification:

```
    /* read the format subchunk */
lFmtSize = (LONG)sizeof( pcmWaveFormat );
if( mmioRead( hmmio, (LPSTR)&pcmWaveFormat, lFmtSize )
    != lFmtSize )
{
    ReportError( hWnd,IDS_CANTREADFORMAT );
    mmioClose( hmmio, 0 );
    return( FALSE );
}
    /* ascend out of the format subchunk */
if( mmioAscend( hmmio, &mmckinfoFmt, 0 ) != 0 )
{
    ReportError( hWnd, IDS_CANTREADFORMAT );
    mmioClose( hmmio, 0 );
    return( FALSE );
}
```

```
    /* make sure the sound file is an 8-bit mono PCM WAVE file */
if( ( pcmWaveFormat.wf.wFormatTag != WAVE_FORMAT_PCM ) ||
    ( pcmWaveFormat.wf.nChannels != 1 ) ||
    ( pcmWaveFormat.wBitsPerSample != 8 ) )
{
    ReportError( hWnd, IDS_UNSUPPORTEDFORMAT );
    mmioClose( hmmio, 0 );
    return( FALSE );
}
```

mmioRead expects a file handle, a pointer to a memory buffer, and a byte quantity. lFmtSize contains the number of bytes in a PCMWAVEFORMAT structure, and mmio-Read loads that many bytes from the disk.

The Ascend command advances the file position pointer past the last byte of the format chunk, ready for the next file operation. mmioAscend takes only three parameters because it never needs to think about the enclosing superchunk in order to find the end of a subchunk.

For clarity, we've limited ShowWave to one-channel sounds with 8 bits per pixel. To allow other ratings, you could add a few variables and modify the scrollbar code. (More on that in the section "Scrolling While Playing or Recording" later in this chapter.)

We've verified the data format. Now we can load it into memory. We'll find the data subchunk, determine its size, allocate a memory buffer for it, and read the data into the buffer.

```
    /* find the data subchunk */
mmckinfoData.ckid = mmioFOURCC('d','a','t','a');
if( mmioDescend( hmmio, &mmckinfoData, &mmckinfoWave,
                MMIO_FINDCHUNK ) != 0 )
{
    ReportError( hWnd, IDS_CORRUPTEDFILE );
    mmioClose( hmmio, 0 );
    return( FALSE );
}
    /* get the size of the data subchunk */
lDataSize = (LONG)mmckinfoData.cksize;
if( lDataSize == 0 )
{
```

```
      ReportError( hWnd,IDS_NOWAVEDATA );
      mmioClose( hmmio, 0 );
      return( FALSE );
   }
      /* allocate and lock memory for the waveform data */
   lpData = GlobalAllocPtr( GMEM_MOVEABLE, lDataSize );
   if( ! lpData )
   {
      ReportError( hWnd, IDS_OUTOFMEMORY );
      mmioClose( hmmio, 0 );
      return( FALSE );
   }
      /* read the data subchunk */
   if( mmioRead( hmmio, (LPSTR)lpData, lDataSize ) != lDataSize )
   {
      ReportError( hWnd, IDS_CANTREADDATA );
      GlobalFreePtr( lpData );
      mmioClose( hmmio, 0 );
      return( FALSE );
   }
```

Finding the `data` chunk is just like finding the `fmt` chunk. `mmioDescend` fills the `mmckinfoData` variable with information that includes the size of the data. `lData-Size` tells us how much space to allocate from memory and how many bytes to read from the file.

To finish `ReadWaveData`, we close the file and return through the procedure's parameters three values: a pointer to the new memory object, the number of data bytes in the object, and the sampling rate:

```
      /* close the file */
   mmioClose( hmmio, 0 );
      /* set return variables */
   *lplpWaveData = lpData;
   *lpdwWaveDataSize = (DWORD)lDataSize;
   *lpdwSamplesPerSec = pcmWaveFormat.wf.nSamplesPerSec;
   return( TRUE );
   }
```

WARNING After closing the .WAV audio file, do not free the pointer to the retrieved data, because the data is retained in memory for further use. When the audio waveform is replayed, instead of reopening the file to read the data again, the audio player plays from memory.

Writing the .WAV File

WriteWaveData transfers a wave sound from a memory buffer to a disk file. When the user modifies an existing sound or records a new one, WriteWaveData saves the result. It performs these steps:

1. Opens the file.

2. Creates the RIFF superchunk with a WAVE format type.

3. Creates the fmt subchunk; fills in its size and data fields.

4. Creates the data subchunk; fills in its size and data fields.

5. Ascends to the end of the file, causing the total size to be written in for the superchunk.

6. Closes the file.

```
/*-------------------------------------------------------------------
    WRITE WAVE DATA
    Transfer waveform data from a memory buffer to a disk file
   ---------------------------------------------------------------*/
BOOL WriteWaveData( HWND hWnd,              // main window
                    LPSTR lpszFileName,    // destination file
                    LPSTR lpWaveData,      // data source buffer
                    DWORD dwWaveDataSize,  // buffer data size
                    DWORD dwSamplesPerSec  // sampling rate
{
    HMMIO         hmmio;           // file handle
    MMCKINFO      mmckinfoWave;    // description of "WAVE" chunk
    MMCKINFO      mmckinfoFmt;     // description of "fmt " chunk
    MMCKINFO      mmckinfoData;    // description of "data" chunk
    PCMWAVEFORMAT pcmWaveFormat;   // contents of "fmt " chunk
    LONG          lFmtSize;        // size of "fmt " chunk
    LONG          lDataSize;       // size of "data" chunk
```

```
      /* open given file for writing using multimedia file I/O */
hmmio = mmioOpen( lpszFileName, NULL,
                  MMIO_ALLOCBUF | MMIO_WRITE | MMIO_CREATE );
if( hmmio == NULL )
{
   ReportError( hWnd, IDS_CANTOPENFILE );
   return( FALSE );
}
      /* create a "RIFF" chunk with a "WAVE" form type */
mmckinfoWave.fccType = mmioFOURCC( 'W','A','V','E' );
if( mmioCreateChunk( hmmio, &mmckinfoWave, MMIO_CREATERIFF )
               != 0 )
{
   ReportError( hWnd, IDS_CANTWRITEWAVE );
   mmioClose( hmmio, 0 );
   return( FALSE );
}
```

This `mmioOpen` command tells the system we want to buffer our file operations, write without reading, and create the file if it doesn't already exist. `mmioCreate-Chunk` expects three parameters: a file handle, a structure describing the new chunk, and an optional flag for creating superchunks.

The `MMCKINFO` structure has a field called `dwDataOffset`. `mmioCreateChunk` returns a value there telling where in the file the new chunk's data area begins. It also leaves the file pointer on the first byte of the new data area.

`mmioCreateChunk` cannot insert new chunks into the middle of a file. If the file pointer is not at the end of the file, old data will be overwritten.

Having established the main `RIFF` chunk, we next create and initialize the format subchunk:

```
      /* store size of the format subchunk */
lFmtSize = (LONG)sizeof( pcmWaveFormat );
   // Create the format subchunk.
   // Since we know the size of this chunk, specify it in the
   // MMCKINFO structure so MMIO doesn't have to seek back and
   // set the chunk size after ascending from the chunk.
mmckinfoFmt.ckid = mmioFOURCC( 'f', 'm', 't', ' ' );
mmckinfoFmt.cksize = lFmtSize;
if (mmioCreateChunk( hmmio, &mmckinfoFmt, 0 ) != 0)
{
```

```
        ReportError( hWnd, IDS_CANTWRITEFORMAT );
        mmioClose( hmmio, 0 );
        return( FALSE );
}
    /* initialize PCMWAVEFORMAT structure */
pcmWaveFormat.wf.wFormatTag      = WAVE_FORMAT_PCM;
pcmWaveFormat.wf.nChannels       = 1;
pcmWaveFormat.wf.nSamplesPerSec  = dwSamplesPerSec;
pcmWaveFormat.wf.nAvgBytesPerSec = dwSamplesPerSec;
pcmWaveFormat.wf.nBlockAlign     = 1;
pcmWaveFormat.wBitsPerSample     = 8;
    /* write the format subchunk */
if( mmioWrite( hmmio, (LPSTR)&pcmWaveFormat, lFmtSize )
    != lFmtSize )
{
    ReportError( hWnd, IDS_CANTWRITEFORMAT );
    mmioClose( hmmio, 0 );
    return( FALSE );
}
    /* ascend out of the format subchunk */
if( mmioAscend( hmmio, &mmckinfoFmt, 0 ) != 0 )
{
    ReportError( hWnd, IDS_CANTWRITEFORMAT );
    mmioClose( hmmio, 0 );
    return( FALSE );
}
```

Remember that every chunk contains a tag, a size, and some data. mmioCreate-Chunk leaves a space for the size, but if the cksize field is 0, then the space remains blank until the next mmioAscend seals off the new chunk. Normally, mmioAscend must calculate the data size, move back to the size field and fill it in, and then move forward to the end of the data. By providing the size, we avoid the extra backward motion, saving the time of two disk accesses.

The value in the global variable dwSamplesPerSecond defaults to 22,050 (22.05 kHz), but it changes whenever ReadWaveData loads a new file. (Choosing New from the File menu resets the value.) Because ShowWave restricts itself to one-channel sounds with 8 bits per sample, every sample always contains 1 byte. This is why we can put the same value in the nSamplesPerSecond and nAvgBytesPer-Second fields of the pcmWaveForm variable.

The nBlockAlign field tells how many bytes one sample fills. The size of a sample must be rounded up to the nearest byte. A 12-bit-per-sample sound, for example, would align on 2-byte boundaries. Four bits would be wasted in each block, but when loaded into memory the extra padding speeds up data access. The CPU always fetches information from memory in whole bytes and words, not bits.

You may wonder why we call mmioAscend when the write operation has already moved the file position to the end of the format data. Again, the answer has to do with alignment and access speed. A chunk's data area must always contain an even number of bytes so that it aligns on word (2-byte) boundaries. If the data contains an odd number of bytes, the final mmioAscend adds padding. Otherwise it has no effect. mmioCreateChunk should nearly always be followed eventually by mmioAscend.

The format chunk written, we next perform the same steps to create the data chunk:

```
    /* store size of the "data" subchunk */
lDataSize = (LONG)dwWaveDataSize;
    /* create the "data" subchunk that holds waveform samples */
mmckinfoData.ckid  = mmioFOURCC( 'd', 'a', 't', 'a' );
mmckinfoFmt.cksize = lDataSize;
if( mmioCreateChunk( hmmio, &mmckinfoData, 0 ) != 0 )
{
    ReportError( hWnd, IDS_CANTWRITEDATA );
    mmioClose( hmmio, 0 );
    return( FALSE );
}
    /* write the "data" subchunk */
if( mmioWrite( hmmio, lpWaveData, lDataSize ) != lDataSize )
{
    ReportError( hWnd, IDS_CANTWRITEDATA );
    mmioClose( hmmio, 0 );
    return( FALSE );
}
    /* ascend out of the "data" subchunk */
if( mmioAscend( hmmio, &mmckinfoData, 0 ) != 0 )
{
    ReportError( hWnd, IDS_CANTWRITEDATA );
    mmioClose( hmmio, 0 );
    return( FALSE );
}
```

That `mmioAscend` command moves to the end of the `data` subchunk, but remember we are still inside the `RIFF` superchunk. We've called `mmioCreateChunk` three times but `mmioAscend` only twice. One more to go:

```
    /* ascend out of "WAVE" chunk--causes size to be written */
    if( mmioAscend( hmmio, &mmckinfoWave, 0 ) != 0 )
    {
        ReportError( hWnd, IDS_CANTWRITEWAVE );
        mmioClose( hmmio, 0 );
        return( FALSE );
    }
    /* close the file */
    mmioClose( hmmio, 0 );
    return( TRUE );
}
```

Before creating each subchunk, we put a size value in the `cksize` field, so that WinMM knew the chunk size from the beginning. But for the first chunk, the parent chunk, we provided only a format type (`WAVE`). The final `mmioAscend` completes the creation of the first chunk. It computes the size and records it right after the "`RIFF`" tag at the beginning of the file.

Handling Errors

`mciGetErrorString` works only with the error returns from `mciSendCommand`; the file I/O procedures have no equivalent function for error messages. We put our own messages in ShowWave.RC and write `ReportError` to display them:

```
/*-----------------------------------------------------------
    REPORT ERROR
    Report given error to the user
-----------------------------------------------------------*/
static void ReportError( HWND hWnd, int iErrorID )
{
    HINSTANCE hInstance;
    char szErrStr[MAX_RSRC_STRING_LEN];
    char szCaption[MAX_RSRC_STRING_LEN];

    hInstance = GetWindowInstance( hWnd );
    LoadString( hInstance, iErrorID, szErrStr, sizeof(szErrStr) );
    LoadString( hInstance, IDS_CAPTION, szCaption, sizeof(szCap-
tion) );
```

```
        MessageBox( hWnd, szErrStr, szCaption,
                MB_ICONEXCLAMATION | MB_OK );
        return;
    }
```

The WinMain Module

WinMain registers window classes for the main window and the sound graph control. The custom window classes let us paint the control window and assign an icon to the dialog window. This module also contains the About box procedure.

The ShowWave Module

The MCI and MMIO modules provide a modular set of tools that any program might use to manipulate .WAV files. The ShowWave.C module runs the program's main window and a modal dialog box. In response to commands from the user, it calls functions from the other modules to play and record sounds.

ShowWave_WndProc mixes characteristics of a window procedure and a dialog procedure. Like a window procedure, it calls DefWindowProc and returns an LRESULT; like a dialog procedure, it receives WM_INITDIALOG rather than WM_CREATE. Because the window is launched by the DialogBox command, it initializes like a dialog box. Because the window has its own custom window class, it must have its own window procedure and does not use the default DefDlgProc processing.

ShowWave stores newly recorded sounds in the temporary file until they have names, so the dialog initialization handler generates a name for the file by calling GetTempPath and GetTempFileName. These commands generate a full path with a unique filename suitable for storing temporary data. If the environment defines a TEMP variable, the path takes it into account. The second and third parameters of GetTempFileName are for alphabetic and numeric elements to be combined in the filename.

SWT stands for ShowWave Temporary. Since we haven't provided a number, Windows will append digits drawn from the current system time to create a unique name. The new name is returned in the final parameter.

Responding to Commands

Some of the WM_COMMAND messages come from the menu, some from buttons on the dialog box. A different procedure handles each command. StopPlay appeared earlier in the MCI module.

```
/*--------------------------------------------------------------------
    SHOWWAVE_ONCOMMAND
        Handle WM_COMMAND messages here.  Respond to actions from
        each dialog control and from the menu.
    -------------------------------------------------------------------*/
static void ShowWave_OnCommand( HWND hDlg, int  iCmd,
                                      HWND hCtl, UINT uCode )
{
    switch( iCmd )
    {
        case IDM_NEW:                           // clear data buffer
            NewWaveFile( hDlg );
            break;

        case IDM_OPEN:                          // load a disk file
            OpenWaveFile( hDlg );
            break;

        case IDM_SAVE:                          // save to disk file
        case IDM_SAVEAS:
            SaveWaveFile( hDlg, (iCmd==IDM_SAVEAS) );
            break;

        case IDM_EXIT:                          // end program
            FORWARD_WM_CLOSE( hDlg, PostMessage );
            break;

        case IDM_MIXWITHFILE:                   // mix two sounds
            MixWithFile( hDlg );
            break;

        case IDM_INCREASEVOLUME:                // make louder
        case IDM_DECREASEVOLUME:                // make softer
            ChangeVolume( hDlg, iCmd==IDM_INCREASEVOLUME );
            break;

        case IDM_ABOUT:                         // show About box
            DialogBox( GetWindowInstance(hDlg),
                       MAKEINTRESOURCE(DLG_ABOUT),
                       hDlg, About_DlgProc );
            break;
```

```
        case IDD_PLAY:                    // play a sound
            PlayWaveFile( hDlg );
            break;

        case IDD_RECORD:                  // record a sound
            RecordWaveFile( hDlg );
            break;

        case IDD_STOP:                    // interrupt device
            if( mciDevice )
            {
                StopPlay( hDlg, mciDevice );
            }
            break;

        default:
            break;
    }
    return;
    UNREFERENCED_PARAMETER( hCtl );
    UNREFERENCED_PARAMETER( uCode );
}
```

Scrolling the Wave Image

Windows translates scrollbar input into one of eight SB_ notification codes delivered through the first parameter of a WM_HSCROLL message. The eight signals reflect the actions described in Figure 36.3.

Each program decides for itself what the signals mean. The SB_ signals are named for their most common application, paging through a document. SB_TOP and SB_BOTTOM indicate opposite ends of the data. SB_LINEUP and SB_LINEDOWN move through the data by the smallest permissible increment, usually 1. The page-scrolling messages move at whatever intermediate increment the programmer decides is convenient.

The range of ShowWave's scrollbar measures the current sound in hundredths of a second. Line commands scroll in tenths of a second; page commands scroll in full seconds. When the new position is reached, we store it in dwCurrentSample, move the scrollbar thumbpad, update the dialog text that says how many seconds we have progressed into the file, and call another procedure to repaint the wave graph. The value in dwCurrentSample measures the current position in samples.

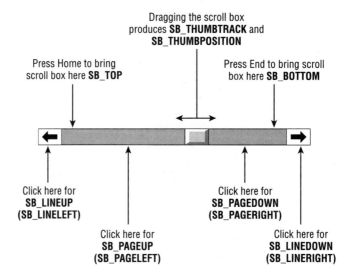

FIGURE 36.3

Scrollbar commands

Dragging the scroll box produces **SB_THUMBTRACK** and **SB_THUMBPOSITION**

Press Home to bring scroll box here **SB_TOP**

Press End to bring scroll box here **SB_BOTTOM**

Click here for
SB_LINEUP
(SB_LINELEFT)

Click here for
SB_PAGEDOWN
(SB_PAGERIGHT)

Click here for
SB_PAGEUP
(SB_PAGELEFT)

Click here for
SB_LINEDOWN
(SB_LINERIGHT)

The assignment statement converts hundredths of a second to samples. It assumes each sample contains 8 bits.

```
/*-----------------------------------------------------------------
   SHOWWAVE_ONHSCROLL
       Process WM_HSCROLL messages here.  Advance through the sound
       file according to the user's signals from the scrollbar.
   -----------------------------------------------------------------*/

static void ShowWave_OnHScroll( HWND hDlg,  HWND hCtl,
                                UINT uCode, int  iPos )
{
   int iMinPos, iMaxPos;

   ScrollBar_GetRange( hCtl, &iMinPos, &iMaxPos );
   switch( uCode )
   {
      case SB_LINEUP:
         iHScrollPos -= 11;
         break;

      case SB_LINEDOWN:
         iHScrollPos += 11;
         break;
```

```
        case SB_PAGEUP:
            iHScrollPos -= 101;
            break;

        case SB_PAGEDOWN:
            iHScrollPos += 101;
            break;

        case SB_TOP:
            iHScrollPos = iMinPos;
            break;

        case SB_BOTTOM:
            iHScrollPos = iMaxPos;
            break;

        case SB_THUMBPOSITION:
        case SB_THUMBTRACK:
            iHScrollPos = iPos;
            break;

        default:
            return;
    }
        /* update scrollbar thumb */
    iHScrollPos = max( iMinPos, min(iHScrollPos, iMaxPos) );
    ScrollBar_SetPos( hCtl, iHScrollPos, TRUE );
        /* set current sample */
    dwCurrentSample = (iHScrollPos*dwSamplesPerSec) / 100;
        /* set position and length text */
    UpdateTimeText( hDlg );
        /* paint the waveform data */
    PaintWaveData( hDlg );
    return;
}
```

Scrolling While Playing or Recording   While ShowWave plays or records a sound, we want the scrollbar thumbpad to move forward and the sound wave to scroll with it. As you'll see in a minute, ShowWave always begins a timer at the same time it begins playing or recording. ShowWave_OnTimer responds to the WM_TIMER messages.

```
/*--------------------------------------------------------------
    SHOWWAVE_ONTIMER
        Handle WM_TIMER messages here.  Update display to show
        current position in sound file.
    ----------------------------------------------------------*/
void ShowWave_OnTimer( HWND hDlg, UINT uID )
{
    int   iMaxPos;
    HWND  hwndScrollBar = GetDlgItem( hDlg, IDD_SCROLLBAR );
    if( uID == TMRPLAY )
    {
        /* set the new scrollbar position */
        FORWARD_WM_HSCROLL( hDlg, hwndScrollBar, SB_LINEDOWN, 0,
                            SendMessage );
    }
    else
    {
        /* set the new waveform data */
        dwWaveDataSize += dwSamplesPerSec/10;
        /* set the new scrollbar range */
        iMaxPos = (int)((dwWaveDataSize*100) / dwSamplesPerSec );
        ScrollBar_SetRange( hwndScrollBar, 0, iMaxPos, FALSE );
        /* set the new scrollbar position */
        FORWARD_WM_HSCROLL( hDlg, hwndScrollBar, SB_BOTTOM, 0,
                            SendMessage );
    }
    return;
}
```

The timer messages arrive ten times each second. The uID value is set when the timer begins and will be either TMRPLAY or TMRRECORD. If the timer is marking progress during a Play operation, we send ourselves a scroll message to advance the thumbpad one-tenth of a second further into the sound wave.

While ShowWave records, the size of the file through which we're scrolling changes. The scrollbar thumbpad is always at the right end of the bar because we're always at the end of the recorded data, but as more data comes in, the file size increases and the scrollbar range must increase, too. First we update the global variable dwWaveDataSize, adding to it the number of bytes received every tenth of a second. (Remember that with 8 bits per sample, each sample adds 1 byte to the file size.) Then we convert the new file size into hundredths of a second and set that as the scrollbar's new maximum range. And again we send ourselves another scroll message to keep the thumbpad at the end of the bar.

Ending a Play or Record Operation

Playing and recording continue in the background until the user clicks on Stop or the device reaches the end of its input element. When the action ends, WinMM sends the MM_MCINOTIFY message that we requested with the MCI_NOTIFY flag. The Windowsx.H file does not include message-handler macros for any multimedia messages, so we wrote HANDLE_MM_MCINOTIFY and put it in ShowWave.H. When the notify message comes, we need to close the device and kill the timer.

```
/*-------------------------------------------------------------------

   SHOWWAVE_ONMCINOTIFY
      Handle MM_MCINOTIFY messages here.  Clean up after a playback
      or recording operation terminates.
   -----------------------------------------------------------------*/

static void ShowWave_OnMCINotify( HWND hDlg, UINT uCode,
                                        MCIDEVICEID mciDevice )
{
    int  iMaxPos;
    HWND hwndScrollBar = GetDlgItem( hDlg, IDD_SCROLLBAR );
    if( uTimerID == TMRPLAY )
    {
        /* close devices */
        CloseAudioDevice( hDlg );
        CloseTimerDevice( hDlg );
        if( uCode == MCI_NOTIFY_SUCCESSFUL )
        {
            FORWARD_WM_HSCROLL( hDlg, hwndScrollBar, SB_BOTTOM, 0,
                            SendMessage );
        }
    }
    else
    {
        /* save recording and close devices */
        SaveRecord( hDlg, mciDevice, szTempFileName );
        CloseAudioDevice( hDlg );
        CloseTimerDevice( hDlg );
        /* set file dirty flag */
        bIsFileDirty = TRUE;
        /* read new waveform data */
        ReadWaveData( hDlg, szTempFileName, &lpWaveData,
                    &dwWaveDataSize, &dwSamplesPerSec );
```

```
        /* set the new scrollbar range */
iMaxPos = (int)((dwWaveDataSize * 100 )/dwSamplesPerSec);
ScrollBar_SetRange( hwndScrollBar, 0, iMaxPos, FALSE );
    /* set the new scrollbar position */
FORWARD_WM_HSCROLL( hDlg, hwndScrollBar, SB_BOTTOM, 0,
                    SendMessage );
}
return;
UNREFERENCED_PARAMETER( mciDevice );
}
```

This time, we determine which action has stopped by testing a global variable, uTimerID, which we set when the timer started. If the device was playing sound and the sound ended successfully, we finish the scroll action by advancing the thumbpad to the end of the bar.

When ShowWave records a sound, the new data accumulates in a temporary file. When the recording ends, the program lifts the entire sound into a memory buffer so it can be the current sound. Since the user has not yet given the new sound a name and saved it, we mark the current file "dirty." And again we finish the scroll operation by updating the scroll range and moving the thumbpad to the end.

Ending the Program

The last few message-handling functions help the program close down without losing data or leaving objects behind.

```
/*-----------------------------------------------------------
    SHOWWAVE_ONQUERYENDSESSION
        Handle WM_QUERYENDSESSION messages here.  Give the user a
        chance to save any open file before program ends.
-------------------------------------------------------------*/
static BOOL ShowWave_OnQueryEndSession ( HWND hDlg )
{
    return( QuerySave(hDlg) );
}


/*-----------------------------------------------------------
    SHOWWAVE_ONDESTROY
        Handle WM_DESTROY message here.  Close all devices.
-------------------------------------------------------------*/
static void ShowWave_OnDestroy ( HWND hDlg )
```

```
{
    OFSTRUCT of;

    DeleteBrush( hbrBackgnd );
    FreeGlobalWaveData( );                          // release buffer
    CloseAudioDevice( hDlg );                       // close devices
    CloseTimerDevice( hDlg );
    OpenFile( szTempFileName, &of, OF_DELETE );// delete temp file
    PostQuitMessage( 0 );                           // send WM_QUIT
    return;
}
```

To clean up, we delete the background brush created in ShowWave_OnInitDialog, release the buffer where the current sound is held, close the audio device if it's open, kill the timer if it's running, and delete the temporary file we opened on initializing. Here are the cleanup functions:

```
/*------------------------------------------------------------
    QUERY SAVE
        Ask user to confirm loss of unsaved file before closing
    -------------------------------------------------------------*/
BOOL QuerySave ( HWND hDlg )
{
    HINSTANCE hInstance;
    char szText[MAX_RSRC_STRING_LEN];
    char szCaption[MAX_RSRC_STRING_LEN];
    char szFormat[MAX_RSRC_STRING_LEN];
    int  iRet;

        /* is file dirty? */
    if( ! bIsFileDirty )
    {
        return( TRUE );
    }
        /* see if user wants to save the modifications */
    hInstance = GetWindowInstance( hDlg );
    LoadString( hInstance, IDS_CAPTION, szCaption,
                sizeof(szCaption) );
    LoadString( hInstance, IDS_CONFIRMCLOSE, szFormat,
                sizeof(szFormat) );
    wsprintf( szText, szFormat, (LPSTR)szFileTitle );
    iRet = MessageBox( hDlg, szText, szCaption,
```

```
                              MB_YESNOCANCEL | MB_ICONQUESTION );
   if( iRet == IDYES )
   {
      FORWARD_WM_COMMAND( hDlg, IDM_SAVE, NULL, 0, SendMessage );
   }
   return( iRet != IDCANCEL );
}


/*-------------------------------------------------------------------
   FREE GLOBAL WAVE DATA
      Free storage associated with the global waveform data
   ----------------------------------------------------------------*/
static void FreeGlobalWaveData( void )
{
   if( lpWaveData )
   {
      GlobalFreePtr( lpWaveData );
      lpWaveData = NULL;
   }
   return;
}


/*-------------------------------------------------------------------
   CLOSE AUDIO DEVICE
      Close an opened waveform audio device
   ----------------------------------------------------------------*/
static void CloseAudioDevice ( HWND hDlg )
{
   if( mciDevice )
   {
      CloseDevice( hDlg, mciDevice );
      mciDevice = 0;
   }
   return;
}


/*-------------------------------------------------------------------
   CLOSE TIMER DEVICE
      Kill an active timer; stop receiving WM_TIMER messages
   ----------------------------------------------------------------*/
static void CloseTimerDevice ( HWND hDlg )
```

```
{
    if( uTimerID )
    {
        KillTimer( hDlg, uTimerID );
        uTimerID = 0;
    }
    return;
}
```

QuerySave tests bIsFileDirty to see whether the current sound has been saved. If not, we put up a message box asking the user what to do. The user chooses Yes (to save), No (to end without saving), or Cancel (to avoid ending after all). The function returns TRUE unless the user cancels.

Displaying Information in Static Controls

The next procedures change static controls in the dialog box to make them show current information.

```
/*- - - - - - - - - - - - - - - - - - - - - - - - - - - - - - - - - - - - - - - - - - - - - - - - -
    PAINT WAVE DATA
        Repaint the dialog box's GraphClass display control
    - - - - - - - - - - - - - - - - - - - - - - - - - - - - - - - - - - - - - - - - - - - - - - - -*/

static void PaintWaveData ( HWND hDlg )
{
    HWND hwndShowWave = GetDlgItem( hDlg, IDD_SHOWWAVE );
    InvalidateRect( hwndShowWave, NULL, TRUE );
    UpdateWindow( hwndShowWave );
    return;
}


/*- - - - - - - - - - - - - - - - - - - - - - - - - - - - - - - - - - - - - - - - - - - - - - - -
    UPDATE FILE TITLE TEXT
        Set a new filename in the dialog box's static filename control
    - - - - - - - - - - - - - - - - - - - - - - - - - - - - - - - - - - - - - - - - - - - - - - - -*/
static void UpdateFileTitleText ( HWND hDlg )
{
    Static_SetText( GetDlgItem(hDlg, IDD_FILETITLE), szFileTitle );
    return;
}
```

```
/*------------------------------------------------------------------
   UPDATE TIME TEXT
      Update the static dialog controls that show the scroll
      thumb's current position and the playing time for the
      current .WAV file
------------------------------------------------------------------*/
static void UpdateTimeText ( HWND hDlg )
{
    DWORD dwFrac;
    UINT  uSecs, uTenthSecs;
    char  szText[MAX_RSRC_STRING_LEN];
    char  szFormat[MAX_RSRC_STRING_LEN];

       /* get the format string */
    LoadString( GetWindowInstance(hDlg), IDS_TIMEFMT, szFormat,
                sizeof(szFormat) );
       /* update position text */
    dwFrac     = ((dwCurrentSample*100) / dwSamplesPerSec) / 10;
    uSecs      = (UINT)(dwFrac / 10);
    uTenthSecs = (UINT)(dwFrac % 10);
    wsprintf( szText, szFormat, uSecs, uTenthSecs );
    Static_SetText( GetDlgItem(hDlg, IDD_POSITION), szText );
       /* update length text */
    dwFrac     = ((dwWaveDataSize*100) / dwSamplesPerSec) / 10;
    uSecs      = (UINT)(dwFrac / 10);
    uTenthSecs = (UINT)(dwFrac % 10);
    wsprintf( szText, szFormat, uSecs, uTenthSecs );
    Static_SetText( GetDlgItem(hDlg, IDD_LENGTH), szText );
    return;
}
```

Resetting the Program

When the user chooses New from the File menu, the program must discard any current data and reset all its variables. NewWaveFile also updates the static dialog box controls and effectively disables the scrollbar by making its range very small.

```
/*------------------------------------------------------------------
   NEW WAVE FILE
      Start work on a new .WAV file.  Reset variables and update
      display.  Called in response to the New command.
------------------------------------------------------------------*/
```

```
static void NewWaveFile ( HWND hDlg )
{
    HINSTANCE hInstance;
    HWND hwndScrollBar = GetDlgItem( hDlg, IDD_SCROLLBAR );

        /* close the old Wave file */
    if( ! QuerySave( hDlg ) )
    {
        return;
    }
        /* set filename and title */
    hInstance = GetWindowInstance( hDlg );
    LoadString( hInstance, IDS_UNTITLED, szFileTitle,
                sizeof(szFileTitle) );
    szFileName[0] = '\0';
    FreeGlobalWaveData();           // delete old waveform data
    bIsFileDirty = FALSE;           // set file dirty flag
    UpdateFileTitleText( hDlg );    // set filename text
        /* set the new waveform data */
    dwCurrentSample = 0;
    lpWaveData      = NULL;
    dwWaveDataSize  = 0;
    dwSamplesPerSec = 22050;
        /* set the new scrollbar range */
    ScrollBar_SetRange( hwndScrollBar, 0, 1, FALSE );
        /* set the new scrollbar position */
    FORWARD_WM_HSCROLL( hDlg, hwndScrollBar, SB_TOP,
                        0, SendMessage );
    return;
}
```

Getting a Filename

GetFileName calls the common dialog box for opening or saving files.

```
/*-----------------------------------------------------------------
    GET FILE NAME
        Invoke the File Open or File Save As common dialog box.
        If the bOpenName parameter is TRUE, the procedure runs
        the OpenFileName dialog box.

    RETURN
```

```
              TRUE if the dialog box closes without error.  If the dialog
              box returns TRUE, then lpszFile and lpszFileTitle point to
              the new file path and name, respectively.
    ----------------------------------------------------------------*/
    static BOOL GetFileName ( HWND hDlg,
                              BOOL bOpenName,      // open file or save as
                              LPSTR lpszFile,      // buffer for file path
                              int iMaxFileNmLen,   // max file path length
                              LPSTR lpszFileTitle,  // buffer for filename
                              int iMaxFileTitleLen ) // max filename length
    {
        OPENFILENAME ofn;

        /* initialize structure for the common dialog box */
        lpszFile[0] = '\0';
        ofn.lStructSize       = sizeof( OPENFILENAME );
        ofn.hwndOwner         = hDlg;
        ofn.hInstance         = NULL;
        ofn.lpstrFilter       = szOFNFilter[0];
        ofn.lpstrCustomFilter = NULL;
        ofn.nMaxCustFilter    = 0;
        ofn.nFilterIndex      = 1;
        ofn.lpstrFile         = lpszFile;
        ofn.nMaxFile          = iMaxFileNmLen;
        ofn.lpstrFileTitle    = lpszFileTitle;
        ofn.nMaxFileTitle     = iMaxFileTitleLen;
        ofn.lpstrInitialDir   = NULL;
        ofn.lpstrTitle        = NULL;
        ofn.nFileOffset       = 0;
        ofn.nFileExtension    = 0;
        ofn.lpstrDefExt       = szOFNDefExt;
        ofn.lCustData         = 0;
        ofn.lpfnHook          = NULL;
        ofn.lpTemplateName    = NULL;
        /* invoke the common dialog box */
        if( bOpenName )                                 // open a file
        {
            ofn.Flags = OFN_HIDEREADONLY | OFN_PATHMUSTEXIST |
                        OFN_FILEMUSTEXIST;
            return( GetOpenFileName(&ofn) );
        }
        else                                            // Save As...
```

```
        {
            ofn.Flags = OFN_HIDEREADONLY | OFN_OVERWRITEPROMPT;
            return( GetSaveFileName(&ofn) );
        }
    }
```

Opening a Data File

When the user chooses Open from the File menu, the procedure asks the user to
choose a file and then passes the name to ReadWaveData in the MMIO module.
When the program loads new data, it resets the scrollbar range and pushes the
thumbpad back to 0.

```
/*-------------------------------------------------------------------
    OPEN WAVE FILE
        Open a new .WAV file
-------------------------------------------------------------------*/
static void OpenWaveFile ( HWND hDlg )
{
    int  iMaxPos;
    HWND hwndScrollBar = GetDlgItem( hDlg, IDD_SCROLLBAR );

        /* close the old Wave file */
    if( !QuerySave( hDlg ) )
    {
     return;
    }
        /* get a Wave file to open */
    if( ! GetFileName( hDlg, TRUE, szFileName, sizeof(szFileName),
                    szFileTitle, sizeof(szFileTitle) ) )
    {
        return;
    }
    FreeGlobalWaveData();           // delete old waveform data
    bIsFileDirty = FALSE;           // set file dirty flag
    UpdateFileTitleText( hDlg );    // set filename text
        /* read new waveform data */
    dwCurrentSample = 0;
    ReadWaveData( hDlg, szFileName, &lpWaveData, &dwWaveDataSize,
                &dwSamplesPerSec );
        /* set the new scrollbar range */
    iMaxPos = (int)(( dwWaveDataSize * 100 ) / dwSamplesPerSec );
    ScrollBar_SetRange( hwndScrollBar, 0, iMaxPos, FALSE );
```

```
        /* set the new scrollbar position */
    FORWARD_WM_HSCROLL( hDlg, hwndScrollBar, SB_TOP,
                        0, SendMessage );
    return;
}
```

Saving New Data

With the procedures we've already defined, writing a wave file to disk is easy. SaveWaveFile spends most of its time ensuring that we have a filename and that we don't write over important data.

```
/*------------------------------------------------------------------
   SAVE WAVE FILE
      Save waveform data to disk.  If the second parameter is TRUE,
      or if the current data does not yet have a filename, this
      procedure will request a name.
   ----------------------------------------------------------------*/
static void SaveWaveFile( HWND hDlg, BOOL bAskForName )
{
    HINSTANCE hInstance;
    BOOL bSave;
    char szText[MAX_RSRC_STRING_LEN];
    char szCaption[MAX_RSRC_STRING_LEN];
    int  iRet;

        /* anything to save? */
    if( ! lpWaveData )
    {
        return;
    }
        /* if renaming or no name, prompt user for name */
    if( ( bAskForName ) || ( szFileName[0] == '\0' ) )
    {     /* get the name of the wave file to save as */
        bSave = GetFileName( hDlg, FALSE,
            szFileName,  sizeof(szFileName),
            szFileTitle, sizeof(szFileTitle) );
    }
    else
    {     /* no new name; confirm overwriting old file */
        hInstance = GetWindowInstance( hDlg );
        LoadString( hInstance, IDS_OVERWRITE, szText,
                    sizeof(szText) );
```

```
        LoadString( hInstance, IDS_CAPTION, szCaption,
                    sizeof(szCaption) );
        iRet = MessageBox( hDlg, szText, szCaption,
                           MB_YESNO | MB_ICONQUESTION );
        bSave = (iRet == IDYES);
    }
       /* save to the wave file */
    if( bSave )
    {
        bIsFileDirty = FALSE;        /* set file dirty flag */
        UpdateFileTitleText( hDlg );  /* set filename text */
           /* write out the waveform data */
        WriteWaveData(hDlg, szFileName, lpWaveData, dwWaveDataSize,
                      dwSamplesPerSec );
    }
    return;
}
```

Mixing Two Sounds Together

ShowWave's Edit menu includes a Mix command. To mix one sound with another, you average them; that is, you add together each pair of samples and divide by two. When you play the combined sounds, you should hear both components simultaneously.

```
/*-------------------------------------------------------------
    MIX WITH FILE
        Mix a .WAV file into the current waveform data, combining
        the data from both into a single recording.  Mixing begins
        at the current point in the current file.  Mixing stops if
        we reach the end of the current file; it will not extend
        the current file.
-------------------------------------------------------------*/
static void MixWithFile ( HWND hDlg )
{
    HINSTANCE hInstance;
    char   szMixFile[_MAX_FNAME];     // name of second .WAV file
    LPSTR  lpMix;                     // data from second file
    DWORD  dwMixSize;                 // size of new data
    DWORD  dwMixSPS;                  // samples per second
    char   szErrStr[MAX_RSRC_STRING_LEN];
    char   szCaption[MAX_RSRC_STRING_LEN];
    LPSTR  lpDest, lpSrc;             // pointers for data transfer
```

```
DWORD dw;                           // loop variable
int   iMaxPos;                      // scrollbar range
HWND  hwndScrollBar = GetDlgItem( hDlg, IDD_SCROLLBAR );

   /* get a .WAV file to mix with */
if( !GetFileName( hDlg, TRUE, szMixFile, sizeof(szMixFile),
               NULL, 0 ) )
{
   return;                          // no filename
}
   /* read waveform data */
if( ! ReadWaveData( hDlg, szMixFile, &lpMix,
                  &dwMixSize, &dwMixSPS ) )
{
   return;                          // error reading data
}
   /* mix data */
if( ! lpWaveData )
{
   bIsFileDirty = TRUE;       /* set file dirty flag */
      /* set the new waveform data */
   dwCurrentSample = 0;
   lpWaveData      = lpMix;
   dwWaveDataSize  = dwMixSize;
   dwSamplesPerSec = dwMixSPS;
      /* set the new scrollbar range */
   iMaxPos = (int)((dwWaveDataSize*100) / dwSamplesPerSec );
   ScrollBar_SetRange( hwndScrollBar, 0, iMaxPos, FALSE );
      /* set the new scrollbar position */
   FORWARD_WM_HSCROLL( hDlg, hwndScrollBar, SB_TOP,
                     0, SendMessage );
}
else
{
       /* for demo, use only matching frequencies */
   if( dwSamplesPerSec != dwMixSPS )
   {
      hInstance = GetWindowInstance( hDlg );
      LoadString( hInstance, IDS_BADFREQUENCY, szErrStr,
                  sizeof(szErrStr) );
      LoadString( hInstance, IDS_CAPTION, szCaption,
```

```
                        sizeof(szCaption) );
        MessageBox( hDlg, szErrStr, szCaption,
                    MB_ICONEXCLAMATION | MB_OK );
        GlobalFreePtr( lpMix );
        return;
    }
        /* mix new file into waveform at current position */
    lpSrc  = lpMix;
    lpDest = lpWaveData + dwCurrentSample;
    for( dw = 0; dw < (dwWaveDataSize-dwCurrentSample); dw++ )
    {
        /* merge one source and destination sample */
       *lpDest = (BYTE)(((int)(BYTE)*lpDest + (BYTE)*lpSrc) / 2);
        lpSrc++;                     // increment transfer pointers
        lpDest++;
        if( lpSrc >= ( lpMix + dwMixSize ) )
        {
            break;                   // reached end of original data
        }
    }
        /* clean up */
    GlobalFreePtr( lpMix );       // free memory
    bIsFileDirty = TRUE;          // set file dirty flag
    PaintWaveData( hDlg );        // paint the new waveform data
    }
    return;
}
```

MixWithFile begins by asking for the name of a .WAV file to open and reading the data into a second memory buffer, lpMix. If there is no current sound (the user has not already opened another file), the new "mix" sound simply becomes the current sound. We mark the new file as unsaved, set the global variables, and give the scrollbar new range values based on the length of the new sound.

But normally, the user will already have loaded a sound and we'll need to combine two sets of data. For demonstration purposes, ShowWave mixes only sounds that have the same sampling rate. To mix sounds with different rates, you would skip over some samples in the faster sound. For example, if one had a sampling rate of 11 and the other of 22, you would average every other sample from the second sound with one sample from the first.

The for loop that averages bytes together starts with the current position in the current sound. The user may already have played or scrolled partway through the file. The loop continues averaging bytes until it reaches the end of either sound and then stops. The new sound is cut off if it extends past the end of the old one. You could allow mixing to expand the current sound by calling `GlobalReallocPtr` to expand the `lpWaveData` buffer.

The line that averages two samples performs some typecasting to ensure that the compiler uses integers (which have 2 bytes) when it multiplies and divides. Even though the answer always fits in a byte, the intermediate product of two samples often overflows that limit.

Changing the Volume

The Effects menu lets the user make the current sound louder or softer. Like mixing, this effect involves modifying the samples mathematically. To understand the calculation, consider the diagram of a sound wave in Figure 36.4. The wave undulates above and below a middle point, called the *baseline*. When the wave swings very high and low, far away from the baseline, the sound it makes is loud. Quiet sounds have low peaks and shallow troughs. You can make a quiet sound loud by raising the peaks and lowering the troughs.

FIGURE 36.4

A sound wave undulates around its baseline

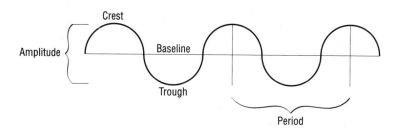

When a digitizer samples a sound wave, it notes where the wave falls in relation to the baseline at any given moment. When recording with 8 bits per sample, the range of the largest wave is divided into 256 different regions. Each sample names one of the regions. Sixteen-bit samples perceive 65,536 regions in the same amplitude and so record much finer distinctions. ShowWave works with 8-bit samples, so a value of 128 represents the baseline.

To change the volume of a sound sample, first determine its distance from the baseline:

WaveHeight = sample – baseline

Samples with values less than 128 produce negative heights, indicating a trough in the wave. To increase the volume by 25 percent, multiply each height by 1.25:

LouderHeight = (WaveHeight * 125) / 100;

Finally, we need to be sure the new value doesn't fall outside the possible range of 8-bit values. Amplitudes greater than 255 or less than 0 are not permitted.

LouderSample = LouderHeight + baseline

LouderSample = max(0, min(LouderSample, 255))

For 16-bit samples, make *LouderSample* type LONG and change the second calculation to this:

LouderSample = max(– 32768, min(LouderSample, 32767))

ShowWave can either increase or decrease the volume by 25 percent. To decrease the volume, multiply each height by 0.75.

```
/*----------------------------------------------------------
    CHANGE VOLUME
        Increase/decrease the volume of the waveform data playback
-----------------------------------------------------------*/
static void ChangeVolume( HWND hDlg, BOOL bIncrease )
{
    LPSTR lp;
    DWORD dw;
    int   iTmp, iFactor;

        /* anything to change? */
    if( ! lpWaveData )
    {
        return;
    }
        /* change the volume of the waveform data */
    lp      = lpWaveData;
    iFactor = (bIncrease ? 125 : 75);
    for( dw = 0; dw < dwWaveDataSize; dw++ )
    {
        iTmp = (((int)(BYTE)(*lp) - MIDVALUE) * iFactor) / 100;
        *lp = (BYTE)max( MINVALUE, min(iTmp+MIDVALUE, MAXVALUE) );
        lp++;
    }
}
```

```
        /* set file dirty flag */
    bIsFileDirty = TRUE;
        /* paint the new waveform data */
    PaintWaveData( hDlg );
    return;
}
```

Playing a Sound

BeginPlay from the MCI module plays a sound, but PlayWaveFile performs some additional housekeeping chores before calling that core function.

```
/*-------------------------------------------------------------------
    PLAY WAVE FILE
        Play waveform data
-----------------------------------------------------------------*/
static void PlayWaveFile ( HWND hDlg )
{
    LPSTR lpsz;
    DWORD dwFrom;
    int   iMinPos, iMaxPos;
    HWND  hwndScrollBar = GetDlgItem( hDlg, IDD_SCROLLBAR );

        /* anything to play? */
    if( ! lpWaveData )
    {
        return;
    }
        /* get waveform file to play */
    if( ! bIsFileDirty )
    {
        lpsz = szFileName;
    }
    else
    {
        /* temporarily store waveform data to disk for playing */
        WriteWaveData( hDlg, szTempFileName, lpWaveData,
                      dwWaveDataSize, dwSamplesPerSec );
        lpsz = szTempFileName;
    }
        /* if current position is end of sound, reset to beginning */
    ScrollBar_GetRange( hwndScrollBar, &iMinPos, &iMaxPos );
```

```
    if( iHScrollPos == iMaxPos )
    {
        FORWARD_WM_HSCROLL( hDlg, hwndScrollBar, SB_TOP,
                            0, SendMessage );
    }
        /* convert current sample position to milliseconds */
    dwFrom = (dwCurrentSample*1000) / dwSamplesPerSec;
        /* play waveform file */
    if( OpenDevice( hDlg, lpsz, &mciDevice ) )
    {
        if( ! BeginPlay( hDlg, mciDevice, dwFrom) )
        {
            CloseAudioDevice( hDlg );
            return;
        }
            /* set timer to update display */
        uTimerID = TMRPLAY;
        SetTimer( hDlg, uTimerID, 100, NULL );
    }
    return;
}
```

Since `BeginPlay` must play from a disk file, first we need to decide which file to pass it. If the sound in memory has not changed since the user loaded it, Show-Wave reads from the sound's original file. But if the user has changed the sound by mixing it or adjusting its volume, ShowWave deposits the sound in the temporary file we created on initialization.

If the user has scrolled partway through the current sound, we should start playing at the current position. The static variable `iHScrollPos` remembers where the scrollbar thumbpad is. If the user has scrolled to the end of the file, `PlayWaveFile` sends a message to reset the thumbpad at the beginning. `ShowWave_OnHScroll` answers the message, updating both `iHScrollPos` and `dwCurrentSample` to reflect the new file position.

Having guaranteed that the starting point is not the end of the file, `PlayWave-File` opens the audio device and calls `BeginPlay`. The sound starts, and `Begin-Play` returns immediately. The `SetTimer` command causes Windows to send us `WM_TIMER` messages every tenth of a second while the sound continues to play. You already saw how `ShowWave_OnTimer` responds to each message by advancing the scrollbar thumbpad and scrolling the wave graph.

Recording a Sound

The code for recording closely resembles the code for playing sound. The opening chores differ, however. Although the high-level audio commands allow you to insert newly recorded sound into an existing wave sound, not all devices support the MCI_RECORD_INSERT flag with the MCI_RECORD command. For simplicity, ShowWave insists on recording to an empty file, and the opening if statement enforces the restriction.

We have also somewhat arbitrarily limited the recording to 20 seconds. The user can interrupt the recording any time before that by clicking on the Stop button. If you prefer to leave the recording time open-ended, modify BeginPlay by removing the MCI_TO flag. (Or you might conditionally remove the flag only if the dwTo parameter is 0.)

```
/*----------------------------------------------------------------
   RECORD WAVE FILE
      Record waveform data
------------------------------------------------------------*/
static void RecordWaveFile ( HWND hDlg )
{
    HINSTANCE hInstance;
    char szErrStr[MAX_RSRC_STRING_LEN];
    char szCaption[MAX_RSRC_STRING_LEN];

    /* for demo purposes, record only onto new wave files */
    if( lpWaveData )
    {
        hInstance = GetWindowInstance( hDlg );
        LoadString( hInstance, IDS_BADRECORDFILE, szErrStr,
                    sizeof(szErrStr) );
        LoadString( hInstance, IDS_CAPTION, szCaption,
                    sizeof(szCaption) );
        MessageBox( hDlg, szErrStr, szCaption,
                    MB_ICONEXCLAMATION | MB_OK );
        return;
    }
    /* record waveform data into a new file */
    if( OpenDevice( hDlg, "", &mciDevice ) )
    {
        /* set recording to stop after 20 seconds */
        if( ! BeginRecord( hDlg, mciDevice, 20000 ) )
```

```
        {
           CloseAudioDevice( hDlg );
           return;
        }
           /* set timer to update display */
        uTimerID = TMRRECORD;
        SetTimer( hDlg, uTimerID, 100, NULL );
     }
     return;
}
```

The GraphWin Module

The ShowWave application uses a custom window class GraphClass to display the sound wave. The custom control is defined in the resource script thus:

```
CONTROL    "", IDD_SHOWWAVE, "GraphClass", 0x0000, 53, 22, 76, 23
```

GraphClass names a window class that ShowWave registers when it initializes. The Graphwin.C module contains the three procedures that support our Graph-Class window: RegisterGraphClass tells the system about the new class when the program begins, Graph_WndProc receives messages for the control, and Graph_OnPaint draws the sound wave.

```
/*-------------------------------------------------------------
    REGISTER GRAPH CLASS
        Register the window class for the dialog box's wave graph
        control window.  The main dialog box's resource template
        names this window class for one of its controls.  This
        procedure must be called before CreateDialog.
    -------------------------------------------------------------*/

BOOL RegisterGraphClass ( HINSTANCE hInstance )
{
    WNDCLASS wc;

    wc.style        = 0;
    wc.lpfnWndProc  = Graph_WndProc;
    wc.cbClsExtra   = 0;
    wc.cbWndExtra   = 0;
    wc.hInstance    = hInstance;
```

```
        wc.hIcon          = NULL;
        wc.hCursor        = LoadCursor( NULL, IDC_ARROW );
        wc.hbrBackground  = GetStockBrush( BLACK_BRUSH );
        wc.lpszMenuName   = NULL;
        wc.lpszClassName  = szGraphClass;
        return( RegisterClass(&wc) );
    }


    /*-------------------------------------------------------------
       GRAPH WNDPROC
         Receive messages for the main dialog box's sound graph window.
       -----------------------------------------------------------*/

    LRESULT WINAPI Graph_WndProc( HWND    hWnd,    UINT   uMsg,
                                  WPARAM wParam, LPARAM lParam )
    {
        switch (uMsg)
        {
            /* paint the green sound graph line */
            HANDLE_MSG( hWnd, WM_PAINT, Graph_OnPaint );
            default:
                return( DefWindowProc(hWnd, uMsg, wParam, lParam) );
        }
    }
```

The window procedure intercepts only one message, WM_PAINT, and in every other case the window accepts the standard message responses from the default window procedure. (Dialog box controls are not themselves dialog boxes, so they call DefWindowProc and not DefDlgProc.)

Our GraphClass window isn't really a full-blown control. Real controls must be careful with global or static variables because, unlike child windows, they do not have separate data segments for each window instance. Changing one static variable for one control would change that variable for all controls of the same class. Also, a control should answer the WM_GETDLGCODE message to tell the parent dialog box what keyboard input it wants. (GraphClass doesn't want any and would respond with DLGC_STATIC.)

TIP
A tightly designed custom control can be compiled into a DLL and made available to all applications, including a dialog editor. To do this, you would need to write and export a small set of standard control functions.

Drawing the Sound Wave

Rather than connecting points on the wave curve, ShowWave represents each sample as a vertical line. The wave height indicated in the sample determines the height of the vertical line. Each line extends an equal distance above and below the baseline, coloring in the space over and under each wave. Solid shapes show up better in the small graph window than a single wave line could. In Figure 36.5, you can see how the vertical lines fill the wave.

FIGURE 36.5

How ShowWave draws the sound wave

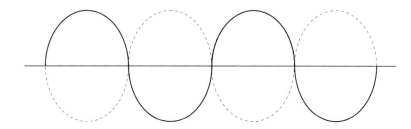

```
/*------------------------------------------------------------------
    GRAPH_ONPAINT
        Handle WM_PAINT messages for the Graph window.  Draw
        the green wave graph.
    -------------------------------------------------------------*/
static void Graph_OnPaint ( HWND hWnd )
{
    PAINTSTRUCT ps;
    HDC    hDC;
    HPEN   hPen, hpenOld;      // green pen for drawing columns
    RECT   rClient;            // size of graph control window
    int    iBase;              // vertical position of baseline
    LPSTR  lp;                 // points to one sample in wave data
    DWORD  dwMaxStart;         // maximum value for starting point
    int    iYScale;            // vertical scaling factor
    int    iCol;               // horizontal position of a column
    int    iColHeight;         // height of a column
```

```
      /* begin paint processing */
hDC = BeginPaint( hWnd, &ps );
   /* create a pen for drawing graph */
if( GetDeviceCaps(hDC, NUMCOLORS) > 2 )
{
   hPen = CreatePen( PS_SOLID, 1, RGB_GREEN ); // color
}
else
{
  hPen = CreatePen( PS_SOLID, 1, RGB_WHITE );    // mono display
}
if( hPen )
{
     /* select the pen */
   hpenOld = SelectPen( hDC, hPen );
      /* draw the waveform baseline */
   GetClientRect( hWnd, &rClient );
   iBase = RECTHEIGHT(rClient) / 2;
   MoveToEx( hDC, 0, iBase, NULL );
   LineTo( hDC, (int)rClient.right, iBase );
      /* graph waveform data */
   if( lpWaveData )
   {
      /* set the current sample position in the waveform data */
      dwMaxStart = dwWaveDataSize - RECTWIDTH(rClient) - 1;
      lp = lpWaveData + min( dwCurrentSample, dwMaxStart );
         /* determine the height scaling factor */
      iYScale = ( ( MAXVALUE - MINVALUE) + 1 ) /     // amplitude
              ( RECTHEIGHT(rClient) - 4 );      // control height
         // Subtracting 4 from the height ensures a small
         // margin above and below the biggest waves
         /* paint samples from the waveform data */
      for( iCol = (int)rClient.left;
          iCol <= (int)rClient.right; iCol++ )
         {
         iColHeight = ( (int)(BYTE)(*lp++) - MIDVALUE ) / iYScale;
            if( iColHeight != 0 )
            {
               /* figure absolute value of column height */
               if( iColHeight < 0 )
               {
```

```
                            iColHeight = -iColHeight;
                    }
                        /* draw line from below base to above base */
                    MoveToEx( hDC, iCol, iBase - iColHeight, NULL );
                    LineTo( hDC, iCol, iBase + ( iColHeight + 1 ) );
                }
            }
        }
        /* restore the DC and delete the pen */
        SelectPen( hDC, hpenOld );
        DeletePen( hPen );
    }
        /* end paint processing */
    EndPaint( hWnd, &ps );
    return;
}
```

`Graph_OnPaint` represents the baseline with a horizontal line bisecting the graph window. The first vertical line on the left side of the control window will represent the current sample. If the user has scrolled to a point near the end of the file and only a few samples remain, the wave graph might not extend all the way across the window. To avoid leaving part of the graph empty, the program imposes a maximum value for the starting point. If the graph control is, for example, 50 pixels wide, the graph must not begin less than 50 samples from the end.

The heights must be scaled to fit inside the window. A line extending the full height of the window must represent the maximum possible amplitude. With 8-bit samples, the maximum is 256. ShowWave calculates the line height with the following formulas:

Scale factor = maximum amplitude / window height

Column height = sample height / scale factor

To preserve a small margin of 2 pixels below and above the tallest waves, Show-Wave subtracts 4 from the window height when figuring the scale factor.

The loop that draws each column begins by figuring the sample height and scaling it down to fit in the window. It draws each column by moving to a point below the baseline and drawing upward to a point an equal distance above the baseline. Because the columns extend on both sides of the baseline, the height of each column is twice the height of the sample.

We could call the C library function `abs` to get the absolute value of `iColHeight`, but then the compiler would add library code to the .EXE file. The `if` statement takes up less memory.

Some Improvements for the ShowWave Program

You might want to do some experimenting to see how you can improve our demo multimedia program. Here, we present some ideas, but you probably can think of some others.

Although the 8-bit sample size is common, you might want to allow ShowWave to work with 16-bit samples as well. We've described several places where Show-Wave makes calculations that assume 8-bit samples, such as in changing the volume, drawing the sound wave, and moving the scrollbar thumbpad. Any place that assumes a sample is a `BYTE` or refers to the manifest constants `MINVALUE`, `MIDVALUE`, and `MAXVALUE` would need to be changed. The 16-bit samples range in value from -32,768 to 32,767, with a midpoint of 0.

You also know enough to add stereo sound. `MixWithFile` and `ChangeVolume` would need to do everything twice, once for the left channel and once for the right. To draw the sound wave, you could average both channels together or let the user choose which channel to see. In a stereo data chunk, the channels are interleaved:

Sample one: channel 0 sample, channel 1 sample

Sample two: channel 0 sample, channel 1 sample

...

`MixWithFile` might be modified to permit expanding the original sound. To do this, you would need to reallocate the buffer periodically.

The `MCI_OPEN` command reloads the `waveaudio` driver each time you open the device. From working with printers, you know that loading the driver causes a noticeable lag. ShowWave could load the driver once on opening and close it once at the end. In between, it would open and close individual device elements. The very first Open command would specify a device type but no device element; subsequent commands would open and close with an element name. The final close would again omit the element. Several programs may open one device simultaneously, so holding it open won't cause trouble. (Whether different programs can share the same device *element* depends on the flags they use with `MCI_OPEN`.)

With `EnableWindow` and `EnableMenuItem`, you could disable buttons and menu commands not currently available. For example, all the buttons should be disabled until the user loads a sound. Stop should be disabled unless a playback or record message is in progress.

Finally, you could add `MessageBeep` commands to the program's error messages. Those who favor restraint in interface design will limit audio signals to the more critical errors or allow the user to choose whether and when to hear error sounds.

This chapter began with a general discussion of the hardware for multimedia applications and the WinMM translation layer that permits Windows programs to manipulate multimedia files in a device-independent manner. Windows works with files that contain data for wave sounds, MIDI music, animation, and analog video, among other formats.

For a sample program, we chose to work with waveform audio because its hardware requirements are less demanding; many machines now have inexpensive sound cards. The ShowWave program demonstrates a full range of MCI command messages for opening and closing a device, playing and recording sounds, and interrupting operations. The MMIO module demonstrates the group of WinMM functions that facilitate reading and writing chunks of a RIFF file. The complete program is included on the CD that accompanies this book.

Having read this far, you have passed well beyond the beginning stages of Windows programming and have come to understand such advanced topics as threads, processes, synchronization, pipes, virtual memory, exception handling, enhanced metafiles, DDEML, and multimedia. Thorough as we have been, more remains. Windows NT/95 is too large a system for one book to explain everything.

However, you are now prepared to proceed into new fields on your own, exploring even more mysteries. After all, the best applications cannot be described here; they are still waiting for you—not me—to think of them.

INDEX

Note to the Reader: First level entries are in **bold**. Page numbers in **bold** indicate the principal discussion of a topic or the definition of a term. Page numbers in *italic* indicate illustrations.

B

(

D

E

F

G

H

I

J

K

L

M

O

X

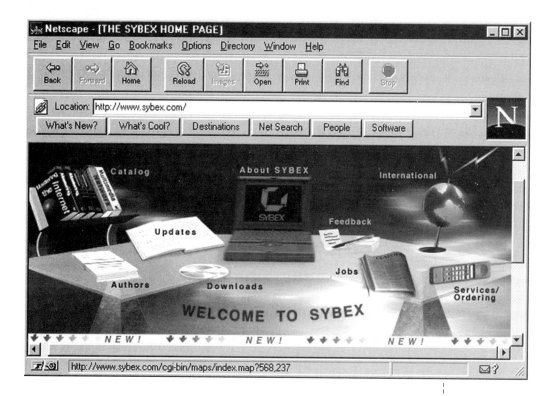

PenDraw1: Demonstrates drawing mode operations and color interactions. (Chapter 22)

PenDraw2: Demonstrates drawing using standard shapes (arc, chord, ellipse, pie, and rectangle). (Chapter 23)

PenDraw3: Demonstrates the polygon and polypolygon drawing tools for multisided figures. (Chapter 23)

PenDraw4: Demonstrates using bitmapped brushes to fill shapes. (Chapter 24)

PenDraw5: Demonstrates retrieving and displaying bitmap images. (Chapter 24)

PenDraw6: Demonstrates using metafile operations to store and replay previous calculated sequences and how to exchange metafiles between applications. (Chapter 32)

PieGraph: Shows how pie graphs are created. (Chapter 23)

RPClient: Demonstrates an RPC (Remote Procedure Calls) client. (Chapter 20)

RPCServ: Demonstrates an RPC server. (Chapter 20)

Shades: Provides simple methods for manipulating images, enhancing or decreasing contrast, and using elementary edge-detection algorithms. (Chapter 27)

SVGA_Win: Demonstrates color palettes under SVGA video. (Chapter 22)

Target: Demonstrates using nondestructive overlays for graphics images. (Chapter 28)

Threads: Demonstrates using multiple threads to carry out several tasks independent of the main process. A second version also shows how to use exceptions. (Chapters 14 and 16)

Unwind: Demonstrates using a filter function to modify variables causing an exception and how to replay the code where an error would have occurred. (Chapter 16)

ViewPCX: Demonstrates loading and displaying .PCX (PaintBrush) images. (Chapter 26)

WebView: Demonstrates Internet tools and toolkits. (Chapter 19)

WinHello: Demonstrates the basic requirements of any Windows NT/95 application and introduces the Template. I include file. (Chapter 2)

WNetDemo: Demonstrates mapping a user-specified network resource to a local device name. (Chapter 20)

Please note:
If you are using NT 3.5x, you will not be able to use the CD that accompanies this book.